mediaguardian

Media Directory

2006

Edited by **Chris Alden**

Researched by **Toni Hanks, Pauline Hughes, Rick Peters, Mo Smith, Janice Wood**

First published in 2005 by GuardianBooks,
an imprint of Guardian Newspapers Ltd.

Copyright in main text © Chris Alden 2005

Copyright in comment pages and database
© Guardian Newspapers Ltd 2005

Austin cartoons © David Austin

The Guardian and MediaGuardian are trademarks
of the Guardian Media Group plc and Guardian
Newspapers Ltd.

A CIP record for this book is available from
the British Library.

ISBN: 1-84354-059-2

Cover design: Two Associates
Text Design: Byrony Newhouse

Proofread by Amelia Hodsdon

Data researched and updated on behalf of
Guardian Newspapers by Toni Hanks

Disclaimer
We have taken all steps possible to ensure the
accuracy of the data in this directory. If any
information is incorrect, please send an email with
updated details to mediadirectory@guardian.co.uk

Printed by Cambridge University Press

Contents

INDEPENDENT RADIO NEWS

the big news on radio

274 stations – 27 million listeners
Source: Rajar

How to use this book

Welcome to the MediaGuardian Media Directory 2006, the indispensable handbook
for journalists, students and media professionals.

This book is not merely a directory. In addition to those 13,000 contact phone numbers
and listings of the great and good, we also include 40,000 words of analysis and advice
on how the media industry works.

For a general introduction to media in the UK, turn to the **State of the Media** section
on page 1. You'll find a guide to the top stories in the media over the past year, with
analysis of key trends, and a guide to the financial performance of the media.

If you know which part of the media you're interested in, turn to our chapters on
individual media sectors. Each chapter comes in two parts: first, a guide to the sector
with a roundup of trends, plus comment from Guardian journalists and other industry
figures; and second, at the end of each chapter, those all-important contacts. To help
you find your way around, we've divided the chapters into **The News Media** (page 9),
which means press, TV, radio, new media and global media; **Creative Media** (page 255),
including books and, new to the book this year, film and music; and **Media Services** (page 311),
by which we mean advertising, PR and media law. Together, the chapters include about
7,000 media contacts.

The book is also a guide to your career in media. This year, we've put all the advice
on how to get on in media – including job-finding tips, a guide to media diversity,
and how to get an agent – into one easy-to-use section, **A Career in Media** (page 355).
Again, we list all the contacts you need: including, most usefully for students, courses
in press, broadcasting, marketing, advertising, new media, film and music. We also list
media recruitment agencies for the first time.

At the back of the handbook, you will find a **Contacts Book** (page 403) aimed particularly
at journalists – with more than 6,000 contacts for the most high-profile public and private
organisations in the UK. Whether you want a government department, police force,
football team, charity, airline or FTSE-listed company, you will find a number and
a website here. If they have a press office, we've done our best to list that too.

We hope you find the book useful.

Chris Alden

State of the media

Rupert Murdoch is not usually a man to admit his mistakes. So when, in April 2005, the boss of News Corporation – the eighth largest media company in the world, and the owner of the Sun, the Times and Sky – told a conference of newspaper editors that he and others had been "remarkably complacent" about the digital revolution, the rest of the media sat up and took notice. The youth of today, he said, "don't want to rely on the morning paper for their up-to-date information. They don't want to rely on a God-like figure from above to tell them what's important. And to carry the religion analogy a bit further, they certainly don't want news presented as gospel."

Murdoch was talking about the newspaper business; journalists, he said, had not done enough thinking about how the next generation accesses its news. But he need not have stopped there. For the pressures wrought by the digital economy – the fragmentation of media, ease of access to the media industry, citizen journalism, iPods, podcasts, search engines, digital radio, digital television – are wreaking havoc. No media sector has been left untouched by what in effect has been a rapid liberalisation of the industry; and few sectors have reacted with the speed they might.

Look first at the **BBC**. The corporation has been a leader in promoting digital technologies: in the past four years it has launched four new digital TV channels and dozens of new digital radio stations; it spent around £70m on its websites in 2004 and continues to invest in interactive TV. The BBC is rightly looking forward to a time when there is no such thing as just the five terrestrial channels; when BBC2 must compete on an equal footing with Living TV and the Discovery channels and hundreds more services. Given that future, it's no surprise that the question is asked: what do we pay our licence fee for? What should the corporation's public service remit be? How can its commercial competitors be protected at the same time? It is against that background that the BBC director general, Mark Thompson, announced about 4,000 job cuts at the corporation, even as it negotiates over the renewal of its licence. The message coming from government seems to be: in a digital future, we want a leaner, more focused BBC; see page 142 for more on that.

Now look back at Rupert Murdoch. The internet, he realises, is changing the way people consume their news; they want it on demand, they want it an easy-to-swallow format, and they want it cheap or for free. It's lessons like these that led to the launch of free morning tabloids such as Metro; bland it may be, but it's a valuable service and it's eating into the circulations of paid-for newspapers nationwide. And it's because of that kind of competition that Murdoch, a newspaperman to his bones, took the decision to take the Times, of all papers, **tabloid** for the first time in its history (page 13). Look forward to a moment, years hence, when it updates its editions throughout the morning too.

Across other media sectors, the story is the same. The commercial radio industry, dependent on advertising as it is, is struggling to compete with internet advertising; so GWR and Capital Radio have merged and, unthinkable at one time, the competition commission waved the deal through (page 195). The music industry has been revolutionised by digital downloads to iPods and other digital audio players, and has had to include them in its charts for the first time (page 300). The books industry is worried about technologies such as Google Print, unimaginable a couple of years back, that allow users to search books on the world wide web (page 258); what will that mean for libraries and traditional copyright deals? And talking of Google, in July of 2005 we had the spectacle of a seven-year-old internet company being worth an astonishing £45.8bn on the Nasdaq stock exchange – making it, at that moment at least, the third largest media company in the world, with Microsoft just ahead of it and Yahoo! just behind.

Of course, anyone who has played Guardian Unlimited's Fantasy Chairman football game will know that, in any market where humans are involved, reputations will come and go. Six years ago, new media was trendy; three years ago you couldn't touch it; now it's trendy again, and the markets will keep over-correcting. But take a look at the stats in the box. Multichannel TV households are up 16%; broadband connections are up more than 80%; and sales of digital radio sets are up 175%; but newspaper circulations and radio audiences are down. Whatever the markets may say, those figures will have the biggest impact on the media industry for years to come.

Stock market performance, 2004–05

The FTSE media and photography index is, generally speaking, a short-term barometer of consumer performance in the UK as a whole; and at the moment, that outlook is cautious. Shares fell in September 2004 but recovered quickly, and at the time of writing were hovering at about the same level as in summer 2004.

On the London stock exchange, advertising group **WPP**'s shares remained steady at about £6; **Reuters** slipped slightly in 2004 but recovered in 2005 to about £4; while the **Daily Mail and General Trust** and **Johnston Press** both outperformed the market slightly in late 2004 only to slip back in 2005, at about £6.50 and £5 respectively. All these share prices were largely similar to last year's.

BSkyB shares took a jolt in July 2004 as the company rethought its digital strategy, but remained steady thereafter at between £3.50 and £4.

Whole-year trends	2004	2003
Total national newsaper circulation (per week)	86.3 million	89.2 million
Total regional newspaper circulation/distribution	67.2 million	68.4 million
Total consumer magazine circulation (per issue, July to June)	62.4 million†	56.5 million§
Total households with multichannel TV*	15.6 million	13.4 million
Total radio reach	43.9 million	44.0 million
*total number of DAB digital radios sold**	*1.2 million*	*435,000*
Total households with internet access*	16 million	12.5 million
*total broadband connections**	*6.2 million*	*3.4 million*
Total volume of books sold	282 million	286 million
Total measured ad spend	£18.4bn	£17.2bn

* Figures at the end of year. For statistics for spring and summer 2005, see individual chapters of the book.
†July 2004 to June 2005   § July 2003 to June 2004
Sources: ABC, Newspaper Society, PPA, Ofcom, Books and the Consumer survey, Advertising Association

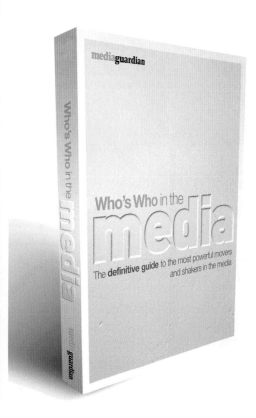

MediaGuardian 100

The MediaGuardian 100 is our annual guide to the most powerful figures in one of the UK's most vibrant industries. The 2005 list – the fifth – was drawn up by an experienced panel of media watchers from politics, journalism, advertising, PR and the internet. Our ambition is to take a snapshot of the individuals who run or influence the UK media in 2005.

Candidates are judged on three criteria – their cultural, economic and political clout in the UK. Political influence dominated 2004's election-year discussion, but cultural and economic power determined most of the choices in this year's list, made up from all sectors of the media – broadcasting, publishing, advertising, new media, marketing and PR. With 35 new entrants and only three people retaining the same position from 2004, it's all change.

Mark Thompson (right) and Michael Grade... steering the BBC through charter renewal

Dan Chung

1= Mark Thompson and Michael Grade

Jobs: BBC director general; BBC chairman
Ages: Thompson 47, Grade 62 *Industry:* broadcasting *Total group income:* £3.835bn *Staff:* 27,264
Salary: Thompson £453,000 (£459,000 including benefits); Grade £72,000 (£96,000 including benefits)
2004 rankings: Thompson 6, Grade 2

They make for something of an odd couple – the showbiz impresario and the hard-nosed strategist. Yet Mark Thompson and Michael Grade have guided the BBC through a perilous 12 months in which its future funding and the very nature of its existence have been called into question.

It is the peculiar nature of charter renewal that the corporation must justify itself every 10 years under the fiercest cross-examination. This year it has been tougher than ever, yet Thompson and Grade will be delighted by the outcome.

The licence fee? Secured for the next 10 years. External regulation of the BBC? Rejected. Proposals to "top slice" its public funding? Thrown out by Tessa Jowell's green paper on the future of the BBC in March. It has been a remarkable turnaround in the fortunes of the corporation, reeling less than 18 months ago from the Hutton report and rudderless following the double departure of Gavyn Davies and Greg Dyke.

Not that the intervening period has been without pain. Far from it. Thompson's radical three-year plan to axe around 4,000 jobs, saving £355m a year, is the biggest single reorganisation in its history. Staff anger manifested itself in a 24-hour strike in May that brought the giant BBC News machine to a virtual standstill.

3. Rupert Murdoch

Job: chairman and chief executive, News Corporation
Age: 74 *Industry:* broadcasting, publishing, new media
Annual revenue: US$20.96bn *Staff:* 35,000
Salary: US$4.5m (US$17m including bonuses)
2004 ranking: 1

Head of a $48bn media empire, Murdoch's interests range from the Sun, the Times and BSkyB in the UK to Fox TV in the US, Star TV in Asia, publishing house HarperCollins and 175 newspapers around the world. He also owns Foxtel in Australia and Sky Italia. On a global scale, Murdoch is more powerful than anyone else on this list.

4. Charles Allen

Job: chief executive, ITV *Age:* 47 *Industry:* broadcasting
Turnover: £2.08bn *Salary:* £1m (£1.88m including bonus and benefits) *2004 ranking:* 30

The unofficial award for survivor of the year goes to... Charles Allen. At the beginning of 2004 it was looking bleak for the ITV chief executive, encircled by sniping institutional investors and potential predators. But Allen remains at the helm of ITV plc and looks more secure than for a long time. The network's first year of operations surpassed expectations, with profits up 7% to £340m. Even better, Allen secured a multimillion-pound windfall from Ofcom, slashing ITV's licence fee payments by an unprecedented £135m a year.

5. Tessa Jowell

Job: culture secretary *Age:* 57 *Industry:* politics *Staff:* 530
Salary: £133,997 *2004 ranking:* 5

As rivalries at the heart of government go, it was almost enough to put Tony Blair and Gordon Brown in the shade. The running battle between culture secretary Tessa Jowell and the prime minister's adviser Lord Birt has been one of the ever-presents of the media landscape. But when the long-awaited green paper on the future of the BBC was published in March, it was clear there was only one winner. And it wasn't John Birt.

6. Steve Jobs

Job: co-founder and chief executive, Apple Computer and Pixar Animation *Age:* 50 *Industry:* new media, music, film
Turnover: $8.28bn (Apple) *2004 ranking:* 29

No one has done more to change the way we listen to music in the modern era than Steve Jobs. The iPod phenomenon has transformed Apple's fortunes. More than 16m have been sold and Apple has four-fifths of the legal download market. But iPod and the new generation of portable digital players are having an impact on the media industry far beyond Apple's bottom line.

7. Kevin Lygo

Job: director of television, Channel 4 *Age:* 46
Industry: broadcasting *Annual programming budget:*
£493m *Staff:* 185 *Salary:* £418,000 (£589,000 including bonuses) *2004 ranking:* 23

He might not be able to boast the biggest audience or the biggest budget, but Kevin Lygo is the most powerful channel controller in British television. At a time of fierce multichannel competition, Lygo's Channel 4 grew its audience share last year to 9.8%

8. Sir Martin Sorrell

Job: group chief executive, WPP *Age:* 60
Industry: advertising, marketing *Turnover:* £4.3bn
Staff: 59,932 *Salary:* £840,000 (£2.42m including bonus and benefits) *Worth:* £111m *2004 ranking:* 9

Sir Martin Sorrell is the country's most influential advertising man, in charge of the world's second-largest ad group, worth £7.7bn. One of the biggest success stories in British business, Sorrell's WPP has been on a five-year spending spree, buying up ad agencies Young & Rubicam, Cordiant and Grey Global, and media buyer Tempus.

9. Sergey Brin and Larry Page

Job: co-founders and directors, Google *Age:* Brin 31, Page 32 *Industry:* new media *Turnover:* $3.19bn
Staff: 3,021 *Salary:* $1 *Worth:* $10bn *2004 ranking:* 20

Google is the ultimate new media success story. The value of the company has risen relentlessly since it was floated on the New York stock exchange, peaking last month at more than $84bn, dwarfing rival media outfits such as Time Warner, Walt Disney and Viacom. Not bad for a couple of Stanford university upstarts who dreamed up the idea in a garage in 1998.

10. Paul Dacre

Job: editor-in-chief, Associated Newspapers *Age:* 56
Industry: publishing *Circulation:* Daily Mail 2.38m; Mail on Sunday 2.34m; London Evening Standard 344,145 (Jan-June 2005) *Salary:* £885,000 (£1.16m including bonus and benefits) *2004 ranking:* 7

Paul Dacre is the most powerful newspaper editor in Britain. His Daily Mail sets the news agenda like no other and having long overtaken the ailing Daily Mirror, it has now set its sights on the Sun in its bid to become the country's biggest selling daily paper.

a or an before h? use an only if the h is silent: an hour, an heir, an honourable man, an honest woman; but a hero, a hotel, a historian (but don't change a direct quote if the speaker says, for example, "an historic") • **abattoir** • **abbeys** cap up, eg Rievaulx Abbey, Westminster Abbey • **Aborigines, Aboriginal** cap up when referring to native Australians • **aborigines, aboriginal** lc when referring to indigenous populations • **accents** use on French, German, Spanish and Irish Gaelic words (but not anglicised French words such as cafe, apart from exposé, resumé) • **access** has been known as contact since the 1989 Children Act • **acknowledgment** not acknowledgement • **acronyms** take initial cap, eg Aids, Isa, Mori, Nato • **act** uc when using full name, eg Criminal Justice Act 1998, Official Secrets Act; but lc on second reference, eg "the act", and when speaking in more general terms, eg "we need a radical freedom of information act"; bills remain lc until passed into law • **acting** always lc: acting prime minister, acting committee chair, etc • **actor** male and female: avoid actress except when in name of award, eg Oscar for best actress. One 27-year-old actor contacted the Guardian to say "actress" has acquired a faintly pejorative tinge and she wants people to call her actor (except for her agent who should call her often) • **AD, BC** AD goes before the date (AD64), BC goes after (300BC); both go after the century, eg second century AD, fourth century BC • **adaptation** not adaption • **addendum** plural addendums • **addresses** 119 Farringdon Road, London EC1R 3ER

> **This stuff matters. Rules do not limit; they liberate**
> **John Humphrys**

> **Valuably insists on the writing of good English**
> **Tom Paulin**

Dan Chung

Matt Lucas (left) and David Walliams... in at number 21

53. Paul Merrill editor, Zoo PUBLISHING *(new entry)*

55. Simon Kelner editor, Independent PUBLISHING *(58)*

56. Martin Newland editor, Daily Telegraph PUBLISHING *(68)*

57. Roly Keating controller, BBC2 BROADCASTING *(50)*

58. Liz Forgan chair, Scott Trust PUBLISHING, NEW MEDIA *(new entry)*

59. Richard Reed co-founder and marketing director, Innocent MARKETING *(new entry)*

60. Brian Sullivan director of customer products and services, BSkyB BROADCASTING *(new entry)*

61. James Purnell minister for creative industries and tourism POLITICS *(new entry)*

62. Max Clifford founder, Max Clifford Associates PUBLIC RELATIONS *(65)*

63. Nicholas Coleridge managing director, Condé Nast PUBLISHING *(76)*

64. Robert Thomson editor, the Times PUBLISHING *(62)*

65. Lesley Douglas controller, BBC Radio 2 and 6 Music BROADCASTING *(75)*

66. David Mannion editor-in-chief, ITV News BROADCASTING *(new entry)*

67. Duncan Edwards managing director and chief executive officer, National Magazine Company PUBLISHING *(88)*

68. Andrew Gowers editor, Financial Times PUBLISHING *(69)*

69. Alison Sharman controller, Children's BBC BROADCASTING *(new entry)*

70. Nick Pollard head of Sky News BROADCASTING *(87)*

71. Sir Christopher Meyer chairman, Press Complaints Commission REGULATION *(41)*

72. Richard Scudamore chief executive, Premier League FOOTBALL *(new entry)*

73. Paul Potts chief executive, Press Association PUBLISHING, NEW MEDIA *(new entry)*

74. Richard Wallace editor, Daily Mirror PUBLISHING *(44)*

75. Trevor Beattie founder, Beattie McGuinness Bungay ADVERTISING *(new entry)*

76. Paul O'Grady TV presenter BROADCASTING *(new entry)*

77. Roger Alton editor, Observer PUBLISHING *(74)*

78. Andy Parfitt controller, Radio 1 BROADCASTING *(new entry)*

79. Jane Tranter controller of drama commissioning, BBC BROADCASTING *(new entry)*

80. Sarah Sands editor, Sunday Telegraph PUBLISHING *(new entry)*

81. Johnny Hornby managing partner, Clemmow Hornby Inge ADVERTISING *(81)*

82. Simon Shaps chief executive, Granada BROADCASTING *(new entry)*

83. Andrew Neil newspaper executive, TV presenter BROADCASTING, PUBLISHING *(85)*

84. Jane Lighting chief executive, Five BROADCASTING *(60)*

85. Richard Woolfe director of television, Living TV, Living TV2, Ftn BROADCASTING *(93)*

86. Peter Hill editor, Daily Express PUBLISHING *(87)*

87. Stuart Murphy controller, BBC3 BROADCASTING *(new entry)*

88. Robert Saville partner and creative director, Mother ADVERTISING *(new entry)*

89. Sir Robert Phillis chief executive, Guardian Media Group PUBLISHING, BROADCASTING, NEW MEDIA *(82)*

90. Peter Bennett-Jones chairman, Tiger Aspect Productions and PBJ Management BROADCASTING *(new entry)*

91. David Elstein chairman, Sparrowhawk BROADCASTING *(new entry)*

92. Bob Shennan controller, BBC Radio 5 Live BROADCASTING *(98)*

93. Natalka Znak controller of factual entertainment, Granada BROADCASTING *(new entry)*

94. Nick Robinson political editor, BBC BROADCASTING *(new entry)*

95. Anurag Dikshit founder, group operations director, Partygaming NEW MEDIA *(new entry)*

96. Matthew Freud chairman, Freud Communications PUBLIC RELATIONS *(new entry)*

97. David Chance co-founder, chairman, Top Up TV BROADCASTING *(new entry)*

98. Jeremy Dear general secretary, National Union of Journalists INDUSTRIAL RELATIONS *(new entry)*

99. Holy Moly internet content provider NEW MEDIA *(new entry)*

100. Lord Birt Job: special adviser to No 10 GOVERNMENT *(80)*

The Wharf/ Phil Adams

Sarah Sands (80th)... new editor of Sunday Telegraph

■ Panellists

Lord Alli A member of Labour's "kitchen cabinet", Lord Alli became the youngest peer in parliament aged 34. Co-founder of Big Breakfast and TFI Friday producer Planet 24; chairman of media rights company Chorion.

Emily Bell Editor-in-chief of Guardian Unlimited. Previously worked for the Observer as advertising correspondent, media business editor and finally business editor.

Mark Bolland As deputy private secretary to the Prince of Wales, Bolland was credited for rebuilding his profile after the death of Diana. Voted PR professional of the year four years ago, he quit royal service to set up his own PR company. Former director of the Press Complaints Commission.

Wayne Garvie As the BBC's head of entertainment, Garvie was responsible for rejuvenating BBC1's Saturday-night schedule with its unlikely retro hit, Strictly Come Dancing. A former producer on This Morning, he produced The Krypton Factor and Lily Savage at Granada before switching to the BBC.

Janine Gibson Editor-in-chief of MediaGuardian, Janine Gibson has previously written for the Independent, Broadcast magazine and Televisual magazine. Oversees all of the Guardian's weekday G3 sections – Society, Media, Life and Education.

Jim Hytner Group brand and UK marketing director of Barclays. As marketing chief of ITV he oversaw a £100m facelift for the channel; previously at Five, he developed a reputation for high-profile publicity stunts. He also worked at BSkyB under Sam Chisholm.

Mark Lawson Journalist, broadcaster and author, perhaps best known as presenter of the weekly BBC2 arts show, Newsnight Review. A Guardian columnist since 1995, his last novel, Going Out Live, featured the story of a workaholic talkshow host and anti-hero. His credits include BBC2's The Late Show and Radio 4's Front Row. He has twice been voted TV critic of the year.

Naresh Ramchandani Beginning his copywriting career at a fledgling HHCL in 1990, Naresh Ramchandani's first TV commercial for Maxell won the grand prix at Cannes. In 1995 he became a founding creative director of St Luke's, where he helped to relaunch Boots No7, make Radio 1 credible again and asked the country to chuck out its chintz for Ikea. In 2000 he set up Karmarama.

Janet Street-Porter Janet Street-Porter's career has spanned TV and publishing as editor of the Independent on Sunday, controller of Live TV, head of youth at the BBC and creator of the Bafta-winning Network 7. Now editor-at-large for Independent newspapers, she has appeared on I'm a Celebrity… Get Me Out of Here!.

News media

THE NATIONALS

Britain is famous for the quality, energy and diversity of its national press. According to the Newspaper Marketing Agency, some 85% of UK adults say they read a national paper on a monthly basis; and according to ABCs, between 80 and 90 million national papers are sold each week. But the market is crowded: there are now 10 daily papers and 11 Sundays, as listed in the table on page 14; and over the past few decades, national dailies have lost millions from their circulations under the challenge of competing media. Many of the changes in national papers over the past decades – increased pagination, ever more supplements, price wars and now the "compact" broadsheet – have been efforts to reverse this long-term circulation decline.

About half the daily papers sold in the UK are red-top tabloids: that is, the Sun, the Daily Mirror and the Daily Star. Of these, the Sun is biggest seller. The midmarket tabloids – the Daily Mail and the Daily Express – account for more than a quarter of daily sales: of these, the Mail sells more than twice as many papers as its rival, and outsells the Daily Mirror too. In the quality press, the Independent and the Times are fully tabloid, the Guardian is moving to a "Berliner"-style midsize version in autumn 2005, while the Telegraph and the FT remain broadsheets. The Telegraph leads the market.

The Sunday market is similar. The News of the World leads the popular sales march, far outselling Trinity Mirror's Sunday Mirror and Sunday People, and Richard Desmond's Daily Star Sunday. In the middle market, the Mail on Sunday outstrips the Sunday Express; and the Sunday Times leads broadsheet sales ahead of the Sunday Telegraph, the Observer – which also plans to move to a midsize format in early 2006 – and the Independent on Sunday.

Throughout this chapter, circulation figures for national newspapers exclude bulks (see explainer on ABCs, opposite).

Red-tops

The Sun, Britain's biggest-selling newspaper, celebrated its 40th birthday in September 2004 – but there was not much public celebration. The newspaper's 80s heyday is behind it: these days the newspaper is losing circulation in line with the other red-tops, falling to below 3.3 million for the six months to June 2005, almost 3%. Free online news, and the rise of free papers such as Metro, were blamed for the decline.

In July 2005 the Sun announced 20 editorial job cuts; this after losing

■ Explainer: ABCs

What are ABCs? ABCs are circulation figures published by the Audit Bureau of Circulation, an independent company that monitors and verifies sales of newspapers and magazines.

How often do ABCs come out? National newspaper ABCs are published each month. Regional newspaper and magazine ABCs are published every six months, covering January–June and July–December each year.

What do the ABCs include? The ABC publishes the number of copies of a publication sold at full price and sent to subscribers. They sometimes include "bulks" – copies distributed free to targeted places such as hotels and airlines – but now bulks must be reported by target audience, and the number of "actively purchased" copies is more often considered the headline figure. The figures in this book exclude bulks.

its star columnist in May 2005 when Richard Littlejohn left to join the Daily Mail. The month before, MediaGuardian.co.uk reported that the Sun's political editor, Trevor Kavanagh, would be working on his last general election for the paper. The newspaper had flirted with the Tories and published critical leading articles about Tony Blair – but, ever ready to back a winner, it swung behind Labour in the run-up to the poll.

In June 2005, the Sun showed it had not lost its knack for irreverence and controversy by publishing a photo of the former Iraqi dictator Saddam Hussein in his underpants. The White House and much of the world's press reacted angrily to the picture's publication; while the Sun described it as "an extraordinary iconic news image", lawyers for Saddam threatened to sue.

The Sun was also ready to redress its mistakes of the past: in July 2004 it issued an apology to the people of Liverpool for its coverage of the Hillsborough disaster in 1989 – after Wayne Rooney, then playing for Everton, was criticised for selling his story to the paper.

The Sun's sister paper, the **News of the World**, lost about 170,000 readers, its circulation falling to 3.66 million in the first six months of 2005; but its diet of celebrity sex scoops won it the title of newspaper of the year at the British Press Awards.

Figures might look bad in Wapping, but at the Mirror Group they have been worse. The **Daily Mirror**'s sales, which plunged through the 2 million barrier in 2002, have continued to fall almost every month to date, and for January to June 2005 stood at 1.74 million. Two high-profile journalists left the paper in 2005: the news editor, Chris Boffey, quit in March after he was only offered a two-month contract on the end of his six-month probation at the paper, while 3am girl Jessica Callan announced she was leaving in September to go travelling. In December 2004, it had been announced that the 3am celeb magazine was being axed because it was losing too much money.

The Mirror's editor, Richard Wallace, may have been in the job for more than a year, but the newspaper continues to be reminded of the events of former editor Piers Morgan's reign. In August 2004, Morgan won a £1.7m payoff from the company in compensation for the loss of his job; and then received £1.2m from the Random House imprint Ebury Press to write The Insider, his memoirs of his life in the newspaper industry. Next month, Morgan's former deputy, Des Kelly, won a settlement thought to be worth around £400,000 after suing the paper for unfair dismissal. Then in April 2005, two former Daily Mirror writers – the so-called City Slickers – pleaded not guilty to charges of share-ramping for financial gain; while court proceedings against a reservist suspected of faking photos of Iraqi prisoner abuse, which led to Morgan's sacking, were delayed.

The **Sunday Mirror**'s circulation fell 3% in the 12 months to June 2005, just about keeping its head over the 1.5 million barrier. But it experienced every newspaper's nightmare when, as the presses were running one Sunday morning in April 2005, journalists realised they had identified the wrong man as so-called "Lotto rapist" Iorworth Hoare. Presses were stopped and papers pulped, but thousands of copies had already been distributed to urban areas. Retired security foreman George Ayling, the man it incorrectly identified, won £100,000 in damages and costs.

The circulation of Trinity Mirror's other Sunday paper, the **People**, is in a parlous state. The newspaper lost almost one-tenth of its readers in the

year to June 2005, falling below a million for the first time in its history. The People sells just over 956,000 papers, less than half the number of copies it sold a decade ago. In June 2005, Trinity Mirror said that revenues across its three titles – the Daily Mirror, the Sunday Mirror and the People – were set to fall by 7% in the first six months of the year.

The **Daily Star**, Richard Desmond's red-top, cut its price to 15p for a period in January 2005 – but still lost around 5% of its readers year on year, and was overtaken again by its sister paper the Daily Express. The **Daily Star Sunday** lost more than 14% of its circulation, which fell to just over 440,000.

Quality press

This year it was **The Times**' turn to win plaudits for going tabloid. The newspaper, which had been publishing broadsheet and tabloid editions together, scrapped the broadsheet version on Monday November 1 2004. The plans had been kept secret even from the newspaper's own journalists – who, MediaGuardian reported, had been working on pages for the broadsheet edition as late as the Friday before.

Tabloid Times... boosted circulation

Going fully tabloid gave the paper an immediate circulation boost – up by around 4% in the first month, a trend which continued year-on-year into the first six months of 2005. In December, the paper had overtaken the Daily Telegraph in full-rate sales for the first time, though total sales were still well behind its rival; the Telegraph sells a significant number of papers though reduced-rate subscriptions. But the Times' success came at a cost: combined losses at the Times and the Sunday Times rose more than threefold to £40.1m in the year to March 2005, a reflection of the increased promotion and the job of putting out a newspaper at two different sizes for half the year.

The Times continued to tweak its Saturday supplements, scrapping the Weekend Review and replacing it with a books section, and taking The Knowledge nationwide.

The **Sunday Times** is also reported to be eyeing the benefits of the tabloid format in some of its supplements. Its circulation held steady in the six months to June 2005 at about 1.35 million, a good performance in a declining market.

The **Independent** spent about £6m going tabloid, it was reported in November 2004. Its short-term reward was being named newspaper of the year at the What the Papers Say awards in December; but what the Independent News & Media boss, Tony O'Reilly, really wants is for the newspaper to turn a profit, something he hopes to do by 2006. In spring 2005 the Independent redesigned, switching to a seven-column grid and bringing supplements into the main body of the paper; but there was no change to editor Simon Kelner's stock-in-trade stunt and opinion-led front pages, often left-leaning with an internationalist bent. The paper's circulation reached 225,700 in the six months to June 2005 – up only 0.5% year on year, suggesting that the period of dramatic circulation rises is over. Nevertheless, of all the daily papers, only the two quality tabloids, the Independent and the Times, posted a circulation rise.

The **Independent on Sunday** was thought to be considering a tabloid move back in July 2004; the company chief executive, Ivan Fallon, admitted nine months later that the paper looked "a bit of a fish out of water" as a broadsheet, although circulation slipped only 1% to 172,600. Fallon said the paper would one day become tabloid, but did not say when.

Next paper to change size will be the **Guardian**, which will relaunch

in a midsize format in autumn 2005, roughly when this book goes to press – with its sister paper the **Observer** following suit early in 2006. Carolyn McCall, the chief executive of Guardian Newspapers, said the aim was to "position our papers as the first of a new generation of full-colour national newspapers". The Guardian will also be hoping to reverse a 4.6% circulation decline to 342,000 in the first six months of 2005.

The Guardian's website, Guardian Unlimited, won two online newspaper awards in May 2005. It picked up a coveted Webby for best newspaper on the internet, beating the New York Times, the Washington Post and the Wall Street Journal; and the next week it won the UK-based Newspaper Awards gong for best website for the sixth successive year.

At the Observer, circulation slipped by a couple of percentage points year-on-year to around 415,000; headcount dipped in summer 2005 as 10 staff took voluntary redundancy and a further three jobs were not replaced.

Although the **Daily Telegraph** will soon be the only general news-led daily broadsheet left, life at the Telegraph Group under the Barclay brothers has hardly been quiet – except, perhaps, on the editorial floors. Ninety jobs were lost at the paper in March 2005, of which 15 were sackings and 75 were voluntary redundancies. Among those who left were

National daily circulations

	Editor	Jan–Jun 05	Jan–Jun 04	% change
Popular & midmarket				
Sun	Rebekah Wade	3,268,449	3,365,844	−2.89
Daily Mail	Paul Dacre	2,284,086	2,322,970	−1.67
Daily Mirror	Richard Wallace	1,737,872	1,883,274	−7.72
Daily Express	Peter Hill	867,291	892,388	−2.81
Daily Star	Dawn Neesom	854,344	898,692	−4.93
Quality press				
Daily Telegraph	Martin Newland	861,042	878,030	−1.93
Times	Robert Thomson	641,163	616,706	3.97
Financial Times	Andrew Gowers	397,799	414,377	−4.00
Guardian	Alan Rusbridger	342,039	358,625	−4.62
Independent	Simon Kelner	225,706	224,499	0.54

National Sunday circulations

	Editor	Jan–Jun 05	Jan–Jun 04	% change
Popular & midmarket				
News of the World	Andy Coulson	3,665,944	3,840,584	−4.55
Mail on Sunday	Peter Wright	2,261,407	2,269,271	−0.35
Sunday Mirror	Tina Weaver	1,540,574	1,594,143	−3.36
People	Mark Thomas	956,328	1,029,364	−7.10
Sunday Express	Martin Townsend	892,876	889,973	0.33
Daily Star Sunday	Gareth Morgan	440,824	515,200	−14.44
Quality press				
Sunday Times	John Witherow	1,351,872	1,347,665	0.31
Sunday Telegraph	Sarah Sands	652,492	672,554	−2.98
Observer	Roger Alton	415,526	425,317	−2.30
Independent on Sunday	Tristan Davies	172,463	174,573	−1.21
The Business	Publisher: Andrew Neil	20,007	61,144	−67.28

Source: ABC. All figures exclude bulks

foreign affairs writer Robin Gedye and leader writer Daniel Johnson. They followed the group executive editor, Brenda Haywood, who left in February, and the news editor, Fiona Barton; she joined Associated Newspapers the same month, to be replaced by the features editor, Richard Preston. Arriving at Canary Wharf were Lawrence Sear, who came out of retirement in January to be managing editor; the former Tory press chief Guy Black, who joined as communications boss after the election; and 40 staff from the paper's newly closed City office. The newspaper also closed its media desk, putting the media editor, Tom Leonard, and correspondent Matt Born to work in the newsroom. Circulation slipped a couple of points to 861,000 excluding bulks.

The axe was also wielded in dramatic fashion at the **Sunday Telegraph**, where the editor, Dominic Lawson, was sacked in June after 10 years in the job; circulation had fallen almost 3% to about 652,500 for the six months to June 2005. Lawson was replaced by Sarah Sands, the deputy editor of the daily title, who had made the Saturday section her own. Kim Fletcher, Sands' husband and the Telegraph's editorial director, fell on his sword to avoid any perceived conflict of interest.

Negative headlines continued to follow the former boss of the Telegraph titles, Conrad Black. A Hollinger International investigation, filed with the New York Securities and Exchange Commission in August 2004, accused him and his wife Barbara Amiel of treating the company, then the Telegraph titles' parent company, as if it were their "piggy bank": the report alleged that they ran the company as a "corporate kleptocracy", using its money to fund a £23,000 birthday party menu involving Beluga caviar, lobster ceviche and 69 bottles of fine wine. Black, who resigned in June 2005, faces lawsuits totalling £1bn in the US; he denied the charges in the report.

Life is happier at the **Financial Times** after a judge threw out a City firm's £230.5m libel claim against the newspaper in October (though the case continued for a smaller claim; see media law, page 337, for more on that). The FT broke even in the final quarter of 2004, reducing losses

Awards

to £9m over the course of the year; and its owner, Pearson, said it would break even in 2005 if the advertising upturn continued. Part of the money was saved through cost-cutting: 30 editorial staff members left as a result of a voluntary redundancy scheme announced in February 2005; and the newspaper folded its weekly media section, Creative Business, in December 2004. Instead, it launched an afternoon freesheet for corporate subscribers, FTpm, in April 2005. Circulation was 4% down and fell below 400,000.

Midmarkets

The **Daily Mail** found itself in an unusual position in 2005 – having to deal with a fall in circulation. Sales were 2.28 million in the six months to June 2005, down almost 1.7% on the year before. It was not for the want of investment: the editor, Paul Dacre, was paid £1.16m in 2004, up almost 30% on the £899,000 he earned in 2003; and in November 2004, the Daily Mail & General Trust invested £90m in eight new London presses, enabling it to deliver 128-page editions of the paper with 64 pages of colour.

The newspaper lost two key writers in the past year. In October 2004, Lynda Lee-Potter – the columnist known as "the First Lady of Fleet Street" – died at 69 after suffering a brain tumour. Ross Benson, a war reporter and diarist, died in March 2005 at the age of 56.

The **Mail on Sunday** held its circulation steady, at about 2.26 million for the six months to June 2005.

Cost-cutting measures continued at the **Daily Express** and **Sunday Express**. The daily had increased its pagination towards the end of 2004 in an effort to compete with the Daily Mail, but then reversed that decision; and then in March 2005 it closed the Sunday Express's S2 entertainment supplement. In June and July 2005, the papers' owner, Richard Desmond, announced he was stopping sending bulk copies of both newspapers to hotels, trains and airlines, and closed the Express Newspapers office in Manchester; the Express also endured the embarrassment of having the phone lines cut off at its parliamentary office.

Staff at the newspapers took industrial action in April 2005, when the

I'm sorry, I haven't a Sudoku

A year ago, no one had heard of it: now almost every UK newspaper carries it. Sudoku, a Japanese puzzle created in the 1980s, swept through the British press in 2005 after the Times became the first paper to carry the puzzle.

The puzzle itself is deceptively simple. You are given a nine-by-nine grid, divided into nine three-by-three boxes; and you fill the grid so that every row, column and three-by-three box contains the numbers 1 to 9. You are given a few numbers to start you off; just enough, in fact, to ensure that there is only one possible solution.

Papers took to the publishing the puzzles in different ways. The Sun called its puzzle the "Sun Doku"; the Guardian chose to source its versions from a Japanese publisher who creates them manually rather than computer-generating them; and the Independent launched a competition to find the country's first Sudoku grand master. That was won by Edward Billig, a 23-year-old transcriber from – of all places – Wapping.

NUJ called a mandatory meeting between 4pm and 6pm on a Friday as part of a pay dispute. About 90 journalists joined the meeting, at a nearby wine bar, and rejected a 3.3% pay offer. There was also a row over staff at the Express being asked to file copy to the Daily Star as well.

Further embarrassment came as the Daily Express had to compensate 2,500 readers who were offered a £10 cruise as part of a travel promotion. The promotion, run by travel company MKM, attracted 40,000 readers but a shortage of cabins and a Caribbean hurricane meant not all readers got what they were promised. The newspaper said readers would be offered an alternative cruise, a holiday or a long-haul flight as compensation.

The Daily Express circulation was about 867,600 in the six months to June 2005, down 2.8% on the year before; this was significantly below its 2000 figure and 1.4 million adrift of the Daily Mail. Sunday Express circulation rose very slightly to about 893,000.

The bottom line

Spending on newspaper advertising remained steady. The first quarter of 2005 saw national newspaper spend rise to £521m, according to the Advertising Association – a rise of just 0.1% if inflation is taken into account. This represented a decline of one percentage point in the share of the total advertising market, to about 13%. If all press is taken into account, display advertising rose by 0.8% in real terms, but classified declined by 1.6%.

The PCC

The self-regulatory body for the newspaper industry is the Press Complaints Commission, or PCC: it operates a code of practice by which newspapers agree to abide, and according to which members of the public may complain. According to its annual report, the commission dealt with almost 130 breaches of its privacy code last year, out of a total 3,649 complaints.

Despite recent reforms, some think the PCC does not have enough teeth. The Labour MP, Peter Bradley, launched a private members bill in

Major PCC rulings

- **October 2004:** The PCC rejects a complaint from footballer Rio Ferdinand over a Daily Star article about SMS messages it alleged he sent to fellow celeb Abi Titmuss; no further action was thought necessary because the newspaper had offered to publish Ferdinand's denial.

- **October 2004:** EastEnders star Leslie Grantham has a complaint to the PCC rejected, after reports that the BBC ordered him to have treatment for sex addiction.

- **November 2004:** The publisher of the Spectator, Kimberly Quinn, complains to the PCC that a photograph of her published in the Sunday Mirror intruded into her privacy and had been taken following harassment; but the commission rejects the complaint, saying there was nothing to suggest the photographer had "persisted unduly in his attentions, or had acted in an intimidating fashion".

- **December 2004:** The PCC condemns the Sun for printing a front-page "confession" by the footballer Stan Collymore in which he appeared to admit that he was a liar, saying the paper hadn't made it clear enough that the confession was fiction.

- **March 2005:** The Mail on Sunday is reprimanded for a "flagrant and fundamental breach" of the PCC code after it revealed details about the health of Louise Miliband, wife of minister David Miliband. The details appeared in an article about the couple's recent adoption of a child.

The shrinking world of the red-tops **Peter Preston**

If there's a thin line between love and hate, there's an even thinner one between optimism and pervasive gloom about the future of newspapers. Being too cheerful gets press pundits down.

"It's been an extraordinarily positive year for the global industry," said the director of the World Association of Newspapers, Timothy Balding, opening WAN's Seoul conference the other day. Here was a "renaissance", fuelled by new approaches and better marketing. Total sales around the globe were up year-on-year by 2.1% and the total number of new daily titles by 2%. Advertising revenue had risen 5.3%.

Hail Asian circulations, up 4.1%; South American sales, up 6.3%; Africa with 6%. Praise Indian circulations, up 8% in a year; Indonesia at 6.5%; not to mention Mongolia, posting a steppe-shivering 31% rise. If this is industrial death, we should all be so lucky.

And yet, put down your bugle and pick up the nearest stethoscope. Nothing in printland is ever quite as simple as it seems, and Balding's glummer critics rather relish it that way. For every upside, there's a downside. For every tale of third world readerships rising with increasing education and development, there's one in which first world readers in America and Europe bale out. Exit, pursued by apathy and internet.

Of course, that's true up to a point. US daily sales have dropped 1% in a year and 2.6% over the past five years: EU sales were 0.7% down in 2004 and 0.4% less than they were in 1999. But the most fascinating shifts are between countries rather than continents. Eight EU countries – as opposed to just one in 2003 – saw circulations bounce higher, Poland (at 15.2%),

Portugal (5.8%) and Spain (1.3%) among them.

It wasn't a universal triumph. France, Germany and the Netherlands were big losers, with Ireland, Slovakia, Hungary and Denmark deep in the red column, too. But worst of all? Yes: the UK, down 4.4% on 2003 and a whopping 11.4% over the past five years.

Apparently, something's particularly rotten in the state of Fleet Street. It isn't a Europe-wide affliction, because much of Europe has barely lost anything. It isn't wholly an internet blight, either. Why, if rampant technology is the enemy, are Singapore newspaper sales up 3% and Malaysian up 4%? Why are US circulations, though weakening, actually still much stronger than ours?

No simplicities here, either. The British weekly press, targeting local communities and offering a service beyond individual blogging, isn't suffering any sort of recession: ad revenues and many sales figures are healthy. Quality morning dailies are also a relatively stable sector – down only a couple of points or so and actually up year on year last (election) month by more than 3% as gains on compact conversion broadly balance broadsheet ailments.

The sharpest, longest problems of decay, in fact, exist only in two main sectors. One is evening newspaper production, beset by changing big-city work patterns, traffic congestion and the growth of new media. The other, most cataclysmic of the lot, afflicts our supposedly mass-market red-tops.

This year so far, the red-tops are running around 5% down on 2004 – not so far off a half-million copies gone in 12 months; tens of thousands set with the Sun (which fell again, even in election month) or cracked with the Mirror.

You can, in part, blame the mushroom growth of celebrity and lads' mags. Somebody's stealing the erstwhile emperor's clothes. Add in a youth market losing the reading habit and TV sprouting new channels by the minute and there's trouble looming huge on the horizon.

When WAN's strategic adviser, Jim Chisholm, talked to top people in the regional press recently, he laid out some key principles for sales success. Here are three of them:

- "Circulation winners think and act long-term – they regard circulation growth as the thing that drives every other aspect of success." No short-term gimmicks, no management churn. Think long and play long.

- Believe, too, that "growing circulation delivers profit". Too often the "profitability margin comes in inverse proportion to circulation growth". But you need to sacrifice short-term profits to secure sales stability. And you need to invest. A typical 2.5% of turnover spent on marketing would be laughed out of other industries' boardrooms. "We are a mature market, but we are under-investing in marketing by 50%."

- Then there's "moment of truth" time. "For many circulation winners there was a do-or-die decision that forced them to think differently and radically." See how the Daily Mail came back from the brink of bankruptcy in the 70s. So have the guts to discover your moment of truth now, rather than five years down the road.

These aren't the only keys to the kingdom, of course: but they do jangle loudly when you look at current figures.

Why is Poland soaring upwards on the world table? Because new tabloids, with fresh verve and polish, are expanding the market, reaching audiences nobody has touched before. Why is Spain moving forwards? Because innovation and investment have been relentless through the past 10 years. And you can tell that story over and over again when sales go up.

The immediate problem in Britain is not widespread collapse but sectoral slump. It's Trinity Mirror not quite knowing where to go next with its national titles. It's the Star stuck in a Desmond groove. It's a Sun in growing need of reinvention.

The Mail still piles in marketing and branding cash, the Independent, Times and Guardian change shape, hard-working weeklies try different editions for different villages, evening papers permutate free and paid-for copies in innovative ways and start totally free contenders. (The Evening Standard, with added Lite, is beginning to claim some free plus paid-for total figures that push it way over 400,000 again.)

There is a long view here. There's still belief in an industry with a future worth investing in. Is there nothing equivalent to be done in the red-top world? Seoul's buoyant figuring shows there is always something to be done. The difficulty is finding the fire and invention (and, yes, the prudent optimism) to get on with it.

This article appeared in the Observer on June 12 2005

February calling for the commission to be replaced with a system giving citizens the statutory right to correct significant factual inaccuracies about them in the press. In response, Tim Toulmin, the chairman of the commission, wrote in the Guardian: "The PCC grants no privileges to editors. We are acutely aware that a complainant, who has never been in the media's glare before, may require from us special support and advice in what can be a deeply intimidating situation, confronted by the Goliath of a major newspaper."

Then in July, the Liberal Democrat peer Lord Taverne accused the PCC of acting like a "paper tiger" with regard to newspaper coverage of Maxine Carr, who was given a secret identity after emerging from the jail sentence she had received for lying to protect the Soham murderer, Ian Huntley. Home Office ministers had called a crisis meeting over stories that reported Carr's alleged activities.

The PCC did agree to extend its one-month time limit for people to complain to the commission about stories, promising "more rigorous" controls on newspapers that try to delay the process.

Joining the commission in 2004 and 2005 were the Good House-keeping editor, Lindsay Nicholson, Condé Nast executive Harriet Wilson, and two lay members. They replaced the former Maxim editor Tom Loxley, Arthur Hearnden, James Bishop of the Illustrated London News, and the former chairman, Robert Pinker.

National newspaper ownership

Group name	Market share		Titles	Executive control
	Jan–Jun 05	Jan–Jun 04		
News International	35.0%	34.6%	Sun Times Sunday Times News of the World	Rupert Murdoch
Daily Mail and General Trust	19.7%	19.3%	Daily Mail Mail on Sunday	Lord Rothermere
Trinity Mirror	15.9%	16.6%	Daily Mirror Sunday Mirror People	Victor Blank
Northern and Shell	14.4%	14.5%	Daily Express Daily Star Sunday Express Daily Star Sunday	Richard Desmond
Telegraph Group (& The Business)	7.2%	7.2%	Daily Telegraph Sunday Telegraph The Business	Barclay brothers
Guardian Media Group	3.0%	3.1%	Guardian Observer	Scott Trust
Pearson	2.9%	3.0%	Financial Times	Pearson board
Independent Newspapers	1.9%	1.8%	Independent Independent on Sunday	Tony O'Reilly

THE REGIONALS

Regional newspaper circulations continue to slide alarmingly. Just over 66 million newspapers were sold or distributed in the six months to July 2005, compared with more than 70 million five years before. The problems are most noticeable at the top end of the market: none of the top 20 regional papers posted an increase in circulation in the same period, and most posted significant falls; while none of the top four newspaper groups – Trinity Mirror, Newsquest, the Daily Mail & General Trust and Johnston Press, who together control more than 60% of regional newspaper circulation – increased their circulation either.

The Newspaper Society, which lobbies for the publishers of regional and local papers, argues the case for the regional press. More than 85% of British adults read a regional newspaper, it says; this compares with just 70% who read a national. There are 1,283 regional and local newspapers in the UK, of which about 100 are dailies, 22 Sundays, 530 paid-for weeklies, and 629 free weekly newspapers. But it warns that the BBC's plans to expand into local and regional media – including digital news channels and local websites – could have a damaging effect on the regional press.

It was a busy year for the **Evening Standard**, the London evening title. It had two of the UK's biggest stories in consecutive days in July, with the news that London had won the 2012 Olympic bid, then the tragic reports of the tube and bus bombs that killed 52 people plus four suicide bombers. The paper put up £100,000 as part of a fund for those affected by the tragedy, backed by London's mayor, Ken Livingstone.

But the Standard's relationship with the mayor in 2005 had not always been so constructive. In February, Livingstone attracted accusations of anti-semitism when he likened a Jewish reporter from the newspaper to a "concentration camp guard" for working for the Standard, saying staff at the paper – which is owned by Associated Newspapers, publishers of the Daily Mail – were "a load of scumbags and reactionary bigots". The Commission for Racial Equality and the local government standards board for England and Wales began investigations, and politicians called on Livingstone to apologise; but the most the Standard got was an expression of "regret".

That row came against the background of Livingstone's attempts to break the Standard's exclusive deal to distribute papers in London's tube and rail network. In March, the mayor invited bids to distribute a free afternoon newspaper in stations; and then in April the Office of Fair Trading decided that another paper should indeed be allowed to compete against the Standard in the afternoon and evening (though not in the morning, when Associated distributes early editions of its free paper, Metro). The Express owner, Richard Desmond, and the News International owner, Rupert Murdoch, are thought to be watching the market with interest.

2005 also saw the launch of Standard Lite, a free afternoon paper with a limited distribution. It was thought that the free spin-off might hit the Standard's sales, but in fact its paid-for circulation held steady throughout the spring.

If bosses thought the Standard Lite had no effect on circulation, they couldn't say the same about the Evening Standard's website,

ThisisLondon.com. Up to 10 staff were thought to have left the site in July 2005, as bosses worried that the site was damaging newspaper revenues.

Another newspaper to launch a "lite" edition was the **Manchester Evening News**. The paper, owned by the Guardian Media Group, launched a free evening version in March 2005, to add to the new morning edition it announced in September 2004.

The biggest-selling regional daily was again the tabloid **Daily Record** in Scotland; the paper's circulation slid to 450,000 by June 2005, from above 500,000 18 months before. By contrast, the **Scotsman**, a quality paper that went tabloid in August 2004 – some 170 years after it abandoned the format – has a circulation of just under 70,000. There was an editorial merry-go-round in autumn 2004 when Iain Martin left the Scotsman to become editor of the sister **Scotland on Sunday**, replacing John McLellan who had joined the **Edinburgh Evening News**; he in turn replaced Ian Stewart, who became deputy editor at the Scotsman under its new editor, John McGurk.

At the Sunday Herald, the deputy editor Richard Walker was promoted to the top job in September 2004, after Andrew Jaspan had left to become editor-in-chief of the Melbourne Age.

The bottom line

Advertising revenues continued to hold steady in the regional press, despite declining circulations: the value of the market reached £806m in the first quarter of 2005, up 0.6% in real terms on 2004. The second quarter, however, was hit hard by the ban on government advertising during the general election campaign.

Mergermania came to a halt in the regional newspaper industry in 2004 and 2005. **Archant** was the only group making major acquisitions: it bought 27 papers worth £62m in north London and Kent from the Independent group in 2004, and spent £6.1m in March 2005 for a group of London magazines from Highbury House. Its profits in 2004 rose almost 17% to £32.4m.

Profits were also up at the **Daily Mail & General Trust**, but in June 2005 the newspaper group announced it would be cutting jobs in an effort to save £20m a year after investment in IT and presses.

Johnston Press, so frequently the darling of media investors after a series of acquisitions, continued to perform well: its profits rose 18% –

Top 10 regional publishers			
	Number of papers	Weekly circulation (m)	Share
Trinity Mirror	230	14.4	21.8%
Newsquest	214	10.1	15.3%
Northcliffe Newspapers Group	112	8.6	13.0%
Johnston Press	241	8.1	12.2%
Associated Newspapers	9	6.8	10.3%
Archant	79	2.9	4.4%
Guardian Media Group	43	2.5	3.8%
The Midland News Association	19	2.1	3.2%
Scotsman Publications	7	1.1	1.7%
DC Thomson	3	1.1	1.7%
Top 10	**957**	**57.7**	**87.2%**
All regional publishers	**1,286**	**66.2**	

Data for 1 July 2005

Source: Newspaper Society

although it admitted in 2004 that it would not be acquiring any more newspapers for a while. The group, which owns 244 newspapers including the Yorkshire Post, did hit something of a plateau in 2005, with falling advertising revenues thanks to the general election.

It was **Trinity Mirror** who announced plans to buy more regional newspapers, as it reported a 21% increase in profits to £216.8m – despite what it called a "disappointing" performance by the Daily Mirror. But its regional newspaper boss, Stephen Parker, left the company in July 2004 with a pay-off of around £320,000.

Newsquest, Britain's second largest regional newspaper group, posted improved results in 2004, according to its US owner Gannett. The US company posted record earnings of £753m, a rise of 8.7%.

With rising profits at most companies, **low pay** was a grievance for regional newspaper journalists. The NUJ staged protests in May outside the Newspaper Society's annual lunch at the Savoy Hotel, reminding executives that regional paper journalists often start on a salary of £12,000 or less.

Regional newspaper circulations

	Average net circulation Jul–Dec 2004	% change	Frequency	Editor
Top 20 paid regionals				
Sunday Mail, Scotland	584,671	−5.4	Sunday	Allan Rennie
Sunday Post, Dundee	497,800	−6.1	Sunday	David Pollington
Daily Record, Scotland	478,980	−4.9	morning	Bruce Waddell
Evening Standard, London	361,340	−9.4	evening	Veronica Wadley
West Midlands Express & Star	157,783	−3.5	evening	Adrian Faber
Manchester Evening News	141,737	−7.4	evening	Paul Horrocks
Liverpool Echo	129,681	−4.5	evening	Mark Dickinson
Birmingham Evening Mail	96,143	−10.5	evening	Roger Borrell
Belfast Telegraph	94,540	−8.3	evening	Edmund Curran
Evening Times, Glasgow	91,613	−1.2	evening	Charles McGhee
Newcastle Evening Chronicle	89,074	−0.3	evening	Paul Robertson
Aberdeen Press & Journal	87,858	−2.8	morning	Derek Tucker
Leicester Mercury	84,419	−9.4	evening	Nick Carter
Sunday Life, Belfast	82,850	−4.9	Sunday	Martin Lindsay
Dundee Courier & Advertiser	81,002	−2.5	morning	Arthur Adrian
Scotland on Sunday	80,975	−2.7	Sunday	Iain Martin
Sunday Sun, Newcastle	80,066	−7.3	Sunday	Peter Montellier
Shropshire Star	79,460	−4.1	evening	Sarah Jane Smith
Herald, Glasgow	78,746	n/a	morning	Mark Douglas–Home
Sunday Mercury, Birmingham	75,049	−12.7	Sunday	David Brookes

Source: Newspaper Society, ABC

	Average net circulation Jul–Dec 2004	% change	Frequency	Editor
Top 10 frees				
Metro London	490,434		morning	Kenny Campbell
Manchester Metro News	308,589		weekly	Richard Butt
Nottingham & Long Eaton Topper	208,876		weekly	John Howarth
Nottingham Recorder	154,324		weekly	Graham Glen
The Glaswegian	148,806		weekly	Garry Thomas
Southampton Advertiser*	146,517		weekly	Ian Murray
Herald & Post Edinburgh †	144,968		weekly	Gail Milne
Wirral Globe	134,458		weekly	Leigh Marles
Derby Express	122,847		weekly	Andy Machin
Coventry Observer	120,674		weekly	Mike Green

*Nov 15–Jan 2   † Aug 2–Jan 2

Sources: Newspaper Society, VFD

Making Lite work

You can say what you like about the MEN Lite, says Paul Horrocks, editor of the Manchester Evening News; just don't call it a freesheet.

MEN Lite is the latest in a series of free offshoots of regional and national newspapers launched in 2005, following the success of Associated's morning Metro.

Like the Evening Standard's Standard Lite and the Financial Times' FTpm, the mantra is: make it short, make it free – but make it a quality paper.

"You wouldn't call the morning Metro a freesheet; it's a good newspaper. They've tapped it into a market that wasn't buying newspapers; how can it be wrong for a million people now to be reading the Metro, who weren't reading a paper before? It can't be. The stigmatisation of free is wrong."

The MEN Lite may not have the same amount of content as the paid-for – it largely dispenses with features, comment and analysis – but Horrocks stresses that it is still an edition of the Manchester Evening News.

Taken together with the other editions, the point is to maintain circulation – so important to advertisers – without relying on short-term promotions. The result, he says, could be a solution that addresses the "underlying year-on-year grind of decline" in the regional press.

"We're not convinced yet, and we don't know for sure, but I think we might be on the edge of a longer-term fix than some of the giveaways and promotions we've relied on in the past," he says.

But doesn't giving away a newspaper undermine the paid-for sale? Perhaps. At the Standard – where the strategy is to distribute the Lite at lunchtime – paid-for sales slipped slightly in its first few months, although the finance director, Peter Williams, denied that the free paper was responsible; sales then rose in the aftermath of the London bombings, muddying the picture.

At the Manchester Evening News, which so far circulates 10,000 Lites after 4pm in the city centre (and plans to expand into other areas of the city), Horrocks says a figure of 2% sales lost – what he calls "cannibalisation" – is worst-case.

Against that, he says, are the benefits of being able to offer advertisers a stable circulation.

"The underlying strategy is this. We are now able to say to advertisers: look, we have a portfolio of products. Within that portfolio of web, of TV, of radio, and of print, if you just want the print option and you just want the Manchester Evening News, you will now get a certain number of paid-for topped up by at least 10,000 frees.

"So we guarantee you that you will never fall below 150,000-per-night circulation made up of paid and free. We're offering stability to advertisers – and I think it's that stability that is going to see us through."

It's not been easy getting to this stage. The Manchester Evening News is now available in three paid-for editions – the first at 6am, with overnight printing for the first time – making the newspaper effectively a 24-hour publisher.

But now that the Manchester Evening News has both a free and a paid-for element to its circulation, Horrocks is adamant that that should be reflected in the ABCs.

He is calling for a joint certificate that lists a total distribution figure, broken down to include the circulation of the paid-for and the distribution of the Lite.

"Clearly the Standard, who started this first, will want to drive it in that direction. If other papers join this experiment – and we've had a huge amount of interest in it – then the pressure will become too great."

If the ABC is swayed, then the battle to rid the stigma from free newspapers may already have been won.

The Manchester Evening News is part of Guardian Media Group

MAGAZINES

The magazine market is booming. There are almost 8,500 separate periodical titles in Britain, up almost a quarter over the past decade; about two-thirds are business titles and one-third consumer.

Consumer magazines are leading the march: circulation rose 9% year on year in the six months to December 2004, although ad spend dipped slightly in real terms to £194m.

TV magazines continued to top the newsstand ABCs: What's On TV, published by IPC, remained the number one seller, cutting its price to 35p from 45p to stay on top of the competition. The publisher also spent £10m in spring 2005 on the launch of TV Easy, the first "handbag-sized" paid-for TV guide. Faced with a price war among the cheaper magazines, the BBC put £1m into promoting and redesigning the Radio Times.

Celebrity magazines continued to be the biggest growth area of the market: Now, Heat, Closer and Hello! all grew their circulation in the six months to December 2004. Closer broke though the psychologically important 500,000 barrier; and Natmags launched Reveal, with a combination of real-life stories and celebrity gossip. But OK! lost a vital round of its court battle with Hello! over Catherine Zeta Jones' wedding pictures, when the appeal court ruled it would have to pay back damages to Hello! totalling almost £2m (see media law, page 338).

In women's magazines, the most high-profile launch was Grazia, which reached newsstands in February 2005. The style weekly launched with Jane Bruton, the former editor of Eve, as its editor, and with a £16m budget. In July, it raised its cover price by 20p as circulation topped 150,000. In the six months to June 2005, Good Housekeeping overtook Cosmopolitan in the monthly market to take second place behind Glamour; this after falling to fourth six months before, behind Emap's Yours.

All the attention in the men's market focused on the continued scrap between IPC's Nuts and Emap's Zoo. In July 2004 Nuts had a 90,000 lead over Zoo, with its editor, Phil Hilton, named launch editor of the year at the British Society of Magazine Editors awards. By the end of the year that lead had been cut to 30,000, so in March 2005 Nuts moved its publication day forward two days and cut its cover price to 60p from the usual £1.20. Zoo fought back, adding an 11-page entertainment guide, but the gap grew to just under 45,000 copies in the first six months of 2005.

One casualty of the weeklies' success was IPC's Loaded, which fell to sixth place in the men's market at the end of 2004; but after a £2m spring relaunch and a price cut, it fought back to fourth. In August 2004, Loaded had suffered some embarrassment when it accidentally let a tiny picture of an erect penis slip through a page in its sex industry advertising, causing WHSmith to withdraw it from the shelves. Worse was to come when Tesco said in 2005 it would obscure the front covers of men's magazines with sexually explicit content – including Nuts and Zoo – and place them on higher shelves.

At the news magazines, all eyes were on the Spectator, where the editor, Boris Johnson, had to resign as shadow arts minister after an alleged affair with fellow writer Petronella Wyatt, reports of which he had described as "an inverted pyramid of piffle". That followed the affair between Kimberly Quinn, the magazine's publisher, and the home

Major launches

- February 2005: Grazia (Emap)
  Big-budget glossy monthly
- January 2005: Pick Me Up (IPC)
  Real-life weekly
- October 2004: Reveal (Natmags)
  Glossy/real-life weekly

secretary, David Blunkett; and columnist Rod Liddle's relationship with fellow employee Alicia Monckton, leading commentators to surmise that there was something in the water. Some of the revelations followed Johnson's public apology to the people of Liverpool, after a controversial editorial accusing Liverpudlians of wallowing in "victim status" was published in the wake of the killing of Ken Bigley in Iraq.

The goings-on at the Spectator utterly eclipsed the editorial reshuffle at the left-leaning New Statesman, where John Kampfner replaced Peter Wilby as editor in May 2005. The magazine's deputy editor, Cristina Odone, had quit a few months before.

In the overgrown schoolboy market, Viz celebrated its 25th anniversary in October 2004.

As far as **market moves** were concerned, Future Publishing agreed in April to buy 38 titles from Highbury House – including Fast Car magazine – for £30.5m. The competition commission had ruled out an earlier move for all of Highbury House's magazines. Future also bought Spanish Homes Magazine from husband and wife team Roger and Susan Faulks, who made £1.5m on the magazine a decade after buying it for a "pittance".

BBC Worldwide is waiting to see if the government will force it to sell off more of its magazines. A green paper in March 2005 expressed "concerns" about the BBC's strategy for its magazines unit; for more on the background, see TV, page 142.

Business press

Perhaps two-thirds of magazines in the country are business titles: Brad lists more than 5,300 business magazines that accept advertising, but some estimates say there are as many as 10,000, if every journal and newsletter is taken into account.

The business press depends on advertising for most of its revenue – so it was disappointing to see that ad spend in business magazines fell from £227m to £221m, some 4.3% if inflation is taken into account.

Big news in the business press last year was the sale of Press Gazette, the weekly trade magazine for journalists, from Quantum Business Media to the former Daily Mirror editor, Piers Morgan. One of Morgan's first jobs will be to rescue the reputation of the annual Press Awards, which Press Gazette organises; in 2005 11 newspaper editors withdrew their support from the event after a public row between Bob Geldof and the Mirror editor, Richard Wallace. That followed a punch-up two years ago involving the motoring journalist Jeremy Clarkson and one Piers Morgan.

Quantum also sold Media Week, the weekly magazine for media agencies, ad agencies and marketers, to Haymarket, owners of Campaign, PR Week and Marketing.

Customer magazines

Customer magazines – magazines published on contract for companies, and often distributed free of charge for marketing purposes – are still a growing part of the industry. According to Mintel research for the Association of Publishing Agencies, the sector was worth £344m in 2004, up from £328m in 2003.

In October 2004 John Brown, the founder of John Brown Publishing – which produces the most widely distributed customer title, Sky The Magazine – made a personal £20m from the sale of the company in a £33m management buyout.

Magazine distribution

The magazine industry is facing a shake-up, after the Office of Fair Trading said in February 2005 that it considered its distribution arrangements to be anti-competitive, because publishers deal with only one distributor in a region. Publishers are up in arms, wholesalers are sceptical, and even newsagents reckon it could create a "worst-case scenario", because greater competition might mean less incentive to deliver to remote parts of the country. In July, publishers, wholesalers and retailers met government officials to register their protest.

Top 10s

		Average circulation/issue		
		Jan–Jun 05	Jan–Jun 04	Year-on-year (%)
Top 10 women's weeklies				
1	Take a Break	1,200,397	1,208,473	−0.7
2	Chat	609,163	606,559	0.4
3	Now	591,795	580,007	2.0
4	That's Life	569,631	573,996	−0.8
5	Heat	560,438	540,556	3.7
6	Closer	540,044	480,187	12.5
7	OK!	532,843	553,777	−3.8
8	Pick Me Up	503,950	–	–
9	Woman	485,463	536,364	−9.5
10	Woman's Weekly	425,568	451,690	−5.8
Top 10 women's lifestyle				
1	Glamour	609,626	608,734	0.1
2	Good Housekeeping	475,838	417,893	13.9
3	Cosmopolitan	462,943	456,447	1.4
4	Yours	440,070	413,855	6.3
5	Marie Claire	381,281	380,760	0.1
6	Woman & Home	327,554	303,701	7.9
7	Prima	326,231	330,179	−1.2
8	Candis	319,914	315,803	1.3
9	Company	302,127	325,185	−7.1
10	New Woman	270,686	290,913	−7.0
Top 10 men's lifestyle – including weeklies				
1	FHM	560,167	573,713	−2.4
2	Nuts	304,751	290,337	5.0
3	Zoo	260,317	200,125	30.1
4	Loaded	237,083	235,140	0.8
5	Men's Health	228,108	221,049	3.2
6	Maxim	227,377	227,017	0.2
7	GQ	125,050	124,685	0.3
8	Front	88,154	100,259	−12.1
9	Stuff	77,373	70,230	10.2
10	Bizarre	76,328	87,331	−12.6

*Not in last year's top 10

Top 50 consumer magazines

	Title	Average circulation/issue		Year-on-year (%)
		Jan–Jun 05	Jan–Jun 04	
1	Sky The Magazine	6,783,581	6,600,677	2.8
2	Asda Magazine	2,631,293	2,453,133	7.3
3	Boots Health & Beauty	1,765,387	1,834,270	−3.8
4	What's on TV	1,673,790	1,635,023	2.4
5	The National Trust Magazine	1,655,088	1,573,615	5.2
6	U (Magazine for Unison members)	1,465,833	–	–
7	Saga Magazine	1,245,006	1,244,002	0.1
8	Take a Break	1,200,397	1,208,473	−0.7
9	TV Choice	1,157,622	1,082,654	6.9
10	The Somerfield Magazine	1,134,364	1,130,743	0.3
11	Radio Times	1,080,199	1,104,767	−2.2
12	Eyes Down	984,946	–	–
13	Reader's Digest	776,902	822,780	−5.6
14	Debenhams Desire	745,126	–	–
15	Birds	620,780	616,477	0.7
16	Glamour	609,626	608,734	0.1
17	Chat	609,163	606,559	0.4
18	Now	591,795	580,007	2.0
19	That's Life	569,631	573,996	−0.8
20	Heat	560,438	540,556	3.7
21	FHM	560,167	573,713	−2.4
22	Closer	540,044	480,187	12.5
23	OK!	532,843	553,777	−3.8
24	Pick Me Up	503,950	–	–
25	Woman	485,463	536,364	−9.5
26	Good Housekeeping	475,838	417,893	13.9
27	Cosmopolitan	462,943	456,447	1.4
28	Yours	440,070	413,855	6.3
29	Woman's Weekly	425,568	451,690	−5.8
30	Legion	425,462	456,744	−6.8
31	Woman's Own	424,292	446,194	−4.9
32	TV Times	418,192	473,379	−11.7
33	Emma's Diary Pregnancy Guide	416,140	–	–
34	Homebase Ideas	399,348	447,500	−10.8
35	Best	398,289	401,678	−0.8
36	The Vauxhall Magazine	394,846	422,907	−6.6
37	Auto Exchange	392,598	420,167	−6.6
38	Hello!	392,481	361,225	8.7
39	Bella	389,100	414,984	−6.2
40	Marie Claire	381,281	380,760	0.1
41	New!	373,039	403,864	−7.6
42	Motoring & Leisure	371,940	365,010	1.9
43	People's Friend	363,638	369,430	−1.6
44	National Geographic Magazine	350,253	340,605	2.8
45	The Garden	348,567	332,033	5.0
46	Sainsbury's The Magazine	346,898	280,947	23.5
47	TV Easy	340,018	–	–
48	Unlimited	338,000	330,520	2.3
49	Caravan Club The Magazine	328,305	322,820	1.7
50	Woman & Home	327,554	303,701	7.9

Newsstand titles in bold

Sources: ABC/PPA. Top 50 excludes groups of titles

Further reading

■ Press

MediaGuardian
media.guardian.co.uk/presspublishing
Press Gazette: weekly trade magazine
www.pressgazette.co.uk

■ Books

The Shipping News E ANNIE PROULX, FOURTH ESTATE 1993
The tale of Quoyle, who finds his peace by writing about car crashes
Scoop EVELYN WAUGH, PENGUIN MODERN CLASSICS 1938
Classic Fleet Street satire
In Print: A Career in Journalism CHRIS ALDEN, GUARDIAN BOOKS 2004
Essential guide to a career in newspapers and magazines
The Guardian Stylebook DAVID MARSH AND NIKKI MARSHALL,
GUARDIAN BOOKS 2004
Orwell: The Observer Years GUARDIAN BOOKS 2004
**The Elements of Journalism: What the people should know and what the
public should expect** BILL KOVACH, GUARDIAN BOOKS 2003

■ Film

All The President's Men, 1976
Dustin Hoffman and Robert Redford star as Carl Bernstein and Bob Woodward,
the Washington Post journalists whose investigation into Watergate brought down
the Nixon presidency

■ Web only

World News: newspaper search engine
www.worldnews.com
journalism.co.uk
www.journalism.co.uk

■ Other resources

Audit Bureau of Circulations
www.abc.org.uk
Newspaper Society
www.newspapersoc.org.uk
Periodical Publishers Association
www.ppa.org.uk
Association of Publishing Agencies
www.apa.co.uk

British magazines go global **Tim Burrowes**

With the UK magazine market so viciously competitive, little wonder the products that survive the Darwinian process often go on to be world-beaters too.

And in 2005, the process accelerated like never before, with UK publishers throwing themselves into the international market.

The bravest have gone into new markets and launched editions themselves. Others license their brands to local partners, while the safest route of all is to simply syndicate content.

Perhaps because every day sees more than three million travellers enter a new country, familiar brands tend to do well in new places.

The economic benefits for both sides are clear. For UK-based publishers, licensing is virtually free money for content that has already been produced. And for local publishers, they get to offer readers high production values that will stand out against under-resourced local products.

Among the most successful of expansions has been the UK brand FHM, published by Emap. With well over 20 editions around the world, from Taiwan to Germany to South Africa to China, the cocktail of babes and laddish fun has blown away local competitors. Almost the only market where it is struggling to take off is Estonia.

One of the few markets identified by Emap as unsuitable for FHM is the Middle East, where cultural sensitivities are such that a local version of the magazine would be virtually unrecognisable compared to its racy international sibling.

Yet the Middle East, with its fast-growing but undeveloped media market, has been a major target for international editions.

Throughout the year, there was a steady trickle of UK-inspired launches. Consumer titles from the UK market like OK!, Hello!, Grazia – originally Italian but reinvented in the UK – and Time Out all either launched, increased frequency or spun off further local language editions during the year.

The region also saw one of the first international spin-offs of a UK trade title, with the launch of Campaign Middle East, in opposition to a monthly title that takes content from the US-based Advertising Age. Campaign's UK-based owner Haymarket has also successfully licensed the magazine to Romania.

But geographically, the hottest action has been occurring in China, with its billion-plus population and fast growing economy. With barriers coming down, publishers have been quick to spot the potential.

As FHM publishing director James Carter told Media Week during 2005: "There are about 100 million adults out of that billion that could afford to read and are in the right demographic for FHM. A similar market position in China to the one we have in the UK would mean selling a million copies." That's worth taking seriously.

Dennis Publishing was also getting ready to take on the Chinese market with its men's title Maxim, which took the US by storm when it came across from the UK. The Week is another Dennis title that is successfully building an audience in the US.

BBC Worldwide's Top Gear magazine is yet another that has looked east, with a title that is understood to have been a successful launch in China.

And Emap clearly believes its weekly title Zoo will offer further fuel for foreign growth, with senior staff, including former editor Paul Merrill, working on its international development and an early launch in Spain.

The growth is just as big in the women's glossy market. InStyle, published in the UK by IPC, is in around 10 international markets. The handbag-sized Glamour, launched in the UK and already massive in the US, is another seeing success in European markets.

And Bath-based Future shows that for UK publishers, international growth means serious cash. The company has 144 licensees in 41 different countries; 15% of the company's revenues and 40% of its profits come from its exports. With figures like those, UK magazines are worldwide big business.

Tim Burrowes is the editor of Campaign Middle East

National press Contacts

National daily newspapers

Daily Express
Express Newspapers
The Northern & Shell Building
Number 10 Lower Thames Street
London EC3R 6EN
0871 434 1010
www.express.co.uk
firstname.surname@express.co.uk
Editor: Peter Hill

- *Deputy editor: Hugh Whittow; news: Greg Swift; political: Patrick O'Flynn*
- *Section editors – city: Stephen Kahn; comment: Laura Kibby; defence: John Ingham; features: Fergus Kelly; foreign: Gabriel Milland; health: Victoria Fletcher; money: Holly Thomas; showbiz: Mark Jagasia; sport: Bill Bradshaw; transport: John Ingham; TV: Charlotte Civil*
- *Production editor: Bob Smith; chief sub: Keith Ging*

Daily Mail
Associated Newspapers
Northcliffe House, 2 Derry Street
Kensington, London W8 5TT
020 7938 6000
www.dailymail.co.uk
firstname.surname@dailymail.co.uk
Editor: Paul Dacre

- *Deputy editor: Alistair Sinclair; news: Tony Gallagher; political: Ben Brogan*
- *Sections – city: Alex Brummer; diplomatic: Rebecca English; diary: Richard Kay; features: Leaf Kalfayan; Money Mail: Tony Hazell; showbiz: Nicole Lampert; sport: Tim Jotischky; transport: Ray Massey*
- *Correspondents – consumer affairs: Sean Poulter; education: Sarah Harris; health: Jenny Hope; industry: Becky Barrow; political: James Chapman, Graeme Wilson; social affairs: Steve Doughty*
- *Production editor: Harbans Baga; chief subs: Matthew Gocher (news); Robin Popham (features)*
- *Publicity: Charles Garside, 020 7938 6000*

Daily Mirror
MGN, One Canada Square
Canary Wharf, London E14 5AP
020 7293 3000
www.mirror.co.uk
firstname.surname@mirror.co.uk
Editor: Richard Wallace

- *Deputy editor: Conor Hanna; news: Anthony Harwood; political: Oonagh Blackman. Group political editor: David Seymour*
- *Sections – business: Clinton Manning; consumer: Ruki Sayid; fashion: Amber Graafland; features: Matt Kelly; foreign: Mark Ellis; health: Caroline Jones; money: John Husband; sport: Dean Morse; TV: Nicola Methven*
- *Executive editor (production): Jon Moorhead; chief news sub: Pratima Sarwate; chief features sub: James Rettie; assistant editor (pictures): Ian Down; picture editor: Greg Bennett*
- *Publicity: Sarah Vaughan-Brown, 020 7293 3222*

Daily Sport
Sport Newspapers
19 Great Ancoats Street
Manchester M60 4BT
0161 236 4466
www.dailysport.net
firstname.surname@ sportsnewspapers.co.uk

- *Publicity: Jane Field, 0161 238 8135*

Daily Star
Express Newspapers
The Northern & Shell Building
Number 10 Lower Thames Street
London EC3R 6EN
0871 434 1010
www.dailystar.co.uk
firstname.surname@dailystar.co.uk
Editor: Dawn Neesom

- *Deputy editor: Jim Mansell; news: Kieron Saunders; political: Macer Hall; features: Samantha Taylor; sport: Howard Wheatcroft; Cashpoint: Michelle Carter*
- *Production editor: Bob Hadfield*

Daily Telegraph
Telegraph Group
1 Canada Square, Canary Wharf
London E14 5DT
020 7538 5000
www.telegraph.co.uk
firstname.surname@telegraph.co.uk
Editor: Martin Newland

- *News: Richard Preston; political: George Jones; home affairs: Philip Johnston; managing editor: Sue Ryan; executive editor: Neil Darbyshire; night editor: David Lucas*
- *Sections – arts: Sarah Crompton; city: TBA; diplomatic: Anton La Guardia; fashion: Clare Coulson; features: Rachel Simhon; foreign: Alan Philps; health: Celia Hall; legal: Joshua Rozenberg; literary: Sam Leith; money: Ian Cowie; science: Roger Highfield; sport: Keith Perry; Weekend: Jon Stock*
- *Production editor: Steve Greaves*
- *Publicity: Danielle Howe, 020 7528 6263*

Financial Times
The Financial Times Group
1 Southwark Bridge
London SE1 9HL
020 7873 3000
www.ft.com
firstname.surname@ft.com
Editor: Andrew Gowers

- *Deputy editor: Chrystia Freeland; news: Tracy Corrigan, Deborah Hargreaves; political: James Blitz*
- *Sections – Saturday edition: Michael Skapinker; Asia edition: John Ridding; FT magazine: Graham Watts; Europe: John Thornhill; comment: Brian Groom; public policy: Nicholas Timmins*
- *Production editors: Ken Tough (day), Andy Anderson (operations); night UK news editor: Jeremy Hart*
- *Director of communications/PR: Jo Manning-Cooper; PR manager: Lucy Ellison*

The Guardian
Guardian Newspapers Limited
119 Farringdon Road
London EC1R 3ER
020 7278 2332
www.guardian.co.uk
firstname.surname@guardian.co.uk
Editor: Alan Rusbridger

- *Deputy editor: Georgina Henry; deputy editor (news): Paul Johnson; home affairs: Alan Travis; home news: Ed Pilkington, Andrew Culf; political: Michael White*
- Sections - *arts: Charlie English (Friday Review: Merope Mills); books: Claire Armitstead; city: Julia Finch; economics: Larry Elliott; education: Will Woodward; environment: John Vidal; features: Ian Katz; foreign: Harriet Sherwood; health: Sarah Boseley; media: Matt Wells; northern: Martin Wainright; obituaries: Phil Osborne; regional affairs: Peter Hetherington; social affairs: John Carvel; sport: Ben Clissit; travel: Andy Pietrasik; Weekend magazine: Katharine Viner; women's page: Clare Margetson*
- *Assistant editor (production): David Marsh; production editor, G2: Paul Howlett; production editor, Weekend: Bill Mann; chief sub, city: Rob Firth*
- *Publicity: Anna Sinfield, 020 7239 9818*

The Independent
Independent News and Media (UK)
Independent House, 191 Marsh Wall
London E14 9RS
020 7005 2000
www.independent.co.uk
firstletter.surname@independent.co.uk
firstname.surname@independent.co.uk
Editor-in-chief: Simon Kelner

- *Deputy editor: Ian Birrell; news: Danny Groom; political: Andrew Grice*
- Sections - *city: Jeremy Warner; diplomatic: Ann Penketh; education: Richard Garner; environment: Michael McCarthy; features: Adam Lee; foreign: Leonard Doyle; health: Jeremy Laurance; labour: Barrie Clement; media: Ian Burrell; science: Steve Connor; sport: Matt Tench; transport: Barrie Clement*
- *Production editor: Carl Reader*
- *Marketing manager: David Greene, 020 7005 2000*

The Sun
News Group Newspapers
1 Virginia St, London E98 1SN
020 7782 4000
www.thesun.co.uk
firstname.surname@the-sun.co.uk
Editor: Rebekah Wade

- *Deputy editor: Fergus Shanahan; executive editor: Chris Roycroft-Davis; managing editor: Graham Dudman; political: Trevor Kavanagh (deputy: George Pascoe-Watson, Whitehall: David Wooding); news: Christopher Pharo; chief reporter: John Kay*
- Sections - *Bizarre: Victoria Newton; business: Ian King; crime: Mike Sullivan; defence: Tom Newton Dunn; features: Dominic Mohan; motoring: Ken Gibson; sport: Steve Waring; Sun Woman: Sharon Hendry; TV: Sara Nathan*
- *Chief editorial production editor: Mike Fairbairn; chief sub, news: Jim Holgate*
- *Publicity: Lorna Carmichael, 020 7782 5000*

The Times
Times Newspapers
1 Pennington St, London E98 1TT
020 7782 5000
www.timesonline.co.uk
firstname.surname@thetimes.co.uk
Editor: Robert Thomson

- *Deputy editor: Ben Preston; home: John Wellman; home news: Oliver Wright; political: Philip Webster (deputy: Rosemary Bennett; assistant: Peter Riddell); Washington correspondent: Tom Baldwin; Whitehall: Jill Sherman; chief political corr: David Charter*
- Sections - *business: Patience Wheatcroft; comment: Daniel Finkelstein; countryside: Valerie Elliott; diplomatic: Richard Beeston; education: Tony Halpin; features: Michael Harvey; financial: Graham Searjeant; foreign: Bronwen Maddox; health: Nigel Hawkes; money: Anne Ashworth; sport: Tim Hallissey*
- *Executive editors/chief subs: Chris McKane, Simon Pearson*
- *Communications director: Anoushka Healy, 020 7782 5000*

National Sunday newspapers

The Business
PA News Centre
292 Vauxhall Bridge Road
London SW1V 1AE
020 7961 0000
www.thebusinessonline.com
firstinitialsurname@thebusiness.press.net
Also published on Monday
Publisher and editor-in-chief: Andrew Neil; editor: Ian Watson

- *Deputy editor: Allister Heath*
- Sections - *Economics: Allister Heath; media and retail: Rupert Steiner; technology: Tony Glover; transport (and chief reporter): Tracey Boles; utilities and energy: Richard Orange*
- *Production: Graham Penn; chief sub: Phil Swift*

Daily Star Sunday
Express Newspapers
The Northern & Shell Building
Number 10 Lower Thames Street
London EC3R 6EN
0871 434 1010
www.megastar.co.uk
firstname.surname@dailystar.co.uk
Editor: Gareth Morgan

- *Deputy editor: David Harbord; news: Michael Booker; political: Macer Hall*
- Sections - *Features: Victoria Lissaman; sport: Ray Ansbro*
- *Chief sub: Mike Woods; picture editor: Tomassina Brittain*

The Independent on Sunday
Independent News and Media (UK)
Independent House, 191 Marsh Wall
London E14 9RS
020 7005 2000
www.independent.co.uk
initial.surname@independent.co.uk
Editor: Tristan Davies

- *Deputy editor: Michael Williams; political: Andy McSmith (deputy: Francis Elliott)*
- Sections - *education: Richard Garner; environment: Geoffrey Lean; features: Nick Coleman; sport: Neil Morton; travel: Kate Simon; women's: Elizabeth Heathcote*
- *Production editor: Keith Howitt*
- *Marketing manager: Jonathan Grogan, 020 7005 2000*

The Mail on Sunday

Associated Newspapers
Northcliffe House, 2 Derry Street
Kensington, London W8 5TT
020 7938 6000
www.mailonsunday.co.uk
firstname.surname@
    mailonsunday.co.uk
Editor: Peter Wright

- *Deputy editor: Rod Gilchrist; news: Sebastian Hamilton; home affairs: Christopher Leake; political: Simon Walters*
- *Sections – education: Glen Owen; defence: Christopher Leake; environment: Jo Knowsley; features: Sian James; showbusiness: Katie Nicholl; sport: Malcolm Vallerius*
- *Production editor: Tim Smith; executive production editors: Nic Petkovic, Derek Whitfield*
- *Managing editor: John Wellington, 020 7938 7015*

News of the World

News Group Newspapers
1 Virginia St, London E98 1NW
020 7782 4000
www.thenewsoftheworld.co.uk
firstname.surname@notw.co.uk
Editor: Andy Coulson

- *Deputy editor: Neil Wallis; news: James Weatherup; assistant editor (news): Ian Edmondson; political: Ian Kirby; investigations: Mazher Mahmood; senior associate editor: Harry Scott*
- *Production editor: Richard Rushworth*
- *Publicity: Hayley Barlow, 020 7782 4529*

The Observer

Guardian Newspapers Limited
3–7 Herbal Hill
London EC1R 5EJ
020 7278 2332
www.observer.guardian.co.uk
firstname.surname@observer.co.uk
Editor: Roger Alton

- *Deputy editors: John Mulholland, Paul Webster; executive editor, news: Kamal Ahmed; political: Gaby Hinsliff*
- *Sections – arts: Sarah Donaldson; books: Robert McCrum; business: Frank Kane; comment: Barbara Gunnell; foreign affairs: Peter Beaumont; health: Jo Revill; media: Vanessa Thorpe; money: Jill Insley; Observer Food Monthly: Nicola Jeal; Observer Music Monthly: Caspar Llewellyn Smith; Observer Sport Monthly: Jason Cowley; public affairs: Antony Barnett; Review: Jane Ferguson; social affairs: Jamie Doward; sport: Brian Oliver*
- *Production editor: Bob Poulton; chief news sub: David Pearson*
- *Publicity: Diane Heath, 020 7239 9936*

The People

MGN, One Canada Square
Canary Wharf, London E14 5AP
020 7293 3000
www.people.co.uk
firstname.surname@people.co.uk
Editor: Mark Thomas

- *Deputy editor: Alan Edwards; news: Ben Proctor; associate news editor: David Jeffs; political: Nigel Nelson*
- *Features: Chris Bucktin; investigations: Roger Insall; showbiz: Debbie Manley; sport: Lee Horton*
- *Chief sub: Trisha Harbord; night editor: Matt Clarke; picture editor: Paula Derry*
- *Publicity: Sarah Vaughan-Brown, 020 7293 3222*

The Sunday Express

Express Newspapers
The Northern & Shell Building
Number 10 Lower Thames Street
London EC3R 6EN
0871 434 1010
www.express.co.uk
firstname.surname@express.co.uk
Editor: Martin Townsend

- *Deputy editor: Richard Dismore; news: James Murray; political: Julia Hartley-Brewer*
- *Sections – arts: Rachel Jane; business: Lawrie Holmes; crime: Andrea Perry; defence & diplomatic: Kirsty Buchanan; environment: Stuart Winter; features: Giulia Rhodes; health: Hilary Douglas; royal: Keith Perry; sport: Scott Wilson; travel: Jane Memmler*
- *Night editor: Andy Hoban; assistant night editor (features): Stuart Kershaw; chief news sub: Keith Ging*

Sunday Mirror

MGN, One Canada Square
Canary Wharf, London E14 5AP
020 7293 3000
www.sundaymirror.co.uk
firstname.surname@sundaymirror.co.uk
Editor: Tina Weaver

- *Deputy editor: James Scott; associate editor: Mike Small; assistant editor (news): Nick Buckley; news: James Saville; political: Paul Gilfeather; chief reporter: Euan Stretch*
- *Sections – features: Nicky Dawson; investigations: Graham Johnson; show business: Ben Todd; sport: David Walker*
- *Chief subs: Brian Hancill (news and features); Phil Davies (sport). Picture editor: Mike Sharp*
- *Publicity: Sarah Vaughan-Brown, 020 7293 3222*

Sunday Sport

Sport Newspapers
19 Great Ancoats St
Manchester M60 4BT
0161 236 4466
www.sundaysport.com
Editor: Paul Carter

- *News editor: Jane Field; features: John Warburton; sports: Mark Smith*

The Sunday Telegraph

Telegraph Group, 1 Canada Square
Canary Wharf, London E14 5DT
020 7538 5000
www.telegraph.co.uk
firstname.surname@telegraph.co.uk
Editor: Sarah Sands

- *Deputy editor: Matthew d'Ancona; news: Richard Ellis; political: Patrick Hennessy*
- *Sections – city: Robert Peston; foreign: Topaz Amoore; Review: Susannah Herbert; sport: Jon Ryan*
- *Publicity: Danielle Howe, 020 7538 6263*

The Sunday Times

Times Newspapers
1 Pennington St, London E98 1ST
020 7782 5000
www.sunday-times.co.uk
firstname.surname@
    sunday-times.co.uk
Editor: John Witherow

- *Deputy editor: Martin Ivens; managing editor: Richard Caseby; news: Nick Hellen; associate editor: Bob Tyrer; managing editor, news: Charles Hymas; political: David Cracknell (deputy: Andrew Porter)*
- *Sections – arts: Richard Brooks; books: Caroline Gascoigne; business: Will Lewis; city: Richard Fletcher; culture: Helen Hawkins; driving: Nick Rufford; Doors: David Johnson; economics: David Smith; financial editor: Paul Durman; Focus: Paul Nuki; foreign: Sean Ryan; home: Carey Scott; home affairs: David Leppard; Insight: Jonathan Culvert; Ireland: Fiona McHugh; medical: Lois Rogers; money: Bill Kay; News Review: Mark Skipworth; science: Jonathan Leake; Scotland: Les Snowdon; sport: Alex Butler; Sunday Times Magazine: Robin Morgan; Style: Tiffanie Darke; travel: Christine Walker; TV: David Hutcheon.*
- *Managing editor (production): Ian Coxon; chief subs: David Paton; Denise Boutall (arts and leisure); Arnis Biezais (business)*
- *Publicity: Sophie Bickford*

Regional press Contacts

Main publishers

Archant
Prospect House, Rouen Road
Norwich NR1 1RE
01603 772803
www.archant.co.uk
Chairman: Richard Jewson;
chief executive: John Fry; corporate
communications manager: Keith
Morris, 01603 772814
Archant Regional
01603 772824
MD: Nigel Websper

Daily Mail & General Trust
Northcliffe House, 2 Derry Street
London W8 5TT
020 7938 6000
www.dmgt.co.uk
Chairman: Viscount Rothermere;
chief executive: CJF Sinclair
Associated Newspapers
Northcliffe House, 2 Derry Street
London W8 5TT
020 7938 6000
www.associatednewspapers.co.uk
MD: Kevin Beatty;
editor-in-chief: Paul Dacre
Northcliffe Newspapers Group
31–32 John St, London WC1N 2QB
020 7400 1100
www.nng.co.uk
MD: Michael Pelosi

DC Thomson
185 Fleet St, London EC4A 2HS
020 7400 1030
www.dcthomson.co.uk

Guardian Media Group
75 Farringdon Road
London EC1M 3JY
020 7713 4452
www.gmgplc.co.uk
Chairman: Paul Myners;
CEO, regionals: Ian Ashcroft

Independent News and Media
Independent House
2023 Bianconi Avenue
Citywest Business Campus
Naas Road, Dublin 24, Ireland
00 353 1 466 3200
www.inmplc.com
Chief executive: Sir Anthony O'Reilly;
CEO, Ireland: Vincent Crowley;
CEO, UK: Ivan Fallon

Johnston Press
53 Manor Place
Edinburgh EH3 7EG
0131 225 3361
www.johnstonpress.co.uk
Non-executive chairman: Roger Parry;
CEO: Tim Bowdler

Midland News Association/
Express & Star
51–53 Queen St
Wolverhampton WV1 1ES
01902 313131
www.mna-insite.co.uk
www.expressandstar.com

Newsquest Media
58 Church Street, Weybridge
Surrey KT13 8DP
01932 821212
www.newsquest.co.uk
Chairman and chief executive: Paul
Davidson

Scotsman Publications
Barclay House, 108 Holyrood Road
Edinburgh EH8 8AS
0131 620 8620
www.scotsman.com
Publisher: Andrew Neil;
MD: Steven Walker

Trinity Mirror
One Canada Square, Canary Wharf
London E14 5AP
020 7293 3000
www.trinitymirror.com
Chairman: Sir Victor Blank;
chief executive: Sly Bailey

Regional newspapers – England

Major paid-for regionals

The Argus (Brighton)
Argus House, Crowhurst Road
Hollingbury, Brighton BN1 8AR
01273 544544
www.theargus.co.uk
Daily. Owner: Newsquest. Editor:
Michael Beard; news: Melanie
Dowding; night news editor: David
Wells; features: Jacqui Phillips;
production: Chris Heath

Birmingham Evening Mail
PO Box 78, Weaman St, Birmingham
West Midlands B4 6AY
0121 236 3366
www.icbirmingham.co.uk
Daily. Owner: Trinity Mirror. Editor:
Steve Dyson; news: Andy Richards;
features: Alison Handley

Blackpool Gazette & Herald
Avroe House, Avroe Crescent
Blackpool Business Park
Blackpool FY4 2DP
01253 400888
www.blackpoolonline.co.uk
Daily. Owner: Johnston Press.
Editor: David Halliwell; news: James
Higgins; features: Paul McKenzie; chief
sub: Linda Chatburn

Bolton Evening News
Newspaper House, 1 Churchgate
Bolton, Lancs BL1 1DE
01204 522345
www.thisisbolton.co.uk
Daily. Owner: Newsquest. Editor-in-
chief: Steve Hughes; news: James
Higgins; features: Andrew Mosley;
production: John Bird

Bristol Evening Post
Temple Way, Bristol BS99 7HD
0117 934 3000
www.thisisbristol.co.uk
Daily. Owner: Northcliffe Newspapers.
Editor: Mike Norton; news: Kevan
Blackadder; features: Bill Davis; chief
sub: Helen Lawrence

Coventry Evening Telegraph
Corporation St, Coventry CV1 1FP
024 7663 3633
www.iccoventry.co.uk
Daily. Owner: Trinity Mirror. Editor:
Alan Kirby; news: John West; features:
Steven Chilton; head of production:
Barry Mathew

Daily Echo
Richmond Hill
Bournemouth BH2 6HH
01202 554601
www.thisisbournemouth.co.uk
Daily. Owner: Newsquest. Editor: Neal
Butterworth; news: Andy Martin;
features: Kevin Nash

Derby Evening Telegraph
Northcliffe House, Meadow Rd
Derby, Derbyshire DE1 2DW
01332 291111
www.thisisderbyshire.co.uk
Daily. Owner: Northcliffe Newspapers.
Editor: Steve Hall; news: Nicola
Hodgson; features: Cheryl Hague; chief
sub: Peter Pheasant

East Anglian Daily Times
Press House, 30 Lower Brook Street
Ipswich IP4 1AN
01473 230023
www.eadt.co.uk
Daily. Owner: Archant. Editor: Terry
Hunt; news: Aynsley Davidson;
features: Julian Ford

Eastern Daily Press
Prospect House, Rouen Road
Norwich NR1 1RE
01603 628311
www.edp24.co.uk
Daily. Owner: Archant. Editor: Peter
Franzen; deputy editor: James Ruddy

Evening Chronicle (Newcastle)
Groat Market
Newcastle Upon Tyne NE1 1ED
0191 232 7500
www.icnewcastle.co.uk
Daily. Owner: Trinity Mirror. Editor:
Paul Robertson; news: John Howe;
features: Jennifer Bradbury; chief sub:
Beverley Pearson

Evening Gazette
Borough Road
Middlesbrough TS1 3AZ
01642 234227
www.icteesside.co.uk
Daily. Owner: Gazette Media Company
(Trinity Mirror). Editor: Darren
Thwaites; news: Jim Horsley; acting
features: Barbara Argument

Evening Standard
Northcliffe House, 2 Derry Street
London W8 5TT
020 7938 6000
www.thisislondon.co.uk
Daily. Owner: Associated Newspapers.
Editor: Veronica Wadley; news: Ian
Walker; features: Simon Davies

Express & Star
51–53 Queen St, Wolverhampton
West Midlands WV1 1ES
01902 313131
www.expressandstar.com
Daily. Owner: Midland News
Association. Editor: Adrian Faber;
news: Mark Drew; features: Dylan
Evans; chief sub: Tony Reynolds

Hull Daily Mail
Blundell's Corner, Beverley Road
Hull HU3 1XS
01482 327111
www.hulldailymail.co.uk
Daily. Owner: Northcliffe Newspapers.
Editor: John Meehan; news: Jeremy
Deacon; deputy news editor: Paul
Baxter; features: Paul Johnson; chief
sub: Daniel Urben

The Journal (Newcastle)
Groat Market
Newcastle Upon Tyne NE1 1ED
0191 201 6230
www.thejournal.co.uk
Daily. Owner: Newcastle Chronicle &
Journal (Trinity Mirror).
Editor: Brian Aitken; night editor:
Richard Kirkman; news: Matt
McKenzie; features: Jane Hall

Lancashire Evening Post
Oliver's Place, Preston PR2 9ZA
01772 838103
www.prestontoday.net
Daily. Owner: Johnston Press.
Editor: Simon Reynolds

Lancashire Evening Telegraph
1 High Street, Blackburn
Lancashire BB1 1HT
01254 298220
www.thisislancashire.co.uk
Daily. Owner: Newsquest.
Editor-in-chief: Kevin Young; news:
Andrew Turner; features: John Anson

Leicester Mercury
St George St, Leicester LE1 9FQ
0116 251 2512
www.thisisleicestershire.co.uk
Daily. Owner: Northcliffe Newspapers.
Editor: Nick Carter; news: Mark
Charlton; features: Alex Dawson

Liverpool Daily Post
Old Hall St, Liverpool L6 9JQ
0151 227 2000
www.icliverpool.co.uk
Daily. Owner: Trinity Mirror. Acting
editor: Rob Irvine; news: Greg Fray

Liverpool Echo
Old Hall St, Liverpool L6 9JQ
0151 227 2000
www.icliverpool.co.uk
Daily. Owner: Trinity Mirror. Editor:
Alastair Machray; news: Alison Gow

Manchester Evening News
164 Deansgate
Manchester M3 3RN
0161 832 7200
www.manchesteronline.co.uk
Daily. Owner: Guardian Media Group.
Editor: Paul Horrocks; news: Ian Woods;
deputy features editor:John Whittaker

The News (Portsmouth)
Portsmouth Publishing & Printing
The News Centre, London Rd
Hilsea, Portsmouth
Hampshire PO2 9SX
023 9266 4488
www.portsmouth.co.uk
Daily. Owner: Johnston Press.
Editor: Mike Gilson; news: Colin
McNeill; features: John Millard

Northern Echo (Darlington & South West Durham)
Priestgate, Darlington
County Durham DL1 1NF
01325 381313
www.thisisthenortheast.co.uk
Daily. Owner: Newsquest. Editor: Peter
Barron; news: Nigel Burton; features:
Nick Morrison; chief sub: Dave Horsley

Nottingham Evening Post
Castle Wharf House
Nottingham NG1 7EU
0115 948 2000
www.thisisnottingham.co.uk
Daily. Owner: Northcliffe Newspapers.
Editor: Graham Glen; news: Claire
Catlow; features: Jeremy Lewis

Plymouth Evening Herald
17 Brest Road
Derriford Business Park
Plymouth PL6 5AA
01752 765529
www.thisisplymouth.co.uk
Daily. Owner: Northcliffe Newspapers.
Editor: Alan Qualtrough; news: James
Garnett; features: Mike Bramhall

The Sentinel (Stoke-on-Trent)
Staffordshire Sentinel Newspapers
Sentinel House, Etruria
Stoke-on-Trent ST1 5SS
01782 602525
www.thesentinel.co.uk
Daily. Owner: Northcliffe Newspapers.
Editor: Sean Dooley; news: Robert
Cotterill; features: Charlotte Little-
Jones; chief sub: Chris Smith

Shropshire Star
Shropshire Newspapers, Ketley
Telford, Shropshire TF1 5HU
01952 242424
www.shropshirestar.com
Daily. Owner: Midland News
Association. Editor: Sarah Jane Smith;
news: John Simcock; features: Carl Jones

Southern Daily Echo
Newspaper House, Test Lane
Redbridge, Southampton SO16 9JX
023 8042 4777
www.dailyecho.co.uk
Daily. Owner: Newsquest.
Editor: Ian Murray; news: Gordon
Sutter; chief sub: Colin Jenkins

The Star (Sheffield)
York Street, Sheffield
South Yorkshire S1 1PU
0114 276 7676
www.sheffieldtoday.net
Daily. Owner: Johnston Press.
Editor: Alan Powell; news: Bob
Westerdale; features: John Highfield;
head of content: Paul License

Sunday Mercury
Weaman St, Birmingham
West Midlands B4 6AT
0121 236 3366
www.icbirmingham.co.uk
Sunday. Owner: Trinity Mirror.
Editor: David Brookes; deputy: Paul
Cole; news: Tony Larner

Sunday Sun (Newcastle)
Groat Market
Newcastle upon Tyne NE1 1ED
0191 232 7500
www.icnewcastle.co.uk
Sunday. Owner: Trinity Mirror.
Editor: Peter Montellier; news: Mike
Kelly; production: Colin Patterson;
chief sub: Lesley Oldfield

Telegraph and Argus (Bradford)
Hall Ings, Bradford BD1 1JR
01274 729511
www.thisisbradford.co.uk
Daily. Owner: Newsquest. Editor:
Perry Austin-Clarke; news: Martin
Heminway; features: David Barnett;
chief sub: Mel Jones

Western Daily Press (Bristol)
Temple Way, Bristol BS99 7HD
0117 934 3223
www.westpress.co.uk
Daily. Owner: Northcliffe Newspapers.
Editor: Terry Manners; backbench
executive editor: Dave Webb; news:
Cathy Ellis; features: Steve White; chief
sub: Tom Nicholson; production: Dave
Edler

Western Morning News
17 Brest Road
Derriford Business Park
Plymouth PL6 5AA
01752 765500
www.westernmorningnews.co.uk
Daily. Owner: Northcliffe Newspapers.
Editor-in-chief: Alan Qualtrough;
news: Mark Hughes, Steve Grant

York Evening Press
76–86 Walmgate, York YO1 9YN
01904 653051
www.yorkandcountypress.co.uk
Daily. Owner: Newsquest.
Editor: Kevin Booth; news: Scott
Armstrong; features: Chris Titley;
chief sub: Simon Ritchie

Yorkshire Evening Post
PO Box 168, Wellington Street
Leeds LS1 1RF
0113 243 2701
www.leedstoday.net
Daily. Owner: Johnston Press.
Editor: Neil Hodgkinson; news:
Gillian Howorth; features: Anne
Pickles; production: Howard Corry

Yorkshire Post
PO Box 168, Wellington St
Leeds LS1 1RF
0113 243 2701
www.yorkshireposttoday.co.uk
Daily. Owner: Johnston Press.
Editor: Peter Charlton; news: Hannah
Start; features: Catherine Scott

Other local and regional papers – England

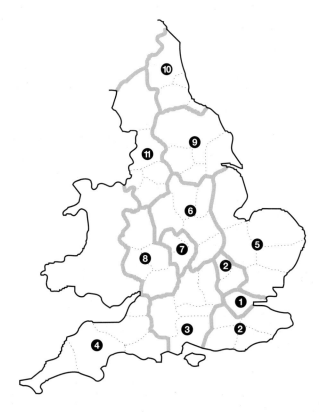

1 **London** page 37

2 **South-east England** page 40

3 **South England** page 46

4 **South-west England** page 49

5 **East England** page 52

6 **Midlands** page 56

7 **West Midlands** page 60

8 **West England** page 61

9 **North England** page 63

10 **North-east England** page 65

11 **North-west England** page 67

London

Barnes, Mortlake & Sheen Times
020 8940 6030
www.richmondandtwickenham
times.co.uk
*Weekly (Fri). Owner: Newsquest. Editor:
Paul Mortimer; news: Andrew Raine*

Barnet & Potters Bar Times
020 8203 0411
www.barnetandpottersbartimes.co.uk
*Weekly (Thu). Owner: Newsquest.
Editor: John Killeen; news: Colin O'Toole*

Barnet & Whetstone Press
020 8367 2345
www.icnorthlondononline.co.uk
*Weekly free (Thu). Owner: Trinity
Mirror Southern. Editor: Simon Jones;
news: Kerry Sheehan*

Brent & Wembley Leader
020 8427 4404
www.icharrow.co.uk
*Weekly free (Fri). Owner: Trinity Mirror
Southern. Editor: Jo Makosinski; news:
Claire Garner; features: Victoria
Prewer; production: Andre Erasmus*

Brentford, Chiswick & Isleworth Times
020 8940 6030
www.richmondandtwickenham
times.co.uk
*Weekly (Fri). Owner: Newsquest. Editor:
Paul Mortimer; news: Andrew Raine*

Bromley & Beckenham Times
020 8269 7000
www.archant.co.uk
*Weekly (Thu). Owner: Archant.
Editor: Melody Ryall; production:
Sarah McLeod*

Bromley & Orpington Express
020 8269 7000
www.archant.co.uk
*Weekly free (Wed). Owner: Archant.
Editor: Melody Ryall; production:
Sarah McLeod*

Bromley News
01959 564766
www.bromley-today.co.uk
*Weekly (Thu). Owner: Tindle
Newspapers. Editor: Bridger Hogan*

Bromley News Shopper
020 8646 5772
www.newsshopper.co.uk
*Weekly (Thu). Owner: Newsquest. Editor:
Andrew Parkes; news: Matthew Ramsden*

Camden Chronicle
020 8340 6868
www.london24.net
*Weekly (Thu). Owner: Archant.
Editor: Tony Allcock; news: Ollie Lane*

Camden New Journal
020 7419 9000
www.camdennewjournal.co.uk
*Weekly (Thu). Owner: New Journal
Enterprises. Editor: Eric Gordon; news:
Dan Carrier; features: Sunita Rappai;
production: Sarah Roberts*

Camden Times
020 8962 6868
www.wbtimes.co.uk
*Weekly (Wed). Owner: Archant.
Editor: Tim Cole*

Caterham & District Advertiser
020 8763 6666
www.icsurrey.co.uk
*Weekly (Fri). Owner: Trinity Mirror
Southern. Editor: Ian Carter; news:
Andy Worden*

Chingford Guardian
020 8498 3400
www.chingfordguardian.co.uk
*Weekly (Thu). Owner: Newsquest.
Editor: Pat Stannard*

The Chiswick
020 8940 6030
www.richmondandtwickenham
times.co.uk
*Weekly (Wed). Owner: Newsquest. Editor:
Paul Mortimer; news: Andrew Raine*

City of London & Dockland Times
020 7247 2524
*Fortnightly (Mon).
Editor: Mr D Delderfield*

Croydon Advertiser
020 8763 6666
www.iccroydon.co.uk
*Weekly (Fri). Owner: Trinity Mirror
Southern. Editor: Ian Carter; news:
Andy Worden*

Croydon Borough Post
020 8763 4433
www.iccroydon.co.uk
*Weekly (Wed). Owner: Trinity Mirror
Southern. Editor: Ian Carter; news:
Andy Worden*

Croydon Guardian
020 8774 6565
www.croydonguardian.co.uk
*Weekly (Wed). Owner: Newsquest. Editor:
Alison Hepworth; news: Helen Barnes*

Docklands News
0870 751 7212
www.docklandsnews.co.uk
*Weekly (Thu). Editor: Cherry Martin;
senior reporter: Afsheen Latif*

Ealing & Acton Gazette
020 8579 3131
www.icealing.co.uk
*Weekly (Fri). Owner: Trinity Mirror
Southern. Editor: Sarah Graham;
news: Paul Ryan; features: Victoria
Prewer*

Ealing Informer
020 8579 3131
www.icealing.co.uk
*Weekly (Wed). Owner: Trinity Mirror
Southern. Editor: Sarah Graham;
news: Paul Ryan; features: Victoria
Prewer*

Ealing Leader
01895 451000
www.icuxbridge.co.uk
*Weekly (Fri). Owner: Trinity Mirror
Southern. Editor: Sarah Graham;
news: Paul Ryan; features: Victoria
Prewer; chief sub: Joyce McKim*

Ealing Times
01494 755000
www.ealingtimes.co.uk
*Weekly (Thu). Owner: Newsquest.
Editor: Steve Cohen; news: James Young*

East End Life
020 7364 3059
*Sunday free. Owner: London Borough
of Tower Hamlets. Editor: Laraine
Clay; news: Helen Watson*

East London Advertiser
020 7791 7799
*Weekly (Thu). Owner: Archant. Editor:
Malcolm Starbrook; news: Mike Brooke*

East London Enquirer
01277 627300
Weekly (Thu). Editor: Carol Driver

Edgware & Mill Hill Press
020 8367 2345
www.icnorthlondononline.co.uk
*Weekly free (Thu). Owner: Trinity
Mirror Southern. Editor: Simon Jones;
news: Kerry Sheehan*

Edgware & Mill Hill Times
020 8203 0411
www.edgwaretimes.co.uk
*Weekly (Thu). Owner: Newsquest.
Editor: John Killeen; news: Colin O'Toole*

Eltham and Greenwich Times
020 8269 7000
www.archant.co.uk
*Weekly (Wed). Owner: Archant.
Editor: Melody Ryall; production:
Sarah McLeod*

Enfield Advertiser
020 8367 2345
www.icnorthlondononline.co.uk
*Weekly (Wed). Owner: Trinity Mirror
Southern. Editor: Simon Jones; news:
Kerry Sheehan*

Enfield Gazette
020 8367 2345
www.icnorthlondononline.co.uk
*Weekly (Thu). Owner: Trinity Mirror
Southern. Editor: Simon Jones; news:
Kerry Sheehan*

Enfield Independent
020 8362 1431
www.enfieldindependent.co.uk
*Weekly (Wed). Owner: Newsquest.
Editor: Kate Russell*

Erith & Crayford Times
020 8269 7000
www.archant.co.uk
*Weekly (Wed). Owner: Archant.
Editor: Melody Ryall; production:
Sarah McLeod*

Evening Standard
See page 35

Fulham Gazette
020 8579 3131
www.icealing.co.uk
*Weekly (Fri). Owner: Trinity Mirror
Southern. Editor: Sarah Graham*

Greater London Advertiser
024 7668 9878
*Weekly free (Wed). Owner: Northcliffe
Newspapers. Editor: Michael Masih*

Green Lanes Express
020 7241 1666
www.greenlanesexpress.com
*Weekly free (Thu). Editor: Derya Filiz;
news: Catrin Rogers*

Greenford & Northolt Gazette
020 8579 3131
www.icealing.co.uk
Weekly (Fri). Owner: Trinity Mirror Southern. Editor: Sarah Graham

Greenwich Borough Mercury
020 8769 4444
www.icsouthlondon.co.uk
Weekly (Wed). Owner: Trinity Mirror Southern. Editor-in-chief: Hannah Walker

Hackney Gazette
020 7791 7799
hackneygazette.co.uk
Weekly (Thu). Owner: Archant. Editor: Mick Ferris; news: Russ Lawrence

Hammersmith & Fulham Chronicle
020 8572 1816
www.trinitymirrorsouthern.co.uk
Weekly (Thu). Owner: Trinity Mirror Southern. News editor: Jenny Eagle; features: Gerri Besgrove; content editor: Janice Raycroft

Hammersmith & Shepherd's Bush Gazette
020 8579 3131
www.icealing.co.uk
Weekly (Fri). Owner: Trinity Mirror Southern. Editor: Sarah Graham

Hampstead and Highgate Express
020 7433 0000
www.hamhigh.co.uk
Weekly (Fri). Owner: Archant. Editor: Geoff Martin; news: Bridget Galton; features: Melanie Smith

Harefield Gazette
01895 451000
www.icuxbridge.co.uk
Weekly (Wed). Owner: Trinity Mirror Southern. Editor-in-chief: Adrian Seal; content editor: Liz Bellchambers

Haringey Advertiser
020 8367 2345
www.icnorthlondononline.co.uk
Weekly (Wed). Owner: Trinity Mirror Southern. Editor: Simon Jones; news: Kerry Sheehan

Harrow Leader
020 8427 4404
www.icharrow.co.uk
Weekly free (Fri). Owner: Trinity Mirror Southern. Editor: Jo Makosinski; news: Claire Garner; features: Victoria Prewer; production: Andre Erasmus

Harrow Observer
020 8427 4404
www.icharrow.co.uk
Weekly (Thu). Owner: Trinity Mirror Southern. Editor: Jo Makosinski; news: Claire Garner; features: Victoria Prewer; production: Andre Erasmus

Harrow Times
01923 216216
www.harrowtimes.co.uk
Weekly (Thu). Owner: Newsquest. Editor: Charlie Harris

Hayes & Harlington Gazette
01895 451000
www.icuxbridge.co.uk
Weekly (Wed). Owner: Trinity Mirror Southern. Editor-in-chief: Adrian Seal; content editor: Liz Bellchambers

Hendon & Finchley Press
020 8367 2345
www.icnorthlondononline.co.uk
Weekly free (Thu). Owner: Trinity Mirror Southern. Editor: Simon Jones; news: Kerry Sheehan

Hendon Times
020 8359 5959
www.hendontimes.co.uk
Weekly (Thu). Owner: Newsquest. Editor: John Killeen; news: Colin O'Toole

Highbury & Islington Express
020 7433 0000
www.islingtonexpress.co.uk
Weekly (Fri). Owner: Archant. Editor: Geoff Martin; features: Melanie Smith

Hillingdon & Uxbridge Times
01494 755000
www.hillingdontimes.co.uk
Weekly free (Thu). Owner: Newsquest. Editor: Steve Cohen; news: James Young

Hornsey & Crouch End Journal
020 8340 6868
www.london24.net
Weekly (Thu). Owner: Archant. Editor: Tony Allcock; news: Alison Campsie

Hounslow, Brentford & Chiswick Informer
020 8572 1816
www.trinitymirrorsouthern.co.uk
Weekly free (Fri). Owner: Trinity Mirror Southern. News editor: Ben Harvey

Hounslow Chronicle
020 8572 1816
www.trinitymirrorsouthern.co.uk
Weekly (Thu). Owner: Trinity Mirror Southern. News editor: Ben Harvey; features: Gerri Besgrove

Hounslow, Feltham & Hanworth Times
020 8940 6030
www.hounslowguardian.co.uk
Weekly (Fri). Owner: Newsquest. Editor: Paul Mortimer; news: Andrew Raine

Hounslow Guardian
020 8940 6030
www.hounslowguardian.co.uk
Weekly (Thu). Owner: Newsquest. Editor: Paul Mortimer; news: Andrew Raine

Hounslow Informer
020 8572 1816
www.trinitymirrorsouthern.co.uk
Weekly free (Fri). Owner: Trinity Mirror Southern. Features editor: Gerri Besgrove; content editor: Janice Raycroft

Ilford Recorder
020 8478 4444
www.ilfordrecorder.co.uk
Weekly (Thu). Owner: Archant. Editor: Chris Carter; production: Mike Cubitt

Islington Gazette
020 8340 6868
www.london24.net
Weekly (Thu). Owner: Archant. Editor: Tony Allcock; news: Ollie Lane

Islington Tribune
020 7419 9000
www.camdennewjournal.co.uk
Weekly (Fri). Owner: New Journal Enterprises. Editor: Eric Gordon; news: Dan Carrier; features: Sunita Rappai; production: Sarah Roberts

Kensington & Chelsea Informer
020 8572 1816
www.trinitymirrorsouthern.co.uk
Weekly (Fri). Owner: Trinity Mirror Southern. News editor: Jenny Eagle; features: Gerri Besgrove; content editor: Janice Raycroft

Kilburn Times
020 8962 6868
www.wbtimes.co.uk
Weekly (Wed). Owner: Archant. Editor: Tim Cole

Kingston & Surbiton Times
020 8940 6030
www.hounslowguardian.co.uk
Weekly (Fri). Owner: Newsquest. Editor: Paul Mortimer; news: Chris Briddon

Kingston Guardian
020 8940 6030
www.kingstonguardian.co.uk
Weekly (Thu). Owner: Newsquest. Editor: Sean Duggan

Kingston Informer
020 8572 1816
www.trinitymirrorsouthern.co.uk
Weekly (Fri). Owner: Trinity Mirror Southern. News: Jenny Eagle; features: Gerri Besgrove; content editor: Janice Raycroft

Lewisham & Greenwich Mercury
020 8769 4444
www.icsouthlondon.co.uk
Weekly free. Owner: Trinity Mirror Southern. Editor-in-chief: Hannah Walker; news: Shujaul Azam

Lewisham Borough Mercury
020 8769 4444
www.icsouthlondon.co.uk
Weekly (Wed). Owner: Trinity Mirror Southern. Editor-in-chief: Hannah Walker; chief reporter: Keely Sherbird

Lewisham News Shopper
020 8646 5772
www.newsshopper.co.uk
Weekly (Thu). Owner: Newsquest. Editor: Andrew Parkes; news: Matthew Ramsden; chief sub: Tim Miles

Leyton & Leytonstone Guardian
020 8498 3400
www.leytonguardian.co.uk
Weekly (Thu). Owner: Newsquest. Editor: Pat Stannard

Marylebone & Paddington Informer
020 8572 1816
www.trinitymirrorsouthern.co.uk
Weekly (Fri). Owner: Trinity Mirror Southern. News: Jenny Eagle; features: Gerri Besgrove; content editor: Janice Raycroft

Marylebone & Paddington Mercury
020 8572 1816
www.trinitymirrorsouthern.co.uk
Weekly (Fri). Owner: Trinity Mirror
Southern. News: Jenny Eagle; features:
Gerri Besgrove; content editor: Janice
Raycroft

Mayfair Times
020 7259 1050
www.pubbiz.com
Monthly free (1st Mon). Editor-in-chief:
Eric Brown; editor: Thelma Day

Metro London
020 7651 5200
www.metro.co.uk
Daily. Owner: Associated Newspapers.
Editor: Kenny Campbell; news: Mark
Dorman; features: Kieran Meeke;
production: Jason Kent

Mitcham, Morden & Wimbledon Post
020 8769 4444
www.icsouthlondon.co.uk
Weekly free (Fri). Owner: Trinity
Mirror Southern. Editor-in-chief:
Hannah Walker; news: Shujaul Azam

Muswell Hill & Crouch End Times
020 8359 5959
Weekly (Thu). Owner: Newsquest.
Editor: John Killeen; news: Colin O'Toole

Muswell Hill Journal
020 8340 6868
www.london24.net
Weekly (Thu). Owner: Archant. Editor:
Tony Allcock; news: Alison Campsie

New Addington Advertiser
020 8763 6666
www.icsurrey.co.uk
Weekly (Fri). Owner: Trinity Mirror
Southern. Editor: Ian Carter; news:
Andy Worden

Newham Recorder
020 8472 1421
www.recorderonline.co.uk
Weekly (Wed). Owner: Archant.
Editor: Colin Grainger; deputy editor:
John Finn; news: Pat Coughtrey

Pinner Observer
020 8427 4404
www.icharrow.co.uk
Weekly (Thu). Owner: Trinity Mirror
Southern. Editor: Jo Makosinski; news:
Claire Garner; features: Victoria
Prewer; production: Andre Erasmus

The Press (north London)
020 8364 4040
Weekly free (Thu). Owner: Trinity
Mirror Southern. Editor: Simon Jones;
news: Kerry Sheehan; arts editor:
Jonathan Lovett

Richmond & Twickenham Informer
020 8572 1816
www.trinitymirrorsouthern.co.uk
Weekly (Fri). Owner: Trinity Mirror
Southern. News editor: Jenny Eagle;
features: Gerri Besgrove; content editor:
Janice Raycroft

Richmond & Twickenham Times
020 8940 6030
www.richmondandtwickenham
times.co.uk
Weekly (Fri). Owner: Newsquest. Editor:
Paul Mortimer; news: James Adlam

Richmond Borough Guardian
020 8940 6030
www.kingstonguardian.co.uk
Weekly (Fri). Owner: Newsquest. Editor:
Paul Mortimer; news: James Adlam

Ruislip & Northwood Gazette
01895 451000
www.icuxbridge.co.uk
Weekly (Wed). Owner: Trinity Mirror
Southern. Editor-in-chief: Adrian Seal;
content editor: Liz Bellchambers

St John's Wood & Maida Vale
Express (Wood & Vale)
020 7433 0000
www.islingtonexpress.co.uk
Weekly (Fri). Owner: Archant.
Editor: Geoff Martin; news: Bridget
Galton; features: Melanie Smith

South Bucks Star
01494 755000
www.southbucksstar.co.uk
Weekly free (Thu). Owner: Newsquest.
Editor: Steve Cohen; news: Julie Voyce;
features: Lindy Bilgorri

South London Press
020 8769 4444
www.icsouthlondon.co.uk
Twice-weekly (Tue, Fri). Owner: Trinity
Mirror Southern. Editor-in-chief:
Hannah Walker; news: Shujaul Azam

Southall Gazette
020 8579 3131
www.icealing.co.uk
Weekly (Fri). Owner: Trinity Mirror
Southern. Editor: Sarah Graham

Southwark Weekender
020 7231 5258
Weekly free (Fri). Editor: Chris
Mullany and Kevin Quinn

Stanmore Observer
020 8427 4404
www.icharrow.co.uk
Weekly (Thu). Owner: Trinity Mirror
Southern. Editor: Jo Makosinski; news:
Claire Garner; features: Victoria
Prewer; production: Andre Erasmus

Stratford & Newham Express
020 7791 7799
Weekly (Wed). Owner: Archant. Editor:
Pat O'Connor; reporter: Charlotte Smith

Stratford Guardian
020 8478 4444
Weekly (Thu). Owner: Archant. Editor:
Chris Carter; production: Mike Cubitt

Streatham Guardian
020 8646 6336
www.streathamguardian.co.uk
Weekly (Thu). Owner: Newsquest.
Editor: Dave Tilley; features: June
Sampson

Streatham, Clapham & West
Norwood Post
020 8769 4444
www.icsouthlondon.co.uk
Weekly free (Thu). Owner: Trinity
Mirror Southern. Editor-in-chief:
Hannah Walker; news: Shujaul Azam

Sudbury Times
020 8962 6868
www.sudburytimes.co.uk
Weekly (Wed). Owner: Archant. Editor:
Tim Cole

Teddington & Hampton Times
020 8940 6030
Weekly (Fri). Owner: Newsquest. Editor:
Paul Mortimer; news: James Adlam

Tottenham & Wood Green Journal
020 8340 6868
www.london24.net
Weekly (Thu). Owner: Archant. Editor:
Tony Allcock; news: Alison Campsie

Tottenham Independent
020 8362 1432
www.tottenhamindependent.co.uk
Weekly (Fri). Owner: Newsquest.
Editor: Kate Russell

Tower Hamlets Recorder
020 8472 1421
www.recorderonline.co.uk
Weekly (Thu). Owner: Archant.
Editor: Colin Grainger; deputy editor:
John Finn; news: Pat Coughtrey

Uxbridge & Hillingdon Leader
01895 451000
www.icuxbridge.co.uk
Weekly free (Thu). Owner: Trinity
Mirror Southern. Editor-in-chief:
Adrian Seal; content editor: Liz
Bellchambers

Uxbridge & W Drayton Gazette
01895 451000
www.icuxbridge.co.uk
Weekly (Tue). Owner: Trinity Mirror
Southern. Editor-in-chief: Adrian Seal;
content editor: Liz Bellchambers

Walthamstow Guardian
020 8498 3400
www.walthamstowguardian.co.uk
Weekly (Thu). Owner: Newsquest.
Editor: Pat Stannard

Wandsworth Guardian
020 8646 6336
www.wandsworthguardian.co.uk
Weekly (Thu). Owner: Newsquest. News
editor: Laura Simpson; features: June
Sampson

Wembley & Kingsbury Times
020 8962 6868
www.wbtimes.co.uk
Weekly (Wed). Owner: Archant.
Editor: Tim Cole

Wembley Leader
020 8427 4404
www.icharrow.co.uk
Weekly (Thu). Owner: Trinity Mirror
Southern. Editor: Jo Makosinski; news:
Claire Garner; features: Victoria
Prewer; production: Andre Erasmus

Wembley Observer
020 8427 4404
www.icharrow.co.uk
Weekly (Thu). Owner: Trinity Mirror
Southern. Editor: Jo Makosinski; news:
Claire Garner; features: Victoria
Prewer; production: Andre Erasmus

West End Extra
020 7419 9000
www.camdennewjournal.co.uk
Weekly (Fri). Owner: New Journal
Enterprises. Editor: Eric Gordon; news:
Joel Taylor; features: Sunita Rappai;
production: Sarah Roberts

Westender
020 7607 6060
*Monthly free (last week in month).
Editor: Eileen Martin; news: Bina
Gowrea; features: Eileen Duff;
production: Jason Kent*

Westminster & Pimlico News
020 8572 1816
www.trinitymirrorsouthern.co.uk
*Weekly (Fri). Owner: Trinity Mirror
Southern. News editor: Jenny Eagle;
features: Gerri Besgrove; content editor:
Janice Raycroft*

Westminster Independent
020 8961 3345
www.londonlocals.co.uk
*Monthly (last Fri).
Editor: Jan Mappin; news: Jaz Walia*

The Wharf
020 7510 6306
www.icthewharf.co.uk
*Weekly free (Thu). Owner: Trinity Mirror
Southern. Editor: Tom Derbyshire;
deputy editor: Debra Killalea*

Willesden & Brent Times
020 8962 6868
www.wbtimes.co.uk
*Weekly (Wed). Owner: Archant.
Editor: Tim Cole*

Willesden Observer
020 8427 4404
www.icharrow.co.uk
*Weekly (Thu). Owner: Trinity Mirror
Southern. Editor: Jo Makosinski; news:
Claire Garner; features: Victoria
Prewer; production: Andre Erasmus*

Wimbledon Guardian
020 8646 6336
www.wimbledonguardian.co.uk
*Weekly (Thu). Owner: Newsquest. Editor:
Dave Tilley; features: June Sampson*

Wimbledon News
020 8646 6336
www.wimbledonnews.co.uk
*Weekly (Wed). Owner: Newsquest. Editor:
Dave Tilley; features: June Sampson*

South-east England

Bedfordshire, East Sussex,
Hertfordshire, Kent, Surrey, West
Sussex

Addlestone and Byfleet Review
01483 508700
www.surreyad.co.uk
*Weekly (Wed). Owner: Guardian
Media Group. Group editorial director:
Marnie Wilson; editor: Penny Bray*

Adscene (Ashford & Tenterden)
01227 767321
www.trinitymirrorsouthern.co.uk
*Weekly free (Fri). Owner: Trinity
Mirror Southern. Editor-in-chief:
Lesley Finlay; features: Julia Rogers;
chief sub: Mark Silva*

Adscene (Canterbury)
01227 767321
www.trinitymirrorsouthern.co.uk
*Weekly free (Thu). Owner: Trinity
Mirror Southern. Editor: John Nurden;
features: Julia Rogers; chief sub: Paul
Taylor; production: Mark Silva*

Adscene (Folkestone & Dover)
01227 767321
www.trinitymirrorsouthern.co.uk
*Weekly free (Wed). Owner: Trinity
Mirror Southern. Editor: Simon Finlay*

Adscene (Maidstone)
01622 690339
www.kent-online.co.uk
*Weekly free (Thu). Owner: Trinity
Mirror Southern. Editor: Diane Nicholls*

Adscene (Medway)
01227 767321
www.trinitymirrorsouthern.co.uk
*Weekly free (Thu). Owner: Trinity
Mirror Southern. Editor: Diane Nicholls*

Adscene (Sittingbourne & Sheppey)
01227 767321
www.trinitymirrorsouthern.co.uk
*Weekly free (Thu). Owner: Trinity
Mirror Southern. Editor: Christine
Rayner*

Adscene (Thanet)
01227 767321
www.trinitymirrorsouthern.co.uk
*Weekly free (Wed). Owner: Trinity
Mirror Southern. Editor: Rebecca
Smith; news: Jenny De Freitas*

Aldershot News
01483 508700
www.aldershot.co.uk
*Weekly (Tue). Owner: Guardian Media
Group. Group editorial director:
Marnie Wilson; editor: James Taylor*

The Argus (Brighton)
See page 34

Ashford KM Extra
01233 623232
www.kentonline.co.uk
*Weekly (Tue). Owner: Kent Messenger
Group. Editor: Leo Whitlock; news:
Simon Alford; chief sub: Claire Stevens;
production: Gary Barker*

Baldock Crow
01763 245241
www.royston-crow.co.uk
*Weekly (Thu). Owner: Archant.
Editor: Les Baker*

Barnet & Potters Bar Times
020 8359 5959
www.barnettimes.co.uk
*Weekly (Thu). Owner: Newsquest.
Group editor: John Kileen; chief
reporter: Colin O'Toole*

Bedford Times & Citizen
01234 405060
www.bedfordtoday.co.uk
*Weekly (Fri). Owner: Johnston Press.
Editor: Chris Hall; deputy editor: Olga
Norford; news: Mark Lewis*

Bedfordshire on Sunday
01234 300888
www.seriousaboutnews.com
*Sunday. Owner: LSN Media. Editor:
Steve Lowe; news: Liz O'Reilly;
production: Phil Umney*

Bexhill AdNews
01424 730555
www.bexhilltoday.co.uk
*Weekly free (Wed). Owner: Johnston
Press. Deputy editor: John Dowling;
news: Daniel Collins*

Bexhill-on-Sea Observer
01424 730555
www.bexhilltoday.co.uk
*Weekly (Fri). Owner: Johnston Press.
Deputy editor: John Dowling; news:
Daniel Collins*

Bexley Express
020 8269 7000
www.bexleyexpress.co.uk
*Weekly free (Wed). Owner: Archant.
Editor: Melody Ryall; production:
Mick Taylor*

**Bexley Dartford & Gravesham News
Shopper**
01689 885701
www.newsshopper.co.uk
Weekly (Wed). Editor: Andrew Parkes

Bexley Mercury
020 8769 4444
www.icsouthlondon.co.uk
*Weekly free (Wed/Thu). Owner: Trinity
Mirror Southern. Editor: Hannah
Walker*

Bexleyheath & Welling Times
020 8269 7000
*Weekly (Wed). Owner: Archant. Editor:
Melody Ryall; production: Mick Taylor*

Biggin Hill News
01959 564766
www.biggin-hill-today.co.uk
*Weekly (Thu). Owner: Tindle
Newspapers. Editor: Charlotte
McDonald*

Biggleswade & Sandy Comet
01462 420120
www.thecomet.net
*Weekly (Thu). Owner: Archant. Editor:
Darren Isted; news: John Adams*

Biggleswade Advertiser
01462 441020
www.hitchinadvertiser.co.uk
*Weekly (Wed). Owner: Observer
Standard Newspapers. General
manager: Ricky Allan*

Biggleswade Chronicle
01767 222333
www.biggleswadetoday.co.uk
*Weekly (Fri). Owner: Johnston Press.
Editor: Jim Stewart*

Bishops Stortford Citizen
01992 572285
www.eppingforestguardian.co.uk
Weekly (Thu). Owner: Newsquest.
Editor: David Jackman.
Bishops Stortford Herald
01279 624331
www.herald24.co.uk
Weekly (Thu). Owner: Archant. Editor:
Barry Hunt; reporter: Tracey Hubbard
Bognor Regis Guardian
01243 534133
www.chichester.co.uk
Weekly free (Wed). Owner: Johnston
Press. Editor: Alicia Denny
Bognor Regis Observer
01243 828777
www.chichester.co.uk
Weekly (Thu). Owner: Johnston Press.
Editor: Keith Newberry; features:
Kevin Smith
Borehamwood & Elstree Times
020 8359 5959
www.borehamwoodtimes.co.uk
Weekly (Fri). Owner: Newsquest.
Group editor: John Kileen; chief
reporter: Colin O'Toole
Brighton & Hove Leader
01273 544544
www.thisisbrightonandhove.co.uk
Weekly (Fri). Owner: Newsquest. Editor:
Chris Chandler; news: Mike Dunford
Camberley Courier
01252 339760
www.camberley.co.uk
Weekly free (Wed). Owner: Guardian
Media Group. Editor: James Taylor;
news: Adam Clark
Camberley News & Mail
01252 339760
www.camberley.co.uk
Weekly (Fri). Owner: Guardian Media
Group. Editor: James Taylor; news:
Adam Clark
Canterbury KM Extra
01227 768181
www.kentonline.co.uk
Weekly (Tue). Owner: Kent Messenger
Group. Editor: Bob Bounds; news: Trisha
Jamieson; production: Gary Barker
Cheshunt & Waltham Mercury
01992 414141
www.herts-essex-news.co.uk
Weekly (Fri). Owner: Herts & Essex
Newspapers. Editor: Ian Rogerson;
news: Pat Roberts
Chichester & Selsey Journal
01243 534133
www.chichester.co.uk
Weekly free (Wed). Owner: Johnston
Press. Editor: Alicia Denny
Chichester Observer
01243 539389
www.chiobserver.co.uk
Weekly (Thu). Owner: Johnston Press.
Editor: Keith Newberry; features: Peter
Homer
Chislehurst Times
020 8269 7000
Weekly (Thu). Owner: Archant. Editor:
Melody Ryall; production: Mick Taylor

Cranleigh Times
01483 508700
Weekly free (Wed). Owner: Guardian
Media Group. Group editorial director:
Marnie Wilson; news: Debby Thompson
Crawley News
01737 732000
www.icsurrey.co.uk
Weekly (Wed). Owner: Trinity Mirror
Southern. Editor-in-chief: Ian Carter;
content editor: Lesley Hickson
Crawley Observer
01293 562929
www.crawleyobserver.co.uk
Weekly (Wed). Owner: Johnston Press.
Editor: Graham Campbell; news: Allan
Norbury; chief sub: Mark Dunford
Crowborough Courier
01892 681000
www.thisiskentandeastsussex.co.uk
Weekly (Fri). Owner: Northcliffe
Newspapers. Editor: Giles Broadbent;
news: Melanie Whittaker; Today editor:
Lucia Blash; production: Richard Page
Croydon Advertiser
020 8763 6666
www.iccroydon.co.uk
Weekly (Fri). Owner: Trinity Mirror
Southern. Editor-in-chief: Ian Carter;
content editor: Andy Worden
Croydon Guardian
020 8774 6590
www.croydonguardian.co.uk
Weekly (Wed). Owner: Newsquest.
Editor: Alison Hepworth; news: Helen
Barnes; chief sub: Ali Masud
Croydon Post
01737 732000
www.iccroydon.co.uk
Weekly (Thu). Owner: Trinity Mirror
Southern. Editor-in-chief: Ian Carter;
content editor: Andy Worden
Dartford & Swanley Extra Informer
01322 220791
www.kent-online.co.uk
Weekly (Thu). Owner: Kent Messenger
Group. Editor: Sandra Hembury;
news: Louise Edwards
Dartford Express
020 8269 7000
www.dartfordexpress.co.uk
Weekly free (Wed). Owner: Archant.
Editor: Melody Ryall; production:
Mick Taylor
Dartford Messenger
01322 220791
www.kent-online.co.uk
Weekly (Thu). Owner: Kent Messenger
Group. Editor: Sandra Hembury;
news: Denise Eaton
Dartford Times
020 8269 7000
www.dartfordtimes.co.uk
Weekly (Thu). Owner: Archant. Editor:
Melody Ryall; production: Mick Taylor
Dover & Deal Extra
01233 623323
www.kentonline.co.uk
Weekly (Wed). Owner: Kent Messenger
Group. Editor: Leo Whitlock; news:
Simon Alford; chief sub: Claire Stevens;
production: Gary Barker

Dover Express
01227 767321
www.trinitymirrorsouthern.co.uk
Weekly (Thu). Owner: Trinity Mirror
Southern. Editor: Simon Finlay
Dover Mercury
01304 240380
Weekly (Thu). Owner: Kent Messenger
Group. Editor: Graham Smith
Downs Mail
01622 630330
www.downsmail.co.uk
Monthly (variable). Editor: Dennis Fowle
Dunstable Gazette
01582 526000
www.lutontoday.co.uk
Weekly (Wed). Owner: Johnston Press.
Editor: Geoff Cox
East Grinstead Courier
01892 681000
www.thisiskentandeastsussex.co.uk
Weekly (Thu). Owner: Northcliffe
Newspapers. Editor: Giles Broadbent;
news: Melanie Whittaker; Today editor:
Lucia Blash; production: Richard Page
East Grinstead Observer
01737 732000
www.icsurrey.co.uk
Weekly (Wed). Owner: Trinity Mirror
Southern. Editor-in-chief: Ian Carter
East Kent Gazette
01227 767321
www.trinitymirrorsouthern.co.uk
Weekly (Thu). Owner: Trinity Mirror
Southern. Editor: Christine Rayner
East Kent Mercury
01304 365526
www.eastkentmercury.co.uk
Weekly (Thu). Owner: Kent Messenger
Group. Editor: Graham Smith;
production: Gary Barker
Eastbourne & District Advertiser
01323 722091
www.eastbournetoday.co.uk
Weekly free (Thu). Owner: Johnston
Press. Editor: Peter Austin; commercial
editor: Andrew Bennett; sports editor:
Ken McEwan
Eastbourne Gazette
01323 722091
www.eastbournetoday.co.uk
Weekly (Wed). Owner: Johnston Press.
Editor: Peter Austin; commercial
editor: Andrew Bennett; sports editor:
Ken McEwan
Eastbourne Herald
01323 722091
www.eastbournetoday.co.uk
Weekly (Fri). Owner: Johnston Press.
Editor: Peter Austin; commercial
editor: Andrew Bennett; sports editor:
Ken McEwan
Edenbridge Chronicle
01959 564766
www.edenbridge-today.co.uk
Weekly (Thu). Owner: Tindle
Newspapers. Editor: Signid Sherrell
Edenbridge County Border News
01959 564766
www.edenbridge-today.co.uk
Weekly (Thu). Owner: Tindle
Newspapers. Editor: Kevin Black

41

Edenbridge Courier
01892 681000
www.thisiskentandeastsussex.co.uk
Weekly (Fri). Owner: Northcliffe
Newspapers. Editor: Giles Broadbent;
news: Melanie Whittaker; Today editor:
Lucia Blash; production: Richard Page

Edgware & Mill Hill Times
020 8359 5959
www.edgwaretimes.co.uk
Weekly (Thu). Owner: Newsquest.
Group editor: John Kileen; chief
reporter: Colin O'Toole

Elmbridge Guardian
020 8646 6336
www.elmbridgeguardian.co.uk
Weekly (Thu). Owner: Newsquest.
Editor: Sean Duggan

Epsom, Ewell & Banstead Post
020 8763 6666
www.icsurrey.co.uk
Weekly (Fri). Owner: Trinity Mirror
Southern. Editor: Ian Carter; news:
Andy Worden

Epsom Guardian
020 8646 6336
www.epsomguardian.co.uk
Weekly (Thu). Owner: Newsquest.
Editor: Sean Duggan

Esher News & Mail
01483 508700
www.esher.co.uk
Weekly (Fri). Owner: Guardian Media
Group. Group editorial director:
Marnie Wilson; editor: Elaine Cole

Farnham Herald
01252 725224
www.farnham-herald-today.co.uk
Weekly (Fri). Owner: Tindle
Newspapers. Editor: Sandy Baker; chief
reporter: Corina Larby

Farnham Post
01420 88949
Fortnightly free (Mon). Owner:
Guardian Media Group. General
manager: Alan Wooler

Faversham KM Extra
01227 768181
www.kentonline.co.uk
Weekly (Tue). Owner: Kent Messenger
Group. Editor: Bob Bounds; news:
Trisha Jamieson; production: Gary
Barker

Faversham News
01227 475901
www.kentonline.co.uk
Weekly (Thu). Owner: Kent Messenger
Group. Editor: Bob Bounds; news:
Trisha Jamieson; production: Gary
Barker

Faversham Times
01227 767321
www.trinitymirrorsouthern.co.uk
Weekly (Thu). Owner: Trinity Mirror
Southern. Editor: Christine Rayner;
features: Julia Rogers

Folkestone & Hythe Extra
01303 850676
Weekly (Wed). Owner: Kent Messenger
Group. Editor: Leo Whitlock;
production: Gary Barker

Folkestone Express
01233 623232
www.kentonline.co.uk
Weekly (Wed). Owner: Kent Messenger
Group. Editor: Leo Whitlock; news:
Simon Alford; chief sub: Claire Stevens

Folkestone Herald
01227 767321
www.trinitymirrorsouthern.co.uk
Weekly (Thu). Owner: Trinity Mirror
Southern. Editor: Simon Finlay

Friday-Ad
0870 162 9999
www.friday-ad.co.uk
Weekly (Fri). Editor: David Sommerville

Gatwick Skyport
020 8538 2236
www.trinitymirrorsouthern.co.uk
Weekly free (Fri). Owner: Trinity
Mirror Southern. Editor: Liz Billings;
news: Lucy Walters

Godalming Times
01483 508700
Weekly free (Wed). Owner: Guardian
Media Group. Group editorial director:
Marnie Wilson; news: Debby Thompson

Gravesend Express
020 8269 7000
www.gravesendexpress.co.uk
Weekly free (Wed). Owner: Archant.
Editor: Melody Ryall; production:
Mick Taylor

Gravesend KM Extra
01474 333381
www.kent-online.co.uk
Weekly (Fri). Owner: Kent Messenger
Group. Editor: Sandra Hembury;
news: Denise Eaton

Gravesend Messenger
01474 333381
www.kent-online.co.uk
Weekly (Thu). Owner: Kent Messenger
Group. Editor: Sandra Hembury;
news: Denise Eaton

Gravesend Reporter
020 8269 7000
www.gravesendreporter.co.uk
Weekly (Thu). Owner: Archant.
Editor: Melody Ryall; production:
Mick Taylor

Guildford Times
01483 508700
www.surreyad.co.uk/news
/guildford-times.html
Weekly free (Wed). Owner: Guardian
Media Group. Group editorial director:
Marnie Wilson; news: Debby Thompson

Hailsham Gazette
01323 722091
www.eastbournetoday.co.uk
Weekly (Wed). Owner: Johnston Press.
Editor: Peter Austin; commercial
editor: Andrew Bennett; sports editor:
Ken McEwan

Harpenden Observer
01727 834411
www.stalbansobserver.co.uk
Weekly (Wed). Owner: Newsquest.
Editor: Claire Bourke

Haslemere Times & Mail
01252 716444
www.haslemere-herald-today.co.uk
Weekly free (Tue). Owner: Tindle
Newspapers. Editor: Sandy Baker;
subeditor: Tony Short

Hastings & St Leonards Observer
01424 854242
www.hastingstoday.co.uk
Weekly (Fri). Owner: Johnston Press.
Associate editor: Russell Claughton;
news: Ann Terry

Hastings AdNews
01424 854242
www.hastingstoday.co.uk
Weekly (Fri). Owner: Johnston Press.
Associate editor: Russell Claughton;
news: Ann Terry

Hemel Hempstead Gazette
01442 262311
www.hemelonline.co.uk
Weekly (Wed). Owner: Johnston Press.
Editor: David Feldstein; sports editor:
Graham Caygill

Hendon & Finchley Times
020 8359 5959
www.hendontimes.co.uk
Weekly (Thu). Owner: Newsquest.
Group editor: John Kileen; chief
reporter: Colin O'Toole

Herne Bay Gazette
01227 475901
www.kentonline.co.uk
Weekly (Thu). Owner: Kent Messenger
Group. Editor: Bob Bounds; news:
Trisha Jamieson; production: Gary
Barker

Herne Bay KM Extra
01227 768181
www.kentonline.co.uk
Weekly (Tue). Owner: Kent Messenger
Group. Editor: Bob Bounds; news:
Trisha Jamieson; production: Gary
Barker

Herne Bay Times
01227 771515
Weekly (Thu). Owner: Trinity Mirror
Southern. Editor: John Nurden;
features: Julia Rogers; chief sub: Paul
Taylor; production: Mark Silva

Hertford Times
01707 327551
www.whtimes.co.uk
Weekly (Wed). Owner: Archant. Editor:
Terry Mitchinson; news: Chris Lennon

Hertfordshire Mercury
01992 526625
www.herts-essex-news.co.uk
Weekly (Fri). Owner: Herts & Essex
Newspapers. Editor: Paul Winspear

Hertfordshire on Sunday
01234 308603
Sunday. Owner: LSN Media.
Editor: Judy Reilly

Hertfordshire Star
01992 526625
www.herts-essex-news.co.uk
Weekly (Wed). Owner: Herts & Essex
Newspapers. Editor: Chris Bristow

Herts & Essex Observer
01279 866355
www.herts-essex-news.co.uk
Weekly (Thu). Owner: Archant.
Editor: Val Brown; news: Sandra Perry

Herts Advertiser
01727 865165
www.hertsad.co.uk
Weekly (Thu). Owner: Observer
Standard Newspapers. Editor: Noel
Cantillon

Hitchin Advertiser
01462 441020
www.hitchinadvertiser.co.uk
Weekly (Wed). Owner: Observer
Standard Newspapers. General
manager: Ricky Allan

Hitchin Comet
01438 866200
www.thecomet.net
Weekly (Thu). Owner: Archant. Editor:
Darren Isted; news: John Adams

Hoddesdon & Broxbourne Mercury
01992 414141
www.herts-essex-news.co.uk
Weekly (Fri). Owner: Herts & Essex
Newspapers. Editor: Ian Rogerson;
news: Pat Roberts

Horley Life
01273 544544
www.thisisbrightonandhove.co.uk
Weekly (Thu). Owner: Newsquest.
Editor: Chris Chandler; news: Mike
Dunford

Horsham Advertiser
01403 751200
www.horshamtoday.co.uk
Weekly (Fri). Owner: Johnston Press.
Editor: Gary Shipton; chief sub: Steve
Payne; production: Jonathan Taylor

Hythe Herald
01227 767321
www.trinitymirrorsouthern.co.uk
Weekly (Thu). Owner: Trinity Mirror
Southern. Editor: Simon Finlay

Isle of Thanet Gazette
01227 767321
www.trinitymirrorsouthern.co.uk
Weekly (Thu). Owner: Trinity Mirror
Southern. Editor: Rebecca Smith; news:
Jenny De Freitas

Kent & Sussex Courier
01892 681000
www.thisiskentandeastsussex.co.uk
Weekly (Fri). Owner: Northcliffe
Newspapers. Editor: Giles Broadbent;
news: Melanie Whittaker; Today editor:
Lucia Blash; production: Richard Page

Kent Messenger
01622 695666
www.kent-online.co.uk
Weekly (Fri). Owner: Kent Messenger
Group. Editor: Bob Dimond;
community editor: Cathy Tyce

Kent on Sunday
01303 817000
www.kentonsunday.co.uk
Sunday. Owner: KOS Media
(Publishing). Editor: Ian Patel; news:
Gary Wright; chief sub: Dave Hobday;
production: Jason Pyne

Kentish Express
01233 623232
www.kentonline.co.uk
Weekly (Thu). Owner: Kent Messenger
Group. Editor: Leo Whitlock; news:
Simon Alford; chief sub: Claire Stevens;
production: Gary Barker

Kentish Gazette
01227 768181
www.kentonline.co.uk
Weekly (Thu). Owner: Kent Messenger
Group. Editor: Bob Bounds; news:
Trisha Jamieson; production: Gary
Barker

Kingston Guardian
020 8646 6336
www.kingstonguardian.co.uk
Weekly (Thu). Owner: Newsquest.
Editor: Sean Duggan

Lea Valley Star
01992 526625
www.herts-essex-news.co.uk
Weekly (Wed). Owner: Herts & Essex
Newspapers. Editor: Chris Bristow

Leatherhead Advertiser
01737 732000
www.icsurrey.co.uk
Weekly (Thu). Owner: Trinity Mirror
Southern. Editor-in-chief: Ian Carter;
content editor: Monica Hawley

Leatherhead Guardian
020 8646 6336
www.leatherheadguardian.co.uk
Weekly (Thu). Owner: Newsquest.
Editor: Sean Duggan

Leighton Buzzard & Linslade Citizen
01908 651200
www.miltonkeynestoday.co.uk
Weekly free (Thu). Owner: Johnston
Press. Editor: Alan Legg

Leighton Buzzard Observer
01525 858400
www.miltonkeynestoday.co.uk
Weekly (Tue). Owner: Johnston Press.
Editor: Nick Wormley; news: Mike King

Leighton Buzzard On Sunday
01908 809000
www.seriousaboutnews.com
Sunday. Owner: LSN Media. Editor:
Gaynor Selby; news: Martin Bughair

Letchworth & Baldock Comet
01462 420120
www.thecomet.net
Weekly (Thu). Owner: Archant. Editor:
Darren Isted; news: John Adams

Limited Edition (Hertfordshire)
01923 216220
Monthly (1st Tue). Owner: Newsquest.
Editor: Deborah Aspinall

Littlehampton Gazette
01903 230051
www.littlehamptontoday.co.uk
Weekly (Thu). Owner: Johnston Press.
Editor: Roger Green

Luton & Dunstable on Sunday
01582 707707
www.seriousaboutnews.com
Sunday. Owner: LSN Media. Editor:
Gaynor Selby; news: Martin Bughair;
production: Phil Umney

Luton Herald & Post
01582 700600
www.lutontoday.co.uk
Weekly (Thu). Owner: Johnston Press.
Editor: John Francis

Luton News
01582 526000
www.lutontoday.co.uk
Weekly (Wed). Owner: Johnston Press.
Assistant editor: Geoff Cox

Maidstone KM Extra
01622 695666
www.kent-online.co.uk
Weekly free (Fri). Owner: Kent
Messenger Group. Editor: Bob Dimond;
community editor: Cathy Tyce

Medway Messenger (Rochester,
Chatham, Gravesend)
01622 717880
www.kent-online.co.uk
Weekly (Mon, Fri). Owner: Kent
Messenger Group. Editor: Bob Dimond;
news: Nikki White; features: Lynn Cox;
chief sub: Digby Kennard

Medway News
01227 767321
www.trinitymirrorsouthern.co.uk
Weekly (Thu). Owner: Trinity Mirror
Southern. Editor: Diane Nicholls

Medway Standard
01227 767321
www.trinitymirrorsouthern.co.uk
Weekly (Fri). Owner: Trinity Mirror
Southern. Editor: Diane Nicholls

The Messenger (Haslemere)
01428 653999
www.messenger-online.co.uk
Weekly free (Wed). Editor: Guy
Butchers; news: Sheila Checkley

Mid Sussex Citizen
01444 452201
www.midsussextoday.co.uk
Weekly free (Wed). Owner: Johnston
Press. Editor: Paul Watson

Mid Sussex Leader
01273 544544
www.thisismidsussex.co.uk
Weekly (Thu). Owner: Newsquest.
Editor: Chris Chandler; news: Mike
Dunford

Mid Sussex Times
01444 452201
www.midsussextoday.co.uk
Weekly (Thu). Owner: Johnston Press.
Editor: Paul Watson

Midhurst & Petworth Observer
01730 813557
www.midhurstandpetworth.co.uk
Weekly (Thu). Owner: Johnston Press.
Editor: Keith Newberry; news: Jane Hunt

News & Mail
01483 508900
www.surreyad.co.uk
Weekly (Wed). Owner: Guardian
Media Group. Group editorial director:
Marnie Wilson

News in Focus
01732 228000
www.thisiskentandeastsussex.co.uk
Weekly (Tue). Owner: Northcliffe
Newspapers. Editor: Frank Baldwin

News Shopper Guide
01689 885701
www.newsshopper.co.uk
Weekly (Thu). Owner: Newsquest.
Editor: Andrew Parkes; news: Matthew
Ramsden; chief sub: Tim Miles

Orpington & Petts Wood Times
020 8269 7000
Weekly (Thu). Owner: Archant. Editor:
Melody Ryall; production: Mick Taylor

Paddock Wood Courier
01892 681000
www.thisiskentandeastsussex.co.uk
Weekly (Fri). Owner: Northcliffe
Newspapers. Editor: Giles Broadbent;
news: Melanie Whittaker; Today editor:
Lucia Blash; production: Richard Page

Redhill & Reigate Life
01689 885701
www.redhillandreigatelife.co.uk
Weekly (Wed). Owner: Newsquest. Editor:
Alison Hepworth; chief sub: Ali Masud

Reigate Post
020 8770 7171
www.icsurrey.co.uk
Weekly (Thu). Owner: Trinity Mirror
Southern. Editor: Ian Carter; news:
Helen Backway

Reigate, Redhill & Horley Post
01737 732000
www.icsurrey.co.uk
Weekly (Wed). Owner: Trinity Mirror
Southern. Editor-in-chief: Ian Carter;
content editor: Glen Mitchell

Romney Marsh Herald
01227 767321
www.trinitymirrorsouthern.co.uk
Weekly (Wed). Owner: Trinity Mirror
Southern. Editor: Diane Nicholls

Royston & Buntingford Mercury
01992 526600
www.herts-essex-news.co.uk
Weekly (Fri). Owner: Herts & Essex
Newspapers. Editor: Paul Winspear;
news: Paul Brackley; features: Bridget
McAlpine

Royston Crow
01763 245241
www.royston-crow.co.uk
Weekly (Thu). Owner: Archant.
Editor: Les Baker

Rye & Battle Observer
01424 854242
www.ryeandbattletoday.co.uk
Weekly (Fri). Owner: Johnston Press.
Associate editor: Russell Claughton;
news: Ann Terry

St Albans & Harpenden Review
01727 834411
www.stalbansobserver.co.uk
Weekly free (Wed). Owner: Newsquest.
Editor: Claire Bourke

St Albans Observer
01727 834411
www.stalbansobserver.co.uk
Weekly (Thu). Owner: Newsquest.
Editor: Claire Bourke

Seaford Gazette
01323 722091
www.eastbournetoday.co.uk
Weekly (Wed). Owner: Johnston Press.
Editor: Peter Austin; commercial
editor: Andrew Bennett; sports editor:
Ken McEwan

Sevenoaks Chronicle
01732 228000
www.thisiskentandeastsussex.co.uk
Weekly (Thu). Owner: Northcliffe
Newspapers. Editor: Frank Baldwin

Sheerness Times Guardian
01795 580300
Weekly (Thu). Owner: Kent Messenger
Group. Editor: Duncan Marsh; news:
Linda Mitchell

Sheppey Gazette
01227 767321
www.trinitymirrorsouthern.co.uk
Weekly (Thu). Owner: Trinity Mirror
Southern. Editor: Christine Rayner

Shoreham Herald
01903 230051
www.shorehamtoday.co.uk
Weekly (Thu). Owner: Johnston Press.
Editor: Michelle Neville

Sittingbourne KM Extra
01795 580300
www.kentonline.co.uk
Weekly (Wed). Owner: Kent Messenger
Group. Editor: Duncan Marsh; news:
Linda Mitchell

South Coast Leader
01273 544544
www.thisisbrightonandhove.co.uk
Weekly (Fri). Owner: Newsquest. Editor:
Chris Chandler; news: Mike Dunford

Staines & Ashford News
01932 561111
www.trinitymirrorsouthern.co.uk
Weekly free (Wed). Owner: Trinity
Mirror Southern. Editor: Liz Dixon;
news: Judy Parsons

Staines & Egham News
01932 561111
www.trinitymirrorsouthern.co.uk
Weekly free (Wed). Owner: Trinity
Mirror Southern. Editor: Liz Dixon;
news: Judy Parsons

Staines Guardian
020 8940 6030
www.stainesguardian.co.uk
Weekly (Thu). Owner: Newsquest. Editor:
Paul Mortimer; news: James Adlam

Staines Informer
01932 561111
www.trinitymirrorsouthern.co.uk
Weekly (Thu). Owner: Trinity Mirror
Southern. Editor: Liz Dixon; news:
Judy Parsons

Staines Leader
01932 561111
www.trinitymirrorsouthern.co.uk
Weekly (Thu). Owner: Trinity Mirror
Southern. Editor: Liz Dixon

Star Classified (Bishops Stortford)
01279 866355
www.herts-essex-news.co.uk
Weekly (Thu). Owner: Archant.
Editor: Val Brown; news: Sandra Perry

Stevenage Advertiser
01462 441020
www.hitchinadvertiser.co.uk
Weekly (Wed). Owner: Observer
Standard Newspapers. General
manager: Ricky Allan

Stevenage Comet
01462 420120
www.thecomet.net
Weekly (Thu). Owner: Archant. Editor:
Darren Isted; news: John Adams

Stevenage Herald
01462 420120
www.thecomet.net
Weekly free (Wed). Owner: Archant.
Editor: Darren Isted; news: John Adams

Stevenage Mercury
01992 526600
www.herts-essex-news.co.uk
Weekly (Fri). Owner: Herts & Essex
Newspapers. Editor: Paul Winspear;
news: Paul Brackley; features: Bridget
McAlpine

Surrey & Hants News
01252 716444
www.farnham-herald-today.co.uk
Weekly free (Tue). Owner: Tindle
Newspapers. Editor: Sandy Baker;
sub: Tony Short

Surrey Advertiser
01483 508700
www.surreyad.co.uk
Weekly (Fri). Owner: Guardian Media
Group. Group editorial director: Marnie
Wilson; news: Debby Thompson

Surrey Comet
020 8646 6336
www.surreycomet.co.uk
Weekly (Wed). Owner: Newsquest.
Editor: Sean Duggan

Surrey Hants Star
01252 316311
www.shstar.co.uk
Weekly free (Thu). Owner: Guardian
Media Group. Editor: Joanne Jones

Surrey Herald
01932 561111
www.trinitymirrorsouthern.co.uk
Weekly (Wed). Owner: Trinity Mirror
Southern. Editor: Liz Dixon

Surrey Mirror
020 8770 7171
www.icsurrey.co.uk
Weekly (Wed). Owner: Trinity Mirror
Southern. Editor: Ian Carter; news:
Glen Mitchell; features: Caroline
Harrap; chief sub: Sherif El Alfay

Sussex Express
01273 480601
www.sussexexpress.co.uk
Weekly (Fri). Owner: Johnston Press.
Editor: Peter Austin; deputy editor:
Kevin Penfold

Sutton Advertiser
020 8763 6666
www.icsurrey.co.uk
Weekly (Fri). Owner: Trinity Mirror
Southern. Editor: Ian Carter; news:
Andy Worden

Sutton Borough Post
020 8763 6666
www.icsurrey.co.uk
Weekly (Wed). Owner: Trinity Mirror
Southern. Editor: Ian Carter; news:
Andy Worden

Sutton Guardian
020 8646 6336
www.suttonguardian.co.uk
Weekly (Thu). Owner: Newsquest.
Editor: Sean Duggan

Swanley Messenger
01322 220791
www.kent-online.co.uk
Weekly (Thu). Owner: Kent Messenger
Group. Editor: Sandra Hembury; news:
Louise Edwards

Swanley Times
020 8269 7000
Weekly (Thu). Owner: Archant. Editor:
Melody Ryall; production: Mick Taylor

Tandridge Chronicle
01959 564766
www.tandridge-today.co.uk
Weekly (Thu). Owner: Tindle
Newspapers. Editor: Signid Sherrell

Tandridge County Border News
01959 564766
www.tandridge-today.co.uk
Weekly (Thu). Owner: Tindle
Newspapers. Editor: Kevin Black

Tenterden Express
01233 623232
www.kentonline.co.uk
Weekly (Tue). Owner: Kent Messenger
Group. Editor: Leo Whitlock; news:
Simon Alford; chief sub: Claire Stevens

Tenterden KM Extra
01233 623232
www.kentonline.co.uk
Weekly (Tue). Owner: Kent Messenger
Group. Editor: Leo Whitlock; news:
Simon Alford; chief sub: Claire Stevens

Thanet KM Extra
01622 717880
www.kentonline.co.uk
Weekly (Wed). Owner: Kent Messenger
Group. Editor: Carol Davies

Thanet Times
01227 767321
www.trinitymirrorsouthern.co.uk
Weekly (Thu). Owner: Trinity Mirror
Southern. Editor: Rebecca Smith; news:
Jenny De Freitas

Tonbridge Courier
01892 681000
www.thisiskentandeastsussex.co.uk
Weekly (Fri). Owner: Northcliffe
Newspapers. Editor: Giles Broadbent;
news: Melanie Whittaker; Today editor:
Lucia Blash; production: Richard Page

Tunbridge Wells Courier
01892 681000
www.thisiskentandeastsussex.co.uk
Weekly (Fri). Owner: Northcliffe
Newspapers. Editor: Giles Broadbent;
news: Melanie Whittaker; Today editor:
Lucia Blash; production: Richard Page

Tunbridge Wells Extra
01732 364596
www.kentonline.co.uk
Weekly (Fri). Owner: Kent Messenger
Group. Editor: Bob Dimond; news:
Nigel Jarrett

Virginia Water Villager
01753 523355
Fortnightly (Thu). Owner: Clyde &
Forth Press. Editor: Sally Stevens;
news: Mike Sim

Walton & Weybridge Informer
01932 561111
www.trinitymirrorsouthern.co.uk
Weekly free (Thu). Owner: Trinity
Mirror Southern. Editor: Liz Dixon;
news: Abbi Dornan

Watford Free Observer
01923 216216
www.watfordobserver.co.uk
Weekly (Thu). Owner: Newsquest.
Editor: Peter Wilson-Leary; news:
Frazer Ansell

Watford Review
01923 216212
www.stalbansobserver.co.uk
Weekly free (Wed). Owner: Newsquest.
Editor: Peter Wilson-Leary

Watford Times
01788 543077
Weekly free (Wed). Editor: Stephen
Williams; news: Stuart Platt

Weald Courier
01892 681000
www.thisiskentandeastsussex.co.uk
Weekly (Fri). Owner: Northcliffe
Newspapers. Editor: Giles Broadbent;
news: Melanie Whittaker; Today editor:
Lucia Blash; production: Richard Page

Wealden Advertiser
01580 753322
www.wealdenad.co.uk
Weekly free (Fri). Editor: Graham Thorn

Weekend Herald (Crawley,
Horsham, Horley)
01293 562929
www.crawleyobserver.co.uk
Weekly free (Fri). Owner: Johnston
Press. Editor: Graham Campbell; news:
Allan Norbury; chief sub: Mark Dunford

Welwyn & Hatfield Review
01727 834411
www.stalbansobserver.co.uk
Weekly (Thu). Owner: Newsquest.
Editor: Claire Bourke

Welwyn & Hatfield Times
01707 327551
www.whtimes.co.uk
Weekly (Wed). Owner: Archant. Editor:
Terry Mitchinson; news: Chris Lennon

Westerham County Border News
01959 564766
www.westerham-today.co.uk
Weekly (Thu). Owner: Tindle
Newspapers. Editor: Kevin Black

West Sussex County Times
01403 751200
www.horshamonline.co.uk
Weekly (Fri). Owner: Johnston Press.
Editor: Gary Shipton; chief sub: Steve
Payne; production: Jonathan Taylor

West Sussex Gazette
01243 534155
www.chichester.co.uk
Weekly (Wed). Owner: Johnston Press.
Editor: Dorothy Blundell; news: Jeannie
Knight; chief sub: Zoe Shardlow

Weybridge Villager
01753 523355
Fortnightly (Thu). Owner: Clyde &
Forth Press. Editor: Sally Stevens;
news: Mike Sim

Whitstable Gazette
01227 768181
www.kentonline.co.uk
Weekly (Thu). Owner: Kent Messenger
Group. Editor: Bob Bounds; news: Trisha
Jamieson; production: Gary Barker

Whitstable KM Extra
01227 768181
www.kentonline.co.uk
Weekly (Tue). Owner: Kent Messenger
Group. Editor: Bob Bounds; news: Trisha
Jamieson; production: Gary Barker

Whitstable Times
01227 771515
Weekly (Thu). Owner: Trinity Mirror
Southern. Editor: John Nurden;
features: Julia Rogers; chief sub: Paul
Taylor; production: Mark Silva

Woking Informer
01932 561111
www.trinitymirrorsouthern.co.uk
Weekly free (Thu). Owner: Trinity
Mirror Southern. Editor: Liz Dixon;
news: Irlene Watchmore

Woking News & Mail
01483 755755
www.woking.co.uk
Weekly (Thu). Owner: Guardian Media
Group. Editor: Penny Bray; news: Paul
Barry

Woking Review
01483 755755
www.surreyad.co.uk
Weekly (Wed). Owner: Guardian Media
Group. Editor: Penny Bray; news: Paul
Barry

Worthing Advertiser
01903 230051
www.worthingtoday.co.uk
Weekly (Wed). Owner: Johnston Press.
Editor: Tony Mayes

Worthing Guardian
01903 282401
www.worthingtoday.co.uk
Weekly (Fri). Owner: Johnston Press.
Editor: Nikki Jeffrey

Worthing Herald
01903 230051
www.worthingtoday.co.uk
Weekly (Thu). Owner: Johnston Press.
Editor: John Buss; news: Harriet Shelley

South England

Berkshire, Buckinghamshire, Hampshire, Oxfordshire, Wiltshire

Abingdon Herald
01865 425262
www.thisisoxfordshire.co.uk
Weekly (Thu). Owner: Newsquest.
Editor: Derek Holmes

The Advertiser (Newbury)
01635 524111
www.newburynews.co.uk
Weekly (Tue). Owner: Blacket Turner.
Editor: Brien Beharrell; news: Martin Robertshaw

Aldershot Courier
01252 339760
www.aldershot.co.uk
Weekly free (Wed). Owner: Guardian Media Group. Editor: James Taylor; news: Adam Clark

Aldershot Mail
01252 339760
www.surreyad.co.uk
Weekly (Tue). Owner: Guardian Media Group. Editor: James Taylor; news: Adam Clark

Aldershot News
01252 339760
www.aldershot.co.uk
Weekly (Fri). Owner: Guardian Media Group. Editor: James Taylor; news: Adam Clark

Alresford Gazette
01420 84446
Weekly (Tue). Owner: Tindle Newspapers. Editor: Christine McDerment; news: Paul Ferguson

Alton Gazette
01420 84446
Weekly (Wed). Owner: Tindle Newspapers. Editor: Christine McDerment; news: Paul Ferguson

Alton Times & Mail
01252 716444
www.alton-herald-today.co.uk
Weekly free (Tue). Owner: Tindle Newspapers. Editor: Tony Short; features: Angie Williamson

Amersham & Chesham Free Press
01494 755081
www.bucksfreepress.co.uk
Weekly (Fri). Owner: Newsquest. Editor: Steve Cohen; news: Julie Voyce; features: Lind Bilgorri

Amersham Examiner
01753 888333
www.buckinghamtoday.co.uk
Weekly (Thu). Owner: Trinity Mirror Southern. Editor: Peter Krinks; news: Estelle Sinkins

Andover Advertiser
01264 323456
www.andoveradvertiser.co.uk
Weekly (Fri). Owner: Newsquest. Editor: Joe Scicluna; deputy editor: Judy Belbin; features: Simon Reeve; chief sub: Judith Hughes

Andover Advertiser Midweek
01264 323456
www.andoveradvertiser.co.uk
Weekly (Wed). Owner: Newsquest. Editor: Joe Scicluna; deputy editor: Judy Belbin; features: Simon Reeve; chief sub: Judith Hughes

Ascot News
01344 456611
www.icberkshire.co.uk
Weekly (Thu). Owner: Trinity Mirror Southern. Editor: Joe Wise; chief reporter: James Osborne

Ash & Farnham Mail
01252 339760
www.aldershot.co.uk
Weekly (Tue). Owner: Guardian Media Group. Editor: James Taylor; news: Adam Clark

Banbury Cake
01295 256111
www.thisisoxfordshire.co.uk
Weekly (Thu). Owner: Newsquest. Editor: Derek Holmes; news: Stephanie Preece; features: Julian Dancer

Banbury Citizen
01295 227777
www.banburyguardian.co.uk
Weekly free (Fri). Owner: Johnston Press. Editor: Bridget Dakin; news: Cally Reynolds

Banbury Guardian
01295 227777
www.banburyguardian.co.uk
Weekly (Thu). Owner: Johnston Press. Editor: Bridget Dakin; news: Cally Reynolds

Basingstoke & Northampton Gazette
01256 461131
www.thisishampshire.net
Weekly (Fri). Owner: Newsquest. Editor: Mark Jones; news: Emma Morton; chief sub: Jonathan Lee; production manager: Alan Cranham

Basingstoke Extra
01256 461131
www.thisishampshire.net
Weekly free (Wed). Owner: Newsquest. Editor: Mark Jones; news: Emma Morton; chief sub: Jonathan Lee; production manager: Alan Cranham

Basingstoke Observer
01256 694121
Weekly (Thu). Owner: Milestone Group. Editor: Steve Davies; head of production: Tom McGowran

Beaconsfield Advertiser
01753 888333
www.buckinghamtoday.co.uk
Weekly (Thu). Owner: Trinity Mirror Southern. Editor: Peter Krinks; news: Estelle Sinkins

Berkhamsted & Tring Gazette
01442 262311
www.hemelonline.co.uk
Weekly (Wed). Owner: Johnston Press. Editor: David Feldstein; news: Ann Traynor; sports editor: Graham Caygill

Bicester Advertiser
01865 425262
www.thisisoxfordshire.co.uk
Weekly (Fri). Owner: Newsquest. Editor: Derek Holmes

Bicester Review
01280 813434
www.buckinghamtoday.co.uk
Weekly (Fri). Owner: Buckingham Advertiser Group. Editor: Rob Gibbard; assistant editor: Mark Pendred; deputy editor: Clare Wale

Bordon Post
01730 264811
www.petersfield.co.uk
Weekly (Wed). Owner: Johnston Press. Editor: Graeme Moir; features: Will Parsons

Bordon Times & Mail
01252 716444
Weekly free (Tue). Owner: Tindle Newspapers. Editor: Tony Short; features: Angie Williamson

Brackley & Towcester Advertiser
01280 813434
www.buckinghamtoday.co.uk
Weekly (Fri). Owner: Buckingham Advertiser Group. Editor: Rob Gibbard; assistant editor: Mark Pendred; deputy editor: Clare Wale

Bracknell & Ascot Times
0118 936 6180
www.getbracknell.co.uk
Weekly (Thu). Owner: Guardian Media Group. Editor: Adam D Smith; deputy editor: Matt Blackman; news: Adam J Smith; sports editor: Steve Skerry

Bracknell Midweek News
01344 456611
www.icberkshire.co.uk
Weekly (Thu). Owner: Trinity Mirror Southern. Editor: Joe Wise; chief reporter: James Osborne

Bracknell News
01344 456611
www.icberkshire.co.uk
Weekly (Thu). Owner: Trinity Mirror Southern. Editor: Joe Wise; chief reporter: James Osborne

Bracknell Standard
0118 936 6180
www.getbracknell.co.uk
Weekly (Thu). Owner: Guardian Media Group. Editor: Adam D Smith; deputy editor: Matt Blackman; news: Adam J Smith; sports editor: Steve Skerry

Buckingham & Winslow Advertiser
01280 813434
www.buckinghamtoday.co.uk
Weekly (Fri). Owner: Buckingham Advertiser Group. Editor: Rob Gibbard; assistant editor: Mark Pendred; deputy editor: Clare Wale

Buckinghamshire Advertiser
01753 888333
Weekly (Thu). Owner: Trinity Mirror Southern. Editor: Peter Krinks; news: Estelle Sinkins

Buckinghamshire Echo
0116 233 3635
Weekly (Tue). Owner: Journal Publishing Company. Editor: Elaine Ellis

Buckinghamshire Examiner
01753 888333
www.buckinghamtoday.co.uk
Weekly (Thu). Owner: Trinity Mirror Southern. Editor: Peter Krinks; news: Estelle Sinkins

Bucks Free Press
01494 755000
www.bucksfreepress.co.uk
Weekly (Fri). Owner: Newsquest. Editor: Steve Cohen; news: Julie Voyce

Bucks Free Press Midweek
01494 755081
www.bucksfreepress.co.uk
Weekly (Tue). Owner: Newsquest. Editor: Steve Cohen; news: Julie Voyce; features: Lind Bilgorri

Bucks Herald
01296 318300
www.bucksherald.co.uk
Weekly (Wed). Owner: Johnston Press. Editor: David Summers; news: Sarah Young; features: Rachel Woodbridge

Chippenham, Corsham Advertiser
01225 760945
www.wiltshirepublications.com
Weekly (Thu). Owner: Northcliffe Newspapers. Editor: David Gledhill; news: Paul Wiltshire; features: George McCready; production: Marion Wild

Crowthorne & Sandhurst Times
0118 936 6180
www.getbracknell.co.uk
Weekly (Wed). Owner: Guardian Media Group. Editor: Adam D Smith; news: Matt Blackman; sport: Steve Skerry

Crowthorne, Sandhurst, Owlsmoor Newsweek
01344 456611
www.icberkshire.co.uk
Weekly (Wed). Owner: Trinity Mirror Southern. Editor: Joe Wise; chief reporter: James Osborne

Devizes, Melksham & Vale of Pewsey News
01793 528144
www.thisisswindon.co.uk
Weekly free (Wed). Owner: Newsquest. Editor: Mark Waldron; news: Cath Turnbull

Didcot Herald
01865 425262
www.thisisoxfordshire.co.uk
Weekly (Thu). Owner: Newsquest. Editor: Derek Holmes

Eastleigh News Extra
01962 841772
www.thisishampshire.net
Weekly free (Thu). Owner: Newsquest. Editor: Mary Payne; news: Kit Neilson

Eton Observer
01753 523355
www.thisisslough.com
Weekly (Fri). Owner: Clyde & Forth Press. Editor: Sally Stevens; assistant editor: Mike Sim

Evening Advertiser (Swindon)
01793 528144
www.thisisswindon.co.uk
Daily. Owner: Newsquest. Editor: Mark Waldron; news: Cath Turnbull

Fareham & Gosport Journal
023 9266 4488
www.thisisportsmouth.co.uk
Weekly free (Thu). Owner: Johnston Press. Editor: Mike Gilson; news: Colin McNeill; features: John Millard

Fareham & Gosport News
See The News, page 35

Farnborough News & Mail
01252 339760
www.farnborough.co.uk
Weekly (Tue). Owner: Guardian Media Group. Editor: James Taylor; news: Adam Clark

Fleet News & Mail
01252 339760
www.fleet-online.co.uk
Weekly (Tue). Owner: Guardian Media Group. Editor: James Taylor; news: Adam Clark

Frome Times and White Horse News
01225 704761
www.wiltshirepublications.com
Fortnightly free (Thu). Owner: Wiltshire Publications. Editor: Ian Drew; news: Lorraine Williams

Hamble Valley Journal
023 9266 4488
www.thisisportsmouth.co.uk
Weekly free (Thu). Owner: Johnston Press. Editor: Mike Gilson; news: Colin McNeill; features: John Millard

Hampshire Chronicle
01962 841772
www.thisishampshire.net
Weekly (Fri). Owner: Newsquest. Editor: Keith Redbourn; news: Kit Neilson

Hants & Dorset Avon Advertiser
01722 426500
www.thisiswiltshire.co.uk
Weekly (Wed). Owner: Newsquest. Editor: Bill Browne; news: David Vallis; features: Lesley Bates; chief sub: Sarah Elderkin

Hants & Surrey Post Dispatch
01420 88949
Fortnightly free (Mon). Owner: Tindle Newspapers. Editor: Alan Wooler

Hart Courier
01252 339760
www.surreyad.co.uk
Weekly (Fri). Owner: Guardian Media Group. Editor: James Taylor; news: Adam Clark

Havant & Waterlooville Journal
023 9266 4488
www.thisisportsmouth.co.uk
Weekly free (Thu). Owner: Johnston Press. Editor: Mike Gilson; news: Colin McNeill; features: John Millard

Havant & Waterlooville News
See The News, page 35

Hemel Hempstead Herald & Express
01442 262311
www.hemelonline.co.uk
Weekly (Thu). Owner: Johnston Press. Editor: David Feldstein; news: Ann Traynor; sports editor: Graham Caygill

Henley Standard
01491 419444
www.henleystandard.co.uk
Weekly (Fri). Editor: George Tuckfield; news: David Dawson

Isle of Wight County Press
01983 521333
www.iwcp.co.uk
Weekly (Fri). Editor: Brian Dennis; news: Phil Wolsey

Liphook Times & Mail
01252 716444
Weekly free (Tue). Owner: Tindle Newspapers. Editor: Tony Short; features: Angie Williamson

Lymington Times
01425 613384
Weekly (Fri). Editor: Charles Curry

Maidenhead Advertiser
01628 680680
www.maidenhead-advertiser.co.uk
Weekly (Fri). Editor: Martin Trepte; news: Glenn Mitchell

Maidenhead Express
01753 825111
www.icberkshire.co.uk
Weekly (Fri). Owner: Trinity Mirror Southern. Editor: Paul Thomas; news: Francis Batt

Marlow Free Press
01494 755081
www.bucksfreepress.co.uk
Weekly (Fri). Owner: Newsquest. Editor: Steve Cohen; news: Julie Voyce; features: Lind Bilgorri

Melksham Independent News
01225 704761
www.melkshamnews.com
Fortnightly free (Thu). Owner: Wiltshire Publications. Editor: Ian Drew; news: Lorraine Williams

Meon Valley News
023 9263 2767
www.meonvalleynews.org.uk
Monthly (Mon). Owner: Tindle Newspapers. Editor: Christine Miller; assistant editor: Angela Ennis

Mid Hampshire Observer
01962 859559
www.hantsmedia.co.uk
Weekly (Wed). Owner: Hampshire Media. Editor: Pete Harvey

Milton Keynes Citizen
01908 371133
www.miltonkeynes.co.uk
Weekly free (Thu). Owner: Johnston Press. Editor: Jan Henderson; news: Steve Larner

Milton Keynes Journal
0116 233 3635
Weekly (Tue). Owner: Journal Publishing Company. Editor: Susan Davis

Milton Keynes News
01908 809000
www.seriousaboutnews.co.uk
Weekly (Wed). Owner: LSN Media. Editor: David Gale

47

Monday Gazette
01256 461131
www.thisishampshire.net
Weekly (Mon). Owner: Newsquest.
Editor: Mark Jones; news: Emma
Morton; chief sub: Jonathan Lee;
production manager: Alan Cranham

New Forest Post
01590 613888
www.thisishampshire.net
Weekly (Thu). Owner: Newsquest.
Editor: Ian Murray

New Milton Advertiser
01425 613384
Weekly (Fri). Editor: Charles Curry

Newbury & Thatcham Chronicle
01635 32812
www.icberkshire.co.uk
Weekly free (Wed). Owner: Trinity
Mirror Southern. Editor: Morris O'Brien

Newbury Weekly News
01635 524111
www.newburynews.co.uk
Weekly (Thu). Owner: Blacket Turner.
Editor: Brien Beharrell; news: Martin
Robertshaw

The News (Portsmouth)
See page 35

Oxford Courier
01235 553444
www.courier-newspapers-oxford.co.uk
Weekly (Thu). Owner: Northcliffe
Newspapers. Editor: Lawrence Web;
production: Howard Taylor

Oxford Journal
01235 553444
www.courier-newspapers-oxford.co.uk
/journal.htm
Weekly (Fri). Owner: Northcliffe
Newspapers. Editor: Lawrence Web;
production: Howard Taylor

Oxford Mail
01865 425262
www.thisisoxfordshire.co.uk
Daily. Owner: Newsquest.
Editor: Simon O'Neill

Oxford Star
01865 425262
www.thisisoxfordshire.co.uk
Weekly (Thu). Owner: Newsquest.
Editor: Simon O'Neill

Oxford Times
01865 425262
www.thisisoxfordshire.co.uk
Weekly (Fri). Owner: Newsquest.
Editor: Derek Holmes; news: Stephanie
Preece; chief sub: Marc Evans

Oxfordshire Weekly
01865 425262
www.thisisoxfordshire.co.uk
Weekly (Wed). Owner: Newsquest.
Editor: Derek Holmes

Petersfield Mail
01252 716444
Weekly free (Tue). Owner: Tindle
Newspapers. Editor: Tony Short;
features: Angie Williamson

Petersfield Post
01730 264811
www.petersfield.co.uk
Weekly (Wed). Owner: Johnston Press.
Editor: Graeme Moir; features: Will
Parsons

Portsmouth & Southsea Journal
023 9266 4488
www.thisisportsmouth.co.uk
Weekly free (Thu). Owner: Johnston
Press. Editor: Mike Gilson; news: Colin
McNeill; features: John Millard

Property Chronicle (Berkshire)
0118 950 3030
www.icberkshire.co.uk
Weekly (Wed, Thu). Owner: Trinity
Mirror Southern. Editor: Anthony
Longden; news: Maurice O'Brien;
features: Zenia Poole; production:
Jeremy Drakes

Reading Central
0118 918 3000
www.readingcentral.co.uk
Weekly (Thu). Owner: Guardian Media
Group. Editor: Hiliary Scott; chief sub:
Jenny Laurence

Reading Chronicle
0118 950 3030
www.icberkshire.co.uk
Weekly (Thu). Owner: Trinity Mirror
Southern. Editor: Anthony Longden;
news: Maurice O'Brien; features: Zenia
Poole; production: Jeremy Drakes

Reading Evening Post
0118 918 3000
www.getreading.co.uk
Daily (Mon–Fri). Owner: Guardian
Media Group. Editor: Andy Murrill;
news: Jason Collie; features: Kate
Magee; chief sub: Alan Blayney

Romsey Advertiser
023 8042 4777
www.thisishampshire.net
/hampshire/romsey
Weekly (Fri). Owner: Newsquest.
Editor: Ian Murray; news: Gordon
Sutter; chief sub: Colin Jenkins

Salisbury Avon Advertiser
01722 426500
www.thisiswiltshire.co.uk
Weekly (Wed). Owner: Newsquest.
Editor: Bill Browne; news: David
Vallis; features: Lesley Bates; chief sub:
Sarah Elderkin

Salisbury Journal
01722 426500
www.thisissalisbury.co.uk
Weekly (Thu). Owner: Newsquest.
Editor: Bill Browne; news: David
Vallis; features: Lesley Bates; chief sub:
Sarah Elderkin

Sandhurst & Crowthorne Mail
01252 339760
www.aldershot.co.uk
Weekly (Tue). Owner: Guardian Media
Group. Editor: James Taylor; news:
Adam Clark

Sandhurst & Crowthorne News
01252 339760
www.aldershot.co.uk
Weekly (Fri). Owner: Guardian Media
Group. Editor: James Taylor; news:
Adam Clark

Slough Express
01753 825111
www.icberkshire.co.uk
Weekly (Thu). Owner: Trinity Mirror
Southern. Editor: Paul Thomas; news:
Francis Batt

Slough Observer
01753 523355
www.thisisslough.com
Weekly (Wed). Owner: Clyde & Forth
Press. Editor: Sally Stevens; assistant
editor: Mike Sim

Southern Daily Echo
See page 35

South Bucks, Wycombe & Chiltern
Star and Midweek
01494 755000
www.hillingdontimes.co.uk
Weekly (Tue, Thu). Owner: Newsquest.
Editor: Steve Cohen; news: Sharon
Walters

Southampton Advertiser
023 8042 4777
Weekly (Thu). Owner: Newsquest.
Editor: Ian Murray; news: Gordon
Sutter; chief sub: Colin Jenkins

South Oxfordshire Courier
01235 553444
www.courier-newspapers-oxford.co.uk
Weekly (Thu). Owner: Northcliffe
Newspapers. Editor: Lawrence Web;
production: Howard Taylor

Surrey & Hampshire Guardian
024 7663 1911
Daily. Owner: Journal Publishing
Company. Editor: Jag Basra; news:
Keith Brailford; features: Andrew Woods

Swindon Star
01793 528144
www.thisisswindon.co.uk
Weekly free (Thu). Owner: Newsquest.
Editor: Mark Waldron; news: Cath
Turnbull

Tadley Gazette
01256 461131
www.thisishampshire.net
Weekly free (Wed). Owner: Newsquest.
Editor: Mark Jones; news: Emma
Morton; chief sub: Jonathan Lee;
production manager: Alan Cranham

Thame Gazette
01296 318300
www.aylesburytoday.co.uk
Weekly (Fri). Owner: Johnston Press.
Editor: David Summers; news: Sarah
Young; features: Rachel Woodbridge

Thatcham News
01635 524111
www.newburynews.co.uk
Weekly (Thu). Owner: Blacket Turner.
Editor: Brien Beharrell; news: Martin
Robertshaw

Trowbridge, Melksham,
Bradford-on-Avon Advertiser
01225 760945
www.wiltshirepublications.com
Weekly (Thu). Owner: Northcliffe
Newspapers. Editor: David Gledhill;
news: Paul Wiltshire; features: George
McCready; production: Marion Wild

Twyford Times
0118 936 6180
www.getbracknell.co.uk
Weekly (Wed). Owner: Guardian
Media Group. Editor: Adam D Smith;
news: Matt Blackman; sports editor:
Steve Skerry

Wallingford Herald
01865 425262
www.thisisoxfordshire.co.uk
Weekly (Thu). Owner: Newsquest.
Editor: Derek Holmes

Wantage Herald
01865 425262
www.thisisoxfordshire.co.uk
Weekly (Thu). Owner: Newsquest.
Editor: Derek Holmes

Warminster & Westbury Standard
01373 462379
www.thisissomerset.co.uk
Weekly (Thu). Owner: Northcliffe
Newspapers. Editor: Joanne Roughton

Warminster Journal
01985 213030
Weekly (Fri).
Editors: RC Shorto and DJ Watkins

West & North Wilts Star
01225 777292
www.thisiswiltshire.co.uk
Weekly free (Thu). Owner: Newsquest.
Editor: Andy Sambidge; news: Craig
Evry; features: Sarah Seamarks

Westbury, Warminster Advertiser
01225 760945
www.wiltshirepublications.com
Weekly (Thu). Owner: Northcliffe
Newspapers. Editor: David Gledhill;
news: Paul Wiltshire; features: George
McCready; production: Marion Wild

Wilts & Gloucestershire Standard
01285 642642
www.thisiscirencester.com
Weekly (Thu). Owner: Newsquest.
Editor: Peter Davidson; news: Simon
Davis

Wiltshire Gazette and Herald
01793 528144
www.thisisswindon.co.uk
Weekly (Thu). Owner: Newsquest.
Editor: Mark Waldron; news: Gary
Lawrence

Wiltshire Guardian
024 7663 1911
Weekly free (Thu). Owner: Journal
Publishing Company. Editor: Jag
Basra; news: Keith Brailford; features:
Andrew Woods

Wiltshire Times
01225 777292
www.thisiswiltshire.co.uk
Weekly (Fri). Owner: Newsquest.
Editor: Andy Sambidge; news: Craig
Evry; features: Sarah Seamarks

Winchester News Extra
01962 841772
www.thisishampshire.net
Weekly free (Thu). Owner: Newsquest.
Editor: Mary Payne; news: Kit Neilson

Winchester Shopper
023 8042 4777
www.thisishampshire.net
Sunday. Owner: Newsquest.
Editor: Ian Murray; news: Gordon
Sutter; chief sub: Colin Jenkins

Windsor, Ascot & Maidenhead Observer
01753 523355
www.thisiswindsor.com
Weekly (Fri). Owner: Clyde & Forth
Press. Editor: Sally Stevens; assistant
editor: Mike Sim

Windsor Express
01753 825111
www.icberkshire.co.uk
Weekly free (Thu). Owner: Trinity
Mirror Southern. Editor: Paul Thomas;
news: Francis Batt

Witney & West Oxfordshire Gazette
01865 425262
www.thisisoxfordshire.co.uk
Weekly (Wed). Owner: Newsquest.
Editor: Derek Holmes

Wodley Times
0118 936 6180
www.getbracknell.co.uk
Weekly (Wed). Owner: Guardian
Media Group. Editor: Adam D Smith;
news: Matt Blackman; sports editor:
Steve Skerry

Woking Midweek
01344 456611
www.icberkshire.co.uk
Weekly (Wed). Owner: Trinity Mirror
Southern. Editor: Joe Wise; chief
reporter: James Osborne

Wokingham News
01344 456611
www.icberkshire.co.uk
Weekly (Wed). Owner: Trinity Mirror
Southern. Editor: Joe Wise; chief
reporter: James Osborne

Wokingham Standard
0118 936 6180
www.getbracknell.co.uk
Weekly (Thu). Owner: Guardian Media
Group. Editor: Adam D Smith; deputy
editor: Matt Blackman; news: Adam J
Smith; sports editor: Steve Skerry

Wokingham Times
0118 936 6180
www.getbracknell.co.uk
Weekly (Thu). Owner: Guardian Media
Group. Editor: Adam D Smith; deputy
editor: Matt Blackman; news: Adam J
Smith; sports editor: Steve Skerry

Woodley & Earley Chronicle
0118 963 3030
www.icberkshire.co.uk
Weekly (Thu). Owner: Trinity Mirror
Southern. Editor: Anthony Longden;
news: Maurice O'Brien; features: Zenia
Poole; production: Jeremy Drakes

Yateley Mail
01252 339760
www.aldershot.co.uk
Weekly (Tue). Owner: Guardian Media
Group. Editor: James Taylor; news:
Adam Clark

Yateley News
01252 339760
www.aldershot.co.uk
Weekly (Fri). Owner: Guardian Media
Group. Editor: James Taylor; news:
Adam Clark

South-west England

Cornwall, Devon, Dorset,
Somerset & Avon

Bath Chronicle
01225 322322
www.thisisbath.co.uk
Daily. Owner: Northcliffe Newspapers.
Editor: Sam Holliday; news: Paul
Wiltshire; features: Georgette
McCready; chief sub: Graham Holburn

Bath Times
01225 322322
www.thisisbath.co.uk
Weekly (Wed). Owner: Northcliffe
Newspapers. Editor: Sam Holliday;
news: Paul Wiltshire

Bournemouth Advertiser
01202 554601
www.thisisdorset.net
Weekly free (Thu). Owner: Newsquest.
Editor: Neal Butterworth; news: Andy
Martin; features: Kevin Nash

Bridgwater Mercury
01823 365151
www.thisisthewestcountry.co.uk
Weekly (Tue). Owner: Newsquest.
Editor-in-chief: Ken Bird; deputy
group editor: Bob Drayton

Bridgwater Star
01823 365151
www.thisisthewestcountry.co.uk
Weekly (Thu). Owner: Newsquest.
Editor-in-chief: Ken Bird; deputy
group editor: Bob Drayton

Bridgwater Times
01275 335100
www.thisissomerset.co.uk
Weekly (Thu). Owner: Northcliffe
Newspapers. Editor: Carol Deacon;
news: Juliette Auty

Bridport & Lyme Regis News
01308 425884
www.thisisdorset.net/dorset
/bridportandlyme
Weekly (Fri). Owner: Newsquest.
Editor: Holly Robinson

Bristol Evening Post
See page 34

Bristol Observer
0117 934 3401
www.thisisbristol.co.uk
Weekly free (Fri). Owner: Northcliffe
Newspapers. Editor: Peter O'Reilly

Brixham News
01803 864212
Weekly free (Wed). Owner: Tindle
Newspapers. Editor: Gina Coles

Bude & Stratton Post
01566 772424
Weekly (Thu). Owner: Tindle
Newspapers. Editor: Geoff Seccombe;
news: Keith Whitford

Burnham & Highbridge Mercury
01823 365151
www.thisisthewestcountry.co.uk
Weekly (Tue). Owner: Newsquest.
Editor-in-chief: Ken Bird; deputy
group editor: Bob Drayton

Burnham & Highbridge Times
01275 335100
www.thisissomerset.co.uk
*Weekly (Thu). Owner: Northcliffe
Newspapers. Editor: Carol Deacon;
news: Juliette Auty*

Burnham & Highbridge Weekly News
01823 365151
www.thisisthewestcountry.co.uk
*Weekly (Thu). Owner: Newsquest.
Editor-in-chief: Ken Bird; deputy
group editor: Bob Drayton*

Camborne and Redruth Packet
01326 213333
www.thisisthewestcountry.co.uk
*Weekly free (Wed). Owner: Newsquest.
Editor: Terry Lambert; news: Stephen
Ivall; chief sub: David Robinson*

**Camelford & Delabole Journal
Gazette**
01566 772424
*Weekly (Fri). Owner: Tindle
Newspapers. Editor: Geoff Seccombe;
news: Keith Whitford*

Camelford & Delabole Post
01566 772424
*Weekly (Thu). Owner: Tindle
Newspapers. Editor: Geoff Seccombe;
news: Keith Whitford*

Central Somerset Gazette
01749 832300
www.thisissomerset.co.uk
*Weekly (Fri). Owner: Northcliffe
Newspapers. Editor: Philip Welch*

Chard & Ilminster News
01823 365151
www.thisisthewestcountry.co.uk
*Weekly (Wed). Owner: Newsquest.
Editor-in-chief: Ken Bird; deputy
group editor: Bob Drayton*

Chard & Ilminster News (Somerset)
01460 67474
www.thisisthewestcountry.co.uk
*Weekly (Wed). Owner: Newsquest.
Editor: Ken Bird; chief reporter: Alex
Cameron*

Chard Advertiser
01297 357504
www.chard-today.co.uk
*Weekly free (Fri). Owner: Tindle
Newspapers. Editor: Tony Woodman*

Cheddar Valley Gazette
01749 832300
www.thisissomerset.co.uk
*Weekly (Thu). Owner: Northcliffe
Newspapers. Editor: Philip Welch*

Chew Valley Gazette
01275 332266
www.chewvalleygazette.co.uk
*Monthly (last Fri). Owner: Northcliffe
Newspapers. Editor: Rowland Janes;
features: Anne Collier*

Clevedon Mercury
01275 335142
www.thisissomerset.co.uk
*Weekly (Thu). Owner: Northcliffe
Newspapers. Editor: Carol Deacon;
news: Juliette Auty; chief sub: Kevin Lee*

Cornish & Devon Post
01566 772424
*Weekly (Thu). Owner: Tindle
Newspapers. Editor: Geoff Seccombe;
news: Keith Whitford*

Cornish Guardian
01208 78133
www.cornishguardian.co.uk
*Weekly (Thu). Owner: Northcliffe
Newspapers. Editor: Alan Cooper; news:
Ian Sheppard; chief sub: Anna Witney*

The Cornishman
01736 362247
www.thisiscornwall.co.uk
*Weekly (Thu). Owner: Northcliffe
Newspapers. Editor: Jeremy Ridge;
features: Joyce Channon*

Cornish Times
01579 342174
www.liskeard-today.co.uk
*Weekly (Fri). Owner: Tindle
Newspapers. Editor: John Noble*

Crewkerne Advertiser
01297 631120
www.crewkerne-today.co.uk
*Weekly free (Fri). Owner: Tindle
Newspapers. Editor: Tony Woodman*

Culm, Crediton & Tiverton Gazette
01884 252725
*Weekly (Tue). Owner: Northcliffe
Newspapers. Editor: Mary-Ann
Bloomfield*

Daily Echo
See page 35

Dartmouth Chronicle
01548 853101
www.dartmouth-today.co.uk
*Weekly (Fri). Owner: Tindle
Newspapers. Editor: Gina Coles; chief
sub: Lucy Baker-Kind*

Dawlish Gazette
01626 353555
www.dawlish-today.co.uk
*Weekly (Fri). Owner: Tindle
Newspapers. Editor: Ruth Davey; news:
John Belment; chief sub: Steven Taylor*

Dawlish Post
01626 353555
www.dawlish-today.co.uk
*Weekly (Fri). Owner: Tindle
Newspapers. Editor: Ruth Davey; news:
John Belment; chief sub: Steven Taylor*

Dorchester Advertiser
01305 830930
www.thisisdorset.net
*Weekly (Thu). Owner: Newsquest.
Editor: David Murdock; news: Paul
Thomas; features: Dirmaid
Macdonagh; chief sub: Nick Horton*

Dorset Echo
01305 830930
www.thisisdorset.net
*Weekly (Thu). Owner: Newsquest.
Editor: David Murdock; news: Paul
Thomas; features: Dirmaid Macdonagh*

Exeter Express and Echo
01392 442211
www.thisisexeter.co.uk
*Daily. Owner: Northcliffe Newspapers.
Acting editor: Tim Dixon; news: Sue
Kemp; features: Lynne Turner;
production: Jerry Charge*

Exeter Leader
01392 442211
www.thisisexeter.co.uk
*Weekly free (Wed). Owner: Northcliffe
Newspapers. Acting editor: Tim Dixon;
news: Sue Kemp; features: Lynne Turner*

Exmouth Herald
01392 888444
www.exmouthherald.co.uk
*Weekly free (Fri). Owner: Archant.
Chief sub: Mary Evans*

Falmouth Packet
01326 213333
www.thisisthewestcountry.co.uk
*Weekly (Thu). Owner: Newsquest.
Editor: Terry Lambert; news: Stephen
Ivall; chief sub: David Robinson*

Frome & Somerset Standard
01225 322322
www.thisissomerset.co.uk
*Weekly (Thu). Owner: Northcliffe
Newspapers. Editor: Joanne Roughton;
features: Aliya Frostick*

Frome Times
01225 704761
www.frometimes.co.uk
*Fortnightly free (Thu). Editor: Ian
Drew; news: Lorraine Williams*

Hayle Times
01736 795813
www.stivesnews.co.uk
*Weekly (Fri). Editor: Toni Carver; news:
Paul Pocock; features: Tricia Carver*

Helston Gazette
01326 213333
www.thisisthewestcountry.co.uk
*Weekly free (Wed). Owner: Newsquest.
Editor: Terry Lambert; news: Stephen
Ivall; chief sub: David Robinson*

Holsworthy Post
01566 778220
*Weekly (Fri). Owner: Tindle
Newspapers. Editor: Keith Whitford*

Honiton Advertiser
01297 33034
www.pulmansweekly.co.uk
*Weekly (Wed). Owner: Tindle
Newspapers. General manager: Keith
Hawkins; editorial manager: Tony
Woodman*

**Ivybridge, South Brent & South
Hams Gazette**
01548 853101
www.ivybridge-today.co.uk
*Weekly (Fri). Owner: Tindle
Newspapers. Editor: Gina Coles; chief
sub: Lucy Baker-Kind*

Journal (Exmouth)
01392 888444
www.archantdevon.co.uk/journal.asp
*Weekly (Thu). Owner: Archant.
Editor: Mary Evans*

Kingsbridge & Salcombe Gazette
01548 853101
*Weekly (Fri). Owner: Tindle
Newspapers. Editor: Gina Coles; chief
sub: Lucy Baker-Kind*

Launceston Journal Gazette
01566 772424
*Weekly (Fri). Owner: Tindle
Newspapers. Editor: Geoff Seccombe;
news: Keith Whitford*

Liskeard Gazette & Journal
01579 342174
Weekly (Wed). Owner: Tindle
Newspapers. Editor: Mary Richards

Mid Cornwall Advertiser
01726 66755
www.midcornwall-today.co.uk
Monthly (middle of month). Owner:
Tindle Newspapers. Editor: Fiona Jolley

Mid Devon Advertiser
01626 353555
www.newton-abbot-today.co.uk
Weekly (Fri). Owner: Tindle
Newspapers. Editor: Ruth Davey; news:
John Belment; chief sub: Steven Taylor

Mid Devon Star
01823 365151
www.thisisthewestcountry.co.uk
Weekly (Fri). Owner: Newsquest.
Editor-in-chief: Ken Bird; deputy
group editor: Bob Drayton

Midweek Herald
01392 888444
www.archantdevon.co.uk
Weekly (Wed). Owner: Archant.
Editor: Peter Le Riche

Newquay Voice
01637 878298
www.newquayvoice.co.uk
Weekly (Wed). Editor: Andrew Laming;
deputy editor: Matt Bond

North Cornwall Advertiser
01208 815096
www.northcornwall-today.co.uk
Monthly free (1st Wed). Owner: Tindle
Newspapers. Editor: Tony Gregan

North Devon Gazette & Advertiser
01271 344303
www.northdevongazette.co.uk
Weekly (Wed). Owner: Archant.
Editor: David Tanner

North Devon Journal
01271 347420
www.thisisnorthdevon.co.uk
Weekly (Thu). Owner: Northcliffe
Newspapers. Managing editor: Andy
Cooper; deputy editor: Richard Best;
features: Sue Robinson

North Somerset Times
01934 422622
www.thewestonmercury.co.uk
Weekly (Wed). Owner: Archant.
Editor: Heather Pickstock; news: Andy
Ridgeway

Okehampton Times
01822 613666
www.okehampton-today.co.uk
Weekly (Thu). Owner: Tindle
Newspapers. Editor: Colin Brent

Ottery Advertiser
01297 33034
Weekly (Wed). Owner: Tindle
Newspapers. General manager: Keith
Hawkins; editorial manager: Tony
Woodman

Penwith Pirate
01326 213333
www.thisisthewestcountry.co.uk
Weekly free (Wed). Owner: Newsquest.
Editor: Terry Lambert; news: Stephen
Ivall; chief sub: David Robinson

Plymouth Evening Herald
See page 35

Plymouth Extra
01752 765525
www.thisisthewestcountry.co.uk
Weekly free (Thu). Owner: Northcliffe
Newspapers. Editor: Paul Atkins; news:
Pam Guyatt

Plympton Plymstock & Ivybridge
News
01548 853101
Weekly (Fri). Owner: Tindle
Newspapers. Editor: Gina Coles; chief
sub: Lucy Baker-Kind

Poole Advertiser
01202 675413
Weekly free (Thu). Owner: Newsquest.
Editor: Neal Butterworth; news: Andy
Martin; features: Kevin Nash

Post Advertiser
01305 830900
Monthly free (Mon). Owner: Newsquest.
Editor: Bob Conway

Princetown Times
01822 613666
www.thisisthewestcountry.co.uk
Weekly (Thu). Owner: Tindle
Newspapers. Editor: Colin Brent

St Ives Times & Echo
01736 795813
www.stivesnews.co.uk
Weekly (Fri). Editor: Toni Carver; news:
Paul Pocock; features: Tricia Carver

Shepton Mallet Journal
01749 832300
www.thisissomerset.co.uk
Weekly (Thu). Owner: Northcliffe
Newspapers. Editor: Philip Welch

Sidmouth Herald
01392 888444
www.archantdevon.co.uk
Weekly (Fri). Owner: Archant.
Editor: Emma Silverthorne

Somerset County Gazette
01823 365151
www.thisisthewestcountry.co.uk
Weekly (Fri). Owner: Newsquest.
Editor-in-chief: Ken Bird; deputy
group editor: Bob Drayton

Somerset Guardian
01225 322322
www.thisissomerset.co.uk
Weekly (Thu). Owner: Northcliffe
Newspapers. Editor: Joanne Roughton;
features: Aliya Frostick

South Devon & Plymouth Times
01584 856353
www.thisisthewestcountry.co.uk
Weekly (Thu). Owner: Tindle
Newspapers. Editor: Gina Coles

Sunday Independent
01752 206600
www.thisisthewestcountry.co.uk
Sunday. Owner: Tindle Newspapers.
Editor: John Noble; news: Nikki Belso

Swanage and Wareham District
Advertiser
01929 427428
www.thisisdorset.net
Weekly free (Thu). Owner: Newsquest.
Editor: Neal Butterworth; news: Paula
Tegerdine

Taunton Star
01823 365151
www.tauntonstar.co.uk
Weekly (Wed). Owner: Newsquest.
Editor: Neal Butterworth; deputy
group editor: Bob Drayton

Taunton Times
01823 250500
www.thisissomerset.co.uk
Weekly free (Thu). Owner: Northcliffe
Newspapers. Editor: Debbie Rundle;
news: Steve Weatherill

Tavistock Times Gazette
01822 613666
www.tavistock-today.co.uk
Weekly (Thu). Owner: Tindle
Newspapers. Editor: Colin Brent

Teignmouth News
01626 353555
www.teignmouth-today.co.uk
Weekly (Fri). Owner: Tindle
Newspapers. Editor: Ruth Davey; news:
John Belment; chief sub: Steven Taylor

Teignmouth Post & Gazette
01626 353555
www.teignmouth-today.co.uk
Weekly (Fri). Owner: Tindle
Newspapers. Editor: Ruth Davey; news:
John Belment; chief sub: Steven Taylor

Torbay Weekender
01803 676000
www.thisissouthdevon.co.uk
Weekly (Thu). Owner: Northcliffe
Newspapers. Editor: Brendan
Hanrahan; news: Jim Parker; features:
Nick Pannell; chief sub: Nigel Lines

Torquay Herald Express
01803 676000
www.thisissouthdevon.co.uk
Daily. Owner: Northcliffe Newspapers.
Editor: Brendan Hanrahan; news: Jim
Parker; features: Nick Pannell; chief
sub: Nigel Lines

Totnes News
01548 853101
Weekly (Fri). Owner: Tindle
Newspapers. Editor: Gina Coles; chief
sub: Lucy Baker-Kind

Totnes Times Gazette
01584 856353
www.thisisthewestcountry.co.uk
Weekly (Thu). Owner: Tindle
Newspapers. Editor: Gina Coles

Trader News (West Somerset)
01984 632731
Weekly free (Wed). Owner: Northcliffe
Newspapers. Editor: Gareth Purcell

Truro Packet
01326 213333
www.thisisthewestcountry.co.uk
Weekly (Wed). Owner: Newsquest.
Editor: Terry Lambert; news: Stephen
Ivall; chief sub: David Robinson

Wellington Weekly News
01823 250500
www.thisissomerset.co.uk
Weekly (Wed). Owner: Northcliffe
Newspapers. Editor: Debbie Rundle;
news: Steve Weatherill

Wells Journal
01749 832300
www.thisissomerset.co.uk
Weekly (Thu). Owner: Northcliffe
Newspapers. Editor: Philip Welch

The West Briton
01872 271451
www.thisiscornwall.co.uk
Weekly (Thu). Owner: Northcliffe
Newspapers. Editor: Richard
Vanhinsberg; chief reporter: Lyn Barton

West Somerset Free Press
01984 632731
www.west-somerset-today.co.uk
Weekly (Fri). Owner: Northcliffe
Newspapers. Editor: Gareth Purcell

Western Daily Press (Bristol)
See page 36

Western Gazette
01935 700500
www.westgaz.co.uk
Weekly (Thu). Owner: Northcliffe
Newspapers. Editor: Martin Heal; news:
Zena O'Rourke; features: Carla Gale

Western Morning News (Plymouth)
See page 36

Weston & Worle News
01275 335140
www.thisissomerset.co.uk
Weekly (Thu). Owner: Northcliffe
Newspapers. Editor: Carol Deacon;
news: Juliette Auty; chief sub: Kevin Lee

Weston Mercury
01934 422622
www.thewestonmercury.co.uk
Weekly (Fri). Owner: Archant. Editor:
Judy Kisiel; news: Andy Ridgeway

Weston-super-Mare Admag
01934 422622
www.thewestonmercury.co.uk
Weekly (Wed). Owner: Archant. Editor:
Judy Kisiel; news: Andy Ridgeway

Weymouth & Portland Advertiser
01305 830930
www.thisisdorset.net
Weekly (Thu). Owner: Newsquest.
Editor: David Murdock; news: Paul
Thomas; features: Dirmaid Macdonagh

Yeovil and Clarion
01752 206600
www.yeovil-clarion-today.co.uk
Weekly free (Fri). Owner: Tindle
Newspapers. Editor: John Noble

Yeovil Express
01823 365151
www.thisisthewestcountry.co.uk
Weekly (Thu). Owner: Newsquest.
Editor-in-chief: Ken Bird; deputy
group editor: Bob Drayton

Yeovil Times
01935 700500
Weekly free (Wed). Owner: Northcliffe
Newspapers. Editor: Martin Heal; news:
Zena O'Rourke; features: Carla Gale

East England

Cambridgeshire, Essex, Lincolnshire,
Norfolk, Suffolk

Alford Standard
01754 897120
www.skegnesstoday.co.uk
Weekly (Wed). Owner: Johnston Press.
Editor: John Coupe

Axholme Herald
01427 874417
Weekly (Fri). Owner: Northcliffe
Newspapers. Editor: Ron Shipley

Barking & Dagenham Post
0845 070 0161
www.bdpost.co.uk
Weekly (Thu). Owner: Archant.
Editor: Amanda Patterson; news:
Wayne Tuckfield

Barking & Dagenham Recorder
020 8478 4444
www.recorderonline.co.uk
Weekly (Thu). Owner: Archant.
Editor: Chris Carter

Barking & Dagenham Weekender
0845 070 0161
Weekly (Fri). Owner: Archant. Editor:
Amanda Patterson; news: Wayne
Tuckfield; chief sub: Graham Whitmore

Barking & Dagenham Yellow Advertiser
01268 503400
www.trinitymirrorsouthern.co.uk
Weekly (Thu). Owner: Trinity Mirror
Southern. Editor: Paula Dady;
features: Pat Jones

Basildon & Wickford Recorder
01268 522792
www.thisisessex.co.uk
Daily. Owner: Newsquest. Editor:
Martin McNeill; news: Chris Hatton;
chief sub: Neal Reeve

Basildon Yellow Advertiser
01268 503400
www.trinitymirrorsouthern.co.uk
Weekly (Thu). Owner: Trinity Mirror
Southern. Editor: Paula Dady; features:
Pat Jones

Beccles & Bungay Journal
01603 628311
www.edp24.co.uk
Weekly (Fri). Owner: Archant.
Editor: Terry Redhead

Billericay & Wickford Gazette
01277 219222
www.thisisessex.co.uk
Weekly (Wed). Owner: Northcliffe
Newspapers. Editor: Roger Watkins;
news: Sheelagh Bree; features: Josie
Stephenson

Boston Citizen
01205 311433
www.bostontoday.co.uk
Weekly (Fri). Owner: Johnston Press.
Editor: Julia Ogden; news: Pam
Browne; chief sub: Warren Moody

Boston Focus
01205 354547
www.bostonuk.com/focus
Monthly free. Owner: Northcliffe
Newspapers. Editor: Irene Kettle; news:
Sally Teatheredge; features: Iris Clapp;
chief sub: Will Bramhill

Boston Standard
01205 311433
www.bostontoday.co.uk
Weekly (Wed). Owner: Johnston Press.
Editor: Julia Ogden; news: Pam
Browne; chief sub: Warren Moody

Boston Target
01522 820000
www.thisislincolnshire.co.uk
Weekly (Wed). Owner: Northcliffe
Newspapers. Editor: Glyn Belsher

Braintree & Witham Times
01376 343344
www.thisisessex.co.uk
Weekly (Thu). Owner: Newsquest.
Editor: James Wills; news: Veronica Balls

Braintree Chronicle
01245 600700
www.thisisessex.co.uk
Weekly (Wed/Thu). Owner: Northcliffe
Newspapers. Editor: Stuart Rawlins;
news: Matt Adams; features: Darryl
Webber

Brentwood, Billericay & Havering Recorder
01708 771500
www.romfordrecorder.co.uk
Weekly (Fri). Owner: Archant. Editor:
Mark Sweetingham; news: Eden Black

Brentwood Gazette
01277 219222
www.thisisessex.co.uk
Weekly (Wed). Owner: Northcliffe
Newspapers. Editor: Roger Watkins;
news: Sheelagh Bree; features: Josie
Stephenson

Brentwood Weekly News
01268 522792
www.thisisessex.co.uk
Weekly (Thu). Owner: Newsquest.
Editor: Martin McNeill; news: Chris
Hatton; chief sub: Neal Reeve

Brentwood Yellow Advertiser
01268 503400
www.trinitymirrorsouthern.co.uk
Weekly free (Fri). Owner: Trinity
Mirror Southern. Editor: Paula Dady;
features: Pat Jones

Bury Free Press
01284 768911
www.buryfreepress.co.uk
Weekly (Fri). Owner: Johnston Press.
Editor: Barry Peters; news: Lesley
Anslow; features: Sue Green

Bury St Edmunds Citizen
01284 768911
Weekly (Fri). Owner: Johnston Press.
Editor: Barry Peters; news: Lesley
Anslow; features: Sue Green

Bury St Edmunds Mercury
01284 702588
www.edp24.co.uk
Weekly (Fri). Owner: Archant. Editor:
Paul Couch; news: Will Grahame-Clarke

Cambridge Crier
01223 434434
www.cambridge-news.co.uk
Weekly (Fri). Owner: Cambridge
Newspapers. Editor: Nigel Brookes;
features: James Fuller

Cambridge Evening News
01223 434434
www.cambridge-news.co.uk
Daily. Owner: Cambridge Newspapers.
Editor: Murray Morse; news: John
Deex; features: Paul Kirkley

Cambridge Weekly News
01223 434434
www.cambridge-news.co.uk
Weekly (Wed). Owner: Cambridge
Newspapers. Editor: Nigel Brookes

Cambridgeshire Times
01354 652621
Weekly (Thu). Owner: Archant.
Editor: Brian Asplin; news: John
Elworthy; features: Maggie Gibson

Castle Point Yellow Advertiser
01268 503400
www.trinitymirrorsouthern.co.uk
Weekly free (Thu). Owner: Trinity
Mirror Southern. Editor: Paula Dady;
features: Pat Jones

Castlepoint & Rayleigh Standard
01268 522792
www.thisisessex.co.uk
Weekly (Wed). Owner: Newsquest.
Editor: Martin McNeill; news: Chris
Hatton; chief sub: Neal Reeve

Chatteris Times
01354 652621
www.cambs-times.co.uk
Weekly (Thu). Owner: Archant.
Editor: Brian Asplin; news: John
Elworthy; features: Maggie Gibson

Chelmsford Chronicle
01245 600700
www.thisisessex.co.uk
Weekly (Wed, Thu). Owner: Northcliffe
Newspapers. Editor: Stuart Rawlins;
news: Matt Adams; features: Darryl
Webber

Chelmsford Weekly News
01245 493444
www.thisisessex.co.uk
Weekly (Thu). Owner: Newsquest.
Editor: Neil Thomas; news: Denise Rigby

Chelmsford Yellow Advertiser
01268 503400
www.trinitymirrorsouthern.co.uk
Weekly free (Thu). Owner: Trinity
Mirror Southern. Editor: Paula Dady;
features: Pat Jones

Clacton & Frinton Gazette
01255 221221
www.thisisessex.co.uk
Weekly (Fri). Owner: Newsquest.
Chief sub: Nigel Brown

Colchester Evening Gazette
01206 506000
www.nqe.info
Daily. Owner: Newsquest.
Editor-in-chief: Irene Kettle; news:
Sally Teatheredge; features: Iris Clapp;
chief sub: Will Bramhill

Dereham & Fakenham Times
01603 628311
www.edp24.co.uk
Weekly (Thu). Owner: Archant.
Editor: Terry Redhead

Diss Express
01379 642264
www.dissexpress.co.uk
Weekly (Fri). Owner: Johnston Press.
Editor: Terry Redhead

Diss Mercury
01603 628311
www.edp24.co.uk
Weekly (Fri). Owner: Archant.
Editor: Terry Redhead

Dunmow & Stansted Chronicle
01245 600700
www.thisisessex.co.uk
Weekly (Wed/Thu). Owner: Northcliffe
Newspapers. Editor: Stuart Rawlins;
news: Matt Adams; features: Darryl
Webber

Dunmow Broadcast and Recorder
01371 874537
www.dunmow-broadcast.co.uk
Weekly free (Thu). Owner: Archant.
Editor: Mike Almond; reporter: Jenny
Oliveira

Dunmow Observer
01279 866355
www.herts-essex-news.co.uk
Weekly (Thu). Owner: Herts & Essex
Newspapers. Editor: Val Brown; news:
Sandra Perry

East Anglian Daily Times
See page 35

East Herts Herald
01279 624331
www.herald24.co.uk
Weekly (Thu). Owner: Archant. Editor:
Barry Hunt; news: Tracey Hubbard

Eastern Daily Press
See page 35

Ely Standard
01353 667831
www.ely-standard.co.uk
Weekly (Thu). Owner: Archant.
Editor: John Ison; news: Debbie Davies

Epping & Waltham Yellow Advertiser
01268 503400
www.trinitymirrorsouthern.co.uk
Weekly free (Thu). Owner: Trinity
Mirror Southern. Editor: Paula Dady;
features: Pat Jones

Epping Guardian
01992 572285
www.eppingguardian.co.uk
Weekly (Thu). Owner: Newsquest.
Editor: David Jackman

Epping Independent
020 8498 3400
www.newsquest.co.uk
Weekly (Thu). Owner: Newsquest.
Editor: David Jackman

Epping Star
01279 838111
www.thisisessex.co.uk
Weekly (Thu). Owner: Herts & Essex
Newspapers. Editor: Ken Morley;
news: Mark Fletcher

Epworth Bells & Crowle Advertiser
01427 872202
www.epworthtoday.co.uk
Weekly (Thu). Owner: Johnston Press.
Editor: Janet Harrison

Essex Chronicle
01245 600700
www.thisisessex.co.uk
Weekly (Wed/Thu). Owner: Northcliffe
Newspapers. Editor: Stuart Rawlins;
news: Matt Adams; features: Darryl
Webber

Essex County Standard
01206 506000
www.nqe.info
Weekly (Fri). Owner: Newsquest.
Editor: Jo Robinson; news: David
Grocott; features: Iris Clapp; chief sub:
Will Bramhill

Essex Enquirer
01277 627300
www.thisisessex.co.uk
Weekly (Thu). Owner: Newsquest.
Editor: Carol Driver

Evening Echo (Essex)
01268 522792
www.thisisessex.co.uk
Daily. Owner: Newsquest. Editor:
Martin McNeill; news: Chris Hatton;
chief sub: Neal Reeve

Evening News (Norwich)
01603 628311
www.eveningnews24.co.uk
Daily. Owner: Archant.
Editor: David Bourn

Evening Star (Ipswich)
01473 324788
www.eveningstar.co.uk
Daily. Owner: Archant. Editor: Nigel
Pickover; news: Martin Davey;
features: Tracy Sparling

Fenland Citizen
01945 586100
www.fenlandtoday.co.uk
Weekly (Wed). Owner: Johnston Press.
Editor: Keith Drayton

Gainsborough Standard
01427 615323
www.gainsboroughtoday.co.uk
Weekly (Thu). Owner: Johnston Press.
Editor: Janet Harrison

Gainsborough Target
01427 810148
www.thisislincolnshire.co.uk
Weekly (Fri). Owner: Northcliffe
Newspapers. Editor: Mike Sassi

Goole Courier
01405 782400
www.gooletoday.co.uk
Weekly (Thu). Owner: Johnston Press.
Editor: Janet Harrison; news:
Stephanie Bateman

Goole Times/Selby Post
01405 720110
www.horshamonline.co.uk
Weekly (Thu). Owner: Northcliffe
Newspapers. Editor: Peter Butler

Grantham Citizen
01476 562291
www.granthamtoday.co.uk
Weekly (Tue). Owner: Johnston Press.
Editor: Nick Woodhead; news: John
Pinchbeck

Grantham Journal
01476 562291
www.granthamtoday.co.uk
Weekly (Fri). Owner: Johnston Press.
Editor: Nick Woodhead; news: John
Pinchbeck

Great Yarmouth & Gorleston Advertiser
01493 601206
www.advertiser-online.co.uk
Weekly (Thu). Owner: Archant.
Editor: Nick Woodhead; senior
reporter: Leanne Boast

Great Yarmouth Mercury
01603 628311
www.edp24.co.uk
Weekly (Tue). Owner: Archant.
Editor: Terry Redhead

Grimsby Evening Telegraph
01472 360360
www.thisisgrimsby.co.uk
Daily. Owner: Northcliffe Newspapers
Editor: Michelle Lalor; news: Dave
Atkin; features: Steve Richards;
production: Barrie Farnsworth

Grimsby Target
01472 360360
www.thisisgrimsby.co.uk
Weekly free (Wed). Owner: Northcliffe
Newspapers. Editor: Michelle Lalor;
news: Dave Atkin; features: Steve
Richards; production: Barrie
Farnsworth

Halstead Gazette
01376 343344
www.thisisessex.co.uk
Weekly (Fri). Owner: Newsquest. Editor:
James Wills; news: Veronica Balls

Harlow Herald
01279 624331
www.herald24.co.uk
Weekly (Thu). Owner: Archant. Editor:
Barry Hunt; news: Tracey Hubbard

Harlow Star
01279 838111
www.herts-essex-news.co.uk
Weekly (Thu). Owner: Herts & Essex
Newspapers. Editor: Barry Hunt; news:
Mark Fletcher

Harold Gazette
01277 219222
www.thisisessex.co.uk
Weekly (Wed). Owner: Northcliffe
Newspapers. Editor: Roger Watkins;
news: Sheelagh Bree; features: Josie
Stephenson

Harold Recorder
01708 771500
www.recorderonline.co.uk
Weekly (Fri). Owner: Archant. Editor:
Mark Sweetingham; news: Eden Black

Haverhill Echo
01440 703456
www.buryfreepress.co.uk
Weekly (Thu). Owner: Johnston Press.
News editor: David Hart

Haverhill Weekly News
01223 434434
www.cambridge-news.co.uk
Weekly (Thu). Owner: Cambridge
Newspapers. Editor: Nigel Brookes

Havering Herald
0845 070 0161
Weekly free (Fri). Owner: Archant.
Editor: Richard Thompson

Havering Yellow Advertiser
01268 503400
www.trinitymirrorsouthern.co.uk
Weekly (Wed). Owner: Trinity Mirror
Southern. Editor: Paula Dady;
features: Pat Jones

Horncastle News
01507 353200
www.horncastletoday.co.uk
Weekly (Wed). Owner: Johnston Press.
Managing editor: Tim Robinson;
editor: Janet Richardson

Huntingdon Town Crier
01480 402100
www.cambridge-news.co.uk
Weekly (Thu). Owner: Johnston Press.
Editor: Richard Yetman

Huntingdon Weekly News
01223 434434
www.cambridge-news.co.uk
Weekly (Wed). Owner: Newsquest.
Editor: Murray Morse; news: John Deex

Hunts Post
01480 411481
www.huntspost.co.uk
Weekly (Wed). Owner: Archant.
Editor: Paul Richardson; deputy
editor: Angela Singer

Ilford & Redbridge Post
0845 070 0161
Weekly free (Wed). Owner: Archant.
Editor: Amanda Patterson; news: Wayne
Tuckfield; chief sub: Graham Whitmore

Ipswich Advertiser
01473 324700
www.advertiser-online.co.uk
Weekly (Thu). Owner: Archant. Editor:
Paul Couch; news: Nicola Durrant

Island Times (Canvey Island)
01702 477666
Monthly (Tue). Owner: Archant.
Editor: Michael Guy

Leigh Times
01702 477666
Fortnightly (Tue). Owner: Archant.
Editor: Michael Guy

Lincoln Target
01522 820000
www.thisislincolnshire.co.uk
Weekly (Wed). Owner: Northcliffe
Newspapers. Editor: Mike Sassi

Lincolnshire Echo
01522 820000
www.thisislincolnshire.co.uk
Daily. Owner: Northcliffe Newspapers.
Editor: Mike Sassi

Lincolnshire Free Press
01775 725021
www.spaldingtoday.co.uk
Weekly (Tue). Owner: Johnston Press.
Editor: Alan Salt; news: David Crossley;
features: Julie Williams; chief sub:
Tracey Vale

The Local (Bourne)
01778 425876
Weekly (Fri). Owner: Ashwell Associates.
Editor: Lisa Bruen

**Loughton, Chigwell & Buckhurst
Hill Guardian**
01992 572285
www.eppingguardian.co.uk
Weekly (Thu). Owner: Newsquest.
Editor: David Jackman

Louth Citizen
01507 353200
www.louthtoday.co.uk
Weekly (Fri). Owner: Johnston Press.
Managing editor: Tim Robinson;
editor: Charles Ladbrooke

Louth Leader
01507 353200
www.louthtoday.co.uk
Weekly (Wed). Owner: Johnston Press.
Managing editor: Tim Robinson;
editor: Charles Ladbrooke

Lowestoft Journal
01603 628311
www.edp24.co.uk
Weekly (Fri). Owner: Archant.
Editor: Terry Redhead

Lynn News
01553 761188
www.lynnnews.co.uk
Weekly (Tue, Fri). Owner: Johnston
Press. Editor: Malcolm Powell; news:
Donna Semmens

Maldon & Burnham Chronicle
01245 600700
www.thisisessex.co.uk
Weekly (Wed/Thu). Owner: Northcliffe
Newspapers. Editor: Stuart Rawlins;
news: Matt Adams; features: Darryl
Webber

Maldon & Burnham Standard
01621 852233
Weekly (Thu). Owner: Newsquest.
Editor: Neil Thomas

Market Rasen Mail
01507 353200
www.marketrasentoday.co.uk
Weekly (Wed). Owner: Johnston Press.
Managing editor: Tim Robinson;
editor: Jason Hipsley

Newmarket Journal
01638 564104
www.newmarketjournal.co.uk
Weekly (Thu). Owner: Johnston Press.
Assistant editor: Alison Hayes

Newmarket Weekly News
01223 434434
www.cambridge-news.co.uk
Weekly (Thu). Owner: Cambridge
Newspapers. Editor: Nigel Brookes

Norfolk Citizen
01553 761188
Weekly (Fri). Owner: Johnston Press.
Editor: Chris Hornby

Norfolk North Advertiser
01603 740222
www.advertiser-online.co.uk
Weekly (Fri). Owner: Archant.
Editor: Miles Germy

Norfolk South Advertiser
01603 740222
www.advertiser-online.co.uk
Weekly (Fri). Owner: Archant.
Editor: Sara Hardman

North Essex Advertiser
01473 324700
www.advertiser-online.co.uk
Weekly (Fri). Owner: Archant. Editor:
Paul Couch; news: Nicola Durrant

**North Norfolk & Broadland Town
& Country News**
01692 582287
Monthly (Fri nearest 1st).
Editor: Lawrence Watts

North Norfolk News
01603 628311
www.edp24.co.uk
Weekly (Thu). Owner: Archant.
Editor: Terry Redhead

Norwich Advertiser
01603 740222
www.advertiser-online.co.uk
Weekly (Fri). Owner: Archant.
Editor: Sarah Wade

Ongar & North Weald Gazette
01277 219222
www.thisisessex.co.uk
Weekly (Wed). Owner: Northcliffe
Newspapers. Editor: Roger Watkins;
news: Sheelagh Bree; features: Josie
Stephenson

Ongar Guardian
01992 572285
www.eppingguardian.co.uk
Weekly (Thu). Owner: Newsquest.
Editor: David Jackman

Peterborough Citizen
01733 555111
www.peterboroughnow.co.uk
Weekly (Wed). Owner: Johnston Press.
Editor: Rebecca Stephens; news:
Rebecca Goding; features: Rachel
Gordon; production: Brad Barnes

Peterborough Evening Telegraph
01733 555111
www.peterboroughnow.co.uk
Daily. Owner: Johnston Press
Editor: Rebecca Stephens; news:
Rebecca Goding; features: Rachel
Gordon; production: Brad Barnes

Peterborough Herald & Post
01733 318600
www.peterborough.net/heraldandpost
Weekly (Thu). Owner: Midlands
Weekly Media (Trinity Mirror). Editor:
Steve Rose; features: Amanda Franklin

Ramsey Post
01480 411481
Weekly (Thu). Owner: Archant.
Editor: Paul Richardson; deputy
editor: Angela Singer

Rayleigh Times
01702 477666
Monthly. Owner: Archant.
Editor: Michael Guy

Redbridge Yellow Advertiser
01268 503400
www.trinitymirrorsouthern.co.uk
Weekly (Thu). Owner: Trinity Mirror
Southern. Editor: Paula Dady;
features: Pat Jones

Redbridge, Waltham Forest & West
Essex Guardian
020 8498 3400
www.newsquest.co.uk
Weekly (Thu). Owner: Newsquest.
Editor: Pat Stannard

Romford & Havering Post
0845 070 0161
www.haveringpost.co.uk
Weekly free (Wed). Owner: Archant.
Editorial director: Richard Thompson;
editor: Amanda Patterson

Romford Recorder
01708 771500
www.recorderonline.co.uk
Weekly (Fri). Owner: Archant. Editor:
Mark Sweetingham; news: Eden Black

Royston Weekly News
01223 434434
www.cambridge-news.co.uk
Weekly (Thu). Owner: Cambridge
Newspapers. Editor: Nigel Brookes

Rutland & Stamford Mercury
01780 762255
www.stamfordmercury.co.uk
Weekly (Fri). Owner: Johnston Press.
Editor: Eileen Green; news: Suzanne
Moon

Saffron Walden Observer
01279 866355
www.herts-essex-news.co.uk
Weekly (Thu). Owner: Herts & Essex
Newspapers. Editor: Val Brown; news:
Sandra Perry

Saffron Walden Weekly News
01223 434434
www.cambridge-news.co.uk
Weekly (Thu). Owner: Cambridge
Newspapers. Editor: Nigel Brookes

Saffron Walden, Stansted &
Sawston Reporter
01763 245241
www.thisisessex.co.uk
Weekly (Thu). Owner: Archant.
Editor: Les Baker

St Ives Town Crier
01480 402100
www.stivestoday.co.uk
Weekly (Thu). Owner: Johnston Press.
Editor: Richard Yetman

St Ives Weekly News
01223 434434
www.cambridge-news.co.uk
Weekly (Thu). Owner: Cambridge
Newspapers. Editor: Nigel Brookes

St Neots Town Crier
01480 402100
www.stneotstoday.co.uk
Weekly (Thu). Owner: Johnston Press.
Editor: Richard Yetman

St Neots Weekly News
01223 434434
www.cambridge-news.co.uk
Weekly (Wed). Owner: Newsquest.
Editor: Nigel Brookes

Sawbridgeworth Star
01279 838111
www.thisisessex.co.uk
Weekly (Thu). Owner: Herts & Essex
Newspapers. Editor: Ken Morley; news:
Mark Fletcher

Scunthorpe Target
01724 273273
www.thisisscunthorpe.co.uk
Weekly (Thu). Owner: Northcliffe
Newspapers. Editor: John Grubb; chief
sub: John Curtis

Scunthorpe Telegraph
01724 273273
www.thisisscunthorpe.co.uk
Daily. Owner: Northcliffe Newspapers.
Editor: John Grubb; chief sub: John
Curtis

Skegness Citizen
01507 353200
Weekly (Fri). Owner: Johnston Press.
Managing editor: Tim Robinson;
editor: John Calpe

Skegness Standard
01507 353200
www.skegnesstoday.co.uk
Weekly (Wed). Owner: Johnston Press.
Managing editor: Tim Robinson;
editor: Charles Ladbrooke

Skegness Target
01205 315000
Weekly (Wed). Owner: Northcliffe
Newspapers. Editor: Glyn Belsher

Sleaford Citizen
01529 413646
Weekly (Fri). Owner: Johnston Press.
Editor: John Lavery; news: Andy
Hubbert

Sleaford Standard
01529 413646
Weekly (Wed). Owner: Johnston Press.
Editor: John Lavery; news: Andy
Hubbert

Sleaford Target
01522 820000
www.thisislincolnshire.co.uk
Weekly (Wed). Owner: Northcliffe
Newspapers. Editor: Glyn Belsher

Soham Standard
01353 667831
www.ely-standard.co.uk
Weekly (Thu). Owner: Archant.
Editor: John Ison; news: Debbie Davies

South Woodham & Maldon Weekly
News
01621 852233
www.thisisessex.co.uk
Weekly (Thu). Owner: Newsquest.
Editor: Neil Thomas

Southend Standard
01268 522792
www.thisisessex.co.uk
Weekly (Thu). Owner: Newsquest.
Editor: Martin McNeill; news: Chris
Hatton; chief sub: Neal Reeve

Southend Times
01702 477666
Weekly (Tue). Owner: Archant.
Editor: Michael Guy

Southend Yellow Advertiser
01268 503400
www.trinitymirrorsouthern.co.uk
Weekly free (Thu). Owner: Trinity
Mirror Southern. Editor: Paula Dady;
features: Pat Jones

Spalding Guardian
01775 725021
www.spaldingtoday.co.uk
Weekly (Thu). Owner: Johnston Press.
Editor: Alan Salt; news: David Crossley;
features: Julie Williams; chief sub:
Tracey Vale

Spalding Herald
01775 713723
www.spaldingherald.co.uk
Monthly free (1st of month).
Editor: Natalie Ward

Spilsby Standard
01754 897120
www.skegnesstoday.co.uk
Weekly (Wed). Owner: Johnston Press.
Editor: John Coupe

Spilsby Target
01205 315000
Weekly (Wed). Owner: Northcliffe
Newspapers. Editor: Glyn Belsher

Stamford Citizen
01780 762255
www.stamfordmercury.co.uk
Weekly free (Tue). Owner: Johnston
Press. Editor: Eileen Green; news:
Suzanne Moon

55

Stamford Herald & Post
01733 318600
*Weekly (Thu). Owner: Midlands
Weekly Media (Trinity Mirror). Editor:
Steve Rose; features: Amanda Franklin*

Stansted Observer
01279 866355
www.herts-essex-news.co.uk
*Weekly (Thu). Owner: Herts & Essex
Newspapers. Editor: Val Brown; news:
Sandra Perry*

Sudbury Mercury
01284 702588
www.edp24.co.uk
*Weekly (Fri). Owner: Archant. Editor:
Paul Couch; reporter: Will Wright*

Suffolk Advertiser
01473 324700
www.advertiser-online.co.uk
*Weekly (Fri). Owner: Archant. Editor:
Paul Couch; news: Nicola Durrant*

Suffolk Free Press
01787 375271
www.sudburytoday.co.uk
*Weekly free (Thu). Owner: Johnston
Press. Editor: Phil Minett; news:
Nick Wells*

Swaffham Mercury
01603 628311
www.edp24.co.uk
*Monthly. Owner: Archant.
Editor: Terry Redhead*

Swaffham News
01553 761188
*Weekly (Fri). Owner: Johnston Press.
Editor: Malcolm Powell; news: Donna
Semmens*

Tendring Weekly News
01206 506000
www.thisisessex.co.uk
*Weekly free (Wed). Owner: Newsquest.
Editor-in-chief: Irene Kettle; news:
Sally Teatheredge*

Thetford & Brandon Times
01603 628311
www.edp24.co.uk
*Weekly (Wed). Owner: Archant.
Editor: Terry Redhead*

Thetford Citizen
01284 768911
www.johnstonpress.co.uk/anglia
*Weekly. Owner: Johnston Press.
Editor: Barry Peters; news: Lesley
Anslow; features: Sue Green*

Thurrock Gazette
01375 411502
www.thisisessex.co.uk
*Weekly free (Fri). Owner: Newsquest.
Editor: Neil Speight*

Thurrock, Lakeside & Grays Post
0845 070 0161
*Weekly (Thu). Owner: Archant.
Editor: Amanda Patterson; news:
Wayne Tuckfield; chief sub: Graham
Whitmore*

Thurrock Recorder
01708 771500
www.recorderonline.co.uk
*Weekly (Fri). Owner: Archant. Editor:
Mark Sweetingham; news: Eden Black*

Thurrock Yellow Advertiser
01268 503400
www.trinitymirrorsouthern.co.uk
*Weekly free (Thu). Owner: Trinity
Mirror Southern. Editor: Paula Dady;
features: Pat Jones*

Walden Local
01799 516161
www.thisisessex.co.uk
Weekly (Wed). Editor: John Brooker

Waltham Forest Guardian
020 8498 3400
www.newsquest.co.uk
*Weekly (Thu). Owner: Newsquest.
Editor: Pat Stannard*

Waltham Forest Independent
020 8498 3400
www.newsquest.co.uk
*Weekly (Fri). Owner: Newsquest.
Editor: Pat Stannard*

Watton & Swaffham Times
01603 628311
www.edp24.co.uk
*Weekly (Fri). Owner: Archant.
Editor: Terry Redhead*

Waveney Advertiser
01493 601206
www.advertiser-online.co.uk
*Weekly (Fri). Owner: Archant.
Managing editor: Leanne Boost*

Whittlesey Times
01354 652621
www.cambs-times.co.uk
*Weekly (Thu). Owner: Archant.
Editor: Brian Asplin; news: John
Elworthy; features: Maggie Gibson*

Wisbech Standard
01354 652621
www.wisbech-standard.co.uk
*Weekly (Thu). Owner: Archant.
Editor: Brian Asplin; news: John
Elworthy; features: Maggie Gibson*

Witham Chronicle
01245 600700
www.thisisessex.co.uk
*Weekly (Wed/Thu). Owner: Northcliffe
Newspapers. Editor: Stuart Rawlins;
news: Matt Adams; features: Darryl
Webber*

Woodham Chronicle
01245 600700
www.thisisessex.co.uk
*Weekly (Wed/Thu). Owner: Northcliffe
Newspapers. Editor: Stuart Rawlins;
news: Matt Adams; features: Darryl
Webber*

**Wymondham & Attleborough
Mercury**
01603 628311
www.edp24.co.uk
*Weekly (Fri). Owner: Archant.
Editor: Terry Redhead*

Midlands
Derbyshire, Leicestershire,
Northamptonshire, Nottinghamshire,
Staffordshire

The Advertiser (Staffordshire)
01782 602525
www.thisisthesentinel.co.uk
*Weekly free (Thu). Owner: Northcliffe
Newspapers. Editor: Sean Dooley;
news: Robert Cotterill; features:
Charlotte Little-Jones*

Alfreton & Ripley Echo
01773 834731
www.derbyshiretoday.com
*Weekly (Fri). Owner: Johnston Press.
Editor: David Hopkinson*

Alfreton Chad
01623 456789
www.johnstonpress.co.uk
/yorkshire.asp
*Weekly (Fri). Owner: Johnston Press.
Editor: Jeremy Plews; news: Joy
Thompson; chief sub: Karen Robinson*

Ashbourne News Telegraph
01283 512345
www.ashbournenewstelegraph.co.uk
*Weekly (Wed). Owner: Staffordshire
Newspapers. Editor: Paul Hazeldine;
news: Steve Doohan; features: Bill
Pritchard; production: Diane Finn*

Ashby & Coalville Mail
0116 251 2512
www.thisisleicestershire.co.uk
*Weekly (Tue). Owner: Northcliffe
Newspapers. Editor: Nick Carter; news:
Mark Charlton; features: Alex Dawson*

Ashby Times
01530 813101
*Weekly (Fri). Owner: Trident Midland
Newspapers. News editor: Nick Hudson*

Ashfield Chad
01623 456789
www.ashfieldtoday.co.uk
*Weekly (Wed). Owner: Johnston Press.
Editor: Jeremy Plews; news: Joy
Thompson; chief sub: Karen Robinson*

Atherstone Herald
01827 848535
*Weekly (Thu). Owner: Northcliffe
Newspapers. Editor: Sam Holliday*

Belper Express
01332 291111
*Weekly free (Tue). Owner: Northcliffe
Newspapers. Editor: Andy Machin*

Belper News
01629 582432
www.matlocktoday.co.uk
*Weekly (Wed). Owner: Johnston Press.
Editor: Amanda Hatfield; news: Helen
Taylor*

Biddulph Advertiser
01260 281012
www.thisisthesentinel.co.uk
*Weekly (Thu). Owner: Northcliffe
Newspapers. Editor: Paul Dutton*

Biddulph Chronicle
01260 273737
www.chronicleseries.com
Weekly (Fri). Editor: Jeremy Condliffe

Birstall Post
0116 267 4213
www.birstallpost.co.uk
Monthly free (1st of month). Owner: The Birstall Post Society. Editor: Jerry Jackson

Bolsover & District Advertiser
01246 202291
www.chesterfieldtoday.co.uk
Fortnightly free (Wed). Owner: Johnston Press. Editor: Mike Wilson; assistant editor: Phil Bramley; news: Tracy Mitchell; assistant news editor: Sean Boyle

Brackley Post
01604 614600
www.midlandweeklymedia.co.uk
Weekly (Fri). Owner: Midlands Weekly Media (Trinity Mirror). Editor: Richard Howarth; production: Julie Fisher

Burntwood Mercury
01827 848535
Weekly (Thu). Owner: Northcliffe Newspapers. Editor: Sam Holliday

Burton & South Derbyshire Advertiser
01283 512345
www.uttoxeteradvertiser.co.uk
Weekly (Wed). Owner: Staffordshire Newspapers. Editor: Paul Hazeldine; news: Steve Doohan; features: Bill Pritchard; production: Diane Finn

Burton Mail
01283 512345
www.burtonmail.co.uk
Daily. Owner: Staffordshire Newspapers. Editor: Paul Hazeldine; news: Steve Doohan; features: Bill Pritchard; production: Diane Finn

Burton Trader
01283 512200
Weekly (Wed). Owner: Midlands Weekly Media (Trinity Mirror). Editor: Pam Thomas; news: Paul Henshall; chief sub: Alan Payne

Buxton Advertiser
01298 22118
www.buxtontoday.co.uk
Weekly (Thu). Owner: Johnston Press. Editor: John Phillips; chief reporter: Emma Downes; subeditor: Alan Charnley

Buxton Times
01298 22118
www.buxtontoday.co.uk
Weekly free (Fri). Owner: Johnston Press. Editor: John Phillips; chief reporter: Emma Downes; subeditor: Alan Charnley

Cannock & Rugeley Chronicle
01543 506311
www.expressandstar.com/chronicle
Weekly (Fri). Owner: Midland News Association. Editor: Mark Ship

Cannock & Rugeley Mercury
01827 848535
Weekly (Thu). Owner: Northcliffe Newspapers. Editor: Linda Young

Cannock Chase & Burntwood Post
01543 501700
Weekly (Thu). Owner: Midlands Weekly Media (Trinity Mirror). Editor: Mike Lockley

Cheadle & Tean Times
01538 753162
Weekly (Wed). Editor: Nigel Titterton

Cheadle Post & Times
01538 750011
www.staffordshiresentinel.co.uk
Weekly (Wed). Owner: Northcliffe Newspapers. Editor: Doug Pickford

Chesterfield Advertiser
01246 202291
www.chesterfieldtoday.co.uk
Weekly free (Fri). Owner: Johnston Press. Editor: Mike Wilson; assistant editor: Phil Bramley; news: Tracy Mitchell; assistant news editor: Sean Boyle

Chesterfield Express
01246 504500
Weekly free (Wed). Owner: Johnston Press. Editor: Mike Wilson; assistant editor: Phil Bramley; news: Tracy Mitchell; assistant news editor: Sean Boyle

Chronicle and Echo (Northampton)
01604 467000
www.northantsnews.com
Daily. Owner: Johnston Press. Editor: Mark Edwards; news: Richard Edmondson; production: Graham Tebbutt

Coalville & Ashby Echo
01509 635807
Weekly (Tue). Owner: Midlands Weekly Media (Trinity Mirror). Editor: Pete Warrington

Coalville Times
01530 813101
Weekly (Fri). Owner: Trident Midland Newspapers. Editor: Nick Hudson

Coleshill Herald
01827 848535
www.tamworthherald.co.uk
Weekly (Thu). Owner: Northcliffe Newspapers. Editor: Sam Holliday

Corby Citizen
01536 506100
www.northantsnews.com
Weekly (Thu). Owner: Johnston Press. Acting deputy editor: Mark Edwards; acting news editor: Kristy Ward; features: Joni Ager; chief sub: Kathryn Dunn

Corby Herald & Post
01604 614600
www.midlandweeklymedia.co.uk
Weekly (Thu). Owner: Midlands Weekly Media (Trinity Mirror). Editor: Richard Howarth; production: Julie Fisher

Daventry Express
01327 703383
www.daventrytoday.co.uk
Weekly (Thu). Owner: Johnston Press. Editor: Jason Gibbons; news: Adam Hollier

Derby Evening Telegraph
See page 35

Derby Express
01332 291111
Weekly free (Tue). Owner: Northcliffe Newspapers. Editor: Andy Machin

Derby Trader
01332 253999
Weekly (Thu). Owner: Midlands Weekly Media (Trinity Mirror). Editor: Patrick O'Connor; features: Steve Eyley; chief sub: Richard Taylor

Derbyshire Times
01246 504500
www.derbyshiretimes.co.uk
Weekly (Thu). Owner: Johnston Press. Editor: Mike Wilson; assistant editor: Phil Bramley; news: Tracy Mitchell; assistant news editor: Sean Boyle

Dronfield Advertiser
01246 202291
www.chesterfieldtoday.co.uk
Weekly free (Wed). Owner: Johnston Press. Editor: Mike Wilson; assistant editor: Phil Bramley; news: Tracy Mitchell; assistant news editor: Sean Boyle

Dukeries Advertiser
01636 681234
Weekly (Fri). Editor: Harry Whitehouse; news: Lucy Millard; chief sub: Chris Prine

Eastwood & Kimberley Advertiser
01773 713563
www.eastwoodadvertiser.co.uk
Weekly (Fri). Owner: Johnston Press. Editor: John Shawcroft

Eckington Leader
01246 434343
Weekly (Fri). Owner: Johnston Press. Editor: Mike Wilson; assistant editor: Phil Bramley; news: Tracy Mitchell; assistant news editor: Sean Boyle

The Evening Telegraph (Northants)
01536 506100
www.northantsnews.com
Daily. Owner: Johnston Press. Acting deputy editor: Mark Edwards; acting news editor: Kristy Ward; features: Joni Ager; chief sub: Kathryn Dunn

Glossop Chronicle
0161 304 7691
www.tamesidereporter.com
Weekly (Thu). Owner: Ashton Weekly Newspapers. Editor: Nigel Skinner

Harborough Mail
01858 462626
www.harboroughmail.co.uk
Weekly (Thu). Owner: Johnston Press. Editor: Brian Dodds; news: Maria Thompson

High Peak Courier
01298 22118
www.buxtontoday.co.uk
Weekly free (Fri). Owner: Johnston Press. Editor: John Phillips; chief reporter: Emma Downes; subeditor: Alan Charnley

Hinckley Herald & Journal
01455 891981
www.hinckley-times.co.uk
Weekly (Wed). Owner: Coventry Newspapers (Trinity Mirror). Editor: Andrew Punchon

Hinckley Times
01455 891981
www.hinckley-times.co.uk
*Weekly (Thu). Owner: Coventry
Newspapers (Trinity Mirror).
Editor: Andrew Punchon*

Hucknall & Bulwell Dispatch
01623 456789
www.hucknalltoday.co.uk
*Weekly (Fri). Owner: Johnston Press.
Editor: Richard Silverwood*

Ilkeston & Ripley Trader
01332 253999
*Weekly (Fri). Owner: Midlands Weekly
Media (Trinity Mirror). Editor: Patrick
O'Connor; features: Steve Eyley; chief
sub: Richard Taylor*

Ilkeston Advertiser
0115 944 4411
www.derbyshiretimes.co.uk
*Weekly (Thu). Owner: Johnston Press.
Editor: David Horne*

Ilkeston Express
01332 291111
*Weekly free (Tue). Owner: Northcliffe
Newspapers. Editor: Andy Machin*

Ilkeston Shopper
0115 944 4411
www.derbyshiretimes.co.uk
*Weekly free (Tue). Owner: Johnston
Press. Editor: David Horne*

Kenilworth Citizen
024 7663 3633
*Weekly free (Thu). Owner: Coventry
Newspapers (Trinity Mirror).
Editor: Jonathan Sever*

Kettering Citizen
01536 506100
www.northantsnews.com
*Weekly (Thu). Owner: Johnston Press.
Acting deputy editor: Mark Edwards;
acting news editor: Kristy Ward;
features: Joni Ager; chief sub: Kathryn
Dunn*

Kettering Evening Telegraph
01536 506100
www.northantsnews.com
*Daily. Owner: Johnston Press.
Acting deputy editor: Mark Edwards;
acting news editor: Kristy Ward;
features: Joni Ager; chief sub: Kathryn
Dunn*

Kettering Herald & Post
01604 614600
www.midlandweeklymedia.co.uk
*Weekly (Thu). Owner: Midlands
Weekly Media (Trinity Mirror).
Editor: Richard Howarth; production:
Julie Fisher*

Leek Post & Times
01538 399599
www.staffordshiresentinel.co.uk
*Weekly (Wed). Owner: Northcliffe
Newspapers. Editor: Doug Pickford;
news: Jane Griffiths*

Leicester Mail
0116 251 2512
www.thisisleicestershire.co.uk
*Weekly free (Tue). Owner: Northcliffe
Newspapers. Editor: Nick Carter; news:
Mark Charlton; features: Alex Dawson*

Leicester Mercury
See page 35

Leicestershire Times Today
0115 982 7338
www.leicestertimestoday.com
*Weekly (Fri). Owner: Journal
Publishing Company.
Editor: Matthew Palmer*

**Lichfield & Burntwood Edition
Express and Star**
01902 313131
www.expressandstar.com
*Daily. Owner: Midland News
Association. Editor: Adrian Faber*

Lichfield Mercury
01827 848535
www.lichfieldmercury.co.uk
*Weekly (Thu). Owner: Northcliffe
Newspapers. Editor: Sam Holliday*

Lichfield Post
01543 258523
www.iclichfield.co.uk
*Weekly (Thu). Owner: Midlands
Weekly Media (Trinity Mirror).
Editor: Pam Thomas*

Long Eaton Advertiser
0115 946 2837
*Weekly (Wed). Owner: Midlands
Weekly Media (Trinity Mirror).
Editor: David Godsall*

Long Eaton Recorder
0115 948 2000
www.thisisnottingham.co.uk
*Weekly free (Thu). Owner: Northcliffe
Newspapers. Editor: Graham Glen; news:
Claire Catlow; features: Jeremy Lewis*

Long Eaton Trader
0115 946 9909
*Weekly (Thu). Owner: Midlands
Weekly Media (Trinity Mirror). Editor:
Patrick O'Connor; features: Steve Eyley*

Loughborough Echo
01509 232632
*Weekly (Thu). Owner: Midlands
Weekly Media (Trinity Mirror). Editor:
Andy Rush; news: John Brindley*

Loughborough Mail
0116 251 2512
www.thisisleicestershire.co.uk
*Weekly (Tue). Owner: Northcliffe
Newspapers. Editor: Nick Carter; news:
Mark Charlton; features: Alex Dawson*

Lutterworth Mail
01858 462626
www.harboroughtoday.co.uk
*Weekly (Thu). Owner: Johnston Press.
Editor: Brian Dodds; news: Maria
Thompson*

Mansfield & Ashfield Observer
01623 456789
*Weekly free (Thu). Owner: Johnston
Press. Editor: Tony Spittles*

Mansfield & Ashfield Recorder
01623 420000
*Weekly free (Wed). Owner: Northcliffe
Newspapers. Editor: Graham Glen*

Mansfield Chad
01623 456789
www.mansfieldtoday.co.uk
*Weekly (Wed). Owner: Johnston Press.
Editor: Jeremy Plews; news: Joy
Thompson; chief sub: Karen Robinson*

Market Harborough Herald & Post
01604 614600
www.midlandweeklymedia.co.uk
*Weekly (Thu, Fri). Owner: Midlands
Weekly Media (Trinity Mirror). Editor:
Richard Howarth; production: Julie
Fisher*

Matlock Mercury
01629 582432
www.matlocktoday.co.uk
*Weekly (Thu). Owner: Johnston Press.
Editor: Amanda Hatfield; news: Helen
Taylor*

Melton Citizen
01664 410041
www.meltontoday.co.uk
*Weekly free (Tue). Owner: Johnston
Press. Editor: Michael Cooke*

Melton Times
01664 410041
www.meltontoday.co.uk
*Weekly (Thu). Owner: Johnston Press.
Editor: Michael Cooke*

Mid Staffs Edition Express and Star
01543 506311
www.expressandstar.com
*Daily. Owner: Midland News
Association. Editor: Adrian Faber;
news: Mark Drew*

Mountsorrel Post
0116 267 4213
*4pa. Owner: The Birstall Post Society.
Editor: Jerry Jackson*

Newark Advertiser
01636 681234
www.newarkadvertiser.co.uk
*Weekly (Fri). Editor: Harry
Whitehouse; news: Lucy Millard*

Newcastle Advertiser
01782 619830
www.staffordshiresentinel.co.uk
*Daily. Owner: Northcliffe Newspapers.
Editor: Sean Dooley; news: Robert
Cotterill; features: Charlotte Little-Jones*

**North West Leics & South
Derbyshire Leader**
01530 813101
*Weekly (Wed). Owner: Trident Midland
Newspapers. Editor: Nick Hudson*

Northampton Herald & Post
01604 614600
www.midlandweeklymedia.co.uk
*Weekly (Thu). Owner: Midlands
Weekly Media (Trinity Mirror).
Editor: Richard Howarth; production:
Julie Fisher*

Northampton Mercury
01604 467000
www.northantsnews.com
*Weekly (Thu). Owner: Johnston Press.
Editor: Mark Edwards; news: Richard
Edmondson; production: Graham
Tebbutt*

Northamptonshire Journal
0116 233 3635
*Weekly (Tue). Owner: Journal
Publishing Company.
Editor: Claire Tipton*

Northants on Sunday
01604 467000
www.northantsnews.com
Sunday. Owner: Johnston Press.
Editor: Steve Scoles; news: Richard
Edmondson; features: Angela Pownall;
production manager: Graham Billing

Nottingham & Trent Valley Journal
0115 982 7337
Weekly (Fri). Owner: Journal Publishing
Company. Editor: Matthew Palmer

Nottingham & Long Eaton Topper
0115 969 6000
www.toppernewspapers.co.uk
Weekly free (Wed). Owner: Topper
Newspapers. Editor: John Howarth

Nottingham Evening Post
See page 35

Nottingham Recorder
0115 948 2000
www.thisisnottingham.co.uk
Weekly free (Wed). Owner: Northcliffe
Newspapers. Editor: Graham Glen;
news: Claire Catlow; features: Jeremy
Lewis

Oadby & Wigston Mail
0116 251 2512
www.thisisleicestershire.co.uk
Weekly (Tue). Owner: Northcliffe
Newspapers. Editor: Nick Carter; news:
Mark Charlton; features: Alex Dawson

Peak Advertiser
01629 812159
Fortnightly free (Thu). Editor: Steve Wild

Peak Times
01629 582432
www.matlocktoday.co.uk
Weekly free (Fri). Owner: Johnston
Press. Editor: Amanda Hatfield; news:
Helen Taylor

Potteries Advertiser
01782 602525
www.thisisthesentinel.co.uk
Weekly free (Thu). Owner: Northcliffe
Newspapers. Editor: Sean Dooley;
news: Robert Cotterill; features:
Charlotte Little-Jones

Retford & Bawtry Guardian
01909 500500
www.retfordtoday.co.uk
Weekly (Thu). Owner: Johnston Press.
Editor: George Robinson; news: Jackie
Laver

Retford, Gainsborough & Worksop
Times
01777 702275
Weekly (Thu). Owner: Northcliffe
Newspapers. Editor: Nick Purkiss

Retford Trader
01909 500500
www.retfordtoday.co.uk
Weekly free (Thu). Owner: Johnston
Press. Editor: George Robinson; news:
Jackie Laver

Ripley & Heanor News
01629 582432
www.matlocktoday.co.uk
Weekly (Thu). Owner: Johnston Press.
Editor: Amanda Hatfield; news: Helen
Taylor

Rothley Post
0117 267 4213
6pa. Owner: The Birstall Post Society.
Editor: Jerry Jackson

Rugeley Mercury
01543 414414
www.thisisstaffordshire.co.uk
Weekly (Thu). Owner: Northcliffe
Newspapers. Editor: Tim Hewitt; news:
Andy Kerr

Rugeley Post
01543 258523
Weekly (Thu). Owner: Midlands
Weekly Media (Trinity Mirror).
Editor: Pam Thomas

Rutland Times
01572 757722
www.rutlandtimes.co.uk
Weekly (Thu). Editor: Andy Plaice

The Sentinel (Stoke-on-Trent)
See page 35

Sentinel Sunday
See The Sentinel, page 35

Shepshed Echo
01509 232632
Weekly (Thu). Owner: Midlands Weekly
Media (Trinity Mirror). Editor: Andy
Rush; news: John Brindley

Sherwood/Rainworth Chad
01623 456789
Weekly (Wed). Owner: Johnston Press.
Editor: Jeremy Plews; news: Joy
Thompson; chief sub: Karen Robinson

Shirebrook & Bolsover Chad
01623 456789
Weekly (Wed). Owner: Johnston Press.
Editor: Jeremy Plews; news: Joy
Thompson; chief sub: Karen Robinson

South Notts Advertiser
01636 681234
Weekly (Fri). Editor: Harry
Whitehouse; news: Lucy Millard

Stafford & Stone Chronicle
01785 247290
www.expressandstar.com/chronicle
Daily. Owner: Midland News
Association. Editor: Klooran Wills

Stafford Post
01543 501700
www.icstafford.co.uk
Weekly (Thu). Owner: Midlands
Weekly Media (Trinity Mirror).
Editor: Mike Lockley

Staffordshire Newsletter
01785 257700
www.staffordshirenewsletter.co.uk
Weekly (Thu). Owner: Staffordshire
Newspapers. Editor: Klooran Wills

Stapleford & Sandiacre News
0115 946 2837
Weekly (Wed). Owner: Midlands
Weekly Media (Trinity Mirror).
Editor: David Godsall

Stratford & Banbury Why
0845 600 9742
Weekly free (Fri). Owner: Northcliffe
Newspapers. Editor: Claire Smith

Swadlincote Times
01530 813101
Weekly (Fri). Owner: Trident Midland
Newspapers. News editor: Nick Hudson

Tamworth Herald
01827 848535
www.tamworthherald.co.uk
Weekly (Thu). Owner: Northcliffe
Newspapers. Editor: Sam Holiday

Tamworth Times
01827 308000
Weekly (Thu). Owner: Midlands
Weekly Media (Trinity Mirror).
Editor: Pam Thomas

Towcester Post
01604 614600
www.midlandweeklymedia.co.uk
Weekly (Fri). Owner: Midlands Weekly
Media (Trinity Mirror). Editor: Richard
Howarth; production: Julie Fisher

Trader Pictorial
01636 681234
www.newarkadvertiser.co.uk/trader
Weekly (Wed). Editor: Harry
Whitehouse; news: Lucy Millard

Uttoxeter Advertiser
01889 562050
www.uttoxeteradvertiser.co.uk
Weekly (Tue). Owner: Staffordshire
Newspapers. Editor: Alan Harris

Uttoxeter Post & Times
01889 568999
Weekly (Thu). Owner: Northcliffe
Newspapers. Editor: Doug Pickford;
news: Jane Griffiths

Warsop Chad
01623 456789
Weekly (Wed). Owner: Johnston Press.
Editor: Jeremy Plews; news: Joy
Thompson; chief sub: Karen Robinson

Wellingborough & East Northants
Evening Telegraph
01536 506100
www.northantsnews.com
Daily. Owner: Johnston Press.
Acting deputy editor: Mark Edwards;
acting news editor: Kristy Ward;
features: Joni Ager; chief sub: Kathryn
Dunn

Wellingborough & Rushden Citizen
01536 506100
www.northantsnews.com
Weekly (Thu). Owner: Johnston Press.
Acting deputy editor: Mark Edwards;
acting news editor: Kristy Ward;
features: Joni Ager; chief sub: Kathryn
Dunn

Wellingborough & Rushden Herald
& Post
01604 614600
www.midlandweeklymedia.co.uk
Weekly (Thu). Owner: Midlands Weekly
Media (Trinity Mirror). Editor: Richard
Howarth; production: Julie Fisher

Worksop Guardian
01909 500500
www.worksoptoday.co.uk
Weekly (Fri). Owner: Johnston Press.
Editor: George Robinson; news: Jackie
Laver

Worksop Trader
01909 500500
Weekly free (Wed). Owner: Johnston
Press. Editor: George Robinson; news:
Jackie Laver

Your Leek Paper
01538 371807
www.yourleekpaper.co.uk
Weekly (Wed). Independent.
Editor: Gary Shenton

West Midlands

West Midlands, Warwickshire

Ad News (Willenhall, Wednesbury & Darlaston)
01543 501700
Weekly (Wed). Owner: Midlands Weekly Media (Trinity Mirror). Editor: Mike Lockley

Bedworth Echo
024 7663 3633
www.iccoventry.co.uk
Weekly (Fri). Owner: Coventry Newspapers (Trinity Mirror). Editor: Alan Kirby; news: John West; features: Steven Chilton

Birmingham Evening Mail
See page 34

Birmingham News
0121 234 5073
www.icbirmingham.co.uk
Weekly (Thu). Owner: Birmingham Post & Mail (Trinity Mirror). Editor: David Brook; news: Damien O'Laughlin

Birmingham Post
0121 236 3366
www.icbirmingham.co.uk
Daily. Owner: Birmingham Post & Mail (Trinity Mirror). Editor: Fiona Alexander; news: Carole Cole; features: Sid Langley

Black Country Bugle
01384 567678
www.blackcountrybugle.co.uk
Weekly (Thu). Owner: Staffordshire Newspapers. Editor: Robert Taylor

Coventry Citizen
024 7663 3633
www.iccoventry.co.uk
Weekly (Thu). Owner: Coventry Newspapers (Trinity Mirror). Editor: Alan Kirby; news: John West; features: Steven Chilton

Coventry Evening Telegraph
See page 34

Coventry Observer
024 7649 5900
www.coventryobserver.co.uk
Weekly free (Thu). Owner: Observer Standard Newspapers. Editor: Mike Green

Daventry Express
01788 535363
www.daventryonline.co.uk
Weekly (Thu). Owner: Johnston Press. Editor: Jason Gibbons

Dudley Chronicle
01384 353211
www.expressandstar.com
Weekly (Fri). Owner: Midland News Association. Editor: John Nash; features: Dave Pearce; chief sub: Jane Reynolds

Dudley Edition Express & Star
01384 355355
www.expressandstar.com
Daily. Owner: Midland News Association. Editor: Adrian Faber; news: Mark Drew; features: Dylan Evans; chief sub: Tony Reynolds

Dudley News
01384 358050
www.dudleynews.co.uk
Weekly (Fri). Owner: Newsquest. Editor: Jeff Gepheott; features: Lynn Taylor

Express & Star
See page 35

Express & Star (Stourbridge)
01384 399914
www.expressandstar.com
Weekly (Fri). Owner: Midland News Association. Editor: John Nash

Express & Star (Walsall)
01922 444444
www.expressandstar.com
Weekly (Thu). Owner: Midland News Association. Editor: Mike Caldicott

Great Barr & Erdington Chronicle
0121 553 7171
www.expressandstar.com
Weekly free (Wed). Owner: Midland News Association. Editor: Leon Burakowski

Great Barr Observer
01827 848535
www.tamworthherald.co.uk
Weekly (Fri). Owner: Northcliffe Newspapers. Editor: Mark Eustace

Halesowen Chronicle
01384 353211
Weekly (Fri). Owner: Midland News Association. Editor: John Nash; features: Dave Pearce; chief sub: Jane Reynolds

Halesowen News
01384 358050
www.halesowennews.co.uk
Weekly (Fri). Owner: Newsquest. Editor: Jeff Gepheott; features: Lynn Taylor

Heartland Evening News
024 7635 3534
www.hen-news.com
Daily. Editor: Tony Parrott; news: Kevin Cooke; features: John Jevons; production: Bob Clemens

Kenilworth Weekly News
01926 457777
www.kenilworthonline.co.uk
Weekly (Fri). Owner: Johnston Press. Editor: Martin Lawson

Leamington Spa Courier
01926 457777
www.leamingtononline.co.uk
Weekly (Fri). Owner: Johnston Press. Editor: Martin Lawson

Leamington Spa Observer
01926 451900
www.leamington-now.com
Weekly free (Thu). Owner: Observer Standard Newspapers. Editor: Ian Hughes

Leamington Spa Review
01926 457777
www.leamingtonspatoday.co.uk
Weekly (Thu). Owner: Johnston Press. Editor: Martin Lawson

Metro (Birmingham)
020 7938 6000
www.metrobirmingham.co.uk
Daily. Owner: Associated Newspapers. Editor: Kenny Campbell; news: Mark Dorman; features: Kieran Meeke

Nuneaton Weekly Tribune
024 7663 3633
www.iccoverntry.co.uk
Weekly (Thu). Owner: Coventry Newspapers (Trinity Mirror). Editor: Alan Kirby; news: John West; features: Steven Chilton

Rugby Advertiser
01788 535363
www.rugbyadvertiser.co.uk
Weekly (Thu). Owner: Johnston Press. Editor: Peter Hengenheister

Rugby Observer
01788 535147
www.therugbyobserver.co.uk
Weekly free (Thu). Owner: Observer Standard Newspapers. Editor: Chris Smith

Rugby Review
01788 535363
www.rugbyreviewtoday.co.uk
Weekly (Thu). Owner: Johnston Press. Editor: Peter Hengenheister

Sandwell Chronicle
0121 553 7171
www.expressandstar.com
Weekly free (Wed). Owner: Midland News Association. Editor: Leon Burakowski

Solihull News
0121 711 5723
www.midlandweeklymedia.co.uk
Weekly (Fri). Owner: Midlands Weekly Media (Trinity Mirror). Editor: Ross Crawford

Solihull Times
0121 711 5723
www.midlandweeklymedia.co.uk
Weekly (Fri). Owner: Midlands Weekly. Media (Trinity Mirror)

Stourbridge Chronicle
01384 399914
www.expressandstar.com
Weekly (Fri). Owner: Midland News Association. Editor: John Nash; features: Dave Pearce; chief sub: Jane Reynolds

Stourbridge News
01384 358050
www.thisisstourbridge.co.uk
Weekly (Thu). Owner: Newsquest. Editor: Jeff Gepheott; features: Lynn Taylor

Stratford-upon-Avon Herald
01789 266261
www.stratford-herald.co.uk
Weekly (Thu). Owner: Stratford Herald. Editor: Chris Turner; news: Dale Levack

Stratford-upon-Avon Midweek
01789 266261
www.stratford-herald.co.uk
Weekly (Tue). Owner: Stratford Herald. Editor: Chris Turner; news: Dale Levack

Stratford-upon-Avon Observer
01789 415717
www.stratfordstandard.co.uk
Weekly free (Thu). Owner: Observer Standard Newspapers. Editor: Clare Fitzsimmons

Sunday Mercury (Birmingham)
0121 236 3366
www.icbirmingham.co.uk
Sunday. Owner: Birmingham Post & Mail (Trinity Mirror). Editor: David Brookes; news: Tony Larner; features: Paul Cole

Sutton Coldfield News
0121 355 7070
www.icsuttoncoldfield.co.uk
Weekly (Fri). Owner: Midlands Weekly Media (Trinity Mirror). Editor: Pam Thomas

Sutton Coldfield Observer
01827 848535
www.tamworthherald.co.uk
Weekly (Fri). Owner: Northcliffe Newspapers. Editor: Gary Phelps

Walsall Advertiser
01827 848535
www.tamworthherald.co.uk
Weekly (Thu). Owner: Northcliffe Newspapers. Editor: Natalie Missenden

Walsall Chronicle
01922 444444
www.expressandstar.com
Weekly (Thu). Owner: Midland News Association. Editor: Mike Caldicott

Walsall Observer
01922 636666
www.thisiswalsall.co.uk
Weekly (Fri). Owner: Midlands Weekly Media (Trinity Mirror). Editor: Mike Lockley

Why Coventry, Nuneaton & Hinckley
0845 600 9742
Weekly free (Fri). Owner: Northcliffe Newspapers. Editor: Claire Smith

Why Solihull & District
0845 600 9742
Weekly free (Fri). Owner: Northcliffe Newspapers. Editor: Claire Smith

Why Warwick & Leamington
0845 600 9742
Weekly free (Fri). Owner: Northcliffe Newspapers. Editor: Claire Smith

Wolverhampton Ad News
01543 501700
Weekly (Wed). Owner: Midlands Weekly Media (Trinity Mirror). Editor: Mike Lockley

Wolverhampton Chronicle
01902 313131
www.yourchronicle.com
Weekly free (Thu). Owner: Midland News Association. Editor: Adrian Faber; news: Mark Drew; features: Dylan Evans; chief sub: Tony Reynolds

West England

Gloucestershire, Herefordshire, Shropshire, Worcestershire

Alcester Chronicle
01527 453500
www.thisisworcestershire.co.uk
Weekly (Wed). Owner: Newsquest. Editor: Paul Walker; news: Emily Bridgwater

Berrow's Worcester Journal
01905 748200
www.berrowsjournal.co.uk
Weekly. Owner: Newsquest. Editor: Stewart Gilbert; news: Sala Lloyd; chief sub: Jim Collins

Bridgnorth Journal
01746 761411
www.bridgnorthjournal.co.uk
Weekly (Fri). Owner: Midland News Association. Editor: John Griffiths

Bromsgrove Advertiser
01527 837000
www.thisisworcestershire.co.uk
Weekly (Wed). Owner: Newsquest. Editor: Alan Wallcroft; chief reporter: Peter Lammas

Bromsgrove Messenger
01527 837000
www.thisisworcestershire.co.uk
Weekly (Wed). Owner: Newsquest. Editor: Alan Wallcroft; chief reporter: Peter Lammas

Bromsgrove Standard
01527 574111
www.bromsgrovestandard.co.uk
Weekly free (Fri). Owner: Observer Standard Newspapers. Editor: Tristan Harris

Cheltenham Independent
01453 762412
www.thisisstroud.com
Weekly (Wed). Owner: Newsquest. Editor: Skip Walker; news: Sue Smith

Cheltenham News
01452 424442
www.thisisgloucestershire.co.uk
Weekly (Thu). Owner: Northcliffe Newspapers. Editor: Anita Syvret

Cheltenham/Tewkesbury News
01452 420632
www.thisisgloucestershire.co.uk
Weekly free (Thu). Owner: Northcliffe Newspapers. Editor: Chris Hill

Chipping Sodbury/Yate Gazette
01453 544000
www.thisisthesouthcotswolds.co.uk
Weekly (Fri). Owner: Newsquest. Editor: Skip Walker; news: Carole Taylor

Cotswold Journal
01608 651456
www.thisistewkesbury.com
Weekly (Thu). Owner: Newsquest. Editor: John Murphy; news: Pat Smith

County Independent
01453 762412
www.thisisstroud.com
Weekly (Wed). Owner: Newsquest. Editor: Skip Walker; news: Sue Smith

Droitwich Spa Advertiser
01905 795097
www.thisisdroitwichspa.co.uk
Weekly (Wed). Owner: Newsquest. Editor: Alan Wallcroft; news: Peter Lammas

Droitwich Standard
01527 574111
www.bromsgrovestandard.co.uk/droitwich
Weekly (Fri). Owner: Observer Standard Newspapers. Editor: Tristan Harris

Evesham Journal
01608 651456
www.thisisworcestershire.co.uk
Weekly (Thu). Owner: Newsquest. Editor: John Murphy; news: Pat Smith

Express and Star (Kidderminster)
01902 313131
www.expressandstar.com
Daily. Owner: Midland News Association. Editor: Adrian Faber; news: Mark Drew; features: Dylan Evans; chief sub: Tony Reynolds

Forest of Dean and Wye Valley Review
01594 841113
www.forest-and-wye-today.co.uk
Weekly free (Wed). Owner: Tindle Newspapers. Editor: John Powell

The Forester
01594 820600
www.thisisgloucestershire.co.uk
Weekly (Thu). Owner: Northcliffe Newspapers. Editor: Viv Hargreaves

Gloucester Citizen
01452 424442
www.thisisgloucestershire.co.uk
Daily. Owner: Northcliffe Newspapers. Editor: Ian Mean

Gloucester Independent
01453 762412
www.thisisstroud.com
Weekly (Wed). Owner: Newsquest. Editor: Skip Walker; news: Sue Smith

Gloucester News
01452 424442
www.thisisgloucestershire.co.uk
Weekly free (Thu). Owner: Northcliffe Newspapers. Editor: Chris Hill

Gloucestershire County Gazette
01453 544000
www.thisisthesouthcotswolds.co.uk
Weekly (Fri). Owner: Newsquest. Editor: Skip Walker; news: Carole Taylor

Gloucestershire Echo
01242 271821
www.thisisgloucestershire.co.uk
Daily. Owner: Northcliffe Newspapers. Editor: Anita Syvret; news: Tanya Gledhill; features: Ian Akerman; chief sub: Peter Gavan

Hereford Admag
01432 376120
Weekly (Wed). Owner: Northcliffe Newspapers. Features editor: Clare Fry

Hereford Journal
01432 355353
www.herefordjournal.co.uk
Weekly free (Wed). Owner: Midland News Association. Editor: Colin Osborne; news: Neil Tippten; newsdesk: Debbie Collins

61

Hereford Times
01432 274413
www.thisisherefordshire.co.uk
Weekly (Thu). Owner: Newsquest.
Editor: Liz Griffin; news: Nigel Heins

Jobs Today (Cheltenham & Gloucester)
01453 544000
www.thisisthesouthcotswolds.co.uk
Daily. Owner: Newsquest. Editor: Skip
Walker; news: Carole Taylor

Kidderminster Chronicle
01562 829500
www.thisisworcestershire.co.uk
   /worcestershire/kidderminster
Weekly (Wed). Owner: Newsquest.
Reporter: Jonathan Wood

Kidderminster Shuttle and Times and Stourport News
01562 633333
www.thisisworcestershire.co.uk
   /worcestershire/kidderminster
Weekly (Thu). Owner: Newsquest.
Editor: Clive Joyce

Ledbury Reporter
01684 892200
www.thisisworcestershire.co.uk
Weekly (Fri). Owner: Newsquest.
Editor: Nick Howells; news: Ally Hardy

Leominster Journal
01432 355353
www.leominsterjournal.com
Weekly free (Wed). Owner: Midland
News Association. Editor: Colin
Osborne; news: Neil Tippten; newsdesk:
Debbie Collins

Ludlow Advertiser
01584 873796
www.thisisludlow.co.uk
Weekly (Thu). Owner: Newsquest.
News editor: Jean Kingdon; general
reporter: Michael Baws

Ludlow Journal
01743 248248
www.ludlowjournal.co.uk
Weekly free (Fri). Owner: Midland
News Association. Editor: Mike
Robinson; chief reporter: Vince Buston

Malvern Gazette
01684 892200
www.thisisworcestershire.co.uk
Weekly (Fri). Owner: Newsquest.
Editor: Nick Howells

Market Drayton Advertiser
01630 698113
www.marketdraytonadvertiser.co.uk
Weekly (Fri). Owner: Midland News
Association. Editor: Sam Taylor

Newport Advertiser
01952 811500
www.newportadvertiser.co.uk
Weekly (Fri). Owner: Midland News
Association. Editor: Samantha Taylor;
news: Terry Morris

North Shropshire Chronicle
01743 248248
www.northshropshirechronicle.com
Weekly (Thu). Owner: Midland News
Association. Editor: John Butterworth

Oswestry & Border Counties Advertiser
01691 655321
www.bordercountiesadvertiser.co.uk
Weekly (Wed). Owner: North Wales
Newspapers. Editor: Sue Perry

Redditch Advertiser
01527 453500
www.thisisworcestershire.co.uk
   /worcestershire/redditch
Weekly (Wed). Owner: Newsquest.
Editor: Paul Walker; news: Emily
Bridgwater

Redditch Standard
01527 588688
www.redditchstandard.co.uk
Weekly free (Fri). Owner: Observer
Standard Newspapers. Editor: Andrew
Powell

Ross Gazette
01989 562007
www.ross-today.co.uk
Weekly (Thu). Owner: Tindle
Newspapers. Editor: Chris Robertson;
chief reporter: Jo Scriven

Ross-on-Wye Journal
01432 355353
www.rossonwyejournal.com
Weekly free (Wed). Owner: Midland
News Association. Editor: Colin
Osborne; news: Neil Tippten; newsdesk:
Debbie Collins

Shrewsbury Admag
01743 241414
www.northshropshirechronicle.com
Weekly (Thu). Owner: Northcliffe
Newspapers. General manager: Jan
Edwards

Shrewsbury Chronicle
01743 248248
www.shrewsburychronicle.co.uk
Weekly (Thu). Owner: Midland News
Association. Editor: John Butterworth

Shropshire Star
See page 35

South Shropshire Journal
01584 876311
www.southshropshirejournal.co.uk
Weekly (Fri). Owner: Midland News
Association. Editor: Mike Robinson;
news: Vince Buston

Stourport News
01562 633330
Weekly free (Thu). Owner: Newsquest.
Editor: Clive Joyce; deputy editor:
Alison Grange; news: Peter McMillan

Stratford Observer
01789 415717
www.stratfordobserver.co.uk
Weekly (Fri). Owner: Observer
Standard Newspapers. Editor: Clare
Fitzsimmons

Stroud News & Journal
01453 762142
www.thisisstroud.com
Weekly (Wed). Owner: Newsquest.
Editor: Skip Walker; news: Sue Smith

Telford Journal
01743 248248
www.telfordjournal.co.uk
Weekly free (Thu). Owner: Midland
News Association. Editor: David Sharpe

Tenbury Wells Advertiser
01584 873796
www.thisistenbury-wells.co.uk
Weekly (Thu). Owner: Newsquest.
Editor: Sophie Bignall

Thornbury Gazette
01453 544000
www.thisisthesouthcotswolds.co.uk
Weekly (Fri). Owner: Newsquest. Editor:
Skip Walker; news: Carole Taylor

Why Evesham
0845 600 9742
Weekly free (Fri). Owner: Northcliffe
Newspapers. Editor: Jackie Keeling

Why Redditch & District
0845 600 9742
Weekly free (Fri). Owner: Northcliffe
Newspapers. Editor: Jackie Keeling

Why Worcester, Malvern & Kidderminster
0845 600 9742
Weekly free (Fri). Owner: Northcliffe
Newspapers. Editor: Jackie Keeling

Wilts & Gloucestershire Standard
01285 642642
www.thisiscirencester.com
Weekly (Thu). Owner: Newsquest.
Editor: Peter Davidson; news: Simon
Davies

Worcester Evening News
01905 748200
www.thisisworcestershire.co.uk
Daily. Owner: Newsquest. Editor:
Stewart Gilbert; news: Sala Lloyd; chief
sub: Jim Collins

Worcester Standard
01905 726200
www.worcesterstandard.co.uk
Weekly free (Thu). Owner: Observer
Standard Newspapers. Editor: James
Illes; news: David Dunham

North England

East, North, South & West Yorkshire

Aire Valley Target
01274 729511
*Weekly (Thu). Owner: Newsquest.
Editor: Perry Austin-Clarke; news:
Martin Heminway; features: David
Barnett; chief sub: Mel Jones*

Axholme Herald
01427 874417
*Weekly (Fri). Owner: Northcliffe
Newspapers. Editor: Ron Shipley*

Barnsley Chronicle
01226 734734
www.barnsley-chronicle.co.uk
*Weekly (Fri). Editor: Robert Cockroft;
news: Stephanie Daley; features:
Maureen Middleton; chief sub: John
Threlkeld*

Barnsley Independent
01226 734734
www.barnsley-chronicle.co.uk
*Weekly (Tue). Editor: Robert Cockroft;
news: Stephanie Daley; features:
Maureen Middleton; chief sub: John
Threlkeld*

Batley News
01924 468282
www.dewsburytoday.co.uk
*Weekly (Thu). Owner: Johnston Press.
Editor: John Wilson; news: Anna
Locking*

Beverley Advertiser
01482 327111
*Weekly (Thu). Owner: Northcliffe
Newspapers. Editor: Alex Leys*

Beverley Guardian
01377 241122
www.beverleytoday.co.uk
*Weekly free (Fri). Owner: Johnston
Press. Editor: Dennis Sissons; news:
Steve Petch; chief sub: Gill Pick*

Birstall News
01924 468282
www.dewsburytoday.co.uk
*Weekly (Thu). Owner: Johnston Press.
Editor: John Wilson*

Bradford Target
01274 729511
*Weekly (Tue). Owner: Newsquest.
Editor: Perry Austin-Clarke; news:
Martin Heminway; features: David
Barnett; chief sub: Neal Jones*

Bridlington Free Press
01262 606606
www.bridlingtontoday.co.uk
*Weekly (Thu). Owner: Johnston Press.
Editor: Nick Procter; news: Simon
Haldenby; features: John Edwards*

Bridlington Gazette & Herald
01262 606606
www.bridlingtontoday.co.uk
*Weekly free (Tue). Owner: Johnston
Press. Editor: Nick Procter; news: Simon
Haldenby; features: John Edwards*

Brighouse Echo
01422 260200
www.brighousetoday.co.uk
*Weekly (Fri). Owner: Johnston Press.
Editor: Stephen Firth*

Calderdale News
01422 260200
www.halifaxtoday.co.uk
*Weekly free (Wed). Owner: Johnston
Press. Editor: John Furbisher;
production: Gordon Samson*

Colne Valley Chronicle
01484 437747
www.ichuddersfield.co.uk
*Weekly (Fri). Owner: Trinity Mirror
Huddersfield. Editor: Chris Burgess*

Craven Herald & Pioneer
01756 794117
www.cravenherald.co.uk
*Weekly (Fri). Owner: Newsquest.
Editor: Ian Lockwood; deputy editor:
Lindsey Moore*

Dearne Advertiser
01709 303050
www.doncastertoday.co.uk
*Weekly (Fri). Owner: Johnston Press.
Editor: Linda Waslidge; news: Lee
Siggs; features: Kevin Rogers*

Dearne Valley Weekender
01709 571111
www.rotherhamadvertiser.com
*Weekly (Fri). Owner: Garnet Dickinson
Publishing. Editor: Doug Melloy*

Dewsbury Reporter
01924 468282
www.dewsburytoday.co.uk
*Weekly (Fri). Owner: Johnston Press.
Editor: John Wilson; news: Anna
Locking*

Dinnington & Maltby Guardian
01909 550500
www.dinningtontoday.co.uk
*Weekly (Fri). Owner: Johnston Press.
Editor: George Robinson; news: Jackie
Laver*

Dinnington & Maltby Trader News
01909 550500
*Weekly (Thu). Owner: Johnston Press.
Editor: George Robinson; news: Jackie
Laver*

Doncaster Advertiser
01302 347213
*Weekly (Fri). Owner: Johnston Press.
Editor: Martin Edmunds; news: John
Hepperstall*

Doncaster Free Press
01302 348501
www.doncastertoday.co.uk
*Weekly (Thu). Owner: Johnston Press.
Editor: Graham Huston; news: Kath
Finlay; features: Eddie Mardell;
production: David Crossland*

Doncaster Star
01302 348501
www.doncastertoday.co.uk
*Daily. Owner: Johnston Press.
Reporter: David Kessen*

Driffield Post
01377 241122
www.driffieldtoday.co.uk
*Weekly (Fri). Owner: Johnston Press.
Editor: Dennis Sissons; news: Steve
Petch; chief sub: Gill Pick*

Driffield Times
01377 241122
www.driffieldtoday.co.uk
*Weekly (Wed). Owner: Johnston Press.
Editor: Dennis Sissons; news: Steve
Petch; chief sub: Gill Pick*

**Easingwold Advertiser & Weekly
News**
01347 821329
www.ghsmith.com/advertiser
*Weekly (Thu). Owner: Newsquest.
Editor: Margery Smith*

East Hull Advertiser
01482 327111
*Weekly (Wed). Owner: Northcliffe
Newspapers. Editor: Alex Leys*

East Riding Advertiser
01482 327111
*Weekly (Thu). Owner: Northcliffe
Newspapers. Editor: Alex Leys*

East Riding News
01482 887700
www.eastridinggov.co.uk
*Monthly (1st week).
Editor: Andrew Milner*

Elmsall & South Elmsall Express
01977 640107
www.wakefieldexpress.co.uk
*Weekly free (Fri). Owner: Johnston
Press. Editor: Delia Kitson*

Epworth Bells & Crowle Advertiser
01427 615323
*Weekly (Thu). Owner: Johnston Press.
Editor: Janet Harrison; deputy editor:
Andy Staples; news: Stephanie Bateman*

Filey & Hunmanby Mercury
01723 363636
www.scarboroughtoday.co.uk
*Weekly (Sat). Owner: Johnston Press.
Editor: Ed Asquith; news: Neil
Pickford; chief sub: Steve Banbridge;
production: Pete Hodgson*

Gainsborough News
01427 872202
*Weekly free (Fri). Owner: Johnston
Press. Editor: Janet Harrison; deputy
editor: Andy Staples; news: Stephanie
Bateman*

Gainsborough Standard
01427 615323
*Weekly (Thu). Owner: Johnston Press.
Editor: Janet Harrison; deputy editor:
Andy Staples; news: Stephanie Bateman*

Halifax Evening Courier
01422 260200
www.halifaxtoday.co.uk
*Daily. Owner: Johnston Press.
Editor: John Furbisher*

Harrogate Advertiser
01423 564321
www.harrogatetoday.co.uk
*Weekly (Fri). Owner: Johnston Press.
Editor: Jean Macquarrie; assistant
editor: Rita Sobot; chief sub: Michael
Molsher*

Harrogate Herald
01423 564321
www.harrogatetoday.co.uk
*Weekly (Tue). Owner: Johnston Press.
Editor: Jean Macquarrie; assistant
editor: Rita Sobot; chief sub: Michael
Molsher*

Hebden Bridge Times
01422 260200
www.halifaxtoday.co.uk
*Weekly (Fri). Owner: Johnston Press.
Editor: Sheila Tordoff.*

Heckmondwike Herald
01924 468282
www.dewsburytoday.co.uk
*Weekly (Fri). Owner: Johnston Press.
Editor: John Wilson*

Holderness & Hornsea Gazette
01964 612777
www.holderness-online.com
*Weekly (Thu). Publisher: Brian Adcock;
news: David McAughtrie*

Holderness Advertiser
01482 327111
*Weekly (Wed). Owner: Northcliffe
Newspapers. Editor: Alex Leys*

Holme Valley Express
01484 430000
www.ichuddersfield.co.uk
*Weekly (Tue). Owner: Trinity Mirror
Huddersfield. Editor: Chris Burgess*

Huddersfield Daily Examiner
01484 430000
www.ichuddersfield.co.uk
*Daily. Owner: Trinity Mirror
Huddersfield. Editor: Roy Wright; news:
Neil Atkinson; features: Andrew Flynn*

Huddersfield District Chronicle
01484 437747
www.ichuddersfield.co.uk
*Weekly (Fri). Owner: Trinity Mirror
Huddersfield. Editor: Chris Burgess*

Hull Daily Mail
See page 35

Ilkley Gazette
01943 607022
www.ilkleygazette.co.uk
*Weekly (Thu). Owner: Newsquest.
Editor: Mel Vasey; chief reporter: Paul
Langan*

The Journal (Hull)
01482 327111
*Monthly (24th). Owner: Northcliffe
Newspapers. Editor: Roy Woodcock*

Keighley & Craven Target
01274 729511
*Weekly (Tue). Owner: Newsquest.
Editor: Perry Austin-Clarke; news:
Martin Heminway; features: David
Barnett; chief sub: Mel Jones*

Keighley News
01535 606611
www.keighleynews.co.uk
*Weekly (Thu). Owner: Newsquest.
Editor: Malcolm Hoddy; news: Alistair
Shand; chief sub: Ralph Badham*

Knaresborough Post
01423 564321
www.knaresboroughtoday.co.uk
*Weekly (Fri). Owner: Johnston Press.
Editor: Jean Macquarrie; assistant
editor: Rita Sobot; chief sub: Michael
Molsher*

Leeds Weekly News
0113 243 2701
*Weekly (Thu). Owner: Johnston Press.
Editor: Sheila Holmes*

Look Local (Sheffield)
0114 283 1100
www.looklocal.org.uk
*Weekly (Wed). Editor: Phil Dolby; head
of production: Adrian von Werzbach*

Malton & Pickering Mercury
01723 363636
www.maltontoday.co.uk
*Weekly (Wed). Owner: Johnston Press.
Editor: Ed Asquith; news: Neil
Pickford; chief sub: Steve Banbridge;
production: Pete Hodgson*

Metro Yorkshire
020 7651 5200
www.metro.co.uk
*Daily. Owner: Associated Newspapers.
Editor: Kenny Campbell; news: Mark
Dorman; features: Kieran Meeke*

Mirfield Reporter
01924 468282
www.dewsburytoday.co.uk
*Weekly (Fri). Owner: Johnston Press.
Editor: John Wilson*

Morley Advertiser
0113 252 4020
www.morleytoday.co.uk
*Weekly (Wed). Owner: Johnston Press.
Editor: Robert Evans; news: Sarah Hall*

Morley Observer
01924 468282
www.dewsburytoday.co.uk
*Weekly (Fri). Owner: Johnston Press.
Editor: John Wilson*

North Yorkshire Advertiser
01325 381313
www.thisisdarlington.co.uk
/the_north_east/advertiser
*Weekly free (Tue). Owner: Newsquest.
Editor: Peter Barron; news: Nigel
Burton; features: Nick Morrison; chief
sub: Ken Farrier*

North Yorkshire Herald & Post
01642 245401
www.ncjmediainfo.co.uk
*Weekly (Fri). Owner: Gazette Media
Company (Trinity Mirror). Editor: Sue
Giles*

North Yorkshire News
01765 601248
www.northallertontoday.co.uk
*Weekly free (Wed). Owner: Johnston
Press. Editor: Steve Barton; news:
Stephen Pass*

Northallerton, Thirsk & Bedale Times
01765 601248
www.northallertontoday.co.uk
*Weekly (Fri). Owner: Johnston Press.
Editor: Steve Barton; news: Stephen Pass*

Ossett Observer
01924 375111
www.wakefieldtoday.co.uk
*Weekly free (Fri). Owner: Johnston
Press. Editor: Mark Bradley; news:
Lisa Rookes*

Pateley Bridge & Nidderdale Herald
01423 564321
www.nidderdaletoday.co.uk
*Owner: Johnston Press. Editor: Jean
Macquarrie; assistant editor: Rita
Sobot; chief sub: Michael Molsher*

Pocklington Post
01759 301003
www.pocklingtontoday.co.uk
*Weekly (Fri). Owner: Johnston Press.
Editor: Kay Darley; news: Neil
Pickford; chief sub: Steve Banbridge;
production: Pete Hodgson*

Pontefract & Castleford Express
01977 737200
www.wakefieldexpress.co.uk
*Weekly (Thu). Owner: Johnston Press.
Editor: David Ward; news: Julie
Hawksworth*

Pontefract & Castleford Extra
01977 737200
www.wakefieldexpress.co.uk
*Weekly free (Fri). Owner: Johnston
Press. Editor: David Ward; news: Julie
Hawksworth*

Pudsey Times
01943 466750
*Weekly (Thu). Owner: Johnston Press.
Editor: Kate Evans*

**Ripon Gazette & Boroughbridge
Herald**
01423 564321
www.ripontoday.co.uk
*Weekly (Fri). Owner: Johnston Press.
Editor: Jean Macquarrie; assistant
editor: Rita Sobot; chief sub: Michael
Molsher*

**Rotherham & South Yorkshire
Advertiser**
01709 364721
www.rotherhamadvertiser.com
*Weekly (Fri). Owner: Garnet Dickinson
Publishing. Editor: Doug Melloy; news:
Ann Charlton*

Rotherham Record
01709 364721
www.rotherhamadvertiser.com
*Weekly (Wed). Owner: Garnet
Dickinson Publishing. Editor: Doug
Melloy; news: Ann Charlton*

Scarborough Evening News
01723 363636
www.scarborougheveningnews.co.uk
*Daily. Owner: Johnston Press.
Editor: Ed Asquith; news: Neil
Pickford; chief sub: Steve Banbridge;
production: Pete Hodgson*

Scarborough Trader
01723 352269
www.tradertoday.co.uk
*Weekly free (Thu). Owner: Johnston
Press. Editor: Ed Asquith*

Selby Chronicle
01757 702198
www.selbytoday.co.uk
*Weekly free (Fri). Owner: Johnston
Press. Editor: Chris Page; news:
Richard Parker*

Selby Post
01405 720110
www.selbypost.co.uk
*Weekly (Thu). Owner: Northcliffe
Newspapers. Editor: Peter Butler*

Selby Star
01904 653051
www.yorkandcountypress.co.uk
/york/ycp/star
*Weekly free (Wed). Owner: Newsquest.
Editor: Lynne Martin*

Selby Times
01757 702802
www.selbytoday.co.uk
*Weekly (Thu). Owner: Johnston Press.
Editor: Chris Page; news: Richard Parker*

Sheffield & South Yorkshire Times Today
0115 956 8858
*Weekly free (Wed). Owner: GPC General
Publishing Company.
Editor: Matthew Palmer*

Sheffield Journal
0114 276 7676
www.sheffieldtoday.net
*Weekly free (Thu). Owner: Johnston
Press. Editor: Alan Powell; news: Bob
Westerdale; features: John Highfield;
head of content: Paul License*

Sheffield Mercury
0114 276 3633
Weekly (Fri). Editor: David Hayes

Sheffield Telegraph
0114 276 7676
www.sheffieldtoday.net
*Weekly (Fri). Owner: Johnston Press.
Editor: David Todd; news: Peter Kay;
head of content: Paul License*

Sheffield Weekly Gazette
0114 276 7676
www.sheffieldtoday.net
*Weekly (Thu). Owner: Johnston Press.
Editor: Alan Powell; news: Bob
Westerdale; features: John Highfield;
head of content: Paul License*

South Yorkshire Times
01709 303050
www.dearnetoday.co.uk
*Weekly (Thu). Owner: Johnston Press.
Editor: Linda Waslidge*

Spenborough Guardian
01924 468282
www.dewsburytoday.co.uk
*Weekly (Fri). Owner: Johnston Press.
Editor: John Wilson*

The Star (Sheffield)
See page 35

Telegraph and Argus (Bradford)
See page 36

Todmorden News & Advertiser
01422 260200
www.halifaxtoday.co.uk
*Weekly (Fri). Owner: Johnston Press.
Editor: Sheila Tordoff*

The Town Crier (Bradford)
01274 729511
*Weekly (Thu). Owner: Newsquest.
Editor: Perry Austin-Clarke; news:
Martin Heminway; features: David
Barnett; chief sub: Mel Jones*

Wakefield Express
01924 375111
www.wakefieldexpress.co.uk
*Weekly free (Fri). Owner: Johnston
Press. Editor: Mark Bradley; news:
Lisa Rookes*

Wakefield, Rothwell & Alton Extra
01924 375111
www.wakefieldexpress.co.uk
*Weekly free (Thu). Owner: Johnston
Press. Editor: Mark Bradley; news:
Lisa Rookes*

Weekly Advertiser
01924 468282
www.dewsburytoday.co.uk
*Weekly free (Fri). Owner: Johnston
Press. Editor: John Wilson*

West Hull Advertiser
01482 327111
*Weekly (Wed). Owner: Northcliffe
Newspapers. Editor: Alex Leys*

Wetherby, Boston Spa & Tadcaster News
01423 564321
www.harrogatetoday.co.uk
*Weekly (Fri). Owner: Johnston Press.
Editor: Jean Macquarrie; assistant
editor: Rita Sobot; chief sub: Michael
Molsher*

Wharfe Valley Times
01943 466750
*Weekly (Thu). Owner: Johnston Press.
Editor: Kate Evans*

Wharfedale & Airedale Observer
01943 465555
www.wharfedaleobserver.co.uk
*Weekly (Thu). Owner: Newsquest.
Editor: Mel Vasey; chief reporter:
Jim Jack*

Whitby Gazette
01947 602836
www.whitbytoday.co.uk
*Twice weekly (Tue, Fri). Owner:
Johnston Press. Editor: Damien
Holmes*

York Evening Press
See page 36

York Star
01904 653051
www.yorkandcountypress.co.uk
/york/ycp/star
*Weekly free (Wed). Owner: Newsquest.
Editor: Lynne Martin*

Yorkshire Evening Post
See page 36

Yorkshire Express
0115 956 8858
*Weekly free (Wed). Owner: GPC General
Publishing Company.
Editor: Matthew Palmer*

Yorkshire Gazette & Herald
01904 653051
www.thisisryedale.co.uk
*Weekly (Wed). Owner: Newsquest.
Editor: Chris Buxton*

Yorkshire Post
See page 36

North-east England

Cleveland, Durham,
Northumberland, Tyne & Wear

Berwick Advertiser
01289 306677
www.berwicktoday.co.uk
*Weekly (Thu). Owner: Johnston Press.
Editor: Janet Workershaw; news: Ian
Smith; features: Thomas Baldwin;
chief sub: Keith Hamblin*

Berwick Gazette
01289 306677
www.tweedalepress.co.uk
*Weekly free. Owner: Johnston Press.
Editor: Willie Mack*

Chester-le-Street Advertiser
01325 381313
www.thisisthenortheast.co.uk
*Weekly free (Thu). Owner: Newsquest.
Editor: Peter Barron; news: Nigel
Burton; features: Nick Morrison; chief
sub: Ken Farrier*

Citylife (Newcastle)
0191 211 5093
www.newcastle.gov.uk/citylife
*Monthly (last week of month). Editor:
Jane Byrne*

Consett & Stanley Advertiser
01325 381313
www.thisisthenortheast.co.uk
*Weekly free (Thu). Owner: Newsquest.
Editor: Peter Barron; news: Nigel
Burton; features: Nick Morrison; chief
sub: Ken Farrier*

Darlington & Stockton Times
01325 381313
www.thisisthenortheast.co.uk
*Weekly (Fri). Owner: Newsquest.
Editor: Malcolm Warne; news: Mike
Bridgen; chief sub: Andy Brown*

Darlington, Aycliffe & Sedgefield Advertiser
01325 381313
www.thisisthenortheast.co.uk
*Weekly free (Wed). Owner: Newsquest.
Editor: Peter Barron; news: Nigel
Burton; features: Nick Morrison; chief
sub: Ken Farrier*

Darlington Herald & Post
01325 262000
www.icteesside.co.uk
*Weekly (Fri). Owner: Johnston Press.
Editor: Sue Giles*

Durham Advertiser
01325 381313
www.thisisthenortheast.co.uk
*Weekly free (Thu). Owner: Newsquest.
Editor: Peter Barron; news: Nigel
Burton; features: Nick Morrison; chief
sub: Ken Farrier*

East Cleveland Advertiser
01325 381313
www.theclarion.co.uk
*Weekly free (Fri). Owner: Newsquest.
Editor: Peter Barron; news: Nigel
Burton; features: Nick Morrison; chief
sub: Ken Farrier*

East Cleveland Herald & Post
01642 234227
www.icteesside.co.uk
Weekly (Wed). Owner: Gazette Media Company (Trinity Mirror).
Editor: Sue Giles

Evening Chronicle (Newcastle)
See page 35

Evening Gazette
See page 35

Gateshead Herald and Post
0191 201 6405
Weekly (Wed). Owner: Newcastle Chronicle & Journal (Trinity Mirror).
Editor: Catherine Welford; news: Zoe Burn

Hartlepool Mail
01429 239333
www.hartlepoolmail.co.uk
Daily. Owner: Johnston Press.
Editor: Paul Napier; deputy editor: Brian Nuttley

Hartlepool Star
01429 239333
www.hartlepoolmail.co.uk
Weekly free (Thu). Owner: Johnston Press. Editor: Paul Napier; deputy editor: Brian Nuttley

Hexham Courant
01434 602351
www.hexham-courant.co.uk
Weekly (Fri). Owner: Cumbrian News Group. Editor: Collin Tapping; news: Brian Tilley

Houghton Star
0191 501 5800
Weekly free (Thu). Owner: Johnston Press. Editor: Betty Long

The Journal (Newcastle)
See page 35

Metro North East
0191 477 7445
www.metro.co.uk
Daily. Owner: Newcastle Chronicle & Journal (Trinity Mirror).
Editor: Deane Hodgson

Middlesbrough Herald & Post
01642 234227
www.icteesside.co.uk
Weekly (Wed). Owner: Gazette Media Company (Trinity Mirror).
Editor: Sue Giles

Morpeth Herald
01670 510522
www.morpethtoday.co.uk
Weekly (Thu). Owner: Johnston Press.
Editor: Terry Hackett

Newcastle Herald & Post
0191 201 6405
www.icnewcastle.co.uk
Weekly (Wed). Owner: Newcastle Chronicle & Journal (Trinity Mirror).
Editor: Catherine Welford; news: Zoe Burn

Newcastle Times
01332 205900
www.regional-media.co.uk
Weekly (Thu). Owner: Journal Publishing Company. Editor: Sonia Walters; news: Simon Howorth; features: Katie Doherty; production: Fiona Smith

News Post Leader (Whitley Bay)
0191 251 8484
www.blyth-wansbecktoday.co.uk
Weekly. Owner: Johnston Press.
Editor: Ross Weeks

North Tyneside Herald & Post
0191 201 6405
www.icnewcastle.co.uk
Weekly (Wed). Owner: Newcastle Chronicle & Journal (Trinity Mirror).
Editor: Catherine Welford; news: Zoe Burn

Northern Echo
See page 35

Northumberland Gazette
01665 602234
www.northumberlandtoday.co.uk
Weekly (Thu). Owner: Johnston Press.
Editor: Andrew Smith

Northumberland Herald and Post
0191 201 6405
Weekly (Wed). Owner: Newcastle Chronicle & Journal (Trinity Mirror).
Editor: Catherine Welford; news: Zoe Burn

Peterlee Star
0191 501 5800
Weekly free (Thu). Owner: Johnston Press. Editor: Betty Long

Seaham Star
0191 501 5800
Weekly free (Thu). Owner: Johnston Press. Editor: Betty Long

South Durham Herald & Post
01642 234227
www.icteesside.co.uk
Weekly (Fri). Owner: Gazette Media Company (Trinity Mirror).
Editor: Sue Giles

South Shields Gazette
0191 455 4661
www.southtynesidetoday.co.uk
Daily. Owner: Johnston Press.
Editor: John Syzmanski

South Tyne Star
0191 455 4661
Weekly free (Thu). Owner: Johnston Press. Editor: John Syzmanski

South Tyneside Herald & Post
0191 201 6405
www.icnewcastle.co.uk
Weekly (Wed). Owner: Newcastle Chronicle & Journal (Trinity Mirror).
Editor: Catherine Welford; news: Zoe Burn

Stockton & Billingham Herald & Post
01642 234227
www.icteesside.co.uk
Weekly (Wed). Owner: Gazette Media Company (Trinity Mirror).
Editor: Sue Giles

Sunday Sun (Newcastle)
See page 36

Sunderland Echo
0191 501 5800
www.sunderland-today.co.uk
Daily. Owner: Johnston Press.
Editor: Rob Lawson; news: Gavin Foster; features: Paul Taylor; production: Paul Larkin

Sunderland Star
0191 501 5800
Weekly free (Thu). Owner: Johnston Press. Editor: Betty Long

Teesside Focus
01332 365811
www.regional-media.co.uk
Weekly free (Mon). Owner: Journal Publishing Company. Editor: Sean Peaty

Teesside Herald & Post
01642 234227
www.icteesside.co.uk
Weekly (Wed). Owner: Gazette Media Company (Trinity Mirror).
Editor: Sue Giles

Wallsend News Guardian
0191 251 8484
www.northtynesidetoday.co.uk
Weekly free (Thu). Owner: Johnston Press. Editor: Ross Weeks

Washington Star
0191 501 5800
Weekly free (Thu). Owner: Johnston Press. Editor: Betty Long

Whitley Bay News Guardian
0191 251 8566
www.northtynesidetoday.co.uk
Weekly free (Thu). Owner: Johnston Press. Editor: Ross Weeks

North-west England

Cheshire, Cumbria, Lancashire, Manchester, Merseyside

Accrington Observer
01254 871444
www.accringtonobserver.co.uk
Weekly (Fri). Owner: Guardian Media Group. Editor: Mervyn Kay; news: Michelle McKenna

Advertising Times
01200 422324
Weekly (Fri). Owner: Trinity Mirror Cheshire. Editor: Vivien Meath; news: Duncan Smith; features: Barry Bradshaw; production: Paul Watson

Anfield and Walton Star
0151 236 2000
Weekly (Thu). Owner: Trinity Mirror Merseyside. News editor: Kevin Mathews

Ashton-under-Lyne Reporter
0161 303 1910
Weekly (Thu). Editor: Nigel Skinner

Asian News
01706 354321
www.theasiannews.co.uk
Monthly (4th Fri). Owner: Guardian Media Group. Editor: Steve Hammond

Barnoldswick & Earby Times
01282 612561
www.eastlancashireonline.co.uk
Weekly (Fri). Owner: Johnston Press. Editor: Roy Prenton; news: Peter Dewhurst

Barrow Advertiser
01229 840150
www.cumbria-online.co.uk
Weekly free (Thu). Owner: Cumbrian News Group. Editor: Steve Brauner; news: Don Townend; features: Bill Myers; chief sub: Sarah Farrell

Bentham Guardian
01524 32525
Weekly (Fri). Owner: Johnston Press. Editor: Sue Riley; news: Louise Bryning; features: Paul Collins; chief sub: Bryan Carter

Birkenhead News
0151 647 7111
www.icwirral.co.uk
Weekly (Wed). Owner: Trinity Mirror Merseyside. Editor: Sue McCann; news: Louise Powney

Blackburn Citizen
01254 678678
www.thisislancashire.co.uk
Weekly (Thu). Owner: Newsquest. Editor-in-chief: Kevin Young; news: Andrew Turner; features: John Anson

Blackpool & Fylde Citizen
01253 292005
www.thisislancashire.co.uk
Weekly (Thu). Owner: Newsquest. Editor: Greg Morgan; news: Steve Dunthorne; features: Nikki Masters

Blackpool Gazette & Herald
See page 34

Blackpool Reporter
01253 400800
www.blackpoolonline.co.uk
Daily. Owner: Johnston Press. Editor: David Halliwell; news: James Higgins; chief sub: Linda Chatburn

Bolton Evening News
See page 34

Bolton Journal
01204 522345
www.thisisbolton.co.uk
Weekly (Thu). Owner: Newsquest. Editor-in-chief: Steve Hughes; editor: Derrick Grewcock; news: James Higgins; features: Andrew Mosley; production: John Bird

Bootle Times
0151 932 1000
www.icliverpool.co.uk
Weekly (Thu). Owner: Trinity Mirror Merseyside. Editor: Peter Harvey; news: Lloyd Jones

Bromborough & Bebington News
0151 647 7111
Weekly (Wed). Owner: Trinity Mirror Merseyside. Editor: Sue McCann; news: Louise Powney

Burnley Citizen
01254 678678
www.thisislancashire.co.uk
Weekly (Thu). Owner: Newsquest. Editor-in-chief: Kevin Young; news: Andrew Turner; features: John Anson

Burnley Express
01282 426161
www.burnleytoday.co.uk
Weekly (Tue, Fri). Owner: Johnston Press. Editor: Chris Daggett; news: Margaret Parsons; features: Barry Bradshaw; production: Paul Watson

Bury Journal
0161 764 9421
www.thisisbury.co.uk
Weekly (Wed). Owner: Newsquest. Editor: Bill Allen; news: Steve Orrell; chief sub: John Ellavy

Bury Times
0161 764 9421
www.thisisbury.co.uk
Weekly (Tue, Fri). Owner: Newsquest. Editor: Bill Allen; news: Steve Orrell; chief sub: John Ellavy

Buy Sell Cheshire
0151 330 4991
www.cheshirenews.co.uk
Weekly (Thu). Owner: Trinity Mirror Cheshire. Editor: Nigel White

Carnforth Guardian
01524 32525
Weekly (Fri). Owner: Johnston Press. Editor: Sue Riley; news: Louise Bryning; features: Paul Collins; chief sub: Bryan Carter

Chester & District Standard
01244 304500
www.chesterstandard.co.uk
Weekly (Thu). Owner: North Wales Newspapers. Editor: Jonathan White

Chester Chronicle
01244 340151
www.cheshirenews.co.uk
Weekly (Fri). Owner: Trinity Mirror Cheshire. Editor: Barry Ellans

Chester Mail
01244 340151
www.cheshirenews.co.uk
Weekly (Fri). Owner: Trinity Mirror Cheshire. Editor: Barry Elans

Chorley Citizen
01257 269313
www.thisislancashire.co.uk
/lancashire/chorley
Weekly (Wed). Owner: Johnston Press. Editor-in-chief: Kevin Young

Chorley Guardian
01257 264911
www.chorleytoday.co.uk
Weekly (Thu). Owner: Johnston Press. Editor: Tracy Bruce; news: Vanessa Taylor; chief sub: Mal Morris

Chronicle Weekend (Oldham)
0161 633 2121
www.oldham-chronicle.co.uk
Daily. Editor: Jim Williams; news: Mike Attenborough; chief sub: Steve Sutcliffe

Clitheroe Advertiser & Times
01200 422324
www.clitheroe.co.uk
Weekly (Thu). Owner: Johnston Press. Editor: Vivien Meath; news: Duncan Smith

Colne Times
01282 612561
www.eastlancashireonline.co.uk
Weekly (Fri). Owner: Johnston Press. Editor: Roy Prenton; news: Peter Dewhurst

Community News (Macclesfield)
01625 503322
Weekly (Thu). Owner: Northcliffe Newspapers. Editor: Jean Ellis

Congleton Advertiser
01782 602525
Weekly free (Thu). Owner: Northcliffe Newspapers. Editor: Sean Dooley; news: Robert Cotterill; features: Charlotte Little-Jones

Congleton Chronicle
01260 273737
www.chronicleseries.com
Weekly (Fri). Editor: Jeremy Condliffe

Congleton Guardian
01260 280686
www.thisischeshire.co.uk
Weekly (Fri). Owner: Newsquest. Editor: Paul Smith; news: Ian Ross

Crewe & Nantwich Guardian
01925 434000
www.thisischeshire.co.uk
Weekly (Thu). Owner: Newsquest. Editor: Nicola Priest

Crewe Chronicle
01270 256631
www.cheshirenews.co.uk
Weekly (Wed). Owner: Trinity Mirror Cheshire. Editor: Dave Fox; news: Jan Roberts

Crewe Mail
01270 211767
www.cheshirenews.co.uk
Weekly (Fri). Owner: Trinity Mirror
Cheshire. Editor: Dave Fox; news: Jan
Roberts

Crosby Herald
0151 932 1000
www.icseftonandwestlancs.co.uk
Weekly (Thu). Owner: Trinity Mirror
Merseyside. Editor: Peter Harvey;
news: Lloyd Jones

Cumberland and Westmorland Herald
01768 862313
www.cwherald.com
Weekly (Sat). Editor: Colin Maughan;
news: Liz Stannard; features: Helen
Phillips

Cumberland News
01228 612600
www.cumberland-news.co.uk
Weekly (Fri). Owner: Cumbrian News
Group. Editor: Keith Sutton; news: Sue
Crawford; features: Mary Ingham;
production: Andy Nixon

Deeside Chronicle
01244 340151
www.cheshirenews.co.uk
Weekly (Fri). Owner: Trinity Mirror
Cheshire. Editor: Paul Cook

East Cumbrian Gazette
01228 612600
www.cumbria-online.co.uk
Weekly free (Thu). Owner: Cumbrian
News Group. Editor: Keith Sutton;
news: Sue Crawford; features: Mary
Ingham; production: Andy Nixon

Ellesmere Port Pioneer
0151 355 5181
www.cheshirenews.co.uk
Weekly (Wed). Owner: Trinity Mirror
Cheshire. Editor: Phil Robinson

Ellesmere Port Standard
01244 304500
www.ellesmereportstandard.co.uk
Weekly (Thu). Owner: North Wales
Newspapers. Editor: Jonathan White

Evening Leader (Chester)
01352 707707
Daily. Editor: Barry Jones; features:
Joanne Shone; chief sub: Joanne Shone;
production: Karen Perry

Fleetwood Weekly News and Chronicle
01253 772950
www.fleetwoodtoday.co.uk
Weekly (Wed). Owner: Johnston Press.
Editor: Gary Miller; news: Karen
Evans; chief sub: Linda Chatburn

Flint & Holywell Chronicle
01244 821911
www.cheshirenews.co.uk
Weekly (Fri). Owner: Trinity Mirror
Cheshire. Editor: Paul Cook; news:
Kevin Hughes

Formby Champion
01704 392392
www.championline.net
Weekly (Wed). Owner: Champion
Media Group. Editor: Martin Hovden

Formby Times
01704 872237
www.icseftonandwestlancs
.co.uk/icformby
Weekly (Thu). Owner: Trinity Mirror
Merseyside. Editor: Hazel Shaw

Freestyle
01704 392392
www.championline.net
Monthly (Fri). Owner: Champion
Media Group. Editor: Erica Dillon

Frodsham & Helsby Chronicle
01244 340151
www.cheshirenews.co.uk
Weekly (Fri). Owner: Trinity Mirror
Cheshire. Editor: Paul Cook

Garstang Courier
01995 602494
www.garstangtoday.co.uk
Weekly (Fri). Owner: Johnston Press.
Editor: Richard Machin; news: Tony
Coppin

Garstang Guardian
01524 32525
www.prestontoday.net
Weekly (Fri). Owner: Johnston Press.
Editor: Sue Riley; news: Louise
Bryning; features: Paul Collins; chief
sub: Bryan Carter

Heswall News
0151 647 7111
Weekly (Wed). Owner: Trinity Mirror
Merseyside. Editor: Sue McCann; news:
Louise Powney

Heywood Advertiser
01706 360626
www.heywoodadvertiser.co.uk
Weekly (Wed). Owner: Guardian Media
Group. Editor: Margaret Cheesebrough

Hoylake & West Kirby News
0151 647 7111
Weekly (Wed). Owner: Trinity Mirror
Merseyside. Editor: Sue McCann; news:
Louise Powney

Huyton & Roby Star
0151 236 2000
Weekly (Thu). Owner: Trinity Mirror
Merseyside. News editor: Kevin Mathews

Keswick Reminder
01768 772140
www.keswickreminder.co.uk
Weekly (Fri). Editor: Jane Grave

Kirkby Extra
07831 090566
Monthly (1st Wed). Editor: Chris O'Shea

Kirkham Express
01253 724236
Weekly (Thu). Owner: Johnston Press.
Editor: Gary Miller; news: Chris Dixon

Knowsley Challenge
0151 236 2426
www.knowsleychallenge.co.uk
Monthly (15th). Owner: Trinity Mirror
Merseyside. Editor: Alan Birkett

Knutsford Guardian
01925 434000
www.thisischeshire.co.uk
Weekly (Wed). Owner: Newsquest.
Editor: Nicola Priest

Lakeland Echo
01524 833111
www.lakelandtoday.co.uk
Weekly (Fri). Owner: Johnston Press.
Editor: David Waddington

Lancashire Evening Post
See page 35

Lancashire Evening Telegraph
See page 35

Lancaster & Morecambe Citizen
01524 382121
www.thisislancashire.co.uk
Weekly (Thu). Owner: Johnston Press.
Editor: Phil Fleming

Lancaster Guardian
01524 32525
www.lancastertoday.co.uk
Weekly (Fri). Owner: Johnston Press.
Editor: Sue Riley; news: Louise
Bryning; features: Paul Collins; chief
sub: Bryan Carter

Leigh Journal
01942 672241
www.thisislancashire.co.uk
Weekly (Thu). Owner: Newsquest.
Editor: Mike Hulme

Leigh Reporter
01942 603334
www.leightoday.co.uk
Weekly free (Thu). Owner: Johnston
Press. Editor: Wendy Moss

Leyland Guardian
01257 264911
www.leylandtoday.co.uk
Weekly (Wed). Owner: Johnston Press.
Editor: Tracy Bruce; news: Vanessa
Taylor; chief sub: Mal Morris

Liverpool Post & Echo
See page 35

Longridge News
01772 783265
www.thisislancashire.co.uk
Weekly (Thu). Owner: Johnston Press.
Editor: Richard Machin

Lytham St Annes & Fylde Express
01253 724236
Weekly (Thu). Owner: Johnston Press.
Editor: Gary Miller; news: Chris Dixon

Macclesfield Express
01625 424445
www.macclesfield-express.co.uk
Weekly (Wed). Owner: Guardian
Media Group. Editor: Mike Quilley;
news: Pat Hills

Macclesfield Times
01625 424445
www.manchesteronline.co.uk/news
papers/macctimes.html
Weekly (Thu). Owner: Guardian Media
Group. Editor: Mike Quilley; news: Pat
Hills

Maghull & Aintree Star
0151 236 2000
www.icseftonandwestlancs
.co.uk/icmaghull
Weekly (Thu). Owner: Trinity Mirror
Merseyside. News editor: Kevin Mathews

Maghull Champion
01704 392392
www.championline.net
Weekly (Wed). Owner: Champion
Media Group. Editor: Martin Hovden

Manchester Evening News
See page 35
Manchester Metro News
0161 832 7200
www.metronews.co.uk
Marketplace (Wirral)
0151 906 3000
Weekly (Thu). Owner: Newsquest.
Editor: Leigh Marles
Metro North West
0161 836 5152
www.metro.co.uk
Daily free. Owner: Associated
Newspapers
Middleton & North Manchester
Guardian
0161 643 3615
www.middletonguardian.co.uk
Weekly (Thu). Owner: Guardian Media
Group. Editor: Gerry Sammon
Middlewich Chronicle
01244 340151
www.cheshirenews.co.uk
Weekly (Fri). Owner: Trinity Mirror
Cheshire. Editor: Paul Brown
Middlewich Guardian
01925 434000
www.thisischeshire.co.uk
Weekly (Wed). Owner: Newsquest.
Editor: Nicola Priest
Midweek Advertiser
01695 572501
Weekly (Thu). Owner: Trinity Mirror
Merseyside. Editor: Rob Hopkins;
news: Clifford Birchall
Mold & Buckley Chronicle
01244 340151
www.cheshirenews.co.uk
Weekly (Fri). Owner: Trinity Mirror
Cheshire. Editor: Paul Cook
Morecambe Guardian
01524 32525
Weekly (Fri). Owner: Johnston Press.
Editor: Sue Riley; news: Louise
Bryning; features: Paul Collins; chief
sub: Bryan Carter
Morecambe Visitor
01524 833111
www.morecambetoday.co.uk
Weekly (Wed). Owner: Johnston Press.
Editor: Glen Cooper; news: Ingrid Kent
Nantwich Chronicle
01244 340151
www.cheshirenews.co.uk
Weekly (Fri). Owner: Trinity Mirror
Cheshire. Editor: Alan Jarvis
Nelson Leader
01282 612561
www.burnleytoday.co.uk
Weekly (Fri). Owner: Johnston Press.
Editor: Roy Prenton; news: Peter
Dewhurst
Neston News
0151 647 7111
Weekly (Wed). Owner: Trinity Mirror
Merseyside. Editor: Sue McCann; news:
Louise Powney

News & Star (Carlisle)
01228 612600
www.news-and-star.co.uk
Daily (Mon–Thu). Owner: Cumbrian
News Group. Editor: Keith Sutton;
news: Sue Crawford; features: Mary
Ingham; production: Andy Nixon
Newton & Golborne Guardian
01925 434000
www.thisischeshire.co.uk
Weekly (Thu). Owner: Newsquest.
Editor: Nicola Priest
Northwest Evening Mail (Barrow)
01229 821835
www.nwemail.co.uk
Daily. Owner: Cumbrian News Group.
Editor: Steve Brauner; news: Don
Townend; features: Bill Myers; chief
sub: Sarah Farrell
Northwich & District Guardian
01925 434000
www.thisischeshire.co.uk
Weekly (Wed). Owner: Newsquest.
Editor: Nicola Priest
Northwich Chronicle
01244 340151
www.cheshirenews.co.uk
Weekly (Fri). Owner: Trinity Mirror
Cheshire. Editor: Paul Brown
Northwich Herald & Post
01244 340151
www.cheshirenews.co.uk
Weekly (Fri). Owner: Trinity Mirror
Cheshire. Editor: Paul Brown
Northwich Mail
01606 42272
Weekly (Thu). Owner: Trinity Mirror
Cheshire. Editor: Paul Brown
Oldham Evening Chronicle
0161 633 2121
www.oldham-chronicle.co.uk
Daily. Editor: Jim Williams; news:
Mike Attenborough; chief sub: Steve
Sutcliffe
Ormskirk Advertiser
01695 572501
Weekly (Thu). Owner: Trinity Mirror
Merseyside. Editor: Rob Hopkins;
news: Clifford Birchall
Ormskirk Champion
01704 392392
www.championline.net
Weekly (Wed). Owner: Champion
Media Group. Editor: Malcolm Hindle
Padiham Express
01282 426161
www.burnleytoday.co.uk
Weekly (Tue, Fri). Owner: Johnston
Press. Editor: Chris Daggett; news:
Margaret Parsons
Pendle & Burnley Reporter
01282 612561
Weekly free (Fri). Owner: Johnston
Press. Editor: Roy Prenton; news: Peter
Dewhurst
Pendle Express
01282 612561
www.burnleytoday.co.uk
Weekly (Tue, Fri). Owner: Johnston
Press. Editor: Roy Prenton; news: Peter
Dewhurst

Poynton Times
01625 424445
www.manchesteronline.co.uk
Weekly (Wed). Owner: Guardian
Media Group. Editor: Mike Quilley;
news: Pat Hills
Preston & Leyland Reporter
01772 838103
Weekly free (Thu). Owner: Johnston
Press. Editor: Simon Reynolds
Preston & Leyland Citizen
01772 824631
www.thisislancashire.co.uk
Weekly (Thu). Owner: Newsquest.
Editor: Gill Ellis; news: Jane Willis
Prestwich & Whitefield Guide
0161 764 9421
www.thisisbury.co.uk
Weekly (Fri). Owner: Newsquest.
Editor: Bill Allen; news: Steve Orrell;
chief sub: John Ellavy
Prestwich Advertiser
0161 789 5015
www.prestwichadvertiser.co.uk
Weekly (Fri). Owner: Guardian Media
Group. Editor: Vince Hale
Radcliffe Times
0161 764 9421
www.thisisbury.co.uk
Weekly (Thu). Owner: Newsquest.
Editor: Bill Allen; news: Steve Orrell;
chief sub: John Ellavy
Rochdale Express
01706 354321
www.manchesteronline.co.uk/news
          papers/rochdaleexpress.html
Weekly free (Fri). Owner: Guardian
Media Group. Editor: Claire Mooney
Rochdale Observer
01706 354321
www.rochdaleobserver.co.uk
Weekly (Wed, Sat). Owner: Guardian
Media Group. Editor: Claire Mooney
Rossendale Free Press
01706 213311
www.therossendalefreepress.co.uk
Weekly (Thu). Owner: Guardian Media
Group. Editor: Adrian Purslow
Runcorn and Widnes Herald & Post
0151 424 5921
Weekly (Fri). Owner: Trinity Mirror
Cheshire. Editor: Ian Douglas; news:
Simon Drury
Runcorn Weekly News
0151 424 5921
www.cheshireonline.icnetwork.co.uk
Weekly (Thu). Owner: Trinity Mirror
Cheshire. Editor: Ian Douglas; news:
Simon Drury
Runcorn World
0151 907 8525
www.runcornworld.co.uk
Weekly (Wed). Owner: Newsquest.
Editor: Jeremy Craddock; news:
Barbara Jordan
St Helens Star
01925 434000
www.thisisst-helens.co.uk
Weekly (Thu). Owner: Newsquest.
Editor: Nicola Priest

69

St Helens, Prescot & Knowsley Reporter
01744 22285
www.sthelenstoday.net
Weekly (Wed). Owner: Johnston Press. Editor: Julie McCormick

Sale & Altrincham Messenger
0161 908 3360
www.thisistrafford.co.uk/trafford/sale_altrincham
Weekly (Thu). Owner: Newsquest. Editor: Lynn Hughes

Salford Advertiser
0161 789 5015
www.salfordadvertiser.co.uk
Weekly (Fri). Owner: Guardian Media Group. Editor: Vince Hale

Skelmersdale Advertiser
01695 572501
www.icseftonandwestlancs.co.uk
Weekly (Thu). Owner: Trinity Mirror Merseyside. Editor: Rob Hopkins; news: Clifford Birchall

Skelmersdale Champion
01704 392392
www.championline.net
Weekly (Wed). Owner: Champion Media Group. Editor: Malcolm Hindle

South Cheshire Advertiser
01782 602525
Weekly free (Thu). Owner: Northcliffe Newspapers. Editor: Sean Dooley; news: Robert Cotterill; features: Charlotte Little-Jones

South Cheshire Guardian
01925 434000
www.thisischeshire.co.uk
Weekly (Wed). Owner: Newsquest. Editor: Nicola Priest

South Cheshire Mail
01270 256631
www.cheshirenews.co.uk
Weekly (Wed). Owner: Trinity Mirror Cheshire. Editor: Dave Fox; news: Jan Roberts

South Lakes Citizen
01539 720555
www.thisisthelakedistrict.co.uk
Weekly free (Wed). Owner: Newsquest. Editor: Mike Glover; news: Mike Addison; chief sub: Richard Belk

South Liverpool Merseymart
0151 734 4000
Weekly (Thu). Owner: Trinity Mirror Merseyside. News editor: Kevin Mathews

South Manchester Reporter
0161 446 2213
www.southmanchesterreporter.co.uk
Weekly (Thu). Owner: Guardian Media Group. Editor: Laurence Matheson; news: Andy Cranshaw

South Wirral News
0151 355 5181
Weekly free. Owner: Trinity Mirror Cheshire. Editor: Phil Robinson

Southport Champion
01704 392392
www.championline.net
Weekly (Wed). Owner: Champion Media Group. Editor: Martin Hovden

Stockport Citizen
0161 491 5700
Fortnightly (Thu). Independent. Editor: Mike Shields

Stockport Express
0161 480 4491
www.stockportexpress.co.uk
Weekly (Wed). Owner: Guardian Media Group. Editor: Mandy Leigh; news: Duncan Ponter; features: Lisa Woodhouse

Stockport Times East
0161 475 4834
www.manchesteronline.co.uk/newspapers/stockporttimeseast.html
Weekly (Thu). Owner: Guardian Media Group. Editor: Mandy Leigh; news: Duncan Ponter; features: Lisa Woodhouse

Stockport Times West
0161 475 4834
www.manchesteronline.co.uk/newspapers/stockporttimeswest.html
Weekly (Thu). Owner: Guardian Media Group. Editor: Mandy Leigh; news: Duncan Ponter; features: Lisa Woodhouse

Stretford & Urmston Messenger
0161 908 3360
www.thisistrafford.co.uk/trafford/stretford_urmston
Weekly (Thu). Owner: Newsquest. Editor: Lynn Hughes

Tameside Advertiser
0161 339 7611
www.tamesideadvertiser.co.uk
Weekly free (Thu). Owner: Guardian Media Group. Editor: David Porter

Tameside Reporter
0161 304 7691
www.tamesidereporter.com
Weekly (Thu). Owner: Ashton Weekly Newspapers. Editor: Nigel Skinner

Thornton, Cleveleys & Poulton Citizen
01253 292005
www.thisislancashire.co.uk
Weekly (Thu). Owner: Newsquest. Editor: Greg Morgan; news: Steve Dunthorne; features: Nikki Masters

Village Visiter (Lancashire)
01695 572501
Weekly (Thu). Owner: Trinity Mirror Merseyside. Editor: Rob Hopkins; news: Clifford Birchall

Wallasey News
0151 647 7111
Weekly (Wed). Owner: Trinity Mirror Merseyside. Editor: Sue McCann; news: Louise Powney

Warrington Guardian
01925 434000
www.thisischeshire.co.uk
Weekly (Thu). Owner: Newsquest. Editor: Nicola Priest; news: Gareth Dunning

Warrington Guardian Midweek
01925 434000
www.thisischeshire.co.uk
Weekly free (Tue). Owner: Newsquest. Editor: Nicola Priest

Warrington Mercury
01925 434000
www.thisischeshire.co.uk
Weekly free (Fri). Owner: Newsquest. Editor: Nicola Priest

West Cumberland Times and Star
01900 607600
www.times-and-star.co.uk
Weekly (Fri). Owner: Cumbrian News Group. Editor: Stephen Johnson; deputy editor: Ian Brogden

West Cumbrian Gazette
01228 612600
www.cumbria-online.co.uk
Weekly free (Thu). Owner: Cumbrian News Group. Editor: Keith Sutton; news: Sue Crawford; features: Mary Ingham; production: Andy Nixon

West Derby & Tuebrook Star
0151 236 2000
Weekly (Thu). Owner: Trinity Mirror Merseyside. News editor: Kevin Mathews

Westmorland Gazette
01539 720555
www.thisisthelakedistrict.co.uk
Weekly (Fri). Owner: Newsquest. Editor: Mike Glover; news: Mike Addison; chief sub: Richard Belk

Westmorland Messenger
01539 720555
www.thisisthelakedistrict.co.uk
Weekly (Wed). Owner: Newsquest. Editor: Mike Glover; news: Mike Addison; chief sub: Richard Belk

Whitchurch Herald
01948 662332
Weekly (Thu). Owner: Trinity Mirror Cheshire. Editor: Andrew Bowan

Whitehaven News
01946 595100
www.whitehaven-news.co.uk
Weekly (Thu). Owner: Cumbrian News Group. Editor: Colin Edgar; deputy editor: Alan Cleaver; news: David Siddall

Widnes Weekly News
0151 424 5921
www.iccheshire.co.uk
Weekly (Thu). Owner: Trinity Mirror Cheshire. Editor: Ian Douglas; news: Adrian Short

Widnes World
0151 907 8525
www.widnesworld.co.uk
Weekly (Wed). Owner: Newsquest. Editor: Jeremy Craddock; news: Barbara Jordan

Wigan Courier
01257 400026
www.wigancourier.co.uk
Monthly (last Fri). Independent. Editor: Mark Ashley

Wigan Evening Post
01772 838103
www.wigantoday.net
Daily. Owner: Johnston Press. Editor: Simon Reynolds; news: Gillian Gray

Wigan Observer
01772 838103
www.wigantoday.net
Weekly (Tue). Owner: Johnston Press. Editor: Gillian Gray

Wigan Reporter
01772 838103
www.wigantoday.net
Weekly (Thu). Owner: Johnston Press.
Editor: Gillian Gray
Wilmslow Citizen
0161 491 5700
Fortnightly (Thu). Independent.
Editor: Mike Shields
Wilmslow Express
01625 529333
www.thewilmslowexpress.co.uk
Weekly (Wed). Owner: Guardian
Media Group. Editor: Mike Quilley;
news: Betty Anderson
Winsford Chronicle
01244 340151
www.cheshirenews.co.uk
Weekly (Fri). Owner: Trinity Mirror
Cheshire. Editor: Richard Ault
Winsford Guardian
01925 434000
www.thisischeshire.co.uk
Weekly (Wed). Owner: Newsquest.
Editor: Nicola Priest
Wirral Chronicle
01244 340151
www.cheshirenews.co.uk
Weekly (Fri). Owner: Trinity Mirror
Cheshire. Editor: Richard Ault
Wirral Globe
0151 906 3000
www.thisiswirral.co.uk
Weekly (Wed). Owner: Newsquest.
Editor: Leigh Marles
Wirral Target
0151 906 3000
www.thisiswirral.co.uk
Fortnightly free (Wed). Owner:
Newsquest. Editor: Leigh Marles
Wythenshawe World
0161 998 4786
Fortnightly free (Fri). Editor: John
Oatway

Isle of Man

Isle of Man Courier
01624 695695
www.iomonline.co.im
Weekly (Thu). Owner: Johnston Press.
Editor: Lionel Cowin; news: Jo Overty;
chief sub: Dave Corbett
Isle of Man Examiner
01624 695695
www.iomonline.co.im
Weekly (Tue). Owner: Johnston Press.
Editor: Lionel Cowin; news: Jo Overty;
chief sub: Dave Corbett
The Manx Independent
01624 695695
www.iomonline.co.im
Weekly (Fri). Owner: Johnston Press.
Editor: Lionel Cowin; news: Jo Overty;
chief sub: Dave Corbett

Regional newspapers – Wales

Major regionals

Wales on Sunday
Thomson House, Havelock Street
Cardiff CF10 1XR
029 2058 3583
www.icwales.co.uk
Sunday. Owner: Western Mail & Echo
(Trinity Mirror). Editor: Tim Gordon;
news: Laura Kemp
Western Mail
Thomson House, Havelock Street
Cardiff CF10 1XR
029 2058 3583
www.icwales.co.uk
Daily. Owner: Western Mail & Echo
(Trinity Mirror). Editor: Alan
Edmunds; news: Paul Carey
South Wales Echo
Thomson House, Havelock Street
Cardiff CF10 1XR
029 2058 3583
www.icwales.co.uk
Daily. Owner: Western Mail & Echo
(Trinity Mirror). Editor: Richard
Williams; news: Cathy Owen
South Wales Evening Post
PO Box 14, Adelaide Street
Swansea SA1 1QT
01792 510000
www.swep.co.uk
Daily. Owner: Northcliffe Newspapers.
Editor: Spencer Feeney; news: Peter
Slee; features: Catherine Ings; chief sub:
Lynne Fernquest

North Wales

Abergele Visitor
01492 584321
www.icnorthwales.co.uk
Weekly (Thu). Owner: Trinity Mirror
North Wales. Editor: Alan Davies;
news: Steve Stratford
Bangor Chronicle
01248 387400
www.northwaleschronicle.co.uk
Weekly (Thu). Owner: North Wales
Newspapers. Editor: Emlyn Roberts;
news: Claire Hart; features: Tony Coates
Bangor/Anglesey Mail
01286 671111
www.icnorthwales.co.uk
Weekly (Wed). Owner: Trinity Mirror
North Wales. Editor: Jeff Eames; news:
Linda Roberts; production: Mark Jones
Buy Sell (Flintshire Edition)
01978 290400
Weekly (Wed). Owner: Trinity Mirror
Cheshire. No editorial

Caernarfon & Denbigh Herald
01286 671111
www.icnorthwales.co.uk
Weekly (Thu). Owner: Trinity Mirror
North Wales. Editor: Jeff Eames; news:
Linda Roberts; production: Mark Jones
Y Cymro
01970 615000
www.y-cymro.co.uk
Weekly (Mon). Owner: Tindle
Newspapers. Editor: Ioan Hughes
Daily Post
01492 574455
www.icnorthwales.co.uk
Daily. Owner: Trinity Mirror North
Wales. Editor: Rob Irvine
Denbighshire Free Press
01745 813535
www.denbighshirefreepress.co.uk
Weekly (Thu). Owner: North Wales
Newspapers. Editor: Alistair Syme
Flintshire Chronicle
01244 821911
www.icnorthwales.co.uk
Weekly (Fri). Owner: North Wales
Newspapers. Editor: Paul Cook; news:
Kevin Hughes
Flintshire Leader
01244 304500
www.chesterstandard.co.uk
Weekly (Thu). Owner: North Wales
Newspapers. Editor: Barrie Jones
Flintshire Leader & Standard
01352 707707
www.flintshirestandard.co.uk
Weekly (Thu). Editor: Barrie Jones;
features: Joanne Shone; chief sub:
Joanne Shone; production: Karen Perry
Gwynedd Chronicle
01248 387400
www.chroniclenow.co.uk
Weekly (Thu). Owner: North Wales
Newspapers. Editor: Emlyn Roberts;
news: Claire Hart; features: Tony Coates
Yr Herald
01286 671111
www.icnorthwales.co.uk
Weekly (Sat). Owner: Trinity Mirror
North Wales. Editor: Jeff Eames; news:
Linda Roberts; production: Mark Jones
Holyhead & Anglesey Mail
01286 671111
www.icnorthwales.co.uk
Weekly (Wed). Owner: Trinity Mirror
North Wales. Editor: Jeff Eames; news:
Linda Roberts; production: Mark Jones
North Wales Chronicle
01248 387400
www.chroniclenow.co.uk
Weekly (Thu). Owner: North Wales
Newspapers. Editor: Emlyn Roberts;
news: Claire Hart; features: Tony Coates
North Wales Pioneer
01492 531188
www.northwalespioneer.co.uk
Weekly (Thu). Owner: North Wales
Newspapers. Editor: Steve Rogers

North Wales Weekly News
01492 584321
www.icnorthwales.co.uk
*Weekly (Thu). Owner: Trinity Mirror
North Wales. Editor: Alan Davies;
news: Steve Stratford*

Rhyl, Prestatyn & Abergele Journal
01745 357500
www.rhyljournal.co.uk
*Weekly (Thu). Owner: North Wales
Newspapers. Editor: Steve Rogers;
deputy editor: Catherine Murphy*

Rhyl & Prestatyn Visitor
01745 334144
www.icnorthwales.co.uk
*Weekly free (Wed). Owner: Trinity
Mirror North Wales. Editor: Alan
Davies; news: Dave Jones*

Vale Advertiser
01492 584321
icnorthwales.icnetwork.co.uk
/news/valeadvertiser
*Weekly (Fri). Owner: Trinity Mirror
North Wales. Editor: Alan Davies;
news: Steve Stratford*

Wrexham Evening Leader
01978 355151
www.eveningleader.co.uk
*Daily. Owner: North Wales Newspapers.
Editor: Barrie Jones*

Wrexham Leader
01978 355151
www.bigleader.co.uk
*Weekly free (Fri). Owner: North Wales
Newspapers. Editor: Barrie Jones*

Wrexham Mail
01978 351515
www.icnorthwales.co.uk
*Weekly (Thu). Owner: Trinity Mirror
Cheshire. Editor: Paul Cook; news:
Kevin Hughes*

Ynys Mon Chronicle
01248 387400
www.chroniclenow.co.uk
*Weekly (Thu). Owner: North Wales
Newspapers. Editor: Emlyn Roberts;
news: Claire Hart; features: Tony Coates*

South Wales

Abergavenny Chronicle
01873 852187
www.abergavenny.co.uk
*Weekly (Thu). Owner: Tindle
Newspapers. Editor: Liz Davies*

Abergavenny Free Press
01873 857497
www.thisismonmouthshire.co.uk
*Weekly (Wed). Owner: Newsquest.
Editor: Andy Downie; news: Lesley Flynn*

Barry & District News
01446 704981
www.thisisbarry.co.uk
*Weekly (Thu). Owner: North Wales
Newspapers. Editor: Shira Valek*

Barry Gem
01446 774484
www.barry-today.co.uk
*Weekly (Thu). Owner: Tindle
Newspapers. Editor: Don John*

Brecon & Radnor Express
01874 610111
www.brecon-radnor.co.uk
*Weekly (Wed). Owner: Tindle
Newspapers. Editor: Dave Meechan*

Bridgend & District Recorder
01446 774484
*Weekly (Tue). Owner: Tindle
Newspapers. Editor: Don John*

Cambrian News
01970 615000
www.aberystwyth-today.co.uk
*Weekly (Wed). Owner: Tindle
Newspapers. Editor: Beverly Davies;
news: Simon Middlehurst*

Campaign Blackwood
01633 777212
www.thisisgwent.co.uk
*Weekly (Fri). Owner: North Wales
Newspapers. Editor: Andy Downie;
chief sub: Gina Robertson*

Campaign Caerphilly
01633 777212
www.thisisgwent.co.uk
*Weekly (Fri). Owner: North Wales
Newspapers. Editor: Andy Downie;
chief sub: Gina Robertson*

Campaign North Gwent
01633 777212
www.thisisgwent.co.uk
*Weekly (Fri). Owner: North Wales
Newspapers. Editor: Andy Downie;
chief sub: Gina Robertson*

Campaign Pontypridd
01633 777212
www.thisisgwent.co.uk
*Weekly (Fri). Owner: North Wales
Newspapers. Editor: Andy Downie;
chief sub: Gina Robertson*

Cardiff Advertiser & Property Times
029 2030 3900
www.thecardiffandsouthwales
advertiser.co.uk
*Weekly (Fri). Independent. Editor:
David Hynes*

Cardigan & Tivyside Advertiser
01239 614343
www.thisistivyside.net
*Weekly (Wed). Owner: Newsquest.
Editor: Areurin Evans; news: Sue Lewis*

Carmarthen Herald
01267 227222
www.carmarthenjournal.co.uk
*Weekly free (Fri). Owner: Northcliffe
Newspapers. Editor: David Hardy;
news: Diane Williams*

Carmarthen Journal
01267 227222
www.carmarthenjournal.co.uk
*Weekly (Wed). Owner: Northcliffe
Newspapers. Editor: David Hardy;
news: Diane Williams*

Chepstow Free Press
01291 621882
www.thisismonmouthshire.co.uk
*Weekly (Wed). Owner: Newsquest.
Editor: Andy Downie; news: Jacqui
Carole*

County Echo (Newport)
01348 874445
www.newport-today.co.uk
*Weekly (Fri). Owner: Tindle
Newspapers. Editor: Bev Davies*

County Times & Gazette (Brecon)
01938 553354
www.countytimes.co.uk
*Weekly (Thu). Owner: North Wales
Newspapers. Editor: Martin Wright*

Courier (Neath)
01792 510000
*Weekly (Tue). Owner: Northcliffe
Newspapers. Editor: Paul Turner*

Cowbridge Gem
01446 774484
www.cowbridge-today.co.uk
*Weekly (Thu). Owner: Tindle
Newspapers. Editor: Don John*

Cynon Valley Leader
01685 873136
www.icwales.co.uk
*Weekly (Wed). Owner: Western Mail
& Echo (Trinity Mirror).
Editor: Gary Marsh*

Glamorgan Gazette
01656 304924
www.icwales.co.uk
*Weekly (Thu). Owner: Western Mail
& Echo (Trinity Mirror).
Editor: Deborah Rees*

Gwent Gazette
01495 304589
www.icwales.co.uk
*Weekly (Tue). Owner: Western Mail
& Echo (Trinity Mirror).
Editor: Sarah Harris*

Heart of Wales Chronicle
01874 610111
*Weekly (Mon). Owner: Tindle
Newspapers. Editor: Dave Meechan*

Llanelli Star
01554 745300
www.thisissouthwales.co.uk
*Weekly (Wed, Thu). Owner: Northcliffe
Newspapers. Editor: Andy Pearson;
news: Laura Grime*

Llantwit Major Gem
01446 774484
www.llantwit-major-today.co.uk
*Weekly (Thu). Owner: Tindle
Newspapers. Editor: Don John*

Merthyr Express
01685 856500
*Weekly (Fri). Owner: Western Mail
& Echo (Trinity Mirror).
Editor: Gordon Caldicott*

Mid Wales Journal
01597 828060
www.midwalesjournal.co.uk
*Weekly (Fri). Owner: Midland News
Association. Editor: Mike Robinson;
news: Karen Evans*

Milford & West Wales Mercury
01646 698971
www.thisismilfordhaven.co.uk
*Weekly (Thu). Owner: Newsquest.
News editor: Richard Harris*

Monmouth Free Press
01600 713631
www.thisismonmouthshire.co.uk
*Weekly (Wed). Owner: Newsquest.
Editor: Andy Downie; news: Sarah Wood*

Monmouthshire Beacon
01600 712142
www.monmouth-today.co.uk
*Weekly (Thu). Owner: Tindle
Newspapers. Editor: Robert Williams*

Narbeth & Whitland Observer
01834 843262
Weekly (Fri). Owner: Tindle Newspapers. Editor: Neil Dickinson

Neath & Port Talbot Guardian
01639 778885
Weekly (Thu). Owner: Western Mail & Echo (Trinity Mirror). Editor: Rhodri Evans

Neath & Port Talbot Tribune
01792 510000
Monthly (2nd Fri). Owner: Northcliffe Newspapers. Editor: Paul Turner

Penarth Times
029 2070 7234
www.thisispenarth.co.uk
Weekly (Thu). Owner: North Wales Newspapers. News editor: Shira Valek

Pontypool Free Press
01495 751133
www.thisismonmouthshire.co.uk
Weekly (Wed). Owner: Newsquest. Editor: Andy Downie; news: Adrian Osmond

Pontypridd Observer
01443 665161
www.icwales.com
Weekly (Wed). Owner: Western Mail & Echo (Trinity Mirror). Editor: Dean Powell

Rhondda Leader
01443 665151
Weekly (Thu). Owner: Western Mail & Echo (Trinity Mirror). Editor: Kayrin Davies; news: Dave Edwards

South Wales Argus
01633 810000
www.thisisgwent.co.uk
Daily. Owner: Newsquest. Editor: Gerry Keightley; news: Mark Templeton; chief sub: Caroline Woolard

South Wales Guardian
01269 592781
www.thisisammanford.co.uk
Weekly (Wed). Owner: Newsquest. Editor: Elizabeth Cartwright; news: Emma Evans; features: Richard Sharpe

Swansea Herald
01792 514630
Weekly (Thu). Owner: Northcliffe Newspapers. Editor: David Robbins

Tenby Observer
01834 843262
www.tenby-today.co.uk
Weekly (Fri). Owner: Tindle Newspapers. Editor: Neil Dickinson

Tenby Times
01834 843262
Monthly free (1st Wed). Owner: Tindle Newspapers. Editor: Neil Dickinson

Weekly Argus
01633 810000
www.thisisgwent.co.uk
Weekly (Thu). Owner: Newsquest. Editor: Gerry Keightley; news: Mark Templeton; chief sub: Caroline Woolard

Western Telegraph
01437 763133
www.thisispembrokeshire.net
Weekly (Wed). Owner: Newsquest. Editor: Fiona Philips

Regional newspapers – Scotland

Main regionals

Aberdeen Press and Journal
Aberdeen Journals, Lang Stracht
Mastrick, Aberdeen AB15 6DF
01224 690222
www.thisisnorthscotland.co.uk
Daily. Owner: Northcliffe Newspapers. Editor: Derek Tucker; news: Fiona McWhirr; features: Richard Neville; chief sub: Jim Urquart

Courier and Advertiser
80 Kingsway East, Dundee DD4 8SL
01382 223131
www.thecourier.co.uk
Daily. Owner: DC Thomson. Editor: Bill Hutcheon; news: Arliss Rhind; features: Catriona Macinnes; production: Brian Clarkson

Daily Record
One Central Quay, Glasgow G3 8DA
0141 309 3000
www.dailyrecord.co.uk
Daily. Owner: Mirror Group. Editor: Bruce Waddell; news: Tom Hamilton; features: Melanie Harvey

Edinburgh Evening News
Barclay House, 108 Holyrood Road
Edinburgh EH8 8AS
0131 620 8620
www.edinburghnews.com
Daily. Owner: Scotsman Publications. Editor: John McLellan; news: Euan McGrory; features: Gina Davidson; chief sub: Howard Dorman; production: Mark Eadie

Glasgow Evening Times
200 Renfield St, Glasgow G2 3QB
0141 302 7000
www.eveningtimes.co.uk
Daily. Owner: Newsquest. Editor: Charles McGhee; news: Hugh Boag; features: Garry Scott; chief sub: Andy Clark

Glasgow Herald
200 Renfield St, Glasgow G2 3QB
0141 302 7000
www.theherald.co.uk
Daily. Owner: Newsquest. Editor: Mark Douglas-Home; news: Magnus Llewellin; features: Mark Smith; chief sub: Chris Macrae

Scotland On Sunday
Barclay House, 108 Holyrood Road
Edinburgh EH8 8AS
0131 620 8620
www.scotlandonsunday.com
Sunday. Owner: Scotsman Publications. Editor: Ian Martin; news: Peter Laing; features: Claire Hay; chief sub: Martin Allen; production: Chris Dry

The Scotsman
Barclay House, 108 Holyrood Road
Edinburgh EH8 8AS
0131 620 8620
www.scotsman.com
Daily. Owner: Scotsman Publications. Editor: John McGurk; news: James Hall; assistant features editor: Gaby Soutar; production editors: John Ellingham and Alistair Norman (subs), Alastair Clark (opinion)

Scottish Daily Mirror
1 Central Quay, Glasgow G3 8DA
0141 221 2121
www.mirror.co.uk
Daily. Owner: Trinity Mirror. News: Shaun Milne

Sunday Herald
200 Renfield St, Glasgow G2 3QB
0141 302 7800
www.sundayherald.com
Sunday. Owner: Newsquest. Editor: Richard Walker; news: Charlene Sweeney; features: Susan Flockhart; production: Roxanne Sorooshian

Sunday Mail
One Central Quay, Glasgow G3 8DA
0141 309 3000
www.sundaymail.co.uk
Sunday. Owner: Mirror Group. Editor: Allan Rennie; news: Brendan McGinty; features: Susie Cormack; chief sub: George Welsh

Sunday Post
DC Thomson & Co, 2 Albert Square
Dundee DD1 9QJ
01382 223131
www.thesundaypost.co.uk
Sunday. Owner: DC Thomson. Editor: David Pollington; news: Tom McKay; features: Bruce Allan; chief sub: Alastair Bennett

Other Scottish newspapers

Aberdeen & District Independent
01224 618300
www.aberdeen-indy.co.uk
Weekly (Thu). Independent. Editor: Derek Piper; news: Donna Morrison

Aberdeen Citizen
01224 690222
Weekly (Wed). Owner: Northcliffe Newspapers. Editor: Donald Martin

Aberdeen Evening Express
01224 690222
www.eveningexpress.co.uk
Daily. Owner: Northcliffe Newspapers. Editor: Donald Martin; deputy: Richard Prest; news: Lee Mackay; chief sub: James Donaldson

The Advertiser (Midlothian)
0131 561 6600
Weekly (Wed). Owner: Johnston Press. Editor: Roy Scott; news: Alex Hogg

Airdrie & Coatbridge Advertiser
01236 748648
www.icscotland.co.uk
Weekly (Wed). Owner: Scottish & Universal Newspapers (Trinity Mirror). Editor: John Murdoch

Alloa & Hillfoots Advertiser
01259 214416
Weekly (Thu). Owner: Dunfermline Press Group. Editor: Kevin McRoberts; news: Lindsey Reid

Annandale Herald
01461 202078
Weekly (Thu). Owner: Dumfriesshire Newspapers. Editor: Bryan Armstrong; news: Alan Hall

Annandale Observer
01461 202078
Weekly (Fri). Owner: Dumfriesshire Newspapers. Editor: Bryan Armstrong; news: Alan Hall

Arbroath Herald
01241 872274
Weekly (Fri). Owner: Johnston Press. Editor: Craig Nisbet; news: Brian Forsythe

Ardrossan & Saltcoats Herald
01294 464321
www.threetowners.com /herald/herald_files.htm
Weekly (Fri). Owner: Scottish & Universal Newspapers (Trinity Mirror). Editor: Alex Clarke; news: Craig Nisbet

Argyllshire Advertiser
01631 563058
www.argyllshireadvertiser.co.uk
Weekly (Fri). Owner: Oban Times. Editor: Stewart Mackenzie; news: Joanne Simms

Arran Banner
01631 568000
www.obantimes.co.uk
Weekly (Sat). Owner: Oban Times. Editor: Stewart Mackenzie

Ayr Advertiser
01292 267631
Weekly (Wed). Owner: Ayrshire Weekly Press. Editor: Alex Clarke; news: Caroline Paterson

Ayrshire Extra
01292 611666
Weekly (Thu). Owner: Archant. Editor: John Matthews

Ayrshire Post
01292 261111
www.icscotland.co.uk
Weekly (Wed). Owner: Scottish & Universal Newspapers (Trinity Mirror). Editor: Alan Woodison; deputy editor: Cheryl McEvoy; features: Yonnie McInnes

Ayrshire Weekly Press
01294 464321
Weekly (Fri). Owner: Scottish & Universal Newspapers (Trinity Mirror). Editor: Alex Clarke; news: Craig Nisbet

Ayrshire World
01294 272233
www.icscotland.co.uk
Weekly free (Wed). Owner: Scottish & Universal Newspapers (Trinity Mirror). Editor: Alan Woodison; news: Lex Brown; chief sub: Murray Stevenson

Banffshire Herald
01542 886262
www.bannfshireherald.com
Weekly (Fri). Owner: J&M Publishing. Editor: Morven Macneil

Barrhead News
0141 887 7055
Weekly (Wed). Owner: Clyde & Forth Press. Editor: Tom McConigley

Bearsden, Milngavie & Glasgow Extra
0141 427 7878
www.icscotland.co.uk
Weekly (Thu). Owner: Archant. Editor: Allan Hodge; news: Colin Macdonald; chief sub: Jim Cameron

Bellshill Speaker
01698 264611
Weekly (Thu). Owner: Johnston Press. Editor: Archie Fleming

Berwick Gazette
01289 306677
www.berwicktoday.co.uk
Weekly (Thu). Owner: Johnston Press. Editor: David Johnstone; news: Sandy Brydon; features: Janice Gillie; chief sub: Diane Smith

Berwickshire News
01289 306677
www.berwickshiretoday.co.uk
Weekly (Fri). Owner: Johnston Press. Editor: David Johnstone; news: Sandy Brydon; features: Janice Gillie; chief sub: Diane Smith

Blairgowrie Advertiser
01250 872854
www.icscotland.co.uk
Weekly (Thu). Owner: Scottish & Universal Newspapers (Trinity Mirror). Editor: Alison Lowson

Border Telegraph
01896 758395
www.bordertelegraph.com
Weekly (Tue). Owner: Border Weeklies. Editor: Atholl Innes

Brechin Advertiser
01356 622767
www.brechinadvertiser.com
Weekly (Thu). Owner: Angus County Press. Editor: Alan Ducat; news: Gregor Wilson; features: Jenny Hill

Buchan Observer
01779 472017
www.buchanie.co.uk
Weekly (Tue). Owner: Archant. Editor: Ken Duncan

The Buteman
01700 502503
www.icscotland.co.uk
Weekly (Fri). Owner: Angus County Press. Editor: Craig Borland

Caithness Courier
01955 602424
www.caithness-courier.co.uk
Weekly (Wed). Owner: North of Scotland Newspapers. Editor: Alan Henry; news: Karen Macdonald

Campbell Times Courier
01631 563058
Weekly (Sat). Owner: Oban Times. Editor: Stewart Mackenzie; news: Joanne Simms

Campbeltown Courier & Argyllshire Advertiser
01586 554646
www.campbeltowncourier.co.uk
Weekly (Fri). Owner: Oban Times. Editor: Ranald Watson

Carrick Gazette
01671 402503
Weekly (Thu). Owner: Angus County Press. Editor: Peter Jeal

Central Fife Times & Advertiser
01383 728201
Weekly (Wed). Owner: Dunfermline Press Group. Editor: Jim Stark; chief sub: Susan Dryburgh

Clydebank Post
0141 952 0565
Weekly (Thu). Owner: Clyde & Forth Press. Editor: James Walsh

Clyde Post
01475 726511
Weekly free (Wed). Owner: Clyde & Forth Press. Editor: Martin Biddle

Clyde Weekly News
01294 273421
www.icScotland.co.uk
Weekly (Wed). Owner: Scottish & Universal Newspapers (Trinity Mirror). Editor: Alex Clarke

Craigmillar Chronicle
0131 661 0791
www.craignet.org.uk/chronicle
Monthly free (1st of month). Editor: Sally Fraser

Cumbernauld News & Advertiser
01236 725578
www.falkirktoday.co.uk
Weekly free (Fri). Owner: Johnston Press. Editor: Alistair Blyth; chief sub: Neil Smith

Cumbernauld News & Kilsyth Chronicle
01236 725578
www.falkirktoday.co.uk
Weekly (Wed). Owner: Johnston Press. Editor: Alistair Blyth; chief sub: Neil Smith

Cumnock Chronicle
01290 421633
Weekly (Wed). Owner: Ayrshire Weekly Press. Editor: Douglas Skelton

Deeside Piper
01330 824955
www.deesidepiper.com
Weekly (Fri). Owner: Angus County Press. Editor: Phil Allan

Donside Piper & Herald
01330 824955
www.donsidepiper.com
Weekly (Fri). Owner: Angus County Press. Editor: Phil Allan

Dumbarton & Vale Of Leven Reporter
01436 673434
Weekly (Tue). Owner: Clyde & Forth Press. Editor: David Morrison; news: Steve MacIlroy

Dumfries & Galloway Standard
01387 240342
www.icscotland.co.uk
Weekly (Wed). Owner: Scottish & Universal Newspapers (Trinity Mirror). Editor: Elizabeth Martin; news: Ian Pollock

Dumfries and Galloway Today
01387 240342
www.icscotland.co.uk
Weekly (Wed). Owner: Scottish & Universal Newspapers (Trinity Mirror). Editor: Elizabeth Martin; news: Ian Pollock

Dumfries Courier
01461 202078
Weekly free (Fri). Owner:
Dumfriesshire Newspapers. Editor:
Bryan Armstrong; news: Alan Hall

Dunfermline Press & West of Fife Advertiser
01383 728201
www.snpa.org.uk
Weekly (Thu). Owner: Dunfermline
Press Group. Editor: Tom Davidson;
news: Simon Harris

Dunoon Observer & Argyllshire Standard
01369 703218
www.dunoon-observer.co.uk
Weekly (Fri). Owner: E&R Ingles.
Editor: Bill Jardin

East Fife Mail
01592 261451
www.fifenow.co.uk
Weekly free (Wed). Owner: Johnston
Press. Editor: Ian Muirhead

East Kilbride News
01355 265000
www.iclanarkshire.co.uk
Weekly (Wed). Owner: Scottish &
Universal Newspapers (Trinity
Mirror). Editor: Gordon Bury; news:
Lynda Nichol

East Kilbride World
01698 283200
Weekly free (Fri). Owner: Scottish &
Universal Newspapers (Trinity Mirror).
Editor: Joseph Kelly

East Lothian Courier
01620 822451
www.eastlothiancourier.com
Weekly (Fri). Owner: Dunfermline
Press Group. Editor: Elaine Reid

East Lothian Herald
01289 306677
www.berwickshire-news.co.uk
Weekly (Thu). Owner: Johnston Press.
Editor: David Johnstone; news: Sandy
Brydon; features: Janice Gillie; chief
sub: Diane Smith

East Lothian News
0131 561 6600
www.eastlothiantoday.co.uk
Weekly (Thu). Owner: Johnston Press.
Editor: Roy Scott; news: Alex Hogg

East Lothian Times
0131 561 6600
Weekly free (Fri). Owner: Johnston Press.
Editor: Roy Scott; news: Alex Hogg

Ellon Advertiser
01888 563589
Weekly (Fri). Owner: W Peters & Son.
Editor: Joyce Summers

Ellon Times & East Gordon Advertiser
01779 472017
Weekly (Thu). Owner: Archant. Acting
editor: Ken Duncan

Eskdale and Liddesdale Advertiser
01387 380012
Weekly (Thu). Owner: Cumbrian News
Group. Editor: Keith Sutton; news:
Rachael Norris

Evening Telegraph (Dundee)
01382 223131
Daily. Owner: DC Thomson. Editor:
Gordon Wishart; news: Elaine
Harrison; features: Phillip Smith

The Extra (Ayrshire)
01292 611666
www.theextra24.co.uk
Weekly (Thu). Owner: Archant.
Editor: John Matthews

Falkirk Herald
01324 624959
www.falkirktoday.co.uk
Weekly (Thu). Owner: Johnston Press.
Editor: Colin Hume; assistant editor:
Duncan McCallum; chief reporter:
Alan Muir

Falkirk, Grangemouth & Linlithgow Advertiser
01324 638314
Weekly (Wed). Owner: Johnston Press.
Editor: Colin Hume; assistant editor:
Duncan McCallum; chief reporter:
Alan Muir

Fife & Kinross Extra
01383 728201
Weekly free (Fri). Owner: Dunfermline
Press Group. Editor: Andrew Cowie

Fife Free Press
01592 261451
www.fifenow.co.uk
Weekly (Thu). Owner: Johnston
Press. Editor: Allen Crow

Fife Herald
01592 261451
www.fifenow.co.uk
Weekly free (Fri). Owner: Johnston
Press. Editor: Graham Scott

Fife Leader
01592 261451
www.fifenow.co.uk
Weekly free (Tue). Owner: Johnston
Press. Editor: Jack Snedden

Forfar Dispatch
01307 464899
www.forfardispatch.com
Weekly (Tue). Owner: Angus County
Press. Editor: Alan Ducat

Forres Gazette
01309 672615
www.forres-gazette.co.uk
Weekly (Wed). Scottish Provincial Press.
Editor: Ken Smith

Fraserburgh Herald
01779 472017
Weekly (Fri). Owner: Archant.
Editor: Alex Shand

Galloway Gazette
01671 402503
www.gallowaygazette.com
Weekly (Thu). Owner: Angus County
Press. Editor: Peter Jeal

Galloway News
01556 504141
www.icscotland.co.uk
Weekly (Thu). Owner: Scottish &
Universal Newspapers (Trinity
Mirror). Editor: Elizabeth Martin;
chief sub: Chris McIntyre

The Gazette (Paisley)
0141 887 7055
Weekly (Wed). Owner: Clyde & Forth
Press. Editor: Tom McConigley

Glasgow East News
0141 573 5060
Weekly free (Fri). Owner: Johnston
Press. Editor: Christine McPherson;
chief sub: Jim Holland

Glasgow South & Eastwood Extra
0141 427 7878
www.icscotland.co.uk
Weekly (Thu). Owner: Archant.
Editor: Allan Hodge; news: Colin
Macdonald; chief sub: Jim Cameron

Glasgow West Extra
0141 427 7878
www.icscotland.co.uk
Weekly (Thu). Owner: Archant.
Editor: Allan Hodge; news: Colin
Macdonald; chief sub: Jim Cameron

The Glaswegian
0141 309 3132
Weekly free. Owner: Scottish Daily
Record & Sunday Mail (Trinity
Mirror). Editor: Garry Thomas

Glenrothes Gazette
01592 261451
www.fifenow.co.uk
Weekly free (Wed). Owner: Johnston
Press. Editor: Brian Stormont

Gorgie Dalry Gazette
0131 337 2457
Monthly (Fri). Independent.
Editor: Brian Montgomery

Greenock Telegraph
01475 726511
www.greenocktelegraph.co.uk
Weekly (Wed). Owner: Clyde & Forth
Press. Editor: Martin Biddle

Hamilton Advertiser
01698 283200
www.icScotland.co.uk
Weekly (Thu). Owner: Scottish &
Universal Newspapers (Trinity
Mirror). Editor: Joseph Kelly

Hamilton Extra People
01698 261321
Weekly (Fri). Owner: Archant.
Editor: Martin Clark

Hawick News
01750 21581
www.hawicktoday.co.uk
Weekly (Fri). Owner: Johnston Press.
Editor: Michael Mee

Helensburgh Advertiser
01436 673434
Weekly (Thu). Owner: Clyde & Forth
Press. Editor: David Morrison; news:
Steve MacIlroy

Herald & Post Edinburgh
0131 620 8620
Weekly free (Thu). Owner: Scotsman
Publications. Editor: Gail Milne

Highland News
01463 732222
www.highland-news.co.uk
Weekly (Thu). Owner: Scottish
Provincial Press. Editor: Helen Macrae

Huntly Express
01466 793622
Weekly (Fri). Owner: J&M Publishing.
Editor: Pat Scott

Ileach (Islay & Jura)
01496 810355
www.ileach.co.uk
Fortnightly (Sat). Independent.
Editor: Carl Reavey

Inverness & Nairnshire Herald
01463 732222
Weekly (Thu). Owner: Scottish
Provincial Press. Editor: Helen Macrae

Inverness Courier
01463 233059
www.inverness-courier.co.uk
Weekly (Tue, Fri). Owner: Scottish Provincial Press. Editor: Jim Love

Inverurie Advertiser
01888 563589
Weekly (Fri). Owner: W Peters & Son. Editor: Joyce Summers

Inverurie Herald
01467 625150
www.inverurieherald.com
Weekly (Thu). Owner: Angus County Press. Editor: David Duncan

Irvine & North Ayrshire Extra
01292 611666
www.theextra24.co.uk
Weekly (Thu). Owner: Archant. Editor: John Matthews

Irvine Herald
01294 222288
www.icscotland.co.uk
Weekly (Wed). Owner: Scottish & Universal Newspapers (Trinity Mirror). Editor: Alan Woodison; news: Lex Brown; chief sub: Murray Stevenson

Irvine Times
01294 273421
Weekly (Wed). Owner: Scottish & Universal Newspapers (Trinity Mirror). Editor: Alex Clarke

John O'Groat Journal
01955 602424
www.johnogroat-journal.co.uk
Weekly (Fri). Owner: North of Scotland Newspapers. Editor: Alan Henry; news: Karen Macdonald

Kilmarnock & District Extra
01292 611666
www.theextra24.co.uk
Weekly (Thu). Owner: Archant. Editor: John Matthews

Kilmarnock Standard
01563 525115
www.icscotland.co.uk
Weekly (Wed). Owner: Scottish & Universal Newspapers (Trinity Mirror). Editor: Alan Woodison; news: Lex Brown

Kincardineshire Observer
01561 377283
Weekly (Fri). Owner: Angus County Press. Editor: Charles Wallace

Kirkintilloch Herald
0141 775 0040
www.kirkintillochtoday.co.uk
Weekly (Wed). Owner: Johnston Press. Editor: Christine McPherson; chief sub: Jim Holland

Kirriemuir Herald
01307 464899
www.kirriemuirherald.com
Weekly (Wed). Owner: Angus County Press. Editor: Alan Ducat

Lanark Gazette
01555 663937
Weekly (Thu). Owner: Johnston Press. Editor: Aileen McCulloch

Lanarkshire Extra
01698 261321
www.icscotland.co.uk
Weekly (Thu). Owner: Archant. Editor: Martin Clark

Lanarkshire World
01698 283200
www.icscotland.co.uk
Weekly (Wed). Owner: Scottish & Universal Newspapers (Trinity Mirror). Editor: Joseph Kelly

Largs & Millport Weekly News
01475 689009
Weekly (Wed). Owner: Clyde & Forth Press. Editor: Andrew Cochrane

Lennox Herald
01389 742299
www.icscotland.co.uk
Weekly (Wed). Owner: Scottish & Universal Newspapers (Trinity Mirror). Editor: Alan Woodison

Linlithgowshire Journal & Gazette
01506 844592
www.icscotland.co.uk
Weekly (Fri). Owner: Johnston Press. Editor: Jack Shennan; features: Julie Currie

Lochaber News
01463 732222
www.lochaber-news.co.uk
Weekly (Thu). Owner: Scottish Provincial Press. Editor: Helen Macrae

Lothian Times East
0131 561 6600
Weekly free (Fri). Owner: Johnston Press. Editor: Roy Scott; news: Alex Hogg

Mearns Leader
01569 762139
www.mearnsleader.com
Weekly (Thu). Owner: Angus County Press. Editor: John McIntosh

Metro Scotland
020 7651 5200
www.metroscot.co.uk
Daily. Owner: Associated Newspapers. Editor: Kenny Campbell; news: Mark Dorman; features: Kieran Meeke

Mid Lothian Times
0131 561 6600
Weekly free (Fri). Owner: Johnston Press. Editor: Roy Scott; news: Alex Hogg

Midlothian Advertiser
0131 561 6600
Weekly (Wed). Owner: Johnston Press. Editor: Roy Scott; news: Alex Hogg

Milngavie & Bearsden Herald
0141 956 3533
Weekly (Fri). Owner: Johnston Press. Editor: Robert Wilson; news: Rena O'Neill

Moffat News
01461 202078
Weekly (Thu). Owner: Dumfriesshire Newspapers. Editor: Bryan Armstrong; news: Alan Hall

Montrose Review
01674 672605
www.montrosereview.net
Weekly (Thu). Owner: Angus County Press. Editor: Douglas Hill

Motherwell Extra
01698 261321
Weekly (Fri). Owner: Archant. Editor: Martin Clark

Motherwell Times
01698 264611
Weekly (Thu). Owner: Johnston Press. Editor: Archie Fleming

Musselburgh News
0131 561 6600
Weekly (Thu). Owner: Johnston Press. Editor: Roy Scott; news: Alex Hogg

North Ayrshire World
01294 272233
www.icScotland.co.uk
Weekly (Wed). Owner: Scottish & Universal Newspapers (Trinity Mirror). Editor: Alan Woodison; news: Lex Brown; chief sub: Norman Reid

North East Gazette
01224 618300
www.aberdeen-indy.co.uk
Weekly (Fri). Editor: Derek Piper; news: Donna Morrison

North Edinburgh News
0131 467 3972
www.northedinburghnews.co.uk
Monthly free (2nd Wed). Editor: Mary Burnside

North Star
01463 732222
www.highland-news.co.uk
Weekly (Thu). Owner: Scottish Provincial Press. Editor: Helen Macrae

North West Highlands Bratach
01641 521227
www.bratach.co.uk
Monthly (1st Thu). Editor: Donald McCloud

Northern Scot
01343 548777
www.northern-scot.co.uk
Weekly (Fri). Owner: Scottish Provincial Press. Editor: Pauline Taylor

Northern Times
01408 633993
www.northern-times.co.uk
Weekly (Thu). Owner: Scottish Provincial Press. Editor: Duncan Ross

Oban Times
01631 563058
www.obantimes.co.uk
Weekly (Thu). Owner: Oban Times. Editor: Stewart Mackenzie; news: Joanne Simms

The Orcadian
01856 879000
www.orcadian.co.uk
Weekly (Thu). Editor: Stuart Laundy

Paisley & District People
0141 887 7055
Weekly free (Fri). Owner: Clyde & Forth Press. Editor: Tom McConigley

Paisley & Renfrewshire Extra
0141 427 7878
www.icscotland.co.uk
Weekly (Thu). Owner: Archant. Editor: Allan Hodge; news: Colin Macdonald; chief sub: Jim Cameron

Paisley Daily Express
0141 887 7911
www.icscotland.co.uk
Daily. Owner: Scottish & Universal Newspapers (Trinity Mirror). Editor: Jonathan Russell; news: Anne Dalrymple; chief sub: Wendy Slavin

Peebles Times
0131 561 6600
Weekly free (Fri). Owner: Johnston Press. Editor: Roy Scott; news: Alex Hogg

Peeblesshire News
01896 758395
www.peeblesshirenews.com
*Weekly (Fri). Owner: Border Weeklies.
Editor: Atholl Innes*

Perth Shopper
01738 626211
*Weekly free. Owner: Scottish &
Universal Newspapers (Trinity
Mirror). Editor: Alison Lowson*

Perthshire Advertiser
01738 626211
www.icperthshire.co.uk
*Weekly (Tue, Fri). Owner: Scottish &
Universal Newspapers (Trinity
Mirror). Editor: Alison Lowson*

Ross-shire Herald
01463 732222
*Weekly (Thu). Owner: Scottish
Provincial Press. Editor: Helen Macrae*

Ross-shire Journal
01349 863436
www.rsjournal.co.uk
*Weekly (Fri). Owner: Scottish
Provincial Press. Editor: Caroline
Rham; features: Jacqui McKenzie*

Rutherglen Reformer
0141 647 2271
www.icscotland.co.uk
*Weekly (Thu). Owner: Scottish &
Universal Newspapers (Trinity
Mirror). Editor: Gordon Bury; deputy
editor: Louise Reilly*

St Andrews Citizen
01592 261451
www.fifenow.co.uk
*Weekly free (Fri). Owner: Johnston
Press. Editor: Mike Rankin*

Selkirk Advertiser
01750 21581
www.selkirktoday.co.uk
*Weekly (Fri). Owner: Johnston Press.
Editor: Susan Windram*

Shetland Life
01595 693622
www.shetlandtoday.co.uk
*Monthly (1st Fri). Editor: Andrew
Morrison*

Shetland News
01806 577332
www.shetland-news.co.uk
Daily, online. Editor: John Daly

Shetland Times
01595 693622
www.shetlandtoday.co.uk
Weekly. Editor: Viala Wishart

Southern Reporter
01750 21581
www.borderstoday.co.uk
*Weekly (Fri). Owner: Johnston Press.
Editor: Susan Windram*

Stirling News
01259 214416
*Weekly free (Wed). Owner: Dunfermline
Press Group. Editor: Andrew Cowie*

Stirling Observer
01786 451110
www.icstirlingshire.co.uk
*Twice-weekly free (Wed, Fri). Owner:
Scottish & Universal Newspapers
(Trinity Mirror). Editor: Alan Rennie;
deputy editor: Donald Morton*

Stirling/Alloa & Hillfoots Shopper
01786 451110
*Weekly free (Fri). Owner: Scottish &
Universal Newspapers (Trinity
Mirror). Editor: Alan Rennie; deputy
editor: Donald Morton*

**Stornoway Gazette & West Coast
Advertiser**
01851 702687
www.stornowaygazette.co.uk
Weekly (Thu). Editor: Melinda Gillen

Stranraer & Wigtownshire Free Press
01776 702551
www.stranraer.org/freepress
Weekly (Wed). Editor: John Neil

Strathearn Herald
01738 626211
www.icperthshire.co.uk
*Weekly (Fri). Owner: Scottish &
Universal Newspapers (Trinity
Mirror). Editor: Alison Lowson*

Strathkelvin Advertiser
0141 775 0040
*Weekly (Sat). Owner: Johnston Press.
Editor: Christine McPherson; chief sub:
Jim Holland*

Strathspey Herald
01479 872102
www.sbherald.co.uk
*Weekly (Wed). Owner: Scottish
Provincial Press. Editor: Gavin
Musgrove*

Turriff Advertiser
01888 563589
*Weekly (Fri). Owner: W Peters & Son.
Editor: Joyce Summers*

Wee County News
01259 724724
www.wee-county-news.co.uk
*Weekly (Thu). Editor: Joan McCann;
chief sub: Susan Carden; production:
Bryan Watson*

West Highland Free Press
01471 822464
www.whfp.co.uk
Weekly (Thu). Editor: Ian McCormack

West Lothian Courier
01506 633544
www.icscotland.co.uk
*Weekly (Thu). Owner: Scottish &
Universal Newspapers (Trinity
Mirror). Acting editor: Joe Kelly*

West Lothian Herald & Post
0131 620 8620
*Weekly free (Thu). Owner: Scotsman
Publications. Editor: Stuart Farquhar*

Wishaw Press
01698 373111
www.icscotland.co.uk
*Weekly (Wed). Owner: Scottish &
Universal Newspapers (Trinity
Mirror). Editor: John Murdoch*

Wishaw World
01698 283200
www.icscotland.co.uk
*Weekly (Fri). Owner: Scottish &
Universal Newspapers (Trinity
Mirror). Editor: Joseph Kelly*

Regional newspapers – Northern Ireland

Main regionals

Belfast Telegraph
124–144 Royal Avenue
Belfast BT1 1EB
028 9026 4000
www.belfasttelegraph.co.uk
*Daily. Owner: Independent News &
Media. Editor-in-chief: Edmund
Curran; news: Paul Connolly; features:
Gail Walker*

Sunday Life
124–144 Royal Avenue
Belfast BT1 1EB
028 9026 4000
www.sundaylife.co.uk
*Sunday. Owner: Independent News &
Media. Editor: Martin Lindsay; news:
Martin Hill; features: Audrey Watson*

Daily Ireland
028 9061 2345
www.dailyireland.com
*Daily. Owner: Andersonstown News
Group. Editor: Maria McCourt; deputy
editor: Colin O'Carroll*

The Daily Mirror (NI)
028 9056 8000
www.mirror.co.uk
*Daily. Owner: Mirror Group.
Editor: Jerry Miller; news: Morris
Fitzmaurice; features: Jilly Beattie*

Irish News
028 9032 2226
www.irishnews.com
*Daily. Owner: Morton Group.
Editor: Noel Doran; news: Steven
O'Reilly; features: Joanna Braniff*

News Letter
028 9068 0000
www.newsletter.co.uk
*Daily. Owner: Century Newspapers.
Editor: Austin Hunter; news: Rick
Clarke; features: Jeff Hill*

The People (Northern Ireland edition)
028 9056 8000
www.people.co.uk
*Sunday. Owner: Mirror Group. Editor:
Stephen McQuire; news: Liz Trainor*

Sunday Mirror
028 9056 8000
www.sundaymirror.co.uk
*Sunday. Owner: Mirror Group. Editor:
Christian McCashin; assistant editor:
Donna Carton*

Other newspapers

Andersonstown News
028 9061 9000
www.irelandclick.com
Weekly (Mon, Thu). Owner: Andersonstown News Group. Editor: Robin Livingstone

Antrim Guardian
028 9446 2624
www.ulster-ni.co.uk
Weekly (Wed). Owner: Alpha Group. Editor: Liam Hesfron

Antrim Times
028 3839 3939
www.mortonnewspapers.com
Weekly (Wed). Owner: Morton News Group. Editor: David Armstrong; assistant editor: Desmond Blackadder

Armagh Observer
028 8772 2557
Weekly (Wed). Independent. Editor: Desmond Mallon; news: Desmond Mallon Junior

Armagh-Down Observer
028 8772 2557
Weekly (Thu). Independent. Editor: Desmond Mallon; news: Desmond Mallon Junior

Ballycastle Chronicle
028 7034 3344
www.ulsternet-ni.co.uk/chronicle
/pages/ballycastle.htm
Weekly (Wed). Owner: Northern News Group. Editor: John Fillis

Ballyclare Advertiser
028 9336 3651
www.ulster-ni.co.uk
Weekly (Wed). Owner: Alpha Group. Editor: Raymond Hughes

Ballymena Chronicle
028 8772 2557
Weekly (Wed). Independent. Editor: Desmond Mallon; news: Desmond Mallon Junior

Ballymena Guardian
028 2564 1221
www.ulsternet-ni.co.uk
Weekly (Wed). Owner: Alpha Group. Editor: Maurice O'Neil; assistant editor: Shaun O'Neil

Ballymena Times
028 2565 3300
www.mortonnewspapers.com
Weekly (Tue). Owner: Morton News Group. Editor: Desmond Blackadder; features: Stephanie Manson

Ballymoney & Coleraine Chronicle
028 7034 3344
www.ulsternet-ni.co.uk/chronicle
/pages/ballymoney.htm
Weekly (Wed). Owner: Northern News Group. Editor: John Fillis

Ballymoney Times
028 2766 6216
www.mortonnewspapers.com
Weekly (Wed). Owner: Morton News Group. Editor: Lyle McMullen; news: Clare Smith; features: Rachael Stamford

Banbridge Chronicle
028 4066 2322
Weekly (Wed). Independent. Editor: Bryan Hooks

Banbridge Leader
028 4066 2745
www.banbridgeleader.com
Weekly (Wed). Independent. Editor: Damien Wilson; features: Cathy Wilson

Bangor Spectator
028 9127 0270
Weekly (Thu). Owner: DE Alexander & Sons. Editor: Paul Flowers

Belfast News
028 9068 0000
www.icnorthernireland.co.uk
Weekly (Thu). Owner: Century Newspaper. Editor: Julie McClay; news: Rick Clarke; features: Jeff Hill

Carrick Gazette
028 9336 3651
www.ulster-ni.co.uk
Weekly (Wed). Owner: Alpha Group. Editor: Raymond Hughes

Carrick Times
028 3839 3939
www.mortonnewspapers.com
Weekly (Thu). Owner: Morton News Group. Editor: David Armstrong; assistant editor: Lyle McMullen

Carrickfergus Advertiser
028 8772 2274
www.ulsternet-ni.co.uk/carrick
/cpages/cmain.htm
Weekly (Wed). Owner: Alpha Group. Editor: Raymond Hughes

City News
028 7127 2200
www.derryjournal.com
Weekly (Wed). Owner: Local Press. Editor: Pat McArt; deputy editor: Siobhan McEleney

Coleraine Times
028 7035 5260
www.mortonnewspapers.com
Weekly (Wed). Owner: Morton News Group. Editor: David Rankin

County Down Spectator
028 9127 0270
Weekly (Thu). Owner: Spectator Newspapers. Editor: Paul Flowers

Craigavon Echo
028 3839 3939
www.mortonnewspapers.com
Weekly free (Wed). Owner: Morton News Group. Editor: David Armstrong; assistant editor: Hugh Vance

Derry Journal
028 7127 2200
www.derryjournal.com
Weekly (Tue, Fri). Owner: Local Press. Editor: Pat McArt; news: Bernie Mullan

Derry Journal (Sunday)
028 7127 2200
www.derryjournal.com
Sunday. Owner: Local Press. Editor: Pat McArt; deputy editor: Siobhan McEleney

Derry News
028 7129 6600
Twice-weekly (Thu, Mon). Independent. Editor: Joanne McCool; news: Mark Mullen; head of production: Ann Breslin

Derry on Monday
028 7127 2200
www.derryjournal.com
Weekly (Mon). Owner: Local Press. Editor: Pat McArt; deputy editor: Siobhan McEleney

Down Democrat
028 4461 4400
www.downdemocrat.com
Weekly (Tue). Owner: TCH Group. Editor: Terry McLaughlin; sales editor: Tina McGuire

Down Recorder
028 4461 3711
www.thedownrecorder.co.uk
Weekly (Wed). Independent. Editor: Paul Symington

Dromore Leader
028 3839 3939
www.mortonnewspapers.com
Weekly (Wed). Owner: Morton News Group. Editor: David Armstrong

Dungannon News & Tyrone Courier
028 8772 2271
www.ulsternet-ni.co.uk/courier
/cpages/cmain.htm
Weekly (Wed). Owner: Alpha Group. Editor: Ian Grear

Dungannon Observer
028 8772 2557
Weekly (Fri). Independent. Editor: Desmond Mallon; news: Desmond Mallon Junior

East Antrim Advertiser
028 2827 2303
www.mortonnewspapers.com
Monthly. Owner: Morton News Group. Editor: David Armstrong; assistant editor: Hugh Vance

East Antrim Guardian
028 2564 1221
www.macunlimited.net
Weekly (Wed). Owner: Northern Alpha Group. Editor: Maurice O'Neil; assistant editor: Shaun O'Neil

Farming Life
028 9068 0000
www.farminglife.com
Weekly (Wed, Sat). Owner: Century Newspaper. Editor: David McCoy; news: Rick Clarke; features: Jeff Hill

Fermanagh Herald
028 8224 3444
www.fermanaghherald.com
Weekly (Wed). Owner: North West of Ireland Printing Co. Editor: Pauline Leary

Fermanagh News
028 8772 2557
Weekly (Fri). Independent. Editor: Desmond Mallon; news: Desmond Mallon Junior

Foyle News
028 7127 2200
www.derryjournal.com
Weekly (Wed). Editor: Pat McArt; deputy editor: Siobhan McEleney

Impartial Reporter
028 6632 4422
www.impartialreporter.com
Weekly (Thu). Independent. Editor: Denzil McDaniel

The Journal (Derry)
028 7127 2200
www.derryjournal.com
Weekly (Thu). Owner: Local Press
Lakeland Extra
028 6632 4422
www.impartialreporter.com
Monthly free (3rd Mon). Independent.
Editor: Denzil McDaniel; news: Sarah
Sanderson; features editor Lily Dane;
head of production: Tony Quinn
Larne Gazette
028 9336 3651
www.ulster-ni.co.uk
Weekly (Wed). Owner: Alpha Group.
Editor: Raymond Hughes
Larne Times
028 3839 3939
www.mortonnewspapers.com
Weekly (Thu). Owner: Morton News
Group. Editor: David Armstrong;
assistant editor: Hugh Vance
The Leader (Banbridge/Dromore)
028 2827 2303
www.mortonnewspapers.com
Weekly (Wed). Owner: Morton News
Group. Editor: David Armstrong;
assistant editor: Damien Wilson
The Leader (Coleraine)
028 7034 3444
www.ulsternet-ni.co.uk/leader
/pages/leader.htm
Weekly (Mon). Owner: Northern News
Group. Editor: John Fillis
Limavady Chronicle
028 7034 3444
www.ulsternet-ni.co.uk/chronicle
/pages/limavady.htm
Weekly (Wed). Owner: Northern News
Group. Editor: John Fillis
Lisburn Echo
028 3839 3939
www.mortonnewspapers.com
Weekly free (Wed). Owner: Morton
News Group. Editor: David Armstrong;
assistant editor: Hugh Vance
Londonderry Sentinel
028 7134 8889
www.mortonnewspapers.com
Weekly (Wed). Owner: Morton News
Group. Editor: Robin Young; assistant
editor: Donna Deeney
Lurgan & Portadown Examiner
028 8772 2557
Weekly (Wed). Independent. Editor:
Desmond Mallon; news: Desmond
Mallon Junior
Lurgan Mail
028 3832 7777
www.mortonnewspapers.com
Weekly (Thu). Owner: Morton News
Group. Editor: Clint Aitken; assistant
editor: John Bingham; news: Richard
Burton; head of production: Lesley Wiley
Magherafelt & Limavady Constitution
028 7034 3444
www.ulsternet-ni.co.uk/ncon
/pages/limavady.htm
Weekly (Wed). Owner: Northern News
Group. Editor: John Fillis

Mid-Ulster Echo
028 8676 2288
www.mortonnewspapers.com
Weekly free (Wed). Owner: Morton
News Group. Editor: Mark Bain;
assistant editor: Alan Rogers
Mid-Ulster Mail
028 8676 2288
www.mortonnewspapers.com
Weekly (Thu). Owner: Morton News
Group. Assistant editor: Alan Rogers
Mid-Ulster Observer
028 8772 2557
Weekly (Wed). Independent. Editor:
Desmond Mallon; news: Desmond
Mallon Junior
Mourne Observer & County Down News
028 4372 2666
www.mourneobserver.com
Weekly (Wed). Independent.
Editor: Terrance Bowman
Newry Advertiser
028 8772 2557
Monthly free. Independent. Editor:
Desmond Mallon; news: Desmond
Mallon Junior
Newry Democrat
028 3025 1250
www.newrydemocrat.com
Weekly (Tue). Owner: Thomas Crosby
Holdings. Editor: Caroline McEvoy;
features: Patrick Ryan; head of
production: Stephen Burns
Newtownabbey Times
028 3839 3939
www.mortonnewspapers.com
Weekly (Thu). Owner: Morton News
Group. Editor: David Armstrong;
assistant editor: Desmond Backadder
Newtownards Chronicle
028 9127 0270
Weekly (Thu). Owner: Spectator
Newspapers. Editor: Paul Flowers
Newtownards Spectator
028 9127 0270
Weekly (Thu). Owner: Spectator
Newspapers. Editor: Paul Flowers
North Belfast News
028 9058 4444
www.irelandclick.com
Weekly (Fri). Owner: Andersonstown
News Group. Editor: John Ferris;
news: Andrea McKernon; features:
Aine McEntee
North West Echo
028 3839 3939
www.mortonnewspapers.com
Weekly free (Wed). Owner: Morton
News Group. Editor: David Armstrong;
assistant editor: John Fillis
Northern Constitution
028 7034 3444
www.ulsternet-ni.co.uk/ncon
/pages/coleraine.htm
Weekly (Wed). Owner: Northern News
Group. Editor: John Fillis
The Outlook (Portadown)
028 4063 0202
www.ulsternet-ni.co.uk
Weekly (Wed). Owner: Alpha Group.
Editor: Ruth Rogers

Portadown Times
028 3833 6111
www.mortonnewspapers.com
Weekly (Fri). Owner: Morton News
Group. Editor: David Armstrong
Roe Valley Sentinel
028 3839 3939
www.mortonnewspapers.com
Weekly (Wed). Owner: Morton News
Group. Editor: David Armstrong;
assistant editor: John Fillis
South Belfast News
028 9024 2411
www.irelandclick.com
Weekly (Fri). Owner: Andersonstown
News Group. Editor: Alison Morris
Strabane Chronicle
028 8224 3444
www.strabanechronicle.com
Weekly (Thu). Owner: North West of
Ireland Printing Co. Editor: Michelle
Canning
Strabane Weekly News
028 8224 2721
www.ulsternet-ni.co.uk
Weekly (Thu). Owner: Alpha Group.
Editor: Wesley Atchison; features:
Geraldine Wilson
Tyrone Constitution
028 8224 2721
www.ulsternet-ni.co.uk
Weekly (Thu). Owner: Alpha Group.
Editor: Wesley Atchison; features:
Geraldine Wilson
Tyrone Herald
028 8224 3444
www.tyroneherald.com
Weekly (Mon). Owner: The North West
of Ireland Printing & Publishing Co.
Editor: Morris Kennedy
Tyrone Times
028 8775 2801
www.mortonnewspapers.com
Weekly (Fri). Owner: Morton News
Group. Editor: Peter Bayne
Ulster Gazette & Armagh Standard
028 3752 2639
www.ulstergazette-ni.co.uk
Weekly (Thu). Owner: Alpha Group.
Editor: Richard Stewart
Ulster Herald
028 8224 3444
www.ulsterherald.com
Weekly (Thu). Owner: North West of
Ireland Printing Co. Editor: Darach
McDonald
Ulster Star
028 9267 9111
www.mortonnewspapers.com
Weekly (Fri). Owner: Morton News
Group. Editor: David Fletcher; news:
Mary McGee

Magazines Contacts

Main magazine & contract magazine publishers

Archant
Prospect House, Rouen Road
Norwich NR1 1RE
01603 772803
www.archant.co.uk
Chief executive: John Fry; MD, Archant Life: Johnny Hustler, 01603 772101; general manager, Archant Dialogue customer publishing: Chris Rainer, 01603 772532

Archant Specialist
The Mill, Bearwalden Business Park
Royston Road, Wendens Ambo
Essex CB11 4GB
01799 544200
MD: Farine Clarke

PRESS: *Keith Morris, 01603 772814*

Brooklands Group
Westgate, 120–128 Station Road
Redhill, Surrey RH1 1ET
01737 786800
mail@brooklandsgroup.com
www.brooklandsgroup.com
Chief executive: Darren Styles; account director: Matthew Jenns

BBC Worldwide
Woodlands, 80 Wood Lane
London W12 0TT
020 8433 2000
www.bbcworldwide.com
MD: Peter Phippen

Cedar
Pegasus House, 37–43 Sackville St
London W1S 3EH
020 7534 2400
info@cedarcom.co.uk
www.cedarcom.co.uk
MD: Jules Rastelli; editorial director: Mark Jones

Centaur
50 Poland St, London W1F 7AX
020 7970 4000
firstname.secondname@centaur.co.uk
www.centaur.co.uk
Publishing directors: Robin Coates, Roger Beckett, Howard Sharman, Tim Potter, Nigel Roby, Annie Swift

CMP Information
Ludgate House, 245 Blackfriars Rd
London SE1 9UY
020 7921 5000
www.cmpinformation.com
Part of United Business Media.
MD: Bernard Grey

Condé Nast
Vogue House, Hanover Square
London W1S 1JU
020 7499 9080
www.condenast.co.uk
MD: Nicholas Coleridge

DC Thomson
185 Fleet St, London EC4A 2HS
020 7400 1030
shout@dcthomson.co.uk
www.dcthomson.co.uk

Dennis
30 Cleveland St, London W1T 4JD
020 7907 6000
firstname_secondname@dennis.co.uk
www.dennis.co.uk
CEO: Alistair Ramsay; group publishing director, consumer division: Kerin O'Connor

Emap
Wentworth House, Wentworth Street
Peterborough PE1 1DS
020 7278 1452
www.emap.com
Group chief executive: Tom Maloney

Emap Communications
Scriptor Court, 155 Farringdon Rd
London EC1R 3AD
020 7841 6600
Chief executive: Derek Carter

Emap Consumer Media
Endeavour House
189 Shaftesbury Avenue
London WC2H 8JG
020 7437 9011
Chief executive: Paul Keenan; MD: Dharmash Mistry

Emap Performance
Mappin House, 4 Winsley St
London W1W 8HF
020 7436 1515

Future
Beauford Court, 30 Monmouth St
Bath BA1 2BW
01225 442244
firstname.secondname@futurenet.com
www.futurenet.com
Chief executive: Greg Ingham; MD: Robert Price

London office
99 Baker Street
London W1U 6FP
020 7317 2600
PRESS: *01225 732235 / 822517*

H Bauer
Academic House, 24–28 Oval Rd
London NW1 7DT
020 7241 8000
www.bauer.co.uk
MD: David Goodchild

Hachette Filipacchi
64 North Row, London W1K 7LL
020 7150 7000
www.hf-uk.com
Chairman: Kevin Hand; general manager women's group: Julie Harris

Haymarket
174 Hammersmith Road
London W6 7JP
020 8267 5000
hpg@haymarketgroup.com
www.haymarketgroup.com
Group MD: Eric Verdon-Roe; joint MDs, Haymarket Magazines: Kevin Costello, Simon Daukes; chairman and MD, Haymarket Business Publications: Martin Durham

Haymarket Customer Publishing
38–42 Hampton Rd
Teddington, Middlesex TW11 0JE
020 8267 5411
haycustpub@haynet.com
www.haycustpub.com
MD: Patrick Fuller

Highbury House Communications
Jordan House, 47 Brunswick Place
London N1 6EB
020 7608 6700
www.hhc.co.uk
Chief executive: Mark Simpson; MD: Mike Frey; divisional publishing director: Mark Salmon. Account manager, customer publishing: Katherine Punch; editor, customer publishing: Dawn Freeman
PRESS: *020 7608 6600*

Highbury Entertainment
Paragon House, St Peter's Road
Bournemouth BH1 2JS
01202 299900

Highbury Leisure
Berwick House, 8–10 Knoll Rise
Orpington, Kent BR6 0PS
01689 887200
email@highburyleisure.co.uk
www.highburyleisure.co.uk

IPC Media
King's Reach Tower, Stamford St
London SE1 9LS
0870 444 5000
www.ipcmedia.com
Owned by Time Warner. CEO: Sylvia Auton; editorial director: Mike Soutar

John Brown Citrus
The New Boathouse
136–142 Bramley Rd
London W10 6SR
020 7565 3000
www.jbcp.co.uk
MD: Dean Fitzpatrick, 020 7565 3202; editorial director: Paul Colbert

National Magazine Company
National Magazine House
72 Broadwick St, London W1F 9EP
020 7439 5000
www.natmags.co.uk
MD: Duncan Edwards

New Crane Publishing
20 Upper Ground
London SE1 9PD
020 7633 0266
enquiries@newcrane.co.uk
www.newcrane.com
Owned by Delia Smith and Michael
Wynn Jones

Publicis Blueprint
Whitfield House
83–89 Whitfield Street
London W1A 4XA
020 7462 7777
www.publicis-blueprint.com
MD: Jason Frost

Rare Publishing
102 Sydney Street, London SW3 6NJ
020 7368 9600
Bristol office 0117 929 7680
www.rarecontent.co.uk
Part of Chime Communications.
MD: Julian Downing; publishing and
commercial director: Sarah Kermode;
editorial director: Maureen Rice;
editor-in-chief: Matthew Cowen

Redwood
7 St Martin's Place
London WC2N 4HA
020 7747 0700
info@redwoodgroup.net
www.redwoodgroup.net
MD: Keith Grainger

Reed Business Information
Quadrant House, The Quadrant
Sutton SM2 5AS
020 8652 3500
www.reedbusiness.co.uk
Part of Reed Elsevier. Chief executive:
Peter Jones

River Group
Victory House, Leicester Square
London WC2H 7QH
020 7306 0304
info@river.co.uk
www.therivergroup.co.uk
Joint MD and sales and marketing
director: Nicola Murphy; joint MD and
editorial director: Jane Wynn

VNU Business
VNU House, 32–34 Broadwick St
London W1A 2HG
020 7316 9000
firstname_secondname@vnu.co.uk
www.vnunet.com
MD: Brin Bucknor

Consumer magazines

Adult

Erotic Review
020 7907 6000
www.theeroticreview.co.uk
Monthly. Owner: Dennis.
Editor: Rowan Pelling

Escort
020 7292 8000
Monthly. Owner: Paul Raymond.
Editor: James Hundleby

Fiesta
01376 534549
www.fiesta.co.uk
13pa. Owner: Galaxy.
Editor: Ross Gilfillan

For Women
020 7308 5363
9pa. Owner: Fantasy Publications.
Editor: Liz Beresford

Knave
01376 534549
www.knave.co.uk
13pa. Owner: Galaxy.
Editor: Ross Gilfillan

Mayfair
020 7292 8000
Monthly. Owner: Paul Raymond.
Editor: David Rider

Men Only
020 7292 8000
Monthly. Owner: Paul Raymond.
Editor: Pierre Perrone

Skin Two
020 7498 5533
www.skintwo.co.uk
4pa. Owner: Tim Woodward.
Editor: Tony Mitchell

Viz
020 7907 6000
www.viz.co.uk
Monthly. Owner: Dennis

Arts, music, film & TV

247
01752 294130
www.twenty4-seven.co.uk
Monthly. Owner: Afterdark Media.
Editor: Lucy Griffiths

All About Soap
020 7150 7000
www.allaboutsoap.co.uk
Fortnightly. Owner: Hachette Filipacchi
UK. Editor: Jonathan Hughes

Amateur Photographer
020 7261 5100
www.amateurphotographer.co.uk
Weekly. Owner: IPC Media.
Editor: Garry Coward-Williams

AN Magazine
0191 241 8000
www.a-n.co.uk
Monthly. Owner: F22The Artists
Information Company.
Editor: Gillian Nicol

The Art Book
01323 811759
www.blackwellpublishing.com
4pa. Owner: Blackwell Publishing.
Editor: Sue Ward, Marion Arnold

The Art Newspaper
020 7735 3331
www.theartnewspaper.com
Monthly. Independent. Group editor:
Anna Somers Cocks

Art Quarterly
020 7225 4818
www.artfund.org
4pa. Owner: National Art Collection
Fund. Editor: Caroline Bugler

Art Review
020 7246 3350
www.art-review.com
Monthly. Owner: ArtReview.
Editor: Daniel Kunitz

The Artist
01580 763315
www.theartistmagazine.co.uk
Monthly. Owner: The Artists' Publishing
Company. Editor: Sally Bulgin

Artists & Illustrators
020 7700 8500
www.aimag.co.uk
Monthly. Owner: Quarto Magazines.
Editor: John Swinfield

Arts East
01223 434434
www.cambridgenewspapers.co.uk
Monthly. Owner: Cambridge
Newspapers. Editor: Louise Cummings

BBC Music Magazine
0117 927 9009
www.bbcmagazines.com/music
Monthly. Owner: Origin Publishing.
Editor:Oliver Condy

The Big Cheese
020 7607 0303
www.bigcheesemagazine.com
Monthly. Independent.
Editor: Eugene Butcher

Billboard
020 7420 6000
www.billboard.com
Weekly. Owner: VNU.
Editor: Emmanuel Legrand

Blues & Soul
020 7402 6897
www.bluesandsoul.com
Fortnightly. Owner: Blues & Soul.
Editor: Bob Killbourn

The Brighton Source
01273 561617
www.brightonsource.co.uk
Monthly. Owner: Newsquest.
Editor: Marcus O'Dair

Buzz Magazine
029 2025 6883
www.buzzmag.co.uk
Monthly. Editor: Emma Clark

Cineworld
01225 737300
www.cineworld.co.uk
Bi-monthly. Owner: Concept.
Editor: Sally Thomson

Classic FM – The Magazine
020 8267 5000
www.haymarketpublishing.co.uk
Monthly. Owner: Haymarket.
Editor-in-chief: John Evans

Classic Rock
020 7317 2654
www.classicrockmagazine.com
13pa. Owner: Future.
Editor: Scott Rowley

Classical Music
020 7333 1742
www.rhinegold.co.uk
Fortnightly. Owner: Rhinegold.
Editor: Keith Clarke

Country Music People
020 8854 7217
www.countrymusicpeople.com
Monthly. Owner: Music Farm.
Editor: Craig Baguley

Country Music Round-up
01472 821707
www.cmru.co.uk
Monthly. Owner: CMRU.
Editor: John Emptage

The Crack
0191 230 3038
www.thecrackmagazine.com
Monthly. Editor: Robert Meddes

Cult Times
020 8875 1520
www.visimag.com
Monthly. Owner: Visual Imagination.
Editor: Paul Spragg

Dance Europe
020 8985 7767
www.danceeurope.net
Monthly. Editor: Emma Manning

Dance Gazette
020 7326 8000
www.rad.org.uk
3pa. Owner: Royal Academy of Dance.
Editor: David Jays

DJ
020 7608 6500
www.djmag.com
Fortnightly. Owner: Highbury House.
Editor: Lesley Wright

DMC Update
020 7262 6777
www.dmcworld.com/update
Weekly. Owner: DMC.
Publisher: Tony Prince

DVD Monthly
01392 434477
www.predatorpublishing.co.uk
Monthly. Owner: Predator.
Editor: Tim Isaac

DVD Review
020 7331 1000
www.dvdreview.net
13pa. Owner: Future.
Editor: Paul Morgan

DVD World
020 7331 1000
www.highburywv.com
13pa. Owner: Highbury House.
Editor: Richard Marshall

Early Music Today
020 7333 1744
www.rhinegold.co.uk
6pa. Owner: Rhinegold.
Editor: Lucien Jenkins

Empire
020 7182 8000
www.empireonline.co.uk
Monthly. Owner: Emap.
Editor: Colin Kennedy

Entertainer
01302 347225
www.doncastertoday.co.uk
Weekly. Owner: Johnston Press.
Editor: Martin Edmonds

EP Magazine
0845 644 5513
www.vigilante.co.uk
10pa. Owner: Vigilante Publications.
Editor: Jon Ewing

Film Review
020 8875 1520
www.visimag.com
Monthly. Owner: Visual Imagination.
Editor: Grant Kempster

The Fly
020 7691 4555
www.the-fly.co.uk
Monthly. Owner: Channelfly
Enterprises. Editor: Will Kinsman

Freetime
01252 621513
www.freetimemag.co.uk
4pa. Owner: VRA. Editor: Vic Robbie

fRoots
020 8340 9651
www.frootsmag.com
Monthly. Owner: Southern Rag.
Editor: Ian Anderson

Future Music
01225 442244
www.futuremusic.co.uk
13pa. Owner: Future. Editor: Andy Jones

The Gazette
01782 575569
Monthly. Owner: Potteries Publications.
Editor: Terry Winter

Gramophone
020 8267 5136
www.gramophone.co.uk
Monthly. Owner: Haymarket.
Editor: James Jolly

Granta
020 7704 9776
www.granta.com
4pa. Owner: Granta. Editor: Ian Jack

Guitar
020 8726 8303
www.ipcmedia.com
Monthly. Owner: IPC Media.
Editor: Marcus Leadley

Guitar Buyer
01353 665577
Monthly. Owner: MB Media.
Editor: Mick Taylor

Guitar Techniques
01225 442244
www.futurenet.com/guitartechniques
13pa. Owner: Future.
Editor: Neville Marten

Guitarist
01225 442244
www.futurenet.com/guitarist/
13pa. Owner: Future.
Editor: Michael Leonard

Hip Hop Connection
01223 210536
www.hiphop.co.uk
Monthly. Owner: Infamous Ink.
Editor: Andy Cowan

Hollywood Reporter
020 7420 6004
www.hollywoodreporter.com
Weekly. Owner: VNU.
Editor: Robert Dowling

Home Cinema Choice
020 7331 1000
www.homecinemachoice.com
Monthly. Owner: Future.
Editor: Steve May

Hotdog
01690 887200
13pa. Owner: Highbury House.
Editor: Tom Hawker

Impact
01484 435011
www.martialarts.co.uk
Monthly. Owner: MAI Publications.
Editor: John Mosby

Inside Soap
020 7150 7000
www.insidesoap.co.uk
Weekly. Owner: Hachette Filipacchi UK.
Editor: Steven Murphy

It's Hot
020 8433 3910
www.bbcmagazines.com/hot
13pa. Owner: BBC Worldwide.
Acting editor: Shelley Moulden

Jazz at Ronnie Scott's
020 7485 9803
www.ronniescotts.co.uk
Bi-monthly. Editor: Jim Godbolt

Jazz Guide
01908 312392
Monthly. Editor: Bernie Tyrrell

Jazz UK
029 2066 5161
www.jazzservices.org.uk
Bi-monthly. Owner: Jazz Services.
Editor: John Fordham

Kerrang!
020 7182 8000
www.kerrang.com
Weekly. Owner: Emap.
Editor: Paul Brannigan

Knowledge
020 8533 9300
www.knowledgemag.co.uk
10pa. Owner: Vision Publishing.
Editor: Colin Steven

Leisure Painter
01580 763315
www.leisurepainter.co.uk
Monthly. Owner: The Artists' Publishing
Company. Editor: Ingrid Lyon

The List
0131 550 3050
www.list.co.uk
Fortnightly; extra festival issues in
August. Editor: Nick Barley

London Review of Books
020 7209 1101
www.lrb.co.uk
Fortnightly. Owner: LRB.
Editor: Mary-Kay Wilmers

London Theatre Guide
020 7557 6700
www.officiallondontheatre.co.uk
Fortnightly. Owner: The Society of
London Theatre. Editor: Philippa Smart
M8
0141 840 5980
www.m8magazine.com
Monthly. Editor: Kevin McFarlane
Magpie
0870 071 1611
www.magpiedirect.com
Bi-monthly. Editor: Mark Rye
Metal Hammer
020 7317 2691
www.metalhammer.co.uk
13pa. Owner: Future.
Editor: Jamie Hibbard
Mixmag
020 7817 8805
www.mixmag.net
Monthly. Owner: Emap.
Features editor: Gavin Herlihy
Mojo
020 7436 1515
www.mojo4music.com
Monthly. Owner: Emap.
Editor: Phil Alexander
Movie Mag International
020 8567 3662
www.movie-mag.net
Monthly. Editor: Bharathi Pradhan
Music Tech
01249 716557
www.musictechmag.co.uk
Monthly. Owner: Anthem Publishing.
Editor: Neil Worley
National Gallery Season Guide
020 7747 2836
www.nationalgallery.org.uk
3pa. Owner: National Gallery.
Editor: Andrea Easey
NME
020 7261 5564
www.nme.com
Weekly. Owner: IPC Media.
Editor: Conor McNicholas
Official Elvis Presley Fan Club
Magazine
0844 800 6881/2
www.elvisweb.co.uk
Bi-monthly. Editor: Todd Slaughter
Opera
020 8563 8893
www.opera.co.uk
Monthly. Editor: John Allison
Opera Now
020 7333 1740
www.rhinegold.co.uk
6pa. Owner: Rhinegold.
Editor: Ash Khandekar
Piano
020 7333 1724
www.rhinegold.co.uk
6pa. Owner: Rhinegold.
Editor: Jeremy Siepmann
The Potteries Post
01782 575569
Monthly. Owner: Potteries Publications.
Editor: Terry Winter

Q4Music
020 7436 1515
www.q4music.com
Monthly. Owner: Emap.
Editor: Paul Rees
RA Magazine
020 7300 5820
www.ramagazine.org.uk
4pa. Owner: Royal Academy of Arts.
Editor: Sarah Greenberg
Radio Times
020 8433 2235
www.radiotimes.com
Weekly. Owner: BBC Worldwide.
Editor: Gill Hudson
Record Buyer
01522 511265
Monthly. Owner: Aceville.
Editor: Paul Rigby
Rhythm
01225 442244
www.futurenet.com/rhythm
13pa. Owner: Future. Editor: Louise King
Rock Sound
020 7877 8770
www.rock-sound.net
Monthly. Editor: Darren Taylor
Rolling Stone
00 1 212 484 1616
www.rollingstone.com
26pa. Owner: Rolling Stone Magazine.
Editor: Jann S Wenner
Satellite and Digital Choice
020 7331 1000
www.highburywv.com
8pa. Owner: Highbury House.
Editor: Grant Rennell
Satellite TV Monthly
020 7351 3612
www.satellitetvtoday.com
Monthly. Owner: Highbury House.
Editor: Paul Hirons
Screen International
020 7505 8096
www.screendaily.com
Weekly. Owner: Emap.
Editor: Michael Gubbins
SFX
01225 442244
www.sfx.co.uk
13pa. Owner: Future.
Editor: Dave Bradley
Shivers
020 8875 1520
www.visimag.com
Monthly. Owner: Visual Imagination.
Editor: David Miller
Sight & Sound
020 7957 8963
www.bfi.org.uk/sightandsound
Monthly. Owner: British Film Institute.
Editor: Nick James
Smash Hits
020 7436 1515
www.smashhits.net
Fortnightly. Owner: Emap.
Editor: Lara Palamoudian
Soaplife
020 7261 7568
www.ipcmedia.com
Fortnightly. Owner: IPC Media.
Editor: Hellen Gardner

Songlines
020 7371 2777
www.songlines.co.uk
Bi-monthly. Editor: Simon Broughton
Sound on Sound
01954 789888
www.soundonsound.com
Monthly. Owner: SOS Publications
Group. Editor: Paul White
The Stage
020 7403 1818
www.thestage.co.uk
Weekly. Editor: Brian Attwood
Starburst
020 8875 1520
www.visimag.com
Monthly. Owner: Visual Imagination.
Editor: Stephen Payne
Stardust International
020 7224 2600
www.stardustindia.com
Monthly. Owner: Magna.
Editor: Ashwin Varde
The Strad
020 7618 3095
www.thestrad.com
Monthly. Owner: Newsquest.
Editor: Naomi Sadler
Straight No Chaser
020 8533 9999
www.straightnochaser.co.uk
Bi-monthly. Editor: Paul Bradshaw
Theatregoer
020 7439 2777
www.theatregoer.net
Monthly. Owner: Whatsonstage.
Editor: Terri Paddock
This is London Magazine
020 7434 1281
www.thisislondontickets.co.uk
Weekly. Editor: Julie Jones
Time Out
020 7813 3000
www.timeout.com
Weekly. Owner: Time Out Group.
Editor: Gordon Thomson
Time Out Student Guide
020 7813 3000
www.timeout.com
Annually. Owner: Time Out Group.
Editor: Sharon Lougher
Times Literary Supplement
020 7782 3000
www.the-tls.co.uk
Weekly. Owner: TSL Education.
Editor: Peter Stothard
Top of the Pops Magazine
020 8433 3910
www.bbcmagazines.com/totp
Fortnightly. Owner: BBC Worldwide.
Editor: Peter Hart
Total DVD
020 7331 1000
www.totaldvd.net
13pa. Owner: Highbury House.
Editor: Chris Jenkins
Total Film
020 7317 2449
www.totalfilm.co.uk
13pa. Owner: Future.
Editor: Matt Mueller

Total Guitar
01225 442244
www.totalguitar.co.uk
13pa. Owner: Future.
Editor: Stephen Lawson

Total TV Guide
020 7241 8000
www.bauer.co.uk
Weekly. Owner: H Bauer.
Editor: Jon Peake

TV & Satellite Week
020 7261 7534
www.tvandsatelliteweek.com
Weekly. Owner: IPC Media.
Editor: Jonathan Bowman

TV Choice
020 7241 8000
www.bauer.co.uk
Weekly. Owner: H Bauer.
Editor: Jon Peake

TV easy
020 7261 7776
www.ipcmedia.com
Weekly. Owner: IPC Media.
Editor: Richard Clark

TV Hits!
020 7150 7000
www.tvhits.co.uk
Monthly. Owner: Hachette Filipacchi
UK. Editor: Fran Babb

TV Quick
020 7241 8000
www.bauer.co.uk
Weekly. Owner: H Bauer.
Editor: Jon Peake

TV Times
08704 445000
www.ipcmedia.com
Weekly. Owner: IPC Media.
Editor: Mike Hollingsworth

TV Zone
020 8875 1520
www.visimag.com
Monthly. Owner: Visual Imagination.
Editor: Jan Vincent-Rudzki

Ultimate DVD
020 8875 1520
www.visimag.com
Monthly. Owner: Visual Imagination.
Editor: David Richardson

Uncut
020 7261 6992
www.uncut.co.uk
Monthly. Owner: IPC Media.
Editor: Allan Jones

Un
0117 927 9009
www.un.com
10pa. Owner: Origin Publishing.
Editor: Pat Reid

Unreel
0870 220 4350
www.unreelmovies.co.uk
Bi-monthly. Owner: Concept
Publishing. Editor: Sally Thomson

V&A Magazine
020 7942 2505
www.vam.ac.uk
3pa. Owner: Culture Shock.
Editor: Charlotte Mullins

Variety
020 7611 4580
www.variety.com
Daily and weekly.
Owner: Reed Business Information.
Editor-in-chief: Peter Bart

What's on in London
020 7278 4393
www.whatsoninlondon.co.uk
Weekly. Editor: Michael Darvell

What's on TV
020 7261 7535
www.ipcmedia.com
Weekly. Owner: IPC Media.
Editor: Colin Tough

Where London
020 7611 7885
Monthly. Owner: Where Publications.
Editor: Mary Anne Evans

The Wire
020 7422 5014
www.thewire.co.uk
Monthly. Editor: Chris Bohn

Word
020 7520 8625
www.wordmagazine.co.uk
Monthly. Owner: Development Hell.
Editor: Mark Ellen

Writers' News
0113 200 2929
www.writersnews.co.uk
Monthly. Owner: Warners.
Editor: Derek Hudson

The X Files
020 7620 0200
www.titanmagazines.com
Monthly. Owner: Titan Publishing.
Editor: Martin Eden

X-pose
020 8875 1520
www.visimag.com
Monthly. Owner: Visual Imagination.
Editor: Anthony Brown

The Zone
01983 865668
www.zone-sf.com
Website. Owner: Pegasus Press.
Editor: Tony Lee

Children and teenage

2000 AD
01865 200603
www.2000adonline.com
Weekly. Owner: Rebellion.
Editor: Matt Smith

Action Man
01892 500100
www.paninicomics.co.uk
18pa. Owner: Panini UK.
Editor: Simon Frith

Angel Magazine
020 7250 0750
Monthly. Owner: Metropolis
Publishing. Editor: Mark Kebble

Animal Action
0870 010 1181
www.rspca.org.uk
Bi-monthly. Owner: RSPCA.
Editor: Sarah Evans

Animals and You
01382 223131
www.dcthomson.co.uk
Monthly. Owner: DC Thomson.
Editor: Margaret Monaghan

Aquila Children's Magazine
01323 431313
www.aquila.co.uk
Monthly. Owner: New Leaf Publishing.
Editor: Jackie Berry

Art Attack
01892 500100
www.paninicomics.co.uk
18pa. Owner: Panini UK.
Editor: Karen Brown

Balamory Magazine
020 8433 2356
www.bbcmagazines.com
13pa. Owner: BBC Worldwide.
Editor: Siobhan Keeler

Barbie
020 7380 6452
www.egmontmagazines.co.uk
Fortnightly. Owner: Egmont
Magazines. Editor: Claire Noonan

BBC Toybox
020 8433 2356
www.bbcmagazines.com/toybox/
13pa. Owner: BBC Worldwide. Editors:
Nora Kerezovic, Paddy Kempshall

Beano
01382 223131
www.beanotown.com
Weekly. Owner: DC Thomson.
Editor: Euan Kerr

Bliss
020 7437 9011
www.blissmag.co.uk
Monthly. Owner: Emap.
Editor: Lisa Smosarski

Breakout
01235 553444
www.couriergroup.com
6pa. Owner: Courier Newspaper Group.
Editor: Lawrence Webb

CosmoGirl!
020 7439 5000
www.cosmogirl.co.uk
Monthly. Owner: National Magazine
Company. Editor: Celia Duncan

Dandy
01382 223131
www.dandy.com
Weekly. Owner: DC Thomson.
Editor: Morris Heggie

Disney & Me
020 7380 6449
www.egmontmagazines.co.uk
Fortnightly. Owner: Egmont Magazines.
Editor: Jeanette Ryall

Disney Princess
020 7380 6449
www.egmontmagazines.co.uk
Fortnightly. Owner: Egmont Magazines.
Editor: Jeanette Ryall

Elle Girl
020 7150 7000
www.hf-uk.com
Monthly. Owner: Hachette Filipacchi
UK. Editor: Claire Irvin

Fimbles Magazine
020 8433 2000
www.bbcmagazines.com
13pa. Owner: BBC Worldwide.
Editor: Nora Kerezovic

Girl
01392 664141
Monthly. Owner: LCD Publishing.
Editor: Joanne Trump

Girl Talk
020 8433 1846
www.bbcmagazines.com/girltalk
Fortnightly. Owner: BBC Worldwide.
Editor: Samantha McEvoy

Go Girl
020 7380 6471
www.egmontmagazines.co.uk
Fortnightly. Owner: Egmont Magazines.
Editor: Sarah Delmege

Guiding
020 7592 1821
www.girlguiding.org.uk
Monthly. Owner: GirlGuiding UK.
Editor: Wendy Kewley

Hot Wheels
020 7380 6467
www.egmontmagazines.co.uk
Monthly. Owner: Egmont Magazines.
Editor: Matt Crossick

Mizz
08704 445000
www.ipcmedia.com
Weekly. Owner: IPC Media.
Editor: Sharon Christal

Pokemon World
01202 299900
5-weekly. Owner: Highbury
Entertainment. Editor: Nick Roberts

Pony
01428 601020
www.ponymag.com
Monthly. Owner: DJ Murphy
Publishers. Editor: Janet Rising

Power Rangers
020 7380 6449
www.egmontmagazines.co.uk
Monthly. Owner: Egmont Magazines.
Editor: Jeanette Ryall

Rugrats
0161 624 0414
13pa. Owner: Toontastic Publishing.
Editor: Emma Boff

Scouting Magazine
020 8433 7219
www.scoutingmagazine.org
Bi-monthly. Owner: Redactive
Publishing. Editor: Chris James

Shout Magazine
01382 223131
www.dcthomson.co.uk
Fortnightly. Owner: DC Thomson.
Editor: Ria Welch

Simpsons Comic
020 7620 0200
www.titanmagazines.com
Monthly. Owner: Titan Publishing.
Editor: Paul Terry

Sneak
020 7436 1515
www.sneakmagazine.com
Weekly. Owner: Emap.
Editor: Simon Harper

Spectacular Spiderman
01892 500100
www.paninicomics.co.uk
17pa. Owner: Panini UK.
Editor: Tom O'Malley

Sugar
020 7150 7000
www.sugarmagazine.co.uk
Monthly. Owner: Hachette Filipacchi
UK. Editor: Annabel Brog

Thomas & Friends
020 7380 6454
www.egmontmagazines.co.uk
Fortnightly. Owner: Egmont Magazines.
Editor: Audrey Wong

Toxic
020 7380 6465
www.egmontmagazines.co.uk
Fortnightly. Owner: Egmont Magazines.
Editor: Matt Yeo

Tweenies Magazine
020 8433 2356
www.bbcmagazines.com
Fortnightly. Owner: BBC Worldwide

Winnie the Pooh
020 7380 6449
www.egmontmagazines.co.uk
Monthly. Owner: Egmont Magazines.
Editor: Jeanette Ryall

Wolverine & Gambit
01892 500100
www.paninicomics.co.uk
13pa. Owner: Panini UK.
Editor: Scott Gray

Young Scot
0131 313 2488
www.youngscot.org
Monthly. Editor: Fiona McIntyre

Computing & gadgets

.net
01225 442244
www.netmag.co.uk
13pa. Owner: Future.
Editor: Lisa Jones

3D World
01225 442244
www.3dworldmag.co.uk
13pa. Owner: Future.
Editor: Jim Thacker

Computer Arts
01225 442244
www.computerarts.co.uk
13pa. Owner: Future.
Editor: Gillian Carson

Computer Arts Projects
01225 442244
www.computerarts.co.uk
13pa. Owner: Future.
Editor: Rob Carney

Computer Buyer
020 7907 6000
www.computerbuyer.co.uk
Monthly. Owner: Dennis.
Editor: James Nixon

Computer Shopper
020 7907 6000
www.computershopper.co.uk
Monthly. Owner: Dennis.
Editor: Paul Sanders

Computer Upgrade
01225 442244
www.computerupgrademag.co.uk
13pa. Owner: Future.
Editor: Adam Evans

ComputerActive
020 7316 9000
www.computeractive.co.uk
Fortnightly. Owner: VNU.
Editor: Dylan Armbrust

Computing Which?
020 7770 7564
www.computingwhich.co.uk
Bi-monthly. Owner: Which?
Editor: Jessica Ross

Cube
01202 299900
www.totalgames.net
13pa. Owner: Highbury Entertainment.
Editor: Miles Guttery

Digital Camcorder Buyer
01202 299900
6pa. Owner: Highbury Entertainment.
Editor: Paul Newman

Digital Creative Arts
01202 299900
6pa. Owner: Highbury Entertainment.
Editor: Thomas Watson

Digital Home
01225 442244
www.digitalhomemag.co.uk
13pa. Owner: Future.
Editor: Dean Evans

Digital Music Maker
01202 299900
Monthly. Owner: Highbury
Entertainment. Editor: Karl Foster

Digital Photo
01733 264666
www.emap.com
Monthly. Owner: Emap.
Editor: Jon Adams

Digital Video
020 7331 1000
www.camuser.co.uk
13pa. Owner: Future.
Editor: Robert Hull

Digital Video Made Easy
01202 299900
13pa. Owner: Highbury Entertainment.
Editor: Mark Hattersley

Edge
01225 442244
www.edge-online.co.uk
13pa. Owner: Future. Editor: Tony Mott

Essential Home Cinema
020 7331 1000
13pa. Owner: Highbury House.
Editor: Rob Lane

Games Domain
0121 326 0900
www.gamesdomain.com
Website, updated daily. Owner: Yahoo!

Games TM
01202 299900
www.gamestm.co.uk
13pa. Owner: Highbury Entertainment.
Editor: Simon Phillips

GamesMaster
01225 442244
www.futurenet.com/gamesmaster
13pa. Owner: Future.
Editor: Robin Alway

GigaHZ
01202 299900
8pa. Owner: Highbury Entertainment.
Editor: Paul Lester

Hi-Fi Choice
020 7317 2600
www.hifichoice.co.uk
13pa. Owner: Future.
Editor: Tim Bowern

Hi-Fi News
020 8726 8311
www.hifinews.com
Monthly. Owner: IPC Media.
Editor: Steve Harris

Hi-Fi World
01275 371386
www.hi fiworld.co.uk
Monthly. Editor: David Price

Home Cinema Choice
020 7317 2600
www.homecinemachoice.co.uk
Owner: Future. Editor: Steve May

iCreate
01202 299900
9pa. Owner: Highbury Entertainment.
Editor: Paul Newman

Internet and Broadband Advisor
01225 442244
www.netadvisor.co.uk
13pa. Owner: Future.
Editor: Alex Summersby

Internet User
01202 299900
13pa. Owner: Highbury Entertainment.
Editor: Dominic Brookman

Internet World
020 8232 1600
www.internetworld.co.uk
Monthly. Owner: Penton Media Europe.
Editor: Mark Dye

Jetix
01225 442244
www.myfavouritemagazines.co.uk
13pa. Owner: Future.
Editor: Cavan Scott

Linux Format
01225 442244
www.linuxformat.co.uk
13pa. Owner: Future.
Editor: Nick Veitch

Login Magazine
01702 589169
Monthly. Owner: Enterbrain.
Editor: Rick Haynes

MacFormat
01225 442244
www.macformat.co.uk
13pa. Owner: Future.
Editor: Graham Barlow

MacUser
020 7907 6000
www.macuser.co.uk
Fortnightly. Owner: Dennis.
Editor: Nick Rawlinson

Macworld
020 7071 3615
www.macworld.co.uk
13pa. Owner: IDG London.
Editor: David Fanning

Micro Mart
0121 233 8707
www.micromart.co.uk
Weekly. Owner: Trinity Publications.
Editor: Simon Brew

NGC
01225 442244
www.futurenet.com/ngc
13pa. Owner: Future.
Editor: Thomas East

Official Playstation 2 Magazine
01225 442244
www.playstation.co.uk
13pa. Owner: Future.
Editor: Stephen Pierce

Official Xbox Magazine
020 7317 2477
www.officialxboxmagazine.co.uk
13pa. Owner: Future.
Editor: Gavin Ogden

P2
01202 299900
www.totalgames.net
13pa. Owner: Highbury Entertainment.
Editor: Roy Kimber

PC Advisor
020 7071 3615
www.pcadvisor.co.uk
Monthly. Owner: IDG London.
Editor: Guy Dixon

PC Answers
01225 442244
www.pcanswers.co.uk
13pa. Owner: Future.
Editor: Simon Pickstock

PC Basics
01202 299900
13pa. Owner: Highbury Entertainment.
Editor: Geoff Spick

PC Format
01225 442244
www.pcformat.co.uk
13pa. Owner: Future.
Editor: Adam Oxford

PC Gamer
01225 442244
www.pcgamer.co.uk
13pa. Owner: Future.
Editor: Mark Donald

PC Home
01202 299900
13pa. Owner: Highbury Entertainment.
Editor: Paul Lester

PC Plus
01225 442244
www.pcplus.co.uk
13pa. Owner: Future.
Editor: Ian Robson

PC Pro
020 7907 6000
www.pcpro.co.uk
Monthly. Owner: Dennis.
Editor: James Morris

PC Utilities
01625 855000
www.pc-utilities.co.uk
13pa. Owner: Live Publishing
International. Editor: Gavin Burrell

PC Zone
020 7317 2600
www.pczone.co.uk
13pa. Owner: Future. Editor: Jamie Sefton

PDA Buyer
01202 299900
Bi-monthly. Owner: Highbury
Entertainment. Editor: Dave Harfield

PDA Essentials
01202 299900
13pa. Owner: Highbury Entertainment.
Editor: Dave Harfield

Personal Computer World
01858 438881
www.pcw.co.uk
Monthly. Owner: VNU. Editor: Rob Jones

Play
01202 299900
www.totalgames.net
13pa. Owner: Highbury Entertainment.
Editor: Nick Jones

Powerstation
01202 299900
13pa. Owner: Highbury Entertainment.
Editor: Mike O'Sullivan

Practical Web Projects
01202 299900
13pa. Owner: Highbury Entertainment.
Editor: James Thronton

PSM2
01225 442244
www.futurenet.com/psm2
13pa. Owner: Future.
Editor: Daniel Griffith

PSW
020 7317 2600
www.myfavouritemagazines.co.uk
13pa. Owner: Future.
Editor: Lee Nutter

Solutions
01202 299900
www.totalgames.net
13pa. Owner: Highbury Entertainment.
Editor: Phil King

Stuff
020 8267 5036
www.stuffmagazine.co.uk
Monthly. Owner: Haymarket.
Editor: Oliver Irish

T3
020 7317 2600
www.t3.co.uk
13pa. Owner: Future.
Editor: James Beechinor-Collins

Total Games.net
01202 299900
www.totalgames.net
Bi-monthly. Owner: Highbury
Entertainment. Editor: Nick Roberts

Total Mobile
020 7331 1000
www.camuser.co.uk
13pa. Owner: Future.
Editor: Phil Lattimore

Web Designer
01202 299900
13pa. Owner: Highbury Entertainment.
Editor: Thomas Watson

Web Pages Made Easy
01202 299900
13pa. Owner: Highbury Entertainment.
Editor: Rob Clymo

Web User
020 7261 7294
www.webuser.co.uk
Fortnightly. Owner: IPC Media.
Editor: Andrew Craig

What Digital Camcorder
020 7331 1000
www.whatcamcorder.net
13pa. Owner: Future.
Editor: Ali Upham
What Hi-Fi? Sound and Vision
020 8267 5000
www.whathifi.com
Monthly, plus awards issue.
Owner: Haymarket
What Home Cinema
020 7331 1000
www.homecinemachoice.com
 /whathomecinema/magazine
Monthly. Owner: Future.
Editor: Adrian Justins
What Satellite and Digital TV
020 7331 1000
www.wotsat.com
Monthly. Owner: Future.
Editor: Alex Lane
What Video and Widescreen TV
020 7331 1000
www.whatvideomag.com
Monthly. Owner: Future.
Editor: Danny Phillips
Windows XP Made Easy
01202 299900
13pa. Owner: Highbury Entertainment.
Editor: Stuart Tarrant
Windows XP: The Official Magazine
01225 442244
www.windowsxpmagazine.co.uk
13pa. Owner: Future.
Editor: Richard Keith
XBM
01202 299900
www.totalgames.net/pm/148
13pa. Owner: Highbury Entertainment.
Editor: Ian Dean
Xbox World
01225 442244
www.xboxworld.co.uk
13pa. Owner: Future.
Editor: Tim Weaver

Current affairs

AFF Families Journal
01980 615525
www.aff.org.uk
4pa. Owner: Army Families Federation.
Editor: Sue Bonney
The American
01297 561147
Monthly. Owner: Acnorbry.
Editor: Catherine Russell
Big Issue
020 7526 3388
www.bigissue.com
Weekly. Editor: Matt Ford
Big Issue in Scotland
0141 418 7000
www.bigissuescotland.com
Weekly. Editor: Claire Black
Big Issue in the North
0161 834 6300
www.bigissueinthenorth.com
Weekly. Editor: Ato Erzan

Challenge Newsline
01903 241975
Monthly. Owner: Verité.
Editor: Debbie Bunn
Connect Magazine
020 7865 8100
www.greenpeace.org.uk
4pa. Owner: Greenpeace.
Editor: Stokeley Webster
Diplo
020 7833 9766
www.diplo-magazine.co.uk
Monthy. Owner: Editor: Charles Baker
EarthMatters
020 7490 1555
www.foe.co.uk
3pa. Owner: Friends of the Earth.
Editors: Adam Bradbury, Nicola Baird
Ecologist
020 7351 3578
www.theecologist.org
10pa. Editor: Zac Goldsmith
Economist
020 7830 7000
www.economist.com
Weekly. Owner: The Economist
Newspaper. Editor: Bill Emmott
Glasgow Magazine
0141 287 0901
www.glasgow.gov.uk
Bi-monthly. Owner: Glasgow City
Council. Editor: John Brown
Granta
020 7704 9776
www.granta.com
4pa. Owner: Granta Publications.
Editor: Ian Jack
Green Futures
020 7324 3660
www.greenfutures.org.uk
Bi-monthly. Owner: Forum for the
Future. Editor: Martin Wright
The House Magazine
020 7091 7530
www.epolitix.com
Weekly. Owner: Dods Parliamentary
Communications.
Editor: Sir Patrick Cormack
Impact International
020 7263 1417
www.impact-magazine.com
Monthly. Owner: News and Media.
Editor: Ahmad Irfan
Index on Censorship
020 7278 2313
www.indexoncensorship.org
4pa. Owner: Taylor & Francis.
Editor: Judith Bidal-Hall
The Liberty Newsletter
020 7403 3888
www.liberty-human-rights.org.uk
4pa. Owner: Liberty, The National
Council for Civil Liberties.
Editor: Zoe Gillard
Middle East Expatriate
020 8943 3630
www.middleeastexpatonline.com
Monthly. Owner: Al Hilal Publishing
& Marketing Group.
Editor: Babu Kalyanpur

New African
020 7713 7711
www.africasia.com
Monthly. Owner: IC Publications.
Editor: Baffour Ankomah
New Internationalist
01865 811400
www.newint.org
Monthly.
Editorial contact: David Ransom
New Statesman
020 7730 3444
www.newstatesman.com
Weekly. Editor: John Kampfner
News Africa
020 7713 8135
www.newsafrica.net
Monthly. Editor: Moffat Ekoriko
Newsweek
020 7851 9799
www.newsweek.com
Weekly. Editor: Fareed Zakaria
Outrage – magazine of Animal Aid
01732 364546
www.animalaid.co.uk
4pa. Editor: Mark Gold
Parliamentary Brief
020 7381 1611
www.thepolitician.org
Monthly. Editor: Roderick Crawford
Party Politics
020 7324 8500
www.sagepub.co.uk
6pa. Owner: Sage Publications.
Editor: Lucy Robinson
Private Eye
020 7437 4017
www.private-eye.co.uk
Fortnightly. Owner: Pressdram.
Editor: Ian Hislop
Prospect
020 7255 1281
www.prospect-magazine.co.uk
Monthly. Owner: Prospect Publishing.
Editor: David Goodhart
Red Pepper
020 7281 7024
www.redpepper.org.uk
Monthly. Owner: Socialist Newspaper
(Publications).
Editor: Hilary Wainwright
Report
020 7930 6441
www.askatl.org.uk
10pa. Owner: Association of Teachers
and Lecturers. Editor: Heather Pinnell
SchNEWS
01273 685913
www.schnews.org.uk
Weekly. Editor: Jo Makepeace
Socialism Today
020 8988 8773
www.socialismtoday.org
Monthly. Editor: Lynn Walsh
The Socialist
020 8988 8770
www.socialistparty.org.uk
Weekly. Owner: Eastway Offset.
Editor: Ken Smith

Socialist Review
020 7538 3308
www.socialistreview.org.uk
11pa. Owner: Socialist Workers Party
(Britain). Editor: Peter Morgan

Socialist Worker
020 7538 0828
www.socialistworker.co.uk
Weekly. Owner: Newsfax.
Editor: Chris Bambery

Spectator
020 7405 1706
www.spectator.co.uk
Weekly. Editor: Boris Johnson

The Sticks Magazine
01462 486810
www.the-sticks.com
Monthly. Owner: The Plain English
Publishing Company.
Editor: John Boston

Time
020 7499 4080
www.time.com
Weekly. Owner: Time.
Editor: James Geary

Tribune
020 7433 6410
www.tribuneweb.co.uk
Weekly. Editor: Chris McLaughlin

Unite
01582 663880
www.pensioneronline.com
8pa. Owner: National Federation
of Royal Mail and BT Pensioners.
Editor: Lee Wilson

The Week
020 7907 6000
www.theweek.co.uk
Weekly. Owner: Dennis.
Editor: Jeremy O'Grady

The World Today
020 7957 5712
www.theworldtoday.org
Monthly. Owner: The Royal Institute
of International Affairs.
Editor: Graham Walker

WWF News
01483 426444
www.wwf.org.uk
Quarterly. Owner: WWF.
Editor: Guy Jowett

Food & drink

BBC Good Food
020 8433 3342
www.bbcmagazines.com/goodfood
Monthly. Owner: BBC Worldwide.
Editor: Gillian Carter

Decanter
020 7471 2010
www.decanter.com
Monthly. Owner: IPC Media.
Editor: Amy Wislocki

Delicious
020 7775 7757
www.deliciousmagazine.co.uk
Monthly. Owner: Seven Publishing.
Editor: Mitzie Wilson

Easy Cook
020 8433 2000
www.bbcmagazines.com
4pa. Owner: BBC Worldwide.
Editor: Sara Buenfeld

Food & Travel
020 8332 9090
www.fox-publishing.com
Monthly. Owner: Green Pea Publishing.
Editor: Laura Tennant

Food Chain
01603 274130
www.foodchain-magazine.com
Bi-monthly. Owner: Schofield
Publishing. Editor: Libbie Hammond

Foodie Magazine
01527 61122
www.thefoodie.co.uk/magazine.php
Monthly. Owner: CW Corporate
Communications.
Editor: Alison Davison

Italian Wines & Spirits
020 8458 4860
www.iwines.it
Website updated monthly.
Editor: Pino Khail

Olive
020 8433 1389
www.olivemagazine.co.uk
Monthly. Owner: BBC Worldwide.
Editor: Christine Hayes

Sainsbury's Magazine
020 7633 0266
www.sainsburysmagazine.co.uk
Monthly. Owner: New Crane Publishing.
Editor: Sue Robinson

Somerfield Magazine
0117 989 7808
www.somerfield.co.uk
13pa. Owner: Rare Publishing.
Editor: Hannah Smith

The Vegetarian
0161 925 2000
www.vegsoc.org
4pa. Owner: The Vegetarian Society of
the United Kingdom.
Editor: Jane Bowler

Waitrose Food Illustrated
020 7565 3000
www.jbcp.co.uk
Monthly. Owner: John Brown Publishing
Group. Editor: William Sitwell

What's Brewing
01727 867201
www.camra.org.uk
Monthly. Owner: Camra.
Editor: Ted Bruning

Whisky Magazine
01603 633808
www.whiskymag.com
8pa. Owner: Paragraph Publishing.
Editor: Dominic Roskrow

Wine
020 7549 2567
www.wineint.com
Monthly. Owner: Quest Magazines &
Events. Editor: Catharine Lowe

Your M&S Magazine
020 7747 0700
www.redwoodgroup.net
4pa. Owner: Redwood.
Editor: Diane Kenwood

Gay and lesbian

▶▶ See page 119

General interest

American in Britain
020 8661 0186
www.americaninbritain.co.uk/
4pa. Owner: The American Hour.
Editor: Helen Elliott

Another Magazine
020 7336 0766
www.anothermag.com
2pa. Owner: Dazed Group.
Editor: Jefferson Hack

Asian Image
01254 298263
www.asianimage.co.uk
Monthly. Owner: Newsquest.
Editor: Shuiab Khan

Astronomy Now
01903 266165
www.astronomynow.com
Monthly. Owner: Pole Star Publications.
Editor: Stuart Clark

BBC History Magazine
0117 927 9009
www.bbchistorymagazine.com
Monthly. Owner: Origin Publishing.
Editor: Greg Neale

Brighton & Hove Life
01903 604209
www.archantlife.co.uk
Monthly. Owner: Archant.
Editor: Jonathan Keeble

Cambridge Agenda
01223 309224
www.thecambridgeagenda.co.uk
Monthly. Owner: Life Publishing.
Editor: Nick Jordan

Cambridgeshire Life
01799 544273
www.archantlife.co.uk
Monthly. Owner: Archant.
Editor: Robyn Bechelet

Cheshire Life
01772 722022
www.archantlife.co.uk
Monthly. Owner: Archant.
Editor: Patrick O'Neill

Choice
01733 555123
www.choicemag.co.uk
Monthly. Editor: Norman Wright

Contemporary
020 7740 1704
www.contemporary-magazine.com
Monthly. Owner: Art 21.
Editor: Michele Rebecchi

Cornwall Life
01803 860910
www.archantlife.co.uk
Monthly. Owner: Archant.
Publisher: Anita Newcombe

Cotswold Life
01242 216050
www.archantlife.co.uk
Monthly. Owner: Archant.
Publisher: Peter Waters

Dazed & Confused
020 7336 0766
www.confused.co.uk
Monthly. Owner: Dazed Group.
Editor: Callum McGeoch

Der Spiegel
020 8605 3893
www.spiegel.de
Weekly. Editor: Stefan Aust

Devon Life
01803 860928
www.archantlife.co.uk
Monthly. Owner: Archant.
Editor: Jan Barwick

Dorset
01305 211840
www.archantlife.co.uk
Monthly. Owner: Archant.
Editor: Bridget Swann

DV8
01202 388388
www.dv8online.co.uk
Monthly. Editor: Helen Mayson

EDP Norfolk Magazine
01603 772469
www.EDP24.co.uk
Monthly. Owner: Archant.
Editor: Carolyn Bowden

Epicurean Life
020 7376 5959
www.epicureanlife.co.uk
4pa. Editor: Azzy Asghar

Essex Life & Countryside
01799 544273
www.archant.co.uk
Monthly. Owner: Archant.
Editor: Robyn Bechelet

Expression
01392 263052
www.exeter.ac.uk/alumni
2pa. Owner: University of Exeter Alumni
Network. Editor: Karen Lippoldt

Focus Magazine
0117 927 9009
www.focus.com
Monthly. Owner: Origin Publishing.
Editor: Paul Parsons

Folio
0117 942 8491
www.foliomag.com
Monthly. Owner: Venue Publishing.
Editor: Ali Stevens

Forward
0118 983 8243
www.guidedogs.org.uk
4pa. Editor: Tracey Gurr

Freemasonry Today
01284 754155
www.freemasonrytoday.co.uk
4pa. Editor: Michael Baigent

Fresh Direction
020 7424 0400
www.freshdirection.co.uk
3pa. Owner: Antonville.
Editor: Paul Russell

The Green
020 7792 2626
www.archantlife.co.uk
Monthly. Owner: Archant.
Editor: Sarah Hodgson

The Guide Magazine
020 8297 0809
www.archantlife.co.uk
Monthly. Owner: Archant.
Editor: Lee Cheshire

H&E Naturist
01405 760298
www.henaturist.co.uk
Monthly. Owner: New Freedom
Publications. Editor: Sara Backhouse

Hampshire Life
01242 216053
www.archantlife.co.uk
Monthly. Owner: Archant.
Publisher: Peter Waters

Harrods
020 7499 9080
2pa. Owner: Condé Nast.
Editor: Nicola Davidson

Harvey Nichols Magazine
020 7747 0700
www.redwoodgroup.net
4pa. Owner: Redwood.
Editor: Deborah Bee

Hertfordshire Life
01799 544273
www.archantlife.co.uk
Monthly. Owner: Archant.
Editor: Robyn Bechelet

The Hill
020 7792 2626
www.archantlife.co.uk
Monthly. Owner: Archant.
Editor: Jane Turney

History Today
020 7534 8000
www.historytoday.com
Monthly. Owner: History Today.
Editor: Peter Furtado

Hot Press
00 353 1 241 1500
www.hotpress.com
Fortnightly. Owner: Osnovina.
Editor: Niall Stokes

Hotline (Virgin Trains)
020 7306 0304
www.therivergroup.co.uk
Quarterly. Owner: River Publishing.
Editor: Rod Stanley

i-D
020 7490 9710
www.i-dmagazine.co.uk
Monthly. Editor: Glenn Waldron

Illustrated London News
020 7805 5555
www.ilng.co.uk
Bi-annual. Owner: Illustrated London
News. Editor: Alison Booth

The Insight
01273 245956
www.theinsight.co.uk
Monthly. Owner: The Insight.
Editor: Nic Compton

Kent Life
01622 762818
www.archantlife.co.uk
Monthly. Owner: Archant.
Editor: Sarah Sturt

Kindred Spirit
01803 866686
www.kindredspirit.co.uk
6pa. Editor: Richard Beaumont

Lancashire Life
01772 722022
www.archantlife.co.uk
Monthly. Owner: Archant.
Editor: Anthony Skinner

Let's Talk! Norfolk
01603 772413
www.EDP24.co.uk
Monthly. Owner: Archant.
Editor: Cathy Brown

Let's Talk! Suffolk
01473 324795
www.archant.co.uk
Monthly. Owner: Archant.
Editor: Anne Gould

The Lifeboat
01202 662254
www.rnli.org.uk
4pa. Owner: RNLI. Editor: Liz Cook

Limited Edition
01689 885661
www.thisisedition.co.uk
Monthly. Owner: Newsquest.
Editor: Andrew Parkes

Living South
020 7223 0022
www.archant.co.uk
Monthly. Owner: Archant.
Editor: Pendle Harte

Magnet – The Village Communicator
01825 732796
www.magnetpublications.com
Monthly. Editor: Mary Hillyar

Majesty
020 7436 4006
www.majestymagazine.com
Monthly. Owner: Rex Publications.
Editor-in-chief: Ingrid Seward

Mayfair and St James's Life
020 7344 9121
www.mayfairlife.co.uk
Monthly. Editor: Stephen Goringe

MQ – Masonic Quarterly
020 7793 4140
www.mqmagazine.co.uk
Quarterly. Owner: Grand Lodge
Publications. Editor: John Jackson

New Humanist
020 7436 1151
www.newhumanist.org.uk
Bi-monthly. Owner: Rationalist Press
Association. Editor: Frank Jordans

Nexus
01342 322854
www.nexusmagazine.com
Bi-monthly. Editor: Duncan Roads

Norfolk Roots
01603 772198
www.norfolkroots24.co.uk
Bi Monthly. Owner: Archant.
Editor: Robin Vyrnwy-Pierce

North Magazine
020 7250 0750
Monthly. Owner: Metropolis Publishing.
Editor: Mark Kebble

NW
020 7792 2626
www.archantlife.co.uk
Monthly. Owner: Archant.
Editor: Cathy Levy

Occasions
020 7650 2000
www.occasions-mag.com
*4pa. Owner: Ethnic Media Group.
Editor: Sheri Mill*

The Oldie
020 7436 8801
www.theoldie.co.uk
*Monthly. Owner: Oldie Publications.
Editor: Richard Ingrams*

Oxfordshire Life
01242 216050
www.archantlife.co.uk
*Monthly. Owner: Archant.
Publisher: Peter Waters*

Password
020 7261 9878
Bi-monthly. Editor: Alistair Gordon

Perth Life
01738 567700
Monthly. Editor: Stephen Lavery

Platform
0115 848 1510
www.su.ntu.ac.uk
      /your-union/exec/platform.php
*Fortnightly. Owner: Nottingham Trent
Students Union. Editor: Loay El Hady*

Quicksilver Magazine
020 7747 9390
www.quicksilvermagazine.co.uk
*Bi-monthly. Owner: PSP
Communications. Editor: Alex Johnson*

Reader's Digest
020 7715 8000
www.readersdigest.co.uk
*Monthly. Owner: Reader's Digest.
Editor: Katherine Walker*

Reform
020 7916 8630
www.urc.org.uk
*11pa. Owner: United Reformed Church.
Editor: David Lawrence*

The Resident
020 7384 9124
www.theresident.co.uk
*Monthly. Owner: Metropolis Publishing.
Editor: Amanda Constance*

Royal Berkshire Life
01242 216050
www.archantlife.co.uk
*Monthly. Owner: Archant.
Publisher: Peter Waters*

Royalty
020 8201 9978
www.royalty-magazine.com
*Monthly. Owner: Sena Julia Publicatus.
Editor: M Houston*

Salvationist
020 7367 4890
www.salvationarmy.org.uk/salvationist
*Weekly. Owner: Salvation Army.
Editor: Dean Pallant*

Scots Magazine
01382 223131
www.scotsmagazine.com
*Monthly. Owner: DC Thomson.
Editor: John Methven*

Sixer
0114 250 6300
www.northernlifestyle.com
*Monthly. Owner: Regional Magazine
Company. Editor: Chris Wilson*

Somerset Life
01803 860910
www.archantlife.co.uk
*Monthly. Owner: Archant.
Editor: Nicki Lukehurst*

The Spark
0117 914 3434
www.thespark.co.uk
4pa. Editor: John Dawson

Surrey Life
01737 247188
www.archantlife.co.uk
*Monthly. Owner: Archant.
Editor: Katherine Simmons*

Sussex Life
01903 604209
www.archantlife.co.uk
*Monthly. Owner: Archant.
Editor: Jonathan Keeble*

SW
020 7223 0022
www.archantlife.co.uk
*Monthly. Owner: Archant.
Editor: Sarah Hodgson*

Tank
020 7434 0110
www.tankmagazine.com
*Quarterly. Owner: Tank Publications.
Editor: Masoud Golsorkhi*

Toni & Guy
020 7462 7777
www.publicis-blueprint.co.uk
*4pa. Owner: Publicis Blueprint.
Editor: Scarlett Brady*

Town & Country News
01692 582287
*Monthly. Owner: Leisure Publishing.
Editor: Laurence Watts*

Trafford Magazine
020 7387 9888
www.babersmith.co.uk
*2pa. Owner: Baber Smith.
Editor: Debbie Hyams*

The Village
020 7792 2626
www.archantlife.co.uk
*Monthly. Owner: Archant.
Editor: Jane Turney*

The Visitor
01963 351256
Monthly. Editor: Helen Dunion

Wavelength
01872 247546
www.wavelengthmag.co.uk
*Monthly. Owner: Cornwall & Devon
Media. Editor: Steve Bough*

Weekly News
01382 223131
www.dcthomson.co.uk
*Weekly. Owner: DC Thomson.
Editor: Dave Burness*

Which?
020 7770 7373
www.which.co.uk
*Monthly. Owner: Which?
Editor: Malcolm Coles*

**The World of Yachts & Boats
(pan-Arab)**
020 7328 3334
www.worldofyachts.com
*Bi-monthly. Owner: The World of
Yachts & Boats. Editor: Nabil Farhat*

Yorkshire Life
01772 722022
www.archantlife.co.uk
*Monthly. Owner: Archant.
Editor: Esther Leach*

You Can! Magazine
01242 544905
*3pa. Owner: Independent News & Media
(UK). Editor: Anthony McClaran*

Your Family Tree
01225 442244
www.yourfamilytreemag.co.uk
*13pa. Owner: Future.
Editor: Garrick Webster*

Yours
01733 264666
www.emap.com
*Monthly. Owner: Emap.
Editor: Valerie McConnell*

Home and garden

25 Beautiful Gardens
020 7261 5015
www.ipcmedia.com
*Bi-annual. Owner: IPC Media.
Editor: John Smigielski*

25 Beautiful Homes
020 7261 5015
www.ipcmedia.com
*Monthly. Owner: IPC Media.
Editor: John Smigielski*

25 Beautiful Kitchens
020 7261 5015
www.ipcmedia.com
*Bi-monthly. Owner: IPC Media.
Editor: John Smigielski*

Amateur Gardening
01202 440840
www.ipcmedia.com
*Weekly. Owner: IPC Media.
Editor: Tim Rumball*

BBC Gardeners' World
020 8433 3959
www.gardenersworld.com
*Monthly. Owner: BBC Worldwide.
Editor: Adam Pasco*

BBC Good Homes
0870 444 2607
www.bbcmagazines.com
      /goodhomes
*Monthly. Owner: BBC Worldwide.
Editor: Lisa Allen*

BBC Homes & Antiques
020 8433 3483
www.bbcmagazines.com
      /homesandantiques
*Monthly. Owner: BBC Worldwide.
Editor: Mary Carroll*

Country Homes & Interiors
020 7261 6434
www.ipcmedia.com
*Monthly. Owner: IPC Media.
Editor: Rhoda Parry*

Country Living
020 7439 5000
www.countryliving.co.uk
*Monthly. Owner: National Magazine
Company. Editor: Susy Smith*

Country Market
0870 162 9999
www.country-mkt.co.uk
Monthly. Editor: David Somerville

Easy Gardening
020 8433 2950
www.bbcmagazines.com
/easygardening
10pa. Owner: BBC Worldwide.
Editor: Ceri Thomas

Elle Decoration
020 7150 7000
www.hf-uk.com
Monthly. Owner: Hachette Filipacchi UK.
Editor: Michelle Ogunadehin

The English Garden
020 7751 4800
www.theenglishgarden.co.uk
Monthly. Owner: Archant.
Editor: Janine Wookey

The English Home
020 7751 4800
www.theenglishhome.co.uk
Monthly. Owner: Archant.
Editor: Charlotte Coward-Williams

The Essential Kitchen, Bathroom & Bedroom Magazine
01206 851117
www.essentialpublishing.co.uk
Monthly. Owner: Essential Publishing.
Acting editor: Natalie Kelly

Essential Water Garden
01206 505977
www.essentialwatergarden.co.uk
10pa. Owner: Aceville Publications.
Editor: Georgina Wroe

Fabric
020 7747 0700
www.redwoodgroup.net
Monthly. Owner: Redwood.
Editor: Steven Short

The Garden
01733 775775
www.rhs.org.uk
Monthly. Owner: RHS Publications.
Editor: Ian Hodgson

Garden Answers
01733 264666
www.emap.com
Monthly. Owner: Emap.
Editor: Kevin Wilmott

Garden News
01733 264666
www.emap.com
Weekly. Owner: Emap.
Editor: Sarah Page

Gardening Which?
020 7770 7564
www.which.co.uk/gardeningwhich
10pa. Owner: Which? Editor: Julia Bolton

Gardens Illustrated
0870 444 2611
www.bbcmagazines
.com/gardensillustrated
10pa. Owner: BBC Worldwide.
Editor: Clare Foster

Gardens Monthly
01689 887200
www.highburyleisure.co.uk
Monthly. Owner: Highbury House.
Editor: Helen Griffin

Good Housekeeping
020 7439 5000
www.goodhousekeeping.co.uk
Monthly. Owner: National Magazine Company. Editor: Lindsay Nicholson

Home & Country
020 7384 2194
www.womens-institute.co.uk
Monthly. Owner: Women's Institute.
Editor: Joanna Remmer

Home Efficiency
01753 884216
www.4ecotips.com
Bi-monthly. Owner: Bucks House Publications. Editor: Andrew Leech

Home Furnishing News (HFN)
020 7240 0420
www.hfnmag.com
Weekly. Owner: Fairchild.
Editor: Warren Shoulberg

Home Life Magazine
028 3832 4006
Monthly. Editor: M Kinsella

Home View
01277 366134
www.homeviewpropertymagazine.com
Bi-monthly. Editor: Garry Clarke

Homebase Ideas
020 7462 7777
www.publicis-blueprint.co.uk
Quarterly. Owner: Publicis Blueprint.
Editor: Ward Hellewell

Homebuilding & Renovating
01527 834400
www.centaur.co.uk
Monthly. Owner: Centaur.
Editor: Jason Orme

Homes & Gardens
020 7261 5678
www.homesandgardens.com
Monthly. Owner: IPC Media.
Editor: Deborah Barker

Homes & Interiors Scotland
0141 221 5559
www.homesandinteriorsscotland.com
Bi-monthly. Owner: International Magazines. Editor: Sandra Colamartino

Homes Overseas
020 7002 8300
www.homesoverseas.co.uk
Monthly. Owner: Blendon Communications. Editor: Mike Hayes

Homes Review
01206 506249
Monthly. Owner: MS Publications

HomeStyle
01206 851117
www.essentialpublishing.co.uk
Monthly. Owner: Essential Publishing.
Editor: Sarah Gallaher

House & Garden
020 7499 9080
www.houseandgarden.co.uk
Monthly. Owner: Condé Nast.
Editor: Susan Crewe

House Beautiful
020 7439 5000
www.housebeautiful.co.uk
Monthly. Owner: National Magazine Company. Editor: Kerryn Harper

Ideal Home
020 7261 6474
www.ipcmedia.com
Monthly. Owner: IPC Media.
Editor: Susan Rose

International Homes
01245 358877
www.international-homes.com
Monthly. Editor: Jill Keene

Ireland's Homes Interiors & Living
028 9147 3979
Monthly. Editor: Judith Robinson

KBB – Kitchens, Bedrooms & Bathrooms Magazine
020 8515 2000
www.dmgworldmedia.com
Monthly. Owner: DMG World Media.
Editor: Rosalind Anderson

Key
020 7494 3155
www.21carrot.com
2pa. Owner: 21 Carrot.
Editor: Clare Weatherall

Livingetc
020 7261 6603
www.ipcmedia.com
Monthly. Owner: IPC Media.
Editor: Suzanne Imre

Location, Location, Location
01737 786853
www.brooklandsgroup.com
Monthly. Owner: Brooklands Media.
Editor: Martyn Hocking

Period House
01206 851117
www.essentialpublishing.co.uk
Monthly. Owner: Essential Publishing.
Editor: Charlotte Barber

Period Ideas
01206 505976
www.periodideas.com
Monthly. Owner: Aceville Publications.
Editor: Jeannine McAndrew

Period Living & Traditional Homes
020 7182 8775
www.emap.com
Monthly. Owner: Emap.
Editor: Sharon Parsons

Real Homes Magazine
020 7150 7000
www.hhc.co.uk
Monthly. Owner: Hachette Filipacchi.
Editor: Karen Williams

Renovations
020 7384 1985
4pa. Editor: Liz Cowley

Scottish Home & Country
0131 225 1724
www.swri.org.uk
Monthly. Owner: Scottish Women's Rural Institutes. Editor: Liz Ferguson

Traditional Homes & Interiors
01795 599191
www.cplmedia.co.uk
10pa. Owner: CPL Media.
Editor: Vicki Watson

Wallpaper
020 7322 1592
www.wallpaper.com
Monthly. Owner: IPC Media.
Editor: Jeremy Langmead

What House?
020 7939 9888
www.whathouse.co.uk
*Monthly. Owner: Blendon
Communications. Editor: Lisa Isaacs*

World of Interiors
020 7499 9080
www.worldofinteriors.co.uk
*Monthly. Owner: Condé Nast.
Editor: Rupert Thomas*

Your Home
01206 851117
www.essentialpublishing.co.uk
*Monthly. Owner: Essential Publishing.
Editor: Hayley Chilver*

Your New Home
01732 878800
www.yournewhome.co.uk
*Bi-monthly. Owner: New Concept Group.
Editor: Karen Keeman*

Leisure

Absolute Horse
01473 731220
www.ahmagazine.com
*Monthly. Owner: PCD Media.
Editor: Sandy Lee*

Aeroplane
020 7261 5849
www.aeroplanemonthly.com
*Monthly. Owner: IPC Media.
Editor: Michael Oakey*

Air Enthusiast
01780 755131
www.airenthusiast.com
*Bi-monthly. Owner: Key Publishing.
Editor: Ken Ellis*

Air Transport World
01628 477775
www.atwonline.com
*Monthly. Owner: Penton Media.
Editor: Perry Flint*

Aircraft Illustrated
01932 266600
www.aircraftillustrated.com
*Monthly. Owner: Ian Allan Publishing.
Editor: Alan Burney*

Airliner World
01780 755131
www.airlinerworld.com
*Monthly. Owner: Key Publishing.
Editor: Tony Dixon*

Animal Life
0870 010 1181
www.rspca.org.uk
*Quarterly. Owner: RSPCA.
Editor: Amanda Bailey*

Antique Collecting
01394 389950
www.antique-acc.com
*10pa. Owner: Antique Collectors Club.
Editor: Susan Wilson*

Antique Dealer & Collectors Guide
020 8691 4820
www.antiquecollectorsguide.co.uk
*Bi-monthly. Owner: Status Court.
Editor: Philip Bartlam*

At Home in Cardiff Bay
029 2045 0532
*4pa. Owner: City Publications.
Editor: Andy Meredith*

Aviation News
01424 720477
www.aviation-news.co.uk
*Monthly. Owner: HPC Publishing.
Editor: Barry Wheeler*

Aviation Week & Space Technology
020 7434 3126
www.aviationnow.com
*Weekly. Owner: McGraw-Hill.
Editor-in-chief: Anthony Velocci;
London bureau chief: Douglas Barrie*

Award Journal
01753 727470
www.theaward.org
3pa. Editor: Dave Wood

BBC Wildlife Magazine
0117 927 9009
www.bbcwildlifemagazine.com
*Monthly. Publisher: Origin Publishing.
Editor: Sophie Stafford*

Bird Keeper
020 7261 6201
www.ipcmedia.com
*Monthly. Owner: IPC Media.
Editor: Donald Taylor*

Bird Life
01767 680551
www.rspb.org.uk
*Bi-monthly. Owner: RSPB.
Editor: Derek Niemann*

Birds
01767 680551
www.rspb.org.uk
4pa. Owner: RSPB. Editor: Rob Hume

Birdwatch
020 8881 0550
www.birdwatch.co.uk
*Monthly. Owner: Solo Publishing.
Editor: Dominic Mitchell*

Bird Watching
01733 264666
www.emap.com
*Monthly. Owner: Emap.
Editor: David Cromack*

BMFA News
0116 244 0028
www.bmfa.org/news
Bi-monthly. Editor: Eric Clark

Boat International
020 8547 2662
www.boatinternational.com
*Monthly. Owner: Edisea.
Editor: Amanda McCracken*

Boats & Yachts for Sale
01243 533394
www.boats-for-sale.com
*Monthly. Owner: Marine Trader Media.
Editor: Sue Milne*

Book & Magazine Collector
0870 732 8080
13pa. Editor: Jonathan Scott

Bridge Magazine
020 7388 2404
www.bridgemagazine.co.uk
Monthly. Editor: Mark Horton

British Birds
01580 882039
www.britishbirds.co.uk
Monthly. Editor: Roger Riddington

British Horse
0870 120 2244
www.bhs.org.uk
*Bi-monthly. Owner: The British Horse
Society. Editor: David Prince*

British Naturism
01604 620361
www.british-naturism.org.uk
4pa. Editor: Tracey Major

Budgerigar World
01678 520262
*Monthly. Owner: County Press.
Editor: G Evans*

Buy a Boat (for under £20,000)
01243 533394
www.boats-for-sale.com
*Monthly. Owner: Marine Trader Media.
Editor: Sue Milne*

Cage & Aviary Birds
020 7261 6201
www.ipcmedia.com
*Weekly. Owner: IPC Media.
Editor: Donald Taylor*

Camping & Caravanning
024 7647 5270
www.campingandcaravanningclub
.co.uk
*Monthly. Owner: The Camping &
Caravanning Club. Editor: Nick Harding*

Camping Magazine
01778 391000
www.campingmagazine.co.uk
*10pa. Owner: Warners.
Editor: Mike Cowton*

Canal & Riverboat
01603 708930
www.canalandriverboat.com
*Monthly. Owner: Morgan Publications.
Editor: Chris Cattrall*

Canal Boat
0118 977 1677
www.canalboatmagazine.com
*Monthly. Owner: Archant.
Editor: Emrhys Barrell*

Caravan Club Magazine
01342 336804
www.caravanclub.co.uk
*Monthly. Owner: The Caravan Club.
Editor: Barry Williams*

Caravan Magazine
020 8726 8249
www.ipcmedia.com
*Monthly. Owner: IPC Media.
Editor: Steve Rowe*

The Cat
0870 209 9099
www.cats.org.uk
*4pa. Owner: Cats Protection.
Editor: Clare Jeater*

Cat World
01903 884988
www.catworld.co.uk
*Monthly. Owner: Ashdown.co.uk.
Editor: Jo Rothery*

Chess
020 7388 2404
www.chess.co.uk
Monthly. Editor: Jimmy Adams

Church Music Quarterly
01306 872800
www.rscm.com
*4pa. Owner: Royal School of Church
Music. Editor: Esther Jones*

Classic Boat
020 8726 8130
www.ipcmedia.com
Monthly. Owner: IPC Media.
Editor: Dan Houston

Club News
01322 311600
www.swanpublishing.co.uk
6pa. Owner: Swan Publishing.
Editor: David Tickner

Coast
020 8547 9702
www.coastmagazine.co.uk
Monthly. Editor: Katie Ebben

Coin News
01404 46972
www.tokenpublishing.com
Monthly. Owner: Token Publishing.
Editor: John Mussell

Coin Yearbook
01404 46972
www.tokenpublishing.com
Yearly. Owner: Token Publishing.
Editor: John Mussell

Collect it!
01206 851117
www.collectit.info
Monthly. Owner: Essential Publishing.
Editor: Jo Bates

Collections
020 7870 9000
www.bostonhannah.co.uk
3pa. Owner: Boston Hannah
International. Editor: Charles Ford

Collector
020 8740 7020
www.artefact.co.uk
Bi-monthly. Owner: Barrington
Publications. Editor: Paul Hooper

Collectors Gazette
01778 391000
www.collectorsgazette.com
Monthly. Owner: Warners.
Editor: Denise Burrows

Companions Magazine
01952 290999
www.pdsa.org.uk
4pa. Owner: PDSA. Editor: Clare Evans

Continental Modeller
01297 20580
www.peco-uk.com
Monthly. Owner: Peco Publications &
Publicity. Editor: Andrew Burnham

Country Illustrated
020 7291 8609
www.countryclubuk.com
Monthly. Owner: St Martin's Magazines.
Editor: Julie Spencer

Country Life
020 7261 6400
www.countrylife.co.uk
Weekly. Owner: IPC Media.
Editor: Clive Aslet

Country Market
0870 162 9999
www.country-mkt.co.uk
Monthly. Editor: David Somerville

Country Smallholding
01392 888481
www.countrysmallholding.com
Monthly. Owner: Archant.
Editor: Diane Cowgill

Country Walking
01733 264666
www.emap.com
Monthly. Owner: Emap.
Editor: Jonathan Manning

The Countryman
01756 701033
www.countrymanmagazine.co.uk
Monthly. Owner: Country Publications.
Editor: Bill Taylor

The Countryman's Weekly
01822 855281
www.countrymansweekly.com
Weekly. Owner: Countrywide Periodical
Publishing. Editor: David Venner

Countryside La Vie
0116 212 2555
www.countryside-lavie.com
Bi-monthly. Editor: Marlene Bowley

Crafts
020 7806 2538
www.craftscouncil.org.uk
Bi-monthly. Owner: Crafts Council.
Editor: Geraldine Rudge

Crafts Beautiful
01206 505989
www.crafts-beautiful.com
Monthly. Owner: Aceville Publications.
Editor: Natasha Reed

Crafty Carper
0114 258 0812
www.anglingpublications.co.uk
Monthly. Owner: Angling Publications.
Editorial director: Martin Ford

Cross Stitch Collection
01225 442244
www.crossstitchcollection.co.uk
13pa. Owner: Future. Editor: Cathy Lewis

Cross Stitcher
01225 442244
www.cross-stitchermagazine.co.uk
13pa. Owner: Future.
Editor: Cathy Lewis

Cumbria
01756 701033
www.dalesman.co.uk
Monthly. Owner: Country Publications.
Editor: Terry Fletcher

Dalesman
01756 701033
www.dalesman.co.uk
Monthly. Owner: Country Publications.
Editor: Terry Fletcher

Dartmoor Magazine
01822 614899
www.dartmoormagazine.co.uk
4pa. Owner: Key Publications.
Editor: Elisabeth Stanbrook

Dog World
01233 621877
www.dogworld.co.uk
Weekly. Editor: Stuart Baillie

Dogs Today
01276 858880
www.dogstodaymagazine.co.uk
Monthly. Editor: Beverley Cuddy

Doll Magazine
01903 884988
www.dollmagazine.com
Monthly. Owner: Ashdown.co.uk.
Editor: Emma Brown

Dolls House World
01903 884988
www.dollshouseworld.com
Monthly. Owner: Ashdown.co.uk.
Editor: Laura Quiggan

Engineering in Miniature
01926 614101
www.engineeringinminiature.co.uk
Monthly. Owner: Tee Publishing.
Editor: CL Deith

EOS Magazine
01869 331741
www.eos-magazine.com
4pa. Owner: Robert Scott Associates.
Editor: Angela August

EQ
01986 782368
www.feedmark.com
4pa. Owner: Feedmark UK.
Editorial contact: Jo Gregory

ESP Magazine
01733 253477
www.espmag.co.uk
Monthly. Editor: Sharon McAllister

Evergreen
01242 537900
www.thisengland.co.uk
4pa. Owner: This England.
Editor: Roy Faiers

Everyday Practical Electronics
01202 873872
www.epemag.co.uk
Monthly. Owner: Wimborne Publishing.
Editor: Mike Kenward

Families East
020 8694 8694
www.familiesonline.co.uk
Bi-monthly. Owner: Families Magazines.
Editor: Mewe Mechese

Families Edinburgh
0131 624 0049
www.familiesonline.co.uk
Bi-monthly. Owner: Families Magazines.
Editor: Louise Armour

Families Liverpool
0151 522 9361
www.familiesonline.co.uk
Bi-monthly. Owner: Families Magazines.
Editor: Jennifer-Paige Deenihan

Families North
020 7794 5690
www.familiesonline.co.uk
Bi-monthly. Owner: Families Magazines.
Editor: Cathy Youd

Families Together
01903 821082
www.cfnetwork.co.uk
3pa. Owner: Christian Publishing and
Outreach. Editor: Russ Bravo

Families Upon Thames
01932 254584
www.familiesonline.co.uk
Bi-monthly. Owner: Families Magazines.
Editor: Francis Loates

The Flower Arranger
020 8748 2673
www.theflowerarrangermagazine
.co.uk
4pa. Owner: The National Association
of Flower Arrangement Societies
(NAFAS). Editor: Judith Blacklock

Flyer
01225 481440
www.flyer.co.uk
13pa. Owner: Seager Publishing.
Editor: Philip Whiteman

FlyPast
01780 755131
www.flypast.com
13pa. Owner: Key Publishing.
Editor: Ken Ellis

Fortean Times
020 7907 6000
www.forteantimes.com
13pa. Owner: Dennis.
Editor: David Sutton

Galleries
020 8740 7020
www.galleries.co.uk
Monthly. Owner: Barrington
Publications. Editor: Andrew Aitken

Gibbons Stamp Monthly
01425 472363
www.gibbonsstampmonthly.com
Monthly. Owner: Stanley Gibbons
Publications. Editor: Hugh Jefferies

Good Woodworking
01225 442244
www.futurenet.com
13pa. Owner: Future. Editor: Nick Gibbs

Goodtimes
020 8764 3344
www.arp050.org.uk
6pa. Owner: Association of Retired and
Persons Over 50. Editor: Susi Rogol

Goodwood Magazine
01243 755000
www.goodwood.co.uk
Yearly. Owner: Red Giant Projects.
Editor: Kathryn Bellamy

The Great Outdoors
0141 302 7700
www.newsquest.co.uk
Monthly. Owner: Newsquest.
Editor: Cameron McNaish

Gulliver's World
01228 404350
www.lilliputlane.co.uk
4pa. Owner: Enesco.
Editor: Lynne Thompson

Gun Mart
01702 479884
www.gunmart.net
Monthly. Owner: Aceville Publications.
Editor: Pat Farey

Hali
020 7970 4000
www.hali.co.uk
6pa. Owner: Centaur. Editor: Ben Evans

Heritage Magazine
020 7751 4800
www.heritagemagazine.co.uk
Bi-monthly. Owner: Archant.
Editor: Penelope Rance

Hoofprint
01565 872107
Monthly. Owner: Penn House Publishing.
Editor: Barry Hook

Horoscope
01202 873872
www.horoscope.co.uk
Monthly. Owner: Wimborne Publishing.
Editor: Mike Kenward

Horse
020 7261 5867
www.ipcmedia.com
Monthly. Owner: IPC Media.
Editor: Amanda Williams

Horse & Hound
020 7261 6453
www.horseandhound.co.uk
Weekly. Owner: IPC Media.
Editor: Lucy Higginson

Horse & Rider
01428 601020
www.horseandridermagazine.co.uk
Monthly. Owner: DJ Murphy Publishers.
Editor: Alison Bridge

International Boat Industry
020 8726 8134
www.ibinews.com
Monthly. Owner: IPC Media.
Editor: Ed Slack

K9 Magazine
0870 011 4115
www.k9magazine.com
Quarterly. Owner: K9 Media Solutions.
Editor: Ryan O'Meara

Kew
020 8332 5906
www.rbgkew.org.uk
4pa. Editor: Sue Seddon

Koi Carp
01202 735090
www.koi-carp.com
Monthly. Owner: Freestyle Publications.
Editor: Louise Harper

Lakeland Walker
01778 391000
www.warnersgroup.co.uk
Bi-monthly. Owner: Warners Group.
Editor: Michael Cowton

Legion – Royal British Legion
020 7880 7666
www.britishlegion.org.uk
Bi-monthly. Owner: Redactive
Publishing. Editor: Claire Townley-Jones

Leisure Painter
01580 763315
www.leisurepainter.co.uk
Monthly. Owner: The Artists' Publishing
Company. Editor: Ingrid Lyon

Leisure Scene
01494 888433
www.cssc.co.uk
3pa. Owner: CSSC Sports & Leisure.
Editor: Gemma Thomson

Lifewatch Magazine
020 7449 6363
www.zsl.org
3pa. Owner: Zoological Society of
London. Editor: Debbie Curtis

Marine Modelling International
01684 588500
www.marinemodelmagazine.com
Monthly. Owner: Traplet Publications.
Editor: Chris Jackson

Microlight Flying (The British
Microlight Aircraft Assocation
official magazine)
01524 841010
www.pagefast.co.uk
6pa. Owner: Pagefast.
Editor: David Bremner

Military Illustrated Past & Present
0870 870 2345
www.publishingnews.co.uk
Monthly. Owner: Publishing News.
Editor: Tim Newark

Military in Scale
01684 588500
www.militaryinscale.com
Monthly. Owner: Traplet Publications.
Editor: Spencer Pollard

Military Modelling
01689 887200
www.militarymodelling.com
15pa. Owner: Highbury House.
Editor: Ken Jones

Miniature Wargames
01202 297344
www.miniwargames.com
Monthly. Owner: Pireme Publishing.
Editor: Iain Dickie

Model & Collectors Mart
0121 233 8712
www.modelmart.co.uk
Monthly. Owner: Trinity Publications.
Editor: Dean Shepherd

Model Boats
01525 382847
www.modelboats.co.uk
Monthly. Owner: Highbury House.
Editor: John Cundell

Model Collector
020 8726 8238
www.modelcollector.co.uk
Monthly. Owner: IPC Media.
Editor: Lindsey Amrani

Model Engineer
01689 887200
www.highburyleisure.co.uk
26pa. Owner: Highbury House.
Editor: Mike Chrisp

Model Engineers' Works
01689 887200
www.highburyleisure.co.uk
8pa. Owner: Highbury House.
Editor: David Fenner

Model Helicopter World
01684 588500
www.modelheliworld.com
Monthly. Owner: Traplet Publications.
Editor: Jon Tanner

Motor Boat & Yachting
020 7261 5333
www.ybw.com
Monthly. Owner: IPC Media.
Editor: Hugo Andreae

Motor Boats Monthly
020 7261 7256
www.motorboatsmonthly.com
Monthly. Owner: IPC Media.
Editor: Simon Collis

Motor Caravan Magazine
020 8726 8249
www.motorcaravanmagazine.co.uk
Monthly. Owner: IPC Media.
Editor: Simon Collis

Motor Caravanner
01480 496130
www.motorcaravanners.org.uk
Monthly. Owner: The Motor
Caravanners' Club. Editor: Kate Jones

Motorcaravan & Camping Mart
01778 391000
www.caravanmart.co.uk
11pa. Owner: Warners Group.
Editor: Peter Sharpe
Motorhome Monthly
020 8302 6150
www.stoneleisure.com
Monthly. Owner: Stone Leisure.
Editor: Robert Griffiths
Natural World
01733 264666
www.emap.com
3pa. Owner: Emap. Editor: Rupert Paul
New Stitches
01227 750215
www.newstitches.com
Monthly. Owner: Creative Crafts
Publishing. Editor: Mary Hickmott
Norfolk Afloat
01603 219757
www.archant.co.uk
Bi-Monthly. Owner: Archant.
Editor: John Lawson
Our Dogs
0870 731 6500
www.ourdogs.co.uk
Weekly. Owner: Our Dogs Publishing.
Editor: Anne Williams
Paddles
01202 735090
www.freestyle-group.com
Monthly. Owner: Freestyle Publications.
Editor: Richard Parkin
PaperCraft Inspirations
01225 442244
www.futurenet.com/papercraft
13pa. Owner: Future.
Editor: Jenny Dodd
Park Home & Holiday Caravan
020 8726 8253
www.ipcmedia.com
Monthly. Owner: IPC Media.
Editor: Anne Webb
Patchwork & Quilting
01684 588500
www.pandqmagazine.com
Monthly. Owner: Traplet Publications.
Editor: Di Huck
Paws
020 7627 9293
www.dogshome.org
4pa. Owner: Battersea Dogs Home.
Editor: Helen Tennant
The People's Friend
01382 223131
www.dcthomson.co.uk
Weekly. Owner: DC Thomson.
Editor: Margaret McCoi
Pet Patter
020 7415 7100
www.mediamark.co.uk
Quarterly. Owner: Mediamark
Publishing. Editor: Pip Jones
Pilot
01799 544200
www.pilotweb.co.uk
Monthly. Owner: Archant.
Editor: Dave Calderwood

Popular Crafts
01689 887200
www.popularcrafts.com
13pa. Owner: Highbury House.
Editor: Debbie Moss
Popular Patchwork
01689 887200
www.highburyleisure.co.uk
13pa. Owner: Highbury House.
Editor: Stacey Kerr
Practical Boat Owner
01202 680593
www.pbo.co.uk
Monthly. Owner: IPC Media.
Editor: Sarah Norbury
Practical Caravan
020 8267 5000
www.practicalcaravan.com
Monthly. Owner: Haymarket.
Editor: Carl Rodgerson
Practical Fishkeeping
01733 282764
www.emap.com
Monthly. Owner: Emap.
Editor: Karen Youngs
Practical Wireless
0870 224 7810
www.pwpublishing..uk/pw
Monthly. Owner: PW Publishing.
Editor: Rob Mannion
Practical Woodworking
01689 887200
www.getwoodworking.com
Monthly. Owner: Highbury House.
Editor: Mark Chisholm
Prediction
020 8726 8257
www.predictionmagazine.co.uk
Monthly. Owner: IPC Media.
Editor: Tania Ahsan
Quick & Crafty
01206 505980
www.crafts-beautiful.com
Monthly. Owner: Aceville Publications.
Editor: Lynn Martin
Quick & Easy Cross Stitch
01225 442244
www.futurenet.com
/quickandeasycrossstitch
13pa. Owner: Future.
Editor: Ruth Spolton
RA Magazine
020 7300 5820
www.ramagazine.org.uk
4pa. Owner: Royal Academy of Arts.
Editor: Sarah Greenberg
Racecar Engineering
020 8726 8364
www.racecar-engineering.com
Monthly. Owner: IPC Media.
Editor: Charles Armstrong-Wilson
RadCom
0870 904 7373
www.rsgb.org
Monthly. Owner: Radio Society of
Great Britain. Editor: Alex Kearns
Radio Control Jet International
01684 588500
www.rcjetinternational.com
Bi-monthly. Owner: Traplet Publications.
Editor: Tom Wilkinson

Radio Control Model Flyer
01525 222573
www.modelflyermagazine.com
Monthly. Owner: ADH Publishing.
Editor: Ken Shepherd
Radio Control Model World
01684 588500
www.rcmodelworld.com
Monthly. Owner: Traplet Publications.
Editor: Peter Dawson
Radio Race Car International
01684 588500
www.radioracecar.com
Monthly. Owner: Traplet Publications.
Editor: Chris Deakin
Rail Express
01780 470086
www.railexpress.co.uk
Monthly. Owner: Foursight Publications.
Editor: Philip Sutton
Railway Modeller
01297 20580
www.peco-uk.com
Monthly. Owner: Peco Publications &
Publicity. Editor: John Brewer
Raw Vision
01923 856644
www.rawvision.com
4pa. Editor: John Maizels
RCM & E
01689 887200
www.modelflying.co.uk
Monthly. Owner: Highbury House.
Editor: Graham Ashby
RIB International
01884 266100
www.ribmagazine.com
Bi-monthly.
Editor: Hugo Montgomery-Swan
Routing
01689 887200
www.getwoodworking.com
6pa. Owner: Highbury House.
Editor: Neil Mead
RYA Magazine
023 8060 4100
www.rya.org.uk
Quarterly. Owner: Royal Yachting
Association. Editor: Deborah Cornick
Sailing Today
01489 580836
www.sailingtoday.co.uk
Monthly. Editor: John Goode
Scale Aviation Modeller
0870 733 3373
www.sampublications.com
Monthly. Owner: Sam Publications.
Editor: Neil Robinson
ScrapBook Inspirations
01225 442244
www.myfavouritemagazines.co.uk
13pa. Owner: Future. Editor: Jenny Dixon
Sew Bridal
01243 379009
www.sewbridal.co.uk
Annually. Owner: McCall Butterick &
Vogue. Editor: Julie Watkins
Sewing World
01684 588500
www.sewingworldmagazine.com
Monthly. Owner: Traplet Publications.
Editor: Wendy Gardiner

Sew Today
01243 379009
www.sewdirect.com
10pa. Owner: McCall Butterick & Vogue.
Editor: Julie Watkins

Ships Monthly
01283 542721
www.ipcmedia.com
Monthly. Owner: IPC Media.
Editor: Iain Wakefield

Short Wave Magazine
0870 224 7810
www.pwpublishing..uk/swm
Monthly. Owner: PW Publishing.
Editor: Kevin Nice

Simply Knitting
01225 442244
www.futurenet.com
/simplyknittingmagazine
13pa. Owner: Future.
Editor: Debora Bradley

Stamp Magazine
020 8726 8243
www.stampmagazine.co.uk
Monthly. Owner: IPC Media.
Editor: Steve Fairclough

Steam Days
01202 304849
www.steamdaysmag.co.uk
Monthly. Owner: Redgauntlet
Publications. Editor: Douglas Kennedy

Steam Railway
01733 264666
www.emap.com
Monthly. Owner: Emap.
Editor: Tony Streeter

Styleyes Magazine
020 7747 0700
www.redwoodgroup.net
2pa. Owner: Redwood.
Editor: Laurence Weinberger

Surrey Nature
01483 795440
www.surreywildlifetrust.org
3pa. Owner: Surrey Wildlife Trust.
Editor: Chris Parker

The Teddy Bear Club International
01206 505978
www.planet-teddybear.com
Monthly. Owner: Aceville Publications.
Editor: Melissa Highland

Time Out Shopping Guide
020 7813 3000
www.timeout.com
Annual. Owner: Time Out Group.
Editor: Ismay Atkins

Today's Fishkeeper
01254 236380
Monthly. Owner: Valley Publishing.
Editor: Liz Donlan

Toy Soldier & Model Figure
01403 711511
www.toy-soldier.com
Monthly. Owner: Ashdown.co.uk.
Editor: Stuart Hessney

Treasure Hunting
01376 521900
www.greenlightpublishing.co.uk
Monthly. Owner: Greenlight Publishing.
Editor: Greg Payne

Trends
020 8342 5777
www.independentregionals.com
4pa. Owner: Archant.
Editor: Tony Allcock

Truck Model World
01225 442244
Monthly. Owner: Future.
Editor: Peter White

Used Bike Guide
01507 529300
www.usedbikeguide.com
Monthly. Owner: Mortons Media Group.
Editor: Brian Tarbox

Wag
020 7837 0006
www.dogstrust.org.uk
3pa. Owner: Dogs Trust.
Editor: Deana Selby

Walk
020 7339 8500
www.ramblers.org.uk
Quarterly. Owner: The Ramblers
Association/ Think Publishing.
Editor: Christopher Sparrow

Waterways
01283 790447
www.waterways.org.uk
Quarterly. Owner: Inland Waterways
Association. Editor: Harry Arnold

Waterways World
01283 742951
Monthly. Editor: Hugh Potter

What's It Worth?
01225 786835
www.antiques-collectables.co.uk
13pa. Owner: Merricks Media.
Editor: Rachel Harrison

Which Caravan
01778 391000
www.whichcaravan.co.uk
Monthly. Owner: Warners Group.
Editor: Mark Sutcliffe

Wild Times
01767 680551
www.rspb.org.uk
6pa. Owner: RSPB.
Editor: Derek Niemann

Wildfowl & Wetlands
01453 891187
www.wwt.org.uk
4pa. Owner: Wildfowl & Wetlands
Trust. Editor: Mike Daw

Woodcarving
01273 477374
www.thegmcgroup.com
Bi-monthly. Owner: Guild of Master
Craftsmen. Editor: Stuart Lawson

The Woodturner
01689 887200
www.getwoodworking.com
6pa. Owner: Highbury House.
Editor: Nick Hunton

Woodturning
01273 477374
www.thegmcgroup.com
13pa. Owner: Guild of Master Craftsmen.
Editor: Colin Simpson

The Woodworker
01689 887200
www.getwoodworking.com
Monthly. Owner: Highbury House.
Editor: Mark Ramuz

Workbox
01579 340100
www.ebony.co.uk/workbox
Bi-monthly. Owner: Ebony Media.
Editor: Victor Briggs

The Yellow Book
01483 211535
www.ngs.org.uk
Yearly. Owner: National Garden Scheme.
Editor: Julia Grant

You & Your Vet
020 7636 6541
www.bva-awf.org.uk
4pa. Owner: British Veterinary
Association. Editor: Martin Alder

Your Cat
01780 766199
www.yourcat.co.uk
Monthly. Owner: Bourne Publishing
Group. Editor: Sue Parslow

Your Dog
01780 766199
www.yourdog.co.uk
Monthly. Owner: Bourne Publishing
Group. Editor: Sarah Wright

Your Horse
01733 264666
www.emap.com
Monthly. Owner: Emap.
Editor: Natasha Simmonds

Men's interest

Arena
020 7437 9011
www.emap.com
Monthly. Owner: Emap.
Editor: Anthony Noguera

Arena Homme Plus
020 7437 9011
www.emap.com
2pa. Owner: Emap.
Editor: Joanne Furness

Bizarre
020 7907 6000
www.bizarremag.com
Monthly. Owner: Dennis.
Editor: Joe Gardiner

Boys Toys
01202 735090
www.boystoys.co.uk
Monthly. Owner: Freestyle Publications.
Editor: Duncan Madden

Details
020 7240 0420
www.details.com
10pa. Owner: Fairchild.
Editor: Daniel Peres

DNR
020 7240 0420
www.dnrnews.com
Weekly. Owner: Fairchild.
Editor: Jon Birmingham

Esquire
020 7439 5000
www.esquire.co.uk
Monthly. Owner: National Magazine
Company. Editor: Simon Tiffin

FHM
020 7436 1515
www.fhm.com
Monthly. Owner: Emap.
Editor: Ross Brown
FHM Collections
020 7436 1515
www.fhm.com
Monthly. Owner: Emap.
Editor: Gary Kingsnorth
Front
020 7288 7500
www.hhc.co.uk
Monthly. Owner: Highbury House.
Editor: Ioin McSorley
GQ
020 7499 9080
www.gq.com
Monthly. Owner: Condé Nast.
Editor: Dylan Jones
Loaded
020 7261 5562
www.loaded.co.uk
Monthly. Owner: IPC Media.
Editor: Martin Daubney
Maxim
020 7907 6000
www.maxim-magazine.co.uk
Monthly. Owner: Dennis.
Editor: Greg Gutfeld
Men's Fitness
020 7907 6000
www.mensfitnessmagazine.co.uk
Monthly. Owner: Dennis.
Editor: Peter Muir
Men's Health
020 7439 5000
www.menshealth.co.uk
11pa. Owner: National Magazine
Company. Editor: Morgan Rees
Menz
029 2039 6600
www.hilspublications.com
4pa. Owner: Hils Publications.
Editor: Hilary Ferda
Muscle & Fitness
01423 504516
www.muscle-fitness-europe.com
Monthly. Owner: Weider Publishing.
Editor: Geoff Evans
Musclemag International
0845 345 0916
www.emusclemag.com
Monthly. Owner: Tropicana Health &
Fitness. Editor: Gary Hill
Nuts
020 7261 5660
www.nuts.co.uk
Weekly. Owner: IPC Media.
Editor: Phil Hilton
Zoo Weekly
020 7437 9011
www.zooweekly.co.uk
Weekly. Owner: Emap.
Editor: Paul Merrill

Money and property

Bloomberg Money
020 7484 9771
www.masteringmoney.com
Monthly. Owner: Incisive Media.
Editor: Julian Marr
Business Week
020 7176 6060
www.businessweek.com
Weekly. Owner: McGraw-Hill.
Bureau chief: Stanley Reed
Complete Guide to Homebuying
020 7827 5454
www.homebuying.co.uk
Monthly. Owner: Charterhouse
Communications. Editor: Nia Williams
Country Landowner and Rural Business
01392 447766
www.cla.org.uk
Monthly. Owner: Archant.
Editor: Phil Griffin
Euroslot
01622 687031
www.datateam.co.uk
Monthly. Owner: Datateam Publishing.
Editor: Alan Campbell
Forbes
020 7534 3900
www.forbes.com
Fortnightly. Owner: Forbes.
Editor: Paul Maidment
Fortune
020 7322 1074
www.fortune.com
Fortnightly. European editor, Fortune
Europe: Nelson Schwartz
Investment International
020 7827 5433
www.investmentinternational.com
Monthly. Owner: Charterhouse
Communications. Editor: TBA
Investors Chronicle
020 7775 6292
www.investorschronicle.co.uk
Weekly. Owner: Financial Times
Business. Editor: Matthew Vincent
ISA Direct
020 7409 1111
www.allenbridge.co.uk
2pa. Owner: Allenbridge.
Editor: Anthony Yadgaroff
London Property News
01933 271611
www.londonpropertynews.co.uk
Monthly. Editor: Julia Read
The MBA Career Guide
020 7284 7200
www.topmba.com/careers
2pa. Editor: Nunzio Quacquarelli
Money Observer
020 7713 4188
www.moneyobserver.com
Monthly. Owner: Guardian Media
Group. Editor: Andrew Pitts
Moneywise
020 7382 4300
www.moneywise.co.uk
Monthly. Editor: Ben Livesey

Mortgage Advisor & Home Buyer
020 8334 1691
www.mortgageadvisormag.co.uk
Monthly. Owner: Crimson Publishing.
Editor: Ruth Bell
The Mortgage Edge
020 7430 5129
www.mortgageedge.co.uk
Monthly. Editor: Christina Jordan
Mortgage Finance Gazette
020 7827 5457
www.mfgonline.co.uk
Monthly. Owner: Charterhouse
Communications. Editor: John Murray
Mortgage Introducer
020 7827 5422
www.mortgageintroducer.com
Weekly. Owner: Charterhouse
Communications. Editor: Rob Griffiths
Negotiator
01252 843566
www.negotiator-magazine.co.uk
Fortnightly. Owner: Inside
Communications.
Editor: Rosalind Renshaw
Optima
020 8420 4488
www.optimamagazine.co.uk
Fortnightly. Editor: Kathryn Michaels
Personal Finance Confidential
020 7633 3600
www.fleetstreetpublications.co.uk
Monthly. Owner: Fleet Street
Publications.
Managing editor: Dave Fedash
Personal Finance Magazine
020 7827 5454
www.pfmagazine.co.uk
Monthly. Owner: Charterhouse
Communications. Editor: Martin Fagan
Post Magazine
020 7484 9700
www.postmagazine.co.uk
Weekly. Owner: Incisive Media.
Editor: Jonathan Swift
The Property Magazine
01480 494944
www.property-platform.com
Monthly. Owner: Guild of Professional
Estate Agents. Editor: Malcolm Lindley
Scotland's New Home Buyer
0131 556 9702
4pa. Owner: Pinpoint Scotland.
Editor: Anna Baird
What House?
020 7939 9888
www.whathouse.co.uk
Monthly. Owner: Blendon
Communications. Editor: Lisa Isaacs
What Investment
020 7827 5490
www.what-investment-mag.co.uk
Monthly. Owner: Charterhouse
Communications. Editor: Kieron Root
What Investment Trust
020 7827 5454
www.charterhouse
   -communications.co.uk
3pa. Owner: Charterhouse
Communications. Editor: Kieron Root

What ISA
020 7827 5454
www.charterhouse
-communications.co.uk
*3pa. Owner: Charterhouse
Communications
Editor: Amanda Jarvis*

What Mortgage
020 7827 5454
www.what-mortgage-mag.co.uk
*Monthly. Owner: Charterhouse
Communications.
Editor: Victoria Hartley*

Your Money: Savings & Investments
020 7404 3123
www.yourmoney.com
*Quarterly. Owner: Incisive Media.
Editor: Mike Collins*

Your Mortgage
020 7404 3123
www.yourmortgage.co.uk
*Monthly. Owner: Incisive Media.
Editor: Paula John*

Your New Home
01732 878800
www.yournewhome.co.uk
*6pa. Owner: New Concept.
Editor: Stuart Humphrey*

Motoring

100% Biker
01244 663400
www.100-biker.co.uk
*Monthly. Owner: Jazz Publishing.
Editor: Pat Ringwood*

4x4 Magazine
020 8726 8000
www.4x4i.com
*Monthly. Owner: IPC Media.
Editor: John Carroll*

911 & Porsche World Magazine
01737 814311
www.chp.com
*Monthly. Owner: CH Publications.
Editor: Chris Horton*

Advanced Driving
01483 230300
www.iam.org.uk
*3pa. Owner: Institute of Advanced
Motorists. Editor: Ian Webb*

American Motorcycle Dealer
01892 511516
www.dealer-world.com
*Monthly. Owner: Dealer World.
Editor: Robin Bradley*

Audi Driver
01525 750500
www.autometrix.co.uk
*Monthly. Owner: AutoMetrix
Publications. Editor: Paul Harris*

The Audi Magazine
01590 683222
*2pa. Owner: Clive Richardson
Communications.
Editor: Clive Richardson*

Autocar
020 8267 5630
www.autocarmagazine.co.uk
*Weekly. Owner: Haymarket.
Editor: Rob Aherne*

Auto Express
020 7907 6000
www.autoexpress.co.uk
*Weekly. Owner: Dennis.
Editor: David Johns*

Auto Italia
01707 273999
www.auto-italia.co.uk
*Monthly. Owner: TRMG.
Editor: Philip Ward*

AutoTrader
020 7278 2332
www.autotrader.co.uk
*Weekly. Owner: Guardian Media Group.
Editor: Jerry Fowden*

Auto Weekly
01392 442211
www.autoweekly.co.uk
Weekly. Editor: Steve Hall

The Automobile
01483 268818
www.oldcar-discoveries.com
*Monthly. Owner: Enthusiast Publishing.
Editor: Michael Bowler*

Back Street Heroes
020 7772 8300
www.insidecom.co.uk
*Monthly. Owner: Inside
Communications. Editor: Stu Garland*

Banzai
01732 748000
www.banzaimagazine.com
*Monthly. Owner: Unity Media.
Editor: Joe Clifford*

BBC Top Gear
020 8433 2313
www.topgear.com
*Monthly. Owner: BBC Worldwide.
Editor: Michael Harvey*

Bike
01733 468000
www.emap.com
*12pa. Owner: Emap.
Editor: John Westlake*

BMW Car
01732 748000
www.bmwcarmagazine.com
*Monthly. Owner: Unity Media.
Editor: Bob Harper*

BMW Magazine
020 7534 2400
www.cedarcom.co.uk
*Quarterly. Owner: Cedar.
Editor: Andrew Gillingwater*

Car
01733 468000
www.car-magazine.co.uk
*12pa. Owner: Emap.
Editor: Jason Barlow*

Car Mechanics
01959 541444
www.carmechanicsmag.co.uk
*Monthly. Owner: Kelsey Publishing.
Editor: Peter Simpson*

CarSport Magazine
028 9078 3200
www.carsportmag.net
*Monthly. Owner: Greer Publications.
Editor: Pat Burns*

Classic & Sports Car
020 8267 5000
www.classicandsportscar.com
*Monthly. Owner: Haymarket.
Editor: James Elliott*

Classic American
0161 877 9977
www.classic-american.com
*Monthly. Owner: Guardian Media
Group. Editor: Ben Klemenzson*

Classic Bike
01733 468000
www.emap.com
12pa. Owner: Emap. Editor: Hugo Wilson

The Classic Bike Guide
01507 529300
www.classicbikeguide.com
*Monthly. Owner: Mortons Media
Group. Editor: Tim Britton*

Classic Car
01733 468000
www.emap.com
12pa. Owner: Emap. Editor: Phil Bell

Classic Car Mart
0121 233 8712
www.classic-car-mart.co.uk
*Monthly. Owner: Trinity Publications.
Editor: Frank Westworth*

Classic Car Weekly
01733 347559
www.classic-car-weekly.co.uk
*Weekly. Owner: Kelsey Publishing.
Editor: Russ Smith*

Classic Ford
01225 442244
www.classicfordmag.co.uk
*Monthly. Owner: Future.
Editor: Steve Phillips*

Classic Military Vehicle
01959 541444
www.kelsey.co.uk
*Monthly. Owner: Kelsey Publishing.
Editor: Pat Ware*

Classic Motor Monthly
01204 657212
www.classicmotor.co.uk
Monthly. Editor: John Hodson

Classic Motorcycle
01507 529300
www.classicmotorcycle.co.uk
*Monthly. Owner: Mortons Media
Group. Editor: James Robinson*

Classic Racer
01507 529300
www.classicracer.com
*Bi-monthly. Owner: Mortons Media
Group. Editor: Nigel Clark*

Classics
01689 887200
www.futurenet.com
*13pa. Owner: Future.
Editor: Gary Stretton*

Custom Car
01959 541444
www.kelsey.co.uk
*Monthly. Owner: Kelsey Publishing.
Editor: Kev Elliott*

Dirt Bike Rider
01524 834077
www.dirtbikerider.co.uk
Monthly. Editor: Sean Lawless

Enjoying MG
01954 231125
www.mgcars.org.uk
Monthly. Owner: Polestar Colchester.
Editor: Richard Ladds

Evo
020 7907 6000
www.evo.co.uk
Monthly. Owner: Dennis.
Editor: Peter Tomalin

Fast Bikes
01689 887200
www.fastbikesmag.com
www.futurenet.com
13pa. Owner: Future.
Editor: Richard Newland

Fast Car
01689 887200
www.fastcar.co.uk
www.futurenet.com
13pa. Owner: Future.
Editor: Gez Jones

Fast Ford
01225 442244
www.fastfordmag.co.uk
Monthly. Owner: Future.
Editor: Simon Woolley

GoMini
01225 442244
www.gomini.co.uk
Monthly. Owner: Future.
Editor: Helen Webster

Good Motoring
01342 825676
www.motoringassist.com
Quarterly. Owner: Gem Motoring Assist.
Editor: Derek Hainge

Intersection
020 7608 1166
www.intersectionmagazine.com
Monthly. Owner: Intersection Media.
Editor: Dan Ross

Jaguar Driver
01582 419332
www.jaguardriver.co.uk
Monthly. Owner: Jaguar Drivers Club.
Editor: Steve Fermore

Jaguar World Monthly
01959 541444
www.jaguar-world.com
Monthly. Owner: Kelsey Publishing.
Editor: Matt Skelton

J-Tuner
01225 442244
www.jtunermagazine.co.uk
Monthly. Owner: Future.
Editor: Steve Chalmers

Land Rover Enthusiast
01379 890056
www.landroverenthusiast.com
Monthly. Editor: James Taylor

Land Rover Owner International
01733 468000
www.lro.com
13pa. Owner: Emap. Editor: John Pearson

Land Rover World
020 8726 8000
www.landroverworld.co.uk
Monthly. Owner: IPC Media
Editor: John Carroll

Lexus Magazine
020 7837 8337
www.mccann.com
4pa. Owner: MRM Partners.
Editor: Lucy Reid

LRM – Land Rover Monthly
01359 240066
www.lrm.co.uk
Monthly. Editor: Richard Howell-Thomas

MaxPower
01733 468000
www.maxpower.co.uk
13pa. Owner: Emap.
Editor: John Sootheran

Mazda Magazine
020 7833 7410
www.northstarpublishing.com
4pa. Owner: Northstar Publishing.
Editor: Mark Walton

Mercedes
01789 490530
3pa. Owner: Impact Press & PR.
Editor: Eric Lafone

Mercedes Enthusiast
020 8639 4400
www.mercedesenthusiast.co.uk
Monthly. Owner: Sundial Magazines.
Editor: Dan Trent

MG Enthusiast Magazine
01924 499261
www.mg-enthusiast.com
6pa. Editor: Martyn Wise

Mini Magazine
01225 442244
www.minimag.co.uk
Monthly. Owner: Future.
Editor: Helena Clark

MiniWorld
020 8726 8354
www.ipcmedia.com
Monthly. Owner: IPC Media.
Editor: Monty Watkins

Motor Cycle News (MCN)
01733 468000
www.motorcyclenews.com
Weekly. Owner: Emap.
Editor: Marc Potter

Motor Sport
020 8267 5000
www.haymarketpublishing.co.uk
Monthly. Owner: Haymarket.
Editor: Paul Fearnley

Motorcycle Mechanics
01507 529442
www.classicmechanics.com
Monthly. Owner: Mortons Media Group.
Editor: Rod Gibson

Motorcycle Racer
01353 665577
www.motorcycleracer.net
Monthly. Owner: MB Media.
Editor: Tony Carter

Motorcycle Rider
01652 680060
www.rbp-.co.uk
4pa. Owner: RBP. Editor: Andy Dukes

Motorcycle Sport & Leisure
01353 616100
www.motorcyclemag.co.uk
Monthly. Owner: Motoplay Publications.
Editor: Rod Chapman

Motoring & Leisure
01273 744757
www.csma.uk.com
10pa. Owner: CSMA
Editor: David Arnold

The Motorist
020 8994 3239
Weekly. Owner: New York Publishing &
Media Corporation. Editor: BJ Charig

Performance Bikes
01733 468000
www.emap.com
Monthly. Owner: Emap.
Editor: Tim Thompson

Performance VW
01732 748000
www.performancevwmag.com
Monthly. Owner: Unity Media.
Editor: Elliot Roberts

Peugeot Rapport
0117 925 1696
www.specialistuk.com
3pa. Owner: Specialist.
Editor: Karen Ellison

Porsche Post
01608 652911
www.porscheclubgb.com
Monthly. Editor: Stephen Mummery

Post Office Motoring
0191 418 3970
4pa. Owner: The Post Office Auto Club.
Editor: Alan Fairbairn

Practical Classics
01733 468000
www.emap.com
13pa. Owner: Emap.
Editor: Martyn Moore

Redline
01225 442244
www.redlinemag.co.uk
13pa. Owner: Future.
Editor: Dan Lewis

The Renault Magazine
01737 786800
www.brooklandsgroup.com
4pa. Owner: Brooklands Publishing.
Editor: Ann Wallace

Retro Cars
01225 442244
www.retrocarsmag.co.uk
Monthly. Owner: Future.
Editor: Paul Wager

Ride
01733 468000
www.emap.com
13pa. Owner: Emap.
Editor: Stefan Bartlett

Saab Magazine
01603 664242
www.archant.co.uk
2pa. Owner: Archant. Editor: Zoe Francis

Safety Fast!
01235 555552
www.mgcc.co.uk
Monthly. Editor: Peter Browning

Scootering
01507 529300
www.scootering.com
Monthly. Owner: Mortons Media Group.
Editor: Andy Gillard

Street Fighters
020 7772 8300
www.insidecom.co.uk
Monthly. Owner: Inside
Communications. Editor: Stu Garland

SuperBike Magagzine
020 8726 8445
www.superbike.co.uk
Monthly. Owner: IPC Media.
Editor: Kenny Pryde

Test Drive
020 7907 6000
www.testdrivemag.co.uk
Monthly. Owner: Dennis.
Editor: Mike Askew

Torque
01455 891515
www.triumph.co.uk
Quarterly. Owner: Riders Association
of Triumph. Editor: Neil Webster

Total BMW
01225 442244
www.totalbmag.co.uk
Monthly. Owner: Future.
Editor: Matt Robinson

Total Vauxhall
01225 442244
www.totalvauxhall.co.uk
Monthly. Owner: Future.
Editor: Barton Brisland

Toyota's In Front
020 7837 8337
www.mccann.com
4pa. Owner: MRM Partners.
Editor: Oliver Parsons

Twist & Go Scooter Magazine
01507 529408
www.twistngo.com
Monthly. Owner: Mortons Media Group.
Editor: Mau Spencer

TWO – Two Wheels Only
020 8267 5000
www.haymarketpublishing.co.uk
Monthly. Owner: Haymarket.
Assistant editor: Tim Dickson

Used Bike Guide
01507 529300
www.usedbikeguide.com
Monthly. Owner: Mortons Media Group.
Editor: Brian Tarbox

VM – Vauxhall
01582 426909
www.vauxhall.co.uk/vmmagazine
3pa. Owner: Brooklands Publishing.
Editor: Michelle Howard

Volks World
020 8726 8347
www.volksworld.com
Monthly. Owner: IPC Media.
Editor: Ivan McCutcheon

Volkswagen Driver
01525 750500
www.autometrix.co.uk
Monthly. Owner: AutoMetrix
Publications. Editor: Neil Birkitt

The Volvo Magazine
020 7747 0700
www.redwoodgroup.net
3pa. Owner: Redwood.
Editor: Zac Assemakis

VW Magazine
01778 391000
www.vwmonline.co.uk
Monthly. Owner: Warners Group.
Editors: Richard Copping, Ken
Cservenka

What Car?
020 8267 5000
www.whatcar.co.uk
Monthly. Owner: Haymarket.
Editor: David Motton

Which Kit?
01737 222030
www.which-kit.com
Monthly. Editor: Peter Filby

Photography

Digital Camera Buyer
01202 299900
13pa. Owner: Highbury Entertainment.
Editor: Richard Sutcliffe

Digital Camera Magazine
01225 442244
www.dcmag.co.uk
13pa. Owner: Future.
Editor: Marcus Hawkins

Digital Camera Shopper
01225 442244
www.dcmag.co.uk
13pa. Owner: Future. Editor: Geoff Harris

Digital Photo Effects
01225 442244
www.dcmag.co.uk
13pa. Owner: Future. Editor: Dan Oliver

Digital Photographer
01202 299900
13pa. Owner: Highbury Entertainment.
Editor: Michael Roscoe

Digital Photography Made Easy
01202 299900
www.madeeasy.co.uk
13pa. Owner: Highbury Entertainment.
Editor: Richard Sutcliffe

Digital Photography User
01202 299900
6pa. Owner: Highbury Entertainment.
Editor: Richard Sutcliffe

Photography Monthly
0845 650 1065
www.photographymonthly.co.uk
Monthly. Owner: Archant.
Editor: Daniel Lezano

What Camera
020 7681 1010
www.ipcmedia.com
4pa. Owner: IPC Media.
Editor: Joel Lacey

What Digital Camera
020 7261 5323
www.what-digital-camera.com
Monthly. Owner: IPC Media.
Editor: Nigel Atherton

Which Digital Camera?
01799 544240
www.archant.co.uk
Monthly. Owner: Archant.
Technical editor: Darren Harbar

Puzzles

100 Crosswords
01737 378700
www.puzzler.co.uk
13pa. Owner: Puzzler Media.
Editor: Debbie Hardy

Cross Reference
01737 378700
www.puzzler.co.uk
13pa. Owner: Puzzler Media.
Editor: Charles Sloan

Kriss Kross
01737 378700
www.puzzler.co.uk
13pa. Owner: Puzzler Media.
Editor: Jo MacLeod

Logic Problems
01737 378700
www.puzzler.co.uk
13pa. Owner: Puzzler Media.
Editor: Steve Bull

Pocket Puzzler Crosswords
01737 378700
www.puzzler.co.uk
13pa. Owner: Puzzler Media.
Editor: Maggie Ayres

Puzzle Compendium
01737 378700
www.puzzler.co.uk
10pa. Owner: Puzzler Media.
Editor: Birgitta Bingham

Puzzle Corner Special
01737 378700
www.puzzler.co.uk
10pa. Owner: Puzzler Media.
Editor: Debbie Hardy

Puzzle Selection
020 7241 8000
www.bauer.co.uk
Monthly. Owner: H Bauer.
Editor: Sonia Garner

Puzzler
01737 378700
www.puzzler.co.uk
13pa. Owner: Puzzler Media.
Editor: Catherine Filby

Puzzler Quiz Kids
01737 378700
www.puzzler.co.uk
7pa. Owner: Puzzler Media.
Editor: Jackie Guthrie

Sudoku
01737 378700
www.puzzler.co.uk
8pa. Owner: Puzzler Media.
Contact: Tim Preston

Take a Break
020 7241 8000
www.bauer.co.uk
Weekly. Owner: H Bauer.
Editor: John Dale

Take a Crossword
020 7241 8000
www.bauer.co.uk
13pa. Owner: H Bauer.
Editor: David Moore

Take a Puzzle
020 7241 8000
www.bauer.co.uk
13pa. Owner: H Bauer.
Editor: Michael Jones

Sport

Ace
020 7381 7000
Monthly. Owner: Tennis GB. Editor: Nigel Billen

Adrenalin
0870 732 8080
www.adrenalin.com
4pa. Owner: Metropolis International (UK). Editor: Mike Fordham

Agfis
020 7963 7888
www.sportservicesgroup.com
Bi-annual; also weekly email bulletin, Sport Insider. Owner: Sport Services Group. Editor: Caroline Reid.

Air Gun World
0118 977 1677
www.airgunshooting.org
Monthly. Owner: Archant. Editor: Adam Smith

Air Gunner
0118 977 1677
www.archant.co.uk
Monthly. Owner: Archant. Editor: Nigel Allen

Airgun World
0118 977 1677
www.archant.co.uk
Monthly. Owner: Archant. Editor: Adam Smith

Angler's Mail
020 7261 5829
www.ipcmedia.com
Weekly. Owner: IPC Media. Editor: Tim Knight

Angling Times
01733 237111
www.anglingtimes.co.uk
Weekly. Owner: Emap. Editor: Richard Lee

Angling Times Advanced
01733 465705
www.anglingtimes.co.uk
Monthly. Owner: Emap. Editor: Steve Cole

The Arsenal Magazine
020 7704 4138
www.arsenal.com
Monthly. Owner: Arsenal Football Club. Editor: Andy Exley

Athletics Weekly
01733 898440
www.athletics-weekly.com
Weekly. Owner: Descartes Publishing. Editor: Jason Henderson

Autosport
020 8267 5000
www.autosport.com
Weekly. Owner: Haymarket. Editor: Biranit Goren

Badminton Magazine
01908 268400
www.badmintonengland.co.uk
Quarterly. Owner: Badminton England. Contact: Gerry Cronin

Boxing Monthly
020 8986 4141
www.boxing-monthly.co.uk
Monthly. Owner: Topwave. Editor: Glyn Leach

Boxing News
020 7618 3069
www.boxingnewsonline.net
Weekly. Owner: Newsquest. Editor: Claude Abrams

British Homing World
01938 552360
www.pigeonracing.com
Weekly. Editor: Steven Richards

British Waterski & Wakeboard
01932 570885
www.britishwaterski.org.uk
5pa. Owner: British Water Ski. Editor: Gavin Kelly

Bunkered
0141 950 2216
www.bunkered.co.uk
8pa. Owner: Pro Sports Promotions. Editor: Paul Grant

Calcio Italia
01249 564564
www.calcioitalia.co.uk
Monthly. Owner: Anthem Publishing. Editor: John Taylor

Canoe Focus
01480 465081
www.canoefocus.co.uk
Bi-monthly. Owner: 2B Graphic Design. Editor: Peter Tranter

Carpworld
0114 258 0812
www.anglingpublications.co.uk
Monthly. Owner: Angling Publications. Publishing editor: Tim Paisley

Carve Surfing Magazine
01637 878074
www.orcasurf.co.uk
8pa. Owner: Orca Publications. Editor: Chris Power

Celtic View
0141 551 4218
www.celticfc.net
Weekly. Owner: Cre8. Editor: Paul Cuddihy

Clay Shooting
01264 889533
www.clay-shooting.com
Monthly. Owner: Brunton Business Publications. Editor: Richard Rawlingson

Climb
01298 72801
www.planetfear.com
Monthly. Owner: Greenshires Group. Editor: Neil Pearson

Climber
01778 391000
www.climber.co.uk
Monthly. Owner: Warners. Editor: Bernard Newman

Coarse Fisherman
07971 241484
www.coarse-fisherman.co.uk
Website, updated daily. Editor: Philip Runciman

Combat
0121 344 3737
www.martialartsinprint.com
Monthly. Owner: Martial Arts Publications. Editor: Malcolm Martin

Combat & Survival
01484 435011
www.combatandsurvival.com
Monthly. Owner: MAI Publications. Editor: Bob Morrison

Corporate Golf Magazine
01273 777994
www.golfnews.co.uk
4pa. Owner: Golf News. Editor: Nick Bayly

Country Walking
01733 264666
www.emap.com
Monthly. Owner: Emap. Editor: Jonathan Manning

Cricket World Magazine
01476 561944
www.cricketworld.com
Quarterly. Editor: Alistair Symondson

Cycle
0870 873 0060
www.ctc.org.uk
Bi-monthly. Owner: Cyclists' Touring Club. Editor: Dan Joyce

Cycle Sport
020 8726 8452
www.cyclesport.co.uk
Monthly. Owner: IPC Media. Editor: Robert Garbutt

Cycling Plus
01225 442244
www.cyclingplus.co.uk
13pa. Owner: Future. Editor: Tony Farrelly

Cycling Weekly
020 8726 8452
www.cyclingweekly.co.uk
Weekly. Owner: IPC Media. Editor: Robert Garbutt

Daily Mail Ski & Snowboard Magazine
020 8515 2000
www.skiingmail.com
6pa Sep–Mar. Owner: DMG World Media. Editor: Henry Druce

Darts World
020 8650 6580
www.dartsworld.com
Monthly. Owner: World Magazines. Editor: Tony Wood

Direct Hit
020 7953 7473
www.surreycricket.com
5pa. Owner: Trinorth. Editor: Matt Thacker

Dirt MTB Magazine
01305 251263
www.dirtmag.co.uk
Bi-monthly. Owner: 4130 Publications. Editor: Mike Rose

Distance Running
0141 810 9000
www.inpositionmedia.co.uk
4pa. Owner: In Position Media. Editor: Hugh Jones

DIVE Magazine
020 8940 0555
www.divemagazine.co.uk
Monthly. Editor: Simon Rogerson

Diver
020 8943 4288
www.divernet.com
Monthly. Owner: The Diver Group.
Editor: Steve Weinman

Document Skateboard
01305 251263
www.documentskateboard.com
9pa. Owner: 4130 Publications.
Editor: Percy Dean

Document Snowboard
01733 293250
www.fall-line.co.uk
Monthly Oct–Mar. Owner: Fall-Line
Media. Editor: Ian Sansom

Dog Training Weekly
01348 875011
www.pembrokeshirepress.com
Weekly. Owner: Canine Press.
Editor: Angela Barrah

England Rugby
01707 273999
www.rfu.com
Quarterly. Owner: TRMG.
Editor: Howard Johnson

Equi-Ads
01738 567700
www.equiads.net
Monthly. Editor: Mary Moore

Evening Times Wee Red Book
0141 302 6606
Yearly. Owner: Newsquest.
Editor: Philip Joyce

Eventing
020 7261 5388
www.ipcmedia.com
Monthly. Owner: IPC Media.
Editor: Julie Harding

The Evertonian
0151 285 8412
Monthly. Owner: Trinity Mirror.
Editor: Ken Rogers

F1 Racing
020 8267 5000
www.haymarketpublishing.co.uk
Monthly. Owner: Haymarket.
Editor: Matt Bishop

The Fairway Golfing News
01633 666700
www.fairway.org.uk
Monthly. Editor: John Doherty

Fall-Line Skiing
01733 293250
www.fall-line.co.uk
Monthly Oct–Feb. Owner: Fall-Line
Media. Editor: Ian Sansom

The Field
020 7261 5198
www.thefield.co.uk
Monthly. Owner: IPC Media.
Editor: Jonathan Young

Fighters
0121 344 3737
www.martialartsinprint.com
Monthly. Owner: Martial Arts
Publications. Editor: Malcolm Martin

First Down
020 7005 2000
www.independent.co.uk
Weekly. Owner: Independent News &
Media (UK). Editor: Tony Prince

Fitness First
01932 841450
www.fitnessfirst.com
Quarterly. Owner: Weybridge Press.
Editor: Iain Mackie

FitPro
0870 513 3434
www.fitpro.com
Bi-monthly. Owner: Fitness
Professionals. Editor: Gemma Carr

Flex
01423 504516
www.flex-europe.com
Monthly. Owner: Weider Publishing.
Editor: Geoff Evans

Football First
01430 455305
www.sportfirst.com
Weekly. Owner: Sport First.
Editor: Chris Wiltshire

Football Insider
020 7963 7888
www.sportservicesgroup.com
Bi-annual; also daily email.
Owner: Sport Services Group.
Editor: Andrew Brown

Football Italia
01494 564564
www.channel4.co.uk/sport
/football_italia
Monthly. Owner: Anthem Publishing.
Editor: John Taylor

FourFourTwo
020 8267 5000
www.haymarketpublishing.co.uk
Monthly. Owner: Haymarket.
Deputy editor: Mat Snow

Gamefisher
020 7283 5838
www.salmon-trout.org
2pa. Owner: Salmon & Trout
Association. Editor: Carmel Jorgensen

Glory Glory Man United
01225 442244
www.futurenet.com
13pa. Owner: Future.
Editor: Sarah Shaddick

Going for Golf
01268 554100
www.goingforgolf.com
Quarterly. Editor: Neil Webber

The Golf Guide: Where to Play/
Where to Stay
0141 887 0428
www.holidayguides.com
Yearly. Owner: FHG Guides.
Editor: Anne Cuthbertson

Golf International
020 7828 3003
www.golfinternationalmag.co.uk
10pa. Editor: Robert Green

Golf Monthly
020 7261 7237
www.golf-monthly.co.uk
Monthly. Owner: IPC Media.
Editor: Jane Carter

Golf News
01273 777994
www.golfnews.co.uk
Monthly. Owner: Golf News.
Editor: Nick Bayly

Golf World
01733 288011
www.emap.com
Monthly. Owner: Emap.
Editor: Andy Carlton

Good Ski Guide
020 7332 2000
www.goodskiguide.com
4pa in winter. Owner: Profile Sports
Media. Editor: Kate Langmuir

Greenside
01753 646815
www.foremostonline.com
3pa. Owner: Foremost Golf.
Editor: Jenni O'Connor

The Gymnast
0116 247 8766
www.british-gymnastics.org
Bi-monthly. Editor: Trevor Low

Improve Your Coarse Fishing
01733 237111
www.emap.com
Monthly. Owner: Emap.
Editor: Kevin Green

In The Know
0870 333 2062
www.itkonline.com
Monthly. Editor: Darren Croft

International Rugby News
020 7005 2000
www.independent.co.uk
Monthly. Owner: Independent News &
Media (UK). Editor: Russell Stander

Ireland's Equestrian Magazine
028 3833 4272
www.irelandsequestrian.co.uk
Bi-monthly. Owner: Mainstream
Publishing. Editor: TBA

Irish Golf Review
0161 683 8000
www.worldsfair.co.uk
Quarterly. Owner: World's Fair.
Editor: Mike Appleton

Karting
01689 897123
www.kartingmagazine.com
Monthly. Owner: Lodgemark Press.
Editor: Mark Burgess

The Kop
0151 285 8412
Monthly. Owner: Trinity Mirror.
Editor: Chris McLoughlin

Lady Golfer
01274 851323
Monthly. Owner: Sports Publications.
Editor: Mickey Walker

LFC
0151 285 8412
Weekly. Owner: Trinity Mirror.
Editor: Steve Hanrahan

Liverpool Monthly
01392 664141
Monthly. Owner: LCD Publishing.
Editor: Joanne Trump

London Cyclist
020 7928 7220
www.lcc.org.uk
Bi-monthly. Owner: London Cycling
Campaign. Editors: Jonathan Hewett,
Rebecca Lack

Manchester United Magazine
020 7317 2614
www.manutd.com/magazine/
13pa. Owner: Future.
Editor: Sarah Shaddick
Martial Arts Illustrated
01484 435011
www.martialarts.co.uk
Monthly. Owner: MAI Publications.
Editor: Bob Sykes
Match
01733 237111
www.matchmag.co.uk
Weekly. Owner: Emap.
Editor: Ian Forster
Match Fishing Magazine
01327 311999
www.total-fishing.com
Monthly. Owner: DHP.
Editor: Dave Harrell
Moto
01305 251263
www.motomagazine.co.uk
Bi-monthly. Owner: 4130 Publications.
Editor: Rob Walters
Motor Sport
020 8267 5000
www.haymarketpublishing.co.uk
Monthly. Owner: Haymarket.
Editor: Paul Fearnley
Motorsport News
020 8267 5385
www.haymarketpublishing.co.uk
Weekly. Owner: Haymarket.
Editor: Tim Bowdler
Motorsports Now!
01753 765000
www.msauk.org
Quarterly. Owner: The Really Motoring
Group (TRMG). Editor: Pete Wadsworth
Mountain Bike Rider
020 8726 8000
www.mountainbikerider.co.uk
Monthly. Owner: IPC Media.
Editor: John Kitchiner
Mountain Biking UK
01225 442244
www.mbuk.com
13pa. Owner: Future. Editor: Mat Brett
Muscle & Fitness
01423 504516
www.muscle-fitness-europe.com
Monthly. Owner: Weider Publishing.
Editor: Geoff Evans
Musclemag International
0845 345 0916
www.emusclemag.com
Monthly. Owner: Tropicana Health &
Fitness. Editor: Gary Hill
National Club Golfer
01274 851323
www.nationalclubgolfer.com
Monthly. Owner: Sports Publications.
Editor: Chris Bertram
The Non-League Paper
020 8971 4333
www.thenon-leaguepaper.com
Twice weekly (Aug–May), weekly
(May–Aug). Owner: Greenways Media.
Editor: David Emery

The Official Tour de France Guide
020 7608 6500
www.procycling.com
Yearly. Owner: Highbury House.
Editor: Jeremy Whittle
The Outdoor Adventure Guide
01733 293250
www.fall-line.co.uk
Bi-monthly. Owner: Fall-Line Media.
Editor: Martina Hanlon
PQ International
020 7924 2550
www.pqpolo.com
4pa. Owner: Euromedia Services.
Editor: Roger Chatterton-Newman
Procycling
020 7331 1000
www.procycling.com
Monthly. Owner: Future.
Editor: Jeremy Whittle
Pull!
01780 766199
www.countrypursuits.co.uk
10pa. Owner: Bourne Publishing Group.
Editor: Mike Barnes
Raceform Update
020 7293 3000
www.racingpost.co.uk
Weekly. Owner: Trinity Mirror.
Editor: Bernie Ford
Racing Calendar
0870 871 2000
www.britishcycling.org.uk
Quarterly. Owner: British Cycling
Federation. Editor: Phil Ingham
Racing Pigeon Weekly
01689 600006
www.racingpigeon.co.uk
Weekly. Editor: Steve Dunn
Racing Post
020 7293 3000
www.racingpost.co.uk
Daily. Owner: Racing Post.
Editor: Chris Smith
Ride BMX
01305 251263
www.ridebmxmag.co.uk
9pa. Owner: 4130 Publications.
Editor: Mark Noble
Rugby League World
01484 401895
www.totalrl.com
Monthly. Owner: League Publications.
Editor: Tim Butcher
Rugby Leaguer & League Express
01484 401895
www.totalrl.com
Weekly. Owner: League Publications.
Editor: Martyn Sadler
Rugby Times
01484 401895
www.rugbytimes.com
Weekly. Owner: League Publications.
Editor: Jon Newcombe
Rugby World
020 7261 6810
www.rugbyworld.com
Monthly. Owner: IPC Media.
Editor: Paul Morgan

Runner's World
020 7439 5000
www.runnersworld.co.uk
Monthly. Owner: National Magazine
Company. Editor: Steven Seaton
Running Fitness
01733 347559
www.running-fitness.co.uk
Monthly. Owner: Kelsey Publishing.
Editor: Paul Larkins
Scuba World
01202 735090
www.freestyle-group.com
Monthly. Owner: Freestyle Publications.
Acting editor: Mark Nuttall
Sea Angler
01733 237111
www.emap.com
Monthly. Owner: Emap. Editor: Mel Russ
Seahorse
01590 671899
www.seahorsemagazine.com
Monthly. Owner: Fairmead
Communications. Editor: Andrew Hurst
Shoot Monthly
020 7261 6287
www.shootmonthly.co.uk
Monthly. Owner: IPC Media.
Editor: Colin Mitchell
The Shooting Gazette
01780 485 351
www.ipcmedia.com
Monthly. Owner: IPC Media.
Editor: Will Hetherington
Shooting Sports
01206 525697
www.shooting-sports.net
Monthly. Owner: Aceville Publications.
Editor: Peter Moore
Shooting Times
020 7261 6180
www.shootingtimes.co.uk
Weekly. Owner: IPC Media.
Editor: Robert Gray
Sidewalk Skateboarding Magazine
01235 536229
www.sidewalkmag.com
Monthly. Owner: Permanent
Publishing UK. Editor: Ben Powell
Snooker Scene
0121 585 9188
www.snookersceneshop.co.uk
Monthly. Owner: Evertons News
Agency. Editor: Clive Everton
Speedway Star
020 8335 1100
www.speedwaystar.net
Weekly. Owner: Pinegen.
Editor: Richard Clark
Spin
01689 887200
www.hhc.co.uk
Monthly. Owner: Highbury House.
Editor: Duncan Steer
Sport Cities and Venues
020 7963 7888
www.sportservicesgroup.com
Bi-annual; also weekly email.
Owner: Sport Services Group.
Editor: Caroline Reid

Sport Diver
01799 544200
www.sportdiver.co.uk
Monthly. Owner: Archant.
Editors: Mark Evans, Rebecca Corbally

Sporting Gun
08704 445000
www.ipcmedia.com
Monthly. Owner: IPC Media.
Editor: Robin Scott

Sporting Shooter
020 7751 4800
www.sportingshooter.co.uk
Monthly. Owner: Archant.
Editor: James Marchington

Sportsbetting Update
020 7963 7888
www.sportservicesgroup.com
Weekly email. Owner: Sport Services
Group. Editor: Andrew Gellatly

Sportsmedia
020 7963 7888
www.sportservicesgroup.com
Bi-annual; also daily email. Owner:
Sport Services Group. Editor: Jay Stuart

The Squash Player
01753 775511
www.squashplayer.co.uk
10pa. Owner: McKenzie Publishing.
Editor: Ian McKenzie

Summit
0870 010 4878
www.thebmc.co.uk
Quarterly. Owner: Warners Group.
Editor: Alex Messenger

Super Reds
01392 664141
Monthly. Owner: LCD Publishing.
Editor: Joanne Trump

Surf News
01637 878074
www.britsurf.co.uk
4pa. Owner: Orca Publications.
Editor: Chris Power

The Surfer's Path
01235 536229
www.surferspath.com
Bi-monthly. Owner: Permanent
Publishing UK. Editor: Alex Dick-Read

Swimming
01509 632230
www.britishswimming.org
Monthly. Owner: Amateur Swimming
Association. Editor: Peter Hassall

Swimming Pool News
01353 777 656
www.swimmingpoolnews.co.uk
Bi-monthly. Owner: Archant.
Editor: Christina Connor

**Taekwondo & Korean Martial Arts
Magazine**
0121 344 3737
www.martialartsinprint.com
Monthly. Owner: Martial Arts
Publications. Editor: Malcolm Martin

Thoroughbred Owner and Breeder
020 7408 0903
www.racehorseowners.net
Monthly. Owner: Racehorse Owners
Association. Editor: Richard Griffiths

Today's Golfer
01733 237111
www.emap.com
Monthly. Owner: Emap.
Editor: Paul Hamblin

Today's Pilot
01780 755131
www.todayspilot.co.uk
Monthly. Owner: Key Publishing.
Editor: Dave Unwin

Total Carp
01327 311999
www.total-fishing.com
Monthly. Owner: DHP.
Editor: Mark Coulson

Traditional Karate
0121 344 3737
www.martialartsinprint.com
Monthly. Owner: Martial Arts
Publications. Editor: Malcolm Martin

Trail
01733 264666
www.trailroutes.com
Monthly. Owner: Emap.
Editor: Guy Procter

Trials & Motorcross News
01524 834030
www.tmxnews.co.uk
Weekly. Owner: Johnston Press.
Editor: John Dickinson

Trout & Salmon
01733 237111
www.emap.com
Monthly. Owner: Emap.
Editor: Sandy Leventon

Ultra-Fit
01736 350204
www.ultra-fitmagazine.com
8pa. Editor: Charles Mays

Unity
01993 811181
www.unitymag.co.uk
8pa. Owner: Arcwind.
Editor: Steve Glidewell

Warren Miller's Impact
020 7240 4071
www.warrenmiller.co.uk
Yearly. Editor: Guy Chambers

What Mountain Bike
01225 442244
www.whatmtb.co.uk
13pa. Owner: Future.
Editor: Jane Bentley

When Saturday Comes
020 7729 1110
www.wsc.co.uk
Monthly. Editor: Andy Lyons

White Lines Snowboarding Magazine
01235 536229
www.whitelines.com
6pa (Oct–Mar). Owner: Permanent
Publishing UK. Editor: Matt Barr

Windsurf Magazine
01993 811181
www.windsurf.co.uk
10pa. Owner: Arcwind.
Editor: Mark Kasprowicz

Women & Golf
020 7261 7237
www.ipcmedia.com
Monthly. Owner: IPC Media.
Editor: Jane Carter

World Soccer
020 7261 5714
www.worldsoccer.com
Monthly. Owner: IPC Media.
Editor: Gavin Hamilton

Yachting Monthly
020 7261 6040
www.yachtingmonthly.com
Monthly. Owner: IPC Media.
Editor: Paul Gelder

Yachting World
020 7261 6800
www.ybw.com
Monthly. Owner: IPC Media.
Editor: Andrew Bray

Yachts & Yachting
01702 582245
www.yachtsandyachting.com
Fortnightly. Editor: Gael Pawson

Travel

A Place in the Sun
01737 786820
www.aplaceinthesunmag.co.uk
Monthly. Owner: Brooklands Media.
Editor: Matt Havercroft

Activity Wales
01437 766888
www.activitywales.com
Yearly. Editor: Matthew Evans

Adventure Travel
01789 450000
www.atmagazine.co.uk
Bi-monthly. Editor: Alun Davies

Arab Traveller
01621 842745
Bi-monthly. Owner: Fanar Publishing
WLL. Editor: Jeremy Wright

Australian News
01323 726040
www.australian-news.co.uk
Monthly. Owner: Outbound Publishing.
Editor: Paul Beasley

BA Impressions
020 7269 7480
www.impressions-ba.com
Quarterly. Owner: Ink Publishing.
Editor: Edward Chamberlain

Best of Britain
020 7611 7891
www.morriseurope.com
Yearly. Owner: Morris Visitor
Publications. Editor: Chris Johnson

Bradmans Business Travel Guides
020 7613 8777
www.bradmans.com
Yearly. Owner: Ink Publishing.
Editor: Richard Bence

Canada News
01323 726040
www.canadanews.co.uk
Monthly. Owner: Outbound Publishing.
Editor: Paul Beasley

City to Cities
01322 311600
www.swanpublishing.co.uk
6pa. Owner: Swan Publishing.
Editor: David Tickner

CN Traveller (Condé Nast Traveller)
020 7499 9080
www.cntraveller.com
Monthly. Owner: Condé Nast.
Editor: Sarah Miller

Destination New Zealand
01323 726040
www.destination-newzealand.com
Monthly. Owner: Outbound Publishing.
Editor: Paul Beasley

Easyjet Magazine
020 7613 8777
www.easyjetinflight.com
Monthly. Owner: Ink Publishing.
Editor: Michael Keating

Edinburgh Shopping & Tourist Guide
01506 508001
2pa. Owner: Capital Group.
Editor: Roger Sadler

Education Travel Magazine
020 7440 4025
www.hothousemedia.com
Bi-monthly. Owner: Hothouse Media.
Editor: Amy Baker

Enjoy Dorset & Hampshire Magazine
01202 737678
www.enjoydorset.co.uk
Yearly. Owner: Eastwick Publishing.
Editor: Zoe Wilson

Ensign
01202 414200
Yearly. Editor: Karen Portnall

Essentially America
020 7243 6954
www.phoenixip.com
Quarterly. Owner: Phoenix
International Publishing.
Editor: Mary Moore Mason

Flybe. Uncovered
020 8649 7233
www.bmipublications.com
Bi-monthly. Owner: BMI Publications.
Editor: Alan Orbell

Food & Travel
020 8332 9090
www.fox-publishing.com
Monthly. Owner: Green Pea Publishing.
Editor: Laura Tennant

France
01242 216050
www.francemag.com
Monthly. Owner: Archant.
Editor: Nick Wall

French Property News
020 8543 3113
www.french-property-news.com
Monthly. Owner: Archant.
Editor: Karen Tait

Gap Year
0870 241 6704
www.gapyear.com
Website. Editor: Tom Griffiths

Geographical
020 7170 4360
www.geographical.co.uk
Monthly. Owner: Campion Press.
Editor: Nick Smith

Going USA
01323 726040
www.goingusa.com
Bi-monthly. Owner: Outbound
Publishing. Editor: Paul Beasley

Greece
01225 786835
www.merricksmedia.co.uk
Bi-monthly. Owner: Merricks Media.
Editor: Diana Cambridge

High Life
020 7534 2400
www.cedarcom.co.uk
Monthly. Owner: Cedar.
Editor: Scott Manson

Holiday Which?
020 7770 7564
www.which.co.uk
4pa. Owner: Which?
Editor: Lorna Cowan

Holiday, The RCI Magazine
01536 310101
www.rci.com
3pa. Owner: RCI Europe.
Editor: Simon McGrath

Homes Overseas
020 7002 8300
www.homesoverseas.co.uk
Monthly. Owner: Blendon
Communications. Editor: Mike Hayes

In Britain
020 7751 4800
www.archant.co.uk
Bi-monthly. Owner: Archant.
Editor: Andrea Spain

In London
020 7611 7891
www.morriseurope.com
Bi-monthly. Owner: Morris Visitor
Publications. Editor: Chris Johnson

Italia
01249 716557
www.italia-magazine.com
Monthly. Owner: Anthem Publishing.
Editor: Paul Pettengale

Italy
01305 266360
www.italymag.co.uk
Monthly. Owner: Poundbury
Publishing. Editor: Fiona Tankard

Kuoni World Magazine
01306 744555
www.kuoni.co.uk
4pa. Owner: Kuoni Travel.
Editor: Naomi Wilkinson

Livewire
020 7805 5555
www.ilng.co.uk
Bi-monthly. Owner: The Illustrated
London News Group.
Editor: Claire Roberts

Living France
01242 216050
www.livingfrance.com
Monthly. Owner: Archant.
Editor: Lucy-Jane Cypher

London and More
020 7005 5858
Fortnightly. Owner: Independent News
& Media (UK). Editor: Bill Williamson

The London Guide
020 7611 7891
www.morriseurope.com
Monthly. Owner: Morris Visitor
Publications. Editor: Chris Johnson

London Hotel Magazine
020 7373 7282
www.goodlifemedia.co.uk
Bi-monthly. Owner: Goodlife Media.
Editor: ER Spence

London Planner
020 7751 4848
www.londonplanner.co.uk
Monthly. Owner: Archant.
Editor: Nick Buglione

Med Life
020 7415 7020
www.touchline.com
Quarterly. Owner: Touchline
Publishing. Editor: Glyn Wilmshurst

My Travel Recline & Life Magazines
020 7613 8777
www.mytravelmag.com
Quarterly. Owner: Ink Publishing.
Editor: Chloe Wilson

National Geographic
00 1 813 979 6845
www.nationalgeographic.com
Monthly. Owner: Bill Allen

Orient-Express Magazine
020 7805 5555
www.ilng.co.uk
4pa. Owner: The Illustrated London
News Group. Editor: Alison Booth

Overseas
020 7408 0214 x205
www.rosl.org.uk
4pa. Owner: The Royal Over-Seas
League. Editor: Pat Treasure

Pride of Britain
020 7739 1434
www.prideofbritainhotels.com
2pa. Owner: Freeway Media.
Editor: Sophie MacKenzie

The Railway Magazine
020 7261 5821
www.ipcmedia.com
Monthly. Owner: IPC Media.
Editor: Nick Pigott

Redhot Magazine
020 7613 8777
www.ontoeurope.com
Quarterly. Owner: Ink Publishing.
Editor: Bethen Rider

South Africa News
01323 726040
www.southafricanews.co.uk
Bi-monthly. Owner: Outbound
Publishing. Editor: Paul Beasley

Spain
0131 226 7766
www.spainmagazine.co.uk
Monthly. Owner: The Media Company.
Editor: Sue Hitchen

Spanish Homes
01225 442244
www.buyingabroad.net
Monthly. Owner: Future.
Editor: Mike Shakespeare

Sunday Times Travel
020 7413 9302
www.sundaytimestravel.co.uk
Monthly. Owner: River Publishing.
Editor: Ed Grenby

TNT Magazine
020 7373 3377
www.tntmagazine.com
Twice weekly. Owner: TNT.
Editor: Lyn Eyb

Travel & Leisure
020 8554 4456
www.tlmags.com
4pa. Owner: Travel & Leisure
Magazines. Editor: Terry Stafford

Travel Australia
01424 223111
www.consylpublishing.co.uk
2pa. Owner: Consyl Publishing.
Editor: Bill Deacon

Travel GBI
020 7729 4337
Monthly. Editor: Richard Cawthorne

Traveller
020 7589 3315
www.traveller.org.uk
Quarterly. Owner: WEXAS.
Editor: Jonathan Lorie

Travelmag
01672 810202
www.travelmag.co.uk
Online magazine. Editor: Jack Barker

Trip
0131 226 7766
www.trip-magazine.co.uk
Bi-monthly. Owner: The Media
Company. Editor: Aileen Easton

Wanderlust
01753 620426
www.wanderlust.co.uk
Bi-monthly. Editor: Lyn Hughes

Welcome to London
020 8297 4444
www.welcometolondon.com
Bi-monthly. Owner: Pareto.
Editor: Melanie Armstrong

Where London
020 7611 7891
www.morriseurope.com
Monthly. Owner: Morris Visitor
Publications. Editor: Mary Anne Evans

Women and health

Accent Magazine
0191 284 9994
Monthly. Editor: Kevin Wright

Al-Jamila
020 7831 8181
www.alkhaleejiahadv.com.sa
/srpc/jamila
Weekly. Owner: Saudi Research &
Publishing. Editor: Sanaa Elhadethee

Allergy Magazine
020 7613 8777
www.allergymagazine.com
Bi-monthly. Owner: Ink Publishing.
Editor: Charmaine Yabsley

Asian Woman
0870 755 5501
www.aimplc.co.uk
Bi-monthly. Owner: Asian Interactive
Media. Editor: Nagina London

Asthma
020 7786 5000
www.asthma.org.uk
4pa. Owner: Asthma UK.
Editor: Laura Smith

A–Z of Calories
01984 623014
Bi-monthly. Owner: Octavo
Publications. Editor: Gertude Pertl

B
020 7150 7000
www.bmagazine.co.uk
Monthly. Owner: Hachette Filipacchi
UK. Editor: Frances Sheen

Baby & You
020 7331 1000
www.hhc.co.uk
Monthly. Owner: Highbury House.
Editor: Claire Davies

Balance
020 7424 1010
www.diabetes.org.uk
Bi-monthly. Owner: Diabetes UK.
Editor: Martin Cullen

Be Slim
01984 623014
4pa. Owner: Octavo Publications.
Editor: Gertude Pertl

Beautiful Brides
0117 934 3742
www.thisisbristol.co.uk/beautifulbrides
4pa. Owner: BUP Niche Publications.
Editor: Harry Mottram

Bella
020 7241 8000
www.bauer.co.uk
Weekly. Owner: H Bauer.
Editor: Jayne Marsden

Best
020 7439 5000
www.natmags.co.uk
Weekly. Owner: National Magazine
Company. Editor: Louise Court

Black Beauty & Hair
020 7720 2108
www.blackbeautyandhair.com
Bi-monthly. Owner: Hawker Consumer
Publications. Editor: Irene Shelley

Blackhair
01376 534549
Bi-monthly. Owner: Hairflair
Magazines. Editor: Jane MacArthur

Bliss for Brides
01376 534549
www.blissforbrides.co.uk
Bi-monthly. Owner: For the Bride
Publishing. Editor: Abbey Wade

Brides
020 7499 9080
www.bridesuk.net
Bi-monthly. Owner: Condé Nast.
Editor: Liz Savage

Caduceus Journal
01926 451897
www.caduceus.info
4pa. Editor: Sarida Brown

Candis
0870 745 3002
www.candis.co.uk
Monthly. Owner: New Hall
Publications. Editor: Jenny Campbell

Chat
020 7261 6570
www.ipcmedia.com
Weekly. Owner: IPC Media.
Editor: June Smith-Sheppard

Closer
020 7437 9011
www.emap.com
Weekly. Owner: Emap.
Editor: Jane Johnson

Company
020 7439 5000
www.company.co.uk
Monthly. Owner: National Magazine
Company. Editor: Victoria White

Cosmopolitan
020 7439 5000
www.cosmopolitan.co.uk
Monthly. Owner: National Magazine
Company. Editor: Sam Baker

Cosmopolitan Hair & Beauty
020 7439 5000
www.cosmohairandbeauty.co.uk
Monthly. Owner: National Magazine
Company. Editor: Melanie Goose

Elle
020 7150 7000
www.hf-uk.com
Monthly. Owner: Hachette Filipacchi
UK. Editor: Lorraine Candy

Emma's Diary Pregnancy Guide
enquiries@emmasdiary.net
www.emmasdiary.net
Weekly. Owner: Lifecycle Marketing

Essentials
020 7261 5553
www.ipcmedia.com
Monthly. Owner: IPC Media.
Editor: Julie Barton-Breck

Eve
020 8433 1070
www.evemagazine.co.uk
Monthly. Owner: Haymarket.
Editor: Sara Cremer

Family Circle
020 7261 6193
www.ipcmedia.com
Monthly. Owner: IPC Media.
Editor: Karen Livermore

Family Magazine
01200 453000
www.family-mag.co.uk
Bi-monthly. Owner: RVPL.
Editor: Jeremy Nicholls

For the Bride
01376 534549
www.forthebride.co.uk
Bi-monthly. Owner: For the Bride
Publishing. Editor: Abbey Wade

Glamour
020 7499 9080
www.glamour.com
Monthly. Owner: Condé Nast.
Editor: Jo Elvin

Grazia
020 7437 9011
www.graziamagazine.co.uk
Weekly. Owner: Emap.
Editor-in-chief: Fiona McIntosh;
editor: Jane Bruton

Hair
020 7261 6974
www.ipcmedia.com
Bi-monthly. Owner: IPC Media.
Editor: Zoe Richards

Hair & Beauty
020 7436 9766
Bi-monthly. Owner: Style Media.
Editor: Laura Curtis

Hair Now
020 7436 9766
Bi-monthly. Owner: Style Media.
Editor: Tim Frisby

Hairflair
01376 534549
9pa. Owner: Hairflair Magazines.
Editor: Ruth Page

Hairstyles Only
01376 534549
9pa. Owner: Hairflair Magazines.
Editor: Ruth Page

Happy
0871 434 1010
www.happymagazine.co.uk
Monthly. Owner: Northern and Shell.
Editor: Eilidh Macaskill

Harpers & Queen
020 7439 5000
www.harpersandqueen.co.uk
Monthly. Owner: National Magazine
Company. Editor: Lucy Yeomans

Health & Fitness
020 7331 1000
www.hfonline.co.uk
Monthly. Owner: Future. Editor: Mary
Comber

The Health Store Magazine
020 7385 0074
www.thehealthstore.co.uk
Bi-monthly. Editor: Jane Garton

Healthy
020 7306 0304
www.therivergroup.co.uk
Bi-monthly. Owner: River Publishing.
Editor: Heather Beresford

Healthy Times
020 7819 1111
www.squareonegroup.co.uk
Quarterly. Owner: Square One Group.
Editor: Sharon Gray

Heat
020 7437 9011
www.emap.com
Weekly. Owner: Emap.
Editor: Mark Frith

Hello!
020 7667 8901
www.hellomagazine.com
Weekly; website updated daily.
Editor: Ronnie Whelan

Hia
020 7539 2270
Monthly. Owner: Al Madina Printing &
Publishing Company. Editor: Mai Badr

InStyle
020 7261 4747
www.ipcmedia.com
Monthly. Owner: IPC Media.
Editor: Louise Chunn

Jane
020 7240 0420
www.janemag.com
Monthly. Owner: Fairchild.
Editor: Jane Pratt

Junior
020 7761 8900
www.juniormagazine.co.uk
Monthly. Owner: Future.
Editor: Catherine O'Dolan

Junior Pregnancy & Baby
020 7761 8900
www.juniormagazine.co.uk
Monthly. Owner: Future.
Editor: Debora Stottor

Ladies First
029 2039 6600
www.hilspublications.com
4pa. Owner: Hils Publications.
Editor: Hilary Ferda

The Lady
020 7379 4717
www.thelady.co.uk
Weekly. Owner: Arline Usden

Marie Claire
020 7261 5177
www.ipcmedia.com
Monthly. Owner: IPC Media.
Editor: Marie O'Riordan

More!
020 7859 8606
www.moremagazine.co.uk
Fortnightly. Owner: Emap.
Editor: Alison Hall

Mother & Baby
020 7874 0200
www.emap.com
Monthly. Owner: Emap.
Editor: Eleanor Dalrymple

Ms London
020 7005 2000
www.independent.co.uk
Weekly. Owner: Independent News &
Media (UK). Editor: Bill Williamson

MS Matters
020 8438 0700
www.mssociety.org.uk
Bi-monthly. Owner: Multiple Sclerosis
Society. Editor: Debbie Reeves

My Weekly
01382 223131
www.dcthomson.co.uk
Weekly. Owner: DC Thomson.
Editor: Harrison Watson

New Woman
020 7437 9011
www.newwoman.co.uk
Monthly. Owner: Emap.
Editor: Margi Conklin

New!
0871 434 1010
Weekly. Owner: Northern and Shell.
Editor: Kirsty Mouatt

Now
020 7261 6274
www.nowmagazine.com
Weekly. Owner: IPC Media.
Editor: Jane Ennis

Number Ten
020 7439 9100
www.numberten.co.uk
Bi-annual. Owner: Arberry Pink.
Editor: Laura Sheed

OK!
0871 434 1010
www.ok-magazine.com
Weekly. Owner: Northern and Shell.
Editor: Lisa Palta

Parent News UK
020 8337 6337
www.parents-news.co.uk
Monthly. Editor: Penny McCarthy

Parent Talk
020 7450 9072/3
www.parentalk.co.uk
Website updated weekly.
Editor: Maggie Doherty

People
020 7322 1134
www.people.com
Weekly. Owner: Time Life.
Editor: Bryan Alexander

Pick Me Up
020 7261 5588
www.pick-me-up.co.uk
Weekly. Owner: IPC Media.
Editor: June Smith-Sheppard

Practical Parenting
020 7261 5058
www.ipcmedia.com
Monthly. Owner: IPC Media.
Editor: Mara Lee

Pregnancy and Birth
020 7347 1885
www.emap.com
Monthly. Owner: Emap.
Editor: Kaye McIntosh

Pregnancy Magazine
020 7331 1000
Monthly. Owner: Future. Editor: Claire
Roberts

Pride Magazine
020 7228 3110
www.pridemagazine.com
Monthly. Owner: Pride Media.
Editor: Sherry Dixon

Prima
020 7439 5000
www.primamagazine.co.uk
Monthly. Owner: National Magazine
Company. Editor: Maire Fahey

Prima Baby
020 7439 5000
www.primababy.co.uk
Monthly. Owner: National Magazine
Company. Editor: Julia Goodwin

Real
01206 851117
www.essentialpublishing.co.uk
Fortnightly. Owner: Essential
Publishing. Editor: Sian Rees

Real Health & Fitness
020 7306 0304
www.therivergroup.co.uk
Bi-monthly. Owner: River Publishing.
Editor: Andy Darling

Red
020 7150 7000
www.redmagazine.co.uk
Monthly. Owner: Hachette Filipacchi
UK. Editor: Trish Halpin

Reveal
020 7439 5000
www.natmags.co.uk
Weekly. Owner: National Magazine
Company. Editor: Sarah Edwards

Rosemary Conley Diet & Fitness Magazine
01509 620444
www.conley.co.uk/magazine
9pa. Owner: Quorn House Publishing.
Editor: Geri Hosier

She
020 7439 5000
www.she.co.uk
Monthly. Owner: National Magazine
Company. Editor: Terry Tavner

Slimmer, Healthier, Fitter
01206 505972
www.slimmerrecipes.co.uk
10pa. Owner: Aceville Publications.
Editor: Helen Mulley

Slimming Magazine
020 7874 0200
www.emap.com
Monthly. Owner: Emap.
Editor: Marie Farqharson

Slimming World
01773 546360
www.slimming-world.com
7pa. Editor: Christine Michael

Star
0871 434 1010
Weekly. Owner: Northern and Shell.
Editor: Busola Odulate

Take a Break
020 7241 8000
www.bauer.co.uk
Weekly. Owner: H Bauer.
Editor: John Dale

Tatler
020 7499 9080
www.tatler.co.uk
Monthly. Owner: Condé Nast.
Editor: Geordie Greig

That's Life!
020 7241 8000
www.bauer.co.uk
Weekly. Owner: H Bauer.
Editor: Jo Checkley

Tiara
029 2039 6600
www.hilspublications.com
3pa. Owner: Hils Publications.
Editor: Hilary Ferda

Top Santé Health & Beauty
020 7437 9011
www.emap.com
Monthly. Owner: Emap.
Editor: Lauren Libbert

Twins, Triplets & More Magazine
0870 770 3305
www.tamba.org.uk
4pa. Owner: The Twins and Multiple
Births Association. Editor: Jane Williams

Ulster Bride
028 9066 3311
www.ulstertatler.com
Bi-monthly. Owner: Ulster Talter
Publications. Editor: Christopher Sherry

Ulster Tatler
028 9066 3311
www.ulstertatler.com
Monthly. Owner: Ulster Talter
Publications. Editor: Richard Sherry

Ultra-Fit
01736 350204
www.ultra-fitmagazine.com
8pa. Editor: Charles Mays

Vanity Fair
020 7499 9080
www.vanityfair.co.uk
Monthly. Owner: Condé Nast.
Editor: Henry Porter

Vogue
020 7499 9080
www.vogue.com
Monthly. Owner: Condé Nast.
Editor: Alexandra Shulman

W
020 7240 0420
www.wmagazine.com
Monthly. Owner: Fairchild.
Editor: Patrick McCarthy

Wave
01273 818160
www.thelatest.co.uk/wave
Monthly. Owner: The Latest.
Editor: Emma Amyatt-Leir

Wedding
020 7261 7470
www.weddingandhome.co.uk
Monthly. Owner: IPC Media.
Editor: Kate Barlow

Wedding Day
020 7761 8980
www.beachpublishing.co.uk
Bi-monthly. Owner: Beach
Publications. Editor: Alice Kodell

Wedding Journal
028 9045 7457
www.weddingjournalonline.com
Quarterly. Owner: Penton Group.
Editor: Tara Craig

WeightWatchers
020 8882 2555
8pa. Owner: Castlebar Publishing.
Editor: Barbara Raine-Allen

WM
029 2022 3333
www.icwales.co.uk
Quarterly. Owner: Trinity Mirror.
Editor: Nina Rabaiotti

Woman
020 7261 7023
www.ipcmedia.com
Weekly. Owner: IPC Media.
Editor: Lisa Burrow

Woman & Home
020 7261 5176
www.womanandhome.com
Monthly. Owner: IPC Media.
Editor: Sue James

Woman Alive
01903 821082
www.womanalive.co.uk
Monthly. Owner: Christian Publishing
and Outreach. Editor: Jackie Stead

Woman's Own
020 7261 5500
www.ipcmedia.com
Weekly. Owner: IPC Media.
Editor: Elsa McAlonan

Woman's Weekly
020 7261 6131
www.ipcmedia.com
Weekly. Owner: IPC Media.
Editor: Gilly Sinclair

Women's Health
020 7226 2222
www.hhc.co.uk
Monthly. Owner: Highbury House.
Editor: Tracey Smith

Women's Wear Daily (WWD)
020 7240 0420
www.wwd.com
Daily. Owner: Fairchild.
Editor: James Fallon

Yoga and Health
020 7480 5456
www.yogaandhealthmag.co.uk
Monthly. Owner: Yoga Today.
Editor: Jane Sill

You & Your Wedding
020 7439 5000
www.youandyourwedding.co.uk
6pa. Owner: National Magazine
Company. Editor: Carole Hamilton

Zest
020 7439 5000
www.zest.co.uk
Monthly. Owner: National Magazine
Company. Editor: Alison Pylkkanen

Major customer magazines

Asda Magazine
020 7462 7777
www.publicis-blueprint.co.uk
Monthly. Publisher: Publicis Blueprint.
Editor: Suzanne Carter

BMW Magazine
020 7534 2400
www.cedarcom.co.uk
Quarterly. Publisher: Cedar.
Editor: Andrew Gillingwater

Boots Health and Beauty
020 7747 0700
www.redwoodgroup.net
6pa. Publisher: Redwood.
Editor: Jan Boxshall

Caravan Club Magazine
01342 336804
www.caravanclub.co.uk
Monthly. Publisher: The Caravan Club.
Editor: Barry Williams

Carlos – Virgin Atlantic Upper Class
020 7565 3000
www.jbcp.co.uk
Monthly. Publisher: John Brown
Publishing Group. Editor: Michael
Jacovides

Debenhams Desire
020 7462 7777
www.publicis-blueprint.co.uk
5pa. Publisher: Publicis Blueprint.
Editor: Amanda Morgan

Heritage Today
020 7565 3000
www.english-heritage-books.org.uk
Quarterly. Publisher: John Brown
Publishing Group. Editor: Francine
Lawrence

High Life
020 7534 2400
www.cedarcom.co.uk
Monthly. Publisher: Cedar.
Editor: Scott Manson

Homebase Ideas
020 7462 7777
www.publicis-blueprint.co.uk
Quarterly. Publisher: Publicis
Blueprint. Editor: Ward Hellewell

Honda Dream
020 7306 0304
www.therivergroup.co.uk
Quarterly. Publisher: River Publishing.
Editor: Chris Hatherill

Hotline (Virgin Trains)
020 7306 0304
www.therivergroup.co.uk
Quarterly. Publisher: River Publishing.
Editor: Rod Stanley

Motoring & Leisure
01273 744757
www.csma.uk.com
10pa. Publisher: CSMA.
Editor: David Arnold

National Trust Magazine
020 7222 9251
www.nationaltrust.org.uk
3pa. Publisher: National Trust.
Editor: Gaynor Aaltonen

O Magazine
020 7565 3000
www.jbcp.co.uk
Monthly. Publisher: John Brown
Publishing Group. Editor: Sean Kearns

The Renault Magazine – Vanguard
020 7462 7777
www.publicis-blueprint.co.uk
Quarterly. Publisher: Publicis
Blueprint. Editor: Jason Day

Saga Magazine
01303 771523
www.saga.co.uk
Monthly. Publisher: Saga Group.
Editor: Emma Soames

Sainsbury's Magazine
020 7633 0266
www.sainsburysmagazine.co.uk
Monthly. Publisher: New Crane
Publishing. Editor: Sue Robinson

Sky The Magazine
020 7565 3000
www.jbcp.co.uk
Monthly. Publisher: John Brown
Publishing Group. Editor: Simon Geller

Somerfield Magazine
0117 989 7808
www.somerfield.co.uk
13pa. Publisher: Rare Publishing.
Editor: Hannah Smith

Spirit of Superdrug
020 7306 0304
www.therivergroup.co.uk
Monthly. Publisher: River Publishing.
Editor: Joani Walsh

Triangle
020 8267 5000
www.haymarketpublishing.co.uk
2pa. Publisher: Haymarket.
Editor: Emma Pearson

Unlimited
0117 927 9009
www.originpublishing.co.uk
10pa. Publisher: Origin Publishing.
Editor: Pat Reid

VM – Vauxhall
01582 426909
http://vauxhall.co.uk/vmmagazine/
3pa. Publisher: Brooklands Publishing.
Editor: Michelle Howard

Waitrose Food Illustrated
020 7565 3000
www.jbcp.co.uk
Monthly. Publisher: John Brown
Publishing Group. Editor: William
Sitwell

Your M&S Magazine
020 7747 0700
www.redwoodgroup.net
4pa. Publisher: Redwood.
Editor: Diane Kenwood

Business and trade press

Business

Accountancy
020 8247 1387
www.accountancymagazine.com
Monthly. Owner: CCH.
Editor: Chris Quick

Accountancy Age
020 7316 9000
www.accountancyage.com
Weekly. Owner: VNU.
Editor: Damian Wild

Accounting & Business
020 7396 5966
www.accaglobal.com
10pa. Owner: Certified Accountants
(Publications). Editor: John Prosser

Accounting Technician
020 7837 8600
www.accountingtechnician.co.uk
Monthly. Owner: Association of
Accounting Agencies. Editor: Fritha
Sutherland

Assessment
020 7801 2884
www.pcs.org.uk/revenue
Monthly. Owner: Public & Commercial
Services Union. Editor: Denis Calnan

Bradmans Business Travel Guides
020 7613 8777
www.bradmans.com
Yearly. Owner: Ink Publishing.
Editor: Richard Bence

Brand Strategy
020 7970 4000
www.mad.co.uk
Monthly. Owner: Centaur.
Editor: Elen Lewis

Business Informer
0191 518 4281
Bi-monthly. Owner: Deneholme
Publishing. Editor: Alan Roxborough

Business Traveller
020 7779 8888
www.businesstraveller.com
10pa. Owner: Panacea Publishing
International. Editor: Tom Otley

CFO Europe
020 7830 1090
www.cfoeurope.com
11pa. Owner: The Economist
Newspaper. Editor: Janet Kersnar

Corporate Citizenship Briefing
020 7940 5610
www.ccbriefing.co.uk
Bi-monthly. Founding editor: Mike
Tuffrey

Creative Review
020 7970 4000
www.mad.co.uk
Monthly. Owner: Centaur.
Editor: Patrick Burgoyne

Design Week
020 7970 4000
www.mad.co.uk
Weekly. Owner: Centaur.
Editor: Lynda Relph-Knight

Director
020 7766 8950
www.iod.com
Monthly. Owner: Director Publications.
Editor: Joanna Higgins

Employee Benefits
020 7970 4000
www.employeebenefits.co.uk
Monthly. Owner: Centaur.
Editor: Debi O'Donovan

Euromoney
020 7779 8888
www.euromoneyplc.com
Monthly. Owner: Euromoney
Institutional Investor. Editor: Peter Lee

Finance Week
020 7970 4000
www.financeweek.co.uk
Weekly. Owner: Centaur.
Editor: Sean Brierly

Financial Advisor
00 1 732 450 8866
www.financialadvisormagazine.com
Weekly. Owner: Charter Financial
Publishing Network.
Senior editor: Raymond Fazzi

Financial Management
020 7368 7177
www.cimaglobal.com
Monthly. Owner: Caspian.
Editor: Ruth Prickett

Financial News
01227 818605
www.efinancialnews.com
Weekly. Editor: William Wright

Financial World
01227 818609
www.financialworld.co.uk
Monthly. Owner: Caspian.
Editor: Denise Smith

First Voice of Business
01223 477411
www.campublishers.com
Bi-monthly. Owner: Cambridge
Publishers. Editor: Mike Sewell

Fund Strategy
020 7970 4000
www.fundstrategy.co.uk
Weekly. Owner: Centaur.
Editor: Daniel Ben-Ami

Growing Business
020 8334 1661
www.gbmag.co.uk
Monthly. Owner: Crimson Publishing.
Features editor: Matt Thomas

Human Resources
020 8267 4641
www.humanresourcesmagazine.com
11pa. Owner: Haymarket.
Editor: Trevor Merriden

Industrial Focus
020 7014 0300
www.industrialfocus.co.uk
Bi-monthly. Owner: Tower Publishing.
Editor: Mike Wearing

Institutional Investor – International Edition
020 7779 8888
www.iilondon.com
Monthly. Owner: Euromoney
Institutional Investor.
Editor: Andrew Capon

In-Store
020 7970 4000
www.mad.co.uk
Monthly. Owner: Centaur.
Editor: Matthew Valentine

Insurance Age
020 7484 9700
www.insuranceage.com
Monthly. Owner: Incisive Media.
Editor: Michelle Worvell

Investor Relations
020 7637 3579
www.ironthenet.com
Monthly. Owner: Cross-Border
Publishing. Editor: Claire Hunte

The Journal
020 7534 2400
www.cedarcom.co.uk
Bi-monthly. Owner: Cedar.
Editor: John Guy

Landscape and Amenity Product Update
01952 200809
www.landscapespecification.com
6pa. Owner: Tanner Stiles Publishing.
Editor: David Stiles

Logistics Manager
020 7970 4000
www.logisticsmanager.co.uk
Monthly. Owner: Centaur.
Editor: Maureen Gaines

Management Today
020 8267 5000
www.mtmagazine.co.uk
Monthly. Owner: Haymarket.
Editor: Matthew Gwyther

Marketing Week
020 7970 4000
www.mad.co.uk
Weekly. Owner: Centaur.
Editor: Stuart Smith

MiD
020 7612 9300
www.infoconomy.com
Bi-monthly. Owner: Infoconomy.
Editor: Graeme Burton

Money Marketing
020 7970 4000
www.centaur.co.uk
Weekly. Owner: Centaur.
Editor: John Lappin

Mortgage Strategy
020 7970 4000
www.mortgagestrategy.co.uk
Weekly. Owner: Centaur.
Editor: Robyn Hall

New Business
020 7407 9800
www.newbusiness.co.uk
Quarterly. Owner: IBMG.
Editor: Nick Martindale

New Media Age
020 7970 4000
www.nma.co.uk/
Weekly. Owner: Centaur.
Editor: Michael Nutley

OS Magazine
0141 567 6000
www.peeblesmedia.com
Bi-monthly. Owner: Peebles Media
Group. Editor: Mike Travers

Overseas Trade
020 7368 9600
www.overseas-trade.co.uk
Monthly. Owner: Rare Publishing.
Editor: Janet Tibble

Pensions & Investments
020 7457 1430
www.pionline.com
Fortnightly. Owner: Crain
Communications. Editor: Nancy
Webman

Pensions Age
020 7426 0424
www.pensions-age.com
Monthly. Owner: Pensions Age
Magazine. Editor: Francesca Fabrizi

People Management
020 7880 6200
www.peoplemanagement.co.uk
Fortnightly. Owner: Redactive
Publishing. Editor: Steve Crabb

Personnel Today
020 8652 3941
www.personneltoday.com
Weekly. Owner: Reed Business
Information. Editor: Jane King

Professional Manager
020 7421 2705
www.managers.org.uk
Bi-monthly. Owner: Chartered
Management Institute. Editor: Sue Mann

Public Private Finance
020 7970 4000
www.publicprivatefinance.co.uk
Monthly. Owner: Centaur.
Editor: Mark Hellowell.

Real Business
020 7368 7177
www.realbusiness.co.uk
Monthly. Owner: Caspian.
Editor: Adam Leyland

Recruiter Magazine
020 7880 6226
www.recruitermagazine.co.uk
Fortnightly. Owner: Redactive
Publishing. Editor: Dee Dee Doke

StartUps.co.uk
020 8334 1721
www.startups.co.uk
Website, updated hourly.
Online editor: Dan Matthews

Supply Management
020 7880 6200
www.supplymanagement.co.uk
Fortnightly. Owner: Redactive
Publishing. Editor: Geraint John

What's New In Industry
020 7970 4000
www.centaur.co.uk
Monthly. Owner: Centaur.
Editor: David Keighley

Construction and engineering

ABC&D
01527 834400
www.abc-d.co.uk
*Monthly. Owner: Centaur. Editors:
Barry Cooke and Claire Mackle*

Architecture Today
020 7837 0143
www.architecturetoday.co.uk
*10pa. Editors: Ian Latham, Mark
Swenarton*

Builder & Engineer
0161 236 2782
www.builderandengineer.co.uk
*Monthly. Owner: Excel Publishing.
Editor: Alex Kearns*

Building
020 7560 4149
www.building.co.uk
*Weekly. Owner: CMP Information.
Editor: Denise Chevin*

Building Design
020 7921 8200
www.bdonline.co.uk
*Weekly. Owner: CMP Information.
Editor: Robert Booth*

Building Products
020 8565 4387
www.buildingproducts.co.uk
*Monthly. Owner: Quantum Business
Media. Editor: Phil Stronach*

Construction Manager
020 7560 4000
www.construction-manager.co.uk
*10pa. Owner: The Builder Group.
Editor: Rod Sweet*

Construction News
020 7505 6868
www.cnplus.co.uk
*Weekly. Owner: Emap.
Editor: Aaron Morby*

Construction Products
020 7505 6868
www.cnplus.co.uk
*Monthly. Owner: Emap.
Editor: Julian Birch*

Contract Journal
020 8652 4761
www.contractjournal.com
*Weekly. Owner: Reed Business
Information. Editor: Rob Willock*

Electronics
01622 699174
www.connectingindustry.com
11pa. Editor: Joanne Bennett

Electronics Weekly
020 8652 3650
www.electronicsweekly.com
*Weekly. Owner: Reed Business
Information. Editor: Richard Wilson*

The Engineer
020 7970 4000
www.e4engineering.com
*Fortnightly. Owner: Centaur.
Editor: Andrew Lee*

Gas Installer
020 7401 4101
*Monthly. Owner: Corgi.
Editor: Nicole Perry*

IEE Review
01438 313311
www.iee.org/review
*Monthly. Owner: The Institution of
Electrical Engineers. Editor: Dickon Ross*

Metal Working Production
020 7970 4000
www.mwp.co.uk
*Monthly. Owner: Centaur.
Editor: Mike Excell*

New Civil Engineer
020 7505 6600
www.nceplus.co.uk
*Weekly. Owner: Emap.
Editor: Antony Oliver*

Offshore
01992 656 657
www.offshore-mag.com
*Monthly. Owner: Penwell Corporation.
Editor: Eldon Ball*

Pipeline World
01494 675139
www.pipemag.com
*Bi-monthly. Owner: Scientific Surveys.
Editor: John Tiratsoo*

PIR Construction
0870 749 0220
www.pirnet.co.uk
*6pa. Owner: The Bellmont Agency.
Editor: Derek Cooper*

Process Engineering
020 7970 4000
www.processengineering.co.uk
*Monthly. Owner: Centaur.
Editor: Mike Spear*

Professional Electrician & Installer
01923 237799
www.hamerville.co.uk
*11pa. Owner: Hamerville Magazines.
Editor: Richard Pagett*

Professional Engineering
020 7973 1299
www.profeng.com
*Fortnightly. Owner: Professional
Engineering Publishing.
Editor: John Pullin*

**Professional Heating & Plumbing
Installer**
01923 237799
www.hamerville.co.uk
*11pa. Owner: Hamerville Magazines.
Editor: Stuart Hamilton*

Public Sector Building
01527 834400
www.centaur.co.uk
*6pa. Owner: Centaur.
Publisher: Derek Rogers*

RIBA Journal
020 7921 8560
www.ribajournal.com
*Monthly. Owner: The Builder Group.
Editor: Amanda Baillieu*

What's New In Building
020 7560 4193
www.wnibonline.com/
*Monthly. Owner: CMP information.
Editor: Mark Pennington*

Defence

Airforces Monthly
01780 755131
www.airforcesmonthly.com
*Monthly. Owner: Key Publishing.
Editor: Malcolm English*

Jane's Defence Weekly
020 8700 3700
www.janes.com
*Weekly. Owner: Jane's.
Editor: Peter Felstead*

Navy News
023 9229 4228
www.navynews.co.uk
Monthly. Editor: Jim Allaway

Soldier
01252 347356
www.soldiermagazine.co.uk
Monthly. Editor: John Elliott

Education

Child Education
0845 850 4411
www.scholastic.co.uk
*Monthly. Owner: Scholastic.
Editor: Michael Ward*

Education Today
020 7947 9536
www.collegeofteachers.ac.uk
*Quarterly. Owner: College of Teachers.
Editor: Brychan Thomas*

Education Travel Magazine
020 7440 4025
www.hothousemedia.com
*Bi-monthly. Owner: Hothouse Media.
Editor: Amy Baker*

FE Now
01458 830033
www.aoc.co.uk
*4pa. Owner: The Association of Colleges.
Editor: Sara Clay*

Gair Rhydd
029 2078 1400
www.cardiffstudents.com
*Weekly. Owner: Cardiff Union Services.
Editor: Tom Wellingham*

Governors' News
0121 643 5787
www.nagm.org.uk
*5pa. Owner: National Association of
School Governors. Editor: TBC*

Higher Education Review
020 8341 1366
www.highereducationreview.com
3pa. Editor: John Pratt

ICT for Education
020 8334 1600
www.ictforeducation.co.uk
*Monthly. Owner: Crimson Publishing.
Editor: Ian Delaney*

The Lecturer
020 7837 3636
www.natfhe.org.uk
*5pa. Owner: NATFHE.
Editors: Brenda Kirsch, Midge Purcell*

LSE Magazine
020 7955 7582
www.lse.ac.uk
*2pa. Owner: London School of
Economics. Editor: Judith Higgin*

The Magic Key
020 8433 2883
www.bbcmagazines.com
Monthly. Owner: BBC Worldwide.
Editor: Stephanie Cooper

Nursery Education
01926 887799
www.scholastic.co.uk
Monthly. Owner: Scholastic.
Editor: Sarah Sodhi

Nursery World
020 7782 3000
www.nurseryworld.co.uk
Weekly. Owner: TSL Education.
Editor: Liz Roberts

Open Learner
01223 400362
www.nec.ac.uk
Website. Editor: Sarah Lawrence

Oxford Today
01865 280545
www.oxfordtoday.ox.ac.uk
3pa. Owner: University of Oxford.
Editor: Georgina Ferry

Report
020 7930 6441
www.askatl.org.uk
10pa. Owner: Association of Teachers
and Lecturers. Editor: Heather Pinnell

Right Start
020 7878 2338
www.rightstartmagazine.co.uk
Bi-monthly. Owner: McMillan-Scott.
Editor: Lynette Lowthian

Scottish Educational Journal
0131 225 6244
www.eis.org.uk
5pa. Owner: Educational Institute of
Scotland. Editor: Simon MacAulay

Sesame
01908 653011
www.open.ac.uk/sesame
4pa. Owner: Open University.
Editor: Yvonne Cook

Special Schools Guide
020 7970 4000
www.centaur.co.uk
Annual. Owner: Centaur.
Publisher: Derek Rogers

Student Direct
0161 275 2943
www.student-direct.co.uk
Weekly during term.
Editor: Alexa Gainsbury

The Teacher
020 7380 4708
www.teachers.org.uk
8pa. Owner: Redactive Publishing.
Editor: Mitch Howard

Teaching Today
0121 457 6248
www.teachersunion.org.uk
5pa. Owner: NASUWT. Editor: Joe Devo

Times Educational Supplement
020 7782 3000
www.tes.co.uk
Weekly. Owner: TSL Education.
Editor: Judith Judd

Times Higher Education Supplement
020 7782 3000
www.thes.co.uk
Weekly. Owner: TSL Education.
Editor: John O'Leary

Farming

British Dairying
01438 716220
Monthly. Owner: WB Publishing.
Editor: Judie Allen

Crop Production Magazine
01743 761739
www.cpm.gb.net
Monthly Feb–Oct.
Editor: Angus McKirdy

Crops
020 8652 4923
www.reedbusiness.co.uk
Fortnightly. Owner: Reed Business
Information. Editor: Charles Abel

Dairy Farmer
01732 377273
16pa. Owner: CMP Information.
Editor: Peter Hollinshead

Farmers Guardian
01772 799411
www.farmersguardian.com
Weekly. Owner: CMP Information.
Editor: Liz Falkingham

Farmers Weekly
020 8652 4912
www.fwi.co.uk
Weekly. Owner: Reed Business
Information. Editor: Stephen Howe

Feed International
00 31 30 659 2236
www.wattnet.com
Monthly. Owner: Watt Publishing.
Editor: Clayton Gill

Living Earth
0117 914 2434
www.soilassociation.org
3pa. Editor: Elisabeth Winkler

NFU Horticulture
020 7331 7359
www.nfuonline.com
3pa. Owner: NFU. Editor: Freya Rodger

Poultry International
00 31 30 659 2234
www.wattnet.com
Monthly. Owner: Watt Publishing.
Editor: Jackie Linden

Scottish Farmer
0141 302 7700
www.newsquest.co.uk
Weekly. Owner: Newsquest.
Editor: Alistair Fletcher

Tractor & Machinery
01959 541444
www.kelsey.co.uk
Monthly. Owner: Kelsey Publishing.
Editor: Peter Love

Health and social care

Ambulance Today
0151 708 8864
Quarterly. Editor: Declan Heneghan

Arthritis News
020 7380 6521
www.arthritiscare.org.uk
Bi-monthly. Owner: Arthritis Care.
Editor: Kate Llewelyn

BMJ
020 7387 4499
www.bmj.com
Weekly. Owner: BMJ Publishing Group.
Editor: Fiona Godlee

Care and Health
0870 901 7773
www.careandhealth.com
Weekly. Editor: Marcia White

Community Care
020 8652 4886
www.communitycare.co.uk
Weekly. Owner: Reed Business
Information. Editor: Polly Neate

Doctor
020 8652 8740
www.doctorupdate.net
Weekly. Owner: Reed Business
Information. Editor: Charles Creswell

Druglink
020 7922 8605
www.drugscope.co.uk
Bi-monthly. Owner: DrugScope.
Editor: Harry Shapiro

GP
020 8267 4846
www.gponline.com
Weekly. Owner: Haymarket.
Editor: Bronagh Miskelly

Health Service Journal
020 7874 0200
www.hsj.co.uk
Weekly. Owner: Emap.
Editor: Alastair McLellan

Hospital Doctor
020 8652 8745
www.hospital-doctor.net
Weekly. Owner: Reed Business
Information. Editor: Mike Broad

The Lancet
020 7424 4910
www.lancet.com
Weekly. Owner: Elsevier.
Editor: Richard Horton

Medeconomics
020 8267 5000
www.gponline.com
Monthly. Owner: Haymarket.
Editor: Julian Tyndale-Biscoe

MIMS
020 8267 5000
www.gponline.com
Monthly. Owner: Haymarket.
Editor: Colin Duncan

Nursing Standard
020 8423 1066
www.nursing-standard.co.uk
Weekly. Owner: RCN Publishing.
Editor: Jean Gray

Nursing Times
020 7874 0500
www.nursingtimes.net
Weekly. Owner: Emap.
Editor: Rachel Downey

The Pharmaceutical Journal
020 7572 2414
www.pjonline.com
Weekly. Owner: Royal Pharmaceutical
Society of Great Britain.
Editor: Olivia Timbs

The Practitioner
020 7921 8113
www.practitioner-i.co.uk
Monthly. Owner: CMP Information.
Editor: Gavin Atkin

The Psychologist
0116 252 9573
www.bps.org.uk/publications
/thepsychologist
Monthly. Owner: The British
Psychological Society.
Editor: Dr Jon Sutton

Pulse
020 7921 8106
www.pulse-i.co.uk
49pa. Owner: CMP Information.
Editor: Phil Johnson

RCN Bulletin
020 8423 1066
www.nursing-standard.co.uk
Weekly. Owner: RCN Publishing.
Editor: Ken Edwards

Update
020 8652 8760
www.doctorupdate.net
Monthly. Owner: Reed Business
Information. Editor: Anna Sayburn

▶▶ SEE ALSO DISABILITY, page 118

Housing

Housing Association Magazine
0121 682 8881
www.wavcoms.co.uk
Bi-monthly. Owner: Waverley
Communications.
Editor: Bruce Meecham

Inside Housing
020 7772 8300
www.insidehousing.co.uk
Weekly. Owner: Inside
Communications. Editor: Kate Murray

Regeneration & Renewal
020 8267 4381
www.regenerationmagazine.com
Weekly. Owner: Haymarket.
Editor: Richard Garlick

Roof
020 7505 2161
www.roofmag.org.uk
Bi-monthly. Owner: Shelter.
Editor: Emma Hawkey

Law

Law Society Gazette
020 7841 5546
www.lawgazette.co.uk
Weekly. Owner: The Law Society.
Editor: Jonathan Ames

The Lawyer
020 7970 4000
www.centaur.co.uk
Weekly. Owner: Centaur.
Editor: Catrin Griffiths

Legal Week
020 7566 5600
www.legalweek.com
Weekly. Owner: Legal Week Global
Media. Editor: John Malpas

Media Lawyer
01229 716622
www.medialawyer.press.net
Bi-monthly. Owner: Press Association.
Editor: Tom Welsh

Media

▶▶ JOURNALISM, page 120

  TV, page 189

  RADIO, page 230

  NEW MEDIA, page 241

  GLOBAL MEDIA, page 252

  BOOKS, page 284

  FILM, page 296

  MUSIC, page 309

  ADVERTISING, page 325

  PR, page 335

  MEDIA LAW, page 349

Police

Constabulary Magazine
0870 350 1892
Monthly. Owner: National Press
Publishers. Editor-in-chief: Christopher
Locke

Police Magazine
020 8335 1000
www.polfed.org
Monthly. Owner: Police Federation of
England & Wales. Editor: Metin Enver

Police Review
020 8276 4729
www.policereview.com
Weekly. Owner: Jane's. Editor:
Catriona Marchant

Property

The Estate Agent
01926 496800
www.naea.co.uk
10pa. Owner: The National Association
of Estate Agents. Editor: June Warner

Estates Gazette
020 7911 1805
www.reedbusiness.co.uk
Weekly. Owner: Reed Business
Information. Editor: Peter Bill

Facilities Management Journal
020 8771 3614
www.fmarena.com
Monthly. Owner: Market Place
Publishing. Editor: Mark Povey

Facilities Management UK
0161 683 8032
www.worldsfair.co.uk
Bi-monthly. Owner: World's Fair.
Editor: Mike Appleton

Sold Out
020 7702 3322
www.soldoutonline.co.uk
Monthly. Owner: CI Publications.
Editor: Philip Cowan

Retail and catering

Asian Trader
020 7928 1234
www.gg2.net
Fortnightly. Owner: Garavi Gujarat
Publications. Editor: R Solanki

Caterer and Hotelkeeper
020 8652 4210
www.reedbusinessinformation.co.uk
Weekly. Owner: Reed Business
Information. Editor: Mark Lewis

Caterer and Licensee News
01202 552333
www.catererlicensee.co.uk
Monthly. Owner: RBC Publishing.
Editor: Peter Adams

Catering Update
020 8652 8307
www.reedbusiness.co.uk
Monthly. Owner: Reed Business
Information. Editor: Kathy Bowry

Chain Leader UK
020 8652 3370
www.chainleaderuk.co.uk
Monthly. Owner: Reed Business
Information. Editor: Forbes Mutch

Class
01293 610442
www.william-reed.co.uk
Monthly. Owner: William Reed
Publishing. Editor: Paul Wootton

Convenience Store
01293 610218
www.william-reed.co.uk
Fortnightly. Owner: William Reed
Publishing. Editor: David Rees

DNR
020 7240 0420
www.dnrnews.com
Weekly. Owner: Fairchild.
Editor: Jon Birmingham

Drapers
020 7812 3700
www.drapersonline.com
Weekly. Owner: Emap.
Editor: Josephine Collins

Eat Out
01474 574436
www.dewberry-boyes.co.uk
Monthly. Owner: Dewberry Boyes.
Editor: David Foad

Food Manufacture
01293 610231
www.foodmanufacture.co.uk
Monthly. Owner: William Reed
Publishing. Editor: Rick Pendrous

Footwear News (FN)
020 7240 0420
www.footwearnews.com
Weekly. Owner: Fairchild. Editor:
Michel Atmore

Forecourt Trader
01293 610219
www.william-reed.co.uk
Monthly. Owner: William Reed
Publishing. Editor: Merril Boulton

The Franchise Magazine
01603 620301
www.franchise-group.com
8pa. Owner: Franchise Development
Services. Editor: Stuart Anderson

The Grocer
01293 610259
www.grocertoday.co.uk
Weekly. Owner: William Reed
Publishing. Editor: Sheila Sheridan

Hospitality
0161 236 2782
www.excelpublishing.co.uk
Monthly. Owner: Excel Publishing.
Editor: Eithne Dunne

Independent Retail News
01322 611240
www.irn-talkingshop.co.uk
Fortnightly. Owner: Nexus Holdings.
Editor: Richard Siddle

Leisure Report
01293 846 559
www.martin-info.com
Monthly. Owner: William Reed
Publishing. Acting editor: Duncan Rowe

MA Scotland
0141 222 5381
www.william-reed.co.uk
Fortnightly. Owner: William Reed
Publishing. Editor: Tom Stainer

MBR
01293 610268
www.william-reed.co.uk
Monthly. Owner: William Reed
Publishing. Editor: Mary Carmichael

Morning Advertiser
01293 610480
www.william-reed.co.uk
Weekly. Owner: William Reed
Publishing. Editor: Andrew Pring

Off Licence News
01293 610226
www.william-reed.co.uk
Weekly. Owner: William Reed
Publishing. Editor: Graham Holter

Party Times
01926 886588
www.partytimes.biz
Bi-monthly. Owner: Plaza Publishing.
Editor: Andrew Maiden

PubChef
01293 610487
www.william-reed.co.uk
Monthly. Owner: William Reed
Publishing. Editor: Jo Bruce

The Publican
020 8565 4200
www.thepublican.com
42pa. Owner: United Advertising
Publications. Editor: Caroline Nodder

Sales Promotion
01799 544200
www.salespromo.co.uk
Monthly. Owner: Archant.
Editor: Jerry Glenwright, Gill Crawley

Shopping Centre
01293 610294
www.william-reed.co.uk
Monthly. Owner: William Reed
Publishing. Editor: Pat Morgan

Supermarket News
020 7240 0420
www.supermarketnews.com
Weekly. Owner: Fairchild.
Editor-in-chief: David Orgel

Toy News
01992 535646
www.toynewsmag.com
Weekly. Owner: Intent Media.
Editor: Ronnie Dungan

The Trader
01202 445320
www.thetrader.co.uk
Monthly. Owner: United Advertising.
Publications

Women's Wear Daily (WWD)
020 7240 0420
www.wwd.com
Daily. Owner: Fairchild.
Editor: James Fallon

WWDBeautyBiz
020 7240 0420
www.wwd.com
9pa. Owner: Fairchild.
Editor: Jenny Fine

Science

Clinical Laboratory International
01442 877777
www.cli-online.com
8pa. Owner: Reed Business Information.
Editor: Frances Bushrod

Nature
020 7833 4000
www.nature.com
Weekly. Owner: Nature Publishing
Group. Editor: Phil Campbell

New Scientist
020 7611 1201
www.newscientist.com
Weekly. Owner: Reed Business
Information. Editor: Jeremy Webb

Science
01223 326500
www.sciencemag.org
Weekly. Owner: American Association
for the Advancement of Science.
Editor: Andrew Sugden

Technology

British Photographic Industry News
01799 544200
www.archant.co.uk
Monthly. Owner: Archant.
Editor: Terry Hope

Computer Business Review
020 7675 7910
www.cbronline.com
Monthly. Owner: Business Review.
Editor: Jason Stamper

Computer Weekly
020 8652 8450
www.computerweekly.com
Weekly. Owner: Reed Business
Information. Editor: Hooman Bassirian

Computing
020 7316 9000
www.computing.co.uk
Weekly. Owner: VNU. Editor: Toby Wolpe

Develop
01992 535646
www.developmag.com
Monthly. Owner: Intent Media.
Editor: Owain Bennallack

Developer Network Journal
0117 930 0255
www.dnjonline.com
Website. Owner: Matt Publishing.
Editor: Matt Nicholson

Information Age
020 7612 9300
www.infoconomy.com
Monthly. Owner: Infoconomy.
Editor: Kenny MacIver

IT Week
020 7316 9000
www.itweek.co.uk
Weekly. Owner: VNU. Editor: Lem Bingley

ITNOW
01793 417474
www.bcs.org
Bi-monthly. Owner: British Computer
Society. Editor: Brian Runciman

Mobile Entertainment
01992 535646
www.mobile-ent.biz
Monthly and website. Owner: Intent
Media. Editor: Stuart O'Brien

PC Retail
01992 535646
www.pcretailmag.com
Monthly. Owner: Intent Media.
Editor: Scott Bicheno

Professional Photographer
01799 544200
www.professionalphotographer.co.uk
Monthly. Owner: Archant.
Editor: Terry Hope

Scientific Computing World
01223 477411
www.europascience.com
Bi-monthly. Owner: Europa Science.
Editor: Tom Wilkie

Transport

Aerospace International
020 7670 4300
www.aerosociety.com
Monthly. Owner: The Royal Aeronautical Society. Editor: Richard Gardner

Air International
01780 755131
www.airinternational.com
Monthly. Owner: Key Publishing. Editor: Malcolm English

Automotive Engineer
020 7304 6809
www.pepublishing.com
Monthly. Owner: Professional Engineering Publishing. Editor: William Kimberley

Autowired
01565 872107
www.autowired.co.uk
Daily. Editor: Barry Hook

Commercial Motor
020 8652 3612
www.reedbusinessinformation.co.uk
Weekly. Owner: Reed Business Information. Editor: Andy Salter

Flight International
020 8652 3885
www.flightinternational.com
Weekly. Owner: Reed Business Information. Editor: Murdo Morrison

Helicopter International
01934 822524
www.helidata.rotor.com
Bi-monthly. Owner: Avia Press Associates. Editor: Elfan ap Rees

Motor Trader
01322 611301
www.motortrader.co.uk
Weekly. Owner: Nexus Holdings. Editor: Curtis Hutchinson

Motor Transport
020 8652 3285
www.reedbusinessinformation.co.uk
Weekly. Owner: Reed Business Information. Editor: Andrew Brown

Professional Motor Mechanic
01923 237799
www.hamerville.co.uk
11pa. Owner: Hamerville Magazines. Editor: Nick Holt

Rail
01733 264666
www.emap.com
Fortnightly. Owner: Emap. Editor: Nigel Harris

Railnews
020 7278 6100
www.railnews.co.uk
Monthly. Owner: Clarity Publishing. Editor: Paul Whiting

Truck & Driver
020 8652 3303
www.reedbusinessinformation.co.uk
Weekly. Owner: Reed Business Information. Editor: Dave Young

Trucking
01225 442244
www.truckingmag.co.uk
Monthly. Owner: Future. Editor: Ivor Carroll

Travel trade

Travel Trade Gazette
020 7921 8029
www.ttglive.com
Weekly. Owner: CMP Information. Editor: John Welsh

Travel Weekly
020 8652 8227
www.travelweekly.co.uk
Weekly. Owner: Reed Business Information. Editor: Martin Lane

Minority press

Cultural and ethnic minorities

Ad-Diplomasi News Report
Focus Press (UK)
020 7286 1372
info@ad-diplomasi.com
www.ad-diplomasi.com
Monthly. Arabic. Editor: Raymond Atallah

Al-Ahram
Al-Ahram
weeklymail@ahram.org.eg
http://weekly.ahram.org.eg
Weekly. English, serving Arab world. Editor in chief: Hani Shukrallah; deputy editor in chief: Mona Anis; managing editor: Galal Nassar; layout editor: Samir Sobhi

Al-Arab
Al Arab Publishing House
020 7274 9381
editor@alarab.co.uk
www.alarabonline.org
Daily and online. Arabic. Editor: AS Elhuni

Al-Jamila
Saudi Research and Marketing UK
020 7831 8181
aljamila@hhsaudi.com
www.arab.net
Monthly. Arabic. Upper and middle-income Arab women. Editor: Sanaa Al-Hadethee

Al-Majalla
Saudi Research and Marketing UK
020 7831 8181
al-majalla@hhsaudi.com
www.al-majalla.com
Weekly. Arabic. Arab matters. Editor: Fahed Al-Tayash

Anandabazar Patrika
subscription@abpmail.com
www.anandabazar.com
Daily. Bengali. Editor: Shrabani Basu

Anglo–Hellenic Review
Anglo–Hellenic League
020 7267 3877
paul.watkins@virgin.net
www.hellenicbookservice
  .com/ahr.htm
2pa. Cultural affairs covering Greece and Britain. Editor: Paul Watkins

Another Generation
07725 608614
contact@
  anothergeneration-mag.com
www.anothergeneration-mag.com
Bi-monthly. Asian. Editor: Farah Damji

Ashraq Al Awsat
Saudi Research and Marketing UK
020 7831 8181
editorial@asharqalawsat.com
www.aawsat.com
Daily. Arabic. Editor: Tariq Al Homayed

Asian Entertainment Guide
020 7723 6797
Weekly. Editor: N Gosai

Asian Leader Midlands
Urban Media
0871 872 9893
zakia@asianleader.com
Fortnightly. English, free. Editor: Zakia Yousaf

Asian News
Guardian Media Group
01706 357086
asiannews@gmwn.co.uk
www.theasiannews.co.uk
Monthly. Editor: Steve Hammond; chief reporter: Shelina Begum

Asian Post
Hussain Media
020 8558 9127
leali@theasianpost.co.uk
Weekly. English. Editor: Murtaza Ali Shah

Asian Times
Ethnic Media Group
020 7650 2000
news@asiantimes.co.uk
www.asiantimesonline.co.uk
Weekly. English. Editor: Burhan Ahmad

Asians in Media
020 8561 6855
sunny.hundal@asiansinmedia.org
www.asiansinmedia.org
Weekly. Guide to the British Asian media industry. Editor: Sunny Hundal

Awaaz
Awaaz Multi Media
01924 510512
info@awaaz.com
www.awaaznews.com
Monthly. English, Urdu and Gujarati. Editor: Ayub Bismillah

Barficulture.com
020 8561 6855
www.barficulture.com
Website. Young British Asians. Editor: Sunny Hundal

Blacknet
0870 746 5000
junior@blacknet.co.uk
www.blacknet.co.uk
Community website for black people in Britain. Editor: Junior Wilson

Black Information Link
020 7582 1990
blink1990@blink.org.uk
www.blink.org.uk
Website. Editor: Lester Holloway

Canada Post
020 8840 9765
info@canadapost.co.uk
www.canadapost.co.uk
Monthly. Managing editor: Paula Adamick

Caribbean Times
Ethnic Media Group
020 7650 2000
caribbeantimes@ethnicmedia.co.uk
www.caribbeantimes.co.uk
Weekly. Editor: Ron Shillingford; editorial director: Michael Eboda; production designer: Kashem Mohammed

Chinatown
CTM Publishing
0161 245 3252
enquiries@
     chinatownthemagazine.com
www.chinatownthemagazine.com
Bi-monthly. English for Chinese. Publisher: William Ong; editor: Davidine Sim

chup magazine
info@chupmagazine.com
www.chupmagazine.com
Bi-monthly. English for British Bengalis. Editor: Jasmine

Clickwalla.com
MeMedia
020 7693 8416
amit@memediagroup.com
www.clickwalla.com
Website. Editor: Amit Daryamani

Daily AUSAF
020 8521 8555
ausaflondon@aol.com
www.dailyausaf.com or
www.dailyausaf.de
Daily. Urdu. Chief editor: Mehtab Khan

Daily Jang London
Jang Publications
020 7403 5833
editor@janglondon.co.uk
www.jang.com.pk
Daily. English and Urdu. Editor: Zahoor Niazi

Des Pardes
020 8571 1127
despadesuk@btconnect.com
Weekly. Punjabi for Indian expatriates. Editor: GS Virk

Dziennik Polski
The Polish Daily (Publishers)
020 8740 1991
editor@dziennikpolski.co.uk
www.polishdailynews.com
Daily. Polish. Editor: Grzegorz Malkiewicz

Eastern Eye
Ethnic Media Group
020 7650 2000
editor@easterneyeuk.co.uk
www.easterneyeonline.co.uk
Weekly. For Indian, Pakistani, Sri Lankan and Bangladeshi communities in Britain. Editor: Amar Singh; subeditor: Jayanti Venkateshwaran; production editor: Koyes Uddin

Echo Me
Multi Ethnic (Aberdeen)
01224 645268 / 645200
info@multiethnic.co.uk
www.multiethnic.co.uk
Bi-monthly. All ethnic groups. Executive managing director: Kemi Adebayo

Eikoku News Digest
News Digest International
020 7616 1100
info@newsdigest.co.uk
www.newsdigest.co.uk
Weekly. Japanese. Editor: Mikiko Toshima

Euro Bangla
Newsfax
020 7377 0311
info@eurobangla.co.uk
www.eurobangla.co.uk
Weekly. Bangla and English. Managing Director: Masaddik Ahmed

Garavi Gujarat
Asian Media & Marketing Group
020 7928 1234
garavi@gujarat.co.uk
www.gg2.net
Weekly. English and Gujarati. Editor: Ramniklal Solanki

The Gleaner
020 7737 7377
www.jamaica-gleaner.com
Weekly. Editor in chief: Deidre Forbes

Gujarat Samachar/ Asian Voice
Asian Business Publications
020 7749 4080
support@abplgroup.com
www.gujarat-samachar.com
Weekly. Editor: C Patel

Hia
HH Saudi Research & Marketing UK
020 7831 8181
hia@hhsaudi.com
Monthly. Arab women. Editor: Mai Badr

Hurriyet
020 7734 1211
www.hurriyetim.com
Daily. Turkish. Editor: Aysegul Richardson

Impact International
020 7263 1417
editor@impact-magazine.com
Monthly. Muslim current affairs. Editor: Ahmed Irfan

India Monitor
shiv@journalist.com
www.indiamonitor.com
Website.

India Times
Times Internet
servicedesk@timesgroup.com
http://timesofindia.indiatimes.com/
Daily and website. Managing director: Mahendra Swarup; general manager, brands: Sumanta Pal

Irish Post
020 8741 0649
irishpost@irishpost.co.uk
www.irishpost.co.uk
Weekly. Editor: Frank Murphy

Irish World
Newsfax
020 8453 7800
sales@theirishworld.com
www.theirishworld.com
Weekly. Acting editor: Tom Griffin

Janomot
Publication 1969
020 7377 6032
janomot@btconnect.com
www.janomotnews.com
Weekly. Bengali. Editor: Nabab Uddin

Jewish Chronicle
020 7415 1500
webmaster@thejc.com
www.thejc.com
Weekly and website. Editor: Ned Temko

Jewish Telegraph
0141 621 4422
mail@jewishtelegraph.com
www.jewishtelegraph.com
Weekly. Editor: Paul Harris

KAL
(see also Spectrum)
020 7439 9100
www.kalmagazine.com
Bi-annual. Careers and recruitment for ethnic minority students. Editor: Laura Sheed

La Voce degli Italiani
redaction@lavoce.com
www.lavoce.com
Fortnightly. Italians in Europe. Editor: Ivo Mazzon

London Turkish Gazette
020 8889 5025
news@londragazete.com
www.londragazete.com
Weekly. Turkish and English. Publisher: Yilmaz Ozyigit; editor: Artun Goksan

London Welsh Magazine
London Welsh Association
020 7837 3722
ddaniel@streamline-cm.co.uk
www.londonwelsh.org
Quarterly. Editor: David Daniel

Maghreb Review
020 7388 1840
maghrab@maghrabreview.com
www.maghrabreview.com
Quarterly. English and French. North Africa, sub-Saharan Africa, Middle East and Islam. Islamic studies: history, geopolitics, environment. Editor: Mohammed Ban-madani

MIL Matchmaker Magazine
Matchmaker International
020 8868 1879
info@perfect-partner.com
www.perfect-partner.com
3pa. Asians seeking partners. Editor: Mr Bharat Raithatha

Mauritian Abroad
Sankris Publishing
01795 539499
eveer77807@aol.com
Quarterly. English and French. Editor: Krish Veeramah

Mauritius News
020 7498 3066
editor@mauritiusnews.co.uk
www.mauritiusnews.co.uk
Monthly. Editor: Peter Chellen

Milap Weekly
020 7385 8966
*Weekly. Urdu-speaking community.
Editor: Ramesh Soni*

Muslim News
Visitcrest
020 8863 8586
editor@muslimnews.co.uk
www.muslimnews.co.uk
Monthly. Editor: Ahmed Versi

Muslim Weekly
020 7377 1919
info@themuslimweekly.com
www.themuslimweekly.com
Weekly. Editor: Ahmed Malik

Navin Weekly
020 7385 8966
Weekly. Hindi. Editor: Ramesh Kumar

New Nation
Ethnic Media Group
020 7650 2000
general@ethnicmedia.co.uk
www.newnation.co.uk
*Weekly. Black African-Caribbean news.
Editorial Director: Michael Eboda;
news editor: Angela Foster; Pulse
editor: Justin Onyeka; Pulse features
editor: Adenike Adenitire; production
editor: Jerome Defrietas*

New World
020 77002673
dhirennewworld@blueyonder.co.uk
*Fortnightly. Editor and publisher:
Dhiren Basu*

The News
Jang Publications
020 7403 5833
thenewsse1@yahoo.com
www.jang.com.pk
*Daily. English and Urdu. Editor:
Shahid Ullah*

New Zealand News UK
Southern Link Media
020 7463 2100
editor@southernlink.co.uk
www.nznewsuk.co.uk
Weekly. Editor: Rachael Walsh

Noir
www.noir-mag.com
*Website. Black culture. Editor: Victoria
Thomas*

Noticias Latin America
020 7686 1633
informacion@noticias.co.uk
www.noticias.co.uk
Monthly. Spanish. Editor: Alberto Rojas

Notun Din Bengali Newsweekly
Din Publishers
020 7247 6280
news@notundin.plus.com
*Weekly. Bengali. Editor: Mohib
Chowdhury*

Occasions Magazine
Ethnic Media Group
020 7650 2000
sheri@occasions.co.uk
www.occasions.co.uk
*Quarterly. Asians worldwide. Editor:
Sheri Mill*

Opportunity
020 7005 2250
*Quarterly. 16–25, all ethnic minority
backgrounds. Magazine manager:
Claire Lavery*

Pakistan Post
Hussain Media
020 8558 9127
editor@thepakistanpost.net
www.thepakistanpost.net
*Weekly. Urdu and English. Editor in
Urdu: Faizan Arif; editor in English:
Murtaza Ali Shah*

Parikiaki
info@parikia.com
www.parikia.com/greek/parikiaki.html
Weekly. Cypriots in UK

Pride Magazine
020 72283110
info@pridemagazine.com
www.pridemagazine.com
*Monthly. Black African, black
Caribbean, mixed race. Publisher: Carl
Cushnie; editor: Sherry Dixon*

Punjabi Guardian
0121 5543995
punjabiguardian@hotmail.com
*Fortnightly. Punjabi and English.
Editor: Indarjit Singh*

Punjab Mail International
020 8522 0901
*Monthly. Punjabi and English. Editor:
Gurdip Singh Sandhu*

Punjab Times International
PTI Derby Media
01332 372851
panjabtimes@aol.com
*Weekly. Punjabi and English. Punjabi
community in UK. Editor: Ms Purewal*

Red Hot Curry
01438 365582
www.redhotcurry.com
*Website. South Asian, British Asian, and
East African Asian. Editor: Lopa Patel*

Sayidaty
Saudi Research and Marketing UK
020 7831 8181
sayidaty@hhsaudi.com
www.sayidaty.net
*Weekly. Arab issues. Editor: Hani
Nakshbandi*

Sikh Courier International
The World Sikh Foundation
020 8864 9228
2pa. Sikhs. Editor: Sukhbir Singh

Sikh Messenger
020 8540 4148
sikhmessenger@aol.com
Quarterly. Editor: Indarjit Singh

Sikh Times
Archline Midland
0121 523 0115
info@thesikh-times.co.uk
www.thesikh-times.co.uk
*Weekly. English, Punjabi. Editor: Jas
Pal Singh*

SomethingJewish.co.uk
07976 220273
editor@somethingjewish.co.uk
www.somethingjewish.co.uk
*Website. UK Jewish. Editor: Leslie
Bunder*

Spectrum
020 7439 9100
laura@arberrypink.co.uk
www.spectrummagazine.co.uk
*Bi-annual. Careers and recruitment for
ethnic minority students. Editor:
Laura Sheed*

Surma
020 7377 9787
info@surmanewsgroup.co.uk
www.surmanewsgroup.co.uk
*Weekly. Bangla. Publisher: Sarz
Ahmed; editor: Mohammed Emadadul
Choudhury*

Ta Nea
020 8806 0169
ta.nea@btconnect.com
Weekly. Greek. Editor: Louis Vrakas

TNT Magazine
Trader Media Group
020 7373 3377
enquiries@tntmag.co.uk
www.tntmagazine.com
*Weekly. International travellers.
Editor: Lyn Eyb*

Travellers' Times
c/o The Rural Media Company
01432 344039
travellerstimes@ruralmedia.co.uk
www.travellerstimes.org.uk
*Quarterly. Gypsies and Travellers.
Editor: Bill Laws*

Ukrainian Thought
Association of Ukrainians in GB
020 7229 8392
administrator@augb.co.uk
www.augb.co.uk/ukrainian
_thought.htm
*Weekly. Ukrainian. Administrator:
Mrs Anna Mikulin*

Ultra Journey
Japan Journals
020 7255 3838
info@japanjournals.com
www.japanjournals.com
Monthly. Japanese. Editor: Ko Tejima

Voice, The
020 7737 7377
www.voice-online.co.uk
*Weekly. English for Jamaican/
Caribbean community. Editor: Deidre
Forbes*

Weekly Journey
Japan Journals
020 7255 3838
lina@japanjournals.com
www.japanjournals.com
Weekly. Japanese in Britain. Editor:
K Tejima

Disability

Big Print
0800 124007
bigprint@rnib.org.uk
www.big-print.co.uk
Weekly. Large print news.

Breathing Space
The British Lung Foundation
020 7688 5555
enquiries@blf-uk.org
www.lunguk.org/
Quarterly. Lung disease. Editor:
Humphrey Couchman

Communication
The National Autistic Society
020 7833 2299
publications@nas.org.uk
www.nas.org.uk
3pa. Autism. Editor: Anne Cooper

Devon Link
Devon County Council and
Torbay Council
01392 382332
joanne.white@devon.gov.uk
www.devon.gov.uk/devonlink
Quarterly. People with physical and
sensory disabilities, and carers. Editor:
Joanne White

Disability Now
Scope
020 7619 7323
editor@disabilitynow.org.uk
www.disabilitynow.org.uk
Monthly. Acting editor: Sarah Hobson

Disabled and Supportive Carer
Euromedia Associates
01254 390066
editorial@euromedia-al.com
6pa. Editor: Richard Cheeseborough

Disabled Motorist
01832 734724
www.ddmc@ukonline.co.uk
Monthly. Editor: David Holding

DISH Update
DISH
01727 813815
info@dish.uk.net
www.dish.uk.net
Quarterly. Disability info for people in
Hertfordshire. Editor: Jane Fookes

Epilepsy Today
Epilepsy Action
0113 2108800
smitchell@epilepsy.org.uk
www.epilepsy.org.uk
Quarterly. Editor: Sue Mitchell

FreeHand
Abucon
020 7834 1066
info@abucon.co.uk
www.abucon.co.uk
4pa. Elderly disabled in their own
homes. Editor: Liza Jones

Jigsaw
DISH
01727 813815
info@dish.uk.net
www.dish.uk.net
Quarterly. Disability info for young
people. Editor: Jane Fookes

MS Matters
MS Society
020 8438 0700
info@mssociety.org.uk
www.mssociety.org.uk
6pa. Editor: Debbie Reeves

New Beacon
Royal National Institute of the Blind
020 7878 2307
beacon@rnib.org.uk
www.rnib.org.uk
11pa. For those with sight problems.
Editor: Ann Lee

New Pathways
The MS Resource Centre
01206 505444
info@msrc.co.uk
www.msrc.co.uk
6pa. MS issues. Editor: Judy Graham

Ouch!
020 8752 5444
ouch@bbc.co.uk
www.bbc.co.uk/ouch
Website. Editor: Damon Rose

One in Seven Magazine
The Royal National Institute for
Deaf People
020 7296 8000
oneinseven@rnid.org.uk
www.rnid.org.uk
6pa. For the deaf. Editor: Dawn Egan

The Parkinson Magazine
Parkinson's Disease Society of the UK
020 7931 8080
lhurst@parkinsons.org.uk
www.parkinsons.org.uk
Quarterly. Editor: Lucy Hurst

Pinpoint
Disability West Midlands
0121 414 1616
pinpoint@dwm.org.uk
www.dwm.org.uk
6pa. All disabled people. Editor: Pete
Millington

Positive Nation
The UK Coalition of People Living
with HIV and Aids (UKC)
020 7564 2121
editor@positivenation.co.uk
www.positivenation.co.uk
11pa. Issues for people with HIV Aids.
Editor: Amanda Elliott; news editor:
Martin Flynn

Pure
The National Kidney Research Fund
01733 704650
marcoms@nkrf.org.uk
www.nkrf.org.uk
Quarterly. Editor: Louise Cox

New Bulletin
Royal Association for Disability
and Rehabilitation
020 7250 3222
radar@radar.org.uk
www.radar.org.uk
11pa. Civil rights issues for the disabled.
Editor: Jim Pollard

Soundaround
Soundaround Associations
020 8741 3332
nigel@soundaround.org
www.soundaround.org
Monthly. Visually impaired,
worldwide. Executive editor: Nigel Vee

Stroke News
The Stroke Association
020 7566 0300
www.stroke.org.uk
Quarterly. Editor: Daisy Thomas

Talk
The National Deaf Children's Society
020 7490 8656
ndcs@ndcs.org.uk
www.ndcs.org.uk
6pa. For deaf children. Editor: Emma
Knight

Talking Sense
Sense, National Deafblind and
Rubella Association
020 7272 7774
enquiries@sense.org.uk
www.sense.org.uk
3pa. Deafblind. Editor: Colin Anderson

Typetalk Update
Paver Downes Associates
0151 293 0505
smith@paverdownes.co.uk
www.paverdownes.co.uk
6pa. Down's syndrome. Editor: Rachel
Smith

Viewpoint
Mencap
020 7696 5599
viewpoint@mencap.org.uk
www.mencap.org.uk/viewpoint
6pa. Learning disabilities. Editor:
Faiza Fareed

Vitalise
(formerly Winged Fellowship Trust)
020 7017 3420
admin@vitalise.org.uk
www.vitalise.org.uk
2pa. Disabled people and their carers.
Editor: James Hale

Gay and lesbian

3sixty
City Pride Publications
01273 570570
info@3sixtymag.co.uk
www.3sixtymag.co.uk
Monthly. Editor: Jamie Hakin

Attitude
Remnant Media
020 7308 5090
attitude@attitude.co.uk
www.attitude.co.uk
Monthly. Editor: Adam Mattera

AXM
Blue Maverick Media
020 7749 1970
m.miles@axm-mag.com
www.axm-mag.com
Monthly. Editor: Matthew Miles

Bent
All Points North Publications
020 7837 2660
editor@bent.com
www.bent.com
11–12pa. Editor: Christopher Amos

Boyz
020 7025 6120
hudson@boyz.co.uk
www.boyz.co.uk
Weekly. Editor: David Hudson

Diva
Millivres-Prowler
020 7424 7400
edit@divamag.co.uk
www.divamag.co.uk
Monthly. Editor: Jane Czyzselska

G3
G3 Magazine
020 7272 0093
info@g3magazine.co.uk
www.g3magazine.co.uk
Monthly. Editor: Sarah Garrett

Gay Times
Millivres-Prowler
020 7424 7400
vicky@millivres.co.uk
www.gaytimes.co.uk
Monthly. Editor: Vicky Powell

Gay.com UK
020 7734 3700
info@uk.gay.com
www.uk.gay.com
Editor: Christine Townsend

Midlands Zone
What's On Magazine Group
01743 281777
info@zonemag.com
www.zonemag.com
Monthly. Editor: Martin Monahan

Outnorthwest
0161 235 8035
editor@outnorthwest.com
www.lgf.org.uk
*Monthly free, published by the Lesbian
and Gay Foundation. Editor: Grahame
Robertson*

Pink Paper
Millivres-Prowler
020 7424 7400
tris@pinkpaper.com
www.pinkpaper.com
*Weekly. Editor: Tris Reid-Smith;
deputy editor: Simon Swift; editorial
designer: Fernando Safont*

Refresh
Swan Publishing
01322 311600
refresh@swanpublishing.co.uk
www.refreshmag.co.uk
Monthly. Editor: David Tickner

Stonewall Newsletter
Stonewall
020 7881 9440
info@stonewall.org.uk
www.stonewall.org.uk
Quarterly. Editor: Jodie West

UKBlackOut.com
www.ukblackout.com
Website. For black lesbians and gays

Religion

All The World
The Salvation Army
020 7332 0101
kevin_sims@salvationarmy.org
www.salvationarmy.org
Quarterly. Editor: Kevin Sims

Baptist Times
Baptist Times
01235 517670
editor@baptisttimes.co.uk
www.baptisttimes.co.uk
*Weekly. Church leaders. Editor: Mark
Woods*

Catholic Herald
020 7588 3101
editorial@catholicherald.co.uk
www.catholicherald.co.uk
Weekly. Acting Editor: Luke Coppen

Catholic Times
Gabriel Communications
0161 236 8856
catholictimes@yahoo.co.uk
www.ctonline.org
Weekly. Editor: Kevin Flaherty

Christian Herald
01903 821082
editor@christianherald.org.uk
www.christianmedia.org.uk
*Weekly. Evangelical Christian
community. Editor: Russ Bravo*

Christianity and Renewal
Premier Media Group (PMG)
020 7316 1450
ccp@premier.org.uk
www.christianitymagazine.com
Monthly. Editor: John Buckeridge

Daily Bread
Scripture Union Publishing
01908 856000
nigelh@scriptureunion.org.uk
www.dailybread.org.uk
*Quarterly. Adult Bible readers. Editor:
James Davies*

Home and Family
The Mothers' Union
020 7222 5533
homeandfamily@themothersunion.org
www.themothersunion.org
Quarterly. Editor: Jill Worth

Jewish Chronicle
020 7415 1500
webmaster@thejc.com
www.thejc.com
Weekly and website. Editor: Ned Temko

Jewish Telegraph
0141 621 4422
mail@jewishtelegraph.com
www.jewishtelegraph.com
Weekly. Editor: Paul Harris

Jewish.net
07976 220273
admin@jewish.net
www.jewish.net
Website

The Life
Scripture Union Publishing
01908 856000
media@scriptureunion.org.uk
www.scriptureunion.org.uk/thelife
Quarterly

Life and Work
Board of Communications
0131 225 5722
magazine@lifeandwork.org
www.lifeandwork.org
*Monthly. Church of Scotland. Editor:
Lynne McNeil*

The Muslim News
Visitcrest
020 8863 8586
editor@muslimnews.co.uk
www.muslimnews.co.uk
Monthly. Editor: A Versi

New Day
The Leprosy Mission
01733 370505
karendup@tlmew.org.uk
www.leprosy.org.uk
2pa. Editor: Karen Duplessis

Presbyterian Herald
Presbyterian Church in Ireland
028 9032 2284
herald@presbyterianireland.org
www.presbyterianireland.org
Monthly. Editor: Rev Arthur Clarke

Scottish Catholic Observer
0141 221 4956
info@scottishcatholicobserver.com
www.scottishcatholicobserver.com
Weekly. Editor: Harry Conroy

Sikh Courier International
World Sikh Foundation
020 8864 9228
thesikhcourier@hotmail.com
www.sikhfoundation.org
2pa. Editor: Sukhbir Singh

SomethingJewish.co.uk
07976 220273
editor@somethingjewish.co.uk
www.somethingjewish.co.uk
UK Jewish website. Editor: Leslie Bunder

Ummah.com
info@ummah.com
www.ummah.org.uk
Website. English. Islam

The Universe
Gabriel Communications
0161 236 8856
newsdesk@the-universe.net
www.totalcatholic.com
Weekly. Roman Catholics and Ireland.
Editor: Joe Kelly

War Cry
Salvation Army
020 7367 4900
warcry@salvationarmy.org.uk
www.salvationarmy.org.uk/warcry
Weekly. Christian current affairs.
Editor: Major Nigel Bovey

Journalism trade press

Best Sellers
020 7689 3357
robin.parker@newtrade.co.uk
www.newtrade.co.uk
2pa. Owner: Newtrade Publishing.
Consumer magazine data and ABC
results. Editor: Robin Parker

British Journalism Review
020 7324 8500
editor@bjr.org.uk
www.bjr.org.uk
Quarterly. Owner: SAGE Publications.
Managing editor: Brian Bass; Editor:
Bill Hagerty

CPU Quarterly
020 7583 7733
cpu@cpu.org.uk
www.cpu.org.uk
Quarterly. Owner: Commonwealth
Press Union. In-house newspaper
of the Association of Commonwealth
Newspapers. Executive director:
Lindsay Ross; editorial contact: Rosie
Vlasto; press officer: Harry Wilson

The Journal
020 7252 1187
memberservices@ioj.co.uk
www.ioj.co.uk
Owner: The Chartered Institute of
Journalists. Quarterly. Editor: Andy
Smith

journalism.co.uk
Mousetrap Media
01273 384293
info@journalism.co.uk
www.journalism.co.uk
Website. Editor/publisher: John
Thompson; news: Jemima Kiss

The Journalist
020 7278 7916
timg@nuj.org.uk
www.nuj.org.uk
10pa. Owner: National Union of
Journalists. Free to union members.
Editor: Tim Gopsill

Magazine Retailer
020 7689 3357
robin.parker@newtrade.co.uk
www.newtrade.co.uk
2pa. Owner: Newtrade Publishing.
Information on magazine sales in all
sectors. Editor: Robin Parker

Magazine World
020 7404 4169
info@fipp.com
www.fipp.com
Quarterly. Owner: FIPP. International
consumer and B2B publishing trends.
Editor: Arif Durrani

News from NewstrAid
01371 874198
oldben@newstraid.demon.co.uk
www.newstraid.org.uk
Annual. Owner: Newstraid Benevolent
Society. Charity for the newspaper
industry. Editorial contact: Tansey Davis

Press Gazette
020 8565 4448
pged@pressgazette.co.uk
www.pressgazette.co.uk
Weekly. Independent. Editor: Ian
Reeves; features editor: Julie Tomlyn

Ulrich's Periodical Directory
01342 310450
sales@bowker.co.uk
www.ulrichsweb.com
Annual; updated quarterly on CD,
monthly on website. Owner: Bowker.
Editor: Laurie Kaplan

Useful associations

Association of American
Correspondents in London
c/o Time Life International
Brettenham House, Lancaster Place
London WC2E 7TL
020 7499 4080
elizabeth_lea@timemagazine.com

Association of British Science
Writers
Wellcome Wolfson Building
165 Queen's Gate
London SW7 5HE
0870 770 3361
absw@absw.org.uk
www.absw.org.uk

Association of Freelance Writers
Sevendale House, 7 Dale Street
Manchester M1 1JB
0161 228 2362
fmn@writersbureau.com
www.writersbureau.com
/resources.htm

Audit Bureau of Circulations (ABC)
Saxon House, 211 High Street
Berkhamsted, Hertfordshire HP4 1AD
01442 870800
marketing@abc.org.uk
www.abc.org.uk

Authors' Club
40 Dover Street, London W1S 4NP
020 7499 8581
circles@author.co.uk
www.author.co.uk

British Copyright Council
29–33 Berners Street
London W1T 3AB
01986 788122
secretary@britishcopyright.org
www.britishcopyright.org

British Guild of Beer Writers
68B Elmwood Rd
London SE24 9NR
07973 465081
peterhaydon@onetel.net.uk
www.beerguild.com

British Guild of Travel Writers
51B Askew Crescent
London W12 9DN
020 8749 1128
charlotte.c@virtualnecessities.com
www.bgtw.org

British Newspaper Library
The British Library
Newspaper Library, Colindale Avenue
London NW9 5HE
020 7412 7353
newspaper@bl.uk
www.bl.uk/catalogues
/newspapers.html

British Society of Magazine Editors
137 Hale Lane, Edgware
Middlesex HA8 9QP
020 8906 4664
admin@bsme.com
www.bsme.com

Broadcasting Press Guild
Tiverton, The Ridge, Woking
Surrey GU22 7EQ
01483 764895
torin.douglas@bbc.co.uk

Bureau of Freelance Photographers
Focus House, 497 Green Lanes
London N13 4BP
020 8882 3315
info@thebfp.com
www.thebfp.com

Campaign for Freedom of Information
Suite 102, 16 Baldwins Gardens
London EC1N 7RJ
020 7831 7477
admin@cfoi.demon.co.uk
www.cfoi.org.uk

Campaign for Press and
Broadcasting Freedom
2nd Floor, Vi and Garner Smith
House, 23 Orford Road
Walthamstow, London E17 9NL
020 8521 5932
freepress@cpbf.org.uk
www.cpbf.org.uk

Chartered Institute of Journalists
2 Dock Offices, Surrey Quays Road
London SE16 2XU
020 7252 1187
memberservices@ioj.co.uk
www.ioj.co.uk

Foreign Press Association in London
11 Carlton House Terrace
London   SW1Y 5AJ
020 7930 0445
secretariat@foreign-press.org.uk
www.foreign-press.org.uk

Garden Writers' Guild
c/o Institute of Horticulture
14/15 Belgrave Square
London   SW1X 8PS
020 7245 6943
gwg@horticulture.org.uk
www.gardenwriters.co.uk

Guild of Agricultural Journalists
Charmwood, 47 Court Meadow
Rotherfield, East Sussex   TN6 3LQ
01892 853187
don.gomery@farmingline.com
www.gaj.org.uk

Guild of Food Writers
020 7610 1180
guild@gfw.co.uk
www.gfw.co.uk

Guild of Motoring Writers
39 Beswick Avenue
Bournemouth   BH10 4EY
01202 518808
gensec@gomw.co.uk
www.guildofmotoringwriters.co.uk

International Newspaper Marketing Association
10300 North Central Expressway
Suite 467, Texas 75231   USA
00 1 214 373 9111
www.inma.org

MediaWise Trust
38 Easton Business Centre
Felix Road, Bristol   BS5 0HE
0117 941 5889
info@mediawise.org.uk
www.mediawise.org.uk
Media ethics charity

Medical Writers' Group
The Society of Authors
84 Drayton Gardens
London   SW10 9SB
020 7373 6642
info@societyofauthors.org
www.societyofauthors.org

National Union of Journalists
Acorn House, 308–312 Gray's Inn Rd
London   WC1X 8DP
020 7278 7916
info@nuj.org.uk
www.nuj.org.uk

Newspaper Marketing Agency
Berkeley Square House
Berkeley Square, London   W1J 6BD
020 7887 6112
enquiries@nmauk.co.uk
www.nmauk.co.uk

Newspaper Society
Bloomsbury House
74–77 Great Russell St
London   WC1B 3DA
020 7636 7014
ns@newspapersoc.org.uk
www.newspapersoc.org.uk

Outdoor Writers' Guild
PO Box 118, Twickenham   TW1 2XB
020 8538 9468
secretary@owg.org.uk
www.owg.org.uk

Periodical Publishers Association (PPA)
Queens House, 28 Kingsway
London   WC2B 6JR
020 7404 4166
info1@ppa.co.uk
www.ppa.co.uk

Picture Research Association
c/o 1 Willow Court, off Willow Street
London   EC2A 4QB
chair@picture-research.org.uk
www.picture-research.org.uk

Press Complaints Commission
1 Salisbury Square
London   EC4Y 8JB
020 7353 1248
complaints@pcc.org.uk
www.pcc.org.uk

Scottish Newspaper Publishers Association
48 Palmerston Place
Edinburgh   EH12 5DE
0131 220 4353
info@snpa.org.uk
www.snpa.org.uk

Scottish Print Employers Federation and Scottish Daily Newspaper Society
48 Palmerston Place
Edinburgh   EH12 5DE
0131 220 4353
info@spef.org.uk
www.spef.org.uk

Society of Editors
University Centre, Granta Place
Mill Lane, Cambridge   CB2 1RU
01223 304080
info@societyofeditors.org
www.societyofeditors.org

Society of Women Writers and Journalists
swwriters@aol.com
www.swwj.co.uk

Sports Journalists' Association of Great Britain
c/o Victoria House
Bloomsbury Square
London   WC1B 4SE
020 7273 1589
petta.naylor@sportengland.org
www.sportsjournalists.co.uk

Press agencies Contacts

National Association of Press Agencies
41 Lansdowne Crescent
Leamington Spa
Warwickshire CV32 4PR
01926 424181
secretariat@napa.org.uk
www.napa.org.uk

24/7 Media (Photography)
200 St Andrews Road
Bordesley Village, Birmingham
West Midlands B9 4JG
0121 753 1329
Photographer covering news, sports, features, PR and commercial

7 Day Press
132 West Nile Street
Glasgow G1 2RQ
0141 572 0060
daypress@aol.com
www.7daypress.co.uk
Scottish sport

AFX News
Finsbury Tower
103–105 Bunhill Row
London EC1Y 8TN
020 7422 4870
john.manley@afxnews.com
www.afxnews.com
International financial news

Agence France-Presse, UK
78 Fleet Street, London EC4Y 1NB
020 7353 7461
london.bureau@afp.com
www.afp.com
Major agency

Agencia EFE
299 Oxford Street, 6th Floor
London W1C 2DZ
020 7493 7313
www.efe.com
Spanish news agency

Airtime Television News
PO Box 258, Maidenhead SL6 9YR
01628 482763
info@airtimetv.co.uk
www.airtimetv.co.uk
Heathrow airport

Allscot News Agency
PO Box 6, Haddington EH41 3NQ
01620 822578
allscotnewsuk@compuserve.com
Scottish news

Anglia Press Agency
17A Whiting Street
Bury St Edmunds, Suffolk IP33 1NR
01284 702421
news@angliapressagency.co.uk
East Anglia, words and pictures

ANSA News Agency
Essex House, 12–13 Essex Street
London WC2R 3AA
020 7240 5514
ansalondra@yahoo.com
www.ansa.it
News worldwide

Apex News and Picture Agency
Priests Court, Main Road
Exminster, Exeter EX6 8AP
01392 824024
info@apexnewspix.com
www.apexnewspix.com
Based in south-west. All news

APTN
The Interchange, Oval Road
Camden Lock, London NW1 7DZ
020 7482 7400
aptninfo@ap.org
www.aptn.com
International newsgathering

Associated Press News Agency
12 Norwich Street
London EC4A 1BP
020 7353 1515
www.ap.org
Worldwide all news

Associated Sports Photography
21 Green Walk, Leicester LE3 6SE
0116 232 0310
asp@sports-photos.co.uk
www.sporting-heroes.net
Worldwide sports, travel

Australian Associated Press
Associated Press Building
12 Norwich Street
London EC4A 1QJ
020 7353 0153
news.london@aap.com.au
www.aap.com.au
European news to Australia

Bellis News Agency
14B Kenelm Road, Rhos on Sea
Colwyn Bay, North Wales LL28 4ED
01492 549503
bellisd@aol.com
North Wales

Big Picture Press Agency
50–54 Clerkenwell Road
London EC1M 5PS
020 7250 3555
picturedesk@bigpictures.co.uk
www.bigpicturesphoto.co.uk
Celebrities

Bloomberg LP
City Gate House
39–45 Finsbury Square
London EC2A 1PQ
020 7330 7500
newsdesk@bloomberg.net
www.bloomberg.com
Worldwide financial

Bournemouth News & Picture Service
1st Floor Offices, 5–7 Southcote Road
Bournemouth BH1 3LR
01202 558833
news@bnps.co.uk
www.bnps.co.uk
News and features

Calyx Multimedia
41 Churchward Avenue
Swindon SN2 1NJ
01793 520131
richard@calyxpix.com
www.calyxpix.com
Stills, news and freelance cameraman

Capital Press Agency
14 Canongate Venture
New Street, Edinburgh EH8 8BH
0131 652 3999
capitalnews@hemedia.co.uk,
capitalpix@hemedia.co.uk
www.hemedia.co.uk
Edinburgh, Lothians and Borders

Capital Pictures
85 Randolph Avenue
London W9 1DL
020 7286 2212
sales@capitalpictures.com
www.capitalpictures.com
International celebrities

Cassidy & Leigh Southern News Service
Exchange House, Hindhead Road
Hindhead GU26 6AA
01428 607330
denis@cassidyandleigh.com
pics@cassidyandleigh.com
News and pictures

Caters News Agency
Queens Gate, Suite 40
121 Suffolk Street Queensway
Birmingham B1 1LX
0121 616 1100
news@catersnews.com
features@catersnews.com
pix@catersnews.com
West Midlands news, featuring pictures and sport

Cavendish Press and CPMedia
3rd Floor, Albert House
17 Bloom Street
Manchester M1 3HZ
0161 237 1066
newsdesk@cavendish-press.co.uk
www.cavendish-press.co.uk
www.cpmedia.co.uk
News and pictures

Celtic News
PO Box 26, Llangadog
Carmarthenshire SA19 9YR
01550 740209
features@celtic-news.co.uk
www.celticnews.co.uk
UK-wide features for nationals and magazines

Central News Network
Suite 7, 350 Main Street
Canelon, Falkirk FK1 4EG
01324 630505
jimdavisofcnn@aol.com
Central Scotland news features

Central Press Features
5th Floor, BEP Building
Temple Way, Bristol BS99 7HD
0117 934 3600
mail@central-press.co.uk
www.central-press.co.uk
Worldwide editorial syndication

Centre Press Agency
2 Clairmont Gardens
Glasgow G3 7LW
0141 332 8888
centrenews@hemedia.co.uk,
centrepix@hemedia.co.uk
www.hemedia.co.uk
Central and southern Scotland

Chapman & Page
Dengate House, Amber Hill
Boston PE20 3RL
01205 290477
chapmanpage@internett.demon.co.uk
Syndicated features agency

Chester News Service
Linen Hall House, Stanley Street
Chester CH1 2LR
01244 345562
news@chesterstandard.co.uk
www.chesterstandardnow.co.uk
North Wales area

Chester Press Bureaux
Riverside House
Brymau 3 Trading Estate, River Lane
Saltney, Chester CH4 8RQ
01244 678575
ron@chesterpb.freeserve.co.uk
*North-west area press agency and
contract publishing*

Computer Wire
Charles House
108–110 Finchley Road
London NW3 5JJ
020 7675 7000
kevin.white@computerwire.co.uk
www.computerwire.com
Worldwide IT index links

Copyline Scotland
70 Tomnahurich Street
Inverness IV3 5DT
01463 231415
copylinescotland@aol.com
Scottish Highlands

Cotswold & Swindon News Service
Oxford House, 101 Bath Road
Swindon SN1 4AX
01793 485461
cotswin@stares.co.uk
www.stares.co.uk
Swindon area

Coventry News Service
7 Queen Victoria Road
Coventry CV1 3JS
024 7663 3777
adent@advent-communications.co.uk
www.advent-communications.co.uk
Coventry area

David Hoffman Photo Library
c/o BAPLA, 18 Vine Hill
London EC1R 5DZ
020 8981 5041
lib@hoffmanphotos.com
www.hoffmanphotos.com
Social issues in UK and Europe

DBSP
112 Cornwall Street South
Glasgow G41 1AA
0141 427 5344
stewart.mcdougall@btclick.com
Worldwide sport

Dobson Agency
20 Seafield Avenue, Osgodby
Scarborough YO11 3QG
01723 585141
pix@dobsonagency.co.uk
www.dobsonagency.co.uk
*Covering Yorkshire, Cleveland,
Humberside and rest of UK*

Double Red Photographic
The Old School, Thorn Lane, Goxhill
Barrow upon Humber DN19 7JE
01469 531416
doublered@atlas.co.uk
www.doublered.co.uk
Motorsport photography

Dow Jones Newswires
10 Fleet Place, Limeburner Lane
London EC4M 7QN
020 7842 9900
djequitiesnews.london@dowjones.com
www.djnewswires.com
International financial news

DPA (German Press Agency)
30 Old Queen Street
St James's Park, London SW1H 9HP
020 7233 2888
london@dpa.com
www.dpa.com
Global media services

Dragon News & Picture Agency
21 Walter Road, Swansea SA1 5NQ
01792 464800
mail@dragon-pictures.com
www.dragon-pictures.com
All news and PR

Emirates News Agency
The Studio, 143 Lavender Hill
London SW11 5QJ
020 7228 1060
mia@mia.gb.com
www.mia.gb.com
News from Arab peninsula

Empics Sports Photo Agency
Pavilion House, 16 Castle Boulevard
Nottingham NG7 1FL
0115 844 7447
info@empics.com
www.empics.com
Sports worldwide, celebrities

Entertainment News
Dragon Court, 27–29 Mackin Street
London WC2B 5LX
020 7190 7795
info@entnews.co.uk
www.entnews.co.uk
Diary for entertainment news

Essex News Service
2 The Street, Great Tay
Colchester CO6 1AE
01206 211413
perfect@teynews.fs.net
Essex area news and features

Evertons News Agency
Cavalier House, Hayley Green Court
130 Hagley Road, Halesowen
Birmingham B63 1DY
0121 585 9188
clive.everton@talk21.com
Snooker and golf. Magazine journalist

Feature Story News
The Interchange, Oval Road
London NW1 7DZ
020 7485 0303
drewc@featurestory.com
www.featurestory.com and
www.featurestorynews.com
*Domestic and international radio and
TV stories*

Ferrari Press Agency
7 Summerhill Road, Dartford
Kent DA1 2LP
01322 628444
news@ferraripress.com
www.ferraripress.com
*Kent, south London, south Essex, East
Sussex, Calais and Boulogne etc*

Fleetline News Service
Southern House, 1a Bedford Road
East Finchley, London N2 9DB
020 8445 7447
fleetlinenews@hotmail.com
*Law courts, magistrates courts, appeals.
Employment tribunals throughout
London*

Foresightnews
Dragon Court, 27–29 Mackin Street
London WC2B 5LX
020 7190 7788
info@foresightnews.co.uk
www.foresightnews.co.uk
Forward planning media news diary

Frank Ryan News Service
Cargenriggs, Islesteps
Dumfries DG2 8ES
01387 253700
smeddum@btinternet.com
*South west Scotland, general news and
features*

Freemans Press Agency
Raleigh House, 1 Mill Road
Barnstable EX31 1JQ
01271 324000
tonyfreemanpressagency@bp.com
www.bipp.com
All news, north Devon

Future Events News Service
FENS House, 8–10 Wiseton Road
London SW17 7EE
020 8672 3191
uk@fensintl.com
www.fens.com
*Diary news service, UK/international.
Entertainment and business*

Getty Images
116 Bayham Street
London NW1 1OG
0800 376 7981
allsportlondon@gettyimages.com
www.gettyimages.com
Images of news

Gloucestershire News Service
Maverdine Chambers
26 Westgate Street
Gloucester GL1 2NG
01452 522270
john.hawkins@glosnews.com
www.glosnews.com
Gloucester general news

Gosnay's Sports Agency
Park House, 356 Broadway
Horsforth, Leeds LS18 4RE
0113 258 5864
gosnays@aol.com
Sports news

Government News Network
London
River Walk House, 157–161 Millbank
London SW1P 4RR
020 7217 3091
london@gnn.gsi.gov.uk
www.gnn.gov.uk
Government press office

West Midlands
5 St Phillips Place
Birmingham B3 2PW
0121 352 5500
birmingham@gsi.gov.uk
www.gnn.gov.uk

East Midlands
Belgrave Centre, Stanley Place
Talbot Street, Nottingham NG1 5GG
0115 971 2780
nottingham@gnn.gov.uk
www.gnn.gov.uk

North-west
27th Floor, Sunley Tower
Picadilly Plaza, Manchester M1 4BD
0161 952 4500
manchester@gnn.gov.uk
www.gnn.gov.uk
All North-west, Carlisle to Stoke

North-east
Citygate, Gallowgate
Newcastle upon Tyne NE1 4WH
0191 202 3600
newcastle@gnn.gov.uk
www.gnn.gov.uk

Yorkshire & Humber
1st Floor, City House
New Station Street, Leeds LS1 4JG
0113 283 6599
leeds@gnn.gsi.gov.uk
www.gnn.gov.uk

Harrison Photography
37/39 Great Northern Street
Belfast BT9 7FJ
028 9066 3100
mail@harrisonphotography.co.uk
www.harrisonphotography.co.uk
All Northern Ireland. Business, PR, photography

Hayters Teamwork
Image House, Station Road
London N17 9LR
020 8808 3300
sport@haytersteamwork.com
www.haytersteamwork.com
Home and international sports

IPS Photo Agency
21 Delisle Road, London SE28 0JD
020 8855 1008
info@ips-net.co.uk
Agents in Japan, Italy, Germany, Spain, France, Scandinavia

Independent Radio News (IRN)
ITN Radio, 200 Gray's Inn Road
London WC1X 8XZ
020 7430 4814
irn@itn.co.uk
www.irn.co.uk
National and international news

Independent Sports Network
London Television Centre
Upper Ground, London SE1 9LT
020 7827 7700
jane.tatnall@isntv.co.uk
www.isntv.co.uk
UK sport transmissions

Islamic Republic News Agency (IRNA)
3rd Floor, Imperial Life House
390–400 High Road
Wembley, Middlesex HA9 6AS
020 8903 5531
irna@irna.ir
www.irna.ir
Islamic Republic news agency

Information Telegraph Agency of Russia (ITAR-TASS)
Suite 12–20, 2nd Floor, Morley House
314–320 Regent Street
London W1B 3BD
020 7580 5543
iborisenko@yahoo.co.uk
www.itar-tass.com
Russian business news agency

Jarrold's Press Agency
68 High Street, Ipswich IP1 3QJ
01473 219193
jarroldspress@cix.compulink.co.uk
Suffolk, north Essex, south Norfolk, East Anglia and football coverage

Jenkins Group
Berkeley House, 186 High Street
Rochester ME1 1EY
01634 830888
nickand marion@hotmail.com
PR worldwide

Jewish Chronicle News Agency
25 Furnival Street, London EC4A 1JT
020 7415 1500
marketing@thejc.com
www.thejc.com
Worldwide all news

JIJI Press
4th Floor, International Press Centre
76 Shoe Lane, London EC4A 3JB
020 7936 2847
edit@jiji.co.uk
www.jiji.co.jp
London economic news

John Connor Press Associates
57a High Street, Lewes BN7 1XE
01273 486851
news@jcpa.co.uk
News and features in Sussex

John Fairfax (UK)
1 Bath Street, London EC1V 9LB
020 7688 2777
linda@fairfaxbn.com
www.f2.com
Worldwide news

John Wardle Agency
Trafalgar House, 5 High Lane
Manchester M21 9DJ
0161 861 8015
iwhittell@aol.com
Sports agency nationwide

Kuwait News Agency (KUNA)
6th Floor, New Premier House
150 Southampton Row
London WC1B 5AL
020 7278 5445
kuwait@btclick.com
www.kuwait-info.com
News around the world

Kyodo News
5th Floor, 20 Orange Street
London WC2H 7EF
020 7766 4400
london@kyodonews.jp
www.kyodo.co.jp
Japan news, worldwide news

Lakeland Press Agency
16 Stonecroft, Ambleside
Lancashire LA22 0AU
01539 431749
craigwilson23@yahoo.co.uk
Cumbria/Lake District. All news and features

Lappas of Exeter
7 Waylands Road, Tiverton
Devon EX16 6UT
01884 254555
lappas@freeuk.com
www.richardlappas.com
Devon, Cornwall, Somerset, Dorset

M&Y News Agency
65 Osborne Road, Southsea
Portsmouth PO5 3LS
023 9282 0311
mynews@dircon.co.uk
www.mynewsagency.co.uk
News, sports and pictures. Hants, Sussex, Dorset

M2 Communications
PO Box 475, Coventry CV1 1ZB
020 7047 0200
m2pw@m2.com
www.m2.com
Global all news

Maghreb Arabe Press
35 Westminster Bridge Road
London SE1 7JB
020 7401 8146
mapldn@aol.com
www.map.co.ma
North Africa, Middle East and Mediterranean. All news

Market News International
Ocean House, 10–12 Little Trinity Lane
London EC4V 2AR
020 7634 1655
ukeditorial@marketnews.com
www.marketnews.com
International economics, politics and financial markets

Marshall's Sports Service
2 Newfield Drive
Kingswinford DY6 8HY
01384 274877
marshall@bham-sport.demon.co.uk
West Midlands sports

Masons News Service
Unit 2, Clare Hall, Parsons Green
St Ives, Cambs PE27 4WY
01480 302302
newsdesk@masons-news.co.uk
www.campix.co.uk
General news from East Anglia

Media Features
36 Holcroft Court, Carburton Street
London W1W 5DJ
020 7436 3678
leozanelli@aol.com
Worldwide press syndication

Mercury Press Agency
7th Floor, Cotton Exchange
Old Hall Street, Liverpool L3 9LQ
0151 236 6707
reporters@mercurypress.co.uk
www.mercurypress.co.uk
Merseyside, Lancashire, Cheshire, parts of North Wales

National News Agency
4–5 Academy Buildings
Fanshaw Street, London N1 6LQ
020 7684 3000
news@nationalnews.co.uk
www.nationalpictures.co.uk
General news. London and south-east

News of Australia
1 Virginia Street, London E98 1NL
020 7702 1355
anne.wall@newsint.co.uk
www.news.com.au
Australian news

News Team International
41–43 Commercial Street
Birmingham B1 1RS
0121 246 5511
commercial@newsteam.co.uk
www.newsteam.co.uk
Midlands, London news

Newsflash Scotland
1st Floor, Viewfield Chambers
Viewfield Place, Stirling FK8 1NQ
01786 477310
news@nflash.co.uk
www.newsflashscotland.com
Scotland

North News and Pictures
The Newgate Centre
69 Grainger Street
Newcastle upon Tyne NE1 5JE
0191 233 0223
pictures@northnews.co.uk;
news@northnews.co.uk
North-east England, Cumbria and borders

North West News Service
10 Broseley Avenue
Manchester M20 6JX
07980 006606
northwestnews@ntlworld.com
www.nw-news.co.uk

Northscot Press Agency
18 Adelphi, Aberdeen AB11 5BL
01224 212141
northnews@hemedia.co.uk;
northpix@hemedia.co.uk
www.hemedia.co.uk
Grampian and Highlands

Nunn Syndication
13a Shade Thames, Butlers Wharf
London SE1 2PU
020 7407 4666
production@nunn-syndication.com
www.nunn-syndication.com
London press agency

Press Association (PA)
292 Vauxhall Bridge Road
London SW1V 1AE
020 7963 7000
information@pa.press.net
www.pa.press.net
National news agency of UK and Ireland; provider of real-time news and sports information and images

PA News Birmingham
312–313 The Custard Factory
Gibb Street, Digbeth
Birmingham B9 4AA
0121 224 7686
pa_birmingham@hotmail.com
www.pa.press.net

PA News Liverpool
PO Box 48, Old Hall Street
Liverpool L69 3EB
0151 472 2548
paliverpool@pa.press.net
www.pa.press.net

PA News Scotland
1 Central Quay, Glasgow G3 8DA
0870 830 6725
pascotland@pa.press.net
www.pa.press.net

Pacemaker Press International
787 Lisburn Road, Belfast BT9 7GX
028 9066 3191
david@pacemakerpressintl.com
www.pacemakerpressintl.com
Northern Ireland, Republic of Ireland

Parliamentary & EU News Service
19 Douglas Street, Westminster
London SW1P 4PA
020 7233 8283
info@parliamentary-monitoring.co.uk
www.parliamentary-monitoring.co.uk
Parliamentary news service

The Picture Library
16 Crescent Road, London N22 7RS
020 8365 8389
joanne@thepicturelibraryltd.net
www.thepicturelibraryltd.net

PPP News Service
109 Conway Road, London N14 7BH
020 8886 2721
wkastor@compuserve.com
Germany and its politics

Press Agency (Gatwick)
1a Sunview Avenue
Peacehaven BN10 8PJ
01273 583103
petershirley2@hotmail.com
Gatwick and south coast, national press

Press Team Scotland
22 St John's Street, Coatbridge
Lanarkshire ML5 3EJ
01236 440077
news@pressteam.co.uk
Lanarkshire, Glasgow and west Scotland

Press Trust of India
Suite 303, Radnor House
93–97 Regent Street
London W1B 4ET
020 7494 0602
ptilondon@aol.com
www.ptinews.com
Worldwide news and photos

Profile Group (UK)
Dragon Court, 27–29 Macklin Street
London WC2B 5LX
020 7190 7777
info@profilegroup.co.uk
www.profilegroup.co.uk
Future events info and business leads

Racenews
85 Blackstock Road
London N4 2JW
020 7704 0326
racenews@compuserve.com
www.racenews.co.uk
Worldwide horse racing

Raymonds Press Agency
3rd Floor Abbots Hill Chambers
Gower Street, Derby DE1 1SD
01332 340404
news@raymondspress.com
www.raymondspress.com
Sports, news and photography

Reuters
30 The Reuters Building
South Colonnade
Canary Wharf E14 5EP
020 7250 1122
robert.woodward@reuters.com
www.reuters.com
Worldwide news and features

Rex Features
18 Vine Hill, London EC1R 5DZ
020 7278 7294
rex@rexfeatures.com
www.rexfeatures.com
International and USA picture agency

Richard Harris News
Woody Glen, How Mill
Branton CA8 9JY
01228 670381
richardwjharris@aol.com
News in north Cumbria

Ross Parry Agency
40 Back Town Street
Farsley, Leeds LS28 5LD
0113 236 1842
newsdesk@rossparry.co.uk
www.rossparry.co.uk
Yorkshire, news features and photos

**Russian Information Agency –
Novosti (RIA-Novosti)**
3 Rosary Gardens, London SW7 4NW
020 7370 3002
ria@novosti.co.uk
www.rian.ru
Russia

Scottish News Agency
Avian House, 4 Lindsay Court
Dundee Technology Park
Dundee DD2 1SW
01382 427035
g.ogilvy@scottishnews.com
*East and central Scotland, Perthshire,
Fife, Edinburgh, Lothians and Borders*

Scottish News & Sport
15 Fitzroy Place, Glasgow G3 7RW
0141 221 3602
info@snspix.com
www.snspix.com
Scotland sport

Smith Davis Press
Queens Chambers
8 Westport Road, Burslem
Stoke on Trent ST6 4AW
01782 829850
smith-davis@smith-davis.co.uk
www.smith-davis.co.uk
*Photography, graphic design and
freelance journalists*

Snowmedia Consultancy
Unit G4, Broadway Studio
28 Tooting High Street
London SW17 0RG
020 8672 9800
info@snowmedia.net
www.snowmedia.net
*Nationwide lifestyle profiles on health
and sport*

Solent News and Photo Agency
23 Mitchell Point, Ensign Way
Hamble, Southampton SO31 4RF
023 8045 8800
news@solentnews.biz
www.solentnews.biz
*Hants, Wilts, Isle of Wight news features
for all media*

Somerset News Service
3 Lewis Road, Taunton
Somerset TA2 6DU
01823 331856
somersetnews@boltblue.com
Contact: Richard Briers

Somerset Photo News
12 Jellalabad Court, The Mount
Taunton, Somerset TA1 3RZ
01823 282053, 07860 207333
somersetphotonews@boltblue.com
Somerset

South Beds News Agency
Bramingham Park Business Centre
Enterprise Way, Bramingham Park
Luton, Beds LU3 4BU
01582 572222
southbedsnews@btconnect.com
Herts, Beds, Bucks, Northants

South West News & Picture Service
Media Centre, Emma-Chris Way
Abbeywood Park, Bristol BS34 7JU
0117 906 6500
news@swns.com
www.swns.com
*South-west general news, features and
photos*

Space Press News and Pictures
Bridge House, Blackden Lane
Goostrey, Cheshire CW4 8PZ
01477 533403
scoop2001@aol.com
*Knutsford, Macclesfield, Crewe,
Nantwich, Wilmslow, Alderley Edge,
Northwich, Cheshire, Shropshire and
North-west*

The Special Photographers Library
236 Westbourne Park Road
London W11 1EL
020 7221 3489
info@specialphotographers.com
www.specialphotographers.com

Specialist News Services
27 Newton Street, London WC2B 5EL
020 7831 3267
desk@snsnews.co.uk
*National. Consumer, media, city, travel
and motor industry, advertising and
marketing, new products, science and
nature*

Speed Media One
3 Kings Court, Horsham RH13 5UR
01403 259661
info@speedmediaone.co.uk
www.speedmediaone.co.uk
*General news and features. Sport, sport
development, education, local
government*

Sport & General Press Agency
63 Gee Street, London EC1V 3RS
020 7253 7705
info@alphapress.com
www.alphapress.com

Sportsphoto
20 Clifton Street
Scarborough YO12 7SR
01723 367264
stewart@sportsphoto.co.uk
www.allstarpl.com
*All sport and entertainment, national
and international*

Tim Wood Agency
Press Room, Central Criminal Courts
London EC4M 7EH
020 7248 3277
*Court cover at Old Bailey and Southwark
and Knightsbridge crown courts*

Tony Scase News Service
Little Congham House
Congham, Kings Lynn PE32 1DR
01485 600650
news@scase.co.uk
www.scase.co.uk
East Anglia news

TV News
Feature Story News, The Interchange
Oval Road, London NW1 7DZ
020 7485 0303
london.bureau@featurestory.com
www.fsntv.com
*TV news for north America, south-east
Asia, southern Africa*

UK Press
Unit 27, The Limehouse Cut
46 Morris Road, London E14 6NQ
020 7515 3878
info@ukpress.com
www.ukpress.com
Europe/UK photography

Unique Entertainment News
50 Lisson Street, London NW1 5DF
020 7453 1650
philip.chryssikos@unique.com
www.ubcmedia.com
Nationwide general news and features

Universal Pictorial Press & Agency
29–31 Saffron Hill
London EC1N 8SW
020 7421 6000
contacts@uppa.co.uk
www.uppa.co.uk
*Press and worldwide commercial
photography*

Wales News & Picture Service
Market Chambers, 5–7 St Mary's Street
Cardiff CF10 1AT
029 2066 6366
news@walesnews.com
www.walesnews.com
Wales. General news and features

Warwickshire News & Picture Agency
41 Lansdowne Crescent
Leamington Spa CV32 4PR
01926 424181
barrie@tracynews.com
*Midlands. General news, features and
pictures*

Wessex Features and Photos Agency
Neates Yard, 108 High Street
Hungerford RG17 0NB
01488 686810
news@britishnews.co.uk
www.britishnews.co.uk
Women's news, nationwide

West Coast News
Renaissance House, Parracombe
Barnstaple, Devon EX31 4QH
01598 763296
westcoast.news@dial.pipex.com
Devon, Cornwall, west Somerset

White's Press Agency
446 London Road
Heeley, Sheffield S2 4HP
0114 255 3975
newsdesk@press-agency.com
Men's sport, south Yorkshire

Wireimage UK
77 Oxford Street, London W1D 2ES
020 7659 2811
jc@wireimage.com
www.wireimage.com
*Worldwide coverage of entertainment
news and sport*

World Entertainment News Network
35 Kings Exchange
Tileyard Road, London N7 9AH
020 7607 2757
sales@wenn.com
www.wenn.com
Worldwide entertainment and photos

Xinhua News Agency of China
8 Swiss Terrace, Belsize Road
Swiss Cottage, London NW6 4RR
020 7586 8437
xinhua@easynet.co.uk
www.xinhuanet.com
News of China

Picture libraries Contacts

British Association of Picture Libraries and Agencies
18 Vine Hill, London EC1R 5DZ
020 7713 1780
enquiries@bapla.org.uk
www.bapla.org

Picture Research Association
c/o 1 Willow Court, Off Willow Street, London EC2A 4QB
020 7739 8544
chair@picture-research.org.uk
www.picture-research.org.uk
Fine arts collection for museums throughout the world

4Corners Images*
12 Larden Road, London W3 7ST
020 8811 1010
info@4cornersimages.com
www.4cornersimages.com

A1PIX*
40 Bowling Green Lane
Finsbury Business Centre
London EC1R 0NE
020 7415 7045
london@a1pix.com
www.a1pix.com
*Travel, business, lifestyle, children,
nature, animals and illustrations. Hi-res
download facility, personal search service*

AA World Travel Library*
16th Floor, Fanum House
Basing View, Basingstoke
01256 491588
travel.images@theaa.com

Abode Interiors Picture Library*
Albion Court, 1 Pierce Street
Macclesfield, Cheshire SK11 6ER
01625 500070
info@abodepix.co.uk
www.abodepix.co.uk

ACESTOCK.COM*
Satellite House, 2 Salisbury Road
Wimbledon, London SW19 4EZ
020 8944 9944
library@acestock.com
www.acestock.com

Action Images*
Image House, Station Road
London N17 9LR
020 8885 3000
info@actionimages.com
www.actionimages.com

Action Library*
Bretton Court, Bretton
Peterborough PE3 8DZ
0870 062 8287
susan.voss@emap.com
www.actionlibrary.com

Action Plus Sports Images*
54/58 Tanner Street
London SE1 3PH
020 7403 1558
osha@actionplus.co.uk
www.actionplus.co.uk

**Adam (Amnesty Digital Asset
Management)***
Audio Visual Resources
Amnesty International
International Secretariat
1 Easton Street, London WC1X 0DW
020 7413 5588
audiovis@amnesty.org

Adams Picture Library*
Unit 50B, Canalot Production Studios
222 Kensal Road
London W10 5BN
020 8964 8007
mail@adamspicturelibrary.com
www.adamspicturelibrary.com

Advertising Archives*
45 Lyndale Avenue
London NW2 2QB
020 7435 6540
library@advertisingarchives.co.uk
www.advertisingarchives.co.uk
*British and American press ads,
magazine illustration*

Aerofilms Photo Library*
32–34 Station Close, Potters Bar
Hertfordshire EN6 1TL
01707 648390
library@aerofilms.com
www.simmonsaerofilms.com

africanpictures.net*
Leighton Street No. 17
Pietermaritzburg
KwaZulu-Natal, South Africa 3201
00 27 33 345 9445
rosanne@africanpictures.net
www.africanpictures.net

Agripicture Images*
1 Bowdens Lane, Shillingford
Tiverton, Devon EX16 9DG
01398 331598
info@agripicture.com
www.agripicture.com

akg-images*
5 Melbray Mews
158 Hurlingham Road
London SW6 3NS
020 7610 6103
enquiries@akg-images.co.uk
www.akg-images.co.uk

Alamy Images*
Central 127 Milton Park
Abingdon, Oxfordshire OX14 4SA
01235 844600
sales@alamy.com
www.alamy.com

Alinari Archives*
Largo Alinari, 15
Florence, Italy 20123
00 39 055 239 5249
fioravanti@alinari.it
www.alinariarchives.it

All Action Digital*
St Johns House, 54 St Johns Square
London EC1V 4JL
020 7250 0350
info@allaction.co.uk
www.allactiondigital.com

AllStar & Sportsphoto*
20 Clifton Street
Scarborough YO12 7SR
01723 367264
library@allstarpl.com
www.allstarpl.com
Worldwide sports, politics, travel

Alpine Club Photo Library*
55 Charlotte Road
London EC2A 3QF
020 7033 0203
photos@alpine-club.org.uk
www.alpine-club.org.uk

Alvey & Towers*
The Springboard Centre
Mantle Lane, Coalville
Leicestershire LE67 3DW
01530 450011
office@alveyandtowers.com
www.alveyandtowers.com
Transport

**Ancient Art & Architecture
Collection Library***
Suite 1, 410–420 Rayners Lane
Pinner, Middlesex HA5 5DY
020 8429 3131
library@aaacollection.co.uk
www.aaacollection.com

Andes Press Agency*
26 Padbury Court, London E2 7EH
020 7613 5417
apa@andespressagency.com
www.andespressagency.com
*Travel and social documentary
worldwide, Latin America, UK, Middle
East*

Andreas von Einsiedel Archive*
72–80 Leather Lane
London EC1N 7TR
020 7242 7674
elisa@einsiedel.com
www.einsiedel.com

* Member of BAPLA, the British Association of Picture Libraries and Agencies

Andrew N Gagg's Photo Flora*
Town House Two, Fordbank Court
Henwick Road, Worcester WR2 5PF
01905 748515
andrew.n.gagg@ntlworld.com
homepage.ntlworld.com
/a.n.gagg/photo/photoflora.html

Angelo Hornak Library*
17 Alwyne Villas, London N1 2HG
020 7354 1790
angelohornak@mac.com
www.angelohornak.co.uk

Animal Photography*
4 Marylebone Mews
New Cavendish Street
London W1G 8PY
020 7935 0503
thompson@animal-photography.co.uk
www.animal-photography.co.uk

Ann & Bury Peerless Picture Library*
22 Kings Avenue, Minnis Bay
Birchington On Sea, Kent CT7 9QL
01843 841428
www.peerlessimages.com

Anthony Blake Photo Library*
20 Blades Court, Deodar Road
Putney, London SW15 2NU
020 8877 1123
info@abpl.co.uk
www.abpl.co.uk

Antiquarian Images*
PO Box 20, Chislehurst
Kent BR7 5SZ
020 8467 6297
enquiries@antiquarianimages.co.uk
www.antiquarianimages.com

AP Photo Archive*
12 Norwich Street
London EC4A 1BP
020 7427 4263
london_photolibrary@ap.org
www.apwideworld.com
Archive of global news agency

Aquarius Library*
PO Box 5, Hastings
East Sussex TN34 1HR
01424 721196
aquarius.lib@clara.net
www.aquariuscollection.com

Arcaid Picture Library*
Parc House, 25–37 Cowleaze Road
Kingston upon Thames
Surrey KT2 6DZ
020 8546 4352
arcaid@arcaid.co.uk
www.arcaid.co.uk

Arcangel Images*
46 Chestnut Avenue, Buckhurst Hill
Essex IG9 6EW
020 8559 1545
info@arcangel-images.com
www.arcangel-images.com

arcblue.com*
93 Gainsborough Road
Richmond TW9 2ET
020 8940 2227
info@arcblue.com
www.arcblue.com

Architectural Association Photo Library*
36 Bedford Square
London WC1B 3ES
020 7887 4066
valerie@aaschool.ac.uk
www.aaschool.ac.uk/photolib

Ardea*
35 Brodrick Road
London SW17 7DX
020 8672 2067
ardea@ardea.com
www.ardea.com
Wildlife, pets, environment

ArenaPAL*
Lambert House, 55 Southwark Street
London SE1 1RU
020 7403 8542
searches@arenapal.com
www.arenapal.com

Arkreligion.com*
57 Burdon Lane, Cheam
Surrey SM2 7BY
020 8642 3593
images@artdirectors.co.uk
www.arkreligion.com

Aroomwithviews*
Bluff House, Stoulgrove Lane
Woodcroft, Chepstow NP16 7QE
01594 529111
aroomwithviews@aol.com
www.aroomwithviews.com

Art Archive, The*
2 The Quadrant, 135 Salusbury Road
London NW6 6RJ
020 7624 3500
artarch@picture-desk.com
www.picture-desk.com

Art Directors and Trip Photo Library*
57 Burdon Lane, Cheam
Surrey SM2 7BY
020 8642 3593
images@artdirectors.co.uk
www.artdirectors.co.uk
Worldwide countries and religion

Artbank Illustration Library
114 Clerkenwell Road
London EC1M 5SA
020 8906 2288
info@artbank.com
www.artbank.com
Online library

artimagedirect.com*
29 High Street, Stalham
Norwich NR12 9AH
01692 580205
enquiries@artimagedirect.com
www.artimagedirect.com

ARWP*
10 Tidcombe, Nr Marlborough
Wiltshire SN8 3SL
01264 731238
sales@andyrouse.co.uk
www.andyrouse.co.uk

Aspect Picture Library*
40 Rostrevor Road
London SW6 5AD
020 7736 1998
aspect.Ldn@btinternet.com
www.aspect-picture-library.co.uk

Atmosphere Picture Library*
Willis Vean, Mullion, Helston
Cornwall TR12 7DF
01326 240180
pix@atmosphere.co.uk
www.atmosphere.co.uk

Auto Express Picture Library*
Dennis Publishing
30 Cleveland Street
London W1T 4JD
020 7907 6132
pictures@dennis.co.uk
www.autoexpressimages.co.uk

Aviation Picture Library*
116 The Avenue, West Ealing
London W13 8JX
020 8566 7712
avpix@aol.com
www.aviationpictures.com

Aviation-Images.com*
42 Queens Road, Wimbledon
London SW19 8LR
020 8944 5225
pictures@aviation-images.com
www.aviation-images.com
Aviation and aerial photography

Axel Poignant Archive*
115 Bedford Court Mansions
Bedford Avenue
London WC1V 3AG
020 7636 2555
rpoignant@aol.com
Anthropology, ethnography

Axiom Photographic Agency*
The Saga Building, 326 Kensal Road
London W10 5BZ
020 8964 9970
jen@axiomphoto.co.uk
www.axiomphoto.co.uk

BAA Aviation Photo Library*
Green Dragon Vaults
Parliament Square
Hertford SG14 1PT
01992 501134
sales@in-press.co.uk
www.baa.com/photolibrary

BananaStock*
Henley House, Howe Road
Watlington, Oxfordshire OX49 5EL
01491 613800
team@bananastock.com
www.bananastock.com

Barnardos'*
Tanners Lane, Bakingside
Ilford, Essex IG6 1QG
020 8498 7345
stephen.pover@barnardos.org.uk
www.barnardos.org.uk

BBC Photo Library*
B116 BBC Television Centre
Wood Lane, London W12 7RJ
020 8225 7193
Research-Central@bbc.co.uk
www.bbcresearchcentral.com

BDI Images*
56 Five Ash Down, Uckfield
East Sussex TN22 3AL
01825 733095
bob@bdi-images.com
www.bdi-images.com

Beachfeature.com*
41 Trebarwith Crescent
Newquay, Cornwall TR7 1DX
01637 870430
info@beachfeature.com
www.beachfeature.com

Beken of Cowes*
16 Birmingham Road, Cowes
Isle of Wight PO31 7BH
01983 297311
beken@beken.co.uk
www.beken.co.uk

The Best of Morocco
Seend Park, High Street
Seend, Wiltshire SN12 6NZ
01380 828533
chris@realmorocco.com
www.realmorocco.com

BFI Stills, Posters and Designs*
21 Stephen Street, London W1T 1LN
020 7957 4797
stills.films@bfi.org.uk
www.bfi.org.uk

Big Glass Eye Stock*
5 Irwin Avenue, Belfast BT4 3AF
028 9059 4748
info@bigglasseye.com
www.bigglasseye.com

Big Pictures*
50–54 Clerkenwell Road
London EC1M 5PS
020 7250 3555
alan.williams@bigpictures.co.uk
www.bigpicturesphoto.com

Birmingham Central Library*
Chamberlain Square
Birmingham B3 3HQ
0121 303 4439
pete.james@birmingham.gov.uk
www.birmingham.gov.uk

Birmingham Museums & Art Gallery Picture Library*
Chamberlain Square
Birmingham B3 3DH
0121 303 3155
picture_library@birmingham.gov.uk
www.bmag.org.uk

Birmingham Picture Library*
14 St. Bernard's Road, Olton
Solihull B92 7BB
0121 765 4114
office@bplphoto.co.uk
www.bplphoto.co.uk

Bluegreen Pictures*
11 Bath Road, Cowes
Isle of Wight PO31 7QN
01983 282233
info@bluegreenpictures.com
www.bluegreenpictures.com

BM Totterdell Photography*
Constable Cottage, Burlings Lane
Knockholt, Sevenoaks TN14 7PE
01959 532001
btrial@btopenworld.com

Bridgeman Art Library*
17–19 Garway Road
London W2 4PH
020 7727 4065
pictureresearch@bridgeman.co.uk
www.bridgeman.co.uk

Britain on View*
Image Resource Library
Thames Tower (4th Floor)
Black's Road, Hammersmith
London W6 9EL
020 8563 3120
bovsales@visitbritain.org
www.britainonview.com

British Antarctic Survey*
High Cross, Madingley Road
Cambridge CB3 OET
01223 221412
pictures@bas.ac.uk
www.antarctic.ac.uk

British Library Imaging Services*
96 Euston Road, London NW1 2DB
020 7412 7614
imagesonline@bl.uk
www.bl.uk/imagesonline
Images, maps, historical and engravings

British Motor Industry Heritage Trust*
Heritage Motor Centre
Banbury Road, Gaydon
Warwick CV35 0BJ
01926 645 073
bmiht@tiscali.co.uk
www.heritage.org.uk

British Museum Photography and Imaging*
The British Museum
Great Russell Street
London WC1B 3DG
020 7323 8633
photography@thebritishmuseum.ac.uk
from autumn 2005:
www.bmimages.com

Bryan and Cherry Alexander Photography*
Higher Cottage, Manston
Sturminster Newton
Dorset DT10 1EZ
01258 473006
alexander@arcticphoto.co.uk
www.arcticphoto.co.uk
Arctic and Antarctic specialists

Bubbles Photolibrary*
3 Rose Lane, Ipswich IP1 1XE
01473 288605
info@bubblesphotolibrary.co.uk
www.bubblesphotolibrary.co.uk

Built Vision*
49 Lucknow Drive
Nottingham NG3 5EU
0115 962 1112
office@builtvision.co.uk
www.builtvision.co.uk

Burall Floraprint*
Oldfield Lane, Wisbech
Cambridgeshire PE13 2TH
0870 728 7222
zbrown@burall.com

Buzz Pictures*
14 Shanklin Road, London N8 8TJ
020 8374 2596
office@buzzpictures.co.uk
www.buzzpictures.co.uk

Camera Press*
21 Queen Elizabeth Street
London SE1 2PD
020 7378 1300
sales@camerapress.com
www.camerapress.com
Worldwide photographic library

Capital Pictures*
85 Randolph Avenue
London W9 1DL
020 7286 2212
sales@capitalpictures.com
www.capitalpictures.com

CartoonStock*
Unit 2, Lansdown Mews
Bath BA1 5DY
01225 789600
admin@cartoonstock.com
www.cartoonstock.com

Celebrity Pictures*
98 De Beauvoir Road
London N1 4EN
020 7275 2700
steve@celebritypictures.co.uk
www.celebritypictures.co.uk

Cephas Picture Library*
Hurst House, 157 Walton Road
East Molesey, Surrey KT8 0DX
020 8979 8647
pictures@cephas.co.uk
www.cephas.com
Wine and vineyards, whisky and brandy, food and drink

Chatsworth Photo Library*
Chatsworth, Bakewell
Derbyshire DE45 1PP
01246 565300
photolibrary@chatsworth.org
www.chatsworth.org

Chris Bonington Picture Library*
Badger Hill, Hesket Newmarket
Wigton, Cumbria CA7 8LA
01697 478286
frances@bonington.com
www.bonington.com

Chris Howes/Wild Places Photography
51 Timber Square, Cardiff CF24 3SH
029 2048 6557
photos@wildplaces.co.uk
Travel, topography and natural history, plus action sports and caving

Christian Aid Photo Section*
PO Box 100, London SE1 7RT
020 7523 2235
jcabon@christian-aid.org

Christian Him's Jazz Index*
26 Fosse Way, London W13 0BZ
020 8998 1232
christianhim@jazzindex.co.uk
www.jazzindex.co.uk

Christie's Images*
1 Langley Lane, Vauxhall
London SW8 1TJ
020 7582 1282
imageslondon@christies.com
www.christiesimages.com
Fine and decorative art

Christopher Hill Photographic Library*
17 Clarence Street, Belfast BT2 8DY
028 9024 5038
sales@scenicireland.com
www.scenicireland.com

Chrysalis Images
The Chrysalis Building
Bramley Road, London W10 6SP
020 7314 1469
Tforshaw@chrysalisbooks.co.uk
www.chrysalisbooks.co.uk
History, transport, cookery, crafts, space

CIRCA Photo Library*
ICOREC, 3 Wynnstay Grove
Fallowfield, Manchester M14 6XG
0161 248 5731
joanne@icorec.net

Collections*
13 Woodberry Crescent
London N10 1PJ
020 8883 0083
collections@btinternet.com
www.collectionspicturelibrary.co.uk
*Britain and Ireland: people and
traditional culture*

Construction Photography*
3 Morocco Street, London SE1 3HB
020 7403 8866
Lucy@constructionphotography.com
www.constructionphotography.com

Corbis*
111 Salusbury Road
London NW6 6RG
0800 731 9995
info@corbis.com
www.corbis.com

Cornish Picture Library*
Trelawney Lodge, Keveral Lane
Seaton, Cornwall PL11 3JJ
01503 250673
info@imageclick.co.uk
www.imageclick.co.uk

Country Life Picture Library*
King's Reach Tower
Stamford Street, London SE1 9LS
020 7261 6337
camilla_costello@ipcmedia.com
www.clpicturelibrary.co.uk
*Architecture, country pursuits, gardens,
crafts, black and white pictures*

**Countryside Agency Photographic
Library***
John Dower House, Crescent Place
Cheltenham
Gloucestershire GL50 3RA
01242 521381

**Courtauld Institute of Art Image
Libraries***
Somerset House, Strand
London WC2R 0RN
020 7848 2879
galleryimages@courtauld.ac.uk
www.courtauld.ac.uk
and www.artandarchitecture.org.uk

Crafts Council Picture Library*
44a Pentonville Road, Islington
London N1 9BY
020 7806 2503
photostore@craftscouncil.org.uk
www.craftscouncil.org.uk/photostore

Crash Picture Agency*
No1 Innovation Centre
Silverstone Circuit, Silverstone
Northants NN12 8GX
0870 350 5044
images@crash.net
www.crashpa.net

Creatas*
5 Finch Drive
Springwood Industrial Estate
Braintree, Essex CM7 2SF
0800 056 7533
sales@creatas.co.uk
www.creatas.co.uk

Create Online*
The Mansion, Bletchley Park
Milton Keynes MK3 6EB
01980 372727
enquiries@createonline.net
www.createonline.net

Creative Image Library*
Brook Cottage, Hale Oak Road
Weald, Sevenoaks TN14 6NQ
01732 462001
sales@creativeimagelibrary.com
www.creativeimagelibrary.com

Culture Archive, The*
193 Ditchling Road
Brighton BN1 6JB
01273 552929
culture@pavilion.co.uk
www.fulltable.com/index.htm

Cumbria Photo*
Ashleigh, Holly Road
Windermere, Cumbria LA23 2AQ
01539 444444
bbarden@gocumbria.org
www.cumbriaphoto.co.uk

**Dance Picture Library and Circus
Images***
4 Ongar Place, Addlestone
Surrey KT15 1JF
07956 319362
linda-rich@dancepicturelibrary.com
www.dancepicturelibrary.com

David Hoffman Photo Library*
c/o Bapla office, 18 Vine Hill
London EC1R 5DZ
020 8981 5041
lib@hoffmanphotos.com
www.hoffmanphotos.com
*Social issues, built from journalistic
work since 1970s*

David King Collection*
90 St Pauls Road, London N1 2QP
020 7226 0149
davidkingcollection@btopenworld.com
www.davidkingcollection.com
*Soviet Union and other Communist
movements*

David Noble Photography*
Longleigh, 28 Coolinge Lane
Folkestone, Kent CT20 3QT
01303 254263
djn@noblepics.co.uk
www.noblepics.co.uk

David Tipling Photo Library*
84 Dolphin Quays, Clive Street
North Shields, Tyne & Wear NE29 6HJ
0191 270 8646
dt@windrushphotos.demon.co.uk
www.davidtipling.com

David Williams Picture Library*
50 Burlington Avenue
Glasgow G12 0LH
0141 339 7823
david@scotland-guide.co.uk

**Dee Conway Ballet & Dance Picture
Library***
110 Sussex Way, London N7 6RR
020 7272 7845
www.ddance.co.uk

The Defence Picture Library*
8 Creykes Court, The Millfields
Plymouth, Devon PL1 3JB
01752 312061
pix@defencepictures.com
www.defencepictures.com

Digital Vision*
India House, 45 Curlew Street
London SE1 2ND
020 7378 5685
kieran.mahon@digitalvision.com
www.digitalvision.com

DIY Photolibrary*
The Covert, Pickhurst Rise
West Wickham, Kent BR4 0AA
020 8777 5025
info@diyphotolibrary.com
www.diyphotolibrary.com

DK Images*
80 Strand, London WC2R 0RL
020 7010 4500
enquiries@dkimages.com
www.dkimages.com

DN – Images*
Cambridge Lodge, Gate Lane
Freshwater Bay
Isle of Wight PO40 9QD
01983 759918
info@dn-images.com
www.dn-images.com

Dominic Photography*
4b Moore Park Road
London SW6 2JT
020 7381 0007
dominicphoto@
    catherineashmore.co.uk

dopeshots.com*
27 Orchard Park, Holmer Green
Bucks HP15 6QX
01494 717 118
info@dopeshots.com
www.dopeshots.com

Double Red Photographic*
The Old School, Thorn Lane, Goxhill
Barrow upon Humber DN19 7JE
01469 531416
doublered@atlas.co.uk
www.doublered.co.uk
Motorsport photography

E&E Picture Library*
Beggars Roost, Woolpack Hill
Brabourne Lees, Ashford
Kent TN25 6PR
01303 812608
isobel@picture-library.freeserve.co.uk
http://picture-library.mysite
      .wanadoo-members.co.uk
World religion

Ecoscene*
Empire Farm, Throop Road
Templecombe BA8 0HR
01963 371700
pictures@ecoscene.com
www.ecoscene.com

Edifice*
Cutterne Mill, Southwood
Evercreech, Somerset BA4 6LY
01749 831400
info@edificephoto.com
www.edificephoto.com
Buildings and architecture

Education Photos*
April Cottage, Warners Lane
Albury Heath, Guildford GU5 9DE
01483 203846
johnwalmsley@educationphotos.co.uk
www.educationphotos.co.uk
Education, work, homes, signs

Elizabeth Whiting & Associates*
70 Mornington Street
London NW1 7QE
020 7388 2828
ewa@elizabethwhiting.com
www.elizabethwhiting.com

EMPICS*
Pavilion House, 16 Castle Boulevard
Nottingham NG7 1FL
0115 844 7447
info@empics.com
www.empics.com

English Heritage Photo Library*
23 Savile Row, London W1S 2ET
020 7973 3338
photo.library@english-heritage.org.uk
www.english-heritage.org.uk

**English Heritage, National
Monuments Record***
English Heritage, Kemble Drive
Swindon SN2 2GZ
01793 414600
nmrinfo@english-heritage.org.uk
www.english-heritage.org.uk

Environmental Investigation Agency*
62–63 Upper Street, London N1 0NY
020 7354 7968
tomthistlethwaite@
      eia-international.org
www.eia-international.org

ePicscotland.com*
Unit 5 Hathaway Business Centre
21/29 Hathaway Street
Glasgow G20 8TD
0141 945 0000
info@epicscotland.com
www.epicscotland.com

**Eric Hepworth Golf Course Picture
Library***
72 Apley Road, Hyde Park
Doncaster DN1 2AY
01302 322674
eric@hepworthgolfphotography.com
www.hepworthgolfphotography.com

Esler Crawford Photography*
37a Lisburn Road, Belfast BT9 7AA
028 9032 6999
esler.crawford@btclick.com
www.eslercrawford.com

Everynight Images*
Top Floor Studio
127 Strathleven Road, Brixton
London SW2 5JS
020 7738 7297
info@everynight.co.uk
www.everynight.co.uk

Exile Images*
1 Mill Row, Weston Hill Road
Brighton BN1 3SU
01273 208741
pics@exileimages.co.uk
www.exileimages.co.uk
*Refugees, protest, asylum seekers, conflict.
Middle East, Balkans, south-east Asia*

Eye Ubiquitous / Hutchison*
65 Brighton Road
Shoreham-by-sea
West Sussex BN43 6RE
01273 440113
library@eyeubiquitous.com
www.eyeubiquitous.com

eyevine*
3 Mills Film Studios, Three Mill Lane
London E3 3DU
020 8709 8709
info@eyevine.com
www.eyevine.com

Fairfaxphotos.com*
201 Sussex Street, Sydney 2000
00 61 2 9282 2442
fairfaxphotos@fairfax.com.au
www.fairfaxphotos.com

Famous*
13 Harwood Road, London SW6 4QP
020 7731 9333
info@famous.uk.com
www.famous.uk.com

ffotograff
10 Kyveilog Street, Cardiff CF11 9JA
029 2023 6879
ffotograff@easynet.co.uk
www.ffotograff.com
*Travel, exploration, arts, architecture,
culture, Wales, Middle East, Far East*

FilmMagic*
Suite 501, 77 Oxford Street
London W1D 2ES
020 7659 2827
vicky@filmmagic.com
www.filmmagic.com

Financial Times Pictures
1 Southwark Bridge, London SE1 9HL
020 7873 3000
photosynd@ft.com
www.ft.com

Fine Art Photographic Library*
2a Milner Street, London SW3 2PU
020 7589 3127
info@fineartphotolibrary.com
www.fineartphotolibrary.com

Firepix International*
68 Arkles Lane, Anfield
Liverpool L4 2SP
0151 260 0111
info@firepix.com
www.firepix.com

The Flight Collection*
Quadrant House, The Quadrant
Sutton SM2 5AS
020 8652 8888
qpl@rbi.co.uk
www.theflightcollection.com

Flowerphotos*
71 Leonard Street, London EC2A 4QU
020 7684 5668
sales@flowerphotos.com
www.flowerphotos.com

FLPA – Images of Nature*
Pages Green House
Wetheringsett
Stowmarket IP14 5QA
01728 860789
pictures@flpa-images.co.uk
www.flpa-images.co.uk

Fogden Wildlife Photographs*
16 Locheport, North Uist
Western Isles HS6 5EU
01876 580245
susan.fogden@virgin.net
www.fogdenphotos.com

Food Features*
Stream House, West Flexford Lane
Wanborough, Guildford GU3 2JW
01483 810840
frontdesk@foodpix.co.uk
www.foodpix.co.uk

foodanddrinkphotos*
Studio 4, Sun Studios
30 Warple Way, London W3 0RX
020 8740 6610
info@foodanddrinkphotos.com
www.foodanddrinkphotos.com

**Forest Commission Life Picture
Library**
231 Corstorphie Road
Edinburgh EH12 7AT
0131 314 6411
neil.campbell@forestry.gsi.gov.uk
www.forestry.gov.uk

Fortean Picture Library*
Henblas, Mwrog Street
Ruthin LL15 1LG
01824 707278
janet.bord@forteanpix.demon.co.uk
www.forteanpix.demon.co.uk

Fotografique*
43a Gunter Grove, Chelsea
London SW10 0UN
020 7376 5843
duncan@fotografique.com
www.fotografique.com

fotoLibra*
22 Mount View Road
London N4 4HX
020 8348 1234
professionals@fotolibra.com
www.fotolibra.com

Fotomas Index UK*
12 Pickhurst Rise
West Wickham BR4 0AL
020 8776 2772

Framed Picture Library*
18 Vine Hill, London EC1R 5DZ
020 7713 1780

Francis Frith Collection, The*
Frith's Barn, Teffont
Salisbury SP3 5QP
01722 716376
sales@francisfrith.co.uk
www.francisfrith.co.uk

Frank Lane Picture Agency
Pages Green House, Pages Green
Wetheringsett, Suffolk IP14 5QA
01728 860789
pictures@flpa-images.co.uk
www.flpa-images.co.uk
Natural history, environment, pets, weather

FremantleMedia Stills Library, The*
Unit 5, Teddington Business Park
Station Road, Teddington
Middlesex TW11 9BQ
020 8977 2134
stills.library@fremantlemedia.com
www.fremantlemediastills.com

Galaxy Picture Library*
34 Fennels Way, Flackwell Heath
High Wycombe HP10 9BY
01628 521338
robin@galaxypix.com
www.galaxypix.com
Astronomy and the sky

Garden and Wildlife Matters Photo Library*
Marlham, Watermill Lane
Henley's Down, Battle
East Sussex TN33 9BN
01424 830566
gardens@gmpix.com
www.gardenmatters.uk.com

Garden Exposures Photo Library*
316 Kew Road, Kew Gardens
Richmond, Surrey TW9 3DU
020 8287 0600
pictures@gardenexposures.co.uk
www.gardenexposures.com

Garden Photo Library*
239a Hook Road, Chessington
Surrey KT9 1EQ
020 8397 3761
Derek@GardenPhotoLibrary.com
www.gardenphotolibrary.com

Garden Picture Library*
Unit 12, Ransome's Dock
35 Parkgate Road
London SW11 4NP
020 7228 4332
info@gardenpicture.com
www.gardenpicture.com
Gardening

GardenWorld Images*
Grange Studio, Woodham Road
Battlesbridge
Wickford, Essex SS11 7QU
01245 325725
info@gardenworldimages.com
www.gardenworldimages.com

Geo Aerial Photography*
4 Christian Fields, London SW16 3JZ
020 8764 6292
geo.aerial@geo-group.co.uk
www.geo-group.co.uk

Geo Science Features Picture Library
6 Orchard Drive, Wye
Kent TN25 5AU
01233 812707
gsf@geoscience.demon.co.uk
www.geoscience.demon.co.uk

Geoff Wilkinson Image Library*
The Old Stables
rear of 84 Nightingale Lane
Wanstead, London E11 2EZ
020 8530 4612
mjw@gwimlib.com
www.gwimlib.com

GeoScience Features Picture Library*
6 Orchard Drive, Wye
Kent TN25 5AU
01233 812707
gsf@geoscience.demon.co.uk
www.geoscience.demon.co.uk

Geoslides Photography*
4 Christian Fields, London SW16 3JZ
020 8764 6292
geoslides@geo-group.co.uk
www.geo-group.co.uk
Landscape and human interest

Getty Images*
101 Bayham Street
London NW1 0AG
0800 376 7977
sales@gettyimages.co.uk
www.gettyimages.co.uk
Live feed photo agency

Glasgow Museums Photo Library*
The Burrell Collection
Pollok Country Park
2060 Pollokshaws Road
Glasgow G43 1AT
0141 287 2595
photolibrary@cls.glasgow.gov.uk
www.glasgowmuseums.com

Golf Picture Library*
24 New Road, Aston Clinton
Buckinghamshire HP22 5JD
01296 630914
requests@golfpicturelibrary.com
www.golfpicturelibrary.com

Great Stock Photo Library*
PO Box 87622, Houghton
Johannesburg, South Africa 2041
00 27 11 880 7826
enquiries@greatstock.co.za
www.greatstock.co.za

Greenpeace Images*
Canonbury Villas, London N1 2PN
020 7865 8294
pix@uk.greenpeace.org
www.greenpeace.org.uk

Greenpeace International Images*
Photo Library, Otto Heldringstraat 5
Amsterdam 1066 AZ
00 31 20 718 2116
julieanne.wilce@int.greenpeace.org
www.greenpeace.org

Guzelian*
5 Victoria Road, Saltaire, Bradford
Yorkshire BD18 3LA
01274 532300
pictures@guzelian.co.uk
www.guzelian.co.uk

Hali Archive*
Hali Publications Ltd., St Giles House
50 Poland Street, London W1F 7AX
020 7970 4600
hali@centaur.co.uk
www.hali.com

Harpur Garden Library*
44 Roxwell Road, Chelmsford
Essex CM1 2NB
01245 257527
harpur.garden.library@dsl.pipex.com
www.harpurgardenlibrary.co.uk

Heather Angel/Natural Visions*
6 Vicarage Hill, Farnham
Surrey GU9 8HG
01252 716700
hangel@naturalvisions.co.uk
www.naturalvisions.co.uk
Online images of worldwide wildlife

Heritage Image Partnership*
Finsbury Business Centre
40 Bowling Green Lane
London EC1R 0NE
020 7970 5665
info@heritage-images.com
www.heritage-images.com

Heseltine Archive*
Mill Studios, Frogmarsh Mills
South Woodchester
Gloucestershire GL5 5ET
01453 873792
john@heseltine.co.uk
www.heseltine.co.uk

Historic Royal Palaces*
Apartment 25, Hampton Court Palace
East Molesey, Surrey KT8 9AU
020 8781 9775
annie.heron@hrp.org.uk
www.hrp.org.uk

Historic Scotland Photographic Library*
Historic Scotland, Longmore House
Salisbury Place, Edinburgh EH9 1SH
0131 668 8647
hs.photolibrary@scotland.gsi.gov.uk
www.historic-scotland.gov.uk

History of Advertising Trust Archive (HAT)*
HAT House, 12 Raveningham Centre
Raveningham, Norwich NR14 6NU
01508 548623
archive@hatads.demon.co.uk
www.hatads.org.uk

Historystore*
29 Churton Street
London SW1V 2LY
020 7976 6040
claire@historystore.ltd.uk
www.historystore.ltd.uk

Hobbs Golf Collection*
5 Winston Way, New Ridley
Stocksfield
Northumberland NE43 7RF
01661 842933
info@hobbsgolfcollection.com
www.hobbsgolfcollection.com

Holt Studios*
Coxes Farm, Branscombe, Seaton
Devon EX12 3BJ
01297 680569
library@holt-studios.co.uk
www.holt-studios.co.uk
World agriculture and horticulture.
Wildlife, pests and diseases

Houghton's Horses*
Radlet Cottage, Spaxton, Bridgwater
Somerset TA5 1DE
01278 671362
kit@enterprise.net
www.houghtonshorses.com

Hungry Eye Images*
504 Queens Quay, 58 Upper Street
London EC4V 3EH
020 7329 6855
info@hungryeye.co.uk
www.hungryeyeimages.com

Hutchison Picture Library
65 Brighton Road, Shoreham on sea
West Sussex BN43 6RE
01273 440113
library@hutchisonpictures.co.uk
www.hutchisonpictures.co.uk
Worldwide contemporary images

ICCE Photolibrary*
Burcott House, Wing
Leighton Buzzard LU7 0JU
01296 688245
jacolyn@iccephotolibrary.co.uk
www.iccephotolibrary.co.uk

Idarta Travel Images*
522 The Greenhouse
Custard Factory
Birmingham B9 4AA
sales@idartatravelimages.com
www.idartatravelimages.com

Idols Licensing and Publicity*
593–599 Fulham Road
London SW6 5UA
020 7385 5121
info@idols.co.uk
www.idols.co.uk

Illustrated London News Picture Library*
20 Upper Ground, London SE1 9PF
020 7805 5585
research@ilnpictures.co.uk
www.ilnpictures.co.uk

Image Option*
73 Jarrow Road, Chadwell Heath
Essex RM6 5RL
01708 732336
info@imageoption.co.uk
imageoption.co.uk

Image Quest Marine*
The Moos, Poffley End, Witney
Oxfordshire OX29 9UW
01993 704050
info@imagequestmarine.com
www.imagequestmarine.com

Image Solutions*
P.O Box 62429, UAE
00 971 4 340 4092
info@gulfimages.com
www.gulfimages.com

Image Source*
1 Sekforde Street, London EC1R 0BE
020 7075 6789
info@imagesource.com
www.imagesource.com

image100*
4th Floor, 79 New Cavendish Street
London W1W 6XB
020 7612 1550
info@image100.com
www.image100.com

Images of Africa Photobank*
11 The Windings, Lichfield
Staffordshire WS13 7EX
01543 262898
info@imagesofafrica.co.uk
www.imagesofafrica.co.uk
130,000 images of 20 African countries

Imagestate*
Ramillies House, 1–2 Ramillies Street
London W1F 7LN
020 7734 7344
sales@imagestate.co.uk
www.imagestate.com

Impact Photos*
18–20 St John Street
London EC1M 4NX
020 7251 5091
library@impactphotos.com
www.impactphotos.com

Imperial War Museum*
Photograph Archive
All Saints Annexe, Austral Street
London SE11 4SL
020 7416 5333
photos@iwm.org.uk
www.iwm.org.uk

Infoterra*
Atlas House, 41 Wembley Road
Leicester LE3 1UT
0116 273 2314
info@infoterra-global.com
www.infoterra-global.com

Inpho Sports Photography*
15A Lower Baggot Street, Dublin 2
00 353 1 7088 084
norman@inpho.ie
www.inpho.ie

Institution of Mechanical Engineers*
1 Birdcage Walk, London SW1H 9JJ
020 7304 6836
m_claxton@imeche.org.uk
www.imeche.org.uk

Interior Archive*
1 Ruston Mews, London W11 1RB
020 7221 9922
karen@interior-archive.netkonect.co.uk
www.interiorarchive.com

International Photobank*
Unit D, Roman Hill Business Park
Broadmayne, Dorset BT2 8LY
01305 854145
peter@internationalphotobank.co.uk
www.internationalphotobank.co.uk
400,000 travel images

Irish Image Collection*
Ballydowane East, Bunmahon
Kilmacthomas, Co Waterford
00 353 51 292020
george@theirishimagecollection.ie
www.theirishimagecollection.ie

Irish Picture Library*
69b Heather Road
Sandyford Industrial Estate, Dublin 18
00 353 1 2950 799
info@fatherbrowne.com
www.fatherbrowne.com/ipl

Jacqui Hurst
66 Richford Street, London W6 7HP
020 8743 2315
jacquih@dircon.co.uk
www.jacquihurstphotography.co.uk
Designers and applied artists, regional
food producers and markets

Jaguar Daimler Photographic Library*
B/1/002, Browns Lane, Allesley
Coventry CV5 9DR
024 7620 2743
kram4@jaguar.com
www.jdht.com

James Davis Worldwide
65 Brighton Road, Shoreham on sea
West Sussex BN43 6RE
01273 452252
library@eyeubiquitous.com
www.eyeubiquitous.com
Travel collection

Janine Wiedel Photo Library*
8 South Croxted Road
London SE21 8BB
020 8761 1502
wiedelphoto@compuserve.com
www.wiedel-photo-library.com

Jessica Strang*
504 Brody House, Strype Street
London E1 7LQ
020 7247 8982
jessica@jessicastrang.plus.com
Architecture, interiors and gardens

JGA*
7 Holborn View, Woodhouse
Leeds LS6 2RD
0113 295 0446
sales@canalstock.co.uk
www.canalstock.co.uk

Jim Henderson Photography*
Crooktree, Kincardine O'Neil
Aboyne, Aberdeenshire AB34 4JD
01339 882149
JHende7868@aol.com
www.jimhendersonphotography.com
Aberdeenshire, aurora borealis, ancient
Egypt

John Birdsall Social Issues Photo Library*
89 Zulu Road, New Basford
Nottingham NG7 7DR
0115 978 2645
photos@JohnBirdsall.co.uk
www.johnbirdsall.co.uk

Member of BAPLA, the British Association of Picture Libraries and Agencies

133

John Cleare/Mountain Camera Picture Library*
Hill Cottage, Fonthill Gifford
Salisbury SP3 6QW
01747 820320
cleare@btinternet.com
mountaincamera.com
Landscapes fot UK and worldwide – mountains and trekking

John Heseltine Archive
Mill Studio, Frogmarsh Mills
South Woodchester
Gloucester GL5 5ET
01453 873792
john@heseltine.co.uk
www.heseltine.co.uk
Landscapes, architecture, food and travel: Italy and UK

John Warburton-Lee Photography*
The Grange, Walcot, Sleaford
Lincolnshire NG34 0ST
01529 497223
info@johnwarburtonlee.com
www.johnwarburtonlee.com

Jon Arnold Images*
7 Rydes Avenue, Guildford GU2 9SR
01483 451245
info@jonarnoldimages.com
www.jonarnold.com

Katz*
109 Clifton Street, London EC2A 4LD
020 7749 6012
info@katzpictures.com
www.katzpictures.com

Kennel Club, The*
1–5 Clarges Street, London WIJ 8AB
020 7518 1009
picturelibrary@the-kennel-club.org.uk
www.the-kennel-club.org.uk

Kobal Collection*
2 The Quadrant, 135 Salusbury Road
London NW6 6RJ
020 7624 3500
info@picture-desk.com
www.picture-desk.com

Kos Picture Source*
7 Spice Court, Ivory Square
Plantation Wharf, London SW11 3UE
020 7801 0044
images@kospictures.com
www.kospictures.com
Water-based images

LAT Photographic*
Somerset House, Somerset Road
Teddington, Middlesex TW11 8RU
020 8251 3000
zoe.mayho@haynet.com
www.latphoto.co.uk

Latent Light*
P.O Box 1426, Mangotsfield
Bristol BS16 9ZJ
0870 043 5536
enquiries@latentlight.com
www.latentlight.com

Lebrecht Music and Arts Photo Library*
58b Carlton Hill, London NW8 0ES
020 7625 5341
pictures@lebrecht.co.uk
www.lebrecht.co.uk

Lee Miller Archives*
Farley Farmhouse, Muddles Green
Chiddingly, East Sussex BN8 6HW
01825 872691
archives@leemiller.co.uk
www.leemiller.co.uk

Leonard Smith Collection*
Greenacre, Brantham Hill, Brantham
Manningtree, Essex CO11 1TB
01206 393321
library@leonardsmith.co.uk
www.leonardsmith.co.uk

Lesley & Roy Adkins
10 Acre Wood, Whitestone
Exeter EX14 2HW
01392 811357
mail@adkinsarchaeology.com
www.adkinarchaeology.com
Archaeology and heritage

Lickerish*
36 Eastcastle Street
London W1W 8DP
020 7323 1999
emma@lickerish.biz
www.lickerish.biz

Lindley Library, Royal Horticultural Society*
80 Vincent Square
London SW1P 2PE
020 7821 3051

Link Picture Library*
33 Greyhound Road
London W6 8NH
020 7381 2433
lib@linkpicturelibrary.com
www.linkpicturelibrary.com

London Aerial Photo Library*
Studio D1, Fairoaks Airport
Chobham, Surrey GU24 8HU
01276 855997
info@londonaerial.co.uk
www.londonaerial.co.uk
Aerial imagery (oblique and vertical) covering most UK

Londonstills.com*
Flat 3, 5 Keswick Road
Putney, London SW15 2HL
020 8874 4905
ricky@londonstills.com
www.londonstills.com

Lonely Planet Images*
72–82 Rosebery Avenue
Clerkenwell, London EC1R 4RW
020 7841 9062
lpi@lonelyplanet.co.uk
www.lonelyplanetimages.com

MacQuitty International Photographic Collection*
7 Elm Lodge, River Gardens
Stevenage Road, London SW6 6NZ
020 7385 5606
miranda.macquitty@btinternet.com

Magnum Photos*
2nd Floor Moreland Buildings
5 Old Street, London ECIV 9HL
020 7490 1771
magnum@magnumphotos.co.uk
www.magnumphotos.com

Manchester Art Gallery Picture Library*
Mosley Street, Manchester M2 3JL
0161 235 8863
t.walker@manchester.gov.uk
www.manchestergalleries.org

Mander and Mitchenson Theatre Collection*
Jerwood Library of the Performing Arts
Trinity College of Music
King Charles Court
Old Royal Naval College
London SE10 9JF
020 8305 4426
rmangan@tcm.ac.uk
www.mander-and-mitchenson.co.uk

Marianne Majerus Photography*
1 Mason's Place, off Moreland Street
London EC1V 8DU
020 7253 5551
mm@mariannemajerus.com
www.mariannemajerus.com

Marsden Archive, The*
The Presbytery, Hainton
Market Rasen, Lincolnshire LN8 6LR
01507 313646
info@marsdenarchive.com
www.marsdenarchive.com

Marx Memorial Library Pictures*
37a Clerkenwell Green
London EC1R 0DU
020 7253 1485
marx.library@britishlibrary.net
www.marxlibrary.net

Mary Evans Picture Library*
59 Tranquil Vale, Blackheath
London SE3 0BS
020 8318 0034
pictures@maryevans.com
www.maryevans.com
Historical images

Massive Pixels*
07956 505186
info@massivepixels.com
www.massivepixels.com

mattonimages.co.uk*
2 Western Avenue Business Park
Mansfield Road, London W3 0BZ
020 8753 7000
info@mattonimages.co.uk
www.mattonimages.co.uk

M-Dash*
Tower House, 25 Wollaton Road
Beeston, Nottingham NG9 2NG
0115 925 8802
info@m-dash.com
www.m-dash.com

Mediscan*
2nd Floor, Patman House
23–27 Electric Parade, George Lane
London E18 2LS
0871 220 5256
info@mediscan.co.uk
www.mediscan.co.uk

Merseyside Photo Library*
Suite 6 , Egerton House, Tower Road
Birkenhead, Wirral CH41 1FN
0151 666 2289
ron@rja-mpl.com
merseysidephotolibrary.com

Michael Cole Camerawork*
The Coach House, 27 The Avenue
Beckenham, Kent BR3 5DP
020 8658 6120
mikecole@dircon.co.uk
www.tennisphotos.com

**Military Picture Library
International, The***
PO BOX 3350, Shepton Mallet
Somerset BA4 4WX
01749 850560
info@mpli.co.uk
www.militarypicturelibrary.com

**Millbrook House Picture Library
(Railphotos)***
Unit 1, Oldbury Business Centre
Pound Road, Oldbury
West Midlands B68 8NA
0121 544 2970

Millennium Images*
48 Belsize Square, London NW3 4HN
020 7794 9194
mail@milim.com
www.milim.com

Mirrorpix*
22nd Floor, One Canada Square
Canary Wharf, London E14 5AP
020 7293 3700
.desk@mirrorpix.com
www.mirrorpix.com

Monitor Picture Library*
The Forge, Roydon, Harlow
Essex CM19 5HH
01279 792700
sales@monitorpicturelibrary.com
www.monitorpicturelibrary.com
UK and international personalities

Mooney Photo*
25 Armitage Bridge Mills
Armitage Bridge
Huddersfield HD4 7NR
01484 663698
keely@mooney-photo.co.uk
www.mooney-photo.co.uk

Mother & Baby Picture Library*
Emap Esprit, Greater London House
Hampstead Road, London NW1 7EJ
020 7347 1867
mother.baby.pl@emap.com
www.motherandbabypicturelibrary.com

Motoring Picture Library*
National Motor Museum, Beaulieu
Brockenhurst, Hampshire SO42 7ZN
01590 614656
motoring.pictures@beaulieu.co.uk
www.motoringpicturelibrary.com

Moviestore Collection*
2nd Floor, Chartwell House
61–65 Paulet Road
London SE5 9HW
020 7733 9990
sales@moviestorecollection.com
www.moviestorecollection.com

Museum of Antiquities*
The University, Newcastle NE1 7RU
0191 222 7846
www.museums.ncl.ac.uk

Museum of English Rural Life*
The University of Reading
Redlands Road, Reading RG1 5EX
0118 378 8660
merl@reading.ac.uk
www.ruralhistory.org

Museum of London Picture Library*
London Wall, London EC2Y 5HN
020 7814 5604/12
picturelib@museumoflondon.org.uk
www.museumoflondon.org.uk

nagelestock.com*
Parkgate, West Approach Drive
Cheltenham GL52 3AD
01242 242952
look@nagelestock.com
www.nagelestock.com

Narratives (Interiors Food Travel)*
11 Gibraltar Walk, London E2 7LH
020 7366 6658
pictures@narratives.co.uk
www.narratives.co.uk

**National Archives Image Library
(Public Record Office)***
Ruskin Avenue, Kew
Richmond TW9 4DU
020 8392 5225
image-library@nationalarchives.gov.uk
www.nationalarchives.gov.uk
British and colonial history

National Army Museum*
Royal Hospital Road, Chelsea
London SW3 4HT
020 7730 0717
photo@national-army-museum.ac.uk
www.national-army-museum.ac.uk

National Galleries of Scotland*
Picture Library, The Dean Gallery
73 Belford Road, Edinburgh EH4 3DS
0131 624 6258
picture.library@nationalgalleries.org
www.nationalgalleries.org

**National Gallery of Ireland Picture
Library***
Merrion Square West, Dublin 2
00 353 1 6633 526/7
mmcfeely@ngi.ie
www.nationalgallery.ie

National Gallery Picture Library*
St Vincent House, 30 Orange Street
London WC2H 7HH
020 7747 5994
picture.library@nationalgallery.co.uk
www.nationalgallery.co.uk/library

National Maritime Museum*
Picture Library
National Maritime Museum
Greenwich, London SE10 9NF
020 8312 6645
picturelibrary@nmm.ac.uk
www.nmm.ac.uk/picturelibrary

National Museums Liverpool*
PO Box 33 127, Dale Street
Liverpool L69 3LA
0151 478 4657
Photography@liverpoolmuseums.org.uk
www.liverpoolmuseums.org.uk

**National Museums of Scotland
Picture Library***
Chambers Street, Edinburgh EH1 1JF
0131 247 4236
h.osmani@nms.ac.uk
www.nms.ac.uk

**National Portrait Gallery Picture
Library***
St Martin's Place
London WC2H 0HE
020 7312 2475
picturelibrary@npg.org.uk
www.npg.org.uk/picturelibrary
Portraits

National Trust for Scotland, The*
28 Charlotte Square
Edinburgh EH2 4ET
0131 243 9315
irobertson@nts.org.uk
www.nts.org.uk

National Trust Photo Library*
36 Queen Anne's Gate
London SW1H 9AS
020 7447 6788
photo.library@nationaltrust.org.uk
www.nationaltrust.org.uk/photolibrary

**Natural History Museum Picture
Library***
Cromwell Road, South Kensington
London SW7 5BD
020 7942 5401
nhmpl@nhm.ac.uk
www.nhm.ac.uk/piclib

Nature Photographers*
West Wit, New Road Little London
Tadley, Hampshire RG26 5EU
01256 850661
paul@naturephotographers.co.uk
www.naturephotographers.co.uk
Worldwide natural history

Nature Picture Library*
BBC Broadcasting House
Whiteladies Road, Bristol BS8 2LR
0117 974 6720
info@naturepl.com
www.naturepl.com
Wildlife

Neil Williams Classical Collection
22 Avon Hockley, Tamworth
Staffordshire B77 5QA
01827 286086
neil@classicalcollection.co.uk
Classical music

**Neill Bruce's Automobile Photo
Library***
Grange Cottage, Harts Lane
Burghclere, Newbury RG20 9JN
01635 278342
neillb@brucephoto.co.uk
www.brucephoto.co.uk

Network Photographers*
32 Paul Street, London EC2A 4LF
020 7739 9000
info@networkphotographers.com
www.networkphotographers.com

News Team International*
41–43 Commercial Street
Birmingham B1 1RS
0121 246 5111
syndication@newsteam.co.uk
www.newsteam.co.uk

*Member of BAPLA, the British Association of Picture Libraries and Agencies

135

NewsCast*
PO BOX 10, London EC1V 0PQ
020 7608 1000
photo@newscast.co.uk
www.newscast.co.uk

Newsquest (Herald & Times)*
200 Renfield Street, Glasgow G2 3QB
0141 302 7364
rights@glasgow.newsquest.co.uk
www.thepicturedesk.co.uk

NHPA*
Little Tye, 57 High Street
Ardingly, Sussex RH17 6TB
01444 892514
nhpa@nhpa.co.uk
www.nhpa.co.uk
Natural history

NI Syndication*
1 Virginia Street, London E98 1SY
020 7711 7888
enquiries@nisyndication.com
www.nisyndication.com

Novosti Photo Library*
3 Rosary Gardens, London SW7 4NW
020 7370 1873
photos@novosti.co.uk
http://en.rian.ru
Russia

Nunn Syndication*
13a Shad Thames, Butlers Wharf
London SE1 2PU
020 7407 4666
enquiries@nunn-syndication.com
www.nunn-syndication.com

Oceans-Image Pictures*
2nd Floor, 83–84 George Street
Richmond TW9 1HE
020 8332 8422
matthew@oceans-image.com
www.oceans-image.com

Offside Sports Photography*
11 Mary Street, Islington
London N1 7DL
020 7354 0477
mail@welloffside.com
www.welloffside.com

OnAsia*
C/O Creative Digital Services
6th Floor Vanissa Building
29 Soi Chidlom, Ploenchit Road
Pathumwan, Bangkok 10330
00 66 2655 4680
sales@onasia.com
www.onasia.com

Organics Image Library*
The Studios, 27 Hogarth Road
Brighton & Hove BN3 5RH
01273 701557
info@organicsimagelibrary.com
www.organicsimagelibrary.com

Original Double Red Photographic, The*
The Old School, Thorn Lane
Goxhill, North Lincolnshire DN19 7JE
01469 531416
doublered@atlas.co.uk
www.doublered.co.uk

Oxford Picture Library*
15 Curtis Yard, North Hinksey Lane
Oxford OX2 0LX
01865 723404
opl@cap-ox.com
www.cap-ox.com

Oxford Scientific (OSF)*
Ground Floor, Network House
Station Yard, Thame
Oxfordshire OX9 3UH
01844 262370
enquiries@osf.co.uk
www.osf.co.uk

PA Photos
292 Vauxhall Bridge Road
London SW1V 1AE
020 7963 7990
paphotos@pa.press.net
www.paphotos.com
News, entertainment, celebrity and sports

Panos Pictures*
Studio 3B, 38 Southwark Street
London SE1 1UN
020 7234 0010
pics@panos.co.uk
www.panos.co.uk
Documentary library specialising in developing world

Papilio*
155 Station Road, Herne Bay
Kent CT6 5QA
01227 360996
library@papiliophotos.com
www.papiliophotos.com
Natural history subjects worldwide

Patrick Eagar Photography*
1 Queensberry Place, Richmond
Surrey TW9 1NW
020 8940 9269
patrick@patrickeagar.com
www.patrickeagar.com

PBPA – Paul Beard Photo Agency*
PBPA House, 33 Sanctuary Close
St John's, Worcester WR2 5PY
0845 644 7975
Paul@pbpa.co.uk
photos.pbpa.co.uk

Peter Dazeley Photography*
The Studios, 5 Heathman's Road
Parsons Green, London SW6 4TJ
020 7736 3171
studio@peterdazeley.com

Peter Sanders Photography*
24 Meades Lane, Chesham
Buckinghamshire HP5 1ND
01494 773674
photos@petersanders.com
www.petersanders.com

PGI-Images*
14 Windsor Road, Ducks Island
Barnet EN5 2PR
020 8364 9506
pgi.images@virgin.net
pgi.images.com

Phil Sheldon Golf Picture Library*
Southcroft, 40 Manor Road
Barnet EN5 2JQ
020 8440 1986
Phil@philsheldongolfpics.co.uk
Gill@philsheldongolfpics.co.uk
www.philsheldongolfpics.co.uk
More than 500,000 images of golf

Photega*
Telford Way
Waterwells Business Park
Quedgeley, Gloucester GL2 2AB
01452 541221
images@photega.com
www.photega.com

Photofusion Picture Library*
17a Electric Lane, Brixton
London SW9 8LA
020 7733 3500
library@photofusion.org
www.photofusion.org
Contemporary social and environmental issues

Photogold
40 Dunvegan Place, Polmont
Falkirk FK2 0NX
01324 720038
sales@photogold.co.uk
www.castlepictures.com
Scotland

Photolibrary Wales*
2 Bro-Nant, Church Road
Pentyrch, Cardiff CF15 9QG
029 2089 0311
info@photolibrarywales.com
www.photolibrarywales.com

photolibrary.com*
81a Endell Street, Covent Garden
London WC2H 9AJ
020 7836 5591
uksales@photolibrary.com
www.photolibrary.com

Photomax Specialist Aquarium Picture Library*
118–122 Magdalen Road
Oxford OX4 1RQ
01865 372981
info@photomax.org.uk
www.photomax.org.uk

Photonica*
10 Regents Wharf, All Saints Street
London N1 9RL
020 7278 4117
info@photonica.co.uk
www.photonica.com

Photos 12*
20, Rue Lalande, Paris 75014
00 33 1 5680 1440
meurin@photo12.com
www.photo12.com

Photos Horticultural*
PO Box 105, Ipswich IP1 4PR
01473 257329
library@photos-horticultural.com
www.photos-horticultural.com

Photostage*
PO Box 65, Shenley Lodge
Milton Keynes MK5 7YT
01908 262324
info@photostage.co.uk
www.photostage.co.uk

Pictoreal*
The Westall Centre, Hoberrow Green
Redditch, Worcestershire B96 6JY
01386 793600
peter.smith@pictoreal.com
www.pictoreal.com

Picture Business*
67 Maltings Place, Bagleys Lane
Fulham, London SW6 2BY
020 7731 6076
picturebusiness@easynet.co.uk
www.picturebusiness.co.uk

PictureBank Photo Library*
Parman House, 30–36 Fife Road
Kingston Upon Thames KT1 1SY
020 8547 2344
info@picturebank.co.uk
www.picturebank.co.uk

Pictures Colour Library*
10 James Whatman Court
Turkey Mill, Ashford Road
Maidstone ME14 5SS
01622 609809
enquiries@picturescolourlibrary.co.uk
www.picturescolourlibrary.co.uk

Pictures of Britain*
Alma House, 73 Rodney Road
Cheltenham GL50 1HT
01242 537923
info@picturesofbritain.co.uk
www.picturesofbritain.co.uk

picturesofmanchester.com*
13 Alan Road, Withington
Manchester M20 4NQ
0161 448 2034
info@picturesofmanchester.com
www.picturesofmanchester.com

PPL Photo Agency*
Booker's Yard, The Street, Walberton
near Arundel, Sussex BN18 0PF
01243 555561
ppl@mistral.co.uk
www.pplmedia.com
*Watersports, sub-aqua, business, travel,
Sussex scenes and historical images*

Premaphotos Wildlife*
Amberstone, 1 Kirland Road
Bodmin, Cornwall PL30 5JQ
01208 78258
enquiries@premaphotos.com
www.premaphotos.com
Natural history worldwide

Professional Sport UK *
18–19 Shaftesbury Quay
Hertford SG14 1SF
01992 505000
pictures@prosport.co.uk
www.professionalsport.com

Proper Gander Imaging*
94 Leonard Street
London EC2A 4RH
020 7729 6789
info@proper-gander.co.uk
www.proper-gander.co.uk

Pulse Picture Library*
CMP Information Ltd., Ludgate House
245 Blackfriars Road
London SE1 9UY
020 7921 8099
mcollard@cmpinformation.com
www.cmpimages.com

Punch Cartoon Library*
87–135 Brompton Road
Knightsbridge, London SW1X 7XL
020 7225 6710
punch.library@harrods.com
www.punch.co.uk

PunchStock*
Sherwood House, Forest Road
Kew, Surrey TW9 3BY
0800 073 0760
service@punchstock.co.uk
www.punchstock.co.uk

PYMCA*
St John's Building, 2nd Floor
43 Clerkenwell Road
London EC1M 5RS
020 7251 8338
jon@pymca.com
www.pymca.com

QA Photos*
Terlingham Manor Farm
Gibraltar Lane, Hawkinge
Folkestone, Kent CT18 7AE
01303 894141
pix@qaphotos.com
www.qaphotos.com

Rail Images*
5 Sandhurst Crescent
Leigh-on-Sea, Essex SS9 4AL
01702 525059
info@railimages.co.uk
www.railimages.co.uk

Railways – Milepost 92 ½*
Milepost 92 ½, Newton Harcourt
Leicestershire LE8 9FH
0116 259 2068
contacts@milepost92-half.co.uk
www.railphotolibrary.com

Raleigh International*
Raleigh House
27 Parsons Green Lane
London SW6 4HZ
020 7371 8585
www.raleighinternational.org

**Raymond Mander & Joe
Mitchenson Theatre Collection**
Jerwood Library of Performing Arts
Trinity College of Music
King Charles Court
Old Royal Naval College
London SE10 9JF
020 8305 4426
rmangan@tcm.ac.uk
www.mander-and-mitchenson.co.uk

Red Cover*
Unit 7, Aura House
53 Oldridge Road, London SW12 8PP
020 8772 1110
info@redcover.com
www.redcover.com

Redferns Music Picture Library*
7 Bramley Road, London W10 6SZ
020 7792 9914
info@redferns.com
www.redferns.com

Repfoto London*
74 Creffield Road, Acton
London W3 9PS
020 8992 2936
repfoto@btinternet.com
www.repfoto.com

Report Digital*
4 Clarence Rd
Stratford upon Avon CU37 9DL
01789 262151
info@reportdigital.co.uk
www.reportdigital.co.uk

reportphotos.com*
Chocolate Factory Two
4 Coburg Road, London N22 6UJ
020 8340 8855
library@reportphotos.com
www.reportphotos.com

Reservoir*
Willow Grange, Church Road
Watford WD17 4QA
01923 201218
bruce.harding@britishwaterways.co.uk
British Waterways online image library

Retna Pictures*
Pinewood Studios, Pinewood Road
Iver Heath, Buckinghamshire SL0 0NH
01753 785450
ukinfo@retna.com
www.retna.co.uk
Celebrity music and lifestyle

Retrograph Archive Collection
10 Hanover Street, Brighton
East Sussex BN2 9SB
01273 687554
retropix1@aol.com
www.retrograph.com
*Vintage consumer advertising, art,
decorative art*

Reuters*
85 Fleet Street, London EC4P 4AJ
020 7542 5050
kim.lee@reuters.com
www.reuters.com/pictures

Rex Features*
18 Vine Hill, London EC1R 5DZ
020 7278 7294
rex@rexfeatures.com
www.rexfeatures.com

Rex Interstock*
18 Vine Hill, London EC1R 5DZ
020 7278 6989
interstock@rexfeatures.com
www.rexinterstock.com

Robbie Jack Photography*
45 Church Road, Hanwell
London W7 3BD
020 8567 9616
robbie@robbiejack.com
www.robbiejack.com
Performing arts

Robert Estall Photo Agency*
12–14 Swan Street, Boxford
Sudbury, Suffolk CO10 5NZ
01787 210111
robertestall@mac.com
www.africanceremonies.com

Robert Forsythe Picture Library
16 Lime Grove, Prudhoe
Northumberland NE42 6PR
01661 834511
robert@forsythe.demon.co.uk
www.forsythe.demon.co.uk
*Original ephemera and transparencies
of industrial and transport heritage*

*Member of BAPLA, the British Association of Picture Libraries and Agencies

Robert Harding World Imagery*
58–59 Great Marlborough Street
London W1F 7JY
020 7478 4000
info@robertharding.com
www.robertharding.com

Ronald Grant Archive*
The Masters House
The Old Lambeth Workhouse
2 DugardWay, off Renfrew Road
London SE11 4TH
020 7840 2200
pixdesk@rgapix.com

Royal Air Force Museum*
Grahame Park Way, Hendon
London NW9 5LL
020 8205 2266
photographic@rafmuseum.org
www.rafmuseum.org

Royal Armouries Image Library*
Royal Armouries, Armouries Drive
Leeds LS10 1LT
0113 220 1891
image.library@armouries.org.uk
www.armouries.org.uk

Royal Collection Enterprises*
Photographic Services
Windsor Castle, Windsor SL4 1NJ
01753 868286
photoservices@royalcollection.org.uk
www.the-royal-collection.org.uk
Royal family

Royal Geographical Society Picture Library*
1 Kensington Gore
London SW7 2AR
020 7591 3060
pictures@rgs.org
www.rgs.org/picturelibrary

RSPB Images*
PO Box 7515, Heath Road
Ramsden Heath, Billericay
Essex CM11 1HR
01268 711471
rspb@thatsgood.biz
www.rspb-images.com

RSPCA Photolibrary*
Wilberforce Way, Southwater
Horsham, West Sussex RH13 9RS
0870 754 0150
pictures@rspcaphotolibrary.com
www.rspcaphotolibrary.com

Russia and Eastern Images*
Sonning, Cheapside Lane, Denham
Uxbridge, Middlesex UB9 5AE
01895 833508
easteuropix@btinternet.com
www.easteuropix.com

S&O Mathews Photography*
Little Pit Place, Brighstone
Isle of Wight PO30 4DZ
01983 741098
oliver@mathews-photography.com
www.mathews-photography.com
Gardens, plants and landscapes

Sally and Richard Greenhill*
357 Liverpool Road, London N1 1NL
020 7607 8549
sr.greenhill@virgin.net
www.srgreenhill.co.uk

Scala, London*
1 Willow Court, off Willow Street
London EC2A 4QB
020 7782 0044
info@scala-art.demon.co.uk
www.scalarchives.it
Art and culture

Science & Society Picture Library*
Science Museum, Exhibition Road
London SW7 2DD
020 7942 4400
piclib@nmsi.ac.uk
www.scienceandsociety.co.uk
Science Museum, National Railway Museum; photography, film and television

Science Photo Library*
327–329 Harrow Road
London W9 3RB
020 7432 1100
info@sciencephoto.com
www.sciencephoto.com

Scope Features & Scope Beauty*
26–29 St Cross Street
Hatton Garden, London EC1N 8UH
020 7405 2997
images@scopefeatures.com
www.scopefeatures.com

Scott Polar Research Institute Picture Library*
University of Cambridge
Lensfield Road, Cambridge CB2 1ER
01223 336547
picture.library@spri.cam.ac.uk
www.spri.cam.ac.uk/lib/pictures

Scottish Viewpoint*
64 Polwarth Gardens
Edinburgh EH11 1LL
0131 622 7174
info@scottishviewpoint.com
www.scottishviewpoint.com

Shell Photographic Services and Library*
Shell International Limited
Shell Centre, London SE1 7NA
020 7934 4820
photographicservices@shell.com

SIN*
89a North View Road, Crouch End
London N8 7LR
020 8348 8061
sales@sin-photo.co.uk
www.sin-photo.co.uk

Skishoot-Offshoot
Hall Place, Upper Woodcott
Whitchurch, Hampshire RG28 7PY
01635 255527
skishootsnow@aol.com
www.skishoot.co.uk
Winter sports

Skyscan Photolibrary*
Oak House, Toddington
Cheltenham GL54 5BY
01242 621357
info@skyscan.co.uk
www.skyscan.co.uk
Aviation and aerial sports

Snookerimages (Eric Whitehead Photography)
25 Oak Street, Windermere
Cumbria LA23 1EN
015394 48894
eric@snookerimages.co.uk
www.snookerimages.co.uk

SNS Group*
15 Fitzroy Place, Glasgow G3 7RW
0141 221 3602
info@snspix.com
www.snspix.com

SOA Photo Agency*
Lovells Farm, Dark Lane
Stoke St Gregory, Taunton TA3 6EU
0870 333 6062
info@soaphotoagency.com
www.soaphotoagency.com
Humour, sports, travel, modern European

Société Jersiaise Photographic Archive*
7 Pier Road, St Helier, Jersey JE2 4XW
01534 633 398
photoarchive@societe-jersiaise.org
www.societe-jersiaise.org

Sonia Halliday Photographs*
22 Bates Lane, Weston Turville
Buckinghamshire HP22 5SL
01296 612266
info@soniahalliday.com
www.soniahalliday.com

Sotheby's Picture Library*
34–35 New Bond Street
London W1A 2AA
020 7293 5383
piclib.london@sothebys.com
www.sothebys.com

South American Pictures*
48 Station Road, Woodbridge
Suffolk IP12 4AT
01394 383963
morrison@southamericanpictures.com
www.southamericanpictures.com

SplashdownDirect.com*
1 Glen Cottages, Sandy Lane
Abbots Leigh, Bristol BS8 3SE
01275 375520
info@splashdowndirect.com
www.splashdowndirect.com

Stay Still*
The Jerwood Space
171 Union Street, London SE1 0LN
020 7922 1313
staystill@staystill.com
www.staystill.com

Steve Bloom Images*
Middlefield House, Olantigh Road
Wye, Ashford, Kent TN25 5EP
01233 813777
kathy@stevebloom.com
www.stevebloom.com

Still Moving Picture Company
1c Castlehill, Doune
Edinburgh FK16 6BU
01786 842790
info@stillmovingpictures.com
www.stillmovingpictures.com
Scotland and sport

Still Pictures – The Whole Earth Photo Library*
199 Shooters Hill Road
Blackheath, London SE3 8UL
020 8858 8307
info@stillpictures.com
www.stillpictures.com
Environment, nature, social and developing world issues

Stock Scotland*
The Croft Studio, Croft Roy
Crammond Brae, Tain
Ross-shire IV19 1JG
01862 892298
info@stockscotland.com
www.stockscotland.com

Stockbyte*
Kerry Technology Park, Tralee
County Kerry
0800 909190
info@stockbyte.com
www.stockbyte.com

Stockfile*
5 High Street, Sunningdale SL5 OLX
01344 872249
info@stockfile.co.uk
www.stockfile.co.uk
Mountain biking and cycling

StockShot*
2b St Vincent Street
Edinburgh EH3 6SH
0131 557 6688
pictures@stockshot.co.uk
www.stockshot.co.uk

Sue Anderson Island Focus Scotland*
Pony Park, Letterwalton, Benderloch
Oban, Argyll PA37 1SA
01631 720078
info@islandfocus.co.uk
www.islandfocus.co.uk

Sue Cunningham Photographic*
56 Chatham Road
Kingston Upon Thames KT1 3AA
020 8541 3024
pictures@scphotographic.com
www.scphotographic.com

Superstock*
G10 59 Chilton Street
London E2 6EA
020 7729 7473
info@superstock.co.uk
www.superstock.co.uk

Surfpix*
1 High Street, St Davids
Pembrokeshire SA62 6SA
01437 721188
info@surfpix.co.uk
www.surfpix.co.uk

Sutton Motorsport Images*
The Chapel, 61 Watling Street
Towcester, Northants NN12 6AG
01327 352188
customerservices@sutton-images.com
www.sutton-images.com

Swift Imagery*
The Old Farm House, Hexworthy
Yelverton, Devon PL20 6SD
01364 631101
info@theswiftgroup.co.uk
www.theswiftgroup.co.uk

Sylvia Cordaiy Photo Library*
45 Rotherstone, Devizes
Wiltshire SN10 2DD
01380 728327
info@sylvia-cordaiy.com
www.sylvia-cordaiy.com
170 countries, from obscure to stock images

Tate Picture Library*
The Lodge, Millbank
London SW1P 4RG
020 7887 8890
picture.library@tate.org.uk
www.tate.org.uk

Tessa Traeger*
7 Rossetti Studios, 72 Flood Street
London SW3 5TF
020 7352 3641
tessatraeger@solutions-inc.co.uk
www.tessatraeger.com

Theimagefile.com*
Long Barn, Hillgrove
Stonehill Road, Ottershaw
Weybridge, Surrey KT16 0EN
0870 224 2454
sales@theimagefile.com
www.theimagefile.com

Thoroughbred Photography *
The Hornbeams, 2 The Street
Worlington, Suffolk IP28 8RU
01638 713 944
mail@thoroughbredphoto.com
www.thoroughbredphoto.com

Tibet Images*
3rd Floor, 5 Torrens Street
London EC1V 1NQ
020 7278 2377
info@tibetimages.co.uk
www.tibetimages.co.uk

Tim Graham*
London
020 7435 7693
mail@timgraham.co.uk
www.royalphotographs.com

TimeArts Picture Library*
29–31 Distons Lane, Chipping Norton
Oxfordshire OX7 5NY
01608 643334
info@3sco.co.uk
www.3sco.co.uk

TIPS Images *
1st Floor, 7 Kensington Church Court
London W8 4SP
ossie@tipsimages.com
www.tipsimages.com

Tom Hanley*
41 Harefield, Hinchley Wood
Esher, Surrey KT10 9TG
020 8972 9165
tomhanley31@hotmail.com
www.cooperowen.com

TopFoto*
PO Box 33, Edenbridge
Kent TN8 5PF
01732 863939
requests@topfoto.co.uk
www.TopFoto.co.uk

Travel Ink Photo Library*
The Old Coach House
14 High Street, Goring on Thames
Reading RG8 9AR
01491 873011
info@travel-ink.co.uk
www.travel-ink.co.uk

Travel Library, The*
Unit 7, The Kiln Workshops
Pilcot Road, Crookham Village
Fleet GU51 5RY
01252 627233
info@travel-library.co.uk
www.travel-library.co.uk

travel-shots.com*
3b Uplands Close, London SW14 7AS
020 8878 2226
sales@travel-shots.com
www.travel-shots.com

Trevillion Images*
75 Jeddo Road, London W12 9ED
020 8740 9005
info@trevillion.com
www.trevillion.com

TRH Pictures*
Bradley's Close
74–77 White Lion Street
London N1 9PF
020 7520 7647
trh@trhpictures.co.uk
www.trhpictures.co.uk

TROPIX Photo Library*
44 Woodbines Avenue
Kingston upon Thames
Surrey KT1 2AY
020 8546 0823
veronica@tropix.co.uk
www.tropix.co.uk

True North Photo Library
26 New Road, Hebden Bridge
West Yorkshire HX7 8ER
07941 630420
john@trunorth.demon.co.uk
Landscape and life of the North

UKstockimages*
St Cross, Havant, Hants PO9 2QR
023 9247 8643
grant@ukstockimages.com
www.ukstockimages.com

Ulster Museum Picture Library*
Botanic Gardens, Belfast BT9 5AB
028 9038 3113
patricia.mclean.um@nics.gov.uk
www.ulstermuseum.org.uk
Art, archaeology, ethnography, natural history, Irish history

Universal Pictorial Press and Agency*
29–31 Saffron Hill, London EC1N 8SW
020 7421 6000
ctaylor@uppa.co.uk
www.uppa.co.uk

Untitled*
Radar Studio, Coldblow Lane
Thurnham, Maidstone ME14 3LR
01622 737722
info@untitled.co.uk
www.untitled.co.uk

Member of BAPLA, the British Association of Picture Libraries and Agencies

V&A Images*
Victoria and Albert Museum
Cromwell Road, South Kensington
London SW7 2RL
020 7942 2966
vaimages@vam.ac.uk
www.vandaimages.com

Valley Green
Barn Ley, Valley Lane, Buxhall
Stowmarket IP14 3EB
01449 736090
pics@valleygreen.co.uk
Perennials

Vaughan Williams Memorial Library
Cecil Sharpe House
Regents Park Road
London NW1 7AY
020 7485 2206
library@efdss.org
www.efdss.org
Traditional music and culture

Venturepix *
29 London Road, Sawbridgeworth
Hertfordshire CM21 9EH
07970 262505
images@venturepix.com
www.venturepix.com

View Pictures*
14 The Dove Centre
109 Bartholomew Road
London NW5 2BJ
020 7284 2928
info@viewpictures.co.uk
www.viewpictures.co.uk

VinMag*
84–90 Digby Road, London E9 6HX
020 8533 7588
piclib@vinmag.com
www.vinmagarchive.com
20th-century history. Books, newspapers,
posters, adverts, photos, film, ephemera

Vision Vault*
123–125 Curtain Road
Shoreditch, London EC2A 3BX
020 7739 4488
visionvault@taylorjames.com
www.taylorjames.com/visionvault

VK Guy *
Silver Birches, Troutbeck
Windermere, Cumbria LA23 1PN
01539 433519
vic@vkguy.co.uk
www.vkguy.co.uk

Volunteering England Image Bank*
Regent's Wharf, 8 All Saints Street
London N1 9RL
0845 305 6979
marketing@volunteeringengland.org
www.volunteering.org.uk/imagebank

WalesPics (Cambrian Images)*
The Arches, West Street
Rhayader, Powys LD6 5AB
01597 810915
sales@cambrian-images.co.uk
www.cambrian-images.co.uk

Waterways Photo Library*
39 Manor Court Road, Hanwell
London W7 3EJ
020 8840 1659
watphot39@aol.com
www.waterwaysphotolibrary.com
Inland waterways

**Wellcome Trust Medical
Photographic Library***
210 Euston Road, London NW1 2BE
020 7611 8348
medphoto@wellcome.ac.uk
medphoto.wellcome.ac.uk

Werner Forman Archive *
36 Camden Square
London NW1 9XA
020 7267 1034
wfa@btinternet.com
www.werner-forman-archive.com

Wilderness Photographic Library*
4 Kings Court, Kirkby Lonsdale
Cumbria LA6 2BP
01524 272149
wildernessphoto@btinternet.com
www.photosource.co.uk
/wildernessphoto.htm

Window on the World Picture Library*
Mantis Studio, 124 Cornwall Road
London SE1 8TQ
020 7928 3448
usill@winworld.co.uk
www.winworld.co.uk

WireImage*
77 Oxford Street, London W1D 2ES
020 7659 2815
jc@wireimage.com
www.wireimage.com

Woodfall Wild Images*
17 Bull Lane, Denbigh LL16 3SN
01745 815903
wwimages@woodfall.com
www.woodfall.com

Woodland Trust*
Autumn Park, Dysart Road
Grantham, Lincolnshire NG31 6LL
01476 581111
photolibrary@woodland-trust.org.uk
www.woodland-trust.org.uk

World Pictures*
3rd Floor, 43–44 Berners Street
London W1T 3ND
020 7580 1845
worldpictures@btinternet.com
www.worldpictures.co.uk
Travel

World Religions Photo Library*
53a Crimsworth Road
London SW8 4RJ
020 7720 6951
co@worldreligions.co.uk
www.worldreligions.co.uk

WWF-UK Photo-Library*
Panda House, Weyside Park
Godalming, Surrey GU7 1XR
01483 412336
PSunters@wwf.org.uk
www.wwf-uk.org

**York Archaeological Trust Picture
Library**
Cromwell House, 13 Ogleforth
York YO1 7FG
01904 663000
enquiries@yorkarchaeology.co.uk
www.yorkarchaeology.co.uk
Archaeology in York area

Zoological Society of London*
Regents Park, London NW1 4RY
020 7449 6293
library@zsl.org
www.zsl.org

* Member of BAPLA, the British Association of Picture Libraries and Agencies

The television industry is in a state of rapid change. More viewers than ever before are watching multichannel services, with hundreds of channels available on platforms such as Freeview, satellite and cable, and the switchoff of the analogue signal planned to begin in 2008; there is increased competition from services on broadband-enabled computers and mobile devices; and independent production companies are becoming more powerful, having won control over the rights in the programmes they produce.

Those changes are taking their toll on the three major players, the BBC, ITV and BSkyB. The BBC, the main public service broadcaster, announced severe job cuts as it faces the renewal of its charter; the immediate result was a one-day strike in May 2005, but the main challenge remains defining what constitutes "public service" in these days of multiple competing channels and platforms. ITV plc, the biggest commercial terrestrial broadcaster, celebrated its 50th anniversary in 2005 amid rising profits but falling ratings, and public concern over cuts to its regional services; while BSkyB, the main satellite broadcaster, faces the challenge of attracting more subscribers against the challenge of free-to-air digital terrestrial television. The two smaller terrestrial broadcasters, Channel 4 and Five, are hoping to use their terrestrial channels as a springboard for a multichannel future.

With the exception of the BBC, television is regulated by Ofcom – the watchdog formed by the merger of the two former television regulators, the ITC and the Broadcasting Standards Commission, and three other bodies in December 2003. The BBC, for its part, is regulated by its governors; but under the terms of the charter renewal green paper published in 2005, the government plans to replace them with a BBC Trust.

Television audiences are measured by Barb, the Broadcasters Audience Research Board.

Analogue terrestrial ownership

BBC	BBC1, BBC2	publicly owned; board of governors answerable to government
ITV	ITV Anglia, ITV Border, ITV Central, ITV Granada, ITV London, ITV Meridian, ITV Wales, ITV West, ITV Westcountry, ITV Yorkshire, Tyne Tees TV, GMTV (75%)	ITV plc
	Grampian, Scottish	Scottish Media Group
	Ulster	Ulster TV
	Channel	Channel TV
Channel 4	Channel 4, S4C	semi–public
Channel 5	Five	RTL, owned by Bertelsmann

THE BBC

The BBC is the nation's public broadcaster. In television, it runs the two national terrestrial channels, BBC1 and BBC2; plus other channels including BBC3, BBC4, the rolling news service BBC News 24, children's channels CBBC and CBeebies, and specialist channels such as BBC Parliament. It has its own programme-making departments, and a division called BBC Resources that provides production and post-production support both internally and on a commercial basis. It also has extensive interests in radio, new media and, commercially, magazines.

It has been, however, another difficult year for the corporation, as it has undergone **charter review**: in other words, renewal of the terms of its licence to broadcast, which expires in December 2006. The main issues at stake have been the licence fee, its system of regulation – and, at the heart of both, how the BBC's public service remit is defined.

The licence fee is the BBC's main system of funding. Every person who watches television must buy a TV licence, which cost £126.50 in 2005; this licence made up £2.94bn of the BBC's income in 2004, with the rest coming from commercial enterprises (£624m) and a Foreign Office grant to run the World Service (£247m). But the system has been under threat: in a multichannel market, commercial competitors are worried about a publicly funded BBC's impact on their revenues. They have proposed a "top-slicing" of the fee, by which rival broadcasters – for example, ITV or Channel 4 – could pitch for funding for public service broadcasts. Yet in the March 2005 green paper on the future of the corporation, the government said it thought the licence fee "remains the best way to fund the BBC"; but said that toward the end of the switchover process in 2012, a review would "reconsider whether there is a case for the wider use of public funding, including licence fee money, to fund public service broadcasting beyond the BBC".

The green paper also set out plans for a change in the way the BBC is run. The BBC governors, the report said, would be replaced by a "BBC Trust" to handle the licence fee and the corporation's public service obligations. The plan followed criticism in February from Ofcom, the broadcasting regulator, saying the "BBC governors have up to now not been sufficiently independent of the BBC's executive".

Against the background of those changes, the director general, Mark Thompson, announced a series of **job losses**. In one day in March 2005, more than 2,000 job cuts were unveiled in news and the regions, with unions calling it the "worst in the history" of the corporation; in total, 3,780 job losses are planned. On May 23 2005, a **24-hour strike** was held in protest; management reckoned that more than 60% of staff returned to work, but this figure was around 35% in the BBC's network newsrooms, forcing flagship shows such as the Today programme off the air. High-profile faces who turned up for work in the morning included the presenter Terry Wogan, the breakfast business journalist Declan Curry and Radio 5's Shelagh Fogarty. A planned 48-hour strike was then averted at the end of May, when unions noted "significant movement" in the BBC's position; and in July, Thompson waived a performance-related payment that could have netted him more than £135,000.

Austin

I'M GETTING WHIP-ROUND FATIGUE.

LEAVING-DO

BBC NEWS

Strike action... picket lines outside
the BBC in May 2005

That move followed the bizarre revelation in March that, 18 years ago, the current director general had bitten a BBC newsroom colleague in the arm. The incident emerged when an email from the journalist concerned, Anthony Massey, to the Newsnight presenter Jeremy Paxman, was leaked to the Guardian. A BBC spokesman said: "There were some high jinks going on and Mark leant forward and did something like a biting gesture... Our view is that it was a long time ago, there was an apology at the time, and it was high jinks and horseplay."

BBC programming and channels

If you include digital services, BBC channels attracted about 36% of the total television audience in 2004/05, according to the corporation's annual report. Terrestrial channels still accounted for the vast majority of this; but their share of the overall market has been slipping. BBC1's share was 24.4%, down from 25.2% in the previous year; while BBC2's was 9.6%, down from 10.9%.

BBC1 aims to be "the UK's most valued television channel, with the broadest range of quality programmes of any UK mainstream network", according to the annual report. Success of the year was Doctor Who, which dominated Saturday nights in a series written by Russell T Davies; Christopher Eccleston starred as the Time Lord, with Billie Piper as his trusty assistant. The BBC also commissioned a Christmas special and a second series, with David Tennant as the regenerated Doctor. EastEnders, ever the BBC's most popular show, had a more troubled year: one episode in March equalled the record low audience for the soap, just 6.2 million. In the annual report, governors expressed concern at the fall in "serious factual programmes in peak time", while praising the success of Strictly Come Dancing and Doctor Who in helping to "reinvigorate" Saturday nights. The report also showed that BBC1 had aired more repeats in 2004/05 than the year before: 2,683 hours, compared with 2,595.

In May 2005, Peter Fincham took over as BBC1 controller from Lorraine Heggessey.

BBC2's surprise success was The Apprentice, a reality show in which 12 hopefuls vied for a job at Sir Alan Sugar's Amstrad. Overall, some of the channel's drop in share was attributed to the loss of The Simpsons,

while the governors said current affairs was "proving a challenge". Newsnight, the flagship news programme, celebrated its 25th anniversary in June 2005; but months later viewers inundated the programme with protests after a business update was replaced by a 30-second weather forecast. The editor, Peter Barron, put the issue to a public vote, and the weather report was dropped after just a couple of weeks.

It was also a BBC2 programme that attracted the largest number of complaints, when the channel chose to broadcast the controversial musical Jerry Springer: The Opera. The corporation received more than 16,800 complaints about the broadcast in January 2005, which included scenes portraying Jesus as a man in a nappy. But media watchdog Ofcom cleared the BBC of flouting broadcasting guidelines.

Digital-only BBC3 is becoming the home of much of the BBC's home-grown output. Spending on BBC-originated programmes rose to more than £157,000 – more than the corporation spent on in-house programming for BBC1 the previous year. Little Britain won a series of comedy awards, while Casanova was critically praised. The channel's audience share rose to 0.5%. In June 2005, though, the channel attracted criticism from Tory culture spokeswoman Theresa May, who noted that in one week it broadcast "15 episodes of an old American documentary, The Brothel, and nine episodes of the comedy Two Pints of Lager and a Packet of Crisps".

BBC4's audience share rose from 0.1% to 0.2%. Among its successes was political comedy The Thick of It, recommissioned in June 2005.

Both BBC3 and BBC4 had been criticised by Patrick Barwise, the man charged with writing an independent review into the BBC's digital strategy, who said they represent "poor value for money" because the BBC considered them as "niche channels". But CBeebies, the BBC's channel for very young children, was considered a "triumph".

The BBC launched a £1m redesign of its weather coverage in May 2005, and immediately found itself facing a storm of criticism (and other similar headlines). The new bulletins involved a camera sweeping from region to region of a 3D map of the UK, allowing forecasters to show more precise information about cloud cover and rain. Hundreds complained, saying the forecasts were confusing; others thought the oblique angle of view meant the bulletins under-represented Scotland and the north of the England. At one point in July 2005 the system even stopped working during the Six O'Clock News.

Commercial divisions

BBC Worldwide, which exports TV programmes and has magazine and new media interests, increased its profits from £37m to £55m according to the annual report; as charter review progresses, there remains speculation that the division may be sold. BBC Resources, the post-production, studio and costume outfit, made a £7m profit.

BBC Broadcast, the channel management services division, also made £7m, but was sold in June 2005 to Creative Broadcast Services, a subsidiary of an Australian investment bank, for £166m.

BBC executive pay, 2004–05

	Responsibility	Salary £k	bonus £k	benefits £k	2005 £k	2004 £k
Current board members						
Mark Thompson	director general	453	–	6	459	–
Jenny Abramsky	radio and music	233	58	13	304	276
Jana Bennett	television	255	63	16	334	305
Mark Byford	deputy director general	351	92	14	457	384
Stephen Dando	human resources	245	65	3	313	294
Tim Davie (appointed April 2005)	marketing	salary not yet known				
Ashley Highfield	new media	245	57	18	320	308
Zarin Patel (appointed Jan 2005)	finance	59	10	3	72	–
John Smith	chief operating officer	287	72	28	387	327
Caroline Thomson	policy and legal; charter review	210	64	16	290	250
Former board members						
Glenwyn Benson (resigned Jun 2003)	factual and learning	–	–	–	–	39
Greg Dyke (resigned Jan 2004)	director general	–	–	–	–	321
Andy Duncan (resigned July 2004)	marketing	82	–	5	87	309
Carolyn Fairbairn	strategy and distribution (resigned Dec 2004)	162	–	12	174	271
Roger Flynn (resigned March 2004)	BBC Ventures	–	–	–	–	315
Rupert Gavin*	BBC Worldwide	146	–	10	156	373
Pat Loughrey*	nations and regions	48	13	8	69	287
Peter Salmon*	sport	49	14	7	70	289
Richard Sambrook*	World Service	54	13	4	71	292
John Willis*	factual and learning	51	12	5	68	321
Alan Yentob*	drama, entertainment, children	54	13	4	71	301
Incentive plans					47	39
TOTAL		**2,984**	**546**	**172**	**3,749**	**5,301**

* left executive committee in June 2004

A public service publisher

Does the BBC need more public competition? The media regulator, Ofcom, certainly thinks so; it has drawn up proposals for a new, £300m "public service publisher" to compete with it in the digital age.

Ofcom reckons the publicly funded organisation, which would have a programming budget about double that of Five and two-thirds that of Channel 4, is necessary because existing terrestrial broadcasters are having to pursue more commercial strategies in a multichannel market. Many people have criticised the move, saying it allows ITV to cut its commitments to regional news broadcasting.

But as media converges, it's not just the broadcasters with whom the proposed channel will compete. The Newspaper Society already complains that its plans to expand its regional websites are hamstrung by the BBC; plans for a public service publisher are perhaps another danger sign for a press struggling to grapple with the new media age.

ITV

Dan Chung

Financial success...
ITV boss Charles Allen

ITV celebrates its 50th anniversary in September 2005; but is still undergoing change after the creation of ITV plc in February 2004. The company, formed from the merger of Carlton and Granada, owns 11 of the 15 regional franchises that together make up ITV1 – that is, all the franchises in England and Wales, plus Border in Scotland – and also controls ITV2, ITV3, ITV News and GMTV.

Two measures of ITV's success are its profits and its ratings. Its annual report for 2004 showed healthy profits; but in the first half of 2005 its ratings for ITV1 were in decline.

The company made a profit of £340m in 2004; that was an increase on 2003, though the merger of Carlton and Granada meant like-for-like figures were unavailable. The company's share of advertising revenues across all its channels also rose, by 4.7% to £1.59bn. That relieved the pressure on the chief executive, Charles Allen, who in the same year was paid more than £1.8m in salary and bonuses. And in June 2005, Ofcom cut the cost of the company's licence to broadcast to below £80m – down from £215m in 2004.

Much of ITV's financial success can be attributed to job losses and regional cost-cutting. After cutting jobs at Meridian and Central the previous year, ITV announced it would axe 50 jobs at Anglia in Norwich and close its Magdalen Street studio there. ITV said it would outsource its regional peak time output instead. Despite opposition from MPs such as Peter Hain, Ofcom allowed the broadcaster to cut the minimum weekly number of hours of non-news regional programming.

ITV1's ratings were markedly down in 2005; in the first week of June it had its second-worst ever week, with an audience share of just 19%. That poor performance came just a month after the launch of the reality show Celebrity Love Island, which was derided by critics and deserted by viewers; the channel also lost ground with the lucrative youth audience.

But the broadcaster's other channels performed well. Ratings showed in July 2005 that ITV2, with its focus on sport and entertainment, was catching up with Sky One. Golden oldies channel ITV3, launched in November 2004, was a runaway success in multichannel terms, with an audience share of 1.1% after its first six months, just behind its rival UK Gold. ITV4, aimed mainly at male viewers, was due to launch in November 2005.

Changes in the multichannel landscape led ITV to consider altering its digital strategy. In January 2005 the channel complained to Ofcom about the £17m charged by BSkyB for appearing on its satellite service; its options include joining the BBC in a rival Freesat service, or it may negotiate a reduced fee with BSkyB. And in May 2005, the success of Freeview led ITV to consider promoting it more forcefully; ITV-branded channels account for more than a quarter of Freeview viewing.

In ITV News, Tom Bradby was appointed political editor after Nick Robinson left for the BBC; while Daisy Sampson, presenter of BBC2's Daily Politics, became ITV's chief political correspondent.

Regional franchises

Such is ITV plc's dominance over the ITV network that it is easy to forget that, in Northern Ireland, the Channel Islands and parts of Scotland, other companies control the franchises.

In Northern Ireland, **Ulster TV** posted a 29% rise in television profits in 2004; while overall, its profits were up 46% to £13.9m. At SMG, which owns **Scottish TV** and **Grampian**, operating profits in TV were up 28% to £23m. The other regional franchise is **Channel Television**.

CHANNEL 4

Channel 4 was created in 1982 as a publicly owned corporation, with a remit to foster diversity and innovation. These days it finds itself caught on the horns of a dilemma: seek public funding for its services, or chase margins as part of a multichannel future?

Commercially, the company posted a record £46m in profit for 2004, up 34% on the year before; while its share of ratings rose to 9.8%. 4Ventures, the channel's commercial arm, made £12.1m in profits, almost a fourfold rise; though revenues were threatened by the government's decision to hand programming rights to independent producers. In December 2004, it was revealed that 4Ventures would be broken up following the departure of its director, Rob Woodward; E4 and FilmFour would be integrated into the broadcaster's core public service operation, leaving 4Ventures to concentrate on hitting profit targets. As a signal of its new direction, 4Ventures announced a phone-in quiz channel in June 2005.

The immediate effect of Channel 4's profit rise is a £188m fund to invest in its digital channels. At the start of summer 2005, it launched E4 on the Freeview platform, a move which immediately increased the entertainment channel's viewing figures. It also launched the documentary channel 4Docs, and planned an October launch for More4, an "accessible and down-to-earth" channel for the over-35s. The Channel 4 chairman, Luke Johnson, also announced that it planned to break away from television to become an "entertainment brand" active in everything from mobile phones to computer games.

Despite these plans, Channel 4 turned to the government for funding in November 2004, arguing that it faces a £100m-a-year deficit by 2009. In February, though, Ofcom said there was "no immediate case"

for direct public funding of the channel. Earlier, the Channel 4 chief executive, Andy Duncan, had suggested Channel 4 could merge its education and new media operations with the BBC. But the channel abandoned the idea of a merger with its rival broadcaster, Five.

Programming

In line with the launch of its 4Docs channel, Channel 4 increased its focus on documentaries. In November 2004 it outbid the BBC to the UK rights to Fahrenheit 9/11; while in May 2005 it won rights to broadcast Downfall, the critically acclaimed film about Hitler's final days in his Berlin bunker in 1945.

In sport, Channel 4 lost the rights to broadcast England's home cricket Test matches from 2006 to Sky, sparking protests from traditionalists. But racing is set to stay on the channel; Channel 4 had threatened to stop broadcasting racing, but the Tote and a number of racecourses eventually agreed to pay £4.8m for the channel to maintain its association with racing – albeit with a cut of 10 racing days from its schedule.

Channel 4 lost its first-ever presenter in June 2005, when Richard Whiteley – the host of quiz show Countdown since 1982 – died of pneumonia aged 61. The presenter, described by the Guardian as "deceptively bumbling", had become a firm favourite of daytime TV viewers. Kevin Lygo, Channel 4's director of programmes, said he hoped the show would try "revolving hosts for a while and then take stock".

FIVE

Five, the national terrestrial channel launched in 1997, is as of July 2005 completely owned by RTL – a subsidiary of Bertelsmann – after United Business Media sold its 35.4% stake in the channel for almost £250m. The channel had made an operating profit of £19m in 2004, and in 2005 reduced the amount it pays for its licence to £9m from £13m last year.

As a result of coming under single ownership, Five is thought to be in a stronger position to move into the multichannel market. It is thought to be about to bid for Flextech, the Telewest-owned company that owns channels such as Living TV. But in the first half of 2005, its terrestrial audience share fell for the first time, to 6.6% – down from 6.8% the year before.

Most column inches were attracted by The Farm, a farm-based reality show, which in October 2004 achieved the uneasy distinction of becoming the first TV programme to show a celebrity masturbating a pig. The show was later criticised by the RSPCA. At the time, the show also hit headlines for its celebrity bust-ups, after Paul Daniels and Stan Collymore walked out in successive weeks.

Also in October, the daytime TV host Trisha Goddard quit ITV to start a new career at Five.

In 2005, the contract for Five News passed from ITN to Sky News. James Bays was just one high-profile reporter who lost his job as a result of the switch.

MULTICHANNEL TV

The number of people watching multichannel television continues to increase. By the end of March 2005, according to Ofcom, more than 15.4 million households had access to digital TV, through satellite, cable or digital terrestrial; the reach of almost 62% compares with 53% the year before, and 43% the year before that. Add the 744,000 households who subscribe to analogue cable services, and the reach is almost 65%.

The government aims to complete digital switchover – switching off the terrestrial analogue TV signal – by the end of 2012. In April 2005, the Labour party included the plan in its manifesto; while the same month, SwitchCo – a not-for-profit organisation charged with coordinating the switchover effort – was established. This followed the start of a pilot scheme in Wales, when the government switched off analogue transmission to two Carmarthenshire villages, Ferryside and Llansteffan. Berlin, in Germany, and the two Welsh villages became the only areas in Europe with digital-only TV signals. The current plan is to switch off signals in Wales, the West and the Scottish borders first in 2008, with the Channel Islands last in 2012.

Needless to say, a row is already brewing over the cost and implications of the scheme. Freeview said the cost to consumers of converting Britain to digital TV would be around £1bn; Which? magazine claimed that the cost could be up to £3bn; while one analyst, Chris Goodall, told the Guardian he thought the bill could be almost £7bn over 20 years, including the increased energy demands of set-top boxes. An independent report for Ofcom, meanwhile, said the government would have to spend up to £400m to protect vulnerable members of society from losing access to TV altogether; and in May, another Ofcom report warned that more than seven out of 10 people in the UK knew nothing about the government's plans for digital switchover. In July 2005, the culture, media and sport committee announced an inquiry into the plans.

Interactive TV – the plethora of camera angles and services available to digital viewers who "press the red button" – is growing slowly; according to Ofcom, 46% of those who used satellite TV as their main platform

Digital & multichannel TV: the options				
	Main operators	**Connected homes**		
		31–Mar–05	**31–Mar–04**	**Year-on-year rise**
Satellite	Sky Digital	7.35m	6.96m	5.6%
	Free–to–view	445,000	231,000	92.6%
Digital terrestrial	Freeview	5.06m	3.47m	45.8%
Cable	NTL, Telewest	3.29m	3.33m	–1.3%
of which digital:		2.54m	2.41m	5.4%
ADSL		20,000	9,000	122.0%
Total digital		**15.42m**	**13.07m**	**18.0%**
Total multichannel		**16.16m**	**13.99m**	**15.5%**

*plus 355,000 homes in Republic of Ireland   Sources: Ofcom, BSkyB

in 2004 have used interactive services, a figure that falls to 38% for Free-view; only 17% in total said they had bought products or services via their TVs. That said, the number of advertising campaigns is growing steadily; there had been more than 600 by the end of 2004.

Digital terrestrial

Freeview remains the biggest digital success story. The digital terrestrial service – launched in October 2002, as a joint venture between the BBC, BSkyB, and transmitter operator Crown Castle – currently offers 30 TV channels and more than 20 digital radio stations for the cost of a set-top box, prices of which have now fallen below £40. In the first quarter of 2005, the number of subscribers reached more than 5 million, up from 3.5 million the year before. A total of 6.7 million set-top boxes have been sold; Ofcom reckons the rest are being used on second sets.

BSkyB and satellite

Satellite services provided by BSkyB still lead the way in digital TV. Sky Digital offers more than 375 channels, more than any other platform; more than 20 are Sky own-brand or spin-off channels. The company had about 7.7 million subscribers in the first three months of 2005; and also had 770,000 users for its premium Sky Plus service, which offers the facility to pause live TV or record one channel while watching another. Its average revenue per subscriber was £382; in the nine months to the end of March 2005, BSkyB's profits rose to £574m, a year-on-year increase of 31%.

Early criticism of chief executive James Murdoch, son of the company's ultimate owner Rupert Murdoch, has seen the company focus its efforts on growth. In June 2005, Sky Digital announced a new pricing structure offering a greater selection of basic channels at a slightly higher cost, but also broadband services for higher-paying subscribers, with access to goals, match clips and around 200 films.

In October 2004 Sky also launched "Freesat" – by which customers can access around 200 TV and radio channels for a one-off payment of about £150 – but, despite attracting 445,000 subscribers, it had stopped advertising the service by summer 2005.

In January, BSkyB patented technology allowing TV viewers to record favourite programmes without any ad breaks, which ruffled feathers in the ad industry. In June, it announced that three of its TV channels would be available to 1,000 Virgin Mobile customers as part of a pilot project. In November, the company started broadcasting a pint-glass logo into its sport broadcasts to pubs, in an attempt to stop publicans dodging higher subscription charges aimed at the pub trade.

Cost-cutting was also planned, with an announcement of a series of job cuts expected in 2005.

Ratings suffered at Sky One, but the channel headed upmarket in an attempt to attract more advertising revenue. US-bought dramas such as Nip/Tuck and 24 attracted viewers, while homegrown drama Hex – a kind of British Buffy – was recommissioned.

Sky's Sports channels scored a cricketing coup in December 2004, when they won the right to broadcast England's home Test matches from 2006.

Cable

Cable television is a subscription-based service, usually offered in conjunction with telephone or internet, all broadcast through a digital or analogue cable into the home. Just under 3.3 million households subscribed in March 2005, representing a decline of about 37,000 households since the year before. The number of digital cable subscribers actually rose by about 140,000 to just over 2.5 million households; but the fall in the number of analogue subscribers, from about 916,000 to about 744,000, more than offset this. NTL and Telewest, the two main cable operators, are thought to be on the brink of a merger in an effort to compete with their rivals.

BT, meanwhile, is considering delivering cable television via ADSL broadband. At the end of 2004, the only company offering ADSL television was Homechoice, with about 20,000 subscribers.

INDEPENDENT PRODUCTION COMPANIES

The brave new world of independent television production is here. Under the Communications Act 2003, independent producers can now exploit the rights in the ideas they sell. This makes the returnable format – a programme that, like RDF's Faking It and Wife Swap, can be sold internationally as well as in Britain – ever more valuable to the independent producer. British TV exports grew by 6% in 2004 to reach £534m, according to trade body Pact and the government. Add to that the fact that the BBC announced in 2005 that 50% of its output would now be produced by independents, up from 25%, and the indies are in a very healthy position indeed.

Where there is cash, of course, the City will take an interest; and so a process of consolidation is continuing in the independent sector. Although there are 1,000 independent TV producers, according to Pact, only 20 or 30 have the resources to compete regularly for the major programming budgets; and the really big "superindies" are now more powerful than ever.

The most notable recent acquisition was the October 2004 purchase of Company TV, producers of Shameless, by All3Media, the company that already owns Cactus and Lion, and is now the biggest of the superindies. Hat Trick, meanwhile, was reported in April 2005 to be in talks to acquire IWC, the production outfit headed by the Newsnight presenter Kirsty Wark; while Diverse TV, makers of Operatunity, was sold in October 2004 to Fact Based Communications.

In spring 2005, two indies floated on Aim, the Alternative Investment Market. Shed Productions, the company set up by Eileen Gallagher – once a press officer for Scottish TV – floated with a £44m valuation in March; its four owners pocketed £5.5m each. The company, which makes Bad Girls and Footballers' Wives, made £2.8m in gross profits for the six months to the end of February, up from around £900,000 for the same period a year earlier. In June, the BBC commissioned it to produce a drama called Waterloo Road.

Eileen Gallagher... £5.5m richer after Shed float on Aim

Frank Baron

Further reading

■ **Press**

MediaGuardian
media.guardian.co.uk/broadcast

Broadcast: weekly trade magazine
www.broadcastnow.co.uk

Televisual: monthly trade magazine
www.mad.co.uk/publication/tv

■ **Web only**

Digital Spy
www.digitalspy.co.uk

■ **Books**

Strange Places, Questionable People JOHN SIMPSON, PAN 1999 Autobiography of the ubiquitous BBC television journalist

Life On Air DAVID ATTENBOROUGH, BBC 2002 Autobiography of the ubiquitous BBC television naturalist

Broadcast Journalism ANDREW BOYD, FOCAL PRESS 2000 Widely recommended guide

John Birt: the Harder Path TIME WARNER PAPERBACKS 2003 Autobiography of a former director general

On Air: A Career in TV & Radio CHRIS ALDEN, GUARDIAN BOOKS 2004 Essential guide to broadcasting career

■ **Other resources**

Barb
www.barb.co.uk

Digital television
www.digitaltelevision.gov.uk

Pact
www.pact.co.uk

Next to float was RDF Media, the company behind Wife Swap and Faking It. It was valued at almost £50m.

Meanwhile, Telefónica, the Spanish owner of the Big Brother producer Endemol, said it would float a minority stake in the company in late 2005 or early 2006. It had been reported in October 2004 that Time Warner had offered £1.1bn for the company.

TV Corporation, the big indie now headed by former BBC director of sport Peter Salmon, announced profits of £866,000 in 2004 – a good turnaround after it lost almost £9m in 2003. It sold Visions, a facilities company responsible for its sports contracts, to a US outside broadcast firm for almost £17m.

The new dawn for the indies, it seems, comes with new responsibilities. In May, Pact drew up a revised code of practice on work experience, after MediaGuardian published reports about young "runners" in the TV industry who, according to anecdotal evidence, were expected to work long hours for little or nothing, sometimes for months on end. The code limits unpaid work experience to four weeks, after which the job should become a training post, subject to the minimum wage.

Top 20 independent production companies

	Company	Credits
1	TWI	Japan's War, Wimbledon, The Olympics, Premier League
2=	All3media	Black Books, Midsomer Murders, Richard and Judy
2=	RDF	Faking It, Wife Swap
4	Endemol	Big Brother, Fame Academy, Ground Force
5	Talkback Thames	Jamie's Kitchen, The Apprentice, Bo'Selecta!
6	The TV Corporation	Robot Wars, Britain's Worst Driver
7=	Tiger Aspect	Teachers, Murphy's Law
7=	Tinopolis	P'nawn Da, Wedi 7, Le Rygbi
9	Zig Zag	Fashion is Football Challenge, Inside the Mind of Frank Bruno
10	Princess	Back to Reality, Ri:se, The Wright Stuff
11	Shine	Dispatches, Fit to Eat, Masterchef Goes Large
12	IWC	Location, Location, Location
13	Wall to Wall	Regency House Party
14	At It	T4, LA Pool Party, Sun Sea and Silicone
15=	Diverse	Musicality
15=	Leopard Films	Car Booty, Cash in the Attic, Money Spinners
17	Celador	You Are What You Eat, Who Wants To Be a Millionaire?
18	Ricochet	Supernanny, Living in the Sun
19	Objective	Derren Brown: Trick of the Mind, Peep Show
20=	Hat Trick	Have I Got News For You, Room 101, The Kumars at No 42
20=	Pioneer	Naked Science, Danger Man, Tycoon Toys
20=	Twofour	G Girls, Gardens Through Time, The City Gardener

Source: Televisual magazine, October 2005. Rank based on five criteria: turnover, size, output, commissions and an industry peer poll

Thompson's first year at the BBC **Emily Bell**

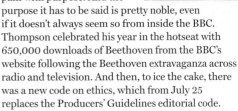

TV

A year ago Channel 4 agreed to release Mark Thompson from his contract so that he could take up his post as the new director-general of the BBC. A small detail about the transaction that is entertaining in hindsight is that C4 extracted an undisclosed five-figure sum from the BBC to recruit Thompson's replacement.

This, as we know, turned out to be the then BBC marketing director, Andy Duncan. So, effectively, the BBC paid to have its own staff poached – a farcical irony if ever there was one. Has the desire to hasten Thompson's arrival led the corporation to subsequently repent at leisure?

At the time, the appointment as chairman of Michael Grade had lifted the BBC's morale post-Hutton to the rafters, and the signing of Thompson represented the completion of the dream team. Since then, the Beeb has ridden a fairly wild rollercoaster of corporate upheaval – a wide-ranging redundancy programme slashing thousands of jobs from the payroll, key departures on its two main television channels, a shake-up in news, a new head for Radio 4 and the World Service, the threat (or promise) of a relocation to Manchester for two key departments, a strike, and the first glimpse of a renewed charter.

It has given Thompson the internal reputation of a man who is protecting the corporation's future but not necessarily that of its staff, of entering the post-Greg Dyke party with a binbag and Marigolds to set about cleaning up the debris of indulgence. One can almost believe Thompson really believed the "Jacuzzi of cash" jibe he made at the BBC during his time at C4.

While one can question the scale and speed of Thompson's reforms, one cannot question that a Thompson imprimatur is beginning to appear. His BBC is a mean machine in many senses of the words – there is a strong sense that the organisation is about turning itself into a future-proof bulldozer, an emperor Dalek with intimations of its own mortality.

Last week the corporation's in-house magazine, Ariel, carried a front-page call to arms from one of the BBC's key new media thinkers, Tom Loosemore. In a space where there would normally be a matey picture of Bill Oddie pursuing a reed warbler, there was a cartoon of a burning BBC logo. "The platform on which the BBC was built is on fire," thunders Ariel, and, says Loosemore, "my job is to get them to smell the smoke and then persuade them not to panic".

This, it seems, is very much the core of Thompson's BBC: pain with purpose. And the purpose it has to be said is pretty noble, even if it doesn't always seem so from inside the BBC. Thompson celebrated his year in the hotseat with 650,000 downloads of Beethoven from the BBC's website following the Beethoven extravaganza across radio and television. And then, to ice the cake, there was a new code on ethics, which from July 25 replaces the Producers' Guidelines editorial code.

Here again, there is the Thompson touch, although the review that created it started well before he arrived – for the first time, news producers are definitively directed that being right is better than being first with the news. This raises a great deal of philosophical questions for the newsroom, though in reality it is only a public statement of what editors have always practised at the BBC.

Dyke's BBC was about swagger and competitiveness, about beating ITV in primetime. Thompson may be making a more conservative start in terms of the high-profile, high-cost areas of television (notwithstanding Doctor Who), but it is interesting that the competitive noise about the threat of the BBC, which rose to a din around Dyke, has died down.

In truth, Thompson's engagement with the idea that the BBC is going beyond television, beyond broadcasting, beyond national borders and beyond the licence fee even, contains more long-term threat to all manner of industries than Dyke's nightly battle with ITV ever did.

Barring accidents and acts of God, Thompson will be at the BBC during one of its most challenging periods – the switch from analogue to digital, the rise of programming available over the internet, the redefinition of what constitutes a television and, therefore, one supposes, a redefinition of the licence fee. A large number of BBC employees have already perished in the smoke, but Thompson, it seems, is almost enjoying the smell of a good fire. The rest of us have plenty of time to panic.

This article appeared in MediaGuardian on June 27 2005

News media

BBC

BBC
020 8743 8000
info@bbc.co.uk
www.bbc.co.uk
Chairman of governors: Michael Grade; vice-chairman: Anthony Salz; governors: Deborah Bull, Dame Ruth Deech, Dermot Gleeson, Professor Merfyn Jones, Professor Fabian Monds, Angela Sarkis, Ranjit Sondhi, Richard Tait; director-general: Mark Thompson
PRESS: *020 8576 1865*
press.office@bbc.co.uk
www.bbc.co.uk/pressoffice

ADDRESSES

Television Centre
Wood Lane, London W12 7RJ
BBC White City
201 Wood Lane, London W12 7TS
Broadcasting House
Portland Place, London W1A 1AA

BBC TV

Television Centre
020 8743 8000
www.bbc.co.uk/television
Director of television: Jana Bennett; controller, programme acquisition: George McGhee
PRESS: *020 8576 9900*
publicity.frontdesk@bbc.co.uk

Nations and regions

Director of nations and regions:
Pat Loughrey

BBC Northern Ireland
Broadcasting House
Ormeau Avenue, Belfast BT2 8HQ
028 9033 8000
www.bbc.co.uk/northernireland
Controller: Anna Carragher

BBC Scotland
Broadcasting House
Queen Margaret Drive
Glasgow G12 8DG
0141 339 8844
www.bbc.co.uk/scotland
Controller: Ken MacQuarrie

BBC Wales
Broadcasting House
Llandaff, Cardiff CF5 2YQ
029 2032 2000
www.bbc.co.uk/wales
Controller: Menna Richards

BBC ENGLISH REGIONS

Controller: Andy Griffee
BBC London
35c Marylebone High Street
London W1U 4QA
020 7224 2424
yourlondon@bbc.co.uk
www.bbc.co.uk/london
Head of regional and local programmes:
Michael MacFarlane

BBC East
The Forum, Millennium Plain
Norwich NR2 1BH
01603 619 331
look.east@bbc.co.uk
www.bbc.co.uk/england/lookeast
Head of regional and local programmes:
Tim Bishop

BBC East Midlands
London Road, Nottingham NG2 4UU
0115 955 0500
emt@bbc.co.uk
www.bbc.co.uk/england
/eastmidlandstoday
Head of regional and local programmes:
Alison Ford

BBC North
Broadcasting Centre
Woodhouse Lane, Leeds LS2 9PX
0113 244 1188
look.north@bbc.co.uk
www.bbc.co.uk/england
/looknorthyorkslincs
Head of regional and local programmes:
Colin Philpott

BBC North East and Cumbria
Broadcasting Centre, Barrack Road
Newcastle upon Tyne NE99 2NE
0191 232 1313
look.north.northeast.cumbria@
bbc.co.uk
www.bbc.co.uk/england
/looknorthnecumbria
Head of regional and local programmes:
Wendy Pilmer

BBC North West
New Broadcasting House
Oxford Road, Manchester M60 1SJ
0161 200 2020
nwt@bbc.co.uk
www.bbc.co.uk/manchester
Head of regional and local programmes:
Martin Brooks

BBC South
Broadcasting House, Havelock Road
Southampton SO14 7PU
023 8022 6201
south.today@bbc.co.uk
www.bbc.co.uk/england/southtoday
Head of regional and local programmes:
Eve Turner

BBC South East
The Great Hall, Mount Pleasant Road
Tunbridge Wells TN1 1QQ
01892 670000
southeasttoday@bbc.co.uk
www.bbc.co.uk/england
/southeasttoday
Head of regional and local programmes:
Laura Ellis

BBC South West
Broadcasting House, Seymour Road
Mannamead, Plymouth PL3 5BD
01752 229201
spotlight@bbc.co.uk
www.bbc.co.uk/england/spotlight
Head of regional and local
programmes: John Lilley

BBC West
Broadcasting House
Whiteladies Road, Bristol BS8 2LR
0117 973 2211
pointswest@bbc.co.uk
www.bbc.co.uk/england/pointswest
Head of regional and local programmes:
Andrew Wilson

BBC West Midlands
The Mailbox, Birmingham B1 1XL
0121 567 6767
midlands.today@bbc.co.uk
www.bbc.co.uk/birmingham
Head of regional and local programmes:
David Holdsworth

Channels

BBC One
Television Centre
020 8743 8000
www.bbc.co.uk/bbcone
Controller: Peter Fincham

BBC Two
Television Centre
020 8743 8000
www.bbc.co.uk/bbctwo
Controller: Roly Keating; controller of daytime: Jay Hunt

BBC Three
Television Centre
020 8743 8000
www.bbc.co.uk/bbcthree
Controller: Stuart Murphy

BBC Four
Television Centre
0870 010 0222
www.bbc.co.uk/bbcfour
Controller: Janice Hadlow

CBBC
Television Centre
020 8743 8000
www.bbc.co.uk/cbbc
Controller: Alison Sharman; chief operating officer: Richard Deverell

CBeebies
Television Centre
020 8743 8000
www.bbc.co.uk/cbeebies
Controller: Alison Sharman

BBC America
PO Box 6266, Florence
KY 41022-6266, USA
00 1 859 342 4070
www.bbcamerica.com
Programme executive: Alison Fredericks

BBC Canada
121 Bloor Street East, Suite 200
Toronto, Ontario, Canada M4W 3M5
00 416 967 3249
feedback@bbccanada.com
www.bbccanada.com

BBC Food
PO Box 5054, London W12 0ZY
020 8433 2221
www.bbcfood.com
Editor: David Weiland

BBC News 24
Television Centre
020 8743 8000
bbcnews24@bbc.co.uk
www.bbc.co.uk/bbcnews24
Editoral director: Mark Popescu

BBC Parliament
4 Millbank, London SW1P 3JA
020 7973 6216
parliament@bbc.co.uk
www.bbc.co.uk/bbcparliament

BBC Prime
PO Box 5054, London W12 0ZY
020 8433 2221
bbcprime@bbc.co.uk
www.bbcprime.com
Editor: David Weiland

BBC World
PO Box 5054, London W12 0ZY
020 8433 2221
bbcworld@bbc.co.uk
www.bbcworld.com
Editorial director: Sian Kevill

BBC Japan
PO Box 5054, London W12 0ZY
www.bbcjapan.tv

Interactive TV

BBCi
Television Centre
020 8743 8000
www.bbc.co.uk/digital/tv
Controller: Rahul Chakkara; head, interactive TV programming: Emma Somerville

---

Ceefax

Television Centre
020 8743 8000

GENRES

BBC News

Television Centre
020 8743 8000
www.bbc.co.uk/news
Director of BBC News: Helen Boaden; deputy: Mark Damazer; head of newsgathering: Adrian Van Klaveren

- Editors – *business: Jeff Randall; diplomatic: Brian Hanrahan; home: Mark Easton; Middle East: Jeremy Bowen; political: Nick Robinson; world affairs: John Simpson*

- UK correspondents – *defence: Paul Adams; diplomatic: Jonathan Marcus; education: Mike Baker; health: Karen Allen; home affairs: Margaret Gilmore; political: Laura Trevelyan; royal: Nicholas Witchell, Peter Hunt; rural affairs: Tom Heap; security: Frank Gardner; social affairs: Daniel Sandford*

- Special correspondents – *Fergal Keane, Gavin Hewitt; TV news: Ben Brown; BBC News 24: Philippa Thomas*

- World correspondents – *world affairs: Peter Biles. Europe: Tim Franks, Chris Morris, Stephen Sackur; Paris: Alan Little, Caroline Wyatt; Berlin: Ray Furlong; Rome: David Willey; Greece: Richard Galpin; Moscow: Damian Grammaticas; south Europe: Brian Barron; central Europe: Nick Thorpe. Middle East: Orla Guerin, James Reynolds, Paul Wood; Turkey: Jonny Dymond. Americas – Washington: Nick Bryant, Matt Frei, Jon Leyne, Clive Myrie, Ian Pannell, Justin Webb; California: David Willis; Mexico and central America: Claire Marshall; South America: Elliott Gotkine. Other – Africa: Hilary Andersson; east Africa: Andrew Harding; south Asia: Adam Mynott; south-east Asia: Kylie Morris; central Asia: Monica Whitlock. World media: Sebastian Usher. Also Dominic Hughes, Jill McGivering, Matthew Price*

Political programmes unit
BBC Westminster, 4 Millbank
London SW1P 3JA
020 7973 6000
Head of political programmes: Fran Unsworth; political editor: Nick Robinson

TV News
Room 1502, Television Centre
020 8624 9043
Head of television news: Roger Mosey; deputy: Rachael Attwell

PROGRAMMES

Breakfast
Room 1605, News Centre
Television Centre
020 8624 9700
breakfasttv@bbc.co.uk
Editor: Richard Porter; presenters: Dermot Murnaghan, Natasha Kaplinsky

Newsnight
Television Centre
020 8624 9800
Editor: Peter Barron; presenters: Jeremy Paxman, Kirsty Wark, Gavin Esler

Panorama
Room 1118, BBC White City
020 8752 7152
panorama@bbc.co.uk
Editor: Mike Robinson; deputy editors: Andrew Bell and Sam Collyns

Politics Show
4 Millbank, London SW1P 3JQ
020 7973 6199
politicsshow@bbc.co.uk
Presenter: Jeremy Vine

Question Time
Mentorn, 43 Whitfield Street
London W1T 4HA
020 7258 6800
Presenter: David Dimbleby

Six O'Clock News
Television Centre
020 8624 9996
Presenters: George Alagiah, Sophie Raworth

Ten O'Clock News
Television Centre
020 8624 9999
Editor: Kevin Bakhurst; presenters: Huw Edwards, Fiona Bruce

Factual and learning

Director of factual and learning
John Willis 020 8752 6501
Controller, factual TV
Glenwyn Benson 020 8743 8000

Arts
2nd Floor, BBC White City
020 8752 4092
claire.lewis.02@bbc.co.uk
Executive producer: Claire Lewis; commissioner, arts and culture: Franny Moyle

Arts (Wales)
Room 4001, BBC Wales
029 2032 2943
paul.islwyn.thomas@bbc.co.uk
Head of arts, Wales: Paul Islwyn Thomas

Classical music
Room EG09, Television Centre
020 8895 6541
Head of TV, classical music and performance: Peter Maniura

Current affairs
Room 1172, BBC White City
020 8752 7005
Head of current affairs: Peter Horrocks

Documentaries and contemporary factual
Room 3559, BBC White City
020 8743 8000
genfact.proposals@bbc.co.uk
Head of documentaries: Alan Hayling; development executives: Nicky Colton, Sara Brailsford

Education
Room 3416, BBC White City
020 8752 5241
Executive editor: Karen Johnson

Education (Northern Ireland)
Education Unit, First Floor
BBC Northern Ireland
028 9033 8445
Editor, learning, NI: Kieran Hegarty

Education (Scotland)
Room 230, BBC Scotland
0141 338 1507
Editor, education, Scotland: Moira Scott

Education (Wales)
Room E3106, BBC Wales
029 2032 2834
Head of education and learning, Wales: Dr Eleri Wyn Lewis

Factual (Northern Ireland)
2nd Floor, BBC Northern Ireland
028 9033 8553
Editor, factual TV: Paul McGuigan; head of factual network production, NI: Fiona Campbell, 020 8752 6074

Factual (Scotland)
Room 3178, BBC Scotland
0141 338 3646
andrea.miller.01@bbc.co.uk
Head of factual programmes, Scotland: Andrea Miller

Factual (Wales)
Room 4020, BBC Wales
029 2032 2976
Head of factual programmes, Wales: Adrian Davies

Lifeskills TV
Room 2308, BBC White City
020 8752 4574
Head of Lifeskills TV: Seetha Kumar

Music (Wales)
Room E4113, BBC Wales
029 2032 2111
davidm.jackson@bbc.co.uk
Head of music, Wales: David Jackson

Specialist factual, current affairs and arts
Room 2156, BBC White City
020 8743 8000
specfact.proposals@bbc.co.uk
Head of independent commissioning: Adam Kemp; commissioner, specialist factual: Emma Swain; senior commissioning executives: Krishan Arora, Lucy Hetherington; executive editor: Jacquie Hughes

PROGRAMMES

Arena
Room 2168, BBC White City
020 8752 5172
Series editor: Anthony Wall

Everyman
Room 5048, BBC Manchester
Broadcasting House, Oxford Road
Manchester M60 1SJ
0161 244 3321
ruth.pitt@bbc.co.uk
Creative director: Ruth Pitt

Horizon
Room 4523, BBC White City
020 8752 6134
horizon@bbc.co.uk
Editor: Matthew Barrett

Imagine
Arts Department, 2nd Floor
BBC White City
020 8752 4092
ian.macmillan@bbc.co.uk
Series producer: Ian Macmillan

Money programme
Room 4116, BBC White City
020 8752 7400
Executive editor: Clive Edwards

One Life
Room 5503, BBC White City
020 8752 6608
todd.austin@bbc.co.uk
Commissioning editor: Todd Austin

Panorama
Room 1118, BBC White City
020 8752 7152
Editor: Mike Robinson

Storyville
Room 201, 1 Mortimer Street
London W1T 3JA
020 7765 5211
storyville@bbc.co.uk
Commissioning editor: Nick Fraser

This World
Room 1362, BBC White City
020 8752 7500
thisworld@bbc.co.uk
Editor: Karen O'Connor

Timewatch
Room 3150, BBC White City
020 8752 7079
Editor: John Farren

Drama and entertainment

Director of drama, entertainment and CBBC
Alan Yentob

Comedy
Room 4045, Television Centre
020 8743 8000
Head of comedy commissioning: Mark Freeland; head of comedy entertainment: Jon Plowman

Comedy and entertainment (Scotland)
Room 3167, BBC Scotland
0141 338 2370
Head of comedy and entertainment, Scotland: Mike Bolland

Daytime
Room 3560
BBC White City
020 8752 6225
Senior commissioning executive, daytime: Dominic Vallely

Daytime entertainment
Room 6070, Television Centre
020 8576 9960
Commissioning executive, daytime entertainment: Gilly Hall

Drama
Room 2145, Television Centre
56 Wood Lane, London W12 7RJ
020 8576 1861

Drama (Northern Ireland)
BBC Northern Ireland
020 8576 1664
Head of drama, NI: Patrick Spence

Drama (Scotland)
Room 2170, BBC Scotland
0141 338 2517
Head of television drama, Scotland: Barbara McKissack

Drama (Wales)
Room E2106, BBC Wales
029 2032 2935
Head of drama, Wales: Julie Gardner

Entertainment
Room 6070, Television Centre
020 8225 6992
Controller, entertainment, commissioning: Jane Lush

Entertainment (Northern Ireland)
Room 229, BBC Northern Ireland
028 9033 8375
mike.edgar@bbc.co.uk
Head of entertainment, events and sport, NI: Mike Edgar

Children

CBBC
Room E1012, Television Centre
020 8576 1280
Director: Alan Yentob; controller: Alison Sharman; chief operating officer: Richard Deverell

Acquisitions
Room 360 DB, Television Centre
020 8576 1105
Head of acquisitions and co-productions: Theresa Plummer Andrews

CBBC Creates
Room E1200, Television Centre
020 8576 1040
Development executive, CBBC Creates: Amanda Gabbitas

CBBC Scotland
Room 2104, BBC Scotland
0141 338 2012
Head of Scotland: Donalda MacKinnon

Drama
Room E817, Television Centre
020 8576 8245
Head of drama: Elaine Sperber

Entertainment
Room E701, Television Centre
020 8225 9269
Head of entertainment: Anne Gilchrist

News and factual
Room E111, Television Centre
020 8576 3118
Head of news and factual: Roy Milani

Pre-school
Room N105, Neptune House
BBC Elstree, Clarendon Road,
Borehamwood, Herts WD6 1JF
020 8228 7072
Head of pre-school: Clare Elstow

Sport

Director of sport
Roger Mosey

Live sport and highlights
Room 5060, Television Centre
020 8225 8400
andrew.thompson.01@bbc.co.uk
Head of new media, sports news and development: Andrew Thompson

Films

BBC Films
1 Mortimer Street, London W1T 3JA
020 7765 0251
Head of BBC Films: David Thompson, 020 7765 0113; executive producer and head of development: Tracy Scoffield 020 7765 0475

▶▶ See page 294

Radio

▶▶ See page 200

New media

BBC New Media
Broadcast Centre, Media Village
202 Wood Lane, London W12 7TP
020 8008 1300
www.bbc.co.uk
Director of new media and technology: Ashley Highfield; controller, internet: Tony Ageh; controller, emerging platforms: Angel Gambino

▶▶ MORE NEW MEDIA see page 236

Business services

BBC Costumes and Wigs
Victoria Road, London W3 6UL
020 8576 1761
costume@bbc.co.uk
wigs@bbc.co.uk
www.bbcresources.com

BBC International Unit
020 8576 1963
international.unit@bbc.co.uk
www.bbc.co.uk/international
Supplies TV facilities to overseas broadcasters transmitting from UK Manager: Peter James

BBC Monitoring
Marketing Unit, Caversham Park
Reading RG4 8TZ
0118 948 6289
csu@mon.bbc.co.uk
www.bbcmonitoringonline.com,
www.monitor.bbc.co.uk
Monitors world media

BBC Outside Broadcasts
Kendal Avenue, London W3 0RP
020 8993 9333
ob@bbc.co.uk
www.bbcresources.com

BBC Post-Production
Television Centre
020 8225 7702
postproduction@bbc.co.uk
www.bbcresources.com
Bristol
Broadcasting House
White Ladies Road, Bristol BS8 2LR
0117 974 6666
Birmingham
The Mailbox, Birmingham B1 1XL
0121 567 6767

BBC R&D
BBC Kingswood Warren
Tadworth, Surrey KT20 6NP
01737 839500
info@rd.bbc.co.uk
www.bbc.co.uk/rd
Head of research: Ian Childs

BBC Research Central
Broadcasting House
research-central@bbc.co.uk
www.bbcresearchcentral.com
Information, footage, pronunciation, radio and photo research services Senior researchers: Helen Turner, Huw Martin, Guy Watkins, Angie Francis, Kyla Thorogood, Richard Jeffery, Jacqueline Faulkner, Michael Paige

BBC Studios
Television Centre
020 8576 7666
tvstudio.sales@bbc.co.uk
www.bbcresources.com

BBC Training and Development
35 Marylebone High Street
London W1U 4PX
0870 122 0216
training@bbc.co.uk
www.bbctraining.co.uk
Training for programme-making, broadcasting and new media
PRESS: *01993 823011*
    louise@energypr.co.uk
    (Louise Findlay-Wilson)
Elstree
Clarendon Road, Borehamwood
Herts WD6 1JF
Wood Norton Training Centre
Evesham, Worcestershire WR11 4YB

BBC Worldwide
Woodlands, 80 Wood Lane
London W12 0TT
020 8433 2000
www.bbcworldwide.com
Commercial arm: businesses include distribution, TV channels, magazines, books, videos, spoken word, music, DVDs, licensed products, CD-ROMs, English language teaching, videos for education and training, interactive telephony, co-production, library footage Chief executive: John Smith

Advisory bodies

Broadcasting Council for Scotland
The Secretary, Broadcasting House
Queen Margaret Drive
Glasgow G12 8DG
0141 339 8844

Broadcasting Council for Wales
The Secretary, Broadcasting House
Llandaff, Cardiff CF5 2YQ
029 2032 2000

Broadcasting Council for Northern Ireland
Head of Public Affairs and Secretary
Broadcasting House,
Ormeau Avenue, Belfast BT2 8HQ
028 9033 8000

Central Religious Advisory Committee
The Secretary, Broadcasting House
London W1A 1AA
020 7580 4468

English National Forum
Head of Press and Public Affairs
English Regions, BBC Birmingham
The Mailbox, Birmingham B1 1XL
0121 567 6767

Governors' World Service Consultative Group
BBC World Service, Bush House
Strand, London WC2B 4PH
020 8743 8000

News media

ITV Network (ITV1)

200 Grays Inn Road
London WC1X 8HF
020 7843 8000
www.itv.com/itv1
www.itvregions.com
*Controllers run commissioning and
scheduling across ITV1 national network
– including non-ITV plc regions.
Network controllers – acquisitions:
Jeremy Boulton, 020 7843 8120; arts,
current affairs and religion: Dominic
Crossley-Holland; children's and youth:
Steven Andrew, 020 7843 8132; comedy:
Sioned Wiliam, 020 7843 8093; drama:
Nick Elliot, 020 7843 8202
(head of continuing series: Corrine
Hollingworth); entertainment: Claudia
Rosencrantz, 020 7843 8105; factual:
Bridget Boseley, 020 7843 8297
(editor: factual programmes: Daniella
Neumann, 020 7843 8101); sport:
Mark Sharman; ITV 50th anniversary:
Liam Hamilton; 020 7843 810*

ITV PLC

London Television Centre
Upper Ground, London SE1 9LT
020 7843 8000
*Controls 11 of the 15 ITV1 franchises,
ITV2, ITV3, ITV News Channel, and
Granada production company.
Chief executive: Charles Allen;
chairman: Sir Peter Burt; director of
regional affairs: Susan Woodward;
controller of regional affairs: Jane Luca.*
PRESS: *020 7620 1620*
COMMUNICATIONS DIRECTOR:
Brigitte Trafford

ITV Broadcast

020 7843 8000
*Runs ITV plc's 11 regional ITV1
franchises; runs ITV2 and ITV3
Chief executive: Mick Desmond;
head of programmes: Nigel Pickard*

ITV1 FRANCHISES

ITV Anglia

Anglia House, Norwich NR1 3JG
01603 615151
firstname.lastname@itv.com
www.angliatv.com
*MD: Graham Creelman; controller
of programmes and regional news:
Neil Thompson; head of regional
affairs: Jim Woodrow*

News at Anglia
0870 240 6003
news@angliatv.com

Cambridge regional office
26 Newmarket Road
Cambridge CB5 8DT
01223 467076

Chelmsford regional office
64–68 New London Road
Chelmsford CM2 0YU
01245 357676

Ipswich regional office
Hubbard House
Ipswich IP1 2QA
01473 226157

Luton regional office
16 Park Street
Luton LU1 2DP
01582 729666

Northampton regional office
77b Abington Street
Northampton NN1 2BH
01604 624343

Peterborough regional office
6 Bretton Green
Peterborough PE3 8DY
01733 269440

ITV Border

The Television Centre
Durranhill, Carlisle CA1 3NT
01228 525101
www.border-tv.com
*MD: Paddy Merrall; production
controller: Neil Robinson; head of news:
Ian Proniewicz; head of features: Jane
Bolesworth.*
PRESS AND REGIONAL AFFAIRS
MANAGER: *Louise Maving*

ITV Central

Gas Street, Birmingham B1 2JT
0121 643 9898
firstname.lastname@itv.com
www2.itv.com/central
*MD: Ian Squires; controller of news and
operations: Laurie Upshon; head of
regional programming: Duncan Rycroft;
editor, Central News West: Dan Barton*
PRESS OFFICER: *Christopher Strange*

Central News East
Terry Lloyd House, 1 Regan Way,
Chetwynd Business Park
Nottingham NG9 6RZ
0115 986 3322
News editor: Mike Blair

Central News South
9 Windrush Court, Abingdon
Business Park, Abingdon
Oxford OX14 1SA
01235 554123
News editor: Ian Rumsey

ITV Granada
Quay Street, Manchester M60 9EA
0161 832 7211
firstname.lastname@itv.com
www.granadatv.com
*MD: Susan Woodward; controller
of programmes: Duncan Ryecroft;
executive producer regional
programmes: Eamonn O'Neal;
controller of regional affairs: Jane
Luca; news editor: Richard Frediani*

Liverpool news centre
Albert Dock, Liverpool L3 4BA
0151 709 9393

Lancaster regional news centre
White Cross, Lancaster LA1 4XQ
01524 60688

ITV London

London Television Centre
Upper Grounds, London SE1 9LT
020 7620 1620
firstname.lastname@itv.com
www2.itv.com/london
*MD: Christy Swords; controller of
regional programming: Emma Barker;
head of regional affairs: Helen Andrews*

London News Network
200 Grays Inn Road
London WC1X 8HF
020 7430 4000
firstname.lastname@itvlondon.com
www.itvlondon.co.uk
*Planning editor: Arti Lukha; head of
news: Stuart Thomas; news editors:
Brendan McGowan, Robin Campbell*

ITV Meridian

Forum One, Parkway
Solent Business Park, Whiteley
Hampshire PO15 7PA
01489 442000
news@meridiantv.com
www.meridiantv.co.uk

Maidstone news office
Maidstone Studios, Vinters Park
Maidstone, Kent ME14 5NZ
01489 442000

Newbury news office
Strawberry Hill House
Strawberry Hill, Newbury
Berkshire RG14 1NG
01635 552266

ITV Tyne Tees

Television House, The Watermark
Gateshead NE11 9SZ
0191 4048700
news@tynetees.tv
firstname.lastname@itv.com
www.tynetees.tv
*MD and controller of programmes:
Graeme Thompson; head of regional
affairs: Norma Hope; head of news:
Graham Marples*

*Tees Valley & North Yorkshire news
office*
Belasis Hall Technology Park
Billingham, Teesside TS23 4EG
01642 566999
newstoday@tynetees.tv
Senior editor: Bill Campbell

ITV Wales

The Television Centre
Culverhouse Cross, Cardiff CF5 6XJ
029 2059 0590
info@itvwales.com
news@itvwales.com
firstname.lastname@itvwales.com
www.itvwales.com
*MD: Roger Lewis; controller of
programmes: Elis Owen; head of
regional affairs: Mansel Jones; head
of news: John G Williams*
PRESS CONTACT: *Mansel Jones*

Carmarthen news office
Coopers Chambers, Lammas Street
Carmarthen
01267 236806
West Wales correspondent: Giles Smith

Colwyn Bay news office
Celtic Business Centre, Plas Eirias
Heritage Gate, Abergele Road
Colwyn Bay LL29 8BW
01492 513888
colwyn@itvwales.com
*North Wales correspondents: Carole
Green, Ian Lang*

Newtown news office
St David's House
Newtown SY16 1RB
01686 623381
Mid-Wales correspondent: Rob Shelley

Wrexham news office
Crown Buildings, 31 Chester Street
Wrexham LL13 8BG
01978 261462
North Wales correspondent: Paul Mewies

ITV West
Television Centre, Bath Road
Bristol BS4 3HG
0117 972 2722
reception@itv.com
firstname.lastname@itv.com
www.itv1west.com
*MD: Mark Haskell; controller of
programmes: Jane McCloskey; head of
features and current affairs: James
Garrett; head of regional affairs:
Richard Lister*
PRESS: *0117 972 2214*

Newsdesk
0117 972 2151/2
itvwestnews@itv.com
Head of news: Liz Hannam

ITV Westcountry
Langage Science Park
Western Wood Way
Plymouth PL7 5BQ
01752 333333
firstname.lastname@itv.com
www.westcountry.co.uk
*MD: Mark Haskell; director of
programmes: Jane McCloskey;
controller, business affairs: Peter
Gregory; director of production
technology: Mark Chaplin; regional
affairs: Rebecca Payne*

Main newsdesk
01752 333329
news@westcountry.co.uk
Controller of news: Phil Carrodus

Barnstaple news office
1 Summerland Terrace
Barnstaple EX32 8JL
01271 324244

Exeter news office
St Luke's Campus
Magdalene Road, Exeter EX4 4WT
01392 499400

Penzance news office
Parade Chambers, 10 Parade Street
Penzance TR18 4BU
01736 331483

Taunton news office
Foundry Cottage, Riverside Place
St James Street, Taunton TA1 1JH
01823 322335

Truro news office
Courtleigh House, Lemon Street
Truro TR1 2PN
01872 262244

Weymouth news office
8 King Street
Weymouth DT4 7BP
01305 760860

ITV Yorkshire
The Television Centre, Kirkstall Road
Leeds, West Yorkshire LS3 1JS
0113 243 8283
firstname.lastname@itv.com
www.yorkshiretv.com
*MD: David Croft, 0113 222 7184;
controller of regional programmes: Clare
Morrow, 0113 222 8724; head of regional
affairs: Mark Covell, 0113 222 7091*
PRESS: *0113 222 7129*

Grimsby office
Immage Studios, Margaret Street
Immingham, Grimsby DN40 1LE
01469 510661
Head of news: Will Venters

Hull office
23 The Prospect Centre
Hull HU2 8PM
01482 324488

Lincoln office
88 Bailgate, Lincoln LN1 3AR
01522 530738

Sheffield office
23 Charter Square, Sheffield S1 4HS
0114 272 7772

York office
York St John's College
Lord Mayors Walk, York YO31 7EX
01904 610066

CHANNELS

ITV2
020 7843 8000
www.itv.com/itv2
*Editor: Zai Bennett, 020 7843 8332;
controller of commissioned programmes:
Daniella Neumann, 020 7843 8101*

ITV3
020 7843 8000
www.itv.com/itv3
*Editor: Steve Arnell, 020 7843 8337;
controller of commissioned programmes:
Daniella Neumann, 020 7843 8101*

ITV News Group
020 7396 6000
*Includes ITV1's national and
international news output, and
regional news for ITV plc franchises (see
above); plus ITV plc's 40% stake in ITN
Chief executive: Clive Jones*

ITV News
ITN, 200 Grays Inn Road
London WC1X 8XZ
020 7833 3000
www.itv.com/news
*ITN is 40% owned by ITV plc
Editor-in-chief: David Mannion;
editor: Deborah Turness; deputy editor:
Jonathan Munro; managing editor:
Robin Elias*

- Key presenters: *Sir Trevor McDonald;
  Mary Nightingale; Katie Derham;
  Mark Austin; Nicholas Owen; Alastair
  Stewart; Andrea Catherwood*
- Editors – *business: Lauren Taylor;
  consumer affairs: Chris Choi;
  international: Bill Neely; political:
  Tom Bradby; science: Lawrence
  McGinty; sport: Tim Ewart; UK: Tom
  Bradby*
- UK correspondents – *news: Adrian
  Britton, Paul Davies, Shiulie Ghosh,
  Lauren Taylor, Mark Webster, Helen
  Wright; political: Angus Walker, Libby
  Wiener, John Ray; north of England:
  Tim Rogers; south of England: Adrian
  Britton; Wales and west of England:
  Geraint Vincent; Scotland: Martin
  Geissler; medical: Sue Saville; crime:
  Dan Rivers; media and arts: Nina
  Nannar; sport: Felicity Barr*
- World correspondents – *international:
  Andrea Catherwood, Penny Marshall,
  James Mates; Europe: Juliet Bremner;
  Washington: Robert Moore; Middle
  East: Julian Manyon; Africa: Neil
  Connery; Asia: John Irvine*
  PRESS: *020 7430 4825
  saskia.wirth@itn.co.uk*
  PRESS RELEASES TO:
  itvplanning@itn.co.uk

ITV News Channel
ITN, 200 Grays Inn Road
London WC1X 8XZ
020 7833 3000
Editor: Ben Rayner

Regional news offices
Part of ITV News Group; listed under
ITV franchises, above

Other ITV plc divisions

Granada
020 7620 1620
*Production arm
Chief executive: Simon Shaps*
PRESS: *020 7843 8218/9*

ITV Consumer
020 7396 6051
*Builds direct consumer revenues
Chief executive officer: Jeff Henry*

ITV Sales
020 7396 6000
*MD: Graham Duff; director of ITV sales:
Gary Digby; director of sales operations:
Jill Kerslake; director of knowledge
management: Andy Bagnall; director of
customer relationship management:
Justin Sampson*

Other ITV1 franchise-holders

SCOTTISH MEDIA GROUP

Chief executive: Andrew Flanagan

Grampian TV
Television Centre
Craigshaw Business Park
West Tullos, Aberdeen AB12 3QH
01224 848848
firstname.lastname@smg.plc.uk
www.grampiantv.co.uk
*MD and controller of regional
programmes: Derrick Thomson; head
of news: Henry Eagles*
PRESS: *Lyndsay Scatterty
01224 848820
lyndsay.scatterty@grampiantv.co.uk*

Scottish TV
200 Renfield Street, Glasgow G2 3PR
0141 300 3000
firstname.lastname@smg.plc.uk
www.scottishtv.co.uk
*MD and controller of regional
programmes: Bobby Hain; head of
news: Paul Mckinney. Newsdesk: 0141
300 3360*
PRESS: *Kirsten Elsby, 0141 300 3670
kirstin.elsby@smg.plc.uk*

INDEPENDENT FRANCHISES

Channel Television
Television Centre, La Pouquelaye
St Helier, Jersey JE1 3ZD
01534 816816
broadcast@channeltv.co.uk
www.channeltv.co.uk
*MD: Michael Lucas; director of
programmes: Karen Rankine
(karen.rankine@channeltv.co.uk);
director of special projects: Gordon de Ste
Croix (gordon@channeltv.co.uk);
director of resources and transmission:
Kevin Banner. Newsroom: 01534 816688*
Guernsey office
Television House, Bulwer Avenue
St Sampson, Guernsey GY2 4LA
01481 241888
broadcast.gsy@channeltv.co.uk
London office
Enterprise House, 1-2 Hatfields,
London SE1 9PG
020 7633 9902

UTV
Ormeau Road, Belfast BT7 1EB
028 9032 8122
info@utvplc.com
www.u.tv
*Group chief executive: John McCann;
director of television: Alan Bremner*
PRESS: *028 9026 2187*

Channel 4

124 Horseferry Road
London SW1P 2TX
020 7396 4444
www.channel4.co.uk
*Chief executive: Andy Duncan, 020
7306 8700; commercial director: Andy
Barnes, 020 7306 8200; director of
television: Kevin Lygo, 020 7306 3775*
PRESS: *Matt Baker, 020 7306 8666*

COMMISSIONING

Managing editor: Janey Walker,
020 7306 8623 (assistant: Melissa
Hameed, 020 7306 8282); Editorial
manager, cultural diversity:
Mary Fitzpatrick, 020 7306 6454;
Disability advisor: Alison Walsh,
020 7306 8125

Comedy
Head of comedy and comedy films:
Caroline Leddy, 020 7306 8718

Daytime and features
Commissioning editor, daytime:
Adam MacDonald, 020 7306 8033;
editor, daytime and features: Mark
Downie, 020 7306 5150

Documentaries
Head: Danny Cohen, 020 7306
6912; commissioning editors:
Meredith Chambers, 020 7306
5571; Simon Dickson, 020 7306
3799; Dominique Walker, 020 7306
3763

E4
Head: Julian Bellamy, 020 7306
6436; commissioning editor: Angela
Jain, 020 7306 8515; head of
scheduling: David Booth, 020 7306
6582; planner: Shireen Tayabali, 020
7306 5591

Education
Head: Heather Rabbatts, 020 7306
5125; commissioning editors:
Deborah Ward, 020 7306 8499, and
Adam Gee, 020 7306 8306

Entertainment
Head: Andrew Newman, 020 7306
6382

Factual entertainment
Head: Julian Bellamy, 020 7306 6436;
editors: Nav Raman, 020 7306 8746,
and Andrew Mackenzie, 020 7306
3680

Features
Head: Sue Murphy, 020 7306 8279;
commissioning editors: Emma
Westcott, 020 7306 8476, Philippa
Ransford, 020 7306 8424, and Liam
Humphreys, 020 7306 6932

Film and drama
Head: Tessa Ross, 020 7306 6455;
senior commissioning editor: Francis
Hopkinson, 020 7306 6970; editor
(series): Camilla Campbell, 020 7306
3783; deputy commissioning editor
(events): Hannah Weaver, 020 7306
5536; assistant editor: Liz Pilling, 020
7306 6621; head of development:
Katherine Butler; head of Filmfour
Lab: Peter Carlton

History, science, religion and arts
Head: Hamish Mykura, 020 7306
1036; commissioning editors: Aaqil
Ahmed, 020 7306 8065, and Jan
Younghusband, 020 7306 5153.
Editor: Louise Bolch, 020 7306 8039

Nations and regions
Director: Stuart Cosgrove, 0141 568
7105

News and current affairs
Head: Dorothy Byrne, 020 7306
8568; commissioning editor
(investigations): Kevin Sutcliffe, 020
7306 1068

**Programming planning and
strategy**
Head: Jules Oldroyd, 020 7306
8229; editor: Neil McCallum, 020
7306 8588; assistant editor: Cath
Lovesey, 020 7306 5622

Sport
Deputy commissioning editor:
Deborah Poulton, 020 7306 8501

Programme acquisition
Jeff Ford, 020 7306 8747

BROADCASTING

Controller: Rosemary Newell, 020 7306
8620; head of schedules: Jules
Oldroyd, 020 7306 8229; deputy
scheduler: John Williams, 020 7306
8257; planner: Lynne Jarrett, 020
7306 8231; senior planner: Lucy
Rogers, 020 7306 8401
Sales and marketing – agency sales:
Matt Shreeve, 020 7306 8240; airtime
management: Merlin Inkley, 020 7306
8254; marketing director: Polly
Cochrane, 020 7306 6446; research
and insight: Claire Grimmond, 020
7306 8779; sponsorship: David
Charlesworth, 020 7306 8043;
strategic sales: Mike Parker 020 7306
8242; strategy: Jonathan Thompson,
020 7306 8799

Business services

124 Facilities
Tony Chamberlain, 020 7306 8110
Channel Four International
Graeme Mason, 020 7306 3796
Consumer products
Mike Morris, 020 7306 5364
Digital channels
Dan Brooke, 020 7306 6497

E4

Julian Bellamy, 020 7306 6436

FilmFour channel

Tom Sykes, 020 7306 6442

New media

Andy Taylor, 020 7306 3651

Channel 4 News

ITN

200 Grays Inn Road
London WC1X 8XZ
020 7833 3000
www.channel4.com/news
*Editor: Jim Gray; deputy editor:
Martin Fewell; managing editor: Gay
Flashman. Newsdesk: 020 7430 4601
Press: 020 7430 4220,
fiona.railton@itn.co.uk*

- Presenters – *anchor: Jon Snow; noon
  anchor: Krishnan Guru-Murthy;
  senior reporter: Sue Turton; presenter:
  Samira Ahmed*

- Senior editors – *home: Evette
  Edwards; foreign: Deborah Rayner.
  International editor: Lindsey Hilsum*

- Commissioning editor, independent
  productions: *Fiona Campbell*

- Chief correspondent: *Alex Thomson.
  Other correspondents – Asia: Ian
  Williams; arts: Nicholas Glass;
  economics: Liam Halligan; foreign
  affairs: Jonathan Miller; home affairs:
  Simon Israel; Midlands: Carl Dinnen;
  political: Gary Gibbon; science: Tom
  Clarke; science/defence: Julian Rush;
  social affairs: Victoria Macdonald;
  Washington: Jonathan Rugman.
  Correspondent: Sarah Smith*

Five

22 Long Acre, London WC2E 9LY
020 7550 5555
firstname.lastname@five.tv
www.five.tv
*Director of programmes: Dan
Chambers, 020 7550 5673 (PA: Sarah
Jackson, 020 7550 5522); controller of
broadcast services: David Burge, 020
7691 6260; history: Alex Sutherland*

- Controllers – *arts, daytime and
  religion: Kim Peat, 020 7421 7107;
  children's programmes: Nick Wilson;
  factual entertainment: Steve Gowans
  (deputy commissioning editor: Ian
  Dunkley, 020 7550 5659); features
  and entertainment: Ben Frow,
  020 7421 7118; news: Chris Shaw,
  020 7421 7122 (deputy: Ian Russell,
  020 7550 5529); science: Justine
  Kershaw, 020 7421 7112; sport:
  Robert Charles, 020 7421 7185;
  special events and pop features:
  Sham Sandhu, 020 7421 7184*

- Drama editor: *Abigail Webber*

- Press: *020 7550 5533; head of press
  and corporate affairs: Paul Leather,
  020 7550 5541; deputy: Tracey
  O'Connor, 020 7550 5553; marketing
  and publicity executive: Louise
  Bowers, 020 7550 5662*

- Heads of publicity – *acquisitions and
  drama: Tamara Bishopp, 020 7550
  5539; factual and features: Louise
  Plank, 020 7550 5659*

- Publicists – *arts, history and daytime:
  Allison Broodie, 020 7550 5587;
  entertainment: Nick Dear, 020 7550
  5634; factual and features: Stephanie
  Faber, 020 7550 5589; science and
  pop features: Elin Rees, 020 7550
  5538*

five news

Unit 1, Sky News, Grant Way,
Isleworth, Middlesex TW7 5QD
020 7800 2705
www.five.tv/news
*Editor: Mark Calvert; deputy editor:
Josie MacRae; head of newsgathering:
Andy Bell*

- Presenters: *Kirsty Young, Kate
  Sanderson, Lara Lewington*

- Political editor: *Michael Wilson*

- Chief correspondent: *Stuart Ramsay*

- Correspondents – *northern: Peter
  Lane; sport: Alex Thomas*

- Reporters and correspondents: *Cathy
  Jones, Catherine Jacob, Lindley
  Gooden, Jason Farrel*

- PRESS: *020 7800 4289. Senior
  publicist: Stella Tooth*

Other departments

Acquisitions
Director: Jay Kandona, 020 7421 7166

Interactive
Producer: Steven Bonner, 020 7550
5663

Scheduling and planning
Director: Susanna Dinnage,
020 7550 5588

RTÉ (Ireland)

Radio Telefís Éireann
Donnybrook, Dublin 4, Ireland
00 353 1 208 3111
info@rte.ie
www.rte.ie
*Irish national broadcaster. Managing
director of television: Noel Curran;
managing director of news: Ed
Mulhall; director of communications:
Bride Rosney*

PRESS: *00 353 1 208 3434
press@rte.ie*

- Press contacts
  *(firstname.lastname@rte.ie) –
  acquisitions and drama: Sharon
  Brady; entertainment: Dympna
  Clerkin; factual: Dervla Keating; Fair
  City (soap): Tara O'Brian; music, sport
  and young people: Richie Ryan; news
  and current affairs: Carolyn Fisher*

KEY GOVERNMENT CONTACTS
FOR DIGITAL TV

Department for Culture, Media and Sport
2–4 Cockspur Street
London SW1Y 5DH
020 7211 6000
digitaltelevision@culture.gov.uk
www.digitaltelevision.gov.uk
Culture secretary: Tessa Jowell
PRESS: *020 7211 6267*
    mark.devane@culture.gsi.gov.uk
SWITCHCO PRESS OFFICE:
    020 7737 7008

DTI
1 Victoria Street, London SW1H 0ET
020 7215 5000
dti.enquiries@dti.gsi.gov.uk
www.dti.gov.uk/industries
    /broadcasting
Head of broadcasting policy and director of digital television project: Jane Humphreys; deputy project manager, digital television: David Fuhr; head of broadcasting technology: Ian Dixon
PRESS: *020 7215 6403*
    nic.fearon-low@dti.gsi.gov.uk

BSkyB

British Sky Broadcasting
Grant Way, Isleworth TW7 5QD
0870 240 3000
www.sky.com
Chief executive: James Murdoch; chief operating officer: Richard Freudenstein; chief marketing officer: Jon Florsheim; MD, Sky Sports: Vic Wakeling Director of corporate communications: Julian Eccles; director of publicity: Adrian Lee; head of programme publicity: Richard Turner; Sky One: Chris Aylott; Sky Movies: Phil Evans; Sky Sports: Chris Haynes; consumer PR: Gabby Bennett
PRESS: *0870 240 3000*

SKY CHANNELS

Grant Way, Isleworth TW7 5QD
0870 240 3000

Sky Bet
www.skybet.com
Marketing director: Simon Miller Consumer PR manager: Heidi Bruckland
PRESS: *020 7705 3275*

Sky Box Office
www.skymovies.com
Head of pay-per-view: Karen Saunders Publicity manager: Phil Evans
PRESS: *020 7800 4252*
    skymoviespublicity@bskyb.com

Sky Cinema 1 & 2
www.skymovies.com
Director of film channels and acquisitions: Sophie Turner-Laing Publicity manager: Phil Evans
PRESS: *020 7800 4252*
    skymoviespublicity@bskyb.com

Sky Customer Channel
Consumer PR manager: Heidi Bruckland
PRESS: *020 7705 3275*

Sky Movies 1–9
www.skymovies.com
Director of film channels and acquisitions: Sophie Turner-Laing Publicity manager: Phil Evans
PRESS: *020 7800 4252*
    skymoviespublicity@bskyb.com

Sky News
Newsdesk: news.plan@bskyb.com
www.skynews.co.uk
Head of Sky News: Nick Pollard

- Key presenters – *Afternoon: Kay Burley, Mark Longhurst; Live at Five: Anna Botting, Jeremy Thompson*
- Correspondents – *business: Michael Wilson; crime: Martin Brunt; entertainment: Neil Sean, Matt Smith; foreign: Richard Bestic, Rachel Amatt, Emma Hurd, Laurence Lee, Tim Marshall, David Chater, Dominic Waghorn, Andrew Wilson, Ian Woods; health: Nicola Hill, Thomas Moore; political: Adam Boulton, Jon Craig, Jenny Percival, Peter Spencer, Glen O'Glaza; royal: Geoff Meade; other: David Bowden, Michelle Clifford, Lisa Holland, Peter Sharp*
- PRESS: *020 7800 4289*
SENIOR PUBLICIST: *Stella Tooth;*
HEAD OF PROGRAMME PUBLICITY:
Richard Turner

Sky One
www.skyone.co.uk
Controller: James Baker
PRESS: *020 7805 7276*
Acting publicity manager: Chris Aylott; head of programme publicity: Richard Turner. Publicists for programmes – 24: Tom Mackey; Battlestar Galactica, Law & Order, Enterprise: Chris Aylott; Cold Case, Malcolm in the Middle: Gayle Hemmings and Melanie Adorian; Nip/Tuck, The Simpsons: Lee Robson)

Sky Mix
www.skyone.co.uk
Controller: James Baker
PRESS: *020 7805 7276.* ACTING
PUBLICITY MANAGER: *Chris Aylott;*
HEAD OF PROGRAMME PUBLICITY:
Richard Turner

Sky Sports 1, 2 & 3
www.skysports.com
MD: Vic Wakeling
PRESS: *020 7800 4254.* HEAD OF
PRESS AND PUBLICITY: *Chris Haynes*

Sky Sports Extra
www.skysports.com
MD: Vic Wakeling
PRESS: *020 7800 4254.* HEAD OF
PRESS AND PUBLICITY: *Chris Haynes*

Sky Sports News
www.skysports.com
MD: Vic Wakeling
PRESS: *020 7800 4254.* HEAD OF
PRESS AND PUBLICITY: *Chris Haynes*

Sky Travel
www.skytravel.co.uk
General manager: Barbara Gibbon
PRESS: *richard.turner@bskyb.com*

Sky Travel Extra
www.skytravel.co.uk
General manager: Barbara Gibbon
PRESS: *richard.turner@bskyb.com*

Sky Travel Shop
www.skytravel.co.uk
General manager: Barbara Gibbon
PRESS: *richard.turner@bskyb.com*

Sky Travel +1
www.skytravel.co.uk
General manager: Barbara Gibbon
PRESS: *richard.turner@bskyb.com*

Sky Vegas Live
www.skyvegaslive.com
Executive producer: Peter Ward
PRESS: *020 7705 3416.*
CONSUMER PR EXECUTIVE: *Tara Hicks*

DEPARTMENTS

Sky Active
www.sky.com/skyactive
MD, Sky Interactive: Ian Shepherd

Sky Business
www.sky.com/business
Sales to non-domestic clients. Commercial marketing director: Iain Holden

Sky Ventures
www.sky.com/ventures
Joint venture channels and services. Director of Sky Ventures: Matthew Imi

Cable

NTL
NTL House
Bartley Wood Business Park
Bartley Way, Hook
Hampshire RG27 9UP
01256 752000
www.ntl.com
CEO: Simon Duffy
PRESS: *01256 752663.* HEAD OF
CORPORATE PR: *Justine Smith;* HEAD
OF CONSUMER PR: *Malcolm Padley*

Cablecom Investments
The Coach House, Bill Hill Park
Wokingham, Berks RG40 5QT
0845 230 0028
customer@cablecom.co.uk
www.cablecom.co.uk
MD: Charles Tompkins

Telewest Global
Export House, Cawsey Way
Woking, Surrey GU21 6QX
01483 750900
www.telewest.co.uk
Acting chief executive: Barry Elson
PRESS: *020 7299 5888*
HEAD OF MEDIA RELATIONS: *Kirstine Cox*

WightCable
56 Love Lane, Cowes
Isle of Wight PO31 7EU
01983 242424
enquiries@wightcable.com
www.wightcable.com
CEO: Duncan Kerr

WightCable North
3 Chalmers Place
Riverside Business Park
Irvine, North Ayrshire KA11 5DH
01294 230000
enquiries@wightcablenorth.com
www.wightcablenorth.com
MD: Sandra Ayres
PRESS: *01294 231145*
    pr@wightcablenorth.com
CONTACT: *Gillian Gordon*

Video Networks
205 Holland Park Avenue
London W11 4XB
020 7348 4000
info@videonetworks.com
www.videonetworks.com+G35
Chairman and CEO: Roger Lynch
PRESS: *020 7348 4110*
HEAD OF PR: *Nick Southall*

Digital terrestrial

Freeview
Broadcast Centre, (BC3 D5)
201 Wood Lane, London W12 7TP
020 8743 8000
www.freeview.co.uk
*Free-to-view digital terrestrial service,
owned by Crown Castle, BBC and BSkyB.
General manager: Lib Charlesworth*
PRESS: *020 7229 4400.* CONSUMER:
Lucy Mayo; CORPORATE: *Hannah
Bailey – both firstname.lastname@
nelsonbostock.com*

Arqiva
Crawley Court, Winchester
Hampshire SO21 2QA
01962 823434
firstname.surname@arqiva.com
www.arqiva.com
*Formerly NTL Broadcast. CEO: Tom
Bennie; MD, media solutions: Steve
Holebrook*
PRESS: *01962 822582*
COMMUNICATIONS MANAGER: *Bruce
Randall*

Crown Castle UK
Warwick Technology Park
Gallows Hill, Heathcote Lane
Warwick CV34 6TN
01926 416000
MarketingUK@crowncastle.co.uk
www.crowncastle.co.uk
*Digital terrestrial transmitter
operator; part-owner of Freeview
MD: Peter Abery*
PRESS: *01926 416870.*
COMMUNICATIONS MANAGER: *Stephen
Arnold*

Top-Up TV
PO Box 208, Twickenham TW1 2YF
0870 054 5354
enquiries@topuptv.com
www.topuptv.com
*Offers top-up pay channels for Freeview
viewers. Chairman: David Chance*

TV channels

ABC1
Chiswick Park, Building 12
566 Chiswick High Road
London W4 5AN
020 8636 2000
VP programming: James Neal
PRESS: *rachel.babington@disney.com*

Adventure One
Grant Way, Isleworth TW7 5QD
0870 240 3000
www.nationalgeographic.co.uk
Contact: Emma Moloney

African and Caribbean TV
28F Lawrence Road
London N15 4EG
020 8809 7700
actv4@yahoo.com
www.actv.org.uk
Programme controller: Dawn Grant

The Amp
Chart Show, 37 Harwood Road
London SW6 4QP
020 7371 5999
www.theamp.tv
Head of music: Sarah Gaugham

Animal Planet
Discovery House, Chiswick Park
Building 2, 566 Chiswick High Road
London W4 5YB
020 8811 3000
www.discoverychannel.co.uk
Channel director: Eliza Burrows
PRESS: *delyth_hughes@
        discovery-europe.com*

Artsworld
Great West House (15th floor)
Great West Road, Brentford
Middlesex TW8 9DF
020 7805 2404
www.artsworld.com
Scheduling manager: Kate Potter
PRESS: *alyssa.bonic@artsworld.com*

AsiaNet
Asianet Complex, Puliyarakonam PO
Trivandrum 695 573 India
00 91 471 237 8407
www.asianetglobal.com

ATN Bangla
WASA Bhaban, 1st Floor
98 Kazi Nazrul Islam Avenue
Kawran Bazar, Dhaka 1215
Bangladesh
00 880 811 1207/08/09/10
info@atnbangla.tv
www.atnbangla.tv

attheraces
11–13 Charlotte Street
London W1T 1RH
020 7566 8911
studio@attheraces.co.uk
www.attheraces.co.uk
MD: Matthew Imi

Authentic TV
www.authentictv.tv

AVAGO
PO Box 42514, London E1W 2WA
0845 006 0235
www.avago.tv
Head of gaming: Damian Cope

B4
37 Harwood Road, London SW6 4QP
020 7371 5999
sarah@chartshow.tv
Head of channels: Chris Boardman

B4U
Transputec House
19 Heather Park Drive
Wembley HA0 1SS
020 8795 7171
www.b4utv.com
Programme controller: Anita Roy
PRESS: *sajnit@b4unetwork.com*

B4U Music
Transputec House
19 Heather Park Drive
Wembley HA0 1SS
020 8795 7171
www.b4utv.com
Programme controller: Anita Roy
PRESS: *sajnit@b4unetwork.com*

Bad Movies
179–181 The Vale, London W3 7RW
020 8600 9700
www.sit-up.tv
MD: Chris Manson

BBC America
PO Box 6266, Florence
KY 41022-6266 USA
00 1 859 342 4070
www.bbcamerica.com
Programme executive: Alison Fredericks

BBC Canada
121 Bloor Street East, Suite 200
Toronto, Ontario, Canada M4W 3M5
00 416 967 3249
feedback@bbccanada.com
www.bbccanada.com

BBC Food
PO Box 5054, London W12 0ZY
020 8433 2221
www.bbcfood.com
Editor: David Weiland

BBC Four
Television Centre
0870 010 0222
www.bbc.co.uk/bbcfour
Controller: Janice Hadlow

BBC Japan
PO Box 5054, London W12 0ZY
www.bbcjapan.tv

BBC News 24
Television Centre
020 8743 8000
bbcnews24@bbc.co.uk
www.bbc.co.uk/bbcnews24
Editorial director: Mark Popescu

BBC One
Television Centre
020 8743 8000
www.bbc.co.uk/bbcone
Controller: Peter Fincham

BBC Parliament
4 Millbank, London SW1P 3JA
020 7973 6216
parliament@bbc.co.uk
www.bbc.co.uk/bbcparliament

BBC Prime
PO Box 5054, London W12 0ZY
020 8433 2221
bbcprime@bbc.co.uk
www.bbcprime.com
Editor: David Weiland

BBC Three
Television Centre
020 8743 8000
www.bbc.co.uk/bbcthree
Controller: Stuart Murphy

BBC Two
Television Centre
020 8743 8000
www.bbc.co.uk/bbctwo
*Controller: Roly Keating; controller of
daytime: Jay Hunt*

BBC World
PO Box 5054, London W12 0ZY
020 8433 2221
bbcworld@bbc.co.uk
www.bbcworld.com
Editorial director: Sian Kevill

BBCi (interactive TV)
Television Centre
020 8743 8000
www.bbc.co.uk/digital/tv
*Controller: Rahul Chakkara; head,
interactive TV programming: Emma
Somerville*

BEN
25 Ashley Road, London N17 9LJ
020 8808 8800
info@bentelevision.com
www.bentelevision.com
Head of programming: Ife Akim

Best Direct
Sentinel House, Poundwell
Modbury PL21 0ZZ
0871 555 5252
www.bestdirect.tv
Account manager: Mary Hastings

Bid TV
Sit-Up House, 179–181 The Vale,
London W3 7RW
0870 165 1647
www.bid.tv

Big Game TV
PO Box 5372, London W1A 8WN
020 7432 7300
www.biggame.tv

Biography Channel
Grant Way, Isleworth TW7 5QD
020 7371 5399
www.thebiographychannel.co.uk
Channel director: Richard Melman
PRESS: *020 7941 5199*
biographychannelpress@bskyb.com

Bloomberg
City Gate House
39–45 Finsbury Square
London EC2A 1PQ
020 7330 7797
newsalert@bloomberg.net
www.bloomberg.com/tv
Executive editor, broadcast: Ken Cohn

Boomerang
Turner House
16 Great Marlborough Street
London W1F 7HS
020 7693 1000
www.cartoonnetwork.co.uk
Channel manager: Dan Balaam
PRESS: *alastair.edwards@turner.com*
PRESS WEBSITE:
www.europe.turnerinfo.com

The Box
Mappin House, 4 Winsley Street
London W1W 8HF
020 7182 8000
www.emap.com
*Programme director: Dave Young;
director of music: Simon Sadler*
PRESS: *maureen.corish@emap.com*

Bravo
160 Great Portland Street
London W1W 5QA
020 7299 5000
www.bravo.co.uk
Programme controller: Jonathan Webb
PRESS: *jakki_lewis@flextech.co.uk*

British Eurosport
Eurosport TV
Heathrow West Business Park
Heron Drive, Langley SL3 8XP
020 7468 7777
www.eurosport.co.uk
Programming director: Pierre Jean Sebert
PRESS: *01753 452500*
mhorler@eurosport.com

British Eurosport 2
Eurosport TV
Heathrow West Business Park
Heron Drive, Langley SL3 8XP
020 7468 7777
www.eurosport.com
*Programming director: Pierre Jean
Sebert*
PRESS: *mhorler@eurosport.com,
01753 452500*

Channel 4
124 Horseferry Road
London SW1P 2TX
020 7396 4444
www.channel4.com
*Chief executive: Andy Duncan, 020
7306 8700; commercial director: Andy
Barnes, 020 7306 8200; director of
television: Kevin Lygo, 020 7306 3775*

Cartoon Network
Turner House
16 Great Marlborough Street
London W1F 7HS
020 7693 1000
www.cartoonnetwork.co.uk
Channel manager: Don Gardiner
PRESS: *alastair.edwards@turner.com*
PRESS WEBSITE:
www.europe.turnerinfo.com

CBBC
Television Centre
020 8743 8000
www.bbc.co.uk/cbbc
*Controller: Alison Sharman; chief
operating officer: Richard Deverell*

CBeebies
Television Centre
020 8743 8000
www.bbc.co.uk/cbeebies
Controller: Alison Sharman

CCTV9
cctv-9-mail1@cctv-9.com
www.cctv9.tv

CFC TV
The Christian Family Channel
2 Silver Rd, Shepherds Bush
London W12 7SG
www.cfctv.com

Challenge
160 Great Portland Street
London W1W 5QA
020 7299 5000
www.challenge.co.uk
Programme controller: Jonathan Webb
PRESS: *jakki_lewis@flextech.co.uk*

Channel U
Video Interactive Television
Studio4, 3 Lever Street
London EC1V 3QU
020 7054 9010
info@vitv.co.uk
www.u-music.tv

Chart Show TV
37 Harwood Road, London SW6 4QP
020 7371 5999
info@chartshow.tv
www.chartshow.tv
Music coordinator: Sarah Gaughan

Chelsea TV
Stamford Bridge, Fulham Road
London SW6 1HS
020 7915 1980
chelseatv@chelseafc.com
www.chelseafc.com
MD: Chris Tate

Chinese Channel
Teddington Studios, Broom Road
Teddington TW11 9NT
020 8614 8364
newseditor@chinese-channel.co.uk
www.chinese-channel.co.uk
Head of programming: Desmond Ng

Classic FM TV
7 Swallow Place, London W1B 2AG
020 7343 9000
classicfmtv@classicfm.com
www.classicfm.com/tv
Station manager: Darren Henley

Classics TV
The Media Centre
131–151 Great Titchfield Street
London W1W 5BB
020 7663 3651
www.classicstv.co.uk
Contact: Petra Oblak

CNBC Europe
10 Fleet Place, London EC4M 7QS
020 7653 9300
www.cnbceurope.com
Executive producers: Harry Fuller,
John Casey
PRESS: *cblenkinsop@cnbceurope.com*

CNN
Turner House
16 Great Marlborough Street
London W1F 7HS
020 7693 1000
www.cnn.com
International managing editor for
EMEA: Nick Wrenn
PRESS: *020 7693 0942*
chris.dwyer@turner.com

Community Channel
3–7 Euston Centre, Regent's Place
London NW1 3JG
020 7874 7626
info@communitychannel.org
www.communitychannel.org
Channel controller: Nick Ware

Create and Craft
Ideal Home House
Newark Road, Peterborough
Cambridgeshire PE1 5WG
08700 777002
customerservices@
idealshoppingdirect.co.uk
www.createandcraft.tv
CEO: Andrew Fryatt

Dating Channel
130 City Road, London EC1V 2NW
020 7748 1500
info@thedatingchannel.com
www.thedatingchannel.com
Mobile technical manager: Paul Doyle

Digital Broadcasting Company
Radio House, 19 Clifftown Road
Southend-on-Sea SS0 1AB
01702 337321
www.digitalbroadcastingcompany
.co.uk

Discovery Channel
Discovery House, Chiswick Park
Building 2, 566 Chiswick High Road
London W4 5YB
020 8811 3000
www.discoverychannel.co.uk
Channel director, senior vice-president:
Jill Offman
PRESS:
lynn_li@discovery-europe.com

Discovery Civilisation
Discovery House, Chiswick Park
Building 2, 566 Chiswick High Road
London W4 5YB
020 8811 3000
www.discoverychannel.co.uk
Channel director, senior vice-president:
Jill Offman
PRESS:
kate_buddle@discovery-europe.com

Discovery Home & Health
Discovery House, Chiswick Park
Building 2, 566 Chiswick High Road
London W4 5YB
020 8811 3000
www.discoverychannel.co.uk
Channel director: Clare Laycock
PRESS:
libby_rowley@discovery-europe.com

Discovery Kids
Discovery House, Chiswick Park
Building 2, 566 Chiswick High Road
London W4 5YB
020 8811 3000
www.discoverychannel.co.uk
Channel director: Clare Laycock
PRESS:
libby_rowley@discovery-europe.com

Discovery Real Time
Discovery House, Chiswick Park
Building 2, 566 Chiswick High Road
London W4 5YB
020 8811 3000
www.realtimetv.co.uk
Channel director, vice-president: Paul
Welling
PRESS:
claire_phillips@discovery-europe.com

Discovery Science
Discovery House, Chiswick Park
Building 2, 566 Chiswick High Road
London W4 5YB
020 8811 3000
www.discoverychannel.co.uk
Channel director, senior vice-president:
Jill Offman
PRESS:
kate_buddle@discovery-europe.com

Discovery Travel and Living
Discovery House, Chiswick Park
Building 2, 566 Chiswick High Road
London W4 5YB
020 8811 3000
www.travelandliving.co.uk
Channel director, vice-president: Paul
Welling
PRESS:
claire_phillips@discovery-europe.com

Discovery Wings
Discovery House, Chiswick Park
Building 2, 566 Chiswick High Road
London W4 5YB
020 8811 3000
www.discoverychannel.co.uk
Channel director, senior vice-president:
Jill Offman
PRESS:
kate_buddle@discovery-europe.com

Disney Channel
Chiswick Park, Building 12
566 Chiswick High Road
London W4 5AN
020 8636 2000
www.disneychannel.co.uk
VP programming: James Neal
PRESS: *rachel.babington@disney.com*

DM Digital
Lower Ground Floor
33/35 Turner Street
Manchester M4 1DW
0161 795 4844
zahidh76@yahoo.com
Contact: Zahidh Hussain

DW-TV
Voltastr. 6, D-13355 Berlin, Germany
00 49 30 4646 0
www.dw-world.de/dw
Head DW-TV: Christoph Lanz

E!
www.eonline.com

E4
124 Horseferry Road
London SW1P 2TX
020 7396 4444
www.channel4.com/e4
Head: Julian Bellamy, 020 7306 6436

eeZee TV
Regis Road, Kentish Town
London NW5 3EG
0870 1287 288
www.eezeetv.co.uk
PRESS: *020 7691 3822*
press@eeZeetv.com

Escape
681 Falmouth Road, Mashpee
MA 02649 USA
00 1 508 477 9385
info@escapetv.tv
www.escapetv.tv

Euro News
60, Chemin des Mouilles, BP 131
F-69131 Lyon-Ecully, France
00 33 4 7218 8000
www.euronews.net
PRESS: *00 33 4 72 18 80 56*

Exchange & Mart TV
Link House, 25 West Street, Poole
Dorset BH15 1LL
01202 445000
tim.brown@unitedadvertising.co.uk
www.exchangeandmart.co.uk/tv
Business development manager: Tim
Brown

Express Shopping Channel
Griffin House, 40 Lever Street
Manchester M60 6ES
020 7308 5283
expressyourself@expressshopping.tv
www.expressshopping.tv
Channel controller: David Holmans

Extreme Sports Channel
The Media Centre, 19 Bolsover Street
London W1W 5NΛ
020 7886 0770
www.extreme.com
Head of acquisitions: Alex Barnes
PRESS:
stuart@extremesportschannel.com

Fantasy Channel
Suite 14, Burlington House
St Saviours Road, St Helier
Jersey JE2 4LA
01534 703700
pfarell@nasnet.je
Programme controller: Peter Farell

Fashion TV
Production Paris, 49
rue Jules Guesde
92300 Levallois Perret – France
00 33 1 4505 4545
info@ftv.com
www.ftv.com
London office: jessica@ftv.com

FilmFour
124 Horseferry Road
London SW1P 2TX
020 7396 4444
www.channel4.com/film/ffchannel
Head: Tom Sykes, 020 7306 6442

five
22 Long Acre, London WC2E 9LY
020 7550 5555
firstname.lastname@five.tv
www.five.tv
Director of programmes: Dan
Chambers, 020 7550 5673 (PA Sarah
Jackson, 020 7550 5522); controller of
broadcast services: David Burge, 020
7691 6260
PRESS: *020 7550 5533*

Fizz
Video Interactive Television
Studio4, 3 Lever Street
London EC1V 3QU
020 7054 9010
info@vitv.co.uk
Contact: Darren Platt

Flaunt
Grant Way, Isleworth TW7 5QD
0870 240 3000
www.flaunt.tv

Fox News
1211 Avenue of the Americas
New York NY 10036
00 1 888 369 4762
foxaroundtheworld@foxnews.com
www.foxnews.com
Senior vice president, corporate
communications: Brian Lewis, 001 212
301 3331, brian.lewis@foxnews.com;
vice president, media relations: Irena
Briganti, 001 212 301 3608,
irena.briganti@foxnews.com

FTN
160 Great Portland Street
London W1W 5QA
020 7299 5000
www.ftn.tv
Programme controller: Richard Woolfe
PRESS: *judy_wells@flextech.co.uk*
jessica_alder@flextech.co.uk

FX and Fox Movie Channel
10000 Santa Monica Blvd
Los Angeles, CA 90067 USA
00 1 310 286 3800
www.fxnetworks.com
Vice president, public relations: John
Solberg, 00 1 310 789 4689; manager,
public relations: Roslyn Bibby, 00 1
310 789 4640

Game Network
Via Bisceglie 71\73, 20152 Milano
Italy
www.game-network.net

Gay Date TV
130 City Road, London EC1V 2NW
020 7748 1500
info@gaydatetv.co.uk
www.gaydatetv.co.uk
Mobile technical manager: Paul Doyle

Gems TV
Eagle Road Studios, Eagle Road
Redditch B98 9HF

GEO TV
geouk@geo.tv
www.geo.tv

Get Lucky TV
www.getlucky.tv

God TV
Angel House, Borough Road
Sunderland, Tyne and Wear SR1 1HW
0191 568 0800
info@god.tv
www.god.tv
UK regional director: Johnny Woodrow

The Golf Channel UK
1 Kingsgate, Bradford Business
Park, Canal Road, Bradford
West Yorkshire BD1 4SJ
www.thegolfchanneluk.com
PRESS: *press@golftvinfo.co.uk*

Golf TV Pro-Shop
1 Kingsgate, Bradford Business
Park, Canal Road, Bradford
West Yorkshire BD1 4SJ
customer@golftvproshop.com
www.golftvproshop.com

Hallmark
234a Kings Road, London SW3 5UA
020 7368 9100
info@hallmarkchannel.co.uk
www.hallmarkchannel.co.uk
Director of acquisitions: Rosy Hill-Davies
PRESS:
janemuirhead@hallmarkchannel.com

History Channel
Grant Way, Isleworth TW7 5QD
020 7371 5399
www.thehistorychannel.co.uk
Channel director: Richard Melman
PRESS: *020 7941 5199*
historychannelpress@bskyb.com

Hits Channel
Mappin House, 4 Winsley Street
London W1W 8HF
020 7182 8000
www.emapadvertising.com
Programme director: Dave Young;
director of music: Simon Sadler
PRESS: *maureen.corish@emap.com*

Hollywood.com Television (HTV)
2255 Glades Road, Suite 219A
Boca Raton, FL 33431 USA
00 1 561 998 8000
www.hollywood.com
Chairman and CEO: Mitchell
Rubenstein; COO: Nicholas Hall

The Horror Channel
info@horrorchannel.com
www.thehorrorchannel.tv

i Sports TV
Television Gaming Group
6–7 Princes Court
Wapping Lane, London E1W 2DA
020 7942 7942
www.isports.tv
MD: Damian Cope

Ideal Vitality
Ideal Home House
Newark Road, Peterborough
Cambridgeshire PE1 5WG
08700 777002
customerservices@
idealshoppingdirect.co.uk
www.idealvitality.tv
CEO: Andrew Fryatt

Ideal World
Ideal Home House
Newark Road, Peterborough
Cambridgeshire PE1 5WG
08700 777002
customerservices@
idealshoppingdirect.co.uk
www.idealworld.tv
CEO: Andrew Fryatt

INI
Charlotte, North Carolina USA
00 1 704 525 9800
info@ini.tv.
www.ini.tv

Islam Channel
14 Bonhill Street, London EC2A 4BX
020 7374 4516
www.islamchannel.tv
PRESS: *pr@islamchannel.tv*

ITV News
200 Grays Inn Road
London WC1X 8XZ
020 7833 3000
www.itv.com/news
Editor: Ben Rayner

ITV1
200 Grays Inn Road
London WC1X 8HF
020 7843 8000
www.itv.com/itv1
ITV Network contacts: see page 158

ITV2
200 Grays Inn Road
London WC1X 8HF
020 7843 8000
www.itv.com/itv2
Channel editor: Zai Bennett; controller
of commissioned programmes:
Daniella Neumann

ITV3
200 Grays Inn Road
London WC1X 8HF
020 7843 8000
www.itv.com/itv3
Channel editor: Steve Arnell; controller
of commissioned programmes:
Daniella Neumann

Jetix
3 Queen Caroline Street
Hammersmith, London W6 9PE
020 7554 9000
www.jetix.co.uk

Kerrang TV
Mappin House, 4 Winsley Street
London W1W 8HF
020 7182 8000
www.emapadvertising.com
Programme director: Dave Young;
director of music: Simon Sadler
PRESS: *maureen.corish@emap.com*

Kiss TV
Mappin House, 4 Winsley Street
London W1W 8HF
020 7182 8000
www.emapadvertising.com
Programme director: Dave Young;
director of music: Simon Sadler
PRESS: *maureen.corish@emap.com*

Living
160 Great Portland Street
London W1W 5QA
020 7299 5000
www.livingtv.co.uk
Programme controller: Richard Woolfe
PRESS: *judy_wells@flextech.co.uk*
jessica_alder@flextech.co.uk

Look4Love TV
Unit 20, Intec 2, Basingstoke
Hampshire RG24 8NE
0871 550 0055
enquiries@look4love.tv
www.look4love.tv

Magic TV
Mappin House, 4 Winsley Street
London W1W 8HF
020 7182 8000
www.emapadvertising.com
Programme director: Dave Young;
director of music: Simon Sadler
PRESS: *maureen.corish@emap.com*

Majestic TV
CC.Comercial La Colonia Edificio II,
Locales 25–27
San Pedro de Alcantara, 29670
Malaga
00 34 952 799 518
www.majestictv.co.uk

Matinee Movies
179–181 The Vale, London W3 7RW
020 8600 9700
www.sit-up.tv
MD: Chris Manson

MATV National
Combine House, 7 Woodboy Street
Leicester LE1 3NJ
0116 2532288
info@matv.co.uk
www.matv.co.uk
MD: Vinod Popat

Men and Motors
200 Grays Inn Road
London WC1X 8HF
020 7843 8000
info@menandmotors.co.uk
www.menandmotors.co.uk
Commissioning editor: Joe Talbot
PRESS: *020 7843 8392*

Motors TV
855, avenue Roger Salengro,
92370 Chaville, France
00 33 1 4115 9852
www.motorstv.com
PRESS: *service.presse@motorstv.com*

MTA – Muslim TV
16 Gressenhall Road
London SW18 5QL
020 8870 0922
info@mta.tv
www.mta.tv

MTV, MTV2, Base, Dance, Hits
MTV, Hawley Crescent
London NW1 8TT
020 7284 7777
www.mtv.co.uk
Head of development (for programme
commissions): Chris Sice
PRESS:
curlewis.samantha@mtvne.com

Music Choice Europe
Fleet House, 57–61 Clerkenwell Road
London EC1M 5AR
020 7014 8700
contactus@musicchoice.co.uk
www.musicchoice.co.uk

Musicians Channel
New Cut Road, Vinters Park
Maidstone ME14 5NZ
01622 684602
info@mchannel.tv
www.musicianschannel.tv

MUTV
4th Floor, 274 Deansgate
Manchester M3 4JB
0161 834 1111
mutv@mutv.com
www.manutd.com/mutv
Editor-in-chief: Bob Farrer

Nation 217
6&7 Princes Court
Wapping Lane, London E1W 2DA
020 7942 7942
william.van.rest@nation217.tv
www.nation217.tv
Channel head: William van Rest

National Geographic Channel
Grant Way, Isleworth TW7 5QD
020 7705 3000
natgeoweb@bskyb.com
www.nationalgeographic.co.uk
General manager: Simon Bohrsmann

Nick Jr
Nickelodeon, 15–18 Rathbone Place
London W1T 1HU
020 7462 1000
abigail.hutton@nickelodeon.co.uk
www.nickjr.co.uk
Director of channels: Howard Litton

Nick Toons TV
Nickelodeon, 15–18 Rathbone Place
London W1T 1HU
020 7462 1000
abigail.hutton@nickelodeon.co.uk
www.nick.co.uk/toons
Director of channels: Howard Litton

Nickelodeon
Nickelodeon, 15–18 Rathbone Place
London W1T 1HU
020 7462 1000
abigail.hutton@nickelodeon.co.uk
www.nick.co.uk
Director of channels: Howard Litton

OBE
Crown House, North Circular Road
London NW10 7PN
020 8961 8909
info@obetv.co.uk
www.obetv.co.uk

Open Access
501 International House
223 Regent Street
London W1B 2QO
0870 744 2041
info@openaccess.tv
www.openaccess.tv

Paramount Comedy
UK House, 4th Floor
180 Oxford Street
London W1D 1DS
020 7478 5300
www.paramountcomedy.co.uk
Director of programming: Heather Jones
PRESS:
zoe.diver@paramountcomedy.com

PCNE Phoenix Chinese News
& Entertainment
The Chiswick Centre
414 Chiswick High Road
London W4 5TF
020 8987 4320/1
info@phoenixcnetv.com
www.phoenixcne.com
MD: Wen Guang

Performance
4 Farleigh Court, Long Ashton
Bristol BS48 1UL
0870 850 8102
info@performancetv.co.uk
www.performance-channel.com
CEO: Steve Timmins; channel
manager: Matthew Clements

Poker Channel
info@thepokerchannel.co.uk
www.thepokerchannel.co.uk
CEO: Crispin Nieboer; head of
programming: James Hopkins;
director of television: Chiara Cipriani
PRESS: *020 7289 4440*
nicole@pagetbaker.com

POP
37 Harwood Road, London SW6 4QP
020 7384 2243
charlotte@chartshow.tv
www.popclub.tv
Head of channels: Chris Boardman

Price Drop TV
Sit-Up House, 179–181 The Vale
London W3 7RW
0870 165 1647
www.price-drop.tv

Q TV
Mappin House, 4 Winsley Street
London W1W 8HF
020 7182 8000
www.emapadvertising.com
Programme director: Dave Young;
director of music: Simon Sadler
PRESS: *maureen.corish@emap.com*

QVC
Marco Polo Hous
346 Queenstown Road
Chelsea Bridge, London SW8 4NQ
020 7705 5600
www.qvcuk.com
Planning manager: Susan Hellyar
PRESS: *020 7886 8440*

Real Estate TV
1–6 Falconberg Court
London W1D 3AB
020 7440 1090
info@realestatetv.tv
www.realestatetv.tv
Head of channel: Mark Dodds

Reality TV
105–109 Salusbury Road
London NW6 6RG
020 7328 8808
www.realitytv.co.uk
PRESS: *jane.wynward@zonevision.com*

Record TV
tvrecord@recordnetwork.net
www.rederecord.com.br

Revelation TV
117a Cleveland Street
London W1T 6PX
020 7631 4446
howard@revelationtv.com
lesley@revelationtv.com
www.revelationtv.com
Head of programming: Howard Conder

RTÉ 1 + 2
Donnybrook, Dublin 4, Ireland
00 353 1 208 3111
info@rte.ie
www.rte.ie/tv
*Commissioning editor, Irish language,
multiculture and education
programmes: Máiread Ní Nuadháin*

S4C
Parc Ty Glas, Llanishen
Cardiff CF14 5DU
Cardiff: 029 20747444
Caernarfon: 01286 674622
www.s4c.co.uk

Sci-Fi
5–7 Mandeville Place
London W1U 3AX
020 7535 3500
www.scifi.com
*Head of programming and acquisitions:
Monica Iglesias*

Screenshop
179–181 The Vale, London W3 7RW
020 8600 9700
www.sit-up.tv
MD: Chris Manson

Scuzz
Grant Way, Isleworth TW7 5QD
0870 240 3000
www.scuzz.tv

Setanta Sport UK
200 Renfield Street, Glasgow G2 3PR
0141 300 3880
setantauk@setanta.com
www.setanta.com
MD, Setanta UK & Ireland: Roger Hall

Shop on TV
020 8453 1120
enquiries@shopon.tv
www.shopon.tv

Shop Vector
64–66 Coleman Street
London EC2R 5BX
020 8104 0493
customerservice@simplymedia.tv
fran.hales@simplymedia.tv
www.vectordirect.tv
Media manager: Fran Hales

Simply Ideas
64–66 Coleman Street
London EC2R 5BX
020 8104 0493
customerservice@simplymedia.tv
fran.hales@simplymedia.tv
www.simplyshoppingtv.co.uk
Media manager: Fran Hales

Simply Shopping
64–66 Coleman Street
London EC2R 5BX
020 8104 0493
customerservice@simplymedia.tv
fran.hales@simplymedia.tv
www.simplyshoppingtv.co.uk
Media manager: Fran Hales

Sky Bet
Grant Way, Isleworth TW7 5QD
0870 240 3000
www.skybet.com
Marketing director: Simon Miller
PRESS: *020 7705 3275.* CONSUMER
PR MANAGER: *Heidi Bruckland*

Sky Box Office
Grant Way, Isleworth TW7 5QD
0870 240 3000
www.skymovies.com
Head of PPV: Karen Saunders
PRESS: *020 7800 4252
        skymoviespublicity@bskyb.com*
PUBLICITY MANAGER: *Phil Evans*

Sky Cinema 1 & 2
Grant Way, Isleworth TW7 5QD
0870 240 3000
www.skymovies.com
*Director of film channels and
acquisitions: Sophie Turner-Laing*
PRESS: *020 7800 4252
        skymoviespublicity@bskyb.com*
PUBLICITY MANAGER: *Phil Evans*

Sky Customer Channel
Grant Way, Isleworth TW7 5QD
0870 240 3000
PRESS: *020 7705 3275.* CONSUMER
PR MANAGER: *Heidi Bruckland*

Sky Mix
Grant Way, Isleworth TW7 5QD
0870 240 3000
www.skyone.co.uk
Controller: James Baker
PRESS: *020 7805 7276.* ACTING
PUBLICITY MANAGER: *Chris Aylott;*
HEAD OF PROGRAMME PUBLICITY:
Richard Turner

Sky Movies 1–9
Grant Way, Isleworth TW7 5QD
0870 240 3000
www.skymovies.com
*Director of film channels and
acquisitions: Sophie Turner-Laing*
PRESS: *020 7800 4252
        skymoviespublicity@bskyb.com*
PUBLICITY MANAGER: *Phil Evans*

Sky News
Grant Way, Isleworth TW7 5QD
0870 240 3000
NEWSDESK: news.plan@bskyb.com
www.skynews.co.uk
*Head of Sky News: Nick Pollard
Presenters and correspondents: see
page 162*
PRESS: *020 7800 4289.*
SENIOR PUBLICIST: *Stella Tooth;*
HEAD OF PROGRAMME PUBLICITY:
Richard Turner

Sky One
Grant Way, Isleworth TW7 5QD
0870 240 3000
www.skyone.co.uk
Controller: James Baker
PRESS: *020 7805 7276.* ACTING
PUBLICITY MANAGER: *Chris Aylott;*
HEAD OF PROGRAMME PUBLICITY:
Richard Turner. PUBLICISTS FOR
PROGRAMMES – *24:* Tom Mackey;
*Battlestar Galactica, Law & Order,
Enterprise:* Chris Aylott; *Cold Case,
Malcolm in the Middle:* Gayle
Hemmings and Melanie Adorian;
Nip/Tuck, The Simpsons: Lee
Robson

Sky Sports 1, 2 & 3
Grant Way, Isleworth TW7 5QD
0870 240 3000
www.skysports.com
MD: Vic Wakeling
PRESS: *020 7800 4254.* HEAD OF
PRESS AND PUBLICITY: *Chris Haynes*

Sky Sports Extra
Grant Way, Isleworth TW7 5QD
0870 240 3000
www.skysports.com
MD: Vic Wakeling
PRESS: *020 7800 4254.* HEAD OF
PRESS AND PUBLICITY: *Chris Haynes*

Sky Sports News
Grant Way, Isleworth TW7 5QD
0870 240 3000
www.skysports.com
MD: Vic Wakeling
PRESS: *020 7800 4254.* HEAD OF
PRESS AND PUBLICITY: *Chris Haynes*

Sky Travel
Grant Way, Isleworth TW7 5QD
0870 240 3000
www.skytravel.co.uk
General manager: Barbara Gibbon
PRESS: *richard.turner@bskyb.com*

Sky Travel +1
Grant Way, Isleworth TW7 5QD
0870 240 3000
www.skytravel.co.uk
General manager: Barbara Gibbon
PRESS: *richard.turner@bskyb.com*

Sky Travel Extra
Grant Way, Isleworth TW7 5QD
0870 240 3000
www.skytravel.co.uk
General manager: Barbara Gibbon
PRESS: *richard.turner@bskyb.com*

Sky Travel Shop
Grant Way, Isleworth TW7 5QD
0870 240 3000
www.skytravel.co.uk
General manager: Barbara Gibbon
PRESS: *richard.turner@bskyb.com*

Sky Vegas Live
Grant Way, Isleworth TW7 5QD
0870 240 3000
www.skyvegaslive.com
Executive producer: Peter Ward.
Consumer PR executive: Tara Hicks
PRESS: *020 7705 3416*

Sky Welcome
Grant Way, Isleworth TW7 5QD
0870 240 3000
Consumer PR executive: Tara Hicks
PRESS: *020 7705 3416*

Smash Hits Channel
Mappin House, 4 Winsley Street
London W1W 8HF
020 7182 8000
www.emapadvertising.com
Programme director: Dave Young;
director of music: Simon Sadler
PRESS: *maureen.corish@emap.com*

Snatch It
Factory Outlet TV
Eagle Road Studios, Eagle Road
Redditch B98 9HF
0845 3 670670
customercare@gemstv.com
www.gemstv.com
MD: Steve Bennett

Sony Entertainment TV Asia
34 Foubert's Place
London W1V 2BH
020 7534 7575
www.setasia.tv
Vice president for international
business: Neeraj Arora
PRESS: *ash_jaswal@spe.sony.com*

Sound TV
21 East Links, Tollgate
Chandlers Ford, Southampton
Hampshire SO53 3TG
023 8065 2777
info@soundtv.co.uk
www.soundtv.co.uk
MD: Richard Digance; head of
programmes for children: Morag
Thorpe; public relations associate:
Steve Blacknell

Soundtrack Channel
1335 Fourth Street, Santa Monica
California 90401 USA
00 1 310 899 1315
contactstc@stcchannel.com
www.stcchannel.com

Star TV/ News/ Plus
Great West House (15th floor)
Great West Road, Brentford
Middlesex TW8 9DF
020 7805 2326
www.uk.startv.com
Senior marketing executive: Gurpreet
Braich
PRESS: *gurpreet.braich@bskyb.com*

SUBtv
140 Buckingham Palace Road
London SW1W 9SA
020 7881 2540
info@subtvweb.com
www.subtvnetwork.com
Commercial manager: Joy Golden;
creative director: Jon Kingdon

Superstore TV
64–66 Coleman Street
London EC2R 5BX
020 8104 0493
customerservice@simplymedia.tv
fran.hales@simplymedia.tv
www.superstore.tv
Media manager: Fran Hales

TBN Europe
PO Box 240, Hatfield
Hertfordshire AL9 6BH
info@tbneurope.org
www.tbneurope.org

TCM
Turner House
16 Great Marlborough Street
London W1V 1AF
020 7693 1000
tcmmailuk@turner.com
www.tcmonline.co.uk
PR: Sophie Hossard

Teachers' TV
16–18 Berners Street
London W1T 3LN
020 7182 7430
info@teachers.tv
www.teachers.tv
Chief executive: Nigel Dacre

Teletext Holidays
Building 10, Chiswick Park
566 Chiswick High Road
London W4 5TS
0870 731 3000
www.teletextholidays.co.uk

TG4
Baile na hAbhann, Co. na Gaillimhe
00 353 91 505050
eolas@tg4.ie
www.tg4.ie
Director of television: Alan Esslemont;
programmes department: Michéal Ó
Meallaigh

Thane Direct
248–250 Tottenham Court Road
London W1T 7RA
020 7580 6110
info@thanedirect.tv
www.thanedirect.co.uk
MD: Richard Whinfrey

Thane Stop and Shop
248–250 Tottenham Court Road
London W1T 7RA
020 7580 6110
info@thanedirect.tv
www.thanedirect.co.uk
MD: Richard Whinfrey

Thomas Cook TV
8 Park Place, Lawn Lane, Vauxhall
London SW8 1UD
020 7820 4470
www.thomascooktv.com

Tiny Pop
37 Harwood Road
London SW6 4QP
020 7371 5999 / 7384 2243
charlotte@chartshow.tv
www.popclub.tv
Head of channels: Chris Boardman

TMF
MTV, Hawley Crescent
London NW1 8TT
020 7284 7777
www.vh1.co.uk
Acting general manager (for programme
commissions): Steve Shannon
PRESS: *hershon.mandy@mtvne.com*

Toonami
Turner House
16 Great Marlborough Street
London W1V 1AF
020 7693 1000
info@toonami.co.uk
www.toonami.co.uk
Channel head: Paul Cackett

Travel Channel
64 Newman Street, London W1T 3EF
020 7636 5401
www.travelchannel.co.uk
Head of programming: Annabelle Parmes
PRESS: *petra@travelchannel.co.uk*

Trouble
160 Great Portland Street
London W1W 5QA
020 7299 5000
www.trouble.co.uk
Programme controller: Jonathan Webb
PRESS: *jakki_lewis@flextech.co.uk*

True Movies
020 7371 5999
charlotte@chartshow.tv

Turner Classic Movies
Turner House
16 Great Marlborough Street
London W1F 7HS
020 7693 1000
www.tcmonline.co.uk
Channel manager: Alan Musa
PRESS: *ann.rosen@turner.com*
　　　　　　www.europe.turnerinfo.com

TV Warehouse
Chalfont Grove, Narcot Lane
Chalfont St Peter
Buckinghamshire SL9 8TW
0800 013 1464
www.tvwarehouseonline.com
MD: John Bramm

TV-Shop
P.O Box 64, Hadleigh IP7 6WF
08700 191019
tvshop-support@portica.co.uk
www.tvshop.com
MD: Ruth Oliver

UCB TV
PO Box 255, Stoke-on-Trent ST4 8YY
0845 604 0401
www.ucb.co.uk
TV broadcasting manager: John Green

Contacts : TV

UKTV Bright Ideas
160 Great Portland Street
London W1W 5QA
020 7299 6200
www.uktv.co.uk
Channel editor: Gareth Williams
PRESS: DORITA.HOLLINS@UKTV.CO.UK

UKTV Documentary
160 Great Portland Street
London W1W 5QA
020 7299 6200
www.uktv.co.uk
Channel editor: James Newton
PRESS: *rebecca.hook@uktv.co.uk*

UKTV Drama
160 Great Portland Street
London W1W 5QA
020 7299 6200
www.uktv.co.uk
Channel editor: Red Johnson
PRESS: *dorita.hollins@uktv.co.uk*

UKTV Food
160 Great Portland Street
London W1W 5QA
020 7299 6200
www.uktvfood.co.uk
Channel editor: Gareth Williams
PRESS: *dorita.hollins@uktv.co.uk*

UKTV G2
160 Great Portland Street
London W1W 5QA
020 7299 6200
www.uktv.co.uk
Channel editor: Steve North
PRESS: *dorita.hollins@uktv.co.uk*

UKTV Gold
160 Great Portland Street
London W1W 5QA
020 7299 6200
www.uktv.co.uk
Channel editor: Red Johnson
PRESS: *dorita.hollins@uktv.co.uk*

UKTV History
160 Great Portland Street
London W1W 5QA
020 7299 6200
www.uktv.co.uk
Channel editor: Adrian Wills
PRESS: *rebecca.hook@uktv.co.uk*

UKTV People
160 Great Portland Street
London W1W 5QA
020 7299 6200
www.uktv.co.uk
Channel editor: Steve North
PRESS: *rebecca.hook@uktv.co.uk*

UKTV Style
160 Great Portland Street
London W1W 5QA
020 7299 6200
www.uktvstyle.co.uk
Channel editor: Catherine Cattion
PRESS: *dorita.hollins@uktv.co.uk*

The Vault
37 Harwood Road, London SW6 4QP
020 7384 2243
sarah@chartshow.tv

Vectone 4U, Bangla, Bolly, Tamil, Urdu and World
Vectone Media, 54 Marsh Wall
Canary Wharf, London E14 9TP
020 7517 4322
a.sharma@vectone.com
CEO: Amitabh Sharma

VH1
MTV, Hawley Crescent
London NW1 8TT
020 7284 7777
www.vh1.co.uk
Acting general manager (for programme commissions): Steve Shannon
PRESS: *hershon.mandy@mtvne.com*

VH1 Classic
MTV, Hawley Crescent
London NW1 8TT
020 7284 7777
www.vh1.co.uk
Acting general manager (for programme commissions): Steve Shannon
PRESS: *hershon.mandy@mtvne.com*

VH2
MTV, Hawley Crescent
London NW1 8TT
020 7284 7777
www.vh1.co.uk
Acting general manager (for programme commissions): Steve Shannon
PRESS: *hershon.mandy@mtvne.com*

Wine Network
88 Kearny Street, Suite 2100
San Francisco CA 94108 USA
00 1 415 772 3639
info@winetv.tv
www.winetv.tv
CEO: Patrick Brunet; COO: Lorie Kim

Wrestling Channel
3rd floor, Welby House
96 Wilton Road, London SW1V 1DW
020 7599 8959
info@thewrestlingchannel.tv
www.thewrestlingchannel.tv

YES661
Harper Road
Sharston Industrial Estate, Sharston
Manchester M22 4RG
0161 947 2580
www.yes661.com
MD: David Ades

YooPlay
Northumberland House
155–157 Great Portland Street
London W1W 6QP
020 7462 0870
oiyoo@yooplay.com
www.yoomedia.com/yooplay

Zee TV
Unit 8, Bellvue Business Centre
Bellvue Road, Northolt UB5 5QQ
020 8839 4000
www.zeetv.co.uk
Programmes manager: Pranab Kapadia
PRESS: *media@zeenetwork.com*

Data services

Ceefax
BBC Television Centre, Wood Lane
London W12 7RJ
020 8743 8000

Teletext
Building 10, Chiswick Park
566 Chiswick High Road
London W4 5TS
0870 731 3000
editor@teletext.co.uk
www.teletext.co.uk
Has a licence to use spare capacity within the Channel 3 (ITV) signal.
Head of TV: Mishma Patel

Other broadcasters

Abacus TV
01508 570970
sales@abacustv.co.uk
www.abacustv.co.uk
Producer: Jane Scarfe

BFBS Forces Radio and TV
01494 878290
sarah.dornford-may@ssvc.com
www.ssvc.com
Controller of television: Helen Williams

BTV – Bloomsbury Television (University College London)
020 7387 3827
btv@ucl.ac.uk
http://welcome.to/btv

BVTV
01582 581753
info@bvtv.co.uk
www.bvtv.co.uk

C4TV
c4tv@cant.ac.uk
www.c4online.co.uk

Capital TV (Wales)
029 2048 8500
enquiries@capital.tv
www.capital.tv
MD: David Morris Jones

Channel M
0161 475 4855
info@channelM.co.uk
www.channelm.co.uk
Operations manager: Susan Steenson

EBS New Media
01462 895999
ben@newmediagroup.co.uk
www.newvisiongroup.co.uk
MD: Ben Tagg

Glasgow University Student Television (GUST)
0141 341 6216
gust@src.gla.ac.uk
www.src.gla.ac.uk/gust
Station controller: Chris Hall

Leeds University Union TV (ls:tv)
0113 380 1423
stationmanager@lstv.co.uk
www.lstv.co.uk

Loughborough Students Union TV (LSUTV)
01509 635045
manager@lsutv.co.uk
www.lsutv.co.uk
Head of media: Anna Bowden

Middlesex Broadcasting Corporation (MATV Channel 6)
0116 253 2288
info@matv.co.uk
www.matv.co.uk
MD: Vinod Popat

Nerve TV
01202 595777
jhawkins@bournemouth.ac.uk
www.nervemedia.net
Media services manager: Jason Hawkins

Nexus UTV
01603 592270
nexusutv@gmail.com
www.uea.ac.uk/~sunexus

North West Television Services (Channel 9 – Coleraine, Limavady, Londonderry/Derry)
028 7131 4400
info@c9tv.tv
www.c9tv.tv
Director: Gary Porter

Northern Visions
028 9024 5495
info@northernvisions.org
www.northernvisions.org

SIX TV – The Oxford Channel
01865 314700
admin@oxfordchannel.com
www.oxfordchannel.com

Solent TV (Isle of Wight)
01983 522344
info@solent.tv
www.solent.tv

STOIC Student Television of Imperial College
020 7594 8100
info@stoictv.com
www.union.ic.ac.uk/media/stoic
Contact: John Anderson

XTV
01392 263598
xtv@ex.ac.uk
www.xtv.org.uk

YCTV – Youth Culture Television
020 8964 4646
stuartr@yctv.org
www.yctv.org

York University St John Student Television (YSTV)
01904 624624
marketing@yorksj.ac.uk
www.yorksj.ac.uk

Independent production companies

Key companies

ALL3MEDIA
87–91 Newman Street
London W1T 3EY
020 7907 0177
www.allthreemedia.com
Chief executive: Steve Morrison; chief operating officer: Jules Burns; creative director: David Liddiment

Assembly TV
Riverside Studios
Crisp Road, London W6 9RL
020 8237 1075
judithmurrell@riversidestudios.co.uk
www.allthreemedia.com
Chief executive: William Burdett-Coutts
• *Black Books; Jo Brand's Hot Potatoes; In Exile*

Bentley Productions
Pinewood Studios, Pinewood Road
Iver, Bucks SL0 0NH
01753 656594
www.allthreemedia.com
MD: Brian True-May
• *Midsomer Murders; Ultimate Force*

Cactus TV
373 Kennington Road
London SE11 4PS
020 7091 4900
touch.us@cactustv.co.uk
www.cactustv.co.uk
MDs: Simon Ross, Amanda Ross
• *Richard & Judy*

Lion Television
Lion House, 26 Paddenswick Road
London W6 0UB
020 8846 2000
Scotland: 0141 331 0450
New York: +1 212 206 8633
LA: +1 310 566 7940
mail@liontv.co.uk
www.liontv.co.uk
MDs: Richard Bradley, Nick Catliff, Shahana Meer, Jeremy Mills; director of production: Patsy Blades; executive producers: Bill Locke, Hilary Rosen
• *Bad Behaviour; Days That Shook the World; Britain's Finest; Castles; Royal Deaths and Diseases; Passport to the Sun*

North One TV
Maywood House
46–52 Pentonville Road
London N1 9HF
020 7502 6000
annelise.unitt@northonetv.com
www.allthreemedia.com
MD: Neil Duncanson; chief executive: John Wohlgemuth; head of production, entertainment: Pip Haddow
• *Formula One; World Rally; The Top Ten series; Speed Sunday; Fifth Gear*

At It Productions
Unit 314, Westbourne Studios
242 Acklam Road, London W10 5YG
020 8964 2122
enquiries@atitproductions.com
www.atitproductions.com
MDs: Martin Cunning, Chris Fouracre
• *T4; LA Pool Party; Sun Sea and Silicone; Perfect Getaway; Chancers; Popworld, 25 Years of Smash Hits; Bride and Grooming; Born Without a Face*

Celador Productions
39 Long Acre, London WC2 9LG
020 7845 6999
tvhits@celador.co.uk
www.celador.co.uk
MDs: Paul Smith, Danielle Lux; head of entertainment: Colman Hutchinson; head of production: Heather Hampson; development executives, comedy: Vanessa Haynes, Humphrey Barclay
• *You Are What You Eat; It's Been A Bad Week; Who Wants To Be a Millionaire?; Winning Lines; Britain's Brainiest; 24 Carrott Gold*

Diverse
Gorleston Street, London W14 8XS
020 7603 4567
reception@diverse.tv
www.diverse.tv
Head of post-production: Paul Bates; director of programmes: Narinder Minhas; creative director: Roy Ackerman; head of production: Janet Smyth; bookings: Fay Searl
• *Musicality: The Winners' Story; Let 'Em All In; Guyana: The Politics of Paradise; If We Could Stop the Violence*

Endemol UK
Shepherds Building Centre
Clarecroft Way, Shepherds Bush
London W14 0EE
0870 333 1700
info@endemoluk.com
www.endemoluk.com
Chief executive: Tom Barnicoat; MD: Nikki Cheetham; director of production: Clare Pickering; heads of production: Petrina Good, Richard Thomson
• *Big Brother; Fame Academy; Orange British Academy Film Awards; Ground Force; Changing Rooms; Restoration; The Salon 2; The Games*

Hat Trick Productions
10 Livonia Street, London W1F 8AF
020 7434 2451
info@hattrick.com
www.hattrick.com
MDs: Denise O'Donoghue, Jimmy Mulville; head of production: Laura Djanogle
• *Have I Got News For You; Bodies; Bromwell High; Room 101; The Kumars at No 42; Father Ted; Jeffrey Archer – The Truth; Underworld; Drop The Dead Donkey*

Hit Entertainment
Maple House, 5th Fl.
149–150 Tottenham Court Rd
London W1T 7NF
020 7554 2500
www.hitentertainment.com
*MD: Charles Burvick; head of
production: Jocelyn Stephenson*
• *Barney and Friends; Art Attack;
Angelina Ballerina; Pingu;
Toddworld; Fireman Sam; Bob the
Builder; Rubbadubbers; Sooty;
Thomas the Tank Engine*

IWC Media
St George's Studio
93–97 St George's Road
Glasgow G3 6JA
0141 353 3222
London: 020 7684 1661
info@iwcmedia.co.uk
www.iwcmedia.co.uk
*Chairman: Alan Clements; MD: Sue
Oriel; creative directors: Zad Rogers,
Hamish Barbour; head of
documentaries: Charlotte Moore;
news editor: Kirsty Walk; head of
factual: Adam Barker*
• *Ultimate Cars; 18th Street; Other Side;
Location, Location, Location; The
Planman; Changemakers; Hunt for Jill
Dando's Killer*

Princess Productions
Whiteley's Centre, 151 Queensway
London W2 4SB
020 7985 1985
reception@princess.tv.com
www.princess.tv.com
*MD: Sebastian Scott; head of
production: Sarah Buckenham*
• *Ruby Does the Business; Back to
Reality; Bump 'n' Grind; Ri:se; The
Wright Stuff*

Prospect Pictures
Wandsworth Plain
London SW18 1ET
020 7636 1234
Capital studios, London:
020 8877 1234
Wales 029 2055 1177
rhys@prospect-uk.com
www.prospect-uk.com
*Company directors: Rhys John, Tony
McAvoy, Barry Lynth; head of
production: Louise Doffman*
• *Saturday Kitchen; Great Food Live;
Under One Roof; Ready Steady Cook*

Ragdoll (UK)
Timothy's Bridge Road
Stratford Upon Avon CV37 9NQ
01789 404100
USA: +1 212 966 4477
pinewood@ragdoll.co.uk
www.ragdoll.co.uk
Director of production: Sue James
• *Open a Door; Rosie and Jim; Tots TV;
Brum; Teletubbies; Teletubbies
Everywhere; Boohbah*

RDF Media
The Gloucester Building
Kensington Village, Avonmore Road
London W14 8RF
020 7013 4000
contactus@rdfmedia.com
www.rdfmedia.com
*Head of production: Jane Wilson;
production executive: Jo Crawley; press
and marketing executive: Alice
Robertson; senior producer: David Wise;
executive producers: Jenny Crowther,
Martin Davidson, Jill Robinson*
• *Faking It 4; Wife Swap; Celebrity Wife
Swap; Scrapheap Challenge 5; Century
of the Self; Holiday Showdown*

September Films
Glen House, 22 Glenthorne Road
London W6 0NG
020 8563 9393
USA: +1 323 960 8085
september@septemberfilms.com
www.septemberfilms.com
*Chief executive: Marcus Plantin;
director of production: Elaine Day;
director of factual and digital channels:
Sam Brick; head of drama and film
development: Nadine Mellor*
• *Holiday Homes Nightmares; Clubbing
on the Frontline; The Bottom Line;
New Tycoons; Secrets and Lies; Instant
Wedding; Making It*

Shine
140 Kensington Church Street
Notting Hill, London W8 4BN
020 7313 8000
info@shinelimited.com
www.shinelimited.com
MD: Elizabeth Murdoch
• *Dispatches; Fit to Eat; Take That;
Masterchef Goes Large*

Talkback Thames Productions
20–21 Newman Street
London W1T 1PG
020 7861 8000
reception@talkbackthames.tv
www.talkbackthames.tv
*Chief executive: Lorraine Heggessey;
executive editor: Daisy Goodwin*
• *Family Affairs; Bo' Selecta!; I'm Alan
Partridge; Jamie's Kitchen; Perfect
Strangers; The Apprentice; Grand
Designs; Green Wing; Nathan Barley;
How Clean Is Your House?; House Doctor*

The Television Corporation
30 Sackville Street, London W1S 3DY
020 7478 7300
Mentorn London: 020 7258 6800
Oxford Mentorn: 01865 318 450
Glasgow Mentorn: 0141 204 6600
tvcorp@tvcorp.co.uk
www.tvcorp.co.uk
*Chief executive: Peter Salmon; director
of programmes: George Carey; MD,
Mentorn: Charles Thompson; head of
programmes, Mentorn Scotland: Jane
Rogerson; head of Mentorn Midlands:
Eamonn Matthews; head of
communications: Mark Ogle*
• *Robot Wars; Britain's Worst Driver;
Botham's Ashes; Gillette World Sport;
Hitler's Legacy; Club Culture;
Question Time; The Real Monty*

Tiger Aspect Productions
7 Soho Street, London W1D 3DQ
020 7434 6700
general@tigeraspect.co.uk
www.tigeraspect.co.uk
*MD: Andrew Zein; executive producer,
entertainment: Anastasia Mouzas;
head of factual: Paul Sommers; head of
comedy: Clive Tulloh; head of history
and features: Charles Brand.
Comedy, drama, entertainment,
factual and animation.*
• *Teachers; Murphy's Law; Streetmate;
Gimme Gimme Gimme*

Tinopolis
Tinopolis Centre, Park Street, Llanelli
Carmarthenshire SA15 3YE
01554 880880
info@tinopolis.com
www.tinopolis.com
Executive chairman: Ron Jones
• *P'nawn Da; Wedi 7; Le Rygbi*

TWI (Trans World International)
Pier House, Strand on the Green
London W4 3NN
020 8233 5000
kmullins@imgworld.com
www.imgworld.com
*MD: Andrew Hampel; head of
production: Graham Fry*
• *Japan's War (in colour series);
Wimbledon; The Olympics; Premier
League; PGA European Tour; Colour
of War*

Twofour Productions
3 Bush Park, Estover
Plymouth PL6 7RG
01752 727400
enq@twofour.co.uk
www.twofour.co.uk
*MD: Charles Wace; director of business
communications: Charles Mills;
director of broadcast programming:
Melanie Leach; director of production:
Shireen Ward*
• *G Girls; Gardens Through Time; Dead
Famous; The City Gardener; Ideal
Home Show*

Wall To Wall
8–9 Spring Place, Kentish Town
London NW5 3ER
020 7485 7424
mail@walltowall.co.uk
www.walltowall.co.uk
Head of production: Helena Ely
• *Life Beyond the Box: Norman Stanley
Fletcher; New Tricks; The Regency
House Party*

Zenith Entertainment
43–45 Dorset Street
London W1U 7NA
020 7224 2440
general@zenith-entertainment.co.uk
www.zenith-entertainment.co.uk
MD of production: Ivan Rendall
• *Byker Grove; 2000 Acres of Sky;
Headliners; Garden Rivals; Room
Rivals; Brian's Boyfriends; Murder
Most Foul*

Zig Zag Productions
13–14 Great Sutton St, Clerkenwell
London EC1V 0BX
020 7017 8755
production@zigzag.uk.com
www.zigzagproductions.tv
*MD: Danny Fenton; head of factual
entertainment: Jes Wilkins; production
executive: Natalie O'Hara; head of
development: Ed Crick*
• *Fashion is Football Challenge; Inside
the Mind of Frank Bruno; Three
Lions; DIY Births; Celebrity
Gladiators; X-Rated: The Ads They
Couldn't Show; That's So Last Week*

Other production companies

12 Yard Productions
020 7432 2929
contact@12yard.com
www.12yard.com
MD: David Young
• *Weakest Link; In It To Win It;
Without Prejudice?; Double Cross;
EggHeads; Here Comes The Sun;
Three's A Crowd*

1A Productions
01360 620855
office@1AProductions.co.uk
MD: Norman Stone
• *Tales From the Madhouse; Man Dancin'*

3BM Television
020 8740 4780
3bmtv@3bmtv.co.uk
www.3bmtv.co.uk
MD: Daniel Korn
• *War Lords; Children of Abraham;
Zero Hour: Ten Days to D-Day*

The 400 Company
020 8746 1400
info@the400.co.uk
www.the400.co.uk
MD: Mark Sloper
• *The Real TT Heroes; Full Throttle
Famous*

Aardman Animations
0117 984 8485
mail@aardman.co.uk
www.aardman.com
MD: Sonia Davis
• *Walkers' Mr Potato Head commercial;
Robinson's Boogie commercial;
Chicken Run*

Absolutely Productions
020 7644 5575
info@absolutely-uk.com
www.absolutely.biz
MD: Miles Bullough
• *Barry Welsh; Stressed Eric; Trigger
Happy TV*

Acacia Productions
020 8341 9392
projects@acaciaproductions.co.uk
www.acaciaproductions.co.uk
MD: J Edward Milner
• *Documentary and news, environment,
current affairs and human rights*

Accomplice Television
00 353 1 660 3235
office@accomplice-tv.com
www.accomplice-tv.com
MD: David Collins
• *Pure Mule; Bachelors Walk Series 1,
2 & 3*

Addictive Television
020 7700 0333
mail@addictive.com
www.addictive.com
*Head of production: Nik Clarke;
Graham Daniels*
• *Spaced Out; Transambient; Night
Shift; The Web Review; Mixmasters
(ITV1); Visual Stings (Magnetic
Channel); Optronica*

Aimimage Production Company
020 7482 4340
atif@aimimage.com
www.aimimage.com
MD: Ahmad Zadeh
• *Terra Circa; Balls to Basra;
The Family Portrait*

Angel Eye
020 7437 0082
office@angeleye.co.uk
www.angeleye.co.uk
MD: Richard Osborne
• *Holy Offensive; Beginners Luck;
Estate Agents; Lady Macbeth; The
Last Chances*

Antelope
01243 370806
mick.csaky@antelope.co.uk
www.antelope.co.uk
*Chief executive and creative director:
Mike Csaky*
• *Docs: Mozart in Turkey; Rebel Music:
The Bob Marley Story; Geiko Girl;
Africa Live; Epic Journey; 13-part
series about Kyoto*

APT Films
020 7284 1695
admin@aptfilms.com
www.aptfilms.com
MD: Jonny Persey
• *Wondrous Oblivion (feature);
Solomon and Gaenor (Oscar
nomination, best foreign film); The
Chosen Ones; Solo One; When I Lived
in Modern Times; Deep Water*

Atlantic Productions
020 7371 3200
info@atlanticproductions.tv
www.atlanticproductions.tv
MD: Anthony Geffen
• *Spartans; The Queen of Sheba;
Nefertiti Resurrected; Mystery of the
Tibetan Mummy; The Real Jules
Verne; Tutankhamen: a murder
mystery; Saladin; Seven Wonders of
Ancient Rome; Who Killed Cleopatra?;
Richard the Lionheart*

Attaboy TV
020 7740 3000
info@attaboytv.com
www.attaboytv.com
MD: Michael Wood
• *The High Road; End of the Line;
A Question of Colin; Life at the Sport;
Vets in Hong Kong*

Avalon
020 7598 7280
enquiries@avalonuk.com
www.avalonuk.com
MD: John Thoday
• *Harry Hill's TV Burp (ITV1); The
Frank Skinner Show (ITV1); Jerry
Springer – The Opera (BBC2); Kelsey
Grammer presents The Sketch Show
(Fox Network USA)*

Betty TV
020 7290 0660
tammy@bettytv.co.uk
www.bettytv.co.uk
MD: Liz Warner
• *Spendaholics; Rude Britannia*

Big Bear Films
020 7229 5982
office@bigbearfilms.co.uk
www.bigbearfilms.co.uk
Directors: John Stroud, Marcus Mortimer
• *My Hero (BBC1); Strange (with BBC1);
Hairy Bikers Cookbook*

Big Heart Media
020 7608 0352
info@bigheartmedia.com
www.bigheartmedia.com
MD: Colin Izod
• *GridClub/music studio; Spin 'n
Groove; Street Corner Symphony;
Rewind; Cape Farewell; Teachers' TV*

Big Umbrella Media
01225 817500
London: 020 7631 2050
production@bigumbrellamedia.co.uk
www.bigumbrellamedia.co.uk
MD: Martin Head
• *Living with the New Cross Fire; Sir
Frank Whittle: The Man who Shrank
the World*

Big Wave Productions
01243 532531
info@bigwavetv.com
www.bigwavetv.com
MD: Sarah Cunliffe
• *Bug Attack; Death on the Amazon;
Secret Weapons*

Black Coral Productions
020 8520 2881
bcp@coralmedia.co.uk
www.m4media.net
MD: Lazell Daley
• *Killing Time; Phil's Job; Which Witch
is Which*

Blackwatch Productions
0141 222 2640
info@blackwatchtv.com
www.blackwatchtv.com
MD: Nicola Black
• *Boys with Breasts; Snorting Coke with
the BBC; Designer Vagina*

Blakeway Productions
020 8743 2040
admin@blakeway.co.uk
www.blakeway.co.uk
MD: Denys Blakeway
• *Empire: how Britain made the modern world; Strike: When Britain Went to War; American Colossus; Prince William; Winston's War; The Major Years*

Blast! Films
020 7267 4260
blast@blastfilms.co.uk
www.blastfilms.co.uk
MD: Edmund Coulthard
• *Principles of Lust; The Death of Klinghoffer; Tales from Pleasure Beach*

Blue Egg Television/Blue Egg Studios
0870 765 0007
info@blueegg.tv
www.blueegg.tv
MD: Jill Scott
• *James Bond: Die Another Day; San Antonio; Orange commercial*

Box TV
020 7297 3333
info@box-tv.co.uk
www.box-tv.co.uk
MD: Justin Thomson-Glover
• *Sunday; Trust; Boudica; Gunpowder, Treason and Plot*

Brechin Productions
020 8876 4333
clive@brechin.com
www.brechin.com
MD: Clive Doij
• *Jigsaw; See it, Saw it; Turnabout; Eureka*

Brian Waddell Productions
028 9042 7646
strand@bwpltv.co.uk
www.bwpltv.co.uk
MD: Brian Waddell
• *The Craig Doyle Show; Carhunt; Chasing Time In... (13-part travel series, National Geographic); Ulster Fly; Boffins; Life After; What Women Really Want; What Kids Really Think; Getaways; Global Flyer*

Brighter Pictures
020 8222 4100
info@brighter.co.uk
www.brighter.co.uk
MD: Gavin Hay
• *Take the Mike; Bombay Blush; Diet Another Day*

Brighter Pictures Scotland
0141 572 0861
scotland@brighter.co.uk
www.brighter.co.uk
MD: Gavin Hay
• *Get a New Life (BBC2); Tabloid Tales (BBC1); Nick Nairn and the Dinner Ladies (BBC Scotland)*

Brighton TV
01273 224260
info@brighton.tv
www.brighton.tv
MD: David Pounds
• *Tales of the Living Dead; Big Boutique*

Brook Lapping Productions
020 7428 3100
info@brooklapping.com
www.brooklapping.com
MD: Brian Lapping
• *I met Osama Bin Laden; The fall of Milosevic; Avenging Terror; Before the Booker; I Met Adolf Eichmann; The Death of Yugoslavia; Israel and the Arabs; Live Aid Remembered (2 parts)*

Cactus TV
020 7091 4900
touch.us@cactustv.co.uk
www.cactustv.co.uk
MDs: Amanda Ross, Simon Ross
• *The Spirit of Diana, The Debate; Songs of Bond; Cliff Richard, The Hits I Missed; Richard & Judy; British Soap Awards*

Caledonia, Sterne And Wyld
0141 564 9100
info@caledonia-tv.com
www.caledonia-tv.com
MD: Seona Robertson
• *Sun Worshippers; King Jamie and the Angel; The Real Tartan Army II*

Carnival (Films and Theatre)
020 8968 0968
info@carnival-films.co.uk
www.carnival-films.co.uk
MD: Brian Eastman
• *Shadowlands; Firelight; Bugs; As If; Poirot; Rosemary and Thyme*

Century Films
020 7378 6106
info@centuryfilmsltd.com
www.centuryfilmsltd.com
MDs: Brian Hill, Katie Bailiff
• *Drinking for England; Feltham Sings; Shot; Men at Fifty*

Chameleon TV
0113 205 0040
www.chameleontv.com
MD: Allen Jewhurst
• *Edge of the City; Love 2 shop; Faith and Music Series*

Channel X
020 7428 3999
info@channelx.co.uk
www.channelx.co.uk
MD: Alan Marke
• *Reeves & Mortimer; Date That; Popetown*

Cicada Films
020 7266 4646
cicada@cicadafilms.com
www.cicadafilms.com
MD: Frances Berrigan
• *Ancient inventions; NYPD Animal Squad; Fat Fiancees; The Abyss; Beyond Pompeii; Bikini*

Circle Multimedia
01243 601482/509501
circlemultimedia@hotmail.com
www.circlemultimedia.com
Director: Jenny Burgess
• *Wire in the Blood; Alchemist's Cat (feature film); Afterlife (feature film); Conqueror (feature film); The Cloak (TV-DVD)*

Clearcut Communications
0161 427 3052
info@clearcut.freeserve.co.uk
MD: Robin Anderson
• *Sex and the Village; On the Edge (Granada); Sense of Place (BBC1); Shanghai'd (BBC2); Proof Positive (pilot for Discovery America)*

Clerkenwell Films
020 7608 2726
andy@clerkenwellfilms.com
MD: Murray Ferguson
• *Quite Ugly One Morning; Dr Jekyll and Mr Hyde (Universal TV); Inspector Rebus; Afterlife*

Collingwood O'Hare Entertainment
020 8993 3666
info@crownstreet.co.uk
www.collingwoodohare.com
MD: Christopher O'Hare
• *Animal Stories; Eddy and the Bear; The King's Beard; Yoko! Jakamoko! Toto!*

The Comedy Unit
0141 305 6666
comedyunit@comedyunit.co.uk
www.comedyunit.co.uk
MDs: Colin Gilbert, April Chamberlain
• *Still Game; The Karen Dunbar Show; Offside; Yo! Diary!; Taxi for Cowan Spanish Special; New Year specials: Chewin' The Fat; Only An Excuse?*

Company Pictures
020 7380 3900
enquiries@companypictures.co.uk
www.companypictures.co.uk
MDs: Charlie Pattinson, George Faber
• *Life and Death of Peter Sellers; Shameless; Forty; White Teeth; Anna Karenina*

Cosgrove Hall Films
0161 882 2500
animation@chf.co.uk
www.chf.co.uk
MD: Lee Marriott
• *Andy Pandy; Bill & Ben; Postman Pat; Enjie Benji; Dangermouse*

CTVC
020 8950 4426
ctvc@ctvc.co.uk
www.ctvc.co.uk
Head of programmes: Ray Bruce
• *Imber, Britain's Lost Village; Tonight; Shariah TV; Victim 001; Bethlehem Year Zero; John Meets Paul; A Mediterranean Journey; Understanding Islam*

Dai4Films
07976 819611
info@dai4films.com
www.dai4films.com
MD: Neil Davies
• *The Montserrat Volcano; Islands in the Sun; Working Machines; Double or Nothing; Raw Spice; Dirty Streets*

Dan Films
020 7916 4771
enquiries@danfilms.com
www.danfilms.com
Director: Julie Baines
• *Creep; Sons of the Wind; The Republic of Love*

Darlow Smithson Productions
020 7482 7027
mail@darlowsmithson.com
www.darlowsmithson.com
MD: John Smithson
• *Touching the Void; We Built this City;
Dragons – A Fantasy Made Real;
Living the Quake; E=MC²*

Darrall Macqueen
020 7407 2322
info@darrallmacqueen.com
www.darrallmacqueen.com
MDs: Maddy Darrall, Billy Macqueen
• *The Crust; Play the Game; Smile series
1, 2, 3 (BBC2); U Get Me series 1, 2, 3
(CBBC)*

Dazed Film and TV
020 7549 6840
info.film&tv@dazegroup.com
www.dazedfilmtv.com
MD: Laura Hastings-Smith
• *Perfect; Stop for a Minute; Untold
Beauty, BBC3; The Lives of the Saints;
Hero2Hero*

DLT Entertainment UK
020 7631 1184
jbartlett@dltentertainment.co.uk
www.dltentertainment.com
MD: John Bartlett
• *As Time Goes By; Love on a Branch
Line; My Family, BBC1; Meet My
Folks, BBC1*

DNA Films
020 7292 8700
info@dnafilms.com
www.dnafilms.com
MD: Andrew MacDonald
• *28 Days Later*

Double Exposure
020 7490 2499
reception@doublex.com
www.doublex.com
MD: Andrew Bethell
• *The House; Culloden; Pleasure Beach*

Eagle and Eagle
020 8995 1884
producer@eagletv.co.uk
www.eagletv.co.uk
Producer: Robert Eagle
• *The Nuclear Boy Scout (C4); Robo
Sapiens (Discovery/TLC); Big
Questions (C4 Learning)*

Eagle Films
01372 844484
enquiries@eaglefilms.co.uk
www.eaglefilms.co.uk
Producer: Katrina Moss
• *Bitter Honey; The Sins of the Father; It
Started with a Kiss; The Road to
Somewhere*

Ecosse Films
020 7371 0290
webmail@ecossefilms.com
www.ecossefilms.com
MD: Douglas Rae
• *Amnesia; Like Father Like Son;
Monarch of the Glen; The Ambassador;
Mrs Brown; Charlotte Gray; Heartless*

**Educational Broadcasting Services
Trust**
020 7613 5082
enquiries@ebst.co.uk
www.ebst.co.uk
Chief executive: Dr Jim Stevenson
• *Looking at Learning; Maths for
Engineers; Maths tutor – Algebra*

Electric Sky
01273 224240
info@electricsky.com
www.electricsky.com
MD: David Pounds
• *Myths of Mankind; Iraq – in the Shadow
of the Palms; First Human Clone*

The Elstree Production Company
01932 572680
enquiries@elsprod.com
www.elsprod.com
Producer: Greg Smith
• *Agnes Brown; George Orwell's Animal
Farm; David Copperfield*

Extreme Production
028 9080 9050
dmalone@extremeproduction.com
www.extremeproduction.com
MD: David Malone
• *Macintyre's Millions; Clash of the
Celtic Giants; Ballykissanything;
Country Practice*

FACE Television
01256 350022
paula@facetv.co.uk
www.facetv.co.uk
MD: Paul Friend
• *Wildlife SOS series 1, 2; Lifeboat
Rescue; Wildlife Photographer*

Faction Films
020 7690 4446
faction@factionfilms.co.uk
www.factionfilms.co.uk
*MDs: David Fox, Sylvia Stevens, Peter
Day*
• *Aphrodite's Drop; Murder in the
Family; Love for Sale (BBC);
Resistencia; Cinematic Orchestra
(C4); Sonic Revolution (C4/Levi's);
Point Annihilation (surf drama)*

The Farnham Film Company
01252 710313
info@farnfilm.com
www.farnfilm.com
MD: Ian Lewis
• *Dance with the Devil; Intergalactic
Kevin; Mona the Vampire; The Druid's
Tune*

Festival Film and TV
020 8297 9999
info@festivalfilm.com
www.festivalfilm.com
MD: Ray Marshall
• *Feature films: Man Dancin'; The Colour*

Film and Music Entertainment
020 7636 9292
info@fame.uk.com
www.fame.uk.com
MD: Mike Downey
• *Guy X; Deathwatch; The Enemy*

Films of Record
020 7286 0333
zoek@filmsofrecord.com
www.filmsofrecord.com
MD: Jane Bevan
• *Malaria; The Protectors; Remember
the Secret Policeman's Ball; Rail Cops*

Fireside Favourites
020 7439 6110
info@firesidefavourites.co.uk
www.firesidefavourites.co.uk
MD: Gavin Claxton
• *House of Rock; Infamous Five series 1
and 2*

Flame Television
020 7713 6868
contact@flametv.co.uk
www.theflamegroup.com
*Chairman: Roger Bolton; MD and head
of production: Clare Featherstone*
• *Discovery Health 2 bulletins; Cage
Combat (Carlton); Crime Team (C4);
Square Planet (Discovery Europe);
Roadies 2 (UK Horizons); Ann Summers
Uncovered (Carlton); Dim Crims (Five);
Jane Goldman Investigates (Living TV);
Wild Prince (C4); Celebrity Love Match;
Celebrities in Therapy*

Flashback Television
020 7490 8996
Bristol: 0117 973 8755
mailbox@flashbacktv.co.uk or
bristol@flashbacktv.co.uk
www.flashbacktv.co.uk
MD: Taylor Downing
• *D-Day: The lost evidence; Regency
Feast; The badness of King George IV;
Nigella Bites; Speed Machines;
Battlestations*

Flick features
020 7855 3697
info@flickfeatures.com
www.flickfeatures.co.uk
Director: John Deery
• *Hell4Leather; Feature film:
Conspiracy of Silence; Pictures of
Anna (in development)*

Flying Elephant Films
020 8230 6920
info@flyingelephant.co.uk
www.flyingelephant.co.uk
MD: Preeyf Nair
• *A Story That Begins at the End; A
Different Life; You Know What I'm
Saying*

Focus Productions
0117 904 6292
Stratford-upon-Avon: 01789 298948
martinweitz@focusproductions.co.uk
or
maddern@focusproductions.co.uk
www.focusproductions.co.uk
MD: Martin Weitz
• *Pharaoh's Holy Treasure (BBC2); This
Sceptred Isle; The Jewish Journey
(BBC R4). Winner, Sony Gold Award.
Projects 2003: Witness on Saint-
making (C4); The Godfather of the
Blues (BBC4)*

Footstep Productions
020 7836 9990
info@footstep-productions.com
www.footstepproductions.com
MD: Collette Thomson
• Worktalk; Voces Espanolas

Free@Last TV
020 7242 4333
barry@freeatlasttv.co.uk
www.freeatlasttv.co.uk
Executive producer: Barry Ryan
• The Spiderman Story; Making Of
Jackass The Movie; Rock 'n' Roll Myths;
Blackadder@20; Adored: The Stone
Roses Story; Mobo Unsung; Dr Who@40

Fresh One Productions
020 7359 1000
www.freemantlemedia.com
MD: Andrew Conran
• Jamie's School Dinners; Oliver's Twist;
Jamie's Kitchen

Fulcrum TV
020 7939 3160
info@fulcrumtv.com
www.fulcrumtv.com
MDs: Christopher Hird, Richard Belfield
• The State of Texas; The Christmas
Truce; The Ultimate Psychic Challenge;
Belonging; The Man from the Met

Genesis Media Group
029 2066 6007
alan@genesis-media.co.uk
www.genesis-media.co.uk
Producer and programme director:
Alan Torjussen
• Peter Warlock; Ceiri and his Music;
Love Talk; Leila Megane; corporate
and government projects plus travel,
arts, music and docs for TV

Ginger Television
020 7663 2300
production@ginger.tv
www.ginger.tv
MD: Elisabeth Partyka
• Czech Mates; High School Projects USA;
Extreme lives – My Right Foot; Don't
Drop the Coffin (ITV), Timewatch – The
Secrets of Enzo Ferrari (BBC2)

Glasshead
020 8740 0024
media@glasshead.co.uk
www.glasshead.co.uk
MD: Lambros Atteshlis
• Blue Dragon; Watch Magic Grandad;
Real Science

Grand Slamm Children's Films
020 7388 0789
info@gscfilms.com
www.gscfilms.com
MD: Ginger Gibbons
• Percy the Park Keeper; Angelina
Ballerina; Kipper; Dot Wot; The
Hairdressers Dog; The Magic Bed

Green Bay Media
029 2064 2370
john-geriant@green-bay.tv
www.green-bay.tv
MD: Phil George, John Geraint
• An Archbishop Like This; A Bloody
Good Friday; Do Not Go Gentle

Green Inc Productions
028 9057 3000
tv@greeninc.tv
MD: Stephen Stewart
• The Afternoon Show; Patrick Kielty
Almost Live; Red Bull DJ Academy;
Anderson In

Green Umbrella
0117 973 1729
postmaster@umbrella.co.uk
www.umbrella.co.uk
MD: Nigel Ashcroft
• Journey to Centre of the Earth; Escape
from Berlin; Galileo's Daughter

Greenlit Productions
020 7287 3545
info@greenlit.co.uk
www.greenlit.co.uk
MD: Jill Green
• Foyle's War; The Swap; Menace; Trust

Greenpoint Films
020 7240 7066
info@greenpointfilms.com
www.greenpointfilms.co.uk
MDs: Patrick Cassavetti, Ann Scott,
Simon Relph
• Only Human; Hideous Kinky; The
Land Girls

Grosvenor Park Productions
020 7529 2500
chris.chrisafis@grosvenorpark.com
www.grosvenorpark.com
MD: Daniel Taylor
• Reign of Fire; Being Julia; Colour Me
Kubrick; Count of Monte Cristo; Spider

Gruber Films
0870 366 9313
office@gruberfilms.com
www.gruberfilms.com
MD: Richard Holmes
• Shooting Fish; Waking Ned; The
Abduction Club

Hand Pict Productions
0131 346 1111
ask@handpict.com
www.handpict.com
Director: George Cathro
• Adoption Stories; East Coast Boy, West
Coast Man; Numero Una

Hanrahan Media
01789 450182
info@hanrahanmedia.com
www.hanrahanmedia.tv
MD: Will Hanrahan
• Your Stars; Renovation Creation;
Star Lives (ITV); World's Biggest
Ghost Hunt; Most Haunted Live
(LivingTV); Men's Health (Bravo)

Hasan Shah Films
020 7722 2419
hsfilms@blueyonder.co.uk
MD: Hasan Shah
• Short: Art Of The Critic. Feature in
development 2003: A Little Scary

Hewland International
020 8215 3345
info@hewland.co.uk
www.hewland.co.uk
MD: Jane Hewland
• Dream Team; Stranger than Fiction;
Dial a Date; Dream Team Retro; Mile
High; Can't Buy Me Love

Hopscotch Films
0141 334 5576
info@hopscotchfilms.co.uk
www.hopscotchfilms.co.uk
MDs: Charlotte Wontner, Clara Glynn,
John Archer
• Writing Scotland; Detox or Die; Last
Train to Beechwood

Hot Shot Films
028 9031 3332
info@hotshotfilms.com
www.hotshotfilms.com
MDs: Brendan J. Byrne, Jimmy
McAleavey
• The Secret Life of Words; Living
History; Blind Vision; Street
Detectives; So You Thought You Knew
the Plantation; Heroes

Hotbed Media
0121 248 3900
mail@hotbedmedia.co.uk
MD: Johannah Dyer
• Under the Hammer; Songs of Praise;
Real Brassed Off; 100 Worst Britons;
Everything Must Go; 100 Worst Pop
Records; Star Portraits with Rolf Harris

Hourglass Productions
020 8540 8786
productions@hourglass.co.uk
www.hourglass.co.uk
MD: Martin Chilcott
• Energy for Nature; DNA and Rocket
Science, Living Donation

HRTV
020 7494 3011
mail@hrtv-online.com
www.hrtv-online.com
MD: Jerry Hibbert
• Tractor Tom; Stressed Eric series II

Hyphen Films
020 7734 0632
nmk@hyphenfilms.com
www.hyphenfilms.com
MD: N.M. Kabir
• Spotlights and Saris; Bollywood
Dancing; Bollywood Women – Intros;
Bismillah of Benaras; Bollywood
Celebrities; Bollywood 2004

I2I Productions
01698 794100
enquiries@ i2itv.com
www.i2itv.com
Director: Gordon Ross
• Crimewatch; Panorama; Holiday
Programme

Icon Films
0117 924 8535
info@iconfilms.co.uk
www.iconfilms.co.uk
MD: Laura Marshall
• Belgrano; King Cobra; Einstein's Brain

Illumina Digital
020 8600 9300
info@illumina.co.uk
www.illumina.co.uk
MD: Andrew Chitty
• DFES; National Theatre; Culture;
Net Cymru

Illuminations Films
020 7288 8400
mail@illumin.co.uk
www.illumin.co.uk
MD: Keith Griffiths
• The Piano Tuner of Earthquakes;
London Orbital; Little Otik

Images Of War
020 7267 9198
derek@dircon.co.uk
www.warfootage.com
MD: Derek Blades
• Mass for Peace; Invasion; D-Day;
Footage for Hitler's Britain; 300 hours
of war-related material

Imago Productions
01603 727600
mail@imagoproductions.tv
www.imagoproductions.tv
MD: Vivica Parsons
• Grudge Match; Perfect Man;
The Coach; Sporty Facts; Bryan's Olde
and Bitter

Independent Image
01883 654867
info@indimage.com
www.indimage.com
MD: David Wickham
• Chefs in the City; Cannabis from the
Chemist; Interpol's Most Wanted

Infinite Pictures
01752 764244
info@infinitepictures.com
www.infinitepictures.com
MD: David Nottage
• Boy's Toys; Civvie to Sailor; Centre Stage

Infonation
020 7370 1082
mail@infonation.org.uk
www.infonation.org.uk
MD: Ron Blythe
• Under One Umbrella; Protected Meal
Times; Challenge UK

Intelfax
020 7928 2727
billskirrow@intelfax.co.uk
www.intelfax.co.uk
MD: Bill Skirrow
• Subtitles for: 21st Century War;
A Band Called Treacle

**Intermedia Film and Video
(Nottingham)**
0115 955 6909
info@intermedianotts.co.uk
www.intermedianotts.co.uk
MD: Ceris Morris
• One For The Road; Slot Art; Shifting
Units; The Entertainer; First Cut

**International Media Productions
(IMP)**
020 8690 9674
improductions@tiscali.co.uk
www.improductions.co.uk
Producer, director: Paul Moody
• Arriva; Tiny Lives; A Beacon for
Culture

ITN factual
020 7430 4511
itn.factual@itn.co.uk
www.itn.co.uk
Head of ITN Factual: Philip Armstrong
• Hunt for The Hood/Bismarck;
Leonardo's Dream Machines; Sars –
Global Killer; Are Your Kids on Drugs?

IWC Media
0141 429 1750
info@iwcmedia.co.uk
www.warkclements.com
MD: Sue Oriel
• Relocation, Relocation, Relocation;
Location, Location, Location;
Jeopardy; The First World War (C4)

Jay Media
media@jaymedia.co.uk
www.jaymedia.co.uk
MD: Nigel Jay
• Skill City; Manchester Evening News;
Preston City Council; Mersey Family
Business Awards; UK Trade &
Investment; Manchester City Council;
Scope

The Jim Henson Company
020 7428 4000
fanmail@henson.com
www.henson.com
MD: Pete Coogan
• Muppet series; Aliens in the Family;
Bear in the Big Blue House

Juniperblue
0117 3305938
richard@juniperblue.com
www.juniperblue.com
MD: Richard Moore
• Tate – Henry Moore Recumbent
Figure; Marine Conservation Society;
Good Beach Guide; Wild Battlefields
Wolf and Polar Bear; Allied Domecq-
Courvoisier XO

Keo Films
020 7490 3580
keo@keofilms.com
www.keofilms.com
MD: Andrew Palmer
• River Cottage Diner; Surviving
Extremes; 10 Years Younger

The Kilroy Television Company
020 7893 7900
info@kilroy.co.uk
Head of production: Graham Walters
• Panorama; Now You're Talking!;
The Kilroy Programme

Kudos
020 7580 8686
info@kudosfilmandtv.com
www.kudosfilmandtv.com
MDs: Stephen Garrett, Jane Featherstone
• Spooks; Life on Mars; Hustle II

Landmark Films
01865 297220
info@landmarkfilms.com
www.landmarkfilms.com
MD: Nick O'Dwyer
• Extraordinary Illness; Beauty School;
Real Life Swap

Landseer Productions
020 7485 7333
mail@landseerfilms.com
www.landseerfilms.com
MD and producer: Derek Bailey
• Resurrecting St Luke's; South Bank
Show – Johnnie Ray; The Magic
Mountain

Leopard Films
0870 420 4232
mail@leopardfilms.com
www.leopardfilms.com
MD: James Burstall
• Car Booty; Cash in the Attic; Money
Spinners; Elvis Mob

Liberty Bell Productions
0191 222 1200
info@libertybell.tv
www.libertybell.tv
MDs: Stuart Prebble, Andrea Wonfor;
head of features: Judith Holder
• Grumpy Old Men; Victoria Wood's Big
Fat Documentary; Stella's Story; For
the Benefit of Mr Parris

Libra Television
0161 236 5599
hq@libratelevision.com
www.libratelevision.com
MDs: Madeline Wiltshire, Louise Lynch
• Gross; Citizen Power; How to be a
Bully; Copycat Kids; History Busters

Little Bird
00 353 1 613 1710
info@littlebird.ie
www.littlebird.ie
Co Chairmen: James Mitchell,
Jonathan Cavendish
• Bridget Jones 2 – The Edge of Reason;
Trauma; Churchill the Hollywood
Years; In my Father's Den

Loose Moose
020 7287 3821
info@loosemoose.net
www.loosemoose.net
MD: Glenn Holberton
• Peperami; Chips Ahoy!; Brisk Iced Tea

Lupus Films
020 7419 0997
info@lupusfilms.net
www.lupusfilms.net
MDs: Camilla Deakin, Ruth Fielding
• Little Wolf's Book of Badness (C4);
Wilde Stories; Little Wolf's Adventure
Academy; Mia, Cool Hunter

Macmillan Media
0870 350 2150
info@macmillanmedia.co.uk
www.macmillanmedia.co.uk
MD: Michael Macmillan
• Corporate video

Malachite
01790 763538
info@malachite.co.uk
www.malachite.co.uk
MD: Charles Mapleston
• Fiore; Children of the Mafia; Dressing
up for the carnival – a portrait of Carol
Shields

Maverick Television
0121 771 1812
London: 020 7631 1062
mail@mavericktv.co.uk
www.mavericktv.co.uk
Chairman: Johnnie Turpie
• *Ten Years Younger; Celebrity Disfigurement*

Maya Vision International
020 7836 1113
john@mayavisionint.com
www.mayavisionint.com
Producer and director: Rebecca Dobbs
• *Hitler's Search for the Holy Grail; Conquistadors; In Search of Shakespeare; Two Moons (feature); In Search of Myths and Heroes*

Mentorn
020 7258 6800
mentorn@mentorn.co.uk
www.mentorn.co.uk
MD: Charles Thompson
• *Robot Wars; Techno Games; Britain's Worst Driver*

Mint Productions
028 9024 0555
Belfast 028 9024 0555
Dublin 00 353 1 491 3333
info@mint.ie
www.mint.ie
MD: Steve Carson
• *Abu Hamza; Two Day Coup; De Lorean; Workers Strike; Crash; Emmet; All the Queen's Men; Who Kidnapped Shergar?*

Monkey
020 7749 3110
info@monkeykingdom.com
www.monkeykingdom.com
MD: Dom Loehnis
• *What Sadie Did Next; Swag; He's Starsky I'm Hutch*

Multi Media Arts
0161 374 5566
info@mmarts.com
www.mmarts.com
MD: Michael Spencer
• *Powerhouse; The Blizzard of Odd; Reality Bites*

Mute Marmalade
020 7449 2552
info@mutemarmalade.com
www.mutemarmalade.com
MD: Jonathan Bentata
• *Black Soles; The Runner; Making Mistakes*

Mykindofshow.com
020 7739 0234
mail@mykindofshow.com
www.mykindofshow.com
MD: Kirsten De Keyser
• *Follow That Tomato; Borscht, Blackbread and Champagne; Bin Sins; Six Degrees of Penetration; Tuscany To Go; Home Health Show*

Nexus Productions
020 7749 7500
info@nexusproductions.com
www.nexusproductions.com
MD: Chris O'Reilly
• *Catch Me if You Can; Goldfrapp; Erasure; Nike; T- Mobile; Aiwa; Monkey Dust*

Objective Productions
020 8846 3950
info@objectiveproductions.com
www.objectiveproductions.net
MDs: Andrew O'Connor, Michael Vine
• *Derren Brown: Trick of the Mind; Peep Show; Dirty Tricks; Balls of Steel; Greatest TV Moments*

October Films
020 7284 6868
info@octoberfilms.co.uk
www.octoberfilms.co.uk
MD: Tom Roberts
• *Suicide Bombers; Rugby World Cup – England's Story; Access to Evil*

Open Mind Productions
020 7437 0624
enquiries@openmind.co.uk
www.openmind.co.uk
MD: Roland Tongue
• *Paz; The Shiny Show; The Number Crew*

Optomen
020 7967 1234
otv@optomen.com
www.optomen.com
MD: Peter Gillbe
• *Ramsay's Kitchen Nightmares Series 2*

Outline Productions
020 7428 1560
mail@outlineproductions.co.uk
MDs: Helen Veale, Laura Mansfield
• *House of Tiny Tearaways; Mongrel Nation; Homefront; Violent Nation; Conspiracies On Trial*

ORTV
020 8614 7200
info@ortv.co.uk
www.ortv.co.uk
MD: Nicholas Claxton
• *John McCarthy – Out of the Shadows; Heart of the Lioness; Saddam's Iraq*

Oxford Film And Television
020 7483 3637
email@oftv.co.uk
www.oftv.co.uk
Creative director: Nicholas Kent
• *Lionheart – The Crusade; Second Generation (C4); Superfly, Terry Jones' Medieval Tales, National Trust (BBC); The Spectator Affair; Vic Reeves: Rogues Gallery; Building Britain; 2003 Visions Of Space*

Paladin Invision
020 7371 2123
pitv@pitv.com
www.pitv.com
MDs: William Cran, Clive Syddall
• *Commanding Heights; Do You Speak American; Dark Star; All Or Nothing At All: The Life of Frank Sinatra*

Pathé Pictures
020 7323 5151
orlaghcollins@pathe-uk.com
www.pathe.com
MD: Francois Ivernel
• *Natural History; Girl With a Pearl Earring; Millions*

Pepper's Ghost Productions
020 8546 4900
enquiries@peppersghost.com
www.peppersghost.com
MD: Paul Michael
• *Tiny Planets; Policecat Fuzz; Bus Stop; Kingfisher Tailor*

Pesky
020 7703 2080
hodge@pesky.com
www.pesky.com
Partners: David Hodgson, Clare Underwood
• *Stress Maniacs; Amazing Adrenalini Brothers; MissyMiss; Invisible INK; CyberPest*

Pilot Film and TV Productions
020 8960 2721
info@pilotguides.com
www.pilotguides.com
Director: John Pilot
• *Globe Trekker; Pilot Guides; Planet Food; Ian Wright Live*

Pioneer Productions
020 8748 0888
pioneer@pioneertv.com
www.pioneertv.com
MD: Stuart Carter
• *Naked Science; Danger Man; Tycoon Toys*

Planet 24 Productions
020 7612 0671
alice@planet24.co.uk
www.planet24.com
MD: Ed Forsdick
• *Mechanick; How to Pull... ; Big Breakfast*

Planet Wild
0161 233 3090
office@planetwild.co.uk
www.planetwild.co.uk
MD: Paula Trafford
• *Cilla in Black and White; George Best's Story; Pushy Parents*

Presentable
029 2057 5729
all@presentable.co.uk
www.presentable.co.uk
MD: Megan Stewart
• *Celebrity Poker Club; Late Night Poker; Conversations with Ronan Williams*

Prism Entertainment
020 8969 1212
info@prism-e.com
www.prismentertainment.co.uk
MDs: Mike Crosby, Amelia Johnson
• *The Stables; FAQ series 3; Beat the Cyborgs*

The Producers
020 7636 4226
jenny@theproducersfilms.co.uk
www.theproducersfilms.co.uk
MDs: Jenny Edwards, Jeanna Polley
• *Belonging; Seeing Red; The Politician's Wife*

Quickfire Media
0117 946 6838
emma.harrison@quickfiremedia.com
www.quickfiremedia.com
MD: Mark Fielder
• *The Last Tommy; In the Footsteps of Churchill; Dispatches: Barrack Room Bullies; Natural World; Wolves of the Barren Lands*

Raw Charm
029 2064 1511
enquiries@rawcharm.tv
www.rawcharm.tv
MD: Pam Hunt
• *War Stories; Grave Detectives; Simon Weston's War Heroes*

Real Life Media Productions
0113 237 1005
info@reallife.co.uk
www.reallife.co.uk
MD: Ali Rashid
• *Mum, I'm a Muslim; Baby Baby; Britain's Most Dangerous Prisoner*

Red Green and Blue Company
020 8746 0616
max@rgbco.com
www.rgbco.com
Directors: Max Whitby, Cathy Collis
• *DNA Interactive*

Red Kite Animations
0131 554 0060
info@redkite-animation.com
www.redkite-animation.com
MD: Ken Anderson
• *The Secret World of Benjamin Bear; The Loch Ness Kelpie; Wilf the Witch's Dog*

Red Production Company
0161 827 2530
info@redlimited.co.uk
www.redproductioncompany.com
MD: Andrew Critchley
• *Blue Blood; Jane Hall Big Bad Bus Ride; Mine All Mine*

Reef Television
020 7836 8595
mail@reeftv.com
www.reef.tv
MD: Richard Farmbrough
• *Sun, Sea & Bargain Spotting; Put Your Money Where Your House Is; Foreign Exchange; Uncharted Territory*

Reel Life Television
020 7713 1585
enquiries@reel-life-tv.co.uk
www.reel-life-tv.co.uk
MDs: Chris Raine, Celine Smith
• *Songs of Praise; Moving On Up; Focus on Fear; Job Bank; Singled Out*

Renting Eyeballs Entertainment
020 7437 4417
malcolm.rasala@rentingeyeballs.com
www.rentingeyeballs.com
MD: Mark Maco
• *Commercials, promos, brand television, motion pictures*

Resource Base
023 8023 6806
post@resource-base.co.uk
www.resource-base.co.uk
MD: Karen Gilchrist, Hilary Durman
• *VEE-TV; Without You; World of Difference (C4); Lion Mountain; Who Cares? (BBC)*

Ricochet Films
020 7251 6966
mail@ricochet.co.uk
www.ricochet.co.uk
MD: Nick Powell
• *Supernanny; Living in the Sun; Flying Heavy Metal; How Not to Decorate; Risking It All; Mirror, Signal, Manoeuvre*

Ronin Entertainment
020 7734 3884
mail@ronintv.com
www.ronintv.com
MDs: Richard Hearsey, Robin Greene
• *The Impressionable Jon Culshaw; Fort Boyard; It's a Knockout*

RS Productions
0191 224 4301
info@rsproductions.co.uk
www.rsproductions.co.uk
MD: Mark Lavender
• *Frozen; Elephants and Angels; Laughter When We're Dead; Thereby Hangs a Tale*

Sally Head Productions
020 8607 8730
admin@shpl.demon.co.uk
MD: Sally Head
• *Forefathers; Plastic Man; Tipping The Velvet; The Cry; Mayor of Casterbridge; The Return*

Samson Films
00 353 1 667 0533
info@samsonfilms.com
www.samsonfilms.com
MD: David Collins
• *Co-producer: Blind Flight; Honeymooners; Abduction Club; Most Fertile Man in Ireland. Feature development: Mir Friends; Immortal; Havoc*

Scream Films
020 8995 8255
info@screamfilms.com
www.screamfilms.com
MD: Susie Dark
• *Famous and Frightened; Dell Winton's Wedding; Terror Alert*

Screenhouse Productions
0113 266 8881
info@screenhouse.co.uk
www.screenhouse.co.uk
Chief executive: Barbara Govan
• *Star Date; Science Shack; Snapshot*

Seventh Art Productions
01273 777678
info@seventh-art.com
www.seventh-art.com
MD: Phil Grabsky
• *Tim Marlow on ... Edward Hopper; Easter in Art; Pelé – World Cup Hero; Great Artists II; The Boy Who Plays on the Buddhas of Bamiyan*

Shed Productions
020 8215 3387
shed@shedproductions.com
www.shedproductions.com
MD: Eileen Gallagher
• *Footballers Wives; Bad Girls*

SMG TV Productions
0141 300 3000
info@smg.plc.uk
www.smgtv.co.uk
Director: Surinder Gautama
• *Taggart; Club Reps: The Workers; Good Bye Mr Chips; Medics of the Glen; Squeak!; How 2*

Slinky Pictures
020 7247 6444
info@slinkypics.com
www.slinkypics.com
MD: Maria Manton
• *Dad's Dead; Don't Do Politics; People's Britain; Super Barrio*

Smith And Watson Productions
01803 863033
info@smithandwatson.com
www.smithandwatson.com
MD: Nick Smith
• *Building a Dream; Bill Wyman's Blues; A Story of Peter Rabbit and Beatrice Potter*

Smoking Dogs Films
020 7249 6644
info@smokingdogsfilms.com
www.smokingdogsfilms.com
MD: David Lawson
• *Urban Soul – Making of Modern R&B; The Wonderful World of Louis Armstrong; Goldie – When Satin Returns*

So Television
020 7960 2000
info@sotelevision.co.uk
www.sotelevision.co.uk
Director: Jon Magnusson
• *Comedy Lab; v Graham Norton (Channel 4)*

Specific Films
020 7580 7476
info@specificfilms.com
www.specificfilms.com
MD: Michael Hamlyn
• *Last Seduction II; Paws; Mr Reliable; Priscilla, Queen of the Desert*

Spire Films
01865 371979
mail@spirefilms.co.uk
www.spirefilms.co.uk
MD: David Wilcox
• *Delia Smith; Romans*

Stampede
01582 727330
dave@stampede.co.uk
www.stampede.co.uk
MD: Mike Chamberlain
- *Putting the Fun in Fundamental;*
  Lin and Ralph – A Love Story;
  Fierce People; Before The Flood

Sunset + Vine
020 7478 7300
reception@sunsetvine.co.uk
www.sunsetvine.co.uk
MD: John Leach
- *Channel 4 Cricket; Gillette World*
  Sport; Gumball 3000; Rad; European
  Poker Tour; Football on Five; John
  Barnes Football Night

Sunstone Films
sunstonefilms@aol.com
www.sunstonefilms.co.uk
- *Before Columbus; Lords of the Maya;*
  Warhorse; Gladiators: The Brutal
  Truth; It Ain't Necessarily So

Talent Television
020 7421 7800
entertainment@talenttv.com
www.talenttv.com
Creative director: John Kaye Cooper
- *Inside Clyde; Best of Friends;*
  Casino, Casino

Telemagination
020 7434 1551
mail@tmation.co.uk
www.telemagination.co.uk
Head of studio: Beth Parker
- *Pongwiffy; Little Ghosts; Something*
  Else; Metalheads; Cramp Twins; Heidi
  (theatrical release)

Television Junction
0121 248 4466
info@televisionjunction.co.uk
www.televisionjunction.co.uk
MDs: Paul Davies, Yvonne Davies
- *Double Act; Seeing Science; Think*
  About It

Tell-Tale Productions
020 8324 2308
info@tell-tale.co.uk
www.tell-tale.co.uk
MD: Karl Woolley
- *Tweenies; Boo*

Ten Alps TV
020 7089 3686
info@tenalps.com
www.tenalps.com
MD: Tim Spencer
- *Peaches Geldof: Inside the Mind of a*
  Teenager; Jeremy Vine Meets... series 2;
  Geldof on Fathers; Geldof on Divorce

Tern Television
0224 211123
Glasgow: 0141 243 5658
info@terntv.com
www.terntv.com
MDs: David Strachan, Gwyneth Hardy
- *Chancers; Fraserburgh; 2003*
  Reloaded; Mapman

Testimony Films
0117 925 8589
mail@testimonyfilms.com
MD: Steve Humphries
- *Lovechild; Sex in a Cold Climate;*
  Britain's Boy Soldiers; Some Liked It
  Hot

Tigress Productions
020 7434 4411
Bristol: 0117 933 5600
general@tigressproductions.co.uk
or general@tigressbristol.co.uk
www.tigressproductions.co.uk
MD: Jeremy Bradshaw
- *Snakemaster; The Jeff Corwin*
  Experience; Dolphin Murders;
  The Science of Combat

Torpedo
029 2076 6117
info@torpedoltd.co.uk
www.torpedoltd.co.uk
Chairman: Mark Jones
- *Fishlock's Sea Stories; Jigsaw;*
  Horatio's Holiday

Touch Productions
01747 828030
enquiries@touchproductions.co.uk
www.touchproductions.co.uk
MD: Malcolm Brinkworth
- *Feeding Martin (Meridian); Beasts of*
  the Roman Games (C4); Life of a Ten
  Pound Note (BBC); The Missing Chink
  (C4); Party Maestro (BBC)

TransAtlantic Films
020 8735 0505
Hereford: 01497 831800
mail@transatlanticfilms.com
www.transatlanticfilms.com
MD: Corisande Albert
- *Amazing Animal Adaptors; Extreme*
  Body Parts; Science of Love

Turn On Television
0161 247 7700
mail@turnontv.co.uk
www.turnontv.co.uk
MD: Angela Smith
- *Viva La Diva; Bangkok Bound;*
  Special Delivery

TV6
020 7610 0266
mail@tv6.co.uk
www.tv6.co.uk
MD: Richard Reisz
- *Horizon: Percy Pilcher's Flying*
  Machines (BBC); Horizon: King
  Solomon's Stone (BBC); Landscape
  Mysteries (BBC); Hidden Egypt
  (National Geographic); Into the Great
  Pyramid (live, Fox Network)

Unique Communications Group
020 7605 1200
ucg@uniquegroup.co.uk
or info@uniquecomms.com
www.uniquecomms.com
MD: Noel Edmonds
- *British Comedy Awards 2003 (ITV);*
  Stars Behind Bars (Five); Harley Street
  (Living TV); I'm the Answer (ITV)

Vera Productions
020 7436 6116
cree@vera.co.uk
www.vera.co.uk
MD: Elaine Morris
- *The Big Impression (BBC1); Between*
  Iraq and A Hard Place (C4); Bremner
  Bird and Fortune (C4)

Vivum Intelligent Media
020 7729 2749
nick@vivum.net
www.vivum.net
MD: Nick Rosen
- *2003 World Trade Centre series (PBS);*
  documentary in Russia (BBC4); high-
  brow factual content

Wag TV
020 7688 1711
post@wagtv.com
www.wagtv.com
MD: Martin Durkin
- *Inter Sex; Divine Designs; Dave*
  Courtney's Underworld; The Great
  Scientist

Wild Dream Films
01273 236168
mail@wild-dream.com
www.wild-dream.com
MD: Stuart Clarke
- *Map Makers; Ancient Discoveries*
  series 1/2

Wild Rover Productions
028 9050 0980
enquiries@wild-rover.com
www.wild-rover.com
MD: Philip Morrow
- *Just For Laughs; A Day In The*
  Westlife of Shane; Would You Pass the
  Eleven Plus?

Wilton Films
020 7749 7282
info@wiltonfilms.com
or cvs@wiltonfilms.com
www.wiltonfilms.com
MD: Paul Mitchell
- *Hotspots; Chechnya; The Alternative*
  Rock 'n' Roll Years; Lords of the Spin

Windfall Films
020 7251 7676
enquiries@windfallfilms.com
www.windfallfilms.com
MD: David Dugan
- *D-Day: The Ultimate Conflict; The*
  Great Escape Revealed; Men of Iron

World Of Wonder
020 7428 3444
wow@wofwonder.co.uk
www.worldofwonder.net
Chief executive: Fenton Bailey
- *Matt's Old Masters; Housebusters;*
  The Art Show – Spoils of War

World Wide Pictures
020 7434 1121
info@worldwidegroup.ltd.uk
www.worldwidegroup.ltd.uk
MDs: Richard King, Ray Townsend,
Chris Courtenay-Taylor
- *Bad Girls; videos for the Office of the*
  Deputy Prime Minister

World's End Productions
020 7751 9880
info@worldsendproductions.com
www.worldsendproductions.com
MDs: Jim Philips, Jerry Drew
• *Shoot Me; Going Down to South Park;*
Dead Casual; Live at Johnny's;
Fighting Talk. Co-production with
Celador: Johnny & Denise

Zeal Television
020 8780 4600
sheila.humphreys@zealtv.net
www.zealtv.net
Chief executive: Peter Christiansen
• *Building the Dream; Come and Have a*
Go if You Think You're Smart Enough;
Resistance; Demolition; Super
Human; Sushi TV

Zeppotron
0870 333 1700
contact@zeppotron.com
www.zeppotron.com
Creative directors: Neil Webster, Ben
Caudell, Charlie Brooker
• *People's Book of Records; Playing*
Tricks; The Cowboy Trap

TV and film studios

124 Facilities
124 Horseferry Road
London SW1P 2TX
020 7306 8040
www.124.co.uk
Part of the Channel 4 group. General
manager: Tony Chamberlain; studio
managers: Tony Kibbles, Tim Moulson

3 Mills Studios
Three Mill Lane, London E3 3DU
020 7363 3336
info@3mills.com
www.3mills.com
MD: Daniel Dark; studio manager:
Jason Taylor

3sixty Media
Quay Street, Manchester M60 9EA
0161 827 2020
enquiry@3sixtymedia.com
www.3sixtymedia.com
Head of studios: Paul Bennett

400 Company
B3 The Workshops
2A Askew Crescent
Shepherds Bush, London W12 9DP
020 8746 1400
info@the400.co.uk
www.the400.co.uk
Studio manager: Christian Riov

Arqiva
Crawley Street, Winchester SO21 2QA
01962 823000
info@arqiva.com
www.arqiva.com
MD: Peter Douglas
Formerly NTL Broadcast

Ascent Media
1 Stephen Street, London W1T 1AL
020 7691 6000
www.ascentmedia.co.uk
Studio manager: Tony Shepherd

APTN
The Interchange, Oval Road
Camden Lock, London NW1 7DZ
020 7482 7580
aptnbookings@ap.org
www.aptn.com
Studio manager: Zara Evans

Ardmore Studios
Herbert Road, Bray
Co Wicklow, Ireland
00 353 1 286 2971
film@ardmore.ie
www.ardmore.ie
MD: Kevin Moriarty

Asylum Studios
Wadsworth Close, Greenford
Perivale UB6 7JS
020 8991 9191
Studio manager: Iain Silvester

BBC Elstree Centre
Clarendon Road, Borehamwood
Herts WD6 1JF
020 8228 7102
www.bbc.co.uk
Senior facility manager: Sue Spree

BBC TV Centre Studios
Wood Lane, Shepherds Bush
London W12 7RJ
020 8743 8000
bbcresources@bbc.co.uk
www.bbcresources.co.uk
Principal facilities manager: Gary
Collins

Box Studios
15 Mandela Street, London NW1 0DU
020 7388 0020
mail@boxstudios.co.uk
www.boxstudios.co.uk
Directors: Philip Bier, Chris Gascoigne;
studio manager: Meredith Howard

Bray Studios
Down Place, Water Oakley
Windsor, Berks SL4 5UG
01628 622111
B.earl@tiscali.co.uk
Studio manager: Beryl Earl

Broadley Studios
Broadley House, 48 Broadley Terrace
London NW1 6LG
020 7258 0324
markfrench@broadleystudios.com
www.broadleystudios.com
MD and studio manager: Mark French

Canalot Production Studios
222 Kensal Road, London W10 5BN
020 8960 8580
andrea.kolokasi@
⠀⠀⠀workspacegroup.co.uk
www.workspacegroup.co.uk
Studio manager: Andrea Kolokasi

Capital Studios
13 Wandsworth Plain
London SW18 1ET
020 8877 1234
louise.prior@prospect-uk.com
www.capitalstudios.co.uk
Studio manager: Bobbi Johnstone

Central Studios
Location House, 5 Dove Lane
Bristol BS2 9HP
0117 955 4777
info@centralstudios.co.uk
www.centralstudios.co.uk
Studio manager: Dave Garbe

Centre Stage
28–30 Osnaburgh Street
London NW1 3ND
020 7388 5225
mail@centrestagestudios.co.uk
www.centrestagestudios.co.uk
MD: Saul Barrington; studio manager:
Toby Gair

Corinthian Television Facilities
Chiswick Park, Building 12
566 Chiswick High Road
London W4 5AN
020 8100 1000
charlotte.alves@ctv.co.uk
www.ctv.co.uk
Studio manager: Shelley Wallis

CTS and Lansdowne Recording Studios
Lansdowne House, Lansdowne Road
London W11 3LP
020 7727 0041
info@cts-lansdowne.co.uk
www.cts-lansdowne.co.uk
Studio manager: Chris Dibble

Depot Studios
29–31 Brewery Road
London N7 9QH
020 7609 1366
info@thedepotstudios.com
www.thedepotstudios.com
Studio manager: Helen Hilton

Desisti Lighting (UK)
15 Old Market Street
Thetford, Norfolk IP24 2EQ
01842 752909
desisti@globalnet.co.uk
www.desisti.co.uk
Director: John Reay-Young

Ealing Studios
Ealing Green, London W5 5EP
020 8567 6655
info@ealingstudios.com
www.ealingstudios.com
Studio manager: Jeremy Pelzer

East Side Studios
40A River Road, Barking
Essex IG11 0DW
020 8507 7572
info@eastsidestudios.com
www.eastsidestudios.com
Studio manager: Susan Noy

Elstree Film and Television Studios
Shenley Road, Borehamwood
Herts WD6 1JG
020 8953 1600
info@elstreefilmtv.com
www.elstreefilmtv.com
Directors: Julie Wicks, Neville Reid

Enfys
Unit 31 Portanmoor Road
East Moors, Cardiff
South Glamorgan, Wales CF2 5HB
029 2049 9988
mail@enfys.tv
www.enfys.tv
Studio manager: Sarah-Jane Salmon

Fountain TV Studios
128 Wembley Park Drive, Wembley
Middlesex HA9 8HQ
020 8900 5800
everyone@ftv.co.uk
www.ftv.co.uk
Studio manager: Tony Edwards

Greenford Studios
5–11 Taunton Road
Metropolitan Centre, Greenford
Middlesex UB6 8UQ
020 8575 7300
studios@panavision.co.uk
www.panavision.co.uk
Studio manager: Kate Tufano

Handstand studios
13 Hope Street, Liverpool L1 9BH
0151 708 7441
info@handstand-uk.com
www.handstand-uk.com
Studio manager: Han Duijvendak

Holborn Studios
49/50 Eagle Wharf Road
London N1 7ED
020 7490 4099
studiomanager@
    holborn-studios.co.uk
www.holborn-studios.co.uk
Studio manager: Marie McCartney

The Hospital
24 Endell Street
Covent Garden, London WC2H 9HQ
020 7170 9112
studio@thehospital.co.uk
www.thehospital.co.uk
Studio manager: Anne Marie Phelan

IAC
Moorside Road, Winchester
Hampshire S23 7US
01962 873000
info@iacl.co.uk
www.iacl.co.uk
Studio manager: Ian Rich

ICA Theatre
The Mall, London SW1Y 5AH
020 7930 0493
info@ica.org.uk
www.ica.org.uk
Technical manager: Lee Curran

Island Studios
9–11 Alliance Road, Acton
London W3 0RA
020 8956 5600
info@islandstudios.net
www.islandstudios.net
MD and studio manager: Steve Guidici

Inmedia Communications
PO Box 2287
Gerrards Cross SL9 8BF
0870 874 8787
www.inmedia.co.uk
Studio manager: Stan Hollins

Lichfield Studios
133 Oxford Gardens
London W10 6NE
020 8969 6161
kate@lichfieldstudios.co.uk
www.lichfieldstudios.com
Studio assistant: Kate Shortt

London Studios
London Television Centre
Upper Ground Floor, London SE1 9LT
020 7737 8888
sales@londonstudios.co.uk
www.londonstudios.co.uk
MD: Debbie Hills; head of sales: Kathy Schulz

London Wall
Studios 3, London Wall Buildings
London EC2M 5SY
020 7216 4740
tellmemore@broadsheeteurope.com
www.broadsheeteurope.com
Studio manager: David Jones

Maidstone Studios
New Cut Road, Vinters Park
Maidstone, Kent ME14 5NZ
01622 691111
info@maidstonestudios.com
www.maidstonestudios.com
MD: Geoff Miles; liaison manager: Denise Buckland

Metro Imaging
76 Clerkenwell Road
London EC1M 5TN
020 7865 0000
katarina@metroimaging.co.uk
www.metroimaging.co.uk
Studio manager: Steve Jackson

Millbank Studios
4 Millbank, London SW1P 3JA
020 7233 2020
facilities@millbank-studios.co.uk
www.millbank-studios.co.uk
Studio manager: Nicola Golding

Millennium Studios
5 Elstree Way, Borehamwood
Herts WD6 1SF
020 8236 1400
info@millenniumstudios.co.uk
www.millenniumstudios.co.uk
MD: Ronan Willson; studio manager: Toni Cullip

Molinare Studios
34 Fouberts Place, London W1F 7PX
020 7478 7000
bookings@molinare.co.uk
www.molinare.co.uk
Studio manager: Richard Mills

Park Royal Studios
1 Barretts Green Road
London NW10 7AE
020 8965 9778
info@parkroyalstudios.com
www.parkroyalstudios.com
Studio manager: Francois van de Langkruis

Phaebus Communications
The Brewery Tower, The Deva Centre
Trinity Way, Manchester M3 7BF
0161 605 9999
solutions@phaebus.co.uk
www.phaebus.co.uk
Studio manager: Steve Bettridge

Picture It Studios
50 Church Road, London NW10 9PY
020 8961 6644
chris@picit.net
www.picit.net
Studio manager: Chris Fellers

Pinewood Studios
Pinewood Road, Iver Heath
Bucks SL0 0NH
01753 651700
firstname.lastname@
    pinewood-studios.co.uk
www.pinewoodshepperton.com
Studio manager: David Wight

Production House NI/ Stage Services North
Unit 5, Prince Regent Retail Park
Prince Regent Road, Belfast BT5 6QP
028 9079 8999
info@productionhouse.net
Studio manager: Neil Lewis

Pylon Studios
Coal Hill Lane, Leeds LS13 1DJ
0113 204 7000
enquiries@pylonstudios.co.uk
www.pylonstudios.co.uk
Studio manager: Jo Scott

Pyramid TV
36 Cardiff Road, Llandaff
Cardiff, Wales CF5 2DR
029 2057 6888
keith@pyramidtv.co.uk
www.pyramidtv.co.uk
Studio manager: Martin Dodwell

Q Broadcast
1487 Melton Road, Queniborough
Leicester LE7 3FP
0116 260 8813
paul@folosite.net
Studio manager: Martin Branson

RC Film & TV Set Construction
Unit C11 Dundonald Enterprise Park
Carrowreagh Road, Dundonald
Northern Ireland BT16 1QT
028 9055 7557
MD: Russell Fulton

Riverside Studios
Crisp Road, Hammersmith
London W6 9RL
020 8237 1000
online@riversidestudios.co.uk
www.riversidestudios.co.uk
Centre manager: Alex Cotterill

Sands Film Studios
Grices Wharf, 119 Rotherhithe Street
London SE16 4NF
020 7231 2209
OStockman@sandsfilms.co.uk
www.sandsfilms.co.uk
MD: Oliver Stockman

Savoy Hill Studios
Savoy Hill House, Savoy Hill
London WC2R 0BU
020 7497 0830
johnherbert@tabard.co.uk
Studio manager: John Herbert

Shepperton Studios
Studios Road, Shepperton
Middlesex TW17 0QD
01932 562611
firstname.lastname@
    pinewood-studios.co.uk
www.pinewoodshepperton.com
Studio manager: David Godfrey

Space Studios
Boden House, 114–120 Victoria Road
London NW10 6NY
020 8961 2412
dja@spacegrp.com
MD: David Johnson

stu-dio
Cabul Road, London SW11 2PR
020 7228 5228
info@the-studio.co.uk
www.the-studio.co.uk
Studio manager: Gemma Masters

Sumners
Suite 401, Barclay House
35 Whitworth Street West
Manchester M1 5NG
0161 228 0330
andy@sumners.co.uk
www.sumners.co.uk
*General manager and chief engineer:
Brian Hardman*

Teddington Studios
Broom Road, Teddington
Middlesex TW11 9NT
020 8977 3252
sales@teddington.tv
www.teddington.co.uk
Studio manager: Ray Gearing

The Worx
10 Heathmans Road, Fulham
London SW6 4TJ
020 7371 9777
enquiries@theworx.co.uk
www.the-worx.co.uk
MDs: Jackie Mallory, Jonathan Mallory

Twickenham Studios
The Barons, St Margarets
Twickenham, Middlesex TW1 2AW
020 8607 8888
caroline@twickenhamfilmstudios.com
www.twickenhamstudios.com
Studio manager: Caroline Tipple

VFX Company
Dukes Island Studios, Dukes Road
London W3 0SL
020 8956 5674
info@thevfxco.co.uk
www.thevfxco.co.uk
Operations manager: Digna Nigoumi

Waterfall Studios
2 Silver Road
Wood Lane, London W12 7SG
020 8746 2000
enquiries@waterfall-studios.com
www.waterfall-studios.com
Studio manager: Samantha Leese

Post-production

3sixty Media
Quay Street, Manchester M60 9EA
0161 839 0360
enquiry@3sixtymedia.com
www.3sixtymedia.com
*Independent. Effects and virtual reality.
Post-production manager: John Mariner*
• *Island at War; Tonight with Trevor
MacDonald; Blue Murder; Vincent;
Coronation Street*

422 Manchester
4th Floor, South Central
11 Peter Street, Manchester M2 5QR
0161 839 6080
cooey@422.com
www.422manchester.com
*Animation, graphics, commercials,
special effects and audio. Production
director: Richard Wallwork*
• *Vimto; Pingu; Mastermind;
A Question of Sport*

422 South
St John's Court, Whiteladies Road
Bristol BS8 2QY
0117 946 7222
debbiet@422.com
www.422south.com
*Factual television and animation,
digital effects, commercials production.
Production director: Andy Davies-
Coward*
• *The British Isles – A Natural History
(BBC); Journey of Life (BBC); Royal
British Legion (TV commercial)*

Ascent Media Camden
13 Hawley Crescent
London NW1 8NP
020 7284 7900
sam.webb@todd-ao.co.uk
www.ascent-media.co.uk
*Nine other sites. Film processing
laboratory; video; tape; DVD.
MD: Sam Webb*
• *Poirot; Auf Wiedersehen Pet; Hustle*

Anvil
Denham Media Park
North Orbital Road, Denham
Uxbridge, Middlesex UB9 5HL
020 8799 0555
mike.anscombe@thomson.net
www.anvilpost.com
*Audio. Part of Technicolor (Thomson
Group). Studio manager: Mike Anscombe*
• *The Brief; Ultimate Force; Midsomer
Murders; Like Father, Like Son; Doc
Martin; Auf Wiedersehen Pet; Heartless*

Arena Digital
74 Newman Street, London W1T 3EL
020 7436 4360
booking@arenadigital.co.uk
www.arenadigital.co.uk
*Part of 2D video facilities. Effects;
audio; documentaries; comedy.
MD: Martin Price*
• *Bo'Selecta!; Trouble at Top;
Scambusters; Brassed off Britain*

Arion Communications
Global House, Denham Media Park
North Orbital Road, Denham
Uxbridge Middlesex UB9 5HL
01895 834484
sales@arion.co.uk
www.arion.co.uk
*Independent. Telecine; DVD
duplication; editing. MD: Neil Mockler*
• *Hitchhiker's Guide to the Galaxy;
Basic Instinct 2; Sahara*

Barcud Derwen
Cibyn, Caernarfon
Gwynedd LL55 2BD
01286 684300
Cardiff 029 2061 1515
enq@barcud-derwen.co.uk
www.barcudderwen.com
Drama, graphics. MD: Tudor Roberts
• *Celebrity Poker; Tracy Beaker series;
Mountains and Man*

Blue
58 Old Compton Street
London W1D 4UF
020 7437 2626
info@bluepp.co.uk
www.bluepp.co.uk
*VTR Group. Special effects; graphics;
commercial; audio. MD: David Cadel*
• *BBC Imagine; Pompeii: The Last Day;
Property People*

Capital FX
3rd Floor, 20 Dering Street
London W1S 1AJ
020 7493 9998
ian@capital-fx.co.uk
www.capital-fx.co.uk
*Independent. Special effects; graphics;
taped film transfer. MD: Ian Buckton*
• *Harry Potter; Troy; Lord of the Rings*

Cine Wessex
Westway House
19 St Thomas Street, Winchester
Hampshire SO23 9HJ
01962 865454
info@cinewessex.co.uk
www.cinewessex.co.uk
*Independent. Editing; camera kit and
crew hire; 2D and 3D graphics; VHS,
CD and DVD. Facilities director: Joe
Conman*
• *City Gardener; Mappin Murder;
Room for Improvement*

Clear
Fenton House
55–57 Great Marlborough Street
London W1F 7JX
020 7734 5557
clear@clear.ltd.uk
www.clear.ltd.uk
*Sister company Finally Cut. Visual
effects, commercials and films. Senior
producer/head of film: Simon Gosling*
• *28 Days Later; BBC Talking Head
preview; Millions*

Clear Cut Hirers
1 Springvale Terrace
London W14 0AE
020 7605 1700
fazal@clearcutpictures.com
www.clearcutpictures.com
Sister company Clear Cut Pictures.
Dry hire post-production equipment.
MD: Fazal Shah
• *Celeb Deck; Glastonbury festival;*
  Liquid News

Clear Cut Pictures
1 Springvale Terrace
London W14 0AE
020 7605 1700
reception@clearcut pictures
www.clearcutpictures.com
Sister company Clear Cut Hirers.
Graphics and digital rostrum; video
and sound. MD: Jo Beighton
• *Crimewatch; Horizon; Money*
  Programme

Clickstream
37 Dean Street, London W1D 4PT
020 7437 0077
info@clickstream.co.uk
www.clickstream.co.uk
Part of VTR Group. Encoding;
telestream; digital asset management.
MD: Neil Lane
• *E-title project for European Union;*
  Paramount; Movie Tone

Code Design
Ingestre Court, Ingestre Place
London W1F 0JL
020 7343 6449
info@codedesign.co.uk
www.codedesign.co.uk
Part of M2 Group. Storyboarding;
direction; studio shooting; graphics.
Production manager: Bryony Evans
• *Troy; Q Channel Broadcasting;*
  Waking the Dead

Component
28 Newman Street. London W1T 1PR
020 7631 4477
mike@component.co.uk
www.component.co.uk
Independent. Pure graphics.
Director: Mike Kenny
• *Hell's Kitchen; Destination D-Day;*
  Without Prejudice; SAS Jungle; Clive
  Anderson Now

Computamatch
117 Wardour Street
London W1F 0NU
020 7287 1316
edl@computamatch.com
www.ascent-media.co.uk
Part of Ascent Group. Film negative
cutting service. MD: Marilyn Sommer
• *5 Children and It; Guinness; Levi's*

Computer Film Services
66b Unit, York Road
Weybridge, Surrey KT13 9DY
01932 850034
enquiries@computerfilm.com
www.computerfilm.com
Independent. Digital disc recorders
and post-production systems. Director:
Peter Holland
• *Harry Potter; Lord of the Rings*

Crow TV
12 Wendell Road, London W12 9RT
020 8749 6071
info@crowtv.com
www.crowtv.com
Independent. Graphics; editing for
television; pogle colour grade; online/
offline editing; audio. MD: Paul Kingsley
• *Vincent, The Full Story; South Bank*
  Show; The Challenge; Mediterranean
  Tales

Cut and Run
Cinema House, 93 Wardour Street
London W1F 0UD
020 7432 9696
editors@cutandrun.co.uk
www.cutandrun.co.uk
Independent. Offline editing. MD: Steve
Gandalphy
• *Commercials: Castrol; Rimmel; Diet*
  Coke; UPS; Lynx

DB Dubbing
4 St Pauls Road
Clifton, Bristol, Avon BS8 1LT
0117 904 8210
miles@dbdubbing.tv
Independent. Audio. MD: Miles Harris
• *Secret Nature; Built for the Kill; Eden*
  Project

De Lane Lea
75 Dean Street, London W1D 3PU
020 7432 3800
info@delanelea.com
www.delanelea.com
Part of Ascent group. Sound for
post-production TV and film. Chief
operating officer: Hugh Penalt-Jones
• *Cold Mountain; Harry Potter, the*
  Prisoner of Azkaban; Two Brothers

DGP
Portland House, 12–13 Greek Street
London W1D 4DL
020 7734 4501
info@dgpsoho.co.uk
www.dgpsoho.co.uk
Independent. Editing; graphics; DVD;
authoring. MD: Julian Day
• *Murder City; Yahoo; Friends; The Last*
  Samurai; Lord of the Rings: Return of
  the King; Six Feet Under

DVA Associates
7/8 Campbell Court, Bramley
Tadley, Hampshire RG26 5EG
01256 882032
info@dva.co.uk
www.dva.co.uk
Independent. Graphics; audio; DVD;
commercials. MD: Barrie Gibson
• *SAS Survival Secrets; Life of David*
  Kelly; Goalrush for Meridian

Editworks
Austin House, 95–97 Ber Street
Norwich, Norfolk NR1 3EY
01603 624402
info@theeditworks.co.uk
Independent. Video. MD: Rob Manson
• *Commercials: Norwich Union; Virgin*
  Money; Essex County Council for
  European Union

Evolution
68 Wells Street, London W1T 3QA
020 7580 3333
bookings@vividpost.com
www.vividpost.com
Independent. Documentaries; audio;
picture. MD: Robin Bextor
• *Dinner Party Inspectors; Inside the*
  Mind of a Suicide Bomber; Horizon
  Stronger

Evolutions Television
5 Berners Street, London W1T 3LF
020 7580 3333
bookings@evolutionstelevision.com
www.evolutionstelevision.com
Independent. Graphics;
documentaries; commercials; audio.
MD: Simon Kanjee
• *Top of the Pops titles; Jump London;*
  Other People's Houses; Top Gear; MTV
  The Lick; MTV Pimp My Ride

The Farm
13 Soho Square, London W1D 3QF
020 7437 6677
info@farmgroup.tv
www.farmgroup.tv
Partner with Home and The Shed.
Online/offline editing; audio dubbing;
high definition edit and grading.
MDs: Nicky Sargent, Vikki Dunn
• *Dunkirk; Friday night with Jonathan*
  Ross; One Life

Films at 59
59 Cotham Hill, Bristol
Avon BS6 6JR
0117 906 4300
info@filmsat59.com
www.filmsat59.com
Independent. Audio; high definition;
equipment hire; online/offline dubbing.
MD: Gina Lee Fucci
• *Teachers; Big Cat Diary; Building the*
  Dream

Finally Cut
1 Springvale Terrace
London W14 0AE
020 7556 6300
fclon@finalcut-edit.com
www.finalcut-edit.com
Sister company Clear. Offline editing.
Producer: Zoe Henderson
• *Commercials: Sony PlayStation;*
  Mountain; Mercedes "movement"

Finishing Post
10, Gilt Way, Giltbrook
Nottingham, Notts NG16 2GN
0115 945 8800
info@finishing-post.co.uk
www.finishing-post.co.uk
Independent. Graphics; editing; DVD
authoring. MD: Mark Harwood
• *Commercials: Jaguar; Peugeot; Heart*
  of the Country; Carlton Country

Flare DVD
Ingestre Court, Ingestre Place
London W1F 0JL
020 7343 6565
sales@flare-DVD.com
www.flare-DVD.com
*Part of M2 group. Short run duplication;
DVD design; authoring; encoding
facility. MD: Tom Jones*
• *Kate Rusby; Hallmark; Fame Academy;
Elton John; Thin Lizzy's Greatest Hits*

4x4
First Floor, 21 Ormeau Avenue
Belfast BT2 8HD
028 9027 1950
4@4x4post.com
www.4x4post.com
*Independent. Effects; graphics;
commercials; audio. Directors: Katy
Jackson; Paula Campbell; Alan Perry;
Jonathan Featherstone*
• *Disability commercials; BTNI
commercial; Just for a Laugh*

Framestore CFC
9 Noel Street, London W1F 8GH
020 7208 2600
info@framestore-cfc.com
www.framestore-cfc.com
*Independent. Effects; computer
generated commercials; films.
Chief executive: William Sergeant*
• *Thunderbirds; Walking with Sea
Monsters*

Frontier Post
67 Wells Street, London W1T 3PZ
020 7291 9191
info@frontierpost.co.uk
www.frontierpost.co.uk
*Independent. Graphics; audio; online/
offline grading. MD: Neil Hatton*
• *Property Dreams; Howard Goodall's
20th Century Greats; Pagans of the
Roman Empire*

Fusion Broadcast
56 Ballynahinch Road, Dromara
Dromore, County Down BT25 2AL
028 9753 1004
sales@fusionbroadcast.co.uk
www.fusionbroadcast.co.uk
*Independent. Crew supplying.
MD: John Morriffey*
• *BBC Northern Ireland; BBC Network*

Frontline Television
35 Bedfordbury, Covent Garden
London WC2 4DU
020 7836 0411
public@frontline-tv.co.uk
www.frontline-tv.co.uk
*Independent. Editing; graphic design;
audio; Avid online/offline; duplication.
MD: Bill Cullen*
• *Bum Fights; VTV programme for the
Deaf; The Curse of Reality TV; Spooks
interactive; Little Britain interactive;
Industrial Revelations*

Fusion Post Production
16 D'Arbly Street, London W1F 8EA
020 7758 0500
edit@fusionpost.co.uk
www.fusionpost.co.uk
*Independent. Audio; online/offline
grading; Symphony online. MD: Adam
de Wolff*
• *BBC Holiday; How Clean is your
House?; The Carrot or the Stick*

Future Post Production
25 Noel Street, London W1F 8GX
020 7434 6655
info@futurefilmgroup.com
www.futurefilmgroup.com
*Part of Future Films Group. Sound; two
dolby mix studios
MDs: Tim Levy, Stephen Margolis*
• *King Arthur; Exorcist, The Beginning;
Harry Potter 3*

Glassworks
33–34 Great Pulteney Street
London W1F 9NP
020 7434 1182
nina@glassworks.co.uk
www.glassworks.co.uk
*Independent. Special effects; animation;
all online. MD: Hector Macleod*
• *Dream Keeper; Bjorkall is Full of Love;
Sprite commercials*

Goldcrest Post-Production
1 Lexington Street
36–44 Brewer Street
London W1F 9LX
020 7437 7972
reception@goldcrest-post.co.uk
www.goldcrest-post.co.uk
*Independent. Sound and telecine.
MD: Peter Joly*
• *Cold Mountain; Lord of Rings, Two
Towers; Girl with a Pearl Earring*

Golden Square
11 Golden Square, London W1F 9JB
020 7300 3555
info@golden-square.co.uk
www.golden-square.co.uk
*Independent. Commercials; special effects
MD: Phil Gillies*
• *Campari; Tomb Raiders; Volkswagen*

Hackenbacker Audio Post Production
10 Bateman Street
London W1D 4AQ
020 7734 1324
reception@hackenbacker.com
www.hackenbacker.com
*Independent. Audio; sound effects;
films; trailers. MDs: Julian Slater,
Nigel Heath*
• *Shaun of the Dead; Girl with a Pearl
Earring; Spooks*

The Hive
37 Dean Street, London W12 4PT
020 7565 1000
contact@hiveuk.com
www.hiveuk.com
*Part of VTR Group. Telecine; online
editing; special effects; 3 DVD and 2D
graphics. MD: Kate Sturgess*
• *Direct Line sponsorship; BBC Bitesize;
Hell's Kitchen promotion*

Home Post Productions
12–13 Richmond Buildings
Soho, London W1D 3HG
020 7292 0200
info@homepost.co.uk
www.farmgroup.tv
*Independent. Graphics; audio; effects;
commercials. MD: Janine Martin*
• *Dunkirk; Friday Night with Jonathan
Ross; One Life*

Lip Sync Post
123 Wardour Street
London W1F 0UU
020 7534 9123
admin@lipsyncpost.co.uk
www.lipsync.co.uk
*Independent. Sound; graphics; editing.
MD: Norman Merry*
• *Silent Witness; Touch the Void;
Trolleywood*

Liquid TV
1–2 Portland Mews
London W1F 8JE
020 7437 2623
info@liquid.co.uk
www.liquid.co.uk
*Independent. Title branding; special
effects. MD: Asra Alikhan*
• *Restoration; Film 2004; Horizon; Troy*

Lola
14–16 Great Portland Street
London W1W 8BL
020 7907 7878
info@lola-post.com
www.lola-post.com
*Independent. Visual effects; commercials;
films and TV. MDs: Grahame Andrew,
Rob Harvey*
• *Troy; 5 children and It; Ancient
Egyptians*

London Post
34–35 Dean Street
London W1D 4PR
020 7439 9080
bookings@londonpost.co.uk
www.londonpost.co.uk
*Part of Arena Digital. Audio; graphics;
sound; editing; telecine. MD: Dave
Thompson*
• *Brassed off Britain; Blag; Celebrity
Penthouse*

M2 Television
Ingestre Court, Ingestre Place
London W1F 0JL
020 7343 6543; Soho 020
73436543; Camden 020 73436789
info@m2tv.com
www.m2tv.com
Edit; visual; audio. MD: Tom Jones
• *Revenge; Human Mind; Bodysnatchers*

The Machine Room
54–58 Wardour Street
London W1D 4JQ
020 7734 3433
info@themachineroom.co.uk
www.themachineroom.co.uk
*Part of VTR Group. Online editing;
telecine suites; DVD; teramix machine;
archive restoration department.
MD: Danny Whybrow*
• *Love Actually; Bad Girls; Footballers
Wives*

185

Mediahouse
Hogarth Business Park
3 Burlington Lane, London W4 2TH
020 8233 5400
info@mediahouse.tv
www.mediahouse.tv/post_production
IMG Mark McCormack Group. Video;
graphics; DVD; transmission studio.
Head of post-production: Karen Mullins
• *Bremner, Bird and Fortune; Planet's*
  Funniest Animals

Men-from-Mars
Unit 6, Walpole Court
Ealing Green, London W5 5ED
020 8280 9000
info@men-from-mars.com
www.men-from-mars.com
Part of Barcud Derwen. Visual effects
for film and TV. Creative director:
Philip Attfield; production director:
Simon Frame
• *Gladiatress; Chasing Liberty; Jekyll*
  and Hyde; Hamburg Cell; Sons of the
  Wind; De-Lovely; Trial and
  Retribution: Blue Eiderdown

Metro Broadcast
5–7 Great Chapel Street
London W1F 8FF
020 7434 7700
Metro Suffolk Street: 020 7202 2000
Metro Ecosse Edinburgh:
  0131 554 9421
Metro Ecosse Glasgow:
  0141 419 1660
info@metrobroadcast.com
www.metrobroadcast.com
Editing inc HD; crewing and equipment
rental; audio and video restoration;
DVD production; webcasting;
duplications and standards conversion.
Directors: Mark Cox, Paul Beale
• *EPKs for Mr Bean; Rugby World Cup*
  promo; NHK various programmes,
  shot and edited in HD

The Mill
40–41 Great Marlborough Street
London W1F 7JQ
020 7287 4041
info@mill.co.uk
www.mill.co.uk
Independent. Commercials;
3d animation; edition. MD: Pat Joseph
• *Commercials: Mercedes; Honda; O2*

MGB Facilities
Capital House, Sheepscar Court
Meanwood Road, Leeds
West Yorkshire LS7 2BB
0113 243 6868
contact@mgbtv.co.uk
www.mgbtv.co.uk
Independent. Graphics; commercials;
DVD; animation. MD: Mike Gaunt
• *Hasbro commercial; Brazilian*
  Football; DFS Furniture

Molinare
34 Fouberts Place, London W1F 7PX
020 7478 7000
bookings@molinare.co.uk
www.molinare.co.uk
Independent. Graphics; DVD; audio.
MD: Mark Foligno
• *Faking It; Make Me Honest; Poirot*

Moving Picture Company
127 Wardour Street
London W1F 0NL
020 7434 3100
mpc@moving-picture.com
www.moving-picture.com
Independent. Commercials; effects;
animation; editing. MD: David Jeffers
• *Troy; Dunkirk; Guinness moth*
  commercial

Nats
10 Soho Square, London W1D 3NT
020 7287 9900
bookings@nats.tv
www.nats.tv
Independent. Editing; audio; telecine;
effects; graphics. MD: Charlie Leonard
• *Seven Wonders of the Industrial*
  World; Grand Designs; The National
  Trust; Property Ladder; Picture of
  Britain; Around the World in 80
  Treasures; The South Bank Show;
  A Place in France; Jamie's Kitchen

Oasis Television
6–7 Great Pulteney Street
London W1F 9NA
020 7434 4133
sales@oasistv.co.uk
www.oasistv.co.uk
Independent. Audio; editing; graphics;
duplication. MD: Gareth Mullaney
• *State of Play; The Young Visitors;*
  May 33rd

One
71 Dean Street, London W1D 3SF
020 7439 2730
info@onepost.tv
www.onepost.tv
Part of Ascent Group. Commercials;
telecine; animation. MD: Paul Jones
• *Jaguar; American Express; Aerosmith*

Optical Image
The Studio, Broome, Stourbridge
West Midlands DY9 0HA
01562 700404
info@optical-image.com
www.optical-image.com
Independent. Animation; DVD;
duplication; effects; graphics.
MD: David Clement
• *Sindy; Jellies; Butt Ugly Martians*

Outpost Facilities
Pinewood Studios, Pinewood Road
Iver, Buckinghamshire SL0 0NH
01753 630770
info@outpostfacilities.co.uk
www.outpostfacilities.co.uk
Independent. Commercials; films;
broadcast; TV. MD: Nigel Gourley
• *My Family; Everything I Know About*
  Men; Teletubbies Everywhere

P3 Post
40–42 Lexington Street
London W1F 0LN
020 7287 3006
reception@p3.tv
www.p3.tv
Independent. Effects; graphics; DVD;
commercials. MD: Martin Price
• *Derren Brown; Celebs Exposed; Audi*

Pepper
3 Slingsby Place, London WC2E 9AB
020 7836 1188
mailuf@pepperpost.tv
www.pepperpost.tv
Independent. Effects; graphics; dramas.
MD: Patrick Holzen
• *Dirty War; Midsomer Murders; White*
  Noise

Phaebus Communications Group
The Brewery Tower, The Deva centre
Trinity Way, Manchester M3 7BF
0161 605 9999
info@phaebus.co.uk
www.phaebus.co.uk
Two branches. DVD; authoring.
MD: Steve Bettridge
• *BBC channel idents; Andy Pandy;*
  Thomas Cook conference events

Pink House
33 West Park Clifton
Bristol, Avon BS8 2LX
0117 923 7087
anita.nandwami@pinkhousepp.com
www.filmsat59.com
Part of Films at 59. Broadcast;
audio; pictures; effects; commercials.
MD: Anita Nandwani
• *Building the Dream; Big Cook Little*
  Cook; Animal Camera

Red Vision
Cambos House, 3 Canal Street
Manchester M1 3HE
0161 907 3764; London 020 7419
2010; Bristol 0117 946 6633
info@redvision.co.uk
www.redvision.co.uk
Computer graphics for film and TV.
MD: David Mousley
• *Touching the Void; D-Day: Men and*
  Machines

Resolution
341 Old Street, London EC1V 9LL
020 7749 9300
London 020 7437 1336
info@resolution.tv
www.resolution.tv
Broadcast; commercials; offline/online;
audio; graphics. MD: Mike Saunders
• *Big Brother; Top Gear; Fame Academy*

Rushes
66 Old Compton Street
London W1D 4UH
020 7437 8676
info@rushes.co.uk
www.rushes.co.uk
Part of Ascent media. Effects; telecine for
commercial video. MD: Joyce Capper
• *Commercials: Hewlett Packard;*
  Offspring; Ford Mondeo (Tom and
  Jerry)

Savalas
333 Woodlands Road
Glasgow G3 6NG
0141 339 0455
all@savalas.co.uk
www.savalas.co.uk
*Independent. Music production; audio;
sound design. MDs: Giles Lamb;
Michael MacKinnon; Karl Henderson*
• *Magdalene Sisters; Relocation,
Relocation, Relocation; Sea of Souls;
Russian Revolution; Asylum;
American Cousins*

2nd Sense Broadcast
Millennium Studios, Elstree Way
Borehamwood, Herts WD6 1SF
020 8236 1133
info@2ndsense.co.uk
www.2ndsense.co.uk
Independent. Audio. MD: Wendy Hewitt
• *Top of the Pops 2; Chuckle Vision; East
Enders Revealed*

Skaramoosh
9–15 Neal Street
London WC2H 9PW
020 7379 9966
reception@skaramoosh.co.uk
www.skaramoosh.com
*Independent. Effects; graphics; audio.
MD: Daniel Slight*
• *Strictly Come Dancing; Football
Factory; Naked Science*

Soho Images
8–14 Meard Street
London W1F 0EQ
020 7437 0831
info@sohoimages.com
www.sohoimages.com
*Part of Ascent Group. Commercials;
telecine transfers; archive restoration;
DVD. MD: Paul Collard*
• *Murder in Mind; Bloody Sunday;
Mrs Brown*

Sound Monsters
4 Grafton Mews, London W1T 5JE
020 7387 3230
info@soundmonsters.com
www.soundmonsters.com
*Independent. Audio; sound; transfer;
animation. MD: Cliff Jones*
• *Death in Gaza; State of Texas; Real
Great Escapes*

St Anne's Post
20 St Anne's Court
London W1F 0BH
020 7155 1500
info@saintannespost.co.uk
www.saintannespost.co.uk
*Part of Ascent Group. Audio; editing;
telecine. MD: Keith Williams*
• *Brothers Grimm; Alfie; Night Detective*

Stream
61 Charlotte Street
London W1T 4PF
020 7208 1567
info@streamdm.co.uk
www.streamdm.co.uk
*Part of Ascent Group. DVD; design
compression; authoring facility.
MD: Paul Kind*
• *The Office; Where We're Calling From;
My Big Fat Greek Wedding*

Strongroom
120-124 Curtain Road, London
EC2A 3SQ
020 7426 5100
luke@strongroom.com
www.strongroom.tv
*Part of Strongroom Studios. Audio post
production for DVD, television and film.
Post-production manager: Luke Colson*
• *New World War; Holiday Exchange;
Pepsi ident; Shaun of the Dead; The
Stone Roses; Little Britain*

Suite
28 Newman Street
London W1T 1PR
020 7636 4488
shelley@suitetv.co.uk
www.suitetv.co.uk
*Independent. Editing for TV.
MD: Shelley Fox*
• *The Office; Swiss Toni; The Lenny
Henry Show; The Sketch Show USA;
Meet the Magoons*

Sumners
Suite 401, Berkeley House
35 Whitworth Street West
Manchester M1 5NG
0161 228 0330
janet@sumners.co.uk
www.sumners.co.uk
*Independent. Online/offline; graphics;
very reality studio. MDs: Janet
Sumner, Andrew Sumner*
• *Best Sitcoms; Songs of Praise; Bank of
Mum and Dad*

Television Set
22 Newman Street, London W1T 1PH
020 7637 3322
terry.bettles@tvsetgroup.co.uk
www.thetelevisionset.co.uk
*2 branches. Restoration of old archives
for reuse; audio; grading; telecine.
MD: Terry Bettles*
• *D-Day plus 60; Poirot remastering;
Let it Be*

Television Services International
10 Grape Street, London WC2H 8TG
020 7379 3435
enquiries@tsi.co.uk
www.tsi.co.uk
*Independent. Longform and shortform in
light entertainment and documentaries.
MD: Simon Peach*
• *Ali G; My New Best Friend; Who Rules
the Roost?*

3 Wise Men
Ingestre Court, Ingestre Place
London W1F 0JL
020 7343 6623
daz@3wisemen.tv
martin@3wisemen.tv
www.3wisemen.tv
*Independent. Offline editing.
MDs: Martin Sage, Darren Jonusas*
• *Seven Industrial Wonders; Battlefield
Britain; Horizon*

Todd-ao creative services
13 Hawley Crescent
London NW1 8NP
020 7284 7900
schedule@todd-ao.co.uk
www.todd-ao.co.uk
*Part of Ascent Group. Telecine grading;
negative film processing; video dailies;
offline/online editing. MD: Samantha
Webb*
• *Monarch of the Glen; Canterbury
Tales; Taggart*

Videosonics
13 Hawley Crescent
London NW1 8NP
020 7209 0209
info@videosonics.com
www.videosonics.com
*Independent. Audio. MD: Denis
Weinreich*
• *Young Adam; Bright Young Things;
Sexy Beast*

VTR
64 Dean Street, London W1D 4QQ
020 7437 0026
reception@vtr.co.uk
www.vtr.co.uk
*Independent. Effects; commercials;
telecine. MD: Kate Sturgess*
• *Christina Aguilera; McDonalds; Persil;
Philadelphia; Rimmel; Dairylea*

Wild Tracks Audio Studio
2nd Floor, 55 Greek Street
London W1D 3DT
020 7734 6331
bookings@wildtracks.co.uk
www.wildtracks.co.uk
*Independent. Audio. MD: Graham
Pickford*
• *Canon; Bob the Builder; Pingu*

Yellow Moon
30 Shaw Road, Holywood
County Down BT18 9HX
028 9042 1826
general@yellowmoon.net
www.yellowmoon.net
Independent. Editing. MD: Greg Darby
• *Citizen Alec; Christine's Children;
Sven-Goran Eriksson*

Film and music libraries

BBC Birmingham, Information & Archives
The Mailbox
Birmingham B1 1RF
0121 567 6767
www.bbc.co.uk
Music, news requests, productions

BFI National Film and TV Archives
Kingshill Way, Berkhamsted
Herts HP4 3TP
01442 876301
darren.long@bfi.org.uk
www.bfi.org.uk
Large collection from 1895 to the present day

East Anglian Film Archive
The Archive Centre, Martineau Lane
Norwich NR1 2DQ
01603 592 664
eafa@uea.ac.uk
www.uea.ac.uk/eafa
Moving images relating to the region of East Anglia

Film and Video Archive, Imperial War Museum
All Saints Annexe, Austral Street
London SE11 4SL
020 7416 5290/1
film@iwm.org.uk
www.iwm.org.uk/collections/film.htm
Images of conflict – 1914 to the present day

Film Institute of Ireland/ Irish Film Archive
6 Eustace Street, Temple Bar
Dublin 2
00 353 1 679 5744
info@irishfilm.ie
www.irishfilm.ie
Films worldwide. Every Irish film ever made

GMTV Library Sales
London TV Centre, Upper Ground
London SE1 9TT
020 7827 7363/6
librarysales@gm.tv
www.gm.tv

Huntley Film Archive
191 Wardour Street
London W1F 8ZE
020 7287 8000
films@huntleyarchives.com
www.huntleyarchives.com
Rare and vintage documentary film from 1895

Images Of War
31a Regents Park Road
London NW1 7TL
020 7267 9198
derek@dircon.co.uk
www.warfootage.com
Images of war archive. 1900 to first Gulf war

ITN Archive
200 Grays Inn Road
London WC1X 8XZ
020 7833 3000
sales@itnarchive.com
www.itnarchive.com
More than 500,000 hours of news and feature material

ITV Central
Gas Street, Birmingham B1 2JT
0121 643 9898
www.itv.com

JW Media Music
4 Whitfield Street, London W1T 2RD
020 7681 8900
info@jwmediamusic.co.uk
www.jwmediamusic.com
Music production and publishing

Media Archive for Central England
The Institute of Television Studies
University of Nottingham
Nottingham NG7 2RD
0115 846 6448
mace@nottingham.ac.uk
www.nottingham.ac.uk/film/mace
East and West Midlands

National Screen and Sound Archive of Wales
Aberystwyth, Ceredigion SY23 3BU
01970 632828
agssc@llgc.org.uk
http://screenandsound.llgc.org.uk
Wales

North West Film Archive
Minshull House, 47–49 Chorlton Street
Manchester M1 3EU
0161 247 3097
n.w.filmarchive@mmu.ac.uk
www.nwfa.mmu.ac.uk
The north-west, 1897 to present day

Northern Region Film and Television Archive
School of Arts & Media
University of Teesside
Middlesbrough TS1 3BA
01642 384022
leo@nrfta.org.uk or
l.enticknap@tees.ac.uk
www.nrfta.org.uk
Public sector moving image archive serving County Durham, Cumbria, Northumberland, Tees Valley and Tyne & Wear

Pathé Pictures
14–17 Market Place
London W1W 8AR
020 7323 5151
www.pathe.co.uk
Worldwide images

Royal Television Society, Library & Archive
info@rts.org.uk
www.rts.org.uk
Archive TV pictures, award ceremonies and monthly dinners

Scottish Screen Archive
1 Bowmont Gardens
Glasgow G12 9LR
0141 337 7400
archive@scottishscreen.com
www.scottishscreen.com/archivelive
Scotland since the 1890s

South East Film & Video Archive
University of Brighton
Grand Parade, Brighton BN2 0JY
01273 643 213
sefva@brighton.ac.uk
www.bton.ac.uk/sefva
/sefilmarchivenews
The south-east: Kent, Surrey, East and West Sussex, Brighton & Hove and Medway

South West Film and Television Archive
Melville Building, Royal William Yard
Stonehouse, Plymouth PL1 3RP
01752 202 650
info@tswfta.co.uk
www.tswfta.co.uk
The south-west from 1890 to the present day

Wessex Film and Sound Archive
Hampshire Record Office
Sussex Street, Winchester SO23 8TH
01962 847742
david.lee@hants.gov.uk
www.hants.gov.uk
/record-office/film/index.html
Central Southern England. Film records 1897 to the present day, sound records 1890 to the present day.

Wiener Library
4 Devonshire Street
London W1W 5BH
020 7636 7247
info@wienerlibrary.co.uk
www.wienerlibrary.co.uk
Modern Jewish history

Yorkshire Film Archive
York Lord St John College
Mayors Walk, York YO31 7EX
01904 716 550
yfa@yorksj.ac.uk
www.yorkshirefilmarchive.com
Moving images of the Yorkshire region

TV & film training and support

BBC Training and development: Broadcast Training
0870 122 0216
training@bbc.co.uk
www.bbctraining.com
All strands of broadcast training

Birds Eye View
020 7288 7444
office@birds-eye-view.co.uk
www.birds-eye-view.co.uk
Emerging women film-makers

Film Education
020 7851 9450
postbox@filmeducation.org
www.filmeducation.org

First Film Foundation
info@firstfilm.co.uk
www.firstfilm.co.uk
Training for new film writers, producers and directors

FT2 – Film and Television Freelance Training
020 7734 5141
info@ft2.org.uk
www.ft2.org.uk
Training for new broadcast freelancers

New Producers Alliance (NPA)
020 7613 0440
queries@npa.org.uk
www.npa.org.uk
Training and support for film-makers

Screenwriters' Workshop
020 7387 5511
screenoffice@tiscali.co.uk
www.lsw.org.uk
Helps writers find work in film and television industries

Shooting People
hello@shootingpeople.org
http://shootingpeople.org
Online network for filmmakers to exchange information and ideas

Skillset: The Sector Skills Council for the Audio Visual Industries
020 7520 5757
info@skillset.org
www.skillset.org
Owned by broadcast industry; accredits courses, publishes handbooks and runs Skillsformedia service (www.skillsformedia.com)

Women in Film and TV
020 7240 4875
emily@wftv.org.uk
www.wftv.org.uk
Membership association open to women with at least one year's professional experience in the television, film and/or digital media industries

▶▶ See also page 386

Trade press

Advance Production News
020 8305 6905
www.crimsonuk.com
Monthly. Listings for production companies. Owner: Crimson Communications. Editor: Alan Williams

BFI Film and Television Handbook
020 7255 1444
eddie.dyja@bfi.org.uk
www.bfi.org.uk/handbook
Annual. Editor: Eddie Dyja

Broadband TV News
01223 464359
office@broadbandtvnews.com
www.broadbandtvnews.com
Free weekly emails and subscription newsletters. Editor, international edition: Julian Clover

Broadcast
020 7505 8000
broadcastnews@emap.com
www.broadcastnow.co.uk
Weekly. TV and radio industry. Owner: Emap Media. Editor: Conor Dignam; news: Colin Robertson; features editor and deputy: Lisa Campbell; chief sub: Angus Walker

Broadcast Hardware International
01628 773935
cathy@hardwarecreations.tv
www.hardwarecreations.tv
10pa. Owner: Hardware Creations. Editor: Dick Hobbs

Cable & Satellite Europe
020 7017 5533
media.enquiries@informa.com
www.telecoms.com
10pa. Owner: Informa Media and Telecoms. Editor: Stuart Thomson

Cable & Satellite International
020 7426 0101
justin@cable-satellite.com
www.cable-satellite.com
6pa. Owner: Perspective Publishing. Editor: John Moulding

Channel 21 International magazine
020 7729 7460
press@c21media.net
www.c21media.net
10pa. Owner: C21 Media. Editor-in-chief: David Jenkinson; editor: Ed Waller

Commonwealth Broadcaster
020 7583 5550
cba@cba.org.uk
www.cba.org.uk
Quarterly of the Commonwealth Broadcasting Association. Editor: Elizabeth Smith

Contacts – The Spotlight Casting Directories
020 7437 7631
info@spotlight.com
www.spotlight.com
Annual. Contacts for stage, film, TV and radio. Editor: Kate Poynton

Crewfinder
028 9079 7902
mail@adleader.co.uk
www.crewfinderwales.co.uk
Annual. Wales's film, TV and video directory. Owner: Adleader Publications. Proprietor: Stan Mairs

Digital Spy
nwilkes@digitalspy.co.uk
www.digitalspy.co.uk
Web. Digital TV. Editor: Neil Wilkes

FilmBang
0141 334 2456
info@filmbang.com
www.filmbang.com
Annual. Scotland's film and video directory. Editor: Marianne Mellin

IBE
01895 421111
info@ibeweb.com
www.ibeweb.com
12pa. International broadcast engineering. Owner: BPL Business Media. Editor: Neil Nixon

Kemps Film, TV, Video Handbook (UK edition)
01342 335861
kemps@reedinfo.co.uk
www.kftv.com
Annual. Guide to international production. Owner: Reed Business Information. Editorial contact: Vivien Carne

The Knowledge
01732 377591
knowledge@cmpinformation.com
www.theknowledgeonline.com
Annual. Production directory. Owner: CMP Information. Editorial contact: Michelle Hathaway

Line Up
01905 381725
editor@lineup.biz
www.lineup.biz
6pa. Journal of the Institute of Broadcast Sound. Owner: Line Up Publications. Editor: Hugh Robjohns

Multichannel News
00 1 646 746 6590
www.multichannel.com
Weekly. Owner: Reed Business Information. Editor-in-chief: Marianne Paskowski; editor: Kent Gibbons; news: Mike Reynolds; copy chief: Michael Demenchuk

Pact directory of Independent producers
020 7067 4367
enquiries@pact.co.uk
www.pact.co.uk
Annual. Directory of independent producers

Pro Sound News Europe
020 7921 8319
david.robinson@cmpinformation.com
www.prosoundnewseurope.com
12pa. Audio industry. Owner: CMP Information. Editor: David Robinson; managing editor: Ben Rosser

The Production Guide
020 7505 8000
theproductionguide@Emap.com
www.productionguideonline.com
Annual. Information on production.
Owner: Emap Media. Editor: Mei Mei
Rogers

Satellite Finance
020 7251 2967
oliver.cann@satellitefinance.com
www.satellitefinance.com
11pa. Finance journal for executives.
Owner: Thompson Stanley Publishers.
Editor: Oliver Cann

Stage Screen and Radio
020 7346 0900
janice@stagescreenandradio.org.uk
www.bectu.org.uk
10pa. Magazine of broadcasting union
Bectu. Editor: Janice Turner

Televisual
020 7970 4000
mundy.ellis@centaur.co.uk
www.mad.co.uk
Monthly. Trade magazine for TV. Owner:
Centaur Holdings. Editor: Mundy Ellis;
news editor: Jonathan Creamer

TV International
020 7017 5533
media.enquiries@informa.com
www.telecoms.com
Daily. International TV listings.
Owner: Informa Media and Telecoms.
Editor: Stewart Clarke

TBI (Television Business International)
020 7017 5533
media.enquiries@informa.com
www.telecoms.com
Annual. Directory of businesses
Owner: Informa Media and Telecoms
Editor: Kevin Scott

TV Technology and Production
01480 461555
www.imaspub.com
6pa. Broadcasting and production
technology. Owner: IMAS Publishing
UK. Editor: Mark Hallinger

TVB Europe
00 353 1 882 4444
tvbeurope@scope.ie
www.tvbeurope.com
Monthly. Broadcasting innovation and
technology. Owner: CMP Information.
Editor-in-chief: Fergal Ringrose

VLV Bulletin
01474 352835
info@vlv.org.uk
www.vlv.org.uk
Quarterly magazine of Voice of the
Listener and Viewer. Advocates citizen
and consumer interests in broadcasting.
Editor: Jocelyn Hay

Zerb
01795 535468
cfox@urbanfox.com
www.gtc.org.uk
2pa. For camera operators. Owner: The
Deeson Group. Editor: Christina Fox

▶▶ CONSUMER FILM AND TV
MAGAZINES see page 81

Events

Bafta Awards
195 Piccadilly, London W1J 9LN
020 7734 0022
www.bafta.org
Film, TV and interactive industries

MediaGuardian Edinburgh International Television Festival
1st Floor, 17–21 Emerald Street
London WC1N 3QN
020 7430 1333
www.mgeitf.co.uk

TV & film associations

Association of Motion Picture Sound
28 Knox Street, London W1H 1FS
020 7723 6727
admin@amps.net
www.amps.net
Film and TV sound technicians

Bafta (British Academy of Film and Television Arts)
195 Piccadilly, London W1J 9LN
020 7734 0022
www.bafta.org
Awards, training and education

Barb (Broadcasters' Audience Research Board)
020 7529 5531
enquiries@barb.co.uk
www.barb.co.uk
Industry-owned audience data
PRESS: *020 7591 9610*

Bectu (Broadcasting, Entertainment, Cinematograph and Theatre Union)
373–377 Clapham Road
London SW9 9BT
020 7346 0900
info@bectu.org.uk
www.bectu.org.uk
Union for broadcasting, entertainment
and theatre

BKSTS – The Moving Image Society
Pinewood Studios, Iver Heath
Bucks SL0 0NH
01753 656656
Info@bksts.com
www.bksts.com
Film foundation, TV and digital tech,
foundation sound for film and video,
broadcasting engineering

British Board of Film Classification
3 Soho Square, London W1D 3HD
020 7440 1570
contact_the_bbfc@bbfc.co.uk
www.bbfc.co.uk

British Film Institute
21 Stephen Street, London W1T 1LN
020 7255 1444
publishing@bfi.org.uk
www.bfi.org.uk
Education, exhibitions and resources

British Universities Film & Video Council
77 Wells Street, London W1T 3QJ
020 7393 1500
ask@bufvc.ac.uk
www.bufvc.ac.uk
To promote the use of media within
higher education

British Video Association
167 Great Portland Street
London W1W 5PE
020 7436 0041
general@bva.org.uk
www.bva.org.uk
Represents the interests of publishers
and rights owners of pre-recorded home
entertainment on video

Broadcasting Press Guild
Tiverton, The Ridge
Woking, Surrey GU22 7EQ
01483 764895
torin.douglas@bbc.co.uk
Promotes professional interests of
journalists who write or broadcast
about the media

Cinema and Television Benevolent Fund
22 Golden Square, London W1F 9AD
020 7437 6567
info@ctbf.co.uk
www.ctbf.co.uk
Trade charity

Drama Association of Wales
The Old Library Building
Singleton Road, Splott
Cardiff CF24 2ET
029 2045 2200
aled.daw@virgin.net
www.amdram.co.uk

DigiTAG (Digital Terrestrial Television Action Group)
17a Ancienne Route
CH-1218 Grand Saconnex, Geneva
Switzerland
00 41 22 717 2735
projectoffice@digitag.org
www.digitag.org
Not-for-profit international association

Digital Television Group
7 Old Lodge Place, St Margarets
Twickenham TW1 1RQ
020 8891 1830
www.dtg.org.uk
International industry-led consortium
Director general: Marcus Coleman

Digital Video Broadcasting Project (DVB)
Project Office, 17a Ancienne Route
CH-1218 Grand Saconnex, Geneva
Switzerland
00 41 22 717 2714
dvb@dvb.org
www.dvb.org
Not-for-profit international association

Directors' Guild of Great Britain
The Directors Centre
8 Flitcroft Street, London WC2H 8DL
020 7836 3602
guild@dggb.org
www.dggb.org

Documentary Film-makers Group
225a Brecknock Road
London N19 5AA
020 7428 0882
info@dfglondon.com
www.dfglondon.com

Equity
Guild House, Upper St Martins Lane
London WC2H 9EG
020 7379 6000
info@equity.org.uk
www.equity.org.uk
Actors' union

Federation of Entertainment Unions
1 Highfield, Twyford, Nr Winchester
Hampshire SO21 1QR
01962 713134
harris.s@btconnect.com

Film Archive Forum
c/o British Universities Film &
Video Council
77 Wells Street, London W1T 3QJ
020 7393 1508
luke@bufvc.ac.uk
www.bufvc.ac.uk/faf

Film Distributors' Association
www.launchingfilms.com
*Trade body representing theatrical film
distributors in the UK*

Focal International
Pentax House, South Hill Avenue
South Harrow HA2 0DU
020 8423 5853
info@focalint.org
www.focalint.org
*Trade association for libraries and
researchers*

Guild of British Camera Technicians
c/o Panavision (UK)
Metropolitan Centre, Bristol Road
Greenford, Middlesex UB6 8GD
020 8813 1999
admin@gbct.org
www.gbct.org

Guild of Television Cameramen
01822 614405
chairman@gtc.org.uk
www.gtc.org.uk

Guild of Vision Mixers
www.guildofvisionmixers.org.uk

Institute of Broadcast Sound
PO Box 932, Guildford GU4 7WW
01483 575450
info@ibs.org.uk
www.ibs.org.uk

**International Federation of Film
Archives (FIAF)**
1 Rue Defacqz
B-1000 Brussels, Belgium
00 322 538 3065
info@fiafnet.org
www.fiafnet.org

**International Visual Communication
Association (IVCA)**
19 Pepper Street, Glengall Bridge
London E14 9RP
020 7512 0571
info@ivca.org
www.ivca.org
*Promotes corporate visual
communication*

MCPS and PRS Alliance
29–33 Berners Street
London W1T 3AB
020 7580 5544
www.mcps-prs-alliance.co.uk
Collects and distributes music royalties

**NaSTA (National Student Television
Association)**
LSUTV, Union Building, Ashby Road
Loughborough
Leicestershire LE11 3TT
01509 635045
media@lborosu.org.uk
www.nasta.org.uk
Student-run TV stations

National Film Theatre
Belvedere Road, South Bank
Waterloo, London SE1 8XT
020 7928 3535
nft@bfi.org.uk
www.bfi.org.uk

Office of Communications (Ofcom)
Riverside House
2A Southwark Bridge Road
London SE1 9HA
020 7981 3000
www.ofcom.org.uk
Press: 020 7981 3033,
mediaoffice@ofcom.org.uk

**Pact (Producers Alliance for
Cinema and Television)**
The Eye, 2nd Floor, 1 Procter Street
Holborn, London WC1V 6DW
020 7067 4367
enquiries@pact.co.uk
www.pact.co.uk
*Trade association for independent
production companies*

The Picture Research Association
c/o 1 Willow Court, off Willow Street
London EC2A 4QB
chair@picture-research.org.uk
www.picture-research.org.uk

Production Guild
N&P Complex, Pinewood Studios
Iver Heath
Buckinghamshire SL0 0NH
01753 651767
patrick@productionguild.com
www.productionguild.com

Production Managers Association
Ealing Studios, Ealing Green
Ealing, London W5 5EP
020 8758 8699
pma@pma.org.uk
www.pma.org.uk

**Professional Lighting and Sound
Association – Plasa**
38 St Leonards Road
Eastbourne BN21 3UT
01323 410335
www.plasa.org

Royal Television Society
1st Floor, Holborn Gate
330 High Holborn
London WC1V 7QT
020 7203 6733
info@rts.org.uk
www.rts.org.uk
Membership and events organisation

**The Satellite & Cable Broadcasters
Group**
29 Harley Street, London W1G 9QR
020 7016 2608
info@scbg.org.uk
www.scbg.org.uk
*The trade association for satellite and
cable programme providers*

Sgrin, Media Agency for Wales
The Bank, 10 Mount Stuart Square
Cardiff Bay, Cardiff CF10 5EE
029 2033 3300
sgrin@sgrin.co.uk
www.sgrin.co.uk
Film, TV and new media in Wales

**Voice of the Listener and Viewer
(VLV)**
101 King's Drive
Gravesend, Kent DA12 5BQ
01474 352835
info@vlv.org.uk
www.vlv.org.uk
*Independent, non-profit society
working to ensure independence,
quality and diversity in broadcasting*

UK Film Council
10 Little Portland Street
London W1W 7JG
020 7861 7861
info@ukfilmcouncil.org.uk
www.ukfilmcouncil.org.uk
Promotes UK as a production centre

UK Post
47 Beak Street, London W1F 9SE
020 7734 6060
info@ukpost.org.uk
www.ukpost.org.uk
*Trade body charged with representing
the post-production and special effects
sector at home and internationally*

Writernet
Cabin V, Clarendon Buildings
25 Horsell Road, Highbury
London N5 1XL
020 7609 7474
info@writernet.org.uk
www.writernet.org.uk
*Information and guidance for
playwrights and performance writers*

Radio

It has been an exciting, but challenging, year for radio. The industry continues to change quickly, thanks to the growth of DAB digital radio, and the arrival of technologies such as 3G radio and podcasting (see glossary, page 399); commercial radio has seen greater consolidation, with the merger in 2004 of GWR and Capital, but a fall in revenues from advertising; and the BBC is trying to plot its future as it undergoes the process of charter review.

Radio listening figures are calculated by Rajar, an independent company owned by both the BBC and commercial radio. According to its figures, the BBC has opened up a significant lead over the commercial stations: in the first quarter of 2005, some 32.5 million people listened to a BBC radio station for at least five minutes a week – a statistic known as a station's "reach" – while some 30.9 million listened to a commercial radio station in the same period. So it was no surprise when, as part of their submissions on the future of the BBC, commercial radio companies called for greater regulation of the corporation's activities.

National listening figures, second quarter 2005			
Top 20 national stations	Reach (m)	Reach (%)	Share (%)
BBC Radio 2	13.3	27	16.0
BBC Radio 1	10.2	21	9.2
BBC Radio 4	9.6	19	11.2
Classic FM	6.3	13	4.3
BBC Radio Five Live	5.7	11	4.4
Heart*	3.1	6	2.2
Magic*	2.9	6	2.0
Galaxy*	2.5	5	1.6
Virgin*†	2.4	5	1.5
Kiss*	2.4	5	1.2
TalkSport	2.2	4	1.8
BBC Radio 3	1.9	4	1.1
Century*	1.7	4	1.3
Jazz/Smooth*	1.4	3	1.0
Capital Gold*†	1.4	3	0.9
BBC World Service	1.1	2	0.5
Kerrang!*	1.0	2	0.4
LBC*	0.9	2	1.0
The Hits	0.8	2	0.3
Classic Gold*†	0.8	2	0.6
Smash Hits	0.6	1	0.2
All BBC national	28.8	58	43.1
All commercial national	13.0	26	10.2

*Total networks. †Jan–Jun 2005   Source: Rajar

BBC stations dominate in the national market, with a reach of 28.6 million to commercial's 13 million; but commercial stations dominate locally, with a reach of 25.4 million to the BBC's 10.2 million.

Not everyone, however, has kept faith with the official figures. In 2004 Kelvin MacKenzie, then the chief executive of the Wireless Group – which owns the national speech station, TalkSport – took Rajar to the high court, saying its pen-and-paper research methods undervalued his station; but the case was thrown out in December, leaving the Wireless Group with a £700,000 legal bill. For its part, Rajar announced in September that a system of electronic measurement would be introduced in 2007.

BBC

BBC radio has five national stations broadcasting via a traditional, analogue signal: Radio 1, for popular and chart music; Radio 2, for slightly older music listeners; Radio 3, for classical, world music and arts; Radio 4, the speech station with flagship news programmes such as Today; and Five Live, for rolling news and sport. The BBC also broadcasts the World Service, the international news station funded separately by the Foreign Office. On digital, it broadcasts all these stations plus five digital-only stations: 6Music, for indie music; 1Xtra, for urban music; the Asian Network, for British Asians; BBC7, for comedy and drama; and Five Live Sports Extra.

Jane Brown

The past few years have seen a reversal in the fortunes of Britain's two most popular stations, Radio 1 and Radio 2. In 1999, Radio 1 held the top spot: it reached 11.3 million listeners in the third quarter of that year, almost 2 million ahead of Radio 2. Now Radio 2 – home to Terry Wogan and Jonathan Ross – is the most popular; it recorded a reach of 13.3 million in the second quarter of 2005, compared to 10.2 million for Radio 1.

Wogan is the most popular breakfast DJ, with 8.1 million listeners in the second quarter of 2005; while Jonathan Ross won the title of "most powerful person in radio" in a Radio Times poll in June. In July 2005, the station also announced that it had attracted Chris Evans to return to the airwaves, with a Saturday afternoon show.

The punters are now returning to Radio 1; Chris Moyles' show attracted 6.3 million listeners in the second quarter of 2005. The BBC annual report praised the station for its commitment to new music, British artists and live music. It suffered a washout in June 2005, though, when a storm flooded its production tent at Glastonbury on the Friday morning; a live show from the festival had to be cancelled as contact was lost. The festival was notable for being the first without John Peel, the broadcaster and champion of new music who died in October; as the tributes showed, Peel will be much missed.

Radio 4's audience rose slightly to about 9.6 million; but the BBC's 2005 annual report warned that the station must not become complacent. "The challenge is to continue to innovate and refresh the network without losing authority and without damaging the valuable sense of ownership that the Radio 4 audience feels towards the station," the governors said.

Radio Five Live's audience slipped to about 5.7 million listeners in the second quarter of 2005; it was praised by the governors for attracting sports fans and young people to the BBC's news coverage. But there are changes planned for the station: according to plans laid out by the

director general, Mark Thompson, most of the station's staff will move to Manchester, probably in 2009 – though much of the news team would remain in London to ensure that the station remained "wired to the 24-hour global news operation", Thompson said.

Radio 3's audience figures remained steady too, with a reach of about 2 million. In June 2005, it cleared the schedules to broadcast every note that Beethoven ever wrote.

The BBC World Service has reached its highest-ever levels in the US, according to the BBC annual report; 5 million tune in each week, up by 300,000 year on year. It is also the biggest speech station in Iraq, with audience of 3.3 million. Globally, it is thought to reach 149 million listeners.

In local news, BBC London's Danny Baker was named DJ of the year at the Sony Radio Academy Awards in May – and then quit the show live on air the next morning. He was replaced by former Heart DJ Jono Coleman.

Good news for the independent radio production sector: the BBC is handing independent radio production the copyright to programmes they make, leaving companies free to resell their formats internationally.

Commercial radio

It is another uncertain period for commercial radio. First, in April 2005 there came the news that radio advertising had been overtaken by online advertising for the first time: ad spend on radio was £637.4m, or 3.8% of the total market, compared to £653.3m (3.9%) from online. Then, over the spring and summer 2005, companies began to announce a further slowdown in ad spend: GCap Media, the group formed from the merger of GWR and Capital in October 2004, announced a 14% fall in revenue in May alone; while Chrysalis Radio, owner of the Heart FM radio stations, issued three profit warnings during the year.

That £771 merger of Capital and GWR was the big industry news in 2004: GCap Media becomes easily the biggest player in commercial radio, with more than one-third of total commercial radio audience. But it was not the only market move. In February 2005, Lord Alli and the venture capital firm 3i launched a £100m takeover bid for Virgin Radio, but its owners, SMG, turned the move down. Then in June 2005 there were two purchases: first Emap took over Scottish Radio Holdings, in a move valuing the company at £391m; and then Ulster TV bought the Wireless Group, owner of TalkSport, in a £98.2m deal. That capped a frustrating year for the then chief executive of Wireless, Kelvin MacKenzie, who had tried and failed to take the company private in a management buyout; Scott Taunton was unveiled as his replacement in July 2005.

Nationally, Classic FM is by far the biggest commercial radio station, with a reach of 6.3 million in the second quarter of 2005.

Twice in the first six months of 2005, all of Britain's commercial radio stations joined together for a simultaneous show. In January, they launched UK Radio Aid, a 12-hour special programme to raise money for child victims of the Asian tsunami; and in June, they joined forces to cover the Live 8 concerts.

London is always the most hotly contested regional radio market. The big mover in the ratings was Heart, which overtook Capital to become the city's top radio station in the first quarter of 2005; it won 7% of the London audience, compared to Capital's 6.1%, with Magic close behind on 6%. Heart's figures included an impressive parting performance

Top 20 local/regional stations by reach

		Reach (m)	Reach (%)	Share (%)
95.8 Capital FM	London	1.94	18	6.1
Magic 105.4	London	1.68	16	5.1
Heart 106.2 FM	London	1.66	16	5.0
Kiss 100 FM	London	1.40	13	4.1
BBC Radio Scotland		0.98	23	10.3
Galaxy 105†	Leeds	0.88	21	7.4
100.7 Heart FM†	Birmingham	0.87	25	9..0
105.4 Century FM	Manchester	0.81	16	5.8
Capital Gold	London	0.78	7	1.7
LBC 97.3	London	0.70	7	3.7
Real Radio†	Scotland	0.69	26	15.4
Jazz FM/Smooth FM	London	0.62	6	1.9
Clyde 1 FM†	Glasgow	0.61	33	15.7
Choice FM	London	0.60	6	2.6
Key 103	Manchester	0.60	22	8.5
BBC Radio Ulster		0.55	40	24.4
Smooth FM	North–west	0.53	10	4.5
Galaxy†	North–east	0.52	25	10.6
XFM 104.9	London	0.51	5	1.6
Radio City 96.7†	Liverpool	0.49	24	12.0
All commercial local		**25,522**	**52**	**33.8**
All BBC local		**10,077**	**20**	**10.9**

†Jan–Jun 2005   Source, Rajar: second quarter 2005

Digital multiplex licence-holders

Holder	Owners	Multiplexes number	location
NATIONAL			
BBC	Public	1	85% to 90% of country
Digital One	GCap, NTL	1	More than 85% of country
Total national:		**2**	
LOCAL AND REGIONAL*			
Capital Radio Digital	GCap	4	South England; Cardiff & Newport
CE Digital	GCap, Emap	3	London, Birmingham, Manchester
The Digital Radio Group	GCap, The Wireless Group, SMG, Carphone Warehouse, Emap	1	London
Emap Digital Radio	Emap	7	North England
MXR	Chrysalis, GCap, Guardian Media Group, UBC Digital, Ford	5	The north, south Wales, West Midlands (all regional)
Now Digital	GCap	13	Throughout the south and the Midlands
Score Digital	Scottish Radio Holdings**	6	Scotland, Northern Ireland
South West Digital Radio	GCap, UKRD	1	Plymouth and Cornwall
Switchdigital	The Wireless Group, GCap, Clear Channel International and The Carphone Warehouse	3	London & Aberdeen (local), central Scotland (regional)
TWG/Emap Digital	The Wireless Group, Emap	2	Swansea, Stoke-on-Trent
TWG Digital	The Wireless Group	1	Bradford/Huddersfield
Total local and regional:		**46**	
TOTAL:		**48**	

*Local licences unless stated   ** Being acquired by Emap

Sources: BBC, Digital Radio Development Bureau.
NB: BBC local and regional stations are carried on commercial multiplexes

from Jono Coleman, who from April 2005 was replaced by Jamie Theakston as breakfast show host. In the second quarter of 2005, however, Heart slipped back to third place with a 5% share; and Capital went back to the top.

XFM's award-winning DJ Christian O'Connell left the station in May 2005, joining Virgin as breakfast show host to replace Pete & Geoff. And in June, Jazz FM – owned by Guardian Media Group – rebranded itself as Smooth 102.2FM.

In the regions, XFM won the much-sought-after licence for a new FM radio station in Manchester, beating 18 rival bids. And Chrysalis bought East Midlands' Century 106 for £30m, promising to rebrand it as Heart.

Digital radio

Digital radio continued to expand in 2004 and 2005. Six years after the launch of the first digital radio service, there are now more than 140 digital radio brands and more than 300 stations, according to the Digital Radio Development Bureau (DDRB), which markets the technology. Consumers can listen to the stations through a DAB digital radio, through their televisions, and through the internet – although by no means all stations are available via all media.

DAB digital radio sets have proved enormously popular. The number of sets sold rose from 547,000 in June 2004 to 1.2 million by the beginning of 2005, said the DDRB; that figure was expected to double over the course of 2005. Using a DAB set, listeners in most major towns can already receive between 30 and 50 radio stations, which in many cases is more than double what is available on analogue. The latest sets allow listeners to record programmes, just as they do with TV; to access radio via an "electronic programme guide", as they do with digital TV; and even to record and rewind live radio. And in December 2004 the media regulator, Ofcom, announced plans for at least 100 more stations, with the figure possibly reaching 370.

In May 2005, it was announced that record numbers of people listen to radio through their TVs and online. More than 30% of over-15s said they listened to radio through their digital TVs, with almost 20% doing so at least once a week; while around 17% said they listened to the radio online.

Other developments include "podcasting", by which radio DJs record shows specifically for download via the internet; and the promised facility to listen to a digital radio station via a 3G mobile phone.

With so many ways to listen, it is not surprising that audiences for digital radio are on the up – especially at the BBC, which is promoting the technology the hardest. In the first quarter of 2005, BBC7's audience reached 556,000, up from below 400,000; while 1Xtra and 6Music both topped 300,000 for the first time. Tim Gardam, the author of an independent government report into the BBC's digital services, gave his backing to the corporation's strategy in launching five stations in 2003; but he did blame the collapse of Oneword, the fledgling commercial station, on the launch of BBC7.

At the time of writing, the government is yet to set a date for switching off the analogue radio signal. In July 2004, Ofcom reckoned it could happen by around 2014; while the BBC has asked the government to wait a few years before making its decision. According to Ofcom, switchover costs would be too high, smaller stations cannot afford the change, and about 100m radios would have to be replaced.

National digital radio stations

On BBC network and Freeview
BBC Radio 1*
BBC 1Xtra
BBC Radio 2*
BBC Radio 3*
BBC Radio 4*
BBC Radio Five Live*
BBC Five Live Sports Extra
BBC 6Music
BBC7
BBC Asian Network
BBC World Service*

On Digital One and Freeview
Oneword
Talksport*

On Digital One only
Classic FM*
Core
Life
Planet Rock
Primetime Radio
Virgin Radio*

On Freeview only
102.2 Smooth FM*
3c
Heat
Kerrang!
The Hits
Kiss*
Magic*
Mojo
Premier Christian Radio
Q
Smash Hits

* Also available on analogue
NB: Most stations are also available online

Community radio

In March 2005, Forest of Dean Community Radio became the first radio station to start broadcasting on a five-year community licence; it was one of 200 stations to apply. The deal is that the government offers cash to those who want to set up non-profit radio stations of their own, with restrictions on sponsorship and advertising to protect commercial radio businesses. The government hopes that some of the hundreds of pirate stations might earn legitimacy by becoming community stations.

Awards

Sony Radio Academy Awards, May 2005

- *Station of the year:* BBC Radio 2
- *Station of the year, audience over 1 million:* Radio City 96.7
- *Station of the year, audience 300,000 to 1 million:* BBC Three Counties Radio
- *Station of the year, audience under 300,000:* BBC Radio Foyle
- *Station of the year, digital terrestrial:* Capital Disney
- *Breakfast show of the year:* Christian O'Connell - Xfm
- *Entertainment award:* Christian O'Connell – Xfm
- *DJ of the year:* Danny Baker – BBC London 94.9
- *Music broadcaster of the year:* Zane Lowe – BBC Radio 1
- *News programme of the year:* Vote Friction – BBC Radio 1
- *Speech broadcaster of the year:* Jeremy Vine – BBC Radio 2

Further reading

■ Press

MediaGuardian
media.guardian.co.uk/radio

■ Books

Travels with My Radio FI GLOVER, EBURY PRESS 2002 Insightful radio travelogue
On Air: A Career in TV & Radio CHRIS ALDEN, GUARDIAN BOOKS 2004
Essential guide to a broadcasting career
Local Radio Journalism PAUL CHANTLER AND SIM HARRIS, FOCAL PRESS 1997
Useful guide

■ Other resources

Digital Radio Development Bureau
www.drdb.org
Radio Academy
www.radioacademy.org
World Radio Network
www.wrn.org

Radio responds **Nick Piggott**

It is perhaps surprising when you look back on it, but commercial DAB digital radio has now been around for six years. Starting in the UK in November 1999, it was one of the most significant investments made by the industry in its future. At the time, DAB was intended to find new revenues for radio, supplementing income from traditional advertising. These days, the imperative for radio to have a digital future remains – but the justifications for doing so are changing.

Advertising agencies, and the clients they represent, are responsible for maximising return on ad spend. "Accountability" has become the watchword for media buyers, ensuring that every pound is spent on the most effective mix of media to communicate a message. Along with accountability come "effectiveness" and "measurability": media buyers want to be able to measure the effect of their campaigns in more detail than ever before.

In this respect, the arrival of the internet has been highly disruptive to the ad industry in general. For many years, assumptions about advertising effectiveness were based on audience measurement from bodies such as Rajar for radio, Barb for TV, and ABC for newspapers. But the internet offered two new opportunities to advertisers: seemingly accurate measurement of delivery and of response rates, and rich media opportunities that demand attention from over-communicated people. As the volumes of people using the internet soar, it is establishing itself as a genuine mass-market medium.

Where does this leave radio? Overall ad spend isn't growing, so the share of where it's being spent is moving around. If agencies perceive one medium to be more effective than other, that's where they will move their spend.

What happens to black-and-white newspaper advertising, sound advertising and TV adverts when consumers expect their advertising to be colourful, interactive and responsive?

The signs are that the internet is attracting share of ad spend from all sectors. What began as careful water-testing is now a substantial business, about as big in turnover – depending on whose numbers you believe – as radio.

But the best internet advertising in the world is worthless without traffic passing by it, and that's where radio is picking up a piece of the action.

Surveys have shown that radio and the internet are highly compatible media: you can listen to the radio while you surf the internet. So radio stations have built great online offerings that fit naturally into their on-air product, bringing two great qualities together in a compelling package. Radio brings mass market numbers and audible messages you can't avoid, and drives traffic into websites that deliver rich media, measurability and interactivity.

Nearly every piece of sponsorship or promotional work executed on commercial radio these days includes an online presence, and some element of text messaging. It's mandatory to offer these as part of the package, or you don't get the business. Being a radio-only sell is not an option any more.

So where does radio go in the future, and what role does digital radio play? DAB is a great technology, and can deliver not only the radio experience, but also rich media experiences such as interactivity, colour and animation. DAB can replicate a "pocket internet" via your radio, delivering essential information linked to the radio station.

Trials show that consumers appreciate and use this content when stations provide it, and receivers that support it should start to appear in the next 18 months. It's a paradigm shift for the radio industry: selling a multimedia experience, delivered with the radio listener in mind.

Digital radio will also improve the consumer proposition of radio. Why does radio need to be time-linear? The surge of interest in "podcasting" shows that people want audio on demand. Digital radio can provide that now, with the ability to record and time-shift programming. Tuning without frequencies, and relevant text information delivered automatically without prodding buttons, keep radio relevant in peoples' lives, a viable competitor against the internet, 3G and interactive TV.

The digitisation of radio started with vision to open brand new revenues to radio. Now the digitisation of radio is about maintaining a vibrant and profitable radio industry in a complex multimedia world.

Nick Piggott is digital content manager in the Future Technologies Team at GCap Media

Radio Contacts

BBC radio

Broadcasting House
Portland Place
London W1A 1AA
020 7580 4468

Director of radio and music:
Jenny Abramsky, 020 7765 4561
Head of radio news:
Stephen Mitchell
Head of radio current affairs:
Gwyneth Williams
Controller, radio production:
Graham Ellis, 020 7765 4809
Controller, interactive radio and music:
Simon Nelson, 020 7765 2545

Press
HEAD OF PRESS AND PUBLICITY, BBC RADIO:
Sue Lynas, 020 7765 4990
NATIONS AND REGIONS:
Tim Brassell, 020 8008 1239
DIGITAL RADIO:
Jamie Austin, 020 7765 0426

Regional press offices
London: 020 7765 4990
Birmingham: 0121 567 6274
Bristol: 0117 974 2130
Manchester: 0161 244 4888
Leeds: 0113 224 7152
Newcastle: 0191 244 1296

See also separate press contacts

Radio stations

BBC Radio 1/1xtra
Yalding House
152–156 Great Portland Street
London W1N 6AJ
www.bbc.co.uk/radio1
www.bbc.co.uk/1xtra
Controller: Andy Parfitt; head of mainstream programmes: Ben Cooper, 020 7765 2236; head of specialist live music: Ian Parkinson, 020 7765 0365; breakfast show: Chris Moyles (Radio 1), Rampage (1xtra)
PRESS: *Alison Hunter, 020 7765 1030*

BBC Radio 2
Western House
99 Great Portland Street
London W1A 1AA
www.bbc.co.uk/radio2
Controller: Lesley Douglas, 020 7765 3493; managing editor: Antony Bellekom, 020 7765 4612; editor, mainstream programmes: Phil Hughes, 020 7765 4159; editor, specialist programmes: Dave Barber, 0121 432 9854; breakfast show: Terry Wogan
PRESS: *Hester Nevill, 020 7765 5712*

BBC Radio 3
Broadcasting House, Portland Place
London W1A 1AA
www.bbc.co.uk/radio3
Controller: Roger Wright, 020 7765 2523; head of speech programmes: Abigail Appleton, 020 7765 3277; head of music programming: John Evans, 020 7765 0481; controller, Proms, live events and TV classical music: Nicholas Kenyon, 020 7765 4928
PRESS: *Sian Davis, 020 7765 5887*

BBC Radio 4
Broadcasting House, Portland Place
London W1A 1AA
www.bbc.co.uk/radio4
Controller: Mark Damazer, 020 7765 3836; network manager: Denis Nowlan, 020 7765 4615; head of radio drama: Alison Hindell, 020 7557 1006; editor, drama and entertainment: Caroline Raphael, 020 7765 1870; editor, radio light entertainment: John Pidgeon, 020 7765 4220; editors, general factual: Jane Ellison (features) 020 7765 0631, Prue Keely (strands) 020 7765 2585; editor, specialist factual: Andrew Caspari, 020 7765 2660
PRESS: *Marion Greenwood, 020 7765 2629*

Today programme
Room G630, Stage 6
Television Centre, Wood Lane
London W12 7RJ
www.bbc.co.uk/radio4/today
Editor: Kevin Marsh; presenters: John Humphrys, James Naughtie, Ed Stourton, Sarah Montague; publicity manager: Peter Roberts, 020 8576 8648
Press: *020 8576 8928*

BBC Radio Five Live & Five Live Sports Extra
Television Centre, Wood Lane
London W12 7RJ
www.bbc.co.uk/fivelive
Controller: Bob Shennan, 020 8624 8956; head of radio sport: Gordon Turnbull, 020 8225 6206; head of news, Radio Five Live: Ceri Thomas, 020 8624 8946; commissioning editor: Moz Dee, 020 8624 8948
PRESS: *Andy Bate, 020 8576 1694*

BBC 6 Music
Western House
99 Great Portland Street
London W1A 1AA
020 7765 3493
www.bbc.co.uk/6music
Controller: Lesley Douglas, 020 7765 3493; head of programmes: Ric Blaxill; breakfast show: Phill Jupitus; see also Radio 2 contacts

BBC Asian Network
Epic House, Charles Street
Leicester LE1 3SH
0116 251 6688
www.bbc.co.uk/asiannetwork
Controller: Bijay Sharma; breakfast: Gagan Grewa
PRESS: *Dimple Poojara, 020 8225 6373*

BBC World Service
Bush House, Strand
London WC2B 4PH
020 7557 2941
www.bbc.co.uk/worldservice
Director: Mark Byford

Nations & regions

BBC Radio Scotland
Queen Margaret Drive
Glasgow G12 8DG
0141 339 8844
scottishplanning@bbc.co.uk
www.bbc.co.uk/scotland
92–95 FM; 810 AM. Controller: Ken MacQuarrie; news editor: Blair Jenkins

BBC Radio Nan Gaidheal
52 Church Street, Stornoway
Isle of Lewis HS1 2LS
01851 705000
feedback@bbc.co.uk
www.bbc.co.uk/scotlandalba/radio
103–105 FM. Editor: Marion MacKinnon; news editor: Norrie Maclennan

BBC Radio Wales/Cymru
Broadcasting House
Llandaff, Cardiff CF5 2YQ
0870 010 0110
radiowales@bbc.co.uk
www.bbc.co.uk/radiowales
93–104 FM. Managing editor: Julie Barton; head of news: Geoff Williams; breakfast show: Richard Ellis/Felicity Evans

BBC Radio Ulster
Broadcasting House
Belfast BT2 8HQ
028 9033 8000
radioulster@bbc.co.uk
www.bbc.co.uk/radioulster
92–95.4 FM. Head of radio: Ana Leddy; head of music: Declan McGovern; head of news: Andrew Colman

BBC Radio Foyle
Northland Road, Derry
Londonderry BT48 7GD
028 7137 8600
radiofoyle@bbc.co.uk
www.bbc.co.uk/radiofoyle
93.1 FM; 792 AM. Head of radio: Ana Leddy; head of news: Eimear O'Callaghan

---

BBC local radio

BBC Radio Berkshire
PO Box 1044, Reading RG4 8FH
0118 946 4200
berkshireonline@bbc.co.uk
www.bbc.co.uk/berkshire
94.6 FM; 95.4 FM; 104.1 FM; 104.4 FM. Editor: Marianne Bell; breakfast show: Jim Cathcart/Maggie Filburn

BBC Radio Bristol and Somerset Sound
PO Box 194, Bristol BS99 7QT
01179 741111
radio.bristol@bbc.co.uk
www.bbc.co.uk/radiobristol and www.bbc.co.uk/bristol
95.5, 94.9 FM; 1548, 1566 AM. Managing editor, Bristol: Jenny Lacey; assistant editors: Dawn Trevett (Bristol), Simon Clifford (Somerset Sound); breakfast show: Nigel Dando/ Rachael Burden

BBC Radio Cambridgeshire
PO Box 96, 104 Hills Road
Cambridge CB2 1LD
01223 259696
cambs@bbc.co.uk
www.bbc.co.uk/cambridgeshire
96 FM; 95.7 FM. News editor: Alison Daws; managing editor: David Martin; breakfast show: Trevor Dann and Emma McLean

BBC Radio Cleveland
PO Box 95FM, Newport Road
Middlesbrough TS1 5DG
01642 225211
bbcradiocleveland@bbc.co.uk
www.bbc.co.uk/tees
95 FM. Managing editor: Andrew Glover; news editor: Peter Harris; breakfast show: Ken Snowdon

BBC Radio Cornwall
Phoenix Wharf
Truro, Cornwall TR1 1UA
01872 275421
radio.cornwall@bbc.co.uk
www.bbc.co.uk/cornwall
103.9 FM; 95.2 FM. Managing editor: Pauline Causey; news editor: Ed Goodrich; breakfast show: Pam Spriggs and James Churchfield

BBC Radio Cumbria
Annetwell Street, Carlisle CA3 8BB
01228 592444
radio.cumbria@bbc.co.uk
www.bbc.co.uk/radiocumbria
95.6 FM; 96.1 FM; 104.1 FM. Managing editor: Nigel Dyson; news editor: Tom Stight; breakfast show: Richard Corrie and Richard Nankivell

BBC Radio Derby
PO Box 104.5, Derby DE1 3HL
01332 361111
radio.derby@bbc.co.uk
www.bbc.co.uk/radioderby
1116 AM; 104.5 AM; 95.3 FM; 96FM. Managing editor: Simon Cornes; news editor: John Atkin; breakfast show: Andy Whitaker

BBC Radio Devon
PO Box 1034, Plymouth PL3 5BD
01752 260323
radio.devon@bbc.co.uk
www.bbc.co.uk/devon
103.4 FM. Managing editor: Robert Wallis; news editor: Emma Clements; breakfast show: Monica Ellis

BBC Essex
198 New London Road
Chelmsford, Essex CM2 9XB
01245 616000
essex@bbc.co.uk
www.bbc.co.uk/essex
103.5 FM; 95.3 FM; 765 AM; 1530 AM; 729 AM. Managing editor: Margaret Hyde; breakfast show: Alison Hodgkins-Brown; breakfast show: Etholle George and John Hayes

BBC Radio Gloucestershire
London Road, Gloucester GL1 1SW
01452 308585
radio.gloucestershire@bbc.co.uk
www.bbc.co.uk/gloucestershire
104.7 FM; 1413 AM. Managing editor: Mark Hurrell; news editor: Ivor Ward-Davis; breakfast show: Vernon Harwood

BBC GMR
PO Box 951, Oxford Road
Manchester M60 1SD
0161 200 2000
gmr.newsdesk@bbc.co.uk
www.bbc.co.uk/england/gmr
95.1 FM; 104.6 FM. Managing editor: Mike Briscoe; news editor: Matt Elliott; breakfast show: Heather Stott and Mark Edwardson

BBC Radio Guernsey
Bulwer Avenue, St Sampsons
Guernsey GY2 4LA
01481 200600
radio.guernsey@bbc.co.uk
www.bbc.co.uk/guernsey
93.2 FM; 1116 AM. Managing editor: David Martin; news editors: Simon Alexander and Kay Longlay; breakfast show: Adrian Gidney

BBC Hereford and Worcester
Hylton Road, Worcester WR2 5WW
01905 748485
bbchw@bbc.co.uk
www.bbc.co.uk/worcester
or www.bbc.co.uk/hereford
104 FM; 104.6 FM; 94.7 FM. Managing editor: James Coghill; news editor: Jo Baldwin; breakfast show: Mike George

BBC Radio Humberside
Queens Court, Queens Gardens
Hull HU1 3RP
01482 323232
radio.humberside@bbc.co.uk
www.bbc.co.uk/humber
95.9 FM; 1485 AM. Managing editor: Simon Pattern; news editor: Kate Slade; breakfast show: Andy Comfort

BBC Radio Jersey
18 Parade Road, St Helier
Jersey JE2 3PL
01534 870000
radio.jersey@bbc.co.uk
www.bbc.co.uk/jersey
88.8 FM. Managing editor: Denzil Dudley; news editor: Sarah Scriven; breakfast show: Tony Gillam

BBC Radio Kent
The Great Hall, Mount Pleasant Road
Tunbridge Wells, Kent TN1 1QQ
01892 670000
radio.kent@bbc.co.uk
www.bbc.co.uk/kent
96.7 FM; 97.6 FM; 104.2 FM. Managing editor: Paul Leaper; news editors: Sally Dunk and Simon Longprice; breakfast show: Steve Ladner

BBC Radio Lancashire and BBC Open Centre
26 Darwen Street, Blackburn
Lancs BB2 2EA
01254 262411
radio.lancashire@bbc.co.uk
www.bbc.co.uk/lancashire
95.5 FM. Managing editor: John Clayton; news editor: Chris Rider; breakfast show: Mike West

BBC Radio Leeds
Broadcasting Centre
2 St Peters Square, Leeds LS9 8AH
0113 244 2131
radio.leeds@bbc.co.uk
www.bbc.co.uk/leeds
92.4 FM. Managing editor: John Ryan; news editor: Andy Evans; breakfast show: Andrew Edwards and Julie Langford

BBC Radio Leicester
Epic House, Charles Street
Leicester LE1 3SH
0116 251 6688
radio.leicester@bbc.co.uk
www.bbc.co.uk/leicester
*104.9 FM. Managing editor: Kate
Squire; breakfast show: Ben Jackson*

BBC Radio Lincolnshire
PO Box 219, Newport
Lincoln LN1 3XY
01522 511411
radio.lincolnshire@bbc.co.uk
www.bbc.co.uk/lincolnshire
*94.9 FM; 1368 FM; 104 FM. Managing
editor: Charlie Partridge; news editor:
Andy Farrant; breakfast show:
William Wright*

BBC London 94.9
35 Marylebone High Street
London W1U 4QA
020 7224 2424
yourlondon@bbc.co.uk
www.bbc.co.uk/london
*94.9 FM. Managing editor: David
Robey; breakfast show: Danny Baker*

BBC Radio Merseyside and BBC Open Centre
55 Paradise Street, Liverpool L1 3BP
0151 708 5500
radio.merseyside@bbc.co.uk
www.bbc.co.uk/liverpool
*95.8 FM. Managing editor: Liam
Fogarty; news editor: Lee Bennion;
breakfast show: Linda McDermot and
Andy Ball*

BBC Radio Newcastle
Broadcasting Centre, Barrack Road
Newcastle upon Tyne NE99 1RN
0191 232 4141
radio.newcastle@bbc.co.uk
www.bbc.co.uk/england/radio
newcastle
*95.4 FM. Managing editor: Graham
Moss; news editor: Doug Morris;
breakfast show: Mike Parr*

BBC Radio Norfolk
The Forum, Millennium Plain
Norwich NR2 1BH
01603 617411
radionorfolk@bbc.co.uk
www.bbc.co.uk/norfolk
*104.1 FM; 95.1 FM; 855 AM; 873 AM.
Managing editor: David Clayton; news
editor: Sarah Kings; breakfast show:
Stephen Bumfrey*

BBC Radio Northampton
Broadcasting House, Abington Street
Northampton NN1 2BH
01604 239100
northampton@bbc.co.uk
www.bbc.co.uk/northamptonshire
*104.2, 103.6 FM. Managing editor:
Laura Moss; news editor: Mark Whall;
breakfast show: Liz Caroll-Wheat*

BBC Radio Nottingham
London Road, Nottingham NG2 4UU
0115 955 0500
radio.nottingham@bbc.co.uk
www.bbc.co.uk/nottingham
*103.8 FM. Managing editor: Gary
Andrews; Mike Bettison; news editor:
Mike Yound; breakfast show: Karl Cooper*

BBC Radio Oxford
PO Box 95.2, Oxford OX2 7YL
01865 311444
radio.oxford@bbc.co.uk
www.bbc.co.uk/radiooxford
*95.2 FM. Managing editor: Steve
Taschini; news editor: Neil Bennett*

BBC Radio Sheffield and BBC Open Centre
54 Shoreham Street, Sheffield S1 4RS
0114 273 1177
radio.sheffield@bbc.co.uk
www.bbc.co.uk/england/radiosheffield
*88.6 FM. Managing editor: Angus
Moorat; news editor: Mike Woodcock;
breakfast show: Antonia Brickell*

BBC Radio Shropshire
2–4 Boscobel Drive
Shrewsbury SY1 3TT
01743 248484
radio.shropshire@bbc.co.uk
www.bbc.co.uk/shropshire
*96 FM; 95.7 FM. Managing editor: Tim
Pemberton; news editor: Sharon Shone;
breakfast show: Eric Smith*

BBC Radio Solent
Broadcasting House, Havelock Road
Southampton SO14 7PW
02380 631311
solent@bbc.co.uk
www.bbc.co.uk/radiosolent
*96.1 FM. Managing editor: Mia
Costello; breakfast show: Julian Clegg*

BBC Southern Counties Radio
Broadcasting Centre
Guildford GU2 7AP
01483 306306
southern.counties.radio@bbc.co.uk
www.bbc.co.uk/southerncounties
*104–104.8 FM; 95–95.3 FM. Managing
editor: Mike Hapgood; news editor:
Mark Carter; breakfast show: Sarah
Gorrell, Ed Douglas, John Radford*

BBC Radio Stoke and BBC Open Centre
Cheapside, Hanley
Stoke on Trent ST1 1JJ
01782 208080
radio.stoke@bbc.co.uk
www.bbc.co.uk/stoke
*94.6 FM. Managing editor: Sue Owen;
breakfast show: Janine Machin*

BBC Radio Suffolk
Broadcasting House
St Matthew's Street, Ipswich
Suffolk IP1 3EP
01473 250000
radiosuffolk@bbc.co.uk
www.bbc.co.uk/suffolk
*105.5 FM; 104.5 FM; 103 FM.
Managing editor: Gerald Main; news
editor: Lis Henderson; breakfast show:
Mark Murphy*

BBC Radio Swindon
PO Box 1234, Swindon SN1 3RW
01793 513626
radio.swindon@bbc.co.uk
www.bbc.co.uk/wiltshire
*103.6 FM. Managing editor: Tony
Worgan; news editor: Kirsty Ward;
breakfast show: Peter Heaton-Jones*

BBC Three Counties Radio
PO Box 3CR, Luton
Bedfordshire LU1 5XL
01582 637400
3cr@bbc.co.uk
www.bbc.co.uk/threecounties
*95.5 FM; 104.5 FM; 103 FM.
Managing editor: Mark Norman;
breakfast show: Roberto Perrone*

BBC Radio Wiltshire
PO Box 1234, Bedfordshire LU1 5XL
01793 513626
radio.wiltshire@bbc.co.uk
www.bbc.co.uk/wiltshire
*103.5 FM; 104.3 FM; 104.9 FM.
Managing editor: Tony Worgan; news
editor: Kirsty Ward; breakfast show:
Sue Davies*

BBC WM (Birmingham)
The Mailbox, Birmingham B1 1RF
0121 567 6000
bbcwm@bbc.co.uk
www.bbc.co.uk/birmingham or
www.bbc.co.uk/blackcountry
*95.6 FM. Managing editor: Keith
Beech; news editor: Raj Ford; breakfast
show: Adrian Goldberg*

BBC WM (Coventry)
1 Holt Court, Greyfriars Road
Coventry CV1 2WR
02476 860086
coventry.warwickshire@bbc.co.uk
www.bbc.co.uk/coventry
*103.7 FM; 94.8 FM; 104 FM.
Managing editor: David Clargo;
breakfast show: Annie Othen*

BBC North Yorkshire – Radio York
20 Bootham Row, York YO30 7BR
01904 641351
northyorkshire.news@bbc.co.uk
www.bbc.co.uk/northyorkshire
*1260 AM; 666 AM; 104.3 FM; 103.7
FM; 95.5 FM. Managing editor: Matt
Youdale; news editor: Anna Evans;
breakfast show: Allan Watkiss, Anna
Wallace, Colin Hazeldon, Sandy
Dunleavy*

Resources

BBC Radio Resources
Brock House, 19 Langham Street
London W1A 1AA
020 7765 3208
radio.facilities@bbc.co.co.uk
www.bbcradioresources.com
*Senior operations manager: Martin
Hollister; head of radio research: Miles
Hosking; communications and
marketing manager: Amanda Bates*

Event Services
Room 112 Brock House
19 Langham Street
London W1A 1AA
020 7765 5100
rr-events-team@bbc.co.uk
www.bbcradioresources.com
Events manager: Mark Diamond;
events assistant: Joanne Surtees, 020
7765 2375

Outside Broadcasts
Room 112 Brock House
19 Langham Street
London W1A 1AA
020 7765 4889
duncan.smith@bbc.co.uk
www.bbcradioresources.com
Operations manager: Will Garrett;
radio outside broadcasts manager:
Duncan Smith

Studios

Birmingham Studios
The Mailbox, Birmingham B1 1RF
0121 567 6767
www.bbc.co.uk/birmingham
Operations co-ordinator: Liz Treacher;
facilities manager: Paul Cook

Bristol Broadcasting House
Whiteladies Road, Bristol BS8 2LR
0117 973 2211
www.bbc.co.uk/bristol
Operations co-ordinator: Maria
Clutterbuck; open team leader: Iain
Hunter

Broadcasting House Studios
Brock House, 19 Langham Street
London W1A 1AA
020 8743 8000
www.bbc.co.uk
Marketing executive in music
management: Amanda Bates; senior
operations manager: Martin Hollister

Maida Vale Studios
1–129 Delaware Road
London W9 2LG
020 7765 2091
www.bbc.co.uk
Facilities manager: John Hakrow

Manchester Studios
New Broadcasting House
PO Box 27, Oxford Road
Manchester M60 1SJ
0161 244 4607
www.bbc.co.uk
Operations co-ordinator: Lilian
O'Callaghan; operations manager:
Richard Savage

Commercial radio

Commercial Radio Companies Association
77 Shaftesbury Avenue
London W1D 5DU
020 7306 2603
info@crca.co.uk
www.crca.co.uk
Chief executive: Paul Brown; research
and communications manager: Alison
Winter

Main commercial radio groups

CN Group
Dalston Road, Carlisle
Cumbria CA2 5UA
01228 612600
news@cumbrian-newspapers.co.uk
www.cumbria-online.co.uk
Chief executive: Robin Burgess; director
of technical services: Peter Simpson;
Director: Christopher Bisco; deputy
managing director: Dave Bowden

Chrysalis Radio Group
The Chrysalis Building
13 Bramley Road, London W10 6SP
020 7221 2213
info@chrysalis.com
www.chrysalis.com
PLC chairman: Chris Wright; chief
executives: Richard Huntingford
(whole group), Phil Riley (radio); head
of network news: Jonathan Richards;
head of press: Huw Davies

Classic Gold Digital
Network Centre, Chiltern Road
Dunstable LU6 1HQ
01582 676200
www.classicgolddigital.com
Managing director: John Baish;
programme controller: Paul Baker

Emap Performance Network
Mappin House, 4 Winsley Street
London W1W 8HF
020 7436 1515
www.emap.com
Group managing director: Marcus
Rich; advertising director: Dave King;
programme director: Phil Roberts

GCap Media
30 Leicester Square
London WC2H 7LA
020 7766 6000
www.gcapmedia.com
Executive chairman: Ralph Bernard;
chief executive: David Mansfield

Lincs FM
Witham Park, Waterside South
Lincoln LN5 7JN
01522 549900
enquiries@lincsfm.co.uk
www.lincsfm.co.uk
Chief executive: Michael Betton;
director of programming: Jane Hill

SMG
200 Renfield Street
Glasgow G2 3PR
0141 300 3300
www.smg.plc.uk
Chief executive: Andrew Flanagan; chief
executive, SMG Radio: John Pearson

Scottish Radio Holdings
Clydebank Business Park
Clydebank, Glasgow G81 2RX
0141 565 2200
www.srhplc.com
Chairman: Lord Gordon of Strathblane;
chief executive, radio: David Goode;
MD, Score Digital: Grae Allan

Tindle Radio Holdings
Old Court House, Union Road
Farnham, Surrey GU9 7PT
01252 735667
www.tindleradio.com
Chairman: Sir Ray Tindle; deputy
chairman: Robert Stiby; directors:
Colin Christmas, Kevin Stewart and
Wendy Craig

UKRD Group
Cam Brea Studios, Wilson Way
Redruth, Cornwall TR15 3XX
01209 310435
enquiries@ukrd.co.uk
www.ukrd.com
Chairman: James St Aubyn; general
managing director: William Rogers;
commercial director: Rob van Pooss;
programme director: Phil Angell;
marketing director: Mark Beever

The Wireless Group
18 Hatfields, London SE1 8DJ
020 7959 7900
www.thewirelessgroup.net
Chief executive: Scott Taunton

National commercial digital radio

Digital One
7 Swallow Place, London W1B 2AG
020 7288 4600
info@digitalone.co.uk
www.ukdigitalradio.com
Joint venture backed by GWR and NTL
Chief executive: Quentin Howard
Press: 07813 783181

Freeview
DTV Services Ltd, PO Box 7630
Mansfield MG18 4YL
020 7792 7412
www.freeview.co.uk
Three shareholders: BBC, Crown Castle
International and BSkyB

Stations on AM, DAB* and Freeview

3c – continuous cool country
Scottish Radio Holdings
Clydebank Business Park,
Clydebank, Glasgow G81 2RX
0141 565 2307
3c@3cdigital.com
www.3cdigital.com
Country music. DAB; Freeview; internet. Station manager, programme controller and breakfast show: Pat Geary. Studio: 08453 450333

The Arrow
Chrysalis Group, 1 The Square
111 Broad Street, Birmingham
West Midlands B15 1AS
0121 695 0000
paul.fairburn@chrysalis.com
www.thearrow.co.uk
Rock. DAB; Freeview. Managing director: Paul Fairburn; programme director: Alan Caruther

Capital Disney
GCap Media, 30 Leicester Square
London WC2H 7LA
020 7766 6000
will.chambers@capitalradiogroup.com
www.capitaldisney.co.uk
Current pop aimed at eight- to 14-year-olds. DAB. Head of Communications Group Radio: Elly Smith; programme controller: Will Chambers. Studio: 08702 027000

Choice FM
GCap Media, 30 Leicester Square
London WC2H 7LA
020 7766 6000
info@choicefm.com
www.choicefm.com
Hip-hop and R&B. DAB; 107.1FM. Managing director: Graham Bryce; programme controller: Ivor Etienne. Studio: 08700 702969

Classic FM
GCap Media, 7 Swallow Place
London W1B 2AG
020 7343 9000
enquiries@classicfm.co.uk
www.classicfm.com
Classical music. DAB; 99.9–102 FM. Editorial contact: Rob Weinberg; managing editor: Darren Henley

Core
GCap Media, PO Box 2000
One Passage Street
Bristol BS99 7SN
020 7911 7342
fresh@corefreshhits.com
www.corefreshhits.com
Pop, dance and R&B. DAB; Sky; cable; internet. Programme services director: Jo Littlehales; digital content manager: Nick Piggott. Studio: 08450 002673

Gaydar Radio
Q Soft Consulting
6th Floor, 2 Holly Road
Twickenham TW1 4EG
020 8744 1287
contact@gaydarradio.com
www.gaydarradio.com
Pop, dance, diva-led house. DAB; Sky; internet. Manager: Gary Frisch; programme controller: Jamie Crick

Heart 106.2
Chrysalis Group
The Chrysalis Building
13 Bramley Road, London W10 6SP
020 7221 2213
www.heart1062.co.uk
70s, 80s and 90s. 106.2 FM. Programme controller: Francis Curry; news editor: Jonathan Richards; breakfast show: Jamie Theakston and Harriet Scott

Heat
Emap Performance Network
Mappin House, 4 Winsley Street
London W1W 8HF
020 7436 1515
www.heatradio.co.uk
Adult contemporary. DAB; Freeview. Managing director: Shaun Gregory; programme controller: Andy Roberts

The Hits
Emap Performance Network
Castle Quay, Castlefield
Manchester M15 4PR
0161 288 5000
studio@thehitsradio.com
www.thehitsradio.com
Contemporary music. DAB in Greater London; Freeview; Sky. Station manager: Phil Mackenzie; programme controller: Anthony Gay. Studio: 08444 158181

Smooth FM
Guardian Media Group
26–27 Castlereagh Street
London W1H 5DL
020 7706 4100
studio@jazzfm.com
www.jazzfm.com
Soul, jazz and R&B. DAB in central Scotland, Greater London, south Wales and Severn estuary; Freeview; 102.2FM in West Midlands. Managing director: John Myers; programme director: Mark Walker. Studio: 08453 451022

Kerrang!
Emap Performance Network
Kerrang! House, 20 Lionel Street
Birmingham B3 1AQ
08450 531052
brendan.moffett@emap.com
http://digital.kerrangradio.co.uk
Rock. Freeview; Sky; cable. Programme controller: Andrew Jefferies; managing director: Adrian Serle. Studio: 08456 880908

Kiss
Emap Performance Network
Mappin House, 4 Winsley Street
London W1W 8HF
020 7436 1515
feedback@kissonline.co.uk
www.kiss100.com
Rhythmic. DAB; Freeview; Sky; 100 FM in Greater London. Managing director: Mark Story; programme director: Andy Roberts. Studio: 020 7617 9100

Capital Life
Capital Radio Group
30 Leicester Square
London WC2H 7LA
020 7766 6000
studio@listentolife.com
www.ukcapitallife.com
Pop. DAB. Programme manager: Kevin Palmer

Magic
Emap Performance Network
Mappin House, 4 Winsley Street
London W1W 8HF
020 7975 8100
studio@magicradio.com
www.magic1054.co.uk
Soft melodic. Freeview; Sky; cable. Managing director: Andria Vidler; programme director: Trevor White. Studio: 020 7436 1054

Mojo
Emap Performance Network
Mappin House, 4 Winsley Street
London W1W 8HF
020 7975 8100
studio@mojo4music.com
www.mojo4music.com
Classic rock and soul. Freeview. Managing director: Dave Henderson; breakfast show: Gary King

Oneword Radio
Landseer House
19 Charing Cross Road
London WC2H OES
020 7976 3030
info@oneword.co.uk
www.oneword.co.uk
Contemporary music. DAB; Freeview; Sky; internet. Managing director: Simon Blackmore

Planet Rock
GCap Media, PO Box 2000
One Passage Street
Bristol BS99 7SN
08450 007625
joinus@planetrock.com
www.planetrock.musicradio.com
Classic radio. DAB. Digital content manager: Nick Piggott

Premier Christian Radio
Premier Media Group
22 Chapter Street
London SW1P 4NP
020 7316 1300
enquiries@premier.org.uk
www.premier.org.uk
Contemporary Christian music. Freeview; Sky; cable; 1305, 1332, 1413 AM. Managing director: Peter Kerrig; programme controller: Sharmaine Noble

* stations with widespread urban coverage

Prime Time Radio
PO Box 5050, London SW1E 6ZR
0870 050 5050
david.atkey@primetimeradio.org
www.primetimeradio.org
Easy listening. DAB; Sky; cable; internet. Managing director: Ron Coles; operations director: David Atkey

Q Radio
Emap Performance Network
Mappin House, 4 Winsley Street
London W1W 8HF
020 7436 1515
brendan.moffett@emap.com
www.q4music.com
Contemporary music. Freeview; Sky; cable. Programme director: Andy Roberts

Smash! Hits
Emap Performance Network
Mappin House, 4 Winsley Street
London W1W 8HF
020 7436 1515
brendan.moffett@emap.com
www.smashhits.net
Chart hits. Freeview; Sky; cable. Programme director: Andy Roberts

TalkSport
The Wireless Group
18 Hatfields, London SE1 8DJ
020 7959 7800
www.talksport.net
Talk, sport and current affairs. Digital One; 1107, 1053, 1089 AM. Managing director: Michael Franklyn; programme director: Bill Ridley. Studio: 08704 202020

Virgin Radio
SMG, No 1 Golden Square
London W1F 9DJ
020 7434 1215
reception@virginradio.co.uk;
studio@virginradio.co.uk
www.virginradio.co.uk
Rock. Digital One; Sky; 1197, 1215, 1233, 1242, 1260 AM. Station manager: Steve Taylor; programme director: Paul Jackson. Studio: 08707 301215

XFM
GCap Media, 30 Leicester Square
London WC2H 7LA
020 7766 6000
www.xfm.co.uk
Alternative music. DAB; Sky; cable; internet; 104.9 FM. Managing director: Graham Bryce; programme controller: Andy Ashton. Studio: 08712 221049

Yarr Radio
Sunrise Radio, Sunrise Radio House
Merrick Road, Southall
Middlesex UB2 4AU
020 8574 6666
info@yaarradio.com
www.yarrradio.com
Asian music. DAB; Sky; internet. Managing director: Doctor Abtarlitt; chief executive: Tony Lit. Studio: 020 8574 6262

News services

ITN Radio
200 Grays Inn Road
London WC1X 8XZ
020 7430 4090
radio@itn.co.uk
www.itn.co.uk
Managing director: John Perkins; editor: Jon Godel. Newsdesk: 020 7430 4814

Independent Radio News (IRN)
200 Grays Inn Road
London WC1X 8XZ
020 7430 4090
irn@itn.co.uk; news@irn.co.uk
www.irn.co.uk
Managing director: John Perkins; editor: Jon Godel. Newsdesk: 020 7430 4814

Commercial local radio: England

LONDON

95.8 Capital FM
30 Leicester Square
London WC2H 7LA
020 7766 6000
info@capitalradio.com
www.capitalfm.com
Pop. Greater London. 95.8 FM. Owner: GCap Media. Managing director: Keith Pringle; head of news: Justin Kings; breakfast show: Johnny Vaughan

107.3 Time FM
2–6 Basildon Road, Abbey Road
London SE2 OEW
020 8311 3112
www.timefm.com
All-time favourites. South-east London. 106.8, 107.3 FM. Owner: London Media Group. Station director: Neil Remain; head of news: Nigel Gooch; breakfast show: Lorna and Will

Capital Gold (1548)
30 Leicester Square
London WC2H 7LA
020 7766 6000
info@capitalradio.com
www.capitalgold.com
Hits of the 60s, 70s and 80s. Greater London. 1548 AM. Owner: GCap Media. Programme director: Andy Turner; head of news: Justin King; breakfast show: Mick Brown

Choice 107.1 FM
291–299 Borough High Street
London SE1 1JG
020 7378 3969
info@choicefm.com
www.choicefm.com
R&B. North London. 107.1 FM. Owner: GCap Media. Programme controller: Ivor Etienne; news editor: Pam Joseph; breakfast show: Martin Jay and Asher

Club Asia
Asia House
227–247 Gascoigne Road
Barking, Essex IG11 7LN
020 8594 6662
info@clubasiaonline.com
www.clubasiaonline.com
Young Asian hit music. Greater London. 972 AM. Independent. Managing director: Humerah Khan; creative director: Sumerah Ahmad; breakfast show: Missy D

Easy Radio
43–51 Wembley Hill Road
London HA9 8AU
020 8795 1035
info@easy1035.com
www.easy1035.com
Easy listening. Greater London. 1035 AM. Owner: Easy Radio. Programme controller and head of music: Natalie King; breakfast show: Chris Townsend

Heart 106.2
The Chrysalis Building, Bramley Road
London W10 6SP
020 7468 1062
www.heart1062.co.uk
Adult contemporary. Greater London. 106.2 FM. Owner: Chrysalis Radio. Programme director: Francis Currie; head of news: Jonathan Richards; breakfast show: Jamie Theakston and Harriet Scott

Smooth FM 102.2
26–27 Castlereagh Street
London W1H 5DL
020 7706 4100
jazzinfo@jazzfm.com
www.jazzfm.com
Smooth jazz and classic soul. Greater London. 102.2 FM. Owner: Guardian Media Group Radio. Managing director: John Myers; programme director: Mark Walker; head of news: Nick Hatfield; breakfast show: Jon Scragg

Kiss 100
Mappin House, 4 Winsley Street
London W1W 8HF
020 7975 8100
firstname.lastname@kiss100.com
www.kiss100.com
Garage, R&B. Greater London. 100 FM. Owner: Emap Performance Network. Managing director: Mark Story; programme director: Andy Roberts; breakfast show: Bam Bam

LBC 97.3 FM
The Chrysalis Building, Bramley Road
London W10 6SP
020 7314 7300
firstname.lastname@lbc.co.uk
www.lbc.co.uk
Talk radio. Greater London. 97.3 FM. Owner: Chrysalis. Managing director: Mark Flanagan; programme director: Scott Solder; head of news: Tom Bateman; breakfast show: Nick Ferrari

LBC News 1152 AM
The Chrysalis Building, Bramley Road
London W10 6SP
020 7314 7309
newsroom@lbc.co.uk
www.lbc.co.uk
*News. Greater London. 1152 AM.
Owner: Chrysalis. Head of network
news: Jonathan Richards*

London Greek Radio
437 High Road, London N12 OAP
0871 288 1000
sales@lgr.co.uk
www.lgr.co.uk
*Greek music. North London. 103.3 FM.
Independent. Programme controller
and head of news: G Gregoriou;
breakfast show: Soula Viola Ri*

London Turkish Radio LTR
185B High Road, Wood Green
London N22 6BA
020 8881 0606
info@londontv.org
www.londonturkishradio.org
*Turkish and English music. North
London. 1584 AM. Independent.
Programme controller: Umit Dandul;
managing director: Erkan
Pastirmacioglu; breakfast show:
Fatos Sarman*

Magic 105.4 FM
Mappin House, 4 Winsley Street
London W1W 8HF
020 7955 1054
firstname.lastname@emap.com
www.magic1054.co.uk
*Adult contemporary. Greater London.
105.4 FM. Owner: Emap Performance
Network. Programming director:
Trevor White; station director: Mark
Storey; breakfast show: Graham Dean*

Premier Christian Radio
22 Chapter Street
London SW1P 4NP
020 7316 1300
premier@premier.org.uk
www.premier.org.uk
*Contemporary Christian music.
Greater London. 1413 AM; 1305 AM;
1413 AM; 1332 AM. Owner: Premier
Media Group. Programme controller:
Charmaine Noble-Mclean; head of
news: Victoria Lawrence; breakfast
show: John Pantry*

Spectrum Radio
4 Ingate Place, Battersea
London SW8 3NS
020 7627 4433
name@spectrumradio.net
www.spectrumradio.net
*Multi-ethnic. Greater London. 558 AM.
Independent. General manager: Paul
Hogan; sales: Millie Bentham*

Sunrise Radio
Sunrise House, Merrick Road
Southall, Middlesex UB2 4AU
020 8574 6666
Reception@sunriseradio.com
www.sunriseradio.com
*Asian music. Greater London. 1458 AM.
Independent. Chief executive: Tony Lit;
MDs: Dr Avtar Lit (London), Andrew
Housley (Midlands); head of news:
David Landau; breakfast show: Tony
Patti*

Virgin 105.8
1 Golden Square, London W1F 9DJ
020 7434 1215
reception@virginradio.co.uk
www.virginradio.co.uk
*Rock. Greater London. 105.8 FM.
Owner: SMG. Programme director:
Paul Jackson; head of news: Andrew
Bailey; breakfast show: Christian
O'Connell*

Xfm
30 Leicester Square
London WC2H 7LA
020 7766 6600
info@xfm.co.uk
www.xfm.co.uk
*Alternative music. Greater London.
104.9 FM. Owner: GCap Media.
Managing director: Graham Bryce;
programme controller: Andrew
Phillips; head of news: Justin King*

SOUTH-EAST

2-Ten FM
PO Box 2020, Calcot, Reading
Berkshire RG31 7FG
0118 945 4400
tim.parker@creation.com
www.musicradio.com
*All types of music. Reading,
Basingstoke, Newbury and Andover.
103.4 FM; 97 FM; 102.9 FM. Owner:
GCap Media. HR development
manager: Jonathan Bradley;
programme controller: Tim Parker;
head of news: Susie Southgate;
breakfast show: The Morning Crew*

96.4 The Eagle
Dolphin House, North Street
Guildford GU1 4AA
01483 300964
onair@964eagle.co.uk
www.964eagle.co.uk
*Adult contemporary. Guildford. 96.4
FM, 1566 AM. Owner: UKRD Group.
Managing director: Valeria Handley;
programme director: Peter Gordon;
head of news: Robert Harris; breakfast
show: Dave Johns*

103.2 Power FM
Radio House, Whittle Avenue
Segensworth
West Fareham PO15 5SH
01489 589911
info@powerfm.co.uk
www.powerfm.com
*20 years to up-to-date pop. South
Hampshire. 103.2 FM. Owner: GCap
Media. Programme controller: Craig
Morris; head of news: Alison Law;
breakfast show: Rick Jackson and
Rachel Brooks*

107.4 The Quay
Flagship Studios PO Box 1074
Portsmouth PO2 8YG
023 9236 4141
mail@quayradio.com
www.quayradio.com
*Pop. Portsmouth. 107.4 FM. Owner:
Radio Investments. Programme
controller and breakfast show: Sam
Matterface*

107.5 Sovereign Radio
14 St Mary's Walk, Hailsham
East Sussex BN27 1AF
01323 442700
info@1075sovereignradio.co.uk
www.1075sovereignradio.co.uk
*Music. Eastbourne. 107.5 FM. Owner:
Radio Investments. Brand manager:
Nigel Ansell; commercial manager:
Karen Dyball; breakfast show: Nigel
Ansell*

107.6 Kestrel FM
Paddington House, Festival Place
Basingstoke RG21 7LJ
01256 694000
studio@kestrelfm.com
www.kestrelfm.com
*70s, 80s, 90s and today. Basingstoke.
107.6 FM. Owner: Milestone Group.
Managing director: Jeff Lee;
programme manager: Andy Green;
head of news: Mel Barham; breakfast
show: Pat Sissons*

107.8 Arrow FM
Priory Meadow Centre, Hastings
East Sussex TN34 1PJ
01424 461177
info@arrowfm.co.uk
www.arrowfm.co.uk
*Adult contemporary. Hastings. 107.8
FM. Owner: Radio Investments.
Managing director: Paul Fairburn;
programme director: Andy Caruthers;
programme controller: Mike Buxton;
head of news: Vicky Jones; breakfast
show: Andy Knight*

107.8 Radio Jackie
The Old Post Office 110–112
Tolworth Broadway
Surbiton, Surrey KT6 7JD
020 8288 1300
info@radiojackie.com
www.radiojackie.com
*Adult contemporary. Kingston-upon-
Thames. 107.8 FM. Independent.
Managing director: Peter Stremes;
programmme controller: Dave Owen;
head of news: Rod Bradbury; breakfast
show: Neil Long*

Bright 106.4
The Market Place Shopping Centre,
Burgess Hill
West Sussex RH15 9NP
01444 248127
reception@bright1064.com
www.bright1064.com
*70s, 80s, 90s and latest. Burgess Hill
and Haywards Heath. 106.4 FM.
Independent. Managing director: Allan
Moulds; sales director: Mak Norman;
programme director: Mark Chapple;
head of news: Alan Lewis; breakfast
show: Mark Chapple*

Capital Gold (1170 and 1557)
30 Leicester Square
London WC2H 7LA
020 7766 6000
info@capitalgold.com
www.capitalgold.com
*Hits of the 60s, 70s and 80s. South
Hampshire. 1557 AM; 1170 AM. Owner:
GCap Media. Programme director:
Andy Turner; head of news: Justin
King; breakfast show: Mick Brown*

Capital Gold (1242 and 603)
30 Leicester Square
London WC2H 7LA
020 7766 6000
info@invictaradio.co.uk
www.capitalgold.com
*Hits of the 60s, 70s and 80s.
Maidstone, Medway and East Kent.
603 AM; 1242 AM. Owner: GCap
Media. Programme director: Andy
Turner; head of news: Justin King;
breakfast show: Neil Winfield*

Capital Gold (1323 and 945)
30 Leicester Square
London WC2H 7LA
020 7766 6000
info@capitalgold.co.uk
www.capitalgold.com
*Hits of the 60s, 70s and 80s. Brighton,
Eastbourne and Hastings. 945 AM;
1323 AM. Owner: GCap Media.
Programme director: Andy Turner;
head of news: Justin King; breakfast
show: Kevin King*

Classic Gold 1431/1485
The Chase, Calcot
Reading RG31 7RB
0118 945 4400
enquiries@classicgolddigital.com
www.classicgolddigital.com
*80s, 90s and modern. Reading,
Basingstoke and Andover. 1431 AM;
1485 AM. Owner: Classic Gold Digital.
Programme controllers: Tim Allen and
Paul Baker; head of news: Susie
Southgate*

Classic Gold 1521
The Stanley Centre, Kelvin Way
Crawley, West Sussex RH10 2SE
01293 519161
studio@musicradio.com
www.musicradio.co.uk
*60s and 70s. Reigate and Crawley. 1521
AM. Owner: Classic Gold Digital.
Station manager: Amanda Masters;
programme controller: Don Douglas;
head of news: Gareth Davies; breakfast
show: Dan Jennings and Emma
Richards*

County Sound Radio 1566 AM
Dolphin House North Street
Guildford GU1 4AA
01483 300964
onair@countysound.co.uk
www.ukrd.com
*Adult contemporary. Guildford. 1566
AM. Owner: UKRD Group. Managing
director: Valerie Handley; programme
director: Peter Gordon; head of news:
Robert Harris; breakfast show: Dave
Johns*

CTR 105.6 FM
6–8 Mill Street, Maidstone ME15 6XH
01622 662500
enq@ctrfm.com
www.ctrfm.com
*Adult contemporary. Maidstone. 105.6
FM. Independent. Managing director:
John Maxfield; head of news: Helen
Fisher; breakfast show: Ant Payne*

Delta FM
65 Weyhill, Haslemere
Surrey GU27 1HN
01428 651971
studio@deltaradio.co.uk
www.deltaradio.co.uk
*Yesterday and today. Alton,
Hampshire. 101.6 FM; 102 FM; 97.1
FM; 101.8 FM. Owner: UKRD Group
and Tindle Newspapers. Managing
director: David Way; sales manager:
Andy Wise; head of news: James
Sloane; breakfast show: Stuart Clark*

FM 103 Horizon
14 Vincent Avenue Crownhill
Milton Keynes MK8 0ZP
01908 269111
reception@horizon.musicradio.com
www.musicradio.com
*80s, 90s and today. Milton Keynes.
103.3 FM. Owner: GCap Media.
Station manager: Trevor Marshall;
programme controller: Trevor
Marshall; breakfast show: Trevor
Cueball and Roz*

Invicta FM
Radio House
John Wilson Business Park
Whitstable, Kent CT5 3QX
01227 772004
info@invictaradio.co.uk
www.invictafm.com
*Pop. Maidstone, Medway and East
Kent. 95.9 FM; 102.8 FM; 96.1 FM;
97 FM; 103.1 FM. Owner: GCap Media.
Programme controller: Max Hailey;
head of news: Nicola Everitt; breakfast
show: The Morning Zoo*

Isle of Wight Radio
Dodnor Park, Newport
Isle of Wight PO30 5XE
01983 822557
admin@iwradio.co.uk
www.iwradio.co.uk
*Adult contemporary and pop. Isle of
Wight. 102 FM; 107 FM. Owner: Radio
Investments. Programme controller:
Tom Stroud; head of news: Andrew
Carter; breakfast show: Andy Shier*

Juice 107.2
170 North Street, Brighton BN1 1EA
01273 386107
info@juicebrighton.com
www.juicebrighton.com
*Commercial dance. Brighton. 107.2
FM. Owner: Brighton & Hove Ltd.
Managing director: Matthew Bashford;
programme controller: Sam Walker;
head of news: Graham Levitt; breakfast
show: Marc Brooks*

Kick FM
The Studios, 42 Bone Lane
Newbury, Berkshire RG14 5SD
01635 841600
mail@kickfm.com
www.kickfm.com
*Adult contemporary. Newbury. 105.6
FM; 107.4 FM. Owner: Milestone
Group. Managing director: Jeff Lee;
head of news: John Statford;
programme controller: Mark Watson;
breakfast show: Mark Watson*

KMfm Canterbury
9 St George's Place, Canterbury
Kent CT1 1UU
01227 475950
reception@kmfm.co.uk
www.kentonline.co.uk/kmfm
*Adult contemporary. Canterbury. 106
FM. Owner: KM Radio. Group
programme controller: Mike Osborne;
head of news: Julia Walsh; breakfast
show: Chris Finn*

KM-FM for Folkestone and Dover
93–95 Sandgate Road
Folkestone, Kent CT20 2BQ
01303 220303
Scork@kmfm.co.uk
www.kentonline/kmfm
*60s, 70s, 80s and 90s. Dover and
Folkestone. 106.8 FM. Owner: KM
Radio. Group programme
controller: Mike Osborne; head of
sales: George Gault; breakfast shoe:
Spencer Cork*

Medway's KM-FM
Medway House, Ginsbury Close
Sir Thomas Longley Road
Stroud ME2 4DU
01634 227808
pcarter@kmfm.co.uk
www.kentonline.co.uk/kmfm
*Adult contemporary. Medway Towns.
100.4 FM; 107.9 FM. Owner: KM Radio.
Group programme controller: Mike
Osborne; breakfast show: Dibbsy and
Amy*

Mercury FM
The Stanley Centre, Kelvin Way
Crawley, West Sussex RH10 9SE
01293 519161
studio@musicradio.com
www.musicradio.com
*60s and 70s. Reigate and Crawley. 97.5
FM; 102.7 FM. Owner: GCap Media.
Programme controller: Don Jennings;
head of news: Gareth Davies; breakfast
show: Dan Jennings and Emma
Richards*

Mix 96
Friars Square Studios
11 Bourbon Street
Aylesbury HP20 2PZ
01296 399396
info@mix96.co.uk
www.mix96.co.uk
*70 to present day. Aylesbury. 96.2 FM.
Owner: Radio Investments. Managing
director: Rachael Faulkner;
programme controller: James O'Neil;
head of news: Penny Harper; breakfast
show: James O'Neil*

Mix 107 FM
PO Box 1107, High Wycombe
Buckinghamshire HP13 6WQ
01494 446611
sales@mix107.co.uk
www.mix107.co.uk
*Adult contemporary. High Wycombe.
107.4 FM. Owner: Radio Investments.
Programme director: Andy Muir; head
of news: Hilary Cogan; breakfast show:
Andy Muir*

Ocean FM
Radio House, Whittle Avenue,
Segensworth
West Fareham PO15 5SH
01489 589911
info@oceanfm.co.uk
www.oceanfm.com
*70s, 80s and 90s. South Hampshire.
96.7 FM; 97.5 FM. Owner: GCap
Media. Programme controller: Stuart
Ellis; head of news: Alison Law;
breakfast show: Richard Williams*

Reading 107 FM
Radio House, Madejski Stadium,
Reading, Berkshire RG2 0FN
0118 986 2555
firstname@reading107fm.com
www.reading107fm.com
*Beatles to Bangles. Reading. 107 FM.
Independent. Managing director: Tony
Grundy; programme controller: Tim
Grundy; marketing director: Joannah
Bishop; breakfast show: Tim Grundy*

The Saint 107.8 FM
Brittania Road
Southampton SO14 5FP
023 8033 0300
studio@saintsfc.co.uk
www.saintsfc.co.uk
*Adult contemporary, Southampton FC.
Southampton. 107.8 FM. Independent.
Programme director: Stewart Dennis;
station director: Tim Manns; head of
news: Will Cope; breakfast show:
Stewart Dennis*

Southern FM
Radio House, PO Box 2000
Brighton BN41 2SS
01273 430111
news@southernfm.co.uk
www.southernfm.com
*Pop. Brighton, Eastbourne and
Hastings. 103.5 FM; 96.9 FM; 102.4
FM; 102 FM. Owner: GCap Media.
Sales director: Jack Manzoor;
programme controller: Tony Aldridge;
news editor: Claire Martin; breakfast
show: Chris Baughen*

Spirit FM
9–10 Dukes Court, Bognor Road
Chichester PO19 8FX
01243 773600
info@spiritfm.net
www.spiritfm.net
*Easy listening. Chichester, Bognor
Regis, Littlehampton. 102.3 FM; 96.6
FM, 106.6 FM. Independent. Managing
director: Stephen Oates; programme
controller: Duncan Barkes; head of
news: Caroline Kingsmill; breakfast
show: Paul Williams*

Splash FM
Guildbourne Centre, Worthing
West Sussex BN11 1LZ
01903 233005
mail@splashfm.com
www.splashfm.com
*60s, 70s, 80s, 90s and today. Worthing.
107.7 FM. Independent. Managing
director: Roy Stannard; programme
controller: Simon Osborne; news editor:
Justin Stacey; breakfast show: Simon
Osborne*

Star 106.6
The Observatory Shopping Centre
Slough SL1 1LH
01753 551066
onair@star1066.co.uk
www.star1066.co.uk
*Adult contemporary. Slough,
Maidenhead, Windsor. 106.6 FM.
Owner: UKRD Group. Programme
controller: Anthony Ballard; head of
news: Rob Harris; breakfast show:
Anthony Ballard*

Thanet's KM-FM
181–183 Northdown Road,
Cliftonville, Kent CT9 2PA
01843 220222
initialsurname@kmgroup.co.uk
www.kentonline.co.uk/kmfm
*Classic hits from 70s and current.
Thanet. 107.2 FM. Owner: KM Radio.
Group programme controller: Mike
Osborne; head of news: Anthony
Masters; breakfast show: Johnny Lewis*

Time 107.5
Lambourne House, 7 Western Road
Romford, Essex RM1 3LD
0870 607 1075
info@timefm.com
www.timefm.com
*Soul. Romford, Barking and
Dagenham. 107.5 FM. Owner: Sunrise
Radio. Managing director: Mark
Reason; programme director: Mark
Dover; breakfast show: Mike Porter*

Wave 105 FM
5 Manor Court, Barnes Wallis Road,
Segensworth East
Fareham, Hampshire PO15 5TH
01489 481057
martin.ball@wave105.com
www.wave105.com
*70s, 80s and 90s hits. Solent. 105.2 FM;
105.8 FM. Owner: ScottishRadio
Holdings. Managing director: Martin
Ball; programme controller: John
Dash; head of news: Jason Beck;
breakfast show: Steve Power*

West Kent's KM-FM
1 East Street, Tonbridge
Kent TN9 1AR
01732 369200
tunbridgestudio@kmfm.co.uk
www.kentonline.co.uk/radio
*Adult contemporary. Tunbridge Wells
and Sevenoaks. 96.2 FM; 101.6 FM.
Owner: KM Radio. Group programme
controller: Mike Osborne; head of news:
Anthony Masters; breakfast show: Rik
and Vanessa*

Win 107.2
PO Box 107
The Brooks Shopping Centre
Winchester, Hants SO23 8FT
01962 841071
jo@winfm.co.uk
www.winfm.co.uk
*Adult contemporary. Winchester. 107.2
FM. Owner: Radio Investments.
Station manager: Jo Talbot; head of
news: Julie Massitter; breakfast show:
David Adams*

SOUTH-WEST

2CR FM
5–7 Southcote Road, Bournemouth
Dorset BH1 3LR
01202 234900
newsbournemouth@creation.com
www.musicradio.com
*80 and 90s and chart music.
Bournemouth and Hampshire. 102.3
FM. Owner: GCap Media. Programme
controller: Graham Mack; sales
director: Jane Suttie; breakfast show:
Graham Mack*

97 FM Plymouth Sound
Earl's Acre, Plymouth PL3 4HX
01752 275600
mail@plymouthsound.musicradio.com
www.musicradio.com
*80s, 90s and today. Plymouth. 97 FM;
96.6 FM. Owner: GCap Media.
Programme controller: Dave Harbour;
head of news: Darryl Jenner; breakfast
show: Leigh-Ann Venning and Martin
Mills*

97.4 Vale FM
Longmead Studios, Shaftesbury
Dorset SP7 8PL
01747 855711
studio@valefm.co.uk
www.vale.fm.co.uk
*Adult contemporary. Shaftesbury.
97.4 FM; 96.6 FM. Owner: Radio
Investments. Programme controller:
Stewart Smith; head of news: Kevin
Gover; breakfast show: Cameron Smith*

104.7 Island FM
12 Westerbrook, St Sampsons
Guernsey GY2 4QQ
01481 242000
firstname@islandfm.guernsey.net
www.islandfm.guernsey.net
*Chart music. Rock show in evenings.
Guernsey. 104.7 FM; 93.7 FM. Owner:
Tindle Radio. Programme controller:
Gary Burgess; head of news: Katie
Collins; breakfast show: Gary Burgess*

107.5 3TR FM
Riverside Studios, Boreham Mill
Bishopstow, Warminster BA12 9HQ
01985 211111
admin@3trfm.com
www.3trfm.com
*Classics. Warminster. 107.5 FM. Owner:
Radio Investments. Brand manager:
Jonathan Fido; sales manager: Will
Brougham; head of news: Louisa
Jackson; breakfast show: Chris Ward*

Bath FM
Station House, Ashley Avenue,
Lower Weston, Bath BA1 3DS
01225 471571
news@bath.fm
www.bath.fm
*Adult contemporary. Bath. 107.9 FM.
Independent. Managing director: Jo
Woods; programme controller and head
of news: Steve Collins; breakfast show:
James Carpenter*

BCRfm
Royal Clarence House
York Buildings High Street
Bridgwater TA6 3AT
01278 727701
studio@bcrfm.co.uk
www.bcrfm.co.uk
*Music from last four decades.
Bridgwater. 107.4 FM. Independent.
Managing director: Mark Painter;
programme controller and breakfast
show: David Englefield*

Channel 103 FM
6 Tunnell Street, St Helier
Jersey JE2 4LU
01534 888103
firstname@channel103.com
www.channel103.com
*Broad mix of pop and rock. Jersey.
103.7 FM. Owner: Tindle Radio.
Managing director: Linda Burnham;
programme director: Spencer Davies;
head of news: Phil Bouchard; breakfast
show: Peter Mac*

Classic Gold 1152 AM
Earl's Acre, Plymouth PL3 4HX
01752 275600
www.classicgolddigital.com
*70s, 80s and 90s. Plymouth. 1152 AM.
Owner: Classic Gold Digital.
Programme controller: Don Douglas;
head of news: Lisa Hay; breakfast
show: Tony Blackburn*

Classic Gold 1260
One Passage Street
Bristol BS99 7SN
0117 984 3200
admin@classicgolddigital.com
www.classicgolddigital.com
*Chart music. Bristol and Bath. 1260
AM. Owner: Classic Gold Digital.
Programme controller: Steve Fountain;
head of news: Cormack McMahon;
breakfast show: Tony Blackburn*

Classic Gold 666/954
Hawthorn House
Exeter Business Park
Exeter EX1 3QS
01392 444444
*Classic hits. Exeter, Torbay. 954 AM;
666 AM. Owner: Classic Gold Digital.
Programme controller: Colin Slade;
breakfast show: Tony Blackburn and
Laura Pittson*

Classic Gold 774
Bridge Studios, Eastgate Centre
Gloucester GL1 1SS
01452 313200
www.classicgolddigital.com
*Various sounds. Gloucester,
Cheltenham. 774 AM. Owner: Classic
Gold Digital. Programme controller:
Marcus Langereiter; head of news and
breakfast show: Neil Vincent*

Classic Gold 828
5 Southcote Road, Bournemouth
Dorset BH1 3LR
01202 234900
newsbournemouth@creation.com
www.classicgolddigital.com
*Popular music. Bournemouth. 828 AM.
Owner: Classic Gold Digital.
Programme controller: Don Douglas;
breakfast show: Tony Blackburn*

Classic Gold 936/1161 AM
Lime Kiln Studio, Lime Kiln
Wooton Bassett, Swindon SN4 7EX
01793 842600
reception@musicradio.com
www.musicradio.com
*Popular music. Swindon. 936 AM; 1161
AM. Owner: Classic Gold Digital.
Managing director: John Baish; head of
programming: Bill Overton; breakfast
show: Tony Blackburn and Laura
Pillson*

Fire 107.6FM
Quadrant Studios
Old Christchurch Road
Bournemouth BH1 2AD
01202 318100
firstname@fire1076.com
www.fire1076.com
*Rhythmic and contemporary.
Bournemouth and Poole. 107.6 FM.
Owner: Radio Investments.
Programme controller: Paul Gerrard;
head of news: Justin Gladdis; breakfast
show: Northern and Gemma*

FOX FM
Brush House, Pony Road
Oxford OX4 2XR
01865 871000
reception@foxfm.co.uk
www.foxfm.co.uk
*Adult contemporary. Oxford and
Banbury. 102.6 FM; 97.4 FM. Owner:
Capital Radio. Programme controller:
Sam Walker; head of news: Hugh
James; breakfast show: Carl and Jo*

Gemini FM
Hawthorn House
Exeter Business Park
Exeter EX1 3QS
01392 444444
gemini@geminifm.musicradio.com
www.musicradio.com
*Top 40. Exeter, Torbay. 97 FM; 103
FM; 96.4 FM. Owner: GWR Group.
Programme controller: Gavin
Marshall; head of news: Michelle
Horsley; breakfast show: Ben Clarke
and Rachael Hicks*

GWR FM and Classic Gold Digital
PO Box 2000
Woottonbassett SN4 7EX
01793 842600
reception@musicradio.com
www.musicradio.com
*70s, 80s and 90s and today. Swindon
and west Wiltshire. 102.2 FM; 96.5
FM; 97.2 FM. Owner: GCap Media.
Programme controller: Sue Carter;
head of news: Deb Evans; breakfast
show: Matt and H and Tony Blackburn*

GWR FM (Bristol and Bath)
PO Box 2000, One Passage Street
Bristol BS99 7SN
0117 984 3200
reception@gwrfm.musicradio.com
www.musicradio.com
*Chart music. Bristol and Bath. 103 FM;
96.3 FM. Owner: GCap Media.
Managing director: Dirk Anthony;
programme controller: Paul Andrew;
head of news: Vickie Brakewell;
breakfast show: Tony and Michaela*

Ivel FM

The Studios, Middle Street
Yeovil, Somerset BA20 1DJ
reception: 01935 848488; studio:
08712 777105
all@ivelfm.co.uk
www.ivelfm.com
*60s, 70s, 80s to present day. Yeovil.
105.6 FM, 106.6 FM. Owner: Local
Radio Company. Programme
controller: Steve Carpenter; heads of
news: Fiona Biggs and Fiona Honan;
breakfast show: Steve Carpenter*

Lantern FM

2b Lauder Lane, Roundswell
Business Park
Barnstable EX31 3TA
01271 340340
jim.trevelyan@creation.com
www.musicradio.com
*Late 90s to present day. Barnstable.
97.3 FM; 96.2 FM. Owner: GCap
Media. Sales director: Jim Trevelyan;
programme controller: Paul Hopper;
head of news: Nicola Rickard; breakfast
show: PJ and Spanky*

Orchard FM

Haygrove House, Taunton
Somerset TA3 7BT
01823 338448
orchardfm@musicradio.com
www.musicradio.com
*Top 40. Yeovil and Taunton. 102.6 FM;
97.1 FM; 96.5 FM. Owner: GCap Media.
Programme controller: Steve Bulley;
journalists: Nicola Maxey and Darren
Bevan; breakfast show: Ian and Laura*

Passion 107.9

270 Woodstock Road
Oxford OX2 7NW
01235 547825
info@passion1079.com
www.passion1079.com
*Dance and pop. Oxford. 107.9 FM.
Owner: Milestone Group. Programme
controller and station manager: Andy
Green; breakfast show: Bodge at
Breakfast*

Pirate FM102

Carn Brea Studios, Wilson Way
Redruth, Cornwall TR15 3XX
01209 314400
enquiries@piratefm102.co.uk
www.piratefm102.co.uk
*Various pop. Cornwall and west Devon.
102.2 FM; 102.8 FM. Owner: UKRD
Group. Managing director: Beverley
Warne; programme director: Bob
McCreadie; head of news: Alistair Jell;
breakfast show: Bob McCreadie*

Quay West Radio

The Harbour Studios
The Esplanade, Watchet
Somerset TA23 0AJ
01984 634900
studio@quaywest.fm
www.quaywest.fm
*Adult contemporary. West Somerset.
102.4 FM. Independent. Programme
director: David Mortimer; head of
news: Spencer Bishop; breakfast show:
David Mortimer*

Severn Sound

Bridge Studios, Eastgate Centre
Gloucester GL1 1SS
01452 313200
reception@musicradio.com
www.musicradio.com
*Various sounds. Gloucester and
Cheltenham. 103 FM; 102.4 FM.
Owner: GCap Media. Programme
controller: Russ Wilcox; sales manager:
Mark Right; head of news: Mark Smith;
breakfast show: Russ, Nicola and Darcy*

South Hams Radio

Unit 1G, South Hams Business Park
Churchstow, Kingsbridge
Devon TQ7 3QH
01548 854595
reception@southhamsradio.com
www.southhamsradio.com
*Adult contemporary. South Hams.
101.9 FM; 100.8 FM; 100.5 FM; 101.2
FM. Owner: GWR Group. Station
manager: David Fitzgerald; head of
news: Louise Henry; breakfast show:
Ian Calvert*

Spire FM

City Hall Studios, Malthouse Lane
Salisbury, Wiltshire SP2 7QQ
01722 416644
admin@spirefm.co.uk
www.spirefm.co.uk
*Chart hits. Salisbury. 102 FM. Owner:
Radio Investments. Managing director:
Ceri Hurford-Jones; programme
controller: Stuart McGinley; breakfast
show: Daren Cee*

Star 107

Unit 3 Brunel Mall, London Road
Stroud, Gloucester GL5 2BP
01453 767369
studio@star1079.co.uk
www.star1079.co.uk
*70s, 80s and 90s and greatest hits.
Stroud. 107.2 FM; 107.9 FM. Owner:
UKRD Group. Head of sales: Rebecca
Tansley; programme controller: Marie
Greenwood; head of news: Simon
Hancock; breakfast show: Ben Store*

Star 107.2

Bristol Evening Post Building
Temple Way, Bristol BS99 7HD
0117 910 6600
dev@star1072.co.uk
www.star1073.co.uk
*Adult contemporary and soul. Bristol.
107.2 FM. Owner: UKRD Group.
Station manager: William Rogers;
head of news: Stephanie Mousey;
breakfast show: Dawn and JP*

Star 107.5

Cheltenham Film Studios, 1st Floor
West Suite Arle Court, Hatherley Lane
Cheltenham GL51 6PN
01242 699555
studio@star1075.co.uk
www.star1075.co.uk
*80s to today. Cheltenham. 107.5 FM.
Owner: UKRD Group. Station
manager: Junie Lewis; programme
manager and head of news: Brody
Swain; breakfast show: Brody Swain
and Louise Bruce*

Star 107.7 FM

11 Beaconsfield Road
Weston Super Mare BS23 1YE
01934 624455
name@star1077.co.uk
www.star1077.co.uk
*70s, 80s and 90s popular music.
Weston Super Mare. 107.7 FM. Owner:
UKRD Group. Programme controller:
Scott Temblett; head of news: Charlotte
Saker; breakfast show: Derek Thompson*

Vibe 101

26 Baldwin Street, Bristol BS1 1SE
0117 901 0101
info@vibe101.co.uk
www.vibe101.co.uk
*Dance and R&B. South Wales and
Severn estuary. 97.2 FM; 101 FM.
Owner: Scottish Radio Holdings.
Managing director: Beverley Cleall-
Harding; programme controller:
Trevor James; head of news: Lucy
Perrett; breakfast show: Darren Daley*

Wessex FM

Radio House, Trinity Street
Dorchester DT1 1DJ
01305 250333
admin@wessexfm.co.uk
www.wessexfm.com
*Hits of 60s, 70s, 80s. Weymouth and
Dorchester. 97.2 FM; 96 FM. Owner:
Radio Investments. Station manager:
Phil Stocks; head of news: Kevin Gover;
breakfast show: Jason Herbert*

EAST ENGLAND

96.9 Chiltern FM

55 Goldington Road
Bedford, Beds MK40 3LT
01234 272400
firstname.surname@musicradio.com
www.musicradio.com
*80s, 90s to today. Bedford. 96.9 FM.
Owner: GCap Media. Sales manager:
Sharon Rush; programme controller:
Simon Marshall; head of news: Mark
Grinnell; breakfast show: Andy Gelder*

97.6 Chiltern FM

Chiltern Road, Dunstable
Beds LU6 1HQ
01582 676200
firstname.surname@musicradio.co.uk
www.musicradio.com
*Easy listening. Herts, Beds, Bucks. 97.6
FM. Owner: GCap Media. Programme
controller: Stuart Davies; head of news:
Mark Grinnell; breakfast show: Gareth
Wesley and Karen Carpenter*

102.7 Hereward FM

PO Box 225 Queensgate Centre
Peterborough PE1 1XJ
01733 460460
firstname.surname@musicradio.com
www.musicradio.com
*Adult contemporary. Greater
Peterborough. 102.7 FM. Owner: GCap
Media. Programme controller: Mickey
Gavin; head of news: Sarah Spence;
breakfast show: Matt and Sarah*

103.4 The Beach
PO Box 103.4
Lowestoft, Suffolk NR32 2TL
0845 345 1035
sue.taylor@thebeach.co.uk
www.thebeach.co.uk
*Chart past and present. Great Yarmouth
and Lowestoft. 103.4 FM. Owner: Tindle
Radio. Managing director: David
Blake; news editor: Kirsty Taylor;
breakfast show: Tom Kay*

Broadland 102
St George's Plain
47–49 Colgate, Norwich NR3 1DB
01603 630621
firstname.surname@musicradio.com
www.musicradio.com
*80s, 90s and today. Norfolk and north
Suffolk. 102.4 FM. Owner: GCap
Media. Programme controller: Steve
Martin; head of news: Harry Mitchell;
breakfast show: Rob and Chrissie*

Classic Gold 1332 AM
PO Box 225, Queensgate Centre
Peterborough PEI IXJ
01733 460460
firstname.surname@
     classicgolddigital.com
www.classicgolddigital.com
*Classic hits. Peterborough. 1332 AM.
Owner: Opus Group/Classic Gold
Digital. Programme controller: Mickey
Gavin; head of news: Sarah Spence;
breakfast show: Tony Blackburn*

Classic Gold 792/828
Chiltern Road
Dunstable, Beds LU6 1HQ
01582 676200
firstname.surname@
     classicgolddigital.com
www.classicgolddigital.com
*60s to modern. Luton, Bedford. 792
AM; 828 AM. Owner: Opus Group/
Classic Gold Digital. Programme
controller: John Baish; head of news:
Mark Grinnell; breakfast show: Tony
Blackburn and Laura Pittson*

Classic Gold Amber
St George's Plain
47–49 Colgate, Norwich NR3 1DB
01603 630621
firstname.surname@
     classicgolddigital.com
www.classicgolddigital.com
*80s, 90s and today. Norwich. 1152 AM.
Owner: GCap Media/Classic Gold
Digital. Programme controller: Paul
Baker; sales centre manager: Rod
Walker; breakfast show: Tony Blackburn*

Classic Gold Amber 1152
Alpha Business Park
6–12 White House Road
Ipswich IP1 5LT
01473 461000
firstname.surname@
     classicgolddigital.com
www.classicgolddigital.com
*70s and 80s. Ipswich and Bury St
Edmunds. 1251 AM; 1170 AM. Owner:
Classic Gold Digital. Programme
controller: Paul Baker; breakfast show:
Tony Blackburn*

Classic Gold Breeze
Radio House, 31 Glebe Road
Stanford, Essex CN1 1QG
01245 524500
firstname.surname@
     classicgolddigital.com
www.classicgolddigital.com
*Classic 60s, 70s, 80s. Southend and
Chelmsford. 1359 AM; 1431 AM.
Owner: Opus Group/Classic Gold
Digital. Programme controller: Paul
Baker; breakfast show: Tony Blackburn*

Dream 100 FM
Northgate House, St Peter's Street
Colchester, Essex CO1 1HT
01206 764466
info@dream100.com
www.dream100.com
*70s to today. North Essex and south
Suffolk. 100.2 FM. Owner: Tindle Radio.
Managing director: Jamie Brodie;
programme controller: Jonathan
Hemmings; head of news: Scott Wilson;
breakfast show: Chris Sturgess*

Dream 107.7
Cater House, High Street
Chelmsford CM1 1AL
01245 259400
firstname.surname@dream107.com
www.dream107.com
*Adult contemporary. Chelmsford. 107.7
FM. Owner: Tindle Radio. Managing
director: Ian Wootton; programme
controller and head of news: Nick Hull;
breakfast show: Tracy Young*

Essex FM
Radio House, 31 Glebe Road
Stanford, Essex CN1 1QG
01245 524500
Lee.murphy@creation.com
www.musicradio.com
*Classic 60s, 70s, 80s. Southend and
Chelmsford. 102.6 FM; 96.3 FM; 97.5
FM. Owner: GCap Media. Programme
controller: Chris Cotton; head of news:
Lee Murphy; breakfast show: Martin
and Sue*

Fen Radio 107.5 FM
5 Church Mews, Wisbech
Cambridgeshire PE13 1HL
01945 467107
studio@fenradio.co.uk
www.sound-wave.co.uk
*70s to today. Fenland. 107.1 FM; 107.5
FM. Owner: UKRD Group. Station
manager and programme director:
Mark Pryke; programme manager:
Richard Grant; sales director: Jason
Smith; breakfast show: Adi Linton*

Hertbeat FM
The Pump House, Knebworth Park
Hertford, Hertfordshire SG3 6HQ
01438 810900
info@hertbeat.com
www.hertbeat.com
*80s/90s, specialist programmes
weekend. Hertfordshire. 106.9 FM;
106.7 FM. Independent. Station
manager: Darrell Thomas; programme
controller: Steve Folland; news editor:
Ruth Gibbon; breakfast show: Steve
Folland*

KL.FM 96.7
18 Blackfriars Street
Kings Lynn, Norfolk PE30 1NN
01553 772777
admin@klfm967.co.uk
www.klfm967.co.uk
*Best of past 30 years. Kings Lynn and
west Norfolk. 96.7 FM. Owner: UKRD
Group. Managing director: William
Rogers; Station manager: Mark Pryke;
programme controller: Simon Rowe;
head of news: Gary Phillips; breakfast
show: Roy Allaway*

Lite FM
2nd Floor, 5 Church Street
Peterborough PE1 1XB
01733 898106
kev@lite1068.co.uk
www.lite1068.co.uk
*Adult contemporary. Peterborough.
106.8 FM. Owner: Forward Media
Group. Managing director: David
Myatt; programme manager: Kevin
Lawrence; head of news: Simon Potter;
breakfast show: Kevin Lawrence*

North Norfolk Radio
PO Box 962 The Studio, Breck Farm
Stody, Norfolk NR24 2ER
01263 860808
info@northnorfolkradio.com
www.northnorfolk.com
*Adult contemporary. North Norfolk.
103.2 FM; 96.2 FM. Independent.
Programme controller: Richard
Lawson; head of news: John Bultitude*

Q103 FM
Enterprise House, The Vision Park
Chivers Way, Histon
Cambridgeshire CB4 9WW
01223 235255
firstname.surname@
     q103.musicradio.com
www.musicradio.com
*Mix of today. Cambridge and
Newmarket. 103 FM. Owner: GCap
Media. Area programme controller:
Paul Green; sales director: Phil Caborn;
head of news: Sarah Spence; breakfast
show: "Q103"*

SGR Colchester
Abbey Gate Two, 9 Whitewell Road
Colchester CO2 7DE
01206 575859
sgrcolchester@musicradio.com
www.musicradio.com
*80s, 90s and today. Colchester. 96.1 FM.
Owner: GCap Media. Programme
controller: Paul Morris; sales director:
Sue Rudland; head of news: Terry
Taylor; senior presenter: Paul Morris;
breakfast show: Louise and Ian*

SGR FM
Alpha Business Park
6–12 White House Road, Ipswich
Suffolk IP1 5LT
01473 461000
firstname.lastname@musicradio.com
www.musicradio.com
*80s, 90s and current hits. Suffolk.
96.4 FM; 97.1 FM. Owner: GCap Media.
Programme controller: Paul Morris;
head of news: Peter Cook; breakfast
show: Frankie and Katie*

Star 107.9
Radio House, Sturton Street
Cambridge CB1 2QF
01223 722300
admin@star107.co.uk
www.star1079.co.uk
*Mainstream adult contemporary.
Cambridge. 107.1 FM, 107.9 FM. Owner:
UKRD Group. Programme controller:
James Keen; head of news: Lynda
Hardy; breakfast show: Andy Gall*

Ten 17
Latton Bush Centre, Southern Way
Harlow, Essex CM18 7BB
01279 431017
firstname.surname@musicradio.com
www.musicradio.com
*Pop. East Herts, west Essex. 101.7 FM.
Owner: GCap Media. Programme
director: Rick Simmonds; news editor:
Lee Murphy; breakfast show: Ian
Burrage*

Vibe FM
Reflection House
The Anderson Centre, Olding Road
Bury St Edmunds IP33 3TA
01284 715300
general@vibefm.co.uk
www.vibefm.co.uk
*Dance and R&B. East of England.
105–108 FM. Owner: ScottishRadio.
Managing director and programme
controller: Gary Robinson; news editors:
Dawn Ferguson and Neil Didsbury;
breakfast show: Stuart Grant*

Watford's Mercury 96.6
Unit 5, The Metro Centre
Dwight Road, Watford WD18 9UP
01923 205470
firstname.surname@musicradio.com
www.musicradio.com
*Popular music. St Albans and Watford.
96.6 FM. Owner: GCap Media.
Programme controller: Rebecca
Dundon; head of news: Tricia Bullen;
breakfast show: Danny Lacey*

EAST MIDLANDS

96 Trent FM
29–31 Castle Gate
Nottingham NG1 7AP
0115 873 1500
firstname.surname@musicradio.com
www.musicradio.com
*All types of music. Nottinghamshire. 96
FM. Owner: GCap Media. Programme
controller: Luis Clark; head of news:
Lewis Scrimshaw; breakfast show: Jo
and Twiggy*

102.8 RAM FM
35–36 Irongate, Derby DE1 3GA
01332 205599
ramfm@musicradio.com
www.musicradiocom
*All current pop music. Derby. 102.8
FM. Owner: GCap Media. Programme
controller: James Daniels; head of
news: Lewis Scrimshaw; breakfast
show: Rachael and Deano*

107 Oak FM
7 Waldron Court
Prince William Road, Loughborough
Leicestershire LE11 5GD
01509 211711
studio@oak107.co.uk
www.oak107.co.uk
*60s to today. Charnwood and
north-west Leicestershire. 107 FM.
Owner: CN Group. Station manager:
Don Douglas; programme manager:
Mike Vitti; head of news: Yvonne
Radley; breakfast show: Dave James*

Centre FM
5–6 Aldergate
Tamworth, Staffordshire B79 7DJ
01827 318000
studio@centrefm.com
www.centre.fm
*80s, 90s and today. South-east
Staffordshire. 101.6 FM; 102.4 FM.
Owner: CN Group. Managing director:
Greg Parker; programme manager:
Stuart Hickman; head of news: Clare
Lavender; breakfast show: Neil Jackson*

106 Century FM
City Link, Nottingham NG2 4NG
0115 910 6100
info106@centuryfm.co.uk
www.106centuryfm.com
*80s, 90s and contemporary. East
Midlands. 106 FM. Owner: GCap
Media. Brand managing director:
Nick Davidson; Brand programme
director: Giles Squire; breakfast show:
Jim and Paula*

Classic Gold 1557
Northamptonshire
19–21 St Edmunds Road
Northampton NN1 5DT
01604 795600
firstname.surname@
classicgolddigital.com
www.classicgolddigital.com
*Classic music. Northampton. 1557 AM.
Owner: Classic Gold Digital.
Programme controller: Chris Rick;
head of news: Sarah Spence; breakfast
show: Tony Blackburn*

Classic Hits
PO Box 262, Worcester WR6 5ZE
01432 360246
info@classicgolddigital.fm
www.classichits.co.uk
*Last four or five decades of hits.
Hereford and Worcester. 954 AM; 1530
AM. Owner: Murfin Media
International. Managing director:
Chris Jefferies; programme controller:
Tim Boswell; head of news: Andrew
Currie; breakfast show: Tim Boswell*

Classic Gold GEM
29–31 Castle Gate
Nottingham NG1 7AP
0115 873 1500
firstname.surname@
classicgolddigital.com
www.classicgolddigital.com
*Classic chart hits. Nottingham, Derby.
999 AM; 945 AM. Owner: Classic Gold
Digital. Managing director: John
Daish; programme controller: Luis
Clark; head of news: Lewis Scrimshaw;
breakfast show: Tony Blackburn*

Connect FM
Unit 1, Centre 2000
Kettering, Northants NN16 8PU
01536 412413
info@connectfm.com
www.connectfm.com
*70s, 80s and 90s and today. Kettering,
Corby. 107.4 FM; 97.2 FM. Owner:
Forward Media Group. Group
managing director: David Myatt;
Station manager: Martin Parr;
programme manager: Danny Gibson;
head of news: John Reading; breakfast
show: Gregg Nunney*

Dearne FM
PO Box 458, Barnsley S71 1XP
01226 321733
enquiries@dearnefm.co.uk
www.dearnefm.co.uk
*60s, 70s, 80s and 90s and current hits.
Barnsley. 97.1 FM; 102 FM. Owner:
Lincs FM Group. Programme controller:
Matt Jones; head of news: Leanne
Goacher; breakfast show: Steve White*

Fosseway Radio
PO Box 107, Hinckley
Leicestershire LE10 1WR
01455 614151
enquiries@fossewayradio.co.uk
www.fossewayradio.co.uk
*70s, 80s and 90s and hits of today.
Hinckley, Nuneaton. 107.9 FM. Owner:
Lincs FM. Chief executive: Michael
Betton; programme manager: Ian Ison;
head of news: James Wall; breakfast
show: Nick Guerney*

Leicester Sound
6 Dominus Way
Meridian Business Park
Leicester LE19 1RP
0116 256 1300
reception@leicesterfm.musicradio.com
www.musicradio.com
*90s and today. Leicester. 105.4 FM.
Owner: GCap Media. Programme
controller: Craig Boddy; head of sales:
Bina Chauhan; head of news: Dean
Roberts; breakfast show: Rae and Kev*

Lincs FM
Witham Park, Waterside South
Lincoln LN5 7JN
01522 549900
enquiries@lincsfm.co.uk
www.lincsfm.co.uk
*Pop. Lincoln. 102.2 FM; 97.6 FM; 96.7
FM. Owner: Lincs FM. Chief executive:
Michael Betton; programme manager:
John Marshall; news editor: Shaun
Dunderdale; breakfast show: John
Marshall*

Mansfield 103.2
The Media Suite
4 Brunts Business Centre
Samuel Brunts Way, Mansfield
Notts NG18 2AH
01623 646666
info@mansfield103.co.uk
www.mansfield103.co.uk
70s, 80s and 90s and present day. Mansfield and District. 103.2 FM. Independent. Managing director: Tony Delahunty; programme director: Katie Trinder; head of news: Ian Watkins; breakfast show: Katie Trinder

Northants 96
19–21 St Edmunds Road
Northampton NN1 5DY
01604 795600
firstname.surname@musicradio.com
www.musicradio.com
Pop. Northampton. 96.6 FM. Owner: GCap Media. Programme controller: Chris Rick; head of news: Sarah Spence; breakfast show: Jagger and Woody

Peak 107 FM
Radio House, Foxwood Road
Chesterfield S41 9RF
01246 269107
info@peak107.com
www.peak107.com
50/50 music mix. Chesterfield, north Derbyshire, south Sheffield and Peak District. 102 FM; 107.4 FM. Owner: The Wireless Group. Group programme controller: Craig Patterson; head of news: Naz Premiji; breakfast show: Sean Goldsmith and Beck Measures

Rutland Radio
40 Melton Road
Oakham, Rutland LE15 6AY
01572 757868
enquiries@rutlandradio.co.uk
www.rutlandradio.co.uk
Last 40 years' hits. Rutland and Stamford. 97.4 FM; 107.2 FM. Owner: Lincs FM. Station manager: Julie Baker; senior journalist: Richard Harding; breakfast show: Rob Persani

Sabras Radio
Sabras Sound, Radio House
63 Melton Road, Leicester LE4 6PN
0116 261 0666
enq@sabrasradio.com
www.sabrasradio.com
Asian music. Leicester. 1260 AM. Independent. Managing director and programme controller: Don Kotak; breakfast show: Mark Spokes

Saga 106.6 FM
Saga Radio House, Alder Court
Riverside Business Park
Nottingham NG2 1RX
0115 986 1066
reception@saga1066fm.co.uk
www.saga1066fm.co.uk
Easy listening from past six decades. East Midlands. 106.6 FM. Owner: Saga Group. Managing director: Phil Dixon; programme director: Paul Robey; head of news: Lisa Teanby; breakfast show: John Peters

Signal 1
Stoke Road, Stoke on Trent ST4 2SR
01782 441300
info@signalradio.com
www.signal1.co.uk
Pop music. Stoke on Trent. 96.4 FM; 102.6 FM; 96.9 FM. Owner: The Wireless Group. Group programme director: John Evington; managing director: Chris Hurst; head of news: Paul Sheldon; breakfast show: Andy Golding and Louise Stone

Signal Two
Stoke Road, Stoke on Trent ST4 2SR
01782 441300
info@signalradio.com
www.signal1.co.uk
Pop music. Stoke on Trent. 1170 AM. Owner: The Wireless Group. ILR group programme director: Kevin Howard; managing director: Chris Hurst; head of news: Paul Sheldon; breakfast show: Johnny Owen

Trax FM
PO Box 444, Worksop
Notts S80 1HR
01909 500611
enquiries@traxfm.co.uk
www.traxfm.co.uk
Adult contemporary. Bassetlaw. 107.9 FM. Owner: Lincs FM. Programme controller: Rob Wagstaff; head of news: Tina Masters; breakfast show: Nick Hancock

WEST MIDLANDS

96.4 FM BRMB
Nine Brindleyplace, 4 Ooozells Square
Birmingham B1 2DJ
0121 245 5000
info@brmb.co.uk
www.brmb.co.uk
Chart music. Birmingham. 96.4 FM. Owner: GCap Media. Commercial controller: Jane Davis; programme controller: Adam Bridge; breakfast show: The Big Brum Breakfast

100.7 Heart FM
1 The Square, 111 Broad Street
Birmingham B15 1AS
0121 695 0000
news@heartfm.co.uk
www.heartfm.co.uk
Easy listening. West Midlands. 100.7 FM. Owner: Chrysalis Radio. Managing director: Paul Fairburn; programme director: Alan Carruthers; head of news: Chris Kowalik; breakfast show: Ed James

107.1 Rugby FM
Dunsmore Business Centre
Spring Street, Rugby CV21 3HH
01788 541100
mail@rugbyfm.co.uk
www.rugbyfm.co.uk
60s, 70s, 80s and 90s and to date. Rugby. 107.1 FM. Owner: Milestone Radio Group. Managing director: Julian Hotchkiss; head of news: Emma Reed; breakfast show: Dale Collins

107.4 Telford FM
PO Box 1074, Telford TF1 5HU
01952 280011
staff@telfordfm.co.uk
www.telfordfm.co.uk
Easy listening. Telford. 107.4 FM. Independent. Programme director: Pete Wagstaff; head of news: Ian Perry; breakfast show: Paul Shuttleworth

107.7 The Wolf
10th Floor, Mander House
Wolverhampton WV1 3NB
01902 571070
firstname@thewolf.co.uk
www.thewolf.co.uk
50/50 mix of yesterday and today. Wolverhampton. 107.7 FM. Owner: Wireless Group. Group programme director: John Evington; breakfast show: Dickie Dodd

Beacon FM
267 Tettenhall Road
Wolverhampton WV6 0DE
01902 461300
firstname.surname@creation.com
www.musicradio.com
Popular mix. Wolverhampton. 97.2 FM; 103.1 FM. Owner: GCap Media. Programme director: Chris Pegg; head of news: Adam Edward; breakfast show: Mark Jeeves and Jo Jesmond

The Bear 102
The Guard House Studios
Banbury Road
Stratford-upon-Avon CV37 7HX
01789 262636
info@thebear.co.uk
www.thebear.co.uk
Classic and current hits. Stratford-upon-Avon. 102 FM. Owner: CN Group. Station director: Chris Arnold; programme controller: Steve Hyden; head of news: Daniel Bruce; breakfast show: Steve Hyden

Capital Gold (1152)
30 Leicester Square
London WC2H 7LA
020 7766 6000
info@capitalgold.co.uk
www.capitalgold.com
Hits of the 60s, 70s and 80s. Birmingham. 1152 AM. Owner: GCap Media. Programme director: Andy Turner; head of news: Justin King; breakfast show: Tom Ross

Classic Gold 1359
Hertford Place, Coventry CV1 3TT
02476 868200
firstname.surname@
classicgolddigital.com
www.classicgolddigital.com
70s, 80s and 90s. Coventry. 1359 AM. Owner: Classic Gold Digital. Programme controller: Russ Williams; breakfast show: Tony Blackburn

Classic Gold WABC
267 Tettenhall Road
Wolverhampton WV6 ODE
01902 461300
firstname.surname@
    classicgolddigital.com
www.classicalgolddigital.com
Classic 80s, 90s onward.
Wolverhampton. 990 AM; 1017 AM.
Owner: Classic Gold Digital.
Programme controller: Chris Pegg; head
of news: Adam Edward; breakfast show:
Tony Blackburn

Galaxy 102.2
1 The Square, 111 Broad Street
Birmingham B15 1AS
0121 695 0000
galaxy1022@galaxy1022.co.uk
www.galaxy1022.co.uk
Easy listening. Birmingham. 102.2 FM.
Owner: Chrysalis Radio. Managing
director: Paul Fairburn; programme
director: Neil Greenslade; head of news:
Chris Kowalik; breakfast show: Dave
Clark

Kix 96
Watch Close Spon Street
Coventry CV1 3LN
024 7652 5656
firstname@kix.fm
www.kix.fm
Pop and Dance. Coventry. 96.2 FM.
Owner: CN Group. Sales director:
Gordon Drummond; programme
manager: Mike Vitti; head of news:
Stuart Everitt; breakfast show: Stefan
Latouche

Mercia FM
Hertford Place, Coventry CV1 3TT
024 7686 8200
merciafm@musicradio.com
www.musicradio.com
80s, 90s and modern. Coventry. 102.9
FM; 97 FM. Owner: GCap Media.
Programme controller: Russ Williams;
head of news: Tony Attwater; breakfast
show: Ru, and James

Radio XL 1296 AM
KMS House Bradford Street
Birmingham B12 OJD
0121 753 5353
arun@radioxl.net
www.radioxl.net
Indian and Asian mixes. Birmingham.
1296 AM. Independent. Managing
director: Arun Bajaj; programme
director: Sukjoinder Ghataore;
breakfast show: Tej

Saga 105.7 FM
3rd Floor, Crown House
Beaufort Court, 123 Hagley Road,
Edgbaston B16 8LD
0121 452 1057
onair@saga1057fm.co.uk
www.saga1057fm.co.uk
40s onwards. West Midlands. 105.7
FM. Owner: Saga Group. Managing
director: Phil Dickson; programme
director: Paul Robey; news editor: Colin
Palmer; breakfast show: Mike Wyer

Wyvern FM
5–6 Barbourne Terrace
Worcester WR1 3JZ
01905 612212
simon.monk@creation.com
www.musicradio.com
Pop music. Hereford and Worcester.
102.8 FM; 97.6 FM; 96.7 FM. Owner:
GCap Media. Programme controller:
Simon Monk; head of news: Jonathan
Dunbar; breakfast show: Lee Stone

NORTH-EAST

Alpha 103.2
Radio House, 11 Woodland Road,
Darlington Co., Durham DL3 7BJ
01325 255552
sales@alpha1032.com
www.alpha1032.com
Classic hits from last 30 years.
Darlington. 103.2 FM. Owner: Radio
Investments. Station manager: Angela
Bridgen; programme manager: Steve
Phillips; head of news: David
Donaldson; breakfast show: James Watt

Century FM
Church Street, Gateshead NE8 2YY
0191 477 6666
info@centuryfm.co.uk
www.100centuryfm.com
80s, 90s and today. North-east
England. 96.2 FM; 96.4 FM; 100.7 FM;
101.8 FM. Owner: GCap Media.
Programme controller: Paul Drogan;
head of news: Rick Martin; breakfast
show: Daryl and Mick

Galaxy 105–106
Kingfisher Way
Silverlink Business Park
Tyne and Wear NE28 9NX
0191 206 8000
matt.mcclure@galaxy1056.co.uk
www.galaxy1056.co.uk
Dance and R&B. North-east England.
105.3 FM; 105.6 FM; 105.8 FM; 106.4
FM. Owner: Chrysalis Radio.
Programme director: Matt McClure;
Journalist: Mandy Simpson; breakfast
show: Kate Fox

Magic 1152
Longrigg, Swalwell
Newcastle upon Tyne NE99 1BB
0191 420 0971
paul.chantler@metroandmagic.com
www.magic1152.co.uk
Classic 60s and 70s. Tyne and Wear.
1152 AM. Owner: Emap Performance
Network. Managing director: Sally
Aitchaison; programme director: Paul
Chantler; breakfast show: Nick Wright

Magic 1170
Radio House, Yales Crescent
Thornaby
Stockton-on-Tees TS17 6AA
01642 888222
colin.paterson@tfmradio.com
www.tfmradio.co.uk
Adult contemporary. Teesside. 1170
AM. Owner: Emap Performance
Network. Managing director: Catherine
Ellington; programme director: Colin
Paterson; head of news: Myles Ashby;
breakfast show: Peter Grant

Metro Radio
Longrigg, Swalwell
Newcastle upon Tyne NE99 1BB
0191 420 0971
paul.chantler@metroandmagic.com
www.magic1152.co.uk
Adult contemporary and chart. Tyne
and Wear. 97.1 FM. Owner: Emap
Performance Network. Managing
director: Sally Aitchison; programme
director: Paul Chantler; breakfast
show: Tony Horn

Sun FM
PO Box 1034, Sunderland SR5 2YL
0191 548 1034
progs@sun-fm.com
www.sun-fm.com
Adult contemporary. Sunderland.
103.4 FM. Owner: Local Radio
Company. Brand controller: Simon
Grundy; head of news: Mark Selling;
breakfast show: Ashley Whitfield

TFM
Radio House, Yales Crescent
Thornaby
Stockton-on-Tees TS17 6AA
01642 888222
colin.paterson@tfmradio.com
www.tfmradio.co.uk
Adult contemporary. Teesside. 96.6 FM.
Owner: Emap Performance Network.
Managing director: Catherine
Ellington; programme director: Colin
Paterson; head of news: Myles Ashley;
breakfast show: Tom Davies and Cara

YORKSHIRE AND HUMBERSIDE

96.3 Radio Aire
51 Burley Road, Leeds LS3 1LR
0113 283 5500
firstname.lastname@radioaire.com
www.radioaire.co.uk
Adult contemporary. Leeds. 96.3 FM.
Owner: Emap Performance Network.
Managing director: Alexis Thompson;
programme director: Stuart Baldwin;
head of news: Richard Pervis; breakfast
show: Cameron and Jamie

96.9 Viking FM
The Boat House, Commercial Road
Hull HU1 2SG
01482 325141
reception@vikingfm.co.uk
www.vikingfm.co.uk
Variety. Hull. 96.9 FM. Owner: Local
Radio Company. Programme director:
Darrell Woodman; head of news: Kirsty
Moore; breakfast show: Foxy and Tom

97.2 Stray FM
The Hamlet, Hornbeam Park Avenue
Harrogate HG2 8RE
01423 522972
mail@972strayfm.co.uk
www.strayfm.com
60s and 70s. Harrogate. 97.2 FM.
Owner: Local Radio Company.
Managing director: Sarah Barry;
programme director: Ray Stroud; head
of news: Patrick Dunlop; breakfast
show: Chris Marsden

Classic Gold 1278/1530 AM
Pennine House, Forster Square
Bradford, West Yorkshire BD1 5NE
01274 203040
general@pulse.co.uk
www.pulse.co.uk
Oldies. Bradford, Halifax and
Huddersfield. 1278 AM; 1530 AM.
Owner: The Wireless Group. ILR group
programme director: John Evington;
managing director: Tony Wilkinson;
head of news: Richard Murie; breakfast
show: Tony Blackburn and Laura Pittson

Compass FM
26a Wellowgate, Grimsby DN32 ORA
01472 346666
enquiries@compassfm.co.uk
www.compassfm.co.uk
Easy listening. Grimsby. 96.4 FM.
Owner: Lincs FM. Programme director:
Jane Hill; programme manager: Andy
Marsh; head of news: Shaun Dunderdale;
breakfast show: Richard Lyon

Fresh Radio
Firth Mill, Firth Street, Skipton
North Yorkshire BD23 2PT
01756 799991
info@freshradio.co.uk
www.freshradio.co.uk
Adult contemporary. Yorkshire Dales
with Skipton. 1431 AM; 1413 AM; 936
AM. Independent. Managing director:
Dave Parker; head of news: James
Wilson; breakfast show: Nick Bewes

Galaxy 105
Joseph's Well, Hannover Walk
off Park Lane, Leeds LS3 1AB
0113 213 0105
mail@galaxy105.co.uk
www.galaxy105.co.uk
Dance and R&B. Yorkshire. 105.8 FM;
105.6 FM; 105.1 FM; 105.6 FM; DAB;
Sky; cable. Owner: Chrysalis Radio.
Managing director: David Lloyd; head
of news and programme director: Mike
Cass; breakfast show: Hirsty, Danny
and JoJo

Hallam FM
Radio House 900 Herries Road
Sheffield S6 1RH
0114 209 1000
Programmes@hallamfm.co.uk
www.hallamfm.co.uk
All types of music. South Yorkshire.
102.9 FM; 103.4 FM; 97.4 FM. Owner:
Emap Performance Network. Managing
director: Iain Clasper; head of news and
programming: Gary Stein; breakfast
show: Big John Breakfast Show

Home 107.9
The Old Stableblock, Lockwood Park
Huddersfield HD1 3UR
01484 321107
info@home1079.com
www.home1079.com
Pop from past three decades.
Huddersfield. 107.9 FM. Owner: Radio
Investments. Programme controller:
John Harding; sales director: Ursula
Johnson; head of news: Steven Naylor;
breakfast show: Patrick Billington

Magic 1161 AM
The Boat House, Commercial Road
Hull HU1 2SG
01482 325141
reception@magic1161.co.uk
www.magic1161.co.uk
60s to present day. Humberside (east
Yorkshire and north Lincolnshire). 1161
AM. Owner: Emap Performance
Network. Managing director: Mike
Bauden; programme director: Darrell
Woodman; head of news: Kirsty Moore;
breakfast show: Steve Jordan

Magic 828
51 Burley Road
Leeds LS3 1LR
0113 283 5500
firstname.lastname@radioaire.com
www.radioaire.co.uk
Adult contemporary. Leeds. 828 AM.
Owner: Emap Performance Network.
Managing director: Alexis Thompson;
programme director: Stuart Baldwin;
head of news: Richard Pervis; breakfast
show: Paul Carrington

Magic AM
Radio House, 900 Herries Road
Sheffield S6 1RH
0114 209 1000
Programmes@magicam.co.uk
www.magicam.co.uk
Popular music. South Yorkshire. 990
AM; 1305 AM; 1545 AM. Owner: Emap
Performance Network. Managing
director: Iain Clasper; head of news and
programming: Gary Stein; breakfast
show: Howie at breakfast

Minster FM
PO Box 123, Dunnington
York YO19 5ZX
01904 488888
general@minsterfm.com
www.minsterfm.com
Past few decades. York. 104.7 FM; 102.3
FM. Owner: Radio Investments.
Commercial station manager: Sarah
Barry; programme controller: Ed
Bretton; head of news: Tristan Hunkin;
breakfast show: Ed Bretton

The Pulse
Pennine House, Forster Square
Bradford, West Yorkshire BD1 5NE
01274 203040
general@pulse.co.uk
www.pulse.co.uk
Oldies. Bradford, Huddersfield and
Halifax. 102.5 FM; 97.5 FM. Owner:
The Wireless Group. ILR group
programme director: John Evington;
managing director: Esther Morton;
head of news: Richard Murie; breakfast
show: Jackie and Steve

Real Radio (Yorkshire)
Sterling Court, Capitol Park
Leeds WF3 1EL
0113 238 1114
info@realradiofm.com
www.realradiofm.com
90s and popular. South and West
Yorkshire. 107.6 FM; 106.2 FM; 107.7
FM. Owner: Guardian Media Group
Radio. Managing director: Shaun
Bowron; programme director: Terry
Underhill; head of news: James Rea;
breakfast show: Guy Harris

Ridings FM
PO Box 333, Wakefield WF2 7YQ
01924 367177
enquiries@ridingsfm.co.uk
www.ridingsfm.co.uk
Popular music. Wakefield. 106.8 FM.
Owner: Lincs FM. Station manager:
Keith Briggs; head of news: Andy
Smith; breakfast show: Kev Wilson

Sunrise FM
Sunrise House, 30 Chapel Street
Little Germany, Bradford BD1 5DN
01274 735043
usha@sunriseradio.fm
www.sunriseradio.fm
Asian music. Bradford. 103.2 FM.
Independent. Managing director and
programme controller: Usha Parmar;
head of news: Gail Papworth; breakfast
show: Gail and Sadia

Trax FM
PO Box 44, Doncaster DN4 5GW
01302 341166
events@traxfm.co.uk
www.traxfm.co.uk
All sorts. Doncaster. 107.1 FM. Owner:
Lincs FM. Programme controller: Rob
Wagstaff; sales manager: Peggy
Watson; head of news: Tina Master;
breakfast show: Mick Hancock

Yorkshire Coast Radio
PO Box 962, Scarborough
North Yorkshire YO11 3ZP
01723 581700
studio@yorkshirecoastradio.com
www.yorkshirecoastradio.com
Chart hits. Bridlington, Scarborough,
Whitby. 96.2 FM; 103.1 FM. Owner:
Radio Investments. Station manager
and programme controller: Chris
Sigsworth; head of news: Al Ross;
breakfast show: Ben Fry

Yorkshire Coast Radio
PO Box 1024, Bridlington, East
Yorkshire YO15 2YW
01262 404400
info@yorkshirecoastradio.com
www.yorkshirecoastradio.com
*Adult contemporary. Bridlington.
102.4 FM. Owner: Radio Investments.
Programme controller: Chris
Sigsworth; sales director: Gaynor
Preston-Routledge; head of news:
Al Ross; breakfast show: Ben Fry*

NORTH-WEST

2BR
Imex Lomeshaye Business Village
Nelson, Lancs BB9 7DR
01282 690000
info@2br.co.uk
www.2br.co.uk
*70s to current. Burnley. 99.8 FM.
Owner: Local Radio Company.
Managing director: Mark Matthews;
breakfast show: Simon Brieley*

96.2 The Revolution
PO Box 962, Oldham OL1 3JF
0161 621 6500
info@therevolution.uk.com
www.revolutiononline.co.uk
*Classic and chart hits. Oldham. 96.2
FM. Owners: UKRD; Hirst Kidd &
Rennie. Managing director: Jackie
Sulkowski; programme controller and
head of news: Chris Gregg; breakfast
show: Sarah Mills*

97.4 Rock FM
PO Box 974, Preston PR1 1YE
01772 477700
firstname.lastname@rockfm.co.uk
www.rockfm.co.uk
*Adult contemporary. Preston and
Blackpool. 97.4 FM. Owner: Emap
Performance Network. Programme
director: Brian Paige; head of news:
Clare Hannah; breakfast show: Dixie*

100.4 Smooth FM
8 Exchange Quay
Manchester M5 3EJ
0161 877 1004
jazzinfo@jazzfm.com
www.jazzfm.com
*Smooth and R&B. North-west England.
100.4 FM. Owner: Guardian Media
Group Radio. Managing director: Roy
Bennett; programming director: Steve
Collins; programme controller: Derek
Webster; breakfast show: Chris Best*

102.4 Wish FM
Orrell Lodge, Orrell Road
Orrell, Wigan WN5 8HJ
01942 761024
studio@wish_fm.com
www.wishfm.net
*80s, 90s, up to date. Wigan. 102.4 FM.
Owner: The Wireless Group.
Programme manager: Jo Heuston;
head of news: Mark McCann; breakfast
show: Danny and Jo*

106.7 FM The Rocket
The Studios, Cables Retail Park
Prescot, Merseyside, L34 5SW
Reception: 0151 290 1501; Studio:
0845 051 1067
www.kcr1067.com
*60s to modern. Knowsley. 106.7 FM.
Owner: Local Radio Company.
Managing director: Mark Matthews;
programme controller: Brian Cullen;
head of news: Sophia Livert; breakfast
show: Dan and Nikki*

106.9 Silk FM
Radio House, Bridge Street
Macclesfield, Cheshire SK11 6DJ
01625 268000
mail@silkfm.com
www.silkfm.com
*Adult contemporary. Macclesfield.
106.9 FM. Owner: Radio Investments.
Commercial manager: Rachael Barker;
programme manager: Andy Bailey;
head of news: Helen Croydon; breakfast
show: Andy Clewes*

107.2 Wire FM
Warrington Business Park, Long Lane
Warrington WA2 8TX
01925 445545
info@wirefm.com
www.wirefm.com
*Adult contemporary. Warrington.
107.2 FM. Owner: The Wireless Group.
Station director: Mathew Allitt; head of
news: Mark Bell; breakfast show:
Dominic Walker*

Asian Sound Radio
Globe House, Southall Street
Manchester M3 1LG
0161 288 1000
info@asiansoundradio.co.uk
www.asiansoundradio.com
*Asian hip-hop. East Lancashire. 963
AM; 1377 AM. Independent. Managing
director and programme director: Shujat
Ali; head of news: Daniyan Paol Shah*

The Bay
PO Box 969, St Georges Quay
Lancaster LA1 3LD
01524 848747
information@thebay.fm
www.thebay.fm
*Adult contemporary. Morecambe Bay,
South Lakes, Cumbria. 102.3 FM; 96.9
FM; 103.2 FM. Station director: Bill
Johnston; programme controller: Sarah
Graham; head of news: Peter Storry;
breakfast show: Darren Milby*

Century 105 FM
Laser House, Waterfront Quay
Salford Quays, Manchester M5O 3XW
0161 400 0105
info1054@centuryfm.co.uk
www.1054centuryfm.com
*Pop. North-west England. 105.4 FM.
Owner: GCap Media. Managing
director: Nick Davidson; Brand
programme director: Giles Squire; head
of news: Matt Bowen; breakfast show:
Darren Proctor*

Classic Gold Marcher 1260 AM
The Studios, Mold Road
Wrexham LL11 4AF
01978 752202
firstname.surname@
classicgolddigital.com
www.classicgolddigital.com
*Classical music. Wrexham and Chester.
1260 AM. Owner: Classic Gold Digital.
Programme controller: Paul Baker;
head of news: Elina Cavanagh;
breakfast show: Tony Blackburn*

Dee 106.3
2 Chantry Court, Chester CH1 4QN
01244 391000
info@dee1063.com
www.dee1063.com
*Adult contemporary. Chester. 106.3 FM.
Independent. Sales manager: Amanda
Hughes; Head of news: Lucy Liddard;
breakfast show: Chris Oakley and
Jennifer McCurry*

Dune FM
The Power Station, Victoria Way
Southport PR8 1RR
01704 502500
studio@dunefm.co.uk
www.dunefm.co.uk
*Adult contemporary. Southport. 107.9
FM. Owner: Local Radio Company.
Programme controller: Jonathan Dean;
head of news: Sophia Levitt; breakfast
show: John Story*

Galaxy 102
5th Floor, The Triangle
Hanging Ditch
Manchester M4 3TR
0161 279 0300
mail@galaxy102.co.uk
www.galaxy102.co.uk
*Dance and R&B. Manchester. 102 FM.
Owner: Chrysalis Radio. Managing
director: David Lloyd; programme
director: Vaughan Hobbs; Editorial:
Lynsey Horn; breakfast show: Nicksy*

Imagine FM
Regent House, Heaton Lane
Stockport SK4 1BX
0161 609 1400
info@imaginefm.com
www.imaginefm.co.uk
*Hits 70s to 90s and today. Stockport.
104.9 FM. Owner: The Wireless Group.
Head of news and programme
controller: Ashley Burne; breakfast
show: Mathew Rudd*

Juice 107.6
27 Fleet Street, Liverpool L1 4AR
0151 707 3107
mail@juiceliverpool.com
www.juice.fm
*R&B. Liverpool. 107.6 FM. Owner:
Absolute Radio. Managing director:
Donna O'Driscoll; programme director:
Grainne Landowski; head of news: Mike
Baker; breakfast show: Louis Hurst*

Key 103
Castle Quay, Castlefield
Manchester M15 4PR
0161 288 5000
first.name@key103.co.uk
www.key103.com
*Mainstream. Manchester. 103 FM.
Owner: Emap Performance Network.
Managing director: Gus McKenzie;
programme director: Anthony Gay;
head of news: John Pickford; breakfast
show: Mike Toolan*

Lakeland Radio
Lakeland Food Park, Plumgarths
Crook Road, Kendal
Cumbria LA8 8QJ
01539 737380
info@lakelandradio.co.uk
www.lakelandradio.co.uk
*60s to modern. Kendal and
Windermere. 100.8 FM; 100.1 FM.
Independent. Managing director: Peter
Fletcher; head of music: Colin Yare;
breakfast show: Sarah Newman*

Magic 1548
St Johns Beacon, 1 Houghton Street
Liverpool L1 1RL
0151 472 6800
firstname@magic1548.com
www.radiocity.co.uk
*Adult contemporary. Liverpool. 1548
AM. Owner: Emap Performance
Network. Managing director: Tom
Hunter; programme director: Richard
Maddock; head of news: Steve
Hothersell; breakfast show: Phil Easton*

Magic 999
St Pauls Square, Preston PR1 1YE
01772 477700
name.surname@magic999.co.uk
www.magic999.co.uk
*Adult contemporary. Preston and
Blackpool. 999 AM. Owner: Emap
Performance Network. Programme
director: Brian Page; head of news: Clare
Hannah; breakfast show: Rob Charles*

Magic 1152
Castle Quay, Castlefield
Manchester M15 4PR
0161 288 5000
first.lastname@key103.co.uk
www.key103.co.uk
*80s, 90s. Manchester. 1152 AM. Owner:
Emap Performance Network.
Managing director: Gus McKenzie;
programme director: Anthony Gay;
head of news: John Pickford; breakfast
show: Spence and Mike*

MFM 103.4
The Studios, Mold Road, Gwersyllt
Nr Wrexham LL11 4AF
01978 752202
sarah.smithard@musicradio.com
www.musicradio.com
*Pop music. Wrexham and Chester.
103.4 FM. Owner: GCap Media.
Managing director: Sarah Smithard;
area programme director: Lisa Marrey;
head of news: Elina Cavenagh;
breakfast show: Dave and Becky*

Radio City 96.7
St Johns Beacon, 1 Houghton Street
Liverpool L1 1RL
0151 472 6800
firstname.surname@radiocity967.com
www.radiocity.co.uk
*Pop. Liverpool. 96.7 FM. Owner: Emap
Performance Network. Managing
director: Tom Hunter; programme
director: Richard Maddock; head of
news: Steve Hothersell; breakfast show:
Kev Seed*

Tower FM
The Mill, Brownlow Way
Bolton BL1 2RA
01204 387000
info@towerfm.co.uk
www.towerfm.co.uk
*Traditional music. Bolton and Bury.
107.4 FM. Owner: Wire Group. Sales
director: Victoria Cullen; programme
director: Kevin McLean; head of news:
Matt Hardman; breakfast show: Bix
and Fairclough*

Wave FM
965 Mowbray Drive, Blackpool
Lancashire FY3 7JR
01253 304965
wave@thewavefm.co.uk
www.wave965.com
*Chart and retro. Blackpool. 96.5 FM.
Owner: The Wireless Group. Regional
MD: Esther Morton; programme
director: Helen Bowden; Station
director: Mel Booth; breakfast show:
Roy Lynch and Hayley Kay*

Wirral's Buzz FM
Media House, Claughton Road
Birkenhead CH41 6EY
0151 650 1700
sarah.smithard@musicradio.com
www.musicradio.com
*Chart 80s and 90s. Wirral. 97.1 FM.
Owner: GWR Group. Programme
controller: Sarah Smithard; head of
news: Alina Cavanagh; breakfast show:
Loraine Gabriel and Jamie Scott*

Commercial local radio: Wales

96.4 FM The Wave
PO Box 964, Swansea SA4 3AB
01792 511964
info@thewave.co.uk
www.thewave.co.uk
*Chart hits. Swansea. 96.4 FM. Owner:
The Wireless Group. ILR group
programme director: John Evington;
station manager: Carrie Mosley; head
of news: Emma Thomas; breakfast
show: Badger and Emma*

Bridge FM
PO Box 1063, Bridgend CF35 6BU
0845 890 4000
firstname.surname@bridge.fm
www.bridge.fm
*Adult contemporary. Bridgend. 106.3
FM. Owner: Tindle Radio. Managing
director: Mark Franklyn; programme
controller: Lee Thomas; head of news:
Kayley Thomas; breakfast show:
Gareth Davies*

Champion FM
Llys y Dderwen Parc Menai
Bangor LL57 4BN
01248 671888
sarah.smithard@musicradio.com
www.musicradio.com
*Modern music. Caenafon. 103 FM.
Owner: GCap Media. Managing
director: Sarah Smithard; Area
programme controller: Graham
Ledger; head of news: David Grundy;
breakfast show: Kevin Williams*

Coast FM
PO Box 963, Bangor LL57 4ZR
01248 671888
firstname.surname@musicradio.com
www.coastfm.co.uk
*Modern music. North Wales coast. 96.3
FM. Owner: GCap Media. Managing
director: Sarah Smithard; Area
programme controller: Graham
Ledger; head of news: David Grundy;
breakfast show: Craig Pilling*

Radio Ceredigion
The Old Welsh School, Alexander Road
Ceredigion SY23 1LF
01970 627999
admin@ceredigionfmf9.co.uk
www.ceredigionradio.co.uk
*Adult contemporary Welsh. Ceredigion.
97.4 FM; 103.3 FM; 96.6 FM.
Independent. Programme controller:
Mark Simon; head of news: Carwyn
Williams; breakfast show: Thomo*

Radio Maldwyn
The Studios, The Park, Newtown
Powys SY16 2NZ
01686 623555
radio.maldwyn@ukonline.co.uk
www.magic756.net
*Adult contemporary. Montgomeryshire.
756 AM. Owner: Murfin Media
International. Managing director and
Operations director and programme
controller: Austin Powell; head of news:
Andrew Curry; breakfast show: Mark
Edwards*

Radio Pembrokeshire

Unit 14 The Old School Estate
Station Road, Narbarth
Pembrokeshire SA67 7DU
01834 869384
enquiries@radiopembrokeshire.com
www.radiopembrokeshire.com
Adult contemporary rock.
Pembrokeshire, West Carmarthenshire.
102.5 FM. Independent. Managing
director and programme controller:
Keri Jones; head of news: Alan Cook;
breakfast show: Keri Jones

Real Radio (South Wales)

PO Box 6105 Ty Nant Court
Cardiff CF15 8YF
029 2031 5100
info@realradiofm.com
www.realradiofm.com
70s to modern. South Wales regional.
105.9 FM; 106 FM; 105.2 FM; 105.4
FM. Owner: Guardian Media Group
Radio. Programme director: Ricky
Durkin; head of news: Gareth Setter;
breakfast show: Angela Jay and Steve
Clark

Red Dragon FM & Capital Gold

Atlantic Wharf
Cardiff Bay CF10 4DJ
029 2066 2066
mail@reddragonfm.co.uk
www.reddragonfm.co.uk
Chart music. Cardiff and Newport.
103.2 FM; 97.4 FM. Owner: GCap
Media. Programme controller: David
Rees; head of news: Angharad Thomas;
breakfast show: Jason Harrold and Ali
Crocker

Sunshine 855

Unit 11, Burway Trading Estate
Bromfield Road, Ludlow
Shropshire SY8 1EN
01584 873795
sunshine855@ukonline.co.uk
www.sunshine855.com
Adult contemporary. Ludlow. 855 AM.
Owner: Murfin Media International.
Managing director: Ginny Murfin;
programme controller: Ginny Murfin;
head of news: Andrew Currie; breakfast
show: Nick Jones

Swansea Sound

PO Box 1170, Swansea SA4 3AB
01792 511170
info@swanseasound.co.uk
www.swanseasound.co.uk
Chart hits. Swansea. 1170 AM. Owner:
The Wireless Group. Station manager:
Carrie Mosley; head of news: Andy
Thomas; head of music: Andy Miles;
breakfast show: Kevin Johns

Valleys Radio

Festival Park Victoria, Beech Grove
Ebbw Vale NP23 8XW
01495 301116
admin@valleysradio.co.uk
www.valleysradio.co.uk
Adult contemporary. Heads of south
Wales valleys. 1116 AM; 999 AM. Owner:
The Wireless Group. Managing director:
Chris Hurst; head of news: Emma
Thomas; breakfast show: Tony Peters

Commercial local radio: Scotland

96.3 QFM

65 Sussex Street, Glasgow G41 1DX
0141 429 9430
sales@q-fm.com
www.q96.net
All types. Paisley. 96.3 FM. Owner: The
Wireless Group. Managing director:
Aaron Shields; head of news: Anna
Lena Winslow; breakfast show: Mike
Richardson

Argyll FM

27–29 Longrow, Campbeltown
Argyll PA28 6ER
01586 551800
argyllradio@hotmail.com
Adult contemporary. Kintyre, Islay
and Jura. 107.7 FM; 107.1 FM; 106.5
FM. Independent. Managing director:
Colin Middleton; programme
controller: Kenny Johnson; head of
news: Ian Henderson; breakfast show:
Bill Young

Beat 106

Four Winds Pavilion, Pacific Quay
Glasgow G51 1EB
0141 566 6106
info@beat106.com
www.beat106.com
Dance. Central Scotland. 106.1 FM;
105.7 FM. Owner: GCap Media.
Programme controller: Claire
Pattenden; news editor: Vicky Lee;
breakfast show: Paul Harper and
Frazier Thompson

Central FM

201 High Street, Falkirk FK1 1DU
01324 611164
mail@centralfm.co.uk
www.centralfm.co.uk
Hits and memories. Stirling and
Falkirk. 103.1 FM. Owner: Radio
Investments. Programme controller:
Tom Bell; head of news: Tadek Pszywa;
breakfast show: Malky Brown

CFM

PO Box 964, Carlisle CA1 3NG
01228 818964
reception@cfmradio.com
www.cfmradio.com
Best mix of music. Carlisle. 96.4 FM;
102.5 FM. Owner: Scottish Radio
Holdings. Managing director: Cathy
Kirk; programme controller: David
Bain; head of news: Bill McDonald;
breakfast show: Robbie Dee

Clan FM

Radio House, Rowantree Avenue
Newhouse Ind. Estate, Newhouses
Lanarkshire ML1 5RX
01698 733107
reception@clanfm.com
www.clanfm.com
Adult contemporary. North
Lanarkshire. 107.9 FM; 107.5 FM.
Owner: Kingdom Group. Station
manager: Janis Melville; programme
controller: Darren Stenhouse; breakfast
show: David Ross; head of news:
Andrew Thompson

Clyde 1 FM

Clydebank Business Park
Glasgow G81 2RX
0141 565 2200
info@clyde1.com
www.clyde1.com
Pop. Glasgow. 97 FM; 103.3 FM; 102.5
FM. Owner: Scottish Radio Holdings.
Managing director: Paul Cooney;
programme controller: Ross
Macfadyen; head of news: Russell
Walker; breakfast show: George Bowie

Clyde 2

Clydebank Business Park
Glasgow G81 2RX
0141 565 2200
info@clyde2.com
www.clyde2.com
Hits from last few decades. Glasgow.
1152 AM. Owner: Scottish Radio
Holdings. Managing director: Paul
Cooney; programme controller: Ross
Macfadyen; head of news: Russell
Walker; breakfast show: Mike Riddoch

Forth Two

Forth House, Forth Street
Edinburgh EH1 3LE
0131 556 9255
info@forth2.com
www.forth2.com
60s, 70s, 80s, 90s and today.
Edinburgh. 1548 AM. Owner: Scottish
Radio Holdings. Managing director:
Adam Findley; programme director:
Luke McCullough; head of news: Paul
Robertson; breakfast show: Scott Wilson

Forth One

Forth House, Forth Street
Edinburgh EH1 3LE
0131 556 9255
info@forthone.com
www.forthone.com
Adult contemporary. Edinburgh. 97.6
FM; 102.2 FM; 97.3 FM. Owner:
Scottish Radio Holdings. Managing
director: Adam Findley; programme
director: Luke McCullough; head of
news: Paul Robertson; breakfast show:
Boogie and Vicky

Heartland FM
Atholl Curling Rink, Lower Oakfield
Pitlochry, Perthshire PH16 5HQ
01796 474040
mailbox@heartlandfm.co.uk
Classic hits. Pitlochry and Aberfeldy.
97.5 FM; 102.7 FM. Independent.
Programme controller: Peter Ramsden;
head of news: Margaret Stevenson;
breakfast show: Hal Stewart

Isles FM
PO Box 333
Stornoway, Isle of Lewis HS1 2PU
01851 703333
studio@isles.fm
www.isles.fm
Adult contemporary. Western Isles. 103
FM. Independent. Director of operations:
David Morrison; head of news: Alex
Kennedy

Kingdom FM
Haig House, Haig Business Park
Markinch, Fife KY7 6AQ
01592 753753
info@kingdomfm.co.uk
www.kingdomfm.co.uk
Across-the-board mix. Fife. 95.2 FM;
105.4 FM; 96.6 FM; 106.3 FM; 96.1
FM. Independent. Chief executive: Ian
Sewell; programme director: Kevin
Brady; head of news: Chris Hodge;
breakfast show: Ian Gilmore

Lochbroom FM
Radio House, Mill Street
Ullapool, Ross-shire IV26 2UN
01854 613131
radio@lochbroomfm.co.uk
www.lochbroomfm.co.uk
Adult contemporary. Ullapool. 96.8
FM; 102.2 FM. Independent.
Chairman: Iain Boyd; head of music
and breakfast show: Tiffany McCaulay

Moray Firth Radio (MFR)
Scorguie Place, Inverness IV3 8UJ
01463 224433
mfr@mfr.co.uk
www.mfr.co.uk
Contemporary and chart. Inverness.
96.6 FM; 96.7 FM; 97.4 FM; 102.5 FM;
102.8 FM. Owner: Scottish Radio
Holdings. Managing director: Danny
Gallagher; senior presenter: Ray
Atkins; breakfast show: Tich McCooey
and Nicky Marr

NECR
The Shed, School Road, Kintore
Aberdeenshire AB51 0UX
01467 632909
necrradio102.1fmsales@supanet.com
Recent hits and classic gold and
specialist country, Irish and Scottish.
Inverurie. 102.1 FM; 102.6 FM; 97.1
FM; 103.2 FM; 101.9 FM; 106.4FM.
Independent. Managing director: Colin
Strong; programme controller: John
Dean; head of news: John Dean;
breakfast show: John Dean

Nevis Radio
Ben Nevis Estate, Claggan
Fort William PH33 6PR
01397 700007
studio@nevisradio.co.uk
www.nevisradio.co.uk
Daily chart music. Evening specialist.
Fort William and parts of Lochaber.
96.6 FM; 102.4 FM; 97 FM; 102.3 FM.
Independent. Head of news, station
manager and programme controller:
Willie Cameron; breakfast show: David
Ogg

Northsound One
Abbotswell Road, West Tullos
Aberdeen AB12 3AJ
01224 337000
northsound@srh.co.uk
www.northsound1.co.uk
Modern music. Aberdeen and north-
east Scotland. 96.9 FM; 97.6 FM; 103
FM. Owner: Scottish Radio Holdings.
Managing director: Iain McKenna;
programme controller: Chris Thomson;
head of news: Neil Metcalf; breakfast
show: Andy James

Northsound Two
Abbotswell Road, West Tullos
Aberdeen AB12 3AJ
01224 337000
northsound@srh.co.uk
www.northsound2.co.uk
Modern music. Aberdeen and north-
east Scotland. 1035 AM. Owner:
Scottish Radio Holdings. Managing
director: Iain McKenna; programme
controller: Chris Thomson; head of
news: Ross Govans; breakfast show:
John McCruvie

Oban FM
132 George Street, Oban
Argyll PA34 5NT
01631 570057
obanfmradio@btconnect.com
www.obanfm.tk
Gaelic to modern pop. Oban. 103.3 FM.
Independent. Managing director:
Cambell Cameron; programme
director: Tina Robertson; head of news:
Coll McDougall

Radio Borders
Tweedside Park, Galashiels TD1 3TD
01896 759444
programming@radioborders.com
www.radioborders.com
Hits and memories. Borders. 96.8 FM;
103.1 FM; 103.4 FM; 97.5 FM. Owner:
Scottish Radio Holdings. Programme
controller: Stuart McCulloch; head of
news: Andrew Thomson; breakfast
show: Keith Clarkson

Real Radio (Scotland)
PO Box 101, Parkway Court
Glasgow Business Park
Glasgow G69 6GA
0141 781 1011
contact.name@realradiofm.com
www.realradiofm.com
Wide variety. Central Scotland. 100.3
FM; 101.1 FM. Owner: Guardian Media
Group Radio. Managing director: Billy
Anderson; programme director: Jay
Crawford; head of news: Heather Kane;
breakfast show: Robin Galloway

River FM
Stadium House, Alderstone Road
Livingstone, West Lothian EH54 7DN
01506 420975
office@river-fm.com
www.river-fm.com
Adult contemporary and charts. West
Lothian. 107.7 FM; 103.4 FM. Owner:
Kingdon Radio Group. Programme
controller: Donny Hughes; sales
director: Susan Dignon; news editor:
Chris Hodge; breakfast show: Alex Boyd

RNA FM
Radio North Angus
Arbroath Infirmary, Rosemount Road
Arbroath, Angus DD11 2AT
01241 879660
info@radionorthangus.co.uk
www.radionorthangus.co.uk
Classic/Scottish and pop. Arbroath,
Carnoustie. 96.6 FM. Independent.
Managing director and head of news:
Malcolm Finlayson

SIBC
Market Street, Lerwick
Shetland ZE1 0JN
01595 695299
info@sibc.co.uk
www.sibc.co.uk
Rock and pop. Shetland. 96.2 FM;
102.2 FM. Independent. Managing
director and programme controller:
Inga Walterson; head of news: Ian
Anderson

South West Sound
Unit 40, The Loreburne Centre
High Street, Dumfries DG1 2BD
01387 250999
info@westsound.co.uk
www.westsound.co.uk
Chart music. Dumfries and Galloway.
96.5 FM; 97 FM; 103 FM. Owner:
Scottish Radio Holdings. Managing
director: Sheena Borthwick;
programme director: Alan Toomey;
head of news: Ian Wilson; breakfast
show: Tommy Jargon

Tay AM
6 North Isla Street, Dundee DD3 7JQ
01382 200800
tayam@radiotay.co.uk
www.radiotay.co.uk
Various music. Dundee and Perth.
1584 AM; 1161 AM. Owner: Scottish
Radio Holdings. Managing director
and programme director: Arthur
Ballingail; head of news: Amanda
Mezullo; breakfast show: Grant Reed

Tay FM

6 North Isla Street, Dundee DD3 7JQ
01382 200800
tayam@radiotay.co.uk
www.radiotay.co.uk
*Various music. Dundee and Perth.
102.8 FM; 96.4 FM. Owner: Scottish
Radio Holdings. Managing director
and programme director: Arthur
Ballingail; head of news: Amanda
Mezullo; breakfast show: Euan
Notman*

Two Lochs Radio

The Harbour Centre, Pier Road
Gairloch IV21 2BQ
01445 712712/ 712106
info@2lr.co.uk
www.2lr.co.uk
*Broad mix and Scottish Gaelic.
Gairloch and Loch Ewe. 106.6 FM.
Independent. Programme director:
Colin Pickering; chairman and station
manager: Alex Gray*

Wave 102

8 South Tay Street, Dundee DD1 1PA
01382 900102
studio@wave102.co.uk
www.wave102.co.uk
*80s, 90s and today. Dundee. 102 FM.
Owner: The Wireless Group. Managing
director: Bill Bowman; programme
controller: Peter Mac; head of news:
Rebecca Wallis; breakfast show:
Peter Mac*

Waves Radio Peterhead

7 Blackhouse Circle
Peterhead AB42 1BW
01779 491012
waves@radiophd.freeserve.co.uk
www.wavesfm.com
*Current and classic. Peterhead. 101.2
FM. Independent. Managing director
and programme controller: Norman
Spence; head of news: Glenn Moir;
breakfast show: Kenny King*

West FM

Radio House, 54a Holmston Road
Ayr KA7 3BE
01292 283662
info@westfm.co.uk
www.westfmonline.com
*Wide variety including music. Ayr.
97.5FM; 96.7 FM. Owner: Scottish
Radio Holdings. Managing director:
Sheena Borthwick; programme director:
Alan Toomey; head of news: Ian Wilson;
breakfast show: Alan Toomey*

West Sound AM

Radio House, 54a Holmston Road
Ayr KA7 3BE
01292 283662
info@westsound.co.uk
www.west-sound.co.uk
*Wide variety of music. Ayr. 1035 AM.
Owner: Scottish Radio Holdings.
Managing director: Sheena Borthwick;
programme director: Alan Toomey;
head of news: Ian Wilson; breakfast
show: Alan Toomey*

Your Radio

Pioneer Park Studios, Unit 1–3
80 Castlegreen Street
Dumbarton G82 1JB
01389 734422
info@yourradio.com
www.yourradiocom
*Popular music. Dumbarton. 103 FM;
106.9 FM. Independent. Station
manager: Derek McIntyre; programme
controller: Steven Scott; head of news:
Gary Pews; breakfast show: Derek
McIntyre*

Commercial local radio: Northern Ireland

City Beat 96.7

PO Box 967, Belfast BT9 5DF
028 9020 5967
misic@citybeat.co.uk
www.citybeat.co.uk
*Commercial chart. Belfast. 96.7 FM.
Owner: CN Group. Station director:
Dorothy McDide; head of news: Mark
Malett; breakfast show: Morris Jay*

Cool FM

PO Box 974, Belfast BT1 1RT
028 9181 7181
music@coolfm.co.uk
www.coolfm.co.uk
*Pop. Northern Ireland. 97.4 FM.
Owner: Scottish Radio Holdings.
Programme controller: David Sloan
MBE; head of news: Harry Castles;
breakfast show: Carl Kinsman*

Downtown Radio

Newtownards, Co Down
Northern Ireland BT23 4ES
028 9181 5555
Programmes@downtown.co.uk
www.downtown.co.uk
*Adult contemporary. Northern Ireland.
97.1 FM; 103.1 FM; 103.4 FM; 102.4
FM; 1026 AM; 96.6 FM; 102.3 FM; 96.4
FM. Owner: Scottish Radio Holdings.
Programme controller: David Sloan
MBE; head of news: Harry Castles;
breakfast show: Caroline and Roy*

Mid FM

2c Park Avenue, Burn Road
Cookstown BT80 8AH
028 8675 8696
firstnamelastname@
    midfm106fm.co.uk
www.mid106fm.co.uk
*80s, 90s mix. Mid-Ulster. 106 FM.
Owner: CN Group. Station director:
Neil McLeod Berriskell; news manager:
James Devlin; senior Presenter: Francie
Quinn; breakfast show: Francie Quinn*

Q101

42A Market Street, Omagh
Co. Tyrone BT78 1EH
028 8224 5777
Manager@q101west.fm
www.q101west.fm
*Chart and pop. Omagh and Enniskillen.
101.2 FM. Owner: Q Radio Network.
Programme controller: Frank
McLaughlin; head of news: Sophie
Wheeler; breakfast show: Stuart Gordon*

Q102

The Riverview Suite
87 Rossdowney Road, Waterside,
Londonderry BT47 5SU
028 7134 4449
Manager@q102.fm
www.q102.fm
*70s to today. Londonderry. 102.9 FM.
Owner: Q Radio Network. Managing
director and programme controller:
Frank McLaughlin; head of news:
Roger Donnelly; breakfast show: Pete
Wilson*

Q97.2 Causeway Coast Radio

24 Cloyfin Road, Coleraine
Co Londonderry BT52 2NU
028 7035 9100
Manager@q972.fm
www.q972.fm
*Adult contemporary. Coleraine. 97.2
FM. Owner: Q Radio Network.
Programme controller: Frank
McLaughlin; head of news: Bob Lee;
breakfast show: Barrie Owler*

Minor stations*

Adventist World Radio
01344 401401
whitegates@AWR.org
www.awr.org
*Community and religious
programmes. Satellite. Programme
director: Yves Senty*

All: Sports Live (instore radio)
0113 399 2043
www.teamtalk.com
In-store. Manager: Mark Woodhead

Amrit Bani
020 8606 9292
info@amritbaniradio.com
www.amritbani.com
*Religious Asian broadcasting. Digital.
Operational director: Surjit Singh
Dusanjh*

Apna Radio
www.apnaradio.com
*Punjabi, Hindi and Pakistani music.
Internet*

Asian Gold
020 8571 7200
info@asiangoldradio.com
www.asiangoldradio.com
*Ethnic Asian. Digital. Chief executive
director: Zorawar Gakhal*

Assalam Radio
00 44 7005 802 897
info@assalam.info
www.assalam.info
French and Arabic. Internet

Bloomberg Radio
020 7330 7575
digitalradio@bloomberg.net
www.bloomberg.co.uk
*Financial news. 1130 AM. Radio editor:
Jack Reed*

Cable Radio
01273 418181
office@cableradio.co.uk
www.cableradio.co.uk
*Adult contemporary. 103.9 FM. Station
manager: R Mustapha*

Calvary Chapel Radio
020 8466 5365; 07779 507032
ccradio@btconnect.com
www.calvarychapelradio.co.uk
*Christian radio. Sky. Managing
director: Brian Brodersen; programme
controller: Alison Johnstone-White;
programmer: Mark Seddon*

Club Asia
020 8594 6662
info@clubasiaonline.com
www.clubasiaonline.com
*Young British Asians. 963 AM, 972
AM. Programme controller: Sumerad
Ahmed*

Easy Radio
020 8574 6666
info@easy1035.com
www.easy1035.com
DAB

ETBC London
020 8795 0045
www.etbclondon.com
Tamil language

Family Radio
00 1 800 543 1495
www.familyradio.com
Christian gospel. Internet

FCUK FM
020 8749 7272
ian@deliciousdigital.com
www.fcuk.com
*Music only. Internet. Managing director:
O Raphael; director: Ian Taylor*

HCJB World Radio
01274 721810
info@hcjb.org.uk
www.hcjb.org
Religious. International shortwave

Holiday FM
www.holidayfmradio.co.uk
*Gran Canaria, Lanzarote, Tenerife,
Costa del Sol, Ibiza, Costa Blanca*

Kool AM
020 8373 1075
pfmnews@email.com
www.koolam.co.uk
*Harlow. 1134 AM. Programme
controller: Joe Bone*

Laser Radio
01342 327842
laser@ukmail.com
www.laserradio.net
*Baltic sea area and Scandinavia. 1350
AM. Managing director: Andrew Yeates*

McColls FM
0113 399 2211
www.teamtalkbroadcast.com
In-store. Manager: Rashida Khan

The Mix
020 7911 7300
mail@themix.musicradio.com
www.musicradio.com
Sky and internet

Music Choice
020 7014 8700
www.musicchoice.co.uk
*Non-stop music compilation channels.
Sky; internet. CEO: Margo Daly*

**NPR Worldwide (National Public
Radio)**
00 1 202 513 2000
www.npr.org/worldwide
*Vice president, communications: Andi
Sporkin*

Panjab Radio
0870 027 2880
info@panjabradio.co.uk
www.panjabradio.co.uk
DAB and internet

Radio Caroline
020 8340 3831
info@radiocaroline.co.uk
www.radiocaroline.co.uk
*Album rock music. Sky and internet.
Programme controller and station
manager: Peter Moore*

Radio France Internationale (RFI)
00 33 1 5640 1212
www.rfi.fr
France's "world service". Internet

Radio Telefis Eireann
info@rte.ie
www.rte.ie
*Ireland's public service broadcaster.
Managing director: Adrian Moynes*

Real Radio
029 2031 5100
ricky.durkin@realradiofm.com
www.realradiofm.com
*60s to present day. 105–106 FM.
Managing director: Andy Carter;
programme director: Ricky Durkin*

Spectrum Digital 1
020 7627 4433
enquiries@spectrumradio.net
www.spectrumradio.net
*Multi-ethnic. 558 AM. General
manager: Paul Hogan*

The Storm
020 7911 7300
reception@stormradio.co.uk
www.stormradio.co.uk
*Modern rock. Digital. Station
manager: Bern Leckie*

Sunrise Radio
020 8574 6666
reception@sunriseradio.com
www.sunriseradio.com
*Asian. 1458 AM. Managing director:
Tony Lit; news editor: David Landau;
programme controller: Tony Patti*

talkGospel.com
020 7316 1300
enquiries@talkgospel.com
www.talkgospel.com
*African and Caribbean churches.
Sky and internet*

TBC Radio
07817 063682
info@tbcuk.com
www.tbcuk.com
*Political analysis, news, Asian music.
Satellite. Managing director: V Ramarag*

TotalRock
info@totalrock.com
www.totalrock.com
*Rock and metal. Sky and internet.
Station manager: Tony Wilson*

Trans World Radio UK
01225 831390
web@twr.org.uk
www.twr.org.uk
*Christian music. Sky and internet;
1467 AM Saturday and Sunday
11.15pm; short-wave 9.87 MHz and
11.865 MHz each morning. Chief
executive: Russell Farnworth;
programme controller: Michael
Pfundner*

Voice of America
00 1 202 401 7000
publicaffairs@voa.gov
www.voanews.com
*News, information, educational and
cultural programming. Satellite*

WorldSpace UK
020 7494 8200
ukservice@worldspace.com
www.worldspace.com
*Music, news. Satellite. Senior vice-
president: Safia Safwat*

*Stations available in UK only on cable, satellite or internet, or on a small number of local DAB licences

Community radio

7 Waves
0151 691 1595
pauline.murphy@merseymail.com
www.7waves.co.uk
*Leasowe, Wirral. Project coordinator:
Pauline Murphy*

209 Radio
01223 700760
getinvolved@209radio.co.uk
www.209radio.co.uk
*Cambridge. Project manager: Karl
Hartland*

ACE Consortium
0115 970 6882
info@ace-consortium.net
*Nottingham. Secretary: Kelbert
Henriques*

Aldershot Garrison FM
01748 830050
hq@garrisonradio.com
www.army.mod.uk/garrisonradio
Programme director: John McCray

Alive in the Spirit of Plymouth FM
01752 242262
chris@cornerstonevision.com
*Programme manager: Christopher
Girdler*

ALL FM
0161 248 6888
alex@allfm.org
www.allfm.org
Manchester. Station manager: Alex Green

Angel Radio Havant
023 9248 1988
angelradiohavant@yahoo.co.uk
Contact: Tony Smith

Angel Radio Isle of Wight
01983 246810
angelradioiw@hotmail.com
Contact: Chris Gutteridge

Asian Star
01753 737474
sbba1@yahoo.co.uk
*Slough. Administration manager: Sbba
Siddique*

Avenues FM
020 8969 9552
Info@avenues.org.uk
*London. Senior youth worker:
Carol Bent (Mr)*

Azhar Community Radio
020 8534 5959
contact@azharacademy.org
London. Contact: Ismail Gangat

Barnsley Community Radio
0871 242 6709
Studio@BarnsleyCommunityRadio
.org.uk
Contact: Darren Holmes

BBA Media
020 8571 9700
amar@bbamedia.com
*London. General manager: Amar
Chadha*

BCB
01274 771677
info@bcb.yorks.com
www.bcb.yorks.com
*Bradford. Director: Mary Dowson;
broadcast manager: Jonathan Pinfield*

Beautiful Bristol FM
0117 946 6673
cserle@aol.com
Contact: Chris Serle

Betar Bangla
020 7729 4333
betarbangla@btconnect.com
*London. Chief executive and director:
Golam Mohammed Chowdhury*

**Bexley Community Media
Association**
01322 447767
andrew.sayers@bcma.biz
www.bcma.biz
Chief executive: Andrew Sayers

Branch FM
01924 454750
steve.hodgson@ntlworld.com
Dewsbury. Contact: Stephen Hodgson

Break FM Newham
020 7474 2111
info@breakfm.com
www.breakfm.com
*London. Station manager: Toby
Harraway; admin: Joanne Hintz*

Bristol Community FM
0117 963 8861
phil@radio19.co.uk
www.bcfm.org.uk
Project manager: Phil Gibbons

BRFM
01795 876045
office@brfm.net
www.brfm.net
*Isles of Sheppey. Station manager:
Danny Lawrence*

Burst FM (Bristol University)
0117 954 5777
info@burstradio.org.uk
www.burstradio.org.uk
Station manager: Martin MacLachlan

Cambridge University Radio
07801 574617
sm@cur1350.co.uk
www.cur1350.co.uk
Station manager: Michael Brooks

Canalside Community Radio FM
01625 576689
nick@ccr-fm.co.uk
www.ccr-fm.co.uk
*Bollington, Macclesfield. Programme
controller and coordinator: Nick Wright*

Carillon Radio
01509 564433
carillonradio@aol.com
*Loughborough. Station manager: Jon
Sketchley*

Castledown Radio
01264 791929
castledownradio@tidworthtrust.co.uk
www.castledownradio.info
*Ludgershall, Wiltshire. Project
manager: Baz Reilly*

Catterick Garrison FM
01748 830050
hq@garrisonradio.com
www.army.mod.uk/garrisonradio/
Programme director: John McCray

Chelmsford Calling
01245 355274
jim.salmon@tiscali.co.uk
Managing director: James Salmon

Cheshire FM
01606 737844
info@cheshirefm.com
www.cheshirefm.com
Northwich. Chairman: David Duffy

Chesterfield Broadcasting Network
01246 851150
info@trustfm.co.uk
Station director: Ivan Spenceley

City Radio Clapham Park
020 8678 5900
hopelinkradio@hotmail.com
www.claphampark.org.uk
*London. Programme director: Angus
Johnson*

City Radio Haringey
020 8809 8505
info@haringeyclc.org.uk
www.haringeyclc.org.uk
London. Centre manager: Andy Segal

Colchester Garrison Radio
01206 782589
colchester@garrisonradio.com
www.garrisonradio.com
Managing director: Mark Page

Crescent Radio
01706 340786
faheem@myself.com
Rochdale. Contact: Faheem Chishti

Cross Rhythms City Radio
08700 118008
steve.perry@crossrhythms.co.uk
www.crossrhythms.co.uk
*Stoke on Trent (Hanley). General
manager: John Bellamy*

Cross Rhythms Teesside
07787 531759
Joel.hauxwell@gmail.com
www.crossrhythmsteesside.co.uk
*Stockton on Tees. General manager:
Joel Hauxwell*

Demo FM
020 8655 7209
gracembailey@yahoo.co.uk
London. Record producer: Charles Bailey

Desi Radio
020 8574 9591
info@desiradio.org.uk
www.desiradio.org.uk
West London. Manager: Amarjit Khera

Difusion 103.1 FM
020 7624 4716
difusion@oosoul.co.uk
www.mediatechnique.co.uk
London. Operations manager: L-J Mair

Diverse FM
01582 654445
diversefm@hotmail.com
www.diversefm.com
Luton. Coordinator: Ashuk Ahmed

Drystone Radio
01535 635392
drystoneradio@fsmail.net
www.drystoneradio.co.uk
Yorkshire Dales. Contact: David Adams

East Africa Star (Eafm)
020 7258 0772
info@eafmradio.com
www.eafmradio.com
London. Contact: Morris Simon Berhane

ECO
020 7223 3129
Geronvision@hotmail.com
London. Manager: Geronimo Palacios

The Edge
radio@theedgefm.co.uk
Suffolk. Contact: Clive Dorrington

Edmonton FM
020 8360 2727
ianmartin@christianaction.org.uk
London. Contact: Ian Martin

Express FM
023 9282 2112
mail@expressfm.com
www.expressfm.com
*South Hampshire. Managing director:
Cheryl Buggy*

Radio Faza FM/ Karimia Institute
0115 8415807
bmccnottingham@hotmail.com
www.karimia.com
*Nottingham. Director: Dr Musharaf
Hussain*

Focus FM Radio
0117 944 4497
info@focusradio.com
www.focusradio.com
Bristol. Director: Theo Stephenson

Forest FM
01202 787740
vwradio@aol.com
www.forestfm.co.uk or
www.forestfm.com
*Verwood Dorset, Managing director:
Steve Saville*

Forest of Dean Community Radio
01594 820722
contactus@fodradio.org
www.fodradio.org
*Cinderford, Glos. Director: Martin
Harrison*

From The Nam FM
07973 677422
ftnradio@yahoo.co.uk
London. Director: Sharon Selvon

Future Radio
01603 250505
info@nr5project.co.uk
www.futurefmradio.co.uk
Norwich. Radio manager: Tom Buckham

Gina FM
020 8571 7353
info@ginafm.com
www.ginafm.com
*East London. Chairman: Jaipreet Kaur
Chohan*

Gloucester FM
01452 396247
Gfmno1@hotmail.com
www.gloucesterfm.com
Chairman: Derrick Francis

GUI
01483 440900
info@starstadium.com
Guildford. Director: Michel Harper

Halton FM
0845 450 7879
kirsty@haltonfm.net
www.haltonfm.net
*Runcorn. General manager: Kirsty
Walker*

Harborough FM
01858 466984
chrishfm@hotmail.com
www.harboroughfm.co.uk
*Market Harborough. Station manager:
Barry Badger*

Hayes Community Radio
020 8573 7992
office@hayesfm.org
www.hayesfm.org
Operations manager: Surish Sharma

Hope FM
01202 780396
bmouthymca@aol.com
www.hopefm.com
*Bournemouth. Executive director: Blair
Crawford*

Indian Muslim Welfare Society
01924 500555
info@imws.org.uk
*Batley. Development manager: Pam
Robinson*

Ipswich Community Radio
01473 418022
info@icrfm.co.uk
www.icrfm.co.uk
Contact: Nick Greenland

Issue FM
020 7274 6700
contactus@issuefm.com
www.issuefm.com
London. Director: Titus Lucas

Life FM
020 7575 3154
Jennifer@bang-ed.com
www.lifefm.org.uk
or www.bang-ed.com
London. Project director: Jennifer Ogole

Lindum Radio
01522 530350
Ray@lindumradio.wanadoo.co.uk
Lincoln. Chairman: Ray Drury

Link FM
01708 378378
dave.butler@haveringbep.co.uk
www.linkfm.net
*Romford. Managing director: Dave
Butler*

Link FM Radio
07050 235630
mikedelb@yahoo.co.uk
*London. Managing director: Mike
Bernard*

Lionheart Radio
01665 602244
studio@lionheartradio.co.uk
www.lionheartradio.co.uk
*Alnwick, Northumberland. Contact:
George Millar*

Lune Valley Radio
01524 271294
paul@lakelandtoday.com
Kirby Lonsdale. Contact: Paul Broadbent

Lyon Radio
01438 234101
craigmaret@yahoo.com
Stevenage. Project manager: Craig Maret

New Style Radio 98.7 FM
0121 456 3826
newstyle@acmccentre.co.uk
www.newstyleradio.co.uk
Birmingham. Chairman: Martin Blissett

NuSound Radio
07909 998927
tari.sian@jpmorgan.com
Ilford. Project director: Tari Sian

Pendle Community Radio
01282 723 455
Shazad.Shaffi@ntlworld.com
Manager: Shazad Shaffi

Phoenix FM (Essex)
01277 234555
studio@phoenixfm.com
www.phoenixfm.com
*Brentwood and Billericay. Station
manager: Paul Golder*

Phoenix FM (Halifax)
0870 9905274
info@phoenixfm.co.uk
www.phoenixfm.co.uk
Contact: Anna Lombardi

The Public FM
0121 525 6861
martyn.haynes@thepublic.com
www.thepublic.com
*West Bromwich. I/C programming:
Martyn Haynes*

Publicmedia UK
01322 223493
vb@publicmedia.co.uk
www.publicmedia.co.uk
*Wigan. Enterprise director: Vince
Braithwaite*

Punjabi Radio
0121 434 4747
ts.patara@punjabiculturalsociety.co.uk
*Black Country. Project director:
Talwinder S Patara*

Pure Radio
0161 474 5961
dave.stearn@stockport.gov.uk
www.pureradio.org.uk
*Stockport. Radio project officer: Dave
Stearn*

Raaj Radio
0116 2756212
infor@raajradio.com
www.raajradio.co.uk
Leicester. Chief executive: Dr CPS Johal

Contacts : Radio

Radio Barnsley
01226 216319
richodr@blueyonder.co.uk
www.ymcaradiobarnsley.co.uk
Barnsley. Training manager: Dave Richardson

Radio CD (Radio Cultural Diversity)
01865 766032
jwoodman@doctors.org.uk
www.radiocd.org
Oxford. Programme director: Dr Woodman

Radio Faza 91.1 FM
0115 844 0052
radiofaza@hotmail.com
www.radiofaza.org.uk
Nottingham .Marketing manager: Javed Mirza

Radio Hartlepool
01429 275222
studio@radiohartlepool.co.uk
www.radiohartlepool.co.uk
Station director: Jason Anderson

Radio La Voz
01580 213588
contact@fernadosobron.com
London. Station manager: Fernando Sobron

Radio Paradise
07830 099199
radioparadise@hotmail.co.uk
Wakefield. Contact: Moheb Khan

Radio Peckham
020 8320 0880
Radiopeckham@yahoo.co.uk
www.eclectic-productions.co.uk
Director: Shane Carey

Radio Reverb
01273 323040
info@earshot.org.uk
www.radioreverb.com
Brighton. Contact: Karen Cass

Radio Scilly
01720 423304
radioscilly@aol.com
www.radioscilly.co.uk
Studio manager: Peter Hobson

Radio Teesdale
01833 696750
alastair@teesdaleenterprise.co.uk
Contact: Alastair Dinwiddie

Radio Ummah
020 8548 4647
www.radioummah.com
Internet. Chief Operating Officer: Saleem Ahmed

Radio Verulam
07711 286488
Philrichards.w@ntlworld.com
www.radio-verulam.co.uk
St Albans and Hemel Hempstead. Station manager: Phil Richards

Raven Sound
020 8466 8060
raven.sound@virgin.net
Bromley. Contact: A Bailey

Regency FM
01246 250230
Studio@Regencyradio.com
www.regencyradio.com
North-east Derbyshire. Station manager: Martin Bancroft

Resonance FM
020 7836 3664
info@resonancefm.com
www.resonancefm.com
London. Station managers: Richard Thomas and Chris Weaver

Salford Community Radio
0161 212 4977
salfordcommunityradio@hotmail.com
www.salfordcommunityradio.org
Manager: Paul Miller

Seaside Radio
01964 611427
lyz@seasideradio.org.uk
Withernsea, E Yorks. Project manager: Lyz Turner

Shalom FM
shalomfm@hotmail.com
www.shalomfm.com
London. Director: Richard Brian Ford

Sheffield Live
0114 2814082
sangita@thedrum.org.uk
Sheffield. Project leader: Sangita Basudev

Siren FM
01522 886270
brudd@lincoln.ac.uk
Lincoln. Contact: Bryan Rudd

Skyline Community Radio
0800 583 5898
Dgi-marketing@supanet.com
Southampton. Managing director: David Algate

Sound Radio
info@soundradio.info
East London. Contact: Lol Gellor

Stourbridge Radio Group
01902 696425
info@stourbridgeradio.com
www.stourbridgeradio.com
Chairman and chief executive: Dr Paul Collins

Sussex Surrey Radio
01737 643767
colin@susyradio.com
www.susyradio.com
Redhill and Reigate. Contact: Colin Pearse

Swale Radio
01795 479326
swaleradio@bibbypublishing.com
Sittingbourne. Project director: Bernard Bibby

Takeover Radio
0116 2999600
Linda@takeoverradio.com
www.takeoverradio.com
Leicester. Contact: Linda Young

Tameside Community Radio
07867 532 850
studio@tcrfm.com
www.tcrfm.com
Contact: Simon Walker

Tidworth Bulford Garrison FM
01748 830050
hq@garrisonradio.com
www.army.mod.uk/garrisonradio
Programme director: John McCray

Touch FM
01908 231777
touchfm@btinternet.com
Milton Keynes. Chief executive: Michael S Johnson

Tyneside Community Broadcast
0191 278 2957
admin@cbit.org.uk
www.cbit.org.uk
Newcastle. Manager: Elaine Parker

Unity Radio 24
023 8023 3239
kelly@unity24.org
www.unity24.org
Southampton. Project manager: Ram Kalyan ("Kelly")

Urban Space
01924 375229
ben@urbanspace.org.uk
Wakefield. Station manager: Ben Brown

Voice of Africa Radio
020 8471 9111
info@voiceofafricaradio.com
www.voiceofafricaradio.com
London. Project manager: Space Clottey

Walsall FM
0154 336 1791
pw004t5791@blueyonder.co.uk
Contact: Pam Weaver

Wayland Community Radio
07769 833868
wayland.radio@tesco.net
Watton, Norfolk. Project manager: David Hatherly

West Hull Community Radio (WHCR FM)
07711 117042
john.harding@btinternet.com
Contact: John Harding

The Weston Point
01928 574593
sec.westonpoint@
   halton-borough.gov.uk
Runcorn. Deputy head: Christopher RJ Bayne

Wetherby Community Radio Group
01937 589088
bobpreedy@yahoo.co.uk
Contact: RE Preedy

Wharfedale FM
01943 463502
nigelfrancis@btinternet.com
Otley, Leeds. Chairman: Nigel Francis

Wirral Christian Media
0151 643 1696
office@flamefmwirral.org.uk
www.flamefmwirral.org.uk
Manager: Norman Polden

Wolverhampton Community Radio Training
0190 257 2260
whitehousep@wolvcoll.ac.uk
www.wcrt.co.uk
Chairman: Peter Whitehouse

Wythenshawe FM
0161 237 5454
phil@radioregen.org
www.radioregen.org
or www.wfm.org
Director: Phil Korbel

Youth Community Media
0845 226 1246
chris@youthcommunitymedia.org.uk
www.youthcommunitymedia.org.uk
Worcester. Radio co-ordinator: Chris Fox

Wales

Afan FM
07791 375999
craig@afanfm.co.uk
www.afanfm.co.uk
Port Talbot. Station manager: Craig Williams

Beats FM
029 2064 0500
john.lenney@immtech.co.uk
www.immtech.co.uk
Cardiff. Director: John Lenny

BRFM
01495 312567
BrynmawrRadio@aol.com
www.brfm.co.uk
Blaenau Gwent. Station manager: Robert Ball

Calon FM
01978 293373
m.wright@newi.ac.uk
www.newi.ac.uk
Wrexham. Head of communications, technology and environment: Michael Wright

Community Media Wrexham
01978 310250
info@wrexhamcra.co.uk
www.wrexhamcra.co.uk
Contact: John Malcolm Humberstone

GTFM
01443 406111
news@gtfm.co.uk
www.gtfm.co.uk
Pontypridd. Station manager: Andrew Jones

Toradio
01495 791599
tormedia@softhome.net
www.tormedia.info/toradio.htm
Torfaen. Contact: Alan Fossey

Scotland

Awaz FM
0141 420 6666
awazfm@hotmail.com
www.radioawaz.com
Glasgow. Contact: Javed Sattar

Black Diamond FM
0131 271 3711
admin@midlothianradio.org.uk
www.midlothianradio.org.uk
Edinburgh. Chairman: John Ritchie

Celtic Music
0141 812 7570
info@celticmusicradio.org.uk
www.celticmusicradio.org.uk
Glasgow. Contact: Robert McWilliam

East End Broadcast
0141 550 3954
spaterson@jwheatley.ac.uk
Glasgow. Project manager: Sam Paterson

Edinburgh Garrison FM
01748 830050
hq@garrisonradio.com
www.army.mod.uk/garrisonradio/
Programme director: John McCray

Faith Radio
0131 555 2290
Worldconquerors1@aol.com
www.wccscotland.org
Edinburgh. Contact: Rev Climate Irungu

The Initiative
0141 429 6314
Info@the-initiative.org.uk
www.the-initiative.org.uk
Glasgow. Community partnership manager: Paul Holmes

Leith FM
0131 553 5304
info@leithmediaworks.com
www.leithmediaworks.co.uk
Edinburgh. Contact: Sandy Campbell

Lowland Radio
01387 253383
jenny@dgaa.net
Dumfries. Director: Jennifer Wilson

Ness Community Radio
01463 731740
colin.macphail@virgin.net
Inverness. Admin director: Colin MacPhail

Radio Asia Scotland
0141 221 4569
Radioasiascotland@hotmail.com
Glasgow. Contact: Mohammed Nasar Moughal

Revival Radio
01236 823810
info@revivalradio.org.uk
www.revivalradio.org.uk
Cumbernauld. Chairman: Ian Dunlop

RNIB Scotland VIP ON AIR
0141 3345530
Kerryn.krige@viponair.com
www.viponair.com
Glasgow. Station manager: Kerryn Krige

Station House Media Unit
01224 487174
info@shmu.org.uk
www.shmu.org.uk
Aberdeen. Co-ordinator: Murray Dawson

Sunny Govan
0141 440 0600
sunnygovanradio@hotmail.com
www.sunnygovan.org
Glasgow. Contact: Heather McMillan

Superstation Orkney
01856 831835
studio@thesuperstation.co.uk
www.thesuperstation.co.uk
Contact: Dave Miller

Northern Ireland

BFBS – Lisburn
01494 878702
march.tyley@ssvc.com
www.ssvc.com
Deputy controller: Marc Tyley

Down FM
028 4461 5815
ian.mccormick@edifhe.ac.uk
www.edifhe.ac.uk
Downpatrick. Head of information and design: Ian McCormick

Drive FM
028 712 71871
enquiries@drivefm.com
www.drive105fm.com
North West. Contact: Richard Moore

Féile FM
028 90 242002
emma@feilebelfast.com
www.feilebelfast.com
Belfast. Station manager: Emma Mullen

Raidió Fáilte
028 9020 8040
mary@aislingghear.tv
Belfast. Contact: Máire Uí Mhaoilchiaráin

Shine FM
028 406 28 406
shinefm@voiceofpeace.fsnet.co.uk
www.shinefm.org.uk
Banbridge. Contact: Annmarie Asiimwe

Hospital, student and sporting event radio

1287 AM Insanity
01784 414268
studio@su.rhul.ac.uk
www.insanityradio.com
Egham. Student radio. 1287 AM.
Station manager: Chris Jackson-Jones

1503 AM Radio Diamonds
01933 652000
mathew.rowe@airwair.co.uk
Matchday service for Rushden and
Diamonds FC. 1503 AM. Contact: Dean
Howells

Auckland Hospital radio
01388 455452
secretary@aucklandradio.com
www.aucklandradio.com
Bishop Auckland. 1386 AM. Station
manager: Craig Robinson

B-1000
01895 203094
www.brunel.ac.uk
Uxbridge. Brunel University. 999 AM

Bailrigg FM
01524 593902
station.manager@bailriggfm.co.uk
www.bailriggfm.co.uk
Lancaster University. 87.7 FM. Station
manager: Vick Kirby

Basildon Hospital Radio
01268 282828
1287am@bhr.co.uk
www.bhr.org.uk
1287 AM. Chairman: Alan Newman

Bedrock AM
01708 738700
Romford. Oldchurch Hospital. 846 AM

BFBS
01494 878701
adminofficer@bfbs.com
www.bfbs.com
Chalfont St Peter. Forces radio.
Northern Ireland only. 1287 AM. Radio
controller: Charles Foster

Big Blue
020 7386 1677
gary@bigbluedigital.co.uk
Chelsea. Matchday service. 96.3 FM.
Contact: Gary Taphouse

Blast 1386
0118 967 5068
blast1386@reading-college.ac.uk
www.blast1386.com
Reading. Student radio. 1386 AM;
internet. Station manager: Bob Goertz

Bridge FM
01382 423000 x25151
studio@bridgefm.org.uk
www.bridgefm.org.uk
Dundee. Hospital, Tayside. 87.7 FM.
Chairman: Barry Hampton;
programme controller: Bob McNally

C4 Radio
01227 767700
c4radio@cant.ac.uk
Canterbury. Christchurch College. 999
AM. Station manager: Ian Eason

Canterbury Hospital Radio
01227 864161
www.chradio.org.uk
Canterbury. 945 AM. Studio manager:
Martin Pauley

Cardiff Stadium Radio
01264 369369
paul.forsyth@sounddec.com
www.sounddeck.com
Cardiff. Rugby referee match
commentary. Sales director: Paul Forsyth

Carillon Radio
01509 564433
carillonradio@aol.com
Loughborough. Loughborough Hospital,
Coalville Hospital. 1386 AM

Carlett Radio
0151 551 7777
enquiries@wmc.ac.uk
Wirral Metropolitan College. 1287 AM

Chichester Hospital Radio
01243 788122 x3000
studio@chr1431.org.uk
www.chr1431.org.uk
St Richard's Hospital. 1431 AM.
Presenter: Bill Barwell

City Hospital Radio
01442 262222
general@hemelradio.com
www.hemelradio.com
Hemel Hempstead. St Albans City
Hospital. 1350 AM; 1287AM.
Chairman: Neil O'Hara

Crush
01707 285005
uhsu.comms@herts.ac.uk
www.uhsu.herts.ac.uk
Hatfield. University of Hertfordshire.
1278 AM. Programme controller: Ollie
Cadman

CUR
01223 501004
committee@cur1350.co.uk
www.cur1350.co.uk
Cambridge. Churchill College,
University of Cambridge. 1350 AM

D:One
01332 590500
http://done.udsu.co.uk/
Derby. University of Derby. 1278 AM

Dorton Radio Station
01732 592500
karen.campbell@rlsb.org.uk
www.rlsb.org.uk
Sevenoaks. Dorton College. 1350 AM.
Station manager: Karen Campbell

Frequency
01772 894895
www.yourunion.co.uk
Preston. University of Central
Lancashire. 1350 AM. Station
manager: Emily Bull

Gara Sound
01623 464220
admin@garibaldi.org.uk
www.garibaldi.org.uk
Mansfield. School radio. 1386 AM.
Station manager: Dave Kenny

GU2
01483 681350
studio@gu2.co.uk
www.gu2.co.uk
Guildford. Student. 1350 AM. Station manager: Tom Knight

Hospital Radio Basingstoke
01256 313521
mail@hrbasingstoke.co.uk
www.hrbasingstoke.co.uk
945 AM. Programme controller: Neil Ogden

Hospital Radio Crawley
01293 534859
1287 AM

Hospital Radio Plymouth
01752 763441
www.hospitalradioplymouth.org.uk
87.7 FM. Communications: Corinne Glen

Hospital Radio Pulse
01527 512048
studio@hospitalradiopulse.com
www.hospitalradiopulse.com
Redditch. 1350 AM. Programme controller: Ian Barstow

Hospital Radio Reading
0118 950 7420
requests@hospitalradioreading.co.uk
www.hospitalradioreading.org.uk
Royal Berkshire and Battle Hospitals. 945 AM. Programme controller: Stephen Ham

Hospital Radio Rossendale
01706 233334
945 AM. Contact: David S Foster

Hospital Radio Yare
01493 842613
jean@birchwell.co.uk
www.radioyare.com
Great Yarmouth. James Paget, Northgate, Lowestoft hospitals. 1350 AM. Chairman: Jean Thorpe; programme controller: Phil Marshall

The Hub
0117 987 1054
hub.radio@uwe.ac.uk
www.thehub1449.com
Bristol. University of the West of England. 1449 AM. Chief engineer: Steve Hagerty

IC Radio
020 7594 8100
info@icradio.com
www.icradio.com
South Kensington. Imperial College halls of residence. 999 AM. Station manager: Mike Jones

Insanity
01784 414268
studio@su.rhul.ac.uk
www.insanityradio.com
Egham. Royal Holloway, University of London. 1287 AM

Jam 1575
01482 466289
email@jam1575.com
www.jam1575.com
Hull. Hull University. 1575 AM. Station manager: Gareth Morris

Junction 11
0118 986 5159
www.1287am.com
Reading. Reading University. 1287 AM. Station manager: Joff Hopkins

Kendal Radio
01539 795420
Info@kendalhospitalradio.com
www.kendalhospitalradio.org.uk
Hospital radio. Studio manager: John Williamson

Kingstown Radio
01482 327711
onair@kingstownradio.com
www.kingstownradio.co.uk
Hull. Hull hospital radio. 1350 AM. Station manager: Nick Palmer

Kool AM
020 8373 1072
pfmnews@email.com
www.koolam.co.uk
Edmonton. 1134 AM. Programme controller: Joe Bone

Livewire
01603 592512
dave@livewire1350.com
www.livewire1350.com
Norwich. UEA students. 1350 AM. Station manager: Alan Milford

Loughborough Campus Radio
01509 635050
studio@lcr1350.co.uk
www.lcr1350.co.uk
Loughborough. Student radio. 1350 AM. Head of media: Lucy Pritchard; station manager: Oliver Folkerd

Mid-Downs Hospital Radio
01444 441350
studio@ndr.org.uk
www.ndr.org.uk
Haywards Heath. Hospital radio. 1350 AM. Station manager: Alan French

Nerve Radio
01202 595765
Jhawkins@bournemouth.ac.uk
www.nervemedia.net
Bournemouth. Bournemouth University. 87.7 FM. Web manager: Jason Hawkins

Nevill Hall Sound
01873 858633
info@nevillhallsound.com
www.nevillhallsound.com
Abergavenny. Nevill Hall Hospital. 1287 AM. Station manager: Colin Palmer

Newbold Radio
01344 454607 x324
www.newbold.ac.uk
Binfield. Newbold College. 1350 AM

Oakwell 1575 AM
enquiries@oakwell1575am.co.uk
www.oakwell1575am.co.uk
Barnsley. Matchday service for Barnsley FC. 1575 AM. Station manager: Stuart Cocker

Palace Radio 1278 AM
020 8653 5796
info@palaceradio.net
www.palaceradio.net
London. Matchday service for Crystal Palace FC. 1278 AM. Communications manager: Terry Byfield

Portsmouth Hospital Broadcasting
023 9262 6299
www.addicks.org/secaudit/phb/
Queen Alexandra Hospital and St Mary's Hospital. 945 AM. Station manager: Barrie Swann

Radio Airthrey
01786 467166
stationManager@airthrey.co.uk
http://susaonline.org.uk
Sterling. Student, music, politics. 1350 AM. Station manager: Niamh Maynard

Radio Branwen
01766 781911
radiobranwen@yahoo.co.uk
Harlech. Student, music. 87.7 FM. Station manager: Trevor Andrews

Radio Brockley
020 8954 6591
studio@radiobrockley.org
www.radiobrockley.org
London. Stanmore's Royal National. Orthopaedic Hospital. 999 AM

Radio Bronglais
01970 635363
office@radiobronglais.co.uk
www.radiobronglais.co.uk
Aberystwyth. Bronglais General Hospital. 87.8 FM. Station manager: Martin Oakes

Radio Cavell
0161 620 3033
info@radiocavell1350.org.uk
www.radiocavell1350.org.uk
Royal Oldham Hospital. 1350 AM. Broadcasting manager: Phil Edmunds

Radio Chelsea and Westminster
London
020 8746 8423
www.chelwest.nhs.uk
Hospital radio. Chairman: Anthony Davis; station manager: James Healy

Radio Glangwili
01267 227504
Carmarthen. West Wales General Hospital. 87.7 FM

Radio Gosh
020 8203 2226
peter@radiogosh.co.uk
www.radiogosh.co.uk
London. Great Ormond Street Hospital. 999 AM. Chairman: Peter Losch

Radio Heatherwood
01344 625818
www.radioheatherwood.org.uk
Ascot. Heatherwood Hospital. 999 AM. Station manager: Dave Smith

Radio Hotspot
01473 326200
www.royalhospitalschool.org
Ipswich. The Royal Hospital School. 1287 AM. Manager: Don Topley

Radio Knockhill
01383 723337
enquiries@knockhill.com
www.knockhill.com
Dunfermline. Motor racing. 1602 AM. Station manager: Garry Stagg

Radio Lonsdale
01229 877877
studio@radiolonsdale.co.uk
www.southlakes-uk.co.uk
Hospital. 87.7 FM. Station manager:
Julian Ackred

Radio Nightingale
01709 304244
Admin@radionightingale.org.uk
www.radionightingale.org.uk
Rotherham District General Hospital.
1350 AM

Radio North Angus
01382 424095
info@radionorthangus.co.uk
www.radionorthangus.co.uk
Arbroath Infirmary and Brechin
Infirmary. 96.6 FM, 87.7 FM.
Managing director: Malcolm Finlayson

Radio North Tees
01642 624337
info@radionorthtees.com
www.radionorthtees.com
Stockton on Tees. Hospital radio.
Station manager: Elliot Kennedy

Radio Northwick Park
020 8869 3959
info@radionorthwickpark.org
www.radionorthwickpark.org
North-west London. Hospital radio.
Programme controller: Matt Blank

Radio Rainbow
01224 552886
www.shrs.org.uk/rainbow/
Aberdeen. Royal Aberdeen Children's
Hospital. 945 AM

Radio Redhill
01737 768511
studio@radioredhill.co.uk
www.radioredhill.co.uk
East Surrey Hospital. 1287 AM. Station
manager: Nigel Gray

Radio Rovers
01254 261413
alan.yardley@creatv.co.uk
www.gjmedia.co.uk/rrovers
Blackburn. Blackburn Rovers
matchday service. 1404 AM. Station
manager: Alan Yardley

Radio Southlands
01273 446084
info@hospitalradiosouthlands.co.uk
www.hospitalradiosouthlands.co.uk
Shoreham. Southlands and Worthing
Hospitals. 846 AM. Programme
controller: Adam James

Radio Tyneside
0191 273 6970
info@radiotyneside.co.uk
www.radiotyneside.co.uk
Newcastle General Hospital. 1575 AM

Radio Warwick
024 7657 3077
studio@radio.warwick.ac.uk
www.radio.warwick.ac.uk
Warwick. Student radio. 1251 AM.
Station manager: James Buckland

Radio West Suffolk
01284 713403
peteowen1350@hotmail.com
www.radiowestsuffolk.co.uk
Bury St Edmunds. West Suffolk
Hospital. 1350 AM. Vice chairman:
P Owen

Radio Wexham
01753 570033
Wexham Park Hospital. 945 AM

Radio Ysbyty Glan Clwyd
01745 584229
Conway. Glan Clwyd District General
Hospital. 1287 AM. Manager: Morag
Jelly

Ram Air
01274 233269
studio@ramair.co.uk
www.ramair.co.uk
Bradford. University of Bradford. 1350
AM. Station manager: Mark Pickering

Range Radio
0161 861 9727
rap@whalleyrange.manchester.sch.uk
www.whalleyrange.manchester.sch.uk
Manchester. Student radio. 1350 AM.
Station manager: Roy Appleby

Red
01206 863211
red@essex.ac.uk
www.essexstudent.com
Colchester. Student radio. 1404 AM.
Station manager: Shruti Budhia

RK1 FM
01691 773671
singletonr@moretonhall.com
Oswestry. Moreton Hall Educational
Trust. 87.7 AM. Head of science:
Richard Singleton

Rookwood Sound Hospital Radio
029 2031 3796
programming@rookwoodsound.co.uk
www.rookwoodsound.co.uk
Llandaff. Rookwood Hospital. 945 AM.
Programme controller: Bryn Stone

Sports! Link-fm
01225 835553
info@sportslinkfm.com
www.sportslinkfm.com
Live sports commentary. 87.7 to 105
FM. Managing director: Peter Downey

SNCR
0115 914 6467
Nottingham. South Nottingham College.
1278 AM

Solar AM
01744 623454
solar1287am@hotmail.com
St Helens. St Helens College. 1287 AM.
Station manager: Terry Broughton

Southside Hospital Broadcasting
01642 854742
info@southsideradio.com
www.southsideradio.com
James Cook University Hospital.
Contact: Alex Lewczuk

Stoke Mandeville Hospital Radio
01296 331575
info@smhr.co.uk
www.smhr.co.uk
1575 AM

Storm FM
01248 383235
admin@stormfm.com
www.stormfm.com
Bangor. University of Wales Bangor.
87.7 FM. Manager: Alex Simpson

Storm Radio
01206 500700
storm@colchsfc.ac.uk
www.colchsfc.ac.uk
Colchester. Student radio. 999 AM.
Station manager: Shirley Hart

Subcity Radio
0141 341 6222
manager@subcity.org
www.subcity.org
Glasgow. Student radio. 1350 AM.
Station manager: Sean Murphy

Surge
0870 357 2287
office@surgeradio.co.uk,
studio@surgeradio.co.uk
www.surgeradio.co.uk
University of Southampton. 1287 AM.
Station manager: Matt Hurst;
programme controller: Thomas
Morgan; head of music: James Hickson

Trust AM
01909 502909
studio@trustam.com
www.trustam.com
Doncaster. Doncaster and Bassetlaw
Foundation Trust group of hospitals.
1278 AM. Programme controllers: Steve
Roberts and Andy Morton

Tunbridge Wells Hospital Radio
01892 528528
info@hrtw.org.uk
www.hrtw.org.uk
Kent and Sussex, Pembury and
Tonbridge Cottage hospitals. 1350 AM.
Programme controller: Mark Burgess

UCA
01292 886358
Marcus.Bowman@paisley.ac.uk
www.ucaradio.paisley.ac.uk
Ayr. University campus, Ayr. 87.7 FM;
DAB. Station manager: Marcus Bowman

UKC Radio 1350 AM
01227 824201
jrgardner@kent.ac.uk
www.ukcradio.co.uk
University of Kent. 1350 AM.
Programme controller: JR Gardner

University Radio Falmer
01273 678999
exec@urfonline.com
www.urfonline.com
Falmer. University of Sussex and
Brighton University Falmer Campus.
1431 AM. Station manager: Daniel
Parslow

University Radio York
01904 433840
ury@ury.york.ac.uk
http://ury.york.ac.uk
York. Student radio. 1350 AM.
Programme controller: Matt Wareham

URB
01225 386611
studio@bath.ac.uk
www.1449urb.com
Bath. Student radio. 1449 AM. Station
manager: Sebastian Mullens

URF
01273 678999
exec@urfonline.com
www.urfonline.com
Brighton. Student radio. 1431 AM.
Station manager: Daniel Parslow

URN
0115 846 8722
manager@urn1350.net
www.urn1350.net
Nottingham. University of Nottingham.
1350 AM. Station manager: Alex Allan;
head of music: Ed Ackerman

Viva AM
01925 722298
head@penketh.warrington.sch.uk
Warrington. Penketh High School. 1386
AM. Programme controller: Jonathan
Kay

VRN
07940 591479
www.victoriaradionetwork.co.uk
Kirkaldy. Victoria Hospital, Kirkaldy.
1287 AM. Programme controller:
Sandy Izatt

WCR AM
01902 572260
training@wcr1350.co.uk
www.wcr1350.co.uk
Wolverhampton. College radio. 1350
AM. Manager: Nicola Stewart

Withybush FM
01437 773564
studio@withybushfm.co.uk
www.withybushfm.co.uk
Withybush Hospital. 87.7 FM. Station
manager: Hilary Raymond

Xpression
01392 263568
stationManager@Xpressionfm.com
www.Xpressionfm.com
Exeter. Student radio. 87.7 FM. Station
manager: Ruth Lovell; programme
controller: Mike Swaine

Xtreme
01792 295989
studio@xtremeradio.info
www.xtremeradio.info
Swansea. Student radio. 1431 AM

Radio associations

Association for International Broadcasting
POBox 990, London SE3 9XL
020 8297 3993
info@aib.org.uk
www.aib.org.uk
Trade organisation

Broadcasting Press Guild
Tiverton, The Ridge
Woking, Surrey GU22 7EQ
01483 764895
torin.douglas@bbc.co.uk
Promotes interests of journalists who
write or broadcast about the media

Commercial Radio Companies Association
The Radiocentre
77 Shaftesbury Avenue
London W1D 5DU
020 7306 2603
info@crca.co.uk
www.crca.co.uk

Creators' Rights Alliance
British Music House
26 Berners Street, London W1T 3LR
020 7436 7296
info@creatorsrights.org
www.creatorsrights.org
Campaigns to protect creators' rights;
operates in all media areas

Digital Radio Development Bureau (DRDB)
The Radiocentre
77 Shaftesbury Avenue
London W1D 5DU
020 7306 2630
info@drdb.org
www.drdb.org
Trade body; funded and supported by
BBC and commercial radio multiplex
operators

Musicians Union
60–62 Clapham Road
London SW9 0JJ
020 7840 5534
london@musiciansunion.org.uk
www.musiciansunion.org.uk

Office of Communications (Ofcom)
Riverside House
2A Southwark Bridge Road
London SE1 9HA
020 7981 3040 or 0845 456 3000
mediaoffice@ofcom.org.uk
www.ofcom.org.uk
Broadcasting super-regulator

Performing Rights Society
29–33 Berners Street
London W1T 3AB
020 7306 4866
press: 020 7306 4803
mediaquery@mcps-prs-alliance.co.uk
www.prs.co.uk
Collects and distributes royalties

Rad10
rad10@rad10.com
www.rad10.com
Free training resource for radio
volunteers looking at going professional;
offers advice for community radio
groups

Radio Joint Audience Research (Rajar)
Gainsborough House
81 Oxford Street, London W1D 2EU
020 7903 5350
info@rajar.co.uk
www.rajar.co.uk
Audience measurement system. Wholly
owned by the Commercial Radio
Companies Association and the BBC

The Radio Academy
5 Market Place, London W1W 8AE
020 7255 2010
info@radioacademy.org
www.radioacademy.org
Professional body for radio; aims to
promote excellence and a greater
understanding of the medium

Voice of the Listener and Viewer (VLV)
101 King's Drive
Gravesend, Kent DA12 5BQ
01474 352835
info@vlv.org.uk
www.vlv.org.uk
Independent, non-profit society
working to ensure independence,
quality and diversity in broadcasting

Women's Radio Group
27 Bath Road, London W4 1LJ
Fax: 020 8995 5442
wrg@zelo.demon.co.uk
www.womeninradio.org.uk
Training and networking charity

World Radio Network
PO Box 1212, London SW8 2ZF
020 7896 9000
email@wrn.org
www.wrn.org
Home to series of global radio networks;
hosts transmission services for world's
leading broadcasters

Radio trade press

Advance Production News
Crimson Communications
211a Station House
Greenwich Commercial Centre
49 Greenwich High Road
London SE10 8JL
020 8305 6905
www.crimsonuk.com
Monthly. Listings for production companies. Editor: Alan Williams

Audio Media
IMAS Publishing UK
Atlantica House, 11 Station Road
St Ives, Cambs PE27 5BH
01480 461555
p.mac@audiomedia.com;
j.miller@audiomedia.com
www.audiomedia.com
Monthly. Professional audio. Editor: Paul Mac; news: Jonathan Miller; editorial manager: Sarah Johnston

Broadcast
Emap Media
33–39 Bowling Green Lane
London EC1R 0DA
020 7505 8000
broadcastnews@emap.com
www.broadcastnow.co.uk
Weekly. TV and radio industry. Editor: Conor Dignam; news: Colin Robertson; features and deputy editor: Lisa Campbell; chief sub: Angus Walker

Broadcast Hardware International
Hardware Creations
48 The Broadway
Maidenhead, Berks SL6 1PW
01628 773935
cathy@hardwarecreations.tv
www.hardwarecreations.tv
10pa. Editor: Dick Hobbs

Commonwealth Broadcaster
Commonwealth Broadcasting
   Association
17 Fleet Street, London EC4Y 1AA
020 7583 5550
cba@cba.org.uk
www.cba.org.uk
Quarterly. Editor: Elizabeth Smith

Contacts – The Spotlight Casting Directories
The Spotlight, 7 Leicester Place
London WC2H 7RJ
020 7437 7631
info@spotlight.com
www.spotlight.com
Annual. Contacts for stage, film, TV and radio. Editor: Kate Poynton

Line Up
Line Up Publications
The Hawthornes, 4 Conference Grove
Crowle WR7 4SF
01905 381725
editor@lineup.biz
www.lineup.biz
Bi-monthly. Journal of the Institute of Broadcast Sound. Editor: Hugh Robjohns

Pro Sound News Europe
CMP Information, Ludgate House
245 Blackfriars Road
London SE1 9UR
020 7921 8319
david.robinson@cmpinformation.com
www.prosoundnewseurope.com
Monthly. Audio industry. Editor: David Robinson; managing editor: Ben Rosser

QSheet
10 Northburgh Street
London EC1V 0AT
020 7253 8888
www.qsheet.com
Monthly. Support material for presenters and producers. Editor: John Reynolds; features and interviews: Nik Harta; art direction and design: Dominic Philcox

Radcom
Radio Society of Great Britain
Lambda House, Cranbourne Road
Potters Bar EN6 3JE
0870 904 7373
radcom@rsgb.org.uk
www.rsgb.org
Monthly. Radio enthusiasts

Radio Magazine
Crown House, 25 High Street
Rothwell, Northants NN14 6AD
01536 418558
info@theradiomagazine.co.uk
www.theradiomagazine.co.uk
Weekly. Radio news for industry. Editor: Paul Boon; features and assistant editor: Collette Hillier; advertising and technical manager: Tom Hooper

Stage Screen and Radio
Bectu, 373–377 Clapham Road
London SW9 9BT
020 7346 0900
janice@stagescreenandradio.org.uk
www.bectu.org.uk
10pa. Broadcasting union. Editor: Janice Turner

VLV Bulletin
Voice of the Listener and Viewer
101 Kings Drive
Gravesend DA12 5BQ
01474 352835
info@vlv.org.uk
www.vlv.org.uk
Quarterly. Advocates citizen and consumer interests in broadcasting. Editor: Jocelyn Hay

New media

Broadband uptake, end of 2004

Internet connections	15.8 million
Total broadband connections	6.2 million
DSL connections	4.2 million
Cable modem connections	1.9 million
Other connections	about 100,000

Source: Ofcom

Online ad spend

Year	Spend £m	Market share %
2004	597	3.2
2003	376	2.2
2002	196.7	1.4
2001	165.7	1.2
2000	154.7	1.1
1999	51.0	0.4
1998	19.4	0.2

Source: Advertising Association

More than five years on from the dotcom crash that left technology entrepreneurs weeping into their keyboards, Britain's new media industry is buoyant. Online advertising reached £653.5m in 2004, according to a report from PricewaterhouseCoopers, the World Advertising Research Centre and the Internet Advertising Bureau – a rise of some 60% – and in October of that year, internet advertising overtook radio advertising for the first time. The value of online shopping, meanwhile, doubled to £39.5bn in 2003, according to the Office for National Statistics.

A major driver for that success, of course, is internet access. Britain is the world's fastest-growing market for broadband services, it was reported in June 2005. There are about 7.1m connections, of which about 5m are DSL connections (requiring a BT line) with the rest using cable or satellite. The then trade and industry secretary, Patricia Hewitt, declared in April that virtually all UK homes would be connected to a broadband-enabled exchange by summer 2005. According to a survey by Continental Research, broadband users are significantly more likely to spend money online.

High-speed internet access is also getting cheaper: Ofcom cut the price that BT charges broadband companies to use its telephone network to £34 in January 2005 – down from £88 at the end of 2004. At least some of those savings are certain to be passed on to the consumer.

Blogs and citizen journalism

Blogs have been around for more than half a decade now – Guardian Unlimited launched its own in April 2000 – but only in the past year or so have mainstream newspapers been using the word "blog" without having to include a lengthy explanation of what one is. It was estimated in May 2005 that there are more than 60 million blogs on the internet, although how many of these get updated regularly is another matter entirely.

The success of the blog, or online journal, has led to plenty of column inches about what effect "citizen journalism" will have on the media industry as a whole. Internet users don't use the media in the same way as newspaper readers or TV viewers; when anyone can keep a blog or post to a message board, then anyone can be a "journalist" and, in theory, anyone can make their voice heard.

In 2005, US bloggers had mainstream media licking their wounds. First bloggers unravelled a CBS News report alleging that George Bush received special treatment during his time in the Texas Air National Guard – forcing the network to admit that it could not say whether the source of its claim could be authenticated, and casting a shadow over its long-serving news anchor Dan Rather, who retired in the wake of the

row. And then CNN's chief news executive, Eason Jordan, resigned after claiming that US forces had "targeted" journalists during the war in Iraq. The remark was made in an off-the-record briefing and ignored by most news organisations – but picked up by bloggers and posted online.

In January 2005, a bookseller became the first blogger in Britain to be "dooced" – that is, sacked for what he wrote in his blog. Joe Gordon, 37, lost his job at the Edinburgh branch of Waterstone's after sounding off about the firm, which he called "Bastardstone's" after his boss refused to give him the week off. The expression comes from the case of Heather Armstrong, who lost her job as a web designer in 2002 after parodying the experience on her blog, Dooce.com.

Search engine wars

From the industry's perspective, the most intriguing battle has been between the makers of the three biggest search engines: Microsoft, Google and Yahoo! **Google** garnered most of the press coverage, as usual: it went public in August 2004 at $85 a share, but these had touched $300 at the end of June 2005. The company reported a more than fivefold increase in profits in the first quarter of 2005, with earnings of £194m. Major launches included the 1Gb webmail service GMail, the Google Maps mapping service (launched after the acquisition of 3D mapmaker Keyhole Corp) and Google Print – the last offering the ability to search and buy printed books.

Google didn't have it all its own way: it was sued for £10m in March 2005 by the French news agency AFP, which claiming the search engine breached its copyright by reproducing its pictures and articles on Google News. Google responded by removing AFP stories from its site.

Yahoo!, meanwhile, has been making even more money: its gross profit rose to more than £1.2bn in 2004, a rise of 80%. The company also offers 1Gb webmail, and in 2005 it bought the trendiest media company on the block, the image organising and sharing application, **Flickr**. In October 2004, it had appointed the former Kelkoo bosses Pierre Chappaz and Dominique Vidal to run its European operations.

Awards

Webby awards

- *Best copy/writing:* McSweeney's Internet Tendency **www.mcsweeneys.net**
- *Blog:* Boing Boing **www.boingboing.net**
- *Community:* Dogster **www.dogster.com**
- *Guides/ratings/reviews:* ConsumerReports.org **www.consumerreports.org**
- *Magazine:* AlterNet.org **www.alternet.org**
- *Film:* The Uninvited **www.postvisual.com/theuninvited**
- *Music:* BBC OneMusic **www.bbc.co.uk/radio1/onemusic**
- *News:* BBC News **http://news.bbc.co.uk**
- *Newspaper:* Guardian Unlimited **www.guardian.co.uk**
- *Politics:* Weapons of Misdirection **www.weaponsofmisdirection.com**
- *Radio:* Virgin Radio **www.virginradio.co.uk**
- *Telecommunications:* Skype **www.skype.com**
- *TV:* Comedy Central's Indecision 2004 **www.comedycentral.com/tv_shows/indecision2004**

Games industry Baftas

- *Racing*: Burnout 3: Takedown
- *Sport*: Pro Evolution Soccer 4
- *Action/adventure*: Half-Life 2
- *Online & multiplayer (sponsored by BT)*: Half-Life 2
- *Handheld:* Colin McRae Rally 2005
- *Best game:* Half-Life 2

As a response to its smaller rivals, **Microsoft** launched its own global search engine, MSN Search, in February 2005. In 2004, though, it had problems of its own: it failed in its challenge to EU antitrust sanctions imposed with regard to bundling its Media Player with Windows, and must now disclose protocols of its Windows software to rivals, and market a version of Windows without Media Player. It had already paid a fine of £347.3m in June 2004.

Dotcom industry

Elsewhere, hype surrounded the public offering in London of Party-Gaming, whose shares closed 11% up at £1.29 on their first day of trading in June. There was also controversy, because online gambling is considered illegal in the US, where most of PartyGaming's customers are based. The company operates out of offices in Gibraltar.

Meanwhile **Lastminute.com**, the long-time darling of Britain's dot-coms, finally sold up in May 2005. Sabre Holdings, the US owner of Travelocity, bought the travel retailer for £577m.

eBay went on a spending spree, spending £340m on Shopping.com in June 2005, and buying London jobs and flats website Gumtree.com the previous month.

Spending on **bbc.co.uk** increased to £69.2m in 2004, according to the BBC annual report; for that outlay, the site attracted an average of 22.8m unique British users a month. But the BBC has had to rethink its digital strategy following criticism in the Graf report of the negative effect of its websites on commercial rivals; sites that were not deemed to be of sufficient public service, such as the BBC Cult website and Fantasy Football, were closed.

Mobile devices

2005 was the year that gadgetry became sexy – and the company that can claim most credit for that is Apple. The company reported £150m in profits in its second quarter, a sixfold increase on the year before – and can attribute much of its success to its iPod MP3 player. The company sold 5.3m iPods and, at the launch of those figures, it accounted for almost one-third of the company's revenues.

For business users, gadget of the year was the BlackBerry, a mobile device offering "push" email direct to a (rather unsightly) phone. Thanks largely to corporate subscriptions, more than 2.5 million people were using the service by the end of March 2005. Research in Motion, the Canadian company behind the gadget, made £530m in revenues in 2004/05.

3G phones finally made their debut in the UK in 2004. Vodafone spent £7bn launching its next-generation phones; while 3, the 3G mobile phone network owned by Hutchison Whampoa, attracted subscribers with the promise of cheap voice calls. In the absence of open internet access, though, 3G services themselves remain relatively unpopular with users; unlike in countries such as Japan, where mobile internet access has taken off using open, third-party services such as iMode.

Perhaps the most popular mobile technology, however, is the humble SMS. Britons are thought to have sent a record 25bn text messages during 2004, according to research by the Mobile Data Association, up 22% on the previous year. The rise in texts can be attributed to the number of mobile phone deals offering bundled SMS messages as standard.

The rise of camera phones has had another, perhaps predictable,

Lastminute.com founders Brent Hoberman and Martha Lane Fox in 2000. They sold up in 2005

Sean Smith

effect: people taking photographs of high-profile news events. So it was that, during the London bomb attacks of July 7 2005 that killed more than 50 people, survivors were able to take photographs of the trains and of people being evacuated through the tunnels – leading Mark Glaser of Online Journalism Review to ask: did the London bombings turn citizen journalists into "citizen paparazzi"? See the Guardian's Neil McIntosh, opposite, for more on that.

The games industry

2005 and 2006 will see the launch of the next generation of gaming consoles: the Microsoft Xbox 360, the Sony PlayStation 3, and the Nintendo Revolution. Of these, the Xbox is due to go on sale before Christmas 2005; the PS3 will come later, but includes integrated WiFi and more USB ports; while the Revolution looks set to compete on price.

In-game advertising also looks set to become important to the gaming industry, as companies launch technologies that allow ads to be delivered and altered in real time.

Top 10 web audiences, July 2005		
Name	**Unique audience (millions)**	
	July 2005	**July 2004**
1 Microsoft	18.9	18.5
2 Google	16.4	12.8
3 Yahoo!	12.5	11.1
4 eBay	11.1	8.5
5 BBC	10.5	7.6
6 Time Warner	8.5	7.2
7 Amazon	7.2	5.6
8 HM Government	5.6	4.1
9 British Telecom	5.4	5.4
10 Wanadoo	5.4	6.0

Source: Nielsen/NetRatings

Further reading

■ **Press**

MediaGuardian: New Media
media.guardian.co.uk/newmedia

Guardian Online
guardian.co.uk/online

New Media Age
www.nma.co.uk

■ **Books**

Boo Hoo: A Dotcom Story ERNST MALMSTEN ET AL, RANDOM HOUSE 2002 Rise and fall of a dotcom dream

Weaving the Web TIM BERNERS-LEE, TEXERE PUBLISHING 2000 History of the world wide web

■ **Web only**

Online Journalism Review
www.ojr.org

The Register
www.theregister.co.uk
Irreverent tech news

ZDNet
www.zdnet.co.uk
IT and tech news

■ **Other resources**

Association of Online Publishers
www.ukaop.org.uk

Listen to the citizen journalist **Neil McIntosh**

Once upon a time, all that readers contributed to media was attention and money. Occasionally they would write a letter. Even more occasionally, it would get printed, after editing from an unseen hand. And the reader would be glad.

How things are changing. We knew they would, of course, with the internet's chatrooms, forums and – latterly – blogs giving new voice to the letter-writing classes.

But fewer predicted what now seems the logical conclusion of this movement; that consumers would themselves become producers on a more regular basis, and start to bypass the censorious red pens that frustrated them so much in the past.

In what seems an absurdly short space of time, the established media has gone from telling its readers, viewers and users what was happening in the world, to asking those readers, viewers and users to tell it what is going on.

From the amateur video that captured the tsunami in south-east Asia at the start of 2005, to the harrowing images from inside London Underground tunnels later in the year, material produced by those that were once called consumers has assumed new importance.

But where did it come from, this change from one-way flow to, in the words of media commentator Jeff Jarvis, "news as a conversation"?

Some of it can be traced to the continued boom in weblogs – most of which publish to tiny audiences of family and friends, but some of which aim for a bigger audience, picking apart arguments they disagree with, research the backgrounds of stories and authors they think suspect, and do it in a tone they regard as infinitely less haughty than the "MSM", or mainstream media.

Some of it can be traced to the availability of technology that the foreign correspondents of yesteryear could only have dreamed of – global mobile phone networks, cheap video cameras capable of broadcast-quality footage, and the ability to transmit words and images anywhere instantly. Meanwhile, tools such as Technorati offer a way to track news as it spread across millions of blogs, with no more effort than a few keystrokes.

Efforts to organise amateur reporting have also grown. The South Korean Ohmynews continues to add to its already huge citizen journalist army. The collaborative Wikinews project, launched in 2004, might have flunked its first big test – the tsunami – but it won widespread praise for its coverage of the terrorist bombings in London.

Indeed, it was 7/7 that did more to bring citizen journalism to the attention of the British media, and

its audience, than anything else before. Broadcasters and websites were quick to spot that some of the audience might have been closer to the story than they were, and used their broadcasts and websites to solicit images and video shot on mobile phones. Then they followed through by placing users' contributions at the heart of the way they told the story.

One of the abiding images of the day – of commuters being escorted out a shattered tube train into a dimly lit tunnel – was taken not by a trained photographer, but by an amateur on a cheap mobile phone, who then posted it on its website. The Flickr site, which organises and displays users' photo collections, became a more vivid portrayal of the day than any one newspaper's spread, or website's gallery, could be.

Where will this lead us? Will it lead to mainstream media fighting over the best amateur images and words? The founders of Scoopt, the first "citizen journalist's photography agency", must surely hope it will – they plan to take 50% of any fees.

But what of the bigger claim – that of the "citizen journalism" zealots, who say the mainstream media is simply a collection of gatekeepers to information, all due to be washed away by the free flow of readers turning to each other to get their news and information?

Traditionalists who believe professional journalism has a future shouldn't worry too much, for now. Much of the debate about citizen journalism remains academic; about whether it works better at an ultra-local level, or more broadly; about whether citizen journalists need to be trained, or just given the freedom to do their thing. Meanwhile, Britain's competitive media landscape at least means it escapes some of the accusations of complacency levelled at our more monopolistic American counterparts.

But the revolution is already beginning, whether we like it or not, because there's only one answer to the fundamental question underpinning it all. When your readers and viewers have more interesting stories to tell than you do, and know more about it than you do, and can tell it faster than you, just how long do you want to keep ignoring them?

Neil McIntosh is assistant editor at Guardian Unlimited

Jeff Jarvis – **www.buzzmachine.com**
Scoopt – **www.scoopt.com**
Wikinews – **http://en.wikinews.org**
Technorati – **www.technorati.com**
Flickr – **www.flickr.com**

New media

New media Contacts

Main search engines/portals

AltaVista/AlltheWeb
New London House
172 Drury Lane
London WC2B 5QR
angela.bloor@overture.com
www.altavista.co.uk
www.alltheweb.com
PRESS: *020 7071 3510*

Ask Jeeves
53 Parker Street
London WG2B 5PT
020 7400 2222
info@askjeeves.co.uk
www.ask.co.uk
PRESS: *020 7400 2222*

Excite UK
Viale G Baccelli, 70
00153 - Roma, Italy
00 39 06 570231
bberger@staff.excite.it
www.excite.co.uk
PRESS: *00 39 06 57023208*

Google UK
European HQ:
Seagrave House
19/20 Earlsfort Terrace, Dublin 02
Ireland
UK sales office:
The Courtyard, 12 Sutton Row
London W1V 5FH
020 7031 3000
UK@google.com
www.google.co.uk
PRESS: *020 7031 3130*

Kelkoo UK
125 Shaftesbury Avenue
London WC2H 8AD
speak2us@kelkoo.co.uk
www.kelkoo.co.uk
PRESS: *press@kelkoo.co.uk*
Shopping search engine owned by Yahoo!

Lycos UK
Lycos House, 3 Sutton Lane
Clerkenwell, London EC1M 5PU
020 7462 9200
www.lycos.co.uk
PRESS:
ukpressoffice@lycos-europe.com

MSN
Microsoft House
10 Great Pulteney Street
London W1R 3DG
0870 6010100
www.msn.co.uk
PRESS: *0870 2077 377*
ukprteam@microsoft.com

Yahoo! UK
10 Ebury Bridge Road
London SW1W 8PZ
020 7131 1000
www.yahoo.co.uk
PRESS: *020 7808 4400*

Main software publishers

Activision UK
Parliament House, St Laurence Way
Slough, Berkshire SL1 2BW
01753 756100
www.activision.com
Games
PRESS: *020 7751 1661*

Adobe
3 Roundwood Avenue
Stockley Park, Uxbridge
Middlesex UB1 1AY
020 8606 4000
www.adobe.co.uk
Design and publishing software

Apple Computer UK
2 Furzeground Way
Stockley Park East, Uxbridge
Middlesex UB11 1BB
020 8218 1000
millar.d@euro.apple.com
www.apple.com/uk
Computer hardware/software
PRESS: *appleuk.pr@euro.apple.com*
apple@bitepr.com

Atari UK
Landmark House
Hammersmith Bridge Road
London W6 9EJ
020 8222 9700
www.atari.co.uk
Games

Codemasters
Stoneythorpe, Southam
Warwickshire CV47 2DL
01926 814132
www.codemasters.co.uk
Games
PRESS: *press@codemasters.co.uk*

Eidos Interactive
Wimbledon Bridge House
1 Hartfield Road
Wimbledon SW19 3RU
020 8636 3000
plc@eidos.co.uk
www.eidos.co.uk
Games

Electronic Arts
2000 Hillswood Drive,
Chertsey, Surrey KT16 0EU
http://uk.ea.com
Independent developer and publisher of interactive entertainment software
PRESS: *01932 450000*

Focus Multimedia
The Studios, Lea Hall Enterprise Park
Wheelhouse Road, Rugeley
Staffordshire WS15 1LH
01889 570156
info@focusmm.co.uk
www.focusmm.co.uk
CD-Roms

IBM Lotus
PO Box 41, North Harbour
Portsmouth, Hampshire PO6 3AU
023 9256 1000
www.lotus.co.uk, www.ibm.com
Office software

Linux
59 East River St, #2
Ogdensburg, NY13669 USA
00 1 315 393 1202
www.linux.org.uk
Free operating system
PRESS: *pr@Linux.org*

Macromedia Europe (UK)
Century Court, Millennium Way
Bracknell RG12 2XN
01344 458600
www.macromedia.com/uk/
Web graphics and design
PRESS: *smowatt@macromedia.com*

Microsoft UK
Microsoft Campus
Thames Valley Park
Reading, Berkshire RG6 1WG
0870 601 0100
www.microsoft.com/uk
Software house
PRESS: *0870 207 7377*
ukprteam@microsoft.com

Network Associates
227 Bath Road
Slough, Berkshire SL1 5PP
01753 217500
www.mcafee.com
Anti-virus

RealNetworks
2nd Floor, 32 Brook Street
London W1K 5DL
020 7290 1206
www.real.co.uk
Audio and video
PRESS: *public_relations@real.com*

Symantec UK
Hines Meadow, St Cloud Way
Maidenhead, Berkshire SL6 8XB
01628 592 222
www.symantec.com
Information security provider
PRESS: *01628 592365*

Main ISPs

AOL UK
80 Hammersmith Road
London W14 8UD
020 7348 8000
www.aol.co.uk
PRESS: *UKMediaOffice@aol.com*

British Telecom
BT Centre, 81 Newgate Street
London EC1A 7AJ
020 7356 5000
www.bt.com
PRESS: *020 7356 5000*

Claranet UK
21 Southampton Row
London WC1B 5HA
020 7685 8310
info@clara.net
www.clara.net
PRESS: *020 7685 8019*

Demon
322 Regents Park Road
Finchley, London N3 2QQ
0845 272 0666
enquiries@demon.net
www.demon.net

Easynet
1 Brick Lane, London E1 6PU
020 7900 4444
business@uk.Easynet.net
www.easynet.net

Entanet
Stafford Park 6, Telford
Shropshire TF3 3AT
0870 770 9588
www.enta.net
PRESS: *0870 770 4996*

Nildram
1 Triangle Business Park
Stoke Mandeville
Buckinghamshire HP22 5BD
0800 197 1490
info@nildram.net
www.nildram.net

NTL UK
NTL House
Bartley Wood Business Park
Hook, Hampshire RG27 9UP
01256 752000
www.ntl.com
PRESS: *020 7466 5000*

One.Tel
3rd Floor, Building 1
Chiswick Park High Road
London W4 5BY
020 7181 9991
www.onetel.co.uk

Pipex
Pipex House, 4 Falcon Gate
Shire Park
Welwyn Garden City AL7 1TW
0845 077 2537
www.pipex.co.uk

PlusNet Technologies
Technology Building
Terry Street, Sheffield S9 2BU
0845 140 0200
www.Plus.net

Surfanytime
38 Queen Street, Glasgow G1 3DX
0870 141 7113
www.surfanytime.co.uk

Telewest
Export House, Cawsey Road
Woking, Surrey GU21 6QX
01483 750900
www.telewest.co.uk
PRESS: *020 7299 5888*

Tiscali UK
20 Broadwick Street
London W1F 8HT
020 7087 2000
www.tiscali.co.uk

Virgin.net
The Communications Building
48 Leicester Square
London WC2H 7LT
www.virgin.net
PRESS: *020 7907 7803*

Vispa Internet
The Courtyard, 160a Moss Lane
Altrincham, Cheshire WA15 8AU
0870 1624 888
info@vispa.net
www.vispa.co.uk

Wanadoo
Nerulam Point, Station Way
St Albans AL1 5HE
0870 909 0666
www.wanadoo.co.uk
PRESS: *020 7553 7566*
mediaqueries@freeserve.com

Yahoo! UK
10 Ebury Bridge Road
London SW1W 8PZ
020 7808 4000
agency@uk.yahoo-inc.com
www.yahoo.co.uk
PRESS: *020 7808 4242*

Main telecoms companies

British Telecom
BT Centre, 81 Newgate Street
PO Box 163, London EC1A 7AJ
020 7356 5000
www.bt.com
PRESS: *020 7356 5000*

Cable and Wireless
Lakeside House, Cain Road
Bracknell, Berks RG12 1XL
01908 845000
peter.eustace@cw.com
www.cableandwireless.co.uk

Colt Communications
Beaufort House, 15 St Botolph Street
London EC3A 7QN
020 7863 5000
info@colt.net
www.colt.co.uk

Energis
Energis House, Forbury Road
Reading, Berkshire RG1 3JH
020 7206 5555
www.energis.co.uk

Hutchinson 3G UK
3 Media Centre, 27b Floral Street
Covent Garden, London WC2E 9DP
0870 733 0333
www.three.co.uk
PRESS: *01628 765000*

Kingston Communications
Carr Lane
Kingston upon Hull HU1 3RE
01482 602000
www.kcom.com
PRESS: *01482 602711*

MCI
Reading International Business Park
Basingstoke Road
Reading, Berkshire RG2 6DA
0118 905 5000
www.mci.com
PRESS: *ukpressoffice@mci.com*

NTL UK
NTL House
Bartley Wood Business Park
Hook, Hampshire RG27 9UP
01256 752000
www.ntl.com
PRESS: *020 7466 5000*

O2
Wellington Street, Slough SL1 1YP
0113 272 2000
www.o2.com
PRESS: *01753 628402*

Orange
St James Court, Great Park Road
Almondsbury, Bristol BS32 4QJ
0870 376 8888
www.orange.co.uk
PRESS: *020 7984 2000*

Telewest
Export House, Cawsey Road
Woking, Surrey TU21 6QX
01483 750900
www.telewest.co.uk
PRESS: *020 7299 5888*

Thus
1/2 Berkley Square
99 Berkley Street, Glasgow G3 7HR
0141 567 1234
www.thus.net

T-Mobile (UK)
Hatfield Business Park
Hatfield, Hertfordshire AL10 9BW
01707 315000
www.t-mobile.co.uk
PRESS: *07017 150150*

Virgin Mobile
5th Floor, Communication Building
48 Leicester Square
London WC2H 7LT
020 7484 4300
www.virginmobile.com

Vodafone
Vodafone House, The Connection
Newbury, Berkshire RG14 2FN
0700 050 0100
www.vodafone.co.uk
PRESS: *07000 500100*
press.office@vodafone.com

UK news online

Ananova
PO Box 36, Leeds LS11 9YJ
0113 367 4600
www.ananova.com

Bbc.co.uk
TV Centre, Wood Lane
London W12 7RJ
020 8743 8000
www.bbc.co.uk

Belfast Telegraph
Independent News and Media
(Northern Ireland)
Internet Department
124–144 Royal Avenue
Belfast BT1 1EB
028 9026 4000
www.belfasttelegraph.co.uk

FT.com
One Southwark Bridge
London SE1 9HL
020 7873 3000
joanna.manning-cooper@ft.com
www.ft.com
PRESS: *020 787 34447*

Guardian Unlimited
119 Farringdon Road
London EC1R 3ER
020 7278 2332
editor@guardianunlimited.co.uk
www.guardian.co.uk
PRESS: *020 7239 9818*

The Independent
Independent House
191 Marsh Wall, London E14 9RS
020 7005 2000
www.independent.co.uk

ITV News
200 Grays Inn Road
London WC1X 8X2
editor@itn.co.uk
www.itv.com/news

Online Mirror
MGN, 1 Canada Square
Canary Wharf, London E14 5AP
020 7293 3000
mirrornews@mgn.co.uk
www.mirror.co.uk
PRESS: *020 7293 3222*

Reuters
30 The Reuters Building
South Colonnade, Canary Wharf
London E14 5EP
020 7250 1122
www.reuters.co.uk
PRESS: *020 7542 7457*

The Scotsman
Barclay House, 108 Holyrood Road
Edinburgh EH8 8AS
0131 620 8620
enquiries@scotsman.com
www.scotsman.com
PRESS: *0131 620 8507*

Sky News
Grant Way, Isleworth TW7 5QD
0870 240 3000
www.sky.com/skynews

The Sun Online
Level 6, 1 Virginia Street
London E98 1SN
020 7782 4000
corporate.info@the-sun.co.uk
www.thesun.co.uk

Telegraph Online
1 Canada Square
Canary Wharf, London E14 5DT
020 7538 5000
corporate.affairs@telegraph.co.uk
www.telegraph.co.uk

The Times
1 Pennington Street
Wapping, London E98 1TA
020 7782 5000
online.editor@thetimes.co.uk
www.timesonline.co.uk

High-profile web-only publishers

Handbag.com
151 Oxford Street, London W1D 2JG
editor@handbag.com
www.handbag.com
Women's consumer site

Motley Fool UK
2nd Floor, Lasenby House
32 Kingly Street
London W1B 5QQ
020 7025 5500
UKWebFool@fool.co.uk
www.fool.co.uk
Personal finance

MyVillage
105 Ladbroke Grove
London W11 1PG
020 7792 0624
info@myvillage.co.uk
www.myvillage.co.uk
Leisure guide

Popbitch
hello@popbitch.com
www.popbitch.com
Celeb gossip email and forum

Salon.com
101 Spear Street, Suite 203
San Francisco, CA 94105, USA
00 1 415 645 9200
www.salon.com
US online magazine

Slate
251 West 57th Street, 19th Floor
New York, NY 10019-1894, USA
00 1 212 445 5330
www.slate.com
US online magazine
PRESS: *press@slate.com*

Upmystreet.com
10th Floor, Portland House
Stag Place, London SW1E 5BH
020 7802 2992
content@upmystreet.com
www.upmystreet.com
Local information
PRESS: *pr@upmystreet.com*

Wikipedia
204 37th Ave North, #330
St Petersburg, FL 33704, USA
00 1 310 474 3223
board@wikimedia.org
www.wikipedia.org
User-edited encyclopaedia
PRESS: *00 1 727 231 0101*

High-profile online traders

Major traders

Amazon UK
Patriot Court 1–9, The Grove
Slough, Berkshire SL1 1QP
www.amazon.co.uk
Books
PRESS: *020 8636 9280*

eBay International
Helvetiastrasse 15/17, 3005 Bern
Switzerland
www.ebay.co.uk
Online marketplace
PRESS: *ebay@77pr.co.uk*

Travel

Ebookers
25 Farringdon Street
London EC4A 4AB
0870 010 7000
www.ebookers.com
PRESS: *020 7958 3784*

Expedia UK
7 Soho Square, London W1D 3QB
020 7019 2000
www.expedia.co.uk
PRESS: *08450 707615*
expediapressoffice@expedia.co.uk

Lastminute.com
Holiday Autos House, Pembroke
Broadway, Canberry GU15 3XD
0871 222 3200
www.lastminute.com

Opodo
Waterfront, Hammersmith
Embankment, London W6 9RU
0870 352 5000
www.opodo.com
www.opodo.co.uk

Teletextholidays.co.uk
Building 10, Chiswick Park
566 Chiswick High Road
London W4 5TS
0870 731 3000
www.teletextholidays.co.uk

Travelocity UK
Western House, Cambridge Road
Stansted, Essex CM24 8BZ
0870 111 7061
www.travelocity.co.uk

Money

Egg
1 Waterhouse Square
138–142 Holborn
London EC1N 2NA
020 7526 2500
www.egg.com
PRESS: *020 7526 2600*
prteam@egg.com

First Direct
40 Wakefield Road, Leeds LS98 1FD
0113 276 6100
www.firstdirect.com
PRESS: *020 7992 1571*

Intelligent Finance
8 Lockside Ave, Edinburgh Park
South Gyle, Edinburgh EH12 9DJ
www.if.com
PRESS: *0131 658 2301*

Interactive Investor
Dashwood House
69 Old Broad Street
London EC2M 1QS
0845 8800 267
www.iii.co.uk
PRESS: *07802 634 695*

Smile
Balloon Street, Manchester M60 4EP
www.smile.co.uk
PRESS: *0161 8295397*

Music

Intomusic.co.uk
PO Box 41071, London SW2 1WT
020 8676 4850
info@intomusic.co.uk
www.intomusic.co.uk/
Independent and alternative music

iTunes UK
iTunes SARL, 8–10 Rue Mathias
Hardt, L-1717 Luxembourg
0800 039 1010
www.apple.com/uk/itunes/
Apple's digital jukebox and music store
PRESS: *appleuk.pr@euro.apple.com*

Napster
20/22 Bedford Row
London WC1R 4JS
www.napster.co.uk
Subscription service
PRESS: *media@napster.co.uk*

OD2
Bush House, 72 Prince Street
Bristol BS1 4QD
0117 910 0150
info@ondemanddistribution.com
www.ondemanddistribution.com
Handles distribution for major online music stores including Big Noise Music, HMV, MSN, MyCokeMusic, Tiscali and Virgin

Playlouder
8–10 Rhoda Street, London E2 7EF
www.playlouder.com
PRESS: *media@playlouder.com*

Sony Connect
Sony, 550 Madison Avenue
New York, NY 10022, USA
00 1 212 833 8000
www.connect-europe.com
Music from all major labels and many indies
PRESS: *01932 816417*

Streets Online
243 Blyth Road, Hayes
Middlesex UB3 1DN
0845 6018330
digital@streetsonline.co.uk
www.streetsonline.co.uk
Owned by Woolworths

Trax2Burn
Proactive, Suite 214
Homelife House, 26–32 Oxford Road
Bournemouth BH8 8EZ
01202 315333
www.trax2burn.com
Three house music labels: End Recordings, Underwater and FatBoy Slim's Southern Fried

Wippit
116 Gloucester Place
London W1U 6HZ
0870 737 1100
info@wippit.com
www.wippit.com
Artists from indie labels

New media agencies

3T Productions
0161 492 1400
queries@3t.co.uk
www.3t.co.uk

Abacus e-media
London: 020 7549 2500
Portsmouth: 023 9289 3600
info@abacusemedia.com
www.abacusemedia.com

Agency Republic
020 7942 0000
chat@agencyrepublic.com
www.agencyrepublic.com/home.asp

AKQA
020 7494 9200
info@akqa.com
www.akqa.com

Amaze
0870 2401700
generalenquiries@amaze.com
www.amaze.com

Arnold Interactive
020 7908 2700
susanna.hurley@ailondon.co.uk
www.ailondon.co.uk

Aspect Group
020 7504 6900
contactus@lbicon.co.uk
www.aspectgroup.co.uk

Babel Media
01273 764100
info@babelmedia.com
www.babelmedia.com

BBC Broadcast
020 8008 0080
www.bbcbroadcast.com

Big Picture Interactive
020 7438 4176
simon@bigpictureblog.com
www.bigpictureblog.com

Bostock and Pollitt
020 7379 6709
david@bostockandpollitt.com
www.bostockandpollitt.com

Brave Marketing
07768 868 697
info@redskin7.com
http://bravemarketing.com

Broadband Communications
0115 959 6455
advertising@broadband.co.uk
www.broadband.co.uk

Carlson Digital
020 8875 0875
www.carlsonmarketing.co.uk

CMW Interactive
020 7224 4050
s-hanneberry@cww-uk.com
www.cmwinteractive.com

Complete Integrated Marketing Communications
020 7383 5300
general@complete.co.uk
www.complete.co.uk

Conchango
01784 222222
www.conchango.com

Corporem Global
01925 413 513
office@corporemglobal.com
www.corporemglobal.com

Craik Jones Digital
020 7734 1650
digital@craikjones.co.uk
www.digital.craikjones.co.uk

cScape
020 7689 8800
m.daniels@cscape.com
www.cscape.com

Dare Digital
020 7612 3600
us@daredigital.com
www.daredigital.com

Deal Group Media
020 7691 1880
www.dgm2.com

Detica
01483 442000
info@detica.comq
www.detica.com

Digit
020 7377 4000
info@digitlondon.com
www.digitlondon.com

Digital TMW
020 7349 4000
info@tmw.co.uk
www.tmw.co.uk

Digitas Europe
020 7494 6700
www.digitas.com

Digiterre
020 7381 7910
info@digiterre.com
www.digiterre.com

DNA
020 7907 4545
info@dna.co.uk
www.dna.co.uk

Dowcarter
London: 020 7689 1200
Edinburgh: 0131 556 1172
jeremy.crowe@dowcarter.com
www.dowcarter.com

Draft London
020 7589 0800
Claire.Wright@draftlondon.com
www.draftlondon.com

DVA
01256 882032
info@dva.co.uk
www.dva.co.uk

E3 Media
0117 9021333
info@E3MEDIA.co.uk
www.e3media.co.uk

EHS Brann
020 7017 1000
www.ehs.co.uk

**Euro RSCG Wnek Gosper
Interaction**
020 7240 4111
info-interaction@eurorscg.com
www.eurorscginteraction.co.uk

Freestyle New Media Group
01926 652832
info@fsnm.co.uk
www.fsnm.co.uk

Global Beach
020 7384 1188
info@globalbeach.com
www.globalbeach.com

Glue London
020 7739 2345
www.gluelondon.com

Good Technology
020 7299 7000
almira.mohamed@
    goodtechnology.com
www.goodtechnology.com

GT Network
01476 514687
info@gtns.co.uk
www.gtns.net

Gurus
023 80231219
info@gurumedia.net
www.gurumedia.net

Haygarth Direct
020 8971 3300
stephen.m@haygarth.co.uk
www.haygarth.co.uk

The Hub Communications
020 8560 9222
www.thehub.co.uk

Hyperlink Interactive
020 7339 8600
info@hyperlink-interactive.co.uk
www.hyperlink-interactive.co.uk

Incepta Online
020 7282 2800
contact@inceptaonline.com
www.inceptaonline.com

Informa Telecoms & Media
020 7017 4852
Kathryn.Bushnell@informa.com
www.arcgroup.com

Intercea
0118 916 9900
www.intercea.co.uk

Interesource New Media
020 7613 8200
www.interesource.com

Ioko365
01904 438 000
info@ioko.com
www.ioko.com

IR Group
020 7436 3140
mark.hill@the-group.net
www.ir-group.com

IS Solutions
01932 893333
www.issolutions.co.uk

iTouch
020 7613 6000
info@itouch.co.uk
www.itouch.co.uk

itraffic
020 7964 8500
www.itraffic.com

Javelin Group
020 7964 8200
info@javelingroup.com
www.javelingroup.com

Lateral
020 7613 4449
www.lateral.net

Lawton eMarketing
023 8082 8522
steve.sponder@lawton.co.uk
www.lawtonemarketing.com

LB Icon (UK)
020 7504 6900
contactus@lbicon.co.uk
www.lbicon.co.uk

Lightmaker Group
01892 615015
sales@lightmaker.com
www.lightmaker.com

Lightmaker Manchester
0161 834 9889
matt.farrar@lightmaker.com
www.lightmaker.com

McCann-i
01625 822 200
info@mccann-i.com
www.mccann-i.com

M-Corp
01425 477766
enquiries@m-corp.com
www.m-corp.com

MediaVest IP
020 7751 1661
www.mediavest.co.uk

MitchellConnerSearson Group
020 7420 7991
london@choosemcs.co.uk
www.mitchellconnersearson.com

Modem Media
020 7874 9400
rmilano@modemmedia.com
www.modemmedia.com

Ogilvy Interactive
020 7345 3000
www.ogilvy.com

Oyster Partners
020 7446 7500
reception@oyster.com
www.oyster.co.uk

PoulterNet
0113 383 4200
enquiries@poulternet.com
www.poulternet.com

Profero
020 7387 2000
contact@profero.com
www.profero.com

Proximity London
020 7298 1000
info@proximitylondon.com
www.chc.co.uk

Reading Room
020 7025 1800
info@readingroom.com
www.readingroom.com

Realise
020 7743 7150
www.realise.com

Recreate Solutions
020 8233 2916
contactus@recreatesolutions.com
www.recreatesolutions.com

Rufus Leonard
020 7404 4490
www.rufusleonard.com

Sapient
020 7786 4500
eu_sales@sapient.com
www.sapient.co.uk

SBI Framfab
020 7071 6300
info.uk@framfab.com
www.framfab.com

Sift Group
0117 915 9600
service@sift.co.uk
www.sift.co.uk

Syzygy UK
020 7460 4080
london@syzygy.net
www.syzygy.net

Tangozebra
020 7535 9850
info@tangozebra.com
www.tangozebra.com

TBG
020 7428 6650
info@tbgltd.co.uk
www.tbgltd.co.uk

TBWA\GGT
020 7440 1100
info@tequila-uk.com
www.tequila-uk.com

Them
020 8392 6868
talktous@themlondon.com
www.themlondon.com
Formerly Head to Head

Tribal DDB
020 7258 4500
www.tribalddb.com

TVF Medical Communications
020 7837 3000
lynette.coetzee@tvf.co.uk
www.tvfcommunications.com

Urbandevcorp
07906 292373
info@urbandevcorp.com
www.urbandevcorp.com

Victoria Real
020 8222 4466
www.victoriareal.com

Wheel
London: 020 7348 1000
Glasgow: 0141 225 6560
www.wheel.co.uk

Wireless Information Network
01494 750500
businessdevelopment@winplc.com
www.winplc.com

Write Image
020 7959 5400
info@write-image.co.uk
www.write-image.com

XM London
020 7724 7228
xminfo@ccgxm.com
www.xmlondon.co.uk

Zentropy
020 7554 0500
aduncan@zentropypartners.com
www.zentropypartners.co.uk

All Response Media
020 7017 1450
www.allresponsemedia.com
www.digit-all.co.uk

Carat Interactive
020 7430 6320
alison.wilde@carat.com
www.carat.com

Cheeze
01473 236892
info@cheeze.com
www.cheeze.co.uk

i-level
020 7340 2700
oracle@i-level.com
www.i-level.com

Isobar UK
020 550 3284
info@isobarcommunications.com
www.isobarcommunications.com

MediaCom North
0161 839 6600
infomcr@mediacomuk.com
www.mediacomnorth.com

MediaVest Manchester
020 7190 8000
ecombe@uk.starcomww.com
www.mediavest.co.uk

Outrider
001 314 209 1005
contact.us@outrider.com
www.outrider.com

PHDiQ
020 7446 0555
callen@phd.co.uk
www.phd.co.uk

Profero
020 7387 2000
contact@profero.com
www.profero.co.uk

Quantum
020 7287 8768
info@quantum-media.co.uk
www.quantum-media.co.uk

Starcom Digital
020 7190 8000
ecombe@uk.starcomww.com
www.starcomww.co.uk

Tribal DDB
020 7258 4500
www.tribalddb.com

Unique Digital Marketing
020 7354 1235
hello@unique-digital.co.uk
www.unique-digital.co.uk

Zed
01923 815 913
design@zed.co.uk
www.zed.co.uk

3G Mobile
Informa Telecoms & Media
020 7017 5537
telecoms.enquiries@informa.com
www.informatm.com
Fortnightly. Editor: Gavin Patterson; news and features: Nick Lane; chief sub: Charles Gordon

Computer Weekly
Reed Business Information
020 8652 3500
editorial@computerweekly.com
www.computerweekly.com
Weekly. Editor: Hooman Bassirian; news and features: Mike Simons; production: Stuart Nissen

Computing
VNU Business Publications
020 7316 9000
katrina_attard@vnu.co.uk
www.computing.vnu.co.uk
Weekly. Editor: Toby Walt; news, features and production: Katrina Attard

EI magazine
Ark Publishing
020 8785 2700
publishing@art-group.com
www.eimagazine.com
Monthly. Editor: Simon Lelic; features and production: Katy Brown

IT Europa
IT BPL
01895 454458
contact@ITEuropa.com
www.ITEuropa.com
20pa. Editor: Andrew Seymour

IT Week
VNU Business Publications
020 7316 9000
itweek_letters@vnu.co.uk
www.itweek.co.uk
Weekly. Editor: Toby Walt; news, features and production: Katrina Attard

Journalism.co.uk
Mousetrap Media, 68 Middle Street
Brighton BN1 1AL
01273 384293
info@journalism.co.uk
www.journalism.co.uk
Website. Editor/publisher: John Thompson; news: Jemima Kiss

NetImperative
020 7071 8707
editorial@netimperative.com
www.netimperative.com
Email and online news service, daily and weekly newsletters
Editor: Mike Butcher

New Media Age
Centaur Communications
020 7970 4000
www.nma.co.uk
Weekly. Editor: Michael Nutely; features: Justin Pearson; production: George Stewart

Contacts : **New media**

241

Online Journalism Review
Annenberg School of Journalism
001 213 740 0948
rniles@usc.edu
www.ojr.org
Online. Publisher: Geoffrey Cowan;
editor: Robert Niles

The Online Reporter
Rider Research
01280 820560
info@riderresearch.com
www.riderresearch.com
Weekly. Editor: Charles Hall

The Register
020 7733 3021
press.releases@theregister.co.uk
www.theregister.co.uk
Website. Editor-in-chief: Drew Cullen;
editor: Joe Fay

Revolution
Haymarket Business Publications
020 8267 4947
revolution.ads@haynet.com
www.revolutionmagazine.com
Monthly. Editor: Philip Smith; news:
Emma Rigby; features: Philip Buxton;
art editor: David Grant; production:
Vic Johnstone

VNUnet.com
VNU Publications
020 7316 9000
newseditor@vnunet.com
www.vnunet.com
Online. Editor: Robert Jaques; chief
sub: Francis Abberley

Wired
001 415 276 8400
www.wired.com
Monthly. Managing editor: Marty
Cortinas; senior reporter: Kim Zetter;
content editor: Leander Kahney; copy
chief: Tony Long; production manager:
Jeremy Barna

World Telemedia
0870 7327 327
info@worldtelemedia.co.uk
www.worldtelemedia.co.uk/wtmag.htm
Quarterly. Publisher: Toby Padgham;
editor: Paul Skeldon

ZDNet UK and Silicon.com
CNet Networks
020 7903 6800
www.cnet.com
Online. Editors: Matt Loney, Tony
Hallett; news: Graham Weirdon

New media associations

Association of Freelance Internet Designers
a.carson@uku.co.uk
www.afid.net

Association of Online Publishers (AOP)
Queens House, 28 Kingsway
London WC2B 6JR
020 7400 7510
alex.white@ukaop.org.uk

British Interactive Media Association
Briarlea House, Southend Road
South Green, Billericay CM11 2PR
01277 658107
info@bima.co.uk
www.bima.co.uk

British Internet Publishers Alliance (BIPA)
49 Park Town, Oxford OX2 6SL
01865 310732
angela.mills@wade.uk.net
www.bipa.co.uk

British Web Design and Marketing Association
PO Box 3227, London NW9 9LX
020 8204 2474
info@bwdma.co.uk
www.bwdma.co.uk

Entertainment and Leisure Software Publishers Association
167 Wardour Street
London W1F 8WL
020 7534 0580
info@elspa.com
www.elspa.com
Trade association for games industry

HTML Writers Guild/ International Webmasters Association (IWA-HWG)
119 E Union Street, Suite F
Pasadena, CA 91103 USA
help@iwanet.org
www.hwg.org/
Training body for web designers

Internet Advertising Bureau
Adam House, 7–10 Adam Street
Strand, London WC2N 6AA
Press: 020 7886 8282
info@iabuk.net
www.iabuk.net

Internet Corporation for Assigned Names and Numbers (ICANN)
4676 Admiralty Way, Suite 330
Marina del Rey
CA 90292-6601, USA
00 1 310 823 9358
icann@icann.org
www.icann.org

Internet Service Providers Association
23 Palace Street
London SW1E 5HW
020 7233 7234
admin@ispa.org.uk
www.ifpa.org.uk

Internet Watch Foundation
East View, 5 Coles Lane
Oakington, Cambridge CB4 5BA
01223 237 700
admin@iwf.org.uk
www.iwf.org.uk
Operate hotline for public to report
inadvertent exposure to illegal internet
content

London Internet Exchange (Linx)
2nd Floor, Geneva House
3 Park Road
Peterborough PE1 2UX
Press: 01733 207700
info@linx.net
www.linx.net

Global media

It's time to unfurl the star-spangled banner. Now that News Corporation has reincorporated itself from Australia to the land of the free, and with the stock of new media companies such as Yahoo! and Google rising, our global media table shows that, at the end of June 2005, nine of the world's biggest 10 media companies were based in the US. The other company, France's Vivendi Universal, came in tenth.

The rewards for being at the top of the media pile are increasing. Microsoft, Google and Yahoo! all turned increased profits in 2004; see the new media section (page 231) for that. Of the traditional groups, **Time Warner** made £1.78bn in 2004, a rise of 27% – and also, despite getting its fingers burned over the 2000 merger with AOL, holds 5m shares in Google. **Comcast**'s operating income was up 48% to £1.64bn. **Viacom**, though, lost £7.3bn – largely thanks to a £10bn charge for writing down the value of its radio and outdoor businesses. In June 2005 the company announced plans to spin off its radio and outdoor businesses into a company called CBS Corp, which will also include the CBS television network, TV production, Simon & Schuster publishing and Paramount theme parks. The move will see Viacom fall out of the global media top 10.

The boardroom wrangles at **Walt Disney** have continued to make headlines. The embattled CEO, Michael Eisner, is set to leave the company in September 2005; Robert Iger was named as his replacement. But in May 2005 two shareholders, Roy Disney and Stanley Gold, sued the company over the selection process; a truce was not agreed until July 2005.

News Corporation made £1.8bn in 2004; it was revealed in September 2004 that Rupert Murdoch earned £9.5m personally from the company in 2003, up 42% on the previous year. In December, though,

Top 10 global media companies

	(Based on market capitalisation at June 30 2005)		
1	General Electric	£208.5bn	80% stake in NBC Universal; significant non–media interests
2	Microsoft	£151.0bn	
3	Google	£45.8bn	
4	Time Warner	£44.0bn	Owns HBO, CNN, Time, Warner Books, AOL
5	Comcast	about £38bn	Owns E! entertainment, Golf Channel
6	Viacom	£29.4bn	Owns CBS, MTV, Nickelodeon, Simon & Schuster, outdoor advertising
7	Walt Disney	£29.0bn	Owns ABC, several US papers, Disney channels, Miramax, theme parks
8	News Corporation	£27.3bn	Owns BSkyB, The Times, The Sun, HarperCollins, DirecTV (US), Star TV (Asia)
9	Yahoo!	£27.2bn	
10	Vivendi Universal	£20.4bn	20% stake in NBC Universal

the Liberty Media boss, John Malone, struck a deal to increase his stake in the company to 17% – leading Murdoch to propose a "poison pill" to ensure a family succession. Under the terms of the move, NewsCorp shareholders would be able to buy new shares at half price if any person or group took a 15% stake in the company. Meanwhile, in January 2005, NewsCorp announced its intention to buy out minority shareholders in the Fox Entertainment Group it already controls.

Vivendi Universal, the French media group, reaped the benefits of selling off its Vivendi Universal Entertainment arm to NBC. It made almost £519m in 2004, compared with a £784m loss in 2003.

World Press Freedom Index 2004 – Reporters Sans Frontières		
Rank / Country	Index	2003 rank and index
Top of the table		
1 Denmark	0.50	(5=, 1.0)
– Finland	0.50	(1=, 0.5)
– Iceland	0.50	(1=, 0.5)
– Ireland	0.50	(17=, 2.83)
– Netherlands	0.50	(1=, 0.5)
– Norway	0.50	(1=, 0.5)
– Slovakia	0.50	(12=, 2.5)
– Switzerland	0.50	(12=, 2.5)
9 New Zealand	0.67	(17=, 2.83)
10 Latvia	1.00	(11, 2.25)
...		
22= US (own territory)	4.00	(31=, 6.0)
...		
28= UK	6.00	(27, 4.25)
...		
36= Israel (own territory)	8.00	(44, 8.0)
Bottom of the table		
108 US (in Iraq)	36.00	(135, 41.0)
...		
115= Israel (occupied territories)	37.50	(146, 49.0)
...		
127 Palestinian Authority	43.17	(130, 39.25)
...		
140 Russia	51.38	(148. 49.5)
...		
148 Iraq	58.45	(124, 37.5)
...		
155= Zimbabwe	67.50	(141, 41.5)
...		
158 Iran	78.30	(160, 89.33)
159 Saudi Arabia	79.17	(156, 71.5)
160 Nepal	84.00	(150, 51.5)
161 Vietnam	86.88	(159, 89.17)
162 China	92.33	(161, 91.25)
163 Eritrea	93.25	(162, 91.5)
164 Turkmenistan	99.83	(158, 82.8)
165 Burma	103.63	(164, 95.5)
166 Cuba	106.83	(165, 97.83)
167 North Korea	107.50	(166 and last, 99.50)

Source: Reporters Sans Frontières. Index drawn up by asking journalists, researchers and legal experts to answer 50 questions about press freedom, covering issues such as murders or arrests of journalists, censorship, pressure, state monopolies in various fields, punishment of press law offences and regulation

How the Guardian reported the unmasking of Deep Throat

Global journalism

Perhaps the biggest news story in global journalism was the news that "Deep Throat", the anonymous source in the Washington Post's coverage of the 1972 Watergate scandal that brought down the Nixon presidency, had finally been exposed. Mark Felt, who was second-in-command at the FBI at the time, revealed his secret to Vanity Fair magazine on May 31, 2005, at the age of 91.

The revelation was somewhat embarrassing for William Gaines, from the department of journalism at the University of Illinois, who over 12 semesters had set his investigative journalism students the task of working out who Deep Throat was – and had concluded on www.deepthroatuncovered.com that the anonymous source was Fred Fielding. "We were wrong," the site reads now.

In October 2004, **Reporters Sans Frontières** published its third annual index of world press freedom, based on a survey of journalists (see table). The table reminded the world that whereas in some countries, freedom to speak and publish is an alienable human right, in other countries it barely exists at all. East Asia and the Middle East emerged as the parts of the world where freedom of the press is threatened most.

In May 2005, the organisation named 2004 "a year of mourning" after reporting that 53 journalists were killed around the world in the course of their job. It was the highest number of deaths since 1955. The International Federation of Journalists reported an even higher figure, saying 129 media staff – the highest on record – were killed doing their jobs in 2004.

Iraq was the deadliest country for journalists: 19 journalists and 12 of their assistants killed there in 2004, and more than a dozen kidnapped. Over the past five years, said the Committee to Protect Journalists, the Philippines, Colombia, Bangladesh and Russia joined Iraq as the most dangerous countries to work in. The IFJ said that those responsible for killing media workers are only half as likely to be caught as burglars in London.

Iraq and the Middle East

The uncomfortable relationship between the **media and the military** in Iraq has grown little clearer, with each blaming the other when things went wrong. Cause celebre for journalists was the killing of two reporters after US troops fired on the Palestine hotel during the 2003 Iraq war: but in November 2004 a US military report concluded that "no fault or negligence" could be ascribed to its soldiers.

Reporters Sans Frontières criticised that investigation, saying it was "extremely disappointed". But in February 2005, CNN news executive Eason Jordan went too far when he said that US forces "targeted" journalists in Iraq; after bloggers reported his comments, he resigned. Jordan later clarified his remarks: "The US military has killed roughly a dozen journalists and in many of those cases journalists were fired upon directly. Now did those soldiers firing their weapons know they were shooting at journalists, per se? No, I have no reason to believe that," he told BBC Radio 4's Today programme.

But according to General Sir Michael Walker, Britain's chief of defence staff, the military is also at risk from journalists. After five members of the Black Watch were killed during a mission to US-controlled areas of Iraq, Sir Michael remarked on BBC2's Newsnight that media coverage of the soldiers could have prompted insurgents to "meet us

with something like a bomb". He added: "And I'm certain, too, that the media coverage would have made it easier for anybody who wanted to conduct those attacks to do so."

The fragile status of the Arabic news channel **al-Jazeera** has also been the matter of much debate. The broadcaster's offices in Baghdad were closed down in September 2004 by Iraq's interim government, a ban that held after the country's elections in spring 2005. More than 20 al-Jazeera journalists had been arrested and jailed by US forces in Iraq by July 2005, and one was killed after a US tank fired a shell at its Baghdad office in 2003. In March 2005, Tayseer Allouni, a Syrian-born al-Jazeera journalist, was placed under house arrest in Spain, where he faced terrorism-related charges.

Reporters Sans Frontières protested in January against what it called the "persistent harassment" of the channel by Arab countries, after the defence minister Hazem Shaalan called al-Jazeera a "terrorist channel".

Yet the channel is changing. In March 2005, Al Antsey and Nick Walshe, formerly foreign news executives at ITN, were appointed to senior roles on al Jazeera's English-language service, for which some 200 journalists are expected to be hired. And the Gulf state of Qatar, which subsidises al-Jazeera, is thought to be considering privatising the channel – because a de facto advertising boycott by Arab countries makes it a drain on the public purse.

It does seem that al-Jazeera will face some competition. The BBC said in June 2004 that it was in talks about launching an Arabic channel of its own.

China – the new frontier

As China opens up to global capitalism – and with the Beijing Olympics just two years away – the rush to profit from its emerging media industry is on. Sir Martin Sorrell, the boss of the advertising supergroup WPP, told a 2005 conference in Beijing that China's ad market – already worth £13bn – would become the world's second largest by 2008. But with the country languishing 162nd out of 167 countries in Reporters Sans Frontières' press freedom index in 2004, the clash between money and civil liberties looks set to be a loud one.

In November 2004, the country relaxed media ownership rules to allow joint media ventures between overseas and licensed Chinese companies – although it later said that would be limited to one venture per company. In summer 2005 BBC Worldwide visited China with plans for a channel there; while in June it was announced that the Condé Nast executive James Woolhouse was relocating to Hong Kong amid plans to launch a Chinese Vogue.

It is China's regulation of the internet, though, that has caused most controversy. It is thought that China operates an internet police force with a staff of many thousands, operating a sophisticated filter system triggered by words such as "democracy"; and in June 2005 authorities announced that websites had to register with the government or be closed down and face a fine. Meanwhile, civil liberties groups have condemned global internet companies for toeing Beijing's line: Microsoft operates a software package that prevents bloggers from using politically sensitive words on its Chinese websites; and Reporters Sans Frontières criticised both it and Yahoo! in 2005 for agreeing to "self-censorship". Google, for its part, opened an office in China in May 2005.

A very corporate dynasty **Chris Alden**

It is a drama fit for any one of Sky Digital's 375 channels. A wealthy patriarch reaches his mid-70s; as he has been blessed with many children, his thoughts turn to the future. He looks at his sons and daughters. Which of you, he thinks, has the wisdom to rule my empire? Or will an outsider usurp the family line?

The story is timeless – but in 2005 it's the dilemma facing Rupert Murdoch, the chairman and chief executive of News Corporation, one of the biggest media companies in the world.

At the heart of the drama is Murdoch himself, who has said that he would like control of NewsCorp to remain within the family.

Murdoch built his business from the brink of extinction to a global operation worth £27bn, controlling some of the world's most famous news and pay-TV operations. But at 74 he is not getting any younger, and the markets want to see plans for a successor for when he steps aside.

At his side for years has been his eldest son, Lachlan Murdoch, groomed to succeed since he was appointed executive director at the age of 24. Lachlan went on to become chairman of Asian pay-TV company Star.

But it seems Lachlan has decided his destiny lies elsewhere. In August, he resigned as deputy chief operating officer (COO) to spend more time with his wife and baby daughter back in Sydney – a decision that his father said left him "disappointed".

At 33, Lachlan perhaps sees independent life more attractive than sitting in a New York office in the shadow of his father's power. If so, he follows his sister Elisabeth Murdoch, who is running her own London production company, Shine.

Lachlan's decision has caused feverish speculation about who will emerge as the pretender to the throne. Some say James Murdoch, the 32-year-old second son, is the man for the job: after a wobbly start,

he has impressed as chief executive of BSkyB. Others say Peter Chernin, News Corp's president and COO, is better-placed in the short term – as a kind of prince regent to James.

A few say the dynastic analogy is a distraction. Rupert Murdoch may want to see a son in charge of the family business, but the reality is that, in any company the size of NewsCorp, it is the markets and shareholders who will have the biggest say.

Look at the struggle it took to get James Murdoch installed as chief executive of BSkyB. Even though James had his father's backing, one in three shareholders still voted against the move.

There are also the rumours of rifts – denied within the family – over the possible roles of Grace and Chloe, his young children by his wife Wendi Deng.

But more important than rumours are the efforts by rival cable TV owner John Malone to increase his stake in NewsCorp – thwarted so far by Murdoch's "poison pill" move to dilute external shareholdings.

That move is being investigated by the Australian Securities and Investments Commission, it was reported in August 2005.

Malone is the chairman of Liberty Media; the thought that News Corporation might fall prey to a rival cable TV company would be anathema to the Murdoch clan.

In that light, an interview given to Bulletin magazine by Murdoch's mother, Dame Elisabeth Murdoch, is telling. She said Rupert might yet retire and hand over to a trusted aide if the time was right.

"If in the future it looked as though somebody else was better for that position, he would be very practical and accept it, and be grateful that there was somebody capable," she said.

They say our corporations are our new nation states. If that is true, then it is wise to remember that, in the western world at least, dynasty has had its day.

Global media

Global media Contacts

Global media groups

Bertelsmann
Carl-Bertelsmann-Strasse 270
33311 Gütersloh, Germany
00 49 5241 800
info@bertelsmann.de
www.bertelsmann.com
PRESS: *00 49 5241 802 466*
oliver.herrgesell@bertelsmann.com

Clear Channel
200 East Basse Road, San Antonio
TX 78209, USA
00 1 210 822 2828
www.clearchannel.com
PRESS:
    isacdollinger@clearchannel.com

ComCast
1500 Market Street, Philadelphia
PA 19102, USA
00 1 866 281 2100
www.comcast.com

Gannett
7950 Jones Branch Drive
McLean VA 22107, USA
00 1 703 854 6000
www.gannett.com
PRESS: *tjconnel@gannett.com*

NewsQuest Media Group
58 Church Street, Weybridge
Surrey KT13 8DP
01932 821212
enquiries@newsquestmedia.co.uk
www.newsquestmedia.co.uk

General Electric/NBC
3135 Easton Turnpike
Fairfield CT 06828, USA
00 1 203 373 2211
www.ge.com/en
PRESS: *gary.sheffer@ge.com*

NewsCorp
1211 Avenue of Americas
8th Floor, New York, NY 10036, USA
00 1 212 852 7017
www.newscorp.com
PRESS: *abutcher@newscorp.com*

Sony
550 Madison Avenue, New York
NY 10022, USA
00 1 212 833 8000
www.sony.com; www.sony.co.uk
PRESS: *press@eu.sony.com*

Time Warner
1 Time Warner Centre
58th and 8th Avenue, New York
NY 10019, USA
00 1 212 484 8000
www.timewarner.com

Viacom
1515 Broadway, New York
NY 10036, USA
00 1 212 258 6000
www.viacom.com
PRESS: *press@viacom.com*

Vivendi Universal
42 avenue de Friedland
75380 Paris Cedex 08, France
00 33 1 7171 1000
New York: 00 1 212 572 7000
www.vivendiuniversal.com
PRESS: *00 33 1 7171 1180*

Walt Disney
500 South Buena Vista Street
Burbank, CA 91521-9722, USA
00 1 818 560 1000
www.disney.go.com
PRESS: *kim.kerscher@dig.com*

Global news outlets

Ireland

Connacht Tribune
15 Market Street, Galway, Ireland
00 353 91 536222
www.connacht-tribune.ie
Weekly. Editor: John Cunningham;
features: Brendon Carol; head of
production: Declan Maguire

Cork Evening Echo
Academy Street
Cork
Ireland
00 353 21 480 2142
www.eveningecho.ie
Daily. Editor: Maurice Gubbins; news:
Emma Connolly; features: John Dolan

Daily Ireland
See page 77

Evening Herald
27–32 Talbot Street, Dublin 1
Ireland
00 353 1 705 5333
www.independent.ie
Daily. Editor: Gerry Oregan; news:
Philip Maloy; features: Dave Lawlor

Ireland on Sunday
50 City Quay, Dublin 2, Ireland
00 353 1 637 5800
Sunday. Editor: Ted Verity; news: Paul
John; features: Drury Cooper; head of
production: Ciaran O'Tuama

Irish Daily Star
62a Terenure Road North
Terenure, Dublin 6W, Ireland
00 353 1 490 1228
www.thestar.ie
Daily. Editor: Gerard Colon; news:
Michael O'Cain; features: Danny Smyth

Irish Examiner
Academy Street, Cork, Ireland
00 353 21 427 2722
www.examiner.ie
Daily. Editor: Jim Vaughan; news:
John O'Mahoney; features: Gill
Germogy

Irish Independent
27–32 Talbot Street, Dublin 1
Ireland
00 353 1 705 5333
www.independent.ie
Daily. Editor: Vincent Doyle; news:
Philip Dunne; features: Peter Carvosso

Irish Times
10–16 D'Olier Street, Dublin 2
Ireland
00 353 1 675 8000
www.ireland.com
Daily. Editor: Geraldine Kennedy;
news: John Maher; features: Shelia
Wayman

Kerryman
Clash, Tralee, County Kerry, Ireland
00 353 66 71 45500
www.kerryman.ie
Weekly. Editor: Declan Malone; news:
Diedre Walsh; features: Marisa Reidy

Leinster Leader
18/19 South Main Street
Naas, County Kildare, Ireland
00 353 45 897302
www.leinsterleader.ie
Weekly. Editor: Michael Sheenan;
features: Sylvia Pownall

Limerick Leader
54 O'Connell Street
Limerick, Ireland
00 353 61 214503/6
www.limerick-leader.ie
Weekly. Editor: Brendon Halligan;
news: Eugene Phelan

Limerick Post
Town Hall Centre, Rutland Street
Limerick, Ireland
00 353 61 413322
www.limerickpost.ie
Weekly. Editor: Billy Ryan; news: Clare
Doyle; features: Rose Rush

RTÉ
New Library Building, Donnybrook
Dublin 4, Ireland
00 353 1 208 3111
info@rte.ie
www.rte.ie
Irish national broadcaster. Press:
00 353 1 208 3434. Acqusitions and
drama: Sharon Brady; entertainment:
Dympna Clerkin; factual: Dervla
Keating; Fair City (soap): Tara O'Brian;
music, sport and young people: Richie
Ryan; news and current affairs:
Carolyn Fisher – all
firstname.lastname@rte.ie

Sunday Business Post
80 Harcourt Street, Dublin 2
Ireland
00 353 1 602 6000
www.sbpost.ie
Sunday. Editor: Cliff Taylor; news:
Gavin Daley; features: Fiona Neff;
head of production: Tom McHale

Sunday Independent
27–32 Talbot Street, Dublin 1
Ireland
00 353 1 705 5333
www.independent.ie
Sunday. Editor: Angus Faning; news:
Willy Kealy; features: Anne Harris

Sunday Tribune
15 Lower Baggot Street, Dublin 2
Ireland
00 353 1 631 4300
www.tribune.ie
Sunday. Editor: Noirin Hegarty; deputy
editor: Diarmuid Doyle; news: Olivia
Doyle; features: Lise Hand; head of
production: Paul Howe

Sunday World
27–32 Talbot Street, Dublin 1
Ireland
00 353 1 884 9000
www.sundayworld.com
Sunday. Editor: Colm McGinty; news:
John Donlon; features: Eamon Dillon;
head of production: John Noonan

TG4
Baile na hAbhann, Co na Gaillimhe
Ireland
00 353 91 505050
www.tg4.ie
Irish-language broadcaster. Director of
television: Alan Esslemont

Europe
- -
Corriere della Sera
28 via Solferino, Milano 20121, Italy
00 39 026 339
www.corriere.it
Italian daily. Editor: Paulo Mieli

Cyprus Mail
24 Vassiliou Voulgaroctonou Street
PO Box 21144, 1502 Nicosia,
Cyprus
00 357 22 818 585
editor@cyprus-mail.com
www.cyprus-mail.com
English-language daily.
Editor: Kosta Pavlowitch

Deutsche Welle
Public Broadcasting Service
Kurt-Schumacher-Str. 3
53113 Bonn, Germany
00 49 228 429 0
www.dw-world.de
German broadcaster. European focus.
Editor: Erik Bettermann

Diario de Noticias
Altzutzate 8, Polígono Industrial Areta
HUARTE-PAMPLONA, Portugal
00 351 948 33 25 33
dnot@dn.pt
www.noticiasdenavarra.com
Portuguese daily. Editor: Pablo Munoz

EuroNews
BP 161, 60 Chemin de Mouilles
69131 Lyon Ecully, France
00 33 4 7218 8000
info@euronews.net
www.euronews.net
Pan-European TV news

Le Figaro
37 rue du Louvre
75002 Paris, France
00 33 1 4221 6200
www.lefigaro.fr
Rightwing quality daily

Frankfurter Allgemeine Zeitung
Hellerhofstraße 2-4
60327 Frankfurt am Main
Germany
00 49 1805 810 811
KaiN.Pritzsche @pri
www.faz.net
Right-leaning daily.
Editor: Kai N. Pritzsche

Gazeta Wyborcza
Szewska, 5
31009 Krakow, Poland
00 48 12 629 5000
www.gazeta.pl
Poland's most popular daily

International Herald Tribune
6 bis, rue des Graviers
92521 Neuilly Cedex, France
00 33 1 4143 9322
iht@iht.com
www.iht.com
Editor: Alison Smale

Kathimerini
D Falireos & E Makariou St 2
185-47 N Faliron, Piraeus, Greece
00 30 210 480 8000
editor@ekathimerini.com
www.ekathimerini.com
English-language daily.
Editor: Nikos Konstandaras

Libération
11, rue Béranger
75154 Paris Cedex 03, France
00 33 1 42 76 17 89
www.libe.com
Left-leaning quality daily.
Editor: Antoine de Grudemar

Le Monde
80 Boulevard Auguste Blanqui
75013 Paris, France
00 33 1 5728 2000
mediateur@lemonde.fr
www.lemonde.fr
France's bestselling quality daily.
Editor: Gerrard Courtoes

Moscow Times
Ulitsa Vyborgskaya 16, Bldg 4
125212 Moscow, Russia
00 7 095 937 3399
editors@themoscowtimes.com
www.moscowtimes.ru
Respected English-language daily.
Editor: Lynn Berry

El Mundo
Calle Pradillo, 42, 28002 Madrid
Spain
00 34 91 586 48 00
www.elmundo.es
Progressive Spanish daily.
Editor: Pedro Ramirez

El País
Miguel Yuste 40
28037 Madrid, Spain
00 34 91 337 8200
redaccion@prisacom.com
www.elpais.es
Spain's biggest daily paper.
Editor: Jesus Ceberio

Prague Post
Stepanska 20, Prague 1
110 00, Czech Republic
00 420 2 9633 4400
info@praguepost.com
www.praguepost.com
The Czech Republic's best English-
language daily. Editor: Will Tizard

Radio France Internationale
116, avenue du President Kennedy
Paris 75016, France
00 33 1 5640 1212
www.rfi.fr
France's "world service"

Radio Netherlands
Box 222, 1200 JG Hilversum
The Netherlands
00 31 35 672 4211
letters@rnw.nl
www.rnw.nl
Holland's best English-language news
service

La Repubblica

Piazza Indipendenza, 11/b
Rome 00185, Italy
00 39 06 49821
larepubblica@repubblica.it
www.repubblica.it
(In Italian.) Liberal Rome-based daily.
Editor: Azio Maruo

Der Standard

Schenkenstrasse 4/6
A-1010 Wien, Austria
00 43 1 53 170
chefredaktion@derStandard.at
www.derstandard.at
(In German.) Liberal daily.
Editor: Oscar Bronnir

Süddeutsche Zeitung

Sendlinger Strasse 8
80331 Munchen, Germany
00 49 89 21830
redaktion@sueddeutsche.de
www.sueddeutsche.de
(In German.) Major Munich-based
paper. Broadly liberal.
Editor: Hans Werner Kilz

De Telegraaf

30 Basisweg, 1043 Amsterdam
The Netherlands
00 31 20 585 9111
redactie-i@telegraaf.nl
www.telegraaf.nl
(In Dutch.) Holland's largest national
daily. Editor: E Bos

Middle East

Al-Ahram

Galaa St., Cairo, Egypt
00 20 2578 6441
weeklyeditor@ahram.org.eg
http://weekly.ahram.org.eg
Editor: Galal Nassar; web editor:
Amira Howeidy

Al-Jazeera

PO Box 22300, Doha, Qatar
00 974 438 2777
info@aljazeera.net.qa
www.aljazeera.com
Arabic-language satellite channel,
based in Qatar

Aljazeera Publishing
London, UK
0870 432 0671
http://english.aljazeera.net

Daily Star

Marine Tower 6th floor
Rue de La Ste Famille, Gemaizeh
Achrafieh, Beirut, Lebanon
00 961 1 587277
www.dailystar.com.lb
Lebanese daily.
Editor: Mr Hanna Anbar

Ha'aretz

21 Schocken St, PO Box 233
Tel Aviv 61001, Israel
00 972 3 512 1212/1204
contact@haaretz.co.il
www.haaretzdaily.com/
English edition of Israel's moderate
national daily, published in Tel Aviv.
Editor: Peter Hirschverg

Jerusalem Post

Jerusalem Post Building
PO Box 81, Jerusalem 91000, Israel
00 972 2531 5666
eedition@jpostmail.com
www.jpost.com
Conservative English-language daily.
Editor: Amotz Asa-El

Jordan Times

Jordan Press Foundation
PO Box 6710
Queen Rania Al Abdullah Street
Amman, Jordan
00 962 6 560 0800
jotimes@jpf.com.jo
www.jordantimes.com
Jordan's only English-language daily.
Editor: Jennifer Hamarneh

Middle East Times

8 Nikis Avenue, Office 201, 2nd Floor
Nicosia 1086, Cyprus
00 357 22 45 47 57
editor@middleastimes.net
www.metimes.com
Quality English-language weekly, based
in Egypt. Editor: Grahame Bennett

US and Canada

CBS Television Network

51 W 52nd St
NY 10019, USA
00 1 212 975 4321
www.cbs.com
News network

CNN

100 International Blvd, Atlanta
GA 30303, USA
00 1 404 827 1500
www.cnn.com
News network

International Herald Tribune

6 bis, rue des Graviers
92521 Neuilly Cedex, France
00 33 1 4143 9322
iht@iht.com
www.iht.com
International daily, owned by the New
York Times. Editor: Alison Smale

LA Times

202 W 1st St, Los Angeles
CA 90012, USA
00 1 213 237 5000
www.latimes.com
Biggest west-coast daily.
Editor: John Carroll

NBC

30 Rockefeller Plaza, New York
NY 10112, USA
00 1 212 664 4444
www.nbc.com
News network

New York Times

229 West 43rd Street, New York
New York 10036, USA
00 1 212 556 1234
editorial@nytimes.com
www.nytimes.com
National paper of record.
Editor: Bill Keller

Wall St Journal

200 Liberty Street, New York
NY 10281, USA
00 1 212 416 2600
wsj.ltrs@wsj.com
www.wsj.com
Conservative financial daily.
Editor: Paul E Steiger

Wall St Journal Europe
87 Boulevard Brand Whitlock
1200 Brussels, Belgium
00 32 2 741 1211
www.europesubs.wsj.com
Global business news for Europe.
Editor: Frederick Kempe

Washington Post

1150 15th Street NW, Washington
DC 20071, USA
00 1 202 334 6000
www.washingtonpost.com
The New York Times' main rival.
Editor: Philip Bennett

Canada

Toronto Globe and Mail

444 Front Street West, Toronto
Ontario M5V 2S9, Canada
00 1 416 585 5000
newsroom@GlobeAndMail.ca
www.theglobeandmail.com
Quality daily, Canada.
Editor: Edward Greenspon

Africa

Daily Mail and Guardian

PO Box 91667, Auckland Park
Johannesburg 2006, South Africa
00 27 11 727 7000
editoronline@mg.co.za
www.mg.co.za
South African daily.
Editor: Ferial Haffejee

Daily Nation

Nation Centre, Kimathi Street
Nairobi, Kenya
00 254 20 320 88 000
www.nationmedia.com
Kenya's biggest daily paper.
Editor: Njerri Rugene

Daily News

PO Box 47549, Greyville, 4023
Zimbabwe, South Africa
00 27 31 308 2107
pather@nn.independent.co.za
www.dailynews.co.za
Daily independent paper.
Editor: Dennis Pather

The East African

Kenya
00 254 20 540 633
comments@nationaudio.com
www.nationaudio
.com/News/EastAfrican/current

East African Standard
Likoni Road, PO Box 30080
Nairobi, Kenya
00 254 20 322 2111
editorial@eastandard.net
www.eastandard.net
Editor: Mr Kwento

Le Matin
1 Rud Birchir Attar, Algiers, Algeria
00 213 216 706 85
(In French.) Moderate, secular paper

Monitor, Uganda
Plot 29-35, 8th Street,
Industrial Area (PO Box 12141)
Kampala, Uganda
00 256 41 232367
info@monitor.co.ug
www.monitor.co.ug
Major independent daily.
Editor: Peter Mwesige

SABC
Private Bag X1, Auckland Park
2006, South Africa
00 27 11 714 5150
feedback@sabcnews.com
www.sabcnews.com
South African broadcaster

Sunday Times (South Africa)
2nd floor, Johnnic Publishing House
4 Biermann Avenue, Rosebank
2196, South Africa
00 27 11 280 3000
suntimes@sundaytimes.co.za
www.suntimes.co.za

Asia

Asahi Shimbun
Tokyo, Japan
00 81 3354 50131
www.asahi.com
Japanese daily

Dawn
Haroon House
Dr Ziauddin Ahmed Road
Karachi 74200, Pakistan
00 92 21 111 444 777
webmaster@dawn.com
www.dawn.com
English-language daily.
Editor: Tahir Mirza

Hindustan Times
Hindustan Times House
18-20, Kasturba Gandhi Marg
New Delhi-110001, INDIA
00 91 11 55561533
salil@hindustantimes.com
www.hindustantimes.com
Editor: Shailesh

Jakarta Post
Jl. Palmerah Selatan 15
Jakarta 10270, Indonesia
00 62 21 5300476
editorial@thejakartapost.com
www.thejakartapost.com
Editor: Endy M Bayuni

JoongAng Ilbo
7, Sunhwa-dong, Jung-gu
Seoul 100-759, Korea
00 82 2 751 9215
iht@joongang.co.kr
http://joongangdaily.joins.com
Korean daily.
Editor: Charles D Sherman

South China Morning Post
16F Somerset House, Taikoo Place
979 King's Road, Quarry Bay
Hong Kong
00 852 2565 2222
peter.dedi@scmp.com
www.scmp.com
English-language daily.
Editor: Peter Dedi

Star News Asia
8th Floor, One Harbourfront,
18 Tak Fung Street, Hunghom
Kowloon, Hong Kong
00 852 2621 8888
http://focusasia.startv
.com/starnewsasia.cfm

Straits Times
Singapore
00 65 6319 5397
STI@sph.com.sg
http://straitstimes.asia1.com.sg
Singapore's most widely circulated
English-language paper: close ties to
the government. Editor: Yeong Ah Seng

Taipei Times
Nanking East Rd, Sec 2, #137, 5Fl
Taipei, ROC - 104, Taiwan
00 886 2 2518 2728
inquiries@taipeitimes.com
www.taipeitimes.com

Latin America and Caribbean

O Estado de Sao Paulo
Av Celestino Bourroul, 68, 1° andar
Bairro do Limão, São Paulo, Brazil
00 55 11 3856 2122
atende@estado.com.br
www.estado.estadao.com.br
Editor: Sandro Vaia

El Mercurio
Santiago, Chile
00 56 2330 1111
www.elmercurio.cl
Daily. Editor: Juan Pablo Illanes

La Nacion
Buenos Aires, Argentina
00 54 11 4319 1600
consultas@lanacion.com.ar
www.lanacion.com.ar
Editor: Hector D'Amico

El Tiempo
Terra Networks Colombia
Diagonal 97 No. 17–60 Oficina 402
Bogotá, Colombia
00 57 160 29898
http://eltiempo.terra.com.co
Editor: Roberto Pombo

El Universal
Mexico City, Mexico
00 52 55 5709 1313/6917
enrique.cardenas@eluniversal.com.mx
www.el-universal.com.mx
Editor: Enrique Cárdenas

Caribbean

Jamaica Gleaner
7 North Street, PO Box 40
Kingston, Jamaica
00 1 876 922 3400
feedback@jamaica-gleaner.com
www.jamaica-gleaner.com
Editor: Garfield Grandison

Pacific

ABS-CBN (Philippines)
Manila, Phillipines
00 63 2 924 4101
newsfeedback@abs-cbn.com
www.abs-cbnnews.com
News network

New Zealand Herald
PO Box 32, Auckland, New Zealand
00 64 9 379 5050
www.nzherald.co.nz
Editor: Tim Murphy

The Age, Melbourne
250 Spencer Street
Melbourne 3000, Australia
00 61 3 9600 4211
inquiries@theage.com.au
www.theage.com.au
Editor: Andrew Jaspan

Sydney Morning Herald
201 Sussex St, GPO Box 506
Sydney NSW 2000, Australia
00 61 2 9282 1569
readerlink@smh.com.au
www.smh.com.au
Quality daily. Editor: Robert Whitehead

Global journalism bodies

AMARC (World Association of Community Broadcasters)
705 Bourget Street, Suite 100
Montreal, Quebec, H4C 2M6
Canada
00 1 514 982 0351
amarc@amarc.org
www.amarc.org

Article XIX
6–8 Amwell Street, London EC1R 1UQ
020 7278 9292
info@article19.org
www.article19.org
Combats censorship

Committee to Protect Journalists
330 7th Avenue 11th Floor
New York NY 10001, USA
00 1 212 465 1004
info@cpj.org
www.cpj.org
Independent, non-profit body defending right of journalists to report without fear of reprisal

Foreign Press Association in London
11 Carlton House Terrace
London SW1Y 5AJ
020 7930 0445
secretariat@foreign-press.org.uk
www.foreign-press.org.uk

Institute for War and Peace Reporting
Lancaster House
33 Islington High Street
London N1 9LH
020 7713 7130
alan@iwpr.net
www.iwpr.net
Training in conflict areas

International Centre for Journalists
1616 H Street NW, Third Floor
Washington DC 20006, USA
00 1 202 737 3700
www.icfj.org

International Consortium of Investigative Journalists
910 17th Street, NW, 7th Floor
Washington, DC 20006, USA
00 1 202 466 1300
www.icij.org

International Federation of Journalists
IPC-Residence Palace, Bloc C
Rue de la Loi 155, B-1040 Brussels
Belgium
00 32 2 235 2200
ifj@ifj.org
www.ifj.org

International Federation of the Periodical Press
Queens House
55–56 Lincoln's Inn Fields
London WC2A 3LJ
020 7404 4169
info@fipp.com
www.fipp.com
Works for benefit of magazine publishers worldwide

International Freedom of Expression
489 College Street, Suite 403
Toronto, Ontario, M6G 1A5
Canada
00 1 416 515 9622
ifex@ifex.org
www.ifex.org

International News Safety Institute
Residence Palace, Block C
International Press Centre
155 Rue de la Loi
1040 Brussels, Belgium
00 32 2 235 2201
info@newssafety.com
www.newssafety.com
Safety network for journalists in conflict zones

International Press Institute
Spiegelgasse 2, A-1010 Vienna
Austria
00 43 1 512 90 11
ipi@freemedia.at
www.freemedia.at
Network of editors, executives and senior journalists

International Women's Media Foundation
1625 K Street NW, Suite 1275
Washington, DC 20006, USA
00 1 202 496 1992
info@iwmf.org
www.iwmf.org
Role of women in news media

InterNews
1640 Rhode Island Avenue NW
7th Floor, Washington DC 20036
USA
00 1 202 833 5740
info@ internews.org
www.internews.org
News around the world

InterWorld Radio
Panos Institute, 9 White Lion Street
London N1 9PD
020 7239 7630/1/2/3
info@interworldradio.org
www.interworldradio.org
Global network for radio stations and journalism

Overseas Press and Media Association
OPMA Secretariat
15 Magrath Avenue
Cambridge CB4 3AH
01223 512631
membership@opma.co.uk
www.opma.co.uk

Panos London
9 White Lion Street, London N1 9PD
020 7278 1111
info@panos.org.uk
www.panos.org.uk
Journalism in developing countries

Reporters Sans Frontières
5 Rue Geoffroy-Marie
75009 Paris, France
00 33 1 4483 8484
rsf@rsf.org
www.rsf.org
Reporters without borders – freedom of the press

World Association of Newspapers
7 Rue Geoffroy St. Hilaire
75005 Paris, France
00 33 1 4742 8500
www.wan-press.org
Senior newsroom editors' forum

World Press Freedom Committee
11690-C Sunrise Valley Drive
Reston, VA 20191, USA
00 1 703 715 9811
freepress@wpfc.org
www.wpfc.org

World Press Photo
Jacob Obrechtstraat 26
1071 KM Amsterdam
The Netherlands
00 31 20 676 6096
office@worldpressphoto.nl
www.worldpressphoto.nl

Global media trade press

The Fourth Estate
00 61 416 178 908
michael@walsh.net
www.fourth-estate.com
Website and weekly newsletter. Editor: Mike Walsh. Digital techology and media

MediaChannel
575 8th Avenue, #2200
New York, NY 10018, USA
00 1 212 246 0202
editor@mediachannel.org
www.mediachannel.org
Website. Executive director: Timothy Karr; executive editor: Danny Schechter

Middle East Media Guide
PO Box 72280, Dubai, UAE
00 971 50 553 0209
editor@middleeastmediaguide.com
www.middleeastmediaguide.com
Annual. Editor: Ben Smalley

Online Journalism Review
3502 Watt Way, Los Angeles
CA 90089, USA
00 1 213 740 0948
rniles@usc.edu
www.ojr.org
Website. Editor: Larry Pryor

PR Week
Haymarket Professional Publications
174 Hammersmith Road
London W6 7JP
020 8267 4429
prweek@haynet.com
www.prweek.com
Weekly. Editor-in-chief: Kate Nicholas; news editor: Ravi Chandiramani

World Press Freedom Review
IPI Headquarters, Spiegelgasse 2
A-1010 Vienna, Austria
00 43 1 512 90 11
ipi@freemedia.at
www.freemedia.at/wpfr/world_m.htm
Website. Director: Johann P Fritz

Global media bodies

Association for International Broadcasting
PO Box 990, London SE3 9XL
020 8297 3993
info@aib.org.uk
www.aib.org.uk
Market intelligence, representation, contacts and other services

Association for Progressive Communications
PO Box 29755, Melville 2109
South Africa
00 27 11 726 1692
webeditor@apc.org
www.apc.org
Internet and ICTs for social justice and development

APC secretariat
Presidio Building 1012
Torney Avenue, PO Box 29904
San Francisco, CA 94129, USA

Committee of Concerned Journalists (CCJ)
Project for Excellence in Journalism, 1850 K St, NW Suite 850, Washington, DC 20006, USA
001 202 293 7394
mail@journalism.org
www.journalism.org
Initiative by journalists to clarify and raise the standards of American journalism

European Audio-Visual Observatory
76, allee de la Robertsau
67000 Strasbourg, France
00 33 388 144400
obs@obs.coe.int
www.obs.coe.int
European media observatory. Operates within framework of Council of Europe

European Broadcasting Union
17A, Ancienne Route
CH-1218 Grand-Saconnex
Switzerland
00 41 22 717 2111
ebu@ebu.ch
www.ebu.ch/en/index.php
Professional association of national broadcasters

International Advertising Association
521 Fifth Avenue, Suite 1807
New York, NY 10175, USA
00 1 212 557 1133
iaa@iaaglobal.org
www.iaaglobal.org
Advocates consumer and advertiser free choice

International Center for Journalists (ICFJ)
1616 H Street, NW, Third Floor, Washington, DC 20006, USA
00 1 202 737 3700
editor@icfj.org
www.icfj.org
Aims to help journalists and raise standards, esp in places with little tradition of a free press

International Classified Media Association (ICMA)
ICMA Head Office, Koggestraat 9H
1012 TA Amsterdam
The Netherlands
00 31 20 638 2336
info@icmaonline.org
www.icmaonline.org
Represents major publishers

International Communications Forum
24 Greencoat Place
London SW1P 1RD
020 7798 6010
icforum@yahoo.co.uk
www.icforum.org
Goodwill network

International Institute of Communications
Regent House, 24–25 Nutford Place
London W1H 5YN
020 7323 9622
enquiries@iicom.org
www.iicom.org
Industry, government and academic forum

International Newspaper Marketing Association
10300 North Central Expressway
Suite 467, Dallas, Texas 75231, USA
00 1 214 373 9111
www.inma.org

International Press Institute (IPI)
Spiegelgasse 2, A-1010 Vienna
Austria
00 43 1 512 90 11
ipi@freemedia.at
www.freemedia.at
Global network of editors, media executives and leading journalists. Supports press freedom, free flow of information, and improved journalism standards

International Public Relations Association
1, Dunley Hill Court
Ranmore Common
Dorking, Surrey RH5 6SX
01483 280 130
iprasec@btconnect.com
www.ipra.org
Network of PR pioneers

International Publishers Association
Ave de Miremont 3
1206 Geneva, Switzerland
00 41 22 346 3018
secretariat@ipa-uie.org
www.ipa-uie.org
NGO with consultative status to UN

International Telecommunication Union
Place des Nations
CH-1211 Geneva 20, Switzerland
00 41 22 730 51 11
itumail@itu.int
www.itu.int
UN body for coordination of global telecom services

International Webcasting Association
4206 F Technology Court
Chantilly, VA 20151, USA
info@webcasters.org
www.webcasters.org

World Associations of Newspapers (WAN)
7 Rue Geoffroy St. Hilaire
75005 Paris, France
00 33 1 4742 8500
contact_us@wan.asso.fr
www.wan-press.org
Defends press freedom and economic independence of newspapers

World Federation of Advertisers
120, Avenue Louise
1050 Brussels, Belgium
00 32 2 502 57 40
www.wfanet.org

World Summit on the Information Society
Executive Secretariat
Place des Nations
1211 Geneva 20, Switzerland
00 41 22 730 60 48
wsis@itu.int
www.itu.int/wsis

Creative media

Books

Despite a slight sales slide in 2004, the UK books industry remains upbeat. Although 2004 wasn't a Harry Potter year – Harry Potter and the Half-Blood Prince was not launched until July 2005 – the industry still profited from bestsellers such as The Da Vinci Code, the growth in online bookselling, and the extraordinary success of the Richard & Judy Book Club.

Book sales

Sales fell 1% to £2.14bn, according to the Books and the Consumer survey, which measures books bought by people aged 12 to 74. The number of books sold fell slightly too: consumers bought 282 million books, down 1% on 2003. Seen in the context of 2002, though, the figures still looked healthy: sales were up 5% on that year, with the number of books up 3%. Including books bought by the under-12s and over-74s, the total value of books sold in 2004 was thought to be about £2.4bn.

That rewards of that success, though, are going into ever fewer pockets. A table of the top British publishers by sales, for example, published in the Bookseller magazine – based on figures compiled by Bookscan – shows that in 2004, just 10 publishers made up 63% of the industry. The biggest is Random House, whose 30 or so imprints take up a full column of the contacts section of this book.

In April 2005, Random House took a 50% stake in Scottish publisher Mainstream; and in the summer of 2004, Hodder Headline was bought by French group Hachette.

Bestsellers

In the absence of a Harry Potter book, the publishing phenomenon of 2004 was The Da Vinci Code, by Dan Brown. The novel, a page-turning thriller about a detective on the trail of a millennium-old religious conspiracy, topped the UK bestseller charts from autumn 2004 until summer 2005. The book was so successful that the Vatican even appointed a cardinal to rebut what it called Brown's "shameful and unfounded errors" – which simply caused more people to go out and buy the book.

July 2005 saw the launch of the sixth book in the Harry Potter series, Harry Potter and the Half-Blood Prince. On its hype-fuelled first day, the book sold more than 2m copies in the UK and 6.9m in the US, beating sales for any of the previous five editions of the book.

Book groups

As if to prove that word-of-mouth is what drives the publishing industry, book groups – in which a group of people meet to decide on a book to read, before sharing their views on it next time – have become

Martin Argles

The Da Vinci Code... bestseller in 2004

WE SEE IT AS THE FIRST STEP TO THE BOOKER PRIZE

C A T

ever more popular in the past few years. Traditionally the territory of bored middle-class housewives, the concept was held up for ridicule in the Channel 4 comedy The Book Group in 2002, but that only served to make it more popular. Then in 2004, the Channel 4 chatshow Richard & Judy launched a TV book group of its own, with celebrity guests reviewing a book a week for 10 weeks. It was hardly a novel idea – the Oprah Book Club had been successful in the US – but it was still a surprise to see the huge effect on sales that the Richard & Judy Book Club had. After Bob Geldof called Joseph O'Connor's historical novel The Star of the Sea a "masterpiece" on the show, for example, the book leapt from number 337 in the UK bestseller chart to number 1. The Guardian even called Richard and Judy "the most powerful people in British publishing". The announcements of which books make the Richard & Judy list now generate as much attention as major literary prizes.

Not to be outdone, the rest of the media soon began to get in on the act. The BBC – whose The Big Read project possibly contributed to the Richard & Judy Book Club's success – responded with the programme Page Turners, presented by Jeremy Vine. The Daily Mail and the Observer, meanwhile, launched book clubs of their own.

Online publishing

The publishing industry woke up to the internet in a big way in 2004, when the search engine Google announced ambitious plans to digitise the back catalogues of major book publishers, and put them into a searchable database. The system, called Google Print, would allow users to search books as well as websites online – with an invitation to buy the book. And the idea does not only include new books: Google already has non-exclusive rights to digitise books from major research libraries, including Harvard, Stanford and the Bodleian library in Oxford.

Emergent readers

Gail Rebuck, the chief executive of Random House, used the Booksellers Association conference in Glasgow in April 2005 to launch a campaign aimed at the millions of UK adults who currently struggle to read. There are some 12 million "emergent readers", according to official figures, who have literacy skills at or below the level expected of a 13-year-old. Random House will target a list of "Quick Reads" at these readers for World Book Day 2006.

Top 10 paperbacks, 2004		
Ranking / Title	**Author**	**RRP**
1 The Da Vinci Code	Dan Brown	£6.99
2 The Curious Incident of the Dog In The Night-Time	Mark Haddon	£6.99
3 A Short History of Nearly Everything	Bill Bryson	£8.99
4 You Are What You Eat	Gillian McKeith	£12.99
5 King of Torts	John Grisham	£6.99
6 Digital Fortress	Dan Brown	£6.99
7 Deception Point	Dan Brown	£6.99
8 Brick Lane	Monica Ali	£6.99
9 Star of the Sea	Joseph O'Connor	£7.99
10 Blow Fly	Patricia Cornwell	£6.99

Industry moves

Among the major publishers, the big news was the trouble at Penguin, where the chief executive, Anthony Forbes Watson, was ousted in February following problems with distribution. He was replaced by John Makinson. Also leaving was David Young chief executive of Time Warner UK – to become boss of Time Warner's global books division, replacing the outgoing Laurence Kirshbaum. Ursula Mackenzie was lined up to replace him.

In journalism news, Nick Clee left his position as the editor of the influential trade title, The Bookseller, in 2005; he was replaced by Philip Jones.

Awards

British Book Awards 2005
www.britishbookawards.com
- *Book of the year:* The Da Vinci Code, by Dan Brown (Corgi)
- *Best read of the year:* Cloud Atlas, by David Mitchell (Sceptre)
- *Literary fiction award:* Cloud Atlas, by David Mitchell (Sceptre)
- *Author of the year:* Sheila Hancock
- *Newcomer of the year:* Susanna Clarke, for Jonathan Strange & Mr Norrell (Bloomsbury)

British book trade awards 2005
- *Publisher of the year:* Orion
- *Imprint and editor of the year:* Atlantic, Toby Mundy
- *Small publisher of the year:* John Blake Publishing

Orange prize 2005
www.orangeindex.co.uk/2005prize
- We Need to Talk About Kevin, by Lionel Shriver (Serpent's Tail)

Orange award for new writers 2005
www.orangeindex.co.uk/oanw05/index.html
- 26a, by Diana Evans (Chatto & Windus)

Man Booker prize 2004
www.themanbookerprize.com
- The Line of Beauty, by Alan Hollinghurst (Picador)

Guardian first book award 2004
http://books.guardian.co.uk/firstbook2004
- Mutants, by Armand Marie Leroi (HarperCollins)

Guardian children's fiction prize 2004
http://books.guardian.co.uk/guardianchildrensfictionprize2004
- How I Live Now, by Meg Rosoff (Puffin)

Whitbread awards 2004
www.whitbread-bookawards.co.uk
- *Book of the year:* Small Island, by Andrea Levy (Review)
- *First novel:* Eve Green, by Susan Fletcher (Fourth Estate)
- *Biography:* My Heart is My Own: The Life of Mary Queen of Scots, by John Guy (Fourth Estate)
- *Children's:* Not the End of the World, by Geraldine McCaughrean (Oxford University Press)
- *Poetry:* Corpus, by Michael Symmons Roberts (Jonathan Cape)

Further reading

■ **Press**

Guardian Review and Guardian Unlimited Books
guardian.co.uk/books

The Bookseller
www.thebookseller.com

Publishing News
www.publishingnews.co.uk

■ **Books**

From Pitch to Publication
CAROLE BLAKE, PAN 1999
Insider's guide by one of Britain's foremost literary agents

On Writing STEPHEN KING, HODDER & STOUGHTON 2001 Part autobiography, part guide to the craft

The Art of Fiction
DAVID LODGE, PENGUIN 1992
Accessible criticism for writers

■ **Web only**

Booksurfer
booksurfer.blogspot.com

Bloomsbury.com writers area
www.bloomsbury.com/WritersArea

■ **Other resources**

Society of Authors
www.writers.org.uk/society

Publishers Association
www.publishers.org.uk

The trade must wake up to the web   **Joel Rickett**

When Google founders Larry Page and Sergey Brin swooped into the 2004 Frankfurt book fair to launch their latest pet project, Google Print, many publishers ducked for cover. Some have still not raised the heads above the parapet.

Not content with indexing some eight billion web pages, Brin and Page had turned their eyes to books. The next step in their declared mission to "organise the world's information and make it universally accessible" was to digitise millions of pages of printed material and open it up for web searches. They wanted publishers from across the world to start posting them copies of books, which Google would scan and add to its main database, as well as a special Google Print archive. In return, they promised to protect the online pages from piracy, give publishers a share of associated advertising revenue, and link to sites to buy the book.

Some publishers, particularly those specialising in academic and scientific work, have embraced the Google Print project. They see the search engine as a vast shop window for their wares. After all, millions of people are going online anyway: why shouldn't they be directed to quality book content? Tens of thousands of titles are already in the Google Print archive: a search for "jobs in journalism" finds about 5,000 pages, including Lynette Sheridan Burns' Understanding Journalism (Sage), Careers in Journalism (Kogan Page), and Ian Hargreaves' Journalism: Truth or Dare? (OUP).

Trade publishers, churning out fiction and non-fiction for a general readership, are more wary. They fear that for an unspecified share of future advertising revenues, they are effectively being asked to give away all their precious content. For areas such as reference works, a reader's needs could easily be met by delving into a few pages of a book online, so where is the impetus to buy? That's not to mention the tricky logistics of author royalties and territorial rights.

At Frankfurt, Page and Brin neglected to say that they were in the advanced stages of finding another route to books. Google has now struck deals with six of the world's most prestigious libraries about digitising swathes of their vast archives, including material still in copyright. After sustained protests from publishing groups, Google backed down in late 2005, modifying its programme so publishers can pull books out. But publishers argue that the opt-out plan turns copyright principles on their head by putting the onus on creators.

Google also insists on retaining ownership of the digital files, making publishers and literary agents paranoid about its ability to suddenly change plans. The strongest critic is Bloomsbury chief executive Nigel Newton, who is no Luddite. "It may lead to a sales increase in the short term, but in 20 years' time it may result in no sales," he warns. "We don't know, once they have this material, what they will do with it." Behind his comments lie a deeper inclination to retain control over the relationship with readers.

But the wider problem for most publishers is that they have failed to digitise their own content. While academic and scientific specialists have invested millions to move into the digital age, trade houses have lacked the profit margins or the long-term strategies to adapt. They now need to build their own online archives, so they can allow Google limited access to books on their own terms. And they need to do it fast.

Joel Rickett is deputy editor of The Bookseller

Books Contacts

Book publishers

A&C Black
(see Bloomsbury Publishing)

AA Publishing
The Automobile Association
14th Floor, Fanum House
Basingstoke, Hampshire RG21 4EA
01256 491519
ian.harvey@theaa.com
www.theaa.co.uk
Maps, atlases and guidebooks

Abacus
(see Time Warner Books)

ABC-Clio
26 Beaumont Street, Oxford OX1 2NP
01865 517222
salesuk@abc-clio.com
www.abc-clio.com
Academic and general reference

Absolute Press
Scarborough House
29 James Street West
Bath BA1 2BT
01225 316013
info@absolutepress.co.uk
www.absolutepress.co.uk
Non-fiction

Abson Books London
5 Sidney Square, London E1 2EY
020 7790 4737
absonbooks@aol.com
www.absonbooks.co.uk
Language glossaries

Acair
7 James Street, Stornoway
Isle of Lewis HS1 2QN
01851 703020
info@acairbooks.com
www.acairbooks.com
Scottish history and culture, Gaelic

Acumen Publishing
15A Lewins Yard, East Street
Chesham, Buckinghamshire HP5 1HQ
01494 794398
steven.gerrard@
    acumenpublishing.co.uk
www.acumenpublishing.co.uk
Philosophy, history and politics

Addison-Wesley
(see Pearson Education)

African Books Collective
Unit 13, Kings Meadow
Ferry Hinksey Road
Oxford OX2 0DP Oxford OX1 1HU
01865 726686
abc@africanbookscollective.com
www.africanbookscollective.com
Publishing and distribution of African books

Age Concern England
1268 London Road
London SW16 4ER
020 8765 7200
media@ace.org.uk
www.ageconcern.org.uk

Aidan Ellis Publishing
Whinfield, Herbert Road
Salcombe, South Devon TQ8 8HN
01548 842755
mail@aidanellispublishing.co.uk
www.aepub.demon.co.uk
General publishing and non-fiction

Albatross Publishing
The Dairy Studios
Runfold St George
Farnham, Surrey GU10 1PL
01252 781994
sbutler@z-guides.com
www.z-guides.com
Reference and non-fiction

Allen & Unwin
(see Orion Publishing Group)

Allen Lane
(see Penguin Books)

Allison & Busby
Suite 111, Bon Marche Centre
241 Ferndale Road
London SW9 8BJ
020 7738 7888
all@alisonandbusby.com
www.alisonandbusby.com
Crime; literary fiction and non-fiction

Allyn & Bacon
(see Pearson Education)

Amber Lane Press
Cheorl House, Church Street
Charlbury, Oxfordshire OX7 3PR
01608 810024
jamberlane@aol.com
www.amberlanepress.co.uk
Plays and theatre

Andersen Press
20 Vauxhall Bridge Road
London SW1V 2SA
020 7840 8701
andersenpress@randomhouse.co.uk
www.andersenpress.co.uk
Children's books and fiction

Anness Publishing
Hermes House
88–89 Blackfriars Road
London SE1 8HA
020 7401 2077
sbaldwin@anness.com
www.annesspublishing.com
General non-fiction

Anthem Press
(see Wimbledon Publishing Press)

Antique Collectors' Club
Sandy Lane, Old Martlesham
Woodbridge, Suffolk IP12 4SD
01394 389950
sales@antique-acc.com
www.antiquecollectorsclub.com

Anvil Press Poetry
Neptune House
70 Royal Hill, London SE10 8RF
020 8469 3033
anvil@anvilpresspoetry.com
www.anvilpresspoetry.com
Poetry

APA Publications
58 Borough High Street
London SE1 1XF
020 7403 0284
berlitz@apaguide.co.uk
www.berlitzpublishing.co.uk
Owned by Langenscheidt Publishing Group. Travel and languages. Imprint: Berlitz Publishing

Appletree Press
The Old Potato Station
14 Howard Street South
Belfast BT7 1AP
028 9024 3074
reception@appletree.ie
www.appletree.ie
Cookery and Celtic interest, bespoke publications

Arc Publications
Nanholme Mill, Shaw Wood Road
Todmorden, Lancashire OL14 6DA
01706 812338
info@arcpublications.co.uk
www.arcpublications.co.uk
Contemporary poetry

Arcadia Books
15–16 Nassau Street
London W1W 7AB
020 7436 9898
info@arcadiabooks.co.uk
www.arcadiabooks.co.uk
Literary fiction, crime, biography, gender studies and travel

Architectural Association Publications
36 Bedford Square
London WC1B 3ES
020 7887 4021
publications@aaschool.ac.uk
www.aaschool.info/publications
Publishing arm of Architectural Association School of Architecture

Arcturus Publishing
26/27 Bickels Yard
151–153 Bermondsey Street
London SE1 3HA
020 7407 9400
info@arcturuspublishing.com
www.arcturuspublishing.com
Non-fiction

Arrow
(see Random House Group)

Ashgrove Publishing
27 John Street, London WC1N 2BX
020 7831 5013
gmo73@dial.pipex.com
www.ashgrovepublishing.com
Owned by Hollydata Publishers.
Mind, body & spirit

Ashley Drake Publishing
PO Box 733, Cardiff CF14 2YX
029 2056 0343
post@ashleydrake.com
www.ashleydrake.com
Imprints: Welsh Academic Press
(academic titles in English); St David's
Press (general trade); Y Ddraig Fach
(children's books in Welsh); Gwasg
Addysgol Cymru (educational in Welsh)

Ashmolean Museum Publications
(see Oxford University)

Atlantic Books
Ormond House
26–27 Boswell Street
London WC1N 3JZ
020 7269 1610
enquiries@groveatlantic.co.uk
www.groveatlantic.co.uk
Literary fiction, non-fiction and
reference. Imprints: Guardian Books,
Observer Books

Atom
(see Time Warner Books)

Aurum Press
25 Bedford Avenue
London WC1B 3AT
020 7637 3225
editorial@aurumpress.co.uk
www.aurumpress.co.uk
Non-fiction

Australian Consolidated Press UK
Moulton Park Business Centre
Red House Road, Moulton Park
Northampton NN3 6AQ
01604 497531
acpukltd@aol.com
www.acpuk.com
Home interest

Authentic Media
9 Holdom Avenue, Bletchley
Milton Keynes MK1 1QR
01908 364200
info@authenticmedia.co.uk
www.authenticmedia.co.uk
Imprints: Authentic (Christian life);
Paternoster (academic and theological
titles and theses)

Autumn Publishing
Appledram Barns
Birdham Road, Near Chichester
West Sussex PO20 7EQ
01243 531660
autumn@autumnpublishing.co.uk
www.autumnpublishing.co.uk
Early learning. Imprint: Byeway Books

Award Publications
1st Floor, 27 Longford Street
London NW1 3DZ
020 7388 7800
info@awardpublications.co.uk
Children's fiction and reference.
Imprint: Horus Editions

Axis Publishing
8C Accommodation Road
London NW11 8ED
020 8731 8080
wallace@axispublishing.co.uk
www.axispublishing.co.uk
Illustrated full colour books

Bantam/Bantam Press
(see Random House Group)

Barefoot Books
124 Walcot Street, Bath BA1 5BG
01225 322400
info@barefootbooks.co.uk
www.barefootbooks.com
Children's picture books

Barny Books
The Cottage, Hough on the Hill
Near Grantham
Lincolnshire NG32 2BB
01400 250246/ 01522 790009
Children's books, adult fiction and
non-fiction

Barrington Stoke
Sandeman House, Trunks Close
55 High Street, Edinburgh EH1 1SR
0131 557 2020
info@barringtonstoke.co.uk
www.barringtonstoke.co.uk
Remedial children's reading

Batsford
(see Chrysalis Books)

BBC Bookshop
PO Box 308, Sittingbourne
Kent ME9 8LW
0870 241 5490
bbcshop@bbc.co.uk
www.bbcshop.com

Benjamin Cummings
(see Pearson Education)

Berg Publishers
1st Floor Angel Court
81 St Clements Street
Oxford OX4 1AW
01865 245104
enquiry@bergpublishers.com
www.bergpublishers.com
Various academic. Imprint: Oswald
Wolff Books

Berghahn Books
3 Newtec Place, Magdalen Road
Oxford OX4 1RE
01865 250011
saleuk@berghahnbooks.com
www.berghahnbooks.com
Academic books and journals

BFI Publishing
British Film Institute, 21 Stephen Street
London W1T 1LN
020 7255 1444
publishing@bfi.org.uk
www.bfi.org.uk/books
Part of the British Film Institute

BFP Books
Focus House, 497 Green Lanes
London N13 4BP
020 8882 3315
info@thebfp.com
www.thebfp.com
Publishing arm of the Bureau of
Freelance Photographers

BIOS Scientific Publishers
(see T&F Informa)

Birlinn
West Newington House
10 Newington Road
Edinburgh EH9 1QS
0131 668 4371
info@birlinn.co.uk
www.birlinn.co.uk
History, folklore, Scottish interest and
fiction

Black & White Publishing
99 Giles Street, Edinburgh EH6 6BZ
0131 625 4500
mail@blackandwhitepublishing.com
www.blackandwhitepublishing.com
General fiction and non-fiction

Black Spring Press
Curtain House, 134–146 Curtain Road
London EC2A 3AR
020 7613 3066
general@blackspringpress.co.uk
www.blackspringpress.co.uk
Fiction and non-fiction

Black Swan
(see Random House Group)

Blackstaff Press
4c Heron Wharf
Sydenham Business Park
Belfast BT3 9LE
028 9045 5006
marketing@blackstaffpress.com
www.blackstaffpress.com
Fiction, non-fiction and poetry

Blackwell Publishing
9600 Garsington Road
Oxford OX4 2DQ
01865 776868
www.blackwellpublishing.com
Journals and textbooks

Bloodaxe Books
Highgreen, Tarset
Northumberland NE48 1RP
01434 240500
publicity@bloodaxebooks.com
www.bloodaxebooks.com
Poetry

Bloomsbury Publishing
38 Soho Square, London W1D 3HB
020 7494 2111
publicity@ bloomsbury.com
www.bloomsbury.com
Adult and children's fiction and
non-fiction (including Harry Potter)

A&C Black (Publishers)
Alderman House, 37 Soho Square
London W1D 3QZ
020 7758 0200
enquiries@acblack.com
www.acblack.com
Reference and non-fiction; Writers' and
Artists' Yearbook

BMJ Books
(incorporated into Blackwell Publishing)

The Bodley Head
(see Random House Group)

Book Guild
Temple House, 25 High Street
Lewes, East Sussex BN7 2LU
01273 472534
info@bookguild.co.uk
www.bookguild.co.uk
Fiction and non-fiction

Boulevard Books & The Babel Guides
71 Lytton Road, Oxford OX4 3NY
01865 712931
raybabel@dircon.co.uk
www.babelguides.com
Contemporary world fiction and guides

Bowker (UK)
3rd Floor, Farringdon House
Wood Street, East Grinstead
West Sussex RH19 1UZ
01342 310450
sales@bowker.co.uk
www.bowker.co.uk
*Part of the Cambridge Information
Group (CIG). Reference and biography*

Boydell & Brewer
PO Box 9, Woodbridge
Suffolk IP12 3DF
01394 610600
boydell@boydell.co.uk
www.boydell.co.uk
Non-fiction, principally medieval studies

Boxtree
(see Macmillan Publishers)

Bradt Travel Guides
23 High Street, Chalfont St Peter
Buckinghamshire SL9 9QE
01753 893444
info@bradtguides.com
www.bradtguides.com
Travel guides

Brasseys
(see Chrysalis Books)

Breedon Books Publishing Co
Breedon House, 3 Parker Centre
Mansfield Road, Derby DE21 4SZ
01332 384235
sales@breedonpublishing.co.uk
www.breedonbooks.co.uk
Local history and heritage, sport

British Academy
10 Carlton House Terrace
London SW1Y 5AH
020 7969 5200
secretary@britac.ac.uk
www.britac.ac.uk

British Library
96 Euston Road
London NW1 2DB
020 7412 7469
blpublications@bl.uk
www.bl.uk

British Museum Press
38 Russell Square
London WC1B 3QQ
020 7323 1234
sales@britishmuseum.co.uk
www.britishmuseum.co.uk

Brooklands Books
PO Box 146, Cobham
Surrey KT11 1LG
01932 865051
sales@brooklands-books.com
www.brooklands-books.com
*Motoring titles and technical
catalogues*

Brown Watson
The Old Mill, 76 Fleckney Road
Kibworth Beauchamp
Leicestershire LE8 0HG
0116 279 6333
books@brownwatson.co.uk
www.brownwatson.co.uk
General children's interest

Brown, Son & Ferguson
4–10 Darnley Street
Glasgow G41 2SD
0141 429 1234
info@skipper.co.uk
www.skipper.co.uk
Nautical textbooks and Scottish plays

Browntrout Publishers
Redland Office Centre
157 Redland Road
Redland, Bristol BS6 6YE
0117 973 9191
sales@browntroutuk.com
www.browntrout.com
Fine art and photography products

Brunner-Routledge
(see T&F Informa)

Bryntirion Press
Bryntirion, Bridgend
Mid-Glamorgan CF31 4DX
01656 655886
office@emw.org.uk
www.emw.org.uk
*Owned by the Evangelical Movement
of Wales. Christian books in English
and Welsh*

Business Education Publishers
The Teleport, Doxford International
Sunderland, Tyne & Wear SR3 3XD
0191 525 2410
info@bepl.com
www.bepl.com

Butterworth
(see Reed Elsevier)

C Hurst & Co
2nd Floor, Africa Centre, 38 King Street
Covent Garden, London WC2E 8JZ
020 7240 2666
hurst@atlas.co.uk
www.hurstpub.co.uk
Contemporary history

Cadogan Guides
Highlands House
165 The Broadway, Wimbledon
London SW19 1NE
020 8740 2050
info@cadoganguides.co.uk
www.cadoganguides.com
*Owned by US firm, Morris
Publications. Travel guides*

Calder Publications
51 The Cut, London SE1 8LF
020 7633 0599
info@calderpublications.com
www.calderpublications.com
*Formerly John Calder (Publishers)
Biography, drama, music, poetry and
translations*

Cambridge University Press
The Edinburgh Building
Shaftesbury Road
Cambridge CB2 2RU
01223 312393
information@cambridge.org
www.cambridge.org

Camden Press
43 Camden Passage
London N1 8EA
020 7226 4673
Social issues. Imprint: Mindfield

Campbell Books
(see Macmillan Publishers)

Canongate Books
14 High Street
Edinburgh EH1 1TE
0131 557 5111
info@canongate.co.uk
www.canongate.net
Literary fiction and non-fiction, music

Capall Bann Publishing
Auton Farm, Milverton
Somerset TA4 1NE
01823 401528
enquiries@capallbann.co.uk
www.capallbann.co.uk
British traditional works and folklore

Capstone Publishing
(see John Wiley & Sons)

Carcanet Press
4th Floor, Alliance House
30 Cross Street
Manchester M2 7AQ
0161 834 8730
info@carcanet.u-net.com
www.carcanet.co.uk
*Poetry, academic works, literary
biography, fiction in translation*

Cardiff Academic Press
St Fagans Road, Fairwater
Cardiff CF5 3AE
029 2056 0333
cap@drakeed.com
www.drakeed.com/cap

Carfax
(see T&F Informa)

Carlton Publishing Group
20 Mortimer Street, London W1T 3JW
020 7612 0400
enquiries@carltonbooks.co.uk
www.carltonbooks.co.uk
*Owned by Carlton Communications
Illustrated entertainment and leisure
titles. Imprints: Carlton Books, Granada
Media, Manchester United Books*

Carroll & Brown Publishers
20 Lonsdale Road, London NW6 6RD
020 7372 0900
mail@carrollandbrown.co.uk
www.carrollandbrown.co.uk
Lifestyle

Cassell Reference/Cassell Military
(see Orion Publishing Group)

Catholic Truth Society (CTS)
40–46 Harleyford Road
London SE11 5AY
020 7640 0042
editorial@cts-online.org.uk
www.cts-online.org.uk
*Roman Catholic books, including
Vatican documents*

Causeway Press
PO Box 13, 129 New Court Way
Ormskirk, Lancashire L39 5HP
01695 576048
causeway.press@btinternet.com
Educational textbooks

Cavendish Publishing
The Glass House, Wharton Street
London WC1X 9PX
020 7278 8000
info@cavendishpublishing.com
www.cavendishpublishing.com
Academic and practitioner law books

CBA (Publishing Department)
St Marys House, 66 Bootham
York YO30 7BZ
01904 671417
info@britarch.ac.uk
www.britarch.ac.uk
*Publishing arm of the Council for
British Archaeology. Archaeology,
practical handbooks*

CBD Research
Chancery House, 15 Wickham Road
Beckenham, Kent BR3 5JS
020 8650 7745
cbd@cbdresearch.com
www.cbdresearch.com
Directories

Century
(see Random House Group)

Chambers Harrap Publishers
7 Hopetoun Crescent
Edinburgh EH7 4AY
0131 556 5929
admin@chambersharrap.com
www.chambersharrap.com
Dictionaries and reference

Channel 4 Books
(see Random House Group)

Chapman Publishing
4 Broughton Place
Edinburgh EH1 3RX
0131 557 2207
chapman-pub@blueyonder.co.uk
www.chapman-pub.co.uk
*Scottish writers including poetry,
drama, short stories*

**Chartered Institute of Personnel
and Development**
151 The Broadway
London SW19 1JQ
020 8263 3387
publish@cipd.co.uk (books) and
editorial@peoplemanagement.co.uk
www.cipd.co.uk
Part of CIPD Enterprises (magazine)

Chatto & Windus
(see Random House Group)

Chicken House Publishing
2 Palmer Street, Frome
Somerset BA11 1DS
01373 454 488
chickenhouse@doublecluck.com
www.doublecluck.com
Children's fiction

Child's Play (International)
Ashworth Road, Bridgemead
Swindon, Wiltshire SN5 7YD
01793 616286
allday@childs-play.com
www.childs-play.com

Chris Andrews Publications
15 Curtis Yard, North Hinksey Lane
Oxford OX2 0LX
01865 723404
chris.andrews1@btclick.com
www.cap-ox.co.uk
*Owns the Oxford Picture Library.
Coffee table books, calendars and diaries*

Christian Focus Publications
Geanies House, Fearn
Tain, Ross-shire IV20 1TW
01862 871011
info@christianfocus.com
www.christianfocus.com
Christian books for adults and children

Chrysalis Books
The Chrysalis Building, Bramley Road
London W10 6SP
020 7314 1400
www.chrysalisbooks.co.uk

Batsford
  *Specialist and technical illustrated
  non-fiction: embroidery, lace, chess,
  bridge, practical art, film and furniture*
Brasseys
  Military
Children's Books
Collins & Brown
  *Illustrated non-fiction: photography,
  crafts and practical arts; national
  magazine branded books; health, mind,
  body & spirit (formerly Vega)*
Conway Maritime
  *Maritime history, ship modelling and
  naval*
Paper Tiger
  *Non-fiction, illustrated: science fiction
  and fantasy art*
Pavilion
  *High-end coffee table books: celebrity,
  lifestyle, interiors, cookery, garden, art
  and photography*
Putnams
  Aeronautical

Robson Books
*Sports, humour and biography, esp.
celebrity; small amount of fiction*

Cicerone Press
2 Police Square, Milnthorpe
Cumbria LA7 7PY
01539 562069
info@cicerone.co.uk
www.cicerone.co.uk
Guidebooks for outdoor enthusiasts

Cico Books
1st Floor, 32 Great Sutton Street
London EC1V 0NB
020 7253 7960
mail@cicobooks.co.uk
Lifestyle and interiors

Cisco Press
(see Pearson Education)

Co & Bear Productions (UK)
565 Fulham Road
London SW6 1ES
020 7385 0888
bvincenzini@cobear.co.uk
www.scriptumeditions.co.uk
*High quality illustrated books.
Imprint: Scriptum Editions*

Colin Smythe
PO Box 6, Gerrards Cross
Buckinghamshire SL9 8XA
01753 886000
sales@colinsmythe.co.uk
www.colinsmythe.co.uk
Anglo-Irish literature and criticism

Collins
(see HarperCollins Publishers)

Collins & Brown
(see Chrysalis Books)

Colourpoint Books
Colourpoint House
Jubilee Business Park
21 Jubilee Road, Newtownards
Co Down BT23 4YH
028 9182 0505
info@colourpoint.co.uk
www.colourpoint.co.uk
School textbooks, transport, Irish interest

Compass Maps
The Coach House, Beech Court
Winford BS40 8DW
01225 445555
info@popoutmaps.com
www.mapgroup.net
Pocket maps and guides

Compendium Publishing
1st Floor, 43 Frith Street
London W1D 4SA
020 7287 4570
compendiumpub@aol.com
Historical

Constable & Robinson
3, The Lanchesters
162 Fulham Palace Road
London W6 9ER
020 8741 3663
enquiries@constablerobinson.com
www.constablerobinson.com
*Fiction and non-fiction: lifestyle,
reference, children's, current affairs and
politics*

Continuum International Publishing Group
Tower Building, 11 York Road
London SE1 7NX
020 7922 0880
info@continuumbooks.com
www.continuumbooks.com
*Academic and religious. Imprints:
Athlone, Pinter, Sheffield Academic
Press, Geoffrey Chapman, Mowbray,
TandT Clark, Burns and Oates,
Morehouse, Claridge Press*

Conway Maritime
(see Chrysalis Books)

Corgi
(see Random House Group)

Countryside Books
Highfield House, 2 Highfield Avenue
Newbury, Berkshire RG14 5DS
01635 43816
info@countrysidebooks.co.uk
www.countrysidebooks.co.uk
Local interest, walking

CRC
(see T&F Informa)

Crecy Publishing
Unit 1a, Ringway Trading Estate
Shadowmoss Road
Manchester M22 5LH
0161 499 0024
enquiries@crecy.co.uk
www.crecy.co.uk
Aviation and naval military history

Cressrelles Publishing Co
10 Station Road Industrial Estate
Colwall, Malvern
Worcestershire WR13 6RN
01684 540154
simonsmith@cressrelles4drama
.fsbusiness.co.uk
*Plays and theatre texts. Imprints:
Actinic Press*

Crowood Press
The Stable Block, Crowood Lane
Ramsbury, Marlborough
Wiltshire SN8 2HR
01672 520320
enquiries@crowood.com
www.crowood.com
*Aviation, military history, country,
sports, hobby and leisure pursuits*

Curzon Press
(see T&F Informa)

CW Daniel Company
(see Random House Group)

Dalesman Publishing Co
The Watermill, Broughton Hall
Skipton, North Yorkshire BD23 3AG
01756 701381
editorial@dalesman.co.uk
www.dalesman.co.uk
*Magazines and regional books
(Yorkshire, Lake District and
Peak District)*

Darton, Longman & Todd
1 Spencer Court
140–142 Wandsworth High Street
London SW18 4JJ
020 8875 0155
mail@darton-longman-todd.co.uk
www.darton-longman-todd.co.uk
Spirituality, theology and Christianity

David & Charles Publishers
Brunel House, Forde Close
Newton Abbot, Devon TQ12 4PU
01626 323200
postmaster@davidandcharles.co.uk
www.davidandcharles.co.uk
*Subsidiary of F&W, USA. Illustrated
non-fiction*

David Fickling Books
(see Random House Group)

David Fulton (Publishers)
(see Granada Learning)

Debrett's
1 Hammersmith Broadway
London W6 9DL
020 8600 8222
people@debretts.co.uk
www.debretts.co.uk
Specialist reference works

Dedalus
Langford Lodge, St Judith's Lane
Sawtry, Cambridgeshire PE28 5XE
01487 832382
info@dedalusbooks.com
www.dedalusbooks.com
*English contemporary fiction and
European fiction in translation,
alternative lifestyle*

Dewi Lewis Publishing
8 Broomfield Road, Heaton Moor
Stockport SK4 4ND
0161 442 9450
mail@dewilewispublishing.com
www.dewilewispublishing.com
Fiction, photography and visual arts

Diva Books
Unit M, Spectrum House
32/34 Gordon House Road
London NW5 1LP
020 7424 7400
www.millivres.co.uk
*Part of the Millivres Prowler Group.
Literary lesbian fiction. Imprint: Red
Hot Diva (lesbian erotic fiction)*

Donhead Publishing
Lower Coombe, Donhead St Mary
Shaftesbury, Dorset SP7 9LY
01747 828422
jillpearce@donhead.com
www.donhead.com
Building, architecture and heritage

Dorling Kindersley
(see Penguin Books)

Doubleday/Doubleday Picture Books
(see Random House Group)

Drake Educational Associates
St Fagans Road, Fairwater
Cardiff CF5 3AE
029 2056 0333
info@drakeav.com
www.drakeav.com
Audio-visual, educational

Dref Wen
28 Church Road, Whitchurch
Cardiff CF14 2EA
029 2061 7860
sales@drefwen.com
Welsh language

Duncan Baird Publishers
Castle House, 75–76 Wells Street
London W1T 3QH
020 7323 2229
enquiries@dbairdpub.co.uk
www.dbponline.co.uk
General non-fiction

Duncan Petersen Publishing
31 Ceylon Road, London W14 0PY
020 7371 2356
dp@macunltd.net
www.charmingsmallhotels.co.uk
Non-fiction

Ebury Press
(see Random House Group)

Eden
(see Random House Group)

Edinburgh University Press
22 George Square
Edinburgh EH8 9LF
0131 650 4218
Timothy.Wright@eup.ed.ac.uk
www.eup.ed.ac.uk

Edward Elgar Publishing
Glensanda House, Montpellier Parade
Cheltenham
Gloucestershire GL50 1UA
01242 226934
info@e-elgar.co.uk
www.e-elgar.com
Economics, business and environment

Egmont Books
239 Kensington High Street
London W8 6SA
020 7761 3500
egmont@egmont.com
www.egmont.com
*Children's entertainment. Imprints:
Heinemann Young Books, Methuen
Children's Books, Hamlyn Children's
Books, Mammoth, Dean*

Eland Publishing
Third Floor, 61 Exmouth Market
Clerkenwell, London EC1R 4QL
020 7833 0762
info@travelbooks.co.uk
www.travelbooks.co.uk
*Travel, poetry, literature and history of
the Islamic world*

Elliot Right Way Books
Kingswood Buildings
Lower Kingswood
Tadworth, Surrey KT20 6TD
01737 832202
info@right-way.co.uk
www.right-way.co.uk
Practical non-fiction paperbacks

Elliott & Thompson
27 John Street, London WC1N 2BX
020 7831 5013
gmo73@dial.pipex.com
www.elliottthompson.com
History, biography, literary and fiction

Elm Consulting
Seaton House, Kings Ripton
Huntingdon
Cambridgeshire PE28 2NJ
01487 773254
sritchie@elm-training.co.uk
www.elm-training.co.uk
Educational aids

Elsevier
(see Reed Elsevier)

Emissary Publishing
PO Box 33, Bicester
Oxfordshire OX26 4ZZ
01869 323447
www.manuscriptresearch.co.uk
Humorous paperbacks

Emma Treehouse
2nd Floor, The Old Brewhouse
Lower Charlton Trading Estate,
Shepton Mallet, Somerset BA4 5QE
01749 330529
treehouse-books@btconnect.com
www.emmatreehouse.com
Children's pre-school

Encyclopaedia Britannica (UK)
2nd Floor, Unity Wharf
Mill Street, London SE1 2BH
020 7500 7800
enquiries@britannica.co.uk
www.britannica.co.uk

English Heritage (Publishing)
Kemble Drive, Swindon SN2 2GZ
01793 414619
customers@english-heritage.org.uk
www.english-heritage.org.uk
General and specialist history

Enitharmon Press
26B Caversham Road
London NW5 2DU
020 7482 5967
books@enitharmon.co.uk
www.enitharmon.co.uk
*Poetry, literary criticism, fiction, art
and photography, memoirs and
translations*

Euromonitor
60–61 Britton Street
London EC1M 5UX
020 7251 8024
info@euromonitor.com
www.euromonitor.com
*Business reference, market analysis
and information directories*

Europa Publications
(see T&F Informa)

Evans Publishing Group
(see Thomson Learning)

Everyman
(see Orion Publishing Group)

Everyman's Library
Northburgh House
10 Northburgh Street
London EC1V 0AT
020 7566 6350
books@everyman.uk.com
*Imprint of Alfred A Knopf (subsidiary
of Random House, USA). Literature,
poetry, children's and travel*

Exley Publications
16 Chalk Hill, Watford
Hertfordshire WD19 4BG
01923 248328
enquiries@exleypublications.co.uk
www.helenexleygiftbooks.com
*Giftbooks, quotation anthologies and
humour*

Expert Books
(see Random House Group)

FA Thorpe (Publishing)
(see Ulverscroft Group)

Faber & Faber
3 Queen Square, London WC1N
3AU
020 7465 0045
info@faber.co.uk
www.faber.co.uk
Fiction, non-fiction and poetry

Facet Publishing
7 Ridgmount Street
London WC1E 7AE
020 7255 0590/ 0505 (text phone)
info@facetpublishing.co.uk
www.facetpublishing.co.uk
*Publishing arm of CILIP (Chartered
Institute of Library and Information
Professionals). Library and
information science*

Fernhurst Books
Duke's Path, High Street
Arundel, West Sussex BN18 9AJ
01903 882277
sales@fernhurstbooks.co.uk
www.fernhurstbooks.co.uk
Sailing and watersports

Findhorn Press
305a The Park, Findhorn, Forres
Morayshire IV36 3TE
01309 690582
info@findhornpress.com
www.findhornpress.com
*New Age, personal development and
alternative health*

First & Best in Education
Unit K, Earlstrees Court
Earlstrees Road, Corby
Northamptonshire NN17 4HH
01536 399004
info@firstandbest.co.uk
www.firstandbest.co.uk
*Educational books for schools.
Imprints: School Improvement Reports*

Fitzwarren Publishing
2 Orchard Drive
Aston Clinton, Aylesbury
Buckinghamshire HP22 5HR
01296 632627
pen2paper@btopenworld.com
Legal handbooks for the layman

Flicks Books
29 Bradford Road, Trowbridge
Wiltshire BA14 9AN
01225 767728
flicks.books@dial.pipex.com
Cinema and related media

Floris Books
15 Harrison Gardens
Edinburgh EH11 1SH
0131 337 2372
floris@florisbooks.co.uk
www.florisbooks.co.uk
*Scientific, religion, holistic health and
children's*

Fodor's
(see Random House Group)

Folens Publishers
Unit 20, Apex Business Centre,
Boscombe Road, Dunstable
Bedfordshire LU5 4RL
0870 609 1237
folens@folens.com
www.folens.com
Educational books. Imprint: Belair

Footprint Handbooks
6 Riverside Court
Lower Bristol Road, Bath BA2 3DZ
01225 469141
pressoffice@footprintbooks.com
www.footprintbooks.com
*Travel. Activity guides to hundreds
of cities and countries*

For Dummies
(see John Wiley & Sons)

Fountain Press
Newpro UK , Old Sawmills Road
Faringdon, Oxfordshire SN7 7DS
01367 242411
sales@newprouk.co.uk
Photography and natural history

Fourth Estate
(see HarperCollins Publishers)

Frances Lincoln Publishers
4 Torriano Mews, Torriano Avenue
London NW5 2RZ
020 7284 4009
reception@frances-lincoln.com
www.franceslincoln.com
Highly illustrated non-fiction

Frank Cass
(see T&F Informa)

Free Association Books
57 Warren Street, London W1T 5NR
020 8906 0396
info@fabooks.com
www.fabooks.com
*Psychoanalysis and psychotherapy,
social science, psychology*

Frommer's
(see John Wiley & Sons)

FT Prentice Hall
(see Pearson Education)

Gaia Books
2–4 Heron Quays, London E14 4JP
020 7531 8439
info@gaiabooks.com
www.gaiabooks.co.uk
*Illustrated natural health, mind body
spirit, natural living and environmental
issues*

Gairm Publications
29 Waterloo Street, Glasgow G2 6BZ
0141 221 1971
Gaelic

Garland Science
(see T&F Informa)

Garnet Publishing
8 Southern Court, South Street
Reading, Berkshire RG1 4QS
0118 959 7847
enquiries@garnet-
ithaca.demon.co.uk
www.garnet-ithaca.co.uk
Imprints: Garnet (Middle East); Ithaca
Press (business books)

Geddes & Grosset
David Dale House
New Lanark ML11 9DJ
01555 665000
info@geddesandgrosset.co.uk
www.geddesandgrosset.co.uk
Children's and reference books.
Imprint: Beanobooks (children's)

Geological Society Publishing House
Unit 7, Brassmill Enterprise Centre
Brassmill Lane, Bath BA1 3JN
01225 445046
sales@geolsoc.org.uk
www.geolsoc.org.uk/bookshop
Publishing arm of the Geological
Society. Undergraduate and
postgraduate texts in the earth sciences

George Mann Books
PO Box 22, Maidstone
Kent ME14 1AH
01622 759591
Original non-fiction and selected
reprints

Gibson Square Books
15 Gibson Square
London N1 0RD
020 7689 4790
publicity@gibsonsquare.com
www.gibsonsquare.com/
Biography and personal experience.
Imprints: Gibson Square; New Editions

Giles de la Mare Publishers
PO Box 25351, London NW5 1ZT
020 7485 2533
gilesdelamare@dial.pipex.com
www.gilesdelamare.co.uk
Art and architecture, biography,
history, music

Gollancz
(see Orion Publishing Group)

GMP (Gay Men's Press)
Unit M, Spectrum House
32/34 Gordon House Road
London NW5 1LP
020 7424 7400
www.millivres.co.uk
Part of the Millivres Prowler Group.
Literary gay fiction. Imprint: Zipper
Books (gay male erotic fiction)

Gomer Press
Llandysul, Ceredigion SA44 4QL
01559 362371
gwasg@gomer.co.uk
www.gomer.co.uk
Adult fiction and non-fiction. Imprint:
Pont Books

Good Web Guide
65 Bromfelde Road
London SW4 6PP
020 7720 8919
marketing@thegoodwebguide.co.uk
www.thegoodwebguide.co.uk

Granada Learning Group
Television Centre, Quay Street
Manchester M60 9EA
0161 827 2927
info@granada-learning.co.uk
www.granada-learning.co.uk

David Fulton Publishers
The Chiswick Centre, 414 Chiswick
High Road
London W4 5PF
020 8996 3610
mail@fultonpublishers.co.uk
www.fultonpublishers.co.uk
Books for Initial Teacher Training
courses, continuing professional
development and for special
educational needs teachers

Leckie and Leckie
8 Whitehill Terrace, St Andrews
Fife KY16 8RN
01334 475656
enquiries@leckieandleckie.co.uk
www.leckieandleckie.co.uk
Study guides for students preparing for
the Scottish Standard Grade and
Higher exams

Letts Educational
The Chiswick Centre
0845 602 1937
mail@lettsed.co.uk
www.lettsed.co.uk
Examination study and revision
guides

nferNelson
The Chiswick Centre
020 8996 8444
information@nfernelson.co.uk
www.nfer-nelson.co.uk
Tests, assessments and assessment
services

SEMERC
Television Centre
0161 827 2927
www.semerc.com
ICT special needs

Granta Books
2–3 Hanover Yard, Noel Road
London N1 8BE
020 7704 9776
lcampbell@granta.com
www.granta.com
Literary fiction and general non-fiction

Green Books
Foxhole, Dartington, Totnes
Devon TQ9 6EB
01803 863260
edit@greenbooks.co.uk
www.greenbooks.co.uk
Green issues

Greenhill Books/ Lionel Leventhal
Park House, 1 Russell Gardens
London NW11 9NN
020 8458 6314
info@greenhillbooks.com
www.greenhillbooks.com
Aviation, military, Napoleonic.
Imprint: Chatham Publishing (naval)

Gresham Books
46 Victoria Road, Summertown
Oxford OX2 7QD
01865 513582
info@gresham-books.co.uk
www.gresham-books.co.uk
Hymn and service books

Griffith Institute
(see Oxford University)

Grub Street
4 Rainham Close
London SW11 6SS
020 7924 3966/ 7738 1008
post@grubstreet.co.uk
www.grubstreet.co.uk
Lifestyle and military

Guild of Master Craftsman
Publications
166 High Street, Lewes
East Sussex BN7 1XU
01273 477374
pubs@thegmcgroup.com
www.gmcbooks.com
Craft and woodworking

Guinness World Records
338 Euston Road, London NW1 3BD
020 7891 4567
press@guinnessworldrecords.com
www.guinnessworldrecords.com

Gullane
(see Pinwheel)

Gwasg Carreg Gwalch
12 Iard yr Orsaf, Llanrwst
Conwy LL26 0EH
01492 642031
books@carreg-gwalch.co.uk
www.carreg-gwalch.co.uk
Welsh fiction and non-fiction; books on
Wales

Halsgrove
Halsgrove House, Lower Moor Way
Tiverton Business Park, Tiverton
Devon EX16 6SS
01884 243242
sales@halsgrove.com
www.halsgrove.com
South-west regional books, cookery,
biography and art

Hambledon and London
102 Gloucester Avenue
London NW1 8HX
020 7586 0817
office@hambledon.co.uk
www.hambledon.co.uk
History and biography

Hamish Hamilton
(see Penguin Books)

Harcourt Education
(see Reed Elsevier)

267

Harlequin Mills & Boon
Eton House, 18–24 Paradise Road
Richmond, Surrey TW9 1SR
020 8288 2800
www.millsandboon.co.uk
Subsidiary of Harlequin, Canada.
Popular fiction

Harley Books
Martins, Great Horkesley
Colchester, Essex CO6 4AH
01206 271216
harley@keme.co.uk
www.harleybooks.com
Natural history

HarperCollins Publishers
77–85 Fulham Palace Road
London W6 8JB
020 8741 7070
webcontact@harpercollins.co.uk
www.harpercollins.co.uk

Collins
Reference books, cartography,
education, dictionaries
www.collins.co.uk

General books
HarperCollins Childrens Books
Picture books, fiction and properties
(Dr Seuss, Paddington Bear, Noddy etc.)
www.harpercollinschildrensbooks.co.uk
• HarperEntertainment
Imprints: Entertainment (media-
related); Collins Willow (sports);
Tolkien and Estates (works by JRR
Tolkien, Agatha Christie, CS Lewis);
HarperCollins Audio
• HarperFiction
Imprints: HarperCollins Fiction (crime
and popular fiction); Voyager (sci-fi and
fantasy)
www.voyager-books.co.uk
www.collins-crime.co.uk
www.readinggroups.co.uk
• HarperPress
Imprints: HarperCollins Non-Fiction
(history, current affairs, travel and
biography); Fourth Estate (innovative
fiction and non fiction);
HarperPerennial (literary paperbacks)
• Thorsons
Health, mind, body & spirit, and
personal development books. Imprint:
Thorsons and Element (colour
illustrated)
www.thorsons.co.uk

Harvard University Press/ MIT Press
Fitzroy House, 11 Chenies Street
London WC1E 7EY
020 7306 0603
info@HUP-MITpress.co.uk
http://mitpress.mit.edu
European office of US company

Harvill Secker
(see Random House Group)

Haynes Publishing
Sparkford, Near Yeovil
Somerset BA22 7JJ
01963 440635
www.haynes.co.uk
Owns Sutton Publishing. Car and
motorcycle service and repair manuals

Heinemann
(see Reed Elsevier)

Helicon Publishing
RM , New Mill House
183 Milton Park, Abingdon
Oxfordshire OX14 4SE
0870 920 0200
helicon@rm.com
www.helicon.co.uk
CD-Roms and online reference and
cartography

Helm Information
The Banks, Mountfield
Nr Robertsbridge
East Sussex TN32 5JY
01580 880561
amandahelm@helm-information.co.uk
www.helm-information.co.uk
Academic

Helter Skelter Publishing
South Bank House
Black Prince Road, London SE1 7SJ
020 7463 2204
info@helterskelterpublishing.com
www.helterskelterbooks.com
Obscure music. Co-imprint with SAF
Publishing: Firefly Publishing
(mainstream rock and pop)

Hesperus Press
4 Rickett Street, London SW6 1RU
020 7610 3331
agallenzi@hesperuspress.com
www.hesperuspress.com
Classic fiction in paperback

Highbury Leisure Publications
Berwick House, 8/10 Knoll Rise
Orpington, Kent BR6 0PS
01689 887200
www.splpublishing.co.uk
Formerly Highbury Nexus. Leisure and
hobbies

Hobsons Publishing
Challenger House, 42 Adler Street
London E1 1EE
020 7958 5000
info@hobsons.co.uk
www.hobsons.com/uk
Part of the Daily Mail & General Trust.
Course and career guides

Hodder Headline Group
338 Euston Road, London NW1 3BH
020 7873 6000
www.hodderheadline.co.uk and
www.madaboutbooks.com
Owned by Hatchett & Every

Hodder Headline Ireland
8 Castlecourt Centre
Castleknock, Dublin 15
00 353 1 824 6288
Adult fiction and non-fiction. Imprint:
HHI Lir (fiction)

Hodder Headline Scotland
2A Christie Street, Paisley PA1 1NB
0141 848 1609
bob.mcdevitt@hodder.co.uk

General
• Hodder & Stoughton *Imprints:*
Sceptre (literary); NEL (crime);
Coronet (commercial fiction); Mobius
(mind, body & spirit); Flame (fiction)

• Headline *Imprints: Review*
(literary); Headline (commercial
fiction and non-fiction)
• John Murray *Fiction, history, travel,*
literature and memoir

Education
• Hodder Arnold *Imprints: teach*
yourself (home reference); Hodder +
Stoughton (reference including FA
Guides and Michelle Thomas)
• Hodder Murray *Curriculum*
materials
• Hodder Gibson *Textbooks and*
revision support for the Scottish
market 0141 848 1609
hoddergibson@hodder.co.uk

Religious
• Hodder Religious *Imprints: Hodder*
& Stoughton (gift and inspirational);
HY [help yourself] (home reference);
HCB (Hodder Christian Books); NIV
[New International Version] (bible
translation)

Children's
• Hodder Children's Books *Fiction for*
children and young adults
• Hodder Wayland *Non-fiction*
educational books
www.hodderwayland.co.uk

Honeyglen Publishing
56 Durrels House, Warwick Gardens
London W14 8QB
020 7602 2876
History and fiction

Honno Welsh Women's Press
c/o Canolfan Merched Y Wawr
Vulcan Street, Aberystwyth
Ceredigion SY23 1JH
01970 623150
post@honno.co.uk
www.honno.co.uk
Reprints of classics, children's, fiction,
poetry, short stories and Welsh women
writers

House of Lochar
Isle of Colonsay, Argyll PA61 7YR
01951 200232
lochar@colonsay.org.uk
www.houseoflochar.com
Mostly Scottish titles. Imprint:
Colonsay Books

House of Stratus
Thirsk Industrial Park
Thirsk, North Yorkshire YO7 3BX
01845 527700
sales@houseofstratus.com
www.houseofstratus.com
Quality literary fiction and non-fiction

How To Books
3 Newtec Place, Magdalen Road
Oxford OX4 1RE
01865 793806
info@howtobooks.co.uk
www.howtobooks.co.uk
Reference and self-help books

Hutchinson
(see Random House Group)

Ian Allan Publishing
Riverdene Business Park
Molesey Road, Hersham
Surrey KT12 4RG
01932 266600
info@ianallanpub.co.uk
www.ianallan.com
*Maritime, road, rail, aviation, militaria
and military history. Imprints:
Midland Publishing, OPC Railway,
Classic Publications, Lewis Masonic*

Ian Henry Publications
20 Park Drive, Romford
Essex RM1 4LH
01708 749119
iwilkes@ianhenry.fsnet.co.uk
History and Sherlock Holmes

IB Tauris
(see Thomson Learning)

Icon Books
The Old Dairy, Brook Road
Thriplow, Cambridge SG8 7RG
01763 208008
info@iconbooks.co.uk
www.iconbooks.co.uk
*History, children's fiction and
non-fiction, adult non-fiction*

IMP Fiction
PO Box 69, Church Stretton
Shropshire SU6 6WZ
0169 4720049
info@impbooks.com
www.impbooks.com
Original fiction

Independent Music Press
PO Box 69, Church Stretton
Shropshire SU6 6WZ
0169 4720049
info@impbooks.com
www.impbooks.com
Music biography and youth culture

Interpet
Interpet House, Vincent Lane
Dorking, Surrey RH4 3YX
01306 873840
kevin@interpet.co.uk
Pet, aquatic and water gardening books

Inter-Varsity Press
38 De Montfort Street
Leicester LE1 7GP
0116 255 1754
ivp@ivp-editorial.co.uk
www.ivpbooks.com
*Christian belief and lifestyle. Imprints:
IVP, Apollos, Crossway*

Isis Publishing
(see Ulverscroft Group)

Ithaca Press
(see Garnet Publishing)

**James Clarke & Co Lutterworth
Press**
PO Box 60, Cambridge CB1 2NT
01223 350865
publishing@jamesclarke.co.uk
www.jamesclarke.co.uk
*Parent company of The Lutterworth
Press. Theological, directory and
reference*

James Currey Publishers
73 Botley Road, Oxford OX2 0BS
01865 244111
editorial@jamescurrey.co.uk
www.jamescurrey.co.uk
*Academic books on Africa and third
world*

Jane's Information Group
163 Brighton Road, Coulsdon
Surrey CR5 2YH
020 8700 3700
info@janes.com
www.janes.com
Defence, aerospace and transport

Janus Publishing Company
105–107 Gloucester Place
London W1U 6BY
020 7580 7664
publisher@januspublishing.co.uk
www.januspublishing.co.uk
*Fiction and non-fiction. Imprint:
Empiricus Books*

Jarrold Publishing
Whitefriars, Norwich, Norfolk NR3 1JR
01603 763300
publishing@jarrold.com
www.jarrold-publishing.co.uk
*Heritage and leisure, walking guides.
Imprints: Pitkin, Unichrome*

Jessica Kingsley Publishers
116 Pentonville Road
London N1 9JB
020 7833 2307
post@jkp.com
www.jkp.com
Social and behavioural sciences

John Blake Publishing
3 Bramber Court, 2 Bramber Road
London W14 9PB
020 7381 0666
words@blake.co.uk
www.blake.co.uk
*General non-fiction, esp true crime,
popular culture, general biography.
Includes Richard Cohen, Smith
Gryphon and Blake Publishing.
Imprints: Metro Books (health, fitness,
cookery and lifestyle)*

John Hunt Publishing
46a West Street, New Alresford
Hampshire SO24 9AU
01962 773768
office@johnhunt-publishing.com
www.johnhunt-publishing.com,
www.o-books.net
*Children's and world religions. Imprint:
O Books (mind, body and spirit)*

John Murray
(see Hodder Headline Group)

John Wiley & Sons
The Atrium, Southern Gate
Chichester PO19 8SQ
01243 779777
cs-books@wiley.co.uk
www.wileyeurope.com
*Scientific, technical and medical;
professional and trade; textbooks and
educational materials*

Capstone Publishing
*Business and personal development
www.capstoneideas.com*
For Dummies
Reference series
Frommer's
Travel guides
Jossey-Bass
Management, education and religion
The Unofficial Guide
Travel, computing
Visual/Redhat Press/ Wrox
Computing
Wiley
*Scientific, technical and medical;
professional and trade; textbooks and
educational materials*
Wiley Interscience
*Scientific, technical and medical; print
and online reference materials*
Wiley-Academy
Architecture
Wiley-Liss
Life and medical
Wiley-VCH
Scientific, technical and medical

Jonathan Cape
(see Random House Group)

Kahn & Averill
9 Harrington Road, London SW7 3ES
020 8743 3278
kahn@averill23.freeserve.co.uk
Books on music

Kenilworth Press
Addington, Buckingham
Buckinghamshire MK18 2JR
01296 715101
editorial@kenilworthpress.co.uk
www.kenilworthpress.co.uk
Equestrian

Kenneth Mason Publications
The Book Barn, Westbourne
Emsworth, Hampshire PO10 8RS
01243 377977
info@researchdisclosure.com
www.researchdisclosure.com
*Lifestyle, nutrition and nautical.
Imprint: Research Disclosure*

Kevin Mayhew Publishers
Buxhall, Stowmarket
Suffolk IP14 3BW
01449 737978
info@kevinmayhewltd.com
www.kevinmayhewltd.com
Religious titles

Kingfisher Publications
New Penderel House
283–288 High Holborn
London WC1V 7HZ
020 7903 9999
sales@kingfisherpub.com
www.kingfisherpub.com
Children's fiction and non-fiction

269

Kluwer Law International
145 London Road
Kingston-on-Thames
Surrey KT2 6SR
020 8247 1694
sales@kluwerlaw.com
www.kluwerlaw.com
*Part of Aspen Publishers, a Wolters
Kluwer company*

Kogan Page
120 Pentonville Road
London N1 9JN
020 7278 0433
kpinfo@kogan-page.co.uk
www.kogan-page.co.uk
Business and management

Kyle Cathie
122 Arlington Road, London NW1 7HP
020 7692 7215
general.enquiries@kyle-cathie.com
www.KyleCathie.com
Lifestyle

Ladybird
(see Penguin Books)

Landmark Publishing
Ashbourne Hall, Cokayne Avenue
Ashbourne, Derbyshire DE6 1EJ
01335 347349
landmark@clara.net
www.landmarkpublishing.co.uk
*Travel guides, and industrial and local
history*

Laurence King Publishing
71 Great Russell Street
London WC1B 3BP
020 7430 8850
enquiries@laurenceking.co.uk
www.laurenceking.co.uk
Illustrated arts

Lawrence & Wishart
99A Wallis Road, London E9 5LN
020 8533 2506
lw@lwbooks.co.uk
www.lwbooks.co.uk
Current and world affairs

Leckie and Leckie
(see Granada Learning)

Lennard Associates
Windmill Cottage, Mackerye End
Harpenden, Hertfordshire AL5 5DR
01582 715866
stephenson@lennardqap.co.uk
*Sporting yearbooks. Imprints and
divisions include: Lennard Publishing,
Queen Anne Press*

Letts Educational
(see Granada Learning)

LexisNexis
(see Reed Elsevier)

Lion Hudson
Mayfield House, 256 Banbury Road
Oxford OX2 7DH
01865 302750
enquiries@lionhudson.com
www.lionhudson.com
*Formed through merger of Lion
Publishing and Angus Hudson
Christian books. Imprints: Lion, Lion
Children's, Candle, Monarch*

Little, Brown
(see Time Warner Books)

Little Tiger Press
Magi Publications
1 The Coda Centre
189 Munster Road, London SW6 6AW
020 7385 6333
info@littletiger.co.uk
www.littletigerpress.com
*Children's picture and novelty books.
Imprints: Little Tiger, Caterpillar Books*

Liverpool University Press
4 Cambridge Street
Liverpool L69 7ZU
0151 794 2233
sbell@liv.ac.uk
www.liverpool-unipress.co.uk

Lonely Planet Publications
72–82 Rosebery Avenue
Clerkenwell, London EC1R 4RW
020 7841 9000
go@lonelyplanet.co.uk
www.lonelyplanet.com
Travel guides

Longman
(see Pearson Education)

Lutterworth Press
(see James Clarke & Co Lutterworth
Press)

Macmillan Publishers
4 Crinan Street, London N1 9XW
020 7843 3600
www.macmillan.com
Nature Publishing Group
4 Crinan Street
020 7843 4000
www.nature.com
*Scientific journals and reference
publishing*
Macmillan Education
Macmillan Oxford
4 Between Towns Road
Oxford OX4 3PP
01865 405700
www.macmillaneducation.com
*ELT learning materials for
international markets*
Palgrave Macmillan
Brunel Road, Houndmills
Basingstoke, Hampshire RG21 6XS
01256 329242
bookenquiries@palgrave.com
www.palgrave.com
*Academic, scholarly and reference
publishing in the social sciences and
humanities*
Pan Macmillan
20 New Wharf Road
London N1 9RR
020 7014 6000
www.panmacmillan.com
*Fiction and non-fiction for adults and
children. Imprints: Macmillan, Pan,
Picador, Young Picador, Boxtree,
Sidgwick and Jackson, Papermac,
Macmillan Children's Books, Campbell
Books, Priddy Books*
• US imprints: *Picador USA; St
Martin's Press; Farrar, Straus and
Giroux Inc.; Henry Holt; Tor*

• Australian imprints: *Pan Macmillan
Australia, Pancake*
• South African imprints: *Pan
Macmillan South Africa, Picador
Africa*
• Irish imprints: *Gill and Macmillan*

Magna Large Print Books
(see Ulverscroft Group)

**Mainstream Publishing Co
(Edinburgh)**
7 Albany Street, Edinburgh EH1 3UG
0131 557 2959
editorial@mainstreampublishing.com
www.mainstreampublishing.com
*General non-fiction and popular
paperbacks*

Management Books 2000
Forge House, Limes Road
Kemble, Cirencester
Gloucestershire GL7 6AD
01285 771441
info@mb2000.com
www.mb2000.com
Working books for working managers

Manchester University Press
Oxford Road, Manchester M13 9NR
0161 275 2310
mucp@manchester.ac.uk
www.manchesteruniversitypress.co.uk

Manson Publishing
73 Corringham Road
London NW11 7DL
020 8905 5150
www.mansonpublishing.com
*Scientific, technical, medical and
veterinary*

Marion Boyars Publishers
24 Lacy Road, London SW15 1NL
020 8788 9522
catheryn@marionboyars.com
www.marionboyars.co.uk
*Formerly Calder and Boyars. Literary
fiction, fiction in translation, social
affairs, film, music, drama*

Marshall Cavendish
119 Wardour Street
London W1F 0UW
020 7565 6000
www.marshallcavendish.co.uk
Adults' and children's and educational

Marston House
Marston House, Marston Magna
Yeovil, Somerset BA22 8DH
01935 851331
alphaimage@marstonhouse.ndo.co.uk
www.marstonhouse.ndo.co.uk
*Fine art, architecture, ceramics and
horticulture*

Martin Dunitz
(see T&F Informa)

McGraw-Hill Education
Shoppenhangers Road
Maidenhead, Berkshire SL6 2QL
01628 502500
www.mcgraw-hill.co.uk
*Business, economics, computing and
engineering*

Professional

Professional, business and general reference books covering computing, science, technical and medical, languages, architecture, careers, politics, management, finance, parenting, health, sports & fitness. Imprints: McGraw-Hill Professional, McGraw-Hill Trade, McGraw-Hill Osborne, McGraw-Hill Medical Publishing, McGraw-Hill Contemporary, Harvard Business School Press, Amacom, Berrett-Koehler, CMP

Higher Education

University textbooks on business, economics, accounting, finance, marketing, computing science, decision sciences. Imprints: McGraw-Hill Education, McGraw-Hill Irwin

Open University Press

Higher education, education, health and social welfare, cultural and media studies, psychology, criminology, sociology, counselling, study guides

Schools

Early childhood, primary and secondary school books. Imprints: Kingscourt, Glencoe and SRA, Macmillan, The Learning Group

Mercat Press

10 Coates Crescent
Edinburgh EH3 7AL
0131 225 5324
enquiries@mercatpress.com
www.mercatpress.com
Fiction and non-fiction of Scottish interest

Merlin Press

PO Box 30705, London WC2E 8QD
020 7836 3020
0845 4581579
info@merlinpress.co.uk
www.merlinpress.co.uk
Economics, history, leftwing politics. Imprints: Green Print, Merlin Press

Merrell Publishers

81 Southwark Street
London SE1 0HX
020 7928 8880
mail@merrellpublishers.com
www.merrellpublishers.com
Art, architecture, design and photography

Methodist Publishing House

4 John Wesley Road
Werrington, Peterborough
Cambridgeshire PE4 6ZP
01733 325002
sales@mph.org.uk
www.mph.org.uk
Owned by the Methodist Church Christian books. Imprint: Epworth Press

Methuen Publishing

11/12 Buckingham Gate
London SW1E 6LB
020 7798 1600
sales@methuen.co.uk
www.methuen.co.uk
Drama and general fiction and non-fiction. Imprint: Politicos (politics)

Michael Joseph

(see Penguin Books)

Michael O'Mara Books

9 Lion Yard, Tremadoc Road
London SW4 7NQ
020 7720 8643
enquiries@michaelomarabooks.com
www.mombooks.com
Biography, popular history, humour, children's and pre-school

Michelin Travel Publications

Hannay House, 39 Clarendon Road
Watford, Hertfordshire WD17 1JA
01923 205240
www.viamichelin.com
Travel books and maps

Microsoft Press

Thames Valley Park, Reading
Berkshire RG6 1WG
0870 601 0100
mspinfo@microsoft.com
www.microsoft.com/mspress/uk
Computing manuals to accompany Microsoft products; also system administration, business solutions and security

Miles Kelly Publishing

Unit 17 & 18, The Bardfield Centre
Great Bardfield, Essex CM7 4SL
01371 811309
info@mileskelly.net
www.mileskelly.net
Children's titles

Milet Publishing

6 North End Parade, London W14 0SJ
020 7603 5477
info@milet.com
www.milet.com
Children's books

Mills & Boon

(see Harlequin Mills & Boon)

MIT Press

(see Harvard University Press/ MIT Press)

Motor Racing Publications

PO Box 1318, Croydon
Surrey CR9 5YP
020 8654 2711
mrp.books@virgin.net
www.mrpbooks.co.uk
Motor racing, road cars, performance and classic cars

MQ Publications

12 The Ivories, 6–8 Northampton St
London N1 2HY
020 7359 2244
kim@mqpublications.com
www.mqpublications.com
Illustrated cookbooks

Multi-Sensory Learning

Highgate House, Groom's Lane
Creaton, Northampton NN6 8NN
01604 505000
info@msl-online.net
www.msl-online.net
Resources on learning difficulties esp. dyslexia

Murdoch Books UK

Erico House, 6th Floor
93–99 Upper Richmond Road
Putney, London SW15 2TG
020 8785 5995
aelliott@murdochbooks.co.uk
Food & drink, craft, gardening, fiction and non fiction

National Trust Publications

36 Queen Anne's Gate
London SW1H 9AS
020 7222 9251
enquiries@thenationaltrust.org.uk
www.nationaltrust.org.uk/bookshop
Publishing arm of The National Trust

Nautical Data

The Book Barn, Westbourne
Emsworth, Hampshire PO10 8RS
01243 389352
info@nauticaldata.com
www.nauticaldata.com

NCVO Publications

Regent's Wharf, 8 All Saints Street
London N1 9RL
020 7713 6161
ncvo@ncvo-vol.org.uk
www.ncvo-vol.org.uk
Publishing imprint of the National Council for Voluntary Organisations Directories, public policy and governance; trusteeship and HR in the voluntary sector

Neil Wilson Publishing

Suite 303, The Pentagon Centre
36 Washington Street
Glasgow G3 8AZ
0141 221 1117
info@nwp.co.uk
www.nwp.co.uk
www.11-9.co.uk
www.vitalspark.co.uk
www.angelshare.co.uk
www.theinpinn.co.uk
Scottish and Irish interest: food and drink, outdoor pursuits, history, humour and biography

Nelson Thornes

Delta Place, 27 Bath Road
Cheltenham
Gloucestershire GL53 7TH
01242 267100
info@nelsonthornes.com
www.nelsonthornes.com
Part of the Wolters Kluwer Group Educational

New Beacon Books

76 Stroud Green Road
London N4 3EN
020 7272 4889
newbeaconbooks@lineone.net
Black-oriented fiction, history, politics, poetry and language

New Holland Publishers (UK)

Garfield House, 86–88 Edgware Road
London W2 2EA
020 7724 7773
postmaster@nhpub.co.uk
www.newhollandpublishers.com
Non-fiction, lifestyle and self-improvement

New Riders
(see Pearson Education)

nferNelson
(see Granada Learning)

Nicholas Brealey Publishing
3–5 Spafield Street
London EC1R 4QB
020 7239 0360
publicity@nbrealey-books.com
www.nbrealey-books.com
Includes Intercultural Press. Cultural business, self-help and travel. US imprint: Intercultural Press

Nick Hern Books
The Glasshouse, 49a Goldhawk Road
London W12 8QP
020 8749 4953
info@nickhernbooks.demon.co.uk
www.nickhernbooks.co.uk
Theatre and film

Nielsen BookData
3rd Floor, Midas House
62 Goldsworth Road, Woking
Surrey GU21 6LQ
0870 7778710
info@bookdata.co.uk
www.nielsenbookdata.com
"The Red Book" directory of publishers

NMS Enterprises
National Museums of Scotland
Chambers Street, Edinburgh EH1 1JF
0131 247 4026
publishing@nms.ac.uk
www.nms.ac.uk
History, art, archaeology, natural history, popular Scottish history, culture, biography and geology

Nottingham University Press
Manor Farm, Church Lane
Thrumpton, Nottingham NG11 0AX
0115 983 1011
editor@nup.com
www.nup.com
Scientific textbooks

Oberon Books
521 Caledonian Road
London N7 9RH
020 7607 3637
oberon.books@btinternet.com
www.oberonbooks.com
Play texts

Octagon Press
PO Box 227, London N6 4EW
020 8348 9392
admin@octagonpress.com
www.octagonpress.com
Philosophy, psychology, travel and Eastern religion

Octopus Publishing Group
2–4 Heron Quays, London E14 4JP
020 7531 8400
info@octopus-publishing.co.uk
www.octopus-publishing.co.uk
www.conran-octopus.co.uk
www.hamlyn.co.uk
www.mitchell-beazley.co.uk
www.philips-maps.co.uk
Owned by Hachette. Illustrated adult reference books

Oldcastle Books
PO Box 394, Harpenden
Hertfordshire AL5 1XJ
01582 761264
info@noexit.co.uk
info@pocketessentials.com
www.noexit.co.uk
www.pocketessentials.com
www.gamblingbooks.co.uk
Imprints: No Exit Press and Crime Time (crime/noir fiction); Pocketessentials (compact reference books on film, tv, literature, ideas and history); High Stakes (gambling)

Omnibus Press
Music Sales, 8–9 Frith Street
London W1D 3JB
020 7434 0066
music@musicsales.co.uk
www.omnibuspress.com
Imprints: Omnibus Press (music-related biography); Vision On (upmarket music-related photo books). US imprint: Schirmer Books (self-help books, music industry)

Oneworld
(see Thomson Learning)

Onlywomen Press
40 St Lawrence Terrace
London W10 5ST
020 8354 0796
onlywomenpress@aol.com
www.onlywomenpress.com
Lesbian and feminist fiction, non-fiction theory and poetry

Open University Press
(see McGraw-Hill Education)

Orbit Press
(see Time Warner Books)

Orion Publishing Group
Orion House
5 Upper Saint Martin's Lane
London WC2H 9EA
020 7240 3444
info@orionbooks.co.uk
www.orionbooks.co.uk
• Gollancz: *Sci-fi and fantasy*
• Orion Children's Books
• Weidenfeld & Nicolson: *History, reference, non-fiction, illustrated and literary fiction, military*
• Cassell Military: *Illustrated and paperback*
• Cassell Reference
• Everyman: *Classics in paperback*
• Phoenix: *Contemporary fiction*

Halban Publishers
22 Golden Square, London W1F 9JW
020 7437 9300
books@halbanpublishers.com
www.halbanpublishers.com
Fiction, memoirs, history, biography and books of Jewish interest

Allen & Unwin (Australian imprint)
www.allen-unwin.com.au

Osprey Publishing
Midland House, West Way
Oxford OX2 0PH
01865 727022
info@ospreypublishing.com
www.ospreypublishing.com
Military history, aviation

Oxford University

Ashmolean Museum Publications
Ashmolean Museum
Beaumont Street, Oxford OX1 2PH
01865 278010
publications@ashmus.ox.ac.uk
www.ashmol.ox.ac.uk
Art and archaeology

Griffith Institute
Sackler Library, 1 St John's Street
Oxford OX1 2LG
01865 278099
griffox@herald.ox.ac.uk
www.ashmol.ox.ac.uk/Griffith.html
Egyptology

Oxford University Press
Great Clarendon Street
Oxford OX2 6DP
01865 556767
enquiry@oup.com
www.oup.com
A department of Oxford University Academic. Imprint: Oxford Children's Books

Palgrave Macmillan
(see Macmillan Publishers)

Pan/Pan Macmillan
(see Macmillan Publishers)

Papermac
(see Macmillan Publishers)

Paper Tiger
(see Chrysalis Books)

Pavilion
(see Chrysalis Books)

Peachpit Press
(see Pearson Education)

Pearson Education
Edinburgh Gate, Harlow
Essex CM20 2JE
01279 623623
HEEnquiriesUK@pearsoned-ema.com
www.pearsoned.co.uk

Allyn & Bacon
Education, humanities and social sciences

Addison-Wesley
Computer programming

Benjamin Cummings
Science

Cisco Press
Cisco systems materials

FT Prentice Hall
Global business

Longman
Educational materials for schools, English language teaching (ELT) materials, higher education textbooks (law, humanities, social sciences)

New Riders
Graphics and design

Peachpit Press
Web development

Penguin Books
(*see separate entry under Penguin Books*)
Penguin Longman
ELT books
Penguin English (for teachers)
www.penguinenglish.com
Penguin Readers (for students)
www.penguinreaders.com
Prentice Hall
Academic and reference textbooks:
business, computer science, engineering
and IT
Prentice Hall Business
Practical and personal development
QUE Publishing
Computing
SAMS Publishing
Reference books for programmers and
developers, web developers, designers,
networking and system administrators
York Notes
Literature guides for students

Pegasus Elliot & Mackenzie Publishers
Sheraton House, Castle Park
Cambridge CB3 0AX
01223 370012
editors@pegasuspublishers.com
www.pegasuspublishers.com
Fiction and non-fiction, crime and
erotica. Imprints: Vanguard Press,
Nightingale Books, Chimera

Pen & Sword Books
47 Church Street, Barnsley
South Yorkshire S70 2AS
01226 734222
enquiries@pen-and-sword.co.uk
www.pen-and-sword.co.uk
Military, naval and aviation history.
Imprints: Leo Cooper, Wharncliffe
Publishing

Penguin Books
80 Strand, London WC2R 0RL
020 7010 3000
penguin@penguin.co.uk
www.penguin.co.uk
Owned by Pearson
Dorling Kindersley
Information books and resources for
children and adults
ePenguin
ebooks
Penguin Audiobooks
Penguin General Books: Imprints:
Penguin Paperbacks; Hamish
Hamilton; Michael Joseph; Viking)
Penguin Ireland
25 St Stephen's Green, Dublin 2
00 353 1 661 7695
info@penguin.ie
www.penguin.ie
Penguin Press
Imprints: Allen Lane (reference inc.
Roget's Thesaurus and Pears
Cyclopaedia); Penguin Classics;
Penguin Modern Classics)
Puffin
Children's

Rough Guides
Travel guides, phrase books, music
guides and reference
roughguide@penguin.co.uk
Warne
Children's, inc. Beatrix Potter,
Spot, Ladybird

Persephone Books
59 Lamb's Conduit Street
London WC1N 3NB
020 7242 9292
info@persephonebooks.co.uk
www.persephonebooks.co.uk
Reprint fiction and non-fiction, focus
on women

Perseus Books Group
69–70 Temple Chambers
3–7 Temple Avenue
London EC4Y 0HP
020 7353 7771
info@perseusbooks.com
www.perseusbooksgroup.com
UK office of US Perseus Books Group.
Non-fiction. Imprints: PublicAffairs
(current affairs), Da Capo Press (music,
history, film and biography), Basic
Books (current affairs, history, popular
science), Counterpoint (literature and
fiction), Basic Civitas Books (African
American studies), Westview Press
(social sciences, humanities, science)

Peter Haddock Publishing
Pinfold Lane, Bridlington
East Yorkshire YO16 6BT
01262 678121
sales@phpublishing.co.uk
www.phpublishing.co.uk
Children's books

Peter Halban Publishers
(see Orion Publishing Group)

Peter Owen Publishers
73 Kenway Road, London SW5 0RE
020 7373 5628
admin@peterowen.com
www.peterowen.com
Biography, non-fiction, literary fiction,
literary criticism, history and the arts

Phaidon Press
18 Regent's Wharf, All Saints Street
London N1 9PA
020 7843 1000
enquiries@phaidon.com
www.phaidon.com
Arts

Pharmaceutical Press
1 Lambeth High Street
London SE1 7JN
020 7735 9141
enquiries@rpsgb.org
www.rpsgb.org
The publications division of the Royal
Pharmaceutical Society of Great
Britain. Medicine

Philip Berrill International
60 Leyland Road, Southport
Merseyside PR9 9JA
01704 534725
philipberrill@hotmail.com
Art and mind, body & spirit guides

Philip Wilson Publishers
109 Drysdale Street
The Timber Yard, London N1 6ND
020 7033 9900
pwilson@philip-wilson.co.uk
www.philip-wilson.co.uk
Art, museums and exhibition materials

Phillimore & Co
Shopwyke Manor Barn, Chichester
West Sussex PO20 2BG
01243 787636
bookshop@phillimore.co.uk
www.phillimore.co.uk
Local and family history

Phoenix
(see Orion Publishing Group)

Piatkus Books
5 Windmill Street, London W1T 2JA
020 7631 0710
info@piatkus.co.uk
www.piatkus.co.uk
Fiction, biography, history, health,
business and personal development

Picador
(see Macmillan Publishers)

Piccadilly Press
5 Castle Road, London NW1 8PR
020 7267 4492
books@piccadillypress.co.uk
www.piccadillypress.co.uk
Children's, teenage and parental books

Pimlico
(see Random House Group)

Pinwheel
Winchester House
259–269 Old Marylebone Road
London NW1 5XJ
020 7616 7200
www.pinwheel.co.uk
Imprints: Gullane (children's picture);
Pinwheel (novelty); Andromeda
(education)

Pluto Press
(see Thomson Learning)

Pocket Books
(see Simon & Schuster UK)

The Policy Press
University of Bristol, Fourth Floor
Beacon House, Queen's Road
Bristol BS8 1QU
0117 331 4054
tpp-info@bristol.ac.uk
www.policypress.org.uk
Social sciences

Politico's Publishing
(see Methuen Publishing)

Polity Press
65 Bridge Street
Cambridge CB2 1UR
01223 324315
info@polity.co.uk
www.polity.co.uk
General academic

Portland Press
3rd Floor, Eagle House
16 Proctor Street
London WC1V 6NX
020 7280 4100
editorial@portlandpress.com
www.portlandpress.com
Biochemistry and medicine

Prentice Hall/ Prentice Hall Business
(see Pearson Education)

Prestel Publishing
4 Bloomsbury Place
London WC1A 2QA
020 7323 5004
sales@prestel-uk.co.uk
www.prestel.com
Art, architecture, photography and design

Priddy Books
(see Macmillan Publishers)

Profile Books
3A Exmouth House, Pine Street,
Exmouth Market, London EC1R 0JH
020 7841 6300
info@profilebooks.com
www.profilebooks.com
Non-fiction. Imprint: Economist Books

Profile Sports Media
5th Floor, Mermaid House
2 Puddledock, London EC4V 3DS
020 7332 2000
info@profilesportsmedia.com
www.profilesportsmedia.com
Sporting annuals and publications

Proquest Information and Learning
The Quorum, Barnwell Road
Cambridge CB5 8SW
01223 215512
marketing@proquest.co.uk
www.proquest.co.uk
Educational

Psychology Press
(see T&F Informa)

Publishing House
Trinity Place, Barnstaple
Devon EX32 9HJ
01271 328892
publishinghouse@
    vernoncoleman.com
www.vernoncoleman.com
Fiction, health, humour, animals and politics

Puffin
(see Penguin Books)

Pushkin Press
12 Chester Terrace
London NW1 4ND
020 7266 9136
info@pushkinpress.com
www.pushkinpress.com
Translated classic and contemporary European literature

Putnams
(see Chrysalis Books)

Quadrille Publishing
Alhambra House
27–31 Charing Cross Road
London WC2H 0LS
020 7839 7117
enquiries@quadrille.co.uk
www.quadrille.co.uk
Lifestyle

Quartet Books
27 Goodge Street, London W1T 2LD
020 7636 3992
quartetbooks@easynet.co.uk
Part of the Namara Group.
Contemporary literary fiction

Quarto Publishing
6 Blundell Street, London N7 9BH
020 77006700
info@quarto.com
www.quarto.com
Highly illustrated non-fiction

QUE Publishing
(see Pearson Education)

Radcliffe Publishing
18 Marcham Road, Abingdon
Oxfordshire OX14 1AA
01235 528820
contact.us@radcliffemed.com
www.radcliffe-oxford.com

Random House Group
Random House
20 Vauxhall Bridge Road
London SW1V 2SA
020 7840 8400
enquiries@randomhouse.co.uk
www.randomhouse.co.uk

Random House Division
- Arrow: *Mass-market paperback fiction and non-fiction*
- Century: *General fiction and non-fiction including commercial fiction, autobiography, biography, history and self-help*
- Chatto & Windus: *Memoirs, current affairs, essays, literary fiction, history, poetry, politics, philosophy and translations*
- Harvill Secker: *Literary fiction, literature in translation, English literature, quality thrillers, some non-fiction*
- Hutchinson: *General fiction and non-fiction including belles-lettres, current affairs, politics, travel and history*
- Jonathan Cape: *Biography and memoirs, current affairs, fiction, history, photography, poetry, politics and travel*
- Pimlico: *Quality non-fiction paperbacks specialising in history, biography, popular culture and the arts*

Random House Business Books
- Vintage: *Quality paperback fiction and non-fiction*
- William Heinemann: *General fiction and non-fiction especially history, literary fiction, crime, science, thrillers and women's fiction*
- Yellow Jersey Press: *Narrative sports books*

Ebury Press Division
- Ebury Press: *Autobiography, biography, popular history, cookery, popular science, humour, diet and health*
- Fodor's: *Travel guides*
- Rider: *Mind, body and spirit*
- Vermilion: *Popular reference, lifestyle, crafts, interior design*

Random House Children's Books
Transworld Publishers
61–63 Uxbridge Road
London W5 5SA
020 8231 6800
Imprints: Hutchinson, Jonathan Cape, The Bodley Head, Doubleday Picture Books, David Fickling Books, Corgi, Red Fox

Transworld Publishers
61–63 Uxbridge Road
London W5 5SA
020 8579 2652
info@transworld-publishers.co.uk
www.booksattransworld.co.uk
Imprints: Bantam, Bantam Press, Corgi & Black Swan, Doubleday, Eden, Expert Books, Channel 4 Books

Ransom Publishing
Rose Cottage, Howe Hill
Watlington, Oxfordshire OX49 5HB
01491 613711
ransom@ransom.co.uk
www.ransom.co.uk
Education

Reader's Digest Association
11 Westferry Circus, Canary Wharf
London E14 4HE
020 7715 8000
gbeditorial@readersdigest.co.uk
www.readersdigest.co.uk
Cookery, history, reference, gardening and DIY

Reaktion Books
79 Farringdon Road
London EC1M 3JU
020 7404 9930
info@reaktionbooks.co.uk
www.reaktionbooks.co.uk
Architecture, Asian and cultural studies, film and travel, art and photography, history and geography

Reardon Publishing
56 Upper Norwood Street
Leckhampton, Cheltenham
Gloucestershire GL53 0DU
01242 231800
reardon@bigfoot.com
www.reardon.co.uk
Member of the Outdoor Writers Guild. Cotswold area local interest

Red Bird Publishing
Kiln Farm, East End Green
Brightlingsea, Colchester
Essex CO7 0SX
01206 303525
info@red-bird.co.uk
www.red-bird.co.uk
Special-effects books for children

Red Fox
(see Random House Group)

Redhat Press
(see John Wiley & Sons)

Reed Elsevier
1–3 Strand, London WC2N 5JR
020 7930 7077
www.reedelsevier.com
PRESS: 020 7166 5657/5670

Science and Medical Division
32 Jamestown Road
Camden Town, London NW1 7BY
020 7424 4200
eurobkinfo@elsevier.com
www.elsevier-international.com
•Elsevier Science and Technology
Imprints: Academic Press (physical, applied and life sciences); Morgan Kaufmann (databases, computer networking, human computer interaction, computer graphics, multimedia information and systems, artificial intelligence, and software engineering); Syngress Media (computing reference works for IT professionals)
•Elsevier Health Sciences *Imprints: Saunders (medical), Mosby (medicine, nursing, allied health and veterinary medicine), Churchill Livingstone (medical), Butterworth-Heinemann (technology, medicine and management), Hanley & Belfus (medical); Bailliere Tindall (nursing and midwifery); BC Decker (medicine, health sciences, and dentistry); GW Medical Publishing (abuse, maltreatment, sexually transmitted diseases, and domestic violence)*
PRESS: PressOffice@elsevier.com

Education Division
Harcourt Education, Halley Court
Jordan Hill, Oxford OX2 8EJ
01865 311366
uk.schools@harcourteducation.co.uk
www.harcourteducation.co.uk
Textbooks and educational resources. Imprints: Ginn, Heinemann (Primary, Secondary, FE and Vocational), Rigby UK

Business Division
Reed Business Information
Quadrant House, The Quadrant,
Sutton, Surrey SM2 5AS
020 8652 3500
PRESS: 020 8652 3296
www.reedbusiness.co.uk
Business directories, magazines, e-newsletters, websites and cd-roms

Legal Division
LexisNexis Butterworths Tolley
Halsbury House, 35 Chancery Lane
London WC2A 1EL
020 7400 2500
competitive.intelligence@
    lexis-nexis.com
www.lexisnexis.co.uk
Legal and business materials in print and online, including The Advertiser Red Books. Butterworths Services provide access to a library of UK law
PRESS: 020 7400 2753

Regency House Publishing
Nial House, 24–26 Boulton Road
Stevenage, Hertfordshire SG1 4QX
01438 314488
regency-house@btconnect.com
Art and transport

Richmond House Publishing Company
70–76 Bell Street, Marylebone
London NW1 6SP
020 7224 9666
sales@rhpco.co.uk
www.rhpco.co.uk
Theatre and entertainment directories

Rider
(see Random House Group)

Robert Hale
Clerkenwell House
45–47 Clerkenwell Green
London EC1R 0HT
020 7251 2661
enquire@halebooks.com
www.halebooks.com

Robson Books
(see Chrysalis Books)

Rodale Books
7–10 Chandos Street
London W1G 9AD
020 7291 6000
www.rodale.co.uk
Lifestyle

Roget's Thesaurus
(see Penguin Books)

RotoVision
Sheridan House
112/116A Western Road, Hove
East Sussex BN3 1DD
01273 727268
sales@rotovision.com
www.rotovision.com
Graphic arts and design

Rough Guides
(see Penguin Books)

Roundhouse Publishing
Millstone, Limers Lane
Northam, North Devon EX39 2RG
01237 474474
roundhouse.group@ukgateway.net
www.roundhouse.net
Cinema and media

Routledge
(see T&F Informa)

Ryland, Peters & Small
Kirkman House
12–14 Whitfield Street
London W1T 2RP
020 7025 2200
info@rps.co.uk
www.rylandpeters.com
Illustrated lifestyle

SAF Publishing
149 Wakeman Road
London NW10 5BH
020 8969 6099
info@safpublishing.com
www.safpublishing.com
Experimental rock and jazz music. Co-imprint with Helter Skelter Publishing: Firefly Publishing (mainstream rock and pop)

Sage Publications
1 Olivers Yard, 55 City Road
London EC1Y 1SP
020 7374 0645
market@sagepub.co.uk
www.sagepub.co.uk
Social sciences and humanities. Imprint: Paul Chapman (education and training)

Saint Andrew Press
Church of Scotland
121 George Street
Edinburgh EH2 4YN
0131 225 5722
standrewpress@cofscotland.org.uk
www.standrewpress.com
Owned by the Church of Scotland. Christian, moral and ethical

Samuel French
52 Fitzroy Street, London W1T 5JR
020 7387 9373
theatre@samuelfrench-london.co.uk
www.samuelfrench-london.co.uk
Plays

SAMS Publishing
(see Pearson Education)

Sangam Books
57 London Fruit Exchange
Brushfield Street, London E1 6EP
020 7377 6399
sangambks@aol.com
Educational textbooks

Saqi Books
26 Westbourne Grove
London W2 5RH
020 7221 9347
editorial@saqibooks.com
www.saqibooks.com
Academic and illustrated; books on Balkans, Middle East and Arab world; Asia and British fiction and fiction in translation

SB Publications
14 Bishopstone Road
Seaford, East Sussex BN25 2UB
01323 893498
sbpublications@tiscali.co.uk
www.sbpublications.co.uk
Local history, travel, guides

Scholastic
Villiers House, Clarendon Avenue
Leamington Spa
Warwickshire CV32 5PR
01926 887799
enquiries@scholastic.co.uk
www.scholastic.co.uk
Education

Scholastic Children's Books
Commonwealth House
1–19 New Oxford Street
London WC1A 1NU
020 7421 9000
scbenquiries@scholastic.co.uk
www.scholastic.co.uk
Fiction. Imprints: Hippo, Point

Scitech Educational
Kent Innovation Centre
Millennium Way
Thanet Reach Business Park
Broadstairs, Kent CT10 2QQ
01843 609300
maria.thompson@scitech-ed.com
www.scitech-ed.com
*Learning resources and e-learning
programs*

SCM Canterbury Press
9–17 St Albans Place
London N1 0NX
020 7359 8033
admin@scm-canterburypress.co.uk
www.scm-canterburypress.co.uk
Theology and hymn books

Scala Publishers
Northburgh House
10 Northburgh Street
London EC1V 0AT
020 7490 9900
info@scalapublishers.com
Art

**Scottish Cultural Press/
Scottish Children's Press**
Unit 6
Newbattle Abbey Business Park
Newbattle Road, Dalkeith EH22 3LJ
Cultural: 0131 660 6366
Children's: 0131 660 4757
info@scottishbooks.com
www.scottishbooks.com
*Scottish-interest books for adult, tourist
and academic readers*

Search Press
Wellwood, North Farm Road
Tunbridge Wells, Kent TN2 3DR
01892 510850
searchpress@searchpress.com
www.searchpress.com
Art and crafts

SEMERC
(see Granada Learning)

Seren
First Floor, 38–40 Nolton Street
Bridgend CF31 3BN
01656 663018
general@seren-books.com
www.seren-books.com
*Wales. Imprint: Border Lines
(biographies)*

Serpent's Tail
4 Blackstock Mews
London N4 2BT
020 7354 1949
info@serpentstail.com
www.serpentstail.com
*Contemporary and gay fiction and
non-fiction*

Severn House Publishers
9–15 High Street, Sutton
Surrey SM1 1DF
020 8770 3930
info@severnhouse.com
www.severnhouse.com
*Hardback fiction for the library
market: romance, science fiction,
horror, fantasy and crime*

Shepheard-Walwyn (Publishers)
Suite 604, The Chandlery
50 Westminster Bridge Road
London SE1 7QY
020 7721 7666
books@shepheard-walwyn.co.uk
www.shepheard-walwyn.co.uk
*Ethical economics, perennial
philosophy, biography, gift books,
books of Scottish interest*

Shetland Times
Gremsta, Lerwick, Shetland ZE1 0PX
01595 693622
adverts@shetland-times.co.uk
www.shetlandtoday.co.uk
Shetland interest

Shire Publications
Cromwell House, Church Street
Princes Risborough
Buckinghamshire HP27 9AA
01844 344301
shire@shirebooks.co.uk
www.shirebooks.co.uk
Original non-fiction paperbacks

Short Books
15 Highbury Terrace
London N5 1UP
020 7226 1607
rebecca@shortbooks.biz
www.shortbooks.co.uk
Non-fiction for adults and children

Sidgwick and Jackson
(see Macmillan Publishers)

Sigma Press
5 Alton Road, Wilmslow
Cheshire SK9 5DY
01625 531035
info@sigmapress.co.uk
www.sigmapress.co.uk
Outdoor, heritage, myth, biography

Simon & Schuster UK
Africa House, 64–78 Kingsway
London WC2B 6AH
020 7316 1900
enquiries@simonandschuster.co.uk
web: www.simonsays.co.uk
*General fiction and non-fiction.
Imprint: Earthlight (science fiction),
Scribner (trade paperback), Pocket
Books (mass-market fiction and
children's), Simon & Schuster Children,
Free Press (literary fiction)*

Skoob Russell Square
10 Brunswick Centre
off Bernard Street
London WC1N 1AE
020 7278 8760
books@skoob.freeserve.co.uk
www.skoob.com
*Literary guides, cultural studies,
esoterica, poetry, new writing from Orient*

Soundings
(see Ulverscroft Group)

Souvenir Press
43 Great Russell Street
London WC1B 3PD
020 7580 9307
souvenirpress@ukonline.co.uk
*Academic. Imprints include: Condor,
Human Horizons, Independent Voices,
Pictorial Presentations, Pop Universal,
The Story-Tellers*

Spellmount
The Village Centre, High Street
Staplehurst, Kent TN12 0BJ
01580 893730
enquiries@spellmount.com
www.spellmount.com
History and military history

Spon Press
(see T&F Informa)

Springer Science & Business Media
100 Borough High Street
London SE1 1LB
020 7863 3000
www.springer-sbm.com
*Owned by Candover & Cinven.
Scientific, technical and medical
textbooks. Imprints: Consultants Bureau*

Springer-Verlag London
Ashbourne House, The Guildway
Old Portsmouth Road, Guildford
Surrey GU3 1LP
01483 734433
postmaster@svl.co.uk
www.springeronline.com
*Computer science, medical,
engineering, astronomy, maths*

Stainer & Bell
PO Box 110, 23 Gruneisen Road
London N3 1DZ
020 8343 3303
post@stainer.co.uk
www.stainer.co.uk
Music and hymns

Stanley Gibbons Publications
7 Parkside, Christchurch Road
Ringwood, Hampshire BH24 3SH
01425 472363
rpurkis@stanleygibbons.co.uk
www.stanleygibbons.co.uk
*Philatelic reference catalogues and
handbooks*

TSO (The Stationery Office)
St Crispins, Duke Street
Norwich, Norfolk NR3 1PD
01603 622211
customer.services@tso.co.uk
www.thestationeryoffice.com

Summersdale Publishers
46 West Street, Chichester
West Sussex PO19 1RP
01243 771107
enquiries@summersdale.com
www.summersdale.com
*Travel, martial arts, self-help, cookery,
humour and gift books*

Summertown Publishing
29 Grove Street, Summertown
Oxford OX2 7JT
01865 454130
chris@summertown.co.uk
www.summertown.co.uk
English-language teaching

Sutton Publishing
Phoenix Mill, Thrupp, Stroud
Gloucestershire GL5 2BU
01453 731114
sales@sutton-publishing.co.uk
www.suttonpublishing.co.uk
Owned by Haynes Publishing.
Biography, countryside, history,
transport, military and aviation

Sweet & Maxwell Group
100 Avenue Road, London NW3 3PF
020 7393 7000
marketinginformation@
    sweetandmaxwell.co.uk
www.sweetandmaxwell.co.uk
Part of the Thomson Corporation.
Legal and professional. Imprints:
W Green (Scotland), Round Hall

T&F Informa
Mortimer House, 37–41 Mortimer
Street
London W1T 3JH
020 7017 5000
www.ir.tfinforma.com
• BIOS Scientific Publishers: *Biology*
  and medicine
• Brunner-Routledge *psychology and*
  counselling
• Carfax: *Social science and humanities*
• CRC: *Science and medical*
• Curzon Press: *Asian and Middle*
  Eastern studies
• Europa Publications: *International*
  affairs, politics and economics
• Frank Cass: *Military and strategic*
  studies. Also Jewish interest imprints:
  Vallentine Mitchell, Jewish Chronicle
  Publications
• Garland Science: *Biology*
• Martin Dunitz: *Medical*
• Psychology Press: *Psychology*
• Routledge: *Humanities & social*
  sciences textbooks/ general non fiction
• Routledge Curzon: *Politics and*
  Middle Eastern studies
• Routledge Falmer: *Education*
• Spon Press: *Architecture and*
  planning
• Taylor & Francis: *Science and reference*
  esp. ergonomics, geographical
  information systems, biotechnology
  and engineering

Taschen UK
1 Heathcock Court, 5th Floor
415 Strand, London WC2R 0NS
020 7845 8585
contact@taschen.com
www.taschen.com
Art and pop culture

Taylor & Francis
(see T&F Informa)

Templar Publishing
Pippbrook Mill, London Road
Dorking, Surrey RH4 1JE
01306 876361
info@templarco.co.uk
www.templarco.co.uk
Illustrated and novelty books for children

Terence Dalton
Water Street, Lavenham
Sudbury, Suffolk CO10 9RN
01787 249290
terence@lavenhamgroup.co.uk
www.terencedalton.com
Part of the Lavenham Group.
Non-fiction: aeronautical, aviation,
maritime and local interest

Thalamus Publishing
4 Attorney's Walk, Bull Ring
Ludlow, Shropshire SY8 1AA
01584 874977
roger@thalamus-books.com
www.thalamus-books.com
Family reference

Thames & Hudson
181A High Holborn
London WC1V 7QX
020 7845 5000
mail@thameshudson.co.uk
www.thamesandhudson.com
Cultural non-fiction

Thomas Cook Publishing
PO Box 227
Unit 15/16 Coningsby Road
Peterborough PE3 8SB
01733 416477
publishing-sales@thomascook.com
www.thomascookpublishing.com
Guide books and timetables

Thomson Learning
50–51 Bedford Row
London WC1R 4LR
020 7067 2500
communications@
    thomsonlearning.com
www.thomsonlearning.co.uk
Part of the Thomson Corporation.
Educational. Imprints: Scientific Press,
Cherry Tree Books (children's), Business
Press, Arden Shakespeare, Computer
Press, Course Technology, Premier
Press, Texere, Wadsworth

Continuum International Publishing
Group
Tower Building, 11 York Road
London SE1 7NX
020 7922 0880
info@continuumbooks.com
www.continuumbooks.com
Academic and religious. Imprints:
Athlone, Pinter, Sheffield Academic
Press, Geoffrey Chapman, Mowbray,
TandT Clark, Burns and Oates,
Morehouse, Claridge Press

Evans Publishing Group
2A Portman Mansions
Chiltern Street, London W1U 6NR
020 7487 0920
sales@evansbrothers.co.uk
www.evansbooks.co.uk
Children's and educational. Imprints:
Cherrytree Books, Evans Brothers, Zero
to Ten

IB Tauris
6 Salem Road, London W2 4BU
020 7243 1225
enquiries@ibtauris.com
www.ibtauris.com
Culture, history and politics. Imprint:
New Press

Oneworld
185 Banbury Road
Oxford OX2 7AR
01865 310597
info@oneworld-publications.com
www.oneworld-publications.com
Religion, history, philosophy and
popular science

Pluto Press
345 Archway Road, Highgate
London N6 5AA
020 8348 2724
pluto@plutobooks.com
www.plutobooks.com
Academic and political non-fiction

Thorsons
(see HarperCollins Publishers)

Time Out Group
c/o L Aldrich Publishing Consultancy
The Studio, 14 Priory Avenue
London W4 1TX
020 7813 3000
www.timeout.com
Guide and travel books

Time Warner Books (UK)
Brettenham House, Lancaster Place
London WC2E 7EN
020 7911 8000
email.uk@twbg.co.uk
www.timewarnerbooks.co.uk
Imprints: Little, Brown (non-fiction);
Abacus (fiction, travel); Time Warner
(paperback fiction); Virago Press
(women authors only: fiction, non-
fiction and poetry); Atom (teen sci-fi);
Orbit Press (sci-fi and fantasy)

Titan Publishing
144 Southwark Street
London SE1 0UP
020 7620 0200
editorial@titanmail.com
www.forbiddenplanet.com
Comic books, graphic novels, spin-offs

Tolkien
(see HarperCollins Publishers)

Top That Publishing
Marine House, Tide Mill Way
Woodbridge, Suffolk IP12 1AP
01394 386651
www.topthatpublishing.com
Children. Imprint: Kudos (adult range)

Transworld Publishers
(see Random House Group)

Travel Publishing
7A Apollo House, Calleva Park
Aldermaston, Berkshire RG7 8TN
0118 981 7777
info@travelpublishing.co.uk
www.travelpublishing.co.uk
Imprints: Hidden Places, Hidden Inns,
Golfers Guides, Country Living Rural
Guides, Off the Motorway

Trentham Books
Westview House, 734 London Road
Stoke-on-Trent
Staffordshire ST4 5NP
01782 745567
tb@trentham-books.co.uk
www.trentham-books.co.uk
Education, culture and law for
professional readers

Trident Press
Empire House, 175 Piccadilly
London W1J 9TB
020 7491 8770
admin@tridentpress.com
www.tridentpress.com
TV tie-ins, history, travel, geography,
culture

Trotman & Co
2 The Green, Richmond
Surrey TW9 1PL
020 8486 1200
mail@trotman.co.uk
www.trotman.co.uk
Careers and education

Ulverscroft Group
The Green, Bradgate Road
Anstey, Leicester LE7 7FU
0116 236 4325
sales@ulverscroft.co.uk
www.ulverscroft.com
FA Thorpe Publishing
Fiction and non-fiction large print books.
Imprints and divisions include: Linford
Romance, Linford Mystery, Linford
Western, Charnwood and Ulverscroft
Isis Publishing
7 Centremead, Osney Mead
Oxford OX2 0ES
01865 250333
sales@isis-publishing.co.uk
www.isis-publishing.co.uk
Large-print books and audio books
Magna Large Print Books
Magna House, Long Preston,
Nr. Skipton
North Yorkshire BD23 4ND
01729 840225
Large-print books; audio fiction and
non-fiction
Soundings
Isis House, Kings Drive, Whitley Bay
Tyne and Wear NE26 2JT
0191 253 4155
mail@gillian2004.plus.com
Audio books
Ulverscroft Large Print Books
The Green, Bradgate Road
Anstey, Leics LE7 7SU
0116 236 4325
Large-print books and audio books

University of Hertfordshire Press
Learning and Information Services
Hatfield Campus Learning
     Resources Centre
College Lane, Hatfield
Hertfordshire AL10 9AB
01707 284681
uhpress@herts.ac.uk
www.herts.ac.uk/UHPress/
Literary criticism and theatre studies,
Romani studies, regional and local
history, parapsychology. Imprints:
Interface Collection, Hertfordshire
Publications

University of Wales Press
10 Columbus Walk, Brigantine Place
Cardiff CF10 4UP
029 2049 6899
press@press.wales.ac.uk
www.wales.ac.uk/press
Imprints: GPC Books, Gwasg Prifysgol
Cymru

University Presses of California,
Columbia & Princeton
1 Oldlands Way, Bognor Regis
West Sussex PO22 9SA
01243 842165
lois@upccp.demon.co.uk
www.ucpress.edu
www.columbia.edu/cu/cup
www.pup.princeton.edu

Unofficial Guides
(see John Wiley & Sons)

Usborne Publishing
83–85 Saffron Hill
London EC1N 8RT
020 7430 2800
mail@usborne.co.uk
www.usborne.com
Non-fiction books for children,
including computer guides, puzzlebooks,
pre-school and books on music

Vallentine Mitchell/ Jewish
Chronicle Publications
(see Frank Cass, T&F Informa)

Vermilion
(see Random House Group)

Viking
(see Penguin Books)

Vintage
(see Random House Group)

Virago Press
(see Time Warner Books)

Virgin Books
Units 5 & 6, Thames Wharf Studios
Rainville Road, London W6 9HA
020 7386 3300
info@virgin-books.co.uk
www.virginbooks.com
TV, film, music, sport and pop culture.
Imprints: Black Lace and Nexus (erotic
fiction)

Vista House
First Century, Suite 72
57 Great George Street
Leeds LS1 3AJ
0906 553 2323
info@first-century.co.uk
www.vistahouse.co.uk
Fiction and non-fiction. Imprint: First
Authors

Visual
(see John Wiley & Sons)

Voyager
(see HarperCollins Publishers)

W Foulsham & Co
The Publishing House
Bennetts Close, Slough
Berkshire SL1 5AP
01753 526769
info@foulsham.com
www.foulsham.com
Lifestyle

Walker Books
87 Vauxhall Walk, London SE11 5HJ
020 7793 0909
enquiry@walker.co.uk
www.walkerbooks.co.uk
Children's big books, book charts, game
books. Series: Giggle Club

Wallflower Press
4th Floor, 26 Shacklewell Lane
London E8 2EZ
020 7690 0115
info@wallflowerpress.co.uk
www.wallflowerpress.co.uk
Film, media and cultural studies

Warne
(see Penguin Books)

Watts Publishing Group
96 Leonard Street
London EC2A 4XD
020 7739 2929
gm@wattspub.co.uk
www.wattspublishing.co.uk
Part of Groupe Lagardere. Children's
non-fiction, reference, fiction, picture
and novelty. Imprints: Franklin Watts,
Orchard Books, Cats Whiskers,
Aladdin/Watts

Weidenfeld & Nicolson
(see Orion Publishing Group)

Wimbledon Publishing Press
75–76 Blackfriars Road
London SE1 8HA
020 7401 4200
enquiries@wpcpress.com
www.wpcpress.com
Textbooks for languages, maths, biology
and accountancy. Imprint: Anthem
Press

Wharncliffe Publishing
(see Pen & Sword Books)

Which?
2 Marylebone Road
London NW1 4DF
020 7770 7000
which@which.net
www.which.net
Publishing arm of the Consumers'
Association

Whittet Books
Hill Farm, Stonham Road, Cotton
Stowmarket, Suffolk IP14 4RQ
01449 781877
annabel@whittet.dircon.co.uk
www.whittetbooks.com
*Natural history, pets and rural interest,
livestock and horticulture*

Whurr Publishers
19B Compton Terrace
London N1 2UN
020 7359 5979
info@whurr.co.uk
www.whurr.co.uk
*Occupational therapy, nursing, special
education, psychology, audiology and
communication disorders*

Wild Goose Publications
Iona Community, 4th Floor
The Savoy House
140 Sauchiehall Street
Glasgow G2 3DH
0141 332 6292
admin@ionabooks.com
www.iona.books.com
*Publishing house of the Iona Community.
Religion, spiritualism and human rights*

Wiley
(see John Wiley & Sons)

William Heinemann
(see Random House Group)

Windhorse Publications
11 Park Road, Moseley
Birmingham B13 8AB
0121 449 9191
info@windhorsepublications.com
www.windhorsepublications.com
Meditation and Buddhism

WIT Press
Ashurst Lodge, Ashurst
Southampton, Hampshire SO40 7AA
023 8029 3223
marketing@witpress.com
www.witpress.com
Scientific and technical

Women's Press
27 Goodge Street
London W1T 2LD
020 7636 3992
sales@the-womens-press.com
www.the-womens-press.com
Part of the Namara Group

Woodhead Publishing
Abington Hall, Abington
Cambridge CB1 6AH
01223 891358
wp@woodhead-publishing.com
www.woodheadpublishing.com
*Formerly Abington Publishing.
Engineering, textiles, finance and
investment, food technology and
environmental science*

Wordsworth Editions
8b East Street, Ware
Hertfordshire SG12 9HJ
01920 465167
enquiries@wordsworth-editions.com
www.wordsworth-editions.com
*Literary classics, reference, poetry,
children's classics, military history and
folklore*

Working White
Chancery Court, Lincolns Inn
Lincoln Road
High Wycombe HP12 3RE
01494 429318
info@workingwhite.co.uk
www.workingwhite.co.uk
*Children's big books, book charts, game
books. Series: Giggle Club*

Wrox
(see John Wiley & Sons)

WW Norton & Company
Castle House, 75–76 Wells Street
London W1T 3QT
020 7323 1579
office@wwnorton.co.uk
Academic and professional non-fiction

X Press
PO Box 25694, London N17 6FP
020 8801 2100
vibes@xpress.co.uk
www.xpress.co.uk
Black interest. Imprints: Nia, 20/20

Y Lolfa Cyf
Talybont, Ceredigion SY24 5AP
01970 832304
ylolfa@ylolfa.com
www.ylolfa.com
*Welsh and Celtic interest. Imprints and
divisions include: Dinas*

Yale University Press (London)
47 Bedford Square
London WC1B 3DP
020 7079 4900
sales@yaleup.co.uk
www.yalebooks.co.uk

Yellow Jersey Press
(see Random House Group)

York Notes
(see Pearson Education)

Young Picador
(see Macmillan Publishers)

Zambezi Publishing
PO Box 221
Plymouth, Devon PL2 2YJ
01752 350453
info@zampub.com
www.zampub.com
New-Age and self-help

Zed Books
7 Cynthia Street, London N1 9JF
020 7837 4014
www.zedbooks.co.uk
*International and third-world affairs
and development studies*

Literary agents

AM Heath & Co*
6 Warwick Court, London WC1R 5DJ
020 7242 2811
www.amheath.com
Fiction, general non-fiction and children's

AP Watt*
20 John Street, London WC1N 2DR
020 7405 6774
apw@apwatt.co.uk
www.apwatt.co.uk
*Full-length typescripts, including
children's books, screenplays for film
and TV*

Abner Stein*
10 Roland Gardens
London SW7 3PH
020 7373 0456
abner@abnerstein.co.uk
*US agents and authors, some full-
length fiction and general non-fiction*

Alan Brodie Representation
6th Floor, Fairgate House
78 New Oxford Street
London WC1A 1HB
020 7079 7990
info@alanbrodie.com
www.alanbrodie.com
Theatre, film and TV scripts

Alexandra Nye
Craigower, 6 Kinnoull Avenue
Dunblane, Perthshire FK15 9JG
01786 825114
*Fiction and topical non-fiction, esp
literary fiction and history*

Andrew Mann*
1 Old Compton Street
London W1D 5JA
020 7734 4751
manscript@onetel.com
*Fiction; general non-fiction; film, TV,
theatre and radio scripts*

Andrew Nurnberg Associates*
Clerkenwell House
45–47 Clerkenwell Green
London EC1R 0QX
020 7417 8800
all@nurnberg.co.uk
Foreign rights

Annette Green Authors' Agency*
1 East Cliff Road
Tunbridge Wells, Kent TN4 9AD
01892 514275
annettekgreen@aol.com
www.annettegreenagency.co.uk
*Literary and general fiction; non-fiction;
fiction for teenagers; upmarket popular
culture*

Artellus
30 Dorset House, Gloucester Place
London NW1 5AD
020 7935 6972
artellus@artellusltd.co.uk
General fiction and non-fiction

* member of the Association of Authors' Agents

The Agency (London)*
24 Pottery Lane, Holland Park
London W11 4LZ
020 7727 1346
info@theagency.co.uk
www.theagency.co.uk
Theatre, film, TV, radio and children's writers and illustrators; also film and TV rights in novels and non-fiction

Andrew Lownie Literary Agency*
17 Sutherland Street
London SW1V 4JU
020 7828 1274
lownie@globalnet.co.uk
www.andrewlownie.co.uk
Non-fiction

Barbara Levy Literary Agency*
64 Greenhill, Hampstead High Street
London NW3 5TZ
020 7435 9046
General fiction, non-fiction, TV presenters, film and TV rights

Bill McLean Personal Management
23B Deodar Road
London SW15 2NP
020 8789 8191
Scripts for all media

Blake Friedmann*
122 Arlington Road
London NW1 7HP
020 7284 0408
carole@blakefriedmann.co.uk
isobel@blakefriedmann.co.uk

BookBlast
PO Box 20184, London W10 5AU
020 8968 3089
info@bookblast.com
www.bookblast.com
Horror, crime, science fiction, fantasy, poetry, short stories, academic, children's books and lifestyle

Brie Burkeman*
14 Neville Court, Abbey Road
London NW8 9DD
0709 223 9113
brie.burkeman@mail.com
Commercial and literary fiction and non-fiction, scripts, poetry, short stories. Independent film and television consultant to literary agents

Bell Lomax Agency
James House, 1 Babmaes Street
London SW1Y 6HF
020 7930 4447
agency@bell-lomax.co.uk
Fiction and non-fiction, biography, children's, business and sport

Campbell Thomson & McLaughlin*
1 King's Mews, London WC1N 2JA
020 7242 0958
Fiction and general non-fiction

Capel & Land*
29 Wardour Street, London W1D 6PS
020 7734 2414
robert@capelland.co.uk
www.capelland.com
Fiction and non-fiction; film, TV, radio presenters

Caroline Davidson Literary Agency
5 Queen Anne's Gardens
London W4 1TU
020 8995 5768
High quality fiction of originality and non-fiction

Caroline Sheldon Literary Agency*
Thorley Manor Farm, Thorley
Yarmouth PO41 0SJ
01983 760205
Fiction, commercial and literary novels, especially women's and children's fiction

Casarotto Ramsay and Associates
National House
60–66 Wardour Street
London W1V 4ND
020 7287 4450
agents@casarotto.uk.com
www.casarotto.uk.com
Scripts for TV, theatre, film and radio

Cat Ledger Literary Agency*
20–21 Newman Street
London W1T 1PG
020 7861 8226
cat.ledger@virgin.net
Non-fiction: popular culture, biography, politics, investigative journalism and fiction (non-genre)

Cecily Ware Literary Agents
19C John Spencer Square
London N1 2LZ
020 7359 3787
info@cecilyware.com
Scripts for TV and film in all areas

Chapman & Vincent*
The Mount, Sun Hill, Royston
Herts SG8 9AT
01763 245005
info@chapmanvincent.co.uk
Non-fiction

Christine Green Authors' Agent*
6 Whitehorse Mews
Westminster Bridge Road
London SE1 7QD
020 7401 8844
info@christinegreen.co.uk
www.christinegreen.co.uk
Literary and general fiction and non-fiction

Conville & Walsh*
2 Ganton Street, Soho
London W1F 7QL
020 7287 3030
sue@convilleandwalsh.com
Literary and commercial fiction; serious and narrative non-fiction; childrens books

Curtis Brown Group*
5th Floor, Haymarket House
28/29 Haymarket
London SW1Y 4SP
020 7396 6600
cb@curtisbrown.co.uk
www.curtisbrown.co.uk
Writers, directors, designers, presenters and actors

The Christopher Little Literary Agency*
10 Eel Brook Studios
125 Moore Park Road
London SW6 4PS
020 7736 4455
christopher@christopherlittle.net
www.christopherlittle.net
Commercial and literary full-length fiction and non-fiction; film scripts for established clients

Darley Anderson Literary, TV & Film Agency*
Estelle House, 11 Eustace Road
London SW6 1JB
020 7385 6652
enquiries@darleyanderson.com
www.darleyanderson.com
Fiction: young male, American, Irish, women's, crime/mystery and humour; non-fiction; children's fiction; selected scripts for film and TV

David Godwin Associates
55 Monmouth Street
London WC2H 9DG
020 7240 9992
assistant@
    davidgodwinassociates.co.uk
Literary and general fiction, non-fiction, biography

David Grossman Literary Agency
118b Holland Park Avenue
London W11 4UA
020 7221 2770
Full-length fiction and general non-fiction, esp controversial

David Higham Associates*
5–8 Lower John Street
Golden Square, London W1F 9HA
020 7434 5900
dha@davidhigham.co.uk
www.davidhigham.co.uk
Fiction; general non-fiction: biography, history, current affairs; children's; scripts

David O'Leary Literary Agents
10 Lansdowne Court
Lansdowne Rise, London W11 2NR
020 7229 1623
d.oleary@virgin.net
Fiction (popular and literary) and non-fiction, esp thrillers, history, popular science, Russia and Ireland (history and fiction)

Deborah Owen*
78 Narrow Street, Limehouse
London E14 8BP
020 7987 51191
do@deborahowen.co.uk
International fiction and non-fiction

Dench Arnold Agency
10 Newburgh Street
London W1F 7RN
020 7437 4551
www.dencharnold.com
Scripts for TV and film

Dinah Wiener*
12 Cornwall Grove, Chiswick
London W4 2LB
020 8994 6011
dinahweiner@enterprise.net
Fiction and general non-fiction:
popular science, cookery

Dorian Literary Agency*
Upper Thornehill, 27 Church Road
St Marychurch, Torquay
Devon TQ1 4QY
01803 312095
General fiction especially popular;
children's (over 10 years)

Dorie Simmonds Agency*
67 Upper Berkeley Street
London W1H 7QX
020 7486 9228
dhsimmonds@aol.com
General fiction and commercial
non-fiction, children's books and
associated rights

Duncan McAra
28 Beresford Gardens
Edinburgh EH5 3ES
0131 552 1558
duncanmcara@hotmail.com
Literary fiction and non-fiction

Ed Victor*
6 Bayley Street, Bedford Square
London WC1B 3HE
020 7304 4100
Mostly commercial fiction and
non-fiction; children's

Edwards Fuglewicz*
49 Great Ormond Street
London WC1N 3HZ
020 7405 6725
julia@efla.co.uk
Fiction: literary, some commercial;
non-fiction: biography, history,
popular culture

Elaine Steel
110 Gloucester Avenue
London NW1 8HX
020 8348 0918
ecmsteel@aol.com
Writers and directors in film, television
and publishing

Elizabeth Puttick Literary Agency*
46 Brookfield Mansions
Highgate West Hill, London N6 6AT
020 8340 6383
agency@puttick.com
www.puttick.com
General non-fiction, esp self-help,
mind, body and spirit, health and
fitness, lifestyle and business

**Elspeth Cochrane Personal
Management**
14/2 Second Floor, South Bank
Commercial Centre
140 Battersea Park Road
London SW11 4NB
020 7819 6256
elspethc@dircon.co.uk
Fiction, non-fiction, biographies,
screenplays, scripts for all media

Eric Glass
25 Ladbroke Crescent
London W11 1PS
020 7229 9500
eglassltd@aol.com
Fiction, non-fiction and scripts

**Eunice McMullen Children's
Literary Agent**
Low Ibbotsholme Cottage
Off Bridge Lane, Troutbeck Bridge
Windermere, Cumbria LA23 1HU
01539 448551
eunicemcmullen@totalise.co.uk
Children's material

Faith Evans Associates*
27 Park Avenue North
London N8 7RU
020 8340 9920
Fiction and non-fiction

Felicity Bryan*
2A North Parade, Banbury Road
Oxford OX2 6LX
01865 513816
agency@felicitybryan.com
Fiction and non-fiction

Felix de Wolfe
Kingsway House, 103 Kingsway
London WC2B 6QX
020 7242 5066
info@felixdewolfe.com
Theatrical agency

Fox & Howard Literary Agency
4 Bramerton Street
London SW3 5JX
020 7352 8691
Non-fiction: biography, history and
popular culture, reference, business and
lifestyle

Frances Kelly Agency*
111 Clifton Road
Kingston Upon Thames
Surrey KT2 6PL
020 8549 7830
Illustrated and academic non-fiction

Futerman, Rose & Associates*
17 Dean Hill Road
London SW14 7DQ
020 8255 7755
guy@futermanrose.co.uk
www.futermanrose.co.uk
Commercial fiction, non-fiction,
biography, film and television scripts
specialising in book-to-film projects

Gillon Aitken Associates*
18–21 Cavaye Place
London SW10 9PT
020 7373 8672
reception@Gillonaitken.co.uk
Fiction and non-fiction

Greene & Heaton*
37 Goldhawk Road
London W12 8QQ
020 8749 0315
info@greeneheaton.co.uk
www.greeneheaton.co.uk
Wide range of fiction and general
non-fiction (clients include Bill Bryson,
Hugh Fearnley-Whittingstall, Michael
Frayn, PD James and Sarah Waters)

Gregory & Co*
3 Barb Mews, London W6 7PA
020 7610 4676
info@gregoryandcompany.co.uk
www.gregoryandcompany.co.uk
Fiction: literary, commercial, crime,
suspense and thrillers; general
non-fiction

ICM
Oxford House, 76 Oxford Street
London W1D 1BS
020 7636 6565
duncanheath@icmlondon.co.uk
Film, TV and theatre scripts

IMG Literary UK
McCormick House, 3 Burlington Lane
Chiswick, London W4 2TH
020 8233 5000
www.imgworld.com
Celebrity books, commercial fiction,
non-fiction, sports-related and
how-to business books

Intercontinental Literary Agency*
33 Bedford Street
London WC2E 9ED
020 7379 6611
ila@ila-agency.co.uk
Translation rights only

Jane Conway-Gordon*
1 Old Compton Street
London W1D 5JA
020 7494 0148
Fiction and general non-fiction

Jane Judd Literary Agency*
18 Belitha Villas, London N1 1PD
020 7607 0273
General fiction and non-fiction:
biography, investigative journalism,
health, women's interests and travel

Janklow & Nesbit (UK)
33 Drayson Mews, London W8 4LY
020 7376 2733
queries@janklow.co.uk
Fiction and non-fiction, commercial
and literary; US and translation rights
handled by Janklow and Nesbit
Associates in New York

Jeffrey Simmons
15 Penn House, Mallory Street
London NW8 8SX
020 7224 8917
jas@london-inc.com
www.jeffreysimmons.com
Biography, cinema and theatre, quality
and commercial fiction, history, law
and crime, politics and world affairs,
parapsychology and sport

Jill Foster
9 Barb Mews, Brook Green
London W6 7PA
020 7602 1263
Scripts for TV, film and radio

JM Thurley Management
Archery House, 33 Archery Square
Walmer, Deal CT14 7JA
01304 371721
jmthurley@aol.com
Full-length fiction, non-fiction, TV and
films

* member of the Association of Authors' Agents

281

Johnson & Alcock*
Clerkenwell House
45/47 Clerkenwell Green
London EC1R 0HT
020 7251 0125
info@johnsonandalcock.co.uk
General fiction and non-fiction

John Welch, Literary Consultant & Agent
Mill Cottage, Calf Lane
Chipping Camden
Gloucestershire GL55 6JQ
01386 840237
johnwelch@waitrose.com
Military, naval and aviation history, general history, and a little biography

Jonathan Clowes*
10 Iron Bridge House
Bridge Approach, London NW1 8BD
020 7722 7674
jonathanclowes@aol.com
Fiction and non-fiction; scripts, especially situation comedy, film and television rights (clients include Doris Lessing, David Nobbs, Len Deighton)

Josef Weinberger Plays
12–14 Mortimer Street
London W1T 3JJ
020 7580 2827
general.info@jwmail.co.uk
www.josef-weinberger.com
Scripts for the theatre; play publisher and licensor of stage rights; publishes plays and acts as UK agent for US agents including the Dramatists Play Service

Judith Chilcote Agency*
8 Wentworth Mansions
Keats Grove, London NW3 2RL
020 7794 3717
judybks@aol.com
Commercial fiction, TV tie-ins, biography and lifestyle

Judith Murdoch Literary Agency*
19 Chalcot Square
London NW1 8YA
020 7722 4197
Full-length fiction only

Judy Daish Associates
2 St Charles Place
London W10 6EG
020 8964 8811
judy@judydaish.demon.co.uk
Scripts for TV, theatre, film and radio

Juri Gabriel
35 Camberwell Grove
London SE5 8JA
020 7703 6186
Quality fiction and non-fiction

Juvenilia
Avington, near Winchester
Hampshire SO21 1DB
01962 779656
juvenilia@clara.co.uk
Baby to teen fiction and picture books; non-fiction and scripts for TV and radio

Knight Features
20 Crescent Grove
London SW4 7AH
020 7622 1467
peter@knightfeatures.co.uk
Motorsports, cartoon books, puzzles, business, history, factual and biographical material

Laurence Fitch
Mezzanine, Quadrant House
80–82 Regent street
London W1B 5AU
020 7734 9911
information@laurencefitch.com
www.laurencefitch.com
Children's and horror books, scripts for theatre, film, TV and radio

Lavinia Trevor Agency*
The Glasshouse
49A Goldhawk Road
London W12 8QP
020 8749 8481
General literary and commercial fiction; non-fiction including popular science

LAW (Lucas Alexander Whitley)*
14 Vernon Street, London W14 0RJ
020 7471 7900
Commercial and literary fiction, non-fiction and children's books; film and TV scripts for established clients

Limelight Management*
33 Newman Street, London W1T 1PY
020 7637 2529
limelight.management@virgin.net
www.limelightmanagement.com
General non-fiction

Lisa Eveleigh Literary Agency*
3rd Floor, 11/12 Dover Street
London W1S 4LJ
020 7399 2803
lisaeveleigh@dial.pipex.com
Literary and commercial fiction and non-fiction

Louise Greenberg Books*
The End House, Church Crescent
London N3 1BG
020 8349 1179
louisegreenberg@msn.com
Literary fiction and non-fiction

Lutyens and Rubinstein*
231 Westbourne Park Road
London W11 1EB
020 7792 4855
susannah@lutyensrubinstein.co.uk
Adult fiction and non-fiction

Maggie Pearlstine Associates*
31 Ashley Gardens
Ambrosden Avenue
London SW1P 1QE
020 7828 4212
post@pearlstine.co.uk
General non-fiction and fiction, history, current affairs, biography, health and politics

Manuscript ReSearch
PO Box 33, Bicester
Oxfordshire OX26 4ZZ
01869 323447
www.manuscriptresearch.co.uk
Scripts for film and TV

Margaret Hanbury Literary Agency*
27 Walcot Square
London SE11 4UB
020 7735 7680
maggie@mhanbury.demon.co.uk
Quality fiction and non-fiction (clients include JG Ballard, Simon Callow, George Alagiah, Judith Lennox); children's books, plays/scripts and poetry

Marjacq Scripts
34 Devonshire Place
London W1G 6JW
020 7935 9499
philip@marjacq.com
luke@marjacq.com
www.marjacq.com
All fiction and non-fiction, screenplays, radio plays and film and tv rights

Mary Clemmey Literary Agency*
6 Dunollie Road, London NW5 2XP
020 7267 1290
Fiction and non-fiction, high quality for an international market

MBA Literary Agents*
62 Grafton Way, London W1T 5DW
020 7387 2076
agent@mbalit.co.uk
Fiction and non-fiction books, TV, film, theatre and radio scripts

Merric Davidson Literary Agency
12 Priors Heath, Goudhurst
Cranbrook, Kent TN17 2RE
01580 212041
authors@mdla.co.uk
www.mdla.co.uk
Fiction especially contemporary (authors include Francesca Clementis, Alison Habens, Simon Scarrow)

Mic Cheetham Literary Agency
11–12 Dover Street
London W1S 4LJ
020 7495 2002
info@miccheetham.com
www.miccheetham.com
General and literary fiction, fantasy and science fiction, crime and some specific non-fiction

Michael Alcock Management (division of Johnson & Alcock)*
Clerkenwell House
45/47 Clerkenwell Green
London EC1R 0HT
020 7251 0125
alcockmgt@aol.com
General non-fiction, literary and commercial mainstream fiction

Micheline Steinberg Associates
Fourth Floor
104 Great Portland Street
London W1W 6PE
020 7631 1310
micheline@steinplays.com
Drama for stage, TV, radio and film

Michelle Kass Associates*
36–38 Glasshouse Street
London W1B 5DL
020 7439 1624
Literary fiction and film

Maggie Noach Literary Agency*
22 Dorville Crescent
London W6 0HJ
020 8748 2926
m-noach@dircon.co.uk
Fiction and general non-fiction

Marsh Agency
11/12 Dover Street, London W1S 4LJ
020 7399 2800
enquiries@marsh-agency.co.uk
www.marsh-agency.co.uk
*International rights specialists selling
English and foreign-language writing*

Narrow Road Company
182 Brighton Road
Coulsdon, Surrey CR5 2NF
020 8763 9895
coulsdon@narrowroad.co.uk
Scripts for TV, theatre, film and radio

Paterson Marsh*
11/12 Dover Street
London W1S 4LJ
020 7399 2800
steph@patersonmarsh.co.uk
www.patersonmarsh.co.uk
*World rights, especially psychoanalysis
and psychotherapy*

Peake Associates*
14 Grafton Crescent
London NW1 8SL
020 7267 8033
peakeassoc@aol.com
www.tonypeake.com
Fiction and non-fiction

Peters Fraser & Dunlop Group (PFD)*
Drury House, 34–43 Russell Street
London WC2B 5HA
020 7344 1000
postmaster@pfd.co.uk
www.pfd.co.uk
*Fiction and children's, plus scripts for
film, theatre, radio and TV*

Pollinger*
9 Staple Inn, Holborn
London WC1V 7QH
020 7404 0342
info@pollingerltd.com
www.pollingerltd.com
*Formerly Laurence Pollinger and
Pearn, Pollinger & Higham. General
trade, non-fiction, children's fiction and
non-fiction*

PVA Management
Hallow Park, Worcester WR2 6PG
01905 640663
books@pva.co.uk
Non-fiction only

Real Creatives Worldwide
14 Dean Street, London W1D 3RS
020 7437 4188
business@realcreatives.com
www.realcreatives.com
*Represents writers and creative media
professionals*

Robert Smith Literary Agency*
12 Bridge Wharf, 156 Caledonian Road
London N1 9UU
020 7278 2444
robertsmith.literaryagency@virgin.net
*Non-fiction; biography, health and
nutrition, lifestyle, showbusiness and
true crime*

Robin Wade Literary Agency
1 Cormorant Lodge
Thomas More Street
London E1W 1AU
020 7488 4171
rw@rwla.com
www.rwla.com
General fiction and non-fiction

Roger Hancock
4 Water Lane, London NW1 8NZ
020 7267 4418
info@rogerhancock.com
*Scripts for comedy, drama and light
entertainment*

Rogers, Coleridge & White*
20 Powis Mews, London W11 1JN
020 7221 3717
Fiction, non-fiction and children's books

Rosemary Sandberg
6 Bayley Street, London WC1B 3HB
020 7304 4110
rosemary@sandberg.demon.co.uk
*Children's picture books and novels,
adult non-fiction*

Rosica Colin
1 Clareville Grove Mews
London SW7 5AH
020 7370 1080
*Full-length manuscripts plus theatre,
film, television and sound broadcasting*

Rupert Crew*
1A King's Mews, London WC1N 2JA
020 7242 8586
info@rupertcrew.co.uk
*Volume and subsidiary rights in fiction
and non-fiction properties*

Rupert Heath Literary Agency
The Beeches, Furzedown Lane
Amport, Hampshire SP11 8BW
01264 771899
theagency@rupertheath.com
www.rupertheath.com
*Fiction, history, biography, science,
arts and popular culture*

Rod Hall Agency
6th Floor, Fairgate House
78 New Oxford Street
London WC1A 1HB
020 7079 7987
office@rodhallagency.com
www.rodhallagency.com
Drama for film, TV and theatre

Sayle Screen
11 Jubilee Place, London SW3 3TD
020 7823 3883
info@saylescreen.com
www.saylescreen.com
*Writers and directors for film, TV,
theatre and radio*

Sheil Land Associates*
52 Doughty Street
London WC1N 2LS
020 7405 9351
info@sheilland.co.uk
*Full-length general, commercial and
literary fiction and non-fiction, including
theatre, film, radio and TV scripts*

Sheila Ableman Literary Agency
122 Arlington Road
London NW1 7HP
020 7485 3409
sheila@ableman.freeserve.co.uk
*Non-fiction including history, science
and biography*

Shelley Power Literary Agency*
13 rue du Pre Saint Gervais
75019 Paris, France
00 33 1 42 383649
shelley.power@wanadoo.fr
*Fiction, business, true crime, film and
entertainment*

Sinclair-Stevenson
3 South Terrace, London SW7 2TB
020 7581 2550
*Biography, current affairs, travel,
history, fiction, the arts*

Sayle Literary Agency*
Bickerton House
25–27 Bickerton Road
London N19 5JT
020 7263 8681
*Fiction, crime and general; general
non-fiction*

Sharland Organisation
The Manor House, Manor Street
Raunds
Northamptonshire NN9 6JW
01933 626600
tsoshar@aol.com
*Scripts for film, TV, theatre and radio;
non-fiction; specialises in national and
international film, television and
theatre negotiations*

Susijn Agency
3rd Floor, 64 Great Titchfield Street
London W1W 7QH
020 7580 6341
info@thesusijnagency.com
www.thesusijnagency.com
*Sells rights worldwide in English and
non-English language literature:
literary fiction and non-fiction*

Tamar Karet Literary Agency
56 Priory Road, Crouch End
London N8 7EX
020 8340 6460
tamar@btinternet.com
*Fiction, leisure, biography, history,
social affairs and politics*

Tanja Howarth Literary Agency*
19 New Row, London WC2N 4LA
020 7240 5553
tanja.howarth@virgin.net
*Fiction and non-fiction from British
writers; represents German authors in
Britain on behalf of German publishers*

* member of the Association of Authors' Agents

The Tennyson Agency
10 Cleveland Avenue
Wimbledon Chase
London SW20 9EW
020 8543 5939
agency@tenagy.co.uk
www.tenagy.co.uk
Theatre, film, radio and TV scripts

Teresa Chris Literary Agency
43 Musard Road, London W6 8NR
020 7386 0633
TeresaChris@litagency.freeserve.co.uk
*Fiction: crime, general, women's,
commercial and literary and non-fiction*

Toby Eady Associates
3rd Floor, 9 Orme Court
London W2 4RL
020 7792 0092
jessica@tobyeady.demon.co.uk
www.tobyeadyassociates.co.uk
*Fiction, non-fiction, especially China,
Middle East, Africa and India*

Valerie Hoskins Associates
20 Charlotte Street
London W1T 2NA
020 7637 4490
vha@vhassociates.co.uk
*Scripts for film, TV and radio, especially
feature films, animation and TV*

Vanessa Holt*
59 Crescent Road, Leigh-on-Sea
Essex SS9 2PF
01702 473787
vanessa@holtlimited.freeserve.co.uk
*General fiction especially crime,
commercial and literary; non-fiction;
non-illustrated children's*

Watson, Little*
Capo Di Monte, Windmill Hill
London NW3 6RJ
020 7431 0770
sz@watsonlittle.com
www.watsonlittle.com
*Commercial and literary fiction and
non-fiction for adults and children*

The Wylie Agency (UK)
17 Bedford Square
London WC1B 3JA
020 7908 5900
mail@wylieagency.co.uk
Fiction and non-fiction

William Morris Agency (UK)*
52/53 Poland Street
London W1F 7LX
020 7534 6800
ldnmailroom@wma.com
www.wma.com
*Fiction; general non-fiction; TV and
film scripts*

William Neill-Hall
Old Oak Cottage, Ropewalk
Mount Hawke, Truro
Cornwall TR4 8DW
01209 891427
wneill-hall@msn.com
*General non-fiction (clients include
George Carey, Philip Yancey and
Eugene Peterson)*

Zebra Agency
Broadland House, 1 Broadland
Shevington, Lancashire WN6 8DH
077193 75575
admin@zebraagency.co.uk
www.zebraagency.co.uk
*Non-fiction and general fiction; scripts
for TV, radio, film and theatre*

* member of the Association of Authors' Agents

**Annual Bibliography of English
Language and Literature**
Modern Humanities Research
Association, Cambridge University
01223 333058
abell@bibl.org
www.mhra.org.uk
    /Publication/Journals/abell.html
*Annual. Editor: Gerard Lowe;
academic editor: Jennifer Fellows*

Books
Publishing News
0870 870 2345
info@publishingnews.co.uk
www.publishingnews.co.uk
Weekly. Editor: Rodney Burbeck

Books in the Media
VNU Entertainment Media
020 7420 6006
www.thebookseller.com
*Weekly. Editor: Neil Denny;
news: Joel Rickett*

The Bookseller
VNU Entertainment Media
020 7420 6006
joel.rickett@bookseller.co.uk
www.thebookseller.com
*Weekly. Editor: Neil Denny;
news: Joel Rickett*

**Booksellers Association Directory
of Members**
The Booksellers Association of
the UK and Ireland
020 7802 0802
mail@booksellers.org.uk
www.booksellers.org.uk
Annual. Editor: Meryl Halls

BookWorld Magazine
Christchurch Publishers
020 7351 4995
leonard.holdsworth@btopenworld.com
*Monthly. Editor: Leonard Holdsworth;
features: James Hughes*

**Digital Demand – The Journal of
Printing and Publishing Technology**
PIRA International
01372 802080
publications@pira.co.uk
www.piranet.com
6pa. Editor: Gareth Blatchford

London Review of Books
Nicholas Spice
020 7209 1141
edit@lrb.co.uk
www.lrb.co.uk
Fortnightly. Editor: Mary-Kay Wilmers

Publishing News
Publishing News
0870 870 2345
mailbox@publishingnews.co.uk
www.publishingnews.co.uk
Weekly. Editor: Liz Thomson

Writers Forum
Writers International
01202 589828
editorial@writers-forum.com
www.writers-forum.com
Monthly. Editor: John Jenkins;
deputy: Mary Hogarth

Writers News/ Writing Magazine
Warner Group Publications
0113 200 2929
derek.hudson@writersnews.co.uk
www.writersnews.co.uk
Monthly. Editor: Derek Hudson

Associations

Academi (Yr Academi Gymreig)
Mount Stuart House
Mount Stuart Square
Cardiff CF10 5FQ
029 2047 2266
post@academi.org
www.academi.org
Welsh national literature promotion
agency

Alliance of Literary Societies
22 Belmont Grove, Havant
Hampshire PO9 3PU
023 9247 5855
rosemary@sndc.demon.co.uk
www.sndc.demon.co.uk

Association for Scottish Literary
Studies
c/o Department of Scottish History
9 University Gardens
University of Glasgow
Glasgow G12 8QH
0141 330 5309
office@asls.org.uk
www.asls.org.uk
Charity promoting language and
literature of Scotland

Association of Christian Writers
All Saints Vicarage
43 All Saints Close, Edmonton
London N9 9AT
020 8884 4348
admin@christianwriters.org.uk
www.christianwriters.org.uk
Support, training and encouragement

Association of Freelance Writers
The Writers Bureau, Sevendale House
7 Dale Street, Manchester M1 1JB
0161 228 2362
studentservices@writersbureau.com
www.writersbureau.com
Correspondence college

Association of Illustrators
150 Curtain Road, London EC2A 3AR
020 7613 4328
info@theaoi.com
www.theaoi.com
Trade association

Association of Learned and
Professional Society Publishers
South House, The Street, Clapham
Worthing, West Sussex BN13 3UU
01903 871686
nick.evans@alpsp.org
www.alpsp.org
For not-for-profit academic and
professional publishers

AuthorsOnline
40 Castle Street, Hertford
Hertfordshire SG14 1HR
0870 7500544
theeditor@authorsonline.co.uk
www.authorsonline.co.uk
Self-publishing and authors' services
worldwide

Authors' Club
40 Dover Street, London W1S 4NP
020 7499 8581
mem@authorsclub.co.uk
www.authorsclub.co.uk
Anyone involved with written words;
administers Best First Novel award
and Sir Banister Fletcher award

Authors' Licensing & Collecting
Society (ALCS)
Marlborough Court, 14–18 Holborn
London EC1N 2LE
020 7395 0600
alcs@alcs.co.uk
www.alcs.co.uk
UK collecting society for writers and
successors

Bibliographical Society
c/o The Institute of English Studies,
University of London
Room 304, Senate House
Mallet Street, London WC1E 7HU
020 7862 8679
admin@bibsoc.org.uk
www.bibsoc.org.uk
Aims to encourage study of
bibliography and history of publishing

Books 4 Publishing
Lasyard House, Underhill Street
Bridgnorth, Shropshire WV16 4BB
0870 777 3339
editor@books4publishing.com
www.books4publishing.com
Online showcase for unpublished writers

Booksellers Association of the UK
& Ireland
Minster House
272 Vauxhall Bridge Road
London SW1V 1BA
020 7834 5477
mail@booksellers.org.uk
www.booksellers.org.uk
Trade association. Coordinates World
Book Day with Publishers Association;
administers Whitbread Book Awards

Booktrust
Book House, 45 East Hill
London SW18 2QZ
020 8516 2977
info@booktrust.org.uk
www.booktrust.org.uk and
www.booktrusted.com
Educational charity

British Centre for Literary
Translation
University of East Anglia, Norwich
Norfolk NR4 7TJ
01603 592134/592785
bclt@uea.ac.uk
www.literarytranslation.com
Translation centre

British Copyright Council
Copyright House
29–33 Berners Street
London W1T 3AB
01986 788122
secretary@britishcopyright.org
www.britishcopyright.org
Liaison committee for copyright interest

British Science Fiction Association
1 Long Row Close, Everdon
Daventry, Northants NN11 3BE
01327 361661
bsfa@enterprise.net
www.bsfa.co.uk
Also publishes Matrix, Vector & Focus
magazines

British Society of Comedy Writers
61 Parry Road, Ashmore Park
Wolverhampton
West Midlands WW11 2PS
01902 722729
info@bscw.co.uk
www.bscw.co.uk
Society of comedy writers

Children's Books Ireland
First Floor
17 North Great Georges Street
Dublin 1, Ireland
00 353 1 872 7475
info@childrensbooksireland.com
www.childrensbooksireland.com
Promotes children's literature

Clé, The Irish Book Publishers'
Association
43/44 Temple Bar
Dublin 2, Republic of Ireland
00 353 1 670 7393
info@publishingireland.com
www.publishingireland.com
Provides expertise and resources;
access to directory of Irish Association
of Freelance Editors, Proofreaders
and Indexers

Combrogos
10 Heol Don, Whitchurch
Cardiff CF14 2AU
029 2062 3359
Arts and media research and editorial
services; books about Wales or by Welsh
authors; contact Dr Meic Stephens

Comedy Writers' Association UK
Wisteria Cottage, Coombe Meadow
Bovey Tracey, Newton Abbot
Devon TQ13 9EZ
info@cwauk.co.uk
www.cwauk.co.uk
Independent comedy writers in the UK
and around the world

Crime Writers' Association (CWA)
media.enquiries@thecwa.co.uk;
info@thecwa.co.uk
www.thecwa.co.uk
Professional group of crime authors

Critics' Circle
c/o Catherine Cooper
69 Marylebone Lane
London W1U 2PH
020 7224 1410
www.criticscircle.org.uk
*Critics of drama, music, cinema &
dance, art and architecture*

**Directory & Database Publishers
Association**
PO Box 23034, London W6 0RJ
020 8846 9707; 020 7405 0836
rosemarypettit@onetel.net.uk
www.directory-publisher.co.uk
Trade association

Drama Association of Wales
The Old Library Building
Singleton Road, Splott
Cardiff CF24 2ET
029 2045 2200
aled.daw@virgin.net
www.amdram.co.uk

English Association
University of Leicester
University Road, Leicester LE1 7RH
0116 252 3982
engassoc@le.ac.uk
www.le.ac.uk/engassoc
*Promotes knowledge, understanding
and enjoyment of English language
and literature*

English PEN
6–8 Amwell Street
London EC1R 1UQ
020 7713 0023
enquiries@englishpen.org
www.englishpen.org
*Association of writers and literary
professionals. Fights for right to
freedom of expression*

**Federation of Worker Writers and
Community Publishers (FWWCP)**
Burslem School of Art, Queen Street
Stoke on Trent ST6 3EJ
01782 822327
thefwwcp@tiscali.co.uk
www.thefwwcp.org uk
*For independent writing workshops
and community publishers*

Fellowship of Authors and Artists
PO Box 158, Hertford SG13 8FA
0870 747 2514
fellowship@
    compassion-in-business.co.uk
www.author-fellowship.co.uk
*Promotes writing and art as therapy
and self-healing*

Garden Writers' Guild
c/o Institute of Horticulture
14/15 Belgrave Square
London SW1X 8PS
020 7245 6943
gwg@horticulture.org.uk
www.gardenwriters.co.uk
*Promotes high-quality garden writing,
photography and broadcasting*

**Gaelic Books Council (Comhairle
nan Leabhraichean)**
22 Mansfield Street
Glasgow G11 5QP
0141 337 6211
brath@gaelicbooks.net
www.gaelicbooks.net

Horror Writers Association
PO Box 50577, Palo Alto
CA 94303, USA
hwa@dcedwards.com
www.horror.org/UK/
*Worldwide organisation of writers and
publishing professionals*

Independent Publishers Guild
P O Box 93, Royston
Hertfordshire SG8 5GH
01763 247014
info@ipg.uk.com
www.ipg.uk.com

Independent Theatre Council
12 The Leathermarket
Weston Street, London SE1 3ER
020 7403 1727
admin@itc-arts.org
www.itc-arts.org
*Offers legal advice and training
opportunities*

Institute of Linguists
Saxon House, 48 Southwark Street
London SE1 1UN
020 7940 3100
info@iol.org.uk
www.iol.org.uk
*Professional association; accredited
exam board; commercial contracts for
government*

**Institute of Translation and
Interpreting (ITI)**
Fortuna House, South Fifth Street
Milton Keynes
Buckinghamshire MK9 2EU
01908 325250
info@iti.org.uk
www.iti.org.uk

International Booksearch Service
8 Old James Street
London SE15 3TS
020 7639 8900
sarah.fordham@btinternet.com
www.scfordham.com
Finds out-of-print books

Irish Writers Centre
19 Parnell Square, Dublin 1
Republic of Ireland
00 353 1 872 1302
info@writerscentre.ie
www.writerscentre.ie
*Promotes Irish writers, living in Ireland,
organises readings and workshops*

*Also houses: Irish Playwrights and
Screenwriters Guild:*
moffats@indigo.ie
www.writerscentre.ie/IPSG.html
*Irish Translators' and Interpreters'
Association*
translation@eircom.net
or secretary-itia@ntlworld.ie
www.translatorsassociation.ie
Irish Writers' Union
words@neteireann.com
www.ireland-writers.com

ISBN Agency
3rd Floor, Midas House
62 Goldsworth Road
Woking GU21 6LQ
0870 777 8712
isbn@nielsenbookdata.co.uk
www.nielsenbookdata.co.uk
Book numbering agency

Manuscript ReSearch
PO Box 33, Bicester
Oxon OX26 4ZZ
01869 323447/322522
www.manuscriptresearch.co.uk
Services for self-publishing authors

Medical Writers' Group
The Society of Authors
84 Drayton Gardens
London SW10 9SB
020 7373 6642
info@societyofauthors.org
www.societyofauthors.org
*Specialist group within Society of
Authors*

National Archives
Kew, Richmond, Surrey TW9 4DU
020 8876 3444
enquiry@nationalarchives.gov.uk
www.nationalarchives.gov.uk
*National resource for documents
relating to British history; brings
together the Public Record Office and the
Historical Manuscripts Commission*

**National Association for Literature
Development**
PO Box 140, Ilkley
West Yorkshire LS29 7WP
01943 862107
steve@nald.org
www.nald.org

**National Association of Writers
Groups**
The Arts Centre, Biddick Lane
Washington, Tyne & Wear NE38 2AB
01262 609228
nawg@tesco.net
www.nawg.co.uk
*Connecting writers' groups around the
country; yearly festivals and
competitions*

**National Association of Writers in
Education**
PO Box 1, Sheriff Hutton
York YO60 7YU
01653 618429
paul@nawe.co.uk
www.nawe.co.uk

New Writing North
2 School Lane, Whickham
Newcastle Upon Tyne NE16 4SL
0191 488 8580
mail@newwritingnorth.com
www.newwritingnorth.com
*Literature development agency for
north-east arts region*

Nielsen BookData
3rd Floor, Midas House
62 Goldsworth Road, Woking
Surrey GU21 6LQ
0870 7778710
info@bookdata.co.uk
www.nielsenbookdata.com
Bibliographic data

Nielsen BookScan
3rd Floor, Midas House
62 Goldsworth Road, Woking
Surrey GU21 6LQ
0870 7778710
info@nielsenbookscan.co.uk
www.nielsenbookscan.co.uk
International sales data monitoring

Player-Playwrights
9 Hillfield Park, London N10 3QT
020 8883 0371
p-p@dial.pipex.com
www.playerplaywrights.co.uk
*Gives opportunities to writers new to
stage, radio and TV*

Public Lending Right
Richard House, Sorbonne Close
Stockton-on-Tees TS17 6DA
01642 604699
registrar@plr.uk.com
www.plr.uk.com
*Distribute government funds to
authors/libraries*

Publishers Association
29B Montague Street
London WC1B 5BH
020 7691 9191
mail@publishers.org.uk
www.publishers.org.uk
Trade association

Publishers Licensing Society
37–41 Gower Street
London WC1E 6HH
020 7299 7730
pls@pls.org.uk
www.pls.org.uk
*Licensing of photocopying materials in
schools and universities*

Publishers Publicity Circle
65 Airedale Avenue, London W4 2NN
020 8994 1881
ppc-@lineone.net
www.publisherspublicitycircle.co.uk
*Forum for book publicists and freelance
PRs*

Romantic Novelists' Association
presssecretary@rna-uk.org;
enquiries@rna-uk.org
www.rna-uk.org

Royal Society of Literature
Somerset House, Strand
London WC2R 1LA
020 7845 4676
info@rslit.org
www.rslit.org
*Holds monthly lectures promoting
literature and spoken word. Annual
prizes*

Science Fiction Foundation
37 Coventry Road, Ilford IG1 4QR
sff@sjbradshaw.cix.co.uk
www.sf-foundation.org
*Writers, academics and critics with an
active interest in science fiction*

Scottish Book Trust
Sandeman House, Trunk's Close
55 High Street, Edinburgh EH1 1SR
0131 524 0160
info@scottishbooktrust.com
www.scottishbooktrust.com
*Arts organiser, promotes reading and
writing in Scotland; holds a resource
library*

Scottish Print Employers Federation
48 Palmerston Place
Edinburgh EH12 5DE
0131 220 4353
info@spef.org.uk
www.spef.org.uk
Advice, expertise, education and training

Scottish Publishers Association
Scottish Book Centre
137 Dundee Street
Edinburgh EH11 1BG
0131 228 6866
info@scottishbooks.org
www.scottishbooks.org
*Networking and information services.
Lobbying organisation for book
publishing issues*

Scottish Youth Theatre
3rd Floor Forsythe House
111 Union Street, Glasgow G1 3TA
0141 221 5127
info@scottishyouththeatre.org
www.scottishyouththeatre.org
*Giving young people in Scotland
opportunity to explore and reach their
creative potential through art*

**Society for Children's Book Writers
& Illustrators**
8271 Beverley Boulevard
Los Angeles, CA 90048, USA
00 1 323 782 1010
scbwi@scbwi.org
www.scbwi.org

**Society for Editors and
Proofreaders (SfEP)**
Riverbank House
1 Putney Bridge Approach
London SW6 3JD
020 7736 3278
admin@sfep.org.uk
www.sfep.org.uk
*Non-profit body promoting high
editorial standards and recognition of
the professional status of its members*

Society of Authors
84 Drayton Gardens
London SW10 9SB
020 7373 6642
info@societyofauthors.org
www.societyofauthors.org
Trade union for professional authors

**Society of Civil and Public Service
Writers**
Adrian Danson, Editor
37 Hollingworth Road
Petts Wood BR5 1AQ
editor@scpsw.co.uk
www.scpsw.co.uk

Society of Indexers
Blades Enterprise Centre
John Street, Sheffield S2 4SU
0114 292 2350
admin@indexers.org.uk
www.indexers.org.uk

**Society of Women Writers &
Journalists**
Calvers Farm, Thelveton, Diss
Norfolk IP21 4NG
01379 740550
zoe@zoeking.com
www.swwj.com

Society of Young Publishers
info@thesyp.org.uk
www.thesyp.org.uk
*Provides a forum, organises readings
and meetings*

**South and Mid-Wales Association
of Writers (SAMWAW)**
c/o IMC Consulting Group
Denham House
Lambourne Crescent
Cardiff CF14 5ZW
029 2076 1170
info@imcconsultinggroup.co.uk
www.samwaw.ik.com
Open to all writers

**Spoken Word Publishing
Association (SWPA)**
c/o Macmillan Audio
20 New Wharf Road
London N1 9RR
020 7014 6041
z.howes@macmillan.co.uk
www.swpa.co.uk

**Sports Writers' Association of Great
Britain**
244 Perry Street, Billericay
Essex CM12 0QP
01277 657708
trevjanbond1@aol.com

Translators Association
84 Drayton Gardens
London SW10 9SB
020 7373 6642
info@societyofauthors.org
www.societyofauthors.org

Welsh Books Council (Cyngor Llyfrau Cymru)
Castell Brychan, Aberystwyth
Ceredigion SY23 2JB
01970 624151
castellbrychan@cllc.org.uk
www.cllc.org.uk and
www.gwales.com
For Welsh writers

West Country Writers' Association
1 Moreton Avenue
Crown Hill, Plymouth PL6 5AZ
01752 785540
www.westcountrywriters.co.uk
Annual congress in May

Women in Publishing
info@wipub.org.uk
www.wipub.org.uk

Writernet
Cabin V, Clarendon Buildings
25 Horsell Road, Highbury
London N5 1XL
020 7609 7474
info@writernet.org.uk
www.writernet.org.uk
*Information and guidance for
playwrights and performance writers*

Writers, Artists and their Copyright Holders (Watch)
David Sutton
Director of Research Projects
University of Reading Library
PO Box 223, Whiteknights
Reading RG6 6AE
0118 931 8783
D.C.Sutton@reading.ac.uk
www.watch-file.com
Database of copyright holders

Writers' Guild of Great Britain
15 Britannia Street
London WC1X 9JN
020 7833 0777
admin@writersguild.org.uk
www.writersguild.org.uk
Trade union for professional writers

The past year has seen a funding crisis in the British film industry. Film production, which reached record levels in 2003, collapsed in 2004 as changes to tax rules and the strong pound made Britain unattractive to investors. Total production investment fell to £800m in 2004, said the lottery-funded UK Film Council in January 2005, down from 2003's record £1.15bn; the number of UK films shooting locally fell from 45 to 27, with co-productions down from 100 to around 80. The troubles came to a head when in June 2005 it was announced that producers behind two of the biggest names in the British film industry, James Bond and Harry Potter, were in talks to produce their next films – Casino Royale, and Harry Potter and the Order of the Phoenix – outside the UK; the same month, the Pinewood Shepperton film studios announced their second profits warning in three months.

Confusion over tax relief for film-makers was one of the reasons why investors fled Britain. In February 2004, the government had announced new rules designed to stop financiers funding films with complex "sale and leaseback" deals – under which financiers would avoid tax by buying a film for more than the production cost, leasing it back to the producer, and then claiming tax relief on the larger amount. About 40 films in production had to reorganise their finances because of the move. Then in December, the Treasury announced plans to combat "double-dipping" – that is, stopping filmmakers from claiming tax relief on both acquisition and production. New rules, allowing tax relief of up to 20% of production costs, were not announced till the budget in March 2005 – during which time many financiers had deserted the British film industry. In May 2005, the film producer Michael Kuhn warned that British filmmaking could die out.

There were also moves to put the situation right. In March 2005, a government green paper urged the BBC to establish a strategy for investing in British film, months after the production company trade body Pact had criticised the corporation for spending less than a seventh of its £70m film budget on British productions. In May, London-based studios and post-production houses – including Pinewood Shepperton – joined forces to create London Plus, a consortium aimed at boosting production activity in London and the south-east. And in July 2005, Skillset announced the Screen Academy Network, a network of seven academies to train a new generation of filmmakers.

Hollywood, by contrast, had a great year. According to the Motion Picture Association of America, which represents the major US studios, worldwide revenues from the film industry rose to £24bn, up 9% from 2003 – with DVD revenues growing at a huge rate.

The major studio news for film fans was that Harvey and Bob Weinstein, the brothers behind Miramax, finally decided to leave Disney, the

US conglomerate that owns the film company. The rights to the Miramax name and its films – which include Shakespeare in Love, The English Patient, Chicago and Fahrenheit 9/11 – will remain with Disney. By June 2005, the Weinsteins looked set to set up their new studio, the Weinstein Company.

In July 2004 Marlon Brando, one of the finest 20th-century film actors, died in Los Angeles at the age of 80.

The film industry continues to tackle DVD and internet film **piracy**. In Hollywood, several executives have advocated releasing DVDs earlier in an effort to combat the problem; while the MPAA has aggressively pursued internet users who upload pirated films to the web. In the UK, the black market in pirate DVDs is expected to reach £1bn by 2008, according to a UK Film Council report.

In the cinemas

In box office terms, UK cinema is growing all the time. UK box office was up 3.5% to £838.7m in 2004, according to Nielsen EDI; while in the first quarter of 2005, UK box office was up 13% – even as figures released in June showed that US cinema audiences had fallen to a 20-year low. Top grossing film of 2004 in Britain was Shrek 2, which made just over £48m. And Fahrenheit 9/11, Michael Moore's satire on George Bush and the American right, had the biggest-ever opening weekend for a documentary, taking more than £1.3m in its opening weekend.

Cinema advertising was worth £34m in the first quarter of 2005, a year-on-year rise of some 16.8% in real terms.

Bouquets and brickbats

The two top grossing British films of 2004, Harry Potter and the Prisoner of Azkaban and Bridget Jones: The Edge of Reason, were both US-UK partnerships, grossing £46m and £36m respectively. But the British film that most stirred the awards judges was Vera Drake, which won three Baftas including best director and best director for Mike Leigh and best actress for Imelda Staunton, and three Oscar nominations. The film also opened the London film festival.

At the Oscars, Martin Scorsese's The Aviator won most awards, with five from 11 nominations. But Clint Eastwood's Million Dollar Baby won the two big awards, best picture and best director, with best actress for Hilary Swank and a supporting gong for Morgan Freeman, to win four out of seven nominations.

At Cannes, Belgian brothers Jean-Pierre and Luc Dardenne won the Palme d'Or for L'Enfant, a story of two street urchins living off crime to buy food for their new baby.

Stirring the critics for different reasons was Michael Winterbottom's 9 Songs, which became the most sexually explicit film in UK mainstream cinema history. The film traced the arc of a relationship from first date to break-up, and included unsimulated sex scenes between its two stars, Kieran O'Brien and Margo Stilley.

One of the worst films of 2004/05 was Fat Slags, the film of the Viz cartoon strip, which was so widely panned that the editors of Viz said they were abandoning the strip in disgust. The Guardian's Peter Bradshaw wrote: "Oh no. Oh, please God, no. Just when we were thinking the British film industry was on the up. Just when we thought that we didn't have to walk around with heads bowed in shame any more. Shaun of the Dead is the toast of Hollywood. It was all going so well. And now this."

Theo van Gogh

The murder of the Dutch filmmaker Theo van Gogh cast a shadow over the global film industry in November 2004. Van Gogh, the great-grand-nephew of Vincent van Gogh, had made Submission, a short film about the status of women within Muslim culture, which featured a woman naked under a transparent veil, with verses from the Koran written on her body. He was shot and stabbed in the street on November 2. In July 2005, a 27-year-old named Mohammed Bouyeri admitted the killing, saying he did it out of "conviction"; "If I ever get free," he said, "I would do it again."

Awards

Oscars
- *Best picture:* Million Dollar Baby
- *Best director:* Clint Eastwood for Million Dollar Baby
- *Best actor:* Jamie Foxx in Ray
- *Best actress:* Hilary Swank in Million Dollar Baby
- *Supporting actor:* Morgan Freeman in Million Dollar Baby
- *Supporting actress:* Cate Blanchett in The Aviator
- *Original screenplay:* Charlie Kaufman for Eternal Sunshine of the Spotless Mind
- *Adapted screenplay:* Alexander Payne and Jim Taylor for Sideways
- *Foreign language film:* The Sea Inside (Spain)
- *Animated film:* The Incredibles

Baftas
- *Best film:* The Aviator
- *Best director:* Mike Leigh for Vera Drake
- *Best actor in a leading role:* Jamie Foxx for Ray
- *Best actress in a leading role:* Imelda Staunton for Vera Drake
- *Best actor in a supporting role:* Clive Owen for Closer
- *Best actress in a supporting role:* Cate Blanchett for The Aviator
- *Outstanding British film of the year:* My Summer of Love
- *Best original screenplay:* Charlie Kaufman for Eternal Sunshine of the Spotless Mind
- *Best adapted screenplay:* Alexander Payne and Jim Taylor for Sideways
- *Best foreign film:* The Motorcycle Diaries

Cannes
- *Palme d'Or:* L'Enfant by Jean-Pierre and Luc Dardenne
- *Grand Prix:* Broken Flowers by Jim Jarmusch

Critically paised...
Imelda Staunton
stars in Vera Drake

Top 10 films released in UK and Ireland, 2004

Rank / Film		Countries	Box office gross (£m)
1	Shrek 2	US	48.1
2	Harry Potter and the Prisoner of Azkaban	UK/US	46.1
3	Bridget Jones: The Edge of Reason	UK/US	36.0
4	The Incredibles	US	32.3
5	Spider–Man 2	US	26.7
6	The Day After Tomorrow	US	25.2
7	Shark Tale	US	22.8
8	Troy	UK/US/Malta	18.0
9	I, Robot	US	18.0
10	Scooby–Doo Too	US	16.5

Source: UK Film Council, Nielsen EDI, RSU

Top 10 UK films released in UK and Ireland, 2004

Rank / Film		Countries	Box office gross (£m)
1	Harry Potter and the Prisoner of Azkaban	UK/US	46.1
2	Bridget Jones: The Edge of Reason	UK/US	36.0
3	Troy	UK/US/Malta	18.0
4	The Phantom of the Opera	UK/US	9.0
5	Wimbledon	UK/US	7.2
6	King Arthur	UK/US/Ire	7.1
7	Shaun of the Dead	UK	6.7
8	Thunderbirds	UK/US	5.4
9	Bride and Prejudice	UK/US	5.2
10	Alien Vs Predator	UK/Cze/Can/Ger	5.2

Source: UK Film Council, Nielsen EDI, RSU

Further reading

■ Press

Guardian Unlimited Film
www.guardian.co.uk/film

Screen International
www.screendaily.com

Sight & Sound
www.bfi.org.uk/sightandsound

■ Web only

Britfilms
www.britfilms.com

IMDb – Internet Movie Database
www.imdb.com

■ Books

The Guerilla Film Makers Handbook
GENEVIEVE JOLIFFE; NEW EDITION OUT
OCTOBER 2005 Guide to amateur
filmmaking

■ Other resources

British Film Institute
www.bfi.org.uk

Shooting People
www.shootingpeople.org

Skillset
www.skillset.com

UK Film Council
www.ukfilmcouncil.org.uk

The quest for British film **Xan Brooks**

To paraphrase Dickens, it is the best times and it is the worst of times for that old warhorse affectionately, and sometimes misleadingly, known as the British film industry. The latest report from the UK Film Council paints an impossibly rosy picture, with cinema admissions at their highest level since that annus mirabilis of 1972, which gave us such classics as Carry on Matron and Mutiny On the Buses. Best of all, some 23% of the most popular films at the UK box office are themselves British movies, as opposed to imported Hollywood behemoths. Taken at face value, this should be cause for celebration. Except it doesn't quite feel that way.

The problem, in a nutshell, is down to the elastic definition of what constitutes a British film these days. As introduced by the government, a newly minted "cultural test" proposes judging movies on the basis on a range of criterion, ranging from the place where they were filmed to the presence of local talent. This allows the statisticians to embrace such big-budget triumphs as Charlie and the Chocolate Factory and Harry Potter and the Goblet of Fire as plucky homegrown heroes, conveniently ignoring the fact that they come bankrolled by the Hollywood studios. Elsewhere, the landscape is rather more troubled, with pureblood British films still struggling to find funding and widespread distribution. For every Shaun of the Dead that defies the odds to become a runaway success, it is possible to point to 10 other pictures, just as worthwhile, that fell between the cracks.

Meanwhile the government was forced to step in to avert what many see as a burgeoning crisis for the UK's studios. In recent years the likes of Pinewood Shepperton and Leavesden have prospered thanks to the government's now defunct Section 42 tax relief scheme, which allowed visiting Hollywood productions to shave 12% off the typical cost of a blockbuster.

But in the summer of 2005 these foreign investors were scared off by combination of a poor exchange rate and a mounting uncertainty over the future of film taxation. Still reeling from Paramount's 11th-hour decision not to shoot a comic-book blockbuster, The Watchmen, at Pinewood, the studio were further stung by a report that the backers of the next James Bond outing were considering relocating to a cheaper base in eastern Europe. For the Cassandras of the British film industry, this news was the equivalent of the ravens leaving the Tower of London. Pinewood, after all, has played host to every Bond movie since the series debuted in 1962.

So what's the solution? Unveiled in July 2005, the new set of tax incentives has the two-pronged aim of safeguarding foreign investment while simultaneously nurturing domestic production. Assuming it scores high enough on the fiendish "cultural test" – the benchmark, apparently, is 15 points out of 30 – a British film with a budget of less than £20m is liable for a 24% tax credit (or £4.8m), with individual producers encouraged to spread this tax break over a range of lower-budgeted productions. In the words of James Purnell, the minister for creative industries: "This is for the Batmans as well as the Vera Drakes. The cultural goals go hand in hand with the industrial goals."

The traditional blockbuster depends on grand resolutions: death or glory, the gallant defeat or glorious victory. But the history of the British film industry sticks to a murkier, art-house template. Its abiding quest is to forge an uneasy truce with the Hollywood titans, a working relationship that enriches UK studios and promotes local talent while preserving the notion of an indigenous British cinema, free from outside interference. It's not a story to set the box office tills alight. But if you can stay the course, and suffer the endless, subtle twists and turns, this ongoing soap opera can be oddly compelling. The final credits, one suspects, are still some way distant.

Xan Brooks is the editor of Guardian Unlimited Film

Film Contacts

Hollywood studios

Buena Vista Motion Pictures Group
owned by Disney
500 S. Buena Vista St
Burbank, CA 91521
00 1 818 560 1000
http://bventertainment.go.com
President: Nina Jacobson

Icon Productions
808 Wilshire Blvd, 4th Fl
Santa Monica, CA 90401
00 1 310 434 7300
www.iconmovies.net
*Partner: Mel Gibson; partner and
president: Bruce Davey*

MGM Pictures
10250 Constellation Blvd
Los Angeles, CA 90067
00 1 310 449 3000
www.mgm.com
Chairman and CEO: Alex Yemenidjian

Miramax Films
owned by Disney
375 Greenwich Street, New York
NY 10013
00 1 212 941 3800
www.miramax.com

Sony Pictures Entertainment
10202 W Washington Blvd
Culver City, CA 90232
00 1 310 244 4000
www.sonypictures.com
Chairman and CEO: Michael Lynton

Touchstone Television Productions
owned by Disney
500 S Buena Vista St, Burbank
CA 91521
00 1 818 560 1000
http://touchstone.movies.go.com
President: Mark Pedowitz

**Twentieth Century Fox Film
Corporation**
10201 West Pico Blvd
Los Angeles, CA 90035
00 1 310 369 1000
www.fox.com
*Co-chairmen: Jim Gianopulos, Tom
Rothman*

Universal Studios
100 Universal City Plaza
Universal City, CA 91608
00 1 818 777 1000
www.universalstudios.com
President and COO: Ron Meyer

Warner Bros Entertainment
4000 Warner Blvd, Burbank
CA 91522
00 1 818 954 6000
www.warnerbros.com
Chairman and CEO: Barry M. Meyer

Major animators and special effects studios

Aardman Animations
Gas Ferry Rd, Bristol BS1 6UN
0117 984 8485
www.aardman.com

Bolexbrothers
Unit 3, Brunel Lock Development
Smeaton Road, Cumberland Basin
Bristol BS1 6SE
0117 985 8000
www.bolexbrothers.co.uk

DreamWorks Animation SKG
1000 Flower St, Glendale, CA 91201
00 1 818 695 5000
www.pdi.com

Industrial Light & Magic
PO Box 2459, San Rafael, CA 94912
00 1 415 448 9000
www.ilm.com

Pixar Animation Studios
1200 Park Ave, Emeryville, CA 94608
00 1 510 752 3000
www.pixar.com

UK film companies

Amber Films
5&9 Side, Newcastle NE1 3JE
0191 232 2000
www.amber-online.com

Bard Entertainments
7 Denmark Street
London WC2H 8LZ
020 7240 7144
office@bardentertainments.co.uk
www.bardentertainments.co.uk

BBC Films
1 Mortimer Street, London W1T 3JA
020 7765 0251
www.bbc.co.uk/bbcfilms
*Head of BBC Films: David Thompson,
020 7765 0113; executive producer and
head of development: Tracy Scoffield
020 7765 0475*

Capitol Films
23 Queensdale Place
London W11 4SQ
020 7471 6000
films@capitolfilms.com
www.capitolfilms.com

Celador Films
39 Long Acre
London WC2E 9LG
020 7845 6800
www.celador.co.uk/films.php

Company Pictures
Suffolk House, 1–8 Whitfield Place
London W1T 5JU
020 7380 3900
enquiries@companypictures.co.uk
www.companypictures.co.uk
MDs: Charlie Pattinson, George Faber

Dan Films
32 Maple Street, London W1T 6HB
020 7916 4771
enquiries@danfilms.com
www.danfilms.com

Ecosse Films
Brigade House, 8 Parsons Green
London SW6 4TN
020 7371 0290
webmail@ecossefilms.com
www.ecossefilms.com
MD: Douglas Rae

Focus Films
Focus Films, The Rotunda Studios
r/o 116–118 Finchley Road
London NW3 5HT
020 7435 9004
focus@focusfilms.co.uk
www.focusfilms.co.uk

Gruber Films
eOffice, 2 Sheraton Street
London W1F 8BH
0870 366 9313
richard.holmes@gruberfilms.com
www.gruberfilms.com

In-Motion Pictures
5 Percy Street, London W1T 1DG
020 7467 6880
enquiries@in-motionpictures.com
www.in-motionpictures.com

Ipso Facto Films
1 Pink Lane
Newcastle upon Tyne NE1 5DW
0191 230 2585
info@ipsofactofilms.com
www.ipsofactofilms.com

Merchant Ivory Productions
46 Lexington Street, London W1F 0LP
020 7437 1200
contact@merchantivory.com

Pathé
Kent House, 14–17 Market Place
Great Titchfield Street
London W1W 8AR
020 7323 5151
www.pathedistribution.com

Picture Palace Productions
13 Egbert Street, London NW1 8LJ
020 7586 8763
www.picturepalace.com

Qwerty Films
42–44 Beak Street
London W1F 9RH
020 7440 5920
info@qwertyfilms.com

Ruby Films
12 Cleveland Row
London SW1A 1DH
020 7925 2999
www.rubyfilms.co.uk

Scion Films
18 Soho Square, London W1D 3QL
020 7025 8003
info@scionfilms.com
www.scionfilms.com

Sigma Films
Film City Glasgow
Summertown Road
Glasgow G51 2LY
0141 445 0400
latenights@sigmafilms.com
www.sigmafilms.com

Vertigo Films
The Big Room Studios
77 Fortress Road
London NW5 1AG
020 7428 7555
mail@vertigofilms.com
www.vertigofilms.com
PRESS: *press@vertigofilms.com*

Working Title Films
Oxford House, 76 Oxford Street
London W1D 1BS
020 7307 3000
www.workingtitlefilms.com

UK film finance

Screen Financiers Association
9 Wimpole Street
London W1G 9SR
info@screenfinanciers.co.uk

TV & film independent production companies

▶▶ see TV, page 171

Post-production

▶▶ see TV, page 183

TV and film studios

▶▶ see TV, page 181

UK distributors

20th Century Fox
Twentieth Century House,
31–32 Soho Square
London W1D 3AP
020 7437 7766
www.fox.co.uk

Arrow Films
18 Watford Road, Radlett
Hertfordshire WD7 8LE
01923 858306
info@arrowfilms.co.uk
www.arrowfilms.co.uk

Artificial Eye
14 King Street, London WC2E 8HR
020 7240 5353
info@artificial-eye.com
www.artificial-eye.com

Blue Dolphin Films
40 Langham Street
London W1W 7AS
020 7255 2494
info@bluedolphinfilms.com
www.bluedolphinfilms.com

Buena Vista International UK/ Filmfactory
3 Queen Caroline Street
London W6 9PE
020 8222 1000
feedback@thefilmfactory.co.uk
www.bvimovies.com

CineFrance
12 Sunbury Place
Edinburgh EH4 3BY
0131 225 6191
info@cinefile.co.uk
www.cinefrance.co.uk

Columbia TriStar UK
25 Golden Square, London W1F 9LU
020 7533 1000
www.sonypictures.co.uk

Dogwoof Pictures
Unit 2 Central Square
27 Saint Mark Street, London E1 8EF
020 7488 0605
info@dogwoofpictures.com
www.dogwoofpictures.com

Entertainment Film Distributors
108–110 Jermeyn Street
London SW1Y 6HB
020 7930 7744

Eros International
customerservice2@
    erosmultimedia.net
www.erosentertainment.com

Feature Film Company
19 Heddon Street, London W1B 4BG
020 7851 6500
www.featurefilm.co.uk

Gala Film Distributors
26 Danbury Street, London N1 8JU
020 7226 5085

Granada International
48 Leicester Square
London WC2H 7FB
020 7491 1441
int.info@granadamedia.com
www.carltonint.co.uk

Icon Film Distribution
180 Wardour St, London W1F 8FX
020 7494 8100
admin@iconmovies.com
www.iconmovies.co.uk

Metrodome
5th Floor, 33 Charlotte Street
London W1T 1RR
020 7153 4421
www.metrodomegroup.com

Momentum Pictures
184–192 Drummond Street
London NW1 3HB
020 7388 1100
info@momentumpictures.co.uk
www.momentumpictures.co.uk

Optimum Releasing
22 Newman Street, London W1T 1PH
020 7637 5403
info@optimumreleasing.com
www.optimumreleasing.com

Pathé Distribution
Kent House, 14–17 Market Place
Great Titchfield Street
London W1W 8AR
020 7323 5151
www.pathedistribution.com

Redbus Film Distribution
Ariel House, 74A Charlotte Street
London W1T 4QJ
020 7299 8800
info@redbus.com
www.redbus.co.uk

Studiocanal
1, Place du Spectacle
92130 Issy-les Moulineaux
00 33 1 71 35 35 35
www.studiocanal.com

Tartan Films Distribution
Atlantic House, 5 Wardour Street
London W1V 3HE
020 7494 1400
www.tartanfilms.com

United International Pictures
UIP House, 45 Beadon Road
Hammersmith, London W6 0EG
020 8741 9041
enquiries@uip.com
www.uip.com

UGC Films UK
34 Bloomsbury Street
London WC1B 3QJ
020 7631 4683

Warner Bros
98 Theobalds Road
London WC1X 8WB
020 7984 5000
www.warnerbros.com

Contacts : Film

Film commissions

UK Film Council
10 Little Portland Street
London W1W 7JG
020 7861 7861
info@ukfilmcouncil.org.uk
www.ukfilmcouncil.org.uk
The government-backed strategic agency working to stimulate a successful UK film industry and culture
PRESS: *020 7861 7508*

Bath Film Office
01225 477711
bath_filmoffice@bathnes.gov.uk
www.visitbath.co.uk

Central England Screen Commission
0121 766 1470
info@screenwm.co.uk
www.screenwm.co.uk

Eastern Screen
01603 767077
productions@
 eastern-screen.demon.co.uk
www.eastern-screen.demon.co.uk

Edinburgh Film Focus
0131 622 7337
info@edinfilm.com
www.edinfilm.com

EM Media
0115 934 9090
info@em-media.org.uk
www.em-media.org.uk

European Film Commission
00 39 067 290 5757
info@europeanfilmcommunication.com
www.europeanfilmcommission.com

Glasgow Film Office
0141 287 0424
info@glasgowfilm.com
www.glasgowfilm.org.uk

Isle of Man Film Commission
01624 687173
iomfilm@dti.gov.im
www.gov.im/dti/iomfilm

Northern Ireland Film and Television Commission
028 9023 2444
info@niftc.co.uk
www.niftc.co.uk

Scottish Highlands and Islands Film Commission
01463 710221
trish@scotfilm.org
www.scotfilm.org

Scottish Screen
0141 302 1700
info@scottishscreen.com
www.scottishscreen.com

Wales Screen Commission
0800 849 8848
enquiries@
 walesscreencommission.co.uk
www.walesscreencommission.co.uk

Regional agencies

Film London
020 7387 8787
info@filmlondon.org.uk
www.filmlondon.org.uk
Strategic agency for film and media in London, to act as catalyst for film-making in London

East Midlands: EM Media
0115 934 9090
info@em-media.org.uk
www.em-media.org.uk

East: Screen East
01603 776920
info@screeneast.co.uk
www.screeneast.co.uk

North-east: Northern Film and Media
0191 269 9200
www.northernmedia.org

North-west: North West Vision
0161 835 6266
info@northwestvision.co.uk
www.northwestvision.co.uk

Screen Yorkshire
0113 294 4410
info@screenyorkshire.co.uk
http://screenyorkshire.co.uk

South-east (not London): Screen South
01303 298222
info@screensouth.org
www.screensouth.org

South-west: South West Screen
0117 952 9977
info@swscreen.co.uk
www.swscreen.co.uk

West Midlands: Screen West Midlands
0121 766 1470
info@screenwm.co.uk
www.screenwm.co.uk

TV & film training and support

▶▶ see TV, page 189

Trade press

Advance Production News
020 8305 6905
www.crimsonuk.com
Monthly. Listings for production companies. Owner: Crimson Communications. Editor: Alan Williams

BFI Film and Television Handbook
020 7255 1444
eddie.dyja@bfi.org.uk
www.bfi.org.uk/handbook
Annual. Editor: Eddie Dyja

British Film Magazine
020 7636 7455
terence@britishfilm-magazine.com
www.britishfilm-magazine.com
Plans to go monthly. Independently owned. Editor: Terence Doyle

Broadcast Hardware International
01628 773935
cathy@hardwarecreations.tv
www.hardwarecreations.tv
10pa. Owner: Hardware Creations. Editor: Dick Hobbs

Channel 21 International magazine
020 7729 7460
press@c21media.net
www.c21media.net
10pa. Owner: C21 Media. Editor-in-chief: David Jenkinson; editor: Ed Waller

Contacts – The Spotlight Casting Directories
020 7437 7631
info@spotlight.com
www.spotlight.com
Annual. Contacts for stage, film, TV and radio. Editor: Kate Poynton

Crewfinder
028 9079 7902
mail@adleader.co.uk
www.crewfinderwales.co.uk
Annual. Wales' film, TV and video directory. Owner: Adleader Publications. Proprietor: Stan Mairs

FilmBang
0141 334 2456
info@filmbang.com
www.filmbang.com
Annual. Scotland's film and video directory. Editor: Marianne Mellin

The Hollywood Reporter
020 7420 6000
london_one@
 eu.hollywoodreporter.com
Daily. Hollywood trade paper. UK bureau chief: Stuart Kemp

IBE
01895 421111
info@ibeweb.com
www.ibeweb.com
12pa. International broadcast engineering. Owner: BPL Business Media. Editor: Neil Nixon

Kemps Film, TV, Video Handbook (UK edition)
01342 335861
kemps@reedinfo.co.uk
www.kftv.com
Annual. Guide to international production. Owner: Reed Business Information. Editorial contact: Vivien Carne

The Knowledge
01732 377591
knowledge@cmpinformation.com
www.theknowledgeonline.com
Annual. Production directory. Owner: CMP Information. Editorial contact: Michelle Hathaway

Pact Directory of Independent Producers
020 7067 4367
enquiries@pact.co.uk
www.pact.co.uk
Annual

Pro Sound News Europe
020 7921 8319
david.robinson@cmpinformation.com
www.prosoundnewseurope.com
12pa. Audio industry. Owner: CMP Information. Editor: David Robinson; managing editor: Ben Rosser

The Production Guide
020 7505 8000
theproductionguide@Emap.com
www.productionguideonline.com
Annual. Information on production. Owner: Emap Media. Editor: Mei Mei Rogers

Screen Digest
020 7424 2820
editorial@screendigest.com
www.screendigest.com
Monthly. Editor: David Fisher; news editor: Guy Bisson; chief analyst: Ben Keen

Screen International
020 7505 8000
screeninternational@emap.com
www.screendaily.com
Weekly. News service for global film industry. Owner: Emap Media. Editor-in-chief: Colin Brown; editor: Michael Gubbins

Stage Screen and Radio
020 7346 0900
janice@stagescreenandradio.org.uk
www.bectu.org.uk
10pa. Magazine of broadcasting union Bectu. Editor: Janice Turner

VLV Bulletin
01474 352835
info@vlv.org.uk
www.vlv.org.uk
Quarterly magazine of Voice of the Listener and Viewer. Advocates citizen and consumer interests in broadcasting. Editor: Jocelyn Hay

Zerb
01795 535468
cfox@urbanfox.com
www.gtc.org.uk
2pa. For camera operators. Owner: The Deeson Group. Editor: Christina Fox

---

Consumer film and TV magazines

▶▶ see page 81

Events

Bafta Awards
195 Piccadilly, London W1J 9LN
020 7734 0022
www.bafta.org
Film, TV and interactive industries

Cannes Film Festival
3, rue Amélie 75007 Paris, France
00 33 1 53 59 61 00
festival@festival-cannes.fr
www.festival-cannes.org

London Film Festival
National Film Theatre, South Bank
London SE1 8XT
020 7815 1322
www.lff.org.uk

Raindance Film Festival
81 Berwick Street
London W1F 8TW
020 7287 3833
info@raindance.co.uk
www.raindance.co.uk

TV & film associations

▶▶ see TV, page 190

297

Music

Dan Chung

Apple's iPod... driving the market for legal digital downloads

The music industry in the UK is emerging from a period of rapid change. At the start of the decade, record companies failed to cotton on quickly enough to the popularity of digital downloads – effectively allowing illegal file-sharers to control the online distribution of their music – but they finally got their act together over the course of 2003 and 2004. By taking a hardline approach to file-sharers – and with a lot of help from portable MP3 players such as the iPod – the industry finally managed to get consumers to start downloading their music legally. The figures speak for themselves: some 500,000 tracks were downloaded legally from UK sites in the first five months of 2005. In the year to March 2005, meanwhile, the industry sold more than 10.3 million singles – a rise of 48% on the previous year; while album sales topped 163 million, a rise of 1.6%.

Digital downloads

The industry's tough approach to file-sharers was always going to be a PR battle; David v Goliath confrontations are a staple for journalists, as the industry was no doubt aware. The BPI tried to concentrate its fire on what it calls "serial uploaders"; that is, it demanded settlements, typically £2,500, from some 60 people who it said were most actively involved in file-sharing. There was, of course, some negative publicity: one of those it named in an action was a single mother who earned £150 a week, whose 14-year-old daughter had been using her computer, and who told the Guardian she could not afford to settle. Nevertheless, in June 2005, the BPI was able to announce that about two-thirds of those it had written to had indeed found the cash to make the case go away. And the results seemed to speak for themselves: the 2005 Digital Music Survey showed that 35% of music consumers now legally download, a huge improvement on even a year or two ago; and the number of legal downloads in Britain rose from about 300,000 in the first quarter of 2004 to 4.6m in the first quarter of 2005. Apple has a huge part of that market: its Europe-wide iTunes service said it sold over 5m tracks in its first 12 weeks after launching in summer 2004. Global sales of music downloads reached the 200m mark in the course of 2004.

In June 2005, meanwhile, a US supreme court decided that file-sharing programs such as Grokster can be held liable for copyright infringement. That could clear the way for the BPI to sue file-sharers, rather than individuals, and save itself a PR nightmare while cutting off the problem at source.

With the rise of digital downloads, another problem facing the industry is how to stop tracks being leaked before their official release date. Coldplay's summer 2005 album, X&Y, was leaked online a week

before its European release; and Oasis tracks accidentally went on sale from a German subsidiary, and could then be found being traded on eBay. In November 2004, leaks from an Eminem album forced the Polydor label to bring forward the release by 11 days.

In July 2004 OD2 – the online track distributor behind sites such as MyCokeMusic – was taken over by US distributor Loudeye.

Charts

With the rise of downloads comes the row over how to represent the phenomenon in the charts. The solution seemed easy enough, when the UK's first download chart was launched in September 2004. Then, in April 2005, the industry changed tack and launched a combined chart for both physical and download sales. The trouble with that was that independent labels, who had been finding it difficult to make an impression on the digital chart – thanks to what the BPI called the "uneasy" relationship between some independents and online distributors – realised that their share of the market was going to fall. The Association of Independent Music (Aim) tried to get the Office of Fair Trading to intervene, but the OFT decided there was no case to answer.

One of the rules of the combined chart is that tracks must be released physically in some form. That led to controversy in 2005 when EMI released a Gorillaz track that was mostly digital, but with a limited-edition seven-inch.

From Band Aid to Live 8

Bob Geldof hardly seemed to be out of the news in 2004 and 2005. First, he celebrated the 20th anniversary of Band Aid by launching Band Aid 20, a remix of Do They Know It's Christmas, which became the Christmas number one. Then in summer 2005, he repeated the trick by organising Live 8, a concert in Hyde Park attracting the likes of Coldplay, REM, Madonna, U2 and Paul McCartney. Tickets were nominally free, but music fans had to enter a charity text message ballot to get their tickets – and with 1.5 million entries for 150,000 tickets, demand outstripped supply by ten to one. The concert did run into controversy, though, for failing to include enough world music acts.

One sign of the times was when tickets for the concert ended up being traded on eBay. At first the auction site allowed the sales to go ahead, but pressure from Geldof – and the accompanying bad publicity – encouraged it to change its mind. Nevertheless, tickets were still being offered for sale on the site with a couple of weeks to go before the concert.

Top 10 singles 2004	
1	Band Aid 20 – Do They Know It's Christmas
2	Eamon – Fuck It (I Don't Want You Back)
3	DJ Casper – Cha Cha Slide
4	Eric Prydz – Call On Me
5	Usher featuring Lil' Jon & Ludacris – Yeah
6	Michelle – All This Time
7	Anastacia – Left Outside Alone
8	Peter Andre – Mysterious Girl
9	Britney Spears – Toxic
10	Frankee – FURB (FU Right Back)

Source: BPI / Official UK Chart Company

Top 10 downloads 2004	
1	U2 – Vertigo
2	Gwen Stefani – What You Waiting For
3	Destiny's Child – Lose My Breath
4	Green Day – American Idiot
5	Band Aid 20 – Do They Know It's Christmas
6	Natasha Bedingfield – These Words
7	Maroon 5 – She Will Be Loved
8	Eminem – Just Lose It
9	Kylie Minogue – I Believe In You
10	Christina Aguilera featuring Missy Elliott – Car Wash

Source: BPI / Official UK Chart Company

Glastonbury

Another hot ticket was the Glastonbury music festival: £125 passes for the famous event sold out online within a couple of hours of going on sale. The festival was undeniably a success, but got off to the worst possible start when torrential rain hit Pilton Farm, washing away tents and cutting off power at the site, meaning the start of the programme had to be delayed. But eBayers still managed to take advantage of the situation: not only were some tickets sold on the site, despite strict security precautions, but at least one entrepreneur started selling "genuine Glastonbury mud".

An OFT report into ticketing arrangements in the UK, meanwhile, called on Trading Standards to enforce laws against ticket touts more vigorously.

Industry news

Big news in the music industry of 2004 was the merger of two of the biggest record companies, Sony and BMG; a deal that meant just four companies controlled 80% of the global music market. The merger was allowed by the EU in July 2004, and the US Federal Trade Commission also waved it through; but independent labels were up in arms. In December 2004, the Brussels-based indies group the Independent Music Companies Association (Impala) launched an appeal against the merger, citing what it called "manifest errors of law, assessment and reasoning".

At Britain's biggest record company, EMI, profits were down 13.1% to £141.9m in the 12 months to the end of March 2005 – but this was better than expected as CD sales held up.

In March, Warner Music Group, the US-based music giant, announced plans to raise almost £400m by listing on Wall Street. The business has been independent from Time Warner since a group of investors bought the company in 2004.

At Universal, Lucian Grainge became CEO of the group's international division; and Korda Marshall was appointed head of Warner Brothers UK, a Warner Music label.

Boating weather... the Glastonbury festival after torrential rain

Richard Harding

Top 20 albums 2004			
1	Scissor Sisters – Scissor Sisters	11	Now That's What I Call Music 59
2	Keane – Hopes And Fears	12	Guns N' Roses – Greatest Hits
3	Robbie Williams – Greatest Hits	13	Now That's What I Call Music 57
4	Maroon 5 – Songs About Jane	14	Ronan Keating – 10 Years Of Hits
5	Katie Melua – Call Off The Search	15	The Streets – A Grand Don't Come For Free
6	Anastacia – Anastacia	16	Now That's What I Call Music 58
7	Usher – Confessions	17	U2 – How To Dismantle An Atomic Bomb
8	Norah Jones – Feels Like Home	18	Eminem – Encore
9	Snow Patrol – Final Straw	19	Joss Stone – The Soul Sessions
10	Il Divo – Il Divo	20	Franz Ferdinand – Franz Ferdinand

Source: BPI / Official UK Chart Company

Awards

Brit awards 2005

- *British album:* Keane – Hopes and Fears
- *British group:* Franz Ferdinand
- *British male solo artist:* The Streets
- *British female solo artist:* Joss Stone
- *International album:* Scissor Sisters – Scissor Sisters
- *International group:* Scissor Sisters
- *International male solo artist:* Eminem
- *International female solo artist:* Gwen Stefani
- *Outstanding contribution to music:* Sir Bob Geldof

Mercury music prize 2004

- Franz Ferdinand

Q awards 2004

- *Best album:* Keane, Hopes and Fears
- *Best live act:* Muse
- *Best new act:* Razorlight
- *Best single:* Jamelia – See It in a Boy's Eyes
- *Best video:* Franz Ferdinand – Take Me Out

MTV Europe music awards 2004

- *Best group:* Outkast
- *Best album:* Usher
- *Best male:* Usher
- *Best female:* Britney Spears

Gramophone awards 2004

- *Baroque vocal:* Opus 111 – Vivaldi, Vespri Solenni per la Festa dell'Assunzione di Maria Vergine
- *Concerto:* Leif Ove Andsnes – Grieg and Schumann, piano concertos
- *Early music:* Phantasm – Gibbons, consorts for viols
- *Historic reissue:* Gérard Souzay – Chausson, Debussy, Duparc, Ravel; Mélodies
- *Orchestral:* BBC Philharmonic – Bax, The Symphonies
- *Opera:* René Jacobs – Mozart, Le nozze di Figaro

Further reading

■ Press

Guardian Unlimited Arts
guardian.co.uk/arts

Music Week
www.musicweek.com

■ Music blogs

Fluxblog
www.fluxblog.org

Music for robots
http://music.for-robots.com

Moistworks
www.moistworks.com

Spoilt Victorian Child
www.spoiltvictorianchild.co.uk

■ Other resources

BBC OneMusic
www.bbc.co.uk/radio1/onemusic

BPI
www.bpi.co.uk

The new sound of music **Alexis Petridis**

It doesn't happen very often, but just occasionally, a development takes place in the world of hi-fi so seismic that it actually changes music itself. It has been going on for over a century, since long before fi was even remotely hi.

One of the reasons pop songs tend to clock in at around three to four minutes is because that's how much music a turn-of-the-century wax cylinder could store. The development of the LP in 1949 had a vast impact on the way jazz sounded: the increased playing time of a 33rpm album allowed musicians to become more adventurous, to stretch out their solos in the studio in the same way as on stage.

The same thing happened again when the album took over from the single as the dominant format of rock music in the mid-60s: longer songs, more experimentation, psychedelia and progressive rock. The advent of the CD in the 80s sparked the boom in the "heritage rock" market. Before CD, record companies paid little attention to their back catalogues, except for the occasional "best of" compilation. Today, heritage rock is a booming industry – digitally re-mastered re-issues of old material, box sets packed with out-takes, ever-more arcane corners of the past dusted down and repackaged for mass consumption - and the public knows more about musical history than ever before, hence all the nostalgia shows and "100 best" programmes on TV.

A few years ago, no one seemed to realise that the rise of the MP3 might have a similar effect on the way music sounds. Attention was focused on the effect it was going to have on the music industry, which was supposed to be ruinous. Five years on, nothing particularly ruinous seems to have happened – the revolutionary new singles chart combining downloads and physical sales looks suspiciously similar to the old unrevolutionary singles chart – and artists and audiences alike seem to have realised that digital sound files have the capacity to dramatically alter rock and pop music.

One thing most people seem to have agreed on is that the ongoing enthusiasm for iPods and downloading spells curtains for the album as we know it. iPod users seem less interested in owning albums than downloading individual tracks, cherry-picking their favourites from what's on offer. Whatever residual affection you may have for the LP, you can't really blame audiences in 2005 for spurning it. It has been looking distinctly peaky for years, ever since the CDs began offering 80 minutes of playing time, which a lot of artists seem determined to fill whether they have 80 minutes of worthwhile material or not. Albums have swelled to twice their original length, become bloated and bad value for money. The MP3 offers fans the opportunity to cut the slack.

As a result, it could be that we're about to enter a new golden age for the single to rival the early 60s or late 70s, with artists concentrating on honing a perfect individual track for download, rather than padding out albums to their requisite length. Alternatively, it could mean that artists release small handfuls of tracks at more regular intervals, instead of concentrating on a biannual cycle of an album followed by a world tour, followed by another album.

There is another factor in digital downloads that could, in theory at least, change music for good. There are no longer any time constraints imposed on how long a piece of music should be. Whether or not this is a good thing is questionable. You don't want to sound old and reactionary, like Kingsley Amis, who went to his grave believing that jazz had been destroyed by the advent of the LP, which "did away with the concentration and concision enforced by the 78 with its three plus minutes" and "encouraged long drum solos and double bass solos". On the other hand, the sort of self-indulgence encouraged by a massively expanded playing time has rarely been good news for rock music, as you find when you listen to a lot of the rather windy music produced in the early 70s, the age when the double and triple album ruled supreme. Perhaps for that reason, few artists took advantage of the CD's 80-minute playing time in order to write 80-minute-long songs: Brian Eno famously had a go on his 1993 album Neroli, but even he could only come up with a 58-minute, rather vague-sounding piece of "thinking music". That's not to say that at some point in the future, a truly fantastic and revolutionary new form of pop music won't emerge in which virtually every song lasts well over an hour: after all, the future of music has never seemed more speculative than it does in light of the advent of MP3. As Eno himself said earlier this year, when asked what he thought was going to happen next in music: "I think that everything is going to happen."

Music Contacts

Major record companies

EMI Group
27 Wrights Lane, London W8 5SW
020 7795 7000
www.emigroup.com
Chairman: Eric Nicoli
• *Labels: Additive Records, EMI Records, Heavenly Records, Mute Records, Parlophone, Positiva Records, Real World, Virgin Records UK*
PRESS: *Amanda Conroy, 020 7795 7529*

Sony BMG Music Entertainment
550 Madison Ave, New York
NY 10022-3211, USA
00 1 212 833 8000
www.sonybmg.com
CEO: Andrew Lack
• *Labels: Arista, BMG Classics, Columbia, Epic, J Records, Jive Records, LaFace Records, Legacy Recordings, Provident Music Group, RCA Records, Sony Classical, Sony Music UK, Sony Wonder, So So Def, Verity*
PRESS: *00 1 212 833 5047*

Sony Music Entertainment (UK)
Bedford House
69–79 Fulham High Street
London SW6 3JW
020 7384 7500
www.sonymusic.co.uk
CORPORATE PRESS: *020 7384 7500*

Universal Music Group
2220 Colorado Avenue
Santa Monica, CA 90404, USA
00 1 310 865 5000
http://new.umusic.com
Chairman and CEO: Jorgen Larsen
• *Labels: Geffen, Island, Lost Highway, MCA, Mercury, Motown Records, Polydor, Universal Classics, Verve Music Group*

Universal Music International
8 St James's Square
London SW1Y 4JU
020 7747 4000
CORPORATE PRESS, UK:
020 7471 5385
CORPORATE PRESS, INTERNATIONAL:
020 7747 4216

Warner Music Group
75 Rockefeller Plaza
New York, NY 10019, USA
00 1 212 275 2000
www.wmg.com
Chairman and CEO, Warner Music Group: Edgar Bronfman Jr; chairman and CEO, US recorded music, Warner Music Group: Lyor Cohen; chairman and CEO, Warner Music International: Paul-René Albertini
• *Labels: 679 Recordings, Asylum, Atlantic, Bad Boy, Code Blue, Elektra, Lava, Maverick, Nonesuch, Reprise,*

Sire, Warner Bros Records, Warner Jazz, Warner Music International, Warner Nashville, Word Label Group
PRESS: *mediainquiries@wmg.com*
UK office
28 Kensington Church Street
London W8 4EP
020 7368 2500
www.warnermusic.co.uk
PRESS: *020 7761 6000*

Record labels

679 Recordings
020 7284 5780
www.679recordings.com
Owner: Warner Music Group

Ace Records
020 8453 1311
www.acerecords.co.uk

Additive Records
020 7605 5000
www.additiverecords.com
Owner: EMI Group
PRESS: *020 7324 6155*

All Around the World
01254 264120
info@aatw.com
www.aatw.com

Aqwa Records
020 8519 4463
www.aqwa.com

Arista Records
020 7384 7500
www.arista.com
Owner: Sony BMG

Asylum Records
020 7761 6000
www.asylumrecords.com
Owner: Warner Music Group

Atlantic Records Group
020 7938 5500
www.atlanticrecords.com
Owner: Warner Music Group
PRESS: *020 7938 5566*

At Large
020 7605 5000
Owner: EMI Group
PRESS: *020 7605 5317*

Audiorec
020 8810 7779
info@audiorec.co.uk
www.audiorec.co.uk

B Unique Records
info@b-uniquerecords.com
www.b-uniquerecords.com

Bad Boy
020 7938 5500
www.badboyonline.com
Owner: Warner Music Group

Baroque Records
024 7636 1001
info@baroquerecords.co.uk
www.baroquerecords.co.uk

Beggars Group
020 8870 9912
beggars@beggars.com
www.beggars.com

Benbecula Records
2005@benbecula.com
www.benbecula.com

BMG Classics
020 7384 7500
www.bmgclassics.com
Owner: Sony BMG

Chandos Records
01206 225200
enquiries@chandos.net
www.chandos-records.com

Chemikal Underground
0141 550 1919
www.chemikal.co.uk

Cherry Red
020 8740 4110
infonet@cherryred.co.uk
www.cherryred.co.uk

Columbia Records
020 7384 7500
www.columbiarecords.com
Owner: Sony BMG

Cooking Vinyl
020 8600 9200
info@cookingvinyl.com
www.cookingvinyl.com

Definite Records
020 8959 0468
Info@definiterecords.net
www.definiterecords.net

Detour Records
01730 815422
detour@btinternet.com
www.detour-records.co.uk

Domino
020 8875 1390
enquiries@dominorecordco.com
www.dominorecordco.com

Dorado Records
020 7287 1689
contact@dorado.net
www.dorado.co.uk

Earache
020 8969 3999
will@earache.com
www.earache.com

Echo
020 7229 1616
info@echo.co.uk
www.echo.co.uk

Elektra
020 7938 5500
www.atlanticrecords.com
Owner: Warner Music Group
PRESS: *020 7938 5566*

EMI Records UK
020 7605 5000
www.emirecords.co.uk
Owner: EMI Group
PRESS: *020 7605 5317*

Epic Records
020 7384 7500
www.epicrecords.com
Owner: Sony BMG

FatCat Records
01273 747433
info@fat-cat.co.uk
www.fat-cat.co.uk

Fierce Panda
mrbongopanda@aol.com
www.fiercepanda.co.uk

Flying Rhino Records
020 8969 6555
info@flying-rhino.co.uk
www.flying-rhino.co.uk

Forever Heavenly
020 7605 5000
www.heavenly100.com
Owner: EMI Group
PRESS: *020 7833 9303*

Geffen Records
020 7471 5400
www.geffen.com
Owner: Universal Music Group

Gorgeous Music
020 7724 2635
velliott@gorgeousmusic.net
www.gorgeousmusic.net

Gut
020 7266 0777
www.gutrecords.com

Heavenly Records
020 7605 5000
www.heavenly100.com
Owner: EMI Group
PRESS: *020 7833 9303*

Hyperion Records
020 8318 1234
info@hyperion-records.co.uk
www.hyperion-records.co.uk

Independiente
020 8747 8111
www.independiente.co.uk

Interscope Geffen A&M
020 7471 5400
www.interscope.com
Owner: Universal Music Group

Def Jam Music
020 7471 5333
www.islanddefjam.com
Owner: Universal Music Group

J Records
020 7384 7500
www.jrecords.com
Owner: Sony BMG

Jeepster
0845 126 0621
info@jeepster.co.uk
www.jeepster.co.uk

Jive Records
020 7384 7500
www.jiverecords.com
Owner: Sony BMG

LaFace Records
020 7384 7500
www.laface.com
Owner: Sony BMG

Lava Records
020 7938 5500
www.lavarecords.com
Owner: Warner Music Group
PRESS: *020 7938 5566*

Legacy Recordings
020 7384 7500
www.legacyrecordings.com
Owner: Sony BMG

Locoz Records
01622 890611
mail@locozrecords.com
www.locozrecords.com

Lost Highway Records
020 7471 5333
www.losthighwayrecords.com
Owner: Universal Music Group

Matador Records
020 8969 5533
www.matadorrecords.com

Maverick Records
020 7761 6000
www.maverick.com
Owner: Warner Music Group

MCA
020 7471 5300
www.umgnashville.com
Owner: Universal Music Group

Mercury
020 7471 5333
www.umgnashville.com
Owner: Universal Music Group

Mi5 Recordings UK
0161 975 6226
info@mi5recordings.co.uk
www.mi5recordings.co.uk

Mighty Atom Productions
01792 367992
dave@mightyatom.co.uk
www.mightyatom.co.uk

Ministry of Sound
0870 060 0010
www.ministryofsound.com

Motown Records
020 7471 5300
www.motown.com
Owner: Universal Music Group

Mute Records
020 8964 2001
www.mute.com
Owner: EMI Group

Nil By Mouth Records
0121 689 0370
info@nil-by-mouth.com
www.nil-by-mouth.com

Nonesuch Records
020 7761 6003
www.nonesuch.com
Owner: Warner Music Group

One Little Indian
020 8772 7600
info@indian.co.uk
www.indian.co.uk

Opera Rara
020 7613 2858
info@opera-rara.com
www.opera-rara.com

Parlophone
020 7605 5000
www.parlophone.co.uk
Owner: EMI Group
PRESS: *020 7605 5437*

Polydor
020 7471 5400
www.polydor.co.uk
Owner: Universal Music Group

Positiva
020 7605 5000
www.positivarecords.com
Owner: EMI Group
PRESS: *020 7324 6155*

Provident Music Group
020 7384 7500
www.providentmusic.com
Owner: Sony BMG

RCA Records
020 7384 7500
www.rcarecords.com
Owner: Sony BMG

Real World
020 7605 5000
www.realworld.on.net
Owner: EMI Group
PRESS: *020 7605 5895*

Reprise Records
020 7761 6000
www.repriserec.com
Owner: Warner Music Group

Riverrun Records
01767 651146
riverrun@rvrcd.co.uk
www.rvrcd.co.uk

Rough Trade Records
020 8960 9888
glen@roughtraderecords.com
www.roughtraderecords.com

Rubicon Records
0181 450 5154
rubiconrecords@btopenworld.com
www.rubiconrecords.co.uk

Sanctuary Classics
020 7300 1888
info@sanctuaryclassics.com
www.sanctuaryclassics.com

Sanctuary Music Group
020 7602 6351
www.sanctuaryrecords.co.uk

Seriously Groovy
020 7439 1947
info@seriouslygroovy.com
www.seriouslygroovy.com

Sire Records
020 7761 6000
www.sirerecords.com
Owner: Warner Music Group

Skint Records
mail@skint.net
www.skint.net

So So Def Records
020 7384 7500
www.soso-def.com
Owner: Sony BMG

Solarise Records
07980 453628
info@solariserecords.com
www.solariserecords.com

Sony Classical
020 7384 7500
www.sonyclassical.com
Owner: Sony BMG

Sony Wonder
www.sonywonder.com

Thirdwave Records
info@thirdwavemusic.com
www.thirdwavemusic.com

Topic Records
020 7263 1240
tony.engle@topicrecords.co.uk
www.topicrecords.co.uk

Universal Classics
020 7471 5000
www.iclassics.com
Owner: Universal Music Group
Universal Records
020 7471 5000
www.universalrecords.com
Owner: Universal Music Group
V2
020 7471 3000
www.v2music.com
Verity Records
020 7384 7500
www.verityrecords.com
Owner: Sony BMG
Verve Music Group
020 7471 5000
www.vervemusicgroup.com
Owner: Universal Music Group
Virgin Records UK
020 8964 6000
www.the-raft.com
Owner: EMI Group
PRESS: *020 8964 6074/*
6085/ 6241/ 6307
Visible Noise
020 7792 9791
julie@visiblenoise.com
www.visiblenoise.com
PRESS: *matt@bluelight.co.uk*
Wall of Sound
general@wallofsound.uk.com
www.wallofsound.net
Warner Bros Records
020 7761 6000
www.wbr.com
Owner: Warner Music Group
Warner Jazz
020 7368 2500
www.warnerjazz.co.uk
Owner: Warner Music Group
PRESS: *020 7368 2542*
Warner Music International
020 7368 2500
www.wmg.com
Owner: Warner Music Group

Music publishers

Big Life
020 7554 2100
www.biglife.co.uk
BMG Music Publishing
020 7835 5200
intl.coregeneral@bmg.com
www.bmgmusicsearch.com
Bucks Music
020 7221 4275
info@bucksmusicgroup.co.uk
www.bucksmusicgroup.com
Carlin Music
020 7734 3251
www.carlinmusic.com
Chrysalis Music Publishing
020 7221 2213
info@chrysalismusic.co.uk
www.chrysalismusic.co.uk
EMI Music Publishing
020 7434 2131
www.emimusicpub.com
Independent Music Group
020 8523 9000
www.independentmusicgroup.com

Kobalt Music Group
020 7434 5155
www.kobaltmusic.com
Memory Lane Music Group
020 8523 8888
www.memorylanemusicgroup.com
Notting Hill
020 7243 2921
info@nottinghillmusic.com
www.nottinghillmusic.com
Sanctuary Music Publishing
020 7300 1866
musicpub@sanctuarygroup.com
www.sanctuarygroup.com
Sony Music Publishing
020 7911 8200
www.sonymusic.co.uk
Universal Music Publishing
020 8752 2600
ukpublishing@umusic.com
www.universalmusicpublishing.com
Warner Chappell UK
020 8563 5800
www.warnerchappell.co.uk

Sheet music publishers

Associated Board of the Royal Schools of Music Publishing
020 7636 5400
publishing@abrsm.ac.uk
www.abrsmpublishing.com
Boosey & Hawkes Music Publishers
020 7054 7200
marketing.uk@boosey.com
www.boosey.com
Brass Wind Publications
01572 737409
www.brasswindpublications.co.uk
Breitkopf & Härtel
01263 768732
www.breitkopf.com
Faber Music
020 7833 7900
information@fabermusic.com
www.fabermusic.com
Music Sales
020 7434 0066
www.musicsales.com
Oxford University Press
01865 353349
music.enquiry.uk@oup.com
www.oup.co.uk
Peters Edition
020 7553 4000
www.editionpeters.com
Stainer & Bell
020 8343 3303
post@stainer.co.uk
www.stainer.co.uk
United Music Publishers
01992 703110
www.ump.co.uk
Universal Edition
020 7439 6678
uelondon@universaledition.com
www.universaledition.com

Production music companies

AKM Music
01926 864068
akm@akmmusic.co.uk
www.akmmusic.co.uk
Amphonic Music
0800 525132
www.amphonic.com
Audio Network
01787 477277
office@audiolicense.net
www.audiolicense.net
Burning Petals
0870 749 1117
enquiries@burning-petals.com
www.burning-petals.co.uk
Extreme Music
020 7485 0111
www.extrememusic.com
KPM Music
020 7412 9111
kpm@kpm.co.uk
www.playkpm.com
Mediatracks
01254 691197
www.mediatracks.co.uk
Music House
020 7412 9111
enquiries@musichouse.co.uk
www.musichouse.co.uk
Primrose Music
020 8946 7808
www.primrosemusic.com
West One Music
020 7292 0000
info@westonemusic.com
www.westonemusic.com

Digital distributors

Amazon
020 8636 9200
www.amazon.co.uk
Free downloadable tracks from high-profile artists
PRESS: *020 8636 9280*
Artist Direct
www.artistdirect.com
Free downloadable tracks from high-profile artists
Connect
00 1 212 833 8000
PRESS: *01932 816417*
service@connect-europe.com
www.connect-europe.com
Sony site, with music from all major labels and many indies
eMusic
00 1 212 201 9240
www.emusic.com
Subscription-based service
PRESS: *00 1 212 561 7454*
pr@emusic.com
Epitonic
00 1 212 320 3624
www.epitonic.com

Insound
00 1 212 777 8056
www.insound.com/mp3
Free indie MP3s

Intomusic.co.uk
020 8676 4850
info@intomusic.co.uk
www.intomusic.co.uk
Independent and alternative music

iTunes UK
0800 039 1010
www.apple.com/uk/itunes
Apple's digital jukebox and music store
PRESS: *appleuk.pr@euro.apple.com*

Mperia.com
00 1 650 388 3000
www.mperia.com
PRESS: *pr@bitpass.com*

Napster
www.napster.co.uk
Subscription service
PRESS: *media@napster.co.uk*

OD2/Loudeye
0117 910 0150
info@ondemanddistribution.com
www.ondemanddistribution.com
*Handles distribution for Big Noise
Music, Freeserve Music Club, HMV,
Ministry of Sound, MSN UK, MTV UK.
MyCokeMusic.com, Tiscali Music Club
and Virgin Megastore*

Playlouder
site@playlouder.com
www.playlouder.com
UK music site
PRESS: *media@playlouder.com*

Streets Online
0845 601 8330
digital@streetsonline.co.uk
www.streetsonline.co.uk
Owned by Woolworths

Trax2Burn
01202 315333
www.trax2burn.com
*Three house music labels: End
Recordings, Underwater and Southern
Fried*

Vitaminic.com
00 1 415 781 7670
info@vitaminic.com
www.vitaminic.com
Pan-European site

Wippit
0870 737 1100
info@wippit.com
www.wippit.com
Specialises in independent label artists

**Association of Professional
Recording Services (APRS)**
PO Box 22, Totnes TQ9 7YZ
01803 868600
info@aprs.co.uk
www.aprs.co.uk

MEMBERS OF APRS:

Abbey Road Studios
3 Abbey Road, London NW8 9AY
020 7266 7000
info@abbeyroad.com
www.abbeyroad.com
Studio manager: Colette Barber

Air Edel Studios
18 Rodmarton Street
London W1U 8BJ
020 7486 6466
trevorbest@air-edel.co.uk
www.air-edel.co.uk
Studio manager: Trevor Best

Air Studios
Lyndhurst Hall, Lyndhurst Road
London NW3 5NG
020 7794 0660
information@airstudios.com
www.airstudios.com
Contact: Alison Burton

British Grove Studios
20 British Grove, Chiswick
London W4 2NL
020 8741 8941
davidstewart@britishgrovestudios.com
www.britishgrovestudios.com
Studio manager: David Stewart

Classic Sound
5 Falcon Park, Neasden Lane
London NW10 1RZ
020 8208 8100
classicsound@dial.pipex.com
www.classicsound.net
Director: Neil Hutchinson

The Dairy
43–45 Tunstall Road
London SW9 8BZ
020 7738 7777
info@thedairy.co.uk
www.thedairy.co.uk
Studio manager: Emily Taylor

Eden Studios
20–24 Beaumont Road
London W4 5AP
020 8995 5432
eden@edenstudios.com
www.edenstudios.com
Studio manager: Natalie Horton

**Gateway School of Recording
& Music Technology**
Kingston Hill Centre
Kingston-upon-Thames
Surrey KT2 7LB
020 8549 0014
info@gsr.org.uk
www.gsr.org.uk
Admin assistant: Jenny Goodwin

ICC Studios
4 Regency Mews, Silverdale Road
Eastbourne, Sussex BN20 7AB
01323 643341/2
info@iccstudios.co.uk
www.iccstudios.co.uk
Technical director: Helmut Kaufman

ICE PR
Unit 5, Acklam Workshops
10 Acklam Road
London W10 5QZ
020 8968 2222
info@ice-pr.com
www.ice-pr.com
MD: Jason Price

Iguana Studio
Unit 1, 88a Acre Lane
London SW2 5QN
020 7924 0496
info@iguanastudio.co.uk
www.iguanastudio.co.uk
Director: Andrea Terrano

Jacobs Studio
Ridgway House, Runwick Lane
near Farnham, Surrey GU10 5EE
01252 715546
andy@jacobs-studios.co.uk
www.jacobs-studios.co.uk
MD: Andy Fernbach

Keynote Studios
Green Lane, Burghfield Bridge
Burghfield, Reading RG30 3XN
01189 599944
keynotestudios@btconnect.co.uk
www.keynotestudios.co.uk
Owner and partner: Noel Newton

Konk Recording Studio
84–86 Tottenham Lane
London N8 7EE
020 8340 7873
linda@konkstudios.com
Station manager: Sarah Lockwood

Lansdowne Recording Studios
Lansdowne House
Lansdowne Road, London W11 3LP
020 7727 0041
info@cts-lansdowne.co.uk
www.cts-lansdowne.co.uk
Client liasion: Sharon Rose

Metropolis
The Powerhouse
70 Chiswick High Road
London W4 1SY
020 8742 1111
studios@metropolis-group.co.uk
www.metropolis-group.co.uk
Station manager: Alison Hussey

Parr Street Studios
33–45 Parr Street, Liverpool L1 4JN
0151 707 1050
info@parrstreet.co.uk
www.parrstreet.co.uk
*Manager: Anne Lewis; bookings
manager: Paul Lewis*

Phoenix Sound
info@phoenixsound.net
www.phoenixsound.net
Contact: Peter Fielder

RAK Recording Studios
42–48 Charlbert Street
St John's Wood, London NW8 7BU
020 7586 2012
trisha@rakstudios.co.uk
www.rakstudios.co.uk
Station manager: Trisha Wegg

Real World Studios
Box Mill, Mill Lane
Box, Corsham, Wiltshire SN13 8PL
01225 743188
studios@realworld.co.uk
www.realworld.on.net
Station manager: Owen Leech

Rockfield Studios
Amberley Court, Rockfield Road
Monmouth NP25 5ST
01600 712449
RockfieldStudios@compuserve.com
Director: Kingsley Ward

Roundhouse Recording Studios
91 Saffron Hill, London EC1N 8PT
020 7404 3333
roundhouse@stardiamond.com
www.stardiamond.com/roundhouse
Contact: Lisa Gunther

Sain
Llandwrog, Caernarfon
Gwynedd LL54 5TG
01286 831111
eryl@sainwales.com
www.sainwales.com
Station manager: Eryl Davies

Sanctuary Studios
150 Goldhawk Road
London W12 8HH
020 8932 3200
julie.bateman@sanctuarygroup.com
www.sanctuarygroup.com
Head of audio studios: Julie Bateman

Sawmills Studio
Golant, Fowey, Cornwall PL23 1LW
01726 833338
ruth@sawmills.co.uk
www.sawmills.co.uk
Station manager: Ruth Taylor

Soho Recording Studios
Basement, The Heals Building
22–24 Torrington Place
London WC1E 7HJ
020 7419 2444
dominic@sohostudios.co.uk
www.sohostudios.co.uk
Manager: Dominic Sanders

Sound Recording Technology
Edison Road, St Ives
Cambs PE27 3LF
01480 461880
srt@btinternet.com
www.soundrecordingtechnology.co.uk
MD: Sarah Pownall

Sphere Studios
2 Shuttleworth Road
Battersea, London SW11 3EA
020 7326 9450
info@spherestudios.com
www.spherestudios.com
MD: Malcolm Atkin

Strongroom Studios
120–124 Curtain Road
London EC2A 3SQ
020 7426 5100
mix@strongroom.co.uk
www.strongroom.co.uk
MD: Richard Boote

Whites Farm Studios
Whites Farm, Wilton Lane
Kenyon Culcheth WA3 4BA
0161 790 4830
whitesfarmstudios@aol.com
www.whitesfarmstudios.com
Manager: Gary White

Whitfield Street Studios
31–37 Whitfield Street
London W1T 2SF
020 7636 3434
david.anderson@whitfield-street.com
www.whitfield-street.com
Operations manager: David Anderson

Promoters

Barfly
49 Chalk Farm Road
London NW1 8AN
020 7691 4244
london.info@barflyclub.com
www.barflyclub.com
*Clubs based in Camden London,
Cardiff, Liverpool, Glasgow and York*

Club Fandango
2 St Pauls Crescent
London NW1 9XS
everyone@clubfandango.co.uk
www.clubfandango.co.uk
*Venues in London, Brighton, Bristol,
Manchester and Glasgow. London
venues include Dublin Castle, Metro, The
Borderline (with BMI) & the Bull & Gate*

Mean Fiddler Music Group
Head office, 16 High Street
Harlesden, London NW10 4LX
020 8961 5490
www.meanfiddler.com
*Astoria, Jazz Cafe, Borderline, The
Garage and Glastonbury festival*

▶▶ **MUSIC VENUES** see page 427

Events

BBC Proms
020 7589 8212
proms@bbc.co.uk
www.bbc.co.uk/proms
PRESS: *020 7765 5575*

Cambridge Folk Festival
The Cambridge Corn Exchange
3 Parsons Court, Wheeler Street
Cambridge CB2 3QE
01223 457555
folkfest@cambridge.gov.uk
www.cambridgefolkfestival.co.uk

Carling Weekend (Reading, Leeds)
Mean Fiddler
16 High Street, Harlseden
London NW10 4LX
020 8961 5490
www.carlinglive.com

Creamfields
Cream Group
Nation, Wolstenholme Square
1–3 Parr Street
0151 707 1309
info@cream.co.uk
www.cream.co.uk/creamfields

**Glastonbury Festival (no festival
in 2006)**
28 Northload Street, Glastonbury
Somerset BA6 9JJ
01458 834 596
office@glastonburyfestivals.co.uk
www.glastonburyfestivals.co.uk

Glyndebourne Festival
Glyndebourne Productions
Glyndebourne, Lewes
01273 812321
info@glyndebourne.com
www.glyndebourne.com

Homelands Festival
Mean Fiddler
16 High Street, Harlseden
London NW10 4LX
020 8961 5490
www.welovehomelands.com

Isle of Wight Festival
info@isleofwightfestival.org
www.isleofwightfestival.org

The London Fleadh
Mean Fiddler
16 High Street, Harlseden
London NW10 4LX
020 8961 5490
www.meanfiddler.com

T in the Park
www.tinthepark.com
PRESS: *Liana Mellotte, 0141 204 7970*

V Festival
www.vfestival.com
PRESS: *vfestival@cakemedia.com*

Orchestras

BBC National Orchestra of Wales
BBC Wales, Broadcasting House
Cardiff CF5 2YQ
0800 052 1812
now@bbc.co.uk
www.bbc.co.uk/wales/now

BBC Philharmonic
New Broadcasting House
Oxford Road, Manchester M60 1SJ
0161 244 4001
philharmonic@bbc.co.uk
www.bbc.co.uk/orchestras
/philharmonic

BBC Scottish Symphony Orchestra
BBC Scotland, Broadcasting House
Queen Margaret Drive
Glasgow G12 8DG
0141 338 2606
bbcsso@bbc.co.uk
www.bbc.co.uk/scotland/music
scotland/bbcsso/concerts

English Symphony Orchestra
Rockliffe House, 40 Church Street
Malvern WR14 2AZ
01684 560696
info@eso.co.uk
www.eso.co.uk

London Philharmonic Orchestra
89 Albert Embankment
London SE1 7TP
020 7840 4200
admin@lpo.org.uk
www.lpo.co.uk

London Symphony Orchestra
Barbican Centre, Silk Street
London EC2Y 8DS
020 7588 1116
admin@lso.co.uk
www.lso.co.uk

Royal Philharmonic Orchestra
16 Clerkenwell Green
London EC1R 0QT
020 7608 8800
info@rpo.co.uk
www.rpo.co.uk

Royal Scottish National Orchestra
73 Claremont Street, Glasgow G3 7JB
0141 226 3868
www.rsno.org.uk

Music schools

Birmingham Conservatoire
Paradise Place
Birmingham B3 3HG
0121 331 5901/5902
conservatoire@uce.ac.uk
www.conservatoire.uce.ac.uk

Leeds College of Music
3 Quarry Hill, Leeds LS2 7PD
0113 222 3400
enquiries@lcm.ac.uk
www.lcm.ac.uk

Royal Academy of Music
Marylebone Road
London NW1 5HT
020 7873 7373
www.ram.ac.uk

Royal College of Music
Prince Consort Road
London SW7 2BS
020 7589 3643
info@rcm.ac.uk
www.rcm.ac.uk

Royal Northern College of Music
124 Oxford Road
Manchester M13 9RD
0161 907 5200
info@rncm.ac.uk
www.rncm.ac.uk

Royal Scottish Academy of Music and Drama
100 Renfrew Street, Glasgow G2 3DB
0141 332 4101
www.rsamd.ac.uk

Royal Welsh College of Music and Drama
Castle Grounds, Cathays Park
Cardiff CF10 3ER
029 2034 2854
music.admissions@rwcmd.ac.uk
www.rwcmd.ac.uk
PRESS: *press@rwcmd.ac.uk*

Trinity College of Music
King Charles Court
Old Royal Naval College
Greenwich, London SE10 9JF
020 8305 4444
info@tcm.ac.uk
www.tcm.ac.uk

Music press

Audience
020 7486 7007
info@audience.uk.com
www.audience.uk.com
Monthly. For live international contemporary music industry. Owner: Audience Media. Executive editor: Gordon Masson; publisher: Steve Harker; sales manager: John Ainsworth

Billboard
020 7420 6000
www.billboard.com
Weekly magazine and daily email. Owner: VNU. Editor: Emmanuel Legrand; news: Lars Brandle; deputy global editor: Tom Ferguson

Five Eight
020 7837 1347
subs@fiveeight.net
www.fiveeight.net
Monthly magazine and daily email. Editor: Eamonn Forde; head of production: Nick Becker

Gramophone
020 8267 5136
www.gramophone.co.uk
Monthly. Owner: Haymarket. Editor: James Jolly

Kerrang!
020 7182 8000
www.kerrang.com
Weekly. Owner: Emap. Editor: Paul Brannigan

Mojo
020 7436 1515
www.mojo4music.com
Monthly. Owner: Emap. Editor: Phil Alexander

Music Industry News Network
00 1 718 278 0662
editor@mi2n.com
www.mi2n.com
News aggregator. Editor-in-chief: Eric de Fontenay

Music Week
020 7921 8390
martin@musicweek.com
www.musicweek.com
Weekly. Owner: CMP Information. Editor: Martin Talbot; news: Paul Williams; features: Adam Webb; chief sub: Dougal Baird; online editor: Nicola Slade

MusicAlly
020 7490 5444
mail@musically.com
www.musically.com
Fortnightly report plus bulletins. Digital music. Editor: Paul Brindley; features: Toby Lewis

Musician
020 7840 5531
info@musiciansunion.org.uk
www.musiciansunion.org.uk
Quarterly. Editor: Keith Ames

NME
020 7261 5564
www.nme.com
Weekly. Owner: IPC Media.
Editor: Conor McNicholas

Q
020 7436 1515
www.q4music.com
Monthly. Owner: Emap.
Editor: Paul Rees

Record of the Day
020 8520 2130
info@recordoftheday.com
www.recordoftheday.com
Daily newsletter. Editor: David
Balfour; music editor: Joe Taylor

▶▶ **MORE CONSUMER MUSIC**
MAGAZINES see page 81

Associations

Association of British Orchestras
20 Rupert Street, London W1D 6DF
020 7287 0333
info@abo.org.uk
www.abo.org.uk

Association of Independent Music
Lamb House, Church Street
London W4 2PD
020 8994 5599
www.musicindie.org

Association of Professional Recording Services
PO Box 22, Totnes TQ9 7YZ
01803 868600
info@aprs.co.uk
www.aprs.co.uk

Association of United Recording Artists
1 York St, London W1U 6PA
0870 8505 200
office@aurauk.com
www.aurauk.com

British Academy of Composers and Songwriters
British Music House
25–27 Berners Street
London W1T 3LR
020 7636 2929
info@britishacademy.com
www.britishacademy.com

British Association of Record Dealers
Colonnade House, 1st Floor,
2 Westover Road
Bournemouth, Dorset BH1 2BY
01202 292063
www.bard.org

British Music Information Centre
1st Floor, Lincoln House
75 Westminster Bridge Road
London SE1 7HS
020 7928 1902
info@bmic.co.uk
www.bmic.co.uk

British Music Rights
British Music House
26 Berners Street, London W1T 3LR
020 7306 4446
britishmusic@bmr.org
www.bmr.org

British Phonographic Industry
Riverside Building, County Hall
Westminster Bridge Road
London SE1 7JA
020 7803 1300
general@bpi.co.uk
www.bpi.co.uk

IFPI
54 Regent Street, London W1B 5RE
020 7878 7900
info@ifpi.org
www.ifpi.org
Represents music industry worldwide

Incorporated Society of Musicians
10 Stratford Place
London W1C 1AA
020 7629 4413
membership@ism.org
www.ism.org

Independent Music Companies Association
Rue du Trône 51
1050 Brussels, Belgium
00 32 2289 2600
impala@kernnet.com
www.impalasite.org
European indie label association

Mechanical-Copyright Protection Society
Copyright House
29–33 Berners Street
London W1T 3AB
020 7580 5544
www.mcps.co.uk

Music Industries Association
Ivy Cottage Offices, Finch's Yard
Eastwick Road, Great Bookham
Surrey KT23 4BA
01372 750600
enquiries@mia.org.uk
www.mia.org.uk

Music Publishers Association
3rd Floor, 20 York Buildings
London WC2N 6JU
020 7839 7779
info@mpaonline.org.uk
www.mpaonline.org.uk

Musicians Union
www.musiciansunion.org.uk
Regional offices
London, east and south-east England
60–62 Clapham Rd, London SW9 0JJ
020 7840 5534
london@musiciansunion.org.uk
Midlands
Benson House, Lombard St
Birmingham B12 0QN
0121 622 3870
birmingham@musiciansunion.org.uk
North of England
40 Canal Street, Manchester M1 3WD
0161 236 1764
manchester@musiciansunion.org.uk

Scotland and Northern Ireland
11 Sandyford Place, Glasgow G3 7NB
0141 248 3723
glasgow@musiciansunion.org.uk
Wales and south-west England
199 Newport Road
Cardiff CF24 1AJ
029 2045 6585
cardiff@musiciansunion.org.uk

Official UK Charts Company
4th Floor
58/59 Great Marlborough Street
London W1F 7JY
020 7478 8500
nadya@theofficialcharts.com
www.theofficialcharts.com

Performing Artists Media Rights Association
UK Performer Services
PO Box 4398, London W1A 7RU
020 7534 1234
team@ukperformerservices.com
www.pamra.org.uk

Performing Rights Society
Copyright House
29–33 Berners Street
London W1T 3AB
020 7580 5544
www.prs.co.uk

Producers and Composers of Applied Music
01886 884204
bobfromer@onetel.com
www.pcam.co.uk

Media services

Advertising

The advertising industry has enjoyed a generally healthy 2004/05, as it puts the media recession of 2002 and 2003 behind it; but things started looking uncertain in the summer of 2005.

Ad spend in the UK was just shy of £4bn in the first quarter of 2005, according to the Advertising Association, which was a healthy 5.3% up on the same period the year before. Internet advertising was the biggest beneficiary – up 51.5% to £210m – while TV and outdoor advertising also performed well. But the outlook for 2005 and 2006 is hazy. The Advertising Association was relatively optimistic, predicting in May 2005 that the UK market would grow by 4.9% in 2005 and 3.8% in 2006. But a slowdown in consumer spending, combined with the lack of a major sporting event in summer 2005, saw many predicting a drop-off in ad spend in the second half of the year.

About the industry

In theory, advertising is split into two main areas: ad agencies, which handle industry accounts and come up with creative ideas; and media agencies, which control the purchase of ad space. There are about 1,600 ad agencies in the UK and more than 300 media agencies. In practice though, many big firms are owned by one of the major, largely US-based, advertising conglomerates, who control not only the main ad and media agencies, but many of the PR and direct marketing agencies as well.

All advertising expenditure, by medium

	2004 £m	2003 £m	2002 £m	2001 £m	2000 £m	1999 £m	1998 £m
National newspapers	1,980	1,906	1,933	2,062	2,252	1,991	1,824
Regional newspapers	3,165	2,986	2,894	2,834	2,762	2,483	2,389
Consumer magazines	819	784	785	779	750	727	709
Business & professional magazines	1,082	1,048	1,088	1,202	1,270	1,195	1,209
Directories	1,086	1,029	990	959	868	831	780
Press production costs	660	634	643	669	702	650	620
TOTAL PRESS	**8,792**	**8,387**	**8,333**	**8,514**	**8,604**	**7,877**	**7,531**
Television	4,740	4,499	4,332	4,147	4,646	4,320	4,029
Direct mail	2,469	2,467	2,378	2,228	2,049	1,876	1,666
Outdoor & transport	986	914	816	788	810	649	613
Radio	604	584	545	541	595	516	460
Internet	597*	408	233	166	155	51	19
Cinema	192	180	180	164	128	123	97
TOTAL ALL MEDIA	**18,379**	**17,439**	**16,817**	**16,548**	**16,988**	**15,412**	**14,415**

*Figures as estimated at March 2005. Internet Advertising Bureau figures are about £50m higher   Source: Advertising Association

Awards

Many ad agencies also offer "below-the-line" marketing services. These services include market research, sales promotion and direct marketing. PR is also traditionally considered a below-the-line service; the industry has such as high profile that it merits a separate chapter (see page 327).

Financial performance

WPP, the London-based advertising supergroup run by Sir Martin Sorrell, had a very healthy 2004. The company, which owns the ad agencies Young & Rubicam, JWT and Ogilvy & Mather, the media buyers MindShare and Mediaedge:cia, and the PR firms Hill & Knowlton and Burson-Marsteller – plus a stake in leading media buyer Carat – saw its profits rise 30% in 2004 to £456.5m. In the first five months of 2005, meanwhile, revenues rose 6% – 16% in the first quarter alone, if you include revenues from its purchase of rival ad firm Grey Global. And the outlook was good, too: in November 2004, WPP won a £700m media buying and planning contract from Unilever.

Other European supergroups had similar successes. Havas, the French advertising group, saw operating profits leap 45% to £135.5m for 2004; though the company faced uncertainty when Alain de Pouzilhac, chairman and chief executive, stepped down after losing control to Vincent Bolloré. **Publicis**, its French rival, which owns Saatchi & Saatchi and Zenith Optimedia, made £406m in 2004, up 6%.

Omnicom, which owns the TBWA and Abbot Mead Vickers BBDO agencies, reported a 17% increase in the three months to September 2004. The US company, which is the biggest advertising group in the world, said its earnings rose to £79m for that quarter.

But there was accounting trouble at **Interpublic**, the US group that owns ad agencies McCann-Erickson and Lowe. The company was unable to file its 2004 annual report on time, and said it may need to restate results with regard to acquisitions made between 1996 and 2001.

Creative performance

Wieden + Kennedy, the ad agency that mysteriously failed to win the overall prize at the 2004 Cannes International Advertising Festival with its Honda "Cog" ad, finally hit the jackpot in 2005. Its ad, "Grrr", saw a Honda diesel engine flying through the sky to the infectious tune "Hate Something, Change Something".

Win something…
Honda's inventive ad "Grrr" took the Grand Prix at Cannes

Creative stunts

It wouldn't be the ad industry if there weren't a couple of creative stunts to get the execs talking. Viral agency Asa Bailey came up with the cheekiest, when it grabbed the domain name OgilvyMather.co.uk from under WPP-owned Ogilvy & Mather's nose. The website showed what looked like the feet of a corpse, with a tag reading: "If you understood the modern brand, you would know how to protect it."

Much less well received was a fake ad, made by London-based advertising creatives Lee Ford and Dan Brooks, which showed a suicide bomber blowing himself up in a VW Polo. The ad was made six months before the July terrorist attack in London, but the duo still ended up having to reach a legal settlement with VW to avoid being sued for damages.

Industry moves

The noisiest startup in the advertising industry came in May, when **Trevor Beattie** – the adman behind the FCUK rebrand, the "Hello Boys" Wonderbra ad and Labour's election campaign – left TBWA/London to start his own agency. Beattie had made the controversial Labour ad representing Michael Howard as a flying pig, which was dropped after accusations of anti-semitism.

Also in May, the French creative duo **Fred & Farid** launched their own agency, Marcel, under the banner of supergroup Publicis. The pair – full names Frederic Raillard and Farid Mokart – had won a series of international awards.

One startup that failed was **Boymeetsgirl**, launched by St Luke's founder Andy Law. The company went into administration in March, but Law returned a few months later under the banner of the global creative network Law & Kenneth. Meanwhile Mark Wnek, whose Ben

Ratecards

£10,000 might buy you:

- Twenty-five 30-second spots in the ITV Anglia North region (10 peak-time, 15 off-peak); includes production

- A full-page colour ad in the Guardian's G2 section

- The outside back cover of a film magazine

- 220,000 page impressions on a "skyscraper" ad on Guardian Unlimited

- 30-second slot at one children's film nationwide (625,000 admissions)

- Seven 30-second breakfast slots every weekday on a London radio station (FM only)

(Based on industry rate cards available in 2005: ITV Anglia, the Guardian and Guardian Unlimited, Emap, Pearl & Dean and Virgin Radio)

Top 20 media agencies 2004 (Media brands ranked by Nielsen Media Research)		
1	MediaCom	£715.3m
2	Starcom UK Group	£673.4m
3	ZenithOptimedia	£622.4m
4	Carat	£577.5m
5	MindShare	£576.9m
6	Initiative	£513.6m
7	OMD UK	£475.9m
8	Universal McCann London	£338.3m
9	Manning Gottlieb OMD	£269.0m
10	PHD	£218.5m
11	Walker Media	£196.7m
12	Vizeum UK	£175.8m
13	Mediaedge:cia	£170.5m
14	MediaVest Manchester	£107.8m
15	Brilliant Media	£83.9m
16	Media Planning Group	£83.0m
17	Booth Lockett Makin	£78.8m
18	Feather Brooksbank	£76.4m
19	BrandConnection	£71.5m
20	The Allmond Partnership	£68.0m

Source: Campaign Report – The Top 300 Agencies, February 2005 (Data supplied by Nielsen Media Research)

Mark Orlando agency failed in January 2004, returned as the chairman and chief creative officer of Lowe in the US.

Meanwhile **Chime Communications**, the advertising group owned by PR man Lord Bell, paid £14.5m to buy Vallance Carruthers Coleman Priest, the ad agency that handles O2's advertising.

Government advertising

The public information film may be a throwback to the 70s, but it's also very much a feature of today. The government spent £158.1m on advertising in the first 11 months of 2004, according to Nielsen Media Research. That record total was more than the £146.4m it spent in the whole of 2003.

Regulation

All eyes were on the Advertising Standards Authority, the self-regulatory body owned by the ad industry, after it gained the power to regulate TV and radio as well as print from July 2004. According to its 2004 report, three of the most four complained-about ads were about religious imagery – including 800 complaints about an ad showing a woman giving birth in a hospital, in a parody of a nativity scene (upheld), 264 complaints about a parody of the Last Supper (rejected), and 182 complaints about an ad for a morning-after pill with the tagline "Immaculate contraception? If only" (upheld).

The most complaints, though, were made about the TV shopping channel Auctionworld. After receiving 1,360 complaints, the ASA fined the channel £450,000 and revoked its licence.

As far as non-broadcast ads were concerned, the number of complaints fell to 12,711, down more than 10%; it investigated 827 ads and upheld complaints against 77% of them.

With ever more headlines about the scourge of binge drinking, alcohol advertising has been restricted. In March 2005, it was announced

Campaign magazine's top 20 UK agencies 2004	
1 Abbott Mead Vickers BBDO	£362.7m
2 JWT	£327.9m
3 McCann Erickson Advertising	£304.6m
4 Publicis	£286.6m
5 M&C Saatchi	£246.3m
6 Ogilvy & Mather	£235.0m
7 Euro RSCG London	£228.6m
8 Saatchi & Saatchi	£221.3m
9 DDB London	£208.9m
10 Leo Burnett	£204.9m
11 Bartle Bogle Hegarty	£202.1m
12 Lowe	£198.2m
13 Grey Worldwide	£194.4m
14 Rainey Kelly Campbell Roalfe/Y&R	£179.2m
15 TBWA\London	£173.1m
16 WCRS	£146.3m
17 Delaney Lund Knox Warren & Partners	£116.7m
18 Mother	£107.8m
19 HHCL/Red Cell	£89.5m
20 Clemmow Hornby Inge	£87.7m

Source: Campaign Report – The Top 300 Agencies, February 2005 (Data supplied by Nielsen Media Research)

ASA rulings

Banned

- **July 2005:** An Accurist ad in Glamour magazine is banned for appearing to depict a naked woman masturbating. The ad showed a naked woman reclining on a chair with her left hand on her stomach and her partly obscured fingers above her crotch, alongside the caption, "Me time". One reader complained that the ad was offensive and demeaning to women.
- **March 2005:** A TV ad for the KFC Mini Chicken Fillet Burger is banned after the ASA rules it misled viewers about the food's size. To test the ad, the ASA bought three of the burgers from a London KFC.
- **February 2005:** The ASA bans a print ad for Ruddles Ale, showing a drawing of a shotgun pointed at the reader. The ad showed the gun between two pub stools, and the tagline: "Excuse me, I believe that's my seat." It formed part of brewer Greene King's "uncompromisingly from the country" campaign.
- **January 2005:** A TV ad featuring Harry Enfield shouting at a Winston Churchill lookalike and calling him a "porky prime minister" is banned before broadcast by the Broadcast Advertising Clearance Centre because it would cause offence. Website Madasafish.com posts the ad online instead.
- **December 2004:** A print ad promoting advertising in national newspapers is banned. The ad, which shows a stiletto heel skewering a man through the stomach, was made by TBWA London for the Newspaper Marketing Agency.
- **December 2004:** Regulators ban a poster ad for the morning-after pill with the tagline "Immaculate Contraception".
- **October 2004:** Condom posters showing the face of a woman apparently having an orgasm are banned. The ASA said the tagline "Come online & play the sex organ" would cause widespread offence, and may tempt children to view unsuitable material.
- **July 2004:** The ASA demands to see all French Connection poster ads before they are displayed in public, after repeatedly warning the company that its FCUK logo was offensive. The watchdog decided on the sanction after upholding a complaint against the company – the tenth in six years – about a poster for its radio station FCUK FM.

Restricted

- **July 2005:** Coca-Cola encouraged antisocial behaviour by producing a TV advert for Fanta showing people spitting, the ASA rules. The ad is banned before 9pm.
- **March 05:** A Marmite advert spoofing the 1950s sci-fi horror The Blob is banned from children's TV after giving toddlers nightmares.

Allowed

- **June 2005:** A KFC TV ad showing people singing with their mouths full is allowed, despite a record 1,671 complaints.
- **May 2005:** The ASA rejects 620 complaints about the "Pot Noodle horn" ad, which shows a large brass horn unfurling from a man's trousers.
- **April 2005:** The Salt Manufacturers' Association fails in its attempt to shoot down a government health campaign linking salt intake to high blood pressure, heart disease and strokes. The poster and TV campaign showed an animated Sid the Slug character warning that "too much salt could lead to a heart attack".
- **February 2005:** In a decision the entire nation willlive to regret, the ASA passes an ad for Crazy Frog after receiving 60 complaints. Some complained about the character's stunted penis, but others merely noted how irritating the ad was.

that the advertising of low-carbohydrate beer would be banned, under a rule preventing companies from making health claims about alcoholic drinks. And in June 2005, it was announced that print ads should not link alcohol with seduction.

There are even tougher rules on advertising tobacco. In December 2004, it was announced that in-shop tobacco advertising would be restricted to an A5 area, of which one-third must include the health warning. Meanwhile in June, the EU health and consumer affairs commissioner, Markos Kyprianou, warned food advertisers that it may ban advertising of junk food to children unless the industry self-regulates.

Further reading

■ **Press**

MediaGuardian
media.guardian.co.uk/advertising

Campaign
www.campaignlive.com

Marketing
www.marketing.haynet.com

Marketing Week
www.mad.co.uk/mw

Media Week
www.mediaweek.co.uk

Promotions & Incentives
www.pandionline.com

Adbusters magazine
www.adbusters.org

■ **Blog**

Ad Rants
www.adrants.com

■ **Books**

How to Get into Advertising
ANDREA NEIDLE, CONTINUUM 2002

Ogilvy on Advertising
DAVID OGILVY, PRION 1995

Shared Beliefs INSTITUTE OF PRACTITIONERS IN ADVERTISING, 2001

■ **Film**

How to Get Ahead in Advertising, 2001 Richard E Grant in post-Withnail black comedy

■ **Other resources**

Advertising Association
www.adassoc.org.uk

Institute of Practitioners in Advertising
www.ipa.co.uk

Driving the online future **Andrew Walmsley**

With internet advertising now bigger than radio, it sounds as if the ad industry has woken up to digital. But in 2005, advertisers will spend less than 6% of their budgets online, compared to around 20% of media being consumed online. And as broadband continues to grow rapidly – almost doubling to a third of all homes in the year to May 2005 – audiences are still growing faster than budgets in gross terms.

In fact, there's a serious polarisation in the market: some advertisers allocate over 20% of their budget online, but many are left dipping their toes in the water, at around 1% spend.

Why the disparity? What are the barriers to changing habits in advertising? Research among larger advertisers just published by the EIAA – the European Interactive Advertising Association: Marketer's Internet Ad Barometer 2005 – is revealing.

Some 50% of advertisers cite "quality of research" and "lack of enthusiasm amongst ad agencies" as barriers to increasing spend. Certainly, the networks have shown little enthusiasm for digital – with few isolated exceptions, failing to invest and succeed in this area. But since there is a great deal of robust research around, and the internet is about the most accountable medium imaginable, it is likely these findings are connected: "unenthusiastic" ad agencies are unlikely to know about, or share, research into digital media.

So is this lack of enthusiasm real, and what is causing it?

While the internet shares some surface characteristics with traditional media, it is used differently by audiences, and often traded in a dissimilar way – reflecting its position as a channel to market, rather than merely a marketing channel.

This makes using it for marketing much more labour-intensive than traditional media, and means it costs more to service. Agencies' usual approach when something new comes along has been to experiment with their clients' money, developing skills along the way. But the digital market has developed differently. When in 2001 a recession struck, traditional agencies cut back their interactive departments, viewing them as a cost, while digital specialists – having nothing else – continued to develop and invest.

Eighteen months after the end of the recession, we have reached an interesting point. Growth is high, but traditional agencies can't catch up. To do so, they'd have to invest to develop the skills and the market position, sacrificing profit in the short term – and that's a tough call, as it would hit their share price.

The normal response is to make acquisitions. But there just aren't the companies to buy, as they've either already been acquired by new and hungrier aggregators, or are building their own empires.

Which brings us back to advertisers.

For many, the internet has now replaced direct mail as their most cost-effective acquisition medium. For these businesses, a straightforward link can be established between investment and return, and it is this that has driven the high growth to date.

These businesses are using search, affiliates and distribution partnerships in combination with online media – using new skills to create a marketing mix that looks quite different to the traditional model. It's a mix that values flexibility, metrics and speed to market as the environment develops at warp speed.

These advertisers have developed a set of new capabilities that are allowing them to create barriers to entry into their markets – an advantage they are exploiting aggressively.

But still largely to be persuaded are FMCG (fast-moving consumer goods) advertisers. With the bulk of budgets devoted to launches, there's a balls-on-the-line feel to this sector that mitigates in favour of tried and tested solutions. Advertisers only have one chance to launch, and they have to get it right.

But as the level of audience continues to increase, matched by continuing falls in audiences to traditional media – Coronation Street down 20% in ten years – it's only a matter of time before a judgment is made that the risk of change is smaller than the risk of staying with TV.

In the meantime, automotive, entertainment and FMCG advertisers with younger audiences are beginning to divert increasing funds to the web. They're attracted by the fact that various surveys show that between 15% and 20% of media consumption is online – much higher for younger, more affluent people. Initiatives such as the use of online ratings have brought new clarity and comparability to the usage of web advertising for brands, and increasingly the use of metrics such as reach and frequency are enabling brand marketers to see better how online fits into the mix they use.

So if anyone is driving the adoption of digital media into the marketing mix, it's advertisers. The medium is seen increasingly as business-critical for direct advertisers, and for many brands there's an awareness that a huge opportunity exists to be tapped. With 49% growth predicted for this year, advertisers aren't going to let agencies' lack of enthusiasm stand in their way.

Andrew Walmsley is co-founder of i-level, the UK's leading online media agency. Link: www.i-level.com

Advertising Contacts

Global supergroups

Aegis
43–45 Portman Square
London W1H 6LY
020 7070 7700
www.aegisplc.com
Aegis Media/Carat
Parker Tower, 43–49 Parker Street
London WC2B 5PS
020 7430 6000
www.carat.co.uk
*Carat MD: Neil Jones; head of
marketing: Nick Gracie; head of PR:
Joe Rudkin*

Grey Global
777 Third Avenue, New York
NY 10017, USA
00 1 212 546 2000
www.grey.com
Bought by WPP in 2005. CEO: Ed Meyer
Grey London
215–227 Great Portland St.
London W1W 5PN
020 7636 3399
www.grey.co.uk
*Chairman: David Alberts; MD: Chris
Hirst; deputy chairman and head of
business development: Nicola
Mendelsohn; head of PR: Cathy
Ditchfield, 020 7413 2317*

Havas
2 Allée de Longchamp
92281 Suresnes Cedex, France
00 33 1 58 47 90 00
www.havas.com
*Chairman and CEO: Alain de
Pouzilhac; corporate communications:
Lorella Gessa, 00 33 1 5847 9036*

Interpublic
1114 Avenue of the Americas
New York, NY 10036, USA
00 1 212 704 1200
www.interpublic.com
*Chairman and CEO: Michael Roth;
senior vice-president and director
of corporate communications:
Philippe Krakowsky,
pkrakowsky@interpublic.com*

Omnicom
437 Madison Avenue, New York
NY 10022, USA
00 1 212 415 3600
PublicAffairs@OmnicomGroup.com
www.omnicomgroup.com
President and CEO: John D Wren

Publicis
133 Avenue des Champs Elysées
75008 Paris, France
00 33 1 44 43 70 00
contact@publicis.com
www.publicis.com

WPP
27 Farm Street, London W1J 5RJ
020 7408 2204
enquiries@wpp.com
www.wpp.com
*CEO: Sir Martin Sorrell; group
communications director: Feona
McEwan*

Advertising agencies

1576 Advertising
0131 473 1576
www.1576.co.uk
Independent
Abbott Mead Vickers BBDO
020 7616 3500
www.amvbbdo.com
Owner: Omnicom
AGA
020 7330 8888
www.aga.co.uk
Independent
Arc Worldwide
020 7751 1662
www.arcww.co.uk
Barnsley office: 01285 740707
Edinburgh: 0131 556 0115
Owner: Publicis
Archibald Ingall Stretton
020 7467 6100
www.archibaldingallstretton.com
40% owned by Havas
ARM Direct
020 7224 3040
www.arm-direct.co.uk
Independent
Artavia Advertising
01271 323333
www.artavia.co.uk
London office: 020 7831 3121
Bournemouth: 01202 293999
Bude: 01288 355646
Exeter: 01392 495529
Manchester: 0161 833 1000
Skipton: 01756 701640
Truro: 01872 223585
Owner: Accord Holdings
Attinger Jack
01225 758222
www.aja.co.uk
Independent
AWA
0161 968 6900
www.awa.uk.net
Independent
Banc
020 7908 2790
www.banc.co.uk
Leeds office: 0113 234 2022
Owner: Media Square

Barkers Scotland
0141 248 5030
www.barkersscotland.co.uk
Edinburgh office: 0131 229 7493
Owner: Barkers
Barrington Johnson Lorains
0161 831 7141
www.bjl.co.uk
Independent
Bartle Bogle Hegarty
020 7734 1677
www.bartleboglehegarty.com
Milton Keynes office: 01908 547815
*Majority owned by employees,
minority stake held by Leo Burnett*
BDH\TBWA
0161 908 8600
www.bdhtbwa.co.uk
Didsbury office: 0161 908 8100
Owner: Omnicom
Beechwood
020 7439 4142
www.beechwood.com
Independent
Bespoke Communications
020 7436 0266
www.bespokecommunications.com
Independent
Big Communications
0116 299 1144
www.bigcommunications.co.uk
Independent
Blac
020 7379 7799
www.blacagency.com
Independent
Black & White Advertising
0191 493 2493
www.blackandwhite.uk.net
Independent
Bray Leino
01598 760700
www.brayleino.co.uk
Independent
The Bridge
0141 552 8384
www.thebridgeuk.com
Independent
Burkitt DDB
020 7320 9300
www.burkittddb.com
Owner: Omnicom
Camp Chipperfield Hill Murray
020 7881 3200
www.cchm.co.uk
Owner: Hill Murry
Campbell Doyle Dye
020 7483 9800
www.cddlondon.com
Independent
Carter Gosling
01225 465415
www.cartergosling.co.uk
Independent

cdp-travissully
020 7437 4224
www.cdp-travissully.com
Owner: Dentsu

Charterhouse Advertising & Marketing
0161 848 9050
www.charterhouse-advertising.co.uk
Independent

Cheetham Bell JWT
0161 832 8884
www.cheethambelljwt.com
Owner: WPP

Chemistry Communications
020 7736 5355
www.chemistrygroup.co.uk
Independent

Citigate
020 7282 8000
www.citigateaf.com
Owner: Incepta

Citigate Smarts
0131 555 0425
www.citigatesmarts.co.uk
Belfast office: 028 9039 5500
Birmingham: 0121 455 8370
Dublin: 00 353 1 642 5889
Glasgow: 0141 222 2040
Manchester: 0161 829 0740
Owner: Incepta

Clark McKay & Walpole
020 7487 9750
www.cmw-uk.com
Leeds office: 0113 234 2022
Independent

Claydon Heeley Jones Mason
020 7924 3000
www.claydonheeley.com
Owner: Omnicom

Clayton Graham Advertising
0141 353 3012
www.claytongraham.co.uk
Independent

Clear Marketing Communications
0161 448 8008
www.clearmarketing.co.uk
Independent

Clemmow Hornby Inge
020 7462 8500
www.chiadvertising.com
Independent

Coltas
0141 204 5665
www.coltas.com
Independent

Connectpoint Advertising
0161 817 4200
www.connectpoint.co.uk
Independent

Craik Jones Watson Mitchell Voelkel
020 7734 1650
www.craikjones.co.uk
Owner: Abbott Mead Vickers

Cravens Advertising
0191 232 6683
www.cravens.co.uk
Leeds office: 0113 384 6030
Independent

CWA Creative
0116 232 7400
www.cwa.co.uk
Christchurch office: 01202 482288
Independent

Da Costa & Co
020 7916 3791
www.dacosta.co.uk
Independent

David Gent Creative
01706 220388
www.davidgentcreative.com
Saffron Walden office: 01799 502662
Independent

DDB London
020 7262 7755
www.ddblondon.com
Owner: Omnicom

Delaney Lund Knox Warren & Partners
020 7836 3474
www.dlkw.co.uk
Independent

Dewynters
020 7321 0488
www.dewynters.com
Independent

DFGW
020 7632 5200
www.dfgw.com
Independent

Dig For Fire
0114 281 1200
www.digforfire.co.uk
Independent

DKA Creative
020 7467 7300
www.dka.uk.com
Independent

Doner Cardwell Hawkins
020 7734 0511
www.doner.co.uk
Part of Doner

Draft London
020 7589 0800
www.draftworldwide.com
Part of Draft Worldwide

Eardrum
020 7287 2211
www.eardrum.com
Independent

EHS Brann
020 7017 1000
www.ehsbrann.com
www.ehsbrannleeds.com
Cirencester office: 01285 644744
Leeds: 0113 207 0400
Part-owned by Euro RSCG

Elliott Borra Perlmutter
020 7836 7722
www.ebpcreative.com
Independent

Euro RSCG
020 7379 3991
www.eurorscg.co.uk
Owner: Havas

Factor 3
01242 254242
www.factor3.co.uk
Independent

Fallon
020 7494 9120
www.fallon.co.uk
Owner: Publicis

Farm Communications
020 7428 1300
www.creativebrief.com
Independent

FCB London
020 7947 8000
www.london.fcb.com
Owner: Interpublic

FEREF
020 7580 6546
www.feref.com
Independent

Fox Kalomaski
020 7691 8090
www.foxkalomaski.co.uk
Independent

Frog Communications
01460 279666
www.4frog.com
Independent

GCAS
028 9055 7700
www.gcasgroup.com
Independent

Genesis Advertising
028 9031 3344
www.genesis-advertising.co.uk
Independent

Gillett & Bevan
0161 228 0023
www.gillett-bevan.com
Independent

Girardot
020 7349 6376
www.girardot.co.uk
Independent

Golley Slater & Partners
029 2078 6000
www.golleyslater.com
Birmingham office: 0121 454 2323
Twickenham: 020 8744 2630
Independent

Goode International
01491 873323
www.goode.co.uk
Independent

Harrison Troughton Wunderman
020 7611 6333
www.htw.wunderman.com
Owner: WPP

HDM Agency
020 7321 2227
www.hdmagency.co.uk
Independent

Heresy
020 7349 6800
www.heresyhq.com
Owner: Chime Communications

HHCL/Red Cell
020 7436 3333
www.hhclredcell.com
Owner: WPP

Hooper Galton
020 7494 6300
www.hoopergalton.co.uk
Independent

Huet & Co
0161 835 3100
www.huet.co.uk
Independent

IC
01772 679383
www.icgonline.co.uk
Independent

Ideas Eurobrand
020 7738 1900
www.ideaseurobrand.com
Independent

Inferno
020 7292 7070
www.inferno-group.com
Independent

JDA
0113 290 4290
www.jda.co.uk
Warrington office: 01925 638899
Independent

Joshua Agency
020 7453 7900
www.joshua-agency.co.uk
Owner: Grey Global

JWT
020 7656 7000
www.jwt.com
Owner: WPP

Kaleidoscope Advertising Design & Marketing
0151 707 2220
www.kadm.co.uk
Independent

Karmarama
020 7612 1777
www.karmarama.com
Independent

Kastner & Partners
020 7689 6989
www.kastnernetwork.co.uk
Independent

Lavery Rowe
020 7378 1780
www.laveryrowe.com
Birmingham office: 0121 212 2230
Independent

Lawton Communications
023 8082 8500
www.lawton.co.uk
Independent

Leagas Delaney
020 7758 1758
www.leagasdelaney.com
Independent

Leith Agency
020 7758 1400
www.leith.co.uk
Edinburgh office: 0131 561 8600
Owner: Cello

Leo Burnett
020 7751 1800
www.leoburnett.co.uk
Owner: Publicis

Levy McCallum
028 9031 9220
www.levymccallum.co.uk
Edinburgh office: 0131 225 9733
Glasgow: 0141 248 7977
Independent

Lowe & Partners
020 7584 5033
www.loweworldwide.com
Owner: Interpublic

M&C Saatchi
020 7543 4500
www.mcsaatchi.com
Independent

Maher Bird Associates
020 7309 7200
www.mba.co.uk
Owner: Omnicom

Marr Associates
01828 632800
www.marr.co.uk
Independent

Martin Tait Redheads
0191 232 1926
www.mtra.co.uk
Independent

Masius
020 7307 9170
www.masius.com
Owner: Publicis

Matters Media
020 7224 6030
Independent

McCann Erickson
020 7837 3737
www.mccann.co.uk
Birmingham office: 0121 713 3500
Bristol: 0117 921 1764
Leeds: 01943 484848
Manchester: 01625 822200
Owner: Interpublic

Mediaedge:cia
020 7803 2000
www.mecglobal.com
Independent

Merle
0141 242 1800
www.merleagency.com
Independent

Miles Calcraft Briginshaw Duffy
020 7073 6900
www.mcbd.co.uk
Independent

Minerva
020 7631 6900
www.minervalondon.com
Owner: Omnicom

Mortimer Whittaker O'Sullivan
020 7379 8844
www.mwo.co.uk
Independent

Mostly Media
01935 478238
www.mostlymedia.co.uk
Independent

Mother
020 7012 1999
www.motherlondon.com
Independent

Mustoes
020 7379 9999
www.mustoes.co.uk
Independent

Nexus/H UK
01892 517777
www.nexus-h.co.uk
Independent

Oakbase
01244 391391
www.oakbase.co.uk
Independent

Ogilvy & Mather
020 7345 3000
www.ogilvy.com
Owner: WPP

Ogilvy Primary Contact
020 7468 6900
www.primary.co.uk
Owner: WPP

Palmer Hargreaves Wallis Tomlinson
01926 452525
www.ph-wt.com
London office: 020 7713 0999
Birmingham: 0121 233 9494
Independent

Peacock Marketing & Design
020 7580 8868
www.peacockdesign.com
Independent

Ping Communications
020 7881 3200
www.pingdirect.com
Independent

Poulter Partners
0113 285 6500
www.poulterpartners.com
Independent

Proximity Media
020 7298 1000
www.proximitylondon.com
Owner: Omnicom

Publicis
020 7935 4426
www.publicis.co.uk
Owner: Publicis

Publicity Bureau
01302 730303
www.publicitybureau.co.uk
Independent

Purity
020 7420 7900
www.puritylondon.com
Independent

PWLC
0113 398 0120
www.pwlc.uk.com
Independent

Quiet Storm
020 7907 1140
www.quietstormltd.com
Independent

Radford Advertising & Marketing
0161 832 8807
www.radfordnet.com
Independent

Radioville
020 7534 5999
www.radioville.co.uk
Independent

Rainey Kelly Campbell Roalfe/Y&R
020 7404 2700
www.rkcryr.com
Owner: Young & Rubicam

Rapier
020 7369 8000
www.rapieruk.com
Independent

Raw Media
01305 259444
www.rawmedia.co.uk
Independent

Redman Jones & Partners
0161 828 2600
www.redmanjones.co.uk
Independent

Rhythmm
0117 942 9786
www.rhythmm.co.uk
Independent

Robson Brown
0191 232 2443
www.robson-brown.co.uk
Manchester office: 0161 877 2004
Independent

RPM3
020 7434 4343
www.rpm3.co.uk
Independent

Saatchi & Saatchi
020 7636 5060
www.saatchi-saatchi.com
Owner: Publicis

Scholz & Friends London
020 7961 4000
www.s-f.com
Owner: S&F Holding GmbH

Sheppard Day Associates
020 7821 2222
www.sheppard-day.com
Independent

Smarter Communications
020 7734 5855
www.smartercomms.com
Independent. Includes Senior King

Sold Out Advertising
020 7704 0409
www.soldout.co.uk
Independent

Soul
020 7292 5999
www.souladvertising.com
Independent

Space City Productions
020 7371 4000
www.spacecity.co.uk
Independent

SPS Advertising
01392 464545
Independent

St Luke's Communications
020 7380 8888
www.stlukes.co.uk
Cooperative

SWK London
020 7734 6933
www.swklondon.co.uk
Independent

Target NMI
020 7436 5000
www.targetnmi.com
Independent

TBA
020 7380 0953
www.tbaplc.co.uk
Independent

Team Saatchi
020 7436 6636
www.teamsaatchi.co.uk
Owner: Publicis

TEQUILA\ London
020 7440 1100
www.tequila-uk.com
Owner: Omnicom

TEQUILA\ Manchester
0161 908 8100
www.tequilamanchester.com
Owner: Omnicom

UK Advertising & Marketing Services
01322 228899
www.ukams.co.uk
Independent

Union Advertising Agency
0131 625 6000
www.union.co.uk
Leeds office: 0113 266 6050
Independent

Vallance Carruthers Coleman Priest
020 7592 9331
www.vccp.com
Independent

Velocity Advertising
020 7436 4433
www.velocityadvertising.co.uk
Independent

WAA
0121 321 1411
www.waa.co.uk
London office: 020 7907 9810
Independent

The Walker Agency
01202 414200
www.thewalkeragency.co.uk
Independent

Walsh Trott Chick Smith
020 7907 1200
www.wtcs.co.uk
Independent

Ware Anthony Rust
01223 566212
www.war.uk.com
Independent

WARL
020 7400 0900
www.warl.com
Independent

WCRS
020 7806 5000
www.wcrs.com
Independent

WFCA Integrated
01892 511085
www.wfca.co.uk
Independent

Wieden & Kennedy
020 7194 7000
www.wklondon.com
Independent

Windmill Partnership
020 7371 2868
www.windmillpartnership.com
Independent

WWAV Rapp Collins
020 8735 8000
www.wwavrc.co.uk
Bristol office: 0117 929 7600
Leeds: 0113 222 6300
Owner: Omnicom

Wyatt International
0121 454 8181
www.wyattinternational.com
Independent

Young & Rubicam EMEA
020 7387 9366
www.yandr.com
Owner: WPP

Young Phillips
01202 298969
Independent

ZenithOptimedia UK
020 7224 8500
www.zenithoptimedia.com
Owner: Publicis

Media agencies

All Response Media
020 7017 1450
www.allresponsemedia.com
Leeds office: 0113 394 4660
Owner: Havas

Allmond Partnership
020 7766 5600
www.theallmondpartnership.com
Independent

AMS Media
020 7843 6900
www.amsgroup.co.uk
Independent

Attinger Jack
01225 758222
www.aja.co.uk
Independent

BJK&E Media
020 7025 3900
www.bjke.co.uk
Owner: WPP

BLM Media
020 7437 1317
www.blm-group.com
Independent

BrandConnection
020 7676 2850
www.brandconnection.com
Owner: Interpublic

Bray Leino
01598 760700
www.brayleino.co.uk
Independent

Brilliant Media
0113 394 0000
www.brilliantmedia.co.uk
Manchester office: 0161 214 7231
Independent

Bygraves Bushell Valladares & Sheldon
020 7734 4445
www.bbvs.co.uk
Independent

Carat
020 7430 6000
www.carat.com
Owner: Aegis

Equinox Communications
020 7580 0186
www.equinoxcomm.co.uk
Owner: Zenith Optimedia

Feather Brooksbank
0131 555 2554
www.featherbrooksbank.co.uk
Glasgow office: 0141 332 3382
Manchester: 0161 834 9793
Owner: Aegis

Initiative Media London
020 7663 7000
www.initiative.co.uk
Owner: Interpublic

John Ayling & Associates
020 7439 6070
Independent

Lavery Rowe Advertising
020 7378 1780
www.laveryrowe.com
Independent

Manning Gottlieb OMD
020 7470 5300
www.manninggottliebomd.com
Owner: Omnicom

Matters Media
020 7224 6030
Leeds office: 0113 209 4495
Independent

Media Campaign Services
020 7389 0800
www.mediacampaign.co.uk
Independent

Media Insight
020 7803 2000
www.mediainsight.com
Manchester office: 0161 930 9000
Owner: WPP

Media Planning
020 7393 9000
www.mpg.com
Owner: Havas

Mediability
01625 441911
www.mediability.co.uk
Independent

MediaCom
020 7874 5500
www.mediacomuk.com
Owner: WPP

MediaCom North
0161 839 6600
www.mediacomnorth.com
Owner: WPP

MediaCom Scotland
0131 555 1500
Owner: WPP

Mediaedge:cia
020 7803 2000
www.mediaedgecia.com
Manchester office: 0161 930 9000
Owner: WPP

MediaVest
020 7190 8000
www.mediavest.co.uk
Manchester office: 0161 211 8032
Owner: Publicis

MediaVision Manchester
0161 838 4444
www.media-vision.co.uk
Edinburgh office: 0131 554 0033
Owner: Publicis

Michaelides and Bednash
020 7468 1168
www.michaelidesandbednash.com
Independent

MindShare
020 7969 4040
www.mindshareworld.com
Owner: WPP

MRM Partners UK
020 7278 3856
www.zentropypartners.co.uk
Owner: Interpublic

Naked
020 7336 8084
www.nakedcomms.com
Independent

OMD
020 7893 4893
www.omdmedia.com
Owner: Omnicom

Outdoor Connection
020 7307 9700
www.outdoorconnection.co.uk
Owner: Omnicom

PHD Compass
020 7446 0555
www.phd.co.uk
Birmingham office: 0121 627 5019
Manchester: 0161 237 7900
Owner: Omnicom

PHD Media
020 7446 0555
www.phd.co.uk
Owner: Omnicom

Rathbone Media
0870 830 1850
www.rathmedia.com
Independent

Robson Brown
0191 232 2443
www.robson-brown.co.uk
Manchester office: 0161 877 2004
Independent

Starcom UK
020 7453 4444
www.smvgroup.com
London office: 020 7190 8000
Owner: Publicis

Target NMI
020 7436 5000
www.targetnmi.com
Independent

Total Media
020 7937 3793
www.totalmedia.co.uk
Warwick office: 01926 840011
Independent

Universal McCann
020 7833 5858
www.mccann.co.uk
Birmingham office: 0121 713 3500
Manchester: 01625 822300
Owner: Interpublic

Vizeum UK
020 7379 9000
www.vizeum.co.uk
Owner: Aegis

Walker Media
020 7447 7500
www.walkermedia.com
Part-owner: M&C Saatchi

Wallace Barnaby
01481 726052
www.wallacebarnaby.com
Jersey office: 01534 759807
Independent

WWAV Rapp Collins
020 8735 8000
www.wwavrc.co.uk
Bristol office: 0117 929 7600
Leeds: 0113 222 6300
Owner: Omnicom

Zed Media
020 7224 8500
www.zedmedia.co.uk
Owner: Publicis

Outdoor media

Clear Channel UK
020 7478 2200
www.clearchannel.co.uk
Independent

JC Decaux
020 7298 8000
www.jcdecaux.co.uk
Birmingham office: 0121 423 3777
Glasgow: 0141 891 8100
Manchester: 0161 873 6366/77
Independent

Maiden
020 7838 4000
www.maiden.co.uk
Birmingham office: 0121 567 2970
Dublin: 00 353 1 29 5233
Glasgow: 0141 779 5250
Leeds: 0113 244 2761
Liverpool: 0151 236 5353
Independent

Primesight
020 7882 1200
www.primesight.co.uk
Erith office: 01322 342028
Owner: SMG

Viacom Outdoor
020 7482 3000
www.viacom-outdoor.co.uk
Belfast office: 028 9032 2333
Birmingham: 0121 233 3400
Bristol: 0117 964 9927
Dublin: 00 353 1669 4500
Edinburgh: 0131 555 1515
Glasgow: 0141 552 5259
Leeds: 0113 242 2294
Manchester: 0161 877 7414
Owner: Viacom

▶▶ NEW MEDIA AGENCIES
see page 239

Direct & promotional marketing

141 Worldwide
020 7706 2306
www.141ww.com
Owner: WPP

Arc Worldwide
020 7751 1662
www.arcww.co.uk
Owner: Publicis

BD-NTWK
020 7749 5500
www.bd-ntwk.com
Glasgow office: 0141 567 8000
Independent

Billington Cartmell
020 7471 1900
www.bcl.co.uk
Independent

Carlson Marketing
020 8875 0875
www.carlson-europe.com
Bristol office: 01454 618811
Northampton: 01604 886000
Independent

Clark McKay and Walpole
020 7487 9750
www.cmw-uk.com
Independent

Claydon Heeley Jones Mason
020 7924 3000
www.chjm.com
Owner: Omnicom

Craik Jones Watson Mitchell Voelkel
020 7734 1650
www.craikjones.co.uk
Owner: Omnicom

Dialogue Marketing
020 8783 3100
www.dialmkg.com
Owner: WPP

Dig For Fire
0114 281 1200
www.digforfire.co.uk
Independent

Draft London
020 7589 0800
www.draftworldwide.com
Part of Draft Worldwide

dunnhumby
020 8832 9222
www.dunnhumby.com
Part-owner: Tesco

Dynamo Marketing
020 7386 0699
www.dynamo.net.uk
Owner: Incepta

EHS Brann
01285 644744
www.ehsbrann.com
www.ehsbrannleeds.com
London office: 020 7017 1000
Leeds: 0113 207 0400
Part-owned by Euro RSCG

Euro RSCG Skybridge
020 8254 1500
www.eurorscgskybridge.com
Owner: Havas

SBG and Finex Communications
020 7326 9191
www.finexgroup.com
Owner: Incepta

Geoff Howe
020 8941 7575
www.geoffhowe.com
Independent

GHA
01903 885672
www.g-h-a.co.uk
Independent

Harrison Troughton Wunderman
020 7611 6333
www.htw.wunderman.com
Owner: WPP

Haygarth
020 8971 3300
www.haygarth.co.uk
Independent

Iris
020 7654 7900
www.irisnation.com
Manchester office: 0161 333 1141
Independent

Joshua Agency
020 7453 7900
www.joshua-agency.co.uk
Owner: Grey Global

Euro RSCG KLP
020 7478 3478
www.klp.co.uk
Owner: Euro RSCG

Marketing Store
020 7745 2100
www.themarketingstore.com
Birmingham office: 01675 467404
Leeds: 0113 246 8266
Owner: Harvey

MRM Partners
020 7837 8337
www.mrmworldwide.com
Manchester office: 01625 822200
Owner: McCann Erickson

OgilvyOne
020 7345 3000
www.ogilvy.com
Owner: WPP

Partners Andrews Aldridge
020 7478 2100
www.andrewsaldridge.com
Independent

Red Cell Response
020 7150 3400
www.redcellresponse.com
Owner: WPP

Proximity Media
020 7298 1000
www.proximitylondon.com
Owner: Omnicom

Rapier
020 7369 8000
www.rapieruk.com
Independent

RMG Connect *(formerly Black Cat)*
020 7656 7310
www.rmgconnect.com
Owner: WPP

SMP
01892 548282
www.smp.uk.com
Independent

TDA
01242 633111
www.tdaltd.com
Independent

TEQUILA\ London
020 7440 1100
www.tequila-uk.com
Owner: Omnicom

TEQUILA\ Manchester
0161 908 8100
www.tequilamanchester.com
Owner: Omnicom

Triangle Communications
020 7071 1500
www.thetrianglegroup.co.uk
Owner: Publicis

Tullo Marshall Warren
020 7349 4000
www.tmw.co.uk
Independent

WDPA
020 7451 9604
www.wdpa.co.uk
Independent

WWAV Rapp Collins
020 8735 8000
www.wwavrc.co.uk
Bristol office: 0117 929 7600
Leeds: 0113 222 6300
Owner: Omnicom

Trade press

Advertising Age
00 1 212 210 0100
editor@adage.com
www.adage.com
Weekly. Owner: Crain Communications. Publishing and editorial director: David Klein; editor: Scott Donaton

Brand Strategy
020 7970 4000
elen.lewis@centaur.co.uk
www.mad.co.uk/bs
Monthly. Owner: Centaur. Editor: Elen Lewis

Campaign
020 8267 4683
campaign@haynet.com
www.brandrepublic.com
Weekly. Owner: Haymarket. Editor: Claire Beale; news: Francesca Newland; features: Larissa Bannister; production: Michael Porter

Cream
020 7796 2211
www.ccsquared.cc/cream
Quarterly. Creative media. Editor: Alastair Ray

Creative Review
020 7970 4000
patrick.burgoyne@centaur.co.uk
www.creativereview.co.uk
Monthly. Owner: Centaur. Editor: Patrick Burgoyne; deputy editor: Paula Carson

Design Week
020 7970 4000
lyndark@centaur.co.uk
www.designweek.co.uk
Weekly. Owner: Centaur. Editor: Lynda Relph-Knight; features: John Stones

Mad.co.uk
020 7970 4000
stuart.aitken@centaur.co.uk
www.mad.co.uk
Online magazine. Owner: Centaur. Deputy editor: Stuart Aitken; news: Sarah Lelic

Marketing
020 8267 5000
marketing@haynet.com
www.brandrepublic.com
Weekly. Owner: Haymarket. Editor: Craig Smith; news: Ben Carter; features: Drew Barrand; production manager: Graham Warren

Marketing Direct
020 8267 5000
noelle.mcelhatton@haynet.com
www.mxdirect.co.uk
Monthly. Owner: Haymarket. Editor: Noelle McElhatton; features: Melanie May

Marketing Week
020 7970 4000
mw.editorial@centaur.co.uk
www.marketing-week.co.uk
Weekly. Owner: Centaur. Editor: Stuart Smith; deputy and news: Amanda Wilkinson

Media Week
020 8267 5000
firstname.surname@haynet.com
www.mediaweek.co.uk
Weekly. Owner: Haymarket. Editor: Philip Smith; news: Hugh Filman; acting features editor: Julia Martin; production: Glenys Trevor

New Media Age
020 7970 4000
mike.nutley@centaur.co.uk
www.nma.co.uk
Weekly. Owner: Centaur. Editor: Mike Nutley; news: Yinka Adegoke

Shots
020 7505 8000
lyndy.stout@shots.net
www.shots.net
International advertising. 6pa. Owner: Emap Communications. Editor: Lyndy Stout; assistant editor: Danny Edwards

Advertising associations

Advertising Association
Abford House, 15 Wilton Road
London SW1V 1NJ
020 7828 2771
aa@adassoc.org.uk
www.adassoc.org.uk
PRESS: *jim.rothwell@adassoc.org.uk*

Advertising Standards Authority
Mid City Place, 71 High Holborn
London WC1V 6QT
020 7492 2222
enquiries@asa.org.uk
www.asa.org.uk

Chartered Institute of Marketing
Moor Hall, Cookham, Maidenhead
Berkshire SL6 9QH
01628 427500
info@cim.co.uk
www.cim.co.uk

Committee of Advertising Practice
Mid City Place, 71 High Holborn
London WC1V 6QT
020 7492 2222
enquiries@cap.org.uk
www.cap.org.uk
PRESS: *press@cap.org.uk*

Direct Marketing Association
DMA House, 70 Margaret Street
London W1W 8SS
020 7291 3300
info@dma.org.uk
www.dma.org.uk

Incorporated Society of British Advertisers
Langham House, 1b Portland Place
London W1B 1PN
020 7291 9020
Media@isba.org.uk
www.isba.org.uk

International Advertising Association
521 Fifth Avenue, Suite 1807
New York, NY 10175 USA
00 1 212 557 1133
iaa@iaaglobal.org
www.iaaglobal.org

Internet Advertising Bureau
Adam House, 7–10 Adam Street
Strand, London WC2N 6AA
Press: 020 7886 8282
info@iabuk.net
www.iabuk.net

Institute of Practitioners in Advertising
44 Belgrave Square
London SW1X 8QS
020 7235 7020
info@ipa.co.uk
www.ipa.co.uk

Market Research Society
15 Northburgh Street
London EC1V 0JR
020 7490 4911
info@mrs.org.uk
www.marketresearch.org.uk

Nielsen/NetRatings
77 St John Street
London EC1M 4AN
020 7014 0590
emeapr@intl.netratings.com
www.nielsen-netratings.com
PRESS: *01865 384108*

Outdoor Advertising Association of Great Britain
Summit House, 27 Sale Place
London W2 1YR
020 7973 0315
enquiries@oaa.org.uk
www.oaa.org.uk

World Federation of Advertisers
120 Avenue Louise
1050 Brussels, Belgium
00 32 2 502 5740
info@wfanet.org
www.wfanet.org

Public relations

Spin machine... Stephen Fry (left) and John Bird as PRs in Absolute Power

The PR industry has reason to congratulate itself: in 2005 it became a pillar of the establishment. The Institute of Public Relations, as it used to be known, is now the Chartered Institute of Public Relations – giving PRs professional status alongside the likes of engineers, surveyors, accountants, and, dare I say it, journalists. The new status is evidence that PR is serious about reinventing itself as a respectable part of the marketing mix. The debate about "spin" has gone off to spend time with its family; these days "return on investment" matters instead.

In 2005, statisticians at the CIPR set themselves the task of proving the value to business of public relations. The body's assistant director and head of marketing and PR, Ann Mealor, has argued that it is time to establish a "standard evaluation process" for PR – so they can define exactly how the industry affects the client's bottom line. Nothing concrete had materialised at the time of writing, but the message was plain: PR is the respectable face of private enterprise, not the sleazy stunt factory it's portrayed as in TV shows such as BBC2's Absolute Power. The hope is that, if good PR is more clearly defined, standards may rise across the board – perhaps meaning that fewer journalists throw news releases in the bin.

But there are those within the industry who think some in PR may be getting above their station. "What on earth were the Privy Council thinking of?" asked PR man Mark Borkowski on his blog, Mark My Words, about the decision to honour the PR industry with a royal charter. "I run a Premiership division team. Further down the league are the waves of people who were too slow for the civil service fast-track, too stupid to read law, too unreliable to be accountants or doctors, too boring and unimaginative to work in an advertising agency, and guess where they all pitch up? My industry, the one where only a tiny handful of people are really any good at it, and the rest run around lying through their teeth and calling it PR."

Perhaps reports of the death of the spin are exaggerated, too. In May, Channel 4 broadcast an investigation into New Labour's PR when it ran a Dispatches documentary, Undercover in New Labour, about the party's election campaign. The programme was shot partly by a reporter wearing hidden cameras who volunteered to help out – and wound up working at the party's London HQ. The documentary showed how the PR team got party members to write on-message letters to local newspapers, to stand behind the prime minister during public TV appearances, and to conduct stunt protests on the road with the opposition campaign.

The name of Max Clifford, meanwhile, is synonymous with a certain kind of celebrity spin. Clifford's client list included Faria Alam, the secretary who bedded both the Football Association boss, Mark Palios, and the England manager, Sven-Goran Eriksson; a Scotsman who was

327

Further reading

■ **Press**

MediaGuardian
media.guardian.co.uk/marketingandpr

PR Week
www.prweek.com

■ **Blogs**

A R Guru's Musings – Stuart Bruce
www.20six.co.uk/stuartbruce

Mark My Words – Mark Borkowski
www.borkowski.co.uk/mark

Rainier PR blog
www.rainierpr.co.uk/blog/blog.html

Stuntwatch – Mark Borkowski
www.borkowski.co.uk/stuntwatch

■ **Films**

The Sweet Smell of Success, 1957
Tom Curtis as a slimy press agent:
unmissable

freed after spending 18 years on death row; but not Michael Jackson. Clifford was one of a few PRs who says he turned down an approach by Jackson to help rebuild his reputation in the wake of the Martin Bashir documentary, in which the star famously admitted he had shared a bed with children.

The bottom line

With the promise of increased accountability, it seems, come increased profits. Chime Communications, the PR group owned by Lord Bell, made an £8m profit in 2004, after losing more than £11m in 2003. It had been in talks with its rival Incepta – owner of Citigate Dewe Rogerson – over a possible merger, but that was scuppered when Incepta chose to agree a £200m merger with Huntsworth, which owns the financial PR firm Hudson Sandler. Incepta, for its part, lost £1.5m before tax in the year to February 2004 – down from a £30.5m loss the year before. Amid the vogue for dealmaking, the French communications group Publicis bought a majority stake in Freud Communications.

New EU regulations, meanwhile, are set to change the way PRs manage companies' internal communications. Since March 2005, companies with more than 150 employees must now communicate with their staff on the way they run their business. A CIPR survey, however, found that more than three-quarters of PR practitioners knew little or nothing about the rules before they were introduced.

PR coups and disasters

PR disasters

- **February 2005 – The Ikea stampede** When Ikea opened in a new store in Edmonton, north London, it took out full-page adverts in the local press to publicise a midnight sale. But 6,000 people turned up and several people were hurt in the rush for a bargain.

- **October 2004 – FT yacht capsizes** As part of the marketing of its launch in Australia, the FT chartered a racing yacht, renamed it the FT Spirit, and organised a trip around Sydney harbour. Sadly for the newspaper, the boat hit a rock next to the Sydney Opera House – and capsized. Local news reports had pictures of the stricken boat, with the FT logo visible on the hull.

- **August 2004 – The Faria Alam affair** Colin Gibson, an ex-Daily Mail sports hack, resigned from his job as the FA's head of PR in August 2004 after it was reported that the PA Faria Alam had had affairs with both the England manager, Sven-Goran Eriksson, and the chief executive, Mark Palios. Gibson had tried to persuade the News of the World not to run details of the Palios story.

PR coup

- **May 2005 – Galloway at the US Congress** Respect MP George Galloway might not be a friend of the UK press, but his performance at a US senate investigation into Iraqi oil had the world's media purring. "I have met Saddam Hussein exactly the same number of times as Donald Rumsfeld met him," he told Congress. "The difference is Donald Rumsfeld met him to sell him guns and to give him maps the better to target those guns … And I told the world that your case for the war was a pack of lies." Galloway had earlier called the investigation a "lickspittle Republican committee" – perhaps the most memorable soundbite of a controversial career.

Politics must learn from business PR **Tim Allan**

Public relations

Time was when business leaders used to admire politicians for their mastery of the media. The intense scrutiny that politicians come under from the press had meant that political parties had become experts in communication techniques. They did not just sit and respond to queries, as some business PRs did; they created a narrative about themselves, and used news stories constantly to reinforce it.

I vividly remember the whole of the 1997 election campaign strategy written as a diagram on a single piece of paper. At the top was the overall theme: Modernising Britain. In the middle were three smaller message boxes supporting the theme. They were: Leadership not Drift; Many not the Few; Future not the Past. Under each of these were a whole series of events, news stories, and speeches, all designed to get one of those messages across.

It was this sort of professionalism and strategic planning that led many UK businesses to wake up to the importance of effective communication. PR departments moved up the corporate hierarchy and salaries went with them. Plenty, like me, trod the path from politics and government to business. Business PR consultancies, of varying quality, mushroomed.

Businesses now have developed their own narratives, their own key messages, and plan intricate communication strategies to help get their key messages across. It is not just consumer PR that is run like a marketing campaign now. The best companies now plan on how to develop a PR "brand" for capital markets or public affairs audiences as well, and they think about which supporting messages will be most effective.

Ironically, as this level of professionalism has taken hold of the business world, political PR has received a good kicking. Accusations of government spin are, I think, hugely overblown, and in effect a shorthand for not liking the government; but the way government communicates has received some stinging, and sometimes justified, criticism. Often the focus on how the message is delivered is more interesting to journalists than the message itself, and this has neutered the effect of communication strategies.

In many ways it is now time for the government to learn from the way business communicates. Business is much more adept, for instance, at communicating to everybody at the same time. A combination of strict disclosure rules and new technology means that much financial and corporate PR is now about simply getting the text and message right, and then pressing the button, rather than spinning a select group of favoured journalists. As the media fragments, it makes no sense to try to tailor messages to particular outlets. Businesses are also better at communicating on their own terms through their own websites, and directly to their shareholders, rather than through the prism of journalists' interpretations.

Yet in politics direct communication is still quite weak. It is ridiculous in my view that the government calls in a group of hacks twice a day to tell them, and no one else, what it is up to. If a business tried that, it would soon get a call from the stock exchange. The result is that the briefing is relayed indirectly through the journalists. I think that lobby briefing should be webcast and broadcast.

Politicians neglect other forms of direct communication at their peril. Many people would, for example, find an interview with the education secretary with a group of teachers on the department's website more illuminating than twelve rounds with a Westminster-obsessed journalist. This type of communication is now a regular feature of many companies' strategies.

In short, the pupil now has much to teach its former master.

Tim Allan worked for Tony Blair from 1992 to 1998. He now runs Portland, a financial PR and public affairs firm

3 x 1
Glasgow
0141 221 0707
info@3x1.com
www.3x1.com

AD Communications
Esher, Surrey
01372 464470
rallen@adcomms.co.uk x
www.adcommunications.co.uk

AS Biss & Co
London
020 7340 6200
tellmemore@asbiss.com
www.asbiss.com

Ashley Communications
Northwood, Middlesex
01923 826150
info@ashleycomms.com
www.ashleycomms.com

Atlas Media Group
Leeds
0113 306 0000
info@atlasmediagroup.co.uk
www.atlasmediagroup.co.uk
London office: 020 7323 7170
Bury St Edmunds: 01284 768935
Nottingham: 0115 934 7340

Attenborough Associates
London
020 7734 4455
info@attenborough.net
www.attenborough.net

August One
London
020 8434 5555
enquiries@augustone.com
www.augustone.com

Aurelia Public Relations
London
020 7351 2227
info@aurelia-london.co.uk
www.aurelia-london.com

Automotive PR
London
020 7494 8050
info@automotivepr.com
www.automotivepr.com

AxiCom
London
020 8392 4050
jtanner@axicom.com
www.axicom.com

B2B Communications
Chessington, Surrey
020 8974 2404
enquiries@b2bcommunications.co.uk
www.b2bcommunications.co.uk

Band & Brown Communications
London
020 7419 7000
nick.band@bbpr.com
www.bbpr.com

Barclay Stratton
London
020 7612 8582
Karen.Sharpes@barclaystratton.co.uk
www.barclaystratton.com

Barkers Scotland
Glasgow
0141 248 5030
ckelly@barkers-scot.com
www.barkersscotland.co.uk

Barrett Dixon Bell
Altrincham, Cheshire
0161 925 4700
info@bdb.co.uk
www.bdb.co.uk

BCLO PR
Bristol
0117 973 1173
info@bclo.co.uk
www.bclo.com

**Beattie Communications Group/
Beattie Media**
London
0207 053 6000
www.beattiemedia.co.uk
London office: 020 7053 6400
Birmingham: 0121 698 8625
Dundee: 01382 562881
Edinburgh: 0131 220 8269
Falkirk: 01324 602550
Glasgow: 01698 787878
Leeds: 0113 213 0300
Manchester: 0161 935 8334

Bell Pottinger
London
020 7861 2400
pbingle@bell-pottinger.co.uk
www.bppa.co.uk

Berkeley PR International
Reading
0118 988 2992
enquiries@berkeleypr.co.uk
www.berkeleypr.co.uk
Bristol office: 01454 203 595
Derbyshire: 01629 826942

BGB & Associates
London
020 7233 2300
pr@bgb.co.uk
www.bgb.co.uk

The Big Partnership
Glasgow
0141 333 9585
alex@bigpartnership.co.uk
www.bigpartnership.co.uk
Aberdeen office: 01224 224433
Edinburgh: 0131 558 3111
Inverness: 01667 464085

Binns & Co Public Relations
London
020 7786 9600
mail@binnspr.co.uk
www.binnspr.co.uk
Bristol office: 0117 920 0092
Edinburgh: 0131 226 8009
York: 01347 844844

Biosector 2
London
020 7016 3300
www.biosector2.com

Biss Lancaster Euro RSCG
London
020 7022 4000
bisslancaster@bisslancaster.com
www.bisslancaster.com

Bite Communications
London
020 8741 1123
moreUK@bitepr.com
www.bitepr.com

BMB Reputation Managers
Luton
01582 725454
email@bmb.uk.com
www.bmb.uk.com

Brahm PR
Leeds
0113 230 4000
www.brahm.com

Brands2Life
London
020 7592 1200
info@brands2life.com
www.brands2life.com

Brave PR
London
020 7802 8111
charlotte.a@bravepr.com
www.bravepr.com

Brazen
Manchester
0161 923 4994
nina@brazenpr.com
www.brazenpr.com

The Bright Consultancy
Henley-in-Arden, West Midlands
01564 795535
ian@bright-consultancy.co.uk
www.bright-consultancy.co.uk

Broadgate
London
020 7726 6111
contact@bgate.co.uk
www.bgate.co.uk

Brower Lewis Pelham PR
London
020 7935 2735
www.blppr.com

Brunswick
London
020 7404 5959
info@brunswickgroup.com
www.brunswickgroup.com

Buchanan Communications
London
020 7466 5000
www.buchanan.uk.com
Leeds office: 01943 883990

Buffalo Communications
London
020 7292 8680
info@buffalo.co.uk
www.buffalo.co.uk

Burson-Marsteller
London
020 7831 6262
Per_Heggenes@bm.com
www.bm.com
Belfast office: 028 9039 3837
Manchester: 0161 228 6677

Cairns & Associates
London
020 7235 7773
jon.meakin@cairnsassociates.co.uk
www.cairnsassociates.co.uk

Camargue
London
020 7636 7366
www.camarguepr.com
Cheltenham office: 01242 577277

Camron PR
London
020 7420 1700
genevieve@camron.co.uk
www.camron.co.uk

Capital MS&L
London
020 7307 5330
steffan.williams@capitalmsl.com
www.capitalmsl.co.uk

Capitalize
London
020 7940 1700
info@capitalize.co.uk
www.capitalize.co.uk

Carat
London
020 7430 6000
nick.gracie@carat.com
www.carat.co.uk

Carrot Communications
London
020 7386 4860
richard.houghton@carrotcomms.co.uk
www.carrotcomms.co.uk

Chambers Cox PR
London
020 7592 3100
info@ccpr.co.uk
www.ccpr.co.uk

Chameleon PR
London
020 7721 7875
www.chameleonmkg.com

Cherton Enterprise
Belfast
028 9065 4007
staff@cherton.co.uk
www.cherton.co.uk

CIB Communications
Leatherhead, Surrey
01372 371800
gavint@cibcommunications.co.uk
www.cibcommunications.co.uk

Citigate Communications
London
020 7282 2880
info@citigatec.co.uk
www.citigatecommunications.co.uk
Birmingham office: 0845 119 9911

Citigate Dewe Rogerson
London
020 7638 9571
perri.taylor@citigatedr.co.uk
www.citigatedr.co.uk

Citigate Northern Ireland
Holywood
028 9039 5500
www.citigateni.co.uk

Citigate Public Affairs
London
020 7838 4800
warwick.smith@citigatepa.co.uk
www.citigatepa.com

Citigate Smarts
Edinburgh
0131 555 0425
www.smarts.co.uk
Belfast office: 028 9039 5500
Birmingham 0121 456 3199
Dublin: 00 353 1 642 5888
Glasgow: 0141 222 2040
Manchester: 0161 829 0740

Citypress PR
Manchester
0161 606 0260
www.citypress.co.uk

Clareville Communications
London
020 7736 4022
mail@clareville.co.uk
www.clareville.co.uk

Clear Communication Consultancy & Training
London
020 7432 2500
clear@clearco.co.uk
www.clearco.co.uk

Cohesive Communications
London
020 7470 8777
www.cohesive.uk.com
Chepstow office: 01291 626200

Cohn & Wolfe
London
020 7331 5300
jonathan_shore@cohnwolfe.com
www.cohnwolfe.com

Colette Hill Associates
London
020 7622 8252
cha@chapr.co.uk
www.chapr.co.uk

College Hill
London
020 7457 2020
pr@collegehill.com
www.collegehill.com

Colman Getty PR
London
020 7631 2666
pr@colmangettypr.co.uk
www.colmangettypr.co.uk
Edinburgh office: 0131 477 7950

The Communication Group
London
020 7630 1411
enquiries@
    thecommunicationgroup.co.uk
www.thecommunicationgroup.co.uk

Communique PR
Manchester
0161 228 6677
www.communiquepr.co.uk
London office: 020 7300 6300

Companycare Communications
Reading
0118 939 5900
www.companycare.com

Consolidated Communications
London
020 7287 2087
sarahr@consol.co.uk
www.consol.co.uk

Corixa Communications
Bristol
0117 949 3394
www.corixa.co.uk

Counsel Public Relations
London
020 7402 2272
nigel.dickie@counsel-huntsworth.com
www.counsel-huntsworth.com

Countrywide Porter Novelli
London
020 7853 2222
www.cpn.co.uk
Banbury office: 01295 224400
Edinburgh: 0131 470 3400
Leeds: 0870 242 4723

Cow Communications
London
020 7684 6969
dirk.singer@cowpr.com
www.cowpr.com

Cubitt Consulting
London
020 7367 5100
www.cubitt.com

Darwall Smith Associates
London
020 7553 3700
gill@dsapr.co.uk
www.dsapr.co.uk

Dialogue Agency
Twickenham
020 8607 0340
enquiry@dialogueagency.com
www.dialogueagency.com

DTW
London
07968 847539
office@dtw.co.uk
www.dtw.co.uk
Canterbury office: 01227 454023
Guisborough, Cleveland:
    01287 610404

Edelman
London
020 7344 1200
london@edelman.com
www.edelman.co.uk

Edson Evers
Stafford
01785 255146
www.edsonevers.com

EHPR (Elizabeth Hindmarch Public Relations)
Windsor, Berkshire
01753 842017
info@ehpr.co.uk
www.ehpr.co.uk
London office: 020 7031 0380

EML
Kingston-upon-Thames, Surrey
020 8408 8000
info@eml.com
www.eml.com

Eulogy!
London
020 7927 9999
pr@eulogy.co.uk
www.eulogy.co.uk

EuroPR Group
London
020 8917 4900
info@europrgroup.com
www.europrgroup.com

Financial Dynamics
London
020 7831 3113
charles.watson@fd.com
www.fd.com

Finsbury PR
London
020 7251 3801
info@finsbury.com
www.finsbury.com

Firefly Communications
London
020 7386 1400
claire.walker@fireflycomms.com
www.fireflycomms.com

Fishburn Hedges
London
020 7839 4321
info@fishburn-hedges.com
www.fishburn-hedges.co.uk

Flagship Group
London
020 7886 8440
www.flagshipgroup.co.uk

Fleishman-Hillard (UK)
London
020 7306 9000
www.fleishman.com
Dublin office: 00 353 1 618 8444
Edinburgh: 0131 226 2162

Focus PR
London
020 7432 9432
vision@focuspr.co.uk
www.focuspr.co.uk

Four Communications
London
07973 893 208
info@fourplc.com
www.fourplc.com

Fox Parrack Hirsch
London
020 7436 4336
tparrack@fphcom.com
www.fphcom.com

Freshwater Marketing Commuications
Cardiff
029 2054 5370
info@freshwater-uk.com
www.freshwater-uk.com
London office: 020 7290 2608
Bristol: 0117 906 6565
Glasgow: 0141 570 0205

Freud Communications
London
020 7580 2626
jackie@freudcommunications.com
www.freudcommunications.com

Galliard Healthcare Communications
London
020 7663 2250
www.galliardhealth.com

Garnett Keeler Public Relations
Surbiton, Surrey
020 8399 1184
pr@garnett-keeler.com
www.garnett-keeler.com

GCI/APCO
London
020 7072 4000
awheeler@gciuk.com
www.gciuk.com

Geronimo PR
London
020 8238 8550
karen.harris@geronimopr.com
www.geronimopr.co.uk

GMX Communications
London
020 7812 6550
www.gmxcommunications.com
Bristol office: 01454 203630
Manchester: 0161 234 0040
Southampton: 023 8071 3000

Golin/Harris Weber
London
020 7067 0600
www.golinharris.com

Golley Slater PR
London
02920 7240 9920
www.golleyslater.com
Birmingham office: 0121 454 2323
Bristol: 0117 921 1131
Cardiff: 029 2038 8621
Cirencester: 01285 741111
Leeds: 0113 297 9737
Manchester: 0161 832 7178
Newcastle: 0191 245 9020
Twickenham: 020 8744 2630

Good Relations
London
020 7861 3030
afossey@goodrelations.co.uk
www.goodrelations.co.uk

Gough Allen Stanley
Bromsgrove, Worcs
01527 579555
info@gough.co.uk
www.gough.co.uk

Grandfield
London
020 7861 3232
enquiries@grandfield.com
www.grandfield.com

Grant Butler Coomber
London
020 8322 1922
www.gbc.co.uk

Grayling
London
020 7255 1100
info@uk.grayling.com
www.grayling.com

Great Circle Communications
Edinburgh
0131 225 4646
info@greatcircle.co.uk
www.greatcircle.co.uk

Green Issues Communications
London
020 7321 3767
www.greenissues.com
Cardiff office: 029 2050 4050
Manchester: 0161 209 3850
Reading: 0118 959 1211

Hallmark Public Relations
Winchester
01962 892900
inspired@hallmarkpr.com
www.hallmarkpr.com

Halogen PR
London
020 7487 9191
www.halogenuk.com
Cheltenham office: 01242 227499

Harrison Cowley
London
020 7404 6777
info@harrisoncowley.com
www.harrisoncowley.com

Haslimann Taylor
Birmingham
0121 355 3446
patzih@haslimanntaylor.com
www.haslimanntaylor.com

Haygarth
London
020 8971 3300
stephen.m@haygarth.co.uk
www.haygarth.co.uk

Henry's House
London
020 7291 3000
www.henryshouse.com

Hill & Knowlton
London
020 7973 5926
wfick@hillandknowlton.com
www.hillandknowlton.co.uk

Hills Balfour
London
020 7922 1100
info@hillsbalfour.com
www.hillsbalfour.com

The Hoffman Agency
Egham, Surrey
01784 487 920
lhoffman@hoffman.com
www.hoffman.com

Hotwire PR
London
020 7608 2500
alexia.sciplino@hotwirepr.com
www.hotwirepr.com

Houston Associates
London
020 8778 1900
info@houston-associates.com
www.houston-associates.com

ICAS PR
Hemel Hempstead
01442 261199
pr@icas.co.uk
www.icas.co.uk
London office: 020 7632 2400

The Ideas Network
London
020 7351 4719
enquiries@ideasnetwork.co.uk
www.ideasnetwork.co.uk

The Impact Agency
London
020 7580 1770
mail@impactagency.co.uk
www.theimpactagency.com

Insight Marketing & Communications
London
020 7861 3999
info@insightmkt.com
www.insightmkt.com
Heathrow office: 020 8564 6397
Manchester: 01625 500800

The ITPR Group
Chertsey, Surrey
01932 578800
www.itpr.co.uk

Jackie Cooper PR
London
020 7208 7208
Info@jcpr.com
www.jcpr.com

JBP Public Relations
0117 907 3400
www.jbp.co.uk

Johnson King
London
020 7357 7799
helenb@johnsonking.co.uk
www.johnsonking.co.uk

Julia Hobsbawm Consulting
London
020 7272 8898
www.juliahobsbawm.com
Communications management consultant

Kaizo
London
020 7580 8852
crispin.manners@kaizo.net
www.kaizo.net

Kavanagh Communications
Cobham, Surrey
01483 238840
anne@kavanaghcommunications.com
www.kavanaghcommunications.com

Keene Public Affairs Consultants
London
020 7287 0652
kpac@keenepa.co.uk
www.keenepa.co.uk

Kelso Consulting
London
020 7388 8886
pr@kelsopr.com
www.kelsopr.com

Kenyon Fraser
Liverpool
0151 706 9931
richardk@kenyons.co.uk
www.kenyons.co.uk

Kestrel WorldCom
London
020 8543 2299
kestrel@kestrelcomms.co.uk
www.kestrelworldcom.com

Ketchum
London
020 7611 3500
david.gallagher@ketchum.com
www.ketchum.com

Kinross & Render
London
020 7592 3105
sr@kinrossrender.com
www.kinrossrender.com

Kysen PR
London
020 7323 3230
contactus@kysenpr.co.uk
www.kysenpr.co.uk

Lansons Communications
London
020 7490 8828
pr@lansons.com
www.lansons.com

Lawson Dodd
London
020 7535 1355
iam@lawsondodd.co.uk
www.lawsondodd.co.uk

Leader Communications
Warwickshire
01564 796200
ms@leader.co.uk
www.leader.co.uk

Leedex Euro RSCG
London
020 7022 4000
www.leedex.com
Edinburgh office: 0131 524 1500
Manchester: 0161 234 9777

Lewis PR
London
207 802 2626
kathp@lewispr.com
www.lewispr.com

Lexis Public Relations
London
020 7908 6488
www.lexispr.com

Lighthouse PR
London
020 7968 4949
www.lighthousepr.com

London Communications Agency
London
020 7479 2830
lca@londoncommunications.co.uk
www.londoncommunications.co.uk

M: Communications
London
020 7153 1530
info@mcomgroup.com
www.mcomgroup.com

MacLaurin *(now part of Trimedia UK)*
London
020 7371 3333
www.trimediauk.com
Glasgow office: 0141 333 6440

Manning Selvage & Lee
London
020 7878 3000
nicholas.walters@mslpr.com
www.mslpr.co.uk

Mantra Public Relations
London
020 7907 7800
info@mantra-pr.com
www.mantra-pr.com

Market Engineering
Banbury, Oxon
01295 277050
www.marketengineering.co.uk

Mary Rahman PR
London
020 7749 1136
www.mr-pr.com

Mason Williams
London
020 7534 6080
info@mason-williams.com
www.mason-williams.co.uk
Manchester office: 0161 273 5923

McCann-Erickson Public Relations
Solihull
0121 713 3500
Contact@mccann.com
www.mccann.com

McCluskey International
London
020 8237 7979
info@mccluskey.co.uk
www.mccluskeyinternational.co.uk

Media Strategy
London
020 7400 4480
clewington@mediastrategy.co.uk
www.mediastrategy.co.uk

Medicom Group
Hampton Court, Surrey
020 8481 8100
enquiries@medicomgroup.com
www.medicomgroup.com

MediTech Media
London
020 7398 0500
info@meditech.co.uk
www.meditech-media.com
Manchester office: 0161 236 2367

Midas PR
London
020 7584 7474
info@midaspr.co.uk
www.midaspr.co.uk

Midnight Communications
Brighton
01273 333 200
enquiries@midnight.co.uk
www.midnight.co.uk

Mulberry Marketing Communications
London
020 7928 7676
info@mulberrymc.com
www.mulberrymc.com

Munro & Forster Communications
London
020 7815 3900
www.munroforster.com

Neesham PR
Berkhamsted
01442 879222
admin@neesham.co.uk
www.neesham.co.uk

Nelson Bostock Communications
London
020 7229 4400
info@nelsonbostock.com
www.nelsonbostock.com

Nexus Communications Group
London
020 7808 9808
www.nexuspr.com

NorthBank Communications
Congleton
01260 296500
info@northbankcommunications.com
www.northbankcommunications.com
London office: 020 7886 8150

Ogilvy
London
020 7309 1000
www.ogilvypr.com

Pagoda PR
Edinburgh
0131 447 8999
info@pagodapr.com
www.pagodapr.co.uk
Belfast office: 028 9032 8291

Partners Group
York
01904 610077
postbox@partners-group.co.uk
www.partners-group.co.uk

Pegasus PR
Worthing, West Sussex
01903 821550
info@pegasuspr.co.uk
www.pegasuspr.co.uk

Penrose Financial
London
020 7786 4888
enquiries@penrose.co.uk
www.penrose.co.uk

PFPR Communications
Maidstone, Kent
01622 691361
info@pfpr.com
www.pfpr.com

Phipps Public Relations
London
020 7759 7400
info@phippspr.co.uk
www.phippspr.com

Pinnacle Marketing Communications
Pinner, Middlesex
020 8869 9339
simon@pinnacle-marketing.com
www.pinnacle-marketing.com

Piranhakid
London
020 7973 5938
www.piranhakid.com

Pleon
London
020 7479 5656
www.pleon.com

Portfolio Communications
London
020 7240 6959
www.portfoliocomms.com

Portland PR
London
020 7404 5344
info@portlandpr.co.uk
www.portlandpr.co.uk

Positive Profile
London
020 7489 2028
info@positiveprofile.com
www.positiveprofile.com

PPS Group
London
020 7629 7377
www.ppsgroup.co.uk
Bristol office: 01454 275 630
Cardiff: 029 2066 0194
Edinburgh: 0131 226 1951
Manchester: 0161 832 2139
Solihull: 0121 767 1863

Prowse & Co
Leatherhead, Surrey
01372 363386
reception@prowse.co.uk
www.prowse.co.uk

Ptarmigan Consultants
Leeds
0113 242 1155
www.ptarmiganpr.co.uk

Public Relations Consultants Association
London
020 7233 6026
pressoffice@prca.org.uk
www.prca.org.uk

Purple PR
London
020 7439 9888
enquiries@purplepr.com
www.purplepr.com

QBO Bell Pottinger
London
020 7861 2424
dwilson@qbo-bellpottinger.co.uk
www.qbo-bellpottinger.co.uk

QuayWest Communications
Coggeshall, Essex
01376 563156
s.morrison@quay-west.co.uk
www.quay-west.co.uk

Radiator PR
London
020 7404 8264
www.radiatorpr.com

Rainier PR
London
020 7494 6570
rainier@rainierpr.co.uk
www.rainierpr.co.uk
Cambridge office: 01359 250641

The Red Consultancy
London
020 7025 6500
red@redconsultancy.com
www.redconsultancy.com

Red Door Communications
London
020 8392 8040
info@rdcomms.com
www.rdcomms.com

Regester Larkin
London
020 7831 3839
enquiries@regesterlarkin.com
www.regesterlarkin.com

Republic
London
020 7379 5000
www.republicpr.com

Resolute Communications
London
020 7357 8187
info@resolutecommunications.com
www.resolutecommunications.com

Revolver Communications
London
020 7251 5599
enquiries@revolvercomms.com
www.revolvercomms.com
Leeds office: 0113 287 0077

Richard Lewis Communications
Southampton
01962 771111
info@crossculture.com
www.crossculture.com

Ruder Finn UK
London
020 7462 8900
mail@ruderfinn.co.uk
www.ruderfinn.com

Salt
London
020 8870 6777
info@saltlondon.com
www.saltlondon.com

Seal Communications
Birmingham
0121 455 7788
www.sealgroup.co.uk
London office: 020 7336 7313

Shine Communications
London
020 7553 3333
brilliance@shinecom.com
www.shineon-line.com

Shire Health Group
London
020 7313 6300
matt.degruchy@shirehealthlondon.com
www.shirehealthlondon.com

Sinclair Mason
Leeds
0870 60 60 960
www.sinclairmason.co.uk

Six Degrees (formerly Roger Staton Associates and Marbles)
Marlow, Buckinghamshire
01628 480280
mail@sixdegreespr.com
www.rsagroup.com

Spark Marketing Communications
London
020 7357 8612
info@sparkcomms.co.uk
www.sparkcomms.co.uk

Spin Media
Manchester
0161 236 9909
www.spinmedia.co.uk

Spreckley Partners
London
020 7388 9988
info@spreckley.co.uk
www.spreckley.co.uk

Staniforth
London
020 7940 7999
urgent@staniforth.co.uk
www.staniforth.co.uk
Manchester office: 0161 274 0100

Starfish Communications
London
020 7323 2121
fearfield@star-fish.net
www.star-fish.net

Storm Communications
London
020 7240 2444
info@stormcom.co.uk
www.stormcom.co.uk
Beaconsfield, Bucks office:
   01494 670444

StrategicAlliance International
Old Amersham, Bucks
01494 434434
nicholasf@strategicpr.net
www.strategicpr.net

Strategy Communications
Bristol
0117 983 6400
enquiries@strategycomms.co.uk
www.strategycomms.co.uk
London office: 020 7849 6663

Target Public Relations
Cheltenham
01242 633100
www.targetgroup.co.uk

Taylor Alden
London
020 8543 3866
pr@tayloralden.co.uk
www.tayloralden.com
Newbury office: 01635 521103

Taylor Herring
London
020 8206 5151
james@taylorherring.com
www.taylorherring.com

TBWA UK Group
London
020 7573 6666
www.tbwa.com
Edinburgh office: 0131 225 3952

Text 100
London
020 8846 0700
michelled@text100.co.uk
www.text100.com

Trimedia Communications
London
020 7371 3333, 020 7898 9036
www.trimediauk.com
Glasgow office: 0141 333 6440

Twelve Consultancy
London
020 7631 0737
mail@twelvepr.co.uk
www.twelvepr.co.uk

Warman Group
Birmingham
0121 605 1111
enquiries@warmangroup.com
www.warmangroup.com

Weber Shandwick
London
020 7067 0000
enquiriesuk@webershandwick.co
www.webershandwick.co.uk
Aberdeen office: 01224 806600
Belfast: 028 9076 1841
Edinburgh: 0131 556 6649
Glasgow: 0141 333 0557
Manchester: 0161 238 9400

Westbury Communications
London
020 7751 9170

What Matters
St Albans, Hertfordshire
01582 793994
www.whatmatters.co.uk

Whiteoaks Consultancy
Farnham, Surrey
01252 727313
comms@whiteoaks.co.uk
www.whiteoaks.co.uk

Wild Card PR
London
0207 355 0655
deck@wildcardpr.co.uk
www.wildcardpr.co.uk

William Murray PR
London
020 8256 1360
www.williammurraypr.co.uk

Willoughby PR
Birmingham
0121 456 3004
joannes@willoughby-pr.co.uk
www.willoughby-pr.co.uk

Write Image
London
020 7959 5400
info@write-image.co.uk
www.write-image.com

Wyatt International
Birmingham
0121 454 8181
info@wyatt-inter.co.uk
www.wyattinternational.com

Yellow Door Creative Marketing
London
020 7580 0707
www.yellow-door.co.uk

PR trade press

Black Book
020 8267 5000
directories@haynet.com
www.prweek.co.uk
Annual. Press and PR contacts.
Formerly known as Contact. Owner:
Haymarket. Publisher of Haymarket
directories: Katherine Davies

Hollis UK Public Relations Annual
020 8977 7711
prannual@hollis-pr.co.uk
www.hollis-pr.co.uk
Annual. Press and PR contacts. Owner:
Hollis Publishing. Editor: Sarah
Hughes

PR Week
020 8267 4520
prweek@haynet.com
www.prweek.com
Weekly. Owner: Haymarket. Editor:
Danny Rogers; news: Ravi
Chandiramani; features: Peter Crush;
sub: Chris Young

Associations

Association of Public Relations
Consultants
Willow House, Willow Place
London SW1P 1JH
020 7233 6026
natasha@prca.org.uk
www.prca.org.uk

British Association of
Communicators in Business
Suite A, 1st floor, Auriga Building
Davy Avenue, Knowlhill
Milton Keynes MK5 8ND
0870 121 7606
enquiries@cib.uk.com
www.cib.uk.com
Professional body for internal and
corporate communications staff

Chartered Institute of
Public Relations
The Old Trading House
15 Northburgh Street
London EC1V OPR
020 7253 5151
info@cipr.co.uk
www.ipr.org.uk
PRESS: *020 7553 3772*

Media law

After a few years of privacy cases dominating the legal agenda, libel lawyers sought to show in 2004 and 2005 that they had not gone out of fashion after all. The Reynolds defence, "no win, no fee" arrangements and so-called "libel tourism" all attracted controversy; while Roman Polanski's £50,000 libel victory against Vanity Fair had headline writers calling London the "libel capital of the world" all over again. Meanwhile, cameras were allowed in court for the first time, while the epic battle between Hello! and OK! looked set to go to the House of Lords.

Libel

The controversy over so-called **libel tourism** – the practice of suing for libel abroad, perhaps in the hope that you have a better chance of winning your case – has rarely been so great. The highest-profile case came in July 2005, when film director Roman Polanski won £50,000 from Vanity Fair, and more than three times as much in costs, after he sued the US edition of the magazine in London. Polanski gave evidence via a video link from Paris: he would not come to the UK for fear of being extradited to the US to face charges of having sex with an under-age girl, which date back to 1979.

Vanity Fair's article alleged that Polanski had made a pass at a woman in a New York restaurant while on the way to the funeral of his murdered wife. Even though the allegations turned out to be untrue, the magazine tried to rely on the defence that the director was a man whose reputation had been damaged "beyond repair" and therefore could not be defamed; but it lost, with the judge, David Eady, directing the jury that this was "not a court of morals". Afterwards the Vanity Fair editor, Graydon Carter, said he thought it "amazing" that "a man who lives in France can sue a magazine published in America in a British court".

But that, these days, is par for the course. In April 2005, the Barclay brothers, owners of the Telegraph, did the reverse – and decided to sue the Times in a French court. The Barclay brothers have houses in France, the articles referred to claims of how they conduct their business in France, and the Times is distributed in France; but, again, there was something bizarre about two British newspapers slugging it out in an overseas court.

In February, though, the high court overturned a libel ruling against the US-based Wall Street Journal – for the Saudi businessman Yousef Jameel, the brother of Mohammed Abdul Latif (see Wall Street Journal Europe case, below) – on the basis that only five people in the UK had read the article online.

Earlier, two cases showed that the **Reynolds defence** – by which journalists can defend a libel action if they have reported responsibly on a matter in the public interest – is a hugely difficult trick to pull off. The

defence, also known as "qualified privilege", was established in a 2001 case brought by the former Irish premier Albert Reynolds against the Sunday Times.

In December 2004, it was the Daily Telegraph that failed to mount the defence successfully, after it reported on documents appearing to show that the MP George Galloway had received money from Saddam Hussein. The High Court judge, David Eady, said Galloway was not given sufficient opportunity to refute the "seriously defamatory" claims, and awarded £150,000 in damages.

In February 2005, the Wall Street Journal Europe failed in the public interest aspect of a Reynolds defence at the court of appeal. It had published an article wrongly suggesting that a company owned by Mohammed Abdul Latif Jameel was being monitored by Saudi authorities as a possible channel for funds to terrorist organisations. The paper had hoped to argue that it had behaved responsibly in publishing the article – having relied, at the time, on five anonymous sources – but it did not, during the libel action, claim that the story was true. But the appeal judge, Lord Phillips, said that not only was "responsible journalism" an insufficiently precise test of the Reynolds defence, but that the original libel jury's findings – rejecting journalist James Dorsey's evidence about four of his sources, and about messages he said he left at Jameel's offices – were such that the newspaper would have failed the test anyway. The paper's lawyer, Mark Stephens, said after the case that "there is a flaw in the qualified privilege defence that is highlighted where you have five anonymous sources that cannot come to court"; but Jameel said he was "delighted" at the ruling.

In an important judgment for freedom of speech, meanwhile, the FT won an action to strike out a record £230.5m libel claim by the City brokers Collins Stewart Tullett. The company had claimed the money on the basis of its drop in share price since an FT article was published in August 2003; had it won such damages, the FT might well have gone out of business. The libel case was still expected to go ahead, with (less substantial) damages for loss of business to be decided if Collins Stewart wins.

Collins Stewart Tullett was also involved in a landmark case in internet law, when Terry Smith, the company's chief executive, won a case against a fund manager who posted allegations on the Motley Fool website in September and October 2003.

Confidentiality

The epic struggle involving OK!, Hello! and the wedding pictures of **Catherine Zeta Jones** took another twist in May 2005, when the court of appeal ordered OK! to pay back damages to Hello! totalling almost £2m. Hello! had taken unauthorised pictures of Zeta Jones' wedding to Michael Douglas, despite an agreement between the OK! and the couple. The court of appeal decided that Hello! would still have to pay £15,000 damages to the couple for breach of confidentiality, but that the confidentiality did not extend to OK! magazine. OK! announced in June that it would take the case to the House of Lords.

Also in May, the Beckhams lost a battle to hold their former nanny, Abbie Gibson, to a confidentiality agreement she had signed – causing some surprise among media lawyers.

In **privacy**, former PCC director Mark Bolland warned in September 2004 that the British media are "perilously close" to having a fully fledged privacy law forced upon them from Europe, after a deadline to

challenge the Princess Caroline of Monaco privacy ruling passed. The European court of human rights had ruled in June that the German press had violated Princess Caroline's right to privacy by publishing photos of her and her children in a public place; a decision that must now be taken into account in the British courts.

Mostly, though, privacy cases go no further than the self-regulatory Press Complaints Commission; see page 17 for more on how the institution works, and the high-profile cases of 2004–05.

No win, no fee

The government agreed in 2004 to review the use of conditional fee agreements (CFAs), after a high court judge said the system has a "chilling effect" on freedom of expression. In a submission to the government in September, 13 media organisations – including Guardian Newspapers, Times Newspapers, the BBC and ITN – demanded a change to rules which mean media companies can pay double the accuser's costs if they lose a case, but still face paying their own costs if they win.

Two examples in May 2005 brought the issue to a head. First, the News of the World claimed it faced a £400,000 legal bill despite winning a high court libel action against Bogdan Maris, the man it accused of plotting to kidnap Victoria Beckham. Andy Coulson, the paper's editor, said: "This case was about as absurd as you can get and highlights what an injustice CFAs are."

Later that month, the Daily Mirror challenged a £594,000 legal bill from model Naomi Campbell in the House of Lords, saying it was a violation of the right to free speech. Under the terms of the CFA, Campbell's lawyers, Schillings, charged the Mirror double the usual costs. Marcus Partington, the Mirror's lawyer, said: "I have never in my professional career in newspapers seen a bill of costs like it, and what makes it worse is that we are being expected to pay effectively a penalty for fighting a case which we won 3-0 in the court of appeal, and which we only lost 3-2 in the House of Lords, simply because Naomi Campbell and her lawyers decided to go on a CFA for her appeal to the House of Lords."

Law and the media, 2004–05

- **June 2005, libel:** Jury fails to reach verdict in Harry Kewell's libel action against Gary Lineker, over an article written in the Sunday Telegraph. "It looks like a replay," Lineker says outside court.

- **June 2005, libel:** The Saudi Arabian businessman, Yousef Jameel, settles his libel action with the Sunday Times over an article alleging he had links with Osama bin Laden. The newspaper issued a statement accepting Jameel had no such links.

- **April 2005, confidentiality:** Hans Martin Tillack, the former Brussels correspondent of the German magazine Stern, fails in a legal bid to stop the European commission looking at his notes and potentially revealing his sources, in a case at the European court of justice.

- **February 2005, courts:** The film director Roman Polanski, a fugitive from justice for 27 years, wins the right to give evidence via video link from Paris during a high court libel action against the US magazine Vanity Fair.

- **November 2004:** The Mail on Sunday wins the right to publish a story alleging links between the restaurateur Martha Greene and convicted fraudster Peter Foster. "Our press is free to get things right and it is free to get things wrong," says the appeal court judge.

- **September 2004, privacy:** Three French photographers who took photographs of Princess Diana and Dodi Fayed on the day of their fatal car crash are cleared in an appeals court of breaking French privacy laws.

Court reporting and contempt

Legal history was made in November 2004 when **cameras** were allowed in an English court for the first time. The scheme at the appeal court was only a pilot, but it coincided with a government consultation on how far the courts should eventually be opened to broadcasters. The constitutional affairs secretary, Lord Falconer, had said in August that a debate was necessary, but added: "We will not have OJ Simpson-style trials in Britain. We must protect witnesses and jurors and victims. We don't want our courts turned into US-style media circuses."

Two months earlier, the government had said it would introduce laws to force media companies to pay legal costs if they publish prejudicial or inaccurate reports that lead to the collapse of a criminal trial. The move follows the 2002 collapse of the trial of footballers Lee Bowyer and Jonathan Woodgate, which was thrown out after an interview in the Sunday Mirror. The paper was fined £75,000 for **contempt of court**, and its editor resigned, but under new rules it could have been liable for a significant proportion of the costs.

In June 2005, the Sun escaped prosecution for allegedly naming the victim of a sexual assault, after a technical error by the Crown Prosecution Service. The CPS brought charges under the **Sexual Offences Act** against "News International", which is indeed the main UK subsidiary of News Corporation; but it should have charged "News Group Newspapers".

In February 2005, Maxine Carr – who was convicted in 2003 of perverting the course of justice by lying to protect the Soham murderer, Ian Huntley – was granted **indefinite anonymity** by a court. The order protects Carr's new identity by banning publication of any details about where she lives or the nature of her work.

Intellectual property

In October 2004 IPC, the publisher of Ideal Home, ended up with a £1.8m costs bill after suing Highbury Publishing for infringement of **copyright** in a rival interiors magazine – and losing. IPC said Home magazine had copied the "design, subject matter, theme and presentational style" of Ideal Home over about four years; but the judge found no copying, reminding the claimants that there is no copyright in "general themes, styles or ideas".

Media law firms

A&L Goodbody
International Financial Services Centre
North Wall Quay, Dublin 1
00 353 1 649 2000
London: 020 7382 0800
law@algoodbody.ie
www.algoodbody.ie
Specialist media and entertainment law group, Ireland. IP and e-commerce; film financing; production law; contracts; defamation

Adlex Solicitors
76A Belsize Lane
London NW3 5BJ
020 7317 8404
adamt@adlexsolicitors.co.uk
www.adlexsolicitors.co.uk
Internet law; co-branding; software licensing; IT; IP; trademark registration

Akin Gump Strauss Hauer and Feld
Citypoint, Level 32
One Ropemaker Street
London EC2Y 9AW
020 7012 9600
londoninfo@akingump.com
www.akingump.com
IP; licensing; finance; media infringement (esp digital music online); defamation; employment inc credit disputes, contracts, confirmation of minors' contracts

Allen and Overy
One New Change
London EC4M 9QQ
020 7330 3000
claire.meeghan@allenovery.com
www.allenovery.com
IP; finance; regulatory and antitrust. For IT, publishing, film, video, radio and TV, programming, live performance, music, sports, ads and PR

Arnold and Porter (UK)
Tower 42, 25 Old Broad Street
London EC2N 1HQ
020 7786 6100
www.arnoldporter.com
Patents, trademarks, copyright and trade secrets

Ashurst
Broadwalk House, 5 Appold Street
London EC2A 2HA
020 7638 1111
enquiries@ashurst.com
www.ashurst.com
Commercial agreements, transactions and litigation; acquisitions, disposals, mergers; advice on European and UK law, licensing, regulation esp pan-European broadcasting; regulators, governments, broadcasters, producers, telecoms, multiplex and satellite operators; specialist film practice

Astburys
210 High Street, Lewes
East Sussex BN7 2NH
01273 403935
jastbury@astburys-law.co.uk
www.astburys-law.co.uk
Services for broadcasting, publishing and advertising

Baily Gibson
30 High Street, High Wycombe
Buckinghamshire HP11 2AG
01494 442661
Beaconsfield: 01494 672661
wycombe@bailygibson.co.uk
www.bailygibson.co.uk
E-commerce; IP

Baker and McKenzie
100 New Bridge Street
London EC4V 6JA
020 7919 1000
info@bakernet.com
www.bakernet.com
E-commerce; IT licensing; broadcast media regulation inc pay-per-view contracts, digital copyright, convergence of media and network technologies

Beachcroft Wansbroughs
100 Fetter Lane, London EC4A 1BN
020 7242 1011
London Eastcheap: 020 7208 6800
Birmingham: 0121 698 5200
Bristol: 0117 918 2000
Manchester: 0161 934 3000
Leeds: 0113 251 4700
Winchester: 01962 705500
info@bwlaw.co.uk
www.bwlaw.co.uk
Interactive commerce and new media inc branding; data protection and privacy; franchising; IP; IT

Beale and Company
Garrick House, 27–32 King Street
Covent Garden, London WC2E 8JB
020 7240 3474
Dublin: 00 353 1 799 6213
reception@beale-law.com
www.beale-law.com
IT inc software, hardware supply and retail; e-commerce; internet; web design; database licensing

Berwin Leighton Paisner
Adelaide House, London Bridge
London EC4R 9HA
020 7760 1000
media@blplaw.com
www.blplaw.com

Bevan Brittan
Head Office, 35 Colston Avenue
Bristol, Avon BS1 4TT
0870 194 1000
info@bevanbrittan.com
www.bevanbrittan.com
IP; IT. Also has offices in Birmingham and London

Bird and Bird
90 Fetter Lane, London EC4A 1JP
020 7415 6000
london@twobirds.com
www.twobirds.com
IP; IT; broadcasting; film finance; advertising; sponsorship; film production; music; publishing

Blake Lapthorn Linnell
Holbrook House
14 Great Queen Street
London WC2B 5DG
020 7430 1709
Oxford: 01865 248607
Southampton: 023 8063 1823
Fareham: 01489 579990
Portsmouth: 023 9222 1122
info@bllaw.co.uk
www.bllaw.co.uk
IP; IT

BM Nyman and Co
181 Creighton Avenue
London N2 9BN
020 8365 3060
bernie.nyman@iname.com
www.bmnyman.co.uk
Publishing law: copyright; defamation; contracts

Bournemouth Media School
Talbot Campus, Fern Barrow
Poole, Dorset BH12 5BB
01202 595191
eforbes@bournemouth.ac.uk
http://media.bournemouth.ac.uk
Media law consultancy to press, broadcast, film and creative industries. See also careers and training

Briffa
Business Design Centre
Upper Street, Islington
London N1 0QH
020 7288 6003
info@briffa.com
www.briffa.com
IP inc brand protection; personality rights in sport; rights for ad industry and designers

Brightley Commercial
Lower Landrine, Mitchell
Newquay, Cornwall TR8 5BB
01872 519087
robert@brightley.com
www.brightley.com
Commercial/company law; contracts; IP; music business agreements

Bristows
3 Lincoln's Inn Fields
London WC2A 3AA
020 7400 8000
info@bristows.com
www.bristows.com
IP and media law inc publishing, ads and marketing. Defamation; sponsorship and merchandising; TV distribution; privacy; competition law

Campbell Hooper
35 Old Queen Street
London SW1H 9JD
020 7222 9070
ch@campbellhooper.com
www.campbellhooper.com
IP; commercial and media dispute resolutions; defamation and media management; theatre; merchandising and sponsorship; advertising and marketing law; brand and domain name management; ICT; e-commerce; software licensing; data protection; licensing agreements

CapitalLaw
Discovery House
Scott Harbour, Cardiff
South Glamorgan CF10 4HA
029 2045 2770
law@capitallaw.co.uk
www.capitallaw.co.uk
Formerly Palser Grossman. IP

Carter-Ruck
International Press Centre
76 Shoe Lane, London EC4A 3JB
020 7353 5005
lawyers@carter-ruck.com
www.carter-ruck.com
Defamation; human rights; IP; employment law

Charles Lucas and Marshall
4 Eastcott House, High Street
Old Town, Swindon
01793 511055
Newbury: 01635 521212
Wantage: 01235 771234
Hungerford: 01488 682506
www.clmsolicitors.co.uk
IT

Charles Russell
8–10 New Fetter Lane
London EC4A 1RS
020 7203 5000
Guildford: 01483 252525
Cheltenham: 01242 221122
enquiry@cr-law.co.uk
www.charlesrussell.co.uk
Telecoms, IT, e-commerce, competition and regulatory law specialists. Data protection team; internet law; entertainment work for film, TV, literary and music sectors inc reputation management and IP

Clarke Willmott
Stoneham Gate, Stoneham Lane
Southampton, Hampshire SO50 9NW
023 8062 4400
Birmingham: 0121 236 0076
Bristol: 0117 941 6600
Taunton: 01823 442266
info@clarkewillmott.com
www.clarkewillmott.com
Media law: Linda Gregory, 023 8062 4443. Sports law: Trevor Watkins, 023 8062 4441

Clifford Chance
10 Upper Bank Street, Canary Wharf
London E14 5JJ
020 7006 1000
info@cliffordchance.com
www.cliffordchance.com
Full IP service: patents, trademarks, copyright, design, trade secrets and unfair competition

Clifford Miller
Burnhill Business Centre
50 Burnhill Road, Beckenham
Kent BR3 3LA
020 8663 0044
mail@millercompany.demon.co.uk
www.cliffordmiller.com
IP; competition (anti-trust); IT law

Clintons
55 Drury Lane, Covent Garden
London WC2B 5RZ
020 7379 6080
info@clintons.co.uk
www.clintons.co.uk
Film and TV: finance; development; IP; production; catalogue acquisition and disposal; distribution and exploitation; rights clearance. Radio: contracts; digital exploitation; IP; licence agreements; licence applications; regulation. Talent agencies: contracts and individual freelance broadcast and bi-media service agreements. Publishing: contracts, libel, disputes, rights exploitation

Cobbetts
Ship Canal House, King Street
Manchester M2 4WB
0845 404 2404
(also offices in Birmingham and Leeds)
enquiries@cobbetts.co.uk
www.cobbetts.co.uk
Software development, outsourcing, data protection, distance selling and ad regulations; defamation; IP; ICT; experience in gaming, music publishing and events, interactive TV, new media, film and TV

Collins Long
24 Pepper Street, London SE1 0EB
020 7401 9800
jamescollins@collinslong.com
www.collinslong.com
Contracts; litigation; development; production; financing; distribution

Collyer-Bristow
4 Bedford Row, London WC1R 4DF
020 7242 7363
cblaw@collyerbristow.com
www.collyerbristow.com
IP; IT and e-commerce; artists and managers, composers and publishers, record producers and distributors, scriptwriters, indies, film producers, actors and performers

Constant and Constant
Sea Containers House
20 Upper Ground, London SE1 9QT
020 7261 0006
iantaylorson@constantlaw.com
www.constantlaw.com
Media and e-commerce: development, production and financing; distribution and sales; broadcasting and publishing; advertising; IP

Couchman Harrington Associates
8 Bloomsbury Square
London WC1A 2LQ
020 7611 9660
enquiries@chass.co.uk
www.chass.co.uk
Sports law, IP and broadcasting

Coudert Brothers
60 Cannon Street
London EC4N 6JP
020 7248 3000
info@london.coudert.com
www.coudert.com
IP; international and domestic film financing and tax planning; international licensing; telecoms

Courts and Co
15 Wimpole Street
London W1G 9SY
020 7637 1651
law@courtsandco.com
www.courtsandco.com
IP inc electronic delivery of AV material; UK trademarks, community trademarks and Madrid Protocol applications; members of International Trademark Association; classical music contracts – recording, film and video

Covington and Burling – Registered Foreign Lawyers and Solicitors – London
265 Strand, London WC2R 1BH
020 7067 2000
www.cov.com
IP and data protection; broadcasting, telecoms, multichannel video distribution, PCS/cellular

Cripps Harries Hall
Wallside House
12 Mount Ephraim Road
Tunbridge Wells, Kent TN1 1EG
01892 515121
reception@crippslaw.com
www.crippslaw.co.uk
IP; technology; copyright and other media rights; defamation, libel and slander

Cumberland Ellis (incorporating Barth and Partners)
Atrium Court, 15 Jockey's Fields
London WC1R 4QR
020 7242 0422
contact@cumberlandellis.com
www.cep-law.co.uk
Specialist sports law team advising on issues such as sponsorship, licensing agreements and media rights; IP; specialist charity law team advising on issues including commercial activities and contracts, donations, constitutions and dispute resolutions

Davenport Lyons
30 Old Burlington Street
London W1S 3NL
020 7468 2600
dl@davenportlyons.com
www.davenportlyons.com
Specialist areas: defamation; film and TV; music; IP; publishing; ads; IT, e-commerce, interactive and new media; sport

David Price Solicitors and Advocates
21 Fleet Street, London EC4Y 1AA
020 7353 9999
enquiries@lawyers-media.com
www.lawyers-media.com
Defamation (libel and slander), breach of confidence and privacy, contempt and copyright, pre-publication advice, internet defamation

Dean Marsh and Co
1892 Building, 54 Kingsway Place,
Sans Walk, London EC1R 0LU
020 7553 4400
info@deanmarsh.com
www.deanmarsh.com
Music and entertainment

Denton Wilde Sapte
Five Chancery Lane, Clifford's Inn
London EC4A 1BU
020 7242 1212
info@dentonwildesapte.com
www.dentonwildesapte.com
IP; services for ads and marketing, broadcasting, IT, live performance, music, publishing, sponsorship, sport and telecoms; film and TV production, film financing

Dickinson Dees
St Ann's Wharf, 112 Quayside
Newcastle Upon Tyne NE99 1SB
0191 279 9000
marketing@dickinson-dees.com
www.dickinson-dees.com
IT and e-commerce

DLA Piper Rudnick Gray Cary
3 Noble Street, London EC2V 7EE
0870 011 1111
(also offices in Birmingham, Liverpool, Manchester, Leeds, Sheffield, Edinburgh, Glasgow)
info@dlapiper.com
www.dlapiper.com
Defamation, confidentiality and privacy, digital media, data protection and freedom of information, publishing, gaming, contractual, IT. Clients include Time Warner Book Group, ITV plc, Thomson and IPC

DMA Legal
4th Foor, 15–16 New Burlington Street
London W1S 3BJ
020 7534 5850
info@dmalegal.com
www.dmalegal.com
IP, defamation, contracts, licensing, distribution, multimedia agreements, royalty arrangements

DMH Stallard
100 Queens Road, Brighton
East Sussex BN1 3YB
01273 329833
Brighton: 01273 329833
Gatwick: 01293 605000
London: 020 7423 1000
        020 7490 5666
enquiries@dmhstallard.com
www.dmhstallard.com
Technology, media and telecoms; charities and public sector

Dorsey and Whitney
21 Wilson Street
London EC2M 2TD
020 7588 0800
Cambridge: 01223 451036
london@dorsey.com
www.dorsey.com
IP litigation

DWF
5 Castle Street, Liverpool
Merseyside L2 4XE
0151 907 3000
Manchester: 0161 603 5000
enquiries@dwf.co.uk
www.dwf.co.uk
IP; contracts

Dyer Burdett and Co
64 West Street, Havant
Hampshire PO9 1PA
023 9249 2472
mail@dyerburdett.com
www.dyerburdett.com
IP; sport; TV, radio, film and theatre production and licensing

Edwin Coe
2 Stone Buildings
London WC2A 3TH
020 7691 4000
mail@edwincoe.com
www.edwincoe.com
IP

Eversheds
Senator House, 85 Queen Victoria St
London EC4V 4JL
020 7919 4500
Birmingham: 0121 232 1000
Cambridge: 01223 443666
Ipswich: 01473 284428
Leeds: 0113 243 0391
Manchester: 0161 831 8000
Cardiff: 029 2047 1147
Newcastle: 0191 241 6000
Norwich: 01603 272727
Nottingham: 0115 950 7000
www.eversheds.com
E-commerce, IT; music, TV and related areas; IP

Farrer and Co
66 Lincoln's Inn Fields
London WC2A 3LH
020 7242 2022
enquiries@farrer.co.uk
www.farrer.co.uk
IP and media law

Fennemores
200 Silbury Boulevard
Central Milton Keynes
Buckinghamshire MK9 1LL
01908 678241
info@fennemores.co.uk
www.fennemores.co.uk
Data protection and contracts in e-business and technology

Ferdinand Kelly
21 Bennetts Hill, Birmingham
West Midlands B2 5QP
0121 643 5228
ferdinand-kelly@dial.pipex.com
www.ferdinandkelly.co.uk
E-commerce, franchising, IT, IP

Field Fisher Waterhouse
35 Vine Street, London EC3N 2AA
020 7861 4000
info@ffw.com
www.ffw.com
Services to broadcasters and publishers esp licensing book and magazine publishing rights in TV programmes; IP

Finers Stephens Innocent
179 Great Portland Street
London W1W 5LS
020 7323 4000
mstephens@fsilaw.co.uk
www.fsilaw.com
Specialist areas: ads and sales promotion; anti-counterfeiting; copyright; cultural property; defamation; design rights; IT and e-commerce; obscenity; publishing; sports law; trademark and brand management; visual arts; photo agencies and libraries; TV and film

Fladgate Fielder
25 North Row, London W1K 6DJ
020 7323 4747
fladgate@fladgate.com
www.fladgate.com
IP, IT and sports law

Foot Anstey
21 Derrys Cross, Plymouth
Devon PL1 2SW
01752 675000
Exeter: 01392 411221
Taunton: 01823 337151
Bridgewater: 01278 452266
tony.jaffa@foot-ansteys.co.uk
www.foot-ansteys.co.uk
*Specialist media, commercial, and
employment advice to newspapers,
publishers and ISPs*

Freshfields Bruckhaus Deringer
65 Fleet Street, London EC4Y 1HS
020 7936 4000
www.freshfields.com
*IP; IT; specialist telecoms, media and
technology (TMT) group*

Gamlins
31–37 Russell Road, Rhyl
Denbighshire LL18 3DB
01745 343500
mike.williamson@gamlins.co.uk
www.gamlins.co.uk
IP

Gateley Wareing
One Eleven Edmund Street
Birmingham B3 2HJ
0121 234 0000
Nottingham: 0115 983 8200
Leicester: 0116 285 9000
gw@gateleywareing.com
www.gateleywareing.co.uk
*IP, esp in computers and software;
technology sector: trademarks, patents,
e-commerce, databases and rights*

George Davies
Fountain Court, 68 Fountain Street
Manchester, Lancashire M2 2FB
0161 236 8992
mail@georgedavies.co.uk
www.georgedavies.co.uk
*IP, contracts and franchising; also
sports personalities and major sporting
bodies*

Gersten and Nixon
National House, 60–66 Wardour Street
London W1F 0TA
020 7439 3961
law@gernix.co.uk
www.gernix.co.uk
*All aspects of media and entertainment
law*

Goodman Derrick
90 Fetter Lane, London EC4A 1PT
020 7404 0606
pherbert@gdlaw.co.uk
www.gdlaw.co.uk
*Media law: disputes and litigation;
contracts and documentation;
programme clearance; regulatory
advice. Film: banking, securitisation;
distribution, writer and talent
contracts; mergers and acquisitions;
sponsorship and merchandising
agreements; script clearance*

Gray and Co
Habib House, 3rd Floor
9 Stevenson Square, Piccadilly
Greater Manchester
Lancashire M1 1DB
0161 237 3360
grayco@grayand.co.uk
www.grayand.co.uk
*Entertainment industry in Manchester
and north-west esp. music and record
companies, film and TV contracts and
finance, sport*

Greenwoods Solicitors
Monkstone House
City Road, Peterborough
Cambridgeshire PE1 1JE
01733 887700
sblackwell@greenwoods.co.uk
www.greenwoods.co.uk
*IP; e-commerce and IT; property and
planning issues for production
companies; corporate and commercial
law*

Grundberg Mocatta Rakison
Imperial House, 15–19 Kingsway
London WC2B 6UN
020 7632 1600
post@gmrlaw.com
www.gmrlaw.com
IP

H2O Law
40–43 Chancery Lane
London WC2A 1JQ
020 7405 4700
enquiries@h2o-law.com
www.h2o-law.com
*Art and photography: advise artists
and photographers on IP, contracts and
licensing; Publishing: manages
authors rights, advises on contract and
dispute issues, IP and libel vetting*

Halliwells
St James's Court, Brown Street
Manchester M2 2JF
0870 365 8000
(also offices in Liverpool, London
and Sheffield)
info@halliwells.com
www.halliwells.com
*Services to music and sports industries;
IP; financing*

Hamlins
Roxburghe House
273–287 Regent Street
London W1B 2AD
020 7355 6000
admin@hamlins.co.uk
www.hamlins.co.uk
IP and copyright

Hammonds
7 Devonshire Square, Cutlers Gardens
London EC2M 4YH
0870 839 0000
enquiries@hammonds.com
www.hammonds.com
*ICT, e-commerce, data protection,
media, sport and entertainment*

Harbottle and Lewis
Hanover House, 14 Hanover Square
London W1S 1HP
020 7667 5000
paul.gower@harbottle.com
www.harbottle.com
*All areas inc film, TV, broadcasting,
IT, sport, music, publishing, fashion,
advertising, marketing and theatre;
IP, defamation, employment, property,
immigration, finance, tax and admin*

Harrison Curtis
8 Jockey's Fields
London WC1R 4BF
020 7611 1720
mail@harrisoncurtis.co.uk
www.harrisoncurtis.co.uk
*Principal areas: music, film and TV,
e-commerce, theatre, advertising and
marketing, sport*

Haynes Phillips
73 Farringdon Road
London EC1M 3JQ
020 7242 2213
hello@haynesphillips.com
www.haynesphillips.com
*IP; music: contracts, rights, licensing,
management, merchandising, music
publishing, videos*

Herbert Smith
Exchange House, Primrose Street
London EC2A 2HS
020 7374 8000
contact@herbertsmith.com
www.herbertsmith.com
*Litigation, competition, corporate, IP,
piracy, copyright and defamation; TV
and radio, IT, books and publishing,
media, music, ads and marketing*

Hewitsons
Shakespeare House
42 Newmarket Road, Cambridge
Cambridgeshire CB5 8EP
01223 461155
Northampton: 01604 233233
Saffron Walden: 01799 522471
mail@hewitsons.com
www.hewitsons.com
IP; IT inc internet, e-commerce, ICT

Hextalls
28 Leman Street, London E1 8ER
020 7488 1424
info@hextalls.com
www.hextalls.com
*Telecoms, media and technology dept
serving music, entertainment,
publishing and telecoms sector*

Hill Dickinson
Pearl Assurance House
2 Derby Square, Liverpool L2 9XL
0151 236 5400
London: 020 7695 1000
Manchester: 0161 817 7200
Chester: 01244 896600
law@hilldickinson.com
www.hilldickinson.com
*broadcasting, theatre and film;
e-commerce; endorsement,
merchandising and sponsorship; IT;
libel and slander; publishing; sports law*

HLW
Princess House, 122 Queen Street
Sheffield, South Yorkshire S1 2DW
0114 276 5555
info@hlwlaw.co.uk
www.hlwlaw.co.uk
IP

Holme Roberts and Owen
5 Chancery Lane, Clifford's Inn
London EC4A 1BU
020 7320 6464
www.hro.com
*IP; film, telecoms, sport and
entertainment*

Howard Kennedy
Harcourt House
19 Cavendish Square
London W1A 2AW
020 7636 1616
Info@howardkennedy.com
www.howardkennedy.com
IP; film, TV, music, theatre, sports

Howell-Jones Partnership
75 Surbiton Road
Kingston upon Thames
Surrey KT1 2AF
020 8549 5186
kingston@hjplaw.co.uk
www.hjplaw.co.uk
IP

Humphreys and Co
14 King Street, Bristol BS1 4EF
0117 929 2662
lawyers@humphreys.co.uk
www.humphreys.co.uk
*IP; sports contracts; IT; also advises
artists, publishers, writers, managers
and record companies in music and
entertainment industries*

Ingram Winter Green
Bedford House, 21A John Street
London WC1N 2BL
020 7845 7400
backchat@iwg.co.uk
www.iwg.co.uk
*E-business and IT; clients in TV, print
media, film, radio, music, printing and
ad industries; film finance,
syndication, distribution, regulation
and broadcasting complaints*

James Chapman and Co
76 King Street, Manchester
Lancashire M2 4NH
0161 828 8000
generalenquiries@
    james-chapman.co.uk
www.james-chapman.co.uk
Sports law

Kemp Little
Cheapside House, 138 Cheapside
London EC2V 6BJ
020 7710 1610
amanda.millar@kemplittle.com
www.kemplittle.com
IP; IT and telecoms regulation

Kent Jones and Done
Churchill House, Regent Road
Stoke-On-Trent
Staffordshire ST1 3RQ
01782 202020
mail@kjd.co.uk
www.kjd.co.uk
*IT, e-commerce, technology licensing,
trademarks and copyright,
entertainment*

Kimbells
Power House, Davy Avenue
Knowlhill, Milton Keynes
Buckinghamshire MK5 8RR
01908 668555
alison.foxton@kimbells.com
www.kimbells.com
IT and IP

Kirkland and Ellis International
Tower 42, 25 Old Broad Street
London EC2N 1HQ
020 7816 8700
info@kirkland.com
www.kirkland.com
*IP inc transactions and litigation
relating to internet and e-commerce*

**Kirkpatrick and Lockhart Nicholson
Graham**
110 Cannon Street
London EC4N 6AR
020 7648 9000
london@klng.com
www.klng.com
IP; IT and technologies

Kuit Steinart Levy
3 St Marys Parsonage, Manchester
Lancashire M3 2RD
0161 832 3434
ksllaw@kuits.com
www.kuits.com
*Licensing and brand acquisitions;
sports merchandising; e-commerce*

Laing & Co
105 Heath Street
London NW3 6FF
020 7794 0555
info@laingandco.com
*Contract renewals, copyright, rights
management, libel and termination
strategies*

Latham and Watkins
11th Floor, 99 Bishopsgate
London EC2M 3XF
020 7710 1000
owen.williams@lw.com
www.lw.com
*IP and technology; acquisition,
financing, licensing and dispute
resolution*

The Law Offices of Marcus J O'Leary
Anvil Court, Denmark Street
Wokingham, Berkshire RG40 2BB
0118 989 7110
moleary@mjol.co.uk
www.mjol.co.uk
*National IT IP firm. Clients include
Microsoft and Dell*

Lawdit Solicitors
Station House, 17 Saxon Road
Southampton, Hampshire SO15 1JJ
0870 950 1122
info@lawdit.co.uk
www.lawdit.co.uk
*IP inc domain names, data protection,
e-commerce, IT contracts, media law,
trademarks and websites*

Laytons
Carmelite, 50 Victoria Embankment
Blackfriars, London EC4Y 0LS
020 7842 8000
Bristol: 0117 930 9500
Guildford: 01483 407000
Manchester: 0161 834 2100
london@laytons.com
www.laytons.com
*IP, IT and related UK and EU
competition law*

Leathes Prior
74 The Close, Norwich
Norfolk NR1 4DR
01603 610911
info@leathesprior.co.uk
www.leathesprior.co.uk
*IP inc counterfeiting, domain names,
passing-off and trade libel; data
protection; employment; e-commerce
and IT*

Lee and Thompson
Greengarden House
15–22 St Christophers Place
London W1U 1NL
020 7935 4665
mail@leeandthompson.com
www.leeandthompson.com
*All aspects of media work covered
(contracts, business structures, IP,
litigation etc) esp in the fields of music,
film and television (finance and
production), sport and celebrity
representation*

Lennox Bywater
9 Limes Avenue, London NW7 3NY
020 8906 1206
lennox.bywater@virgin.net
www.lennoxbywater.com
Sports law

Leonard Lowy and Co
500 Chiswick High Road
London W4 5RG
020 8956 2785
lowy@leonardlowy.co.uk
www.leonardlowy.co.uk
Music industry

Lester Aldridge
Russell House, Oxford Road
Bournemouth, Dorset BH8 8EX
01202 786161
info@LA-law.com
www.lesteraldridge.com
IP

Lewis Silkin
12 Gough Square
London EC4A 3DW
020 7074 8000
mark.king@lewissilkin.com
www.lewissilkin.com
Media brands and technology

Linklaters
One Silk Street, London EC2Y 8HQ
020 7456 2000
rupert.winlaw@linklaters.com
www.linklaters.com
IP; IT and comms law – inc telecoms
and satellites; broadcasting;
e-commerce and internet; outsourcing;
data protection

Lovells
Atlantic House, Holborn Viaduct
London EC1A 2FG
020 7296 2000
information@lovells.com
www.lovells.com
IP; technology, media and telecoms

Macfarlanes
10 Norwich Street
London EC4A 1BD
020 7831 9222
penny.rutterford@macfarlanes.com
www.macfarlanes.com
IP: IT; e-commerce; advertising and
marketing

Maclay Murray and Spens
151 St Vincent Street
Glasgow G2 5NJ
0141 248 5011
London: 020 7606 6130
Edinburgh: 0131 226 5196
Aberdeen: 01224 356130
magnus.swanson@mms.co.uk
www.mms.co.uk
IP; technology (software, electronics
and engineering), film and media,
internet and e-commerce

Magrath and Co
52–54 Maddox Street
London W1S 1PA
020 7495 3003
admin@magrath.co.uk
www.magrath.co.uk
IP; agreements for recording artists and
recording companies, actors, sports
people, TV and filmmakers

Manches
Aldwych House, 81 Aldwych
London WC2B 4RP
020 7404 4433
manches@manches.com
www.manches.com
IT, IP, internet, publishing and media
inc sponsorship, merchandising,
financing, litigation, defamation, data
protection, ad and sales promotion laws

Mann and Partners
New Court Chambers
23–25 Bucks Road, Douglas
Isle Of Man IM99 2EN
01624 695800
law@mannandpartners.com
www.mannandpartners.com
Contracts, disputes and general work
for the film industry

Marks and Clerk Patent and Trademark Attorneys
90 Long Acre, London WC2E 9RA
020 7420 0000
london@marks-clerk.com
www.marks-clerk.com
Patents; trademarks; copyright;
design; domain names; licensing

Marks and Clerk solicitors
90 Long Acre, London WC2E 9RA
020 7420 0250
solicitors@marks-clerk.com
www.marks-clerk.com
IP; IT; publishing

Marriott Harrison
12 Great James Street
London WC1N 3DR
020 7209 2000
www.marriottharrison.co.uk
Corporate finance; media/
entertainment; commercial/IT

Marshall Ross and Prevezer
4 Frederick's Place
London EC2R 8AB
020 7367 9000
mail@mrp-law.co.uk
www.mrp-law.co.uk
IP disputes and data protection

Martineau Johnson
1 Colmore Square
Birmingham B4 6AA
0870 763 2000
lawyers@martjohn.com
www.martineau-johnson.co.uk
IP; IT inc hardware acquisition,
software licensing, internet and
e-commerce

McClure Naismith
Pountney Hill House
6 Laurence Pountney Hill
London EC4R 0BL
020 7623 9155
Glasgow: 0141 204 2700
Edinburgh: 0131 220 1002
london@mcclurenaismith.com
www.mcclurenaismith.com
IP; IT; dispute resolution and litigation

McCormicks
Britannia Chambers, 4 Oxford Place
Leeds, West Yorkshire LS1 3AX
0113 246 0622
Harrogate: 01423 530630
p.mccormick@
   mccormicks-solicitors.com
www.mccormicks-solicitors.com
IP; defamation and media law;
sponsorship; sports law; rights
management and exploitation; charity
law; general commercial and corporate
law

McGrigors
5 Old Bailey, London EC4M 7BA
020 7054 2500
enquiries@mcgrigors.com
www.mcgrigors.com
IP

Memery Crystal Solicitors
44 Southampton Buildings
London WC2A 1AP
020 7242 5905
info@memerycrystal.com
www.memerycrystal.com
Digital technology inc branding,
software development, licensing
agreements, IP, data protection, rights
protection, litigation, domain name
disputes and internet libel

MLM
Pendragon House, Fitzalan Court
Newport Road, Cardiff
South Glamorgan CF24 0BA
029 2046 2562
enquiries@mlmsolicitors.com
www.mlmsolicitors.com
IP; IT, technology companies, TV
companies and broadcasters

Moorcrofts
Mere House, Mere Park
Dedmere Road, Marlow
Buckinghamshire SL7 1PB
01628 470000
info@moorcrofts.com
www.moorcrofts.com
Corporate, IP and regulation. Clients
include RDF, Video Arts and TV
Network

Morgan Cole
Buxton Court, 3 West Way
Oxford, Oxfordshire OX2 0SZ
01865 262600
Cardiff: 029 2038 5385
Reading: 0118 955 3000
London: 020 7822 8000
info@morgan-cole.com
www.morgan-cole.com
IP

Morrison and Foerster MNP
CityPoint, 1 Ropemaker Street
London EC2Y 9AW
020 7920 4000
london@mofo.com
www.mofo.com
IP; new media and technology; telecoms
and other regulation; all aspects of
project and corporate finance

Myers Fletcher and Gordon
15 Cambridge Court
210 Shepherds Bush Road,
Hammersmith, London W6 7NJ
020 7610 4433
mfg@mfglon.co.uk
www.mfg-law.com
Entertainment law, internet, copyright,
appropriation of personality, IP,
dispute litigation

Nabarro Nathanson
Lacon House, Theobalds Road
London WC1X 8RW
020 7524 6000
www.nabarro.com
E-commerce, telecoms, IT

New Media Law
102 Dean Street, London W1D 3TQ
020 7734 9777
ian.penman@newmedialaw.biz
www.newmedialaw.biz
Specialise in media/entertainment law,
including copyright (film, music
and TV) and new media

Nexus Solicitors
Carlton House, 16–18 Albert Square
Manchester, Lancashire M2 5PE
0161 819 4900
help@nexussolicitors.co.uk
www.nexussolicitors.co.uk
Sports and media inc sponsorship,
endorsement agreements,
merchandising and licensing, football
transfers, event regulation, publishing

Norton Rose
Kempson House
35–37 Camomile Street
London EC3A 7AN
020 7283 6000
www.nortonrose.com
All aspects of media law

Olswang
90 High Holborn, London WC1V 6XX
020 7067 3000
london@olswang.com
www.olswang.com
Media communications, technology
and property

Orchard
6 Snow Hill, London EC1A 2AY
020 7246 6100
info@orchardlaw.com
www.orchardlaw.com
Film, marketing, music, publishing,
TV and radio, IT, internet

Osborne Clarke
One London Wall, London EC2Y 5EB
020 7105 7000
www.osborneclarke.com
IP; IT and telecoms; advertising and
marketing

Peachey and Co
95 Aldwych, London WC2B 4JF
020 7316 5200
email@peachey.co.uk
www.peachey.co.uk
Broadcasting; creative media (ads and
marketing); new media; software and
IT services; sport; telecoms

Penningtons
Bucklersbury House
83 Cannon Street
London EC4N 8PE
020 7457 3000
information@penningtons.co.uk
www.penningtons.co.uk
E-business and IP

Pictons
28 Dunstable Road, Luton
Beds LU1 1DY
01582 870870
info@pictons.co.uk
www.pictons.co.uk
Technology IP

Pinsent Masons
Dashwood House, 69 Old Broad
Street, London EC2M 1NR
020 7418 7000
Birmingham: 0121 200 1050
Bristol: 0117 924 5678
Edinburgh: 0131 225 0000
Glasgow: 0141 248 4858
Leeds: 0113 244 5000
Manchester: 0161 250 0100
enquiries@pinsentmasons.com
www.pinsentmasons.com
IP; IT inc resolution of IT and telecoms
disputes

Putsman Solicitors
Britannia House
50 Great Charles Street, Birmingham
West Midlands B3 2LT
0121 237 3000
www.pwlc.co.uk
IP etc for TV production, band and
media managers, celeb agents,
publishers, media personalities, signed
bands and artists, casting agents, venues

Rawlison Butler
Griffin House, 135 High Street
Crawley, West Sussex RH10 1DQ
01293 527744
info@rawlisonbutler.com
www.rawlisonbutler.com
IP and brand protection; IT and
e-commerce; data protection; EU
and UK competition law; contracts

Reed Smith
Minerva House, 5 Montague Close
London SE1 9BB
020 7403 2900
mrutherford@reedsmith.com
www.reedsmith.com
Pre-publication and pre-broadcast inc
libel, invasion of privacy etc; non-
litigation such as protecting IP, general
corporate, negotiation of industry-
related agreements, labour and
employment, comms regulatory, and
ad branding; media management

Reid Minty
Moss House, 15–16 Brooks Mews,
London W1K 4DS
020 7318 4444
lawyers@reidminty.co.uk
www.reidminty.co.uk
Defamation: libel, slander and
malicious falsehood; employment and
litigation

Reynolds Porter Chamberlain
Chichester House
278–282 High Holborn
London WC1V 7HA
020 7242 2877
enquiries@rpc.co.uk
www.rpc.co.uk
Content-related issues for press,
publishers, TV

Richard Howard and Co
45–51 Whitfield Street
London W1T 4HB
020 7831 4511
richard.howard@richardhoward.co.uk
www.richardhoward.tv
TV, paper and electronic publishing,
multimedia and telecoms; IP

Richards Butler International
Beaufort House, 15 St Botolph Street
London EC3A 7EE
020 7247 6555
law@richardsbutler.com
www.richardsbutler.com
IP; telecoms; IT, data protection and
e-business

Ricksons
6 Winckley Square, Preston PR1 3JJ
01772 556677
Leeds: 0113 243 1555
Manchester: 0161 833 3355
info@ricksons.co.uk
www.ricksons.co.uk
E-commerce and computer contracts;
IP; confidentiality agreements and
data protection

Robert Muckle
Norham House
12 New Bridge Street West
Newcastle Upon Tyne NE1 8AS
0191 232 4402
enquiries@robertmuckle.co.uk
www.robertmuckle.co.uk
IP; IT; dispute resolution

Roiter Zucker
Regent House
5–7 Broadhurst Gardens
Swiss Cottage, London NW6 3RZ
020 7328 9111
mail@roiterzucker.co.uk
www.roiterzucker.co.uk
IP and disputes

Rollits
Wilberforce Court, High Street
Hull, North Humberside HU1 1YJ
01482 323239
info@rollits.com
www.rollits.com
IP and telecoms; media and
entertainment law; IT/technology

Rooks Rider
Challoner House
19 Clerkenwell Close
London EC1R 0RR
020 7689 7000
lawyers@rooksrider.co.uk
www.rooksrider.co.uk
IP

Rosenblatt
9–13 St Andrew Street
London EC4A 3AF
020 7955 0880
info@rosenblatt-law.co.uk
www.rosenblatt-law.co.uk
Defamation and IP

Ross and Craig
12a Upper Berkeley Street
London W1H 7QE
020 7262 3077
reception@rosscraig.com
www.rosscraig.com
Co-production arrangements; IP and
copyright; film and TV funding; rights
acquisition; production and artistes'
contracts; defamation; IT and
e-commerce

Rowberry Morris
17 Castle Street, Reading
Berkshire RG1 7SB
0118 958 5611
admin@rowberrymorris.co.uk
www.rowberrymorris.co.uk
All aspects of media law. Specialist unit
advises new bands and writers

RT Coopers Solicitors
Telfords Yard, 6/8 The Highway
London E1W 2BS
020 7488 2985
enquiries@rtcoopers.com
www.rtcoopers.com
Film, TV, music, IP, copyright,
branding, licensing, publishing etc

Salans
Clements House
14–18 Gresham Street
London EC2V 7NN
020 7509 6000
rabrahams@salans.com
www.salans.com
IP; IT and communications law

Schillings
Royalty House, 72–74 Dean Street
London W1D 3TL
020 7453 2500
legal@schillings.co.uk
www.schillings.co.uk
IP and media management

Seddons
5 Portman Square
London W1H 6NT
020 7725 8000
postmaster@seddons.co.uk
www.seddons.co.uk
Entertainment and music industry

Shepherd And Wedderburn
12 Arthur Street
London EC4R 9AB
020 7763 3200
info@shepwedd.co.uk
www.shepwedd.co.uk
IP and trademark litigation, copyright,
sport law

Sheridans
Whittington House, Alfred Place
London WC1E 7EA
020 7079 0100
info@sheridans.co.uk
www.sheridans.co.uk
Agreements; music, book and magazine
publishing; distribution; licensing;
merchandising; sponsorship;
trademarks and domain names

Simmons and Simmons
Citypoint, 1 Ropemaker Street
London EC2Y 9SS
020 7628 2020
enquiries@simmons-simmons.com
www.simmons-simmons.com
IT litigation; technology, media and
telecommunications

Simons Muirhead and Burton
50 Broadwick Street, Soho
London W1F 7AG
020 7734 4499
info@smab.co.uk
www.smab.co.uk
Film and TV regulatory and
production law; dispute resolution,
copyright and libel advice

SJ Berwin
222 Gray's Inn Road
London WC1X 8XF
020 7533 2222
info@sjberwin.com
www.sjberwin.com
IP; film, TV and radio work (content
and carriage), music, telecoms, sport,
animation, digital media, e-commerce
and online

Slaughter and May
One Bunhill Row, London EC1Y 8YY
020 7600 1200
www.slaughterandmay.com
IP; IT; technology, media and telecoms

Spearing Waite
41 Friar Lane, Leicester
Leicestershire LE1 5RB
0116 262 4225
info@spearingwaite.co.uk
www.spearingwaite.co.uk
Franchising, agency and licensing; IP

Spring Law
40 Craven Street
London WC2N 5NG
020 7930 4158
tim.perry@springlaw.co.uk
www.Springlaw.co.uk
IP, franchise arrangements,
sponsorship, rights exploitation,
distribution, merchandising, licensing,
marketing, ads and promotions

Squire Sanders and Dempsey
1st Floor, 60 Cannon Street
London EC4N 6NP
020 7189 8000
ssdinfo@ssd.com
www.ssd.com
Communications law inc IP, internet,
licensing, regulatory restructuring,
satellite communications, broadcasting
and cable

Steeles
Bedford House, 21A John Street
London WC1N 2BL
020 7421 1720
media@steeleslaw.co.uk
www.steeleslaw.co.uk
For record labels, agents, managers,
event organisers, artists, publishers,
writers, broadcasters, unions and
professional bodies

Stringer Saul
17 Hanover Square
London W1S 1HU
020 7917 8500
info@stringersaul.co.uk
www.stringersaul.co.uk
IP; IT and internet; publishing

Tarlo Lyons
Watchmaker Court, 33 St John's Lane
London EC1M 4DB
020 7405 2000
simon.stokes@tarlolyons.com
www.tarlolyons.com
IP; digital media; IT; data protection;
ads; website development and
e-commerce; information security
and fraud; telecoms

Taylor Wessing
Carmelite, 50 Victoria Embankment
London EC4Y 0DX
020 7300 7000
london@taylorwessing.com
www.taylorwessing.com
Patents, copyright and other IP

Teacher Stern Selby
37–41 Bedford Row
London WC1R 4JH
020 7242 3191
g.shear@tsslaw.com
www.tsslaw.com
Defamation and reputation
management; IT; IP; internet and
e-commerce; data protection; telecoms
and risk management

Thompsons
Congress House
23–28 Great Russell Street
London WC1B 3LW
020 7290 0000
info@thompsons.law.co.uk
www.thompsons.law.co.uk
Represents media unions and their
members including NUJ, Bectu and
Amicus

Thomson Snell and Passmore
3 Lonsdale Gardens
Tunbridge Wells, Kent TN1 1NX
01892 510000
info@ts-p.co.uk
www.ts-p.co.uk
E-commerce and IP law

TLT Solicitors
Sea Containers House,
20 Upper Ground, Blackfriars Bridge
London SE1 9LH
020 7620 1311
www.tltsolicitors.com
IT inc internet and e-commerce; sports
law

Travers Smith
10 Snow Hill, London EC1A 2AL
020 7295 3000
travers.smith@traverssmith.com
www.TraversSmith.com
IT and e-commerce; media and IP;
contracts

Truman and Co Solicitors, Truelegal
76 Fore Street, Topsham
Exeter, Devon EX3 0HQ
01392 879414
info@truelegal.co.uk
www.truelegal.co.uk
Commercial, media and e-law for advertising, marketing, PR, web, new media companies in London and South West. Anglo German specialist.

Turner Parkinson
Hollins Chambers, 64a Bridge Street
Manchester, Lancashire M3 3BA
0161 833 1212
tp@tp.co.uk
www.tp.co.uk
IP; computer contracts and e-commerce

Veale Wasbrough
Orchard Court, Orchard Lane
Bristol BS1 5WS
0117 925 2020
anoble@vwl.co.uk
www.vwl.co.uk
IP esp tech, computer systems and e-commerce

Vizards Tweedie
42 Bedford Row, London WC1R 4JL
020 7405 1234
www.vizardstweedie.co.uk
Media and IT law

Wake Smith
68 Clarkehouse Road, Sheffield
South Yorkshire S10 2LJ
0114 266 6660
legal@wake-smith.com
www.wake-smith.co.uk
Media and entertainment law; global tech licensing contracts; agency, distribution and marketing agreements

Watson Farley and Williams
15 Appold Street, London EC2A 2HB
020 7814 8000
info@wfw.com
www.wfw.com
Telecoms, media and tech: for operators, regulators, equipment and maintenance providers, internet services, content providers, e-commerce users and developers

Wiggin
95 Promenade, Cheltenham
Gloucestershire GL50 1WG
01242 224114
law@wiggin.co.uk
www.wiggin.co.uk
Broadcast media, telecoms, e-commerce, advertising, publishing, gaming, music, IP, content and regulation

Willoughby and Partners (Rouse and Co International)
The Isis Building, Thames Quay
193 Marsh Wall, London E14 9SG
020 7345 8888
Oxford: 01865 791990
Harrogate: 01423 850800
rouse@iprights.com
www.iprights.com
IP services worldwide in TV, film, entertainment and publishing sectors inc agreements, rights, licensing and defence of infringement

Wilmer Cutler Pickering Hale and Dorr
Alder Castle House, 10 Noble Street
London EC2V 7QJ
020 7645 2400
www.wilmerhale.com
IP; services for telecoms, internet, e-commerce and software industries

Wollastons
Brierly Place, New London Road
Chelmsford, Esssex CM2 0AP
01245 211211
enquiries@wollastons.co.uk
www.wollastons.co.uk
IP inc agreements, licensing, trademark registration, infringement of copyright, passing off, breach of confidence, warranties and liability, internet trade and portal development

Wragge and Co
55 Colmore Row
Birmingham B3 2AS
0870 903 1000
mail@wragge.com
www.wragge.com
Media business services from content creation and exploitation to financing and corporate development. Offices in London and Brussels

Wright Hassall Solicitors
9 Clarendon Place, Leamington Spa
Warwickshire CV32 5QP
01926 886688
email@wrighthassall.co.uk
www.wrighthassall.co.uk
IP and transactional support to technology, new media and advertising clients. Emphasis on branding, design, merchandising, sponsorship, sales promotion and all copyright issues.

Wright, Johnston and Mackenzie
302 St Vincent Street
Glasgow G2 5RZ
0141 248 3434
Edinburgh: 0131 221 5560
enquiries@wjm.co.uk
www.wjm.co.uk
IP and dispute resolution

Media law journals

Entertainment and Media Law Reports
Sweet and Maxwell
020 7393 7000
gfernando@11southsquare.com;
bbrandreth@11southsquare.com
www.sweetandmaxwell.co.uk
6pa. Editors: Giles Fernando and Benet Brandreth; other editorial contact: Sarah Udell (sarah.udell@thomson.com)

Entertainment Law Review
Sweet and Maxwell
020 7393 7000
Rico.Calleja@Hammonds.com
www.sweetandmaxwell.co.uk
/contact/authors/entlr.html
8pa. Editor-in-chief: Tony Martino; editor: Rico Calleja; house editor: Jane Hyatt (jane.hyatt@thomson.com)

International Journal of Communications Law and Policy
00 49 251 832 8411
IJCLP@digital-law.net
www.digital-law.net/IJCLP
2pa: Jan and July

IP Law and Business
ALM
Editor: 001 212 313 9130
efriedlander@amlaw.com
www.ipww.com
*Monthly, plus annual digest issue
Editor: Emily Friedlander*
PRESS: *001 401 848 5494*

Media Law and Policy
New York Law School
00 1 212 431 2899 x4305
www.nyls.edu/pages/1572.asp

PA Media Lawyer
01229 716622
Medialawyer@pa.press.net
www.medialawyer.press.net
Bi-monthly. Editor: Tom Welsh

Copyright associations

Authors' Licensing and Collecting Society (ALCS)
Marlborough Court, 14–18 Holborn
London EC1N 2LE
020 7395 0600
alcs@alcs.co.uk
www.alcs.co.uk
UK collecting society for writers and their successors

British Copyright Council
Copyright House
29–33 Berners Street
London W1T 3AB
01986 788122
copyright@bcc2.demon.co.uk
Copyright watchdog

Copyright Licensing Agency
90 Tottenham Court Road
London W1T 4LP
020 7631 5555
cla@cla.co.uk
www.cla.co.uk
Administers copyrights

Design and Artists Copyright Society (DACS)
33 Great Sutton Street
London EC1V 0DX
020 7336 8811
info@dacs.org.uk
www.dacs.org.uk
Copyright and collecting society for visual artists

Federation Against Copyright Theft (FACT)
Unit 7, Victory Business Centre
Worton Road, Isleworth
Middlesex TW7 6DB
020 8568 6646
contact@fact-uk.org.uk
www.fact-uk.org.uk
UK film anti-piracy body

Irish Copyright Licensing Agency
25 Denzille Lane, Dublin 2
00 353 1 662 4211
info@icla.ie
www.icla.ie
Ireland's reproduction rights organisation

Mechanical-Copyright Protection Society
29–33 Berners Street
London W1T 3AB
020 7580 5544
www.mcps.co.uk
Collects and distributes music royalties: record companies, broadcasters, novelties, online

Patent Office
Concept House, Cardiff Road
Newport NP10 8QQ
0845 950 0505
enquiries@patent.gov.uk
www.patent.gov.uk
Patents, trademarks, design and copyright

Performing Rights Society
29–33 Berners Street
London W1T 3AB
020 7580 5544
www.prs.co.uk
Collects and distributes music royalties: pubs, clubs, broadcasters, online

Public Lending Right
Richard House, Sorbonne Close
Stockton-on-Tees TS17 6DA
01642 604699
registrar@plr.uk.com
www.plr.uk.com
Library payment scheme for authors

Publishers Licensing Society
37–41 Gower Street
London WC1E 6HH
020 7299 7730
pls@pls.org.uk
www.pls.org.uk
Supports Copyright Licensing Agency

UK Copyright Bureau
110 Trafalgar Road, Portslade
East Sussex BN41 1GS
info@copyrightbureau.co.uk
www.copyrightbureau.co.uk
Copyright service for authors, playwrights, scriptwriters, poets, musicians and associated literary crafts

Writers, Artists and their Copyright Holders (Watch)
David Sutton
Director of Research Projects
University of Reading Library
PO Box 223, Whiteknights
Reading RG6 6AE
0118 931 8783
UK: d.c.sutton@reading.ac.uk
US: rworkman@mail.utexas.edu
www.watch-file.com
Database primarily containing names and addresses of copyright holders and contacts for authors and artists whose archives are housed in libraries in North America and UK

Associations

International Bar Association – Media Law Committee
10th Floor, 1 Stephen Street
London W1T 1AT
020 7691 6868
member@int-bar.org
www.ibanet.org/legalpractice /Media_Law.cfm

Stanhope Centre for Communications Policy Research
Stanhope House, Stanhope Place
London W2 2HH
020 7479 5900
www.stanhopecentre.org/
Media law and policy forum

Media services

Libraries & research

Specialist libraries and archives

Bank of England Information Centre
Threadneedle Street
London EC2R 8AH
020 7601 4715
informationcentre@
   bankofengland.co.uk
www.bankofengland.co.uk
Central banking and finance

Barbican Library
Silk Street, London EC2Y 8DS
020 7638 0569
barbicanlib@corpoflondon.gov.uk
www.cityoflondon.gov.uk
*Lending library with strong arts and
music sections*

BBC Written Archives Centre
Peppard Road, Caversham Park
Reading, Berkshire RG4 8TZ
0118 948 6281
wac.enquiries@bbc.co.uk
www.bbc.co.uk/heritage

BFI National Library
21 Stephen Street, London W1T 1LN
020 7255 1444
library@bfi.org.uk
www.bfi.org.uk/nationallibrary
   /index.html
*World's largest collection of
documentation on film and television*

British Architectural Library
Royal Institute of British Architects
66 Portland Place, London W1B 1AD
020 7580 5533
bal@inst.riba.org
www.architecture.com

British Library
96 Euston Road, London NW1 2DB
0870 444 1500
reader-admissions@bl.uk
www.bl.uk

British Newspaper Library
Colindale Avenue, London NW9 5HE
020 7412 7332
newspaper@bl.uk
www.bl.uk/catalogues/
   newspapers.html

**CAA Library and Information
Centre**
Aviation House, Gatwick Airport
West Sussex RH6 0YR
01293 573725
infoservices@caa.co.uk
www.caa.co.uk

Catholic Central Library
Lancing Street, London NW1 1ND
020 7383 4333
librarian@catholic-library.org.uk
www.catholic-library.org.uk

City Business Library
1 Brewers' Hall Garden
London EC2V 5BX
020 7332 1812
cbl@corpoflondon.gov.uk
www.cityoflondon.gov.uk
   /citybusinesslibrary

City of Westminster Archives Centre
10 St Ann's Street
London SW1P 2DE
020 7641 5180
archives@westminster.gov.uk
www.westminster.gov.uk/archives

DigiReels Media Monitoring
Paramount House
162–170 Wardour Street
London W1F 8ZX
020 7437 7743
peter.godden@digireels.co.uk
www.digireels.co.uk
Online ad database

Foreign and Commonwealth Office
Library and information services E213
King Charles Street
London SW1A 2AH
020 7270 3925
library.enquiries@fco.gov.uk
www.fco.gov.uk

Forestry Commission Library
Forest Research Station
Alice Holt Lodge, Wrecclesham
Farnham, Surrey GU10 4LH
01420 222555
library@forestry.gsi.gov.uk
www.forestry.gov.uk/forest_research

French Institute Library
Institut francais
17 Queensberry Place
London SW7 2DT
020 7073 1350
library@ambafrance.org.uk
www.institut.ambafrance.org.uk

Goethe-Institut Library
50 Princes Gate, Exhibition Road
London SW7 2PH
020 7596 4000
mail@london.goethe.org
www.goethe.de/london
German literature and reference

**Harry Price Library of Magical
Literature**
University of London Library
Senate House, Malet Street
London WC1E 7HU
020 7862 8470
historic@ull.ac.uk
www.ull.ac.uk/historic/collections.shtml
Magic literature

**Institute of Education Library
(London)**
20 Bedford Way, London WC1H 0AL
020 7612 6080
lib.enquiries@ioe.ac.uk
www.ioe.ac.uk
*Over 300,000 volumes including
special sections on educational studies.
2,000 periodicals*

Instituto Cervantes
102 Eaton Square
London SW1W 9AN
020 7201 0757
biblon@cervantes.es
www.cervantes.es
Spain

International Booksearch Service
020 7639 8900
sarah.fordham@btinternet.com
www.scfordham.com
Finds out-of-print books

Italian Cultural Institute
39 Belgrave Square
London SW1X 8NX
020 7396 4425
library@italcultur.org.uk
www.italcultur.org.uk

Linen Hall Library
17 Donegall Square North
Belfast BT1 5GB
028 9032 1707
info@linenhall.com
www.linenhall.com
Ireland and politics

**Llyfrgell Genedlaethol Cymru/
National Library of Wales**
Aberystwyth, Ceredigion SY23 3BU
01970 632800
holi@llgc.org.uk
www.llgc.org.uk

**London Metropolitan Archives
(LMA)**
40 Northampton Road, Clerkenwell
London EC1R 0HB
020 7332 3820
ask.lma@corpoflondon.gov.uk
www.cityoflondon.gov.uk/lma
*Largest local authority archive in the
UK*

Murder Files
Dommett Hill Farm, Hare Lane
Buckland St Mary
Somerset TA20 3JS
01460 234065
enquiry@murderfiles.com
www.murderfiles.com
UK murders since 1400

National Archives
Kew, Richmond, Surrey TW9 4DU
020 8392 3444
enquiry@nationalarchives.gov.uk
www.nationalarchives.gov.uk
11th–20th century national records

National Film and TV Archive
Kingshill Way, Berkhamsted
Herts HP4 3TP
01442 876301
david.pierce@bfi.org.uk
www.bfi.org.uk
*Contains more than 275,000 films and
200,000 TV programmes, dating from
1895 to the present*

National Library for the Blind
Far Cromwell Road, Bredbury
Stockport SK6 2SG
0161 355 2000
enquiries@nlbuk.org
www.nlb-online.org

National Library of Scotland
George IV Bridge
Edinburgh EH1 1EW
0131 226 4531
enquiries@nls.uk
www.nls.uk

National Meteorological Archive
The Scott Building, Sterling Centre,
Eastern Road, Bracknell
Berkshire RG12 2PW
01344 861629
metarc@metoffice.com
www.metoffice.com

National Museum of Scotland
NMS Enterprises, Chambers Street
Edinburgh EH1 1JF
0131 247 4026
nmsphoto@nms.ac.uk
www.nms.ac.uk

Natural History Museum Library
Cromwell Road, London SW7 5BD
020 7942 5460
library@nhm.ac.uk
www.nhm.ac.uk/library/index.html

Office for National Statistics
1 Drummond Gate
London SW1V 2QQ
0845 601 3034
info@statistics.gov.uk
www.statistics.gov.uk

Polish Library
238–246 King Street
London W6 0RF
020 8741 0474
bibliotekapolska@
    posk.library.fsnet.co.uk
www.posk.library.fs.net

**Royal Geographical Society Library
(with the Institute of British
Geographers)**
1 Kensington Gore, London SW7 2AR
020 7591 3000
press@rgs.org
www.rgs.org

Royal Society Library
6 Carlton House Terrace
London SW1Y 5AG
020 7451 2606
library@royalsoc.ac.uk
www.royalsoc.ac.uk
Science

Royal Society of Medicine Library
1 Wimpole Street, London W1G 0AE
020 7290 2940
library@rsm.ac.uk
www.rsm.ac.uk

**Science Fiction Foundation
Research Library**
Liverpool University Library
PO Box 123, Liverpool L69 3DA
0151 794 3142
asawyer@liverpool.ac.uk
www.liv.ac.uk/~asawyer/sffchome.html

Science Museum Library
Imperial College Road
London SW7 5NH
020 7942 4242
smlinfo@nmsi.ac.uk
www.sciencemuseum.org.uk

Theatre Museum Library & Archive
1e Tavistock Street
London WC2E 7PR
020 7943 4700
tmenquiries@vam.ac.uk
www.theatremuseum.org

United Nations Information Centre
Millbank Tower (21st Floor)
21–24 Millbank, London SW1P 4QH
020 7630 1981
info@uniclondon.org
www.unitednations.org.uk

Westminster Music Library
Victoria Library
160 Buckingham Palace Road
London SW1W 9UD
020 7641 4292
musiclibrary@westminster.gov.uk
www.westminster.gov.uk
    /libraries/special/music

Wiener Library
4 Devonshire Street
London W1W 5BH
020 7636 7247
info@wienerlibrary.co.uk
www.wienerlibrary.co.uk
*Modern Jewish history, the Holocaust
and German 20th-century history*

Women's Library
25 Old Castle Street, London E1 7NT
020 7320 2222
moreinfo@thewomenslibrary.ac.uk
www.thewomenslibrary.ac.uk

Zoological Society Library
Regent's Park, London NW1 4RY
020 7449 6293
library@zsl.org
www.zsl.org

Research data

Audit Bureau of Circulations (ABC)
Saxon House, 211 High Street
Berkhamsted
Hertfordshire HP4 1AD
01442 870800
marketing@abc.org.uk
www.abc.org.uk
*Circulation figures for newspapers and
magazines*

**Broadcasters' Audience Research
Board (Barb)**
18 Dering Street, London W1S 1AQ
020 7529 5531
enquiries@barb.co.uk
www.barb.co.uk
TV audience data

Communications Research Group
Anvic House, 84 Vyse Street
Jewellery Quarter
Birmingham B18 6HA
0121 523 9595
research@crghq.com
www.crghq.com
Market and audience research

LemonAd United Kingdom
Nielsen/NetRatings UK, 2nd Floor
4 Elder Street, London E1 6BT
020 7420 9268
barney@netcrawling.com
www.lemonad.com
Advertising monitoring in Europe

National Readership Survey (NRS)
40 Parker Street
London WC2B 5PQ
020 7242 8111
stevemillington@nrs.co.uk
www.nrs.co.uk
*Newspaper and magazine readership
estimates*

Nielsen BookScan
3rd Floor Midas House
62 Goldsworth Road
Woking, Surrey GU21 6LQ
01483 712222
info@nielsenbookscan.co.uk
www.nielsenbookscan.co.uk
*International sales data monitoring
and analysis service for the English-
language book industry worldwide*

Nielsen/NetRatings
ACNielsen House, London Road
Headington, Oxford OX3 9RX
01865 742742
www.acneilson.com
Marketing research worldwide

Rajar
Gainsborough House
81 Oxford Street, London W1D 2EU
020 7903 5350
info@rajar.co.uk
www.rajar.co.uk
*Measures and profiles the audiences of
UK radio stations*

Library associations

Association of Independent Libraries
Leeds Library, 18 Commercial Street
Leeds, West Yorkshire LS1 6AL
0113 245 3071
admin@hlsi.demon.co.uk
www.independentlibraries.co.uk

Association of UK Media Libraries
Editorial Information Services
Financial Times
One Southwark Bridge
London SE1 9HL
020 7873 3920
Margaret.Katny@bbc.co.uk
www.aukml.org.uk
Represents librarians in media industry

**Chartered Institute of Library and
Information Professionals**
7 Ridgmount Street
London WC1E 7AE
020 7255 0500
info@cilip.org.uk
www.cilip.org.uk

**Chartered Institute of Library and
Information Professionals in
Scotland**
1st Floor, Building C, Brandon Gate
Leechlee Road, Hamilton ML3 6AU
01698 458888
cilips@slainte.org.uk
www.slainte.org.uk

Focal International
Pentax House, South Hill Avenue
South Harrow HA2 0DU
020 8423 5853
info@focalint.org
www.focalint.org
*Represents commercial film/
audiovisual, stills and sound libraries,
plus facility houses, film researchers and
producers*

**Museum Libraries & Archives
Council**
16 Queen Anne's Gate
London SW1H 9AA
020 7273 1444
www.mla.gov.uk
*Development agency for museums,
libraries and archives*

A career in media

Careers & training

Salaries from top to bottom

Advertising
- Sir Martin Sorrell, chief executive of WPP: just over £2.4m in 2004, including bonuses
- Trainee account executive: typically £18,000

Newspapers
- Paul Dacre, editor-in-chief of the Daily Mail: £1.1m in year to October 2004
- Graduate trainee, weekly title at Coventry Newspapers: £11,500 (source: NUJ)

Broadcasting
- Mark Thompson, director general of the BBC: £459,000 in 2005 (inc £6,000 benefits)
- Minimum salary, BBC Resources, 2005-06: £12,601 (source: Bectu)

Magazines
- Tom Moloney, chief executive, Emap: £535,600 at 31 March 2005
- Minimum salary, Emap Healthcare: £21,000 (agreed 2003; source: NUJ)

Ask any student if they would like a career in "the media", and they would probably say yes. Ask anyone in the media industry if they would rather still be a student, and they would most likely give the same answer. While a "creative" career might sound glamorous, everyone else thinks so too; and many employers, recognising this, get away with paying low or mediocre salaries for long hours, and even then offer little formal training to help employees develop. To get your foot in the door, most people will probably at some stage have to work for free; to develop professionally, many end up having to train at their own expense. Some give it up and go off to become an accountant instead.

That said, if accountancy is not for you, there are many different kinds of media roles to choose from. In press and publishing, to name but a few roles, you could be a news reporter, a writer of features or specialist articles, a subeditor, a production editor, a commissioning editor, or a writer for the web; in broadcasting, you could be a journalist, a presenter, a researcher, a camera operator, a director or producer. You could be a creative in advertising, a PR agent, or a media buyer whose job it is to know the industry inside out (tip: read this book). And most, if not all these areas, need their designers, graphic artists, production gurus, marketers, sales managers, distributors and managers who – in theory at least – make the whole enterprise tick. Which is better than spending all day sitting in front of a spreadsheet.

Entry-level: courses and work experience

There are two ways of getting into any media career: first, go off and train yourself to do the job; second, do the job. You don't always have to do the first. You always have to do the second.

More and more entrants into the media are well qualified, with good degrees in media studies or other subjects; having such a degree will not necessarily make you stand out from the crowd. Indeed, rightly or wrongly – and partly as a result of articles written by wizened hacks who worked their way up through the regional press – "media studies" still has a poor reputation among employers as a soft option. What can make the difference is a practical qualification which suggests you have the commitment and ability to do the job.

Many parts of the media have accrediting bodies for postgraduate and training courses. In journalism, this is the National Council for the Training of Journalists (NCTJ); the courses it accredits are run either through a training contract at a regional or local paper – the traditional route, with much to recommend it – or, popularly but competitively, at a university. Courses try to be practical as possible: those in newspaper journalism, for example, will include all the knowledge you need plus 100wpm of shorthand; while journalism students at Preston are issued

with a stylebook as if working in a newsroom. Courses will also include work experience, although students usually need work experience to get on the course in the first place.

In broadcasting, journalism courses are accredited by the Broadcast Journalism Training Council (BJTC). There are also a few highly competitive broadcast training schemes, often funded by Skillset – the skills council for the broadcast industry in general. In most parts of TV and radio, many people start as a "runner" or in a similar junior training position and gain experience and qualifications as they progress, often from BBC Training.

In PR, the Chartered Institute of Public Relations approves training courses. Many successful journalism schools now also run PR courses alongside their journalism courses, a trend that started in the US.

The real key to getting any job in the media, though, is work experience. The best way to get work experience is to target an individual in the organisation closest to where you want to work; send them your CV and follow it up a day or two later with a phone call. Be persistent but polite; if they are busy (and they will always say they are), ask when would be the best time to call, or – as a last resort – if there is someone else they think might be able to help you. When doing work experience, dress fairly smartly, put on your most plausible manner, and try to be as helpful as you can. If in doubt, make tea.

The job market

Jobs in the media are advertised in the Guardian on a Monday, on Guardian Unlimited Jobs (jobs.guardian.co.uk) and in other newspapers and the trade press. Most jobs that are advertised nationally attract large numbers of applications, so spend time targeting your CV and covering letter by thinking hard about how your skills and experience best relate to the job description. Keep the CV down to one page (two at most); use a simple font such as Times New Roman (Arial if you love sans serif); and get someone who knows how to spell to read it through (not just Bill Gates).

Remember, most jobs aren't advertised: with the happy exception of the inclusive BBC, many media organisations simply recruit internally or give a job to a freelancer who's been around a while. So if you're looking for a job, the best place to be is working: carry on working for free, or if you are experienced enough, charge freelance rates. So don't apply for jobs simply because they're advertised in the Guardian; better to target the right job for you, or you'll end up back where you started in a few months.

One other problem to bear in mind when looking for a job: the vast majority of media jobs – perhaps up to 80% – are based in London and the south-east. National newspapers, TV production and advertising are based almost exclusively in London; most magazines are in London, with small concentrations elsewhere; only radio, some TV, and (of course) the regional press are truly nationwide.

Journalism at Preston is cutting edge and professional. Our courses cater for all - from the experienced journalist (MA Journalism Leadership) to the next generation of storytellers (BA Hons Digital Journalism Production). With great facilities, outstanding tutors and more than 40 years' experience of teaching journalism, we've earned a national reputation for quality. But don't take our word for it. Ask our alumni. You'll find them in newsrooms across the UK.

Learn it. Do it. Live it.

September 2006

Media Courses

We can prepare you for a variety of exciting careers in the media and cultural industries. Many of our graduates have achieved rewarding and highly successful career opportunities and are employed in organisations such as the BBC, Channel 4, Harper Collins, Transworld Publishing and Saatchi & Saatchi.

BA (Hons) Advertising

BA (Hons) Creative Advertising

BA (Hons) Digital Broadcast Media

BA (Hons) Film: Video Production with Film Studies

HND Media (Moving Image)

BA (Hons) Media Arts

BA (Hons) New Media Journalism

BA (Hons) Photography and Digital Imaging

FdA Photo-imaging*

BA (Hons) Professional Photographic Imaging

BA (Hons) Public Relations

FdA Radio Broadcasting*

MA Media

MA Photography

MA Video Production with Film Studies

* subject to validation

Courses start September and February,
Full-time and Part-time.

Call 0800 036 8888

learning.advice@tvu.ac.uk
www.tvu.ac.uk
apply online at: www.tvu.ac.uk/apply

Thames Valley University
London Reading Slough

Freelancing

Many people who work in the media are freelancers; that is, they are self-employed workers who are paid by the day or by the job. Many experienced journalists and producers become freelancers out of choice, for the relative freedom it offers; there are others who are freelance by necessity because they are looking for a job. In broadcasting, according to the annual Skillset survey, a quarter of the workforce was freelance; though this under-represented the actual freelance population, as many will not have been working on the day of the survey. Many newspaper and magazine journalists also work on a freelance basis, either writing from home or coming into the office to do reporting or subediting shifts.

There are a few major advantages to freelancing: you get to be your own boss, no one tells you what time you have to get up in the morning, and above all you have the freedom to move your career in whatever direction you choose. That's about the size of it. On the other hand, there are many major disadvantages: you never know where the next pay cheque is coming from; you have little power against companies who pay too little, too late, or attempt to appropriate the rights for your work; and you have to fill in a tax return. Remember, you should be entitled to statutory holiday pay in addition to the pay you receive, but many companies will not pay up unless you ask for it.

In broadcasting, you will work a lot of short-term contracts; so ask to see a contract up front, check their rates of pay with broadcasters' union Bectu, and watch out for terms covering intellectual property and statutory holiday pay (companies often try to include holiday pay in the headline figure). In journalism, the biggest issue is rates of pay: publishers are paying reporters and subeditors less and less in real terms each year for a shift, usually by setting arbitrarily low "ceilings" for a day rate. It is up to freelancers and the NUJ to work together to get the pay they deserve.

Further training

Training and professional development, or the lack of it, is a serious problem for the media. In the broadcast industry, Skillset subsidises 60% of the cost a range of short courses for freelances; but freelancers will often have to pay the rest themselves. The BBC also subsidises training, and the industry body Pact can organise training for its members, but regular freelancers will often have less formal training than if they worked for a big in-house team such as the BBC.

10 ways to get that media job **Chris Alden**

1. RESEARCH
It's the number one media skill, so apply it to your job search. Watch plenty of TV; listen to the radio; get digital; read newspapers; surf the web. Read MediaGuardian and MediaGuardian.co.uk, plus the trade press, particularly Broadcast, Televisual and Press Gazette.

2. BUILD CONTACTS
Media is all about contacts. So if you know a friend of a friend who's in the media, call or email, mentioning the person you know in common. Without being pushy or needy, ask them if they can make time for a quick chat – and ask them questions about their work. Don't, however, ask them to find you a job.

3. GET WORK EXPERIENCE
Nothing prepares you better for working in the media than doing the job. So work experience is a useful way in; and in TV, working as a "runner" is the traditional first rung.

4. SHOW OFF YOUR WORK
In journalism and artistic jobs, build a portfolio; in TV or radio, create a showreel or a demo tape to show off what you can do. Work for whatever media outfits you can – newsletters, websites, hospital radio, whoever will use you – to make that portfolio bigger and better.

5. CONSIDER A COURSE
A course with a strong practical element can help you increase your technical knowledge; and in journalism, it may give you skills such as shorthand, law and knowledge of public life. Ultimately, though, it helps you make contacts, get experience, and build that portfolio.

6. CONSIDER A NICHE
Genuine expertise is always bankable. So if you have an interest in and knowledge about a subject – be it arts, travel, health or a region of the country – consider making it your niche.

7. GET THE TECH SKILLS
If you're going for a technical job, you should get some basic experience of the skills involved; if you're not technically minded, you should know how technical concerns affect others. Media is about teamwork: the more knowledge you have, the better the team works, and the more employable you are.

8. TARGET YOUR CV
The traditional CV is not always required to get a job in media, as jobs are often won informally by word of mouth. But if you are using one, then the secret is to prepare a different CV for each job for which you are applying. Use simple, clear design in a well-known font, at a readable point size.

9. PREPARE FOR THE INTERVIEW
Interviews are about the stories you tell, and how you tell them. So remind yourself what you said your skills were; then take time to remember something that happened that backs them up. Other than that, dress smartly, speak slowly, make eye contact and project your voice; come up with intelligent questions – and expect the unexpected.

10. CONSIDER FREELANCING
You do not need a permanent job to have a successful career in media. You could be freelance – that is, paid only for the work you do, or on a short-term contract. Freelancing can be highly stressful and isolating; but once you have been doing it for a while, it can seem like the only way to live.

Adapted from In Print: A Career in Journalism and On Air: A Career in TV & Radio, two MediaGuardian careers guides by Chris Alden

A career in media

360

GOLDSMITHS

Choose MEDIA and COMMUNICATIONS
2006 ENTRY

Choose the following degrees within our internationally-respected, five star RAE rated department.

Undergraduate level: Media and Communications, International Media, or Media combined with Anthropology, Modern Literature, or Sociology.

Postgraduate level: Digital Media; Feature Film; Image and Communication; Journalism; Media and Communications; Radio, Screen Documentary; Script Writing; Television Journalism; Transnational Communications and Global Media; MRes, MPhil and PhD. Plus new for 2006: FilmMaking (January start); Screen Studies* (*subject to regulation).

Attractions include: lively, multi-cultural Department; teaching by internationally leading researchers and media professionals; sessions from visiting professionals from London's media and cultural industries; postgraduate journalism courses accredited by PTC and radio and television journalism by BJTC; excellent employment record - former students work across the sector.

We also offer: a Foundation Certificate: integrated degree in Media and Communications and part-time courses in journalism and media practice, through Professional and Community Education.

FURTHER INFORMATION

Visit the website for more information and application deadlines, or contact Admissions tel 020 7919 7766, e-mail *admissions@gold.ac.uk* or write to AEU, Goldsmiths College, University of London, New Cross, London SE14 6NW.

Goldsmiths
UNIVERSITY
OF LONDON

Goldsmiths aims to be pre-eminent in the study and practice of creative, cognitive, cultural and social processes, and is committed to equal opportunities in all its activities

www.goldsmiths.ac.uk

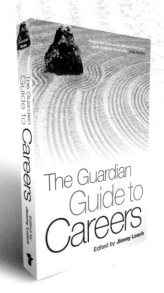

Careers & training Contacts

Universities and training providers

General media See also PR, marketing and advertising
Press, journalism and writing See also publishing and broadcasting
TV, radio and film See also press and multimedia
PR, marketing and advertising
Publishing See also press and multimedia
Multimedia Includes new media, photography, animation, special effects, art and design
Music See also broadcasting

	general media	press, journalism & writing	TV, radio & film	PR, marketing & advertising	publishing	multimedia	music
Aberdeen, University of			●				●
Abertay, Dundee, University of	●			●		●	
Adam Smith College, Fife		●		●		●	
Anglia Polytechnic University			●	●	●	●	●
Arts Institute at Bournemouth			●			●	
Aston University				●		●	
University Centre Barnsley		●				●	●
Basingstoke College of Technology	●					●	
Bath Spa University College	●	●				●	●
Bath, University of			●			●	
Bell College		●	●	●			
Birkbeck, University of London	●	●	●	●		●	●
Birmingham College of Food, Tourism and Creative Studies				●			
Birmingham Conservatoire							●
Birmingham, University of	●	●	●	●		●	●
Blackburn College			●		●	●	●
Bolton, University of	●	●	●	●		●	
Bournemouth University	●	●	●	●		●	●
Bradford College			●	●		●	●
Bradford, University of	●	●	●	●		●	●
Brighton, University of	●	●	●	●		●	●
Bristol, University of		●	●			●	●
Brunel University	●	●	●	●		●	●
Buckingham, University of	●	●		●		●	
Bucks Chilterns University College	●	●	●	●		●	●
Camberwell College of Arts					●	●	
Cambridge, University of							●
Canterbury Christ Church University College	●	●	●	●		●	●
Canterbury College	●		●	●		●	●
Cardiff University	●	●	●	●		●	●
Cardonald College	●	●	●				
Central England in Birmingham, University of	●	●	●	●		●	●
Central Lancashire, University of	●	●	●	●		●	●
Central Saint Martins College of Art and Design	●	●	●			●	
Central School of Speech and Drama		●	●			●	●
Central Sussex College	●	●	●				
Chelsea College of Art and Design				●		●	

Contacts : **Careers & training**

	general media	press, journalism & writing	TV, radio & film	PR, marketing & advertising	publishing	multimedia	music
University College Chester	●	●	●	●		●	●
Chichester College	●		●				
University College Chichester		●	●			●	●
City College Brighton and Hove		●	●			●	●
City Lit		●	●	●	●	●	●
City Of Wolverhampton College	●	●					●
City University, London	●	●	●		●	●	●
Cleveland College of Art & Design			●			●	
Coleg Gwent		●	●			●	●
Coleg Menai						●	
Coleg Sir Gar (Carmarthenshire College)			●			●	●
Conservatoire for Dance and Drama			●				
Cornwall College		●	●			●	
Coventry University	●	●	●	●		●	●
Cumbria Institute of the Arts		●	●			●	
Darlington College Of Technology	●	●	●	●		●	●
De Montfort University	●	●	●	●		●	●
Derby, University of	●	●	●	●		●	●
Doncaster College			●	●		●	●
Dublin Institute of Technology	●	●		●		●	●
Dundee, University of						●	
Durham University							●
Ealing, Hammersmith and West London College	●					●	●
East Anglia, University of	●	●	●	●			●
East London, University of	●	●	●	●	●	●	●
East Surrey College	●		●			●	●
Edge Hill College of Higher Education	●	●	●	●		●	
Edinburgh College of Art				●			
Edinburgh, University of		●	●			●	●
Editorial Centre		●	●			●	
Editorial Training Consultants	●	●	●	●	●	●	
Essex, University of		●	●			●	●
Exeter, University of	●	●	●				
University College Falmouth	●	●	●	●	●	●	
Glamorgan, University of	●	●	●	●		●	●
Glasgow Caledonian University		●	●				●
Glasgow Metropolitan College		●	●	●	●	●	
Glasgow School of Art						●	
Glasgow, University of	●		●			●	●
Gloucestershire, University of		●	●	●	●	●	
Goldsmiths College	●	●	●			●	●
Greenwich, University of	●	●	●	●		●	●
Grimsby Institute of Further & Higher Education	●	●	●	●		●	●
Guildford College	●		●	●		●	●
Harlow College		●				●	●
Harrow College	●	●	●	●		●	●
Henley College Coventry	●		●			●	
Hertfordshire, University of	●	●	●	●		●	●
Highbury College, Portsmouth	●	●	●	●	●	●	●
Hopwood Hall College	●		●				

	general media	press, journalism & writing	TV, radio & film	PR, marketing & advertising	publishing	multimedia	music
Huddersfield, University of	•	•	•	•		•	•
Hull, University of	•	•	•	•		•	•
Journalism Training Centre		•					
Keele, University of	•						•
Kensington and Chelsea College						•	•
Kent Institute of Art and Design			•	•	•	•	
Kent, University of		•	•	•		•	•
King's College London	•		•			•	•
Kingston University	•	•	•	•		•	•
Lambeth College	•	•	•			•	
Lancaster University	•	•	•	•		•	•
Leeds College of Art and Design				•		•	
Leeds College of Music			•				•
Leeds Metropolitan University	•		•			•	•
Leeds Trinity & All Saints	•	•	•				
Leeds, University of		•	•	•		•	•
Leicester, University of			•	•			
Lincoln, University of	•	•	•	•		•	•
Liverpool Community College	•	•	•			•	•
Liverpool Hope University College	•		•	•		•	•
Liverpool John Moores University	•	•	•	•	•	•	•
Liverpool, University of	•		•	•		•	•
London Business School				•			
London College of Communication	•	•	•	•	•	•	•
London College of Fashion		•	•	•		•	
London College of Music & Media							
London Film School			•				
London Metropolitan University	•	•	•	•		•	•
London School of Economics and Political Science	•			•		•	
London School of Journalism		•					
London South Bank University	•	•	•	•		•	•
University College London			•		•		
Luton, University of	•	•	•	•		•	•
Manchester Metropolitan University	•	•	•	•		•	
Manchester, University of	•	•	•				•
Marjon, College of St Mark & St John	•	•	•	•			
Mid-Cheshire College						•	•
Middlesex University	•	•	•	•	•	•	•
Mid-Kent College	•		•		•		•
Napier University	•	•	•	•	•	•	•
National Broadcasting School			•				
National Film and Television School			•			•	•
Neath Port Talbot College			•			•	•
New College Nottingham	•		•			•	•
Newcastle College			•			•	
Newcastle Upon Tyne, University of	•	•	•	•		•	
North East Surrey College of Technology (NESCOT)	•		•			•	•
North East Wales Institute of Higher Education	•	•	•	•		•	•
North East Worcestershire College	•		•			•	•
North West Kent College	•	•				•	•

	general media	press, journalism & writing	TV, radio & film	PR, marketing & advertising	publishing	multimedia	music
Northbrook College Sussex			●	●		●	●
University College Northampton	●	●	●	●			
Northumbria University	●	●	●	●		●	●
Norwich School of Art and Design		●			●	●	
noSweat Journalism Training		●					
Nottingham Trent University	●	●	●	●		●	
Nottingham, University of			●				●
Open University	●						
Oxford Brookes University			●	●	●	●	●
Oxford, University of		●					●
Paisley University	●	●		●		●	●
Peterborough Regional College	●	●	●				●
Plymouth College of Art and Design		●			●	●	●
Plymouth, University of	●	●	●	●	●	●	●
PMA Training	●	●	●	●		●	
Portsmouth, University of	●	●	●	●		●	●
Queen Margaret University College, Edinburgh	●	●	●	●		●	
Queen Mary, University of London			●			●	●
Queen's University Belfast			●				●
Radio and TV School			●				
Ravensbourne College of Design and Communication			●			●	●
Robert Gordon University		●		●	●	●	
Roehampton University	●	●	●	●	●	●	●
Royal Academy of Music							●
Royal College of Music							●
Royal Holloway, University of London		●	●			●	●
Royal Northern College of Music							●
Royal Scottish Academy of Music and Drama	●		●				●
Royal Welsh College of Music and Drama			●	●			●
St Helens College, Merseyside		●	●			●	●
St Martin's College, Lancaster		●					
St Mary's College, Twickenham		●	●			●	
Salford, University of	●	●	●	●		●	●
Salisbury College			●			●	
School of Oriental and African Studies	●		●				●
Sheffield College, The	●	●	●			●	●
Sheffield Hallam University	●	●	●	●		●	●
Sheffield, University of		●	●				●
Solihull College	●			●			
South Birmingham College			●	●		●	●
South Devon College	●		●				●
South East Essex College	●	●	●		●	●	●
South Kent College	●		●	●			●
South Nottingham College			●			●	
South Thames College	●		●			●	●
Southampton Institute	●	●	●	●		●	●
Southampton, University of			●			●	●
Southport College						●	
Staffordshire University	●	●	●			●	●
Stevenson College Edinburgh			●	●			●

	general media	press, journalism & writing	TV, radio & film	PR, marketing & advertising	publishing	multimedia	music
Stirling, University of	●	●	●	●	●		
Stockport College of Further and Higher Education	●	●	●	●		●	
Stratford Upon Avon College	●		●				
Strathclyde, University of		●		●		●	●
Sunderland, University of	●	●	●	●	●	●	●
Surrey Institute of Art and Design	●	●	●	●		●	
Surrey, University of			●			●	●
Sussex, University of	●	●	●			●	●
Sutton Coldfield College	●	●	●			●	●
Swansea Institute of Higher Education		●	●	●		●	●
Swansea University	●	●	●	●			
Tameside College			●			●	
Teesside, University of	●	●	●	●		●	●
Thames Valley University	●	●	●	●		●	●
Trinity College	●	●	●	●		●	
Trinity College of Music							●
Tyne Metropolitan College			●			●	
UHI Millennium Institute	●		●	●		●	●
Ulster, University of	●	●	●	●		●	●
Wakefield College	●					●	●
University of Wales, Aberystwyth	●		●	●			
University of Wales, Bangor	●	●	●	●		●	●
University of Wales Institute, Cardiff		●	●			●	●
University of Wales, Lampeter	●	●	●				
University of Wales, Newport	●	●	●	●	●	●	●
Warwick, University of	●	●	●	●			
Warwickshire College		●		●		●	
West Herts College			●	●		●	
West Kent College	●	●	●				
West of England, University of the	●		●	●		●	●
Westminster, University of		●	●	●		●	●
University College Winchester (formerly King Alfred's College)	●	●	●				
Wirral Metropolitan College	●		●	●		●	●
Wolverhampton, University of	●	●	●	●		●	●
University College Worcester	●		●			●	
York St John College	●	●				●	●
York, University of			●			●	●
Yorkshire Coast College of Further Education						●	

365

Aberdeen, University of
King's College, Aberdeen AB24 3FX
01224 272000
communications@abdn.ac.uk
www.abdn.ac.uk
• MA (ug) film • BMus music

Abertay, Dundee, University of
40 Bell Street, Dundee DD1 1HG
01382 308000
enquiries@abertay.ac.uk
www.abertay.ac.uk
• BA (Hons) media, culture and society • BA (Hons) marketing and
business • BSc (Hons) web design and development. BA (Hons)
computer arts. BSc multimedia development (no year 4)

Adam Smith College, Fife
St Brycedale Avenue, Kirkcaldy, Fife, Scotland KY1 1EX
0800 413280
enquiries@fife.ac.uk
www.fife.ac.uk
Formerly Fife College of Further and Higher Education and Glenrothes
College •HNC/HND practical journalism • HNC/HND communication
with media; events management • HNC/HND interactive multimedia.
AdvDip interactive graphic design. BSc multimedia development

Anglia Polytechnic University
East Road, Cambridge CB1 1PT
Bishop Hall Lane, Chelmsford, Essex CM1 1SQ
0845 271 3333
answers@apu.ac.uk
www.apu.ac.uk
• Fdg media production. BA (Hons) film, TV and theatre design; film with
art history • BA (Hons) advertising design, marketing • MA children's
book illustration • Fdg/BA (Hons) photography; computer games design.
BA (Hons) time-based media; illustration and animation; graphic design;
graphic and web design • Fdg/BA (Hons) pop. BA (Hons) creative music
sound tech with film; creative music tech. BA (Hons) music with drama,
English, psychosocial studies. MA music

Arts Institute at Bournemouth
Wallisdown, Poole, Dorset BH12 5HH
01202 533011
general@aib.ac.uk
www.aib.ac.uk
• BA (Hons) acting for theatre, film and TV; film production • Fdg
commercial photography; interactive media. BA (Hons) graphic design;
photography; commercial photography; animation production;
interactive media

Aston University
Aston Triangle, Birmingham B4 7ET
0121 204 3000
www.aston.ac.uk
• BSc marketing • BSc multimedia tech; multimedia digital systems

University Centre Barnsley
PO Box 266, Church Street, Barnsley S70 2YW
01226 216117
admissions@barnsley.ac.uk
www.barnsley.ac.uk
• Fdg journalism and media production • FdSc multimedia. BSc creative
multimedia tech (top-up) • BA (Hons) creative music tech and sound
recording; pop

Basingstoke College of Technology
Worting Road, Basingstoke RG21 8TN
01256 354141
info@bcot.ac.uk
www.bcot.ac.uk
• BTEC FirstDip/NatDip media • BTEC NatDip/NatCert graphic design;
multimedia. OCN level 3 photography. Short courses: intro to using a
digital camera; web page design with Dreamweaver

Bath Spa University College
Newton Park, Newton St Low, Bath BA2 9BN
01225 875875
enquiries@bathspa.ac.uk
www.bathspa.ac.uk
• BA/BSc (Hons) media communication (joint) • MA creative writing;
writing for young people • Fdg design for digital tech. PgCert/PgDip/MA
interactive multimedia • Fdg commercial music. PgCert/PgDip/
BA(Hons)/MA creative music tech. BA (Hons) music

Bath, University of
Claverton Down, Bath BA2 7AY
01225 388388
admissions@bath.ac.uk
www.bath.ac.uk
• Fdg digital media arts (moving image production) (Wiltshire College,
Chippenham) • Fdg digital media arts (multimedia) (Wiltshire College,
Trowbridge)

Bell College
Almada Street, Hamilton, Lanarkshire ML3 0JB
01698 283100
enquiries@bell.ac.uk
www.bell.ac.uk
• BA journalism*; Prelim journalism (NCTJ). NatCert journalism (NCTJ).
Block-release newspaper journalism. Short courses in subediting,
shorthand, law, freelancing, features • PgDip broadcast journalism.
Short courses: freelance broadcasting, moviemaking without budget,
radio journalism (reporting and interviewing; news and scriptwriting;
production using Cool Edit Pro) • DipHE/CertHE communication. Short
course in marketing

Birkbeck, University of London
Malet Street, Bloomsbury, London WC1E 7HX
0845 601 0174
info@bbk.ac.uk
www.bbk.ac.uk
• Fdg media and business application. Cert/Dip media practice.
BA media and humanities • Cert/MA creative writing. Short courses
in journalism • Cert/Dip/BA film and media. PhD/MPhil film; TV; media.
MA/MRes history of film and visual media. Short courses: film; history
of cinema and screenwriting; radio, docs and video • Dip science
communication. Short courses in PR • Dip multimedia and web
authoring; new media management; web design and development
• Cert/Dip musical techniques and composition; opera studies.
Fcourse/ Dip/AdvDip performance studies: concert singing, opera,
dance. Short courses in music

Birmingham College of Food, Tourism and Creative Studies
Summer Row, Birmingham B3 1JB
0121 604 1000
www.bcftcs.ac.uk
• Fdg/BA(Hons) marketing management; marketing with events/
hospitality management. FdA marketing and PR

Birmingham Conservatoire
Paradise Place, Birmingham B3 3HG
0121 331 5901/2
conservatoire@uce.ac.uk
www.conservatoire.uce.ac.uk
• HND music performance. BMus (Hons) jazz; music. BSc (Hons) music
tech

Birmingham, University of
Edgbaston, Birmingham B15 2TT
0121 414 3344
postmaster@bham.ac.uk
www.bham.ac.uk
• BA culture, society and communication (Europe); media, culture and
society (single and joint) • BA (Hons) creative writing • BA performing
and visual arts. MPhil American film and literature; film; history, film
and TV • MSc marketing • BEng/MEng computer interactive systems
(business management option). BSc/MSc multimedia computer
systems. MEng computer interactive systems with international study.
MSc/PgDip/PgCert comms engineering; multimedia computer systems
• BMus/ BA (joint)/MPhil/MLitt/MMus/PhD music

subject to validation

Blackburn College

Feilden Street, Blackburn BB2 1LH
01254 55144
studentservices@blackburn.ac.uk
www.blackburn.ac.uk
• BTEC NatDip media (moving image). Pre-entry media production. Short courses: makin' music breakin' news; DJ skills Cert/Dip/PgDip marketing professional • BTEC NatDip multimedia; photography. HND photography. Fdg multimedia (Lancaster University) • NOCN IntDip/ AdvDip contemporary and pop

Bolton, University of

Deane Road, Bolton BL3 5AB
01204 900600
enquiries@bolton.ac.uk
www.bolton.ac.uk
• BA (Hons) fashion media * • BA (Hons) media, writing and production; creative writing. MA creative writing • BA (Hons) writing for stage, screen and radio • BA (Hons) marketing; creative advertising. MSc e-marketing • BA (Hons) animation and illustration. HND/BSc (Hons) multimedia and website development. Short courses in internet site design, web site promotion

Bournemouth University

Bournemouth Media School, Weymouth House
Fern Barrow, Poole, Dorset BH12 5BB
01202 965426
bms@bournemouth.ac.uk
www.bournemouth.ac.uk
• BA (Hons) communication and media (University Centre Yeovil) • MA magazine journalism *; journalism (international) * • Fdg video production * (Weymouth College). BA (Hons) scriptwriting for film and TV; TV production; media production * (top-up Bournemouth and Poole College/Weymouth College/University Centre Yeovil); radio production * (Bournemouth and Poole College). MA TV production; radio production; screenwriting; broadcast and film management • Fdg marketing (Bournemouth and Poole College). BA (Hons) PR; ad and marketing comms; marketing; international marketing; international leisure marketing (top-up); international retail marketing (top-up); marketing comms. MA corporate/political comms; PR practice; consumer marketing • Fdg screen design * (University Centre Yeovil); multimedia * (Bournemouth and Poole College); CAD – 3D computer modelling and animation (Bournemouth and Poole College/Salisbury College); CAD – engineering modelling and animation * (Bournemouth and Poole College/Cornwall College); CAD – design engineering * (Cornwall College)/ CAD – graphics and packaging (University Centre Yeovil). BA (Hons) multimedia journalism; interactive media production; computer visualisation and animation; photomedia (top-up at Salisbury College). BSc (Hons) CAD – 3D computer/engineering modelling and animation * (both top-up at Bournemouth and Poole College). MA multimedia journalism; post-production – sound design/editing; interactive media; 3D computer animation; digital effects. MSc computer animation • Fdg music (at Weymouth College); music tech * (at Weymouth College); pop (at Bournemouth and Poole College). BA (Hons) music design (top-up). MA post-production: composing

Bradford College

Great Horton Road, Bradford BD7 1AY
01274 433004
admissions@bradfordcollege.ac.uk
www.bradfordcollege.ac.uk
• PgDip/MA politics of visual representation; representation in film • BTEC HNC advertising and marketing comms. HND marketing comms and advertising. BA (Hons) advertising and marketing comms; marketing comms. MA marketing practice. PgDip/Cert/Dip marketing CIM. NatCert business and marketing. PgDip/MA marketing practice. HE courses in law and marketing • BTEC HND computing (software development). BTEC NatDip multimedia design. Dip digital applications. HND media and special effects (beauty therapy). BA (Hons) graphic media communication; interactive multimedia. Short courses in multimedia design (photography, web page design, animation, CD-Rom design, digital moving image) and Autodesk Inventor • NatDip music performance; music tech

Bradford, University of

Richmond Road, Bradford BD7 1DP
01274 232323
course-enquiries@bradford.ac.uk
www.brad.ac.uk
• BA/BSc media (with options). BSc media tech and production. EurMA media, communication and cultural studies • BA creative writing and identity; creative writing (with options) • BA cinematics (joint); TV (joint). PgDip/MSc entertainment tech; radio frequency comms engineering • BSc marketing (options) • BSc animatronics; computer animation and special effects; e-commerce tech; creative media and tech; internet, law and society; multimedia computing. BA digital media; digital tech (joint). BEng electronic, telecoms and internet engineering. PgDip/MSc personal, mobile and satellite comms; creative media and tech (options). EurMA computer animation and special effects • BA music tech (joint)

Brighton, University of

Mithras House, Lewes Road, Brighton BN2 4AT
01273 644644
admissions@brighton.ac.uk
www.brighton.ac.uk
• BA (Hons) English and sociology (NCTJ) • BA (Hons) sport journalism • Fcert eSystems design and tech. BSc (Hons) digital media development • BA (Hons) communication and media; communication and digital media • FCert graphics communication. FCert/BA (Hons) multimedia. BA (Hons) graphic design • FCert music production. BA (Hons) digital music; music and visual art; music composition for professional media music performance; music production

Bristol, University of

Senate House, Tyndall Avenue, Bristol BS8 1TH
0117 928 9000
www.bristol.ac.uk
• Dip creative writing • BA drama: theatre, film and TV. MA cinema; film and TV production; TV • MSc advanced computing (character animation; global computing and multimedia; internet tech; machine learning and data mining) • BA music. MA music: advanced musical studies; composition of music for film and television

Brunel University

Uxbridge, Middlesex UB8 3PH
01895 274000
admissions@brunel.ac.uk
www.brunel.ac.uk
• MSc health, risk and the media; risk, insecurity and the media • BA English with creative writing. MA creative and transactional writing • BA film and TV; English, drama, music options. MA documentary practice • BSc social anthropology and communication; sociology and communication; communication and media. MSc marketing, business and management; public affairs and lobbying. MA public policy; media and comms • BSc multimedia tech and design. MSc multimedia computing for e-commerce; digital broadcast systems; globalisation and new media; multimedia computing • BA music (also with drama, English, film, TV); creative music tech. MA creative music

Buckingham, University of

Hunter Street, Buckingham MK18 1EG
01280 814080
admissions@buckingham.ac.uk
www.buckingham.ac.uk
• BA (Hons) English with multimedia journalism, media comms and other options • BSc economics with business journalism • BSc (Hons) marketing with media comms (and other options). MSc international marketing management • BA (Hons) English literature with multimedia journalism

*subject to validation

Bucks Chilterns University College

Queen Alexander Road, High Wycombe, Bucks HP11 2JZ
01494 522141
marketing@bcuc.ac.uk
www.bcuc.ac.uk

• BA (Hons) media (joint and with options) • BA (Hons) creative writing (joint and with options); journalism (joint) • HNC/HND live TV production. BA applied performing arts (top-up); applied TV production (top-up). BA (Hons) video production; drama production; film or film studies (all joint and with options) • BA (Hons) ad and promotions management; business and ad management; business and marketing management; business management with marketing; business management with marketing comms; marketing (joint and with options); PR management. PgDip marketing (CIM) • HND internet and multimedia computing; BA applied graphic studies (top-up); applied photography and digital imaging (top-up). BA (Hons) design for digital media; graphic design and advertising. BSc (Hons) multimedia tech (options). Short course: dynamic web page design • BSc (Hons) audio and music tech. BA (Hons) international music management; music entertainment and arts management; music industry management

Camberwell College of Arts

Peckham Road, London SE5 8UF
020 7514 6302
enquiries@camberwell.arts.ac.uk
www.camberwell.arts.ac.uk

• BA/MA conservation; illustration. MA book arts • BA photography. BA/MA graphic design. MA digital arts; digital arts online

Cambridge, University of

The Old Schools, Trinity Lane, Cambridge CB2 1TN
01223 337733
admissions@cam.ac.uk
www.cam.ac.uk

• BA (Hons) music

Canterbury Christ Church University College

Department of Media, North Holmes Road, Canterbury
Kent CT1 1QU
01227 767700
admissions@cant.ac.uk
www.cant.ac.uk

• BA (Hons) media and cultural studies (also joint and with options). MA popular culture and the media • PgDip/MA journalism; MA creative writing • BA (Hons) film, radio and TV (joint and with options). PgDip/MA broadcast journalism. MA media production • BA (Hons) business studies with advertising*; marketing with advertising*; marketing (joint and with options) • DipHE/BA (Hons) digital media. BA (Hons) digital culture, arts and media (joint and with options) • Cert/Dip music. BA (Hons) music (also joint and with options); commercial music. MMus music

Canterbury College

New Dover Road, Canterbury, Kent CT1 3AJ
01227 811111
courseenquiries@cant-col.ac.uk
www.cant-col.ac.uk

• BTEC NatDip media • HND media production. OCN intro to scriptwriting • HND graphic design and advertising. BA (Hons) visual art and communication* • HNC/HND CAD and 3D animation. OCN basic multimedia modelmaking techniques; stop motion animation for beginners • BTEC FirstDip/NatDip music tech. BTEC NatDip music. HND music production. BA (Hons) creative music production. OCN intro to DJ tech; creative DJ tech; intro to music tech for beginners; intro to digital audio; intro to multi-track recording

Cardiff University

Student Recruitment Office, 46 Park Place, Cardiff CF10 3AT
029 2087 4000
prospectus@cardiff.ac.uk
www.cardiff.ac.uk

• BA language and communication. MA teaching and practice of creative writing • BA journalism film and media. PgDip/MA journalism studies. MA international journalism. Short courses: writing, exploring media • BA journalism film and media • PgDip public and media relations. MA international PR; political communication. MSc strategic marketing • Short courses in photography, creative website design, creative digital video production • BMus/BA (Hons – single and joint) music. MA musicology; music, culture and politics; performance studies; composition. Short courses in music

Cardonald College

690 Moss Park Drive, Glasgow G52 3AY
0141 272 3333
enquiries@cardonald.ac.uk
www.cardonald.ac.uk

• HNC/HND media and comms • Prelim Cert journalism (NCTJ). HNC/HND practical journalism • HNC/HND TV operations and production

Central England in Birmingham, University of

Perry Barr, Birmingham B42 2SU
0121 331 5000
info@ucechoices.com
www.uce.ac.uk

• BA (Hons) media and communication • BA (Hons) media and communication (journalism) • BA (Hons) media and communication (radio production; TV and video); TV tech and production • BA (Hons) advertising (joint only); marketing (options); marketing, advertising and PR; media and communication (PR); PR. CIM Dip marketing • HND digital media tech; multimedia; multimedia and networks tech. BA (Hons) media and communication (media photography, multimedia); multimedia tech; sound and multimedia • BSc (Hons) music tech; sound and multimedia; sound engineering and audio production

Central Lancashire, University of

Preston, Lancashire PR1 2HE
01772 201201
cenquiries@uclan.ac.uk
www.uclan.ac.uk

•BA (Hons) creative writing (joint course) • BA (Hons) digital journalism production*; international journalism*; journalism; journalism and English lang or lit*; sports journalism. MA/PgDip broadcast/newspaper/online journalism. MA international journalism; international TV doc production*; journalism leaders; magazine journalism • BA (Hons) film, media and American studies; film, media and visual culture; film and media; TV (minor). BSc (Hons) media production and tech (AV media, journalism options); TV production. MA experimental film • BA (Hons) advertising (options); communication studies; digital comms*; management and PR; marketing (options); press comms*; PR (also with management/marketing). BSc (Hons) marketing. MA/PGDip/PGCert strategic communication. MA marketing. MSc international applied communication; fundraising and sponsorship; marketing management • BSc (Hons) interactive digital media; web and multimedia (also with business information systems) • BA(Hons) multimedia and sonic arts; music practice; music theatre

Central Saint Martins College of Art and Design

12–42 Southampton Row, London WC1B 4AP
020 7514 7022
www.csm.arts.ac.uk

• MA creative practice for narrative environments • BA criticism, communication and curation for arts and design; fashion communication with promotion. MA fashion journalism • BA acting; directing. MA European classical acting; performance (pathways in screen acting, directing, scriptwriting, movement direction); scenography • BA graphic design. PgCert professional studies: photography. PgDip character animation. MA communication design

Central School of Speech and Drama

Embassy Theatre, Eton Avenue, London NW3 3HY
020 7722 8183
enquiries@cssd.ac.uk
www.cssd.ac.uk
• MA writing for stage and broadcast media • MA theatre (inc theatre journalism). MA acting for screen. Short course: intro to acting for screen • MA advanced theatre practice (visual media for performance) • BA theatre practice (theatre sound); acting (music theatre). MA acting musical theatre; advanced theatre practice (sound design and music for performance). Short course in singing; summer school on musical theatre

Central Sussex College

College Road, Crawley, West Sussex RH10 1NR
01293 442200
information@crawley-college.ac.uk
www.crawley-college.ac.uk
• BTEC Dip media • Pre-entry newspaper journalism (NCTJ).
• BTEC NatDip media production

Chelsea College of Art and Design

Millbank, London SW1P 4RJ
020 7514 7751
enquiries@chelsea.arts.ac.uk
www.chelsea.arts.ac.uk
• BA design communication • BA fine art: new media

University College Chester

Parkgate Road, Chester CH1 4BJ
01244 375444
enquiries@chester.ac.uk
www.chester.ac.uk
• BA (Hons) media; cultural studies. MA media and cultural studies
• BA (Hons) journalism • BA (Hons) film; media (TV/radio production)
. MA radio production; screen studies; TV production • BA (Hons) communication studies; advertising; marketing • BA (Hons) graphic design; internet tech; multimedia tech; photography. BSc/BA (Hons) internet tech; multimedia tech; fine art: new media • BA (Hons) media (commercial music production); pop

Chichester College

Westgate Fields, Chichester, West Sussex PO19 1SB
01243 786321
info@chichester.ac.uk
www.chichester.ac.uk
• BTEC FirstDip/NatDip media • BTEC HND media (radio production)

University College Chichester

Bishop Otter Campus, College Lane, Chichester
West Sussex PO19 6PE
01243 816000
admissions@ucc.ac.uk
www.ucc.ac.uk
• BA (Hons) English and creative writing; MA creative writing • Fdg media production & development. BA (Hons) media production and media
• BA (Hons) IT and media; media • Fdg instrumental and vocal teaching; music tech. BA (Hons) music. MA music

City College Brighton and Hove

Pelham Street, Brighton, East Sussex BN1 4FA
01273 667788
info@ccb.ac.uk
www.ccb.ac.uk
• Cert magazine journalism (NCTJ); newspaper journalism (NCTJ). OCN level 3 print journalism • OCN level 3 video production • Short courses: 3D Studio Max, animation, Premiere (desktop video), digital imaging for managers, digital photogaphy, Director, Quark, DVD production, Flash animation, intro to digital imaging, multimedia, web design, PhotoShop for photographers, QTVR production, running a new media company
• Short courses: intro to music tech; Cubase SX for PC; Logic Audio for Apple Mac

City Lit

Keeley Street, London WC2B 4BA
020 7831 7831
infoline@citylit.ac.uk
www.citylit.ac.uk
• Short courses in creative writing, freelance journalism, travel journalism, computer skills for journalists, etc • Short courses in broadcast journalism, writing comedy, scriptwriting, screenwriting
• Short course in how to write a press release • Short course in how to get published • Short courses: HTML, web design and hosting, Dreamweaver and Fireworks, Javascript, using Apple computers, sound and video editing, desktop video and digital editing, Premiere, Final Cut, After Effects, producing animated titles, PhotoShop, digital techniques for printmakers, animation, Maya and 3D animation, digital imaging, digital photography, colour management • Short courses: Cubase sequencing, Pro-tools, Logic Pro, digital music production techniques, Loop-based music using Ableton Live, Reason, Sibelius, Mixing and mastering techniques, drum-and-bass masterclass with Davide Carbone

City Of Wolverhampton College

Wulfrun Campus, Paget Road, Wolverhampton WV6 0DU
01902 836000
mail@wolverhamptoncollege.ac.uk
www.wolverhamptoncollege.ac.uk; www.mediacove.com
• Dip/NatDip media • Pre-entry journalism (NCTJ). BA journalism and editorial design. OCN level 3 art of writing • NatCert music tech

City University, London

Department of Journalism, Northampton Square
London EC1V 0HB
020 7040 5060; journalism: 020 7040 8221
ugadmissions@city.ac.uk; journalism@city.ac.uk
www.city.ac.uk
• MSc media research and analysis. MA transnational media and society
• BA journalism with social science or contemporary history. PGDip newspaper journalism; magazine journalism (PTC). PgDip/MA international journalism. MA creative writing (novels/plays and scripts)
• PGDip broadcast journalism (BJTC)/ TV current affairs journalism
• PgDip/MA publishing studies; electronic publishing. • BSc computer science with games tech; music informatics. BEng media communication systems. BSc/BEng multimedia and internet systems
• BMus/BSc music. MA musicology; music performance studies. PgDip/ MSc music IT

Cleveland College of Art & Design

Green Lane, Linthorpe, Middlesbrough TS5 7RJ
01642 288888
StudentRecruitment@ccad.ac.uk
www.ccad.ac.uk
• BTEC Dip media (moving image). Fdg TV and film production
• BTEC Dip multimedia

Coleg Gwent

The Rhadyr, Usk NP15 2FD
01495 333333
info@coleggwent.ac.uk
www.coleggwent.ac.uk
• OCN writing for the media • BTEC NatDip media (moving image). OCN video and editing production • BTEC Dip multimedia and animation. BTEC NatDip/HNC/HND graphic design. BTEC NatDip photography and digital imaging; multimedia. HND photography and digital imaging. Fdg multimedia. C&G 9231/6922/6923/OCN photography. OCN web design; animation; cartooning and comic strip; CEL animation (traditional); computer graphics and animation; electronic imaging
• BTEC Dip performing arts (music/rock and pop). BTEC NatDip music practice (performing, performance); music tech. OCN music tech; percussion and guitar; level 1 guitar

Coleg Menai

Ffriddoedd Road, Bangor, Gwynedd, North Wales LL57 2TP
01248 370125
student.services@menai.ac.uk
www.menai.ac.uk
• Dip/NatDip e-media

subject to validation

Coleg Sir Gar (Carmarthenshire College)
Graig Campus, Sandy Road, Llanelli
Carmarthenshire SA15 4DN
01554 748000
admissions@colegsirgar.ac.uk
www.colegsirgar.ac.uk
• NatDip media (moving image). EdexcelCert film & TV acting
• OCN web page design • Dip performing arts – music. NatDip music tech. Short courses in musical keyboarding skills and music composition portfolio development

Conservatoire for Dance and Drama
1–7 Woburn Walk, London WC1H 0JJ
020 7387 5101
info@cdd.ac.uk
www.cdd.ac.uk
• MA dance for the screen (London Contemporary Dance School). DipHE costume for theatre, film and TV (Bristol Old Vic Theatre School)

Cornwall College
Trevenson Campus, Pool, Redruth, Cornwall TR15 3RD
01209 611611
enquiries@cornwall.ac.uk
www.cornwall.ac.uk
• HNC media (writing). Fdg newspaper and magazine journalism. PGDip journalism (NCTJ). Short courses in creative writing, writing and selling non-fiction • NatDip media (moving image). Short course: intro to film and video production • BTEC NatDip media (e-media). HNC creative photography in commerical practice. HND multimedia. Fdg animation; multimedia design; graphic and communication design

Coventry University
Priory Street, Coventry CV1 5FB
024 7688 7050
rao.cor@coventry.ac.uk
www.coventry.ac.uk
• BA (Hons) communication, culture and media; media. MA communication, culture and media • BA (Hons) journalism and English; journalism and media. PgCert/PgDip specialist journalism. MA automotive journalism; international media journalism • BA (Hons) media production • BA business and marketing. BA (Hons) advertising and business/media; creative industries management; marketing (joint and options); marketing management. MA marketing. MSc communication management • HND/Fdg/BA multimedia computing. BA crafts and multimedia. BA (Hons) animation and creative computing; digital entertainment tech; English graphic design and media; multimedia computing; multimedia and communication design. BSc/BEng (Hons) internet and broadband comms tech. BEng (Hons) multimedia tech. MA design and digital media; media arts • BA (Hons) music composition and professional practice. BEng (Hons) music tech. BA music and dance. BA (Hons) music and professional practice

Cumbria Institute of the Arts
Brampton Road, Carlisle, Cumbria CA3 9AY
01228 400300; enquiries: 0845 607 6563
info@cumbria.ac.uk
www.cumbria.ac.uk
• BA (Hons) journalism (NCTJ, BJTC); creative writing and contemporary culture; creative writing and film • BA (Hons) media production; film and creative writing; film and contemporary culture • HND graphic design. BA (Hons) photography; graphic design; multimedia design and digital animation

Darlington College Of Technology
Cleveland Avenue, Darlington, County Durham DL3 7BB
01325 503050
enquire@darlington.ac.uk
www.darlington.ac.uk
• Dip media • Pre-entry journalism (NCTJ) • NatDip media production (moving image) • ProfDip marketing (CIM). NatDip multimedia. Level4 Cert digital photo journalism (NCTJ*) • NatCert audio production

De Montfort University
The Gateway, Leicester LE1 9BH
0116 255 1551
enquiry@dmu.ac.uk
www.dmu.ac.uk
• BA (Hons) media • BA (Hons) journalism. PgDip journalism (NCTJ)
• BSc (Hons) media production; media tech; broadcast tech. BA (Hons) film. MA TV scriptwriting • BA (Hons) arts management; marketing; advertising and marketing comms; design management and innovation
• BA (Hons) graphic/interactive/animation/game art design; internet computing; photography and video. BSc (Hons) multimedia computing; tech; video and animation production. MA/PgDip photography. MSc/PgDip/PGCert multimedia comms engineering • HND music tech. BA/BSc (Hons) music, tech and innovation (BA for creative musicians working with technology; BSc for sound technologists with a musical leaning). BSc (Hons) audio and recording tech; radio production

Derby, University of
School of Arts, Design & Technology, Kedleston Road
Derby DE22 1GB
01332 622222
admissions@derby.ac.uk
www.derby.ac.uk
• BA media; popular culture and media (with options) • BA journalism (with options)*; creative writing (single and with options); media writing (with options) • Fdg/BA (top-up) video and photography; video production. BA broadcast media (options); film and TV (single and with options); film and video; film • BA/PgCert/PgDip/MA marketing management. Cert/Dip/PgDip marketing (CIM) • Fdg new media design and production*. BSc computer games programming; design tech; multimedia tech and music production. BA design for digital media (top-up); illustration for animation
• BSc multimedia tech and music production; music tech and audio system design; sound, light and live event tech. BA pop with music tech. PgDip acoustics and noise control. MSc applied acoustics; digital audio systems

Doncaster College
Waterdale, Doncaster DN1 3EX
01302 553553
infocentre@don.ac.uk
www.don.ac.uk
• BA (Hons) scriptwriting • Cert/Dip/PgDip marketing (CIM). MA marketing management • HNC multimedia. Fdg animation and games art. BA (Hons) theatre or dance practice with digital performance. MA digital performance • NCFE InterCert music tech (mix DJ skills); introduction to sound recording. Fdg applied digital media; live performance tech. BA (Hons) music tech (top-up); music (top-up); applied new music; creative music tech

Dublin Institute of Technology
Fitzwilliam House, 30 Upper Pembroke Street, Dublin 2
00 353 1 402 3000
school of media: 00 353 1 402 3098
www.dit.ie
• BA media arts. MA media • BA (Hons) journalism with a language. MA journalism • MA PR • BA (Hons) photography. MA digital media tech
• FCert music. BMus (Hons). MMus performance

Dundee, University of
Nethergate, Dundee DD1 4HN
01382 344000
srs@dundee.ac.uk
www.dundee.ac.uk and www.imaging.dundee.ac.uk
• BA (Hons) animation and electronic media; time-based art; illustration. MSc animation and visualisation; electronic imaging

Durham University
University Office, Old Elvet, Durham DH1 3HP
0191 334 6128
admissions@durham.ac.uk
www.dur.ac.uk
• BA (Hons) music; education studies with music

subject to validation

Ealing, Hammersmith and West London College
Gliddon Road, Barons Court, London W14 9BL
0800 980 2175
Marketing@wlc.ac.uk
www.wlc.ac.uk
• BTEC FirstDip/NatDip media • BTEC NatDip/HND interactive media.
BTEC Dip design. BTEC NatDip graphic design; multimedia; graphics.
Fdg digital animation. Short courses in web page creation and design
• BTEC NatAward/NatDip music tech. BTEC Dip performing arts (music).
BTEC NatDip music practice

East Anglia, University of
Norwich, Norfolk NR4 7TJ
01603 456161
admissions@uea.ac.uk
www.uea.ac.uk
• BA politics with media; society, culture and media. MA economics and
the mass media • BA English literature with creative writing. MA creative
writing • BA film with American studies, English studies, TV. MA film;
film with archiving; studies in fiction • MA culture and communication
• BA music; music with computing; music with mathematics. MMus
music performance studies

East London, University of
Docklands Campus, University Way, London E16 2RD
020 8223 3000
admiss@uel.ac.uk
www.uel.ac.uk
• BA (Hons) media and creative industries; media. MA media; global media
• BA (Hons) creative writing*; journalism • BA (Hons) film and video: theory
and practice/ film history. MA screening history; independent film, video
and new screen media • BA (Hons) media and advertising; communication
studies •BA (Hons) photographic and print media. MA consumer and
promotional culture • HND multimedia tech. BA (Hons) digital arts;
interactive media. BSc (Hons) multimedia; multimedia tech. MA interactive
media practice; cybernetic culture • BA (Hons) music culture: theory and
production. MA sonic culture

East Surrey College
Reigate School of Art Design and Media, Gatton Point
Claremont Road, Redhill, Surrey RH1 2JX
01737 772611
studentservices@esc.ac.uk
www.esc.ac.uk
• FDip art, design and media • HNC/HND 3D media crafts and sculpture;
moving image production. InterDip media: audio, video and photography.
NatDip media (moving image) • InterDip multimedia. NatDip e-media;
photography. HNC/Dip digital photography • NatDip media (audio)

Edge Hill College of Higher Education
St Helen's Road, Ormskirk, Lancashire L39 4QP
01695 584274
enquiries@edgehill.ac.uk
www.edgehill.ac.uk
• BA (Hons) media • BA (Hons) journalism (NCTJ). BSc (Hons) creative
writing. PgDip print journalism • BA (Hons) media (film and TV); film; film
with film and TV production. PgDip broadcast journalism • BA (Hons) media
(advertising); PR • BA (Hons) media (digital media design); animation

Edinburgh College of Art
Lauriston Place, Edinburgh EH3 9DF
0131 221 6000
registry@eca.ac.uk
www.eca.ac.uk
• BA (Hons)/MDes/Dip visual communication – animation; film and TV,
graphic design; illustration; photography

Edinburgh, University of
57 George Square, Edinburgh EH8 9JU
0131 650 4360
sra.enquiries@ed.ac.uk
www.ed.ac.uk
• MSc English literature: creative writing; nation, writing, culture; writing
and cultural politics • MSc film • MSc sound design; design and digital
media • MA (Hons) (undergrad) music; music tech. MSc (postgrad)
research music. Dip music therapy (Nordoff–Robbins). MMus
composition; keyboard performance studies; musicology; organology

Editorial Centre
Hanover House, Marine Court, St Leonards-on-Sea
East Sussex TN38 0DX
01424 435991
enquiries@editorial-centre.co.uk
www.editorial-centre.co.uk
• NatDip journalism (15-week pre-entry newspaper journalism,
Newspaper Qualifications Council). Dip journalism (overseas);
subediting; press photography. Short courses inc reporting, writing,
features, subediting, desk editing, editing, design, law, government,
FoI, photography, pictures, publishing business, marketing, Quark,
InDesign, PhotoShop, etc • Short courses in video camera and editing,
presenting for TV and multimedia, reporting for TV and multimedia,
editing for TV and multimedia, radio • Short course in multimedia
basics, designing for the web, editorial staff and the web

Editorial Training Consultants
13 Petworth Road, Haslemere, Surrey GU27 2JB
01428 644123
info@etc-online.co.uk
www.etc-online.co.uk
• Short tailored courses for businesses. Law: IP inc copyright,
defamation update, IP update. Journalism: interviewing, style, styles
of writing, subbing, research, etc. Broadcast media training; faster,
funnier comic writing. PR: presentation, campaigns, creative thinking,
messaging and positioning, account management, exhibitions, the
sales cycle, management, writing, media training etc. Publishing:
editorial management and craft skills. • New media: online writing
and research; improving site traffic

Essex, University of
Wivenhoe Park, Colchester CO4 3SQ
01206 873333
admit@essex.ac.uk
www.essex.ac.uk
• BA journalism (South East Essex College) • BA film and literature/
history of art; history with film; American studies with film; TV production
and screen theory* (at South East Essex College). MACert film; film
and literature • BSc multimedia production and internet tech (taught in
conjunction with South East Essex College) • BA music production
(South East Essex College)

Exeter, University of
The Queen's Drive, Exeter, Devon EX4 4QJ
01392 661000
www.ex.ac.uk
• BA English, also with film. MA English studies, also with creative writing,
critical theory or film • MA/PhD creative writing • BA film (cinema and
practice)/ film with a modern language; MA film; PhD film by practice

University College Falmouth
Woodlane Campus, Falmouth, Cornwall TR11 4RH
01326 211077
admissions@falmouth.ac.uk
www.falmouth.ac.uk
• BA (Hons) English with media • BA (Hons) English with creative writing;
journalism. PgDip/MA professional writing. MA international journalism*
• BA (Hons) film; broadcasting. PgDip/MA broadcast journalism (BJTC)
(MA options in arts, media, travel/investigative/science/sports journalism;
TV production • PgDip creative advertising • MA illustration: authorial
practice • BA (Hons) graphic design. BA (Hons)/MA photography.
MA interactive art and design

subject to validation

Glamorgan, University of

Pontypridd, Wales CF37 1DL
0800 716925
enquiries@glam.ac.uk
www.glam.ac.uk

• BA (Hons) English, also with media; drama (theatre and media); media and communication studies; media, with options • BA (Hons) creative and professional writing; journalism. MPhil writing • BSc (Hons) digital media and broadcasting tech; lighting tech; live event tech. BA (Hons) film and TV set design; film (joint); film, radio and TV; media production (with options); media production (radio). MPhil/PhD film practice. MSc film producing and business management*. MA scriptwriting (theatre, film, TV and radio) • BA (Hons)/Fdg/MSc/PgD/PgC/CIM Dip marketing. BSC (Hons) media production with marketing • FCert media and information tech. HND/Fdg media tech. BSc (Hons) interactive new media tech; media tech (also as BSc); multimedia; multimedia tech. BA (Hons) media production (photography) • HND/Fdg/BSc/BSc (Hons) music tech; sound tech. BA (Hons) pop. MSc advanced music production; music engineering and production

Glasgow Caledonian University

70 Cowcaddens Road, Glasgow G4 0BA
0141 331 3000
enquiries@gcal.ac.uk
www.gcal.ac.uk

• BA/BA (Hons) journalism (NCTJ). PGDip journalism studies (NCTJ) • BA (Hons) marketing • Dip multimedia visualisation with product design. BSc multimedia tech. MA digital media design • BSc/BSc (Hons) audio tech with electronics; multimedia

Glasgow Metropolitan College

60 North Hanover Street, Glasgow G1 2BP
0141 566 6226
enquiries@glasgowmet.ac.uk
www.glasgowmet.ac.uk

• HNC/HND journalism: broadcast and print • HNC/HND TV operations and production • HNC/HND event management • HNC/HND digital media for publishing and print; publishing. HNC electronic publishing for print media; print media management • HNC/HND interactive multimedia creation; graphic design; visual information: design and illustration. HND professional photography and digital imaging. AdvDip illustrative photography

Glasgow School of Art

167 Renfrew Street, Glasgow G3 6RQ
0141 353 4500
i.johnston@gsa.ac.uk
www.gsa.ac.uk

• MPhil 2D/3D motion graphics

Glasgow, University of

Glasgow G12 8QQ
0141 330 2000
admissions@gla.ac.uk
www.gla.ac.uk

• MA (Hons) creative and cultural studies (undergraduate) • MA (Hons) theatre; film and TV (undergrad). MLitt theatre; film and TV • MA (Hons) arts and media informatics (undergrad) • BMus/MA (Hons) music

Gloucestershire, University of

The Park, Cheltenham GL50 2RH
01242 532700
admissions@glos.ac.uk
www.glos.ac.uk

• BA (Hons) journalism and professional writing; creative writing • BA (Hons) broadcast journalism; film; media comms • BA (Hons) advertising; PR; multimedia marketing • BA (Hons) publishing • BA (Hons) multimedia; design for interactive media; fine art – digital media

Goldsmiths College

Dept of Media and Communications, University of London
New Cross, London SE14 6NW
020 7919 7171
media-comms@gold.ac.uk
www.goldsmiths.ac.uk

• BA media and anthropology/sociology/modern literature/comms; international media; transnational comms and global media. MPhil/PhD/MRes/FCert/BA media and comms. Practice courses in journalism, radio, TV, film, photography, animation, writing and illustration available on most of above • MA journalism (accredited by PTC and recognised by NUJ) • MA feature film; filmmaking; TV journalism; radio (BJTC); screen documentary; scriptwriting • MA digital media: tech and cultural form; image and communication (photography or electronic graphics); interactive media: critical theory and practice • BMus music; music (extension degree); pop studies. PgCert music. MMus composition; contemporary music studies; ethnomusicology; historical musicology; music theory and analysis; performance and related studies; Russian music studies. MPhil/PhD music. Dip jazz and pop. PgDip music teaching to adults. Cert music studies; music workshop skills. FCert integrated degree in music

Greenwich, University of

Old Royal Naval College, Park Row, Greenwich
London SE10 9LS
020 8331 8000
courseinfo@greenwich.ac.uk
www.gre.ac.uk

• BA (Hons) creative industries; media, culture and comms; media and comms • HND professional writing. BA creative writing (options). BA (Hons) media writing (options) • HND TV production tech. BA film (with options) • BA(Hons) international marketing; marketing (options); marketing comms. MA professional services marketing*; sports marketing*; strategic marketing (also executive track); strategic marketing comms • HNC/HND/BA (Hons) graphic and digital design. HND photography. Fdg creative industries (multimedia; image-based media)*. BA (Hons) photography*; 3D digital design and animation. BSc (Hons) multimedia and internet tech; multimedia tech (options); entertainment tech; interactive multimedia games development. BEng (Hons) games and entertainment systems. MA critical studies, new media and practising arts; website architecture. MSc games and entertainment systems software engineering; multimedia and internet tech • Fdg creative industries (music production)

Grimsby Institute of Further & Higher Education

Nuns Corner, Grimsby DN34 5BQ
01472 311222
infocent@grimsby.ac.uk
www.grimsby.ac.uk

• Dip media; bespoke media law training • NatDip media (journalism and publishing). OCN novel/short story writing. BA (Hons) professional writing; digital media production – journalism (both with Lancaster University) • HND media production; media (TV, film and video). NatDip media (moving image). Fdg digital media (broadcast). BA (Hons) digital media production – TV, film, video (with Lancaster University). OCN intro to script writing. ProfCert video journalism; digital video editing • Fdg media and marketing • BTEC NatDip e-media; games media development. HNC photography and digital imaging. HNC/HND interactive media. HND multimedia. BA (Hons) digital media production – photography; multimedia (with Lancaster University) • ProfCert digital audio editing. HND music production. Dip performing arts (music). NatDip music tech. BA (Hons) creative music* (University of Hull)

Guildford College

Stoke Park, Guildford, Surrey GU1 1EZ
01483 448500
info@guildford.ac.uk
www.guildford.ac.uk

• NatCert media • NatDip media (moving image). HND/ BA (Hons) media production. • IntroCert/ ProfCert/Dip/PgDip marketing (CIM) • SROCN level 2 and 3/NatDip photography. Short courses in PhotoShop and Quark Xpress on the Mac • NatCert level 3 music tech. Dip contemporary pop; music production. NatDip pop academy – music practice (vocals)

* subject to validation

Harlow College
Velizy Avenue, Town Centre, Harlow, Essex CM20 3LH
01279 868000
full-time@harlow-college.ac.uk
www.harlow-college.ac.uk
• One-year journalism: newspapers (NCTJ). BA (Hons) journalism
(Middlesex University). Pg journalism: newspapers (NCTJ); magazines
(NCTJ, PTC) • NatDip graphic design. Short courses: Apple Mac
workshop, webpage design, digital photography, advanced digital
photography • NatDip pop. Short course in music tech

Harrow College
Brookshill, Harrow Weald, Middlesex HA3 6RR
020 8909 6000
enquiries@harrow.ac.uk
www.harrow.ac.uk
• BTEC NatCert/NatDip media • Short courses: journalism, journalism
intensive (NCTJ), creative writing • Short courses in film, intro to video
production and editing for beginners, cinematography theory and
practice • Short courses TV presenting, speaking with confidence
 • Short courses in digital video editing for beginners, using digital
photography (PhotoShop), web design using Dreamweaver/Front Page,
animation (Flash) • Short courses: intro to Cubase (music tech), guitar,
music theory beginner to grade 5, piano keyboard, singing and vocal
workout

Henley College Coventry
Henley Road, Bell Green, Coventry CV2 1ED
024 7662 6300
info@henley-cov.ac.uk
www.henley-cov.ac.uk
• BTEC Dip media • BTEC NatDip media – moving image • BTEC NatDip
media – games development; e-media; photography; C&G Level 1
and 2 – photography

Hertfordshire, University of
College Lane, Hatfield AL10 9AB
01707 284000
admissions@herts.ac.uk
www.herts.ac.uk
• BA (Hons) English lang and communication • BA (Hons) English,
available with creative writing or journalism • BSc (Hons) media tech
and digital broadcast • BA (Hons) marketing. BA/Fdg ad and marketing
comms • BA (Hons) English language and communication or English lit
with digital publishing. BA (Hons) digital animation; lens media; model
design and special effects. BA/BSc (Hons) software systems for the
arts and media. BSc (Hons) digital tech; internet tech and e-commerce
 • BSc (Hons) music composition and tech; music; commercial
composition and tech; music tech; sound design tech

Highbury College, Portsmouth
Dept of Media and Journalism, Dovercourt Road
Portsmouth, Hampshire PO6 2SA
023 9238 3131
info@highbury.ac.uk
www.highbury.ac.uk
• BTEC Dip art, design and media; media • Pre-entry newspaper
journalism (NCTJ); magazine journalism (PTC). HND media (journalism).
Short course introduction to newspaper and magazine journalism
• Pre-entry broadcast journalism (BJTC). BTEC NatDip media production
(moving image). HND media (moving image). C&G 7500 TV production.
Short course intro to digital video editing • Short course comms,
advertising and marketing • BTEC NatDip media production (publishing)
• BTEC NatDip multimedia; media production (games design). Short
courses: practical photography skills, using your digital camera,
multimedia design • BTEC NatDip music tech

Hopwood Hall College
St Mary's Gate, Rochdale OL12 6RY
01706 345346
enquiries@hopwood.ac.uk
www.hopwood.ac.uk
• BTEC FirstDip media • BTEC NatDip media (moving image)

Huddersfield, University of
Queensgate, Huddersfield HD1 3DH
01484 422288
admissions@hud.ac.uk
www.hud.ac.uk
• BA (Hons) English (with media, creative writing, journalism); media
and sports journalism; drama and media • BA (Hons) media and print
journalism • BA (Hons) media and TV production • BA (Hons)
advertising with media and design management; creative imaging
(advertising); marketing with innovation; PR with media; PR with media
and design management • HNC/HND multimedia. BA/BSc (Hons) virtual
reality design; interaction design for media tech; multimedia design.
BA (Hons) creative imaging (graphic design/illustration/media and
animation); interactive multimedia; multimedia with installation art;
multimedia (options); video, 3D and popular music; video and 3D for
popular music; virtual reality design with animation. BSc (Hons)/BSc
multimedia computing. BSc (Hons) multimedia computing/tech.
MA creative imaging. MSc electronic and computer based systems
design. MA/MSc innovation for the digital future; interactive multimedia
production. PgCert/PgDip/MSc multimedia and e-learning
• BMus (Hons) music; creative music tech. BA (Hons) drama with music;
music tech; music tech and pop; music with a modern language; music
with English; pop production; media and radio journalism. BSc (Hons)
music tech software development; music tech and audio systems;
pop production. PgDip/MA music (single and joint); music (composition;
electro-acoustic composition; performance; performance;
contemporary music studies; historical musicology). MA music
(musicology)

Hull, University of
Cottingham Road, Hull HU6 7RX
01482 346311
admissions@hull.ac.uk
www.hull.ac.uk
• BA culture, media and society • BA creative writing (options).
Cert creative writing • BA film (with options). MA contemporary literature
and film • BA PR with business/management/marketing; marketing
(options); advertising with management/marketing • BA creative music
tech with digital arts; design for digital media; digital arts. BSc creative
media computing. BSc internal computing with creative media; creative
music tech. BSc computer science with games development.
MSc internet computing; games programming; website design and
development • BA music; creative music tech (single or with digital
arts); drama and music; English and music; music and modern
languages. BSc music tech and computing. BMus music. MMus music
(musicology, composition, performance). MRes creative music tech.
MPhil/PhD music; creative music tech

Journalism Training Centre
29 Harley Street, London W1G 9QR
0845 612 5712
info@jtc.co.uk
www.jtc.co.uk
• Dip periodicals journalism (NUJ). Short courses: subediting, feature
writing, media law

Keele, University of
Keele, Staffordshire ST5 5BG
01782 621111
www.keele.ac.uk
• BA/BSc media, comms and culture • BA/BSc music (options); music
tech (options)

subject to validation

Kensington and Chelsea College

Wornington Centre, Wornington Road, London W10 5QQ
020 7573 5333
enquiries@kcc.ac.uk
www.kcc.ac.uk
• BTEC NatCert/HNC multimedia; graphic design. BTEC interactive use of media (level 2, 3); 3D computer modelling and animation using Lightwave 3D (level 3); video and DVD production (Level 2); graphics (level 2). LOCN web page design Flash, Dreamweaver, Fireworks; e-commerce and business websites with Dreamweaver, PHP and Apache • BTEC FirstDip performing musician* (in partnership with Access to Music). C&G 8008 sound engineering*; creative music producer. LOCN music tech. Music tech with Deep Recording Studios. LOCN studio programming level 1, 2 and 3. C&G sound engineering Level 3

Kent Institute of Art and Design

Oakwood Park, Maidstone, Kent ME16 8AG
01622 620000
info@kiad.ac.uk
www.kiad.ac.uk
• BA (Hons) video media arts; video and photography. MA artists' film, video and photography • BA (Hons) design, branding and marketing; fashion promotion. • BA (Hons) illustration • BTEC NatDip multimedia. Fdg graphic media. BA (Hons) animation; digital 3D design; graphic design; photography; photography and media arts. PgCert contemporary photographic practice; graphic design. MA graphic design; photography

Kent, University of

The Registry, Canterbury, Kent CT2 7NZ
01227 764000
recruitment@kent.ac.uk
www.kent.ac.uk
• BA (Hons) English and American literature and creative writing
• BA (Hons) American studies (art and film); European arts (film); film; film and contemporary arts; visual and performed arts. MA/MPhil/PhD film
• BA (Hons) marketing; business administration (marketing) • BA (Hons) multimedia tech and design. MRes/MPhil/PhD cartoons and caricature. MSc computer animation • BA (Hons) music tech

King's College London

School of Humanities, Strand, London WC2R 2LS
020 7836 5454; enquiries: 020 7848 2929
ceu@kcl.ac.uk
www.kcl.ac.uk
• MA cultural and creative industries • BA English with film; film and American studies; other BA honours programmes with film. MA contemporary cinema cultures. MPhil/PhD opportunities in film
• MA digital culture and tech. MSc information tech and internet law
• BMus music; BA German and music; music with applied computing. Cert advanced musical studies. MMus music. MPhil/PhD opportunities in music

Kingston University

River House, 53–57 High Street, Kingston-upon-Thames Surrey KT1 1LQ
020 8547 2000
admissions-info@kingston.ac.uk
www.kingston.ac.uk
• BA (Hons) visual and material culture; media and cultural studies. BSc (Hons) media tech. MA English: media of the contemporary city
• BA (Hons) creative writing (joint); journalism. MA creative writing
• BA (Hons) history of art, design and film/TV; TV design and production; film. MA production design/screem design for film and TV; contemporary developments in film • Fdg graphic comms. Dip marketing (CIM). MA communication design; marketing; strategic marketing management; political communication, campaigning and advocacy • BA (Hons) graphic design. BA (Hons)/MA illustration and animation • BA (Hons) live arts. BMus (Hons) music. MA composing for film and TV; creative music tech; ethnomusicology; music; music composition; music education; musicology; music performance; pop

Lambeth College

45 Clapham Common South Side, London SW4 9BL
020 7501 5000
courses@lambethcollege.ac.uk
www.lambethcollege.ac.uk
• BTEC FirstDip media • Fdg journalism (London Metropolitan University). Pre-entry newspaper journalism (NCTJ) • BTEC NatDip media (moving image). BTEC NatAward radio. C&G Cert video production techniques.
• LOCN video, photography and digital publishing; web design and animation. C&G Dip/AdvDip web design. BTEC NatAward interactive use of media. BTEC FirstDip multimedia and photography. BTEC NatDip web design and animation (e-media)

Lancaster University

Bailrigg, Lancaster LA1 4YW
01524 65201
ugadmissions@lancaster.ac.uk
www.lancs.ac.uk
• BA (Hons) creative arts; English language and the media; media and cultural studies. MA globalisation and the information age; visual culture
• BA (Hons) English language or literature with creative writing. MA creative writing; women's writing • BA (Hons) film and cultural studies; film and philosophy; sociology. PgDip/MSc media production and distribution • BA (Hons) advertising and marketing. BSc (Hons) marketing; marketing management. MSc advanced marketing management • BSc (Hons) computer science with multimedia systems. BSc (Hons)/MSc communication and computer systems. PgDip/MA/MRes IT, management and organisational change. MSc mobile and ubiquitous computing; multimedia networking. PgDip/MSc mobile game design and m-commerce systems*; multimedia courseware engineering • BA (Hons)/BSc (Hons) computer science and music. BA (Hons) music tech; musicology. BA (Hons)/BMus (Hons) music. MMus music; music theory

Leeds College of Art and Design

Blenheim Walk, Leeds, West Yorkshire LS2 9AQ
0113 202 8000
info@leeds-art.ac.uk
www.leeds-art.ac.uk
• Fdg advertising. BA (Hons) visual comms • BTEC HND multimedia/ photography

Leeds College of Music

3 Quarry Hill, Leeds LS2 7PD
0113 222 3400
enquiries@lcm.ac.uk
www.lcm.ac.uk
• Fdg sound design for film and TV • BA (Hons) jazz studies; music studies; pop studies; music production. MMus jazz studies; music studies. PgCert advanced piano performance

Leeds Metropolitan University

Civic Quarter, Leeds LS1 3HE
0113 283 2600
course-enquiries@leedsmet.ac.uk
www.leedsmet.ac.uk
• BA (Hons) media and popular culture • CertHE/Fdg film and TV production. HND moving image production. BA (Hons) film and moving image production (level 3 top-up). PgCert/PgDip/MA screenwriting (fiction) (Skillset) • HND business and PR; consumer marketing. BA (Hons) PR; PR with a European language; consumer marketing; marketing. BA/BA (Hons) managing cultural and major events. BSc (Hons) marketing media and systems. MA PR management; PR. MSc marketing • Fdg creative tech. HND/BSc (Hons) games design; multimedia tech. BSc (Hons) animation tech and special effects. BA (Hons) web media management. BA/BSc (Hons) education and new media. MSc creative tech; digital imaging tech; web engineering
• BSc (Hons) creative music and sound tech; design tech for music; music tech; music and new media tech. MSc music tech

Leeds Trinity & All Saints

Brownberrie Lane, Horsforth, Leeds LS18 5HD
0113 283 7123
admissions@tasc.ac.uk
www.tasc.ac.uk
• BA English, also with film, media and other options. BA media; media and marketing. Cert media education • BA sports journalism. PgDip/MA bi-media (radio and TV); radio or print journalism (NCTJ) • BA film • PgDip/MA public communication. BA marketing (options)

Leeds, University of

Leeds LS2 9JT
0113 243 1751
enquiry@leeds.ac.uk
www.leeds.ac.uk
• BA creative writing. MA international journalism: production and consumption. PgDip/MA creative writing • BA broadcasting; broadcast journalism; cinema, photography and TV. MA scriptwriting for TV • BA comms. MA comms studies; international comms; media management; political communication • BA new media • BA/BMus music. BA/BSc music, multimedia and electronics. BA popular and world musics; music – philosophy; music – theology and religious studies. MMus music (composition; musicology; performance; pop studies and ethnomusicology; tech and computer music). MA music and education*. PgCert/PgDip/MA music and liturgy

Leicester, University of

University Road, Leicester LE1 7RH
0116 252 2522
admissions@le.ac.uk
www.le.ac.uk
• BA film and the visual arts. MA humanities and film • BSc comms, media and society. MA/PgDip mass comms; globalisation and comms; media and communication research

Lincoln, University of

Brayford Pool, Lincoln LN6 7TS
01522 882000
enquiries@lincoln.ac.uk
www.lincoln.ac.uk
Some courses held at Hull School of Art & Design • BA (Hons) media, culture and comms. MA/MRes/MPhil/PhD media and cultural studies • BA/PgDip/MA journalism • BA (Hons) contemporary lens media; digital and interactive TV; TV and film. BA (Hons)/MA media production. MA documentary and factual programme production • BA (Hons) advertising and art direction; marketing. MSc international marketing strategy. MBA strategic marketing • BA (Hons) animation; games design; interactive and screen-based graphics; interactive multimedia; web design. BSc (Hons) media tech; multimedia tech. BSc (Hons)/MSc games computing • BSc audio tech

Liverpool Community College

Broad Green Road, Old Swan, Liverpool L13 5SQ
0151 252 1515
www.liv-coll.ac.uk
• BTEC FirstDip/HND/Fdg media • Pre-entry journalism (NCTJ). Dip print/periodical journalism (fast-track, NCTJ) • FDip broadcast journalism (BJTC provisional). BTEC NatDip media (moving image) • BTEC NatDip multimedia; photography • BTEC FirstDip/NatAward/NatDip music tech. Cert/Dip video and audio production. ProfDip creative music tech. HND music production

Liverpool Hope University College

Hope Park, Liverpool L16 9JD
0151 291 3000
admission@hope.ac.uk
www.hope.ac.uk
• BA creative and performing arts; media (single and joint) • BA film (joint) • BA marketing (joint) • BA/BSc gaming tech (joint); multimedia tech (joint) • BA music (joint); music, pop, music tech. MA music

Liverpool John Moores University

Roscoe Court, 4 Rodney Street, Liverpool L1 2TZ
0151 231 5090
recruitment@ljmu.ac.uk
www.ljmu.ac.uk
• BA (Hons) media and cultural studies; media, cultural studies and marketing • BA (Hons) journalism (NCTJ); international journalism (NCTJ); imaginative writing. MA journalism; international journalism; writing • BA (Hons) media professional studies; screen studies. MA screen writing • BA (Hons) business and PR; marketing; business and information. BSc (Hons) e-business communication • PgDip/MA information and library management • BA (Hons) English literature and electronic creative tech • BA (Hons) pop studies

Liverpool, University of

Liverpool L69 3BX
0151 794 2000
uksro@liv.ac.uk
www.liv.ac.uk
• BA (Hons) English and communication studies (joint) • BA (Hons) film (European) and a modern language • BA (Hons) communication and business studies (joint); politics and communication studies; marketing. MA politics and the mass media • BSc (Hons) computer and multimedia systems; design and tech with multimedia. BEng (Hons)/MEng (Hons) wireless comms and 3G tech. MSc internet computing • BA (Hons) communication, media and pop (joint). BA (Hons) music/pop. MA music industry studies; pop studies. MMus music

London Business School

Regent's Park, London NW1 4SA
020 7262 5050
www.london.edu
• MBA marketing strategy (full-time executive MBA)

London College of Communication

Elephant & Castle, London SE1 6SB
020 7514 6569
info@lcc.arts.ac.uk
www.lcc.arts.ac.uk
• Fdg media practice. BA media and cultural studies • Fdg/BA/PgDip/MA journalism. GradCert periodical journalism • BA film and video. MA screenwriting; documentary research. PgDip broadcast journalism and documentary photography • Fdg/BA marketing and advertising. BA/MA PR. MA marketing and comms; media management • Dip print production. Fdg cross-media publishing. BA print media, marketing and advertising. GradCert bookbinding and restoration/publishing. Postgraduate programme in publishing/publishing production • Dip animation; pro photography practice; digital design; 3D modelling and animation; new media publishing. NatDip/BA graphic and media design. Fdg studies in art and design; digital media production; interactive games production; photojournalism; design for graphic communication; display design. GradCert photography practice; design for visual communication. BA digital media production; photography. MA/PgDip interactive media. MSc digital colour imaging. MA digital media and print; photography; graphic design. Short courses: digital orientation/media • Dip sound design and music tech. BA sound arts and design. GradCert sonic arts; music publishing

London College of Fashion

20 John Prince's Street, London W1G 0BJ
020 7514 7344
enquiries@fashion.arts.ac.uk
www.fashion.arts.ac.uk
• PgCert fashion and lifestyle journalism. MA fashion journalism • BA costume; make-up and prosthetics; technical effects. MA costume design • Fdg fashion marketing and promotion (also online); fashion design and marketing. GradCert fashion marketing. BA fashion promotion. MA strategic fashion marketing • Fdg fashion styling and photography. BA fashion design tech: illustration; fashion photography. MA fashion photography; digital fashion

London College of Music & Media

see Thames Valley University

subject to validation

375

London Film School
24 Shelton Street, London WC2H 9UB
020 7836 9642
info@lfs.org.uk
www.lfs.org.uk
• MA filmmaking; screenwriting

London Metropolitan University
31 Jewry Street, London EC3N 2EY
020 7320 1616
admissions@londonmet.ac.uk
www.londonmet.ac.uk
• BA (Hons) media* • BA (Hons) creative writing. Fdg/BA (Hons) journalism. MA professional writing • Fdg audio production for broadcast media. BA (Hons) film; film and broadcast production. PgCert/PgDip/MA screenwriting. MA AV production; filmmaking • BA (Hons) ad and marketing communication*; arts management (joint); comms and visual culture; events management and music and media management; marketing; PR. HND/BA (Hons) events management. BSc mass comms. ProfCert/ProfDip/PgDip marketing (CIM). Dip PR (CIPR). AdvCert/HDip marketing comms (Communication Advertising and Marketing Foundation). MA international marketing comms; marketing; mass comms; sport management • Fdg/ BSc (Hons) multimedia. BSc (Hons) digital media; computer animation; computer visualisation and games; digital media and mass comms/multimedia tech and apps; multimedia tech and apps. MA digital entertainment/media/media management/ moving image. MSc multimedia systems • Fdg musical instruments. Fdg*/BA (Hons) music and media management. BSc (Hons) music tech (audio systems). BA (Hons) music education; sound and media*; sound, music and culture. BA/BSc (Hons) music tech (musical instruments). Cert sound recording tech, sound studios and recording

London School of Economics and Political Science
Houghton Street, London WC2A 2AE
020 7405 7686
stu.rec@lse.ac.uk
www.lse.ac.uk
• MSc gender and media • MSc global media and comms; media and comms; media and comms regulation and policy; politics and communication; social and public communication • MSc new media, information and society

London School of Journalism
126 Shirland Road, Maida Vale, London W9 2BT
020 7289 7777
info@lsjournalism.com
www.lsj.org
• PgDip journalism (also online) (NUJ). Short and distance courses inc news/feature/online/freelance journalism, subediting, novel/short story writing, writing for children, law etc

London South Bank University
103 Borough Road, London SE1 0AA
020 7928 8989
enquiries@lsbu.ac.uk
www.lsbu.ac.uk
• BA (Hons) English/ media; BSc (Hons) media and society; MA creative media arts (cultural and media; digital film production; media education; media writing; new media) • BA (Hons) creative writing and English • BA (Hons) digital video production; film (joint) • BA (Hons) arts management; marketing. MSc/PgDip international marketing. ProfDip/ CPD marketing (CIM). E-marketing award (CIM) • HND/BSc (Hons) multimedia computing*. BA (Hons) digital photography/media arts; game cultures. BSc (Hons) special effects. MSc/PgDip/PgCert internet and multimedia information systems/engineering • BA (Hons) sonic media

University College London
Gower Street, London WC1E 6BT
020 7679 2000
www.ucl.ac.uk
• BA film studies Russian/French. MA film studies • MA library and information studies. PgCert/PgDip/MA electronic communication and publishing

Luton, University of
Park Square, Luton, Beds LU1 3JU
01582 734111
enquiries@luton.ac.uk
www.luton.ac.uk
• MA media, culture and tech. MRes media arts • Fdg creative writing. BA (Hons) creative writing; journalism; journalism and public relations. MRes creative writing • Fdg media production (Barnfield/Bedford/ Dunstable/Milton Keynes). BA (Hons) media performance; TV production. MA international cinema; media production (documentary) • Fdg ad and marketing comms. BA (Hons) ad and marketing comms; marketing; marketing and media practices; PR; media advertising; media practices (mass comms). MSc marketing and business management; marketing comms. MA media arts (mass comms) • Fdg creative and editorial photography (Dunstable College); digital imaging and design for media (Milton Keynes College); media art and design. BA (Hons) digital photography and video art; animation. BSc (Hons) computer games development. MA art design and internet tech; new media and internet tech. MSc computer animation • Fdg music tech (Bedford). BA (Hons) music tech

Manchester, University of
Oxford Road, Manchester M13 9PL
0161 306 6000
www.manchester.ac.uk
• BA (Hons) media, culture and society • MA/PhD creative writing • BA (Hons) film with options • BMus (Hons) music. BA (Hons) music and drama. MMus musicology; composition; electroacoustic music composition. MPhil/PhD musicology; composition

Manchester Metropolitan University
All Saints Building, All Saints, Manchester M15 6BH
0161 247 2000
enquiries@mmu.ac.uk
www.mmu.ac.uk
• MA media arts; representation in cinema and media; design and art direction • BA (Hons) English and creative writing • BA (Hons) English and film; contemporary film and video; film and media • BA (Hons) ad and brand management; communication; corporate communication; communication in culture and media; human communication • Fdg new media design. BSc (Hons) multimedia tech; media tech; multimedia computing. BA (Hons) photography; interactive arts. PgCert/PgDip/MSc computing. MSc multimedia systems; internet computing

Marjon, College of St Mark & St John
Derriford Road, Plymouth, Devon PL6 8BH
01752 636700
admissions@marjon.ac.uk
www.marjon.ac.uk
• BA (Hons) media • BA (Hons) writing for the media; creative writing • BA (Hons) creative media practice • BA (Hons) PR

Mid-Cheshire College
Hartford Campus, Chester Road, Northwich
Cheshire CW8 1LJ
01606 74444
info@midchesh.ac.uk
www.midchesh.ac.uk
• HND multimedia; BTEC NatDip multimedia; photography. Fdg new and interactive media. OCN digital photography and image manipulation; photography level 1 and 2 • BTEC NatDip music practice; music tech

Middlesex University
Admissions Enquiries, North London Business Park
London N11 1QS
020 8411 5555
admissions@mdx.ac.uk
www.mdx.ac.uk
• BA (Hons) media and cultural studies • BA (Hons) creative and media
writing; journalism and communication studies; journalism. MA writing
(prose fiction, poetry or scriptwriting) • BA digital film arts/ filmmaking.
BA (Hons) film studies; film video interactive arts; TV production.
MA video and video doc; film and visual cultures • MA media and
comms management. BA marketing • BA (Hons) publishing and media
• HND/HNC multimedia; graphic design. DipHE visual communication
design – graphic design. Fdg graphic design. BA (Hons) graphic/games
design; illustration; multimedia arts; photography. MA/MSc design for
interactive media. MA electronic arts; graphic design • BA (Hons) music;
music and the community; music and arts management; recording arts.
BA/BSc (Hons)/MA sonic arts. MA music; music education

Mid-Kent College
Horsted Centre, Maidstone Road, Chatham, Kent ME5 9UQ
01634 402020
www.midkent.ac.uk
• BTEC IntroDip art, design and media • BTEC NatDip media (moving
image) • BTEC NatDip media (publishing) • BTEC FirstDip pop. BTEC
NatDip music tech. NatDip music practice. BTEC NatAward music tech
(DJ tech)

Napier University
Craiglockhart Campus, Edinburgh EH14 1DJ
0500 353570
info@napier.ac.uk
www.napier.ac.uk
• BA/BA (Hons) culture, media and society • BA/BA (Hons) journalism.
MSc/PgDip international English-language journalism; journalism
• MA screen project development; screenwriting • BA (Hons)
communication; marketing management. MSc/PgDip creative
advertising; international communication; marketing • BA/BA (Hons)
publishing media. MSc/ PgDip publishing • BA/BA (Hons) design futures;
photography, film and imaging. BEng / BEng (Hons) internet computing;
multimedia systems; software engineering. MDes interdisciplinary
design • BMus/ BMus (Hons) music. BA/ BA (Hons) pop

National Broadcasting School
The Innovation Centre, University of Sussex
Brighton BN1 9SB
01273 704510
nbsrory@btinternet.com
www.nationalbroadcastingschool.com
• PgDip NBS radio presentation and production; radio journalism

National Film and Television School
Beaconsfield Studios, Station Road, Beaconsfield
Bucks HP9 1LG
01494 731425/13
info@nftsfilm-tv.ac.uk
www.nftsfilm-tv.ac.uk
• Dip script development; sound recording for film and TV; fundamentals
of fiction direction. MA producing; production design; screenwriting;
sound post-production; cinematography; doc/fiction direction; editing;
producing for TV entertainment*. Doc summer school. Feature
development workshop. Short courses in art and design; camera and
lighting; digital post-production; directing; editing; production; sound;
writing • Dip digital post production; visual and special effects producing.
MA animation direction • MA composing for film and TV

Neath Port Talbot College
Dwr-y-Felin Road, Neath SA10 7RF
01639 648000
enquiries@nptc.ac.uk
www.nptc.ac.uk
• HNC/HND broadcast media • HNC/ HND computing (multimedia)
• HND music performance (pop). BA (Hons) music performance and
production

New College Nottingham
City Campus, Adams Building, Stoney Street
Lace Market, Nottingham NG1 1NG
0115 910 0100
enquiries@ncn.ac.uk
www.ncn.ac.uk
• BTEC FirstDip/NatDip/HND media • C&G TV and video production.
BTEC ProfCert digital video editing • BTEC NatDip e-media production.
Fdg multimedia. Short courses: 3D Studio Max 6 beginner,
intermediate, advanced – character modelling and animation
• HND music performance; music production. FirstDip/NatDip music
practice (pop); music tech. Short courses in FJ skills, music production

Newcastle College
Rye Hill Campus, Scotswood Road, Newcastle NE4 5SA
0191 200 4000
enquiries@ncl-coll.ac.uk
www.newcastlecollege.co.uk
• Fdg TV and media practice • HNC interactive media/graphic design.
Fdg multimedia design; illustration and animation; graphic design;
graphics design for news media

Newcastle Upon Tyne, University of
Newcastle NE1 7RU
0191 222 6000
enquiries@ncl.ac.uk
www.ncl.ac.uk
• BA (Hons) media, communication and cultural studies • PgCert/MA
creative writing. MA literary studies: writing, memory, culture • BA (Hons)
film (options). PgDip/MA film. MA modern and contemporary studies:
British and American literature and film • BA (Hons) marketing and
management. BSc (Hons) marketing • MSc e-business and information
systems; system design for internet apps

North East Surrey College of Technology (NESCOT)
Reigate Road, Ewell, Epsom, Surrey KT17 3DS
020 8394 3038
info@nescot.ac.uk
www.nescot.ac.uk
• FirstDip media • NatDip media production • NatDip multimedia. Fdg
media and multimedia (OUVS); photography and digital imaging (OUVS).
BA (Hons) photography and imaging • NatDip music tech

North East Wales Institute of Higher Education
Plas Coch, Mold Road, Wrexham LL11 2AW
01978 290666
enquiries@newi.ac.uk
www.newi.ac.uk
• BA (Hons) media • BA (Hons) writing • BA (Hons) radio production and
media comms • BA (Hons) media comms; marketing. ProfCert/ProfDip/
PgDip marketing (CIM) • HND internet and multimedia computing;
graphic design. Fdg (Hons) internet and multimedia computing. Fdg
digital media. BA (Hons) animation; graphic/multimedia/moving image
design. BSc (Hons) internet and multimedia computing. MA animation
• Fdg sound/studio tech. BSc (Hons) studio recording and performance
tech

North East Worcestershire College
Peakman Street, Redditch, Worcestershire B98 8DW
01527 570020
info@ne-worcs.ac.uk
www.ne-worcs.ac.uk
• BTEC FirstDip/NatDip media • HNC/HND media (moving image)
• HNC/HND multimedia development • BTEC FirstDip performing arts,
media and music tech. NatDip music tech

North West Kent College
Oakfield Lane, Dartford, Kent DA1 2JT
0800 074 1447
course.enquiries@nwkcollege.ac.uk
www.nwkcollege.ac.uk
• BTEC IntroDip art, design and media; BTEC Dip media; BTEC NatDip
media • HND professional writing • BTEC NatDip graphic design;
multimedia. Short courses: interactive web design, advanced interactive
web design • InterDip music tech; performance. Dip advanced music
tech; advanced acting and music

subject to validation

Northbrook College Sussex

Little Hampton Road, Worthing, West Sussex BN12 6NU
01903 606060; 0800 183 6060
enquiries@nbcol.ac.uk
www.northbrook.ac.uk
• BTEC NatDip performing arts production. HND media, the moving image • BA (Hons) communication design • ABC Dip/ BA (Hons) media arts • BTEC NatDip music tech; music practice – pop; media (audio and radio). HND music performance (pop). Fdg music production. BA (Hons) music composition; performance; production (top-up). BA (Hons) music composition for professional media

University College Northampton

Park Campus, Boughton Green Road
Northampton NN2 7AL
0800 358 2232
study@northampton.ac.uk
www.northampton.ac.uk
• BA (Hons) media and popular culture • HND/BA (Hons) journalism. BA (Hons) creative writing* • HND media production. BA (Hons) contemporary media production*; film and TV; film, TV and popular culture* • BA (Hons) marketing

Northumbria University

Ellison Place, Newcastle Upon Tyne NE1 8ST
0191 232 6002
ca.marketing@northumbria.ac.uk
www.northumbria.ac.uk
• BA (Hons) media, culture and society. BA/MA visual culture • MA creative writing • BA (Hons) English and film; film and TV*; media production; history of modern art, design and film • BSc (Hons) communication. BA (Hons) politics and media • Fdg arts (multimedia design). BA (Hons) contemporary photographic practice/multimedia design. BSc (Hons) multimedia and digital entertainment computing; multimedia computing. MA art practices (media) • BA (Hons) performance. MA music management and promotion

Norwich School of Art and Design

Francis House, 3–7 Redwell Street, Norwich
Norfolk NR2 4SN
01603 610561
info@nsad.ac.uk
www.nsad.ac.uk
• BA (Hons) creative writing. MA writing the visual • BA (Hons) graphic design (design for publishing) • Fdg games art and design; graphic design. BA (Hons) graphic design (graphic design, photography, animation). MA animation and sound design; digital practices

noSweat Journalism Training

16/17 Clarkenwell Close, London EC1R 0AN
020 7490 2006
info@nosweatjt.co.uk
www.nosweatjt.co.uk
• Prelim Cert newspaper journalism (NCTJ). Dip magazine journalism

Nottingham Trent University

Burton Street, Nottingham NG1 4BU
0115 941 8418
cor.web@ntu.ac.uk
www.ntu.ac.uk
• BA (Hons) media and cultural studies. PgDip/MA media and globalisation • BA (Hons) English with creative writing; PGDip/MA newspaper journalism; newspaper journalism (international). PgCert/ PgDip/MA creative writing • BA (Hons) broadcast journalism; design for TV. PGDip/MA TV journalism (also international); radio journalism (also international). PgCert/PgDip/MA cinema • BA (Hons) communication studies. BA(Hons)/MA fashion marketing and communication. ProfDip/ PgDip marketing (CIM) • BA (Hons) photography; photography in Europe. BA/BSc (Hons) multimedia. BSc (Hons) computer science (games tech); imaging and display tech. PGDip/MA online journalism (also international). PgDip/MSc computer games systems; multimedia engineering/games engineering. MA digital products

Nottingham, University of

University Park, Nottingham NG7 2RD
0115 951 5151
undergraduate-enquiries@nottingham.ac.uk
postgraduate-enquiries@nottingham.ac.uk
www.nottingham.ac.uk
• BA film and American studies/cultural sociology/theology. BA (Hons) film and TV. MA/PgDip film. Research opportunities: institute welcomes applications from students interested in analysis of film and TV production and consumption • BA music with film; music; music and philosophy

Open University

Walton Hall, Milton Keynes MK7 6AA
01908 274066
general-enquiries@open.ac.uk
www.open.ac.uk
• MA cultural and media

Oxford Brookes University

Headington Campus, Oxford OX3 0BP
01865 484848
query@brookes.ac.uk
www.brookes.ac.uk
• BA/BSc (Hons) film (joint) • Fdg communication at work. BA/BSc (Hons) arts management and administration (joint); communication, media and culture (single or joint) • BA/BSc (Hons) publishing (single or joint). MA education/educational studies with publishing; international publishing; publishing; publishing and language. MBA (specialism in publishing) • Fdg art and design. BA/ BSc (Hons) fine art (single or joint); multimedia systems (joint). BSc (Hons) media tech (joint); multimedia production (joint). MA interactive media publishing. MSc digital media production; e-commerce computing; web tech • BA/BSc (Hons) music (single or joint). BSc (Hons) sound tech and digital music. MA composition and sonic art; contemporary arts and music

Oxford, University of

Wellington Square, Oxford OX1 2JD
01865 270000
www.music.ox.ac.uk
• Dip/Mstud creative writing • BA (Hons) music

Paisley University

High Street, Paisley, Scotland PA1 2BE
0141 848 3000
info@paisley.ac.uk
www.paisley.ac.uk
• BA (Hons) media • BA (Hons) cinema; screen practice • BA (Hons) marketing; international marketing. MSc international marketing • BSc (Hons) multimedia systems; media tech; multimedia with interactive entertainment tech*; computer games tech; computer animation; digital art • BA (Hons) commercial music; music tech

Peterborough Regional College

Park Crescent, Peterborough PE1 4DZ
01733 767366
info@peterborough.ac.uk
www.peterborough.ac.uk
• BTEC FirstDip/HNC/HND media • C&G 7790 journalism (media techniques). HNC/HND journalism. BTEC NatDip media (publishing; journalism). Fdg print journalism • BTEC NatDip media (moving image, video) • NCFE studio recording and music tech. BTEC NatDip media (audio/radio); music practice

Plymouth College of Art and Design

Tavistock Place, Plymouth PL4 8AT
01752 203434
enquiries@pcad.ac.uk
www.pcad.ac.uk
• NatDip moving image. Fdg media production and the environment* • NatDip media publishing • NatDip electronic media; graphic design; multimedia; photography. BA (Hons) photomedia and design communication. Fdg film and animation; photography and electronic imaging; multimedia design; entertainment and learning tech*; graphic design and production • NatDip audio. NatAward music tech (music for media). Fdg music and sound for media*

A career in media

Plymouth, University of
Drake Circus, Plymouth, Devon PL4 8AA
01752 600600
prospectus@plymouth.ac.uk
www.plymouth.ac.uk
• BA (Hons) media arts (with options); media practice and society. BSc (Hons) science and the media • PgDip/MA creative writing • MA contemporary film practice • BA (Hons) marketing • PgDip/MA publishing • BA (Hons) design: illustration; photography. BA/BSc (Hons) digital art and tech. BSc (Hons) media lab arts; multimedia production and tech. MA/MSc/MRes digital art and tech. MA/MSc digital futures • BA (Hons) music; music with education studies. MA music education

PMA Training
PMA Centre for Media Excellence, 10 Cynthia Street London N1 9JF
020 7278 0606
training@pma-group.com
www.pma-group.com
• One- to three-day short courses. Journalism: news, features, style, subediting and proofing, writing for different mediums, production, investigation, launching a publication etc; also two-day journalism school for school and college leavers; nine-week postgrad course in magazine journalism (PTC).Broadcasting: writing, interviewing and public speaking PR: law, writing, strategy, event management, pitching, internal comms etc. Software: Quark XPress, Adobe Illustrator/ Photoshop/ Acrobat, PowerPoint, HTML, Macromedia Flash/ Dreamweaver, DVD Studio Pro, Adobe Premiere, Final Cut Pro. Also media law; marketing; blogging; public speaking, interviewing and presentation skills

Portsmouth, University of
University House, Winston Churchill Avenue Portsmouth PO1 2UP
023 9284 8484
info.centre@port.ac.uk
www.port.ac.uk
• BA (Hons) English with media, creative writing and film as options • BA (Hons) creative writing and drama; English lang/lit and journalism; languages and creative writing; media and journalism. MA creative writing • BA (Hons) film with options including entertainment tech, creative writing, drama, languages. BA (Hons) media (single or with creative writing, drama, entertainment tech) • BA (Hons) communication and English; marketing. MA communication and language skills; technical communication. MPA masters in public administration • BA (Hons) animation; communication design; design for interactive media; 3D design; video production. BSc (Hons) computer animation; computer games tech; creative computing tech; digital media; digital video tech; enterprise in computer games tech/entertainment tech; entertainment tech; multimedia programming. MA art, design and media; design for digital media; real-time media comms. MSc compositing and special effects; computer animation; digital media; scientific and technical comms • BSc (Hons) music and sound tech. MSc creative and computational sound

Queen Margaret University College, Edinburgh
Corstophine Campus, Clerwood Terrace
Edinburgh EH12 8TS
0131 317 3000
marketing@qmuc.ac.uk
www.qmuc.ac.uk
• BA/BA (Hons) media; media and culture; psychology and media • MFA/MA dramatic writing • BA/BA (Hons) film and media; performance production and management. MFA/MA/PgDip advanced screen practice • BA/BA (Hons) marketing (options); retail business; PR and media/marketing/psychology; event management. CIPR diploma. MSc PR • MBA electronic commerce

Queen Mary, University of London
Mile End Road, London E1 4NS
020 7882 5555
admissions@qmul.ac.uk
www.qmul.ac.uk
• MA/BA film (with options) • BEng/MEng multimedia systems tech • MSc digital music processing

Queen's University Belfast
University Road, Belfast BT7 1NN
028 9024 5133
admissions@qub.ac.uk
www.qub.ac.uk
• BA (Hons)/MA/MPhil film • BSc (Hons) music tech. BA (Hons)/BMus music

Radio and TV School
High Street, Staplehurst, Kent TN12 0AX
01580 895256
mail@radioschool.co.uk
www.radioschool.co.uk
• One-to-one radio courses, covering presentation styles, techniques and production values. Core 1 for beginners with no technical or radio experience; Core 2 for hospital/uni/RSL presenters and nightclub DJs; Core 3 for pro and semi-pro broadcasters working on-air now. One-to-one TV presenter mini-courses for demos and showreels

Ravensbourne College of Design and Communication
Walden Road, Chislehurst, Kent BR7 5SN
020 8289 4900
info@rave.ac.uk
www.ravensbourne.ac.uk
• HECert broadcast post-production. Fdg broadcast post-production; broadcast operations and production; broadcast media tech. BA (Hons) broadcast production (top-up); content creation for broadcasting and new media. BSc (Hons) broadcast tech (top-up) • Fdg computer visualisation and animation. BA (Hons) animation (top-up)/ moving image design. MA interactive digital media; networked media environments • Fdg creative sound design

Robert Gordon University
School Hill, Aberdeen AB10 1FR
01224 262000
admissions@rgu.ac.uk
www.rgu.ac.uk
• BA/BA (Hons) publishing with journalism • BA/BA (Hons) corporate communication • BA/BA (Hons) publishing; publishing with journalism • BA (Hons) photographic and electronic media. BSc (Hons) graphics and animations. BSc/BSc (Hons) computing for internet and multimedia. BDes (Hons) design for digital media; interactive media and gaming design

Roehampton University
Erasmus House, Roehampton Lane, London SW15 5PU
020 8392 3000
enquiries@roehampton.ac.uk
www.roehampton.ac.uk
• BA media and culture. PgDip/MA media and cultural studies • BA/BSc creative writing; journalism and news media. PgDip/MA translation (AV); creative and professional writing; women, gender and writing • BA film and screen practice. BA/BSc film. PgDip/MA cinema. PgDip/MA/MRes performance • BSc marketing; business information management • BA/BSc/PgCert/PgDip/MA children's literature • BA/BSc internet and multimedia computing; computing • BMus/BA/BSc music. PgDip/MA choral education and music education; music and culture

Royal Academy of Music
Marylebone Road, London NW1 5HT
020 7873 7373
go@ram.ac.uk
www.ram.ac.uk
• BMus (4yr) composition; performance. PgDip performance (options in musical theatre and opera). MMus/MPhil/PhD composition; performance

Royal College of Music
Prince Consort Road, London SW7 2BS
020 7589 3643
info@rcm.ac.uk
www.rcm.ac.uk
• BMus (Hons) music. PGDip/MMus integrated masters programme in performance

subject to validation

Royal Holloway, University of London
Egham, Surrey TW20 0EX
01784 434455
admissions@rhul.ac.uk
www.rhul.ac.uk
• MA creative writing • MA doc by practice; feature film screenwriting (MAFFS); producing film and TV; screen studies; screenwriting for TV and film (retreat programme) • BA media arts • BMus music. MMus composition; performance studies (joint with Royal College of Music); advanced musical studies (composition; ethnomusicology; historical musicology; opera studies; performance; performance studies; theory and analysis)

Royal Northern College of Music
124 Oxford Road, Manchester M13 9RD
0161 907 5200
info@rncm.ac.uk
www.rncm.ac.uk
• BMus(Hons). PGDip performance; composition; repetiteur studies. MMus/MPhil performance; composition

Royal Scottish Academy of Music and Drama
100 Renfrew Street, Glasgow G2 3DB
0141 332 4101
registry@rsamd.ac.uk
www.rsamd.ac.uk
• BA acting; technical and production arts • BA (Hons) digital film and TV • BA (Hons) music; Scottish music; Scottish music – piping. MMus performance; opera. Master of opera. MMus composition; conducting. PgDip music. Master of performance in musical theatre

Royal Welsh College of Music and Drama
Castle Grounds, Cathays Park, Cardiff CF10 3ER
029 2034 2854
info@rwcmd.ac.uk
www.rwcmd.ac.uk
• BA (Hons)/PgDip acting; stage management; theatre design • PgDip/MA arts management • HND music performance. BA (Hons) pop: performance and production. BMus (Hons) music. PGDip/MA music therapy

St Helens College
Brook Street, St Helens, Merseyside WA10 1PZ
01744 733766
enquire@sthelens.ac.uk
www.sthelens.ac.uk
• HNC/HND media (writing) • BA (Hons) TV and video production (Liverpool John Moores University). • HNC multimedia (design route). BTEC NatCert multimedia. Fdg interactive multimedia arts and animation (Liverpool John Moores University). BA (Hons) digital arts (LJM Uni) • FirstDip performing arts (music). NatCert music tech. Fdg music tech and sound design* (Huddersfield University)

St Martin's College
Bowerham Road, Lancaster LA1 3JD
01524 384384
www.ucsm.ac.uk
• PgCert/PgDip/MA creative writing

St Mary's College
Waldegrave Road, Twickenham TW1 4SX
020 8240 4000
recruit@smuc.ac.uk
www.smuc.ac.uk
• BA (Hons) professional and creative writing (single or with options) • BA Hons film and TV (joint) • BA (Hons) media arts (joint)

Salford, University of
Salford, Greater Manchester M5 4WT
0161 295 5000
course-enquiries@salford.ac.uk
www.salford.ac.uk
• BA (Hons) media, language and business • BA (Hons) journalism (options); English and creative writing • HND media production; media performance; audio and video systems. BTEC media tech. BA (Hons) media and performance; TV and radio; journalism and broadcasting • BA (Hons) advertising design • BA (Hons) digital 3D design; visual arts; animation. BSc (Hons) computer and video games; multimedia and internet tech • BA (Hons) pop and recording; music. BSc (Hons) audio tech

Salisbury College
Southampton Road, Salisbury, Wiltshire SP1 2LW
01722 344344
enquiries@salisbury.ac.uk
www.salisbury.ac.uk
• BTEC NatAward/Dip/NatDip performing arts. BTEC NatDip media (moving image) • BTEC Dip design; art. BTEC FDip/NatDip art and design. HNC/HND fine art • BTEC Dip/NatDip pop. BTEC NatDip music tech. Cert music tech (DJ skills). Short courses: intro to multitrack recording; sound engineering

School of Oriental and African Studies
Thornaugh Street, Russell Square, London WC1H 0XG
020 7637 2388
study@soas.ac.uk
www.soas.ac.uk
• MA critical media and cultural studies; anthropology of media; global media and postnational communication • MA cinemas of Asia and Africa • BA music. MMus ethnomusicology; performance

Sheffield College, The
The Norton Centre, Dyche Lane, Sheffield S8 8BR
0114 260 3603
course-enquiries@sheffcol.ac.uk
www.sheffcol.ac.uk
• BTEC media • Short courses: journalism reporter (NCTJ), journalism/photography (NCTJ), press photography • HND media production • BTEC NatDip multimedia • BTEC Dip/NatDip music practice

Sheffield Hallam University
City Campus, Howard Street, Sheffield S1 1WB
0114 225 5555
admissions@shu.ac.uk
www.shu.ac.uk
• BA (Hons)/MA/PgDip/PgCert media • MA/PgDip/PgCert broadcast journalism; international broadcast journalism; writing • BA (Hons) film and literature; film and media production; film and history; film. MA/PgDip/PgCert film and media production • BA (Hons) communication studies; visual culture and its management. MA/PgDip/PgCert communication studies; corporate/professional/tech communication • BA (Hons) photographic practice; multimedia and communication design; interactive product design. BSc (Hon) software development (games). MSc/PgDip/PgCert multimedia and internet; entertainment software development

Sheffield, University of
Western Bank, Sheffield S10 2TN
0114 222 2000
www.shef.ac.uk
• BA (Hons)/MA journalism (options). PGDip/MA print journalism. • MA web journalism • PGDip/MA broadcast journalism (BJTC) • MA musicology; music theatre studies

Solihull College
Blossomfield Road, Solihull B91 1SB
0121 678 7000
enquiries@solihull.ac.uk
www.solihull.ac.uk
• BTEC Dip/NatDip media • Cert sales and marketing (Level 2 and 3) (ISMM). FCert marketing (CIM). Cert marketing (Stage 1) (CIM). ProfDip marketing (Stage 2) (CIM). ProfPgDip marketing (Stage 3) (CIM)

subject to validation

South Birmingham College
High Street Deritend, Digbeth, Birmingham B5 5SU
0121 694 5000
info@sbc.ac.uk
www.sbc.ac.uk
• BTEC NatDip media (moving image) • HND media and communication
• BTEC national media (e-media). HND multimedia • BTEC national
media (audio). HND media production – audio pathway

South Devon College
Vantage Point, Long Road, Paignton, Devon TQ4 7BE
01803 400700
enquiries@southdevon.ac.uk
www.southdevon.ac.uk
• FirstDip media • BTEC NatDip media (moving image) • FirstDip music
production. NatDip music tech (audio engineering; studio production)

South East Essex College
Luker Road, Southend-on-Sea, Essex SS1 1ND
01702 220400
learning@southend.ac.uk
www.southend.ac.uk
• BTEC FirstDip media • BA (Hons) journalism. Short courses: writing
your first novel, creative writing • BTEC NatDip moving image. BA (Hons)
TV production and screen media; short course TV presenting skills
• BTEC NatDip publishing • BTEC NatDip digital animation; multimedia.
Short course: basic 3D animation • HND performing arts (music
production). BTEC FirstDip/NatDip contemporary music; music tech.
BTEC NatDip radio. BA (Hons) music production

South Kent College
Folkestone Campus, Shorncliffe Road, Folkestone
Kent CT20 2TZ
01303 858200
www.southkent.ac.uk
• Dip media • FirstDip/NatCert/NatDip performing arts. NatDip media
(moving image) production • IntroCert/ProfCert/ProfDip/PgDip
marketing (CIM) • InterCert/NatCert/NatDip music tech. NatAward
music tech – DJ skills

South Nottingham College
Greythorn Drive, West Bridgford, Nottingham NG2 7GA
0115 914 6400
enquiries@snc.ac.uk
www.snc.ac.uk
• HNC/HND media production • HNC/HND multimedia; photography and
digital imaging; print, media and digital design

South Thames College
Wandsworth High Street, London SW18 2PP
020 8918 7777
studentservices@south-thames.ac.uk
www.south-thames.ac.uk
• BTEC Dip/NatDip media • TRAC foundation filmmaking. ProfDev Cert
16mm film making; film and TV. BTEC NatDip media (moving image).
HNC 16mm film making; TV production; media production • Entry-level
course: design preparation. IntroDip art, design and media. Dip design.
NatCert multimedia (graphics and photography). ProfDev Cert graphic
design. HNC graphic design; photography; art and design (graphic
design) • Entry-level course music, multimedia and video production.
C&G/BTEC Dip/NatCert/NatDip music tech. BTEC NatAward music
production – music for media. BTEC NatAward/NatDip music practice.
NatAward/HNC music production

Southampton Institute
East Park Terrace, Southampton, Hampshire SO14 0RB
023 8031 9000
enquiries@solent.ac.uk
www.solent.ac.uk
• BA (Hons) media with cultural studies. BSc (Hons) environment with
media communication. MA media. • BA (Hons) journalism (NCTJ, PTC,
BJTC); media writing; writing fashion and culture; writing popular fiction *
• BSc (Hons) film and video tech (BKSTS); media tech. BA (Hons) film
and TV; film; screenwriting; TV and video production *. MA independent
film and filmmaking • HND advertising and media comms. Dip marketing
(CIM). BA (Hons) marketing with media and design; PR and
communication. • BA (Hons) animation; digital media; multimedia
design; photography • BSc (Hons) audio tech (BKSTS); music studio
tech (BKSTS). BA (Hons) pop and record production; multimedia sound *

Southampton, University of
University Road, Highfield, Southampton SO17 1BJ
023 8059 5000
www.soton.ac.uk
• BA film (with options) • BA fine art theory and practice (new media);
textiles, fashion and fibre (new media). BSc/MEng computer science
with image and multimedia systems • BSc acoustics and music.
BA music (options). BEng/MEng acoustical engineering

Southport College
Mornington Road, Southport PR9 0TT
0845 006 6236
guidance@southport-college.ac.uk
www.southport-college.ac.uk
• BTEC NatDip multimedia; computing

Staffordshire University
Stoke-on-Trent, Staffordshire ST4 2DE
01782 294000
study@staffs.ac.uk
www.staffs.ac.uk
• BA media   • BA (Hons) English and creative writing; journalism (NCTJ);
sports journalism • BA (Hons)/MA broadcast journalism (BJTC).
BA film; film, TV and radio studies; music broadcasting; TV and radio
documentary; media production; scriptwriting • BA multimedia
graphics; graphics; animation; design innovation; design futures.
MA media futures; interactive multimedia • BA music broadcasting

Stevenson College Edinburgh
Bankhead Avenue, Edinburgh EH11 4DE
0131 535 4600; course enquiries: 0131 535 4700
info@stevenson.ac.uk
www.stevenson.ac.uk
• HNC/HND AV tech. HND TV operations. Fdg film and TV • HNC
advertising and PR • Fdg classical music. HND/Fdg pop

Stirling, University of
Stirling FK9 4LA
01786 473171
admissions@stir.ac.uk
www.stir.ac.uk
• MSc/PGDip media management (available online); media research
• BA (Hons) journalism studies • BA (Hons) film and media; European film
and media • BA (Hons)/PgDip/MSc marketing. PGDip/MSc PR (online
learning available) • MLitt publishing studies

Stockport College of Further and Higher Education
Wellington Road South, Stockport, Cheshire SK1 3UQ
0161 958 3100
enquiries@stockport.ac.uk
www.stockport.ac.uk
• Dip media. IntroDip art, design and media • Dip media techniques radio
and journalism production (level 3) – partnership with CSV Media and
Pure Radio • HND media (moving image – broadcasting). NatDip media
broadcasting. NatCert/NatDip performing arts: media make-up. Dip
production make-up. Cert (level 2) fashion and photographic make-up
• BA advertising • BA graphic design

subject to validation

381

Stratford Upon Avon College

The Willows North, Alcester Road, Stratford-upon-Avon
Warwickshire CV37 9QR
01789 266245
college@stratford.ac.uk
www.stratford.ac.uk
- *BTEC Dip/NatDip/HND media* • *BTEC Dip performing arts – music, dance or acting. BTEC NatDip performing arts (musical theatre)*

Strathclyde, University of

16 Richmond Street, Glasgow G1 1XQ
0141 552 4400
www.strath.ac.uk
- *BA (Hons) journalism and creative writing (joint). MLitt/PgDip in journalism studies (Scottish Centre for Journalism with Glasgow Caledonian – 0141 950 3281)* • *BA/Mres/MSc/PgDip marketing. MSc/PgDip marketing, international. MSc marketing, international (online)* • *BEng/MEng design computing; digital multimedia systems. BSc internet computing; software engineering. MSc/PgDip computer and internet tech. MSc/PgDip/PgCert digital multimedia and communication systems* • *BA applied music*

Sunderland, University of

Edinburgh Building, Chester Road, Sunderland SR1 3SD
0191 515 2112
student-helpline@sunderland.ac.uk
www.sunderland.ac.uk
- *BA (Hons) media, culture and communication. MA/PgDip/PgCert media and cultural studies* • *BA (Hons)/MA journalism (NCTJ)* • *BA (Hons) English and film; broadcast journalism*; film and media; media production (TV and radio). MA/PgDip/PgCert film and cultural studies; media production (TV and video)* • *BA (Hons) marketing; PR (CIPR); ads and design* • *Fdg media design (publishing)* • *Fdg creative multimedia. BA (Hons) photography, video and digital imaging; media production (video and new media); animation and design; design: multimedia and graphics; illustration and design; 3D design innovation; graphic communication; graphic design (top-up). BSc (Hons) product design. MA/PgDip/PgCert design: multimedia and graphics; illustration and design. 3D design innovation; design studies; photography* • *BMus (Hons) jazz, popular and commercial music. BA (Hons) music (top-up). MA/PgDip/PgCert radio (production and management)*

Surrey Institute of Art and Design

Falkner Road, Farnham, Surrey GU9 7DS
01252 722441
registry@surrart.ac.uk
www.surrart.ac.uk
- *BA (Hons) arts and media* • *BA (Hons) journalism (PTC, BJTC, recognised by NUJ); fashion journalism* • *BA (Hons) film and video (BKSTS). MA film and video* • *BA (Hons) ad and brand management* • *BA (Hons) animation; digital screen arts; photography. MA animation; photography; digital games design; graphic communication (branding, printed and interactive media); graphic design and new media*

Surrey, University of

Guildford, Surrey GU2 7XH
01483 689905
information@surrey.ac.uk
www.surrey.ac.uk
- *Fdg TV and radio tech. Dip/NatCert/NatDip media (moving image). MA radio. All at Farnborough College of Technology* • *CIM Cert marketing, e-marketing (Farnborough). CIM Dip/PgDip marketing (Farnborough)* • *Fdg design for interactive new media (Farnborough). BSc (Hons) media tech (Farnborough). MSc digital tech and society* • *BMus (Hons) music (also with professional placement year, or with computer sound design); music and sound recording (Tonmeister). BSc (Hons) mathematics with music. MMus/PgDip/MRes/MPhil/PhD music*

Sussex, University of

Falmer, Brighton BN1 9RH
01273 606755
information@sussex.ac.uk
www.sussex.ac.uk
- *BA media; media practice and theory. PgDip/MA/MPhil/DPhil media and cultural studies. MA gender and media. MSc social research methods (media and cultural studies)* • *MPhil/DPhil creative and critical writing. MA English literature: creative and critical writing; creative writing and personal development; dramatic writing* • *BA film (with options). MA film* • *MA digital media* • *BA music; music and cultural studies; music and film; music with languages. BA/BSc music informatics. MPhil/DPhil composition; music. MA music*

Sutton Coldfield College

Lichfield Road, Sutton Coldfield, West Midlands B74 2NW
0121 355 5671
infoc@sutcol.ac.uk
www.sutcol.ac.uk
- *HND media and communication. BTEC NatDip media* • *Pre-entry Cert newspaper journalism (NCTJ). C&G desktop publishing; 7790 Cert in media techniques: journalism and radio competences* • *C&G 7500 Dip media – TV and video. BTEC Dip media production* • *BTEC NatDip/HND graphic design. BTEC NatDip photography. Short course: intro to web page design. C&G web page design and ICT* • *BTEC NatDip music practice*

Swansea Institute of Higher Education

Mount Pleasant, Swansea SA1 6ED
01792 481000
enquiry@sihe.ac.uk
www.sihe.ac.uk
- *BA (Hons) photojournalism with journalism** • *BA (Hons) English studies, film and TV; video; video with journalism** • *BA (Hons) design for advertising*; marketing. PgDip marketing (CIM)* • *HND/BA/BSc (Hons) 3D computer animation; multimedia. BSc (Hons) computer games development. BA (Hons) creative computer games design; photojournalism (contemporary practice). MA (art and design) photography; visual arts enterprise; visual communication. MA 3D computer animation. MSc multimedia* • *BSc (Hons) music tech*

Swansea University

Singleton Park, Swansea SA2 8PP
01792 205678
admissions@swansea.ac.uk
www.swansea.ac.uk
- *BA (Hons) media (with options). MA media talk* • *MA comparative journalism; creative and media writing* • *BA (Hons) screen studies (options)* • *BA (Hons) public and media relations**

Tameside College

Beaufort Road, Ashton-under-Lyne
Greater Manchester OL6 6NX
0161 908 6600
info@tameside.ac.uk
www.tameside.ac.uk
- *NatDip media (moving image)* • *NatDip multimedia. HNC/NatDip photography. Fdg new media design*

A career in media

Teesside, University of

Middlesbrough, Tees Valley TS1 3BA
01642 218121
registry@tees.ac.uk
www.tees.ac.uk

• BA (Hons) English with media; media; media with history • Fdg journalism • Fdg TV and film production; performance and event production. BA (Hons) media production professional practice; TV production professional practice • BA (Hons) marketing; marketing and retail management/ad management; PR; ad management; ad management and PR; creative advertising and promotions. PgCert professional development: marketing. PgDip marketing (CIM). MSc marketing management • HND web design/development. Fdg digital media. BA (Hons) computer animation; creative digital media/ multimedia/visualisation; computer games art/design; digital character animation; web design. BSc (Hons) computer games programming/ science; computer graphics science; multimedia; tech direction in computer animation; web development. MA computer animation; computer games art; web design; creative digital media. MSc computer animation and graphical tech apps; new media apps; visual and web apps; computer games programming; CGI; web enterprise; web services development • HND music tech. BSc (Hons) media and music tech; digital music. BA (Hons) digital music creation

Thames Valley University

St Mary's Road, Ealing, London W5 5RF
0800 036 8888
learning.advice@tvu.ac.uk
www.tvu.ac.uk

• BA (Hons) media arts; MA/PgDip/MPhil/PhD media • BA (Hons) new media journalism (options). MPhil/PhD journalism • HND media (moving image). Fdg radio broadcasting. BA (Hons) digital broadcast media. BA (Hons)/DipHE/MA film: video production with film. BSc (Hons) radio broadcasting (joint). MA film and the moving image • BA (Hons) advertising (options); creative advertising (options). PR (options); media, creative tech and event management (combinations) • HND multimedia; media tech; photography and digital imaging. Fdg digital animation; photo-imaging. BA (Hons) design for interactive media (options); digital animation (options); media, creative tech and event management (combinations); photography and digital imaging; professional photographic imaging (final year). BA (Hons)/DipHE design for interactive media. BSc (Hons) creative computing; media tech; multimedia computing (options); new media journalism (joint). BA (Hons)/MPhil/PhD digital arts (options). MA photography; computer arts • Fdg live sound (engineering and production); music and multimedia tech; music performance; musical theatre; pop studies. HND music production (music tech); music performance; performing arts (theatre). BA (Hons)/DipHE music tech. BMus (Hons)/DipHE pop performance. BA (Hons) music and creative technologies; music and event management; music and media; combinations of the above; music: performance/ composition (options); music tech (options). BSc (Hons) performance tech. BMus (Hons) music (performance, composition). MA audio tech. MMus composing concert music; composing for film and television; composing for musical theatre. MMus symphonic wind ensemble music; brass band direction. MPhil/PhD music; music tech

Trinity College Carmarthen

Wales SA31 3EP
01267 676767
registry@trinity-cm.ac.uk
www.trinity-cm.ac.uk

• BA media • BA/MA creative writing • BA film • BA advertising. MBA arts management • BA web systems

Trinity College of Music

King Charles Court, Old Royal Naval College, Greenwich
London SE10 9JF
020 8305 4444
admissions@tcm.ac.uk
www.tcm.ac.uk

• BMus (Hons) – intensive performance-centred training. BMus (Hons) Indian classical music (in assoc with Bharatiya Vidya Bhavan Institute of Indian Art and Culture*) – see www.bhavan.net. PgDip/masters – areas of specialisation in creative performance

Tyne Metropolitan College

Embleton Avenue, Wallsend, Tyne and Wear NE28 9NJ
0191 229 5000
enquiries@tynemet.ac.uk
www.tynemet.ac.uk

• HND TV and video • BTEC FirstDip media (e-media)*. BTEC NatDip e-media/graphic design

UHI Millennium Institute

Executive Office, Ness Walk, Inverness IV3 5SQ
01463 279000
eo@uhi.ac.uk
www.uhi.ac.uk

• BA (Hons) Gaelic and media • HNC media production. HND TV and multimedia • HNC/HND advertising and PR • HNC/HND interactive multimedia creation • HNC/HND music performance. BA (Hons) pop performance

Ulster, University of

Cromore Road, Co Londonderry, Northern Ireland BT52 1SA
0870 040 0700
online@ulster.ac.uk
www.ulster.ac.uk

• BA media; media arts. BSc (Hons) business with media; computing with media. BA (Hons) English with media; media (with options). PgDip/MA international media • BSc/BA (Hons) journalism and publishing studies (options). MA newspaper journalism; journalism studies. PgDip newspaper journalism • BA Hons film (options) • BSc (Hons) PR; government/politics with PR; communication (options); communication, advertising and marketing; marketing; government with communication; leisure events and cultural management. BDes design and communication. MSc future communication. PgDip/MDes design and communication • BSc (Hons) interactive multimedia design; multimedia computer games. BDes design for visual communication. BA (Hons) tech and design • Fdg studies in music. BMus (Hons). BA Hons music (options). MMus music

Wakefield College

Margaret Street, Wakefield, West Yorks WF1 2DH
01924 789789
info@wakcoll.ac.uk
www.wakcoll.ac.uk

• HND interactive use of media • HND photography • HND pop

University of Wales, Aberystwyth

Old College, King Street, Aberystwyth, Ceredigion SY23 2AX
01970 623111
ug-admissions@aber.ac.uk
www.aber.ac.uk

• BA/MA/MPhil/PhD media and communication studies • BA/MA/MPhil/ PhD theatre, film and TV • BSc marketing

University of Wales, Bangor

Gwynedd LL57 2DG
01248 351151
admissions@bangor.ac.uk
www.bangor.ac.uk

• BA (Hons) creative studies; Welsh with theatre and media; theatre and media. MA creative studies • BA (Hons) English/Welsh/history with journalism; English/Welsh with creative writing; Welsh communication and journalism; journalism and media. PGCert creative writing. MPhil/PhD creative and critical writing. MA (Welsh) practical journalism • BA Hons English with film; English language with film; film and media (Welsh); history with film; media production (Welsh) • BA (Hons) Communication and media (Welsh) • BA (Hons) (part time) internet, learning and organisations • BA (Hons)/BMus (Hons) music. MA creative music tech; editorial musicology; music; music performance

subject to validation

University of Wales Institute, Cardiff

PO Box 377, Western Avenue, Cardiff CF5 2YB
029 2041 6070
uwicinfo@uwic.ac.uk
www.uwic.ac.uk
▪ BA (Hons) art and creative writing ▪ BA (Hons) broadcast media with popular culture ▪ HND business information tech. BA (Hons) graphic communication; design for interactive media. BSc (Hons) business information systems ▪ HND/BSc (Hons) music and audio electronic systems

University of Wales, Lampeter

Ceredigion SA48 7ED
01570 422351
dept of film and media: 01570 424790
admissions@lamp.ac.uk
www.lamp.ac.uk
▪ BA media. MA/PgDip Welsh media ▪ BA English with creative writing. MA/PgDip creative writing ▪ BA film; film and media. BA/MA/PgDip media production. MA/PgDip screenwriting (bilingual); screen studies

University of Wales, Newport

Caerleon Campus, PO Box 179, Newport
South Wales NP18 3YG
01633 432432
uic@newport.ac.uk
www.newport.ac.uk
▪ MA sports media ▪ BA (Hons) creative writing ▪ BA(Hons) documentary film and TV; film and video; cinema and scriptwriting. MA film
▪ BA (Hons) advertising. BSc marketing ▪ BA (Hons) new media publishing ▪ BA (Hons) animation; multimedia; computer games design. BSc (Hons) digital special effects and animatronics; games development and artificial intelligence. MA animation; design (new media and tech)
▪ BA (Hons) creative sound and music

Warwick, University of

Coventry CV4 7AL
024 7652 3523
www.warwick.ac.uk
▪ BA English literature and creative writing. MA ancient visual and material culture; creative and media enterprises ▪ MA writing ▪ BA film and literature; film with TV. MA film and TV ▪ MSc marketing and strategy

Warwickshire College

Leamington Centre, Warwick New Road, Leamington Spa
Warwickshire CV32 5JE
0800 783 6767
enquiries@warkscol.ac.uk
www.warkscol.ac.uk
▪ Pre-entry journalism (NCTJ) ▪ HND visual communication
▪ HNC graphic design

West Herts College

Watford Campus, Hempstead Road, Watford
Herts WD17 3EZ
01923 812345
admissions@westherts.ac.uk
www.westherts.ac.uk
▪ Fdg/BA (Hons) media production ▪ Fdg business (with advertising, PR, marketing). BA (Hons) advertising and marketing comms ▪ Fdg/BA (Hons) graphic and new media

West Kent College

Brook Street, Tonbridge, Kent TN9 2PW
01732 358101
enquiries@wkc.ac.uk
www.wkc.ac.uk
▪ BA (Hons) media and communication ▪ Pre-entry newspaper journalism (NCTJ) ▪ HND TV production tech. Fdg broadcast journalism.

West of England, University of the

Frenchay Campus, Coldharbour Lane, Bristol BS16 1QY
0117 823 3333
enquiries@uwe.ac.uk
www.uwe.ac.uk
▪ Pre-entry media. BA (Hons)/MA cultural and media. PhD media practice: theory, culture and production ▪ BA (Hons) film. MA film and European cinema; film and European cinema (research); film and video; media (screenwriting) ▪ BA/BSc marketing (options). MA marketing
▪ BA (Hons) drawing and applied arts with animation; graphic design (animation option); illustration with animation; media practice (animation option). BSc (Hons) internet computing; internet systems (joint); internet tech (joint); multimedia computing. MA animation (research); graphic design with animation (research); illustration with animation (research); interactive media (research); media (animation/interactive media/research); multimedia (research) ▪ BSc (Hons) creative music tech; music systems engineering; music systems with maths. MA sound design (research)

Westminster, University of

309 Regent Street, London W1B 2UW
020 7911 5000
www.wmin.ac.uk
▪ BA (Hons) media. PgDip journalism (NCTJ). MA journalism studies (part-time); journalism for international students. All with print and online journalism options ▪ BA (Hons) media (TV/radio production pathways); film and TV production; contemporary media practice. PgDip journalism (broadcast pathway). MA journalism (part-time; broadcast pathway); journalism for international students (broadcast pathway); screenwriting and producing for film and TV; film: culture and industry ▪ BA (Hons) media (PR pathway). MA public comms and PR; communication; communication policy ▪ BSc (Hons) multimedia computing. BA (Hons) animation. MSc interactive multimedia; computer animation ▪ BA (Hons) commercial music. MA audio production; music business management

University College Winchester (formerly King Alfred's College)

Hampshire SO22 4NR
01962 841515
admissions@winchester.ac.uk
www.winchester.ac.uk
▪ Fdg creative industries. BA media; drama, community theatre and media ▪ BA journalism; creative writing (joint). MA creative and critical writing; writing for children ▪ BA film and American culture; film; screen production; media production

Wirral Metropolitan College

Conway Park Campus, Europa Boulevard, Conway Park
Birkenhead, Wirral CH41 4NT
0151 551 7777
enquiries@wmc.ac.uk
www.wmc.ac.uk
▪ BA media ▪ Short courses: writing film scripts, writing scripts for film and TV ▪ ProfCert/ProfDip marketing (CIM) ▪ MOCN art – multimedia
▪ BTEC FirstDip performing arts (music). BTEC NatCert music tech. BTEC NatDip music practice

Wolverhampton, University of

Wulfruna Street, Wolverhampton WV1 1SB
01902 321000
enquiries@wlv.ac.uk
www.wlv.ac.uk
▪ BA (Hons) media and cultural studies ▪ BA (Hons) creative and professional writing; journalism and editorial design ▪ Fdg (arts) broadcast journalism. BA (Hons) film studies; literary, film and theatre studies; TV graphics ▪ BA (Hons) media and comms studies; marketing; PR; public services ▪ HND digital media – design for screen; video production. HNC/HND/ BA (Hons) photography. BA (Hons) animation; computer games design; design; design for multimedia; digital media; graphic comms; multimedia communication; video. BSc (Hons) computer science (games development, software engineering); computing (multimedia); design tech; multimedia apps development; mobile computing; virtual reality design; web computing ▪ BA (Hons) music; music tech and music; music tech and pop; pop; pop (top-up from HND)

subject to validation

University College Worcester
Henwick Grove, Worcester WR2 6AJ
01905 855141
study@worc.ac.uk
www.worc.ac.uk
• HND media. BA (Hons) media and cultural studies • HND filmmaking;
music for the moving image. BA (Hons) drama and performance;
performance costume and make-up (top-up) • BA (Hons) visual arts;
communication design; creative digital media; interactive digital media;
time-based digital media

York St John College
Lord Mayor's Walk, York YO31 7EX
01904 624624
admissions@yorksj.ac.uk
www.yorksj.ac.uk
• BA (Hons) media • PgDip/MA literature studies and creative writing
• Fdg creative industries and tech • BA (Hons) performance: music

York, University of
Heslington, York YO10 5DD
01904 430000
admissions@york.ac.uk
www.york.ac.uk
• BA/MA writing and performance (drama, film, TV). BEng/MEng radio
frequency engineering • BEng/MEng media tech; electronic engineering
with media tech • BA music. BEng/MEng music tech systems; electronic
engineering with music tech systems. MA music; community music.
Dip/MPhil/PhD/MA/MSc music tech

Yorkshire Coast College of Further Education
Lady Edith's Drive, Scarborough, North Yorks YO12 5RN
01723 372105
admissions@ycoastco.ac.uk
www.yorkshirecoastcollege.ac.uk
• Fdg applied digital media (design) (University of Hull/NTI). HND graphic
and multimedia design

In-house training courses

Archant
Prospect House, Rouen Road
Norwich, Norfolk NR1 1RE
paul.durrant@archant.co.uk
www.archant.co.uk
*EDP assistant editor: Paul Durrant. Takes applicants within,
or with strong link to, circulation area. Ask in July for info on
following year's recruitment. After a month's induction,
trainees do a fast-track training course.*

BBC Training and development: Broadcast Training
35 Marylebone High Street
London W1U 4PX
0870 122 0216
training@bbc.co.uk
www.bbctraining.com
*Development executive: Andrew Carmichael. All strands of
broadcast training*

Johnston Training Centre
Upper Mounts
Northampton NN1 3HR
01604 477755
www.johnstonpress.co.uk
*Usually only takes trainees who have preliminary NCTJ
certificate*

Midland News Association
MNA Training Centre
Rock House, Old Hill, Tettenhall
Wolverhampton WV6 8QB
01902 742126
c.clark@expressandstar.co.uk
www.expressandstar.com
*Training coordinator: Crispin Clark. Take non-company
people on the editorial side, usually eight per year depending
on the requirements of the paper at the time.*

Newsquest Media Group
58 Church Street
Weybridge KT13 8DP
01932 821212
www.newsquest.co.uk
Each region operates its own training system

The Press Association
292 Vauxhall Bridge Road
London SW1V 1AE
020 7963 7228
jill.shiel@pressassociation.co.uk
www.pa.press.net
*Editorial support manager: Jill Shiel. In-house trainee
journalist programmes in multimedia, sport and production*

Trinity Mirror Training Centre
Thomson House, Groat Market
Newcastle-upon-Tyne NE1 1ED
0191 201 6043
paul.jones@ncjmedia.co.uk
www.trinitymirror.com
*Foundation course leader: Paul Jones 0191 201 6039.
16-week preliminary course, primarily in-house but external
places available*

Media recruitment companies

Career Moves
London: 020 7292 2900
www.cmoves.co.uk

Davis Company
London: 020 7580 4580
www.daviscompany.co.uk

Hudson Media
London: 020 7187 6000
Aberdeen: 01224 620 262
Birmingham: 0121 633 0010
Edinburgh: 0131 555 4321
Glasgow: 0141 221 8182
Guildford: 01483 303 300
Leeds: 0113 297 9500
Manchester: 0161 832 7728
Milton Keynes: 01908 547 995
Reading: 0118 939 1003
St Albans: 01727 840 660
Woking: 01483 881 000
http://uk.hudson.com

Leed Recruitment
Ipswich: 01473 402627
www.leedrecruitment.com

Marketing Stars
Isleworth: 020 8892 1848
www.marketingstars.co.uk

Media Contacts
London: 020 7359 8244
www.media-contacts.co.uk

The Media Exchange
London: 020 7636 6777
www.themediaexchange.com

The Media Network
London: 020 7637 9227
www.tmn.co.uk

MediaCentrix
London: 020 7812 7180
www.mediacentrix.com

Michael Page Marketing
Birmingham: 0121 230 9350
Bristol: 0117 927 6509
Glasgow: 0141 331 7900
Leeds: 0113 242 3530
London: 020 7831 2000
Manchester: 0161 819 5500
St Albans: 01727 730 111
Weybridge: 01932 264 000
www.michaelpage.co.uk

Moriati Media
London: 020 7307 1280
www.moriati.co.uk

Network Recruitment
London: 020 7580 5151
www.networkdesign.cc

Online Content UK
Harpenden: 0845 123 5717
www.onlinecontentuk.org

Pathfinders
London: 020 7434 3511
www.pathfindersrecruitment.com

Phee Farrer Jones
London, Manchester:
0870 048 9100
Birmingham: 0121 698 2320
www.pheefarrerjones.co.uk

Price Jamieson
London: 020 7580 7702
www.pricejam.com

Profiles Creative
London, Leeds, Reading:
0870 414 6288
www.profilescreative.com

Real Recruitment
London: 020 7499 5955
www.real-recruitment.com/

Recruit Media
London: 020 7758 4550
www.recruitmedia.co.uk

Reilly People
London: 020 7240 8080
www.reillypeople.co.uk

Swindale Parks Recruitment
Halesowen: 0121 585 6079
www.swindaleparks.co.uk

Workstation
London: 020 7371 7161
www.workstation.co.uk

Media training associations

BKSTS – The Moving Image Society
Pinewood Studios, Iver Heath
Bucks SL0 0NH
01753 656656
Info@bksts.com
www.bksts.com
*Film foundation, TV and digital tech,
foundation sound for film and video,
broadcasting engineering*

British Universities Film & Video Council
77 Wells Street, London W1T 3QJ
020 7393 1500
ask@bufvc.ac.uk
www.bufvc.ac.uk
*To promote the use of media within
higher education*

Broadcast Journalism Training Council
The Secretary, 18 Miller's Close
Rippingale, Lincolnshire PE10 0TH
01778 440025
Sec@bjtc.org.uk
www.bjtc.org.uk
Accredits courses

City & Guilds
1 Giltspur Street
London EC1A 9DD
020 7294 2800
enquiry@city-and-guilds.co.uk
www.city-and-guilds.co.uk
Vocational qualifications

FT2 – Film and Television Freelance Training
Fourth Floor, Warwick House
9 Warwick Street, London W1B 5LY
020 7734 5141
info@ft2.org.uk
www.ft2.org.uk
Training for new broadcast freelancers

Film Education
21–22 Poland Street
London W1F 8QQ
020 7851 9450
postbox@filmeducation.org
www.filmeducation.org

First Film Foundation
info@firstfilm.co.uk
www.firstfilm.co.uk
*Training for new film writers,
producers and directors*

National Council for the Training of Journalists
Latton Bush Centre, Southern Way
Harlow, Essex CM18 7BL
01279 430009
info@NCTJ.com
www.nctj.com
*Runs schemes for print journalists.
Accredits courses*

Periodicals Training Council
Queens House, 28 Kingsway
London WC2B 6JR
020 7400 7523
www.ppa.co.uk
Training arm of PPA

Skillset: The Sector Skills Council for the Audio Visual Industries
Prospect House
80–110 New Oxford Street
London WC1A 1HB
020 7520 5757
info@skillset.org
www.skillset.org
*Owned by broadcast industry;
accredits courses, publishes handbooks
and runs Skillsformedia
(www.skillsformedia.com)*

yourcreativefuture.org
education@designcouncil.org.uk
www.yourcreativefuture.org
*Guide to a creative career; sponsored by
government, Design Council and Arts
Council*

386

The more creative your role in the media, the greater the chance that there is an agent to represent you. The best authors, scriptwriters, actors, directors and presenters will always be in demand, but the number of wannabes far exceeds the number of talents. So the agent's role is to be the middle man: to find the talent, sell it, and make themselves a profit into the bargain.

There are more than 200 literary agents in the UK, of which about 75 are members of the association of authors' agents; the agents' association has more than 400 entertainment agencies among its members. Agencies can range from large multinational organisations such as PFD or ICM to tiny operations managed by just one overworked soul. The best agents will have an eye for a talent, a wide range of industry contacts, and above all a hard head for a business deal.

Talent agents

Talent agencies have a reputation – cemented in films such as Little Voice and Some Like It Hot – as a hard-headed, wheeler-dealing bunch. In the real world they come in a vast variety of forms: specialisms include television presenters, voice-overs for radio ads, directors of short films, actors, singers, make-up artists, cruise ship entertainers, lookalikes and of course models; many agencies will handle some but not all of these, even though they work under the broad umbrella of "entertainment". Agents employed by artists charge about 15% commission, rising to 20% for musicians and models in particular; or they may act as talent-brokers, earning their commission as a mark-up charged to the event hirer. There are few hard and fast rules – but the agents' association does have a code of conduct; artists should never, for example, pay a fee to join an agency's books. Other bodies include the personal managers' association, which represents actors' agents; and the association of voice-over agents.

Literary agents

It is increasingly difficult to acquire the services of a good literary agent; but then, it is harder still to sell a novel or a script without one. A good agent will not only advise an author in an editorial capacity, at least in order to make a script more saleable; they will also be able to sell writing for much more than the writer could on their own. In particular, agents aim to separate out rights for different media (such as paperback, film, television, multimedia and novelisation in the case of a script), for different markets (such as potentially lucrative US rights) and even, in this post-Potter world, for merchandising. Thus they hope to earn more for the writer than if all the rights were sold at once. In return, they charge a commission that normally ranges from 10% to 15%.

Agents complain that they are so busy trying to sell their existing authors that they have little time to find new talent. The result is that many agents, at one point or another, are either not accepting new writers or only accepting writers recommended to them by people they know and trust. Those that do receive unsolicited manuscripts are deluged: some agents receive up to 50 a day, which will usually mean the agent is looking for a reason to reject them.

The advice to an author seeking any agent, then, is to make life as easy as possible for them. Don't send work to an agent who doesn't accept unsolicited manuscripts, or who doesn't handle the genre you write in; you'll only be wasting your time and theirs. Check the agent's website to find the authors they already handle: this will help you target to agents who you know will like the kind of work you write. Spend a few moments finding out in what form the agent prefers to see a manuscript: whether complete, or in the form of a few chapters plus synopsis, and how they like the type to be set (normally use a simple font such as Times New Roman, on decent-quality white paper, double-spaced to allow room for notes; don't forget to enclose a stamped addressed envelope). Asked when they like to see a manuscript, many agents will helpfully reply that the best time is when you've improved it as best you can: make of that what you will. Finally, if an agent offers to represent you, trust your instinct: an agent who likes you and your writing will be your best advocate. To put it another way, the better your relationship with your agent, the more likely you are to sell your work.

Finally, don't lose hope: one day it could be your script that is being sold by a top agent such as Jonny Geller for a seven-figure sum at the Frankfurt book fair. It won't be, but it could.

Agents Contacts

Alexander Personal Management
PO Box 834, Hemel Hempstead
Hertfordshire HP3 9ZP
01442 252907
apm@apmassociates.net
www.apmassociates.net
Actors, voiceovers

Amanda Howard Associates
21 Berwick Street
London W1F 0PZ
020 7287 9277
mail@amandahowardassociates.co.uk
www.amandahowardassociates.co.uk
Actors, directors, composers, voiceovers, writers

Andrew Manson
288 Munster Road
London SW6 6BQ
020 7386 9158
post@andrewmanson.com
www.talentroom.com
Actors, voiceovers (for US)

Another Tongue Voices
10–11 D'arblay Street
London W1F 8DS
020 7494 0300
info@anothertongue.com
www.anothertongue.com
Voiceovers

Arlington Enterprises
1–3 Charlotte Street
London W1T 1RD
020 7580 0702
info@arlington-enterprises.co.uk
www.arlingtonenterprises.co.uk
TV presenters

Billy Marsh Associates
76A Grove End Road
St John's Wood, London NW8 9ND
020 7449 6930
talent@billymarsh.co.uk
TV presenters and personalities

Blackburn Sachs Associates
2–4 Noel Street
London W1F 8GB
020 7292 7555
presenters@
    blackburnsachsassociates.com
www.blackburnsachsassociates.com
TV and radio presenters and personalities

Bryan Drew
Mezzanine, Quadrant House
80–82 Regent Street
London W1B 5AU
020 7437 2293
bryan@bryandrewltd.com
Actors, writers, voiceovers

Calypso Voices
25–26 Poland Street
London W1F 8QN
020 7734 6415
calypso@calypsovoices.com
www.calypsovoices.com
Actors for voiceover work

Castaway
7 Garrick Street
London WC2E 9AR
020 7240 2345
sheila@castaway.org.uk
www.castaway.org.uk
Voiceovers

Celebrity Management
12 Nottingham Place
London W1M 3FA
020 7224 5050
info@celebrity.co.uk
www.celebrity.co.uk
Celebrity booking

Chase Personal Management
Model Plan 4th Floor
4 Golden Square, London W1F 9HT
020 7287 8444
leni@modelplanlondon.co.uk
www.modelplan.co.uk
Presenters and celebrities

Complete Talent Agency
200 London Road, Hadleigh
Benfleet, Essex SS7 2PD
01702 427100
info@entertainers.co.uk
www.entertainers.co.uk
Celebrity guests, speakers and comedians
Also at:
The Old Forge, Kingfield Road,
Woking, Surrey GU22 9EG

Conway Van Gelder
3rd Floor, 18–21 Jermyn Street
London SW1Y 6HP
020 7287 1070
fiona@conwayvg.co.uk
www.conwayvangelder.com
Actors, commercials, voiceovers, directors

Crawfords
PO Box 44394, London SW20 0YP
020 8947 9999
info@crawfordsagency.com
www.crawfords.tv
Actors and models for TV commercials

Curtis Brown Group
Haymarket House, 28–29
Haymarket
London SW1Y 4SP
020 7393 4400
info@curtisbrown.co.uk
www.curtisbrown.co.uk
Writers, directors, actors, playwrights and celebrities

David Anthony Promotions
PO Box 286, Warrington
Cheshire WA2 8GA
01925 632496
dave@davewarwick.co.uk
www.davewarwick.co.uk
TV presenters

Downes Presenters Agency
96 Broadway, Bexleyheath
Kent DA6 7DE
020 8304 0541
info@presentersagency.com
www.presentersagency.com
TV presenters

Dynamic FX
Regent House, 291 Kirkdale
London SE26 4QD
020 8659 8130
mail@dynamicfx.co.uk
www.dynamicfx.co.uk
Magical entertainment

Eric Glass
25 Ladbroke Crescent, Notting Hill
London W11 1PS
020 7229 9500
eglassltd@aol.com
Actors, writers

Evans O'Brien
115 Humber Road, London SE3 7LW
020 8293 7077
info@evansobrien.co.uk
www.evansobrien.co.uk
Voiceovers

Excellent Talent Company
19–21 Haverstock Street
London WC2E 7PA
020 7520 5656
ruth@excellentvoice.co.uk
www.excellentvoice.co.uk
Voiceovers and TV presenters

Extras Unlimited
9 Hansard Mews, London W14 8BJ
020 7603 9995
info@extrasunlimited.com
www.extrasunlimited.com
Extras

FBI Agency
PO Box 250, Leeds LS1 2AZ
07050 222747
casting@fbi-agency.ltd.uk
www.fbi-agency.ltd.uk
Models, dancers, walk-ons, presenters, actors, stand-ins

Foreign Legion
62 Blenheim Gardens
London NW2 4NT
020 8450 4451
getem@foreignlegion.co.uk
www.foreignlegion.co.uk
Foreign-language voiceovers and translations

Foreign Versions
60 Blandford Street
London W1U 7JD
020 7935 0993
info@foreignversions.co.uk
www.foreignversions.com
Translators and voiceovers in foreign languages

Fox Artist Management
Concorde House
101 Shepherds Bush Road
London W6 7LP
020 7602 8822
fox.artist@btinternet.com
www.foxartistmanagement.tv
TV presenters

Gordon & French
12–13 Poland Street
London W1F 8QB
020 7734 4818
mail@gordonandfrench.net
Actors and voiceovers

Hobson's Voices
62 Chiswick High Road
London W4 1SY
020 8995 3628
voices@hobson-international.com
www.hobsons-international.com
Actors, voiceovers, children, singers

ICM Artists (London)
4–6 Soho Square
London W1D 3PZ
020 7432 0800
webmaster@icmtalent.com
www.icmtalent.com
Conductors and musicians

Icon Actors Management
Tanzaro House, Ardwick Green North
Manchester M12 6FZ
0161 273 3344
info@iconactors.net
www.iconactors.net
Actors

International Artists
4th Floor, Holborn Hall
193–197 High Holborn
London WC1V 7BD
020 7025 0600
reception@intart.co.uk
www.intart.co.uk
Presenters, actors and comedians

J Gurnett Personal Management
2 New Kings Road
London SW6 4SA
020 7736 7828
mail@jgpm.co.uk
www.jgpm.co.uk
TV and radio presenters

Jacque Evans Management
Suite 1, 14 Holmesley Road
London SE23 1PJ
020 8699 1202
jacque@jacqueevans.com
www.jacqueevans.com
Presenters, journalists, broadcasters and experts

James Grant Management
Syon Lodge, 201 London Road
Isleworth, Middlesex TW7 5BH
020 8232 4100
enquiries@jamesgrant.co.uk
www.jamesgrant.co.uk
TV presenters

Jane Morgan Management
Thames Wharf Studios
Rainville Road, London W6 9HA
020 7386 5345
enquiries@janemorganmgt.com
www.janemorganmgt.com

Jeremy Hicks Associates
11–12 Tottenham Mews
London W1T 4AG
020 7636 8008
info@jeremyhicks.com
www.jeremyhicks.com
Presenters, writers, comedians and chefs

JLA (Jeremy Lee Associates)
4 Stratford Place, London W1C 1AT
020 7907 2800
talk@jla.co.uk
www.jla.co.uk
Presenters, speakers, entertainers

John Miles Organisation
Cadbury Camp Lane
Clapton-in-Gordano
Bristol BS20 7SB
01275 854675
john@johnmiles.org.uk
www.johnmiles.org.uk
Presenters

John Noel Management
2nd Floor, 10A Belmont Street
London NW1 8HH
020 7428 8400
john@johnnoel.com
www.johnnoel.com
TV presenters and radio DJs

Julie Ivelaw-Chapman
The Chase, Chaseside Close
Cheddington, Beds LU7 0SA
01296 662441
jivelawchapman@gmail.com
Broadcasters

KBJ Management
7 Soho Street, London W1D 3DQ
020 7434 6767
general@kbjmgt.co.uk
www.kbjmgt.co.uk
Presenters and comics

Knight Ayton Management
114 St Martin's Lane
London WC2N 4BE
020 7836 5333
info@knightayton.co.uk
www.knightayton.co.uk
TV presenters and news people

Lip Service
60–66 Wardour Street
London W1F 0TA
020 7734 3393
bookings@lipservice.co.uk
www.lipservice.co.uk
Voiceovers

Liz Hobbs Group
1st Floor, 65 London Road
Newark, Notts NG24 1RZ
0870 070 2702
info@lizhobbsgroup.com
www.lizhobbsgroup.com
Musical theatre, actors and presenters

Mark Summer Management & Agency
9 Hansard Mews, London W14 8BJ
0870 443 5621
info@marksummers.com
www.marksummers.com
Choreographers and actors, adults and children

Markham & Froggatt Personal Management
4 Windmill Street, London W1T 2HZ
020 7636 4412
admin@markhamfroggatt.co.uk
www.markhamfroggatt.com
Actors, voiceovers and radio

McLean-Williams Management
212 Piccadilly, London W1J 9HG
020 7917 2806
alex@mclean-williams.com
Actors

MPC Entertainment
MPC House, 15–16 Maple Mews
London NW6 5UZ
020 7624 1184
info@mpce.com
www.mpce.com
Radio, TV and sports personalities

NCI Management
51 Queen Anne Street
London W1G 9HS
020 7224 3960
nicola@nci-management.com
www.nci-management.com
TV presenters

Noel Gay Artists
19 Denmark Street
London WC2H 8NA
020 7836 3941
mail@noelgay.com
www.noelgay.com
TV presenters, voiceovers, writers, directors

Off The Kerb Productions
3rd Floor, Hammer House
113–117 Wardour Street
London W1F 0UN
020 7437 0607
info@offthekerb.co.uk
www.offthekerb.co.uk
Comedians

Also at
22 Thornhill Crescent
London N1 1BJ
020 7700 4477

PFD
Drury House, 34–43 Russell Street
London WC2B 5HA
020 7344 1000
postmaster@pfd.co.uk
www.pfd.co.uk
Writers, directors, producers, actors, technicians, composers, sportsmen and women, public speakers and illustrators

PHA Casting
Tanzaro House, Ardwick Green North
Manchester M12 6FZ
0161 273 4444
info@pha-agency.co.uk
www.pha-agency.co.uk
Models, extras, actors

Princess Talent Management
Princess Studios, Whiteleys Centre
151 Queensway, London W2 4SB
020 7985 1985
talent@princesstv.com
www.princesstv.com
TV and radio presenters

PVA Management
Hallow Park, Hallow
Worcester WR2 6PG
01905 640663
pvamanltd@aol.com
TV and radio presenters and classical musicians

Qvoice
4th Floor, Holborn Hall
193–197 High Holborn
London WC1V 7BD
020 7025 0660
info@qvoice.co.uk
www.qvoice.co.uk
Voiceovers

Rabbit Vocal Management
2nd Floor, 18 Broadwick Street
London W1F 8HS
020 7287 6466
info@rabbit.uk.net
www.rabbit.uk.net
Voiceovers

Rhubarb
Bakerloo Chambers
304 Edgware Road, London W2 1DY
020 7724 1300
enquiries@rhubarb.co.uk
www.rhubarb.co.uk
Voiceovers

Richard Stone Partnership
2 Henrietta Street
London WC2E 8PS
020 7497 0849
all@richstonepart.co.uk
Actors, presenters, voiceovers, comedians

RK Commercials
205 Chudleigh Road
London SE4 1EG
020 8690 6542
enquiries@rkcommercials.com
www.rkcommercials.com
Actors for commercials and presenting work

Roseman Organisation
51 Queen Anne Street
London W1G 9HS
020 7486 4500
info@therosemanorganisation.co.uk
www.therosemanorganisation.co.uk
News and TV presenters

Roxane Vacca Management
73 Beak Street, London W1F 9SR
020 7734 8085
mail@roxanevaccavoices.com
www.roxanevaccavoices.com
Actors and voiceovers

Sally Hope Associates
108 Leonard Street
London EC2A 4XS
020 7613 5353
casting@sallyhope.biz
www.sallyhope.biz
Actors, voiceovers, directors, designers, lighting, hair and make up etc

Shining Management
12 D'Arblay Street, London W1F 8DU
020 7734 1981
info@shiningvoices.com
www.shiningvoices.com
Voiceovers

Speak
59 Lionel Road North, Brentford
Middlesex TW8 9QZ
020 8758 0666
info@speak.ltd.uk
www.speak.ltd.uk
Voiceovers

Speak-Easy
1 Dairy Yard, High Street
Market Harborough, Leics LE16 7NL
0870 013 5126
enquiries@speak-easy.co.uk
www.speak-easy.co.uk
TV presenters and voiceovers

Storm Artists Management
1st Floor, 5 Jubilee Place
London SW3 3TD
020 7368 9967
info@stormartists.co.uk
www.stormmodels.com
Actors, composers and voiceover

Susi Earnshaw Management
68 High Street, Barnet
Herts EN5 5SJ
020 8441 5010
casting@susiearnshaw.co.uk
www.susiearnshaw.co.uk
Actors and musical theatre performers

Susy Wootton Voices
75 Shelley Street, Kingsley
Northampton NN2 7HZ
0870 765 9660
suzy@suzywoottonvoices.com
www.suzywoottonvoices.com
Voiceovers

Take Three Management
110 Gloucester Avenue
Primrose Hill, London NW1 8HX
020 7209 3777
info@take3management.com
www.take3management.co.uk
TV presenters, after dinner speakers

Talking Heads
2/4 Noel Street, London W1F 8GB
020 7292 7575
voices@talkingheadsvoices.com
www.talkingheadsvoices.com
Voiceovers

Tongue & Groove
3 Stevenson Square
Manchester M1 1DN
0161 228 2469
info@tongueandgroove.co.uk
www.tongueandgroove.co.uk
Voiceovers

Unique Management Group
Beaumont House
Kensington Village, Avonmore Road
London W14 8TS
020 7605 1100
celebrities@uniquegroup.co.uk
www.unique-management.co.uk
TV presenters, radio hosts

Upfront Celebrity Services
39–41 New Oxford Street
London WC1A 1BN
020 7836 7702 / 3
info@upfronttv.com
www.celebritiesworldwide.com
Celebrity bookings

Vincent Shaw Associates
51 Byron Road, London E17 4SN
020 8509 2211
info@vincentshaw.com
www.vincentshaw.com
Actors

Vocal Point
25 Denmark Street
London WC2H 8NJ
020 7419 0700
enquiries@vocalpoint.net
www.vocalpoint.net
Voiceovers

Voice & Script International
Aradco House, 132 Cleveland St
London W1T 6AB
020 7692 7700
info@vsi.tv
www.vsi.tv
Translators and voiceovers in foreign languages

Voice Shop
Bakerloo Chambers
304 Edgware Road, London W2 1DY
020 7402 3966
info@voice-shop.co.uk
www.voice-shop.co.uk
Voiceovers

Voice Squad
62 Blenheim Gardens
London NW2 4NT
020 8450 4451
bookem@voicesquad.com
www.voicesquad.com
Voiceovers

Voicebank, The Irish Voice Over Agency
The Barracks, 76 Irishtown Road
Dublin 4
00 353 1 6687234
voicebank@voicebank.ie
www.voicebank.ie
Voiceovers

Voicecall
67A Gondar Gardens, Fortune Green
London NW6 1EP
020 7209 1064
voicecall@blueyonder.co.uk
www.voicecall-online.co.uk
Voiceovers

The Voiceover Gallery
34 Stockton Road, Chorlton
Manchester M21 9ED
0161 881 8844
info@thevoicegallery.co.uk
www.thevoicegallery.co.uk
Voiceovers

Whatever Artists Management
1 York Street, London W1U 6PA
020 7487 3111
wam@agents-uk.com
www.wamshow.biz
Artists in light entertainment

Yakety Yak
8 Bloomsbury Square
London WC1A 2NE
020 7430 2600
info@yaketyyak.co.uk
www.yaketyyak.co.uk
Voiceovers

Literary agents

►► see page 279

Associations

Agents Association
54 Keyes House, Dolphin Square
London SW1V 3NA
020 7834 0515
association@agents-uk.com
www.agents-uk.com
Trade association of entertainment agents

Association of Authors' Agents
A P Watt, 20 John Street
London WC1N 2DR
020 7405 6774
aaa@apwatt.co.uk
www.agentsassoc.co.uk

Personal Managers' Association
1 Summer Road, East Molesey
Surrey KT8 9LX
020 8398 9796
info@thepma.com

A career in media

Media diversity

It has taken Europe to tell us what we already know: that the UK press fosters a "climate of hostility" toward minorities. Time and again over the past year, asylum seekers, refugees, Muslims, Gypsies and Travellers have attracted the attention of rightwing headline-writers – leading the European Commission against Racism and Intolerance to recommend in June 2005 that the authorities do more to combat the problems such reports cause. Journalism in the UK, the report says, includes material that is "racist and inflammatory in its effect".

Perhaps the biggest row came in March 2005, when, under the headline "Stamp on the camps", the Sun newspaper launched a campaign against illegal Traveller settlements, declaring "war" on what it called a "gipsy [sic] free-for all". Gypsy groups reported the Sun to the Commission for Racial Equality and the Press Complaints Commission, saying they feared its campaign might incite racial hatred; the Sun, for its part, denied that its campaign was racist, saying some Travellers had "ruined" householders' lives. The campaign became an election issue when the Tory leader, Michael Howard, proposed to make trespass by Gypsies a criminal offence; but it was left to Dr James Smith, the chief executive of the Holocaust Centre in the UK, to warn against using "populist situations" to political ends.

The row came a few months after the Press Complaints Commission announced it was cracking down on the use of the inaccurate term "illegal asylum seeker", which was used 33 times in British newspapers in 2004 and 38 times in 2003.

But with so few people from ethnic minorities working in UK journalism, it is hardly surprising that problems occur. In 2002, a survey by the Society of Editors showed that 96% of journalists were white – and the other 4% mostly worked in broadcasting, not newspapers.

Broadcasting is certainly ahead of the game: the sector skills council (Skillset) reported in 2005 that 7% in film and TV were from ethnic minorities – though even that was down from 7.4% the previous year. According to figures quoted by the Guardian's Vikram Dodd, Sky says 8.2% of its staff are from ethnic minorities, and 5.2% of its senior management; while Channel 4 says 11% of its staff are from ethnic minorities, with a 9% target for its senior managers by 2006. The BBC, which has focused on this issue since its former director general Greg Dyke called the corporation "hideously white", plans to have 12.5% of its staff from ethnic minorities by the end of 2007, and 7% of senior managers. As Trevor Phillips, the chairman of the Commission for Racial Equality, put it in 2005: "the broadcast side of the industry is at least 20 years ahead of the print media".

So what to do about it? Recruit more black and ethnic minority journalists, it seems. And there are plenty of groups out there trying

to make that happen: see the listings on page 396. The magazine Asians in Media, meanwhile, has produced a list of the top 10 Asians in the British media. These are talented and successful people, but for the most part they are not in the very top jobs: reporting on the list for the Guardian, Vikram Dodd wrote that "board meetings at the big broadcasters and newspapers are about as white as a Klu Klux Klan gathering in the deep South in the 1950s".

In advertising, the Institute of Practitioners in Advertising reported in 2005 that only 4% of agencies' employees are from ethnic minorities; 70% of those, it said, worked in IT departments. "Unless the industry challenges the status quo," it said, "we run the risk of becoming increasingly out of touch with modern day, multicultural Britain." It reminded the industry that 7.9% of the population is of ethnic minority origin – with a combined spending power of £32bn a year.

In January 2005, the ad agency Euro RSCG Life apologised after using a black model to advertise liquorice-flavoured Nicotinell gum. The agency said the ads had been printed in "error", in a move not authorised by the client.

Women

Women still find it more difficult than men to break into the higher echelons of media management: just 15 of the 2005 MediaGuardian 100 were women, although they included the culture and media secretary, the chief executive at Trinity Mirror, the director of television at the BBC, and the editor of the Sun.

In broadcasting, the Skillset 2004 survey showed that women make up just 38% of the workforce, the same amount as in 2003: they were only a significant majority in certain roles, such as make-up and hairdressing (93%) and wardrobe (74%).

Age

Ageism looks set to be a big issue in media from 2006. The issue has always been the media's dirty little secret, with many companies recruiting younger and relatively inexperienced staff in preference to people over 40; and until now, they have been able to get away with it. From October 2006, however, legislation will come into force that makes it unlawful to discriminate on grounds of age, so look out for some high-profile discrimination claims in years to come.

Disability

According to Skillset, the proportion of disabled people employed in the broadcast industries rose from 1% in 2003 to 1.3% in 2004. TV performed best, with 2.3%.

Beyond tokenism **Sunny Hundal**

Diversity" is a word increasingly fraught with complication in the media industry, where encouraging change is akin to trying to part the Red Sea without the help of Moses.

I may be exaggerating, and there are many individuals who have recognised the industry's need to reflect Britain's multi-racial makeup, but there are real concerns about where the drive for diversity heading.

In June 2005 I was at Five's offices in Covent Garden, at an event organised by the Cultural Diversity Network (CDN). There, I heard presenter Trisha Goddard talking about her difficult climb to the top of the chat-show circuit. It was an inspiring story – except that most of the audience already worked in TV, and were more interested in speaking to the sparse smattering of genre commissioners.

After the event, I wrote an article for Asians in Media about the lack of strategic thinking in pushing forward the diversity agenda in broadcasting.

In October 2000, I wrote, the big boys of TV accepted that something needed to be done about "diversity", so they formed the CDN. Five years later they still don't seem to know what direction it should take.

At the end of each year, the CDN publishes a report in which each of the members state what they have done to promote diversity in specific areas over the past year. Unfortunately it is littered with tokenistic statements such as: "We continue to reflect diversity in our programming" or references to one-off shows, such as ITV1's My Life as a Popat, that are meant to reflect diversity on screen.

Events such as the one by Five are organised to give the impression that the TV companies are proactive. More importantly, they can be used to pad out next year's report.

My article drew a fairly muted response from broadcasters, but a strong one from readers. One said: "The whole industry is riddled with cynical box-ticking exercises which would be funny if they weren't so disturbing."

Another pointed out that commissioners had a habit of claiming in the trade press that they were doing plenty to address diversity in programming, even when their own events were full of negative feedback.

When it takes someone like Meera Syal four years to get her popular book Life Isn't All Ha Ha Hee Hee made into a series and be shown at primetime, we know something is wrong.

An Asian executive producer, who has had mainstream comedy success, recently told me that the BBC behaved as if its viewers were all Daily Mail readers who would not watch a drama if a non-white was in a lead role.

Television companies should move on from affirmative-action recruitment policies to more strategic policies. They need to examine which areas of programming require more ethnic minority talent and look to redress the balance.

They need to re-examine issues of portrayal and provide a platform to a wider range of voices from the different communities. They need to learn how to better attract new talent from non-traditional sources.

There are various reasons the current situation is lacking: there is not enough consultation with those who work within the industry – white and non-white; the "diversity events" have little strategic direction or long-term objectives; not many know who is actually leading the CDN with an over-arching plan for everyone.

There is a focus on the TV industry because it remains the principal mass medium in modern society. That is not to say that the problem lies only there.

A recent report by the Institute of Practitioners in Advertising found that nearly 50% of non-white workers within the industry were in back office operations rather than media-buying or selling. Almost two years after the IPA said it had to become more diverse, it is now focused on getting youngsters from a wider range of backgrounds to try and enter the industry.

The Chartered Institute of Public Relations took its own tentative step this year by launching a website focusing on diversity issues, while the UK Film Council recently launched a new charter designed to promote further equality in the film industry.

But the biggest challenge lies within the press. Most newspaper offices would struggle to reflect the racial mix of the UK – let alone that of London, where most of their operations are based.

Only the Guardian publishes an annual and easily accessible document on how many of its employees are from ethnic minority backgrounds. A Society of Editors report last year admitted that even local papers were very behind in reflecting the communities they served.

For example, how can a paper like the Evening Standard reach out to the 40% of non-white London, if its journalists cannot relate to those they are meant to be covering?

In Britain's sometimes constantly evolving race relations, newspapers need to allow non-white communities to effectively represent themselves, if not just to attract new readers but also foster better reporting.

While the intentions are there, the media industry needs to put more thought into how to bring itself into the 21st century.

Sunny Hundal is the editor of Asians in Media

Media diversity

Diversity Contents

Media diversity associations

Age Concern
Astral House, 1268 London Road
London SW16 4ER
020 8765 7200
ace@ace.org.uk
www.ageconcern.co.uk

Age Positive
Department for Work and Pensions
Room W8d, Moorfoot
Sheffield S1 4PQ
agepositive@dwp.gsi.gov.uk
www.agepositive.gov.uk/
Age diversity in employment
PRESS: *020 8238 8550*

Bird's Eye View
Unit 310A, Aberdeen Centre
22–24 Highbury Grove
London N5 2EA
020 7288 7444
office@birds-eye-view.co.uk
www.birds-eye-view.co.uk
*Platform for emerging women film
makers*

Employers' Forum on Disability
Broadcaster and Creative Industries
    Disability Network
Nutmeg House, 60 Gainsford Street
London SE1 2NY
020 7403 3020
jenny.stevens@
    employers-forum.co.uk
www.employers-forum.co.uk
Employers' organisation

**Commission for Racial Equality
(CRE)**
St Dunstan's House
201–211 Borough High Street
London SE1 1GZ
020 7939 0000
info@cre.gov.uk
www.cre.gov.uk

Creative Collective
239a Uxbridge Road
Shepherds Bush, London W12 9DL
020 8576 6305
info@thecreativecollective.com
www.thecreativecollective.com
*Aims to develop social policy on
diversity and to empower community
groups to harness media*

Cultural Diversity Network (CDN)
c/o ITV, London Television Centre
Upper Ground, London SE1 9LT
020 7261 3006
cdnetwork@itv.com
www.itv.com
*Online directory of black, Asian and
other ethnic minority TV freelancers
and staff*

Digital Media Access Group
Applied Computing
University of Dundee
Dundee DD1 4HN
01382 345050
dmag@computing.dundee.ac.uk
www.dmag.org.uk
Promotes new media accessibility

Disability Rights Commission
Freepost MID02164
Stratford upon Avon CV37 9BR
0845 762 2633
enquiry@drc-gb.org
www.drc-gb.org

Emma Awards
67–69 Whitfield Street
London W1T 4HF
020 7636 1233
mail@emma.tv
www.emma.tv
*Multicultural media awards and online
humanitarian information portal*

Equal Opportunities Commission
Arndale House, Arndale Centre
Manchester M4 3EQ
0845 601 5901
info@eoc.org.uk
www.eoc.org.uk

**International Association of Women
in Radio and Television**
nik@netactive.co.za
www.iawrt.org

**International Women's Media
Foundation**
1625K Street NW, Suite 1275
Washington, DC 20006, USA
00 1 202 496 1992
info@iwmf.org
www.iwmf.org

Ligali
PO Box 1257, London E5 0UD
020 8986 1984
mail@ligali.org
www.ligali.org
African British equality organisation

MediaWise Trust
38 Easton Business Centre
Felix Road, Bristol BS5 0HE
0117 941 5889
pw@mediawise.org.uk
www.mediawise.org.uk
Independent media ethics charity

**Society of Women Writers &
Journalists**
Calvers Farm, Thelveton
Diss IP21 4NG
01379 740 550
zoe@zoeking.com
www.swwt.co.uk

**Spoken Word Publishing
Association (SWPA)**
c/o Macmillan Audio
20 New Wharf Road
London N1 9RR
020 7014 6041
audio@penguin.co.uk
www.swpa.co.uk

Women and Equality Unit
35 Great Smith Street
London SW1P 3BQ
0845 001 0029
info-womenandequalityunit@
    dti.gsi.gov.uk
www.womenandequalityunit.gov.uk

Women in Film and Television
6 Langley Street, London WC2H 9JA
020 7240 4875
emily@wftv.org.uk
www.wftv.org.uk

Women in Journalism
wijUK@aol.com
www.womeninjournalism.co.uk

Women in Publishing
info@wipub.org.uk
www.wipub.org.uk

Women's Radio Group
27 Bath Road, London W4 1LJ
020 8995 5442
wrg@zelo.demon.co.uk
www.womeninradio.org.uk
Training, info and production facilities

Media awards

Press

Amnesty International Media Awards
020 7033 1500
www.amnesty.org.uk/mediaawards
Human rights journalism

AOP Online Publishing Awards
020 7400 7532
www.uk.aop.org.uk

BAPLA Picture Editor's Award
020 7713 1780
www.pbf.org.uk//previousshows.html
For nationals that show best practice in crediting images

British Garden Writers Guild
020 7245 6943
www.gardenwriters.co.uk/awards

British Press Awards
020 8565 4392
www.britishpressawards.com
Organised by Press Gazette

British Society of Magazine Editors
020 8906 4664
www.bsme.com

Emmas (Ethnic Multicultural Media Academy awards)
020 7636 1233
www.emma.tv
Multicultural media

Foreign Press Association Annual Media Awards
020 7930 0445
www.foreign-press.org.uk
International journalism by British media

Glenfiddich Food & Drink awards
020 8334 1235
www.glenfiddich.com/foodanddrink

Guardian Student Media Awards
020 7239 9963
www.media.guardian
.co.uk/studentmediaawards
Student journalists, designers and photographers
PRESS: *020 7713 4087*

The Herald Scottish Student Press Awards 2003
0141 302 7000
www.theherald.co.uk
Open to full-time students in Scotland

ICIJ Award for Outstanding International Investigative Reporting
00 1 202 466 1300
www.icij.org

Local Reporting Awards
020 7636 7014
www.newspapersoc.org.uk
Under-30s

Medical Journalism Awards
023 8035 4728
www.norwichunion.co.uk
/medical_journalism_awards

NetMedia European Online Journalism Awards
020 7637 7097
www.net-media.co.uk

Newspaper Awards
01869 340788
www.newspaperawards.newstech
.co.uk
Technical innovation in newspaper and new media production

Observer Hodge Award
01727 799987
www.observer.co.uk/hodgeaward
Young photographers

Picture Editors' Awards
administrator@pictureawards.net
www.pictureawards.net
Photographic journalism

Plain English Media Awards
01663 744409
www.plainenglish.co.uk/mediaawards
Campaign against gobbledygook

PPA Awards
020 7404 4166
www.ppa.co.uk
Periodicals

Press Gazette Student Journalism Awards
020 8565 3056
www.pressgazette.co.uk
Open to students enrolled on a journalism course

Race in the Media Awards
020 7939 0000
www.cre.gov.uk
Organised by Commission for Racial Equality

Regional Press Awards
020 8565 3056
www.regionalpressawards.co.uk
Organised by Press Gazette

What the Papers Say Awards
020 7620 1620
www.granadamedia.com
National newspaper journalists

TV and film

Academy Awards (US)
00 1 310 247 3000
www.oscars.org
Film

Bafta Awards
020 7734 0022
www.bafta.org
Film, TV and interactive industries

British Comedy Awards
020 7605 1200
www.britishcomedyawards.co.uk

British Independent Film Awards
020 7287 3833
www.bifa.org.uk

Broadcast Awards
020 7505 8115
www.broadcastnow.co.uk
Programme ideas and execution

Emmy Awards (US)
00 1 818 754 2800
www.emmys.com
TV
PRESS: *00 1 323 965 1990*

Evening Standard British Film Awards
020 7938 6247
www.thisislondon.co.uk

First Light Film Awards
0121 693 2091
www.firstlightmovies.com
Short films made by 5 to 18-year-olds

Golden Globes (US)
00 1 310 657 1731
www.hfpa.org
TV and film, worldwide

Indie Awards (Pact)
020 7067 4367
www.pact.co.uk
Film, TV, animation and new media producers

National TV Awards
020 7486 4443
Winners picked by viewers

Royal Television Society Awards
020 7691 2470
www.rts.org.uk

Radio

NTL Commercial Radio Awards
020 7306 2603
www.crca.co.uk

Sony Radio Academy Awards
020 7255 2010
www.radioacademy.org/awards

Student Radio Awards
events@studentradio.org.uk
www.studentradio.org.uk

Music

Brits
020 7803 1301
www.brits.co.uk
PRESS: *020 7439 7222*

Broadband from BT Digital Music Awards
louise@dma04.com
www.dma04.com

Classical Brit Awards
020 7803 1301
www.classicalbrits.co.uk

Dancestar
00 1 305 371 2450
www.dancestar.com
Dance music

Grammys (US)
00 1 310 392 3777
www.grammy.com

Gramophone Awards
020 8267 5136
www.gramophone.co.uk
Classical music

Ivor Novello Awards
www.britishacademy
       .com/ivorsmenu/ivorshome.htm
British songwriters, composers and music publishers
PRESS: *020 8621 2345*
TV AND RADIO: *020 7299 7979*

Kerrang Awards
020 7436 1515
www.kerrangawards.com
Rock

Mobo Awards
www.mobo.net
Music of black origin
PRESS: *020 7419 8055,*
press@mobo.com

MTV Europe Awards
www.mtve.com

Music Week Awards
020 7921 8308
www.musicweekawards.com

NME Awards
020 7261 5564
www.nmeawards.com
Voted for by NME readers

Nationwide Mercury Prize
020 8964 9964
www.nationwidemercurys.com
Best album in UK and Ireland

Q Awards
020 7312 8182
www.qawards.co.uk

Radio 3 Awards for World Music
020 7765 5887
www.bbc.co.uk/radio3/awards2006

Books

British Book Design and Production Awards
020 7915 8334
www.britishbookawards2006.com

Guardian First Book Award
020 7278 2332
www.guardian.co.uk/firstbook
First-time writers of fiction, poetry, biography, memoirs, history, politics, science and current affairs
PRESS: *020 7713 4087*

Orange Prize for Fiction
www.orangeprize.co.uk
Women's fiction
PRESS: *020 7471 6893*

The Man Booker Prize
www.themanbookerprize.com
Best novel in English by citizen of Commonwealth, Ireland, Pakistan or South Africa
PRESS: *020 7631 2666*

Whitbread Book Awards
020 7202 2871
www.whitbreadbookawards.co.uk
Contemporary British writing
PRESS: *020 7202 8222*

Advertising & PR

Advertising, Marketing & Digital Media Awards
020 7693 0428
www.newspapersoc.org.uk

British Television Advertising Awards
020 7734 6962
www.btaa.co.uk

Campaign Direct/ Media/ Poster Advertising Awards
020 8267 4090
www.brandrepublic
       .com/magazines/campaign

Cannes Lions International Advertising Festival Awards
020 7239 3400
www.canneslions.com

Communicators in Business Awards
0870 121 7606
www.cib.uk.com

Creative Juice Awards
020 7636 7014
www.newspapersoc.org.uk
Young creative teams with maximum of three years' experience

Institute of Public Relations Excellence Awards
020 7253 5151
www.ipr.org.uk

London International Advertising Awards
020 8426 1670
www.liaawards.com

Marketing Week Effectiveness Awards
020 7970 4772
www.marketingweek.co.uk

Media Week Awards
020 8565 3056
www.mediaweekawards.co.uk

PR Week Awards
020 8267 4017
www.prweek.com

The Pride Awards
01158 419699
www.ipr.org.uk/prideawards

TUC/Bank of Scotland Press and PR Awards
020 7467 1242
www.tuc.org.uk
Journalism about Scottish issues and in Scottish publications

New media

AOP Online Publishing Awards
020 7400 7532
www.uk.aop.org.uk

Bafta Games Awards
020 7734 0022
www.bafta.org
Video games

Bloggies
2005.bloggies.com

New Media Age Awards
020 7970 4848
www.nma.co.uk

New Statesman New Media Awards
020 7730 3444
www.newstatesman.co.uk/nma

Revolution Awards
020 8267 4947
www.revolutionmagazine.com/Awards
Digital marketing and business

Webby Awards
00 1 212 675 3555
www.webbyawards.com
PRESS: *00 1 212 627 8098*

Glossary

Press

ABC: The Audit Bureau of Circulation, the company that monitors and verifies magazines and newspaper sales. "ABCs" is the popular term for the circulation figures it publishes: see explainer on page xx

average issue readership: The number of people who, when surveyed, say they have read a newspaper or magazine within the lifespan of the issue. Also known as AIR

Brad: British Rate and Data, a company that records every periodical that carries advertising in the UK

broadsheet: Larger size of paper, used by the news sections of most quality UK papers; usually 580mm × 380mm

bulks: Copies of newspapers distributed free to targeted places such as hotels and airlines. *See explainer on ABCs*

byline: A journalist's name next to an article. Reporters live for bylines like salesmen live for bonuses

circulation: The number of copies a newspaper or magazines sells or distributes in a defined period (usually a month). Not the same as average issue readership

compact: A less downmarket term for tabloid

copy: Words for publication

DPS: Double-page spread

freesheet: A newspaper or magazine distributed free of charge, and usually paid for by advertising

journalist: Someone who works on the editorial side of a newspaper or magazine

leader: Editorial opinion column expressing the views of the newspaper (or its owner)

masthead: The bit with the title of the newspaper or magazine at the top of the front page

news agency: Company that sells news stories to a newspaper or magazine, usually delivered electronically to each journalist's desktop over the wires. The biggest are Reuters, the UK-based Press Association (PA) and the US-based Associated Press (AP)

Newspaper Society: Body representing the UK's regional press

PPA: The Periodical Publishers Association. Represents magazine publishers in the UK

reporter: Someone who writes news stories. Just one of many kinds of journalist

scoop: The act of printing a news story (or, these days, a celebrity interview) before a rival. The "scoop culture" of the UK press has been criticised for getting in the way of balanced news reporting

standfirst: The short paragraph at the top of a feature article, below the headline, that summarises it for the reader. Usually written by a subeditor

subeditor: Someone who lays out and edits the copy in a newspaper or magazine. Will also write the headline, standfirst and other page furniture such as picture captions

tabloid: Smaller size of paper, until recently used by more downmarket titles and the features sections of some quality papers; usually half the size of broadsheet. Also known as a compact

wires: Electronic delivery of news and pictures, sent by agencies to a journalist's desktop

TV and film

analogue television: Television transmitted in "radio waves"; in other words, not digitally. Most terrestrial TV in the UK is still transmitted in analogue

Barb: The Broadcasters Audience Research Board, which measures television audiences

BBC: The British Broadcasting Corporation. Britain's public service broadcaster

best boy: The second-in-command of a lighting team

BSkyB: Britain's only satellite broadcaster, owned by Rupert Murdoch's News Corporation

cable television: Television delivered through a cable under the ground into the home. Largely concentrated in urban areas. Can be digital or analogue

digital television: Television transmitted in binary format; can be delivered by cable, by satellite or terrestrially. Allows greater choice of channels, better quality and interactive services

EPG: the electronic programme guide

encryption: The encoding of television signals for security purposes, usually so they can only be watched by paying subscribers

free-to-air: A television service that can be received without decoding or paying a fee

Freeview: A commercial free-to-air digital terrestrial service; a partnership between BBC, BSkyB and transmission firm Crown Castle

grip: Someone who handles the equipment that enables a camera to move

HD: High-definition

ITV network: The 15 regional franchises that together make up the ITV1 channel

Glossary

ITV plc: Company, formed from the merger of Carlton and Granada, that controls 11 of the 15 ITV network franchises, including all those in England and Wales

licence fee: How the BBC generates most of its revenue. A colour licence cost £126.50 in 2005

multichannel television: TV that includes more than just the five analogue terrestrial channels. If you receive cable, satellite or digital terrestrial, you are defined as being in a "multichannel home"

multiplex: A single digital terrestrial transmission comprising several channels. There are six television multiplexes in all

Ofcom: Broadcasting super-regulator

Pact: Producers' alliance for cinema and television. Represents independent television production companies

pay-per-view: An individual programme that the viewer has to pay to see

pay-TV: A general term for subscription services that the viewer has to pay to see

radio spectrum: The total capacity of radio frequencies that can be received. A small part of the electromagnetic spectrum, which is made up of a range of phenomena including gamma rays, X-rays, ultraviolet radiation and visible light

satellite television: Television received through a satellite dish, controlled in Britain by BSkyB. BSkyB has switched all its television services to digital

Section 42, Section 48: British tax breaks for the film industry. Until reform of the tax system, film producers wasted no time in claiming both of them, a practice known as "double-dipping"

terrestrial television: Television beamed from a ground transmitter directly to the home; can be analogue or digital

UK Film Council: Lottery-funded body charged with attracting investment to the British film industry

watershed: Before 9pm, nothing may shown on television that is considered unsuitable for children; after 9pm, nothing may shown that is considered unsuitable for adults. 9pm is therefore the "watershed"

Radio

access radio: The old name for community radio

analogue radio: Radio transmitted in waves; in other words, not digitally. Most terrestrial radio in the UK is still transmitted in analogue

audience share: In Rajar figures, the percentage of all radio listening hours that a station accounts for within its transmission area

BBC: The British Broadcasting Corporation. Britain's public service broadcaster

community radio: Not-for-profit, community-based radio. Formerly access radio

DAB digital radio: Digital terrestrial radio

digital radio: Shorthand for digital terrestrial radio. More accurately, refers to any radio transmitted in binary format – either through DAB digital radio, or via a television or the internet

multiplex: A single digital terrestrial transmission, comprising several channels. There are two national and almost 50 local multiplexes

Ofcom: Broadcasting super-regulator

podcasting: A way of publishing audio to the internet; users download podcasts to a PC or portable audio player

Rajar: Radio Joint Audience Research, the company that calculates radio audience figures

radio spectrum: The total capacity of radio signals that can be received

reach: In Rajar figures, the number of people aged 15 or over who tune to a radio station within at least a quarter-hour period over the course of a week, and have listened to the station for at least five minutes within that quarter-hour

New media

3G: Third-generation mobile phones, capable of video messaging, location mapping and other technical wizardry

ADSL: Broadband over a BT phone line (but not necessarily bought from BT)

blog: Diary-style web page in which new entries are added at the top and old ones drift to the bottom; popular among those who want a web page but don't necessarily know much about the internet. Short for "weblog"

broadband: High-speed internet access, usually 512kbps (kilobytes per second) as opposed to the 52kbps of a standard modem

browser: Software usually used to surf, or "browse", the internet. Internet Explorer and Netscape Communicator are the most popular

coverage: The percentage of the country or the population that can be reached by a mobile phone network

search engine: Service allowing you to find a word or image anywhere on the world wide web

short message service (SMS): Text messaging

Wi-Fi: Wireless internet access

Books

A-format, B-format: The two main "sizes" in which paperbacks are published. A-format are smaller (110mm × 178mm) and usually more downmarket; B-format are larger (130mm × 198mm) and usually further upmarket

acquisition editor: Someone in a publishing house who identifies and negotiates to acquire new titles for publication

advance: Initial payment to authors against which any royalties are offset

commissioning editor: Someone in a publishing house who looks for authors to write particular books for publication; sometimes also an acquiring editor

imprint: The name of the publisher; usually a brand operating under the auspices of a large publishing house

literary agent: Person who finds marketable authors and tries to sell rights in their work to publishers, taking a commission in the process

Nielsen Bookscan: Company that produces bestseller lists and other analysis of the UK book industry

royalties: Payment received by the author as a percentage of sales. Usually set off against the advance

rights: The main commodity in the books business. Rights can be separated out to include film, television, multimedia, merchandising and rights to publish abroad

Music

A&R: "Artist and repertoire"; the department of a record label that manages musicians

British Phonographic Industry: Association representing the music industry in the UK

indie: Independent record label

iPod: The most popular digital music (usually MP3) player, manufactured by Apple

label: Organisation that produces music; could be an indie, or a brand operating under the auspices of a large record company

MP3: Most popular digital music format

Advertising & PR

Advertising Association: Body representing the advertising and promotional marketing industries

Advertising Standards Authority: Regulator for advertising

below the line: Marketing services such as PR, direct marketing, market research and sales promotion are said to be "below the line"; advertising directly in media is "above the line"

creatives: In advertising, art directors and copywriters, who often work in pairs on an ad

Chartered Institute of Public Relations: PR professional organisation

display: Advertising in the main body of a publication (as opposed to classified)

demographic data: Information defining a population according to factors such as age, sex and income; used to target an ad or marketing campaign

media agency: Agency that controls the purchase of advertising space, and often the strategic direction of a campaign

pitch: The lifeblood of the advertising industry is the pitch for an account

press release: Information sent by PR agencies and other publicists to journalists

Public Relations Consultants Association: PR trade body

solus: In publishing, the only advert on a page

Media law

contempt of court: A crime that carries imprisonment or a fine. Journalists could be in contempt of a court by publishing information about a defendant or other person granted privacy under a court order or injunction; or by speculating about the guilt or innocence of a defendant; or by publishing a photograph of a defendant when identity is an issue

culture select committee: Influential cross-party parliamentary committee that examines issues in culture, media and sport

European convention on human rights: European Union legislation, incorporated in British law through the Human Rights Act 1998. Includes articles protecting right to freedom of expression, but also the right to privacy

European court of human rights: Highest European court dealing with human rights law

law commission: Senior lawyers who meet to recommend changes in legislation

libel: A civil "tort", for which a complainant may sue for damages. Generally speaking, a journalist commits libel by publishing or broadcasting something that is defamatory, even by implication, to a person or a small enough group of people; *unless* the journalist can prove that what they wrote or published was true, or it was fair comment based firmly in fact, or it was an accurate, contemporaneous report of something said in parliament or court. But that isn't the half of it: see the latest edition of *McNae's Essential Law for Journalists*

Careers and training

Bectu: Broadcasting, entertainment, cinematograph and theatre union. Represents workers in broadcasting, film, theatre, entertainment, leisure and interactive media

BJTC: Broadcast journalism training council. Accredits broadcast journalism courses

FT2: Freelance Training for Film and Television, a respected training body

NCTJ: National council for the training of journalists. Accredits newspaper and magazine journalism courses

NUJ: National union of journalists. Represents journalists

Pact: Producers' alliance for cinema and television. Represents independent television production companies

Skillset: National training organisation for broadcast, film, video and interactive media

A career in media

Contacts book

Downing Street

Prime Minister's Office
10 Downing Street
London SW1A 2AA
020 7270 3000
www.number-10.gov.uk
Prime minister: Tony Blair*
Parliamentary private secretary:
Keith Hill
PRESS: *020 7930 4433*

Government departments

Cabinet Office
70 Whitehall, London SW1A 2AS
020 7276 3000
www.cabinet-office.gov.uk
Cabinet Office minister: John Hutton*
Parliamentary secretary: Jim Murphy
PRESS: *020 7276 1191*

Deputy Prime Minister
26 Whitehall, London SW1A 2WH
020 7944 4400
www.odpm.gov.uk
Deputy prime minister: John Prescott*
Communities and local government
minister: David Miliband*; housing
and planning minister: Yvette Cooper;
local government minister: Phil
Woolas; parliamentary secretaries: Jim
Fitzpatrick, Baroness Andrews
PRESS: *020 7944 4297*

Constitutional Affairs
54 Victoria Street
London SW1E 6QW
020 7210 8614
www.lcd.gov.uk
Constitutional affairs secretary and
Lord Chancellor: Lord Falconer of
Thoroton*
Minister: Harriet Harman;
parliamentary secretaries: Baroness
Ashton of Upholland; Bridget Prentice
PRESS: *020 7210 8512*

Culture, Media and Sport
2–4 Cockspur Street
London SW1Y 5DH
020 7211 6200
www.culture.gov.uk
Culture secretary: Tessa Jowell*
Minister: Richard Caborn;
parliamentary secretaries: David
Lammy, James Purnell
PRESS: *020 7211 6145*

Defence
Horseguards Avenue
London SW1A 2HB
020 7218 9000
www.mod.uk
Defence secretary: John Reid*
Minister: Adam Ingram;
parliamentary secretaries: Don Touhig,
Lord Drayson
PRESS: *020 7218 7907*

Education and Skills
Great Smith Street
London SW1P 3BT
0870 000 2288
www.dfes.gov.uk
Education secretary: Ruth Kelly*
Schools minister: Jacqui Smith;
universities minister: Bill Rammell;
minister for children: Beverley Hughes;
junior minister, children: Maria Eagle;
under secretary for FE and higher
education: Phil Hope; junior minister,
schools: Lord Andrew Adonis
PRESS: *020 7925 6789*

Environment, Food and Rural Affairs
17 Smith Square
London SW1P 3JR
020 7238 6000
www.defra.gov.uk
Environment secretary:
Margaret Beckett*
Minister: Elliot Morley; parliamentary
secretaries: Ben Bradshaw, Lord Bach,
Jim Knight
PRESS – ANIMAL WELFARE: *020 7238*
6044; ENVIRONMENT: *020 7238 6054;*
RURAL AFFAIRS: *020 7238 5608;*
SUSTAINABLE FARMING AND FOOD: *020*
7238 6146

Foreign Office
Whitehall
London SW1A 2AH
020 7270 1500
www.fco.gov.uk
Foreign secretary: Jack Straw*
Europe minister: Douglas Alexander*;
minister for trade: Ian Pearson; Middle
East minister: Kim Howells;
parliamentary secretary: Lord
Triesman
PRESS: *020 7008 3100*

Health
79 Whitehall, London SW1A 2NS
020 7210 4850
www.dh.gov.uk
Health secretary: Patricia Hewitt*
Ministers: Rosie Winterton, Jane
Kennedy, Lord Warner; parliamentary
secretaries: Caroline Flint, Liam Byrne
PRESS: *020 7210 5221*

Home Office
Queen Anne's Gate
London SW1H 9AT
0870 000 1585
www.homeoffice.gov.uk
Home secretary: Charles Clarke*
Ministers: Hazel Blears, Baroness
Scotland of Asthal, Tony McNulty;
parliamentary secretaries: Paul
Goggins, Fiona Mactaggart, Andy
Burnham
PRESS: *020 7035 4381*

International Development
1 Palace Street
London SW1E 5HE
020 7023 0000
www.dfid.gov.uk
International development secretary:
Hilary Benn*
Parliamentary secretary: Gareth Thomas
PRESS: *020 7023 0600*

Law Officers' Department
9 Buckingham Gate
London SW1E 6JP
020 7271 2422
www.lslo.gov.uk
Attorney general: Lord Goldsmith*
Solicitor general: Mike O'Brien;
advocate general for Scotland: Baroness
Clark
PRESS: *020 7271 2440*

Northern Ireland Office
11 Millbank, London SW1P 4PN
028 9052 0700
www.nio.gov.uk
Northern Ireland secretary: Peter Hain*
Ministers: Lord Rooker, David Hanson;
parliamentary secretaries: Angela
Smith, Shaun Woodward
PRESS: *020 7210 6518*
 028 9052 8268

Privy Council
2 Carlton Gardens
London SW1Y 5AA
020 7210 1033
www.privy-council.org.uk
Leader of the Lords and Lord President
of the Council: Baroness Amos*
Leader of the Commons and Lord Privy
Seal: Geoff Hoon*
PRESS: *020 7210 1092*

Scotland Office
Whitehall, London SW1A 2AU
020 7270 6754
www.scottishsecretary.gov.uk
Scotland secretary: Alistair Darling*
Parliamentary secretary: David Cairns
PRESS: *0131 244 9053*

*cabinet minister

Trade and Industry
1 Victoria Street
London SW1H 0ET
020 7215 5000
www.dti.gov.uk
Trade and industry secretary:
  Alan Johnson*
Energy minister: Malcolm Wicks;
minister for trade: Ian Pearson;
minister: Alun Michael;
parliamentary secretaries: Barry
Gardiner, Meg Munn, Lord Sainsbury
of Turville, Gerry Sutcliffe
PRESS: *020 7215 5961 / 5967 / 6405*

Transport
76 Marsham Street
London SW1P 4DR
020 7944 8300
www.dft.gov.uk
Transport secretary: Alistair Darling*
Minister: Dr Stephen Ladyman;
parliamentary secretaries: Derek
Twigg, Karen Buck
PRESS – RAIL: *020 7944 3248;* ROADS:
020 7944 3066; SEA AND AIR: *020*
7944 3232

Treasury
1 Horse Guards Road
London SW1A 2HQ
020 7270 4558
www.hm-treasury.gov.uk
Chancellor of the Exchequer:
  Gordon Brown*
Chief secretary: Des Browne*;
paymaster general: Dawn Primarolo;
financial secretary: John Healey;
economic secretary: Ivan Lewis;
PRESS: *020 7270 5238*

Wales Office
Whitehall, London SW1A 2ER
020 7270 0534
www.walesoffice.gov.uk
Wales secretary: Peter Hain*
Parliamentary secretary: Nick Ainger
PRESS: *020 7270 0565*
  029 2089 8267

Work and Pensions
79 Whitehall, London SW1A 2NS
020 7238 0800
www.dwp.gov.uk
Work and pensions secretary:
  David Blunkett*
Work minister: Margaret Hodge;
pensions minister: Stephen Timms;
parliamentary secretaries: Lord Hunt
of Kingsheath, James Plaskitt, Anne
McGuire
PRESS: *020 7238 0866*

Minister without portfolio
Ian McCartney*

Lords chief whip
Lord Grocott of Telford*

Wales
National Assembly for Wales
Cardiff Bay, Cardiff CF99 1NA
029 2082 5111
www.wales.gov.uk
First minister: Rhodri Morgan
Ministers – business: Jane Hutt;
culture, Welsh language and sport:
Alun Pugh; economic development and
transport: Andrew Davies; education
and lifelong learning: Jane Davidson;
environment, planning and
countryside: Carwyn Jones; finance,
local government and public services:
Sue Essex; health and social services:
Brian Gibbons; social justice and
regeneration: Edwina Hart
PRESS: *029 2089 8099*

Scotland
Scottish Executive
St Andrews House
Edinburgh EH1 3DG
0131 556 8400
www.scotland.gov.uk
First minister: Jack McConnell
Ministers – deputy first minister and
enterprise & lifelong learning: Nicol
Stephen; communities: Malcolm
Chisholm; health and community care:
Andy Kerr; education and young
people: Peter Peacock; environment and
rural development: Ross Finnie;
finance and public service reform: Tom
McCabe; justice: Cathy Jamieson;
parliamentary business: Margaret
Curran; tourism, culture and sport:
Patricia Ferguson; transport and
telecommunications: Tavish Scott
PRESS: *0131 244 1111*

Northern Ireland
Northern Ireland Assembly
(suspended October 2002)
www.niassembly.gov.uk

Northern Ireland Executive
(suspended October 2002)
www.northernireland.gov.uk

Local and regional government
Local Government Association
020 7664 3131
www.lga.gov.uk
PRESS: *020 7664 3333*
County Councils Network
020 7664 3011
www.lga.gov.uk/ccn
Audit Commission for Local
Authorities
020 7828 1212
www.audit-commission.gov.uk
PRESS: *020 7166 2128*
  020 7166 2111
Convention of Scottish Local
Authorities
0131 474 9200
www.cosla.gov.uk
PRESS: *0131 474 9205*
Improvement and Development
Agency
020 7296 6600
www.idea.gov.uk
PRESS: *020 7296 6529*
Local government ombudsman
020 7217 4900
www.lgo.org.uk
Scotland
0870 011 5378
www.scottishombudsman.org.uk
Wales
01656 641150
www.ombudsman-wales.org

Professional bodies
Association of Council Secretaries
and Solicitors
acsesny@cybase.co.uk
www.acses.org.uk
Association of Electoral
Administrators
0151 281 8246
www.aea-elections.co.uk
Association of Local Authority Chief
Executives
www.alace.org.uk

* cabinet minister

406

England

London

Greater London Authority
020 7983 4000
www.london.gov.uk
PRESS: *020 7983 6553*

Association of London Government
020 7934 9999
www.alg.gov.uk
PRESS: *07717 435 184*
07917 227 216

Corporation of London
020 7606 3030
www.corpoflondon.gov.uk
PRESS: *020 7332 1455*

LONDON BOROUGHS

Barking and Dagenham
020 8592 4500
www.barking-dagenham
.gov.uk
PRESS: *020 8227 2107*

Barnet
020 8359 2000
www.barnet.gov.uk
PRESS: *020 8359 7796*

Bexley
020 8303 7777
www.bexley.gov.uk
PRESS: *020 8308 4977*

Brent
020 8937 1234
www.brent.gov.uk
PRESS: *020 8937 1066*

Bromley
020 8464 3333
www.bromley.gov.uk
PRESS: *020 8313 4415*

Camden
020 7278 4444
www.camden.gov.uk
PRESS: *020 7974 5717*

Croydon
020 8686 4433
www.croydon.gov.uk
PRESS: *020 8760 5644*

Ealing
020 8825 5000
www.ealing.gov.uk
PRESS: *020 8825 8686*

Enfield
020 8379 1000
www.enfield.gov.uk
PRESS: *020 8379 4470*

Greenwich
020 8854 8888
www.greenwich.gov.uk
PRESS: *020 8921 5040*

Hackney
020 8356 5000
www.hackney.gov.uk
PRESS: *020 8356 3736*

Hammersmith and Fulham
020 8748 3020
www.lbhf.gov.uk
PRESS: *020 8753 2164*

Haringey
020 8489 0000
www.haringey.gov.uk
PRESS: *020 8489 2997*

Harrow
020 8863 5611
www.harrow.gov.uk
PRESS: *020 8424 1295*

Havering
01708 434343
www.havering.gov.uk
PRESS: *01708 432012*

Hillingdon
01895 250111
www.hillingdon.gov.uk
PRESS: *01895 250534*

Hounslow
020 8583 2000
www.hounslow.gov.uk
PRESS: *020 8583 2180*

Islington
020 7527 2000
www.islington.gov.uk
PRESS: *020 7527 3376*

Kensington and Chelsea
020 7937 5464
www.rbkc.gov.uk
PRESS: *020 7361 2826*

Kingston upon Thames
020 8547 5757
www.kingston.gov.uk
PRESS: *020 8547 4710*

Lambeth
020 7926 1000
www.lambeth.gov.uk
PRESS: *020 7926 2838*

Lewisham
020 8314 6000
www.lewisham.gov.uk
PRESS: *020 8314 7337*

Merton
020 8274 4901
www.merton.gov.uk
PRESS: *020 8274 4901*

Newham
020 8430 2000
www.newham.gov.uk
PRESS: *020 8430 6892*

Redbridge
020 8554 5000
www.redbridge.gov.uk
PRESS: *020 8708 2151*

Richmond upon Thames
020 8891 1411
www.richmond.gov.uk
PRESS: *020 8891 7766*

Southwark
020 7525 5000
www.southwark.gov.uk
PRESS: *020 7525 7306*

Sutton
020 8770 5000
www.sutton.gov.uk
PRESS: *020 8770 5145*

Tower Hamlets
020 7364 5000
www.towerhamlets.gov.uk
PRESS: *020 7364 4969*

Waltham Forest
020 8496 3000
www.lbwf.gov.uk
PRESS: *020 8496 4855*

Wandsworth
020 8871 6000
www.wandsworth.gov.uk
PRESS: *020 8871 6031*

Westminster
020 7641 6000
www.westminster.gov.uk
PRESS: *020 7641 2259*

County councils

Bedfordshire
01234 363222
www.bedfordshire.gov.uk
PRESS: *01234 228888*

Buckinghamshire
01296 395000
www.buckscc.gov.uk
PRESS: *01296 382055*

Cambridgeshire
01223 717111
www.cambridgeshire.gov.uk
PRESS: *01223 717612*

Cheshire
01244 602424
www.cheshire.gov.uk
PRESS: *01244 602216*

Cornwall
01872 322000
www.cornwall.gov.uk
PRESS: *01872 322186*

Cumbria
01228 606060
www.cumbria.gov.uk
PRESS: *01228 606333*

Derbyshire
0845 605 8058
www.derbyshire.gov.uk
PRESS: *01629 585035*

Devon
01392 382000
www.devon-cc.gov.uk
PRESS: *01392 383290*

Dorset
01305 251000
www.dorsetcc.gov.uk
PRESS: *01305 224725*

Durham
0191 383 3000
www.durham.gov.uk
PRESS: *0191 383 3373*

East Sussex
01273 481000
www.eastsussexcc.gov.uk
PRESS: *01273 481552*

Essex
01245 492211
www.essexcc.gov.uk
PRESS: *01245 434979*

Gloucestershire
01452 425000
www.gloscc.gov.uk
PRESS: *01452 425226*

Hampshire
01962 870500
www.hants.gov.uk
PRESS: *01962 847666*

Herefordshire
01432 260000
www.herefordshire.gov.uk/
PRESS: *01432 260224*

Hertfordshire
01438 737555
www.hertsdirect.org
PRESS: *01992 555539*

Kent
0845 824 7247
www.kent.gov.uk
PRESS: *01622 694177*

Lancashire
0845 053 0000
www.lancashire.gov.uk
PRESS: *01772 530726*

Leicestershire
0116 232 3232
www.leics.gov.uk
PRESS: *0116 265 6274*

Lincolnshire
01522 552222
www.lincolnshire.gov.uk
PRESS: *01522 552301*

Norfolk
0844 800 8020
www.norfolk.gov.uk
PRESS: *01603 222716*

North Yorkshire
01609 780780
www.northyorks.gov.uk
PRESS: *01609 532206*

Northamptonshire
01604 236236
www.northamptonshire
.gov.uk
PRESS: *01604 237322*

Northumberland
01670 533000
www.northumberland.gov.uk
PRESS: *01670 534850*

Nottinghamshire
0115 982 3823
www.nottinghamshire.gov.uk
PRESS: *0115 977 3791*

Oxfordshire
01865 792422
www.oxfordshire.gov.uk
PRESS: *01865 810256*

Rutland
01572 722577
www.rutnet.co.uk
PRESS: *01572 758328*

Shropshire
0845 678 9000
www.shropshireonline.gov.uk
PRESS: *01743 252813*

Somerset
0845 345 9166
www.somerset.gov.uk
PRESS: *01823 355020*

Staffordshire
01785 223121
www.staffordshire.gov.uk
PRESS: *01785 276829*

Suffolk
01473 583000
www.suffolkcc.gov.uk
PRESS: *01473 264397*

Surrey
0845 600 9009
www.surreycc.gov.uk
PRESS: *020 8541 9548*

Warwickshire
0845 090 7000
www.warwickshire.gov.uk
PRESS: *01926 412758*
West Sussex
01243 777100
www.westsussex.gov.uk
PRESS: *01243 777408*
Wiltshire
01225 713000
www.wiltshire.gov.uk
PRESS: *01225 713114*
Worcestershire
01905 763763
www.worcestershire.gov.uk
PRESS: *01905 766642*
Isle of Wight
01983 821000
www.iwight.com
PRESS: *01983 823693*

City and district councils

AVON

see Somerset & Avon

BEDFORDSHIRE

Bedford
01234 267422
www.bedford.gov.uk
PRESS: *01234 221622*
Luton
01582 546000
www.luton.gov.uk
Mid Bedfordshire
01525 402051
www.midbeds.gov.uk
South Bedfordshire
01582 472222
www.southbeds.gov.uk

BERKSHIRE

Reading
0118 939 0900
www.reading.gov.uk
PRESS: *0118 939 0957*
Bracknell Forest
01344 352000
www.bracknell-forest.gov.uk
Slough
01753 552288
www.slough.gov.uk
West Berkshire
01635 42400
www.westberks.gov.uk
Windsor and Maidenhead
01628 798888
www.rbwm.gov.uk
Wokingham
0118 974 6000
www.wokingham.gov.uk

BUCKINGHAMSHIRE

Milton Keynes
01908 691691
www.mkweb.co.uk/mkcouncil
PRESS: *01908 252009*
Aylesbury Vale
01296 585858
www.aylesburyvaledc.gov.uk
Chiltern
01494 729000
www.chiltern.gov.uk
South Bucks
01895 837200
www.southbucks.gov.uk
Wycombe
01494 461000
www.wycombe.gov.uk

CAMBRIDGESHIRE

Cambridge
01223 457000
www.cambridge.gov.uk

Peterborough
01733 747474
www.peterborough.gov.uk
East Cambridgeshire
01353 665555
www.eastcambs.gov.uk
Fenland
01354 654321
www.fenland.gov.uk
Huntingdonshire
01480 388388
www.huntsdc.gov.uk
South Cambridgeshire
0845 045 0500
www.scambs.gov.uk

CHANNEL ISLANDS

Isles of Scilly
01720 422537
www.scilly.gov.uk
PRESS: *01720 423371*
States of Jersey
01534 603000
www.gov.je
PRESS: *01534 603430*
States of Guernsey
01481 717000
www.gov.gg
PRESS: *01481 717131*

CHESHIRE

Chester
01244 324324
www.chestercc.gov.uk
PRESS: *01244 402362*
Congleton
01270 763231
www.congleton.gov.uk
Crewe and Nantwich
01270 537777
www.crewe-nantwich.gov.uk
Ellesmere Port and Neston
0151 356 6789
www.ellesmereport-neston.gov.uk
Halton
0151 424 2061
www.halton.gov.uk
Macclesfield
01625 500500
www.macclesfield.gov.uk
Vale Royal
01606 862862
www.valeroyal.gov.uk
Warrington
01925 444400
www.warrington.gov.uk

CLEVELAND

Hartlepool
01429 266522
www.hartlepool.gov.uk
PRESS: *01429 523510*
Middlesbrough
01642 245432
www.middlesbrough.gov.uk
PRESS: *01642 729502*

Redcar and Cleveland
0845 612 6126
www.redcar-cleveland.gov.uk

CORNWALL

Caradon
01579 341000
www.caradon.gov.uk
Carrick
01872 224400
www.carrick.gov.uk
Kerrier
01209 614000
www.kerrier.gov.uk
North Cornwall
01208 893333
www.ncdc.gov.uk
Penwith
01736 362341
www.penwith.gov.uk
Restormel
01726 223300
www.restormel.gov.uk

COUNTY DURHAM

Durham
0191 383 3000
www.durham.gov.uk
PRESS: *0191 383 3373 / 9*
Chester-le-Street
0191 387 1919
www.chester-le-street.gov.uk
Darlington
01325 380651
www.darlington.gov.uk
Derwentside
01207 693693
www.derwentside.gov.uk
Easington
0191 527 0501
www.easington.gov.uk
Sedgefield
01388 816166
www.sedgefield.gov.uk
Teesdale
01833 690000
www.teesdale.gov.uk
Wear Valley
01388 765555
www.wearvalley.gov.uk

CUMBRIA

Carlisle
01228 817000
www.carlisle.gov.uk
PRESS: *01228 817150*
Allerdale
01900 326333
www.allerdale.gov.uk
Barrow-in-Furness
01229 894900
www.barrowbc.gov.uk
Copeland
01946 852585
www.copelandbc.gov.uk
South Lakeland
01539 733333
www.southlakeland.gov.uk

DERBYSHIRE

Derby
01332 293111
www.derby.gov.uk
PRESS: *01332 256207*

Amber Valley
01773 570222
www.ambervalley.gov.uk

Bolsover
01246 240000
www.bolsover.gov.uk

Chesterfield
01246 345345
www.chesterfieldbc.gov.uk

Derbyshire Dales
01629 761100
www.derbyshiredales.gov.uk

Erewash
0115 907 2244
www.erewash.gov.uk

High Peak
0845 129 7777
www.highpeak.gov.uk

North East Derbyshire
01246 231111
www.ne-derbyshire.gov.uk

South Derbyshire
01283 221000
www.south-derbys.gov.uk

DEVON

Exeter
01392 277888
www.exeter.gov.uk
PRESS: *01392 265103*

Plymouth
01752 668000
www.plymouth.gov.uk
PRESS: *01752 304913*

East Devon
01395 516551
www.eastdevon.gov.uk

Mid Devon
01884 255255
www.middevon.gov.uk

North Devon
01271 327711
www.northdevon.gov.uk

South Hams
01803 861234
www.southhams.gov.uk

Teignbridge
01626 361101
www.teignbridge.gov.uk

Torbay
01803 201201
www.torbay.gov.uk

Torridge
01237 428700
www.torridge.gov.uk

West Devon
01822 813600
www.westdevon.gov.uk

DORSET

Bournemouth
01202 451451
www.bournemouth.gov.uk
PRESS: *01202 454668*

Christchurch
01202 495000
www.dorsetforyou.com

East Dorset
01202 886201
www.dorsetforyou.com

North Dorset
01258 454111
www.dorsetforyou.com

Poole
01202 633633
www.poole.gov.uk

Purbeck
01929 556561
www.purbeck-dc.gov.uk

West Dorset
01305 251010
www.dorsetforyou.com

Weymouth and Portland
01305 838000
www.weymouth.gov.uk

EAST SUSSEX

Brighton and Hove
01273 290000
www.brighton-hove.gov.uk
PRESS: *01273 291040*

Eastbourne
01323 410000
www.eastbourne.gov.uk

Hastings
01424 781066
www.hastings.gov.uk

Lewes
01273 471600
www.lewes.gov.uk

Rother
01424 787878
www.rother.gov.uk

Wealden
01892 653311
www.wealden.gov.uk

ESSEX

Southend-on-Sea
01702 215000
www.southend.gov.uk
PRESS: *01702 215020*

Basildon
01268 533333
www.basildon.gov.uk

Braintree
01376 552525
www.braintree.gov.uk

Brentwood
01277 312500
www.brentwood-council.gov.uk

Castle Point
01268 882200
www.castlepoint.gov.uk

Chelmsford
01245 606606
www.chelmsfordbc.gov.uk

Colchester
01206 282222
www.colchester.gov.uk

Epping Forest
01992 564000
www.eppingforestdc.gov.uk

Harlow
01279 446655
www.harlow.gov.uk

Maldon
01621 854477
www.maldon.gov.uk

Rochford
01702 546366
www.rochford.gov.uk

Tendring
01255 686868
www.tendringdc.gov.uk

Thurrock
01375 652652
www.thurrock.gov.uk

Uttlesford
01799 510510
www.uttlesford.gov.uk

GLOUCESTERSHIRE

Gloucester
01452 522232
www.gloucester.gov.uk
PRESS: *01452 396133*

Cheltenham
01242 262626
www.cheltenham.gov.uk
PRESS: *01242 775050*

Cotswolds
01285 623000
www.cotswold.gov.uk

Forest of Dean
01594 810000
www.fdean.gov.uk

South Gloucestershire
01454 868686
www.southglos.gov.uk

Stroud
01453 766321
www.stroud.gov.uk

Tewkesbury
01684 295010
www.tewkesburybc.gov.uk

GREATER MANCHESTER

Manchester
0161 234 5000
www.manchester.gov.uk
PRESS: *0161 234 3534*

Bolton
01204 333333
www.bolton.gov.uk

Bury
0161 253 5000
www.bury.gov.uk

Oldham
0161 911 3000
www.oldham.gov.uk

Rochdale
01706 647474
www.rochdale.gov.uk

Salford
0161 794 4711
www.salford.gov.uk

Stockport
0161 480 4949
www.stockport.gov.uk

Tameside
0161 342 8355
www.tameside.gov.uk

Trafford
0161 912 2000
www.trafford.gov.uk

Wigan
01942 244991
www.wiganmbc.gov.uk

HAMPSHIRE

Portsmouth
023 9283 4092
www.portsmouth.gov.uk
PRESS: *023 9283 4043*

Southampton
023 8022 3855
www.southampton.gov.uk
PRESS: *023 8083 2000*

Basingstoke and Deane
01256 844844
www.basingstoke.gov.uk

East Hampshire
01730 266551
www.easthants.gov.uk

Eastleigh
023 8068 8068
www.eastleigh.gov.uk

Fareham
01329 236100
www.fareham.gov.uk

Gosport
023 9258 4242
www.gosport.gov.uk

Hart
01252 622122
www.hart.gov.uk

Havant
023 9247 4174
www.havant.gov.uk

New Forest
023 8028 5000
www.nfdc.gov.uk

Rushmoor
01252 398398
www.rushmoor.gov.uk

Test Valley
01264 368000
www.testvalley.gov.uk

Winchester
01962 840222
www.winchester.gov.uk

HERTFORDSHIRE

St Albans
01727 866100
www.stalbans.gov.uk
PRESS: *01727 819317 / 6*

Broxbourne
01992 785555
www.broxbourne.gov.uk

Dacorum
01442 228000
www.dacorum.gov.uk

East Hertfordshire
01279 655261
www.eastherts.gov.uk

Hertsmere
020 8207 2277
www.hertsmere.gov.uk

North Hertfordshire
01462 474000
www.north-herts.gov.uk

Stevenage
01438 242242
www.stevenage.gov.uk
Watford
01923 226400
www.watford.gov.uk
Welwyn Hatfield
01707 357000
www.welhat.gov.uk

KENT

Canterbury
01227 862000
www.canterbury.gov.uk
PRESS: *01227 862050*
Ashford
01233 331111
www.ashford.gov.uk
Dartford
01322 343434
www.dartfordbc.gov.uk
Dover
01304 821199
www.dover.gov.uk
Gravesham
01474 337000
www.gravesham.gov.uk
Maidstone
01622 602000
www.digitalmaidstone.co.uk
Medway
01634 306000
www.medway.gov.uk
Sevenoaks
01732 227000
www.sevenoaks.gov.uk
Shepway
01303 850388
www.shepway.gov.uk
Swale
01795 424341
www.swale.gov.uk
Thanet
01843 577000
www.thanet.gov.uk
Tonbridge and Malling
01732 844522
www.tmbc.gov.uk
Tunbridge Wells
01892 526121
www.tunbridgewells.gov.uk

LANCASHIRE

Lancaster
01524 582000
www.lancaster.gov.uk
PRESS: *01524 582041*
Preston
01772 906900
www.preston.gov.uk
PRESS: *01772 906464*
Blackburn with Darwen
01254 585585
www.blackburn.gov.uk
Blackpool
01253 477477
www.blackpool.gov.uk
Burnley
01282 425011
www.burnley.gov.uk

Chorley
01257 515151
www.chorley.gov.uk
Fylde
01253 658658
www.fylde.gov.uk
Hyndburn
01254 388111
www.hyndburnbc.gov.uk
Pendle
01282 661661
www.pendle.gov.uk
Ribble Valley
01200 425111
www.ribblevalley.gov.uk
Rossendale
01706 217777
www.rossendale.gov.uk
South Ribble
01772 421491
www.south-ribblebc.gov.uk
West Lancashire
01695 577177
www.westlancsdc.gov.uk
Wyre
01253 891000
www.wyrebc.gov.uk

LEICESTERSHIRE

Leicester
0116 252 7000
www.leicester.gov.uk
PRESS: *0116 252 6074*
Blaby
0116 275 0555
www.blaby.gov.uk
Charnwood
01509 263151
www.charnwood.gov.uk
Harborough
01858 828282
www.harborough.gov.uk
Hinckley and Bosworth
01455 238141
www.hinckleyandbosworth
online.org.uk
Melton
01664 502502
www.melton.gov.uk
North West Leicestershire
01530 454545
www.nwleics.gov.uk
Oadby and Wigston
0116 288 8961
www.oadby-wigston.gov.uk

LINCOLNSHIRE

Lincoln
01522 881188
www.lincoln.gov.uk
PRESS: *01522 873384*
Boston
01205 314200
www.boston.gov.uk
East Lindsey
01507 601111
www.e-lindsey.gov.uk
North East Lincolnshire
01472 313131
www.nelincs.gov.uk

North Kesteven
01529 414155
www.n-kesteven.gov.uk
North Lincolnshire
01724 296296
www.northlincs.gov.uk
South Holland
01775 761161
www.sholland.gov.uk
South Kesteven
01476 406080
www.skdc.com
West Lindsey
01427 676676
www.west-lindsey.gov.uk

MERSEYSIDE

Liverpool
0151 233 3000
www.liverpool.gov.uk
PRESS: *0151 225 5509*
Knowsley
0151 489 6000
www.knowsley.gov.uk
Sefton
0151 922 4040
www.sefton.gov.uk
St Helens
01744 456789
www.sthelens.gov.uk
Wirral
0151 606 2000
www.wirral.gov.uk

NORFOLK

Norwich
01603 212212
www.norwich.gov.uk
PRESS: *01603 212167 /
212991*
Breckland
01362 695333
www.breckland.gov.uk
Broadland
01603 431133
www.broadland.gov.uk
Great Yarmouth
01493 856100
www.great-yarmouth.gov.uk
**King's Lynn and West
Norfolk**
01553 616200
www.west-norfolk.gov.uk
North Norfolk
01263 513811
www.north-norfolk.gov.uk
South Norfolk
01508 533633
www.south-norfolk.gov.uk

NORTH AND EAST
YORKSHIRE

York
01904 613161
www.york.gov.uk
PRESS: *01904 552005*
Craven
01756 700600
www.cravendc.gov.uk

East Riding of Yorkshire
01482 393939
www.eastriding.gov.uk
Hambleton
0845 121 1555
www.hambleton.gov.uk
Harrogate
01423 500600
www.harrogate.gov.uk
Kingston upon Hull
01482 300300
www.hullcc.gov.uk
Richmondshire
01748 829100
www.richmondshire.gov.uk
Ryedale
01653 600666
www.ryedale.gov.uk
Scarborough
01723 232323
www.scarborough.gov.uk
Selby
01757 705101
www.selby.gov.uk
Stockton-on-Tees
01642 393939
www.stockton-bc.gov.uk

NORTHAMPTONSHIRE

Northampton
01604 837837
www.northampton.gov.uk
Corby
01536 464000
www.corby.gov.uk
Daventry
01327 871100
www.daventrydc.gov.uk
East Northamptonshire
01832 742000
www.east-northampton
shire.gov.uk
Kettering
01536 410333
www.kettering.gov.uk
South Northamptonshire
0845 230 0226
www.southnorthants.gov.uk
Wellingborough
01933 229777
www.wellingborough.gov.uk

NORTHUMBERLAND

Alnwick
01665 510505
www.alnwick.gov.uk
Berwick-upon-Tweed
01289 330044
www.berwickonline.org.uk
Blyth Valley
01670 542000
www.blythvalley.gov.uk
Castle Morpeth
01670 535000
www.castlemorpeth.gov.uk
Tynedale
01434 652200
www.tynedale.gov.uk
Wansbeck
01670 532200
www.wansbeck.gov.uk

NOTTINGHAMSHIRE

Nottingham
0115 915 5555
www.nottinghamcity.gov.uk
PRESS: *0115 915 4686*

Ashfield
01623 450000
www.ashfield-dc.gov.uk

Bassetlaw
01909 533533
www.bassetlaw.gov.uk

Broxtowe
0115 917 7777
www.broxtowe.gov.uk

Gedling
0115 901 3901
www.gedling.gov.uk

Mansfield
01623 463463
www.mansfield.gov.uk

Newark and Sherwood
01636 650000
www.newark-sherwood
dc.gov.uk

Rushcliffe
0115 981 9911
www.rushcliffe.gov.uk

OXFORDSHIRE

Oxford
01865 249811
www.oxford.gov.uk
PRESS: *01865 252616*

Cherwell
01295 252535
www.cherwell-dc.gov.uk

South Oxfordshire
01491 823000
www.southoxon.gov.uk

Vale of White Horse
01235 520202
www.whitehorsedc.gov.uk

West Oxfordshire
01993 861000
www.westoxon.gov.uk

SHROPSHIRE

Bridgnorth
01746 713100
www.bridgnorth-dc.gov.uk

North Shropshire
01939 232771
www.northshropshiredc
.gov.uk

Oswestry
01691 671111
www.oswestrybc.gov.uk

Shrewsbury and Atcham
01743 281000
www.shrewsbury.gov.uk

South Shropshire
01584 813000
www.southshropshire.gov
.uk

Telford & Wrekin
01952 202100
www.telford.gov.uk

SOMERSET AND AVON

Bath and North-east Somerset
01225 477000
www.bathnes.gov.uk

Bristol
0117 922 2000
www.bristol-city.gov.uk
PRESS: *0117 922 2650*

Mendip
01749 648999
www.mendip.gov.uk

North Somerset
01934 888888
www.n-somerset.gov.uk

Sedgemoor
0845 408 2540
www.sedgemoor.gov.uk

South Somerset
01935 462462
www.southsomerset.gov.uk

Taunton Deane
01823 356356
www.tauntondeane.gov.uk

West Somerset
01643 703704
www.westsomersetonline
.gov.uk

SOUTH YORKSHIRE

Doncaster
01302 734444
www.doncaster.gov.uk

Rotherham
01709 382121
www.rotherham.gov.uk

Sheffield
0114 272 6444
www.sheffield.gov.uk
PRESS: *0114 203 9082*

STAFFORDSHIRE

Stoke-on-Trent
01782 234567
www.stoke.gov.uk
PRESS: *01782 232900*

Cannock Chase
01543 462621
www.cannockchasedc
.gov.uk

East Staffordshire
01283 508000
www.eaststaffsbc.gov.uk

Lichfield
01543 250011
www.lichfield.gov.uk

Newcastle-under-Lyme
01782 717717
www.newcastle-staffs
.gov.uk

South Staffordshire
01902 696000
www.sstaffs.gov.uk

Stafford
01785 619000
www.staffordbc.gov.uk

Staffordshire Moorlands
01538 483483
www.staffsmoorlands
.gov.uk

Tamworth
01827 709709
www.tamworth.gov.uk

SUFFOLK

Ipswich
01473 432000
www.ipswich.gov.uk
PRESS: *01473 432031*

Babergh
01473 822801
www.babergh-south-
suffolk.gov.uk

Forest Heath
01638 719000
www.forest-heath.gov.uk

Mid Suffolk
01449 720711
www.midsuffolk.gov.uk

St Edmundsbury
01284 763233
www.stedmundsbury
.gov.uk

Suffolk Coastal
01394 383789
www.suffolkcoastal.gov.uk

Waveney
01502 562111
www.waveney.gov.uk

SURREY

Elmbridge
01372 474474
www.elmbridge.gov.uk

Epsom and Ewell
01372 732000
www.epsom-ewell.gov.uk

Guildford
01483 505050
www.guildford.gov.uk

Mole Valley
01306 885001
www.mole-valley.gov.uk

Reigate and Banstead
01737 276000
www.reigate-banstead
.gov.uk

Runnymede
01932 838383
www.runnymede.gov.uk

Surrey Heath
01276 707100
www.surreyheath.gov.uk

Tandridge
01883 722000
www.tandridgedc.gov.uk

Waverley
01483 523333
www.waverley.gov.uk

Woking
01483 755855
www.woking.gov.uk

TYNE AND WEAR

Newcastle upon Tyne
0191 232 8520
www.newcastle.gov.uk
PRESS: *0191 211 5057*

Gateshead
0191 433 3000
www.gateshead.gov.uk

North Tyneside
0191 200 5000
www.northtyneside.gov.uk

South Tyneside
0191 427 1717
www.s-tyneside-mbc
.gov.uk

Sunderland
0191 553 1000
www.sunderland.gov.uk

WARWICKSHIRE

Warwick
01926 450000
www.warwickdc.gov.uk

North Warwickshire
01827 715341
www.northwarks.gov.uk

Nuneaton and Bedworth
024 7637 6376
www.nuneatonand
bedworth.gov.uk

Rugby
01788 533533
www.rugby.gov.uk

Stratford-on-Avon
01789 267575
www.stratford.gov.uk

WEST MIDLANDS

Birmingham
0121 303 9944
www.birmingham.gov.uk
PRESS: *0121 303 3287*

Coventry
024 7683 3333
www.coventry.gov.uk
PRESS: *024 7683 4848*

Dudley
01384 818181
www.dudley.gov.uk

Sandwell
0121 569 2200
www.laws.sandwell.gov.uk
/ccm/portal/

Solihull
0121 704 6000
www.solihull.gov.uk

Walsall
01922 650000
www.walsall.gov.uk

Wolverhampton
01902 556556
www.wolverhampton
.gov.uk
PRESS: *01902 554077*

WEST SUSSEX

Adur
01273 263000
www.adur.gov.uk

Arun
01903 737500
www.arun.gov.uk

Mid Sussex
01444 458166
www.midsussex.gov.uk

Chichester
01243 785166
www.chichester.gov.uk

Crawley
01293 438000
www.crawley.gov.uk
Horsham
01403 215100
www.horsham.gov.uk
Worthing
01903 239999
www.worthing.gov.uk

WEST YORKSHIRE

Leeds
0113 234 8080
www.leeds.gov.uk
PRESS: *0113 247 4328*
Bradford
01274 431000
www.bradford.gov.uk
Calderdale
01422 357257
www.calderdale.gov.uk
Kirklees
01484 221000
www.kirklees.gov.uk
Wakefield
01924 306090
www.wakefield.gov.uk

WILTSHIRE

Kennet
01380 724911
www.kennet.gov.uk
North Wiltshire
01249 706111
www.northwilts.gov.uk
Salisbury
01722 336272
www.salisbury.gov.uk
PRESS: *01722 434561*
Swindon
01793 463000
www.swindon.gov.uk
PRESS: *01793 463105*
West Wiltshire
01225 776655
www.west-wiltshire-dc
.gov.uk

WORCESTERSHIRE

Worcester
01905 723471
www.cityofworcester.gov.uk
PRESS: *01905 722221*
Bromsgrove
01527 873232
www.bromsgrove.gov.uk
Malvern Hills
01684 862151
www.malvernhills.gov.uk
Redditch
01527 64252
www.redditchbc.gov.uk
Wychavon
01386 565000
www.wychavon.gov.uk
Wyre Forest
01562 732928
www.wyreforestdc.gov.uk

Government offices for the regions

East of England
01223 372500
www.go-east.gov.uk
East Midlands
0115 971 9971
www.goem.gov.uk
London
020 7217 3328
www.go-london.gov.uk
North-east
0191 201 3300
www.go-ne.gov.uk
North-west
0161 952 4000
www.gos.gov.uk/gonw
South-east
01483 882255
www.go-se.gov.uk
South-west
0117 900 1700
www.gosw.gov.uk
West Midlands
0121 212 5050
www.go-wm.gov.uk
Yorkshire and the Humber
0113 280 0600
www.gos.gov.uk/goyh

Government News Network offices

www.gnn.gov.uk

East
01223 372780
East Midlands
0115 971 2780
London
020 7217 3091
North-east
0191 202 3600
North-west
0161 952 4513
South-east
01483 882878
South-west
0117 900 3551
West Midlands
0121 352 5500
Yorkshire and the Humber
0113 283 6599
Scotland
0131 244 9060 / 1
Wales
029 2082 1531
Northern Ireland
020 7276 5166

Regional development agencies

East of England
01223 713900
www.eeda.org.uk
PRESS: *01223 484699*
East Midlands
0115 988 8300
www.emda.org.uk
PRESS: *0115 988 8375*
London
020 7680 2000
www.lda.gov.uk
PRESS: *020 7954 4087*
North-east
0191 229 6200
www.onenortheast.co.uk
PRESS: *0191 229 6311*
North-west
01925 400400
www.nwda.co.uk
PRESS: *01925 400232*
South-east
01483 484220
www.seeda.co.uk
PRESS: *01483 484216*
South-west
01392 214747
www.southwestrda.org.uk
PRESS: *01392 229548*
West Midlands
0121 380 3500
www.advantagewm.co.uk
PRESS: *0121 503 3251 /
3228 / 3242*
Yorkshire
0113 394 9600
www.yorkshire-forward.com
PRESS: *0113 394 9715*

Wales

National Assembly for Wales
See page 406
Cardiff
029 2087 2000
www.cardiff.gov.uk
PRESS: *029 2087 2964*
Swansea
01792 636000
www.swansea.gov.uk
PRESS: *01792 636252*

Carmarthenshire
01267 234567
www.carmarthenshire.gov.uk
Ceredigion
01970 617911
www.ceredigion.gov.uk
Denbighshire
01824 706000
www.denbighshire.gov.uk
Flintshire
01352 752121
www.flintshire.gov.uk
Gwynedd
01286 672255
www.gwynedd.gov.uk
Isle of Anglesey
01248 750057
www.ynysmon.gov.uk
Monmouthshire
01633 644644
www.monmouthshire.gov.uk
Newport
01633 656656
www.newport.gov.uk
Pembrokeshire
01437 764551
www.pembrokeshire.gov.uk
Powys
01597 826000
www.powys.gov.uk

County borough councils

Blaenau Gwent
01495 350555
www.blaenau-gwent.gov.uk
Bridgend
01656 643643
www.bridgend.gov.uk
Caerphilly
01443 815588
www.caerphilly.gov.uk
Conwy
01492 574000
www.conwy.gov.uk
Merthyr Tydfil
01685 725000
www.merthyr.gov.uk
Neath Port Talbot
01639 763333
www.neath-porttalbot.gov.uk
Rhondda Cynon Taff
01443 424000
www.rhondda-cynon-taff.gov.uk
Torfaen
01495 762200
www.torfaen.gov.uk
Vale of Glamorgan
01446 700111
www.valeofglamorgan.gov.uk
Wrexham
01978 292000
www.wrexham.gov.uk

Scotland

Scottish Executive
See page 406
Aberdeen
01224 523406
www.aberdeencity.gov.uk
PRESS: *01224 522821*
Dundee
01382 434000
www.dundeecity.gov.uk
PRESS: *01382 434500*
Edinburgh
0131 200 2000
www.edinburgh.gov.uk
PRESS: *0131 529 4044*
Glasgow
0141 287 2000
www.glasgow.gov.uk
PRESS: *0141 287 0906*

Aberdeenshire
01467 620981
www.aberdeenshire.gov.uk
Angus
0845 277 7778
www.angus.gov.uk
Argyll and Bute
0141 578 8000
www.eastdunbarton.gov.uk
Clackmannanshire
01259 450000
www.clacksweb.org.uk
Dumfries and Galloway
01387 260000
www.dumgal.gov.uk
East Ayrshire
01563 576000
www.east-ayrshire.gov.uk
East Dunbartonshire
0141 578 8000
www.eastdunbarton.gov.uk
East Lothian
01620 827827
www.eastlothian.gov.uk
East Renfrewshire
0141 577 3001
www.eastrenfrewshire.gov.uk
Falkirk
01324 506070
www.falkirk.gov.uk
Fife
01592 414141
www.fife.gov.uk
Highland
01463 702000
www.highland.gov.uk
Inverclyde
01475 717171
www.inverclyde.gov.uk
Midlothian
0131 270 7500
www.midlothian.gov.uk
Moray
01343 543451
www.moray.gov.uk
North Ayrshire
01294 324100
www.north-ayrshire.gov.uk
North Lanarkshire
01698 332000
www.northlan.gov.uk

Orkney Islands
01856 873535
www.orkney.gov.uk
Perth and Kinross
01738 475000
www.pkc.gov.uk
Renfrewshire
0141 842 5000
www.renfrewshire.gov.uk
Scottish Borders
01835 824000
www.scottishborders.gov.uk
Shetland Islands
01595 693535
www.shetland.gov.uk
South Ayrshire
01292 612000
www.south-ayrshire.gov.uk
South Lanarkshire
01698 454444
www.southlanarkshire.gov.uk
Stirling
0845 277 7000
www.stirling.gov.uk
West Dunbartonshire
01389 737000
www.west-dunbarton.gov.uk
West Lothian
01506 775000
www.westlothian.gov.uk
Western Isles
01851 703773
www.w-isles.gov.uk

Northern Ireland

Belfast
028 9032 0202
www.belfastcity.gov.uk
PRESS: *028 9027 0221*
Lisburn
028 9250 9250
www.lisburncity.gov.uk

ANTRIM

Antrim
028 9446 3113
www.antrim.gov.uk
Ballymena
08456 581 581
www.ballymena.gov.uk
Ballymoney
028 2766 0200
www.ballymoney.gov.uk
Carrickfergus
028 9335 8000
www.carrickfergus.org
Larne
028 2827 2313
www.larne.gov.uk
Moyle
028 2076 2225
www.moyle-council.org
Newtownabbey
028 9034 0000
www.newtownabbey.gov.uk

ARMAGH

Armagh
028 3752 9600
www.armagh.gov.uk

Craigavon
028 3831 2400
www.craigavon.gov.uk

Coleraine
028 7034 7034
www.colerainebc.gov.uk
Derry
028 7136 5151
www.derrycity.gov.uk
PRESS: *028 7137 6504*
Limavady
028 7772 2226
www.limavady.gov.uk
Magherafelt
028 7939 7979
www.magherafelt.gov.uk

Ards
028 9182 4000
www.ards-council.gov.uk
Banbridge
028 4066 0600
www.banbridge.com
Castlereagh
028 9049 4500
www.castlereagh.gov.uk
Down
028 4461 0800
www.downdc.gov.uk
Newry and Mourne
028 3031 3031
www.newryandmourne.gov.uk
North Down
028 9127 0371
www.northdown.gov.uk

Fermanagh
028 6632 5050
www.fermanagh.gov.uk

Cookstown
028 8676 2205
www.cookstown.gov.uk
Dungannon and South Tyrone
028 8772 0300
www.dungannon.gov.uk
Omagh
028 8224 5321
www.omagh.gov.uk
Strabane
028 7138 2204
www.strabanedc.com

Parliaments and assemblies

Parliament
020 7219 3000
www.parliament.uk
COMMONS INFORMATION OFFICE:
020 7219 4272; COMMONS PRESS:
020 7219 0898; LORDS INFORMATION
OFFICE: *020 7219 3107*

National Assembly for Wales
029 2082 5111
www.wales.gov.uk
PRESS: *029 2089 8099*

Scottish Parliament
0131 348 5000
www.scottish.parliament.uk
PRESS: *0131 348 5000*

Main political parties

Labour party
0870 590 0200
www.labour.org.uk
Conservative party
020 7222 9000
www.conservatives.com
PRESS: *020 7984 8121*
Liberal Democrat party
020 7222 7999
www.libdems.org.uk
PRESS: *020 7340 4949*

Regional parties

WALES

Plaid Cymru
029 2064 6000
www.plaidcymru.org
PRESS: *01824 709890*
Welsh Labour party
029 2087 7700
www.welshlabour.org.uk
PRESS: *029 2087 7707*
Welsh Conservative party
029 2061 6031
www.welshconservatives.com
PRESS: *029 2089 8395*
Welsh Liberal Democrats
029 2031 3400
www.demrhydcymru.org.uk
PRESS: *029 2089 8426*

SCOTLAND

Scottish Conservative party
0131 247 6890
www.scottishtories.org.uk
PRESS: *0131 247 6874*

Scottish Green party
0870 077 2207
www.scottishgreens.org.uk
PRESS: *0131 348 6360*
Scottish Labour party
0141 572 6900
www.scottishlabour.org.uk
PRESS: *0141 572 6905*
Scottish Liberal Democrats
0131 337 2314
www.scotlibdems.org.uk
PRESS: *0131 348 5810*
Scottish National party
0131 525 8900
www.snp.org.uk
Scottish Socialist party
0141 429 8200
www.scottishsocialistparty.org.uk
PRESS: *0131 348 6382*

NORTHERN IRELAND

Alliance party
028 9032 4274
www.allianceparty.org
Democratic Unionist party
028 9047 1155
www.dup.org.uk
PRESS: *028 9065 4479*
Progressive Unionist party
028 9032 6233
www.pup-ni.org.uk
Sinn Féin
00 353 1 872 6100
www.sinnfein.ie
Social Democratic and Labour party
028 9024 7700
www.sdlp.ie
PRESS: *028 9052 1364*
UK Unionist party
028 9147 9860
www.ukup.org
Ulster Unionist party
028 9076 5500
www.uup.org
PRESS: *028 9076 5521*

Minor parties

British National party
0870 757 6267
www.bnp.org.uk
PRESS: *07074 530267*
Communist League party
mail@communistleague.org.uk
www.communistleague.org.uk
Communist party of Britain
office@communist-party.org.uk
www.communist-party.org.uk
Cooperative party
020 7367 4158
www.co-op-party.org.uk
PRESS: *020 7367 4160*

English Independence party
020 7278 5221
www.englishindependenceparty.com
Green party
020 7272 4474
www.greenparty.org.uk
PRESS: *020 7561 0282*
Liberal party
01562 68361
www.libparty.demon.co.uk
Separate from the Liberal Democrats
National Front
0121 246 6838
www.natfront.com
Natural Law party
020 7821 1813
www.natural-law-party.org.uk
Official Monster Raving Loonies
01252 878382
www.omrlp.com
PRESS: *01484 665226*
Socialist party
020 8988 8777
www.socialistparty.org.uk
PRESS: *020 8988 8778*
Socialist Party of Great Britain
www.worldsocialism.org
UK Independence party
0121 333 7737
www.independence.org.uk
PRESS: *020 7222 9365*
Workers Revolutionary party
020 7232 1101
www.wrp.org.uk

Parliamentary and electoral bodies

Electoral Commission
020 7271 0500
www.electoralcommission.gov.uk
PRESS: *020 7271 0529*
Electoral Reform Society
020 7928 1622
www.electoral-reform.org.uk
PRESS: *07984 644138*
Hansard Society
020 7395 4000
www.hansardsociety.org.uk
PRESS: *020 7395 4010*
Parliamentary Counsel
020 7210 6644
www.parliamentary-counsel.gov.uk
CABINET OFFICE PRESS OFFICE:
020 7276 0317

Thinktanks

Adam Smith Institute
020 7222 4995
www.adamsmith.org
Free market economics
Bow Group
020 7431 6400
www.bowgroup.org
Centre-right
Centre for Economic Policy Research
020 7878 2900
www.cepr.org
European network of research fellows
Centre for Global Energy Studies
020 7235 4334
www.cges.co.uk
Centre for Policy Studies
020 7222 4488
www.cps.org.uk
Established 1974 by Margaret Thatcher and Keith Joseph
Centre for Reform
020 7631 3566
www.cfr.org.uk
Centre for the Study of Financial Innovation
020 7493 0173
www.csfi.org.uk
Civitas
020 7799 6677
www.civitas.org.uk
Civil society
Demos
0845 458 5949
www.demos.co.uk
Everyday democracy
Fabian Society
020 7227 4900
www.fabian-society.org.uk
Centre-left
Federal Trust
020 7735 4000
www.fedtrust.co.uk
Foreign Policy Centre
20 7388 6662
www.fpc.org.uk
Established 1998 by Labour government
International Institute for Environment and Development
020 7388 2117
www.iied.org
Institute for European Environmental Policy
020 7799 2244
www.ieep.org.uk
Institute for Global Ethics
020 7486 1954
www.globalethics.org/uk
HLSP Limited. (formerly Institute for Health Sector Development)
020 7253 5064
www.hlspinstitute.org
Institute for Jewish Policy Research
020 7935 8266
www.jpr.org.uk
Institute for Public Policy Research
020 7470 6100
www.ippr.org.uk
Centre-left
International Institute for Strategic Studies
020 7379 7676
www.iiss.org

Institute of Economic Affairs
020 7799 8900
www.iea.org.uk
UK's original free market thinktank
Institute of Fiscal Studies
020 7291 4800
www.ifs.org.uk
Institute of Ideas
020 7269 9220
www.instituteofideas.com
New Economics Foundation
020 7820 6300
www.neweconomics.org
New Policy Institute
020 7721 8421
www.npi.org.uk
Progressive thinktank
New Politics Network
020 7278 4443
www.new-politics.net
Democracy and participation in politics
Overseas Development Institute
020 7922 0300
www.odi.org.uk
Policy Studies Institute
020 7468 0468
www.psi.org.uk
Politeia
020 7240 5070
www.politeia.co.uk
Role of the state
Royal Institute for International Affairs
020 7957 5700
www.riia.org
Formerly known as Chatham House
Scottish Council Foundation
0131 225 4709
www.scottishcouncilfoundation.org
Smith Institute
020 7823 4240
www.smith-institute.org.uk
Social values and economic imperatives
Social Affairs Unit
020 7637 4356
www.socialaffairsunit.org.uk
Social Market Foundation
020 7222 7060
www.smf.co.uk

Alternative and protest

Anarchist Federation
079 4621 4590
www.afed.org.uk
Anti-Nazi League
020 7924 0333
www.anl.org.uk
Big Green Gathering
01458 834629
www.big-green-gathering.com
British Democracy Campaign
www.britishdemocracycampaign.com
Campaign Against Racism and Facism (CARF)
020 7837 1450
www.carf.demon.co.uk
Charter 88
0845 450 7210
www.charter88.org.uk

Creative Exchange
020 8432 0550
www.creativexchange.org
Democracy Movement
0870 511 0440
www.democracymovement.org.uk
Freedom Association
01746 861267
www.tfa.net
Globalise Resistance
020 7053 2071
www.resist.org.uk
Green Events
020 7424 9100
www.greenevents.fsnet.co.uk
GreenNet
0845 055 4011
www.gn.apc.org
Indymedia
www.indymedia.org.uk
Network of independent media activists
Love Music Hate Racism
020 7924 0333
www.lmhr.org.uk
OneWorld
020 7239 1400
www.oneworld.net
Anti-globalisation
Peoples' Global Action
www.agp.org
Protest Net
rabble-rouser@protest.net
www.protest.net
Reclaim the Streets
rts@gn.apc.org
www.reclaimthestreets.net
Red Star Research
07960 865601
www.red-star-research.org.uk
Revolutionary Communist Group
020 7837 1688
www.revolutionarycommunist.com
Rising Tide
07932 628 269
www.risingtide.org.uk
Squall
squall@squall.co.uk
www.squall.co.uk
The Land is Ours
07961 460171
www.tlio.org.uk
Undercurrents News Network (UNN)
01792 455900
www.undercurrents.org
Alternative news videos
Unite Against Fascism
020 7833 4916, 020 7837 4522
www.uaf.org.uk
Urban 75
www.urban75.com
Wombles
wombles@hushmail.com
www.wombles.org.uk
Anarchist and libertarian

Freemasons

Freemasons
grandsecretary@grandlodge.org.uk
www.grandlodge.org.uk

Government: **Global politics**

Government departments

Foreign Office
020 7270 1500
www.fco.gov.uk
PRESS: *020 7008 3100*
International Development
020 7023 0000
www.dfid.gov.uk
PRESS: *020 7023 0600*

International

United Nations
00 1 212 963 1234
www.un.org
PRESS – SPOKESMAN OF THE
SECRETARY GENERAL: *00 1 212 963
7160;* MEDIA ACCREDITATION: *00 1 212
963 6937 / 7463*
*Regional United Nations Information
Centre*
00 32 2 289 2890
www.runic-europe.org
*UN Commission on International
Trade Law (UNCITRAL)*
00 43 1 26 060 4061
www.uncitral.org
PRESS: *00 43 1 26 060 3325*
*UN Conference on Trade &
Development (UNCTAD)*
00 41 22 917 5809
www.unctad.org
*UN Educational, Scientific & Cultural
Organisation (Unesco)*
00 33 1 4568 1000
www.unesco.org
PRESS: *00 33 1 4568 1743*
*UN High Commissioner for Human
Rights (UNHCHR)*
00 41 22 917 1234
www.unhchr.ch
PRESS: *00 41 22 917 2302*
*UN High Commissioner for Refugees
(UNHCR)*
020 7828 9191, 00 41 22 739 8502
www.unhcr.org.uk
PRESS: *020 7932 1020*
*UN Relief & Works Agency for
Palestinian Refugees (UNRWA)*
00 972 8 677 7333
www.un.org/unrwa
PRESS: *00 972 8 677 7526*
UN World Food Programme
020 7592 9292
www.wfp.org
PRESS: *020 7592 9292*
Unicef
020 7405 5592
www.unicef.org.uk
PRESS: *020 7430 0162*

**International Labour Organisation
(ILO)**
00 41 22 799 6111
www.ilo.org
PRESS: *00 41 22 799 7912*
**International Maritime Organisation
(IMO)**
020 7735 7611
www.imo.org
PRESS: *020 7587 3153*
International Monetary Fund (IMF)
00 1 202 623 7000
www.imf.org
PRESS: *00 1 202 623 7100*
International Whaling Commission
01223 233971
www.iwcoffice.org
Nato
0032 2 707 72 11
www.nato.int
PRESS: *00 32 2 707 5041*
OneWorld
020 7239 1400
www.oneworld.net/uk
PRESS: *020 7239 1424*
World Bank
00 1 202 473 1000
www.worldbank.org
UK PRESS: *020 7930 8511*
World Health Organisation (WHO)
00 41 22 791 2111
www.who.int
PRESS: *00 41 22 791 2222*
World Trade Organisation (WTO)
00 41 22 739 5111
www.wto.org
PRESS: *00 41 22 739 50 07*

EU Institutions

European Parliament
London: 020 7227 4300
Edinburgh: 0131 557 7866
www.europarl.eu.int
PRESS: *00 32 2 284 1448*
European Commission
00 800 6789 1011
www.europa.eu.int/comm/
PRESS: *00 32 2 295 0086*
**Committee of the Regions of the
European Union**
00 32 2 282 2211
www.cor.eu.int
PRESS: *00 32 2 282 2155*
Council of the European Union
00 32 2 285 6111
www.ue.eu.int
PRESS: *00 32 2 285 6309*
**Court of Justice of the European
Communities**
00 352 43031
www.curia.eu.int
PRESS: *00 352 4303 3355 / 66*

European Central Bank
00 49 69 1 3440
www.ecb.int
PRESS: *00 49 69 1344 7454 / 5*
European Court of Auditors
00 352 43 984 5410
www.eca.eu.int
PRESS: *00 352 43 984 5004*
**European Economic and Social
Committee**
00 32 2 546 9011
www.esc.eu.int
PRESS: *00 32 2 546 9396*
European Environment Agency
00 45 33 367100
http://org.eea.eu.int
PRESS: *00 45 33 367160*
European Investment Bank
00 352 4379 3122
www.eib.org
PRESS: *00 352 4379 2159*
The European Ombudsman
00 33 3 8817 2313
www.euro-ombudsman.eu.int
European Police Office
00 31 70 302 5000
www.europol.eu.int
**Office for Official Publications of
the European Communities**
00 352 29291
www.publications.eu.int
**Translation Centre for the Bodies of
the European Union**
00 352 42 17111
www.cdt.eu.int
Western European Union
www.weu.int

Other European contacts

Council of Europe
00 33 3 8841 2033
www.coe.int
PRESS: *00 33 3 8841 2065*
**Council of European Municipalities
and Regions**
00 32 2 511 7477
00 33 1 4450 5959
www.ccre.org
PRESS: *00 32 2 500 0534*
European Court of Human Rights
00 33 3 8841 2018
www.echr.coe.int
PRESS: *00 33 3 9021 4215*
European Space Agency
00 33 1 5369 7654
www.esa.int
PRESS: *00 33 1 5369 7155*
**European University Institute,
Florence**
00 39 055 46851
www.iue.it
PRESS: *00 39 055 468 5313*

European Youth Parliament
00 49 30 9700 5095
www.eyp.org; www.eypuk.com
Organisation for Economic Cooperation and Development
00 33 1 4524 8200
www.oecd.org
PRESS: *00 33 1 4524 9700*
Organisation for Security and Cooperation in Europe
00 43 1 514360
www.osce.org
PRESS: *00 353 1 408 25 50*
Eurocorps
00 33 388 43 20 03
www.eurocorps.org
PRESS: *00 33 388 43 20 06*

Political parties

Confederal Group of the European United Left / Nordic Green Left
00 32 2 284 2683 / 2686
www.europarl.eu.int/gue
PRESS: *00 32 475 646628*
European Liberal Democrats
00 32 2 237 01 40
www.eldr.org
Greens-European Free Alliance
00 32 2 284 2117
00 33 3 8817 5879
www.greens-efa.org
PRESS: *00 32 2 284 4683*
00 33 3 8817 4760
Group for a Europe of Democracies and Diversities
Fax: 00 32 2 284 9144
www.europarl.eu.int/edd
Group of European People's Party (Christian Democrats) and European Democrats
00 32 2 284 2234
www.epp-ed.org
PRESS: *00 32 2284 2228*
00 33 3 8817 4144
Parliamentary Group of the Party of European Socialists
00 32 2 284 2111
www.socialistgroup.org
PRESS: *00 32 2 28 43099*
00 33 3 88 1 74873
Union for Europe of the Nations Group
00 32 2 284 2971
www.europarl.eu.int/uen/
PRESS: *00 32 2 28 444309*
00 33 3 88 17431

Pro-Europe and anti-Europe lobbies

Britain in Europe
020 7725 4200
www.britainineurope.org.uk
Pro-Britain in Europe
PRESS: *020 7940 5213*
Bruges Group
020 7287 4414
www.brugesgroup.com
Eurosceptic thinktank

European Movement
020 7940 5252
www.euromove.org.uk
Pro-European
Federation of Small Businesses
01253 336000
www.fsb.org.uk
Powerful anti-euro lobby
PRESS: *020 7592 8128*
The No Campaign
info@no-euro.com
www.no-euro.com
Pro-Europe, anti-euro

Commonwealth and British international

British Executive Service Overseas
020 8780 7500
www.beso.org
PRESS: *020 8780 7343*
British Council
020 7389 4268
www.britcoun.org
PRESS: *020 7389 4939*
Commonwealth Institute
020 7024 9822
www.commonwealth.org.uk
PRESS: *020 7861 8574*
Commonwealth Secretariat
020 7747 6500
www.thecommonwealth.org
PRESS: *020 7747 6385*

British overseas territories

Anguilla
Governor: 00 1 264 497 2621 / 2
Small east Caribbean island
Bermuda
Governor, Hamilton:
00 1 441 292 3600
100 small islands, 20 inhabited, 600 miles off North Carolina, USA
British Antarctic Territory
Commissioner, London:
020 7008 2614
Uninhabited part of Antarctica, including South Orkney and South Shetland islands
British Indian Ocean Territory
Commissioner, London:
020 7008 2890
Group of Chagos Archipelago islands in central Indian Ocean, south of India
British Virgin Islands
Governor, Tortola:
00 1 284 494 2345 / 2370
Eastern Caribbean group of 46 islands, 11 inhabited, near Anguilla
Cayman Islands
Governor, Georgetown:
00 1 345 244 2434
Three tax-free, wealthy islands south of Cuba
Falkland Islands
Governor, Stanley: 00 500 27433
Largest islands in the south Atlantic

Gibraltar
Governor: 00 350 45440
Promontory of southernmost Spain
Montserrat
Governor, Olveston:
00 1 664 491 2688 / 9
East Caribbean volcanic island
Pitcairn Islands
Governor, Auckland:
00 09 64 366 0186
Eastern group in Pacific, between north New Zealand and Peru. Home of mutineers from HMS Bounty, 1790
St Helena
Governor, Jamestown: 00 290 2555
Island in south Atlantic, 1,100 miles off Angola. Two dependencies
Ascension Island
Administrator: 00 247 7000
700 miles north-west of St Helena
Tristan da Cunha
Administrator: 00 870 764 341 816
Island group 1,850 miles west of Cape Town
South Georgia & Sandwich Islands
Governor, Stanley: 00 500 27433
Scattered islands east and south-east of Cape Horn. South Georgia is military, South Sandwich uninhabited and volcanic
Turks & Caicos Islands
Governor, Grand Turk:
00 1 649 946 2309
30 Caribbean islands, north of Haiti

International aid

ActionAid
020 7561 7561
www.actionaid.org.uk
PRESS: *020 7561 7614*
Baby Milk Action
01223 464420
www.babymilkaction.org
Book Aid International
020 7733 3577
www.bookaid.org
British Leprosy Relief Association
01206 216700, 0845 121 2121
www.lepra.org.uk
British Overseas NGOs for Development (Bond)
020 7837 8344
www.bond.org.uk
British Red Cross
0870 170 7000
www.redcross.org.uk
PRESS: *020 7793 7043 / 2*
Care International
020 7934 9334
www.careinternational.org.uk
PRESS: *020 7934 9315*
Casa Alianza
00 502 2433 9600
www.casa-alianza.org
Catholic Agency for Overseas Development
020 7733 7900
www.cafod.org.uk
PRESS: *020 7326 5557*

Christian Aid
020 7620 4444
www.christian-aid.org.uk
PRESS: *020 7523 2421*

Christian Vision
0121 522 6087
www.christianvision.com

Church Mission Society
020 7928 8681
www.cms-uk.org

Disasters Emergency Committee
020 7387 0200
www.dec.org.uk

International Care and Relief
01892 519 619
www.icrcharity.com

International Committee of Red Cross
00 41 22 734 6001
www.icrc.org
PRESS: *00 41 22 730 2282*

International HIV/Aids Alliance
01273 718900
www.aidsalliance.org

International Rescue Committee
00 1 212 551 3000
www.theirc.org
PRESS: *020 7692 2741*

Islamic Relief
0121 605 5555
www.islamic-relief.org.uk
PRESS: *0121 622 0638*

Médecins sans Frontières (UK)
020 7404 6600
www.uk.msf.org

Methodist Relief and Development Fund
020 7467 5132
www.mrdf.org.uk

Muslim Aid
020 7377 4200
www.muslimaid.org.uk

Oxfam
0870 333 2700, 01865 311311
www.oxfam.org.uk
PRESS: *01865 312498*

Plan UK
020 7482 9777
www.plan-uk.org

Sightsavers
01444 446600
www.sightsavers.org.uk
PRESS: *01444 446655*

Tear Fund
0845 355 8355
www.tearfund.org
PRESS: *020 8943 7779*

Voluntary Services Overseas
020 8780 7200
www.vso.org.uk
PRESS: *020 8780 7285*

WaterAid
020 7793 4500
www.wateraid.org.uk
PRESS: *020 7793 4793*

World Emergency Relief
0870 429 2129
www.wer-uk.org

World Vision UK
01908 841000
www.worldvision.org.uk
PRESS: *01908 841020*

Human rights

ActionAid
020 7561 7561
www.actionaid.org.uk
PRESS: *020 7561 7614*

Amnesty International
020 7033 1500
www.amnesty.org.uk
PRESS: *020 7033 1400*

Anti-Slavery
020 7501 8920
www.antislavery.org
PRESS: *020 7501 8934*

Asian Human Rights Commission
00 852 2698 6339
www.ahrchk.net

Association for Civil Rights in Israel
00 9722 652 1218
www.acri.org.il

British Institute of Human Rights
020 7848 1818
www.bihr.org

British Refugee Council
020 7346 6700
www.refugeecouncil.org.uk
PRESS: *020 7346 1213*

Burma Campaign
020 7324 4710
www.burmacampaign.org.uk
PRESS: *020 7324 4713*

Campaign Against Criminalising Communities
020 7586 5892, 020 7250 1315
www.cacc.org.uk

Campaign Against Sanctions on Iraq
info@casi.org.uk
www.casi.org.uk

Campaign Against the Arms Trade
020 7281 0297
www.caat.org.uk

Centre for Research on Globalisation
00 1 514 425 3814
http://globalresearch.ca

Citizens for Global Solutions
00 1 202 546 3950
www.globalsolutions.org
PRESS: *00 1 202 330 4123*

Coalition for the International Criminal Court
00 1 212 687 2176
00 31 70 363 4484
www.iccnow.org

Concern Worldwide
020 7738 1033
www.concern.net
PRESS: *020 7801 2427 / 77*

Derechos Human Rights
00 34 91 526 7502
www.derechos.org

Eliminate Child Labour in Tobacco
00 41 22 306 1444
www.eclt.org

European Roma Rights Centre
00 36 1 413 2200
http://errc.org

Free Tibet Campaign
020 7324 4605
www.freetibet.org

Gendercide Watch
gendercide_watch@hotmail.com
www.gendercide.org

Global Action to Prevent War
00 1 212 818 1861
www.globalactionpw.org

Global Fund for Women
00 1 415 202 7640
www.globalfundforwomen.org
PRESS: *001 415 202 7640 x338*

Human Rights Watch
020 7713 1995
www.hrw.org

International Fellowship of Reconciliation
00 31 72 512 3014
www.ifor.org

International Physicians for the Prevention of Nuclear War
00 1 617 868 5050
www.ippnw.org

Kurdish Human Rights Project
020 7287 2772
www.khrp.org

Labour Behind the Label
01603 666160
www.labourbehindthelabel.org

One World Action
020 7833 4075
www.oneworldaction.org

Safer World
020 7324 4646
www.saferworld.co.uk
PRESS: *020 7324 4671*

Stop the War Coalition
020 7278 6694
www.stopwar.org.uk
PRESS: *07939 242229*

Transcend
00 40 742 079 716
www.transcend.org

Unrepresented Nations and Peoples Organisation
00 31 70 364 6504
www.unpo.org

War Resistors International
info@wri-irg.org
www.wri-irg.org

Womankind Worldwide
020 7549 0360
www.womankind.org.uk

World Commission for Peace and Human Rights Council
00 92 51 411704
www.worphco.cjb.net

World Organization For Human Rights USA
00 1 202 296 5702
www.humanrightsusa.org

Government: **Overseas embassies in UK**

Afghanistan
020 7509 0091
www.afghanembassy.co.uk
Albania
020 7828 8897
Algeria
020 7221 7800
Andorra
020 8874 4806
Angola
020 7299 9850
www.angola.org.uk
Antigua and Barbuda
020 7486 7073
www.antigua-barbuda.com
Argentina
020 7318 1300
www.argentine-embassy-uk.org
Armenia
020 7938 5435
Australia
020 7379 4334
www.australia.org.uk
Austria
020 7235 3731
www.austria.org.uk
Azerbaijan
020 7938 5482
www.president.az
Bahamas
020 7408 4488
Bahrain
020 7201 9170
Bangladesh
020 7584 0081
www.bangladeshhighcommission
.org.uk
Barbados
020 7631 4975
Belarus
020 7937 3288
http://belembassy.org/uk
Belgium
020 7470 3700
www.diplobel.org/uk
Belize
020 7723 3603
www.bzhc-lon.co.uk
Bolivia
020 7235 4248
www.embassyofbolivia.co.uk
Bosnia and Herzegovina
020 7373 0867
Botswana
020 7499 0031
Brazil
020 7499 0877
www.brazil.org.uk
Brunei
020 7581 0521
Bulgaria
020 7584 9400
www.bulgarianembassy.org.uk
Burma
020 7499 4340
www.myanmar.com

Burundi
00 32 2 230 45 35
Nearest embassy is in Belgium
Cameroon
020 7727 0771
Canada
020 7258 6600
www.dfait-maeci.gc.ca/canada
europa/united_kingdom/
Chile
020 7580 6392
China
020 7299 4049
www.chinese-embassy.org.uk
Colombia
020 7589 9177
www.colombianembassy.co.uk
Congo
020 7622 0419
Congo, Democratic Republic of
020 7278 9825
Costa Rica
020 7706 8844
http://costarica.embassy
homepage.com
Croatia
020 7387 2022
Cuba
020 7240 2488
Cyprus
020 7499 8272
Czech Republic
020 7243 1115
www.mzv.cz/london
Denmark
020 7333 0200
www.denmark.org.uk
Dominica, Commonwealth of
020 7370 5194 / 5
www.dominica.co.uk
Dominican Republic
020 7727 6285
www.serex.gov.do
Ecuador
020 7584 2648
Egypt
020 7499 3304
El Salvador
020 7436 8282
Eritrea
020 7713 0096
Estonia
020 7589 3428
www.estonia.gov.uk
Ethiopia
020 7589 7212-5
www.ethioembassy.org.uk
Fiji
020 7584 3661
Finland
020 7838 6200
www.finemb.org.uk
France
020 7073 1000
www.ambafrance-uk.org
Gabon
020 7823 9986

Gambia, The Republic of
020 7937 6316
Georgia
020 7603 7799
www.embassyofgeorgia.org.uk
Germany
020 7824 1300
www.german-embassy.org.uk
Ghana
020 7235 4142
www.ghana-com.co.uk
Greece
020 7229 3850
www.greekembassy.org.uk
Grenada
020 7631 4277
Guatemala
020 7351 3042
Guinea
020 7078 6087
Guyana
020 7229 7684
Holy See
020 8944 7189
Honduras
020 7486 4880
Hungary
020 7235 5218
www.huemblon.org.uk
Iceland
020 7259 3999
www.iceland.org.uk
India
020 7836 8484
www.hcilondon.org
Indonesia
020 7499 7661
www.indonesianembassy.org.uk
Iraq
020 7581 2264
Iran
020 7225 3000
www.iran-embassy.org.uk
Ireland
020 7235 2171
Israel
020 7957 9500
http://london.mfa.gov.il/
Italy
020 7312 2200
www.embitaly.org.uk
Ivory Coast
020 7201 9601
Jamaica
020 7823 9911
www.jhcuk.com
Japan
020 7465 6500
www.uk.emb-japan.go.jp
Jordan
020 7937 3685
www.jordanembassyuk.org
Kazakhstan
020 7581 4646
www.kazakhstanembassy.org.uk
Kenya
020 7636 2371 / 5

Korea, DPR (North Korea)
020 8992 4965
Korea, Republic of (South Korea)
020 7227 5500
http://korea.embassyhomepage.com
Kuwait
020 7590 3400
www.kuwaitinfo.org.uk
Kyrgyzstan
020 7935 1462
www.kyrgyz-embassy.org.uk
Latvia
020 7312 0040
www.london.am.gov.lv/en
Lebanon
020 7229 7265
Lesotho
020 7235 5686
www.lesotholondon.org.uk
Liberia
020 7388 5489
Libya
020 7201 8280
Lithuania
020 7486 6401
http://amb.urm.lt
Luxembourg
020 7235 6961
Macedonia
020 7976 0535
www.macedonianembassy.org.uk
Madagascar
020 7569 6721
Malawi
020 7491 4172
Malaysia
020 7235 8033
Maldives
020 7224 2135
www.maldiveshighcommission.org
Malta
020 7292 4800
Mauritania
020 7478 9323
Mauritius
020 7581 0294-8
Mexico
020 7499 8586
www.mexicanembassy.co.uk
Moldova
020 8995 6818
Mongolia
020 7937 0150
www.embassyofmongolia.co.uk
Morocco
020 7581 5001
Mozambique
020 7383 3800
Namibia
020 7636 6244
Nepal
020 7229 1594
www.nepembassy.org.uk
Netherlands
020 7590 3200
www.netherlands-embassy.org.uk
New Zealand
020 7930 8422
www.nzembassy.com
Nicaragua
020 7938 2373
http://freespace.virgin.net/emb
.ofnicaragua/

Nigeria
020 7839 1244
www.nigeriahc.org.uk/
Norway
020 7591 5500
www.norway.org.uk
Oman
020 7225 0001
Pakistan
020 7664 9200
www.pakmission-uk.gov.pk
Panama
020 7493 4646
Papua New Guinea
020 7930 0922
Paraguay
020 7610 4180
www.paraguayembassy.co.uk
Peru
020 7838 9223
www.peruembassy-uk.com
Philippines
020 7937 1600
www.philemb.co.uk
Poland
0870 774 2700
www.polishembassy.org.uk
Portugal
020 7235 5331
www.portembassy.gla.ac.uk
Qatar
020 7493 2200
Romania
020 7937 9666
www.roemb.co.uk
Russia
020 7229 2666
Rwanda
020 7224 9832
www.ambarwanda.org.uk
Saint Christopher and Nevis
(St Kitts and Nevis)
020 7460 6500
St Lucia
020 7370 7123
St Vincent and the Grenadines
020 7565 2874
San Marino
020 7823 4762
Saudi Arabia
020 7917 3000
www.saudiembassy.org.uk
Senegal
020 7937 7237
www.senegalembassy.co.uk
Serbia and Montenegro
020 7235 9049
www.yugoslavembassy.org.uk
Sierra Leone
020 7287 9884
www.slhc-uk.org.uk
Singapore
020 7235 8315
www.mfa.gov.sg/london/
Slovakia
020 7243 0803
www.slovakembassy.co.uk
Slovenia
020 7222 5400
www.gov.si/mzz/dkp/vlo/eng
Solomon Islands
00 32 2 732 7085
Nearest embassy is in Belgium

South Africa
020 7451 7299
www.southafricahouse.com
Spain
020 7235 5555
Sri Lanka
020 7262 1841
www.slhclondon.org
Sudan
020 7839 8080
www.sudan-embassy.co.uk
Swaziland
020 7630 6611
Sweden
020 7917 6400
www.swedish-embassy.org.uk
Switzerland
020 7616 6000
www.swissembassy.org.uk
Syria
020 7245 9012
www.syrianembassy.co.uk
Tanzania
020 7569 1470
www.tanzania-online.gov.uk
Thailand
020 7589 2944
Togo
00 33 1 4380 1213
Nearest embassy is in Paris
Tonga
020 7724 5828
Trinidad and Tobago
020 7245 9351
Tunisia
020 7584 8117
Turkey
020 7393 0202
www.turkconsulate-london.com
Turkmenistan
020 7255 1071
Uganda
020 7839 5783
Ukraine
020 7727 6312
www.ukremb.org.uk
United Arab Emirates
020 7581 1281
United States
020 7499 9000
www.usembassy.org.uk
Uruguay
020 7589 8835
Uzbekistan
020 7229 7679
www.uzbekistanembassy.uk.net
Venezuela
020 7584 4206
www.venezlon.co.uk
Vietnam
020 7937 1912
www.vietnamembassy.org.uk
Yemen
020 7584 6607
www.yemenembassy.org.uk
Zambia
020 7589 6655
www.zhcl.org.uk
Zimbabwe
020 7836 7755
http://zimbabwe.embassyhome
page.com

Government: **Overseas diplomatic contacts**

Afghanistan
E: Kabul *00 93 70 102: 000*
www.britishembassy.gov.uk/afghanistan
Albania
E: Tirana *00 355 42 34973/4/5*
www.britishembassy.gov.uk/albania
Algeria
E: Algiers *00 213 2123 0068*
www.britishembassy.gov.uk/algeria
Andorra
C: Andorra La Vella *00 376 839 840 www.ukinspain.com*
Angola
E: Luanda *00 244 2 334582/3, 392991, 387681*
www.britishembassy.gov.uk/angola
Antigua and Barbuda
HC: St John's *00 1 268 462 0008/9, 463 0010*
Argentina
E: Buenos Aires *00 54 11 4808 2200 www.britain.org.ar*
Armenia
E: Yerevan *00 3741 264301 www.britishembassy.am*
Australia
HC: Canberra *00 61 2 6270 6666 www.britaus.net*
CG: Brisbane *00 61 7 3223 3200*
CG: Melbourne *00 61 3 9652 1600*
CG: Perth *00 61 8 9224 4700*
CG: Sydney *00 61 2 9247 7521*
C: Adelaide *00 61 8 8212 7280*
Austria
E: Vienna *00 43 1 716 130 www.britishembassy.at*
C: Bregenz *00 43 5574 78586*
C: Graz *00 43 316 8216 1621*
C: Innsbruck *00 43 512 588320*
C: Salzburg *00 43 662 848133*
Azerbaijan
E: Baku *00 99 412 497 5188/89/90*
www.britishembassy.gov.uk/azerbaijan
Bahrain
E: *00 973 574100 www.ukembassy.gov.bh*
Bangladesh
HC: Dhaka *00 880 2 882 2705 www.ukinbangladesh.org*
Barbados
HC: Bridgetown *00 1 246 430 7800*
www.britishhighcommission.gov.uk/barbados
Belarus
E: Minsk *00 375 172 105920*
www.britishembassy.gov.uk/belarus
Belgium
E: Brussels *00 32 2 287 6211*
www.britishembassy.gov.uk/belgium
Belize
HC: Belmopan *00 501 822 2146 www.britishhighbze.com*
Bolivia
E: La Paz *00 591 2 243 3424*
www.britishembassy.gov.uk/bolivia
Bosnia and Herzegovina
E: Sarajevo *00 387 3328 2200 www.britishembassy.ba*

Botswana
HC: Gaborone *00 267 395 2841*
www.britishhighcommission.gov.uk/botswana
Brazil
E: Brasilia *00 55 61 329 2300 www.uk.org.br*
CG: Rio de Janeiro *00 55 21 2555 9600*
CG: São Paulo *00 55 11 3094 2700 www.gra-bretanha.org.br*
C: Belém *00 55 91 222 5074, 223 0990*
C: Belo Horizonte *00 31 3261 2072*
C: Curitiba *00 55 41 322 1202*
C: Fortaleza *00 55 85 466 8580/2*
C: Manáus *00 55 92 613 1819*
C: Porto Alegre *00 55 51 341 0720*
C: Rio Grande *00 55 53 233 7700*
C: Salvador *00 55 71 243 7399*
C: Santos *00 55 13 3211 2300*
Brunei
HC: Bandar Seri Begawan *00 673 2 222231/223121*
www.britishhighcommission.gov.uk/brunei
Bulgaria
E: Sofia *00 359 2 933 9222 www.british-embassy.bg*
C: Varna *00 359 52 665 5555*
Burma
E: Rangoon *00 95 1 256918, 380322, 370863-5*
Burundi
E-LIAISON: Bujumbura *00 257 827602*
Cambodia
E: Phnom Penh *00 855 23 427124, 428295*
www.britishembassy.gov.uk/cambodia
Cameroon
HC: Yaoundé *00 237 222 0545/0796*
www.britishhighcommission.gov.uk/cameroon
C: Douala *00 237 342 2177/8145*
Canada
HC: Ottawa *00 1 613 237 1530 www.britain-in-canada.org*
CG: Montreal *00 1 514 866 5863*
CG: Toronto *00 1 416 593 1290*
CG: Vancouver *00 1 604 683 4421*
C: Halifax/Dartmouth *00 1 902 461 1381*
C: St John's *00 1 709 579 2002*
C: Winnipeg *00 1 204 896 1380*
C: Quebec City *00 1 418 521 3000*
Chad
E: Ndjamena *00 235 523970*
Chile
E: Santiago *00 56 2 370 4100 www.britemb.cl*
C: Valparaíso *00 56 32 213063*
C: Punta Arenas *00 56 61 211535*
China
E: Beijing *00 86 10 5192 4000 www.britishembassy.org.cn*
CG: Shanghai *00 86 21 6279 7650*
www.britishembassy.org.cn/english/shanghai/bcgs.shtml
CG: Guangzhou *00 86 20 8314 3000 www.uk.cn/gz*
CG: Chongqing *00 86 23 6381 0321*
www.britishcouncil.org.cn
CG: Hong Kong *00 852 2901 3000*
www.britishconsulate.org.hk
CG: Macao *00 852 2901 3000*
Colombia
E: Bogotá *00 57 1 326 8300 www.britain.gov.co*
C: Cali *00 57 2 653 6089*
C: Medellin *00 57 4 377 9966*
Congo, Democratic Republic of
E: Kinshasa *00 243 9816 9100/9111/9200*
Costa Rica
E: San José *00 506 258 2025 www.britishembassycr.com*

Croatia
E: Zagreb *00 385 1 600 9100*
www.britishembassy.gov.uk/croatia
C: Split *00 385 21 341 464*
C: Dubrovnik *00 385 20 324597*
Cuba
E: Havana *00 53 7 204 1771*
www.britishembassy.gov.uk/cuba
Cyprus
HC: Nicosia *00 357 22 861100 www.britain.org.cy*
Czech Republic
E: Prague *00 420 2 5740 2111 www.britain.cz*
Denmark
E: Copenhagen *00 45 3544 5200 www.britishembassy.dk*
C: Aabenraa *00 45 7462 3500*
C: Aalborg *00 45 9811 3499*
C: Aarhus *00 45 8730 7777*
C: Esbjerg *00 45 7911 1900*
C: Fredericia *00 45 7592 2000*
C: Herning *00 45 9627 7300*
C: Odense *00 45 6614 4714*
C: Torshavn, Faroe Islands *00 45 2 9835 9977*
Djibouti
C: *00 253 25 0917*
Dominica, Commonwealth of
HC: Roseau *00 1 246 430 7800*
Dominican Republic
E: Santo Domingo *00 1 809 472 7111*
C: Puerto Plata *00 1 809 586 4244/8464*
East Timor
E: Dili *00 670 332 2838*
Ecuador
E: Quito *00 593 2 2970 800/1 www.britembquito.org.ec*
C: Guayaquil *00 593 4 256 0400 x318*
C: Galápagos *00 593 5 526157/9*
Egypt
E: Cairo *00 20 2 794 0850/2/8 www.britishembassy.org.eg*
CG: Alexandria *00 20 3 546 7001/2, 522 3717, 522 0507*
C: Suez *00 20 62 334102*
El Salvador
C: San Salvador *00 503 281 5555*
Eritrea
E: Asmara *00 291 1 120145*
Estonia
E: Tallinn *00 372 667 4700 www.britishembassy.ee*
Ethiopia
E: Addis Ababa *00 251 1 612354*
www.britishembassy.gov.uk/ethiopia
Fiji
HC: Suva *00 679 322 9100*
www.britishhighcommission.gov.uk/fiji
Finland
E: Helsinki *00 358 9 2286 5100 www.britishembassy.fi*
C: Jyväskylä *00 358 14 446 9211*
C: Kotka *00 358 5 234 4281*
C: Kuopio *00 358 17 265 7777*
C: Åland Islands *00 358 18 13591, 47720*
C: Oulu *00 358 83 310 7117*
C: Rovaniemi *00 358 16 317831*
C: Tampere *00 358 3 256 5701*
C: Turku *00 358 2 274 3410*
C: Vaasa *00 358 6 282 2000*
France
E: Paris *00 33 1 4451 3100 www.amb-grandebretagne.fr*
CG: Bordeaux *00 33 5 5722 2110*
CG: Lille *00 33 3 2012 8272*
CG: Lyon *00 33 4 7277 8170*
CG: Marseille *00 33 4 9115 7210*
C: Amiens *00 33 3 2272 0848*
C: Boulogne-sur-Mer *00 33 3 2187 1680*
C: Calais *00 33 3 2196 3376*
C: Cayenne, French Guiana *00 594 311034*
C: Cherbourg *00 33 2 3388 6560*
C: Dunkirk *00 33 3 2866 1198*

C: Fort de France, Martinique *00 596 618892*
C: Guadeloupe *00 590 825757*
C: La Réunion *00 33 2 6234 7576*
C: Le Havre *00 33 2 3519 7888*
C: Lorient *00 33 2 9787 3620*
C: Montpellier *00 33 4 6715 5207*
C: Nantes *00 33 2 5172 7260*
C: New Caledonia *00 687 273627/282153*
C: Papeete, French Polynesia *00 689 706382*
C: Saumur *00 33 2 4152 9054*
C: St Malo-Dinard *00 33 2 2318 3030*
C: Toulouse *00 33 5 6115 0202*
C: Tours *00 33 2 4743 5058*
Gabon
C: Libreville *00 241 762200/742041*
Gambia, The Republic of
HC: Banjul *00 220 449 5133/4*
www.britishhighcommission.gov.uk/thegambia
Georgia
E: Tbilisi *00 995 32 955497/998447/988796*
www.britishembassy.gov.uk/georgia
Germany
E: Berlin *00 49 30 204570 www.britischebotschaft.de*
CG: Düsseldorf *00 49 211 94480*
www.british-consulate-general.de
CG: Frankfurt *00 49 69 170 0020*
CG: Hamburg *00 49 40 448 0320*
CG: Munich *00 49 89 211090*
CG: Stuttgart *00 49 711 162690*
C: Bremen *00 49 421 590708*
C: Hanover *00 49 511 388 3808*
C: Kiel *00 49 431 331971*
C: Nuremburg *00 49 911 2404 303*
Ghana
HC: Accra *00 233 21 701 0650/ 00 233 21 221665*
www.britishhighcommission.gov.uk/ghana
Greece
E: Athens *00 30 210 727 2600 www.british-embassy.gr*
C: Heraklion (Crete) *00 30 2810 224012*
C: Rhodes *00 30 22410 27247/22005*
C: Thessaloniki *00 30 2310 278006*
VC: Corfu *00 30 26610 30055*
VC: Kos *00 30 22420 21549*
VC: Patras *00 30 2610 277329*
VC: Syros *00 30 22810 82232/88922*
VC: Zakynthos *00 30 26950 22906/48030*
Grenada
HC: St George's *001 473 440 3536/3222*
Guatemala
E: Guatemala City *00 502 2367 5425-9*
Guinea
CG: Conakry *00 224 45 5807/6020*
Guyana
HC: Georgetown *00 592 22 65881-4*
www.britain-in-guyana.org
Haiti
C: Port-au-Prince *00 509 257 3969*
Holy See
E: Rome *00 39 06 699 23561*
www.britishembassy.gov.uk/holysee
Honduras
C: San Pedro Sula *00 504 550 2337*
Hungary
E: Budapest *00 36 1 266 2888 www.britishembassy.hu*
Iceland
E: Reykjavik *00 354 550 5100*
VC: Akureyri *00 354 463 0102*
India
HC: New Delhi *00 91 11 2687 2161*
www.britishhighcommission.gov.uk/india
DHC: Chennai *00 91 44 5219 2151*
DHC: Kolkata *00 91 33 2288 5172-6*
DHC: Mumbai *00 91 22 5650 2222*

Indonesia
E: Jakarta *00 62 21 315 6264*
www.britain-in-indonesia.or.id
C: Medan *00 62 61 821 0559*
Iran
E: Tehran *00 98 21 6705011-9*
www.britishembassy.gov.uk/iran
Iraq
E: Basra *00 964 831000* *www.britishembassy.gov.uk/iraq*
Ireland
E: Dublin *00 353 1 205 3700* *www.britishembassy.ie*
Israel
E: Tel Aviv *00 972 3 725 1222* *www.britemb.org.il*
Italy
E: Rome *00 39 06 4220 0001* *www.britain.it*
CG: Milan *00 39 02 723001*
C: Bari *00 39 080 554 3668*
C: Cagliari *00 39 070 828628*
C: Catania *00 39 095 715 1864*
C: Florence *00 39 055 284133*
C: Naples *00 39 081 423 8911*
C: Palermo *00 39 091 326412*
C: Trieste *00 39 040 347 8303*
C: Turin *00 39 011 650 9202*
C: Venice *00 39 041 505 5990*
Ivory Coast
E: Abidjan *00 225 2030 0800* *www.britaincdi.com*
Jamaica
HC: Kingston *001 876 510 0700*
www.britishhighcommission.gov.uk/jamaica
Japan
E: Tokyo *00 81 3 5211 1100* *www.uknow.or.jp*
C: Sapporo *00 81 11 613 1123*
CG: Osaka *00 81 6 6120 5600*
C: Nagoya *00 81 52 223 5031*
Jerusalem
CG: *00 972 2 541 4100*
CG: West Jerusalem *00 972 2 671 7724*
Jordan
E: Amman *00 962 6 592 3100* *www.britain.org.jo*
Kazakhstan
E: Almaty *00 73272 506191/2*
www.britishembassy.gov.uk/kazakhstan
Kenya
HC: Nairobi *00 254 20 284 4000*
www.britishhighcommission.gov.uk/kenya
Kiribati
HC: Tarawa *00 686 22501*
www.britishhighcommission.gov.uk/fiji
Korea (North)
E: Pyongyang *00 850 2 381 7980-3*
Korea (South)
E: Seoul *00 82 2 3210 5500* *www.uk.or.kr*
Kuwait
E: *00 965 240 3335* *www.britishembassy-kuwait.org/*
Kyrgystan
HC: Bishkek *00 996 312 584245*
Laos
E: Vientiane *00 856 21 413606*
Latvia
E: Riga *00 371 777 4700* *www.britain.lv*
Lebanon
E: Beirut *00 961 1 990400* *www.britishembassy.org.lb*
Lesotho
HC: Maseru *00 266 223 13961* *www.bhc.org.ls*
Liberia
HonC: Freetown *00 231 226056*
Libya
E: Tripoli *00 218 21 335 1084* *www.britain-in-libya.org*
Lithuania
E: Vilnius *00 370 5 246 2900* *www.britain.lt*
Luxembourg
E: *00 352 229864-6* *www.britain.lu*

Macedonia
E: Skopje *00 389 2 3299 299* *www.britishembassy.org.mk*
Madagascar
E: Antananarivo *00 261 20 22 49378/79/80*
C: Toamasina *00 261 20 533 2548/69*
Malawi
HC: Lilongwe *00 265 1 772400*
Malaysia
HC: Kuala Lumpur *00 60 3 2170 2200* *www.britain.org.my*
Malta
HC: Valletta *00 356 2323 0000*
www.britishhighcommission.gov.uk/malta
Mauritania
HC: Nouakchott *00 222 525 8331*
Mauritius
HC: Port Louis *00 230 202 9400*
Mexico
E: Mexico City *00 52 55 5 242 8500*
www.embajadabritannica.com.mx
C: Monterrey *00 52 818 315 2049*
Moldova
E: Chisinau *00 3732 238991*
www.britishembassy.gov.uk/moldova
Monaco
C: *00 377 9350 9954*
Mongolia
E: Ulaanbaatar *00 976 11 458133*
Morocco
E: Rabat *00 212 37 729696* *www.britain.org.ma*
CG: Casablanca *00 212 22 437700*
C: Agadir *00 212 48 823401/2*
C: Marrakech *00 212 44 435095*
C: Tangier *00 212 39 936939/40*
Mozambique
HC: Maputo *00 258 1 320 111*
www.britishhighcommission.gov.uk/mozambique
Namibia
HC: Windhoek *00 264 61 274800*
www.britcoun.org/namibia
Nepal
E: Kathmandu *00 977 1 441 0583/1281/1590/4588*
www.britishembassy.gov.uk/nepal
Netherlands
E: The Hague *00 31 70 427 0427* *www.britain.nl*
CG: Amsterdam *00 31 20 676 4343*
C: Willemstad (Curacao) *00 599 9 747 3322*
New Zealand
HC: Wellington *00 64 4 924 2888* *www.britain.org.nz*
CG: Auckland *00 64 9 303 2973*
C: Christchurch *00 64 3 337 9933*
Nigeria
HC: Abuja *00 234 9 413 2010/2011/2796/2880*
www.ukinnigeria.com
DHC: Lagos *00 234 1 261 9531/9537/9541/9543*
Norway
E: Oslo *00 47 2313 2700* *www.britain.no*
C: Alesund *00 47 7012 4460*
C: Bergen *00 47 5594 4705*
C: Bodo *00 47 7556 5800*
C: Kristiansand *00 47 3812 2070*
C: Stavanger *00 47 5152 9713*
C: Tromso *00 47 7762 4500*
C: Trondheim *00 47 7360 0200*
Oman
E: Muscat *00 968 609000*
www.britishembassy.gov.uk/oman
Pakistan
HC: Islamabad *00 92 51 282 2131/5*
www.britishhighcommission.gov.uk/pakistan
DHC: Karachi *00 92 21 587 2431-6*
Panama
E: Panama City *00 507 269 0866*

Papua New Guinea
HC: Port Moresby *00 675 325 1643/45/59/77*
www.britishhighcommission.gov.uk/papuanewguinea
Paraguay
E: Asunción *00 595 21 612611 www.britain.org.ar*
Peru
E: Lima *00 51 1 617 3000 www.britemb.org.pe*
C: Arequipa *00 51 54 241 340*
C: Cusco *00 51 84 226671/239974*
C: Iquitos *00 51 94 222732*
C: Piura *00 51 74 333300/326233*
C: Trujillo *00 51 44 235548*
Philippines
E: Manila *00 63 2 816 7116*
www.britishembassy.gov.uk/philippines
C: Angeles City *00 63 45 323 4187*
C: Cebu *00 63 32 346 0525*
C: Olongapo *00 63 47 252 2222*
Poland
E: Warsaw *00 48 22 311 0000 www.britishembassy.pl*
C: Gdansk *00 48 58 341 4365, 346 1558*
C: Katowice *00 48 32 206 9801*
C: Kraków *00 48 12 421 7030*
C: Lublin *00 48 81 742 0101*
C: Poznan *00 48 61 851 7290*
C: Szczecin *00 48 91 487 0302*
C: Wroclaw *00 48 71 344 8961*
Portugal
E: Lisbon *00 351 21 392 4000 www.uk-embassy.pt*
C: Oporto *00 351 22 618 4789*
C: Portimão *00 351 282 490 750*
Qatar
E: Doha *00 974 442 1991 www.britishembassy.gov.uk/qatar*
Romania
E: Bucharest *00 40 21 201 7200*
www.britishembassy.gov.uk/romania
Russia
E: Moscow *00 7 095 956 7200 www.britemb.msk.ru*
CG: St Petersburg *00 7 812 320 3200 www.britain.spb.ru*
CG: Yekaterinburg *00 7 343 379 4931*
C: Novorossiysk *00 7 8617 618100*
C: Vladivostok *00 7 4232 411312*
Rwanda
E: Kigali *00 250 584098, 585771, 585773, 586072*
www.britishembassykigali.org.rw
St Kitts and Nevis
HC: Basseterre *001 268 462 0008/9*
St Lucia
HC: Castries *001 758 45 22484/5*
St Vincent
HC: Kingstown *001 784 457 1701*
Samoa
HC: Apia *00 64 4 924 2888*
San Marino
CG: Florence *00 39 055 284133*
São Tomé and Principe
C: São Tomé *00 239 12 21026/7*
Saudi Arabia
E: Riyadh *00 966 1 488 0077*
www.britishembassy.gov.uk/saudiarabia
CG: Jeddah *00 966 2 622 5550/7/8*
Senegal
E: Dakar *00 221 823 7392/9971*
www.britishembassy.gov.uk/senegal
Serbia and Montenegro
E: Belgrade *00 381 11 3060 900 http://britemb.org.yu*
Seychelles
HC: Victoria *00 248 283666*
Sierra Leone
HC: Freetown *00 232 22 232 961/362/563*
Singapore
HC: *00 65 6424 4200 www.britain.org.sg*
Slovakia
E: Bratislava *00 421 2 5998 2000 www.britemb.sk*

Slovenia
E: Ljubljana *00 386 1 200 3910 www.british-embassy.si*
Solomon Islands
HC: Honiara *00 677 21705/6*
Somalia
E: Mogadishu *00 252 1 20288/9*
South Africa
HC: Pretoria *00 27 12 421 7500 www.britain.org.za*
CG: Cape Town *00 27 21 405 2400*
C: Durban *00 27 31 305 3041*
C: East London *00 27 43 726 9380*
C: Port Elizabeth *00 27 41 363 8841*
Spain
E: Madrid *00 34 91 700 8200 www.ukinspain.com*
CG: Barcelona *00 34 93 366 6200*
CG: Bilbao *00 34 94 415 7600/7711/7722*
C: Alicante *00 34 96 521 6022*
C: Las Palmas, Canary Islands *00 34 928 262 508*
C: Málaga *00 34 95 235 23 00*
C: Palma *00 34 971 712445, 712085, 716048, 718501, 712696*
C: Santa Cruz de Tenerife, Canary Islands
00 34 922 28 6863/6653
C: Santander *00 34 942 220000*
C: Vigo *00 34 986 437133*
VC: Ibiza *00 34 971 30 1058/1818/3816*
VC: Menorca *00 34 971 367818*
Sri Lanka
HC: Colombo *00 94 11 2 437336/43*
www.britishhighcommission.gov.uk/srilanka
Sudan
E: Khartoum *00 249 11 777105*
www.britishembassy.gov.uk/sudan
Suriname
C: Paramaribo *00 597 402 558/870*
Swaziland
HC: Mbabane *00 268 404 2581-4*
www.britishhighcommission.gov.uk/swaziland
Sweden
E: Stockholm *00 46 8 671 3000 www.britishembassy.se*
CG: Gothenburg *00 46 31 339 3300*
C: Sundsvall *00 46 60 164000*
Switzerland
E: Berne *00 41 31 359 7700 www.britain-in-switzerland.ch*
CG: Geneva *00 41 22 918 2400*
VC: Basel *00 41 61 483 0977*
VC: Lugano *00 41 91 950 0606*
VC: Montreux/Vevey *00 41 21 943 3263*
VC: Valais *00 41 27 480 3210*
VC: Zurich *00 41 1 383 6560*
Syria
E: Damascus *00 963 11 373 9241-3/7*
C: Aleppo *00 963 21 266 1206, 267 2200*
C: Lattakia *00 963 41 461615*
Tajikistan
E: Dushanbe *00 992 91 901 5079*
www.britishembassy.gov.uk/tajikistan
Tanzania
HC: Dar es Salaam *00 255 22 211 0101*
www.britishhighcommission.gov.uk/tanzania
Thailand
E: Bangkok *00 66 2 305 8333 www.britishemb.or.th*
C: Chiang Mai *00 66 53 263015*
Togo
C: Lomé *00 228 226 4606*
Tonga
HC: Nuku'alofa *00 676 24285/24395*
Trinidad and Tobago
HC: Port of Spain *001 868 6 222748/81234/81068*
www.britain-in-trinidad.org
Tunisia
E: Tunis *00 216 7110 8700*
www.britishembassy.gov.uk/tunisia

425

Turkey
E: Ankara *00 90 312 455 3344 www.britishembassy.org.tr*
VC: Antalya *00 90 242 244 5313*
CG: Istanbul *00 90 212 334 6400*
C: Bodrum *00 90 252 319 0093/4*
C: Izmir *00 90 232 463 5151*
C: Marmaris *00 90 252 412 6486*
Turkmenistan
E: Ashgabat *00 993 12 363462-4*
www.britishembassy.gov.uk/turkmenistan
Uganda
HC: Kampala *00 256 31 312000 www.britain.or.ug*
Ukraine
E: Kiev *00 380 44 490 3660 www.britemb-ukraine.net*
United Arab Emirates
E: Abu Dhabi *00 971 2 610 1100 www.britain-uae.org*
E: Dubai *00 971 4 309 4444*
United States
E: Washington *00 1 202 588 6500 www.britainusa.com*
CG: Atlanta *00 1 404 954 7700*
CG: Boston *00 1 617 245 4500*
CG: Chicago *00 1 312 970 3800*
CG: Houston *00 1 713 659 6270*
CG: Los Angeles *00 1 310 481 0031*
CG: New York *00 1 212 745 0200*
CG: San Francisco *00 1 415 617 1300*
C: Anchorage *00 1 907 786 4848*
C: Charlotte *00 1 704 383 4359*
C: Dallas *00 1 214 521 4090*
C: Denver *00 1 303 592 5200*
C: Kansas City *00 1 913 469 9786*
C: Miami *00 1 305 374 1522*
C: Minneapolis *00 1 612 338 2525*
C: Nashville *00 1 615 743 3061*
C: New Orleans *00 1 504 524 4180*
C: Philadelphia *00 1 215 557 7665*
C: Pittsburgh *00 1 412 624 4200*
C: Portland *00 1 503 227 5669*
C: Puerto Rico *00 1 787 758 9828*
C: St Louis *00 1 636 227 1334*
C: Salt Lake City *00 1 801 297 6922*
C: San Diego *00 1 619 459 8231*
C: San Jose *00 1 408 747 7140 x 1200/1400*
C: Seattle *00 1 206 622 9255*
VC: Orlando *00 1 407 426 7855*
Uruguay
E: Montevideo *00 598 2 622 3630/50*
www.britishembassy.org.uy
Uzbekistan
E: Tashkent *00 99871 120 6451/6288/7852-4*
www.britishembassy.gov.uk/uzbekistan
Vanuatu
HC: Port-Vila *00 678 23100*
www.britishhighcommission.gov.uk/vanuatu
Venezuela
E: Caracas *00 58 212 263 8411 www.britain.org.ve*
C: Maracaibo *00 58 2 61 797 7003*
C: Margarita *00 58 2 95 264 6993*
C: Mérida *00 58 2 74 266 4665*
C: San Cristobal *00 58 2 346 0434, 347 1872*
Vietnam
E: Hanoi *00 84 4 936 0500 www.uk-vietnam.org*
CG: Ho Chi Minh City *00 84 8 829 8433*
Yemen
E: Sana'a *00 967 1 264081-4*
www.britishembassy.gov.uk/yemen
CG: Aden *00 967 2 232712-4*
C: Hodeidah *00 967 3 238130/1*
Zambia
HC: Lusaka *00 260 1 251133*
www.britishhighcommission.gov.uk/zambia
Zimbabwe
E: Harare *00 263 4 77 2990/4700 www.britainzw.org*

Websites

Where a website is not listed, visit
www.britishembassy.gov.uk
for a country list

Arts

Government departments

Culture, Media and Sport
020 7211 6200
www.culture.gov.uk
PRESS: *020 7211 6145*

Arts councils

Arts Council England
0845 300 6200
www.artscouncil.org.uk
PRESS: *020 7973 5321*
Arts Council for Northern Ireland
028 9038 5200
www.artscouncil-ni.org
PRESS: *028 9038 5210*
Arts Council of Wales
029 2037 6500
www.acw-ccc.org.uk
PRESS: *029 2037 6506*
British Council
0161 957 7755
www.britishcouncil.org
PRESS: *020 7389 4268*
Design Council
020 7420 5200
www.design-council.org.uk
PRESS: *020 7420 5286 / 5248*
Scottish Arts Council
0131 226 6051
www.scottisharts.org.uk
PRESS: *0131 240 2404*
UK Film Council
020 7861 7861
www.ukfilmcouncil.org.uk
PRESS: *020 7861 7508*

Galleries and museums

Ashmolean Museum, Oxford
01865 278000
www.ashmol.ox.ac.uk
PRESS: *01865 288298*
Association of Independent Museums
023 9258 7751
www.museums.org.uk/aim
British Library
0870 444 1500
www.bl.uk
PRESS: *020 7412 7110*
British Museum
020 7323 8000
www.thebritishmuseum.ac.uk
PRESS: *020 7323 8583*
Gallery of Modern Art, Glasgow
0141 229 1996
www.glasgowmuseum.com
Geffrye Museum
020 7739 9893
www.geffrye-museum.org.uk

Imperial War Museum
020 7416 5320
www.iwm.org.uk
PRESS: *020 7416 5311*
Institute of Contemporary Arts
020 7930 3647
www.ica.org.uk
PRESS: *020 7930 0493*
Lowry, Salford
0870 787 5780
www.thelowry.com
PRESS: *0161 876 2044*
Modern Art Oxford
01865 722733
www.modernartoxford.org.uk
PRESS: *01865 813813*
Museum of London
0870 444 3852
www.museumoflondon.org.uk
PRESS: *020 7814 5503*
Museums Association
020 7426 6970
www.museumsassociation.org
National Art Collections Fund
020 7225 4800
www.artfund.org
PRESS: *020 7225 4822*
National Galleries of Scotland
0131 624 6200
www.nationalgalleries.org,
www.natgalscot.ac.uk
National Gallery
020 7747 2885
www.nationalgallery.org.uk
PRESS: *020 7747 2865*
National Maritime Museum
020 8858 4422
www.nmm.ac.uk
PRESS: *020 8312 6790*
National Museum and Gallery of Wales
029 2039 7951
www.nmgw.ac.uk
National Museum of Science and Industry
0870 870 4771
www.nmsi.ac.uk
PRESS: *020 7942 4357*
National Museums Liverpool
0151 207 0001
www.liverpoolmuseums.org.uk
PRESS: *0151 478 4612*
National Museums of Scotland
0131 247 4422
www.nms.ac.uk
National Portrait Gallery
020 7306 0055
www.npg.org.uk
PRESS: *020 7312 2452*
Natural History Museum
020 7942 5000
www.nhm.ac.uk
PRESS: *020 7942 5654*

Royal Academy of Arts
020 7300 8000
www.royalacademy.org.uk
PRESS: *020 7300 5615*
Royal College of Art
020 7590 4444
www.rca.ac.uk
PRESS: *020 7590 4114*
Royal Marines Museum
023 9281 9385
www.royalmarinesmuseum.co.uk
Tate
020 7887 8000
www.tate.org.uk
PRESS: *020 7887 8730*
Victoria and Albert Museum
020 7942 2000
www.vam.ac.uk
PRESS: *020 7942 2502*
24 Hour Museum
01273 820044
www.24hourmuseum.org.uk

Performing arts

Almeida Theatre Company
020 7288 4900
www.almeida.co.uk
PRESS: *020 7637 2600*
Barbican Centre
020 7638 4141
www.barbican.org.uk
BBC Proms
proms@bbc.co.uk
www.bbc.co.uk/proms
PRESS: *020 7765 5575*
British Film Institute
020 7255 1444
www.bfi.org.uk
PRESS: *020 7255 1444*
Carling Apollo, Manchester
0161 273 6921
www.getlive.co.uk
Earls Court
020 7385 1200
www.eco.co.uk
Edinburgh Festival Fringe
0131 226 0026
www.edfringe.com
PRESS: *0131 240 1919*
English National Ballet
020 7581 1245
www.ballet.org.uk
English National Opera
020 7836 0111
www.eno.org
PRESS: *020 7845 9378*
Glastonbury Festival
01458 834596
www.glastonburyfestivals.co.uk
No festival in 2006
Glyndebourne Festival
01273 812321
www.glyndebourne.com
PRESS: *01273 812321*

London Astoria
020 7434 9592
www.meanfiddler.co.uk

Millennium Centre, Cardiff
029 2063 6400
www.wmc.org.uk

NEC, Birmingham
0121 780 4141
www.necgroup.co.uk
PRESS: *0121 780 2828*

Ronnie Scott's
020 7439 0747
www.ronniescotts.co.uk

Royal Academy of Dance
020 7326 8000
www.rad.org.uk
PRESS: *020 7326 8003 / 8044*

Royal Albert Hall
020 7589 3203
www.royalalberthall.com

Royal Ballet School
020 7836 8899
www.royal-ballet-school.org.uk
PRESS: *020 7845 7073*

Royal College of Music
020 7589 3643
www.rcm.ac.uk
PRESS: *020 7591 4372*

Royal Concert Hall, Glasgow
0141 353 8080
www.grch.com
PRESS: *0141 353 8016*

Royal National Theatre
020 7452 3333
www.nt-online.org
PRESS: *020 7452 3235*

Royal Opera House, Covent Garden
020 7240 1200
www.royaloperahouse.org

Royal Shakespeare Company
01789 296655
www.rsc.org.uk

Sage, Gateshead
0191 443 4666
www.thesagegateshead.org
PRESS: *0191 443 4613*

South Bank Centre
020 7921 0600
www.sbc.org.uk

Theatres Trust
020 7836 8591
www.theatrestrust.org.uk

Wembley Arena
020 8902 8833
www.whatsonwembley.com
PRESS: *020 8795 8098*

History and heritage

Alexandra Palace and Park
020 8365 2121
www.alexandrapalace.com
PRESS: *020 8365 4328*

Ancient Monuments Society
office@ancientmonumentssociety
.org.uk
www.ancientmonumentssociety.org.uk

Architectural Heritage Fund
020 7925 0199
www.ahfund.org.uk

British Archaeological Association
www.britarch.ac.uk/baa

Civic Trust
020 7539 7900
www.civictrust.org.uk
PRESS: *020 7539 7906*

Council for British Archaeology
01904 671417
www.britarch.ac.uk

English Heritage
0870 333 1181
www.english-heritage.org.uk
PRESS: *020 7973 3250*

Garden History Society
020 7608 2409
www.gardenhistorysociety.org

Historic Royal Palaces
020 8781 9750
www.hrp.org.uk
PRESS: *020 7488 5662 / 3*

Banqueting House
0870 751 5178

Hampton Court Palace
0870 752 7777

Kensington Palace State Apartments
0870 751 5170

Kew Palace and Queen Charlotte's Cottage
0870 751 5179

Tower of London
0870 756 6060

Historical Diving Society
enquiries@thehds.com
www.thehds.com

Historical Metallurgy Society
01792 233223
http://hist-met.org

Institute of Historic Building Conservation
01747 873133
www.ihbc.org.uk

International Council on Monuments & Sites in UK
020 7566 0031
www.icomos.org/uk

Jewish Historical Society of Britain
020 7723 5852
www.jhse.org

Keltek Trust
bells@keltek.org
www.keltek.org
Church bell preservation society

Landmark Trust
01628 825920
www.landmarktrust.org.uk

National Archives
020 8876 3444
www.nationalarchives.gov.uk
PRESS: *020 8392 5277*

National Association of Decorative & Fine Arts Associations
020 7430 0730
www.nadfas.org.uk

National Trust
0870 458 4000
www.nationaltrust.org.uk
PRESS: *0870 609 5380*

National Trust for Scotland
0131 243 9300
www.nts.org.uk
PRESS: *0131 243 9349*

Royal Commisssion on the Ancient & Historic Monuments of Wales
01970 621200
www.rcahmw.org.uk
PRESS: *01970 621201*

Save Britain's Heritage
020 7253 3500
www.savebritainsheritage.org

Scottish Railway Preservation Society
01506 825855
www.srps.org.uk

Society for the Protection of Ancient Buildings
020 7377 1644
www.spab.org.uk
PRESS: *020 7456 0905*

Ulster Architectural Heritage Society
028 9055 0213
www.uahs.co.uk

United Kingdom Institute for Conservation of Historic & Artistic Works
020 7785 3805
www.ukic.org.uk

Vivat Trust
0845 090 0194
www.vivat.org.uk

Business

Government departments

Treasury
020 7270 4558
www.hm-treasury.gov.uk
PRESS: *020 7270 5238*
Trade and Industry
020 7215 5000
www.dti.gov.uk
PRESS: *020 7215 5961 / 5967 / 6405*
Work and Pensions
020 7238 0800
www.dwp.gov.uk
PRESS: *020 7238 0866*

Central banks

Bank of England
020 7601 4444
www.bankofengland.co.uk
PRESS: *020 7601 4411*
European Central Bank
00 49 69 13440
www.ecb.int

Businesses

Business associations

Trade Association Forum
020 7395 8283
www.taforum.org
Confederation of British Industry
020 7379 7400
www.cbi.org.uk
PRESS: *020 7395 8239*
Ethnic Minority Business Forum
embf@sbs.gsi.gov.uk
www.ethnicbusiness.org
Federation of Small Businesses
01253 336000
www.fsb.org.uk
PRESS: *020 75928128*

FTSE 100 companies

3i Group
020 7928 3131
www.3i.com
PRESS: *020 7975 3573*
Alliance & Leicester
0116 201 1000
www.alliance-leicester-group.co.uk
www.newscast.co.uk
PRESS: *0116 200 3355*
Alliance Unichem
01932 870550
www.alliance-unichem.com
PRESS: *01932 870 550*
Allied Domecq
0117 978 5000
www.allieddomecqplc.com
PRESS: *020 7009 3959*

Amvescap
020 7638 0731
www.amvescap.com
PRESS: *00 1 404 479 2886*
Anglo American
020 7698 8500
www.angloamerican.co.uk
PRESS: *020 7698 8555*
Antofagasta
020 7808 0988
www.antofagasta.co.uk
Associated British Foods
020 7399 6500
www.abf.co.uk
AstraZeneca
01582 836000
www.astrazeneca.co.uk
Aviva
020 7283 2000
www.aviva.com
PRESS: *020 7662 8221*
BAA
020 7834 9449
www.baa.co.uk
PRESS: *020 7932 6654*
BAE Systems
01252 373232
www.baesystems.com
PRESS: *01252 384605*
Barclays
020 7699 5000
www.barclays.co.uk
PRESS: *020 7116 64755*
BG Group
0118 935 3222
www.bg-group.com
PRESS: *0118 929 3717*
BHP Billiton
020 7802 4000
www.bhpbilliton.com
PRESS: *020 7802 4177*
BOC Group
01276 477222
www.boc.com
PRESS: *01276 807594*
Boots Group
0115 9506111
www.boots-plc.com
www.newscast.co.uk
PRESS: *0115 959 5995*
BP
020 7496 4000
www.bp.com
PRESS: *020 7496 4076*
British Airways
0870 850 9850
www.britishairways.com
PRESS: *020 8738 5100*
British American Tobacco
020 7845 1000
www.bat.com
PRESS: *020 7845 2888*
British Land
020 7486 4466
www.britishland.com
PRESS: *020 7467 2899*

BSkyB
0870 240 3000
www.sky.com
PRESS: *0870 240 3000*
BT Group
020 7356 5000
www.btplc.com
PRESS – NATIONAL: *020 7356 5369;*
REGIONAL: *0845 726 2624*
Cable & Wireless
01908 845000
www.cw.com
PRESS: *01344 818888*
Cadbury Schweppes
020 7409 1313
www.cadburyschweppes.com
PRESS – GENERAL: *020 7409 1313;*
CADBURY INTERNATIONAL: *0121 458 2000;* CADBURY TREBOR BASSETT: *01923 483483;* CADBURY WORLD: *0121 451 4180;* EUROPEAN BEVERAGES: *01923 250999*
Capita Group
020 7799 1525
www.capita.co.uk
PRESS: *0870 240 0488*
Centrica
01753 494000
www.centrica.co.uk
PRESS: *01753 494085*
Compass Group
01932 573000
www.compass-group.com
PRESS: *01952 573034*
Corus Group
020 7717 4444
www.corusgroup.com
PRESS: *020 7717 4597*
Daily Mail & General Trust
020 7938 6747
www.dmgt.co.uk
PRESS: *020 7938 6000*
Diageo
020 7927 5200
www.diageo.com
Dixons Group
0870 850 3333
www.dixons-group-plc.co.uk
PRESS: *07702 684290*
Emap
020 7278 1452
www.emap.com
PRESS – GENERAL: *020 7278 1452;* EMAP CONSUMER MEDIA: *020 7859 8411;* EMAP PERFORMANCE: *020 7436 1515*
Enterprise Inns
0121 733 7700
www.enterpriseinns.com
Exel Group
01344 302000
www.exel.com
PRESS: *01908 244306*

Friends Provident
0870 6071352
www.friendsprovident.co.uk
CITY AND CORPORATE PRESS:
020 7760 3133

Gallaher Group
01932 859777
www.gallaher-group.com
PRESS: *01932 832531*

Glaxo SmithKline
020 8047 5000
www.gsk.com
PRESS: *020 8047 5502*

Gus
020 7495 0070
www.gus.co.uk
PRESS: *020 7251 3801*

Hanson
020 7245 1245
www.hansonplc.com
PRESS: *01454 316000*

Hays
0191 566 1900
www.hays-travel.co.uk
PRESS: *0191 566 1943*

HBOS
0870 600 5000
www.hbosplc.com
PRESS – GENERAL:
pressoffice@HBOSplc.com;
BANK OF SCOTLAND: *0131 243 7195,*
0845 606 6696; BANK OF SCOTLAND
CORPORATE: *0845 606 6696;*
HALIFAX: *01422 333253*

Hilton Group
020 7856 8000
www.hiltongroup.com
PRESS – GENERAL: *020 7992 1573;*
HILTON: *020 7856 8109;*
LADBROKES: *020 8515 5104;*
LIVINGWELL: *01908 308 854*

HSBC
020 7991 8888
www.hsbc.com
PRESS: *020 7992 1573*

ICI
020 7009 5000
www.ici.com
PRESS: *020 7009 5000*

Imperial Tobacco
0117 963 6636
www.imperial-tobacco.com
PRESS: *0117 933 7241*

Intercontinental Hotel Group
01753 410100
www.intercontinental.com

International Power
020 7320 8600
www.ipplc.com

ITV
020 7843 8000
www.itv.com
PRESS: *020 7620 1620*

J Sainsbury
020 7695 6000
www.j-sainsbury.co.uk
PRESS: *020 7695 7295*

Johnson Matthey
020 7269 8400
www.matthey.com
PRESS: *020 7269 8410*

Kingfisher
020 7372 8008
www.kingfisher.co.uk
PRESS: *020 7644 1030*

Land Securities Group
020 7413 9000
www.landsecurities.co.uk
PRESS: *020 7024 5462*

Legal & General Group
020 7528 6200
www.legalandgeneral.com
PRESS: *01737 375353 / 375351*

Liberty International
020 7960 1200
www.liberty-international.co.uk
PRESS: *020 7887 7029*

Lloyds TSB
020 7626 1500
www.lloydstsb.com
PRESS: *020 7356 2493*

Man Group
020 7144 1000
www.mangroupplc.com
PRESS: *020 7653 6620*

Marks & Spencer
020 7935 4422
www.marksandspencer.com
PRESS: *020 7268 1919*

Morrison Supermarkets
01274 356000
www.morereasons.co.uk
PRESS: *01274 356807*

National Grid Transco
01926 653000
www.nationalgrid.com/uk
PRESS: *01926 656536*

Next
0845 600 7333
www.next.co.uk
PRESS: *0116 284 2503*

Northern Rock
0845 600 8401
www.northernrock.co.uk
PRESS: *0191 279 4676*

O2
0113 272 2000
www.o2.com
PRESS: *01753 628402*

Old Mutual
020 7002 7000
www.oldmutual.com
PRESS: *020 7002 7133*

Pearson
020 7010 2000
www.pearson.com
PRESS – GENERAL: *020 7825 8076;*
CORPORATE: *020 7010 2314 / 07;*
FT GROUP: *020 7873 4447;* PEARSON
EDUCATION: *00 1 212 782 3482;*
PENGUIN UK: *020 7010 3000*

Prudential
020 7220 7588
www.prudential.co.uk
PRESS – GENERAL: *020 7548 3719;*
EGG: *020 7526 2600;* M&G: *020 7548
3222;* UK INSURANCE: *020 7150 2203*

Reckitt Benckiser
01753 217800
www.reckitt.com

Reed Elsevier
020 7930 7077
www.r-e.com
PRESS – GENERAL: *020 7166 5657 / 46;*
BUSINESS PUBLISHING: *020 8652 3296;*
EDUCATIONAL: *00 1 407 345 3987;*
LEGAL: *00 1 937 865 8838;* SCIENCE
AND MEDICAL: *00 31 20 485 2736*

Rentokil Initial
01342 833022
www.rentokil-initial.co.uk
PRESS: *01342 830274*

Reuters Group
020 7250 1122
www.reuters.com
PRESS: *020 7542 8404*

Rexam
020 7227 4100
www.rexam.com
PRESS: *020 7227 4141*

Ri Tinto
020 7930 2399
www.riotinto.com
PRESS: *020 7753 2305*

Rolls Royce
020 7222 9020
www.rolls-royce.com

Royal & Sun Alliance
01403 232323
www.royalsunalliance.com
PRESS – UK: *020 7337 5146;*
WORLD: *020 7111 7047*

Royal Bank of Scotland
020 7250 1122
www.rbs.co.uk
PRESS – GENERAL: *0131 523 4414;*
CORPORATE BANKING AND FINANCIAL
MARKETS: *0131 523 4414;* COUTTS:
020 7957 2427; DIRECT LINE: *0141
308 4100;* LOMBARD: *020 7672 1921;*
NATWEST: *020 7672 1932 / 31 / 27;*
ONE ACCOUNT: *01603 707154;* RBS:
020 7672 1928; RBS CARDS: *020
7672 5086;* RBS INSURANCE: *0845
878 2367;* ULSTER BANK: *00 353 1
608 4573*

SABMiller
020 7659 0100
www.sab.co.za
PRESS: *01483 264156*

Sage Group
0191 294 3000
www.sage.co.uk
PRESS: *0191 294 3036*

Schroders
020 7658 6000
www.schroders.com
PRESS: *020 7658 6000*

Scottish & Newcastle
0131 528 2000
www.scottish-newcastle.com
PRESS: *0131 528 2131*

Scottish & Southern Energy
0845 143 4005
www.scottish-southern.co.uk

Scottish Power
0845 272 7111
www.scottishpower.plc.uk
PRESS: *0141 636 4515*

Severn Trent
0121 722 4000
www.stwater.co.uk
PRESS – GENERAL: *0121 722 4273;*
BIFFA: *01494 521 221;* SEVERN TRENT
WATER: *0121 722 4121*

Shell Transport & Trading Company
020 7934 1234
www.shell.com
PRESS: *020 7934 1234*

Shire Pharmaceuticals
01256 894 000
www.shiregroup.com
PRESS: *01256 894280*

Smith & Nephew
020 7401 7646
www.smith-nephew.com
PRESS: *020 7831 3113*

Smiths Group
020 8458 3232
www.smiths-group.com
PRESS: *020 8457 8403*

Standard Chartered
020 7280 7500
www.standardchartered.com
PRESS: *020 7280 7708*

Tate & Lyle
020 7626 6525
www.tateandlyle.com
PRESS: *020 7977 6143*

Tesco
01992 632222
www.tesco.com
PRESS: *01992 644 645*

Unilever
020 7822 5252
www.unilever.co.uk
PRESS: *020 7822 5252*

United Utilities
01925 237 000
www.unitedutilities.com
PRESS: *01925 537 366*

Vodafone
01635 33251
www.vodafone.co.uk
PRESS – GROUP: *01635 674268;*
UK: *07000 500100*

Whitbread
01582 42 42 00
www.whitbread.co.uk
PRESS – GENERAL: *01582 396 280;*
DAVID LLOYD LEISURE: *01582 844899;*
HOTELS: *01582 396 280;*
RESTAURANTS: *01582 396720;*
MARRIOTT AND TRAVEL INN: *01582 844257*

William Hill
020 8918 3600
www.williamhillplc.co.uk
PRESS: *0780 323 3702*

Wolseley
0118 929 8700
www.wolseley.com

WPP Group
020 7408 2204
www.wpp.com
PRESS: *020 7408 2204*

Xstrata
020 7968 2800
www.xstrata.com
PRESS: *020 7968 2812*

Watchdogs

REGULATORS AND GOVERNMENT AGENCIES

Advertising Standards Authority
020 7492 2222
www.asa.org.uk
PRESS: *020 7492 2123*
020 7492 2222

British and Irish Ombudsman Association
020 8894 9272
www.bioa.org.uk

British Board of Film Classification
020 7440 1570
www.bbfc.co.uk
PRESS: *020 7440 3285*

British Standards Institution
020 8996 9000
www.bsi-global.com
PRESS: *020 7861 3188*

Competition Commission
020 7271 0100
www.competition-commission.org.uk
PRESS: *020 7271 0242*

Council of Mortgage Lenders
020 7437 0075
www.cml.org.uk

Financial Ombudsman Service
020 7964 1000
www.financial-ombudsman.org.uk

Financial Services Authority
020 7066 1000
www.fsa.gov.uk

Food Standards Agency
020 7276 8000
www.foodstandards.gov.uk

Health and Safety Executive
0845 345 0055
www.hse.gov.uk

Health and Safety Executive for Northern Ireland
0800 0320 121, 028 9024 3249
www.hseni.gov.uk

Independent Committee for the Supervision of Telephone Information Services
020 7940 7474
www.icstis.org.uk
PRESS: *020 7940 7408*

Information Commissioner
01625 524 510
www.dataprotection.gov.uk
PRESS: *020 7282 2960*

National Lottery Commission
020 7016 3400
www.natlotcomm.gov.uk
PRESS: *020 7016 3430*

Ofcom
020 7981 3000
www.ofcom.gov.uk
PRESS: *020 7981 3033*

Office of Fair Trading
08457 224499
www.oft.gov.uk

Office of the Rail Regulator
020 7282 2000
www.rail-reg.gov.uk
PRESS: *020 7282 2007*

Ofgem
020 7901 7000
www.ofgas.gov.uk/ofgem
PRESS: *020 7901 7158*

Ofwat
0121 625 1300 / 1373
www.ofwat.gov.uk
PRESS: *0121 625 1442*

Ombudsman for Estate Agents
01722 333306
www.oea.co.uk

Pensions Ombudsman
020 7834 9144
www.pensions-ombudsman.org.uk

Serious Fraud Office
020 7239 7272
www.sfo.gov.uk

Small Business Service
020 7215 5000
www.sbs.gov.uk

Trading Standards Institute
0870 872 9000
www.tsi.org.uk
PRESS: *0870 872 9030*

CONSUMER BODIES

Consumer Support Networks
020 7840 7223
www.csnconnect.org.uk

Consumers' Association
020 7770 7000, 0845 307 4000
www.which.net/corporate
PRESS: *020 7770 7062 / 7373*

General Consumer Council for Northern Ireland
028 9067 2488
www.gccni.org.uk

National Association of Citizens Advice Bureaux
020 7833 7000
www.adviceguide.org.uk

National Consumer Council
020 7730 3469
www.ncc.org.uk

Scottish Consumer Council
0141 226 5261
www.scotconsumer.org.uk

Welsh Consumer Council
029 2025 5454
www.wales-consumer.org.uk

Employment

EMPLOYMENT BODIES

Employment Tribunals
Enquiry line: 0845 795 9775
www.employmenttribunals.gov.uk

Equal Opportunities Commission (EOC)
020 7222 0004
www.eoc.org.uk

Equality Commission for Northern Ireland
028 9050 0600
www.equalityni.org

Investors in People UK
020 7467 1900
www.iipuk.co.uk

Labour Relations Agency
028 9032 1442
www.lra.org.uk
Low Pay Commission
020 7467 7207
www.lowpay.gov.uk
PRESS: *020 7467 7279*
Pay & Employment Rights Service
01924 439587
www.pers.org.uk

UNIONS

Trades Union Congress
020 7636 4030
www.tuc.org.uk
Abbey National Group Union
01442 891122
www.angu.org.uk
Accord
0118 934 1808
www.accord-myunion.org
HBDS Group employees
Alliance and Leicester Group Union of Staff
0116 285 6585
www.algus.org.uk
Amicus
020 8462 7755
www.amicustheunion.org
Manufacturing, technical and skilled workers
Aslef
020 7317 8600
www.aslef.org.uk
Associated Society of Locomotive Engineers and Firemen
PRESS: *020 7317 8600*
Association for College Management
0116 275 5076
www.acm.uk.com
Association of Educational Psychologists
0191 384 9512
www.aep.org.uk
Association of Flight Attendants
001 202 434 1300
www.afanet.org
Association of Magisterial Officers
020 7403 2244
www.amo-online.org.uk
Association of Teachers and Lecturers
020 7930 6441
www.askatl.org.uk
PRESS: *020 7782 1589*
Association of University Teachers
020 7670 9700
www.aut.org.uk
Bakers, Food and Allied Workers Union
01707 260150
www.bfawu.org
Britannia Staff Union
01538 399627
www.britanniasu.org.uk
British Air Line Pilots Association
020 8476 4000
www.balpa.org.uk
PRESS: *020 7924 7555*

British and Irish Orthoptic Society
020 7387 7992
www.orthoptics.org.uk
British Association of Colliery Management – Technical, Energy and Administrative Management
01302 815551
www.bacmteam.org.uk
British Dietetic Association
0121 200 8080
www.bda.uk.com
PRESS: *01626 362473*
Broadcasting, Entertainment, Cinematograph and Theatre Union
020 7346 0900
www.bectu.org.uk
Card Setting Machine Tenters Society
01924 400206
Ceramic and Allied Trades Union
01782 272755
www.catu.org.uk
Chartered Society of Physiotherapy
020 7306 6666
www.csp.org.uk
PRESS: *020 7306 6163*
Communication Workers Union
020 8971 7200
www.cwu.org
Community and District Nursing Association
020 8231 0180
www.cdna.tvu.ac.uk
Community and Youth Workers' Union
0121 244 3344
www.cywu.org.uk
Connect
020 8971 6000
www.connectuk.org
Communications professionals
PRESS: *020 8971 6027*
Diageo Staff Association
020 8978 6069
Staff grades at Diageo, including Guinness, in the UK
Educational Institute of Scotland
0131 225 6244
www.eis.org.uk
Engineering and Fastener Trade Union
0121 420 2204
Equity
020 7379 6000
www.equity.org.uk
Performers and artists
PRESS: *020 7670 0259*
FDA
020 7343 1111
www.fda.org.uk
Senior managers and professionals in public service
PRESS: *020 7343 1121*
Fire Brigades Union
020 8541 1765
www.fbu.org.uk
General Union of Loom Overlookers
01254 51760

GMB
020 8947 3131
www.gmb.org.uk
General union
PRESS: *020 8971 4224*
    07967 273118
Hospital Consultants and Specialists Association
01256 771777
www.hcsa.com
ISTC
020 7239 1200
www.istc-tu.org
Steel and metal industry and communities
Musicians' Union
020 7582 5534
www.musiciansunion.org.uk
NASUWT
0121 453 6150
www.teachersunion.org.uk
National Association of Schoolmasters Union of Women Teachers
NATFHE
020 7837 3636
www.natfhe.org.uk
University and college lecturers
National Association of Colliery Overmen, Deputies and Shotfirers
01226 203743
www.nacods.com
National Association of Cooperative Officials
0161 351 7900
National Association of Educational Inspectors, Advisers and Consultants
01226 383420
www.naeiac.org
National Association of Probation Officers
020 7223 4887
www.napo.org.uk
National Union of Domestic Appliances and General Operatives
020 7387 2578
www.gftu.org.uk
National Union of Journalists
020 7278 7916
www.nuj.org.uk
National Union of Knitwear, Footwear and Apparel Trades
020 7239 1200
www.kfat.org.uk
Manufacturing, retail and logistics
National Union of Lock and Metal Workers
01902 366651
National Union of Marine, Aviation and Shipping Transport Officers
020 8989 6677
www.numast.org
National Union of Mineworkers
01226 215555
www.num.org.uk
National Union of Teachers
020 7388 6191
www.teachers.org.uk
Nationwide Group Staff Union
01295 710767
www.ngsu.org.uk

Prison Officers Association
020 8803 0255
www.poauk.org.uk
Professional Footballers'
Association
0161 236 0575
www.givemefootball.com
Prospect
020 7902 6600
www.prospect.org.uk
Engineers, scientists, managers and
specialists
Public and Commercial Services
Union
020 7924 2727
www.pcs.org.uk
PRESS: *020 7801 2820*
RMT
020 7387 4771
www.rmt.org.uk
Rail, maritime and transport workers
PRESS: *020 7529 8803*
Society of Chiropodists and
Podiatrists
0845 450 3720
www.scpod.org
Society of Radiographers
020 7740 7200
www.sor.org
Transport and General Workers'
Union
020 7611 2500
www.tgwu.org.uk
PRESS: *020 7611 2555*
Transport Salaried Staffs'
Association
020 7387 2101
www.tssa.org.uk
UBAC
01653 697634
Staff at Bradford and Bingley Group
and Alltel Mortgage Solutions
UCAC National Union of Welsh
Teachers
01970 615 577
www.athrawon.com
Union of Construction, Allied
Trades and Technicians
020 7622 2442
www.ucatt.org.uk
PRESS: *020 7622 2422*
Union of Shop, Distributive and
Allied Workers
0161 224 2804 / 249 2400
www.usdaw.org.uk
Unison
0845 355 0845
www.unison.org.uk
Public service union
Writers' Guild of Great Britain
020 7833 0777
www.writersguild.org.uk
Yorkshire Independent Staff
Association
01274 472453
www.ybs.co.uk

Education

Government department

Education and Skills
0870 000 2288
www.dfes.gov.uk
PRESS: *020 7925 6789*

Government agencies

Adult Learning Inspectorate
024 7671 6600
www.ali.gov.uk
PRESS: *024 7671 6703*

Arts and Humanities Research Board
0117 987 6500
www.ahrb.ac.uk
PRESS: *07970 956107*

Council for Science and Technology
020 7215 6518
www.cst.gov.uk

Education and Learning Wales
08456 088 066
www.elwa.ac.uk

Higher Education Funding Council for England (HEFCE)
0117 931 7317
www.hefce.ac.uk
PRESS: *0117 931 7363 / 7431*

Learning and Skills Council
0870 900 6800
www.lsc.gov.uk

Learning and Skills Development Agency
020 7297 9000
www.lsda.org.uk

Learning and Teaching Scotland
0141 337 5000
www.ltscotland.com

National Grid for Learning
www.ngfl.gov.uk

Ofsted
020 7421 6800
www.ofsted.gov.uk
PRESS: *020 7421 6617*

Qualifications and Curriculum Authority
020 7509 5555
www.qca.org.uk
PRESS: *020 7509 6789*

Quality Assurance Agency for Higher Education
01452 557000
www.qaa.ac.uk
PRESS: *01452 557074*

Scottish Qualifications Authority
0845 279 1000
www.sqa.org.uk

Sector Skills Development Agency
01709 765444
www.ssda.org.uk

Student Loans Company
0800 405010
www.slc.co.uk
PRESS: *0141 306 2120*

Teacher Training Agency (TTA)
0845 600 0991
www.canteach.gov.uk

Ucas
01242 222444
www.ucas.com

Professional bodies

Association of Teachers and Lecturers
020 7930 6441
www.askatl.org.uk
PRESS: *020 7782 1541*

Association of University Administrators
0161 275 2063
www.aua.ac.uk

Association of University Teachers
020 7670 9700
www.aut.org.uk
PRESS: *020 7782 1589*

British Educational Research Association
01636 819090
www.bera.ac.uk

National Association of Schoolmasters Union of Women Teachers
0121 453 6150
www.teachersunion.org.uk

National Union of Students
England: 020 7561 6577
Wales: 029 2068 0070
Scotland: 0131 556 6598
Ireland: 028 9024 4641
www.nus.org.uk

National Union of Teachers
020 7388 6191
www.teachers.org.uk

Associations of schools and universities

1994 Group
01273 678208
www.1994group.ac.uk
16 small and medium-sized universities

Boarding Schools' Association
020 7798 1580
www.boarding.org.uk

Girls' Schools Association
0116 254 1619
www.gsa.uk.com

Independent Schools Association
01799 523619
www.isaschools.org.uk

National Association of Independent Schools and Non-Maintained Special Schools
01904 621243
www.nasschools.org.uk

National Grammar Schools Association
0121 567 5222
www.ngsa.org.uk

Russell Group
0151 794 2010
www.russellgroup.ac.uk
19 major research-intensive universities, including Oxford and Cambridge

State Boarding Schools' Association
020 7798 1580
www.sbsa.org.uk

Universities UK
020 7419 4111
www.universitiesuk.ac.uk

Voluntary bodies

Afasic
020 7490 9410
www.afasic.org.uk
Speech, language & communication charity

Campaign for Learning
020 7930 1111
www.campaign-for-learning.org.uk

ContinYou
024 7658 8440
www.continyou.org.uk

Learning Through Action
0870 770 7985
www.learning-through-action.org.uk

Life Education Centres
020 7831 9311
www.lifeeducation.org.uk

National Literacy Trust
020 7828 2435
www.literacytrust.org.uk
PRESS: *020 7828 2435*

UFI/ Learn Direct
0114 291 5000
www.ufi.com

Universities

Aberdeen, University of
01224 272000
www.abdn.ac.uk
PRESS: *01224 272014*

Abertay Dundee, University of
01382 308080
www.abertay.ac.uk

Aberystwyth – University of Wales
01970 623 111
www.aber.ac.uk

Anglia Polytechnic University
0845 271 3333
www.apu.ac.uk

Aston University, Birmingham
0121 204 3000
www.aston.ac.uk

Bangor – University of Wales
01248 351151
www.bangor.ac.uk
PRESS: *01248 38 3298*
Bath Spa University College
01225 875875
www.bathspa.ac.uk
Bath, University of
01225 388388
www.bath.ac.uk
Bell College
01698 283100
www.bell.ac.uk
Birmingham, University of
0121 414 3344
www.bham.ac.uk
PRESS: *0121 414 6680*
Bishop Grossteste College
01522 527347
www.bgc.ac.uk
Bolton Institute of Higher Education
01204 900600
www.bolton.ac.uk
Bournemouth University
01202 524111
www.bournemouth.ac.uk
Bournemouth, Arts Institute at
01202 533011
www.aib.ac.uk
Bradford, University of
01274 232323
www.bradford.ac.uk
PRESS: *1274 233084*
Brighton, University of
01273 600900
www.brighton.ac.uk
PRESS:
  communications@brighton.ac.uk
Bristol, University of
0117 928 9000
www.bris.ac.uk
Brunel University
01895 274000
www.brunel.ac.uk
PRESS: *01895 265585*
Buckingham Chilterns University College
01494 522141
www.bcuc.ac.uk
Buckingham, University of
01280 814080
www.buckingham.ac.uk
PRESS: *01280 820338*
Cambridge, University of
01223 337733
www.cam.ac.uk
PRESS: *01223 332300*
Christ's College: 01223 334900
www.christs.cam.ac.uk
Churchill College: 01223 336000
www.chu.cam.ac.uk
Clare College: 01223 333200
www.clare.cam.ac.uk
Corpus Christi College:
01223 338000
www.corpus.cam.ac.uk
Downing College: 01223 334800
www.downing.cam.ac.uk
Emmanuel College: 01223 334200
www.emma.cam.ac.uk
Fitzwilliam College: 01223 332000
www.fitz.cam.ac.uk

Girton College: 01223 338999
www.girton.cam.ac.uk
Gonville & Caius College:
01223 332447
www.caius.cam.ac.uk
Homerton College: 01223 411141
www.homerton.cam.ac.uk
Hughes Hall: 01223 334898
www.hughes.cam.ac.uk
Jesus College: 01223 339339
www.jesus.cam.ac.uk
Kings College: 01223 331100
www.kings.cam.ac.uk
Lucy Cavendish College:
01223 332190
www.lucy-cav.cam.ac.uk
Magdalene College: 01223 332100
www.magd.cam.ac.uk
New Hall: 01223 762100
www.newhall.cam.ac.uk
Newnham College: 01223 334700
www.newn.cam.ac.uk
Pembroke College: 01223 338100
www.pem.cam.ac.uk
Peterhouse College: 01223 338200
www.pet.cam.ac.uk
Queen's College: 01223 335511
www.quns.cam.ac.uk
Robinson College: 01223 339100
www.rob.cam.ac.uk
St Catharine's College: 01223 338300
www.caths.cam.ac.uk
St Edmund's College: 01223 336250
www.stedmunds.cam.ac.uk
St John's College: 01223 338703
www.joh.cam.ac.uk
Selwyn College: 01223 335846
www.sel.cam.ac.uk
Sidney Sussex College: 01223 338800
www.sid.cam.ac.uk
Canterbury Christ Church University College
01227 767700
www.cant.ac.uk
Cardiff – University of Wales Institute
029 2041 6070
www.uwic.ac.uk
Cardiff University
029 2087 4000
www.cardiff.ac.uk
Central England in Birmingham, University of
0121 331 5595
www.uce.ac.uk
PRESS: *0121 331 6738*
Central Lancashire, University of
01772 201201
www.uclan.ac.uk
Central School of Speech and Drama
020 7722 8183
www.cssd.ac.uk
City University
020 7040 5060
www.city.ac.uk
PRESS: *020 7040 8783*
Conservatoire for Dance & Drama
London Contemporary Dance School
020 7387 0161
www.theplace.org.uk

Royal Academy of Dramatic Art (Rada)
020 7636 7076
www.rada.org.uk
Coventry University
024 7688 7688
www.coventry.ac.uk
Cumbria Institute of the Arts
01228 400300
www.cumbria.ac.uk
Dartington College of Arts
01803 862224
www.dartington.ac.uk
De Montfort University
0116 255 1551
www.dmu.ac.uk
Derby, University of
01332 590500
www.derby.ac.uk
Dundee, University of
01382 344000
www.dundee.ac.uk
Durham, University of
0191 374 2000
www.dur.ac.uk
East Anglia, University of
01603 456161
www.uea.ac.uk
PRESS: *01603 592203*
East London, University of
020 8223 3000
www.uel.ac.uk
Edge Hill College
01695 575171
www.edgehill.ac.uk
Edinburgh College of Art
0131 221 6000
www.eca.ac.uk
Edinburgh, University of
0131 650 1000
www.ed.ac.uk
Essex, University of
01206 873333
www.essex.ac.uk
Exeter, University of
01392 661000
www.ex.ac.uk
Falmouth College of Arts
01326 211077
www.falmouth.ac.uk
Glamorgan, University of
01443 480 480
www.glam.ac.uk
Glasgow Caledonian
0141 331 3000
www.caledonian.ac.uk
Glasgow School of Art
0141 353 4500
www.gas.ac.uk
Glasgow, University of
0141 330 2000
www.gla.ac.uk
Gloucestershire, University of
01242 532825
www.chelt.ac.uk
www.glos.ac.uk
Goldsmiths College, University of London
020 7919 7171
www.goldsmiths.ac.uk
Greenwich, University of
020 8331 8000
www.gre.ac.uk

Harper Adams University College
01952 820820
www.harper-adams.ac.uk

Heriot-Watt University
0131 449 5111
www.hw.ac.uk

Hertfordshire, University of
01707 284000
www.herts.ac.uk
PRESS: *01707 286331*

Huddersfield, University of
01484 422288
www.hud.ac.uk

Hull, University of
01482 346311
www.hull.ac.uk

Imperial College, London
020 7589 5111
www.ic.ac.uk
PRESS: *07803 886248*

Keele University
01782 621111
www.keele.ac.uk

Kent, University of
01227 764000
www.ukc.ac.uk

Kent Institute of Art & Design
01622 757286
www.kiad.ac.uk
PRESS: *01622 620164*

King's College London
020 7836 5454
www.kcl.ac.uk

Kingston University
020 8457 2000
www.kingston.ac.uk

Lampeter – University of Wales
01570 422351
www.lamp.ac.uk

Lancaster University
01524 65201
www.lancs.ac.uk

Leeds Metropolitan University
0113 283 2600
www.lmu.ac.uk

Leeds, University of
0113 243 1751
www.leeds.ac.uk
PRESS: *0113 343 4030*

Leicester, University of
0116 252 2522
www.le.ac.uk

Lincoln, University of
01522 882000
www.lincoln.ac.uk

Liverpool Hope University College
0151 291 3000
www.hope.ac.uk

Liverpool John Moores University
0151 231 2121
www.livjm.ac.uk

Liverpool, University of
0151 794 2000
www.liv.ac.uk
PRESS: *0151 794 2247*

London Metropolitan University
020 7423 0000
www.londonmet.ac.uk

London School of Economics and Political Science (LSE)
020 7405 7686
www.lse.ac.uk

London – University of the Arts
Camberwell College of Arts
020 7514 6302
www.camberwell.arts.ac.uk
Central St Martin's College of Art & Design
020 7514 7000
www.csm.arts.ac.uk
Chelsea College of Art & Design
020 7514 7751
www.chelsea.arts.ac.uk
London College of Communication
020 7514 6500
www.lcc.arts.ac.uk
London College of Fashion
020 7514 7500
www.fashion.arts.ac.uk

Loughborough University
01509 263171
www.lboro.ac.uk

Luton, University of
01582 734111
www.luton.ac.uk

Manchester Metropolitan University
0161 247 2000
www.mmu.ac.uk

Manchester, University of
0161 306 6000
www.man.ac.uk

Middlesex University
020 8411 5000
www.mdx.ac.uk

Napier University
0131 455 6314
www.napier.ac.uk
PRESS: *01698 787844*

Newcastle-upon-Tyne, University of
0191 222 6000
www.ncl.ac.uk

Newman College
0121 476 1181
www.newman.ac.uk
PRESS: *0121 476 1181*

Newport – University of Wales
01633 432432
www.newport.ac.uk

North East Wales Institute of Higher Education
01978 290666
www.newi.ac.uk
PRESS: *01978 293360*

Northern School of Contemporary Dance
0113 219 3000
www.nscd.ac.uk

Northumbria, University of
0191 227 4777
www.unn.ac.uk
PRESS: *0191 227 3477*

Norwich School of Art & Design
01603 610561
www.nsad.ac.uk

Nottingham Trent University
0115 941 8418
www.ntu.ac.uk

Nottingham, University of
0115 951 5151
www.nottingham.ac.uk
PRESS: *0115 846 8092*

Oxford Brookes University
01865 741111
www.brookes.ac.uk

Oxford, University of
01865 288000
www.ox.ac.uk
Admissions: 01865 288000
www.admissions.ox.ac.uk
Balliol College: 01865 277777
www.balliol.ox.ac.uk
Brasenose College: 01865 277510
www.bnc.ox.ac.uk
Christ Church: 01865 276151
www.chch.ox.ac.uk
Corpus Christi College: 01865 276700
www.ccc.ox.ac.uk
Exeter College: 01865 279660
www.exeter.ox.ac.uk
Harris Manchester College:
01865 271006
www.hmc.ox.ac.uk
Hertford College: 01865 279400
www.hertford.ox.ac.uk
Jesus College: 01865 279700
www.jesus.ox.ac.uk
Keble College: 01865 272727
www.keble.ox.ac.uk
Lady Margaret Hall: 01865 274300
www.lmh.ox.ac.uk
Lincoln College: 01865 279800
www.lincoln.ox.ac.uk
Magdalen College: 01865 276063
www.magd.ox.ac.u
Mansfield College: 01865 270999
www.mansfield.ox.ac.uk
Merton College: 01865 276310
www.merton.ox.ac.uk
New College: 01865 279590
www.new.oc.ac.uk
Oriel College: 01865 276555
www.oriel.ox.ac.uk
Pembroke College: 01865 276444
www.pmb.ox.ac.uk
The Queen's College: 01865 279120
www.queens.ox.ac.uk
Regent's Park College: 01865 288120
www.rpc.ox.ac.uk
St Anne's College: 01865 274800
www.stannes.ox.ac.uk
St Catherine's College:
01865 271 701
www.stcatz.ox.ac.uk
St Edmund Hall: 01865 279008
www.she.ox.ac.uk
St Hilda's College: 01865 276884
www.sthildas.ox.ac.uk
St Hugh's College: 01865 274900
www.st-hughs.ox.ac.uk
St John's College: 01865 277318
www.sjc.ox.ac.uk
St Peter's College: 01865 278900
www.spc.ox.ac.uk
Somerville College: 01865 270600
www.some.ox.ac.uk
Trinity College: 01865 279900
www.trinity.ox.ac.uk
University College: 01865 276602
www.univ.ox.ac.uk
Wadham College: 01865 277900
www.wadham.ox.ac.uk
Worcester College: 01865 278300
www.worcester.ox.ac.uk

Paisley, University of
0141 848 3000
www.paisley.ac.uk
Plymouth, University of
01752 600600
www.plymouth.ac.uk
Portsmouth, University of
023 9284 8484
www.port.ac.uk
Queen Margaret University College
0131 317 3000
www.qmuc.ac.uk
Queen Mary, University of London
020 7882 5555
www.qmul.ac.uk
Queen's University Belfast
02890 245133
www.qub.ac.uk
PRESS: *028 9097 3091*
Ravensbourne College of Design & Communication
020 8289 4900
www.rave.ac.uk
Reading, University of
0118 987 5123
www.reading.ac.uk
PRESS: *0118 378 7388*
Robert Gordon University, Aberdeen
01224 262000
www.rgu.ac.uk
Roehampton – University of Surrey
020 8392 3000
www.roehampton.ac.uk
Rose Bruford College
020 8308 2600
www.bruford.ac.uk
Royal Academy of Music
020 7873 7373
www.ram.ac.uk
Royal Agricultural College
01285 652531
www.royagcol.ac.uk
Royal College of Music
020 7589 3643
www.rcm.ac.uk
Royal Holloway, University of London
01784 434455
www.rhul.ac.uk
Royal Northern College of Music
0161 907 5200
www.rncm.ac.uk
Royal Scottish Academy of Music & Drama
0141 332 4101
www.rsamd.ac.uk
Royal Veterinary College
020 74685000
www.rvc.ac.uk
Royal Welsh College of Music & Drama
029 2034 2854
www.rwcmd.ac.uk
St Andrews, University of
01334 476161
www.st-andrews.ac.uk
St George's Hospital Medical School
020 8672 9944
www.sghms.ac.uk

St Mark & St John College
01752 636 700
www.marjon.ac.uk
St Martin's College
01524 384384
www.ucsm.ac.uk
St Mary's College
020 8240 4000
www.smuc.ac.uk
Salford, University of
0161 295 5000
www.salford.ac.uk
School of Oriental and African Studies (SOAS)
020 7637 2388
www.soas.ac.uk
School of Pharmacy, University of London
020 7753 5800
www.ulsop.ac.uk
Scottish Agricultural College
0800 269453
www.sac.ac.uk/education
Sheffield Hallam University
0114 225 5555
www.shu.ac.uk
Sheffield, University of
0114 222 2000
www.sheffield.ac.uk
South Bank University
020 7928 8989
www.sbu.ac.uk
Southampton Institute
023 8031 9000
www.solent.ac.uk
Southampton, University of
023 8059 5000
www.soton.ac.uk
PRESS: *023 8059 3212*
Staffordshire University
01782 294000
www.staffs.ac.uk
Stirling, University of
01786 473171
www.stir.ac.uk
Stranmillis University College
028 9038 1271
www.stran-ni.ac.uk
Strathclyde, University of
0141 552 4400
www.strath.ac.uk
Sunderland, University of
0191 515 2000
www.sunderland.ac.uk
Surrey Institute of Art & Design, University College
01252 722441
www.surrart.ac.uk
Surrey, University of
01483 300800
www.surrey.ac.uk
Sussex, University of
01273 606755
www.sussex.ac.uk
Swansea – University of Wales
01792 205678
www.swan.ac.uk
Swansea Institute of Higher Education
01792 481000
www.sihe.ac.uk

Teesside, University of
01642 218121
www.tees.ac.uk
Thames Valley University
020 8579 5000
www.tvu.ac.uk
Trinity & All Saints College
0113 283 7100
www.tasc.ac.uk
Trinity College, Carmarthen
01267 676767
www.trinity-cm.ac.uk
Trinity College of Music
020 8305 4444
www.tcm.ac.uk
UHI Millennium Institute
01643 27900
www.uhi.ac.uk
Ulster, University of
0870 0400 700
www.ulster.ac.uk
University College Chester
01244 375444
www.chester.ac.uk
University College Chichester
01243 816000
www.ucc.ac.uk
University College London
020 7679 2000
www.ucl.ac.uk
PRESS: *020 7679 9728*
University College Northampton
01604 735500
www.northampton.ac.uk
University College Winchester
01962 841515
www.winchester.ac.uk
University College Worcester
01905 855000
www.worc.ac.uk
Warwick, University of
024 7652 3523
www.warwick.ac.uk
West of England, University of the
0117 965 6261
www.uwe.ac.uk
Westminster, University of
020 7911 5000
www.westminster.ac.uk
Wimbledon School of Art
020 8408 5000
www.wimbledon.ac.uk
Wolverhampton, University of
01902 321000
www.wlv.ac.uk
PRESS: *01902 322003*
Writtle College
01245 424200
www.writtle.ac.uk
York St John College
01904 624624
www.yorksj.ac.uk
York, University of
01904 430000
www.york.ac.uk

Environment

Government and agencies

Department for the Environment, Food and Rural Affairs
020 7238 6000
www.defra.gov.uk
PRESS – ANIMAL WELFARE: *020 7238 6044;* ENVIRONMENT: *020 7238 6054;* RURAL AFFAIRS: *020 7238 5608;* SUSTAINABLE FARMING AND FOOD: *020 7238 6146*

British Waterways Board
01923 201120
www.britishwaterways.co.uk
PRESS: *01923 201329*

Countryside Agency
01242 521381
www.countryside.gov.uk
PRESS: *020 7340 2907*

Environment Agency
08708 506 506
www.environment-agency.gov.uk
PRESS: *020 7863 8710*

Food Standards Agency
020 7276 8000
www.foodstandards.gov.uk
PRESS: *020 7276 8888*

Forestry Commission
0131 334 0303
www.forestry.gov.uk
PRESS: *0131 314 6289*

Meat and Livestock Commission
01908 677577
www.mlc.org.uk
PRESS: *01908 844106*

The Pesticides Safety Directorate
01904 640500
www.pesticides.gov.uk
PRESS: *020 7238 6096*

United Kingdom Atomic Energy Authority
01235 820220
www.ukaea.org.uk
PRESS: *01235 436900*

Rural and environmental bodies

Country Landowners Society
020 7235 0511
www.cla.org.uk
PRESS: *020 7460 7936*

English Heritage
0870 333 1181
www.english-heritage.org.uk
PRESS: *020 7973 3250*

English Nature
01733 455000
www.english-nature.org.uk
PRESS: *01733 455190*

Friends of the Earth
0808 800 1111, 020 7490 1555
www.foe.co.uk
England, Wales and Northern Ireland
PRESS: *020 7566 1649*

Friends of the Earth Scotland
0131 554 9977
www.foe-scotland.org.uk

Game Conservancy Trust
01425 652381
www.gct.org.uk
PRESS: *01425 651000*

Greenpeace
020 7865 8100
www.greenpeace.org.uk
PRESS: *020 7865 8255*

National Farmers Union
020 7331 7200
www.nfu.org.uk
PRESS: *020 7331 7387*

National Trust
0870 242 6620
www.nationaltrust.org.uk

National Trust for Scotland
0131 243 9300
www.nts.org.uk
PRESS: *0131 243 9384*

Ramblers Association
020 7339 8500
www.ramblers.org.uk
PRESS: *020 7339 8531 / 2*

Worldwide Fund for Nature UK
01483 426444
www.wwf-uk.org

National parks

Brecon
01874 624437
www.breconbeacons.org

Dartmoor
01626 832093
www.dartmoor-npa.gov.uk

Exmoor
01398 323665
www.exmoor-nationalpark.gov.uk

Lake District
01539 724555
www.lake-district.gov.uk

Norfolk & Suffolk Broads
01603 610734
www.broads-authority.gov.uk

Northumberland
01434 605555
www.northumberland-national-park.org.uk

North Yorkshire Moors
01439 770657
www.moors.uk.net

Peak District
01629 816200
www.peakdistrict.org

Pembrokeshire Coast
0845 345 7275
www.pembrokeshirecoast.org.uk

Snowdonia
0845 130 6229
www.ccw.gov.uk

Yorkshire Dales
01969 650456, 01756 752748
www.yorkshiredales.org.uk

Voluntary sector

ANIMAL WELFARE

Animal Aid
01732 364546
www.animalaid.org.uk
Animal Defenders
020 8846 9777
www.animaldefenders.org.uk
Animal Health Trust
0870 050 2424
www.aht.org.uk
Bat Conservation Trust
020 7627 2629
www.bats.org.uk
Battersea Dogs Home
020 7622 3626
www.dogshome.org
PRESS: *020 7627 9294*
Blue Cross
01993 822651
www.bluecross.org.uk
Pet welfare charity
British Deer Society
01425 655434
www.bds.org.uk
British Hedgehog Protection Trust
01584 890801
www.software-technics.com/bhps
British Union for Abolition of Vivisection
020 7700 4888
www.buav.org
Brooke Hospital for Animals
020 7930 0210
www.brooke-hospital.org.uk
Working animals in developing world
Butterfly Conservation Trust
0870 774 4309
www.butterfly-conservation.org
Canine Lifeline UK
0870 758 1401
www.caninelifeline.fsnet.co.uk
Cat Action Trust
01555 660784
www.catactiontrust.co.uk
Cats Protection
0870 209 9099
www.cats.org.uk
Celia Hammond Animal Trust
01892 783367
www.celiahammond.org
Dog Trust
020 7837 0006
www.dogstrust.org.uk
Donkey Sanctuary
01395 578222
www.thedonkeysanctuary.org.uk
Farm Animal Welfare Council
020 7904 6721
www.fawc.org.uk
Fauna & Flora International
01223 571000
www.fauna-flora.org
Federation of Zoos
www.zoofederation.org.uk
Feline Advisory Board
0870 742 2278
www.fabcats.org

Humane Slaughter Society
01582 831919
www.hsa.org.uk
Hunt Saboteurs Organisation
0845 450 0727
www.huntsabs.org.uk
International Dolphin Watch
01482 632650
www.idw.org
International Fund for Animal Welfare
020 7587 6700
www.ifaw.org
International League for the Protection of Horses
0870 870 1927
www.ilph.org
League Against Cruel Sports
0845 330 8486
www.league.uk.com
London Wildlife Trust
020 7261 0447
www.wildlondon.org.uk
Mammal Society
020 7350 2200
www.abdn.ac.uk/mammal
Mare & Foal Sanctuary
01626 853085
www.mareandfoal.org.uk
Marine Conservation Society
www.mcsuk.mcmail.com
National Federation of Badger Groups
020 7228 6444
www.nfbg.org.uk
Otter Trust
01986 893470
www.ottertrust.org.uk
People and Dogs Society
01924 897732, 01977 678593
www.padsonline.org
People for the Ethical Treatment of Animals (PETA)
020 7357 9229
www.peta.org
People's Dispensary for Sick Animals (PDSA)
01952 290999
www.pdsa.org.uk
Rare Breeds Survival Trust
024 7669 6551
www.rare-breeds.com
Redwings Horse Sanctuary
01508 481000
www.redwings.co.uk
Royal Society for the Prevention of Cruelty to Animals
0870 555 5999
www.rspca.org.uk
PRESS: *0870 754 0288 / 44*
Royal Society for the Protection of Birds
01767 680551
www.rspb.org.uk
PRESS: *01767 681577*
Save the Rhino
020 7357 7474
www.savetherhino.org
Scottish Society for the Prevention of Cruelty to Animals
0131 339 0222
www.scottishspca.org

Scottish Wildlife Trust
0131 312 7765
www.swt.org.uk
Society for the Protection of Animals Abroad
020 7831 3999
www.spana.org
TRAFFIC
01223 277427
www.traffic.org
Combats damaging trade in plants & animals
Ulster Wildlife Trust
028 4483 0282
www.ulsterwildlifetrust.org
Uncaged
0114 272 2220
www.uncaged.co.uk
Anti-vivisection campaigner
Veteran Horse Society
01239 881300
www.veteran-horse-society.co.uk
Whale & Dolphin Conservation Society
0870 870 0027
www.wdcs.org.uk
Wildfowl & Wetlands Trust
0870 334 4000
www.wwt.org.uk
The Wildlife Trusts
0870 036 7711
www.wildlifetrusts.org
Wood Green Animal Shelters
08701 904090
www.woodgreen.org.uk
World Society for the Protection of Animals
020 7587 5000
www.wspa-international.org
www.wspa.org.uk
WWF UK
01483 426444
www.wwf.org.uk

CONSERVATION

Black Environment Network
01286 870715
www.ben-network.co.uk
British Association for Shooting and Conservation
01244 573000
www.basc.org.uk
PRESS: *01244 573026*
British Trust for Conservation Volunteers
01302 572244
www.btcv.org
Campaign for Real Events
www.c-realevents.demon.co.uk
Provides renewable energy and "alt tech" support for events
Campaign to Protect Rural England
020 7981 2800
www.cpre.org.uk
Centre for Alternative Technology
01654 705950
www.cat.org.uk
Community Composting Network
0114 258 0483, 0114 255 3720
www.communitycompost.org

**Community Service Volunteers –
Environment**
0121 322 2008
www.csv.org.uk
Conservation Foundation
020 7591 3111
www.conservationfoundation.co.uk
**Council for Environmental
Education**
0118 950 2550
www.cee.org.uk
Council for National Parks
020 7924 4077
www.cnp.org.uk
Earth First! In Britain
www.earthfirst.org.uk
Earth Rights
01279 870391
www.earthrights.org.uk
Environmental public interest law firm
Earthwatch Institute
01865 318838
www.uk.earthwatch.org
*Conservation of natural environments
& cultural heritage*
Eco-Village Network
0117 373 0346
www.eco-village.org
Energywatch
0845 906 0708
www.energywatch.org.uk
Environmental Campaigns
01942 612621
www.encams.org
European Rivers Network
00 33 47 102 0814
www.rivernet.org
Based in southern France
Forest Action Network
00 1 250 799 5800
www.fanweb.org
Forum for the Future
020 7324 3630
www.forumforthefuture.org.uk
Future Forests
0870 199 9988
www.futureforests.com
Gaia Energy Centre
01840 213321
www.gaiaenergy.co.uk
Promotes renewable energy
Game Conservancy Trust
01425 652381
www.gct.org.uk
People and Planet
01865 245678
www.peopleandplanet.org
*UK student action on human rights,
poverty and the environment*
Rising Tide
07708 794665
www.risingtide.org.uk
Action against climate change
Royal Society for Nature Conservation
0870 036 1000
www.rsnc.org
Solar Energy Society
07760 163559
www.thesolarline.com
Surfers Against Sewage
0845 458 3001
www.sas.org.uk

**UNEP World Conservation
Monitoring Centre**
01223 277314
www.unep-wcmc.org
Woodland Trust
01476 581135
www.woodland-trust.org.uk

FARMING AND FOOD

Farm
020 7713 9250
www.farm.org.uk
*Campaigners for the future of
independent and family farms*
Farm Animal Welfare Council
020 7904 6721
www.fawc.org.uk
Farming & Wildlife Advisory Group
024 7669 6699
www.fwag.org.uk
Biodynamic Agricultural Association
01453 759501
www.anth.org.uk/biodynamic
Campaign for Real Ale
01727 867201
www.camra.org.uk
Compassion in World Farming
01730 264208
www.ciwf.org.uk
Dig It Up!
www.dig-it-up.uk.net
Action against planting of GM rape crops
Eat the View
01242 533222
www.eat-the-view.org.uk
Food from Britain
020 7233 5111
www.foodfrombritain.com
Promoting sustainable local products
Five Year Freeze Campaign
020 7837 0642
www.fiveyearfreeze.org
Anti-GM activists group
Food & Drink Federation
020 7836 2460
www.fdf.org.uk
Food Dudes
01248 38 3973
www.fooddudes.co.uk
Teaching children about healthy eating
Foundation for Local Food Initiatives
0845 458 9525
www.localfood.org.uk
Free Range Activism Website
www.fraw.org.uk
Future Harvest
00 1 703 548 4540
www.futureharvest.org
*Promoting environmentally sound
agricultural methods*
Henry Doubleday Research Society
024 7630 3517
www.hdra.org.uk
*Researches & promotes organic
methods & produce*
Herb Society
01295 768899
www.herbsociety.co.uk
Herbs for health

**National Association of Farmers
Markets**
0845 458 8420
www.farmersmarkets.net
National Federation of City Farms
0117 923 1800
www.farmgarden.org.uk
Permaculture Society
0845 458 1805
www.permaculture.org.uk
Pesticide Action Network
020 7065 0907
www.pan-uk.org
Soil Association
0117 314 5000
www.soilassociation.org
Sustain
020 7837 1228
www.sustainweb.org
Alliance for better food & farming
UK Food Group
020 7523 2369
www.ukfg.org.uk
*Network for NGOs working on global
food & agriculture issues*
Veggies Catering Campaign
0845 458 9595
www.veggies.org.uk
Willing Workers on Organic Farms
01273 476286
www.wwoof.org/wwoof_uk

GARDENING

Royal Horticultural Society
020 7834 4333
www.rhs.org.uk

Health

Government departments

Department of Health
020 7210 4850
www.dh.gov.uk
PRESS: *020 7210 5221*
Scottish Executive DoH
0131 556 8400
www.scotland.gov.uk
PRESS: *0131 244 2797*
Northern Ireland DoH
028 9052 0500
www.dhsspsni.gov.uk
PRESS: *028 9052 0636*

Government agencies

Centre for Emergency Preparedness and Response
01980 612100
Centre for Infections
020 8200 4400
Centre for Radiation, Chemical and Environmental Hazards
01235 831600
Health and Safety Executive
0870 1545 500
www.hse.gov.uk
PRESS: *020 7717 6700*
OUT OF HOURS: *020 7928 8382*
Health Care Commission
020 7448 9200
www.healthcarecommission.org.uk
PRESS: *020 7448 9401*
Health Professions Council
020 7582 0866
www.hpc-uk.org
Health Protection Agency
020 7759 2700/1
www.hpa.org.uk
Health Service Ombudsman
0845 015 4033
www.ombudsman.org.uk
Human Fertilisation and Embryology Authority
020 7291 8200
www.hfea.gov.uk
Human Genetics Commission
020 7972 1518
www.hgc.gov.uk
PRESS: *020 8675 1066*
Medical Research Council
020 7636 5422
www.mrc.ac.uk
Medicines and Healthcare products Regulatory Agency
020 7084 2000
www.mhra.gov.uk
PRESS: *020 7084 2657*
National Blood Service
0845 7711 711
www.blood.co.uk

National Institute for Health and Clinical Excellence (NICE)
020 7067 5800
www.nice.org.uk
National Patient Safety Agency
020 7927 9500
www.npsa.nhs.uk
NHS Executive
0113 254 5000
www.nhs.uk
PRESS: *020 7210 5221*
NHS Health Scotland
0131 536 5500
www.healthscotland.com
NHS Quality Improvement, Scotland
0131 623 4300
www.nhshealthquality.org
NHS State Hospitals Board for Scotland
01555 840293
www.show.scot.nhs.uk/tsh

Professional bodies

British Medical Association
020 7387 4499
www.bma.org.uk
PRESS: *020 7383 6254*
General Medical Council
0845 357 3456
www.gmc-uk.org
PRESS: *020 7189 5454*
Royal College of Nursing
020 7409 3333
www.rcn.org.uk
PRESS: *020 7647 3633*
Academy of Medical Royal Colleges
020 7408 2244
www.aomrc.org.uk
Royal College of Anaesthetists
020 7813 1900
www.rcoa.ac.uk
Royal College of General Practitioners
020 7581 3232
www.rcgp.org.uk
PRESS: *020 7344 3135 / 6 / 7*
Royal College of Obstetricians & Gynaecologists
020 7772 6200
www.rcog.org.uk
PRESS: *020 7772 6357*
Royal College of Ophthalmologists
020 7935 0702
www.rcophth.ac.uk
Royal College of Paediatrics and Child Health
020 7307 5600
www.rcpch.ac.uk
Royal College of Pathologists
020 7451 6700
www.rcpath.org
PRESS: *020 7451 6752*

Royal College of Physicians of Edinburgh
0131 225 7324
www.rcpe.ac.uk
PRESS: *0131 247 3693*
Royal College of Physicians of Ireland
00 353 1 661 6677
www.rcpi.ie
Royal College of Physicians of London
020 7935 1174
www.rcplondon.ac.uk
PRESS: *x254, x468*
Faculty of Public Health Medicine
020 7935 0243
www.fphm.org.uk
PRESS: *020 7487 1185*
Royal College of Physicians & Surgeons of Glasgow
0141 221 6072
www.rcpsglasg.ac.uk
Royal College of Psychiatrists
020 7235 2351
www.rcpsych.ac.uk
PRESS: *x154, x127*
Royal College of Radiologists
020 7636 4432
www.rcr.ac.uk
PRESS: *x1138*
Royal College of Surgeons of Edinburgh
0131 527 1600
www.rcsed.ac.uk
Royal College of Surgeons of England
020 7405 3474
www.rcseng.ac.uk
PRESS: *020 7869 6045*
Royal College of Surgeons in Ireland
00 353 1 402 2100
www.rcsi.ie
PRESS: *00 353 1 402 8610*
British Dental Association
020 7935 0875
www.bda-dentistry.org.uk
Press: 020 7563 4145/6

Patient groups

Patients Association
020 8423 9111
www.patients-association.com

General health

Action Medical Research
01403 210406
www.action.org.uk
PRESS: *01403 327404*

Alzheimer's Society
020 7306 0606
www.alzheimers.org.uk
PRESS: *020 7306 0813 / 39*

Arthritis Care
020 7380 6500
www.arthritiscare.org.uk
PRESS: *020 7380 6551*

Arthritis Research Campaign
0870 850 5000
www.arc.org.uk
PRESS: *01246 541107*

Association for International Cancer Research
01334 477910
www.aicr.org.uk

Bliss
020 7820 9471
www.bliss.org.uk
National charity for premature or sick babies

Breakthrough Breast Cancer
020 7025 2400
www.breakthrough.org.uk
PRESS: *020 7025 2432*

Breast Cancer Campaign
020 7749 3700
www.bcc-uk.org

Breast Cancer Care
020 7384 2984
www.breastcancercare.org.uk
PRESS: *020 7384 4696*

British Dietetic Association
0121 200 8080
www.bda.uk.com

British Heart Foundation
020 7935 0185
www.bhf.org.uk
PRESS: *020 7487 7172*
OUT OF HOURS: *07764 290381*

British Pregnancy Advisory Service
01564 793225
www.bpas.org
PRESS: *07788 725185*

CLIC Sargent
0845 301 0031
www.clicsargent.org.uk
PRESS: *0117 311 2643*
Children's cancer charity

Cancer Research UK
020 7121 6699
www.cancerresearchuk.org
PRESS: *020 7061 8300*

Consensus Action on Salt and Health
020 8725 2409
www.actiononsalt.org.uk
PRESS: *07711 698984*
020 8853 1349

Cystic Fibrosis Trust
020 8464 7211
www.cftrust.org.uk
PRESS: *020 7940 3800*

Diabetes UK
020 7424 1000
www.diabetes.org.uk
PRESS: *020 7424 1165*

Eating Disorders Association
0870 770 3256
www.edauk.com
PRESS: *0870 770 3221*

Epilepsy Action
0113 210 8800
www.epilepsy.org.uk

Great Ormond St Children's Charity
020 7916 5678
www.gosh.org

Guy's & St Thomas' Charity
020 7955 4996
www.charitablefoundation.org.uk
PRESS: *020 7955 4390*

Healthwise
0870 990 9702
www.healthwise.org.uk
Campaigning and providing helplines

Institute of Cancer Research
020 7352 8133
www.icr.ac.uk
PRESS: *x5312*

International HIV/AIDS Alliance
01273 718900
www.aidsalliance.org

International Obesity Taskforce
020 7691 1900
www.iotf.org

Leukaemia Research Fund
020 7405 0101
www.lrf.org.uk
PRESS: *020 7269 9019*

Macmillan Cancer Relief
020 7840 7840
www.macmillan.org.uk
PRESS: *020 7840 7821*

Marie Curie Cancer Care
020 7599 7777
www.mariecurie.org.uk
PRESS: *020 7599 7700*

Marie Stopes International
020 7574 7400
www.mariestopes.org.uk
Reproductive healthcare worldwide
PRESS: *020 7574 7353*

Meningitis Trust
01453 768000
www.meningitis-trust.org

Mind
020 8519 2122
www.mind.org.uk
National Association for Mental Health
PRESS: *020 8522 1743*

Motor Neurone Disease Association
01604 250505
www.mndassociation.org
PRESS: *01604 611840*

Multiple Sclerosis Society
020 8438 0700
www.mssociety.org.uk
PRESS: *020 7082 0820*

Muscular Dystrophy Campaign
020 7720 8055
www.muscular-dystrophy.org

National Asthma Campaign
020 7786 4900
www.asthma.org.uk
PRESS: *020 7786 4949*

National Heart Forum
020 7383 7638
www.heartforum.org.uk

National Kidney Research Fund
0845 070 7601
www.nkrf.org.uk
PRESS: *01733 704678*

Parkinson's Disease Society of the UK
020 7931 8080
www.parkinsons.org.uk

St John Ambulance
08700 104950
www.sja.org.uk
PRESS: *020 7324 4210*

Stroke Association
020 7566 0300
www.stroke.org.uk
PRESS: *020 7566 1500*

Terrence Higgins Trust
0845 1221 200
www.tht.org.uk
HIV/Aids
PRESS: *020 7816 8622*

The Wellcome Trust
020 7611 8888
www.wellcome.ac.uk
PRESS: *020 7611 7329 / 8612*
Health research charity

World Cancer Research Fund UK
020 7343 4200
www.wcrf-uk.org

Yorkshire Cancer Research
01423 501269
www.ycr.org.uk

Drugs, alcohol and addiction

Addaction
020 7251 5860
www.addaction.org.uk

Adfam
020 7928 8898
www.adfam.org.uk
Families, drugs and alcohol

Alchemy Project
0845 165 1197
www.alchemyproject.co.uk

Alcohol Concern
020 7928 7377
www.alcoholconcern.org.uk

Alcohol Focus Scotland
0141 572 6700
www.alcohol-focus-scotland.org.uk

Alcoholics Anonymous
01904 644026
www.alcoholics-anonymous.org.uk

Arrest Referral Forum
07739 983058
www.drugreferral.org
Support for workers on drugs referral projects

ASH: Action on Smoking and Health
020 7739 5902
www.ash.org.uk

Association of Nurses in Substance Abuse
0870 241 3503
www.ansa.uk.net

Clouds
01747 830733
www.clouds.org.uk
Treatment for addiction
Crew 2000
0131 220 3404
www.crew2000.co.uk
Drug advice service
Drugscope
020 7928 1211
www.drugscope.org.uk
Information resource
European Association for the Treatment of Addiction
020 7922 8753
www.eata.org.uk
Legalise Cannabis Alliance
07984 255015
www.lca-uk.org
Life or Meth
www.lifeormeth.com
Methamphetamine awareness campaign
Narcotics Anonymous
020 7251 4007
www.ukna.org

National Treatment Agency
020 7972 2214
www.nta.nhs.uk
No Smoking Day – March 8
0870 770 7909
www.nosmokingday.org.uk
Parents Against Drug Abuse
0845 702 3867
www.btinternet.com/~padahelp
Promis Recovery Centre
01304 841700
www.promis.co.uk
Multi-addiction awareness and treatment
Release
020 7729 5255
www.release.org.uk
Provides for health, welfare and legal needs of drug users
Re-Solv
01785 817885
www.re-solv.org
Society for prevention of solvent abuse

Ride Foundation
01372 467708
www.ridefoundation.org.uk
Drug awareness programmes for schools
Scottish Drugs Forum
0141 221 1175
www.sdf.org.uk
Substance Misuse Management in General Practice
www.smmgp.org.uk
Transform
0117 941 5810
www.tdpf.org.uk
Anti-prohibition campaign
UK Harm Reduction Alliance
www.ukhra.org
Campaigning for health and ethical treatment of drug users

■ Health helplines

NHS Direct
0845 4647

Alcoholics Anonymous
08457 697555

Alzheimers Helpline
08453 000336

Arthritis Care Helpline
0808 800 4050

Asthma UK Advice Line
08457 010203

British Allergy Foundation Helpline
01322 619898

Carers Line
0808 808 7777

Diabetes UK Careline
0845 120 2960

Doctors' Supportline
0870 765 0001

Drinkline
0800 917 8282

Eating Disorders Association Helpline
0845 634 1414

Eating Disorders Association Youth Helpline
0845 634 7650

Epilepsy Action Helpline
0808 800 5050

Frank (National Drugs Helpline)
0800 776600

Miscarriage Association Helpline
01924 200799

NHS Asian Tobacco Helpline
0800 169 0881 (Urdu)
0800 169 0882 (Punjabi)
0800 169 0883 (Hindi)
0800 169 0884 (Gujerati)
0800 169 0885 (Bengali)

NHS Pregnancy Smoking Helpline
0800 169 9169

NHS Smoking Helpline
0800 169 0169

Organ Donor Line
0845 606 0400

Parents Against Drug Abuse
0845 702 3867

Re-Solv
0808 800 2345

RNID Tinnitus Helpline
0808 808 6666

Sexual Health Direct
08453 101334

Sexual Health Information Line
0800 567123

Smokers Quitline
0800 002200

Still Births and Neonatal Deaths Helpline
020 7436 5881

Women's Health Concern Helpline
0845 123 2319

Women's Health Enquiry Line
0845 125 5254

Strategic health authorities, England

Avon, Gloucestershire and Wiltshire
01249 858500
www.agwsha.nhs.uk
Bedfordshire and Hertfordshire
01727 812929
www.bhha.nhs.uk
Birmingham and the Black Country
0121 695 2222
www.bbcha.nhs.uk
Cheshire and Merseyside
01925 406000
www.cmha.nhs.uk
County Durham and Tees Valley
01642 666700
www.countydurhamteesvalley.nhs.uk
Cumbria and Lancashire
01772 647000
www.clha.nhs.uk
Dorset and Somerset
01935 384000
www.dorsetsomerset.nhs.uk
Essex
01245 397600
www.essex.nhs.uk
Greater Manchester
0161 236 9456
www.gmsha.nhs.uk
Hampshire and Isle of Wight
023 8072 5400
www.hiow.nhs.uk
Kent and Medway
01622 710161
www.kentandmedway.nhs.uk
Leicestershire, Northamptonshire and Rutland
0116 295 7500
www.lnrsha.nhs.uk
Norfolk, Suffolk and Cambridgeshire
01223 597500
www.nscstha.nhs.uk
North and East Yorkshire and Northern Lincolnshire
01904 724500
www.neynlha.nhs.uk

North Central London
020 7756 2500
www.nclondon.nhs.uk
North-east London
020 7655 6600
www.nelondon.nhs.uk
North-west London
020 7756 2500
www.nwlondon.nhs.uk
Northumberland, Tyne and Wear
0191 210 6400
www.ntwha.nhs.uk
Shropshire and Staffordshire
01785 252233
www.sasha.nhs.uk
South-east London
020 7716 7000
www.selondon.nhs.uk
South-west London
020 8545 6000
www.swlha.nhs.uk
South-west Peninsula
01752 315001
www.swpsha.nhs.uk
South Yorkshire
0114 263 0300
www.southyorkshire.nhs.uk
Surrey and Sussex
01293 778899
www.surreysussexsha.nhs.uk
Thames Valley
01865 337000
www.tvha.nhs.uk
Trent
0115 968 4444
www.tsha.nhs.uk
West Midlands South
01527 587500
www.wmssha.nhs.uk
West Yorkshire
0113 295 2000
www.wysha.nhs.uk

Local health boards, Wales

Anglesey
01248 751229
www.angleseylhb.wales.nhs.uk
Blaenau Gwent
01495 325400
www.blaenaugwentlhb.wales.nhs.uk
Bridgend
01656 754400
www.bridgendlhb.wales.nhs.uk
Caerphilly
01443 862056
www.caerphilly.lhb.wales.nhs.uk
Cardiff
029 2055 2212
www.cardifflhb.wales.nhs.uk
Carmarthenshire
01544 744400
www.carmarthenlhb.wales.nhs.uk
Ceredigion
01570 424100
www.ceredigionlhb.wales.nhs.uk
Conwy
01492 536586
www.conwylhb.wales.nhs.uk
Denbighshire
01745 589601
www.denbighshirelhb.wales.nhs.uk
Flintshire
01352 744103
www.flintshirelhb.wales.nhs.uk
Gwynedd
01286 672451
www.gwyneddlhb.wales.nhs.uk
Merthyr Tydfil
01685 358500
www.merthyrtydfillhb.wales.nhs.uk
Monmouthshire
01792 326500
www.monmouthshirelhb.wales.nhs.uk
Neath/Port Talbot
01639 890916
www.neathporttalbotlhb.wales.nhs.uk
Newport
01633 436200
www.newportlhb.wales.nhs.uk
Pembrokeshire
01437 771220
www.pembrokeshirelhb.wales.nhs.uk
Powys
01874 711661
www.powyslhb.wales.nhs.uk
Rhondda Cynon Taff
01443 824400
www.rhonddacynontafflhb.wales.nhs.uk
Swansea
01792 784800
www.swansealhb.wales.nhs.uk
Torfaen
01495 745868
www.torfaenlhb.wales.nhs.uk
Vale of Glamorgan
029 2035 0600
www.valeofglamorganlhb.wales.nhs.uk
Wexham
01978 346500
www.wrexhamlhb.wales.nhs.uk

NHS boards, Scotland

Argyll and Clyde
0141 842 7200
www.scot.nhs.uk/achb
Ayrshire and Arran
01563 577037
www.nhsayrshireandarran.com
Borders
01896 825500
www.nhsborders.org.uk
Dumfries and Galloway
01387 246246
www.nhsdg.scot.nhs.uk
Fife
01592 643355
www.show.scot.nhs.uk/fhb
Forth Valley
01786 463031
www.show.scot.nhs.uk/nhsfv
Grampian
0845 456 6000
www.nhsgrampian.org
Greater Glasgow
0141 201 4444
www.nhsgg.org.uk
PRESS: *0141 201 4429*
Highland
01463 717123
www.show.scot.nhs.uk/nhshighland
Lanarkshire
Acute hospitals: 01236 438100;
primary care: 01698 245000
www.scot.nhs.uk
/nhslanarkshire
Lothian
0131 536 9000
www.nhslothian.scot.nhs.uk
Orkney
01856 888000
www.show.scot.nhs.uk/ohb
Shetland
01595 743060
www.show.scot.nhs.uk/shb
Tayside
01382 818479
www.nhstayside.scot.nhs.uk
Western Isles
01851 702997
www.show.scot.nhs.uk.wihb
Scottish Ambulance Service
0131 446 7000
www.scottishambulance.com

Health & social services boards, Northern Ireland

Eastern
028 9032 1313
www.ehssb.n-i.nhs.uk
Northern
028 2565 3333
www.nhssb.n-i.nhs.uk
Southern
028 3741 0041
www.shssb.org
Western
028 7186 0086
www.whssb.org.uk

NHS foundation trusts

Monitor
020 7340 2400
http://monitor-nhsft.gov.uk
Independent monitor of foundation trusts
PRESS: *020 7340 2440*
Barnsley Hospital NHS Foundation Trust
01226 730000
Basildon and Thurrock Hospitals NHSFT
01268 533911
Bradford Teaching Hospitals NHSFT
01274 542200
Cambridge University Hospitals NHSFT
01223 245151
Chesterfield Royal Hospital NHSFT
01246 277271
City Hospitals Sunderland NHSFT
0191 565 6256
Countess of Chester Hospital NHSFT
01244 365000
Derby Hospitals NHSFT
01332 347141
Doncaster and Bassetlaw Hospitals NHSFT
01302 366666
Frimley Park Hospital NHSFT
01276 604604
Gateshead Health NHSFT
0191 482 0000
Gloucestershire Hospitals NHSFT
08454 222222
Guy's and St Thomas's NHSFT
020 7188 7188
Harrogate and District NHSFT
01423 885959
Heart of England NHSFT
0121 424 2000
Homerton University Hospital NHSFT
020 8510 5555
Lancashire Teaching Hospitals NHSFT
01772 716565
Liverpool Women's NHSFT
0151 708 9988
Moorfields Eye Hospital NHSFT
020 7253 3411
Papworth Hospital NHSFT
01480 830541
Peterborough and Stamford Hospitals NHSFT
01733 874000
Queen Victoria Hospital NHSFT
01342 414000
The Rotherham NHSFT
01709 820000
The Royal Bournemouth & Christchurch Hospitals NHSFT
01202 303626
Royal Devon & Exeter NHSFT
01392 411611
The Royal Marsden NHSFT
020 7352 8171
The Royal National Hospital for Rheumatic Diseases NHSFT
020 7387 9300

Sheffield Teaching Hospitals NHSFT
0114 271 1100
South Tyneside NHSFT
0191 454 8888
Stockport NHSFT
0161 483 1010
University College London Hospitals NHSFT
020 7387 9300
University Hospital Birmingham NHSFT
0121 432 3232

NHS hospitals: England

A

Abingdon Community Hospital, Abingdon
01235 205700
Accrington Victoria Community Hospital, Accrington
01254 687342
Addenbrooke's Hospital, Cambridge
01223 245151
Airedale General Hospital, Keighley
01535 652511
Alcester Hospital, Alcester
01789 762470
Alder Hey Children's Hospital, Liverpool
0151 228 4811
Alderney Hospital, Poole
01202 735537
Alexandra Hospital, Chatham
01634 687166
Alexandra Hospital, Redditch
01527 503030
Alfred Bean Hospital, Driffield
01377 241124
Alnwick Infirmary
0845 811 8118
Altrincham General Hospital, Altrincham
0161 928 6111
Amberstone Hospital, Hailsham
01323 440022
Amersham Hospital, Amersham
01494 526161
Arrowe Park Hospital, Wirral
0151 678 5111
Ashburton & Buckfastleigh Hospital
01364 652203
Ashfield Community Hospital, Kirkby in Ashfield
01636 681681
Ashford Hospital
01784 884488
Ashton House Hospital, Merseyside
0151 653 9660
Ashworth Hospital, Liverpool
0151 473 0303
Axminster Hospital, Axminster
01297 630400

B

Babington Hospital, Belper
01773 824171
Barking Hospital, Essex
020 8983 8000
Barnet Hospital, London
0845 111 4000
Barnsley District General Hospital
01226 730000
Basildon Hospital, Essex
01268 533911
Bassetlaw Hospital, Worksop
01909 500990
Bath Road Day Hospital, Reading
01344 422722
Beacon Day Hospital, Wigan
01695 626034
Beccles & District Hospital
01502 712164
Beckenham Hospital
01689 863000
Bedford Hospital, Bedford
01234 355122
Beeches Hospital, Telford
01952 432963
Beighton Community Hospital, Sheffield
0114 271 7000
Bennetts End Hospital, Hemel Hempstead
01442 215060
Bensham Hospital, Gateshead
0191 482 0000
Berkeley Hospital, Berkley
01453 562000
Berwick Infirmary, Berwick-on-Tweed
08448 118118
Beverley Westwood Hospital
01482 328541
Bexhill Hospital, Bexhill-on-Sea
01424 755255
Bicester Hospital
01869 604000
Bickley Day Hospital, Norfolk
01953 457342
Bingley Hospital
01274 563438
Birch Hill Hospital, Rochdale
01706 377777
Birmingham Children's Hospital
0121 333 9500
Birmingham Dental Hospital
0121 236 8611
Birmingham Heartlands Hospital
0121 424 2000
Birmingham Women's Hospital
0121 472 1377

Bishop Auckland General Hospital
01388 455000
Bishops Castle Community Hospital
01588 638220
Blackberry Hill Hospital, Bristol
0117 965 6061
Blackburn Royal Infirmary, Blackburn
01254 263555
Blackpool Victoria Hospital
01253 300000
Blandford Community Hospital
01258 456541
Blyth Community Hospital
08458 118118
Bodmin Hospital
01208 251301
Bolingbroke Hospital, London
020 7223 7411
Bolitho Hospital, Penzance
01736 575555
Booth Hall Children's Hospital, Manchester
0161 795 7000
Bovey Tracey Hospital, Bovey Tracey
01626 832279
Bradford Royal Infirmary
01274 542200
Bradford-on-Avon Community Hospital
01225 862975
Bradwell Hospital, Newcastle
01782 425400
Brampton War Memorial Community Hospital, Brampton
01697 72534
Brentwood Community Hospital
01277 302893
Bridgnorth Hospital
01746 762641
Bridgwater Community Hospital
01278 451501
Bridlington & District Hospital
01262 606666
Bridport Community Hospital
01308 422371
Brighton General Hospital
01273 696011
Bristol Eye Hospital
0117 923 0060
Bristol General Hospital
0117 926 5001
Bristol Homoeopathic Hospital
0117 973 1231
Bristol Royal Hospital for Children
0117 927 6998
Bristol Royal Infirmary
0117 923 0000

Brixham Hospital
01803 882153
Broadgreen Hospital, Liverpool
0151 282 6000
Broadmoor Hospital
020 8354 8354
Bromyard Community Hospital
01885 485700
Broomfield Hospital, Chelmsford
01245 440761
Buckland Hospital, Dover
01304 201624
Bucknall Hospital, Stoke-on-Trent
01782 273510
Budleigh Salterton Hospital
01395 442020
Burnham-on-Sea War Memorial Hospital
01278 773118
Burnley General Hospital
01282 425071
Bushey Fields Hospital, Dudley
01384 457373
Butleigh Hospital, Glastonbury
01458 850237
Buxton Hospital
01246 277271

C

Calderdale Royal Hospital, Halifax
01422 357171
Calderstones Hospital, Clitheroe
01254 822121
Cambourne/Redruth Community Hospital, Redruth
01209 881688
Cannock Chase Hospital, Cannock
01543 572757
Carlton Court, Lowestoft
01502 538008
Carshalton War Memorial Hospital
020 8647 5534
Cassell Hospital, Richmond
020 8354 8354
Castle Hill Hospital, Cottingham
01482 875875
Castleberg Hospital, Settle
01729 823515
Castleford & Normanton District Hospital
01924 327000
Caterham Dene Hospital
01883 837500
Central Middlesex Hospital, London
020 8965 5733

Chantry House Day
Hospital, Frome
01373 451223

Chapel Allerton Hospital,
Leeds
0113 262 3404

Chard & District Hospital
01460 63175

Charing Cross Hospital,
London
020 8846 1234

Charles Clifford Dental
Hospital, Sheffield
0114 271 7800

Chase Farm Hospital,
Enfield
0845 111 4000

Chase Hospital, Bordon
01420 488801

Cheadle Hospital, Stoke-
on-Trent
01538 487500

Chelsea and Westminster
Hospital, London
020 8746 8000

Cheltenham General
Hospital
08454 222222

Cherry Knowle Hospital,
Sunderland
0191 565 6256

Cherry Tree Hospital,
Stockport
0161 483 1010

Chester le Street Hospital
0191 333 6262

Chesterfield & North
Derbyshire Royal
Hospital, Chesterfield
01246 277271

Chingford Hospital
020 8529 7141

Chippenham Community
Hospital
01249 447100

Chipping Norton
Community Hospital
01608 648450

Chorley & South Ribble
District General Hospital,
Chorley
01257 261222

Christchurch Hospital
01202 486361

Christie Hospital,
Manchester
0161 446 3000

Churchill Hospital,
Headington
01865 741841

Cirencester Hospital
01285 884694

City General Hospital,
Stoke-on-Trent
01782 237510

City Hospital, Birmingham
0121 554 3801

Clacton Hospital
01255 201717

Clatterbridge Hospital,
Wirral
0151 334 4000

Clayton Hospital,
Wakefield
01924 201688

Clifton Hospital, Lytham St
Annes
01253 306204

Clitheroe Hospital
01200 427311

Cobham Cottage Hospital
01932 584204

Cockermouth Cottage
Hospital, Cockermouth
01900 822226

Colchester General
Hospital
01206 747474

Coldeast Hospital,
Southampton
01489 577196

Colman Hospital, Norwich
01603 286286

Congleton & District War
Memorial Hospital,
Congleton
01260 294800

Conquest Hospital, St
Leonards on Sea
01424 755255

Cookridge Hospital, Leeds
0113 267 3411

Coppetts Wood Hospital,
London
020 7794 0500

Coquetdale Cottage
Hospital, Morpeth
0845 811 8118

Corbett House,
Stourbridge
01384 456111

Corby Community Hospital
01536 400070

Coronation Hospital, Ilkley
01943 609666

Cossham Hospital, Bristol
0117 967 1661

Countess of Chester
Hospital
01244 365000

County Hospital, Durham
0191 333 6262

Coventry and Warwickshire
Hospital, Coventry
024 7622 4055

Crawley Hospital
01293 600300

Crediton Hospital
01363 775588

Crewkerne Hospital
01460 72491

Cromer Hospital
01263 513571

Crowborough War
Memorial Hospital
01892 652284

Cumberland Infirmary,
Carlisle
01228 523444

Danesbury Hospital,
Welwyn
01438 714447

Danetre Hospital, Daventry
01327 705610

Darent Valley Hospital,
Dartford
01322 428100

Darlington Memorial
Hospital
01325 380100

Dartmouth & Kingswear
Hospital, Dartmouth
01803 832255

Dawlish Hospital, Dawlish
01626 868500

Delancey Hospital,
Cheltenham
01242 222222

Derby City General
Hospital
01332 340131

Derby Royal Infirmary
01332 347141

Derbyshire Children's
Hospital, Derby
01332 340131

Dereham Hospital
01362 692391

Derriford Hospital,
Plymouth
01752 777111

Devizes Community
Hospital
01380 723511

Devonshire Road Hospital,
Blackpool
01253 303364

Dewsbury and District
Hospital
01924 512000

Diana, Princess of Wales
Hospital, Grimsby
01472 874111

Didcot Hospital
01235 205860

Dilke Memorial Hospital,
Gloucester
01594 598100

Doncaster Gate Hospital,
Rotherham
01709 304802

Doncaster Royal Infirmary
01302 366666

Dorking Hospital
01737 768511

Dorset County Hospital,
Dorchester
01305 251150

Dunston Hill Hospital,
Gateshead
0191 482 0000

Ealing Hospital, Southall
020 8967 5000

Earls House Hospital,
Durham
0191 333 6262

East Ham Hospital, London
020 7540 4380

East Surrey Hospital,
Redhill
01737 768511

Eastbourne District
General Hospital,
Eastbourne
01323 417400

Eastman Dental Hospital,
London
020 7387 9300

Edenbridge & District War
Memorial Hospital,
Edenbridge
01732 862137

Edgware Community
Hospital
020 8952 2381

Edward Hain Hospital, St
Ives
01736 576100

Ellen Badger Hospital,
Shipston-on-Stour
01608 661410

Ellesmere Port Hospital
01244 365000

Elms Day Hospital, Bristol
01225 731731

Elmwood Day Hospital,
Chester
01244 364122

Emi Day Hospital, Reading
01344 422722

Epsom General Hospital
01372 735735

Erith & District Hospital
020 8308 3131

Essex County Hospital,
Colchester
01206 747474

Evesham Community
Hospital
01386 502345

Exmouth Hospital
01395 282000

Fairfield General Hospital,
Bury
0161 764 6081

Fairford Hospital
01285 712212

Faversham Cottage
Hospital
01795 562066

Feilding Palmer Hospital,
Lutterworth
01455 552150

Felixstowe General
Hospital
01394 282214

Fenwick Hospital,
Lyndhurst
023 8028 2782

Health

447

Fieldhead Hospital,
Wakefield
01924 327000
Finchley Memorial
Hospital, London
020 8349 6300
Fleetwood Hospital
01253 306000
Fordingbridge Hospital
01425 652255
Fowey Hospital
01726 832241
Freeman Hospital,
Newcastle-upon-Tyne
0191 233 6161
Frenchay Hospital, Bristol
0117 970 1212
Friarage Hospital,
Northallerton
01609 779911
Frimley Park Hospital,
Frimley
01276 604604
Frome Victoria Hospital
01373 463591
Furness General Hospital,
Barrow-in-Furness
01229 870870

G

George Eliot Hospital,
Nuneaton
024 7635 1351
Glenfield Hospital,
Leicester
0116 287 1471
Gloucestershire Royal
Hospital, Gloucester
01452 528555
Goldie Leigh Hospital,
London
020 8319 7100
Good Hope Hospital,
Sutton Coldfield
0121 378 2211
Goole & District Hospital
01405 720720
Gordon Hospital, London
020 8746 5505
Gorse Hill Hospital,
Leicester
0116 225 6000
Goscote Hospital, Walsall
01922 721172
Gosport War Memorial
Hospital
023 9252 4611
Grantham & District
Hospital
01476 565232
Gravesend & North Kent
Hospital
01474 564333
Great Ormond Street
Hospital for Children,
London
020 7405 9200
Great Western Hospital,
Swindon
01793 604020

Green Lane Hospital,
Devizes
01225 731731
Guest Hospital, Dudley
01384 456111
Guisborough General
Hospital
01642 850850
Guy's Hospital, London
020 7188 7188

H

Halstead Hospital
01787 291022
Halton Hospital, Runcorn
01928 714567
Haltwhistle War Memorial
Hospital
0844 811 8118
Hammersmith Hospital,
London
020 8383 1000
Hammerwich Hospital,
Burntwood
01543 686224
Harefield Hospital
01895 823737
Harold Wood Hospital,
Romford
01708 345533
Harpenden Memorial
Hospital
01582 760196
Harplands Hospital, Stoke-
on-Trent
01782 273510
Harrogate District Hospital
01423 885959
Harry Watton House,
Birmingham
0121 685 6001
Harwich Hospital
01255 201200
Havant War Memorial
Hospital
023 9248 4256
Hawkhurst Cottage
Hospital, Hawkhurst
01580 753345
Haywood Hospital, Stoke-
on-Trent
01782 715444
Heanor Memorial Hospital
01773 710711
Heartlands Hospital,
Birmingham
0121 424 2000
Heath Lane Hospital, West
Bromwich
0121 553 7676
Heatherwood Hospital,
Ascot
01344 623333
Heavitree Hospital, Exeter
01392 411611
Hellesdon Hospital,
Norwich
01603 421421
Helston Hospital
01326 435800

Hemel Hempstead General
Hospital
01442 213141
Herbert Hospital,
Bournemouth
01202 584300
Hereford County Hospital
01432 355444
Hertford County Hospital
01438 314333
Herts & Essex Hospital,
Bishop's Stortford
01279 444455
Hexham General Hospital
0844 811 8118
Highbury Hospital,
Nottingham
0115 977 0000
Highfield Day Hospital,
Chester le Street
0191 333 6262
Highfield Hospital, Widnes
01925 635911
Hill Crest Mental Health
Unit, Redditch
01527 500575
Hillingdon Hospital,
Uxbridge
01895 238282
Hinchingbrooke Hospital,
Huntingdon
01480 416416
Holbeach Hospital,
Spalding
01476 565232
Holme Valley Memorial
Hospital, Holmfirth
01924 327000
Holmelands Hospital, Co
Durham
0191 333 6262
Homeopathic Hospital,
Tunbridge Wells
01892 542977
Homerton University
Hospital, London
020 8510 5555
Honiton Hospital
01404 540540
Hope Hospital, Salford
0161 206 4840
Horn Hall Hospital,
Stanhope
01388 528233
Hornsea Cottage Hospital
01964 533146
Horsham Hospital
01903 843000
Horton Hospital, Banbury
01295 275500
Hospital for Tropical
Diseases, London
020 7387 9300
Hospital of St Cross, Rugby
01788 572831
Huddersfield Royal
Infirmary
01484 342000
Hull Royal Infirmary
01482 328541
Hulton Hospital, Bolton
01204 390390

Hundens Lane Day
Hospital, Darlington
01325 380100
Hunters Moor Hospital,
Newcastle-upon-Tyne
01670 512121
Hurstwood Park
Neurosciences Centre,
Haywards Heath
01444 441881
Hyde Hospital, Cheshire
0161 331 5151
Hythe Hospital,
Southampton
023 8084 5955

I

Ilkeston Community
Hospital
0115 930 5522
Ipswich Hospital
01473 712233

J

James Cook University
Hospital, Middlesbrough
01642 850850
James Paget Hospital,
Great Yarmouth
01493 452452
John Coupland Hospital,
Gainsborough
01476 565232
John Radcliffe Hospital,
Oxford
01865 741166
Johnson Hospital,
Spalding
01476 565232
Julian Hospital, Norwich
01603 421800

K

Kendray Hospital, Barnsley
01226 777811
Kent & Canterbury
Hospital, Canterbury
01227 766877
Kent and Sussex Hospital,
Tunbridge Wells
01892 526111
Kettering General Hospital
01536 492000
Keynsham Hospital, Bristol
0117 986 2356
Kidderminster Hospital
01562 823424
King Edward VII Hospital,
Windsor
01753 860441
King George Hospital,
Ilford
020 8983 8000
King's College Hospital,
London
020 7737 4000
King's Mill Hospital, Sutton
in Ashfield
01623 622515

Kings Park Hospital,
Bournemouth
01202 303757
Kingston Hospital,
Kingston-upon-Thames
020 8546 7711
Knutsford and District
Community Hospital
01565 632112

L

Lady Eden Hospital,
Bishop Auckland
01388 646100
Launceston General
Hospital
01566 765650
Leatherhead Hospital
01372 384384
Leeds Dental Hospital
0113 244 0111
Leeds General Infirmary
0113 243 2799
Leek Moorlands Hospital
01538 487100
Leicester General Hospital,
Leicester
0116 249 0490
Leicester Royal Infirmary,
Leicester
0116 254 1414
Leigh Infirmary, Leigh
01942 672333
Leighton Hospital, Crewe
01270 255141
Leominster Community
Hospital, Leominster
01568 614211
Lewes Victoria Hospital
01273 474153
Lincoln County Hospital
01522 512512
Lings Bar Hospital,
Nottingham
0115 945 5577
Liskeard Community
Hospital
01579 335600
Lister Hospital, Stevenage
01438 314333
Little Brook Hospital,
Dartford
01322 622222
Little Court Day Hospital,
Burnham-on-Sea
01278 786876
Liverpool Women's
Hospital, Liverpool
0151 708 9988
Livingstone Hospital,
Dartford
01322 622222
London Chest Hospital
020 7377 7000
Longton Cottage Hospital,
Stoke-on-Trent
01782 425600
Lord Mayor Treloar
Hospital, Alton
01256 473202

Louth County Hospital
01507 600100
Lowestoft Hospital
01502 587311
Lucy Baldwyn Hospital,
Stourport-on-Severn
01299 827327
Ludlow Hospital
01584 872201
Luton & Dunstable Hospital
0845 127 0127
Lydney and District
Hospital
01594 598220
Lymington Hospital
01590 677011
Lynfield Mount Hospital,
Bradford
01274 494194
Lytham Hospital, Lytham St
Annes
01253 303953

M

Macclesfield District
General Hospital,
Macclesfield
01625 421000
Maiden Law Hospital,
Durham
0191 333 6262
Maidstone Hospital,
Maidstone
01622 729000
Malmesbury Community
Hospital
01666 823358
Malton and Norton
Hospital
01723 368111
Malvern Community
Hospital, Malvern
01684 612600
Manchester Royal Eye
Hospital
0161 276 1234
Manchester Royal
Infirmary
0161 276 1234
Manor Hospital, Walsall
01922 721172
Mansfield Community
Hospital
01623 785050
Market Harborough &
District Hospital, Market
Harborough
01858 410500
Mary Hewetson
Community Hospital,
Keswick
01768 772012
Maudsley Hospital, London
020 7703 6333
Mayday University
Hospital, Croydon
020 8401 3000
Medway Maritime Hospital,
Gillingham
01634 830000

Melksham Community
Hospital
01225 701000
Melton War Memorial
Hospital, Melton
Mowbray
01664 854800
Memorial Hospital, London
020 8856 5511
Mile End Hospital, London
020 7377 7000
Milford-on-Sea Hospital
01590 648100
Mill View Hospital, Hove
01273 696011
Millom Hospital, Cumbria
01229 772631
Milton Keynes General
Hospital
01908 660033
Minehead Hospital
01643 707251
Montagu Hospital,
Mexborough
01709 585171
Monyhull Hospital,
Birmingham
0121 627 1627
Moore Hospital,
Cheltenham
01451 820228
Moorgreen Hospital,
Southampton
023 8047 2258
Moreton-in-Marsh Hospital
01608 650456
Moretonhampstead
Hospital, Newton Abbot
01647 440217
Morpeth Cottage Hospital
0844 811 8118
Moseley Hall Hospital,
Birmingham
0121 678 3890
Mount Gould Hospital,
Plymouth
01752 268011
Mount Vernon Hospital,
Barnsley
01226 777835
Mount Vernon Hospital,
Northwood
01923 217198
Musgrove Park Hospital,
Taunton
01823 333444

N

National Hospital for
Neurology &
Neurosurgery, London
020 7837 3611
Nelson Hospital, London
020 8296 2000
Nevill Hospital, Hove
01273 821680
New Cross Hospital,
Wolverhampton
01902 307999

New Epsom and Ewell
Cottage Hospital
01372 734834
Newark Hospital
01636 681681
Newcastle Dental Hospital,
Newcastle upon Tyne
0191 233 6161
Newcastle General Hospital,
Newcastle upon Tyne
0191 233 6161
Newham General Hospital,
London
020 7476 4000
Newport Hospital,
Shropshire
01952 820893
Newquay and District
Hospital
01637 893600
Newton Abbot Hospital
01626 354321
Newton Community
Hospital, Newton-le-
Willows
0151 426 1600
Newtown Hospital,
Worcester
01905 763333
Norfolk & Norwich
University Hospital
01603 286286
North Devon District
Hospital, Barnstaple
01271 322577
North Hampshire Hospital,
Basingstoke
01256 473202
North Manchester General
Hospital
0161 795 4567
North Middlesex University
Hospital, London
020 8887 2000
North Tyneside General
Hospital, North Shields
0844 811 8118
Northampton General
Hospital
01604 634700
Northern General Hospital,
Sheffield
0114 243 4343
Northgate Hospital, Great
Yarmouth
01493 337652
Northgate Hospital,
Morpeth
01670 394000
Northwick Park Hospital,
Harrow
020 8864 3232
Northwood & Pinner
Hospital, Northwood
01923 824782
Norwich Community
Hospital
01603 776776
Nottingham City Hospital
0115 969 1169

O

Okehampton Community
Hospital
01837 658000
Oldchurch Hospital,
Romford
01708 345533
Ongar War Memorial
Hospital
01277 362629
Orchard Hill Hospital
020 8770 8000
Ormskirk and District
General Hospital,
Ormskirk
01695 577111
Orpington Hospital
01689 863000
Orsett Hospital
01268 533911
Ottery St Mary Hospital
01404 816000
Oxford Community
Hospital
01865 225505

P

Paignton Hospital
01803 557425
Palmer Community
Hospital, Jarrow
0191 451 6000
Papworth Hospital,
Cambridge
01480 830541
Parkside Hospital,
Macclesfield
01625 421000
Patrick Stead Hospital,
Halesworth
01986 872124
Paulton Memorial Hospital,
Bristol
01761 412315
Peasley Cross Hospital, St
Helens
01744 458459
Pembury Hospital,
Tunbridge Wells
01892 823535
Pendle Community
Hospital, Nelson
01282 474900
Penrith Hospital
01768 245300
Pershore Cottage Hospital,
Worcestershire
01386 502070
Peterborough District
Hospital
01733 874000
Peterlee Community
Hospital
01429 266654
Petersfield Hospital
01730 263221
Pilgrim Hospital, Boston
01205 364801
Pinderfields General
Hospital, Wakefield
01924 201688

Plympton Hospital,
Plymouth
01752 314500
Poltair Hospital, Penzance
01736 575570
Pontefract General
Infirmary
01977 600600
Poole Hospital
01202 665511
Portland Hospital, Dorset
01305 820341
Potters Bar Community
Hospital
01707 653286
Preston Hall Hospital,
Aylesford
01622 710161
Primrose Hill Hospital,
Jarrow
0191 451 6375
Princess Alexandra
Hospital, Harlow
01279 444455
Princess Anne Hospital,
Southampton
023 8077 7222
Princess Louise Hospital,
London
020 8969 0133
Princess Marina Hospital,
Northampton
01604 752323
Princess of Wales
Community Hospital,
Bromsgrove
01527 488000
Princess of Wales Hospital,
Ely
01353 652000
Princess Royal Hospital,
Haywards Heath
01444 441881
Princess Royal Hospital,
Hull
01482 701151
Princess Royal Hospital,
Telford
01952 641222
Princess Royal University
Hospital, Orpington
01689 863000
Prospect Park Hospital,
Reading
01344 422722
Prudhoe Hospital
01670 394000
Purley War Memorial
Hospital
020 8401 3000

Q

Queen Alexandra Hospital,
Portsmouth
023 9228 6000
Queen Charlotte's Hospital
020 8383 1111
Queen Elizabeth Hospital,
Gateshead
0191 482 0000

Queen Elizabeth Hospital,
King's Lynn
01553 613613
Queen Elizabeth Hospital,
London
020 8836 6000
Queen Elizabeth II Hospital,
Welwyn Garden City
01707 328111
Queen Elizabeth Medical
Centre, Birmingham
0121 472 1311
Queen Elizabeth The
Queen Mother Hospital,
Margate
01843 225544
Queen Mary's Hospital,
Roehampton, London
020 8789 6611
Queen Mary's Hospital,
Sidcup
020 8302 2678
Queen Victoria Hospital,
East Grinstead
01342 414000
Queen Victoria Hospital,
Morecambe
01524 405700
Queen Victoria Memorial
Hospital, Herne Bay
01227 594700
Queen's Hospital, Burton-
upon-Trent
01283 566333
Queens Medical Centre,
Nottingham
0115 924 9924
Queens Park Hospital,
Blackburn
01254 263555

R

Radcliffe Infirmary, Oxford
01865 311188
Ramsbottom Cottage
Hospital, Bury
0161 331 5151
Ravenscourt Park Hospital,
London
020 8846 7777
Redcliffe Day Hospital,
Wellingborough
01933 440181
Retford Hospital
01777 274400
Ribbleton Hospital, Preston
01772 695300
Richardson Hospital,
Barnard Castle
01833 637436
Ridge Lea Hospital,
Lancaster
01524 586200
Ridley Day Hospital,
Wincanton
01963 32006
Ripley Hospital, Derbyshire
01773 743456
Ripon Community Hospital,
Ripon
01765 602546

Robert Jones and Agnes
Hunt Orthopaedic
Hospital, Oswestry
01691 404000
Roborough Day Hospital,
Eastbourne
01323 638972
Rochdale Infirmary
01706 377777
Romsey Hospital, Romsey
01794 834700
Ross Community Hospital,
Ross-on-Wye
01989 562100
Rossall Hospital,
Fleetwood
01253 655104
Rossendale Hospital
01706 215151
Rotherham District General
Hospital
01709 820000
Rowan House EMI Facility
and Day Hospital,
Malvern
01684 612763
Rowley Regis Hospital
0121 607 3465
Roxbourne Hospital,
Harrow
020 8237 2000
Royal Albert Edward
Infirmary, Wigan
01942 244000
Royal Alexandra Hospital
for Sick Children,
Brighton
01273 328145
Royal Berkshire Hospital,
Reading
0118 322 5111
Royal Bolton Hospital
01204 390390
Royal Bournemouth
General Hospital
01202 303626
Royal Brompton Hospital,
London
020 7352 8121
Royal Cornwall Hospital,
Truro
01872 250000
Royal Devon and Exeter
Hospital
01392 411611
Royal Eye Infirmary,
Plymouth
01752 315123
Royal Free Hospital,
London
020 7794 0500
Royal Hallamshire Hospital,
Sheffield
0114 271 1900
Royal Hampshire County
Hospital, Winchester
01962 863535
Royal Lancaster Infirmary,
Lancaster
01524 65944

Royal Leamington Spa
Rehabilitation Hospital,
Warwick
01926 317700
Royal Liverpool Children's
Hospital, Alder Hey
0151 228 4811
Royal Liverpool University
Dental Hospital
0151 706 2000
Royal Liverpool University
Hospital
0151 706 2051
Royal London
Homeopathic Hospital
020 7391 8833
Royal London Hospital
020 7655 4000
Royal Manchester
Children's Hospital
0161 794 4696
Royal Marsden Hospital,
London
020 7352 8171
Royal Marsden Hospital,
Sutton
020 8642 6011
Royal National Hospital for
Rheumatic Diseases,
Bath
01225 465941
Royal National
Orthopaedic Hospital,
London
020 8954 2300
Royal National Throat,
Nose and Ear Hospital,
London
020 7915 1300
Royal Oldham Hospital
0161 624 0420
Royal Orthopaedic
Hospital, Birmingham
0121 685 4000
Royal Preston Hospital
01772 716565
Royal Shrewsbury Hospital
01743 261000
Royal South Hants
Hospital, Southampton
023 8063 4288
Royal Surrey County
Hospital, Guildford
01483 571122
Royal Sussex County
Hospital, Brighton
01273 696955
Royal United Hospital, Bath
01225 428331
Royal Victoria Hospital,
Folkestone
01303 850202
Royal Victoria Infirmary,
Newcastle-upon-Tyne
0191 233 6161
Royston Hospital
01763 242134
Rushden Hospital
01933 440666
Russells Hall Hospital,
Dudley,
01384 456111

Ruth Lancaster James
Hospital, Alston
01434 381218
Rutland Memorial Hospital,
Oakham
01572 722552
Ryhope General Hospital,
Sunderland
0191 565 6256

S

Saffron Walden Community
Hospital
01799 562900
St Albans City Hospital
01727 866122
St Andrew's Hospital,
London
020 7476 4000
St Ann's Hospital, Poole
01202 708881
St Anne's Hospital,
Altrincham
0161 748 4022
St Anne's Orchard
Psychiatric Day Hospital,
Malvern
01684 561659
St Austell Community
Hospital
01726 291120
St Barnabas Hospital,
Saltash
01752 857400
St Bartholomew's Day
Hospital, Liverpool
0151 489 6241
St Bartholomew's Hospital,
London
020 7377 7000
St Barholomew's Hospital,
Rochester
01634 810900
St Catherine's Hospital,
Birkenhead
0151 678 7272
St Catherine's Hospital,
Bradford
01274 227599
St Charles Hospital,
London
020 8969 2488
St Christopher's Hospital,
Fareham
01329 286321
St Clement's Hospital,
Ipswich
01473 329000
St Clement's Hospital,
London
020 7655 4000
St George's Hospital,
Lincoln
01476 565232
St George's Hospital,
London
020 8672 1255
St George's Hospital,
Morpeth
01670 512121

St George's Hospital,
Stafford
01785 257888
St Helens Hospital
0151 426 1600
St Helier Hospital,
Carshalton
020 8296 2000
St James' Hospital,
Portsmouth
023 9282 2444
St James's University
Hospital, Leeds
0113 243 3144
St John's Hospital,
Chelmsford
01245 440761
St Leonard's Community
Hospital, Ringwood
01202 584200
St Luke's Hospital,
Bradford
01274 542200
St Luke's Hospital, Market
Harborough
01858 410300
St Luke's Hospital,
Middlesbrough
01642 516147
St Margaret's Hospital,
Epping
01992 902010
St Mark's Hospital,
Maidenhead
01628 632012
St Mark's Hospital, Harrow
020 8235 4000
St Martin's Hospital, Bath
01225 831500
St Martin's Hospital,
Canterbury
01227 459584
St Mary's Hospital, Isle of
Wight
01983 524081
St Mary's Hospital, Isles of
Scilly
01720 422392
St Marys Hospital,
Kettering
01536 410141
St Mary's Hospital, London
020 7886 6666
St Mary's Hospital,
Manchester
0161 276 1234
St Mary's Hospital, Melton
Mowbray
01664 411411
St Mary's Hospital,
Portsmouth
023 9228 6000
St Michael's Hospital,
Braintree
01245 440761
St Michael's Hospital,
Bristol
0117 921 5411
St Michael's Hospital,
Hayle
01736 753234

St Michael's Hospital,
Warwick
01926 496241
St Monica's Hospital, York
01347 821214
St Nicholas Hospital,
Newcastle-upon-Tyne
01670 512121
St Pancras Hospital,
London
020 7530 3500
St Peter's Hospital,
Chertsey
01932 872000
St Peter's Hospital, Maldon
01621 725323
St Richard's Hospital,
Chichester
01243 788122
St Thomas' Hospital,
London
020 7188 7188
Salisbury District Hospital,
Salisbury
01722 336262
Sandwell General Hospital,
West Bromwich
0121 553 1831
Savernake Hospital,
Marlborough
01672 514571
Scarborough General
Hospital
01723 368111
Scarsdale Hospital,
Chesterfield
01246 277271
Scott Hospital, Plymouth
01752 314343
Scunthorpe General
Hospital
01724 282282
Seacroft Hospital, Leeds
0113 264 8164
Seasons Day Hospital,
Clevedon
01225 731731
Seaton Hospital
01297 23901
Sedgefield Community
Hospital, Stockton-on-
Tees
01740 626600
Selby War Memorial
Hospital
01757 702664
Selly Oak Hospital,
Birmingham
0121 627 8863
Sevenoaks Hospital
01732 470200
Severalls Hospital,
Colchester
01206 228630
Sheffield Children's
Hospital
0114 271 7000
Shelton Hospital,
Shrewsbury
01743 261000

Sheppey Community
Hospital, Isle of Sheppey
01795 879100
Shepton Mallet Community
Hospital
01749 342931
Shipley Hospital
01274 773390
Shotley Bridge Hospital,
Consett
0191 333 2333
Sir Alfred Jones Memorial
Hospital, Liverpool
0151 494 3198
Sir GB Hunter Memorial
Hospital, Wallsend
0844 811 8118
Sir Robert Peel Hospital,
Tamworth
01827 263800
Sittingbourne Memorial
Hospital
01795 418300
Skegness & District
General Hospital
01476 565232
Skipton General Hospital
01756 792233
Solihull Hospital
0121 424 2000
South Hams Hospital,
Kingsbridge
01548 852349
South Moor Hospital,
Stanley
0191 333 6262
South Petherton Hospital
01460 240333
South Shore Hospital,
Blackpool
01253 306106
South Tyneside District
General Hospital, South
Shields
0191 454 8888
Southampton General
Hospital
023 8077 7222
Southend Hospital,
Westcliff-on-Sea
01702 435555
Southlands Hospital,
Shoreham-by-Sea
01273 455622
Southmead Hospital,
Bristol
0117 950 5050
Southport & Formby
District General Hospital,
Southport
01704 547471
Southport General
Infirmary
01704 547471
Southwold Hospital,
Suffolk
01502 723333
Springfield University
Hospital, London
020 8672 9911

Staffordshire General
Hospital, Stafford
01785 257731
Stamford and Rutland
Hospital
01780 764151
Stead Memorial Hospital,
Redcar
01642 288288
Stepping Hill Hospital,
Stockport
0161 483 1010
Stewart Day Hospital, St
Helens
01744 458393
Stoke Mandeville Hospital,
Aylesbury
01296 315000
Stone House Hospital,
Dartford
01322 622222
Stratford Hospital,
Stratford-upon-Avon
01789 205831
Stratton Hospital, Bude
01288 287700
Stretford Memorial
Hospital, Manchester
0161 881 5353
Stroud General Hospital
01453 562200
Stroud Maternity Hospital
01453 562140
Summerlands Hospital,
Yeovil
01225 731731
Sunderland Eye Infirmary
0191 565 6256
Sunderland Royal Hospital
0191 565 6256
Surbiton Hospital
020 8399 7111
Sussex Eye Hospital,
Brighton
01273 606126
Sutton Hospital, Surrey
020 8644 4343
Swanage Hospital,
Swanage
01929 422282

T

Tameside General Hospital,
Ashton-under-Lyne
0161 331 6000
Tavistock Hospital
01822 612233
Teddington Memorial
Hospital
020 8714 4000
Teignmouth Hospital
01626 772161
Tenbury and District
General Hospital,
Tenbury Wells
01584 810643
Tewkesbury Hospital
01684 293303
Thornbury Hospital, Bristol
01454 412636

Tickhill Road Hospital,
Doncaster
01302 796000
Tiddington Fields,
Stratford-upon-Avon
01789 261455
Tiverton & District Hospital
01884 235400
Tolworth Hospital, Surrey
020 8390 0102
Tonbridge Cottage Hospital
01732 353653
Torbay District General
Hospital, Torquay
01803 614567
Totnes Hospital
01803 862622
Trafford General Hospital,
Manchester
0161 746 2878
Trengweath Hospital,
Redruth
01209 881900
Trowbridge Community
Hospital
01225 752558

U

Uckfield Hospital
01825 769999
Ulverston Hospital
01229 583635
University College
Hospital, London
020 7387 9300
University Dental Hospital,
Manchester
0161 275 6666
University Hospital Aintree,
Liverpool
0151 525 5980
University Hospital
Lewisham, London
020 8333 3000
University Hospital of
Hartlepool
01429 266654
University Hospital of North
Durham
0191 333 2333
University Hospital of North
Tees, Stockton-on-Tees
01429 266654
University of Bristol Dental
Hospital
0117 923 0050
Upton Hospital, Slough
01753 821441

V

Verrington Hospital,
Wincanton
01963 32006
Victoria Central Hospital,
Merseyside
0151 678 7272
Victoria Cottage Hospital,
Havant
01243 376041

Victoria Cottage Hospital,
Maryport
01900 812634
Victoria Hospital, Deal
01304 865400
Victoria Hospital, Lichfield
01543 442000
Victoria Hospital, Sidmouth
01395 512482
Victoria Infirmary,
Northwich
01606 564000

W

Walkergate Hospital,
Newcastle upon Tyne
0191 233 6161
Wallingford Community
Hospital
01491 826037
Walsgrave Hospital,
Coventry
024 7660 2020
Walton Hospital,
Chesterfield
01246 552864
Walton Hospital, Liverpool
0151 525 3611
Wansbeck General
Hospital, Ashington
0844 811 8118
Wantage Hospital
01235 205801
Wareham Community
Hospital
01929 552433
Warminster Community
Hospital
01985 212076
Warrington Hospital
01925 635911
Warwick Hospital
01926 495321
Waterside Mental Health
Day Hospital
01386 502510
Watford General Hospital
01923 244366
Wathwood Hospital,
Rotherham
01709 870800
Welland Hospital, Spalding
01476 565232
Wellington & District
Cottage Hospital
01823 662663
Wells & District Hospital
01749 683200
Wembley Community
Hospital, London
020 8903 1323
Wesham Hospital
Rehabilitation Unit,
Preston
01253 655404
West Berkshire Community
Hospital, Thatcham
01635 273300
West Cornwall Hospital,
Penzance
01736 874000

West Cumberland Hospital,
Whitehaven
01946 693181
West Heath Hospital,
Birmingham
0121 627 1627
West Middlesex University
Hospital, Isleworth
020 8560 2121
West Park Hospital,
Wolverhampton
01902 444000
West Suffolk Hospital, Bury
St Edmunds
01284 713000
West View Hospital,
Tenterden
01580 763677
Westbury Community
Hospital
01373 823616
Western Community
Hospital, Southampton
023 8047 5401
Western Eye Hospital,
London
020 7886 6666
Western House Hospital,
Ware
01920 468954
Westhaven Hospital,
Weymouth
01305 786116
Westminster Memorial
Hospital, Shaftesbury
01747 851535
Westmorland General
Hospital, Kendal
01539 732288
Weston General Hospital,
Weston-super-Mare
01934 636363
Weston Park Hospital,
Sheffield
0114 226 5000
Westwood Hospital,
Beverley
01482 886600
Wexham Park Hospital,
Slough
01753 633000
Weymouth Community
Hospital
01305 760022
Wharfedale Hospital, Otley
01943 465522
Whelley Hospital, Wigan
01942 244000
Whipps Cross University
Hospital, London
020 8539 5522
Whiston Hospital, Prescot
0151 426 1600
Whitby Community
Hospital
01947 604851
Whitby New Hospital
01723 368111
Whitchurch Hospital
01948 666292

Whitstable & Tankerton
Hospital
01227 594400
Whittington Hospital,
London
020 7272 3070
Whitworth Hospital,
Matlock
01246 277271
Wigton Hospital, Cumbria
01697 366600
Willesden Hospital, London
020 8451 8017
William Harvey Hospital,
Ashford
01233 633331
William Julien Courtauld
Hospital, Braintree
01245 440761
Williton Hospital
01984 635600
Wimborne Hospital
01202 858200
Winchcombe Hospital,
Cheltenham
01242 602341
Windsor Day Hospital,
Shepton Mallet
01749 343911
Withernsea Community
Hospital
01964 614666
Withington Hospital,
Manchester
0161 434 5555
Witney Community
Hospital
01993 209400
Woking Community
Hospital
01483 715911
Wokingham Hospital
0118 949 5000
Wolverhampton and
Midland Eye Infirmary
01902 307999
Woodlands Hospital, St
Leonards on Sea
01424 755470
Woods Hospital, Glossop
0161 331 5151
Worcestershire Royal
Hospital, Worcester
01905 763333
Workington Infirmary
01946 693181
Worthing Hospital
01903 205111
Wotton Lawn, Gloucester
01452 891500
Wrightington Hospital,
Wigan
01942 244000
Wycombe Hospital, High
Wycombe
01494 526161
Wythenshawe Hospital,
Manchester
0161 998 7070

Y

Yeatman Hospital,
Sherborne
01935 813991
Yeovil District Hospital
01935 475122
York Hospital
01904 631313

*NHS England hospitals
copyright NHS Connecting
for Health*

Health

NHS hospitals: Wales

Aberbargoed Hospital
01443 828728

Aberdare General Hospital
01685 872411

Abergele Hospital
01745 832295

Abertillery & District
Hospital
01495 214123

Amman Valley Hospital,
Ammanford
01269 822226

Barry Hospital
01446 704000

Blaenavon Hospital
01495 790236

Blaina & District Hospital,
Nantyglo
01495 293250

Bodnant EMI Unit,
Llandudno
01492 862347

Brecon War Memorial
Hospital, Brecon
01874 622443

Bro Cerwyn Day Hospital,
Haverfordwest
01437 773157

Bro Ddyfi Community
Hospital, Powys
01654 702266

Bron y Garth Hospital,
Gwynedd
01766 770310

Bronglais General Hospital,
Aberystwyth
01970 623131

Bronllys Hospital, Brecon
01874 711255

Bryn Beryl Hospital,
Pwllheli
01758 701122

Bryn y Neuadd Hospital,
Conwy
01248 682682

Brynmair Day Hospital,
Llanelli
01554 772768

Bryntirion Hospital, Llanelli
01554 756567

Builth Wells Hospital
01982 552221

Caerphilly and District
Miners' Hospital
029 2085 1811

Cardiff Royal Infirmary
029 2049 2233

Cardigan and District
Memorial Hospital
01239 612214

Cefn Coed Hospital,
Swansea
01792 561155

Cefni Hospital, Anglesey
01248 750117

Chepstow Community
Hospital, Chepstow
01291 636636

Chirk Community Hospital
01691 772430

Cimla Hospital, Neath
01639 862000

Colwyn Bay Community
Hospital
01492 515218

Conwy Hospital
01492 564300

County Hospital, Torfeen
01495 768768

Dan-y-Bryn Unit, Ebbw
Vale
01495 353700

Deeside Community
Hospital, Deeside
01244 830461

Denbigh Infirmary
01745 812624

Dewi Sant Hospital,
Pontypridd
01443 486222

Dobshill Hospital, Deeside
01244 550233

Dolgellau Hospital
01341 422479

Ebbw Vale Hospital
01495 356900

Eryri Hospital, Caernarfon
01286 672481

Fairwood Hospital,
Swansea
01792 203192

Ffestiniog Memorial
Hospital
01766 831281

Flint Community Hospital
01352 732215

Garngoch Hospital,
Swansea
01792 892921

Gellinudd Hospital,
Swansea
01792 862221

Glan Clwyd District General
Hospital, Rhyl
01745 583910

Glanrhyd Hospital,
Bridgend
01656 752752

Glantraeth Day Hospital,
Rhyl
01745 443000

Gorseinon Hospital,
Swansea
01792 702222

Gorwelion Day Hospital,
Aberystwyth
01970 615448

Groeswen Hospital, Port
Talbot
01639 862000

Hill House Hospital,
Swansea
01792 203551

HM Stanley Hospital, St
Asaph
01745 583275

Holywell Community
Hospital
01352 713003

Knighton Hospital
01547 528633

Llandough Hospital,
Penarth
029 2071 1711

Llandovery Hospital
01550 720322

Llandrindod Wells Hospital
01597 822951

Llandudno General
Hospital
01492 860066

Llanfrechfa Grange
Hospital, Cwmbran
01633 623623

Llangollen Community
Hospital
01978 860226

Llanidloes War Memorial
Hospital
01686 412121

Lluesty Hospital, Holywell
01352 710581

Llwynypia Hospital,
Rhondda
01443 440440

Maesteg Community
Hospital
01656 752752

Maindiff Court Hospital,
Abergavenny
01873 735500

Minfordd Hospital, Bangor
01248 352308

Mold Community Hospital
01352 758744

Monmouth Hospital
01600 713522

Montgomery County
Infirmary, Newtown
01686 617200

Morriston Hospital,
Swansea
01792 702222

Mountain Ash General
Hospital
01685 872411

Mynydd Mawr Hospital,
Llanelli
01269 841343

Neath Port Talbot Hospital,
Port Talbot
01639 862000

Oakdale Hospital,
Blackwood
01495 225207

Pontypridd & District
Cottage Hospital
01443 486144

Prestatyn Community
Hospital
01745 853487

Prince Charles Hospital,
Merthyr Tydfil
01685 721721

Prince Phillip Hospital,
Llanelli
01554 756567

Princess of Wales Hospital,
Bridgend
01656 752752

Redwood Memorial
Hospital, Rhymney
01685 840314

Rookwood Hospital,
Cardiff
029 2041 5415

Royal Alexandra Hospital,
Rhyl
01745 443000

Royal Glamorgan Hospital,
Llantrisant
01443 443443

Royal Gwent Hospital,
Newport
01633 234234

Ruthin Hospital
01824 702692

St Brynach's Day Hospital,
Haverfordwest
01437 773157

St Cadoc's Hospital,
Newport
01633 436700

St David's Hospital, Cardiff
029 2053 6666

St David's Hospital,
Carmarthen
01267 237481

St Tydfil's Hospital, Merthyr
Tydfil
01685 723244

St Woolos Hospital,
Newport
01633 234234

Singleton Hospital,
Swansea
01792 205666

South Pembrokeshire
Hospital, Pembroke Dock
01646 682114

Swn-y-Gwynt Day
Hospital, Ammanford
01269 595473

Tenby Cottage Hospital
01834 842040

Tonna Hospital, Neath
01639 862000

Tredegar General Hospital
01495 722271

Tregaron Hospital
01974 298203

Trevalyn Hospital
01244 570446

Ty Sirhowy Health Centre,
Blackwood
01495 229010

Tywyn & District War
Memorial Hospital, Tywyn
01654 710411

University Dental Hospital,
Cardiff
029 2074 7747

University Hospital of
Wales, Cardiff
029 2074 7747

Victoria Memorial Hospital,
Welshpool
01938 553133

Whitchurch Hospital, Cardiff
029 2069 3191
Withybush General
Hospital, Haverfordwest
01437 764545
Wrexham Maelor Hospital,
Wrexham
01978 291100
Ysbyty George Thomas,
Treorchy
01443 440440
Ysbyty Gwynedd, Bangor
01248 384384
Ysbyty Penrhos Stanley,
Anglesey
01407 766000
Ysbyty'r Tri Chwm, Blaenau
Gwent
01495 353200
Ystrad Mynach Hospital,
Hangoed
01443 811411
Ystradgynlais Community
Hospital, Swansea
01639 844777

NHS hospitals: Scotland

Abbotsford Park Hospital,
Edinburgh
0131 447 2674
Aberdeen Maternity
Hospital, Aberdeen
01224 840606
Aberdeen Royal Infirmary
01224 681818
Aberfeldy Community
Hospital
01887 820314
Aboyne Community
Hospital
01339 886433
Acorn Street Day Hospital,
Glasgow
0141 556 4789
Adamson Hospital, Fife
01334 652901
Ailsa Hospital, Ayr
01292 610556
Alexander Hospital,
Coatbridge
01236 422661
Annan Hospital
01461 203425
Arbroath Infirmary
01241 872584
Argyll & Bute Hospital, Argyll
01546 602323
Arran War Memorial
Hospital, Lamlash
01770 600777
Ashludie Hospital, Angus
01382 423000
Astley Ainslie Hospital,
Edinburgh
0131 537 9000
Ayr Hospital
01292 610555
Ayrshire Central Hospital
01294 274191
Balfour Hospital, Kirkwall
01856 888000
Bannockburn Hospital
01786 813016
Belford Hospital, Fort
William
01397 702481
Belhaven Hospital, Dunbar
01368 862246
Benbecula Hospital
01870 603603
Biggart Hospital
01292 470611
Birch Avenue Day Hospital,
Perth
01738 553920
Blairgowrie Community
Hospital
01250 874466
Blawathill Hospital,
Glasgow
0141 954 9547
Bo'ness Hospital
01506 829580

Bonnybridge Hospital
01324 814685
Borders General Hospital,
Melrose
01896 826000
Brechin Infirmary
01356 622291
Brooksby House Hospital,
Largs
01475 672285
Caithness General
Hospital, Wick
01955 605050
Cameron Hospital, Fife
01592 712472
Campbell Hospital, Banff
01261 842202
Campbell House, Gartnavel
Royal Hospital, Glasgow
0141 211 3600
Campbeltown Hospital,
Argyll
01586 552224
Castle Douglas Hospital
01556 502333
Chalmers Hospital, Banff
01261 812567
Chalmers Hospital,
Edinburgh
0131 536 1000
City Hospital, Edinburgh
0131 536 6000
Clackmannan County
Hospital, Alloa
01259 727374
Coathill Hospital,
Coatbridge
01698 245000
Coldstream Cottage
Hospital
01890 882417
Corstorphine Hospital,
Edinburgh
0131 537 5000
County Community
Hospital, Invergordon
01349 852496
Crieff Community Hospital
01764 653173
Crosshouse Hospital,
Kilmarnock
01563 521133
Dalrymple Hospital,
Stranraer
01776 706900
Davidson Cottage Hospital,
Girvan
01465 712571
Dr Gray's Hospital, Elgin
01343 543131
Dr Mackinnon Memorial
Hospital, Isle of Skye
01471 822491
Drumchapel Hospital,
Glasgow
0141 211 6000
Dumbarton Joint Hospital
01389 604100
Dumfries and Galloway
Royal Infirmary, Dumfries
01387 246246

Dunaros Hospital, Isle of
Mull
01680 300392
Dunbar Hospital, Thurso
01847 893263
Dundee Dental Hospital
01382 660111
Dunoon General Hospital
01369 704341
Dunrowan Day Hospital,
Falkirk
01324 639009
Dykebar Hospital, Paisley
0141 884 5122
East Ayrshire Community
Hospital
01290 429429
East Fortune Hospital,
North Berwick
01620 892878
Eastern General Hospital,
Edinburgh
0131 536 7000
Edenhall Hospital,
Musselburgh
0131 536 8000
Edinburgh Dental Hospital,
Edinburgh
0131 536 4900
Edinburgh Orthopaedic
Trauma Unit
0131 536 1000
Edington Cottage Hospital,
North Berwick
01620 892878
Eyemouth Day Hospital
01890 751101
Falkirk & District Royal
Infirmary, Falkirk
01324 624000
Fleming Hospital, Aberlour
01340 871464
Florence Street Day
Hospital, Glasgow
0141 429 2878
Forfar Infirmary, Angus
01307 464551
Forth Park Hospital,
Kirkcaldy
01592 643355
Fraserburgh Hospital
01346 513151
Garrick Hospital, Stranraer
01776 702323
Gartnavel General Hospital,
Glasgow
0141 211 3000
Gilbert Bain Hospital,
Lerwick
01595 743000
Glasgow Dental Hospital
0141 211 9600
Glasgow Homoeopathic
Hospital
0141 211 3000
Glasgow Royal Infirmary
0141 211 4000
Glaxo Day Hospital,
Monifieth
01382 527831

Glen O'Dee Hospital,
Banchory
01330 822233

Glencoe Hospital, Glencoe
01855 811254

Glenrothes Hospital
01592 743505

Hairmyres Hospital, East
Kilbride
01355 585000

Hartwood Hospital, Shotts
01501 823366

Hawick Cottage Hospital
01450 372162

Hawick Day Hospital
01450 370000

Hawkhead Hospital,
Paisley
0141 889 8151

Hawkhill Day Hospital,
Dundee
01382 668300

Hay Lodge Hospital,
Peebles
01721 722080

Herdmanflat Hospital,
Haddington
0131 536 8300

Holmhead Hospital,
Cumnock
01290 422220

Ian Charles Hospital,
Grantown-on-Spey
01479 872528

Insch Hospital
01464 820213

Inverclyde Royal Hospital,
Greenock
01475 633777

Inverurie Hospital
01467 620454

Irvine Memorial Hospital,
Pitlochry
01796 472052

Islay Hospital, Isle of Islay
01496 301000

Johnstone Hospital,
Johnstone
01505 331471

Kello Hospital, Biggar
01899 220077

Kelso Community Hospital
01573 223441

Kildean Hospital, Stirling
01786 446615

Kilsyth Victoria Memorial
Hospital
01236 822172

Kirkcudbright Hospital
01557 330549

Kirklands Hospital,
Bothwell
01698 245000

Knoll Hospital, Duns
01361 883373

Lady Home Hospital,
Lanark
01555 851210

Lady Margaret Hospital,
Isle of Cumbrae
01475 530307

Lawson Memorial Hospital,
Golspie
01408 633157

Leanchoil Hospital, Forres
01309 672284

Leith Hospital, Edinburgh
0131 536 8700

Lightburn Hospital,
Glasgow
0141 211 1500

Little Cairnie Hospital,
Arbroath
01241 872584

Loanhead Hospital,
Edinburgh
0131 440 0174

Lochmaben Hospital
01387 810255

Lorn and Islands District
General Hospital, Oban
01631 567500

Lynebank Hospital, Fife
01383 623623

Mackinnon Memorial
Hospital, Isle of Skye
01471 822491

Macmillan House, Perth
01738 639303

Maud Hospital
01771 613236

Merchiston Hospital,
Johnstone
01505 328261

Mid Argyll Hospital, Argyll
01546 602449

Migdale Hospital, Bonar
Bridge
01863 766211

Moffat Hospital
01683 220031

Monklands Hospital,
Airdrie
01236 748748

Montrose Royal Infirmary
01674 830361

Murray Royal Hospital,
Perth
01738 621151

Netherlea Hospital,
Newport-on-Tay
01382 543223

Newton Stewart Hospital
01671 402015

Ninewells Hospital, Dundee
01382 660111

Orchard House Day
Hospital, Stirling
01786 849717

Orleans Day Hospital,
Dundee
01382 667322

Parkhead Hospital,
Glasgow
0141 211 8331

Perth Royal Infirmary, Perth
01738 623311

Peterhead Community
Hospital
01779 478234

Portree Hospital, Skye
01478 613200

Princes Street Day
Hospital, Stirling
01786 474161

Princess Alexandra Eye
Pavilion, Edinburgh
0131 536 1000

Princess Royal Maternity
Hospital, Glasgow
0141 211 5400

Queen Margaret Hospital,
Dunfermline
01383 623623

Queen Mother's Hospital,
Glasgow
0141 201 0550

Raigmore Hospital,
Inverness
01463 704000

Randolph Wemyss
Memorial Hospital,
Buckhaven
01592 712427

Ravenscraig Hospital,
Greenock
01475 633777

Roadmeetings Hospital,
Carluke
01555 772271

Roodlands Hospital,
Haddington
0131 536 8300

Rosemount Day Hospital,
Arbroath
01241 872584

Ross Memorial Hospital,
Dingwall
01349 863313

Rosslynlee Hospital,
Midlothian
0131 536 7600

Roxburghe House,
Aberdeen
01224 681818

Royal Aberdeen Children's
Hospital
01224 681818

Royal Alexandra Hospital,
Paisley
0141 887 9111

Royal Cornhill Hospital,
Aberdeen
01224 663131

Royal Dundee Liff Hospital
01382 423000

Royal Edinburgh Hospital
0131 537 6000

Royal Hospital for Sick
Children, Edinburgh
0131 536 0000

Royal Hospital for Sick
Children, Glasgow
0141 201 0000

Royal Infirmary of
Edinburgh
0131 536 1000

Royal Northern, Inverness
01463 704000

Royal Scottish National
Hospital, Larbert
01324 570700

Royal Victoria Hospital,
Dundee
01382 423000

Royal Victoria Hospital,
Edinburgh
0131 537 5000

St Andrews Memorial
Hospital, Fife
01334 472327

St Brendan's Hospital, Isle
of Barra
01871 810465

St John's Hospital at
Howden, Livingston
01506 419666

St Margaret's Hospital,
Auchterarder
01764 662246

St Michael's Hospital,
Linlithgow
01506 842053

St Vincent's Hospital,
Kingussie
01540 661219

Sauchie Hospital, Alloa
01259 722060

Seafield Hospital, Buckie
01542 832081

Sister Margaret Hospital,
Jedburgh
01835 863212

Southern General Hospital,
Glasgow
0141 201 1100

Spynie Hospital, Elgin
01343 543131

Stephen Hospital,
Dufftown
01340 820215

Stirling Royal Infirmary,
Stirling
01786 434000

Stobhill Hospital, Glasgow
0141 201 3000

Stracathro Hospital,
Brechin
01356 647291

Strathclyde Hospital,
Motherwell
01698 245000

Stratheden Hospital, Fife
01334 652611

Strathmartine Hospital,
Dundee
01382 423000

Sunnyside Royal Hospital,
Montrose
01674 830361

Thomas Hope Hospital,
Langholm
01387 380417

Thornhill Hospital
01848 330205

Threshold Day Hospital,
Dundee
01382 322026

Tippethill House, West
Lothian
01501 745917

Town & County Hospital,
Caithness
01955 604025

Town & County Hospital,
Nairn
01667 452101
Turner Memorial Hospital,
Keith
01542 882526
Turriff Hospital
01888 563293
Udston Hospital, Hamilton
01698 245000
Ugie Hospital, Peterhead
01779 472011
Uist and Barra Hospital
01870 603603
Vale of Leven District
General Hospital,
Alexandria
01389 754121
Victoria Hospital, Isle of
Bute
01700 503938
Victoria Infirmary, Glasgow
0141 201 6000
Victoria Infirmary,
Helensburgh
01436 672158
Westbank Day Hospital,
Falkirk
01324 624111
Wester Moffat Hospital,
Airdrie
01236 763377
Western General Hospital,
Edinburgh
0131 537 1000
Western Infirmary, Glasgow
0141 211 2000
Western Isles Hospital,
Stornoway
01851 704704
Weston Day Hospital, Fife
01334 652163
Whitehills Hospital, Angus
01307 475222
Whytemans Brae Hospital,
Fife
01592 643355
Wishaw General Hospital
01698 361100
Woodend Hospital,
Aberdeen
01224 663131

NHS hospitals: Northern Ireland

Alexandra Gardens Day
Hospital, Belfast
028 9080 2150
Altnagelvin Area Hospital,
Londonderry
028 7134 5171
Antrim Hospital
028 9442 4000
Ards Hospital,
Newtownards
028 9181 2661
Armagh Community
Hospital
028 3752 2381
Bangor Community
Hospital
028 9151 5304
Belvoir Park Hospital,
Belfast
028 9032 9241
Belfast City Hospital
028 9032 9241
Braid Valley Hospital,
Ballymena
028 2563 5200
Causeway Hospital,
Coleraine
028 7032 7032
Craigavon Area Hospital
028 3833 4444
Daisy Hill Hospital, Newry
028 3083 5000
Dalriada Hospital,
Ballycastle
028 2766 6600
Downe Hospital,
Downpatrick
028 4461 3311
Erne Hospital, Enniskillen
028 6638 2000
Forster Green Hospital,
Belfast
028 9094 4444
Gransha Hospital,
Londonderry
028 7186 0261
Holywell Hospital, Antrim
028 2563 3700
Knockbracken Mental
Health Services, Belfast
028 9056 5656

Lagan Valley Hospital,
Lisburn
028 9266 5141
Longstone Hospital,
Armagh
028 3752 2381
Lurgan Hospital
028 3832 9483
Mater Hospital, Belfast
028 9074 1211
Mid-Ulster Hospital,
Magherafelt
028 7963 1031
Mourne Hospital, Co Down
028 4176 2235
Moyle Hospital, Larne
028 2827 5431
Muckamore Abbey
Hospital, Muckamore
028 9446 3333
Mullinure Hospital, Armagh
028 3752 2381
Musgrave Park Hospital,
Belfast
028 9090 2000
Royal Belfast Hospital for
Sick Children, Belfast
028 9024 0503
Royal Maternity Hospital,
Belfast
028 9024 0503
Royal Victoria Hospital,
Belfast
028 9024 0503
St Luke's Hospital, Armagh
028 3752 2381
Shaftesbury Square
Hospital, Belfast
028 9032 9808
South Tyrone Hospital,
Dungannon
028 8772 2821
Tyrone and Fermanagh
Hospital, Omagh
028 8283 3100
Tyrone County Hospital,
Omagh
028 8283 3100
Ulster Hospital, Dundonald
028 9048 4511
Whiteabbey Hospital,
Newtownabbey
028 9086 5181

Private healthcare

MAIN PRIVATE HEALTHCARE
PROVIDERS

Abbey Hospitals
01772 734444
www.abbeyhospitals.co.uk
BMI Healthcare
020 7009 4500
www.bmihealthcare.co.uk
**British Pregnancy Advisory
Sevice**
01564 793225
www.bpas.org
PRESS: *020 7612 0206*
Bupa Hospitals
020 7656 2000
www.bupahospitals.co.uk
Nuffield Hospitals
020 8390 1200
www.nuffieldhospitals.org.uk
Priory Healthcare
01372 860400
www.prioryhealthcare.co.uk

Law

Government

Home Office
0870 000 1585
www.homeoffice.gov.uk
PRESS: *020 7035 4381*
Attorney General's Office
020 7271 2400
PRESS: *020 7271 2405 / 65*
Department for Constitutional Affairs
020 7210 8614
www.lcd.gov.uk
PRESS: *020 7210 8512*
Scottish Executive
0131 556 8400
www.scotland.gov.uk
PRESS OFFICE, JUSTICE DESK:
0131 244 1111

Government agencies

Law Commission
020 7453 1220
www.lawcom.gov.uk
Legal Services Commission
020 7759 0000
www.legalservices.gov.uk

The legal system

OMBUDSMEN

Legal Services Ombudsman
0845 601 0794
www.olso.org
Scottish Legal Services Ombudsman
0131 556 9123
www.slso.org.uk

LAW ASSOCIATIONS

Administrative Law Bar Association
020 7583 1770
www.adminlaw.org.uk
Association of Personal Injury Lawyers
0115 958 0585
www.apil.com
Association of Women Barristers
020 7842 7070
www.womenbarristers.co.uk
Bar Council
020 7242 0082
www.barcouncil.org.uk
PRESS: *020 7222 2525*
Chancery Bar Association
020 8883 1700
www.chba.org.uk
Commercial Bar Association
020 7404 2022
www.combar.com

Family Law Bar Association
020 7242 1289
www.flba.co.uk
Institute of Barristers' Clerks
020 7831 7144
www.barristersclerks.com
Institute of Legal Executives
01234 841000
www.ilex.org.uk
PRESS: *01234 845715*
Justices' Clerks' Society
0151 255 0790
www.jc-society.co.uk
Law Society
020 7242 1222
www.lawsoc.org.uk
PRESS: *020 7320 5764*
Legal Aid Practitioners' Group
020 7960 6068
www.lapg.co.uk
Magistrates' Association
020 7387 2353
www.magistrates-association.org.uk
Solicitors' Criminal Law Association
01273 676725
www.clsa.co.uk
Solicitors' Family Law Association
01689 850227
www.sfla.org.uk
PRESS: *020 7357 9215*

The judiciary

JUSTICE AGENCIES

Appeals Service
020 7712 2600
www.appeals-service.gov.uk
Children and Family Court Advisory and Support Service (Cafcass)
020 7510 7000
www.cafcass.gov.uk
See website for details of regional offices
Civil Justice Council
020 7947 6670
www.civiljusticecouncil.gov.uk
Court Service, Northern Ireland
028 9032 8594
www.courtsni.gov.uk
PRESS: *028 9041 2345*
Courts Service
020 7189 2000
www.hmcourts-service.gov.uk
PRESS: *020 7210 8512*
Criminal Cases Review Commission
0121 633 1800
www.ccrc.gov.uk
Criminal Records Bureau
0870 909 0811
www.crb.gov.uk
Crown Office and Procurator Fiscal Service, Scotland
0131 226 2626
www.crownoffice.gov.uk

Crown Prosecution Service
020 7796 8000
www.cps.gov.uk
PRESS: *020 7796 8442*
HM Revenue & Customs
0845 010 9000
www.hmrc.gov.uk
PRESS – BUSINESS: *020 7147 2328 / 2324 / 0798;* PERSONAL: *020 7147 2318 / 319 / 333;* LAW ENFORCEMENT: *020 7147 0052 / 2314 / 2331;* SOCIAL: *020 7147 2319 / 2337 / 0051*
Inspectorate of Court Administration
020 7217 4343
www.hmica.gov.uk
Scottish Courts Administration
0131 229 9200
www.scotcourts.gov.uk
PRESS: *0131 556 8400*
Youth Justice Boards for England and Wales
020 7271 3033
www.youth-justice-board.gov.uk
PRESS: *020 7271 3014 / 2988*

Appeal courts

Court of Appeal
Civil cases: 020 7947 6409
Criminal: 020 7947 6014
PRESS – INDIVIDUAL CASES: *020 7947 6000;* POLICY: *020 7210 8512*
High Court
020 7947 6000
Judicial Committee of the Privy Council
020 7276 0483 / 5 / 7
Supreme Courts, Scotland
0131 225 2595
High Court (criminal) and Court of Session (civil)
High Court of Justiciary, Scotland
0131 240 2906
PRESS: *0131 244 2642 / 2656 / 2939 / 3073*
Supreme Court of Northern Ireland
028 9072 4661
PRESS: *028 9041 2385*

Crown courts

Central Criminal Court –
Old Bailey
020 7248 3277
Aylesbury
01296 434401
Barnstaple
01271 373286
Basildon Combined Court
01268 458000
Birmingham
0121 681 3300
Blackfriars
020 7922 5800
Bolton Combined Court
Centre
01204 392881
Bournemouth
01202 502800
Bradford Combined Court
Centre
01274 840274
Bristol
0117 976 3030
Burnley Combined Court
Centre
01282 416899
Cambridge
01223 488321
Canterbury Combined
Court Centre
01227 819200
Cardiff
029 2041 4400
Carlisle Combined Court
Centre
01228 520619
Chelmsford
01245 603000
Chester
01244 317606
Chichester Combined
Court Centre
01243 520742
Coventry Combined Court
Centre
024 7653 6166
Croydon Combined Court
Centre
020 8410 4700
Derby Combined Court
Centre
01332 622600
Doncaster
01302 322211
Durham
0191 386 6714
Exeter Combined Court
Centre
01392 415300
Gloucester
01452 834900
Great Grimsby Combined
Court Centre
01472 311811
Guildford
01483 468500
Harrow
020 8424 2294
Hereford
01432 276118

Hove Trial Centre
01273 229200
Inner London
020 7234 3100
Ipswich
01473 228 585
Isleworth
020 8380 4500
Kingston-upon-Hull
Combined Court Centre
01482 586161
Kingston-upon-Thames
020 8240 2500
Lancaster Crown Court
01772 832300
Leeds Combined Court
Centre
0113 283 0040
Leicester Crown Court
0116 222 5800
Lewes Combined Court
Centre
01273 480400
Lincoln
01522 525222
Liverpool Combined Court
Centre
0151 473 7373
Luton
01582 522000
Maidstone
01622 202000
Manchester (Crown
Square)
0161 954 1702
Manchester at Minshull St
0161 954 7500
Merthyr Tydfil Combined
Court Centre
01685 358222
Middlesex Guildhall
020 7202 0370
Mold
01244 356709
Newcastle upon Tyne
Combined Court Centre
0191 201 2000
Newport (South Wales)
01633 266211
Newport, I.O.W.
01983 821569
Northampton Combined
Court
01604 470400
Norwich Combined Court
Centre
01603 728200
Nottingham
0115 910 3551
Oxford Combined Court
Centre
01865 264200
Peterborough Combined
Court Centre
01733 349161
Plymouth Combined Court
01752 677400
Portsmouth Combined
Court Centre
023 9289 3000

Preston Combined Court
Centre
01772 844700
Reading
0118 967 4400
Salisbury Combined Court
Centre
01722 325444
Sheffield Combined Court
Centre
0114 281 2400
Shrewsbury
01743 355775
Snaresbrook
020 8530 0000
Southampton Combined
Court Centre
023 8021 3200
Southwark
020 7522 7200
St. Albans
01727 753220
Stafford Combined Court
Centre
01785 610730
Stoke-on-Trent Combined
Court
01782 854000
Swansea
01792 484700
Swindon Combined Court
01792 484700
Taunton
01823 326685
Teesside Combined Court
Centre
01642 340000
Truro Combined Court
Centre
01872 222340
Warrington Combined
Court Centre
01925 256700
Warwick Combined Court
Centre
01926 492276
Weymouth and
Dorchester Combined
Court Centre
01305 752510
Winchester Combined
Court Centre
01962 841212
Wolverhampton
Combined Court Centre
01902 48100
Wood Green
020 8826 4100
Woolwich
020 8312 7000
Worcester Combined
Court Centre
01905 730800
York
01904 645121

County courts

Aberdare
01685 888575
Aberystwyth
01970 636370
Accrington
01254 237490
Aldershot & Farnham
01252 796800
Altrincham
0161 975 4760
Ashford
01233 632464
Aylesbury
01296 393498
Banbury
01295 265799
Barnet
020 8343 4272
Barnsley
01226 203471
Barnstaple
01271 372252
Barrow-In-Furness
01229 820046
Basildon Combined Court
01268 458000
Basingstoke
01256 318200
Bath
01225 310282
Bedford
01234 760400
Birkenhead
0151 666 5800
Birmingham Civil Justice
Centre
0121 681 4441
Bishop Auckland
01388 602423
Blackburn
01254 680640
Blackpool
01253 754020
Blackwood
01495 223197
Bodmin
01208 74224 / 73735
Bolton Combined Court
01204 392881
Boston
01205 366080
Bournemouth
01202 502800
Bow
020 8536 5200
Bradford Combined Court
Centre
01274 840274
Brecknock
01685 358222
Brentford
020 8231 8940
Bridgend
01656 768881
Brighton
01273 674421
Brighton County Court
Family Centre
01273 811333

Law

Bristol
0117 910 6700
Bromley
020 8290 9620
Burton Upon Trent County
Court
01283 568241
Burnley Combined Court
01282 416899
Bury
0161 764 1344
Bury St Edmunds
01284 753254
Buxton
01298 23734
Caernarfon
01286 684600
Cambridge
01223 224500
Canterbury Combined
Court
01227 819200
Cardiff Civil Justice Centre
029 2037 6400
Carlisle Combined Court
Centre
01228 520619
Carmarthen
01267 228010
Central London
020 7917 5000
Cheltenham
01242 519983
Chelmsford
01245 264670
Chester Civil Justice
Centre
01244 404200
Chesterfield
01246 501200
Chichester
01243 520700
Chorley
01257 262778
Clerkenwell
020 7359 7347
Colchester
01206 572743
Consett
01207 502854
Conwy & Colwyn
01492 530807
Coventry Combined Court
Centre
01203 536 166
Crewe
01270 539300
Croydon Combined Court
020 8410 4700
Darlington
01325 463224
Dartford
01322 629820
Derby Combined Court
01332 622600
Dewsbury
01924 466135
Doncaster
01302 381730
Dudley
01384 480799

Durham
0191 3865941
Eastbourne
01323 735195
Edmonton
020 8884 6500
Epsom
01372 721801
Evesham
01386 442287
Exeter Combined Court
01392 415300
Gateshead
0191 477 2445
Gloucester
01452 834900
Grantham
01476 539030
Gravesend
01474 321771
Great Grimsby Combined
Court
01472 311811
Guildford
01483 595200
Halifax
01422 344700
Harlow
01279 443291
Harrogate
01423 503921
Hartlepool
01429 268198
Hastings
01424 435128
Haverfordwest
01437 772060
Haywards Heath
01444 456326
Hertford
01992 503954
Hereford
01432 357233
High Wycombe
01494 436374
Hitchin
01462 443750
Horsham
01403 252474
Huddersfield
01484 421043
Huntingdon
01480 450932
Ilford
020 8478 1132
Ipswich
01473 214256
Keighley
01535 602803
Kendal
01539 721218
Kettering
01536 512471
Kidderminster
01562 822480
King's Lynn
01553 772067
Kingston upon Hull
01482 586161
Kingston-upon-Thames
020 8546 8843

Lambeth
020 7091 4410 / 20
Lancaster
01524 68112
Leeds
0113 283 0040
Leicester
0116 222 5700
Leigh
01942 673639
Lewes Combined Court
01273 480400
Lincoln Combined Court
01522 883000
Liverpool Combined Court
0151 473 7373
Llanelli
01554 757171
Llangefni
01248 750225
Lowestoft
01502 586047
Ludlow
01584 872091
Luton
01582 506700
Macclesfield
01625 412800
Maidstone Combined
Court
01622 202000
Manchester
0161 954 1800
Mansfield
01623 656406
Mayor's & City Of London
Court
020 7796 5400
Medway
01634 810720
Melton Mowbray
01634 810720
Merthyr Tydfil Combined
Court
01685 358222
Middlesborough County
Court at Teesside
Combined Court
01642 340000
Milton Keynes
01908 302800
Mold
01352 707330
Morpeth & Berwick
01670 512221
Neath and Port Talbot
01639 642267
Nelson
01282 601177
Newark
01636 703607
Newbury County Court
01635 40928
Newcastle Combined
Court
0191 201 2000
Newport (Gwent) County
Court
01633 227150
Newport (Isle Of Wight)
01983 526821

North Shields
0191 2982339
Northampton Combined
Court
01604 470400
Northwich
01606 42554
Norwich Combined Court
01603 728200
Nottingham
0115 910 3500
Nuneaton
01203 386134
Oldham
0161 290 4200
Oswestry
01691 652127
Oxford Combined Court
Centre
01865 264200
Penrith
01768 862535
Penzance
01736 362987
Peterborough Combined
Court
01733 349161
Plymouth Combined Court
01752 677400
Pontefract
01977 702357
Pontypool
01495 762248
Pontypridd
01443 490800
Poole
01202 741150
Portsmouth Combined
Court
023 9289 3000
Preston Combined Court
01772 844700
Rawtenstall
01706 214614
Reading
0118 987 0500
Redditch
01527 67822
Reigate
01737 763637
Rhyl
01772 844700
Romford
01708 775353
Rotherham
01709 364786
Rugby
01788 542543
Runcorn
01925 256700
St Albans
01727 856925
St Helens
01744 27544
Salford
0161 745 7511
Salisbury
01722 325444
Scarborough
01723 366361
Scunthorpe
01724 289111

Sheffield Combined Court
0114 281 2400
Shoreditch
020 7253 0956
Shrewsbury
01743 289069
Skegness
01205 366080
Skipton
01756 793315
Slough
01753 690300
South Shields
0191 456 3343
Southampton Combined Court
023 8021 3200
Southend
01702 601991
Southport
01704 531541
Stafford
01785 610730
Staines
01784 459175
Stockport
01614 747707
Stoke On Trent Combined Court
01782 854000
Stourbridge
01384 394232
Stratford upon Avon
01789 293056
Sunderland
0191 568 0750
Swansea Civil Justice Centre
01792 510350
Swindon Combined Court
01793 690500
Tameside
0161 331 5614
Tamworth
01827 62664
Taunton
01823 335972
Teesside Combined Court
01642 340000
Telford
01952 291045
Thanet
01843 221722
Torquay & Newton Abbot
01803 616791
Trowbridge
01225 752101
Truro Combined Court
01872 222340
Tunbridge Wells
01892 515515
Uxbridge
020 8561 8562
Wakefield
01924 370268
Walsall
01922 728855
Wandsworth
020 8333 4351
Warrington Combined Court
01925 256700

Warwick Combined Court Centre
01926 492276
Watford
01923 699400 / 1
Wellingborough
01933 226168 / 222393
Welshpool And Newtown
01938 552004
West London
020 7602 8444
Weston Super Mare
01934 626967
Weymouth & Dorchester
01305 752510
Whitehaven
01946 67788
Wigan
01942 246481
Winchester Combined Court
01962 814100
Willesden
020 8963 8200
Wolverhampton Combined Court
01902 481000
Woolwich
020 8854 2127
Worcester Combined Court
01905 730800
Worksop
01909 472358
Worthing
01903 221920
Wrexham
01978 296140
Yeovil
01935 474133
York
01904 629935

Northern Ireland courts

Antrim
028 9446 2661
Armagh
028 3572 2816
Ballymena
028 2564 9416
Banbridge
028 4062 3622
Bangor
028 9147 2626
Belfast
028 9147 2626
Coleraine
028 7034 3437
Craigavon
028 3834 1324
Derry
028 7136 3448
Downpatrick
028 4461 4621
Dungannon
028 8772 2992
Enniskillen
028 6632 2356
Larne
028 2827 2927
Limavady
028 7772 2688
Lisburn
028 9267 5336
Magherafelt
028 7963 2121
Newry
028 7963 2121
Newtownards
028 9181 4343
Omagh
028 8224 2056
Strabane
028 7138 2544

Sheriff courts, Scotland

Aberdeen
01224 657200
Airdrie
01236 751121
Alloa
01259 722734
Arbroath
01241 876600
Ayr
01292 268474
Banff
01261 812140
Campbeltown
01586 552503
Cupar
01334 652121
Dingwall
01349 863153
Dornoch
01862 810224
Dumbarton
01389 763266
Dumfries
01387 262334
Dundee
01382 229961

Dunfermline
01383 724666
Dunoon
01369 704166
Duns
01835 863231
Edinburgh
0131 225 2525
Elgin
01343 542505
Falkirk
01324 620822
Forfar
01307 462186
Fort William
01397 702087
Glasgow
0141 429 8888
Greenock
01475 787073
Haddington
01620 822936
Hamilton
01698 282957
Inverness
01463 230782
Jedburgh
01835 863231
Kilmarnock
01563 520211
Kirkcaldy
01592 260171
Kirkcudbright
01557 330574
Kirkwall
01856 872110
Lanark
01555 661531
Lerwick
01595 693914
Linlithgow
01506 842922
Livingston
01506 462118
Lochmaddy
01876 500340
Oban
01631 562414
Paisley
0141 887 5291
Peebles
01721 720204
Perth
01738 620546
Peterhead
01779 476676
Portree
01478 612191
Rothesay
01700 502982
Selkirk
01750 21269
Stirling
01786 462191
Stonehaven
01569 762758
Stornoway
01851 702231
Stranraer
01776 702138
Tain
01862 892518
Wick
01955 602846

Law centres

Law Centres Federation
020 7387 8570
www.lawcentres.org.uk

Avon & Bristol
0117 924 8662
Barnet
020 8203 4141
Battersea
020 7585 0716
Bradford
01274 306617
Brent Community
020 8451 1122
Bury
0161 272 0666
Cambridge House Law Centre
020 7703 3051
Camden Community
020 7284 6510
Cardiff
029 2049 8117
Carlisle
01228 515129
Central London
020 7839 2998
Chesterfield
01246 550674
Coventry
024 7622 3053
Croydon & Sutton Law Centre (SWLLC)
020 8667 9226
Derby
01332 344557
Devon
01752 519794
Enfield Law Centre
020 8807 8888
Gateshead
0191 478 2847
Gloucester
01452 423492
Greenwich Community
020 8305 3350
Hackney Community
020 8985 8364
Hammersmith & Fulham
020 8741 4021
Harehills & Chapeltown
0113 249 1100
Hillingdon
020 8561 9400
Hounslow
020 8570 9505
Isle of Wight Law Centre
01983 524715
Islington
020 7607 2461
Kingston & Richmond Law Centre (SWLLC)
020 8547 2882
Lambeth
020 7737 9780

Leicester
0116 255 3781
Lewisham
020 8692 5355
Liverpool
0151 709 7222
Luton
01582 481000
Newcastle
0191 230 4777
North Kensington
020 8969 7473
North Manchester
0161 205 5040
Nottingham
0115 978 7813
Oldham
0161 627 0925
Paddington
020 8960 3155
Plumstead Community
020 8855 9817
Rochdale
01706 657766
Saltley & Nechells
0121 328 2307
Sheffield
0114 273 1888
South Manchester
0161 225 5111
Southwark
020 7732 2008
Springfield
020 8767 6884
Stockport
0161 476 6336
Thamesmead
020 8311 0555
Tottenham
020 8800 5354
Tower Hamlets
020 7247 8998
Trafford Law Centre
0161 872 3669
Vauxhall Law and Information Centre
0151 330 0239
Wandsworth & Merton
020 8767 2777
Warrington Community
01925 651104
Wiltshire
01793 486926
Wythenshawe
0161 498 0905 / 6
Northern Ireland: Belfast
028 9024 4401
Northern Ireland: western area
028 7126 2433

Prisons

Prison services

National Offender Management Service
0870 000 1585
www.hmprisonservice.gov.uk
www.homeoffice.gov.uk
PRESS: *020 7035 4381*
Victim helpline: 0845 758 5112
Her Majesty's Inspectorate of Prisons for England and Wales (HMIP)
020 7035 2136
www.homeoffice.gov.uk
Northern Ireland Prison Service
028 9052 5065
www.niprisonservice.gov.uk
Parole Board for England and Wales
0870 420 3505
www.paroleboard.gov.uk
Prisons Ombudsman for England and Wales
020 7035 2876
www.ppo.gov.uk
Scottish Parole Board
0131 244 8373
www.scottishparoleboard.gov.uk
Scottish Prison Service
0131 244 8745
www.sps.gov.uk
Scottish Prisons Inspectorate
0131 244 8481

Professional bodies

Prison Governors Association
020 7217 8591
www.prisongovernors.org.uk
Prison Officers Association
020 8803 0255
www.poauk.org.uk
National Association of Official Prison Visitors
01234 359763
www.brittain.plus.com/naopv
National Association of Probation Officers (Napo)
020 7223 4887
www.napo.org.uk
Trade union and professional association for family court and probation staff

Campaign groups

Action for Prisoners' Families
020 8812 3600
www.prisonersfamilies.org.uk
Apex Trust
020 7920 0317
www.apextrust.com
Campaign for Freedom of Information
020 7831 7477
www.cfoi.org.uk
Committee on the Administration of Justice (Northern Ireland)
028 9096 1122
www.caj.org.uk
Forum for Prisoner Education
020 8525 9599
www.fpe.org.uk
Howard League for Penal Reform
020 7249 7373
www.howardleague.org
Inquest
020 7263 1111
www.inquest.org.uk
Justice
020 7329 5100
www.justice.org.uk
Liberty
020 7403 3888
www.liberty-human-rights.org.uk
Minority Rights Group
020 7422 4200
www.minorityrights.org
National Association for the Care and Resettlement of Offenders
020 7582 6500
www.nacro.org.uk
Prison Reform Trust
020 7251 5070
www.prisonreformtrust.org.uk
Prisoners Advice Service
020 7253 3323
www.prisonersadviceservice.org.uk
Prisoners Family and Friends
020 7403 4091
www.prisonersfamiliesand friends.org.uk
Unit for the Arts and Offenders
01227 470 629
www.a4offenders.org.uk
Unlock
01634 247350
www.unlockprison.org.uk
National association of ex-offenders
Women in Prison
020 7226 5879
www.womeninprison.org.uk

Prisons for men

Acklington
01670 762300
Albany
01983 556300
Altcourse*
0151 522 2000
Ashfield*
0117 303 8000
Ashwell
01572 884100
Aylesbury
01296 444000
Bedford
01234 373000
Belmarsh
020 8331 4400
Birmingham
0121 345 2500
Blakenhurst
01527 400500
Blantyre House
01580 213200
Blundeston
01502 734500
Brinsford
01902 532450
Bristol
0117 372 3100
Brixton
020 8588 6000
Brockhill
01527 552650
Bullingdon
01869 353100
Camp Hill
01983 554600
Canterbury
01227 862800
Cardiff
02920 923100
Castington
01670 382100
Channings Wood
01803 814600
Chelmsford
01245 272000
Coldingley
01483 804300
Dartmoor
01822 892000
Deerbolt
01833 633200
Doncaster*
01302 760870
Dorchester
01305 214500
Dovegate*
01283 829400
Downview
020 8929 3300
Durham
0191 332 3400
Edmunds Hill
01440 743500
Elmley
01795 882000
Erlestoke
01380 814250
Everthorpe
01430 426500

Featherstone
01902 703000
Feltham
020 8844 5000
Ford
01903 663000
Forest Bank*
0161 925 7000
Foston Hall
01283 584300
Frankland
0191 332 3000
Full Sutton
01759 475100
Garth
01772 443300
Gartree
01858 436600
Glen Parva
0116 228 4100
Gloucester
01452 453000
Grendon
01296 443000
Guys Marsh
01747 856400
Haverigg
01229 713000
Hewell Grange
01527 552000
High Down
020 8722 6300
Highpoint
01440 743100
Hindley
01942 855000
Hollesley Bay
01394 412400
Holme House
01642 744000
Hull
01482 282200
Huntercombe
01491 643100
Kingston
023 9295 3100
Kirkham
01772 675400
Kirklevington Grange
01642 792600
Lancaster Castle
01524 565 100
Lancaster Farms
01524 563450
Latchmere House
020 8588 6650
Leeds
0113 203 2600
Leicester
0116 228 3000
Lewes
01273 785100
Leyhill
01454 264000
Lincoln
01522 663000
Lindholme
01302 524700
Littlehey
01480 333000
Liverpool
0151 530 4000

Long Lartin
01386 835100
Lowdham Grange*
0115 966 9200
Maidstone
01622 775300
Manchester
0161 817 5600
Moorland
01302 523000
The Mount
01442 836300
Northallerton
01609 785100
North Sea Camp
01205 769300
Norwich
01603 708600
Nottingham
0115 872 3000
Onley
01788 523400
Parc*
01656 300200
Parkhurst
01983 554000
Pentonville
020 7023 7000
Peterborough*
01733 217500
Portland
01305 825600
Prescoed
01291 675000
Preston
01772 444550
Ranby
01777 862000
Reading
0118 908 5000
Risley
01925 733000
Rochester
01634 803100
Rye Hill*
01788 523300
Send
01483 471000
Shepton Mallett
01749 823300
Shrewsbury
01743 273000
Spring Hill
01296 443000
Stafford
01785 773000
Standford Hill
01795 884500
Stocken
01780 795100
Stoke Heath
01630 636000
Sudbury
01283 584000
Swaleside
01795 804100
Swansea
01792 485300
Swinfen Hall
01543 484000
Thorn Cross
01925 805100

Usk
01291 671600
The Verne
01305 825000
Wakefield
01924 246000
Wandsworth
020 8588 4000
Warren Hill
01394 412400
Wayland
01953 804100
Wealstun
01937 848500
The Weare
01305 825400
Wellingborough
01933 232700
Werrington
01782 463300
Wetherby
01937 544200
Whatton
01949 859200
Whitemoor
01354 602350
Winchester
01962 723000
Wolds*
01430 428000
Woodhill
01908 722000
Wormwood Scrubs
020 8588 3200
Wymott
01772 444000

Prisons for women

Askham Grange
01904 772000
Bronzefield*
01784 425690
Buckley Hall
01706 514300
Bullwood Hall
01702 562800
Cookham Wood
01634 202500
Drake Hall
01785 774100
East Sutton Park
01622 845000
Eastwood Park
01454 382100
Exeter
01392 415650
Holloway
020 7979 4400
Low Newton
0191 376 4000
Morton Hall
01522 666700
New Hall
01924 844200
Peterborough*
01733 217500
Styal
01625 553000

private prisons

Law

Prisons in Scotland

Aberdeen
01224 238300
Barlinnie
0141 7702000
Castle Huntly
01382 319333
Cornton Vale
01786 832591
Dumfries
01387 261218
Edinburgh
0131 444 3000
Glenochil
01259 760471
Greenock
01475 787801
Inverness
01463 229000
Kilmarnock*
01563 548800
Low Moss
0141 7624848
Noranside
01382 319333
Perth
01738 622293
Peterhead
01779 479101
Polmont
01324 711558
Shotts
01501 824000

Prisons in Northern Ireland

Hydebank Wood
028 9025 3666
Maghaberry
028 9261 1888
Magilligan
028 7776 3311

Immigration removal centres

Dover
01304 246400
Haslar
023 9260 4000

private prisons

Legal advice

Activists Legal Project
01865 243772
www.activistslegalproject.org.uk
Legal information for activists
Asylum Aid
020 7377 5123
www.asylumaid.org.uk
Advice line: 020 7247 8741
CHAS Central London
020 7723 5928
www.chascl.org.uk
Housing and debt advice
Children's Legal Centre
01206 872466
www.childrenslegalcentre.com
Community Legal Service
0845 345 4345
www.clsdirect.org.uk
Counsel & Care
020 7241 8555
www.counselandcare.org.uk
Advice line: 0845 300 7585
Detainee Support & Help Unit
020 7358 3655
www.dshu.org.uk
Disability Law Service
020 7791 9800
Environmental Law Foundation
020 7404 1030
www.elflaw.org
Housing Justice
020 7723 7273
www.housingjustice.org.uk
Joint Council for the Welfare of Immigrants
020 7251 8708
www.jcwi.org.uk
Legal Action Group
020 7833 2931
www.lag.org.uk
Legal Services Research Centre
www.lsrc.org.uk
Liberty (the National Council for Civil Liberties)
www.yourrights.org.uk
Advice line: 0845 123 2307
Maternity Alliance
020 7490 7639
www.maternityalliance.org.uk
Information line: 020 7490 7638
National Youth Advocacy Service
0151 649 8700
www.nyas.net
Young people helpline: 0800 616101
Prisoners Advice Service
020 7253 3323
www.prisonersadviceservice.org.uk
Advice line: 0800 018 2156
Prisoners' Families Helpline
0808 808 2003
www.prisonersfamilieshelpline.org.uk
Public Law Project
020 7697 2190
www.publiclawproject.org.uk
Refugee Legal Centre
020 7780 3200
www.refugee-legal-centre.org.uk
Advice line: 020 7780 3220
Scottish Human Rights Centre
0141 332 5960
www.scottishhumanrightscentre.org.uk
UK Legal
0845 2801976
www.uklegal.com

Religion

Inter Faith Network for the UK
020 7931 7766
ifnet@interfaith.org.uk
www.interfaith.co.uk

Anglicanism

Anglican Communion
020 7313 3900
www.anglicancommunion.org
Archbishop of Canterbury
020 7898 1200
www.archbishopofcanterbury.org
Archbishop of York
01904 707021
www.bishopthorpepalace.co.uk
/archbishop.html
Church in Wales
029 2034 8200
suebrookman@churchinwales.org.uk
www.churchinwales.org.uk
Church of England
020 7898 1000
www.cofe.anglican.org
Church of Ireland
00 353 1 497 8422
enquiries@ireland.anglican.org
www.ireland.anglican.org
Record Centre
020 7898 1400
www.lambethpalacelibrary.org
Scottish Episcopal Church
0131 225 6357
office@scotland.anglican.org
www.scotland.anglican.org

Catholicism

Catholic Church
020 7233 8196
www.catholic-ew.org.uk
Media Office
020 7901 4800
Provinces/ Archbishops
Armagh 028 3752 2045
Birmingham 0121 236 5535
Edinburgh 0131 452 8244
Glasgow 0141 226 5898
Cardiff 029 2022 0411
Liverpool 0151 522 1000
Southwark 020 7928 5592
Westminster 020 7798 9055
Catholic Enquiry Office
020 8458 3316
www.life4seekers.co.uk

Other Christian

Baptist Union
01235 517700
www.baptist.org.uk
Church of Christ, Scientist
00 1 617 450 2000
www.themotherchurch.org
Church of Jesus Christ of Latter Day Saints (Mormons)
0121 712 1207
www.lds.org
Church of Scotland
0131 225 5722
www.churchofscotland.org.uk
Churches Together in Britain & Ireland
020 7654 7254
www.ctbi.org.uk
Churches Together in England
020 7529 8141
www.churches-together.org.uk
Congregational Federation
0115 911 1460
www.congregational.org.uk
Council of Churches for Britain
020 7654 7254
www.interchurchfamilies.org
Eastern Orthodox Churches
Greek: 020 7723 4787
Russian: 020 7584 0096
Free Church of England
admin@fce-ec.org.uk
www.fce-ec.org.uk
Free Presbyterian Church of Scotland
daross@donaldalexander.freeserve
.co.uk
www.fpchurch.org.uk
Independent Methodist Churches
wpark@fimc.org.uk
www.fimc.org.uk
International Churches of Christ
info@icoc.org.uk
www.icoc.org.uk
Jehovah's Witnesses
020 8906 2211
www.watchtower.org
Jesus Army
0845 123 5550
www.jesusarmy.org.uk
Lutheran Council of GB
020 7554 2900
www.lutheran.org.uk
Methodist Church
020 7467 5221
www.methodist.org.uk
Moravian Church
020 8883 3409
www.moravian.org.uk
New Testament Church of God
01604 643311
www.ntcg.org.uk
Pentecostal Assemblies of God
0115 921 7272
www.aog.org.uk

Presbyterian Church in Ireland
028 9032 2284
www.presbyterianireland.org
Presbyterian Church of Wales
029 2062 7465
www.ebcpcw.org.uk
Quakers
020 7663 1000
www.quaker.org.uk
Salvation Army
020 7332 0101
www.salvationarmy.org
Seventh Day Adventist Church
01923 672251
www.adventist.org
Unitarian Churches
020 7240 2384
www.unitarian.org.uk
United Free Church of Scotland
0141 332 3435
www.ufcos.org.uk
United Reform Church
020 7916 2020
www.urc.org.uk
World Council of Churches
00 41 22 791 6111
www.wcc-coe.org

Buddhism

BuddhaNet
bdea@buddhanet.net
www.buddhanet.net
London Buddhist Centre (LBC)
0845 458 4716
www.lbc.org.uk
London Buddhist Vihara
020 8995 9493
www.londonbuddhistvihara.co.uk
The Buddhist Society
020 7834 5858
www.thebuddhistsociety.org
Cardiff Buddhist Centre
029 2046 2492
www.cardiffbuddhistcentre.com
Edinburgh Buddhist Centre
0131 228 3333
www.edinburghbuddhistcentre.org.uk
Friends of the Western Buddhist Order
0845 458 4716
www.fwbo.org
Network of Buddhist Organisations
0845 345 8978
www.nbo.org.uk
Potala Buddhist Centre, Belfast
028 9023 8090
www.potalacentre.org.uk
Society Krishna Consciousness
01923 857244
www.iskcon.org.uk

Islam

Islamic Centre of England
020 7604 5501
www.ic-el.org
Islamic Cultural Centre
020 7724 3363
www.islamicculturalcentre.co.uk
Islamic Digest
00 255 744 078830
www.islamicdigest.org
Muslim Council of Britain
020 8432 0585 / 6
www.mcb.org.uk
Muslim Directory
020 8799 4455
www.muslimdirectory.co.uk

Hinduism

Hindu Centre, London
020 7485 8200
Hindunet
hsc@hindunet.org
www.hindunet.org
Hindu Links
www.hindulinks.org

Judaism

Board of Deputies of British Jews
020 7543 5400
www.bod.org.uk
Jewish Network
07976 220273
www.jewish.co.uk
United Synagogue
020 8343 8989
www.unitedsynagogue.org.uk

Sikhism

Sikh Missionary Society
020 8574 1902
www.sikhs.org
Sikhnet
00 505 753 3117
www.sikhnet.com
Sikh Women's Network
info@sikhwomen.com
www.Sikhwomen.com

Spiritualism and paganism

Aetherius Society
020 7736 4187
www.aetherius.org
British Druid Order
sparrowhawk@britishdruidorder.co.uk
www.druidorder.demon.co.uk
Order of Bards, Ovates & Druids
01273 470 888
www.druidry.org
Pagan Federation
0906 3020184
www.paganfed.org
PaganLink
www.paganlink.org
Satanism
HPNadramia@churchofsatan.com
www.churchofsatan.com
Spiritualist Association of Great Britain
info@spiritualuk.com
www.spiritualuk.com
Spiritualists' National Union
0845 4580 768
www.snu.org.uk
Theosophical Society
info@thesociety.org
www.thesociety.org
Transcendental Meditation
08705 143733
www.transcendental-meditation
.org.uk.

Other religions

Baha'i Community of UK
020 7584 2566
www.bahai.org.uk
Church of Scientology
01342 318229
www.scientology.org
Jainism
vinod@jainworld.com
www.jainworld.com
World Zoroastrian Organisation
President@w-z-o.org
www.w-z-o.org

Humanism and atheism

Association of Irish Humanists
00 353 1286 9870
www.irish-humanists.org
British Humanist Assoc
020 7079 3580
www.humanism.org.uk
Gay and Lesbian Humanist Association
01926 858 450
www.galha.freeserve.co.uk/galha.htm
International Humanist and Ethical Union
www.iheu.org
National Secular Society
020 7404 3126
www.secularism.org.uk
Rationalist Press Association
020 7436 1151
www.rationalist.org.uk
South Place Ethical Society
library@ethicalsoc.org.uk
www.ethicalsoc.org.uk

Society

Government

Deputy Prime Minister
020 7944 4400
www.odpm.gov.uk
PRESS: *020 7944 4297*
Health
020 7210 4850
www.dh.gov.uk
PRESS: *020 7210 5221*
Home Office
0870 000 1585
www.homeoffice.gov.uk
PRESS: *020 7035 4381*
Work and Pensions
020 7238 0800
www.dwp.gov.uk
PRESS: *020 7238 0866*

Government agencies

Charity Commission
0870 333 0123
www.charity-commission.gov.uk
PRESS: *020 7674 2323 / 32 / 33*
Children and Family Court Advisory Service
020 7510 7000
www.cafcass.gov.uk
PRESS: *020 7510 7036*
Child Support Agency
08457 133133
www.csa.gov.uk
PRESS: *020 7238 0866*
Commission for Racial Equality (CRE)
020 7939 0000
www.cre.gov.uk
Connexions
0808 001 3219
www.connexions.gov.uk
Advice and support for 13–19 year olds
Housing Corporation
0845 230 7000
www.housingcorp.gov.uk
Funding and regulation of housing associations
Immigration and Nationality Directorate
0870 606 7766
www.ind.homeoffice.gov.uk
Office of the Immigration Services Commissioner
020 7211 1500
www.oisc.gov.uk

Charity association

Institute of Fundraising
020 7840 1000
www.institute-of-fundraising.org.uk

Major charities

Action for Blind People
020 7635 4800
www.afbp.org
PRESS: *020 7635 4898*
ActionAid
020 7561 7561
www.actionaid.org.uk
PRESS: *020 7561 7614*
Age Concern England
020 8765 7200
www.ageconcern.org.uk
PRESS: *020 8765 7200*
Alzheimer's Society
020 7306 0606
www.alzheimers.org.uk
PRESS: *020 7306 0813 / 39*
ARC Addington Fund
024 7669 0587
www.arc-addingtonfund.org.uk
Arthritis Research Campaign
0870 850 5000
www.arc.org.uk
PRESS: *01246 541107*
Association for International Cancer Research
01334 477910
www.aicr.org.uk
Barnardo's
020 8550 8822
www.barnardos.org.uk
PRESS: *020 8498 7555*
Battersea Dogs' & Cats' Home
020 7622 3626
www.dogshome.org
PRESS: *020 7627 9294*
BBC Children in Need Appeal
020 8576 7788
www.bbc.co.uk/pudsey
Benenden Hospital Trust
01580 240333
www.benendenhospital.org.uk
PRESS: *01580 242472*
Birmingham Diocesan Trust
0121 236 5535
www.birminghamdiocese.org.uk
PRESS: *0121 427 2780*
Blue Cross
01993 822651
www.bluecross.org.uk
PRESS: *020 7932 4060*
British and Foreign Bible Society
01793 418100
www.biblesociety.org.uk
PRESS: *01793 418241*
British Heart Foundation
020 7935 0185
www.bhf.org.uk
PRESS: *020 7487 7172*
OUT OF HOURS: *07764 290381*
British Red Cross
0870 170 7000
www.redcross.org.uk
PRESS: *020 7793 7043 / 2*

British Tennis Foundation
020 7381 7000
www.lta.org.uk
PRESS: *020 7381 7009*
Cambridge Foundation
01223 332288
www.foundation.cam.ac.uk
PRESS: *01223 332300*
Cancer Research UK
020 7121 6699
www.cancerresearchuk.org
PRESS: *020 7061 8300*
Catholic Agency for Overseas Development
020 7733 7900
www.cafod.org.uk
PRESS: *020 7326 5557*
Cats Protection
0870 209 9099
www.cats.org.uk
PRESS: *08707 708 612*
ChildLine
020 7650 3200
www.childline.org.uk
PRESS: *020 7650 3240*
Children with Leukaemia Foundation
020 7404 0808
www.leukaemia.org
PRESS: *023 8045 4570*
Children's Society
0845 300 1128
www.childrenssociety.org.uk
PRESS: *020 7841 4422*
Choice Support
020 7261 4100
www.choicesupport.org.uk
Christian Aid
020 7620 4444
www.christian-aid.org.uk
PRESS: *020 7523 2421*
Christian Vision
0121 522 6087
www.christianvision.com
Christie Hospital Charitable Fund
0161 446 3988
www.christies.org
PRESS: *0161 446 3613*
Church of Jesus Christ of Latter Day Saints Great Britain
00 1 801 240 1000
www.lds.org.uk
PRESS: *0121 712 1207*
Church of Scotland Unincorporated Boards and Committees
0131 225 5722
www.churchofscotland.org.uk
PRESS: *0131 240 2243*
Comic Relief
020 7820 5555
www.comicrelief.com
Community Integrated Care
0151 420 3637
www.c-i-c.co.uk
PRESS: *0151 422 5352*

Concern Worldwide
020 7738 1033
www.concern.net
PRESS: *020 7801 2427 / 77*
Diabetes UK
020 7424 1000
www.diabetes.org.uk
PRESS: *020 7424 1165*
Disasters Emergency Committee
020 7387 0200
www.dec.org.uk
Dogs Trust
020 7837 0006
www.dogstrust.org.uk
PRESS: *020 7833 7650 / 70*
Donkey Sanctuary
01395 578222
www.thedonkeysanctuary.org.uk
PRESS: *01395 573097*
Fremantle Trust
01296 393055
www.fremantletrust.org
Great Ormond St Children's Charity
020 7916 5678
www.gosh.org
Guide Dogs for the Blind Association
0118 983 5555
www.guidedogs.org.uk
PRESS: *0118 983 8380*
Help the Aged
020 7278 1114
www.helptheaged.org.uk
PRESS: *020 7239 1942*
020 7837 4570
International Planned Parenthood Federation
020 7487 7900
www.ippf.org
PRESS: *020 7487 7879*
Islamic Relief
0121 605 5555
www.islamic-relief.org.uk
PRESS: *0121 622 0638*
Jewish Care
020 8922 2000
www.jewishcare.org
PRESS: *020 8922 2812*
Leonard Cheshire
020 7802 8200
www.leonard-cheshire.org
Leukaemia Research Fund
020 7405 0101
www.lrf.org.uk
PRESS: *020 7269 9019*
Liverpool Roman Catholic Archdiocesan Trust
0151 522 1020
www.archdiocese-of-liverpool.co.uk
PRESS: *0151 522 1007*
Macmillan Cancer Relief
020 7840 7840
www.macmillan.org.uk
PRESS: *020 7840 7821*
Marie Curie Cancer Care
020 7599 7777
www.mariecurie.uk
PRESS: *020 7599 7700*
Mencap
020 7454 0454
www.mencap.org.uk
PRESS: *020 7696 5524*

Mind
020 8519 2122
www.mind.org.uk
National Association for Mental Health
PRESS: *020 8522 1743*
Motability
01279 635999
www.motability.co.uk
PRESS: *01279 632024*
Multiple Sclerosis Society
020 8438 0700
www.mssociety.org.uk
PRESS: *020 7082 0820*
National Asthma Campaign
020 7786 4900
www.asthma.org.uk
PRESS: *020 7786 4949*
National Council of YMCAs
020 8520 5599
www.ymca.org.uk
PRESS: *020 7421 3008*
National Galleries of Scotland
0131 624 6200
www.nationalgalleries.org
www.natgalscot.ac.uk
National Missing Persons Helpline
020 8392 4545
www.missingpersons.org
PRESS: *020 8392 4510-3*
National Museum of Science and Industry
0870 870 4771
www.nmsi.ac.uk
PRESS: *020 7942 4357*
National Society for the Prevention of Cruelty to Children (NSPCC)
020 7825 2500
www.nspcc.org.uk
PRESS: *020 7825 2514 / 1373*
National Trust
0870 458 4000
www.nationaltrust.org.uk
PRESS: *0870 609 5380*
National Trust for Scotland
0131 243 9300
www.nts.org.uk
PRESS: *0131 243 9349*
NCH
020 7704 7000
www.nch.org.uk
PRESS: *020 7704 7111*
Oxfam
0870 333 2700, 01865 311311
www.oxfam.org.uk
PRESS: *01865 312498*
Parkinson's Disease Society of the UK
020 7931 8080
www.parkinsons.org.uk
PDSA
0800 917 2509
www.pdsa.org.uk
PRESS: *01952 290999*
Plan UK
020 7482 9777
www.plan-uk.org
Portsmouth Roman Catholic Diocesan Trustees Registered (PRCDTR)
01329 835583
www.portsmouth-dio.org.uk
PRESS: *07770 538693*

Prince's Trust
020 7543 1234
www.princes-trust.org.uk
PRESS: *020 7543 1318*
Royal National Institute of the Blind (RNIB)
020 7388 1266
www.rnib.org.uk
PRESS: *020 7391 2223*
Royal National Institute for Deaf People (RNID)
020 7296 8000
www.rnid.org.uk
PRESS: *020 7296 8137*
Roman Catholic Diocese of Hexham & Newcastle
0191 243 3300
www.rcdhn.org.uk
PRESS: *0191 228 0003*
Roman Catholic Diocese of Southwark
020 7928 2495
www.rcsouthwark.co.uk
Royal British Legion
020 7973 7200
www.britishlegion.org.uk
www.poppy.org.uk
PRESS: *020 7973 7296*
Royal Horticultural Society
020 7834 4333
www.rhs.org.uk
PRESS: *020 7821 3043*
Royal Marsden Hospital Charity
020 7352 8171
www.royalmarsden.org
PRESS: *020 7808 2605*
Royal National Lifeboat Institution (RNLI)
0845 122 6999
www.lifeboats.org.uk;
www.rnli.org.uk
PRESS: *01202 662218 /*
663184 / 663127
Royal Society for the Prevention of Cruelty to Animals (RSPCA)
Helpline: 0870 555 5999
enquiries: 0870 333 5999
www.rspca.org.uk
PRESS: *0870 754 0244*
Royal Society for the Protection of Birds (RSPB)
01767 680551
www.rspb.org.uk
PRESS: *01767 681577*
Salford Diocesan Trust
0161 736 1421
www.salforddiocese.org.uk
PRESS: *0161 330 2777*
Salvation Army
020 7367 4500
www.salvationarmy.org.uk
PRESS: *020 7367 4702*
Samaritan's Purse International
020 8559 2044
www.samaritanspurse.org.uk
PRESS: *0131 624 1155*
Save the Children (UK)
020 7012 6400
www.savethechildren.org.uk
PRESS: *020 7012 6841*
Scope
020 7619 7100
www.scope.org.uk
PRESS: *020 7619 7200*

Sense
020 7272 7774
www.sense.org.uk
National deafblind and rubella association
PRESS: *020 7561 3405*

Sheffield City Trust
0114 223 3610
www.sivltd.com
PRESS: *0114 221 0380*

Shelter
0845 458 4590
www.shelter.org.uk
PRESS: *020 7505 2162*

Sightsavers
01444 446600
www.sightsavers.org.uk
PRESS: *01444 446655*

St John Ambulance
08700 10 49 50
www.sja.org.uk
PRESS: *020 7324 4210*

Stroke Association
020 7566 0300
www.stroke.org.uk
PRESS: *020 7566 1500*

Tate
020 7887 8000
www.tate.org.uk
PRESS: *020 7887 8730*

Tear Fund
0845 355 8355
www.tearfund.org
PRESS: *020 8943 7779*

Unicef
020 7405 5592
www.unicef.org.uk
PRESS: *020 7430 0162*

United Jewish Israel Appeal
020 8369 5000
www.ujia.org
PRESS: *020 8369 5028*

United Kingdom Evangelization Trust
08452 26 26 27
www.stewardship.org.uk
PRESS: *020 8502 8599*

Victoria and Albert Museum
020 7942 2000
www.vam.ac.uk
PRESS: *020 7942 2502*

Watch Tower Bible and Tract Society of Britain
020 8906 2211
www.watchtower.org

WaterAid
020 7793 4500
www.wateraid.org.uk
PRESS: *020 7793 4793*

Westminster Roman Catholic Diocesan Trust
020 7798 9036
www.rcdow.org.uk
PRESS: *020 7798 9031*

World Emergency Relief
0870 429 2129
www.wer-uk.org

World Vision UK
01908 841000
www.worldvision.org.uk
PRESS: *01908 841020*

WWF UK
01483 426444
www.wwf.org.uk
PRESS: *01483 412383*

Other charities and campaign groups

Children

Acorns Children's Hospice Trust
0121 248 4800
www.acorns.org.uk

Adoption and Fostering Information Line
0800 783 4086
www.adoption.org.uk

Anna Freud Centre
020 7794 2313
www.annafreudcentre.org
Psychoanalysis for children

Barnardo's
020 8550 8822
www.barnardos.org.uk

BBC Children in Need
020 8576 7788
www.bbc.co.uk/pudsey

Bliss
020 7820 9471
www.bliss.org.uk
National charity for premature or sick babies

Care and Relief For The Young
01489 788300
www.cry.org.uk

Child Concern
0161 832 8113
www.childconcern.org.uk

ChildHope
020 7065 0950
www.childhopeuk.org
Defending street children worldwide

ChildLine
020 7650 3200
www.childline.org.uk

Children and Armed Conflict Unit
01206 873483
www.essex.ac.uk/armedcon

Children with Leukaemia Foundation
020 7404 0808
www.leukaemia.org

Children's Society
0845 300 1128
www.childrenssociety.org.uk

CLIC Sargent
0845 301 0031
www.clicsargent.org.uk
Children's cancer charity

Coram Family
020 7520 0300
www.coram.org.uk
Working with vulnerable children

End Child Poverty
020 7843 1913
www.ecpc.org.uk

EveryChild
020 7749 2468
www.everychild.org.uk

Foyle Foundation
020 7430 9119
www.foylefoundation.org.uk
Distributes grants to arts, health and learning charities

Girlguiding UK
020 7834 6242
www.girlguiding.org.uk

Great Ormond St Children's Charity
020 7916 5678
www.gosh.org

Hope
01442 234561
www.hope-for-children.org
International charity for handicapped, orphaned, poor and exploited children

Hope and Homes for Children
01722 790111
www.hopeandhomes.org

Hyperactive Children's Support Group
01243 551313
www.hacsg.org.uk

International Planned Parenthood Federation
020 7487 7900
www.ippf.org

Kids Clubs Network
020 7512 2112
www.4children.org.uk

National Children's Bureau
020 7843 6000
www.ncb.org.uk

National Youth Agency
0116 242 7350
www.nya.org.uk

NCH
020 7704 7000
www.nch.org.uk
Support for vulnerable children

NSPCC
020 7825 2500
www.nspcc.org.uk

Plan UK
020 7482 9777
www.plan-uk.org
Children in developing countries

Prince's Trust
020 7543 1234
www.princes-trust.org.uk

Relate
0845 1 304016
www.relate.org.uk
Relationship guidance
PRESS: *0845 456 1210*

Ride Foundation
01372 467708
www.ridefoundation.org.uk
Drug awareness, life skills and citizenship programmes for schools

Save the Children (UK)
020 7012 6400
www.savethechildren.org.uk

Second Chance
023 9287 2790
www.second-chance.org.uk
Camping and fishing for disavantaged children

The Site
020 7226 8008
www.thesite.org.uk
Advice and help for young people
PRESS: *020 7288 7309*

Task Brasil Trust
020 7735 5545
www.taskbrasil.org.uk
UK charity for street children in Brazil

Trident Trust
020 7014 1400
www.thetridenttrust.org.uk
Unicef
020 7405 5592
www.unicef.org.uk
United Kingdom Missing Children
www.missingkids.co.uk
Variety Club Children's Charity
020 7428 8100
www.varietyclub.org.uk
War Child UK
020 7916 9276
www.warchild.org.uk
Whizz Kidz
020 7233 6600
www.whizz-kidz.org.uk
Children with disabilities
World Villages for Children
020 7629 3050
www.worldvillages.org
Young Enterprise
01865 776845
www.young-enterprise.org.uk

Citizenship

**Association for Citizenship
Teaching**
020 7367 0510
www.teachingcitizenship.org.uk
*Information and direct action across a
number of areas*
Citizenship Foundation
020 7367 0518
www.citizenshipfoundation.org.uk
Time for Citizenship
www.timeforcitizenship.com

Community

Anchor Trust
020 7759 9100
www.anchor.org.uk
PRESS: *020 7759 9104*
Army Benevolent Fund
020 7591 2000
www.armybenfund.org
Business in the Community
0870 600 2482
www.bitc.org.uk
Changemakers
01458 834767
www.changemakers.org.uk
Citizens Advice Bureaux
020 7833 2181
www.nacab.org.uk
Civil Service Benevolent Fund
020 8240 2400
www.csbf.org.uk
Coalfields Regeneration Trust
0800 064 8560
www.coalfields-regen.org.uk
Common Purpose
020 7608 8100
www.commonpurpose.org.uk
Communities that Care
020 7619 0123
www.communitiesthatcare.org.uk

Community Development Foundation
020 7226 5375
www.cdf.org.uk
Community Foundation
0191 222 0945
www.communityfoundation.org.uk
*Serving Tyne & Wear
and Northumberland*
Community Integrated Care
0151 420 3637
www.c-i-c.co.uk
Community Service Volunteers
020 7278 6601
www.csv.org.uk
Directory of Social Change
0845 077 7707
www.dsc.org.uk
Duke of Edinburgh's Award
01753 727400
www.theaward.org
Erskine Home
0141 812 1100
www.erskine.org.uk
For ex-servicemen
Groundwork
0121 236 8565
www.groundwork.org.uk
*Community improvement schemes in
rundown areas*
Gurkha Welfare Trust
020 7251 5234
www.gwt.org.uk
Nacro
020 7582 6500
www.nacro.org.uk
Crime reduction charity
**National Federation of Community
Organisations**
020 7837 7887
www.communitymatters.org.uk
Neighbourhood Renewal Unit
08450 828383
www.neighbourhood.gov.uk
Norwood Ravenswood Foundation
020 8420 6831
www.nwrw.org
Outward Bound Trust
020 7928 1991
www.outwardbound-uk.org
Police Rehabilitation Centre
01491 874499
www.flinthouse.co.uk
Prince's Trust
020 7543 1234
www.princes-trust.org.uk
Princess Royal Trust for Carers
020 7480 7788
www.carers.org
Quest Trust
01225 466307
www.quest-net.org
Raleigh International Trust
020 7371 8585
www.raleighinternational.org
Rathbone
0161 236 5358
www.rathbonetraining.co.uk
*Learning and training support for the
disadvantaged*
Royal Air Force Benevolent Fund
020 7580 8343
www.rafbf.org.uk

Royal Air Forces Association
020 8286 6667
www.rafa.org.uk
Royal British Legion
08457 725725
www.britishlegion.org.uk
www.poppy.org.uk
**Royal Commonwealth Ex-Services
League**
020 7973 7263
www.bcel.org.uk
Samaritans
020 8394 8300
www.samaritans.org
Scottish Community Foundation
0131 524 0300
www.scottishcommunityfoundation
.com
**Soldiers, Sailors, Airmen and
Families Association – Forces Help**
020 7403 8783
www.ssafa.org.uk
Sue Ryder Care
020 7400 0440
www.sueryedercare.org
*National volunteering campaign for
community welfare*
Time Bank
0845 456 1668
www.timebank.org.uk
Victim Support
020 7735 9166
www.victimsupport.org
Helps victims of crime
Voluntary Service Overseas
020 8780 7200
www.vso.org.uk

Disability

Disability Rights Commission
0845 762 2633
www.drc-gb.org
Independent body established by statute
Action for Blind People
020 7635 4800
www.afbp.org
PRESS: *020 7635 4898*
Afasic
020 7490 9410
www.afasic.org.uk
*For children and young adults with
communication impairments*
**British Wheelchair Sports
Foundation**
01296 395995
www.britishwheelchairsports.org
Christian Blind Mission
01223 484700
www.cbmuk.org.uk
Council for Disabled Children
020 7843 6000
www.ncb.org.uk
Dogs For the Disabled
08700 776600
www.dogsforthedisabled.org
**Elizabeth Foundation for
Pre-School Deaf Children**
023 9237 2735
www.elizabeth-foundation.org

Employment Opportunities for People with Disabilities
020 7448 5420
www.opportunities.org.uk
emPower
020 8355 2341
www.empowernet.org/empower
Aiming to influence policy on disability equipment services
Guide Dogs for the Blind
0118 983 5555
www.guidedogs.org.uk
Leonard Cheshire
020 7802 8200
www.leonard-cheshire.org
Creating opportunities with disabled people
Mencap
020 7454 0454
www.mencap.org.uk
Motability
01279 635999
www.motability.co.uk
National Autistic Society
020 7833 2299
www.nas.org.uk
National Deaf Children's Society
020 7490 8656
www.ndcs.org.uk
National Library for the Blind
0161 355 2000
www.nlb-online.org
Northern Counties School for the Deaf
0191 281 5821
www.northern-counties-school.co.uk
Physically Handicapped and Able Bodied Children
020 8667 9443
www.phabengland.org.uk
Riding for the Disabled
0845 658 1082
www.riding-for-disabled.org.uk
Royal National Institute of the Blind (RNIB)
020 7388 1266
www.rnib.org.uk
Royal National Institute for Deaf People (RNID)
020 7296 8000
www.rnid.org.uk
Royal Hospital for Neuro-disability
020 8780 4500
www.rhn.org.uk
Royal London Society for the Blind
01732 592500
www.rlsb.org.uk
Royal Star and Garter Home
020 8439 8000
www.starandgarter.org
St Dunstan's
020 7723 5021
www.st-dunstans.org.uk
Scope
020 7619 7100
www.scope.org.uk
Sense – National Deafblind and Rubella Association
020 7272 7774
www.sense.org.uk

Sightsavers
01444 446600
www.sightsavers.org.uk
The Shaw Trust
01225 716300
www.shaw-trust.org.uk
Provides training and work opportunities
United Response
020 8246 5200
www.united-response.co.uk
Support for those with learning difficulties and mental health problems
West Midlands Special Needs Transport
0121 333 3107
www.ringandride.org.uk .
Westminster Society for Mentally Handicapped Children and Adults
020 8968 7376
www.wspld.org.uk
World Vision UK
01908 841000
www.worldvision.org.uk

Diversity

Equal Opportunities Commission
0845 601 5901
www.eoc.org.uk

RACE

1990 Trust
020 7582 1990
www.blink.org.uk
Black community organisation
Black Enterprise
08700 76 5656
www.blackenterprise.co.uk
Ethnic Minority Foundation
020 8432 0307
www.emf-cemvo.co.uk

AGE

Age Concern England
020 8765 7200
www.ageconcern.org.uk
Help the Aged
020 7278 1114
www.helptheaged.org.uk
Age Positive
www.agepositive.gov.uk
Age diversity in employment
PRESS: *020 8238 8550*

SEXUALITY

Armed Forces Lesbian and Gay Association
0870 740 7755
www.aflaga.org.uk
Beyond Barriers
0141 574 0242
www.beyondbarriers.org.uk
Gay and Lesbian Association of Doctors and Dentists
0870 765 5606
www.gladd.org.uk

Lesbian and Gay Christian Movement
020 7739 1249
www.lgcm.org.uk
Lesbian and Gay Foundation
0161 235 8035
www.lgf.org.uk
Metro Centre
020 8265 3311
www.themetro.dircon.co.uk
Services for people questioning their sexuality
Outrage
020 8240 0222
http://outrage.nabumedia.com
Direct action for gay rights
Queerspace
info@queerspace.org.uk
www.queerspace.org.uk
Northern Ireland
Stonewall
020 7881 9440
www.stonewall.org.uk
The Gay Vote
webmaster@thegayvote.co.uk
www.thegayvote.co.uk
UK Lesbian and Gay Immigration Group
020 7620 6010
www.uklgig.org.uk

▶▶ DIVERSITY IN THE MEDIA
see page 393

Housing

Broadway
020 7089 9500
www.broadwaylondon.org
Working to house the homeless
Centrepoint
020 7426 5300
www.centrepoint.org.uk
Agency for young homeless
Chartered Institute of Housing
024 7685 1700
www.cih.org
Promoting high standards in housing provision
Connection at St Martin's
020 7766 5544
www.connection-at-stmartins.org.uk
Facilities for London's homeless
Crash
020 8742 0717
www.crash.org.uk
Construction and property industry homeless charity
Crisis
0870 011 3335
www.crisis.org.uk
Homeless charity
Defend Council Housing
020 7987 9989
www.defendcouncilhousing.org.uk
Empty Homes Agency
020 7828 6288
www.emptyhomes.com

Society

FEANTSA
00 32 2 538 6669
www.feantsa.org
European federation of homeless organisations

Foyer Federation
020 7430 2212
www.foyer.net
Accommodation and opportunities for the young

Groundswell
020 7737 5500
www.groundswell.org.uk
Support projects for the homeless

Homeless Link
020 7960 3010
www.homeless.org.uk
UK membership network for homeless agencies

Homes for Homeless People
01582 481426
www.homeline.dircon.co.uk

Housing Quality Network
01723 350099
www.hqnetwork.org.uk
Aims to improve quality of housing services

Joseph Rowntree Foundation
01904 629241
www.jrf.org.uk
Policy research and action on housing and social care

National Housing Federation
020 7067 1010
www.housing.org.uk
Representing the independent social housing sector

Paddington Churches Housing Association
020 8150 4100
www.pcha.org.uk
London housing association founded 1965

Peabody Trust
020 7021 4000
www.peabody.org.uk
London housing association

Room
020 7929 9494
www.room.org.uk
Forum for debate on housing and regeneration issues

Rural Housing Trust
020 7793 8114
www.ruralhousing.org.uk
Affordable housing in English villages

Shelter
0845 458 4590
www.shelter.org.uk

Thames Reach Bondway
020 7702 4260
www.thamesreachbondway.com
London homeless charity
PRESS: *020 7702 5646*

UK Co-Housing Network
coordinator@cohousing.co.uk
www.cohousing.co.uk
Network of resident-developed neighbourhoods

Immigration and refugees

Asylum Aid
020 7377 5123
www.asylumaid.org.uk

Immigration Advisory Service
020 7967 1200
www.iasuk.org

Immigration Law Practitioners' Association
020 7251 8383
www.ilpa.org.uk

Joint Council for the Welfare of Immigrants
020 7251 8708
www.jcwi.org.uk
Human rights for immigrants and asylum seekers in UK

Migration Research Unit
020 7679 7569
www.geog.ucl.ac.uk/mru

Refugee Action
020 7654 7700
www.refugee-action.org.uk

Refugee Council
020 7346 6700
www.refugeecouncil.org.uk

Scottish Asylum Seekers Consortium
0141 248 2396
www.asylumscotland.org.uk

Scottish Refugee Council
0141 248 9799
www.scottishrefugeecouncil.org.uk

Women

Abortion Rights
020 7278 5539
www.abortionrights.org.uk

Breast Cancer Campaign
020 7749 3700
www.bcc-uk.org

Breast Cancer Care
020 7384 2984
www.breastcancercare.org.uk

British Association of Women Entrepreneurs
01786 446044
www.bawe-uk.org

Campaign Against Domestic Violence
020 8520 5881
www.cadv.org.uk

Child and Woman Abuse Studies Unit
020 7133 5014
www.cwasu.org

Emily's List
contact@emilyslist.org.uk
www.emilyslist.org.uk
Campaign for Labour women MPs

European Women's Lobby
00 32 2 217 9020
www.womenlobby.org

Everywoman
0870 746 1800
www.everywoman.co.uk

The Fawcett Society
020 7253 2598
www.fawcettsociety.org.uk
Equality campaign

Feminist Library
020 7928 7789
www.feministlibrary.org.uk

Justice for Women
0113 262 0293
www.jfw.org.uk

League of Jewish Women
020 7242 8300
www.theljw.org

Marie Stopes International
020 7574 7400
www.mariestopes.org.uk
Reproductive healthcare worldwide

Meet A Mum Association
0845 120 6162
www.mama.co.uk

National Association for Premenstrual Syndrome
0870 777 2178
www.pms.org.uk

National Council of Women
01325 367375
www.ncwgb.org

National Federation of Women's Institutes
020 7371 9300
www.womens-institute.co.uk

Older Feminist Network
020 8346 1900
www.ofn.org.uk

Rights of Women
020 7251 6575
www.row.org.uk

Scottish Women's Aid
0131 475 2372
www.scottishwomensaid.co.uk

Single Parent Action Network
0117 951 4231
www.spanuk.org.uk

Suzy Lamplugh Trust
020 8876 0305
www.suzylamplugh.org
Personal safety

Womankind Worldwide
020 7549 0360
www.womankind.org.uk

Women and Manual Trades
020 7251 9192
www.wamt.org

Women's Aid
0117 944 4411
www.womensaid.org.uk

Women's Aid, Ireland
028 2563 2136
www.womens-aid.org.uk

The Women's Library
020 7320 2222
www.thewomenslibrary.ac.uk

Women's Link
020 7248 1200
www.womenslink.org.uk

Women's National Commission
020 7215 6933
www.thewnc.org.uk

YWCA (London)
01865 304200
www.ywca-gb.org.uk

■ Useful helplines

Afasic
0845 355 5577

Benefit Enquiry Line
0800 882200

Childline
0800 1111

Churches Child Protection Advisory Service
0845 120 4550

Deafblind UK
0800 132 320

Disability Living Allowance
0845 712 3456

Elder Abuse Response line
0808 808 8141

Gamblers Anonymous
0870 050 8880

Gingerbread Advice Line
0800 018 4318

Kidscape
0845 120 5204

Learning Disability Helpline
0808 808 1111

National Missing Persons Helpline
0500 700700

NSPCC National Child Protection Helpline
0808 800 5000

Parent Line
0808 800 2222

Refugee Helpline
0800 413 848

Relate
0845 130 4016

Runaway Helpline
0808 800 7070

Samaritans
08457 90 90 90

Saneline
0845 767 8000

Shelter London Line
0808 800 4444

Supportline for Survivors of Professional Abuse
0845 4 500 300

Victim Supportline
0845 303 0900

Welfare Foods Helpline
0800 056 2665

Winter Warmth Advice Line
0800 085 7000

Women's Aid National Domestic Violence Helpline
0845 702 3468

Sport

Government department

Department for Culture, Media and Sport
020 7211 6200
www.culture.gov.uk
PRESS: *020 7211 6145*

Official bodies

UK Sport
020 7211 5100
www.uksport.gov.uk
PRESS: *020 7211 5106*
Sport England
08458 508 508
London: 020 8778 8600
East: 01234 345222
East Midlands: 0115 982 1887
North: 0191 384 9595
North-west: 0161 834 0338
South-east: 0118 948 3311
South-west: 01460 73491
West Midlands: 0121 456 3444
Yorkshire: 0113 243 6443
www.sportengland.org
PRESS: *020 7273 1590*
Sport Scotland
0131 317 7200
Glenmore Lodge: 01479 861256
Cumbrae: 01475 530757
Inverclyde: 01475 674666
www.sportscotland.org.uk
PRESS: *0131 472 3309*
Sports Council for Northern Ireland
028 9038 1222
www.sportni.net
Sports Council for Wales
029 2030 0500
www.sports-council-wales.co.uk
PRESS: *029 2030 0597*

Olympics and Paralympics

London 2012
020 7093 5000
www.london2012.org
PRESS: *020 7093 5100*
British Olympic Association
020 8871 2677
www.olympics.org.uk
PRESS: *020 8871 2677 x233*
British Paralympic Association
020 7211 5222
www.paralympics.org.uk
PRESS: *01225 323518*
International Olympic Committee
00 41 21 621 6111
www.olympic.org
International Paralympic Committee
00 49 228 209 7200
www.paralympic.org

Football

GOVERNING BODIES

Fifa
00 41 222 7777
www.fifa.com
World Cup: Germany 2006
00 49 69 2006 0
www.fifaworldcup.com
Deutsche Fussball-Bund (German FA)
00 49 69 67880
www.dfb.de
UEFA
00 41 22 994 4444
www.uefa.com
PRESS: *00 41 22 99 44559*
Euro 2008, Austria and Switzerland
00 41 848 002008
PRESS: *00 41 22 99 445 9*
FA
020 7745 4545
www.the-fa.org
PRESS: *020 7745 4720*
Women's Football
www.thefa.com/womens
FA Premier League
020 7298 1600
www.premierleague.com
PRESS: *020 7298 1690*
Football League
0870 4420 1888
www.football-league.co.uk
PRESS: *0870 443 9383*
Nationwide Conference
conference@fastwebmedia.co.uk
www.footballconference.co.uk
PRESS:
pressoffice@footballconference.co.uk
Irish Football Association
028 9066 9458
www.irishfa.com
Scottish Football Association
0141 616 6000
www.scottishfa.co.uk
Football Association of Wales
029 2037 2325
www.faw.org.uk

NATIONAL STADIUMS

Millennium Stadium, Cardiff
0870 013 8600
www.millenniumstadium.com
Wembley Stadium
020 8795 9000
www.wembleystadium.com

PREMIERSHIP 2005–06

Arsenal FC
020 7704 4000
www.arsenal.com
PRESS: *020 7704 4010*

Aston Villa FC
0121 327 2299
www.avfc.co.uk
PRESS: *0121 326 1561*
Birmingham FC
0871 226 1875
www.blues.premiumtv.co.uk
PRESS: *0121 244 1501*
Blackburn Rovers FC
0870 111 3232
www.rovers.co.uk
PRESS: *01254 296171*
Bolton Wanderers FC
01204 673673
www.bwfc.co.uk
PRESS: *01204 673675*
Charlton AFC
020 8333 4000
www.cafc.co.uk
PRESS: *020 8333 4000*
Chelsea FC
0870 300 1212
www.chelseafc.co.uk
PRESS: *020 7957 8285*
Everton FC
0151 330 2200
www.evertonfc.com
PRESS: *0151 330 2278*
Fulham FC
0870 442 1222
www.fulham-fc.co.uk
PRESS: *020 8336 7510*
Liverpool FC
0151 263 2361
www.liverpoolfc.net
PRESS: *0151 230 5721*
Manchester City FC
0161 231 3200
www.mcfc.co.uk
PRESS: *0161 438 7631*
Manchester United FC
0161 868 8000
www.manutd.com
PRESS: *0161 868 8720*
Middlesbrough FC
0870 421 1986
www.mfc.co.uk
PRESS: *01325 729916*
Newcastle United FC
0191 201 8400
www.nufc.co.uk
PRESS: *0191 201 8420*
Portsmouth FC
023 9273 1204
www.pompeyfc.co.uk
Sunderland FC
0191 551 5000
www.safc.com
PRESS: *0191 551 5060*
Tottenham Hotspur FC
0870 420 5000
www.spurs.co.uk
PRESS: *020 8506 9043*
West Bromwich Albion FC
0870 066 8888
www.wba.co.uk
PRESS: *0870 066 2860 x4010*

West Ham United FC
020 8548 2748
www.whufc.co.uk
Wigan Athletic FC
01942 774000
www.wiganathletic.tv
PRESS: *01942 770411*

COCA-COLA FOOTBALL LEAGUE
CHAMPIONSHIP

Brighton and Hove Albion FC
01273 695 400
www.seagulls.co.uk
Burnley FC
0870 443 1882
www.burnleyfootballclub.com
Cardiff City FC
029 20 221001
www.cardiffcityfc.co.uk
Coventry City FC
0870 421 1987
www.ccfc.co.uk
Crewe Alexandra FC
01270 213 014
www.crewealex.net
Crystal Palace FC
020 8768 6000
www.cpfc.co.uk
Derby County FC
0870 444 1884
www.dcfc.co.uk
Hull City FC
0870 837 0003
www.hullcityafc.net
Ipswich Town FC
01473 400500
www.itfc.co.uk
Leeds United FC
0113 367 6000
www.lufc.co.uk
Leicester City FC
0870 040 6000
www.lcfc.co.uk
Luton Town FC
01582 411622
www.lutontown.co.uk
Millwall FC
020 723 21222
www.millwallfc.co.uk
Norwich City FC
01603 760 760
www.canaries.co.uk
Plymouth Argyle FC
01752 562561
www.pafc.co.uk
Preston North End FC
0870 442 1964
www.pnefc.net
Queens Park Rangers FC
020 8743 0262
www.qpr.co.uk
Reading FC
0118 968 1100
www.readingfc.co.uk
Sheffield United FC
0870 787 1960
www.sufc.co.uk
Sheffield Wednesday FC
0114 221 2121
www.swfc.co.uk
Southampton FC
0870 220 0000
www.saintsfc.co.uk

Stoke City FC
01782 592 222
www.stokecityfc.com
Watford FC
01923 496000
www.watfordfc.com
Wolverhampton Wanderers FC
0870 442 0123
www.wolves.co.uk

COCA-COLA LEAGUE ONE

AFC Bournemouth
01202 726300
www.afcb.co.uk
Barnsley FC
01226 211211
www.barnsleyfc.co.uk
Blackpool FC
0870 443 1953
www.blackpoolfc.co.uk
Bradford City FC
01274 773355
www.bradfordcityfc.co.uk
Brentford FC
08453 456 442
www.brentfordfc.co.uk
Bristol City FC
0117 963 0630
www.bcfc.co.uk
Chesterfield FC
01246 209765
www.chesterfield-fc.co.uk
Colchester United FC
01206 508800
www.cu-fc.com
Doncaster Rovers FC
01302 539441
www.doncasterroversfc.co.uk
Gillingham FC
01634 300000
www.gillinghamfootballclub.com
Hartlepool United FC
01429 272584
www.hartlepoolunited.co.uk
Huddersfield Town FC
01484 484100
www.htafc.com
Milton Keynes Dons FC
01908 607090
www.mkdons.com
Nottingham Forest FC
0115 982 4444
www.nottinghamforest.co.uk
Oldham Athletic FC
08712 262 235
www.oldhamathletic.co.uk
Port Vale FC
01782 655800
www.port-vale.co.uk
Rotherham FC
01709 512 434
www.themillers.co.uk
Scunthorpe United FC
01724 848077
www.scunthorpe-united.co.uk
Southend United FC
01702 304050
www.southendunited.co.uk
Swansea City FC
01792 616600
www.swanseacity.net
Swindon Town FC
0870 443 1969
www.swindontownfc.co.uk

Tranmere Rovers FC
0151 609 3333
www.tranmererovers.co.uk
Walsall FC
0870 442 0442
www.saddlers.co.uk
Yeovil Town FC
01935 423662
www.ytfc.net

COCA-COLA LEAGUE TWO

Barnet FC
020 8441 6932
www.barnetfc.premiumtv.co.uk
Boston United FC
01205 364406
www.bostonunited.co.uk
Bristol Rovers FC
0117 909 6648
www.bristolrovers.co.uk
Bury FC
0161 764 4881
www.buryfc.co.uk
Carlisle United FC
01228 526 237
www.carlisleunited.premiumtv.co.uk
Cheltenham Town FC
01242 573558
www.ctfc.com
Chester City FC
01244 371376
www.chestercityfc.net
Darlington FC
01325 387000
www.darlington-fc.net
Grimsby Town FC
01472 605050
www.gtfc.co.uk
Leyton Orient FC
020 8926 1111
www.leytonorient.net
Lincoln City FC
01522 880011
www.redimps.com
Macclesfield Town FC
01625 264686
www.mtfc.co.uk
Mansfield Town FC
0870 756 3160
www.mansfieldtown.net
Northampton Town FC
01604 757773
www.ntfc.co.uk
Notts County FC
0115 952 9000
www.nottscountyfc.co.uk
Oxford United FC
01865 337500
www.oufc.co.uk
Peterborough United FC
01733 563947
www.theposh.com
Rochdale FC
01706 644648
www.rochdaleafc.co.uk
Rushden & Diamonds FC
01933 652000
www.thediamondsfc.com
Shrewsbury Town FC
01743 360111
www.shrewsburytown.co.uk
Stockport County FC
0161 286 8888
www.stockportcounty.com

475

Torquay United FC
01803 328666
www.torquayunited.com
Wrexham AFC
01978 262129
www.wrexhamafc.co.uk
Wycombe Wanderers FC
01494 472100
www.wycombewanderers.co.uk

SCOTTISH PREMIER LEAGUE

Aberdeen FC
01224 650400
www.afc.co.uk
PRESS: *01224 650406*
Celtic FC
0845 671 1888
www.celticfc.co.uk
PRESS: *0141 551 4276*
Dundee United FC
01382 833166
www.dundeeunitedfc.co.uk
Dunfermline Athletic FC
01383 724295
www.dafc.co.uk
Falkirk FC
01324 624121
www.falkirkfc.co.uk
Heart of Midlothian FC
0131 200 7200
www.heartsfc.co.uk
Hibernian FC
0131 661 2159
www.hibernianfc.co.uk
Inverness Caledonian Thistle FC
01463 222880
www.caleythistleonline.com
Kilmarnoch FC
01563 545300
www.kilmarnockfc.co.uk
Livingston FC
01506 417000
www.livingstonfc.co.uk
Motherwell FC
01698 333333
www.motherwellfc.co.uk
Rangers FC
0870 600 1972
www.rangers.co.uk

FOOTBALL: OTHER BODIES

Professional Footballers' Association
0161 236 0575
www.givemefootball.com
Referees Association
024 7660 1701
www.footballreferee.org
Football Supporters' Federation
01634 319461
www.fsf.org.uk
Kick It Out
020 7684 4884
www.kickitout.org
football's anti-racism campaign
Show Racism the Red Card
0191 291 0160
www.srtrc.org
Supporters Direct
0870 160 0123
www.supporters-direct.org

Other sports

AMERICAN FOOTBALL

British American Football Association
01661 843179
www.bafa.org.uk

ANGLING

National Federation of Anglers
0115 9813535
www.nfadirect.com
National Federation of Sea Anglers
01364 644643
www.nfsa.org.uk
Salmon and Trout Association
020 7283 5838
www.salmon-trout.org

ARCHERY

The Grand National Archery Society
01952 677888
www.gnas.org

ATHLETICS

British Athletics
0161 406 6320
www.britishathletics.info
International Association of Athletics Federations
00 377 9310 8888
www.iaaf.org

BADMINTON

Badminton Association of England
01908 268400
www.baofe.co.uk
Welsh Badminton Union
029 2022 2082
www.welshbadminton.net
Scottish Badminton Union
0141 445 1218
www.scotbadminton.demon.co.uk
Badminton Union of Ireland
00 353 1 839 3028
www.badmintonireland.com

BALLOONING

British Balloon & Airship Club
0117 953 1231
www.bbac.org

BASEBALL

British Baseball Federation
020 7453 7055
www.baseballsoftballuk.com

BASKETBALL

English Basketball Association
0870 7744225
www.englandbasketball.co.uk
Basketball Association of Wales
07768 044443
www.basketballwales.com

Basketball Scotland
0131 317 7260
www.basketball-scotland.com

BIATHLON

British Biathlon Union
01874 730049
www.britishbiathlon.com
Bobsleigh
British Bobsleigh Association
01225 386802
www.british-bobsleigh.com

BOWLING

English Bowling Association
01903 820222
www.bowlsengland.com
Welsh Bowling Association
01446 733745
Scottish Bowling Association
01292 294623
www.scottish-bowling.co.uk
Irish Bowling Association
028 9065 5076
www.bowlsireland.com

BOXING

Amateur Boxing Association of England
020 8778 0251
www.abae.co.uk
Amateur Boxing Scotland
07900 003206
www.garnockboxing.com
British Boxing Board of Control
029 2036 7000
www.bbbofc.com
International Boxing Federation
00 1 973 414 0300
www.ibf-usba-boxing.com
Irish Amateur Boxing Association
00 353 1 453 3371
www.iaba.ie
World Boxing Association (Venezuela)
00 58 244 663 1584
www.wbaonline.com
World Boxing Organisation
00 1 787 765 4444
www.wbo-int.com

CANOEING

British Canoe Union
0115 982 1100
www.bcu.org.uk

CAVING

British Caving Association
www.british-caving.org.uk

CRICKET

England and Wales Cricket Board
020 7432 1200
www.ecb.co.uk
Cricket Scotland
0131 313 7420
www.scottishcricket.org

Marylebone Cricket Club (Lord's)
020 7616 8500
www.lords.org.uk

CROQUET

Croquet Association
01242 242318
www.croquet.org.uk

CURLING

British Curling Association
01234 315174
www.britishcurlingassociation.org.uk
Royal Caledonian Curling Club
0131 333 3003
www.royalcaledoniancurlingclub.org

CYCLING

British Cycling Federation
0870 871200
www.bcf.uk.com

EQUESTRIANISM

British Equestrian Federation
024 7669 8871
www.bef.co.uk
British Show Jumping Association
024 7669 8800
www.bsja.co.uk

FENCING

British Fencing Association
020 8742 3032
www.britishfencing.com

GOLF

English Golf Union
01526 354500
www.englishgolfunion.org
Welsh Golfing Union
01633 430830
www.welshgolf.org
Scottish Golf Union
01382 549500
www.scottishgolfunion.org
Golfing Union of Ireland, Ulster branch
028 9042 3708
www.gui.ie
Ladies Golf Union
01334 475811
www.lgu.org
R&A, St Andrews
01334 460000
www.randa.org
Open Championship
www.opengolf.com
St Andrews Links
01334 466666
www.standrews.org.uk

GYMNASTICS

British Gymnastics
01952 820330
www.baga.co.uk

HANDBALL

England Handball
01706 229354
www.englandhandball.com

HOCKEY

English Hockey Association
01908 544644
www.englandhockey.co.uk
Welsh Hockey Union
029 2057 3940
www.welsh-hockey.co.uk
Scottish Hockey Union
0131 453 9070
www.scottish-hockey.org.uk
Irish Hockey Assoc
00 353 1 260 0028
www.hockey.ie

HORSE RACING

The Jockey Club
020 7189 3800
www.thejockeyclub.co.uk
Ascot
01344 622211
www.ascot.co.uk
Aintree (Grand National)
0151 523 2600
www.aintree.co.uk
Epsom (Derby)
01372 726311
www.epsomderby.co.uk

ICE HOCKEY

Ice Hockey UK
0115 924 1441
www.icehockeyuk.co.uk

ICE SKATING

National Ice Skating Association of UK
0115 988 8060
www.iceskating.org.uk

MARTIAL ARTS

British Aikido Board
020 8304 8430
www.aikido-baa.org.uk
British Ju-Jitsu Association
0870 774 1122
www.bjjagb.com
British Judo Association
01509 631670
www.britishjudo.org.uk
British Kendo Association
john.howell@kendo.org.uk
www.kendo.org.uk
English Karate Governing Body
01302 337645
www.ekgb.org.uk
Tae Kwon-Do Association of Great Britain
0800 052 5960
www.tagb.biz

KORFBALL

British Korfball Association
020 8395 2306
www.korfball.co.uk

LACROSSE

English Lacrosse Association
07976 258191
www.englishlacrosse.co.uk
PRESS: *07931 376811*

LUGE

Great Britain Luge Association
01684 576604
www.gbla.org.uk

MODERN PENTATHLON

Modern Pentathlon Association of Great Britain
01225 386808
www.mpagb.org.uk

MOTOR SPORTS

Auto-Cycle Union
01788 566400
www.acu.org.uk
Federation Internationale de L'Automobile (FIA)
00 33 1 4312 4455
www.fia.com
Royal Automobile Club Motor Sports Association
01753 765 000
www.msauk.org

MOUNTAINEERING

British Mountaineering Council
0870 010 4878
www.thebmc.co.uk

NETBALL

All England Netball Association
01462 442344
www.england-netball.co.uk
Welsh Netball Association
029 2023 7048
www.welshnetball.co.uk
Netball Scotland
0141 572 0114
www.netballscotland.com

ORIENTEERING

British Orienteering Federation
01629 734042
www.britishorienteering.org.uk

PARACHUTING

British Parachute Association
0116 278 5271
www.bpa.org.uk

PETANQUE

British Petanque Association
024 7645 7815
www.britishpetanque.org.uk

POLO

Hurlingham Polo Association
01367 242828
www.hpa-polo.co.uk

POOL

English Pool Association
01706 642770
www.epa.org.uk

ROUNDERS

National Rounders Association
0114 248 0357
www.nra-rounders.co.uk

ROWING

Amateur Rowing Association
0870 060 7100
www.ara-rowing.org

RUGBY

The Rugby Football League
0113 232 9111
www.rfl.uk.com
**British Amateur Rugby League
Association**
01484 544131
www.barla.org.uk
Rugby Football Union
020 8892 2000
www.rfu.com
Welsh Rugby Union
0870 013 8600
www.wru.co.uk
Scottish Rugby Union
0131 346 5000
www.sru.org.uk
Irish Rugby Union
00 353 1 647 3800
www.irishrugby.ie
Rugby Football Union for Women
020 8831 7996
www.rfu-women.co.uk

SAILING

Royal Yachting Association
08453 450400
www.rya.org.uk

SCUBA DIVING

British Sub-Aqua Club
0151 350 6200
www.bsac.com

SHOOTING

**Great Britain Target Shooting
Federation**
07775 640960
www.gbtsf-worldclass.co.uk

SKIING AND SNOWBOARDING

British Ski & Snowboard Federation
0131 445 7676
www.snowsportgb.com
Snowsport Scotland
0131 445 4151
www.snowsportscotland.org

SOFTBALL

British Softball Federation
020 7453 7055
www.baseballsoftballuk.com

SQUASH

England Squash
0161 231 4499
www.englandsquash.com
Scottish Squash
0131 317 7343
www.scottishsquash.org
Squash Wales
01633 682108
www.squashwales.co.uk
Ulster Squash
028 9038 1222
www.ulstersquash.com

SURFING

British Surfing Association
01673 876474
www.britsurf.co.uk

SWIMMING

**Amateur Swimming Federation of
Great Britain**
01509 618700
www.britishswimming.org

TABLE TENNIS

English Table Tennis Association
01424 722525
www.englishtabletennis.org.uk

TENNIS

Lawn Tennis Association
020 7381 7000
www.lta.org.uk
Tennis and Rackets Association
020 8333 4267
www.irtpa.com

TENPIN BOWLING

British Tenpin Bowling Association
020 8478 1745
www.btba.org.uk

TRIATHLON

British Triathlon Association
01509 226161
www.britishtriathlon.org

VOLLEYBALL

English Volleyball Association
01509 631699
www.volleyballengland.org

WATER SKIING

British Water Ski Federation
01932 575364
www.britishwaterski.co.uk

WEIGHTLIFTING

British Weight Lifting Association
01952 604201
www.bawla.com

WRESTLING

**British Amateur Wrestling
Association**
01246 236443
www.britishwrestling.org

YOGA

British Wheel of Yoga
01529 306851
www.bwy.org.uk

Institutes of sport

English Institute of Sport
0870 759 0400
www.eis2win.co.uk
PRESS: *0870 759 0416*
Scottish Institute of Sport
01786 460100
www.sisport.com
PRESS: *01786 460118*
0131 555 0425

National sports centres

Bisham Abbey, Bucks
01628 476911
www.bishamabbeynsc.co.uk
Crystal Palace, south London
020 8778 0131
www.crystalpalacensc.co.uk
Cumbrae, Ayrshire
0131 317 7200
www.nationalcentrecumbrae.org.uk
Glenmore Lodge, Aviemore
01479 861256
www.glenmorelodge.org.uk
Inverclyde, Largs
01475 674666
www.nationalcentreinverclyde.org.uk
Lilleshall, Shropshire
01952 603003
www.lilleshallnsc.co.uk
**National Water Sports Centre –
Holme Pierrepont, Nottinghamshire**
0115 982 1212
www.nationalsportscentres.co.uk
Plas Menai, Gwynedd
01248 673943
www.plasmenai.co.uk
Plas y Brenin, Conwy
01690 720214
www.pyb.co.uk
Tollymore, County Down
028 4372 2158
www.tollymore.com
Welsh Institute, Cardiff
029 2030 0500
www.welsh-institute-sport.co.uk

Sport and education

**British Universities Sports
Association**
020 7357 8555
www.busa.org.uk
**Central Council of Physical
Recreation**
020 7854 8500
www.ccpr.org.uk
National Council for School Sport
0115 923 1229
www.ncss.org.uk
Physical Education Association of UK
0118 931 6240
www.pea.uk.com
Youth Sport Trust
01509 226600
www.youthsporttrust.org

Sport and disability

**British Amputee and Les Autres
Sports Association**
0120 449 4308
www.balasa.org
British Blind Sport
08700 789000
www.britishblindsport.org.uk
British Deaf Sports Council
Fax: 01268 510621
www.britishdeafsportscouncil.org.uk
**Wheelpower British Wheelchair
Sports**
01296 395995
www.wheelpower.org.uk

Other bodies

The Big Lottery Fund
0845 410 2030
www.biglotteryfund.org.uk
Sports Aid Foundation
020 7273 1975
www.sportsaid.org.uk
Sports Coach UK
0113 274 4802
www.sportscoachuk.org
Women's Sports Foundation
020 7273 1740
www.wsf.org.uk

Travel

Department for Transport
020 7944 8300
www.dft.gov.uk
PRESS –
ROADS: *020 7944 3066;*
MARINE, AVIATION: *020 7944 3232;*
RAILWAYS: *020 7944 3248*
Commission for Integrated Transport
cfit@dft.gsi.gov.uk
www.cfit.gov.uk

Urban transport

London

Transport for London
020 7941 4500
www.tfl.gov.uk/tfl
PRESS: *020 7941 4434*
Congestion charging
0845 900 1234
www.cclondon.com
London Buses
0845 300 7000
www.tfl.gov.uk/buses
London River Services
020 7941 2400
www.tfl.gov.uk/river
London Underground
020 7222 5600
www.tube.tfl.gov.uk
Docklands Light Rail
020 7363 9700
www.tfl.gov.uk/dlr
London Cycling Campaign
020 7928 7220
www.lcc.org.uk
London Transport Users Committee
020 7505 9000
www.ltuc.org.uk
PRESS: *020 7726 9953*

The regions

Centro
0121 200 2787
www.centro.org.uk
West Midlands
PRESS: *0121 214 7073*
GMPTE
0161 242 6000
www.gmpte.gov.uk
Greater Manchester
PRESS: *0161 242 6245*
Merseytravel
0151 227 5181
www.merseytravel.gov.uk
Merseyside
PRESS: *0151 330 1151*

Metro
0113 251 7272
www.wymetro.com
West Yorkshire
PRESS: *0113 251 7213*
Nexus
0191 203 3333
www.nexus.org.uk
Tyne & Wear
PRESS: *0191 203 3112*
South Yorkshire
0114 276 7575
www.sypte.co.uk
PRESS: *0114 221 1335*
Strathclyde
0141 332 6811
www.spt.co.uk
PRESS: *0141 333 3282*
Passenger Transport Executive Group
0113 251 7204
www.pteg.net
Association of all seven passenger transport executives
PRESS: *0113 251 7445*

Rail

Rail companies

Network Rail
020 7557 8000
www.networkrail.co.uk
Infrastructure operator
NATIONAL PRESS: *020 7557 8292 / 3;*
LONDON AND SOUTH-EAST: *020 7557 8107;* MIDLANDS: *0121 345 3100;*
NORTH-EAST: *01904 522825;*
NORTH-WEST: *0161 228 8582;*
SCOTLAND: *0141 555 4109;*
SOUTH AND SOUTH-WEST: *020 7922 4747;* WEST COUNTRY AND WALES: *01793 515267;*
Arriva Trains Wales
0845 6061 660
www.arrivatrainswales.co.uk
PRESS: *029 2072 0522*
C2C
0845 601 4873
www.c2c-online.co.uk
PRESS: *020 7713 2168*
Central Trains
0121 654 2040
www.centraltrains.co.uk
PRESS: *0121 654 1278*
Chiltern Railways
0845 600 5165
www.chilternrailways.co.uk
PRESS: *020 7282 2937*
English Welsh & Scottish Railways
01302 766801
www.ews-railway.co.uk
PRESS: *0870 060 0260*

First Great Western Link
0845 600 5604
www.firstgreatwesternlink.co.uk
PRESS: *01793 499499*
First Scotrail
0845 601 5929
www.firstgroup.com
PRESS: *0141 335 4785*
Freightliner
020 7200 3974
www.freightliner.co.uk
PRESS: *020 7200 3900 / 2*
Gatwick Express
0845 850 15 30
www.gatwickexpress.co.uk
PRESS: *020 8750 6622*
GNER
0845 722 5333
www.gner.co.uk
PRESS: *01904 523072*
Heathrow Express
0845 600 1515
www.heathrowexpress.co.uk
PRESS: *020 8750 6680*
Hull Trains
01482 215745
www.hulltrains.co.uk
PRESS: *01482 867867*
Island Line
01983 812591
www.island-line.co.uk
London Eastern Railway
0845 600 7245
www.onerailway.com
PRESS: *01206 363947 / 8 / 9*
Midland Mainline
0845 722 1125
www.midlandmainline.com
PRESS: *01332 262010*
NI Railways
028 9066 6630
www.nirailways.co.uk
PRESS: *028 9089 9455*
Northern Rail
0845 600 1159
www.northernrail.org
PRESS: *0161 228 4501*
Silverlink
0845 601 4867 / 8
www.silverlink-trains.com
PRESS: *020 7713 2168*
Southern
08451 27 29 20
www.southcentraltrains.co.uk
PRESS: *020 8929 8673*
South West Trains
0845 600 0650
www.swtrains.co.uk
PRESS: *020 7620 5229*
Thameslink
0845 330 6333
www.thameslink.co.uk
PRESS: *020 7620 5253*

Virgin Trains
0870 789 1234
www.virgintrains.co.uk
PRESS: *0870 789 1111*

West Anglia Great Northern Railway (WAGN)
0845 781 8919
www.wagn.co.uk
PRESS: *020 7713 2168*

Wessex Trains
0845 600 0880
www.wessextrains.co.uk

Overseas rail travel

EuRail
www.eurail.com
PRESS: *00 31 30 750 83 92*

Eurostar
01777 77 78 79
www.eurostar.com
PRESS: *020 7922 6030 / 4494*

Rail Europe
0870 584 8848
www.raileurope.co.uk
PRESS: *01732 526729 / 14*
Main distributor of continental rail travel in the UK; including Eurostar, Inter-Rail, Snow Trains, French Motorail and TGV

Rail associations

Association of Train Operating Companies
020 7841 8000
www.atoc.org
Trade association
PRESS: *020 7841 8020*

National Rail Enquiries
08457 484950
www.nationalrail.co.uk

Rail Passengers Council and Committees
08453 022022
www.railpassengers.org.uk

General Consumer Council Northern Ireland
028 9067 2488
www.gccni.org.uk

Government and agencies

Strategic Rail Authority
020 7654 6000
www.sra.gov.uk

Health and Safety Executive: railways
020 7717 6533
www.hse.gov.uk/railways

Office of the Rail Regulator
020 7282 2000
www.rail-reg.gov.uk
PRESS: *020 7282 2007*
LIBRARY: *020 7282 2001*

Rail Safety and Standards Board
020 7904 7777
www.railwaysafety.org.uk

Air travel

Airports

BAA
020 7834 9449
www.baa.co.uk
PRESS: *020 7932 6654*
Operates UK's biggest airports

London City
020 7646 0088
www.londoncityairport.com
PRESS: *020 7646 0054*

London Gatwick
0870 000 2468
www.baa.co.uk/main/airports/gatwick
PRESS: *01293 505000*

London Heathrow
0870 000 0123
www.baa.com/main/airports
/heathrow
PRESS: *020 8745 7224*

London Heliport (Battersea)
020 7228 0181 / 2
www.weston-aviation.com
PRESS: *020 8652 2501*

London Luton
01582 405100
www.london-luton.co.uk
PRESS: *01582 395119*

London Stansted
0870 000 0303
www.baa.com/main/airports/stansted
PRESS: *01279 680534*

Aberdeen
0870 040 0006
www.baa.co.uk/main/airports
/aberdeen
PRESS: *0131 272 2111*

Alderney
01481 822551
www.alderney.gov.gg/index.php
/pid/40

Barrra
01871 890212
www.hial.co.uk/barra-airport.html

Belfast (City)
028 9093 9093
www.belfastcityairport.com
PRESS: *028 9093 5025*

Belfast International Airport (Aldergrove)
028 9448 4848
www.belfastairport.com
PRESS: *07766 475453*

Benbecula
01870 602051
www.hial.co.uk/benbecula
-airport.html

Biggin Hill
01959 578500
www.bigginhillairport.com

Birmingham
0870 733 5511
www.bhx.co.uk
PRESS: *0121 767 7094*

Blackpool
08700 273777
www.blackpoolairport.com

Bournemouth
01202 364000
www.flybournemouth.com
PRESS: *01202 364106*

Bristol
0870 1212747
www.bristolairport.co.uk

RAF Brize Norton
01993 842551
www.raf.mod.uk/rafbrizenorton

Cambridge City Airport
01223 373765
www.cambridgecityairport.com

Campbeltown
01586 553797
www.hial.co.uk/campbeltown
-airport.html

Cardiff International Airport
01446 711111
www.cial.co.uk
PRESS: *01446 712532*

Carlisle
01228 573641
www.carlisleairport.co.uk

Coventry
02476 308600
www.coventryairport.co.uk

RNAS Culdrose
01326 574121
www.royal-navy.mod.uk

Dundee
01382 662200
www.dundeecity.gov.uk/airport

East Midlands
01332 852852
www.eastmidlandsairport.com
PRESS: *01332 852 890 / 1*

Edinburgh
0870 040 0007
www.baa.co.uk/main/airports
/edinburgh
PRESS: *0131 272 2111*

Exeter
01392 367433
www.exeter-airport.co.uk
PRESS: *01392 354945*

Glasgow
0870 040 0008
www.baa.co.uk/main/airports
/glasgow
PRESS: *0131 272 2111*

Gloucester
01452 857700
www.gloucestershireairport.co.uk

Guernsey
01481 237766
www.guernsey-airport.gov.gg

Inverness
01667 464000
www.hial.co.uk/inverness-airport.html

Ipswich
01473 720111

Islay
01496 302361
www.hial.co.uk/islay-airport.html

Isle of Man (Ronaldsway)
01624 821600
www.iom-airport.com

Jersey
01534 492000
www.jersey-airport.com

Kent International, Manston
08707 605755
www.kia-m.com
Lands End
01736 788771
Leeds Bradford International Airport
0113 250 9696
www.lbia.co.uk
PRESS: *0113 391 3333*
Liverpool John Lennon Airport
0870 750 8484
www.liverpooljohnlennonairport.com
PRESS: *0151 907 1622*
Lydd
01797 322411
www.lydd-airport.co.uk
Manchester
0161 489 3000
www.manairport.co.uk
PRESS: *0161 489 2700*
Newcastle
0870 122 1488
www.newcastleairport.com
PRESS: *0191 214 3568*
OUT OF HOURS: *0780 133 5746*
Newquay Cornwall Airport
01637 860600
www.newquayairport.com
Norwich
01603 411923
www.norwichairport.co.uk
Orkney (Kirkwall)
01856 872421
www.hial.co.uk/kirkwall-airport.html
Penzance Heliport
01736 363871
Plymouth City Airport
01752 204090
www.plymouthcity.co.uk/airport.html
PRESS: *01872 276276*
Prestwick
0871 223 0700
www.gpia.co.uk
St Mary's, Isles of Scilly
01720 422677
Sheffield City Airport
0114 201 1998
www.sheffieldcityairport.com
Shetland
01950 460654
Shoreham (Brighton City)
01273 296900
www.shorehamairport.co.uk
Southampton
0870 040 0009
www.baa.co.uk/main/airports
/southampton
PRESS: *023 8062 7141*
Southend
01702 608100
www.southendairport.net
Stornoway
01851 707400
www.hial.co.uk/stornoway-airport.html
Sumburgh
01950 461000
www.hial.co.uk/sumburgh-airport.html
Teesside
01325 332811
www.teessideairport.com

Tiree
01879 220456
www.hial.co.uk/tiree-airport.html
Tresco Heliport
01720 422970
www.tresco.co.uk
Wick
01955 602215
www.hial.co.uk/wick-airport.html

Airlines

Aer Lingus
00 353 1 886 8844
www.aerlingus.ie
PRESS: *00 353 1 886 3420*
Aeroflot
00 1 212 944 2300
www.aeroflot.com
Air Berlin
0870 738 8880
www.airberlin.com
PRESS: *00 49 30 3434 1510*
Air Canada
0871 220 1111
www.aircanada.ca
Air France
0870 142 4343
www.airfrance.com
PRESS: *020 8584 4408*
Air India
020 7495 7950
www.airindia.com
PRESS: *020 8745 1066*
Air Malta
00 356 2169 0890
www.airmalta.com
Air New Zealand
020 8600 7600
www.airnewzealand.com
Air Scotland
0141 222 2363
www.air-scotland.com
Air Seychelles
01293 596656
www.airseychelles.net
Air Wales
0870 777 3131
www.airwales.com
PRESS: *01792 460200*
Alitalia
020 8745 8200
www.alitalia.com
PRESS: *020 8745 8298*
Alaska Airlines
01992 441517
www.alaskaair.com
America West Airlines
00 1 480 693 0800
www.americawest.com
PRESS: *00 1 480 693 5729*
American Airlines
0845 778 9789
www.aa.com
PRESS: *020 8577 4804*
ANA Europe
0870 837 8866
www.anaskyweb.com
PRESS: *020 7808 1356*
ATA
00 1 800 225 2995
www.ata.com

Austrian Airlines
020 7766 0300
www.aua.com
Avianca (Colombia)
0870 576 7747
www.avianca.com
Basiq Air
020 7365 4997
www.basiqair.com
British Airways
0870 850 9850
www.british-airways.com
PRESS: *020 8738 5100*
BMI (British Midland)
01332 854000
www.britishmidland.com
PRESS: *01332 854687*
Cathay Pacific
020 8834 8888
www.cathaypacific.com
PRESS: *020 8834 8800*
China Airlines
020 7436 9001
www.china-airlines.com
PRESS: *00 31 206 463 313*
Continental Airlines
01293 776464
www.continental.com
PRESS: *00 1 713 324 5080*
Cyprus Airways
020 8359 1333
www.cyprusair.com
PRESS: *020 8359 1366*
Delta Express
001 404 715 2600
www.delta.com
PRESS: *020 7932 8376*
EasyJet
0871 244 2366
www.easyjet.com
PRESS: *01582 525252*
El Al Israel Airlines
020 7957 4250
www.elal.com
PRESS: *020 7957 4260*
Emirates
0870 243 2222
www.emirates.com
PRESS: *020 7861 2424*
EUJet
0870 414 1414
www.eujet.com
Finnair
0870 241 4411
www.finnair.com
Flybe
01392 366669
www.flybe.com
PRESS: *0845 675 0681*
Flyglobespan
0870 556 1522
www.flyglobespan.com
GB Airways
01293 664239
www.gbairways.com
PRESS: *01293 664000*
Germanwings
0870 252 1250
www.germanwings.com
PRESS: *presse@germanwings.com*

Gulf Air
0870 777 1717
www.gulfairco.com
Helios
00 357 24 815700
www.flyhelios.com
HLX (Hapag-Lloyd Express)
0870 606 0519
www.hlx.com
Iberia
0870 609 0500
www.iberia.com
PRESS: *00 34 91 587 7205*
Icelandair
00 354 50 50 100
www.icelandair.net
PRESS: *020 78741007*
Japan Airlines
0845 774 7700
www.jal.com
JAT – Yugoslav Airlines
020 7629 2007
www.jat.com
Jet 2
0871 226 1737
www.jet2.com
Kenya Airways
01784 888222
www.kenya-airways.com
KLM Royal Dutch
0870 243 0541
www.klm.com
PRESS: *00 31 20 649 1780*
Kuwait Airways
020 7412 0006
www.kuwait-airways.com
LanChile
0800 917 0572
www.lanchile.com
LOT – Polish Airlines
0870 414 0088
www.lot.com
Lufthansa
0870 837 7747
www.lufthansa.com
PRESS: *020 8750 3415*
Malaysia Airlines
020 7341 2000
www.malaysia-airlines.com
Monarch
01582 400000
www.monarch-airlines.com
PRESS: *01582 398146*
Olympic Airways
0870 606 0460
www.olympic-airways.gr
PRESS: *00 30 210 926 7251*
Portugalia Airlines
0161 250 0385
www.pga.pt
PRESS: *0161 489 5039*
Qantas Airways
0845 774 7767
www.qantas.com.au
PRESS: *020 8846 0501*
Royal Air Maroc
020 7439 4361
www.royalairmaroc.com
Royal Jordanian Airlines
020 7878 6300
www.rja.com.jo
PRESS: *020 7878 6337*

RyanAir
0906 270 5656
www.ryanair.co.uk
PRESS: *00 353 181 21212*
SAS Scandinavian Airlines
00 46 8 797 0000
www.scandinavian.net
PRESS: *00 46 70 997 4893*
Saudi Arabian Airlines
020 7798 9898
www.saudiairlines.com
Singapore Airlines
0870 608 8886
www.singaporeair.com
PRESS: *020 8563 6788 / 41*
Sky Europe
020 7365 0365
www.skyeurope.com
South African Airways
020 8897 3645
www.flysaa.com
Spanair
0870 1266710
www.spanair.com
Sri Lankan Airlines
020 8538 2001
www.srilankan.aero
Swiss
0845 758 1333
www.swiss.com
PRESS: *00 41 848 773 773*
TAP Air Portugal
0870 607 2024
www.tap.pt
PRESS: *00 351 21 841 5000*
Thai Airways
020 7491 7953
www.thaiairways.com
PRESS: *020 7907 9524*
United Airlines
0845 844 4777
www.ual.com
PRESS: *020 8276 6800*
Varig – Brazilian Airlines
0870 120 3020
www.varig.co.uk
Virgin Atlantic
01293 562345
www.virgin-atlantic.com
PRESS: *01293 747 373*
Virgin Express
0870 730 1134
www.virgin-express.com
PRESS: *00 32 2752 0677*
Volare
00 380 44 452 1115
www.volare.kiev.ua
Wizz Air
00 48 22 351 9499
www.wizzair.com
Yemen Airways
020 8759 0385
www.yemenairways.co.uk

Air associations and authorities

Air Accidents Investigation Branch
01252 510300
www.aaib.dft.gov.uk
24-hour accident reporting line:
01252 512299
Air Transport Users Council
020 7240 6061
www.auc.org.uk
Airport Operators Association
020 7222 2249
www.aoa.org.uk
British Airline Pilots Association
020 8476 4000
WWW.BALPA.ORG
PRESS: *020 7924 7555*
Civil Aviation Authority
020 7379 7311
www.caa.co.uk
Regulator
International Air Transport Association
020 8607 6200
www.iata.org
National Air Traffic Services
020 7309 8666
www.nats.co.uk
PRESS: *01489 615945*

Water travel

Ports

Aberdeen
01224 597000
www.aberdeen-harbour.co.uk
Ayr
01292 281687
www.abports.co.uk
Barrow
01229 822911
www.abports.co.uk
Barry
0870 609 6699
www.abports.co.uk
Belfast
028 9055 4422
www.belfast-harbour.co.uk
Boston
01205 365571
www.portofboston.co.uk
Brightlingsea
01206 302200
www.brightlingseaharbour.org
Bristol
0117 982 0000
www.bristolport.co.uk
Brixham
01803 853321
Cardiff
0870 609 6699
www.abports.co.uk
Cowes
01983 293952
www.cowes.co.uk

Dartmouth
01803 832337
www.dartharbour.org.uk
Dover
01304 240400
www.doverport.co.uk
PRESS: *x4806*
Dundee
01382 224121
www.forthports.co.uk
Ellesmore Port (Manchester Ship Canal)
01928 567465
www.shipcanal.co.uk
Eyemouth
01890 750223
Falmouth
01326 312285
www.falmouthport.co.uk
Felixstowe
01394 604500
www.portoffelixstowe.co.uk
Fife
0131 554 2703
www.forthports.co.uk
Fleetwood
01253 872323
www.abports.co.uk
Folkestone
01303 254597
www.folkestoneharbour.com
Garston
0151 427 5971
www.abports.co.uk
Goole
01482 327171
www.abports.co.uk
Grangemouth
01324 482591
www.forthports.co.uk
Great Yarmouth
01493 335500
www.gypa.co.uk
Grimsby
01472 359181
www.abports.co.uk
Harwich
01255 243030
www.hha.co.uk
Heysham
01524 852373
Hull
01482 327171
www.abports.co.uk
Immingham
01472 359181
www.abports.co.uk
Inverness Harbour Trust
01463 715715
www.invernessharbour.co.uk
Ipswich
01473 231010
www.abports.co.uk
Isle of Man
01624 686628
King's Lynn
01553 691555
www.abports.co.uk
Larne
028 2887 2100
www.portoflarne.co.uk

Leith
0131 555 8750
www.forthports.co.uk
Lerwick
01595 692991
www.lerwick-harbour.co.uk
Liverpool
0151 949 6000
www.merseydocks.co.uk
Port of London
020 7743 7900
www.portoflondon.co.uk
Londonderry
028 7186 0555
www.londonderryport.com
Lowestoft
01553 691555
www.abports.co.uk
Medway Ports
01795 596596
www.medwayports.com
Milford Haven
01646 696100
www.mhpa.co.uk
Montrose Port Authority
01674 672302
www.montroseport.co.uk
Mostyn Docks, Holywell
01745 560335
Newport
0870 609 6699
www.abports.co.uk
Peterhead
01779 474020
www.peterhead-bay.co.uk
Plymouth
01752 662191
www.abports.co.uk
Poole
01202 440200
www.phc.co.uk
Portsmouth
023 9229 7395
www.portsmouthand.co.uk
Port Talbot
0870 609 6699
www.abports.co.uk
Ramsgate
01843 587661
www.ramsgatenewport.co.uk
Rosyth
01383 413366
www.forthports.co.uk
Saundersfoot
01834 812094
Scarborough
01947 602354
Seaham
0191 516 1700
www.victoriagroup.co.uk
Shoreham
01273 598100
www.portshoreham.co.uk
Silloth
016973 31358
www.abports.co.uk
Southampton
023 8048 8800
www.abports.co.uk
Stonehaven
01569 762 741

Stornoway
01851 702688
www.stornoway-portauthority.com
Sunderland
0191 553 2100
www.portofsunderland.org.uk
Swansea
0870 609 6699
www.abports.co.uk
Tees & Hartlepool
01642 877000
www.thpal.co.uk
Teignmouth
01626 774044
www.abports.co.uk
Tilbury
01375 852200
www.forthports.co.uk
Troon
01292 281687
www.abports.co.uk
Tyne, Port of
0191 455 2671
www.portoftyne.com
Weymouth
01305 838000
www.weymouth.gov.uk
Whitby, Port of
01947 602354
www.portofwhitby.co.uk

Ferries and cruises

Brittany Ferries
08703 665333
www.brittany-ferries.com
PRESS: *020 7610 4028*
Caledonian MacBrayne
01475 650100
www.calmac.co.uk
Condor Ferries
01202 207207
www.condorferries.co.uk
Cunard Cruise Line
0845 071 0300
www.cunard.com
DFDS Seaways
08702 520524
www.dfdsseaways.co.uk
EasyCruise
0906 292 9000
www.easycruise.com
Fjord Line
0870 143 9669
www.fjordline.com
Hoverspeed
0870 240 8070
www.hoverspeed.com
PRESS: *020 7805 5845*
Hovertravel
01983 811000
www.hovertravel.co.uk
Irish Ferries
08705 171717
www.irishferries.com
Isle of Man Steam Packet Company
01624 645645
www.steam-packet.com
Norfolk Line
00 31 7035 27400
www.norfolkline.com

Orkney Ferries
01856 872044
www.orkneyferries.co.uk
P&O Cruises
023 8065 5000
www.pocruises.com
P&O Ferries
0870 520 2020
www.poferries.com
PRESS: *01304 863833*
Red Funnel Ferries
0870 444 8898
www.redfunnel.co.uk
Sea Containers Irish Sea Operations
020 7805 5000
www.seacontainers.com
SeaFrance
01304 828300
www.seafrance.com
PRESS: *020 7233 2300*
Stena Line
00 46 3185 8000
www.stenaline.com
PRESS: *00 46 3185 8180*
Superfast Ferries Scotland
0870 234 0870
www.superfast.com
Swansea Cork Ferries
01792 456116
www.swansea-cork.ie
Thomson Cruises
0870 607 1642
www.thomson-cruises.co.uk
Wightlink
0870 240 4323
www.wightlink.co.uk
Woolwich Ferry
020 8921 5978

Water travel associations and authorities

Associated British Ports
020 7430 1177
www.abports.co.uk
PRESS: *020 7430 6820 / 60*
Association of Inland Navigation Authorities
0113 243 3125
www.aina.org.uk
British Marine Industries Federation
01784 473377
www.britishmarine.co.uk
British Ports Association
020 7242 1200
www.britishports.org.uk
British Waterways
01923 201120
www.britishwaterways.co.uk
PRESS: *01923 201350*
Hydrographic Office
01823 723366
www.hydro.gov.uk
Inland Waterways Association
01923 711114
www.waterways.org.uk
International Maritime Organisation
020 7735 7611
www.imo.org

Lloyd's Register – Fairplay
01737 379000
www.fairplay.co.uk
Lloyd's Register
020 7709 9166
www.lr.org
Lloyd's List
0220 7017 5531
www.lloydslist.com
Maritime & Coastguard Agency
023 8032 9100
www.mcga.gov.uk
Royal Institute of Navigation
020 7591 3130
www.rin.org.uk
Royal Yachting Association
0845 345 0400
www.rya.org.uk
UK Harbours Directory
www.harbours.co.uk

Road travel

Motoring bodies

AA
0870 600 0371
www.theaa.co.uk
PRESS: *01256 492927*
British Motorcyclists Federation
0116 284 5380
www.bmf.co.uk
British Parking Association
01444 447 300
www.britishparking.co.uk
Coach Operators Federation
01934 832074
http://users.tinyworld.co.uk
/somerbus/index.htm
Confederation of Passenger Transport
020 7240 3131
www.carlton-group.co.uk
/passtransport.html
DVLA (Drivers & Vehicles Licensing Authority)
01792 782341
www.dvla.gov.uk
PRESS: *01792 782318*
Greenflag
0845 246 1557
www.greenflag.com
PRESS: *0113 399 1427*
Institute of Logistics & Transport
01536 740104
www.iolt.org.uk
Institute of the Motor Industry
01992 511 521
www.motor.org.uk
International Road Transport Union
www.iru.org
Licensed Taxi Drivers Association
020 7286 1046
www.ltda.co.uk
Motor Industry Research Association
01268 290123
www.mira.co.uk
National Federation of Bus Users
023 9281 4493
www.nfbu.org

RAC
01628 843888
www.rac.co.uk
PRESS: *020 8917 2742*
Road Haulage Association
01932 841515
www.rha.net
Road Operators Safety Council
01865 775552
www.rosco.org.uk
Society of Motor Manufacturers
020 7235 7000
www.smmt.co.uk
Transport & General Workers Union
020 7611 2500
www.tgwu.org.uk
World Road Association (PIARC)
www.piarc.org

Pedestrians, cyclists and campaign groups

Brake
01484 559909
www.brake.org.uk
Road safety charity
British Cycling Federation
0870 871 2000
www.bcf.uk.com
pressoffice@britishcycling.org.uk
Campaign Against Drinking & Driving
0845 123 5541
www.cadd.org.uk
Cycle Campaign Network
ccn@cyclenetwork.org.uk
www.cyclenetwork.org.uk
Cyclists Touring Club
0870 873 0060
www.ctc.org.uk
PRESS: *0870 873 0063*
Environmental Transport Association
0800 212810
www.eta.co.uk
Environmental campaigner and provider of roadside recovery service
European Federation of Road Victims
fevr@worldcom.ch
www.fevr.org
Lift Share
08700 780225
www.liftshare.com
Online car-sharing scheme
Living Streets
020 7820 1010
www.livingstreets.org.uk
Fighting for cleaner, safer streets
London Cycling Campaign
020 7928 7220
www.lcc.org.uk
Motorcycle Action Group
0870 444 8448
www.mag-uk.org
National Cycle Network
0845 113 0065
www.sustrans.org.uk
PRESS: *0117 927 7555*
Nationwide Cycle Registration
0117 964 2187
www.cycleregistration.com

Ramblers Association
020 7339 8500
www.ramblers.org.uk
PRESS: *020 7339 8531 / 8532*

Reclaim the Streets
rts@gn.apc.org
http://rts.gn.apc.org/

RoadPeace
020 8838 5102
www.roadpeace.org

Slower Speeds Initiative
0845 345 8459
www.slower-speeds.org.uk

Smart Moves
01484 483061
www.smartmoves.co.uk

Sustrans
0845 113 0065
www.sustrans.org.uk
Sustainable transport charity
PRESS: *0117 927 7555*

Buses

Arriva
0191 520 4000
www.arriva.co.uk
PRESS: *0191 520 4106*

Firstgroup
020 7291 0505
www.firstgroup.com
PRESS: *0161 627 7218*

The Go-ahead Group
0191 232 3123
www.go-ahead.com

London United Busways
020 8400 6665
www.lonutd.co.uk

Lothian Buses
0131 554 4494
www.lothianbuses.co.uk
PRESS: *0131 555 6363*

Metroline
020 8218 8888
www.metroline.co.uk

National Express
08705 808080
www.nationalexpress.com
PRESS: *0121 625 1122*

Scottish Citylink
0141 332 9644
www.citylink.co.uk
PRESS: *0141 333 9585*

Stagecoach
01738 442111
www.stagecoachplc.com

Ulsterbus
028 9066 6630
www.ulsterbus.co.uk

Tourism

Major tour operators

First Choice
0870 750 0001
www.firstchoice.co.uk
PRESS: *01293 588762*

MyTravel
01706 742000
www.mytravel.com
PRESS: *0161 232 6464*

Thomas Cook
01733 417100
www.thomascook.com
PRESS: *01733 417272*

Thomson
020 7387 9321
www.thomson.co.uk
PRESS: *020 7383 1484*

Tourism associations

Air Travel Organisers' Licensing (ATOL)
020 7453 6424
www.caa.co.uk/cpg/atol
PRESS: *020 7453 6030*

Association of British Travel Agents
020 7637 2444
www.abtanet.com
PRESS: *020 7307 1900*

British Tourist Authority
020 8846 9000
www.visitbritain.com
PRESS: *020 8563 3220*

Tourism Concern
020 7133 3330
www.tourismconcern.org.uk

Visit London
020 8234 5000
www.visitlondon.com

Youth Hostels Association
01629 592600
www.yha.org.uk
PRESS: *01629 592575*

Utilities

Energy

ENERGY COMPANIES

BNFL
01925 832000
www.bnfl.com
British Nuclear Fuels
PRESS: *01925 832000*

British Gas
0845 600 0560
www.house.co.uk
Gas and electricity supplier. Owned by Centrica
PRESS: *01784 874433*

British Energy
01452 652222
www.british-energy.com
Electricity producer
PRESS: *01506 408801*

Ecotricity
01453 756111
www.ecotricity.co.uk
Electricity supplier
PRESS: *01453 769317*

EDF Energy
020 7242 9050
www.edfenergy.com
Gas and electricity supplier. Owns SWEB, Seeboard and London Energy
PRESS: *020 7752 2266*

Green Energy UK
0845 456 9550
www.greenenergy.uk.com

Good Energy
0845 456 1640
www.good-energy.co.uk
Renewable electricity supplier. Owned by Monkton Group

National Grid Transco
020 7004 3000
www.ngtgroup.com
Energy distribution
PRESS: *020 7004 3147*

Powergen
024 7642 4000
www.powergen.co.uk
Gas and electricity supplier. Owned by E.ON UK
PRESS: *02476 425741*

RWE npower
01793 877777
www.rwenpower.com
Gas and electricity supplier
PRESS: *0845 070 2807*

Scottish and Southern
01738 456000
www.scottish-southern.co.uk
Gas and electricity supplier
PRESS: *0870 900 0410*

Scottish Power
0141 248 8200
www.scottishpower.com
Gas and electricity supplier
PRESS: *0141 636 4515*

ENERGY BODIES AND ASSOCIATIONS

British BioGen
020 8683 6697
www.britishbiogen.co.uk
Bioenergy trade association

British Hydropower Association
01202 886622
www.british-hydro.org
Trade association

British Nuclear Energy Society
020 7222 7722
www.bnes.com

British Photovoltaic Association
01908 442291
www.greenenergy.org.uk/pvuk2/

British Wind Energy Association
020 7689 1960
www.bwea.com
Trade association

Centre for Sustainable Energy
0117 929 9950
www.cse.org.uk
Charity

Energy Retail Association
020 7930 9175
www.energy-retail.org.uk

Energywatch
0845 906 0708
www.energywatch.org.uk
Independent watchdog
PRESS: *08459 060708*

National Energy Foundation
01908 665555
www.natenergy.org.uk
Charity

Nuclear Industry Association
020 7766 6640
www.niauk.org
Trade association
PRESS: *020 7766 6640*

Solar Trade Association
01908 442290
www.greenenergy.org.uk/sta
Trade association

GOVERNMENT AND REGULATION

Defra
08459 335577
www.defra.gov.uk

DTI Energy Group
020 7215 5000
www.dti.gov.uk/energy
PRESS: *020 7215 6407*

Nuclear Decommissioning Authority
01925 802001
www.nda.gov.uk
PRESS: *01925 80 2075*

Ofgem
020 7901 7000
www.ofgem.gov.uk
Official regulator
PRESS: *020 7901 7006*

Water

WATER COMPANIES

Anglian Water
08457 919155
www.anglianwater.co.uk
PRESS: *0870 600 5600*

Dwr Cymru Welsh Water
01443 452300
www.dwrcymru.co.uk
PRESS: *029 2055 6140*

Northumbrian Water
0870 608 4820
www.nwl.co.uk

Scottish Water
0845 601 8855
www.scottishwater.co.uk
PRESS: *01383 848445*

Severn Trent Water
0800 783 4444
www.stwater.co.uk
PRESS: *0121 722 4121*

South West Water
01392 434966
www.southwestwater.co.uk
PRESS: *01392 443020*

Southern Water
01903 264444
www.southernwater.co.uk

Thames Water
020 8213 8451
www.thames-water.com

United Utilities
01925 234000
www.unitedutilities.com
PRESS: *01925 537366*

Wessex Water
01225 526000
www.wessexwater.co.uk
PRESS: *01225 526323 / 9*

Yorkshire Water
01274 691111
www.yorkshirewater.com

WATER ASSOCIATIONS

British Water
020 7957 4554
www.britishwater.co.uk
Trade association

Water UK
020 7344 1844
www.water.org.uk
Trade association

GOVERNMENT AND REGULATION

Defra
08459 335577
www.defra.gov.uk

Drinking Water Inspectorate
020 7082 8024
www.dwi.gov.uk
Watchdog

Ofwat
0121 625 1300 / 73
www.ofwat.gov.uk
Regulator
PRESS: *0121 625 1416 / 96 / 42*
**Water Industry Commissioner for
Scotland**
01786 430200
www.watercommissioner.co.uk

Post

Royal Mail
08457 740740
www.royalmail.com

REGULATOR

**Postcomm (Postal Services
Commission)**
020 7593 2100
www.postcomm.gov.uk
PRESS: *020 7593 2114*

Telecoms

British Telecom
020 7356 5000
www.bt.com
PRESS: *020 7356 5369*
Cable and Wireless
01908 845000
www.cableandwireless.co.uk
PRESS: *01344 818888*
Colt
0207 390 3900
www.colt.co.uk
PRESS: *07017 100100*
Energis
020 7206 5555
www.energis.co.uk
PRESS: *0118 919 3499*
Hutchinson 3G
08707 330 333
www.three.co.uk
PRESS: *01628 765000*
Kingston Communications
01482 602100
www.kcltd.co.uk
PRESS: *01482 602711*
MCI WorldCom
0118 905 5000
www.worldcom.com/uk
mmO2
0113 272 2000
www.mmo2.com
PRESS: *01753 628402*
NTL
0800 052 2000
www.ntl.com
PRESS: *01256 752669*
Orange
01454 624600
www.orange.co.uk
PRESS: *020 7984 2001*

Telewest
01483 750900
www.telewest.co.uk
PRESS: *020 7299 5115*
Thus
0800 0275 8487
www.thus.co.uk
PRESS: *0141 567 1234*
T-Mobile
01707 315000
www.t-mobile.co.uk
PRESS: *07017 150150*
Virgin Mobile
01225 895555
www.virginmobile.com
PRESS: *0845 600 6272*
Vodafone
01635 33251
www.vodafone.co.uk
PRESS: *07000 500100*

REGULATOR

Ofcom
020 7981 3040
www.ofcom.org.uk
PRESS: *020 7981 3033*

Emergency and services

Police

GOVERNMENT AND AGENCIES

Home Office
0870 000 1585
www.homeoffice.gov.uk
PRESS: *020 7035 4381*
Forensic Science Service
01257 224300; 01291 637100
www.forensic.gov.uk
PRESS: *020 7840 2940*
HM Inspectors of Constabulary
01527 882000
www.homeoffice.gov.uk/hmic
/hmic.htm
Independent Police Complaints Commission (IPCC)
0845 300 2002
www.ipcc.gov.uk
PRESS: *020 7166 3214*

POLICE FORCES

▶▶ See panel on page 491

POLICE SERVICES

Police Service
www.police.uk
Centrex
01256 602100
www.centrex.police.uk
National police training
PRESS: *01256 602725*
Interpol
00 33 4 7244 7000
www.interpol.int
National Crime Squad
020 7238 8000
www.nationalcrimesquad.police.uk
PRESS: *0870 268 8100*
National Criminal Intelligence Service
020 7238 8000
www.ncis.gov.uk
PRESS: *0870 268 8100*
Northern Ireland Police Service
028 9065 0222
www.psni.police.uk
PRESS: *028 9070 0084*
Northern Ireland Policing Board
028 9040 8500
www.nipolicingboard.org.uk
PRESS: *028 9040 8539 / 8567*
Police Forces in Scotland
www.scottish.police.uk
Police IT Organisation
020 8358 5555
www.pito.org.uk
National computer
Scottish Drug Enforcement Agency
01224 783289
www.sdea.police.uk

Scottish Police Information Strategy
0141 582 1000
www.spis.police.uk
Civil Nuclear Constabulary (CNC)
www.cnc.police.uk

PROFESSIONAL BODIES

Association of Chief Police Officers
020 7227 3434
www.acpo.police.uk
PRESS: *020 7227 3425*
Association of Chief Police Officers in Scotland
0141 532 2052
www.scottish.police.uk
PRESS: *0141 532 2658*
Association of Police Authorities
020 7664 3185
www.apa.police.uk
PRESS: *use main number*
British Association for Women in Policing
0870 766 4056
www.bawp.org
PRESS: *use main number*
Institute of Traffic Accident Investigators
01332 292447
www.itai.org
PRESS: *use main number*
Police Federation
020 8335 1000
www.polfed.org
PRESS: *use main number*
Police Federation for Northern Ireland
028 9076 4200
www.policefed-ni.org.uk
PRESS: *use main number*
Police Superintendents' Association
0118 984 4005
www.policesupers.com

Fire

Office of the Deputy Prime Minister
020 7944 4400
www.odpm.gov.uk
PRESS: *020 7944 4297*
Fire Policy Division
020 7944 6923
HM Fire Service Inspectorate
020 7944 5569

FIRE AND RESCUE AUTHORITIES

▶▶ See panel on page 491

PROFESSIONAL BODIES

Fire Brigades Union
020 8541 1765
www.fbu.org.uk
PRESS: *07736 818 100*

Chief Fire Officers' Association (CFOA)
01827 302300
www.cfoa.org.uk
Fire Protection Association
01608 812 500
www.thefpa.co.uk

Ambulance

Department of Health
020 7210 4850
www.dh.gov.uk
PRESS: *020 7210 5221*

AMBULANCE SERVICES

▶▶ See panel on page 491

AMBULANCE ASSOCIATIONS

Ambulance Service Association
020 7928 9620
www.the-asa.org
PRESS: *use main number*
Association of Professional Ambulance Personnel
0870 167 0999
www.apap.org.uk

Search and rescue

Maritime and Coastguard Agency
0870 600 6505
www.mcga.gov.uk
Mountain Rescue Council of England and Wales
08702 404024
www.mountain.rescue.org.uk
Network of voluntary rescue teams
RAF Mountain Rescue Association
www.rafmra.org.uk
Search and Rescue Dog Association
chairman@nsarda.org.uk
www.nsarda.org.uk

Military

Ministry of Defence
020 7218 9000
www.mod.uk
PRESS: *020 7218 7907*
British Army
www.army.mod.uk
PRESS: *020 7218 7907*
Royal Air Force
www.raf.mod.uk
PRESS: *020 7218 7907*
Royal Navy
www.royal-navy.mod.uk
PRESS: *020 7218 7907*

Army Training and Recruitment Agency
01980 615041
www.atra.mod.uk

Central Data Management Authority
01793 555391
www.cdma.mod.uk

Computer Emergency Response Team
020 7218 2640
www.mod.uk/cert

Defence Analytical Services Agency
020 7807 8792
www.dasa.mod.uk
UK defence statistics

Defence Procurement Agency
0117 913 0000
www.mod.uk/dpa
PRESS: *0117 913 0000*

Defence Scientific Advisory Council
020 7218 0333
www.mod.uk/dsac
Provides independent advice to the defence secretary

GCHQ (Government Communications Headquarters)
01242 221491
www.gchq.gov.uk
PRESS: *01242 221491 x33847*

International Visits Control Office
0870 607 4455
www.mod.uk/ivco
Provides security clearance and advice for visitors to and from the UK defence industry

Ministry of Defence Police
01371 854000
www.mod.uk/mdp
PRESS: *01371 854416*

Sabre
0800 389 5459
www.sabre.mod.uk
Supports Britain's reservists and employers

Territorial Army
0845 603 8000
www.ta.mod.uk
Reserve force

Veterans Agency
0800 169 2277, 01253 866043
www.veteransagency.mod.uk
MoD contact for veterans and dependants

MI5
www.mi5.gov.uk
UK's defensive security intelligence agency
PRESS: *020 7273 4545 (Home Office)*

MI6
www.fco.gov.uk
Secret intelligence service
PRESS: *020 7008 3100 (Foreign Office)*

MILITARY ASSOCIATIONS

Army Base Repair Organisation
01264 383295
www.abrodev.co.uk

Commonwealth War Graves Commission
01628 634221
www.cwgc.org
PRESS: *01628 507163*

Military Heraldry Society
01952 408830 / 270221

Military Historical Society
020 7730 0717

Orders and Medals Research Society
01295 690009
www.omrs.org.uk

Reserve Forces' and Cadets' Associations' in Scotland
Lowland: 0141 945 4951
Highland: 01382 668283
www.rfca.org.uk

Royal British Legion
020 7973 7200
www.britishlegion.org.uk
www.poppy.org.uk
PRESS: *020 7973 7296*

SSAFA Forces Help
020 7403 8783
www.ssafa.org.uk
National charity helping serving and ex-service men, women and their families

Emergency planning

GOVERNMENT

Air Accidents Investigation Branch
01252 510300
www.aaib.dft.gov.uk
PRESS: *020 7944 3387 / 3232*
24-hour accident reporting line:
01252 512299

Civil Contingencies Secretariat
020 7276 3000
www.ukresilience.info
Formerly the Emergency Planning Division

Emergency Planning College, Easingwold
01347 822877
www.ukresilience.info/college
Government training college
PRESS: *01347 821 406*

London Fire and Emergency Planning Authority
020 7587 2000
www.london-fire.gov.uk

London Prepared
020 7276 3000
www.londonprepared.gov.uk

National Infrastructure Security Co-ordination Centre (NISCC)
020 7821 1330
www.niscc.gov.uk

Health Protection Agency, Centre for Radiation, Chemical and Environmental Hazards, Radiation Protection Division
01235 831600
www.hpa.org.uk/radiation/

Scottish Executive Justice Department
0131 556 8400
www.scotland.gov.uk

Anti-Terrorist Hotline
0800 789321

PROFESSIONAL BODY

Emergency Planning Society
0845 600 9587
www.emergplansoc.org.uk

Voluntary services

Basics
0870 165 4999
www.basics.org.uk
Medical help at disasters

British Red Cross
0870 170 7000
www.redcross.org.uk

Casualties Union
08700 780590
www.casualtiesunion.org.uk
Simulated injuries for emergency exercises

Crimestoppers
020 8254 3200
www.crimestoppers-uk.org
Hotline: 0800 555 111

Royal Life Saving Society
01789 773 994
www.lifesavers.org.uk

Royal National Lifeboat Institution
0845 122 6999
www.rnli.org.uk

St Andrews Ambulance Association
Aberdeen: 01224 877271
Dundee: 01382 322389
Fife: 01592 631758
Edinburgh: 0131 229 5419
Glasgow: 0141 332 4031
www.firstaid.org.uk

St John Ambulance
08700 104950
www.sja.org.uk

Victim Support
020 7735 9166
www.victimsupport.org
Supports victims of crime
PRESS: *020 7896 3809*
Victim support line: 0845 3030 900

▪ Fire, police and ambulance

Avon
FIRE: 0117 926 2061
PRESS: x216
POLICE: 0845 456 7000
PRESS: 01275 816350
AMBULANCE: 0117 927 7046
PRESS: 0117 928 0265,
0870 241 0857

Bedfordshire
FIRE: 01234 351081
PRESS: 01234 326198
POLICE: 01234 841212
PRESS: 01234 842390
AMBULANCE: 01234 408999
PRESS: 01234 408999

Berkshire
FIRE: 0118 945 2888
PRESS: 0118 932 2214 / 83
POLICE: 01865 846000
PRESS: 01865 846699
AMBULANCE: 0118 936 5500
PRESS: 0118 936 5500

Buckinghamshire
FIRE: 01296 424666
PRESS: 01296 424666
POLICE: 01865 846000
PRESS: 01865 846699
AMBULANCE: 01908 262422
PRESS: 01908 262422

Cambridgeshire
FIRE: 01480 444500
PRESS: 01480 444558
POLICE: 0845 456 4564
PRESS: 01480 422393
AMBULANCE: 01603 424255
PRESS: 01603 422729

Cheshire
FIRE: 01606 868700
PRESS: 01606 868657 /
868422 / 868786
POLICE: 01244 350000
PRESS: 01244 612030
AMBULANCE: 0151 260 5220
PRESS: 0151 261 2585

Cleveland
FIRE: 01429 872311
PRESS: x4160 / 4151
POLICE: 01642 326326
PRESS: 01642 301245 / 54
AMBULANCE: 01904 666000
PRESS: 01904 666041

Cornwall
FIRE: 01872 273117
PRESS: 01872 322785
POLICE: 0845 277 7444
PRESS: 01392 452151 / 200
AMBULANCE: 01392 261500
PRESS: 01392 261506

Cumbria
FIRE: 01900 822503
PRESS: 01900 822503
POLICE: 01768 891999
PRESS: 01768 217009
AMBULANCE: 01228 596909
PRESS: 01228 403006

Derbyshire
FIRE: 01332 771221
PRESS: 01332 771221
POLICE: 01773 570100
PRESS: 01773 572033 /
034 / 979
AMBULANCE: 0115 929 6151
PRESS: 0115 929 6151

Devon
FIRE: 01392 872200
PRESS: 01392 872318
POLICE: 0845 277 7444
PRESS: 01392 452151 / 200
AMBULANCE: 01392 261500
PRESS: 01392 261506

Dorset
FIRE: 01305 251133
PRESS: 01305 252040
POLICE: 01202 222222
PRESS: 01202 223893,
07626 932345
AMBULANCE: 01202 851640
PRESS: 01202 851640

Durham
FIRE: 0191 384 3381
PRESS: 0191 384 3381
POLICE: 0191 386 4929
PRESS: 0191 375 2157
AMBULANCE: 0191 273 1212
PRESS: 0191 273 1212

East Sussex
FIRE: 0845 130 8855
PRESS: 01323 462388
POLICE: 0845 607 0999
PRESS: 01273 404173
AMBULANCE: 01273 489444
PRESS: 01273 897859

Essex
FIRE: 01277 222531
PRESS: 01277 222531
POLICE: 01245 491491
PRESS: 01245 452450
AMBULANCE: 01245 443344
PRESS: 01245 444444

Gloucestershire
FIRE: 01452 753333
PRESS: 01452 753333
POLICE: 0845 090 1234
PRESS: 01242 276070
AMBULANCE: 01452 753030
PRESS: 01452 753030

Greater Manchester
FIRE: 0161 736 5866
PRESS: 0161 608 4090
POLICE: 0161 872 5050
PRESS: 0161 856 2220
AMBULANCE: 0161 796 7222
PRESS: 0161 834 9836

Hampshire
FIRE: 023 8064 4000
PRESS: 023 8062 6812
POLICE: 0845 045 4545
PRESS: 01962 871619
AMBULANCE: 01962 863511
PRESS: 01962 843165

Hereford & Worcester
FIRE: 01905 24454
PRESS: 01905 725060
POLICE: 0845 744 4888
PRESS: 01432 347340
AMBULANCE: 01886 834200
PRESS: 01886 834200

Hertfordshire
FIRE: 01992 507507
PRESS: 01992 507546
POLICE: 0845 330 0222
PRESS: 01707 354588
AMBULANCE: 01234 408999
PRESS: 01234 408999

Humberside
FIRE: 01482 565333
PRESS: 01482 567466
POLICE: 0845 606 0222
PRESS: 01482 578372
AMBULANCE: 01904 666000
PRESS: 01904 666041

Isle of Wight
FIRE: 01983 823194
PRESS: 01983 823107
POLICE: 0845 045 4545
PRESS: 01962 871619
AMBULANCE: 01983 534111
PRESS: 01983 534184

Kent
FIRE: 01622 692121
PRESS: 01622 692121
POLICE: 01622 690690
PRESS: 01622 652231-3
PORT OF DOVER POLICE:
01304 240400
AMBULANCE: 01622 747010
PRESS: 01622 740331

Lancashire
FIRE: 01772 862545
PRESS: 01772 866939,
07769 907887
POLICE: 01772 614444
PRESS: 01772 412658 / 444
AMBULANCE: 01772 862666
PRESS: 01772 773005

Leicestershire
FIRE: 0116 287 2241
PRESS: 0116 229 2194
POLICE: 0116 222 2222
PRESS: x2798
AMBULANCE: 0115 929 6151
PRESS: 0115 929 6151

Lincolnshire
FIRE: 01522 582222
PRESS: 01522 552302
POLICE: 01522 532222
PRESS: 01522 558026
AMBULANCE: 0845 045 0422
PRESS: 01522 832638

London
FIRE: 020 7587 2000
PRESS: 020 7587 6100
METROPOLITAN POLICE:
020 7230 1212
PRESS: 020 7230 2171
CITY OF LONDON POLICE:
020 7601 2222
PRESS: 020 7601 2220
AMBULANCE: 020 7921 5100
PRESS: 020 7921 5113

Merseyside
FIRE: 0151 296 4000
PRESS: 0151 296 4419
POLICE: 0151 709 6010
PRESS: 0151 777 8566
AMBULANCE: 0151 260 5220
PRESS: 0151 261 2585

Norfolk
FIRE: 01603 810351
PRESS: 01603 819759
POLICE: 0845 456 4567
PRESS: 01953 423666,
07626 952342
AMBULANCE: 01603 424255
PRESS: 01603 422729

North Yorkshire
FIRE: 01609 780150
PRESS: 01609 788595
POLICE: 0845 606 0247
PRESS: 01609 789959
AMBULANCE: 01904 666000
PRESS: 01904 666041

Northamptonshire
FIRE: 01604 797000
PRESS: 01536 516400
POLICE: 01604 700700
PRESS: 01604 703197
AMBULANCE: 01908 262422
PRESS: 01908 262422

Northumberland
FIRE: 01670 533000
PRESS: 01670 533208
POLICE: 01661 872555
PRESS: 01661 868888
AMBULANCE: 0191 273 1212
PRESS: 0191 273 1212

Nottinghamshire
FIRE: 0115 967 0880
PRESS: 0115 977 4918
POLICE: 0115 967 0999
PRESS: 0115 967 2080
AMBULANCE: 0115 929 6151
PRESS: 0115 929 6151

Oxfordshire
FIRE: 01865 842999
PRESS: 01865 842999
POLICE: 01865 846000
PRESS: 01865 846699
AMBULANCE: 01865 740100
PRESS: 01865 740117

Rutland
FIRE: 0116 287 2241
PRESS: 0116 229 2194
POLICE: 0116 222 2222
PRESS: x2798
AMBULANCE: 0115 929 6151
PRESS: 0115 929 6151

Shropshire
FIRE: 01743 260200
PRESS: 01743 260286
POLICE: 0845 744 4888
PRESS: 01743 237491
AMBULANCE: 01384 215555
PRESS: 01384 246395

Somerset
FIRE: 01823 364500
PRESS: 01823 364582
POLICE: 0845 456 7000
PRESS: 01275 816350
AMBULANCE: 01392 261500
PRESS: 01392 261506

South Yorkshire
FIRE: 0114 272 7202
PRESS: 0114 253 2353
POLICE: 0114 220 2020
PRESS: 0114 252 3848
AMBULANCE: 01709 820520
PRESS: 01709 302026

Staffordshire
FIRE: 01785 813234
PRESS: 01785 285000
POLICE: 0845 330 2010
PRESS: 01785 234864
AMBULANCE: 01785 253521
PRESS: 01785 273309

Suffolk
FIRE: 01473 588888
PRESS: 01473 264392
POLICE: 01473 613500
PRESS: 01473 613996 / 7
AMBULANCE: 01603 424255
PRESS: 01603 422729

Surrey
FIRE: 01737 242444
PRESS: 01737 224027
POLICE: 0845 125 2222
PRESS: 01483 482322
AMBULANCE: 01737 353333
PRESS: 01737 363815

Tyne and Wear
FIRE: 0191 232 1224
PRESS: 0191 235 9470
POLICE: 01661 872555
PRESS: 01661 868888
AMBULANCE: 0191 273 1212
PRESS: 0191 273 1212

Warwickshire
FIRE: 01926 423231
PRESS: 01926 423231
POLICE: 01926 415000
PRESS: North: x3366,
07626 952404;
South: x4266, 07626
955647
AMBULANCE: 01926 881331
PRESS: 01926 881331

West Midlands
FIRE: 0121 359 5161
PRESS: 0121 380 6101
POLICE: 0845 113 5000
PRESS: 0121 626 5858
AMBULANCE: 01384 215555
PRESS: 01384 246395

West Sussex
FIRE: 01243 786211
PRESS: 01243 752448
POLICE: 0845 607 0999
PRESS: 01273 404173
AMBULANCE: 01273 489444
PRESS: 01273 897859

West Yorkshire
FIRE: 01274 682311
PRESS: 01274 655717
POLICE: 0845 606 0606
PRESS: 01924 292045
AMBULANCE: 01924 582000
PRESS: 01924 582204

Wiltshire
FIRE: 01380 723601
PRESS: 01380 723601
POLICE: 01380 722341
PRESS: 01380 734126
AMBULANCE: 01249 443939
PRESS: 01249 443939

Worcestershire
see Hereford & Worcester

Wales

Mid Wales
FIRE: 0870 606 0699
PRESS: 01267 221444
POLICE: 01267 222020
PRESS: 01267 222274
AMBULANCE: 01745 532900
PRESS: 01745 532925

West Wales
FIRE: 0870 606 0699
PRESS: 01267 221444
POLICE: 01633 838111
PRESS: 01267 222274
AMBULANCE: 01745 532900
PRESS: 01745 532925

North Wales
FIRE: 01745 343431
PRESS: 01745 535283
POLICE: 01492 517171
PRESS: 01492 511157-9
AMBULANCE: 01745 532900
PRESS: 01745 532925

South Wales
FIRE: 01443 232000
PRESS: 01443 232164
POLICE: 01656 655555
PRESS: 01656 869291
AMBULANCE: 01745 532900
PRESS: 01495 765466,
01745 532925

Scotland

Central Scotland
FIRE: 01324 716996
PRESS: 01324 716996
POLICE: 01786 456000
PRESS: 01786 456370
AMBULANCE: 0131 446 7000
PRESS: 07974 017937

Dumfries and Galloway
FIRE: 01387 252222
PRESS: 01387 252222
POLICE: 01387 252112
PRESS: 01387 260576
AMBULANCE: 0131 446 7000
PRESS: 07974 017937

Fife
FIRE: 01592 774451
PRESS: x2082 (voicebank),
x2069
POLICE: 01592 418888
PRESS: 01592 418813
AMBULANCE: 0131 446 7000
PRESS: 07974 017937

Grampian
FIRE: 01224 696666
PRESS: 01224 696666
POLICE: 0845 600 5700
PRESS: 01224 386431
AMBULANCE: 0131 446 7000
PRESS: 07974 017937

Highland and Islands
FIRE: 01463 227000
PRESS: 01463 227009
POLICE: 01463 715555
PRESS: 01463 720396
AMBULANCE: 0131 446 7000
PRESS: 07974 017937

Lothian and Borders
FIRE: 0131 228 2401
PRESS: 0131 228 2401
POLICE: 0131 311 3131
PRESS: 0131 311 3423
AMBULANCE: 0131 446 7000
PRESS: 07974 017937

Strathclyde
FIRE: 01698 300999
PRESS: 01698 338207
POLICE: 0141 532 2000
PRESS: 0141 532 2658
AMBULANCE: 0131 446 7000
PRESS: 07974 017937

Tayside
FIRE: 01382 322222
PRESS: 01382 322222
POLICE: 01382 223200
PRESS: 01382 322222
AMBULANCE: 0131 446 7000
PRESS: 07974 017937

Northern Ireland

HQ, Lisburn
FIRE: 028 9266 4221
PRESS: 028 9266 4221
POLICE: 028 9065 0222
PRESS: 028 9070 0084
AMBULANCE: 028 9040 0999
PRESS: 028 9040 0999

British Transport Police

020 7830 8800

PRESS

London and south-east
BREAKING NEWS:
020 7957 1527
FOLLOW-UPS:
LONDON UNDERGROUND:
020 7027 6507
SOUTH LONDON AND SOUTH-
EAST: *020 7983 7231*
NORTH LONDON THROUGH
EAST ANGLIA: *020 7313 1131*

Midlands, Wales and west
BREAKING NEWS:
0121 654 2244
FOLLOW-UPS: *029 2043 0654*

North-east
BREAKING NEWS:
0113 247 9517
FOLLOW-UPS: *0113 247 9575*

North-west
BREAKING NEWS:
0161 228 5685
FOLLOW-UPS: *0161 228 5398*

Scotland
BREAKING NEWS:
0141 335 3198
FOLLOW-UPS: *0141 335 2714*

**National and
policy enquiries**
020 7918 3547

Index

Contacts index

Contacts index

She – Sti

X

Y

Subject index